CJ: Realities and Challenges

CJ

Realities and Challenges

Ruth E. Masters California State University–Fresno

Lori Beth Way California State University–Chico

Phyllis B. Gerstenfeld California State University–Stanislaus

Bernadette T. Muscat California State University–Fresno

Michael Hooper California Commission on Peace Officer Standards and Training

John P. J. Dussich California State University–Fresno

Lester Pincu California State University–Fresno

Candice A. Skrapec California State University–Fresno

Mc Graw Hill
Connect Learn Succeed™

The McGraw-Hill Companies

Connect Learn Succeed™

Published by McGraw-Hill, an imprint of The McGraw-Hill Companies, Inc., 1221 Avenue of the Americas, New York, NY 10020.

This book is printed on acid-free paper.

3 4 5 6 7 8 9 0 DOW/DOW 1 0 9 8 7 6 5 4 3 2 1 0

ISBN: 978-0-07-340151-5
MHID: 0-07-340151-X

Vice President, Editorial: *Michael Ryan*
Executive Editor: *Katie Stevens*
Executive Marketing Manager: *Leslie Oberhuber*
Director of Development: *Rhona Robbin*
Developmental Editors: *Elisa Adams and Betty Slack*
Editorial Coordinators: *Julie Kuljurgis, Erika Lake, and Elena Mackawgy*
Production Editor: *Melissa Williams*
Manuscript Editor: *Kay Mikel*
Permissions Editor: *Marty Moga*
Creative Director: *Jeanne M. Schreiber*
Interior Design: *Amanda Cavanaugh*
Cover Design: *Gearbox*
Cover Photo: *Paul Burns/Blend Images/Getty, Inc.*
Art Manager: *Robin Mouat*
Illustrators: *John and Judy Waller*
Manager, Photo Research: *Brian J. Pecko*
Senior Production Supervisor: *Tandra Jorgensen*
Composition: *10.5/12.5 Adobe Garamond Pro by Lachina Publishing Services*
Printing: *RR Donnelley*

Credits: The credits section for this book begins on page 537 and is considered an extension of the copyright page.

Library of Congress Cataloging-in-Publication Data

Masters, Ruth E.
Criminal justice / Ruth E. Masters…[et al.]—1 ed.
p. cm.
Includes bibliographical references and index
ISBN-13: 978-0-07-340151-5 (alk. paper)
ISBN-10: 0-07-340151-X (alk. paper)
1. Criminal justice, Adminstration of—United States. I. Title.
HV9950.152 2011
364.973—dc22
20090045868

www.mhhe.com

Dedication

Thanks to a dynamite author team that never missed a beat!

—Ruth Masters

Thanks so much to my family, who endured vacations with me at my laptop! Your support is invaluable. On behalf of the author team, I'd also like to thank Dr. Ruth Masters. Her leadership made this process so much smoother than it otherwise might have been. I'd also like to thank Amanda Flanders, Nada Nassar, and Rick Davis for their research support.

—Lori Beth Way

I'd like to thank Dennis, Allison, and Quinn for their continuing support, and for giving up so much of their time so I could work.

—Phyllis Gerstenfeld

Much appreciation for the patience exhibited by my wife, Jill, and son and daughter, Matt and Mollye, as stacks of rough drafts and books competed for space atop both kitchen and dining room tabletops—and for the acceptance of "walk IOUs" by Abbie, our canine guardian of manuscripts.

—Mike Hooper

I would like to thank my wife, Edda, for all the time away from her and the rest of my family, especially for the late night and weekend calls, both at home and while on vacations. She has been an important source of support throughout the entire four-year process.

—John Dussich

I wish to thank Jim McCabe for his support, encouragement, and patience during this entire project. I also wish to acknowledge the leadership of Dr. Ruth Masters, who provided the vision and determination to see this project through and who assembled this group and invited me to join this awesome team. It's been a great experience working with all of you. Thank you all.

—Les Pincu

Brief Contents

Contents

PART 1 CRIME, LAW, AND THE CRIMINAL JUSTICE SYSTEM

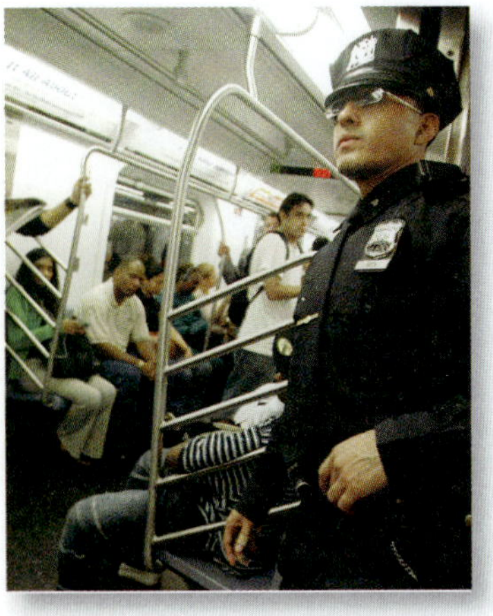

CHAPTER 2 TYPES OF CRIME 24

CHAPTER 3 CAUSES OF CRIME 64

PART 2 LAW ENFORCEMENT

CHAPTER 6 POLICING OPERATIONS 158

CHAPTER 7 LEGAL AND SPECIAL ISSUES IN POLICING 192

PART 3 ADJUDICATION

CHAPTER 8 THE COURTS 224

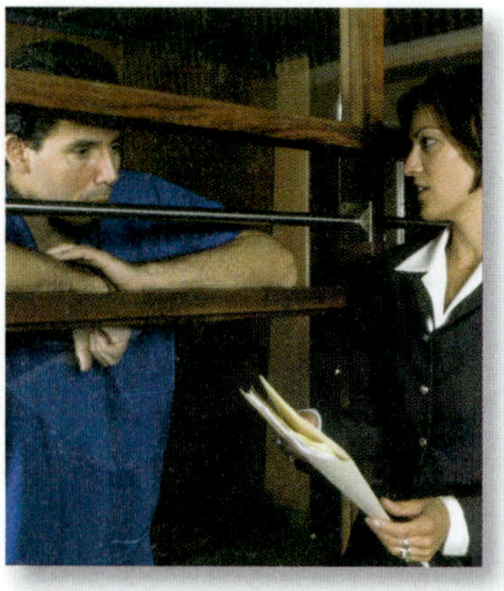

CHAPTER 10 SENTENCING 276

PART 4 CORRECTIONS

CHAPTER 11 OVERVIEW OF CORRECTIONS 300

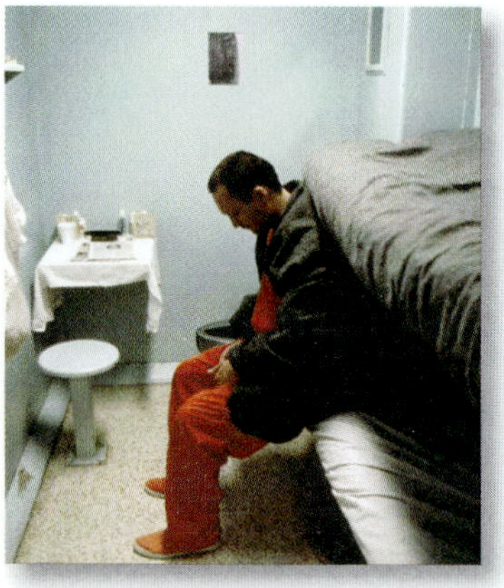

PART 5 SPECIAL ISSUES

List of Boxes

A CASE IN POINT

WHAT ABOUT THE VICTIM?

DISCONNECTS

RACE, CLASS, GENDER

A GLOBAL VIEW

REAL CAREERS

Preface

> "*CJ: Realities and Challenges* is the perfect text for the Intro to CJ course."
>
> –Debra Ross,
> Grand Valley State University

Every student who begins the introduction to criminal justice course believes that he or she knows something about how the system works. Many come from families with a tradition in law enforcement, the courts, or other branches of the criminal justice system. Some are motivated by personal experiences and a desire to right the wrongs that they have experienced in life. Others expect to enter the exciting world of *CSI* investigations and depictions of crime fighting found in the media. What each of these students soon learns is that the realities of the criminal justice system do not always fit their preconceptions.

CJ is a field in which we often ask: What is the truth? What is the reality behind a situation? When examining crime and its consequences, we discover that the answer is more complicated than is often realized. To help students achieve a realistic view of the system, we offer an approach that compares the principles of criminal justice to actual practices.

Underlying every assumption about how the system *should* work is a body of experience showing how it actually *does* work. Examples exist in all branches of the criminal justice system. In law enforcement, how do officers balance the priorities of keeping people safe while upholding their civil liberties? In the courts, why does a change of venue for a jury trial sometimes hurt rather than help a defendant's chance of receiving a fair trial? In prisons, why is illegal drug abuse so pervasive even though such substances are strictly prohibited? The realities revealed by these situations result in challenges that lie at the heart of the criminal justice system–challenges that we explore throughout this text.

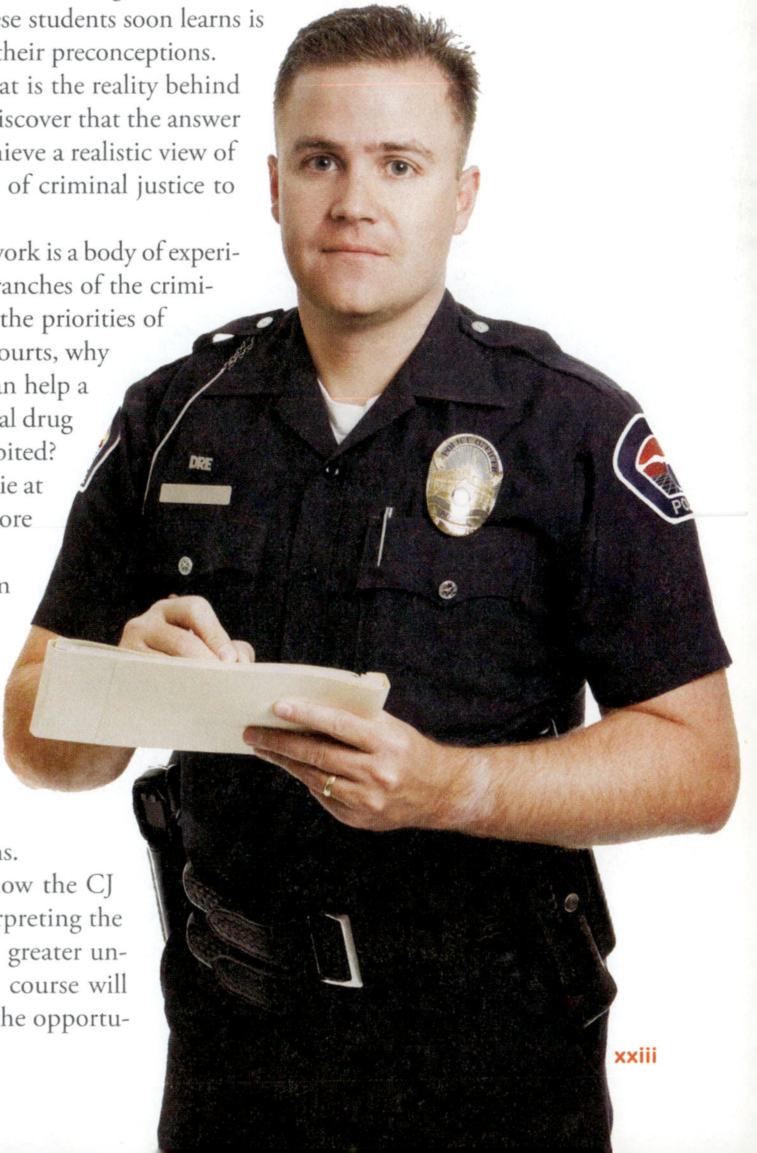

CJ: Realities and Challenges brings together an author team consisting of both practitioners and academics to deliver a contemporary and realistic perspective on vital institutions in American society. We understand that this course is faculty's first chance to engage students in a meaningful exposure to the ideals of the American criminal justice system. *CJ: Realities and Challenges* is designed to translate the passion that we feel in the classroom into a textbook that nourishes the student's enthusiasm for the field while dispelling widely held myths.

This book encourages students to think critically about how the CJ system operates in the real world. Recognizing myths and interpreting the facts underlying the American criminal justice system leads to greater understanding of its complexities. Students who succeed in this course will emerge with a more realistic understanding of the system and the opportunities that await them.

In one sense, the study of criminal justice boils down to learning the components of the system, how laws are enforced, and how crimes and criminals are handled. But there is much more to observe, investigate, and understand. There are longstanding issues in criminal justice that need to be discussed, such as how to balance crime control with deference to due process, how much emphasis should be given to punishment versus rehabilitation, and what the role of the victim should be in the criminal justice process. Any text written in the 21st century must also address current issues and challenges that are altering the face of criminal justice, such as DNA profiling, crime on the Internet, terrorist concerns, and the impact of new technologies on both sides of the law. Can these challenges be integrated into the traditional CJ system or do they require new approaches? We all need to think through these issues.

CJ: Realities and Challenges takes a critical thinking approach to examining traditional and emerging issues in criminal justice. To underscore this approach, we developed a three-part framework for each chapter called *Observe, Investigate, Understand.* Using this approach, we ask students to:

Observe, Investigate, Understand

A Critical Thinking Approach to Criminal Justice

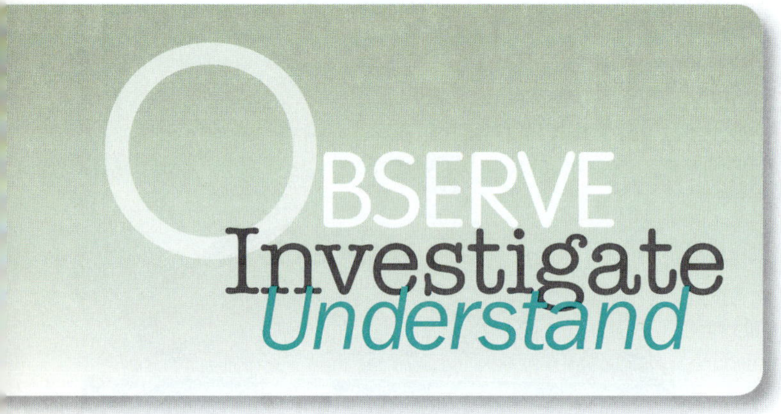

OBSERVE the core principles underlying the criminal justice system.

INVESTIGATE how these foundational principles are applied in the real world.

UNDERSTAND how these principles and practices are still evolving.

Each chapter opens with a series of learning goals tied to this framework. Using vivid examples to reinforce student learning, we explore these goals throughout the chapter. At the chapter's end, we employ this same framework to review and recap key concepts.

The *Observe, Investigate, Understand* framework helps students make logical connections between the principles and practices of criminal justice. As a case in point, in Chapter 7, Legal and Special Issues in Policing, students learn about the concept of police "use of force." While reading the opening vignette, students *observe* how the use of force may become controversial in actual law enforcement situations. The chapter guides students to *investigate* the legal and Constitutional provisions that help society define the limitations of police actions. This discussion leads students to *understand* how law enforcement agencies attempt to regulate the use of force and the many practical outcomes connected to these efforts, from their impact on community relations and city budgets to the evolution of departmental policies and strategies.

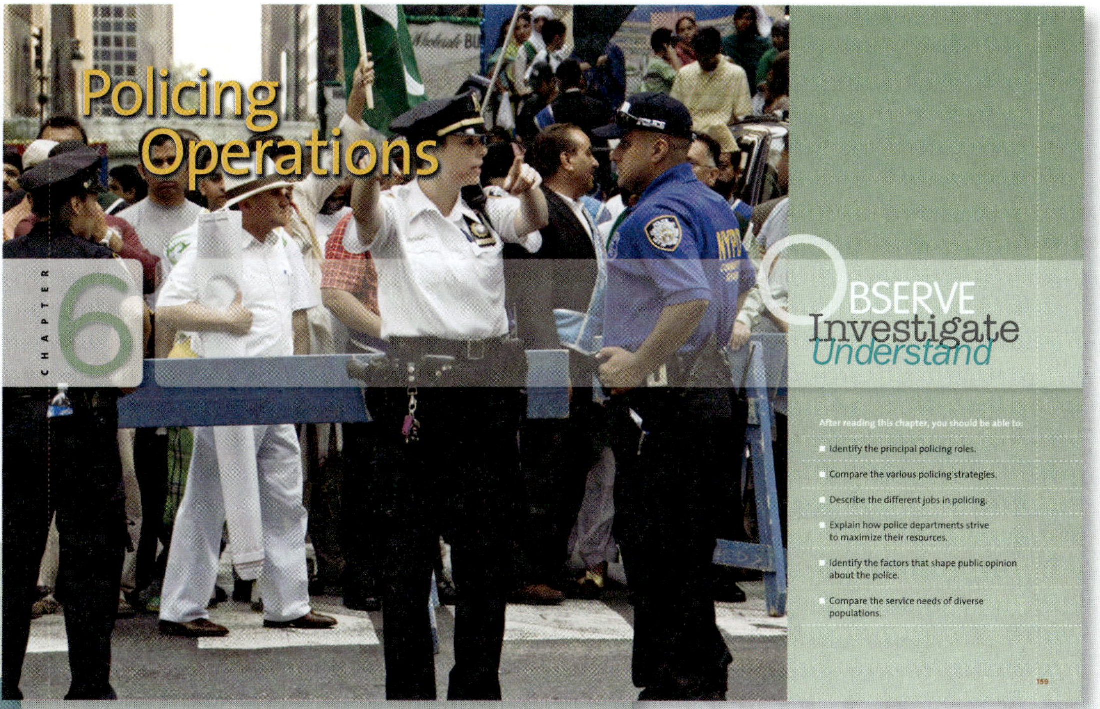

Policing
Operations
CHAPTER 6
OBSERVE
Investigate
Understand
After reading this chapter, you should be able to:
Identify the principal policing roles.
Compare the various policing strategies.
Describe the different jobs in policing.
Explain how police departments strive to maximize their resources.
Identify the factors that shape public opinion about the police.
Compare the service needs of diverse populations.
159

Chapter-opening pages introduce the *Observe-Investigate-Understand* framework. ▶

OBSERVE Investigate Understand

Review

Identify the principal policing roles.

- A major part of the workload of police is maintaining order.
- Police engage in law enforcement when they enforce criminal law and apprehend law breakers.
- Service activities are nonenforcement actions performed on an as-needed basis.

Compare the various policing strategies.

- In preventive patrol, officers are assigned to randomly drive or walk around an area.
- Problem-oriented policing focuses on discovering the underlying causes of problems and encouraging police to find innovative solutions to solve those problems.
- Community-oriented policing focuses on reducing crime and disorder by involving residents in the job of policing.
- Aggressive order maintenance entails police focusing on minor public order offenses that affect residents' quality of life.

Describe the different jobs in policing.

- The rookie police officer quickly learns the realities of police work while working under the guidance of a training officer.
- Patrol officers are the first individuals to respond to a call for service.
- A follow-up investigation occurs after a patrol officer documents the facts of the crime.
- Police are the primary public safety agency in charge of enforcing traffic laws.
- Communications coordinates the performance of law enforcement activities.
- Custody is the incarceration of parties either accused or convicted of a crime.
- Forensics is the application of scientific knowledge and methods to criminal and civil investigations and legal procedures, including criminal trials.

Explain how police departments strive to maximize their resources.

- Departments use geographic information systems (GIS) technology to produce detailed descriptions of crime occurrences and analyze the relationships between variables such as location and time. This information helps police know how to respond to an incident.
- CompStat is a computerized information system that integrates information from crime maps across the city for department leaders' review. This information helps police administrators decide how to allocate their resources.
- Crime analysis can be helpful in reducing the pool of possible suspects, thereby making investigation more efficient.

◀ **Chapters close with a review of key *Observe-Investigate-Understand* learning outcomes.**

"This text is contemporary and fills a void that has existed in the area of criminal justice teaching for a long time. It provides a framework for introducing students to the realities of the criminal justice process and stresses the importance of a comprehensive analysis of the parts, roles, and participants of an evolving criminal justice system."

–William J. Flynn,
Raritan Valley Community College

Discussing **Myths and Realities** about Criminal Justice

Another key goal of this text is to erase misconceptions about the criminal justice system. Appearing throughout the chapters, *Myth and Reality* entries reinforce the reality-based theme of the text by challenging students to think critically about their own beliefs and develop an understanding of the way the system actually works. Each *Myth and Reality* entry relates to a broader discussion that uses supporting data to explain a key principle. A few of the sample myths that we investigate include:

- Police presence reduces crime. (Chapter 6, Policing Operations)
- Eyewitness accounts are the most reliable form of evidence. (Chapter 8, The Courts)
- Incarcerating criminals reduces crime in society. (Chapter 12, Jails and Prisons)
- Victims can make money as a result of the crime(s) committed against them. (Chapter 14, Understanding and Helping Victims)

back story:

WHICH MYTHS NEED DEBUNKING?

To find out, we began with a BIG list of 160 widely-held myths about criminal justice.

We narrowed this list down to 90.

We tested the myths with 25 instructors and 245 students.

THE RESULT:
60 of the most widely-held myths about criminal justice that we use to reveal the realities behind the system.

MYTH/REALITY

MYTH: Police work primarily entails responding to crimes in progress or crimes that have just occurred.

REALITY: The vast majority of calls to police relate to neither violent confrontations nor criminal activities requiring arrest, but rather to minor disputes such as a landlord-tenant disagreement or requests for service such as a vehicle blocking a driveway.[9]

Thematic Features Reinforce the ***Observe, Investigate, Understand*** Framework of the Text.

- **A Case in Point** boxes link key concepts to the world of actual events.
- **A Global View** boxes compare American justice to international justice.
- **Disconnects** boxes explore the gap between the intent of policies and law and their application in the real world.
- **Race, Class, Gender** boxes explore how issues related to race, class, or gender affect the administration of justice.
- **What About the Victim?** boxes remind us that the criminal justice story is also about the victim.
- **Real Careers** profiles tell the story of recent graduates who have chosen a career in criminal justice.
- **Real Crime Tech** entries reveal the way in which technology is currently used throughout the criminal justice network.

Real Careers

STACY SHAMBLIN

Work location: Reno, NV

College(s): University of Nevada, Reno, 2007

Major(s): Criminal Justice (BS)

Job title: Methamphetamine Program Coordinator, Reno Police Department

Salary range for jobs like this: $35,000–$50,000

Time in job: 1.5 years

Work Responsibilities

I coordinate drug education and prevention activities for the Reno Police Department. We educate citizens about the drugs commonly abused in their area, the effects and pa phernalia associated with those drugs, and drug prevent strategies. In general, the program serves middle and h school students, parents, and professionals who work w teens and young adults. My role in the program is to fu requests for instructional materials and presentations a to provide drug awareness training targeted for the spec audience. Trends in substance abuse often change, an adapt our curriculum to provide the most accurate inforr tion possible.

In addition to managing the program, I am responsi for monitoring and reporting quarterly progress to the f eral office that funds our activities—COPS, or Commun Oriented Policing Services (part of the U.S. Department Justice). Although writing reports is not as exciting as pl ning presentations, it is certainly an important aspect of

Why Criminal Justice?

When I was a teenager, I wanted to pursue a career as a criminal prosecutor. As I prepared for college, I realized I wanted to have a more direct impact on crime and public safety through a career in civilian law enforcement. I did not know what careers were possible in law enforcement other than Police Officer, so I consulted my professors and worked two internships while in college.

During my junior year, I applied for the FBI Scholastic Honors Internship Program and was selected to intern in the Economic Crimes Unit at FBI Headquarters in Washington, D.C. My summer with the FBI proved to be a valuable work experience and was certainly a great asset to my resume, but the internship that was most instrumental to my current career was at the Crime Analysis Unit of the Reno Police Department. Shortly after I graduated, my former supervisor, who was impressed with my work as an intern, notified me that the position of Methamphetamine Program Coordinator had become available.

Expectations and Realities of the Job

I have been somewhat surprised by my influence in making key decisions for the program. Even though I am an entry-level employee, I have been encouraged to suggest and even implement new strategies to improve the success of the program. I am impressed with the effectiveness of the

Real Careers boxes provide advice for students from people who have recently begun working in the profession.

DIS Con nects

Junk Science in the Courtroom

Do jurors and judges understand the language used by expert witnesses? Do they know what an expert means when he uses terms such as "consistent with" or "statistically significant"? Do they understand the science that underlies an expert's testimony? The answers to these questions are generally no. How, then, can the triers of fact recognize when expert witnesses present unreliable information based on unscientific methods and analyses? The adversarial nature of judicial proceedings should serve to expose such "junk science" as well as outright fraud in the courtroom. Expert witnesses from the other side should catch it. Even when faulty science is exposed, however, it might not make a difference to jury members.

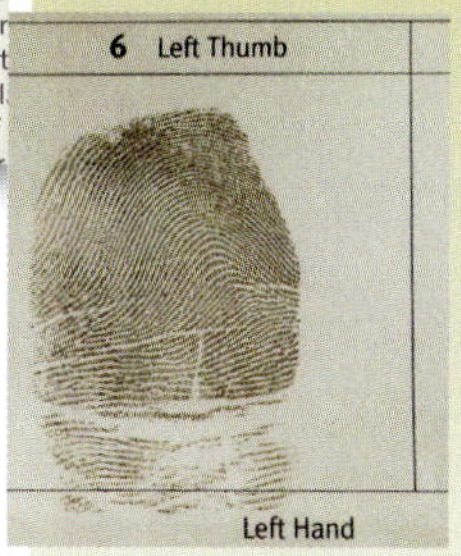

Unfounded scientific opinions may be shrouded by the charismatic presentation of the expert. Huber, for example, discussed the civil case of a woman whose claim of losing her psychic powers after having a CAT scan was supported by expert testimony from a doctor. A Philadelphia jury awarded her $1 million. Although the trial judge threw out that verdict, jurors had been persuaded of an unverifiable claim by an effective courtroom presentation that overruled their common sense.

Sometimes the science itself is good but the person who uses it is mistaken, incompetent, or fraudulent. Despite having flunked organic chemistry in college, Fred Zain became a forensics expert for West Virginia and Texas and testified against defendants in hundreds of cases. Zain was ultimately charged with lying and fabricating evidence, leading to as many as 134 wrongful convictions.

Sometimes the science itself is suspect. Polygraph (lie detector) evidence is generally not admissible because it is considered scientifically unreliable. Even fingerprint evidence has been called into question in recent years. Of course, as scientific techniques advance, what was once considered unreliable may eventually grow strong enough to become acceptable in court.

OBSERVE Investigate Understand

- **Is it necessary for jurors to understand the science that underlies the testimony of expert witnesses?**
- **Why are jurors so willing to believe junk science in a courtroom?**
- **Is the problem of jurors sometimes accepting junk science in criminal trials a valid argument against continuing to use the jury system in American criminal justice?**

SOURCES: P. Huber, "Junk Science in the Courtroom," *Forbes* (July 8, 1991), 68; Supreme Court of Appeals of West Virginia, *Renewed Investigation of the West Virginia State Police Crime Laboratory, Serology Division*, January 2006, www.state.wv.us/wvsca/docs/spring06/32885.htm (retrieved February 23, 2007); Michael Specter, "Do Fingerprints Lie?" *The New Yorker* (May 27, 2002).

Disconnects boxes reveal how practices in the criminal justice system do not always reflect the original intent of the law.

"This text invites students to investigate their own perceptions of the CJ system and look closer at how the system actually works in the real world."

–Terry Pippin,
College of Southern Nevada

An Author Team that's Connected to the Real World

The author team is a blend of academicians and practitioners. They represent all of the key facets of CJ including law enforcement (Mike Hooper and Lori Beth Way), law and the judicial system (Phyllis Gerstenfeld and Candice Skrapec), corrections (Ruth Masters and Lester Pincu), and victim services (Bernadette Muscat and John Dussich).

With backgrounds in law enforcement, the courts, corrections, and victim services, we provide a unique, interdisciplinary view of criminal justice not found in any other textbook. We used a highly collaborative process to write this book. To ensure that we offered a thorough examination of each branch of the criminal justice system, we organized our research, writing, and editing efforts as a peer review circle. Each chapter is the product of an ongoing, iterative review by the entire author team. The result of this synergistic effort is a unified voice providing a balanced, insightful point of view that is informed by the experience of the entire author team and has been affirmed by the feedback of course instructors.

> "The key strength of this text is that it is a product of several experts and professors of criminal justice, giving it both balance and depth."
>
> –Gary Ebels, Grand Rapids Community College

We encourage students to read this text in the spirit in which it was created: have an open mind, think critically, engage in discussion, and exploit the wide knowledge and practical experience represented by the author team. Our collective experience underscores the need for collaboration in addressing the complexity of the criminal justice system.

The Authors

Ruth E. Masters, Ed.D.

Affiliation: Chair and Professor, Department of Criminology, California State University, Fresno. **Expertise:** Ruth E. Masters's specialties are corrections, correctional counseling, drug addiction, criminological theory, and cross-cultural administration of justice. She has worked for the California Department of Corrections (now California Department of Corrections and Rehabilitation) as a Parole Agent supervising addicted adult felons. She has been teaching criminology since 1972.

Lori Beth Way, Ph.D.

Affiliation: Associate Professor and Coordinator of Criminal Justice, California State University, Chico. **Expertise:** Lori Beth Way's research and teaching areas include policing, the courts, and issues of race, class, and gender. Her policing research primarily focuses on police behavior and discretion. She is Project Director for a U.S. Department of Justice Violence Against Women Campus grant to reduce and respond to the crimes of sexual assault, intimate partner violence, and stalking. She also teaches at Butte College Police Academy. While earning her Ph.D., she obtained a master's certificate in Women's Studies.

Phyllis B. Gerstenfeld, J.D., Ph.D.

Affiliation: Chair, Department of Criminal Justice, California State University, Stanislaus. **Expertise:** Phyllis Gerstenfeld has a law degree as well as a Ph.D. in Social Psychology. Her primary areas of research include hate crimes, juvenile justice, and psychology and law. She has published a monograph and co-edited an anthology on hate crimes. She has worked for a large private law firm as well as a public legal services agency and has been teaching criminal justice since 1993.

Bernadette T. Muscat, Ph.D.

Affiliation: California State University, Fresno. **Expertise:** Bernadette Muscat has worked with victims of domestic violence by serving as a legal advocate and by providing counseling, education, and legal advocacy in shelter and court environments. She has worked with law enforcement agencies, victim service programs, and court programs in program and policy development, evaluation, research, and training to ensure effective administration of victim assistance. She works extensively with local, state, and national level multi-disciplinary task force groups to address family violence and violence against women. She has worked with the California Office of Emergency Services (OES) Victim Witness Division on the creation and implementation of the California State Victim Assistance Academy (CVAA) to provide 40-hour training to victim service practitioners throughout California.

Michael Hooper, Ph.D.

Affiliation: Senior Consultant, California Department of Justice, Commission on Peace Officer Standards and Training. **Expertise:** Michael Hooper is currently Chief, Center for Leadership Development, California Commission on Peace Officer Standards and Training (POST). Michael Hooper began his involvement with the criminal justice system as a member of the Los Angeles Police Department. His 23 years of LAPD experience encompassed positions as a patrol officer, field supervisor, and watch commander. This was followed by five years of service on the Criminal Justice Program faculty at Penn State University's Capitol Campus. In his current capacity at POST, he is responsible for the operation of the Institute of Criminal Investigation, Instructor Development Institute, California POST Training Network, Learning Technology Resource Center, and Regional Skills Training Centers.

John P. J. Dussich, Ph.D.

Affiliation: Department of Criminology, California State University, Fresno. **Expertise:** John P. J. Dussich is one of the world's leading authorities on victimology, victim services, criminology, victimological theory, and criminological and victimological research. He has worked as a criminal justice planner, as a police officer, as a warden of a prison, as a director of a program evaluation unit, and is now the director of an international victimology research institute. He has taught criminology since 1966 and victimology since 1976. The American Society of Victimology has named the John P. J. Dussich Award in his honor, and gives it each year to a person who has made significant contributions to the field of victimology.

Lester Pincu, D. Crim.

Affiliation: Professor Emeritus, Department of Criminology, California State University, Fresno. **Expertise:** Lester Pincu has worked in corrections, counseling and group psychotherapy, alcoholism, drug addiction, and treatment programs. He is a California Licensed Marriage and Family Counselor, a Certified Group Psychotherapist, and holds an appointment by the California State Legislature as a member of the California Council on Criminal Justice. He worked as a deputy probation officer for Contra Costa County investigating and supervising juvenile offenders from 1965 to 1970. He was a full-time faculty member at Fresno State from 1970 to 2001.

Candice A. Skrapec, Ph.D.

Affiliation: Associate Professor, Department of Criminology, California State University, Fresno. **Expertise:** Candice Skrapec is a psychologist and criminologist. For the past 20 years she has maintained her research focus on serial murder (particularly in terms of underlying biological and psychological factors) and continues her interviews of incarcerated serial murderers in different countries. Her professional works and academic research result in regular calls from the media, movie and documentary producers, as well as authors of fact and fiction books in the areas of serial murder and investigative profiling. With over 20 years of experience in the law enforcement field working with officers and agencies in Canada, the United States, and Mexico, she is also frequently consulted by police around the world to assist in the investigation of homicide cases. She has taught a wide range of criminology courses since 1988 and has trained police and correctional officers in different countries in the areas related to her academic research and professional experience.

A Complete **Support Package**

CJ: Realities and Challenges includes a dynamic supplements program to meet the needs of both instructors and students.

Student Support:

The Online Learning Center (OLC) for students at **www.mhhe.com/masters1e** provides a wide range of study and assessment tools to reinforce comprehension of the text.

- **Self-quizzes.** Provides multiple-choice, true-false, and critical-thinking questions for each chapter.
- **Observe-Investigate-Understand.** Presents the key learning objectives for each chapter.
- **Careers and Internships.** Offers students additional information about a wide variety of careers in criminal justice and how to prepare for them.
- **Source Connection.** Links to source material for each chapter give the student an opportunity to explore individual cases more deeply.
- **Internet Exercises.** Provides research and interpretive activities associated with Internet sites related to criminal justice.

Instructor Support:

The Online Learning Center (OLC) for instructors at **www.mhhe.com/masters1e** provides teaching aids and tools to help leverage the classroom experience.

- **Instructor's Manual.** Written in partnership with the author team, this instructor's manual provides a comprehensive guide to teaching the introductory course using *CJ: Realities and Challenges*. Part 1 contains extensive materials about teaching the course, with portions tailored for new instructors as well as experienced instructors. Part 2 includes chapter guides that feature learning objectives, chapter previews and reviews, detailed outlines, lecture summaries, additional lecture ideas and class discussion topics.
- **Test Bank.** The Test Bank contains 70 multiple-choice questions per chapter, of which 20 are scenario-based. Each question includes a page reference and topic to tie it to specific sections of a given chapter. Each question is also categorized by level (Basic, Moderate, Difficult) and type (using the following categories of Bloom's Taxonomy: Knowledge, Comprehension, Analysis, Application). McGraw-Hill's computerized EZ Test allows you to create customized exams using the publisher's supplied test items or your own questions. You decide the number, type, and order of test questions with a few simple clicks. EZ Test runs on your computer without a connection to the Internet. A version of the test bank will also be provided in Microsoft Word files for those instructors who prefer this format.
- **PowerPoint Slides.** Two sets of PowerPoint slides provide instructors with dynamic lecture support. The primary set includes chapter outlines, key figures, and online links to supporting video clips such as those provided by NBC News. For those instructors who prefer to create their own lecture outlines, a second set of slides contains only the figures and video links for the text.

- **NBC video clips.** Over an hour's worth of video clips (each between 3–8 minutes long) from NBC news add realism to criminal justice issues and generate discussion. A set of critical thinking questions is provided for each clip to engage students in critical conversation.
- **Online Library of CJ Video Clips.** Instructors frequently request video clips to be used in their CJ classes. Using the Internet as a resource, we provide a dynamically updated annotated index of CJ-related video clips that can be viewed online. The list is organized both by chapter and topic.
- ***Reel Justice.*** *Reel Justice* is an interactive movie produced and distributed by McGraw-Hill for the criminal justice course. Using *Reel Justice*, you enter the world of a police officer and examine issues from an up-close and decision-making perspective. *Reel Justice* is available as a course supplement on CD-ROM and online.
- **Classroom Performance System (CPS).** The Classroom Performance System brings ultimate interactivity to *CJ: Realities and Challenges*. CPS is a wireless polling system that gives you immediate feedback from every student in the class. Use CPS to ask questions during your lecture that have been prepared by McGraw-Hill or enter your own questions. A complete CPS Tutorial is available at **www.einstruction.com.**
- **State Supplements.** A collection of useful background essays on the unique histories and development of laws in key states, including California, Texas, and Florida.
- **CourseSmart eTextbook option.** With the CourseSmart eTextbook version of this title, students can save up to 50% off the cost of a print book, reduce their impact on the environment, and access powerful web tools for learning. Faculty can also review and compare the full text online without having to wait for a print desk copy. CourseSmart is an online eTextbook, which means users need to be connected to the internet in order to access. Students can also print sections of the book for maximum portability. For further details contact your sales representative or go to **www.coursesmart.com**.
- **Course Management Systems.** Whether you use WebCT, Blackboard, e-College, or another course management system, McGraw-Hill will provide you with a *CJ: Realities and Challenges* cartridge that enables you either to conduct your course entirely online or to supplement your lectures with online material.

Contributors

The author team is very appreciative of all the hard work of the McGraw-Hill professionals who worked on this book. Our work is better for their assistance. We would also like to give special thanks to Phil Butcher for his support on this project. Above all, we thank the many contributors for their work in helping shape this text.

Manuscript Reviewers

MIKE ARDIS, Pensacola Jr College
THOMAS BABCOCK, University of Texas at San Antonio
SARAH BACON, Florida State University
ELAINE BARTGIS, University of Central Oklahoma
MICHAEL BISCIGLA, Southeastern Louisiana University
J. PETE BLAIR, University of Texas–San Marcos
MICHAEL BROWN, Ball State University
DIANA BRUNS, Bacone College
KEVIN BUCKLER, University of Texas at Brownsville and Texas Southmost College
DAVID CELESTE, Montgomery College–Rockville
CHARLES CHASTAIN, University of Arkansas at Little Rock
TERE CHIPMAN, Fayetteville Technical Community College
BELINDA CLIFTON, Brookline College
DEXTER CUMMINS, Antelope Valley College
THEODORE DARDEN, College of Dupage
DARIN A. DEFREECE, Sierra College
CLAUDINE RIGAUD DULANEY, Anthem Education Group
STEVE DUNKER, Northeastern State University
ROBERT DURAN, New Mexico State University

GARY EBELS, Grand Rapids Community College
EUGENE EVANS, Camden County College
RICHARD FINN, Western Nevada Community College
BILL FLYNN, Raritan Valley Community College
ALAN FRAZIER, Glendale Community College
HAROLD FROSSARD, Moraine Valley Community College
CRAIG GANSTER, University of Great Falls
ANDY GONIS, Santa Ana College
CHRISTOPHER GORSEK, Mount Hood Community College
CRAIG HEMMENS, Boise State University
VERNA HENSON, Texas State University–San Marcos
CHANG-HUN LEE, University of Arkansas at Little Rock
SHERI JENKINS-CRUZ, University of Southern Mississippi
PATRICIA JOFFER, South Dakota State University
RACHEL JUNG, Mesa Community College
LISA LANDIS, University of South Florida
TONY LAROSE, University of Tampa
SAMANTHA LEWIS, Miami Dade College
THOMAS MAHONEY, Santa Barbara City College
DAVID MARBLE, Collin College
LISA MCBRIDE, Tallahassee Community College
DORRICK MINNIS, Fresno City College
DAN MOESER, East Tennessee State University
KERRY L. MUEHLENBECK, Mesa Community College
ELVAGE MURPHY, Edinboro University (PA)
ELLYN K. NESS, Mesa Community College
ANGELA NICKOLI, Ball State University
RON OLSON, Glendale Community College
ANGELA ONDRUS, Owens Community College
GREGORY OSOWSKI, Henry Ford Community College
MICHAEL PAQUETTE, Middlesex County College
JUSTIN PATCHIN, University of Wisconsin–Eau Claire
BENJAMIN PEARSON-NELSON, Indiana University, Purdue
XAVIER FERNANDO PEREZ, University of Illinois at Chicago
REBECCA PETERSEN, Kennesaw State University
TERRY L. PIPPIN, College of Southern Nevada
NICKY PIQUERO, John Jay College
MICHAEL PITTARO, Cedar Crest College
STEPHEN POLAND, Ferris State University
WAYNE POSNER, East Los Angeles College
STEPHEN REINHART, Western Illinois University
JUDITH REVELS, University of South Florida
DEBRA ROSS, Grand Valley State University
PATTI SALINAS, University of Texas at Brownsville
SHANNON SANTANA, Florida International University
JIM SANTOR, College of Southern Nevada
JOSEPH SCHAFER, Southern Illinois University, Carbondale
WILLIAM SCOLLON, Middle Tennessee State University
WAYNE SEELY, Owens Community College
CHRISTOPHER SHARP, Valdosta State University
WILLIAM SHULMAN, Middle Tennessee State University
SANDRA SKOVRON, Ohio Dominican University
DOMENICK STAMPONE, Raritan Valley Community College
ADAM STEARN, Northeastern University
KEVIN STONE, Montgomery College
MATTHEW O. THOMAS, California State University, Chico
TRACY TOLBERT, California State University, Long Beach
SHARON TRACY, Georgia Southern University
ANGELIA TURNER, University of North Florida
ARNOLD WAGGONER, Rose State College
JAMES WINDELL, Wayne State University
JEFFREY ZACK, Fayetteville Technical Community College

Prospectus Reviewers

STEPHANIE CARMICHAEL, University of Florida
JOHN BROOK, Houston Community College
FRANK BUTLER, Temple University
HAROLD FROSSARD, Moraine Valley Community College
GENNIFER FURST, College of New Jersey
JOHN HAZY, Youngstown State University
CRAIG HEMMENS, Boise State University
PHILLIP HOLLEY, Southwest Oklahoma State
CHARIS KUBRIN, George Washington University
MATTHEW LEONE, University of Nevada–Reno
ELVAGE MURPHY, Edinboro University (PA)
KATHY OBORN, Pierce College (CA)
NICKY PIQUERO, University of Florida–Gainesville
MICHAEL POLAKOWSKI, University of Arizona
MARY ROLLE, Frederick Community College
TONY SMITH, Rowan University
RYAN SPOHN, Kansas State University
STANLEY SWART, University of North Florida
JOHN WHITEHEAD, East Tennessee State

"This text offers a balanced approach to criminal justice that encourages critical thinking."

–Alan Frazier,
Glendale Community College

Preface Reviewers

THOMAS BABCOCK, University of Texas at San Antonio
JOHN BOAL, University of Akron
DHRUBA J. BORA, Marshall University
DAVID CELESTE, Montgomery College–Rockville
STEVEN CHERMAK, Michigan State University
TERE CHIPMAN, Fayetteville Technical Community College
CHARISSE COSTON, University of North Carolina–Charlotte
JEFFREY CZARNEC, Hesser College
THEODORE DARDEN, College of DuPage
STEVE DUNKER, Northeastern State University
ROBERT DURAN, New Mexico State University
GARY EBELS, Grand Rapids Community College
EUGENE EVANS, Camden County College
JANINE FERRARO, Nassau Community College
ALAN FRAZIER, Glendale Community College
ARIC S. FRAZIER, Vincennes University
VERNA HENSON, Texas State University–San Marcos
PATRICIA JOFFER, South Dakota State University
RACHEL JUNG, Mesa Community College
SAMANTHA LEWIS, Miami Dade College
LI YING LI , Metro State College of Denver
JOEL MAATMAN, Lansing Community College
SHANA MAIER, Widener University
LISA MCBRIDE, Tallahassee Community College
DAN MOESER, East Tennessee State University
XAVIER FERNANDO PEREZ, University of Illinois at Chicago
TERRY PIPPIN, College of Southern Nevada–Henderson
JUDITH REVELS, University of South Florida
MANUEL ROMAN, Sierra College
DEBRA ROSS, Grand Valley State University
WAYNE SEELY, Owens Community College
SANDRA SKOVRON, Ohio Dominican University
DAVID WEDLICK, Westchester Community College
JOHN WYANT, Illinois Central College

"One of the major strengths of this manuscript is that it peppers the text with many important myths and realities. Furthermore, the writing is exceptional for a textbook."

–James Windell, Wayne State University

Design Reviewers

TOM ADAMS, Del Mar College
CHARLENE ALLEN, Middle Georgia College
LARRY ANDREWS, Missouri Western State University
THOMAS E. BAKER, University of Scranton
EARL BALLOU, Palo Alto College
ALLEN BARNES, University of Alaska Anchorage
MICHAEL BARRETT, Ashland University
ELAINE BARTGIS, University of Central Oklahoma
SUSAN BEECHER, Aims Community College
TODD BEITZEL, The University of Findlay
MICHAEL BISCIGLA, Southeastern Louisiana University
JOHN BOAL, University of Akron
LES BOGGESS, Fairmont State University
LINDA BOWLIN, Southeastern University
MICHAEL J. BOZEMAN, Mesa State College
GREGORY BRIDGEMAN, Hopkinsville Community College
SARAH BRITTO, Central Washington University
VALERIE BROWN, DeKalb Technical College
HARRY BRUNO, Albany State University & Bainbridge College
MARTHA CAMPBELL, Highland Community College
DAVID CARTER, Southern Oregon University
SAL CATERINA, Niagara County Community College
TIM CHESSER, Gateway Community & Technical College
ANTHONY CHIARLITTI, Pace University–Pleasantville
DAVID CHOATE, Arizona State University
LUCY CRAIG, Motlow State Community College
JAMES CUNNINGHAM, State Fair Community College
JEFFREY CZARNEC, Hesser College
BOB DAVIS, Edgecombe Community College
L. EDWARD DAY, Penn State Altoona
LEE DEBOER, Collin College
JEN DENNIS, Massasoit Community College
TOM DENT, Washington State Community College
JENNIFER DIERICKX, York College of Pennsylvania
KENNETH DONE, Coahoma Community College
THOMAS DRERUP, Clark State Community College
WAYNE DURKEE, Durham Technical Community College
MARTHA EARWOOD, University of Alabama–Birmingham
ROBERT EDDY, Charter Oak State College
SARAH ELHOFFER, St. Louis Community College–Meramec

LIZ ERICKSON, State University of New York at Canton
ELIZABETH ERVIN, Mississippi Valley State University
GREGG ETTER, University of Central Missouri
EUGENE EVANS, Camden County College
LAURA FIDELIE, Midwestern State University
BRANDY FINCH, Piedmont Technical College
IDA FLIPPO, Clackamas Community College
JAMES FORD, College of Saint Elizabeth
PRICE FOSTER, University of Louisville
JANET FOSTER GOODWILL, Yakima Valley Community College
ALAN FRAZIER, Glendale Community College
NATASHA FROST, Northeastern University
CRAIG GANSTER, University of Great Falls
JOHN GRAY, Faulkner University
MICHELE GRILLO, Nova Southeastern University
RANDOLPH GRINC, Caldwell College
MONICA HACK-POLKOSNIK, Herkimer County Community College
AMY HARRELL, Nash Community College
BRIAN HARTE, State University of New York at Canton
SAMANTHA HAUPTMAN, Piedmont Technical College
DANIEL HEBERT, Springfield Technical Community College
JAMES HOULIHAN, Lewis University
DENISE HUGGINS, Central State University
GG HUNT, Wharton County Junior College
MARTHA HURLEY, The Citadel
GERALD JARRETT, Shaw University
CATHERINE JENKS, University of West Georgia
ART JIPSON, University of Dayton
JEAN-GABRIEL JOLIVET, Southwestern College
RACHEL JUNG, Mesa Community College
GREGORY JUSTIS, University of Southern Indiana
STEPHAN KAFTAN, Hawkeye Community College
TRACY KAISER-GOEBEL, Manor College
MICHAEL KAUNE, St. Francis College
JOSEPH L. KIBITLEWSKI, Hodges University
LLOYD KLEIN, St. Francis College
DR. DAVID KOTAJARVI, Lakeshore Technical College
BETSY KREISEL, University of Central Missouri
THOMAS KUROWSKI, Community College of Rhode Island
LISA LANDIS, University of South Florida
BARNEY LEDFORD, Mid Michigan Community College
DAVID LEGERE, Newbury College
FRANK LEONARD, Tallahassee Community College
SAMANTHA LEWIS, Miami Dade College
ERIC LING, York College of Pennsylvania
TRAVIS LINNEMANN, Kansas State University
ROBERT LOUDEN, Georgian Court University
JOEL MAATMAN, Lansing Community College
SEAN MADDAN, University of Tampa
RICHARD MARTIN, Auburn University–Montgomery
MARY ELLEN MASTRORILLI, Boston University–Metropolitan College
CAROLYN McGOVERN, Central Texas College
JOHN MICHAUD, Husson University
MARK MILLER, East Texas Baptist University
DAN MOESER, East Tennessee State University
JACK MONELL, Central Piedmont Community College
ETTA MORGAN, Jackson State University
JANE K. MUNLEY, Luzerne County Community College
GARY NEUMEYER, Arizona Western College
DAVID NICHOLSON, University of Oklahoma
WALTER NIELIWOCKI, Greenfield Community College
MELANIE NORWOOD, Southeastern Louisiana University
TIMOTHY O'DEA, Marist College
PAUL ODEMS, Saint Johns University Queens/Kingsborough Community College
JODY O'GUINN, Lewis & Clark Community College
JAMES O'KEEFE, St. John's University
LYDIA OLSON, University of West Florida
MICHAEL PAQUETTE, Middlesex County College
STACY PARKER, Muskingum College

"The authors have captured the true meaning of the interdisciplinary approach . . . In doing so, one gets a clear sense of statistical reference, theoretical grounding, and substantive issues—all merging to give students a clearer sense of crime, criminal behavior, and the structure, policies, and practices that shape the criminal justice system in post-modern America."

–Tracy Tolbert,
California State University, Long Beach

DAN PARTRICH, MidAmerica Nazarene University
SUSANNE PASTUSCHEK, Crafton Hills Community College
RYAN PATTEN, California State University, Chico
THOMAS PAYNE, The University of Southern Mississippi
MONICA PEREZ, Holyoke Community College

Introductory Criminal Justice Symposium Attendees

MIKE ARDIS, Pensacola Junior College
JOHN AUGUSTINE, Triton College
JOHN BOAL, University of Akron
CHRISTOPHER CHAPMAN, Kingsborough Community College
CHARISSE COSTON, University of North Carolina–Charlotte
PATRICE DAVIS, Essex County College
FRANK DRUMMOND, Modesto Junior College
GARY EBELS, Grand Rapids Community College
PHILIP ETHERIDGE, University of Texas Pan American
RICHARD FINN, Western Nevada Community College
BILL FLYNN, Raritan Valley Community College
ARNETT GASTON, University of Maryland
DOUG HAYNES, Cerritos College
RICHARD KUITERS, Bergen Community College
LI YING LI, Metro State College of Denver
JEFF LONDON, Metro State College of Denver
MIRIAM LORENZO, Miami Dade College
SCOTT MIRE, University of Louisiana at Lafayette
ROSS OLMOS, Harper College
ANGELA ONDRUS, Owens Community College
TERRY PIPPIN, College of Southern Nevada–Henderson
TYRONE POWERS, Anne Arundel Community College
MANUEL ROMAN, Sierra College
KENNETH RYAN, California State University–Fresno
PATTI SALINAS, University of Texas of Brownsville
BILL SHULMAN, Middle Tennessee State University
WILLIAM SONDERVAN, University of Maryland–University College
RON SOPENOFF, Brookdale Community College
PAUL STRETESKY, Colorado State University
KATHRYN SULLIVAN, Hudson Valley Community College
CASEY WELCH, University of North Florida

Supplement Authors

GRACE A. TELESCO WolfBear Institute
Instructor's Manual, YouTubedia
TINA FREIBURGER, University of Wisconsin–Milwaukee
Test Bank, Classroom Performance System
CARLY HILINSKI, Indiana University of Pennsylvania
Test Bank
SAMANTHA LEWIS, Miami Dade College: North Campus
Test Bank
KALIOPI PAPPAS, San Joaquin Delta Community College
Test Bank

Supplement Reviewers

DHRUBA J. BORA, Marshall University
KIMBERLY DETARDO-BORA, Marshall University
GREGG ETTER, University of Central Missouri
BILL FLYNN, Raritan Valley Community College
ARNETT GASTON, University of Maryland
SHANA MAIER, Widener University
TYRONE POWERS, Anne Arundel Community College
DEBRA ROSS, Grand Valley State University
WILLIAM SONDERVAN, University of Maryland–University College

CHAPTER 1

What Is the Criminal Justice System?

OBSERVE Investigate *Understand*

After reading this chapter, you should be able to:

- Illustrate how social norms help us define crime.
- Define crime and explain how it is classified.
- Describe the consequences of crime for the offender and the victim.
- Outline the basic structure of the criminal justice system.
- Describe key models for the workings of the criminal justice system.
- Review the challenges to the criminal justice system today.
- Describe how criminal justice is influenced by public opinion, the media, politics, and policy.

Realities and Challenges

One Man's Journey through the Criminal Justice System

As murders go, it was not remarkable. Twenty-year-old Frederick Hollman was recruited by an older friend to help him "pay back" someone he thought was cheating him. They lured the victim to a desolate road on New York's Long Island on the pretense of buying drugs. While Frederick restrained the victim with a rope, his friend stabbed him multiple times and dumped him out of the car.[1]

The victim managed to reach a house for help and on the way to the hospital, moments before he died, was able to tell the police that "Rick and another guy did it." With this clue, the law enforcement officers were able to track down "Rick" and arrest him. Frederick, meanwhile, had gone to the local police department to claim he was a witness. The detectives questioning him soon determined that Frederick (a.k.a. "Rick") was, in fact, an accomplice in the murder and arrested him.[2]

Within a day Frederick was taken before a judge and charged with second degree murder; soon after that a grand jury indicted him (that is, decided the evidence was sufficient for him to be held under arrest and tried by a jury). Because he could not afford bail, Frederick was confined in a local jail until his jury trial date, nearly a year later. The jury in his trial found him guilty as charged. The prosecutors asked the judge for the maximum sentence of 25 years to life. The judge agreed. Frederick is now in a maximum security prison in New York serving his term and hoping that years from now good behavior in prison will allow him out early to live in the community under supervision of a parole officer.[3]

Police, detectives, victim advocates, judges, lawyers, prosecutors, jurors, correctional officers, parole officers—these are the people who Frederick, the victim and his family, and millions of other offenders, victims, and their families deal with when interacting with the criminal justice system. It is a complex and sometimes lumbering machine, as it tackles the job of taking criminals off the street, ensuring a fair trial, protecting society, and punishing and attempting to rehabilitate offenders.

Of course, there are challenges to match the complexity. Have the police followed proper procedures? Have the victims been treated fairly, and do they understand their rights? Have the prosecutors shared all the relevant evidence with the defending lawyers? Was the jury trial a fair one? What role did the victim and/or the victim's family play in the criminal justice process? Were due process rights protected? Was the sentencing appropriate for the offense? Has the offender been mistreated in prison? Are there opportunities to rehabilitate? Has parole been granted (or denied) in a fair manner? There are many points at which justice may be either served or derailed.

We hope that you, our readers, will learn to think critically about the realities and challenges of the world of criminal justice. We want to help you interpret facts and recognize myths about the criminal justice system so you will have a greater understanding and appreciation of its complexities. We hope you come to understand how the roles of offenders, protectors, and victims are interwoven in a system dedicated to detecting those who violate the rules, determining their guilt, and carrying out an appropriate punishment. We begin in this chapter with a brief exploration of the nature of rules whose violations constitute crime and an introduction to how the criminal justice system is structured and works.

THE RULES THAT BIND: NORMS AND LAWS

Preview

MYTH/REALITY

MYTH: Some behaviors are so wrong that they are crimes in all societies.

REALITY: It is not the nature of an act that makes that act a crime; it is the nature of society that defines a particular act as a crime in that society.

A **norm** is a rule that makes clear what behavior is appropriate and expected in a particular situation. If, for example, it is the norm to arrive at meetings on time, being late violates the norm. The term *abnormal* connotes **deviance**, the violation of a norm. (The prefix "ab" means "away from," so abnormal means "away from the norm."). No behavior is inherently deviant—that is, deviant solely by virtue of its nature. Rather, whether a particular act is considered deviant depends on many factors, including context, place, time, and who is judging it.

Let's consider how a behavior's deviance depends on the context in which it occurs. For example, if you were to spit on 42nd Street in New York City, people might frown at you, but you would not be arrested for it. But if you were to spit in the subway, just under the street, you would be violating a formal regulation of the New York City Transit Authority and could face criminal prosecution in a municipal court. The fact that each week 7 million people pass through the close quarters of the subway system makes hygiene a factor in determining what is deviant in that situation.

Our ideas of deviance also change over time. For example, before the 1970s, being divorced conferred the status of deviant in society. In contrast, today's social norms recognize divorce as acceptable behavior. In other words, there is nothing inherently deviant in getting divorced: society found it deviant until the 1970s, then our attitudes changed.

Norms vary from place to place as well. In Eastern Europe, men greet other men with kisses on the cheek. In the United States this behavior is considered unusual. The Global View box shows how norms about parental behavior can vary from one country to another. Norms also vary from group to group within a society. While some may consider being covered in tattoos deviant, it is the norm within many gangs and among professional athletes.

A **social norm** specifies how people are expected to behave. Informal social norms are social rules that are not written but that we nonetheless know and follow. We learn them from parents, peers, and teachers. In North American society, informal social norms include waiting your turn in line to purchase tickets at a movie theater and not eating mashed potatoes with your fingers.

Formal social norms, also called legal norms, are formally written. Formal norms forbid theft and assault, for instance. Although not all deviance from norms constitutes a crime, violation of formal norms, or laws, sets the criminal justice system in motion. In fact, informal social

norm
A rule that makes clear what behavior is appropriate and expected in a particular situation.

deviance
The violation of a norm.

social norm
A rule that specifies how people are expected to behave.

◀ **Tattoos: Sign of Deviance or Body Art?**

Some groups may consider tattoos a sign of deviance; for others, including many professional athletes, tattoos are a normal means of expression.

▲ Spitting in the subway is a crime that violates a formal regulation of the New York City Transit Authority.

A Global View

Social Norms Differ from Denmark to the United States

Social norms commonly practiced in one locale may not only be unacceptable but illegal in another, as a mother from Denmark discovered. In May 1997, Annette Sorenson, a 30-year-old Danish actress, was pushing her 14-month-old baby daughter in a stroller along the streets of New York City. Sorensen and Exavier Wardlaw, the baby's father, decided to have a drink inside a restaurant and left the baby in the stroller directly outside the establishment. The child was unattended but could easily be seen by the parents from where they sat inside the restaurant.

In the mother's home country of Denmark, it is a common and acceptable practice for adults to leave a baby outside a restaurant or store. They believe that it is good for the baby to get fresh air. This Danish social norm is not only unacceptable in the United States, it is a crime. In New York, those inside the restaurant and walking along the sidewalk were so outraged by the unattended infant in the stroller that the police were called. When the police arrived and located the parents, Sorensen was arrested for endangering the welfare of the child. The baby's father was charged with child endangerment and disorderly conduct.

The charges were eventually dismissed, but the case set off a lengthy legal battle between the parents and the City of New York when the parents sued the city for false arrest. In 1999, a federal jury in Manhattan heard the case and the mother's protests that leaving a baby unattended in a stroller was a common practice in her country. Unmoved by the mother's explanations, the jury rejected the false arrest claim, believing that the police acted in good faith to protect the safety and well-being of an unattended child. The jury further ruled that although the parents were strip-searched by the police, both were entitled to only $1 in damages because they were not falsely arrested. The jury did award Sorensen an additional $66,400 in compensatory and punitive damages because of police actions after her arrest: specifically, police failed to advise her of her right to call the Danish Consulate for assistance. This case highlights how the same action can have very different consequences in different countries.

▲ Annette Sorensen

OBSERVE Investigate Understand

- Should the charges against the parents have been dropped?
- If you were at the restaurant, would you have called the police about the unattended infant? What is your reasoning?
- Were the parents justified in suing the City of New York? Why or why not?

SOURCE: Weiser, B., "Danish Mother's Claim of False Arrest Is Rejected." *New York Times*, December 15, 1999, http://query.nytimes.com/gst/fullpage.html?res=9B03E1D91F31F936A25751C1A96F958260 (retrieved December 22, 2008).

norms can evolve into legal norms. Because it is laws that determine what crimes are, we need to take a closer look at how these legal norms come about.

WHAT IS CRIME?

What constitutes crime? The answer to this question is not as obvious as it may seem. Certainly, a crime is an act that breaks a law. But this description, though concise, does not help us understand the complexity of classifying criminal behavior.

MYTH/REALITY

MYTH: People are either criminal or not.

REALITY: Virtually all people commit crimes at some point in their lives. Whether we consider them criminals depends largely on what offenses they commit.[4]

mala in se
A behavior categorized as morally wrong ("evil in itself").

Experts commonly distinguish two broad categories of crime: *mala in se* and *mala prohibita* crimes.

Can Crimes Be Inherently Wrong?

A crime is referred to as ***mala in se*** if it is categorized, as its Latin name suggests, as an "evil unto itself," a behavior that is morally wrong. This definition implies that a given behavior would be wrong in any context, even if there were no law against it. However, just as there is no such thing as an inherently deviant act, there is no such thing as an inherently criminal act. Society creates crime in the same way it creates deviance—by labeling specific behaviors as such. Thus, behaviors considered criminal in one country may be not only legal in another country but the norm, as we saw in the Global View box.

Because no behavior is criminal until society makes it so, distinguishing a category of crime as *mala in se* can be confusing. We discuss this category of crime here because it is a term often used by researchers and practitioners in the field of criminal justice.

Traditionally, *mala in se* offenses are seen as a violation of a basic universal social value. On the surface, it may seem reasonable to identify acts such as forcible rape as violating some universal code of morality. But no universal social code of justice exists. For example, historically the victim of a sexual assault was not considered the woman herself but rather her husband, father, or brother. What about the Victim? illustrates that the definition of sexual assault crimes is influenced not only by time period but also by the understanding of the victim and her relationship to the perpetrator.

Crimes Prohibited by Law

Mala prohibita crimes, also known as **statutory crimes**, are acts that are criminal because they are prohibited by law. *Mala prohibita* crimes reflect public opinion at a particular moment in time. As standards of social tolerance change, so do the behaviors included in this category.

Laws against adultery provide a case in point. Historically, when a married person had consensual sexual relations with someone outside the marriage, the punishment could be death. Under some laws today, such as strict Islamic law (known as Shariah), adulterers can still be executed. Although adultery remains illegal in many countries today, penalties are relatively minor and are rarely enforced.

What motivates a society to criminalize some behaviors and not others? Two predominant points of view about how crimes become defined capture the essence of this divergence: the consensus perspective and the conflict perspective.

What about the Victim?

Spousal Exemption Laws

In the United States prior to the 1970s, rape was defined as forced or coerced sexual intercourse with a female who was not the defendant's wife. If two people were married, it was assumed that all sexual intercourse between them was consensual, regardless of whether force or coercion occurred. As a result of this spousal exemption from the definition of rape, it was not illegal for a husband to force sexual intercourse on his wife; he could do so without fear of violating the law.

The legal roots of the spousal exemption go back to seventeenth-century England, when Chief Justice Sir Matthew Hale stated that mutual consent was part of the matrimonial contract. According to Hale, the woman gave herself to her husband and did not have the right to refuse his sexual advances. These sentiments remained in place until the 1970s, when the women's rights movement called for a change in the legal definition of rape, removal of the spousal exemption, and equal treatment of all rape victims regardless of marital status. The fight for removal of the spousal exemption continued for more than 20 years; marital rape did not become a crime in all 50 states until 1993.

Thirty states still have partial spousal exemptions for situations in which the wife cannot give consent because she is intoxicated or unconscious, has a mental and/or physical impairment, or is asleep. The legal reasoning is that if the wife is in a state in which she cannot consent, this does not mean she would not have consented. Thus, when the victim is most vulnerable, the law does not protect her because she is married to the perpetrator.

Victims of spousal rape can suffer physical, psychological, and mental scars just like any rape victim. In fact, the closer the relationship between victim and perpetrator, the more difficult the victim's trauma and recovery can be. But because the violation is often prosecuted as a lesser crime, or not prosecuted at all, these rape victims are not treated equally under the law.

Observe Investigate Understand

- **What behaviors, if any, should be understood as part of the marriage contract?**
- **Is partial spousal exemption wrong in all circumstances? In what situations, if any, might it be justified?**
- **What would have to happen for any of the partial spousal exemption states to change their law?**

SOURCES: Raquel Kennedy Bergen, "Marital Rape: New Research and Directions." Applied Research Forum: National Online Resource Center on Violence Against Women, February 2006, http://new.vawnet.org/Assoc_Files_VAWnet/AR_Marital RapeRevised.pdf (retrieved January 3, 2009); Sheryl Grana, *Women and (In)Justice* (Boston, MA: Allyn and Bacon, 2002).

mala prohibita
A statutory crime that reflects public opinion at a moment in time.

statutory crime
An act that is criminal because it is prohibited by law.

Consensus and Conflict Perspectives

consensus perspective
A view of crime that sees laws as the product of social agreement or consensus about what criminal behavior is.

conflict perspective
A view of crime as one outcome of a struggle among different groups competing for resources in their society.

The **consensus perspective** of crime views laws defining crime as the product of social agreement or consensus about what criminal behavior is. Criminals are individuals whose behavior expresses values and beliefs at odds with those of mainstream society. For example, they rob banks while most of us work for a living. Laws, as the product of social consensus, promote solidarity: "We're all together on this." In this perspective, murder is a crime because it violates a consensus belief in the sanctity of life. We agree that killing is wrong, so we criminalize this act. Those who subscribe to the consensus perspective believe that defining some behaviors as criminal is necessary (or functional) because it is in everyone's interest to control those who deviate.

The **conflict perspective**, on the other hand, views the definition of crime as one outcome of a struggle among different groups competing for resources in society. The people who own and control the resources of society (land, power, money) are able to influence those who determine what laws are passed. Rather than looking at individual wrongdoers to understand crime, the conflict perspective looks at the process that determines who is a criminal and who is not. It asks, for example, why we apply more law enforcement resources to the bank robber than to the stockbroker who steals millions of dollars through insider trading on Wall Street.

The conflict perspective holds that laws are influenced and created by those who control the political and economic power within the society. The unequal distribution of resources in society generates competition and, hence, conflict among the groups vying for power. The Disconnects box illustrates how powerful corporate interests may have aided, if not been largely responsible for, passage of laws prohibiting marijuana use. An overview of marijuana's long and complicated history reveals that nothing about the nature of the act itself makes marijuana use a crime. But whether laws against it are consensus or conflict based is a matter of debate. Is using marijuana illegal because we agree it should be (consensus model) or because powerful interests are served by making it so (conflict model)? Or do both models apply?

Source Connection
SPOUSAL EXEMPTION LAW

www.ncvc.org/ncvc/main.aspx?dbName=DocumentViewer&DocumentID=32701

For more information on the history of the spousal exemption law, read "Spousal Rape Laws: 20 Years Later," from the National Center for Victims of Crime.

The conflict perspective is well illustrated in the case of vagrancy laws in England.[5] Vagrancy laws were passed in the fourteenth century to prevent peasants from leaving the employ of wealthy landowners to seek independent work in neighboring towns. Because it took time to develop a trade and become established in the towns, peasants who wandered would, at least initially, lack any apparent means of support. Laws defining unemployed wanderers as vagrants targeted those peasants. Given the choice of being imprisoned for vagrancy or returning to the landowners, many returned to work the land.

Vagrancy laws served the interest of the wealthy by preserving the status quo and their position of power and privilege. Such laws could also, however, be seen as a protection for society because the wandering unemployed would eventually have to commit crimes to support themselves.

Source Connection
U.S. MARIJUANA LAWS

www.druglibrary.org/Schaffer/LIBRARY/studies/vlr/vlrtoc.htm

For more information about the history of marijuana laws in the United States, please read Richard J. Bonnie and Charles H. Whitehead II, "The Forbidden Fruit and the Tree of Knowledge: An Inquiry Into the Legal History of American Marijuana Prohibition," *Virginia Law Review* 56, no. 6 (October 1970), 971–1203.

Using the evolution of vagrancy laws as a model can help us understand many of today's laws in the United States. Most of our laws and the resources of the criminal justice system focus on "crime in the streets," at the expense of attention to corporate crime and government corruption, the so-called crime in the suites, which costs society billions of dollars each year. Like the wealthy landowners of feudal England, today's large corporations get their interests translated into laws. Those who come to be identified as "criminals" are often, like the peasants of medieval society, those who lack power and wealth.

The basis for a particular law also may change over time. For example, we could argue that laws against theft were initially consistent with the conflict model because the will of the more powerful "haves" dictated the passage of laws against theft to protect their own property. The "have-nots" had less in the way of material goods and tended to be the ones identified as the criminals. With the passage of time and a decrease in the previously massive disparity in economic well-being, however, most people came to a consensus about laws against theft.

DIS Connects

Evolution of Marijuana Laws

The evolution of marijuana laws illustrates that laws are mere social constructions that change as we and our social landscape change.

In the United States from the mid-1800s until 1937, marijuana was largely a medicinal drug legally available by prescription. Few knew it as a recreational drug beyond the Mexican American communities close to the Mexican border. Growing anti-Mexican sentiment in various regions of the country spread fear of Mexicans bringing their "loco weed" into the United States and fueled the call for marijuana prohibition. Legislation proposed to control marijuana cited its alleged harmful effects. In fact, the Commissioner of the Federal Bureau of Narcotics, Harry Anslinger, testified before Congress that "marijuana is an addictive drug that produces in its users insanity, criminality, and death." Such claims made it appear marijuana laws would be for the good of the whole society—reflecting a consensus view.

But there was a conflict view at work as well. Powerful corporate interests joined the crusade against marijuana when they recognized that hemp—the plant from which the drug is derived—could be used to make textiles and paper, thereby posing a threat to already established U.S. industries. Fears of the economic potential of the hemp plant—not its psychoactive properties—largely fueled calls for passage of the Marijuana Tax Act of 1937. Under this law, anyone who imported, distributed, or sold marijuana was required to register with the Internal Revenue Service and pay a prohibitive tax. Although the act did not outlaw marijuana, it made it virtually impossible for anyone legally to have anything to do with the drug.

OBSERVE Investigate Understand

- **In what ways did the laws against marijuana reflect a consensus perspective? In what ways did they represent a conflict perspective?**
- **What might make the campaign against marijuana different from campaigns against other recreational drugs, such as cocaine?**
- **Do you think a tax is a better way to control marijuana use than a law against it? State your reasons.**

SOURCES: John Galliher, David Keys, and Michael Elsner, "*Lindesmith v. Anslinger:* An Early Government Victory in the Failed War on Drugs," *Journal of Criminal Law and Criminology* 88 (Winter 1988): 66; Richard Bonnie and Charles Whitehead, *The Marijuana Conviction: A History of Marijuana Prohibition in the United States* (New York: Lindesmith Center, 1999).

THE CONSEQUENCES OF CRIME

Sanctions

There is no sense in having rules if there are no consequences for those who break them. **Sanctions** are prescribed consequences intended to reinforce people's conformity to norms; they can be positive or negative. Although we are well acquainted with the rationale behind punishing bad behavior, we tend not to associate the term *sanction* with rewards for good

sanctions
Prescribed consequences intended to reinforce people's conformity to norms.

behavior. In fact, positive sanctions for behaving appropriately can be just as effective—if not more so—in shaping people's behavior to conform as negative sanctions for deviance. Rewarding an ex-convict's efforts to learn to read and write, for example, may prove more effective in changing his criminal ways than sending him to jail a second time.

Sanctions can be formal or informal. For example, someone who behaves badly in public is likely to be met with disapproving glances, an informal response designed to encourage the deviant to cease and desist. Even though informal sanctions generally do not carry the weight of their formal counterparts, they can have a major impact on behavior.

Our criminal justice system delivers a range of formal negative sanctions in response to criminal behavior. If the crime is relatively minor—say, driving 10 miles per hour over the speed limit—the offender may be given a fine. A criminal infraction of a more serious nature—vandalizing a park—is likely to be sanctioned by a harsher penalty such as probation, which restricts personal freedom by requiring regular meetings with a probation officer and avoidance of drugs, alcohol, and other people on probation. For more serious crimes—such as robbery or assault—the court may set a term of incarceration. Prison inmates are removed from society and deprived of their liberty. For the most serious crimes, in 35 states the offender can be executed.[6]

We have discussed the formal and informal sanctions that offenders face as consequences of their criminal behavior. As would be expected, victims also suffer consequences from criminal behavior; however, often these consequences are not as well understood given our criminal justice system's focus on offenders.

Impact of Crime on Victims

Victims are the targets of illegal actions by others. As a result of those illegal actions, victims suffer physical, sexual, or emotional injury, death, or a combination of ills.

More often than not, criminals and their victims are of the same race and in the same age range, live in the same neighborhood, belong to the same socioeconomic strata, and, with the important exception of rapists and most of their victims, are the same sex. Victims tend to occupy the same social space as do offenders. Would-be criminals notice the victims' vulnerabilities, seize the opportunity, and commit a crime.[7]

Victims are often neglected and even abused by the criminal justice system, making their suffering significantly worse. Some become fearful and less willing to cooperate with the prosecution. It is normal to want to avoid pain. That is why many victims choose not to report their crime, not to cooperate with criminal justice officials, or not to serve as key witnesses.

The plight of victims gave rise to the victim rights movement (see Chapter 14). This movement began to have an effect on the criminal justice system, initiating reforms in the early 1970s. As a result, victims are being treated better and can receive compensation for their injuries and losses. Most suffer fewer hardships and recover more quickly from monetary losses. However, much remains to be done before all victims are treated with the respect, dignity, and care they deserve.

THE STRUCTURE OF THE CRIMINAL JUSTICE SYSTEM

criminal justice system
The interrelation of law enforcement agencies, the courts, the correctional system, and victim services.

As we saw at the beginning of the chapter, the **criminal justice system** consists of a wide array of actors and agencies. The major institutional components of the traditional criminal justice system include law enforcement, the judiciary, and corrections. A contemporary view of the system also considers victim services as an emerging component of the system because of the collaborative effort to incorporate victim services into law enforcement agencies, the courts, and corrections (see Figure 1-1). Generally, we think of law enforcement as kicking off the process of the administration of justice, the courts deciding guilt and punishment, and correctional agencies carrying out that punishment. Victim services,

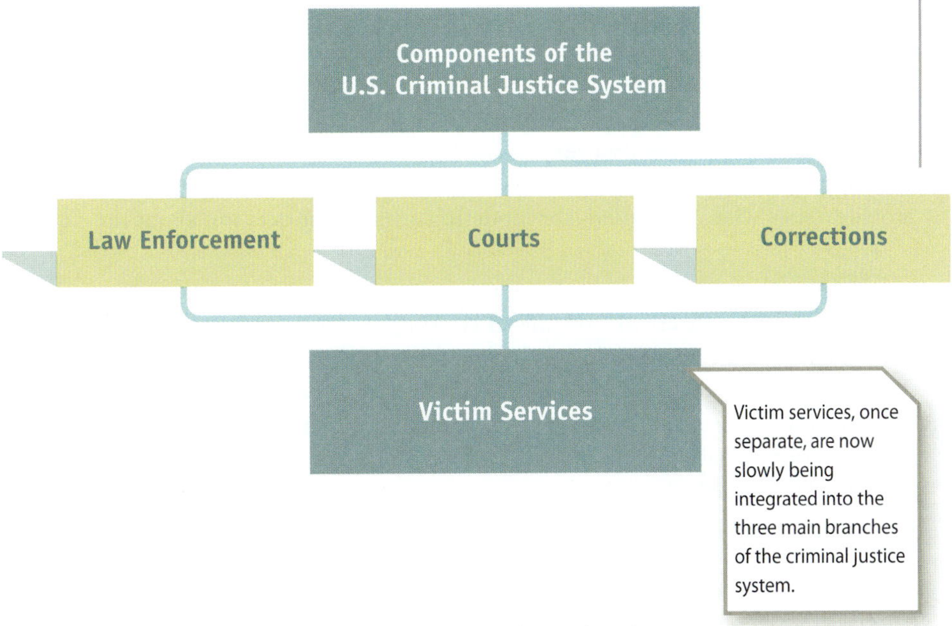

FIGURE 1-1 Components of the U.S. Criminal Justice System

although not traditionally considered a major branch of the criminal justice system, are an important determinant of whether justice is served. The criminal justice system is the sum of all these parts and more.

Law Enforcement

The part of the criminal justice system familiar to most U.S. citizens is law enforcement. From childhood, we can identify a police officer and an officer's car and understand the basic functions of the police—to protect the community and arrest the criminal.

But realistically, the police are called upon to do far more than protect and arrest. They are dispatched to deal with a host of matters ranging from the mundane (checking on the security of a home while the owner is traveling, or writing a traffic ticket), to the bizarre (finding ghosts in a home), to the most serious (homicide), and nearly any imaginable incident in between. Law enforcement officers are expected to resolve many of society's problems and are entrusted to use force only when necessary. Ideally, they make decisions quickly, use discretion, show courage and sacrifice in the face of danger, and treat individuals with dignity and respect even when threatened, harassed, abused, or assaulted.[8]

In recent years, police responsibilities have moved into the educational setting as school resource officers and educators raise awareness about crime, drugs, and prevention. Community-based initiatives have tried to foster a more collaborative relationship between police and citizens to address crime control and prevention.[9]

Courts

The United States has a dual court system made up of **state courts** and **federal courts.** As their names suggest, crimes against state laws are prosecuted in state courts and crimes violating federal statutes in the federal court. State courts differ from state to state, but all have trial courts and appellate courts, where cases can be appealed. The federal system consists of district courts (comparable to the state trial courts), appellate courts or circuit courts where appeals are heard, and the Supreme Court (see Chapter 9).

state courts
The system in which state crimes are prosecuted; it includes both trial and appellate courts.

federal courts
The system in which federal crimes are prosecuted consisting of district courts, appellate courts or circuit courts, and the Supreme Court.

▼ **School Resource Officer with Elementary School Students**

corrections
The systematic, organized effort by society to punish offenders, protect the public, and change an offender's behavior.

alternative sentence
A sentence that is served in a treatment facility or in community service.

probation
An alternative to jail or prison in which the offender remains in the community under court supervision, usually within the caseload of a probation officer.

parole
An early release from prison conditional on complying with certain standards while free.

victim services
The promotion of victims' rights to participate in criminal proceedings and to enjoy personal safety; services include shelters and transitional housing programs, counseling services, and 24-hour hotlines.

Within each of these settings a prosecutor first decides whether to prosecute a case. If so, he or she presents the case against the defendant on behalf of the state or federal government. A grand jury decides whether a case should go to trial. The prosecutor is then responsible for arguing that case at trial. Defense attorneys, hired by a client or assigned by the court, protect the legal rights of the defendant. If the case goes to trial, the defendant is entitled to fair and proper procedures. Finally, judges are the arbiters in the courtroom and are responsible for ensuring that the rules of evidence and law are not violated. They also provide a jury with instructions for rendering a verdict or decision about the case.

Corrections

Corrections is the systematic, organized effort by society to punish offenders, protect the public, and change an offender's behavior. These efforts are realized through programs, services, and facilities that deal with the offender before and after conviction. The purpose of corrections is to achieve the goals of sentencing, which include retribution, deterrence, incapacitation, rehabilitation, (re)integration, and restitution (see Chapter 11).

Once convicted of a crime, offenders may be imprisoned or serve their sentences under supervision within the community while on probation. An offender also may be given an **alternative sentence** that can be served in a treatment facility or carried out in community service. **Probation** is an alternative to jail or prison in which the offender remains in the community under court supervision, usually within the caseload of a probation officer. Offenders who have been sent to prison can be freed on **parole**, an early release based on complying with certain standards while free. A parole officer supervises the offender, who can be sent back to prison if he violates the terms or conditions of the parole (see Chapter 13).

When most people think of corrections and the corrections system, they think of the prison system. The general practice of using imprisonment as punishment for crime is less than two centuries old. The Bureau of Justice Statistics of the U.S. Department of Justice reported that as of midyear 2008 almost 2.4 million prisoners were held in federal or state prisons or in local jails. If we add in the number of individuals on probation and parole, the total number of people under correctional supervision as of midyear 2008 was 7.2 million.[10]

▼ Demonstration for Victim Rights

The victim rights movement began in the 1970s and pushed for more involvement of the victim in the criminal justice process.

Victim Services

Until the late twentieth century, the U.S. criminal justice system focused primarily on the criminal rather than the victim. Since the 1970s, under pressure from the law-and-order movement, the civil rights movement, the women's movement, and other victim-oriented coalitions, the pendulum began to swing the other way. The promotion of victims' rights to participate in criminal proceedings and to enjoy personal safety contributed to the formation of an array of **victim services** inside and outside the criminal justice system, including shelters and transitional housing programs, counseling services, and 24-hour hotlines.[11]

Other services focus on the legal needs of the victim, including the appointment of a **victim advocate** to assist the victim with every aspect of the postvictimization period, from the initial crisis and investigation through case adjudication and ultimately to the offender's release. Two important goals of victim services are to lessen victims' suffering and to facilitate their recovery.

Today, victim advocates work in nonprofit organizations and in all sectors of the criminal justice system. Some work within the system in the district attorney's office, others are in victim/witness units within probation departments, and still others are part of special units in police departments or within correctional institutions.[12] When victims are also family members of the offender, legal services are available to assist with divorce and custody concerns, supervised visitation requests, orders of protection, and mediation.[13]

Victim services may also include helping victims apply for victim compensation and write **victim impact statements** about how their victimization affected them. These statements are generally read in open court prior to sentencing and at probation and parole hearings. In other cases, victim advocates work with **secondary victims** or witnesses to help them cope with the victimization of a loved one. Victim services also include removing a dependent individual from a violent environment and conducting site visits at the new location, assisting victims to obtain a job, and a host of other activities to ensure that victims are able to live a life free of the violence they once experienced.[14]

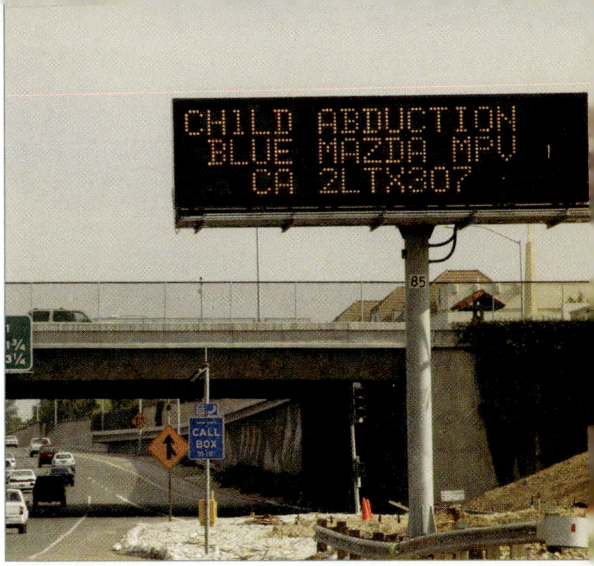

RealCrime Tech

AMBER ALERT SYSTEM

The U.S. Department of Justice created the Amber Alert program to foster partnership between law enforcement agencies, transportation agencies, and broadcast and wireless companies. The goal of the program is to return missing children to their caregivers by widely broadcasting information that would help recover the children. Information such as a description of the suspect's car can be scrolled across electronic highway signs and television screens. The Amber Alert program has been used in the successful recovery of more than 400 missing children.

SOURCE: United States Department of Justice, Office of Justice Programs. "Amber Alert," www.amberalert.gov/index.htm (retrieved January 3, 2009).

HOW CRIMINAL JUSTICE WORKS: THE REALITIES

There are a variety of explanations for—and debates about—how the criminal justice system works in reality rather than its theoretical ideal, or how it *should* work. This section outlines some of those explanations and debates.

MYTH/REALITY

MYTH: Almost all criminal cases go to trial.

REALITY: A high percentage of cases drop out of the criminal justice system without ever getting to trial or before a trial is complete.[15]

If every case were to go to a trial, the criminal justice system would collapse from the overload. There has to be a filtering of cases. All criminal justice professionals have a high level of discretion and can filter out cases along the way. For example, a police officer can decide not to arrest someone who has committed a crime. A prosecutor can decide not to charge someone the police arrested. A judge can dismiss a case. When any of those decisions are made, the suspect drops out of the criminal justice process. A guilty plea by a suspect keeps the offender within the system but also results in no need for a trial.

The result of such discretionary decisions by both criminal justice professionals and suspects creates what is often referred to as the *criminal justice funnel.* Many people begin the process by being arrested, but many fewer ultimately go to trial or are sentenced (see Figure 1-2).

Some people use the **wedding cake model** to help explain why some cases make it through the funnel and some do not. Figure 1-3 depicts the four different layers of the criminal justice wedding cake. The vast majority of cases, about 90 percent, are contained within the base of the cake, Layer 4. These offenses are largely misdemeanor and infraction cases. Misdemeanor cases are those that can result in a sentence of one year incarceration or less, probation, or other alternative sentences. Infractions are even more minor offenses, such as traffic violations. These cases are generally considered not serious or worth much of the system's time. The focus in this layer is to minimize the amount of resources expended on these cases. To that end, there is a very high level of guilty pleas in exchange for lenient treatment.

The next three layers account for the other 10 percent of cases. Layer 3 includes felony cases of a less serious nature (such as car theft) or ones in which the defendant has not previously had trouble with the law. These cases are also dispatched with rather quickly. The system starts slowing down with Layer 2. This tier includes serious felonies. Here you would find murder cases, defendants with many prior offenses, and cases that include

victim advocate
A professional who assists the victim with every aspect of the postvictimization period.

victim impact statement
A victim's statement about how his experiences with crime affected him.

secondary victims
Family and friends of an individual who has been victimized.

wedding cake model
An explanation of the workings of the criminal justice system that shows how cases get filtered according to the seriousness of the offense.

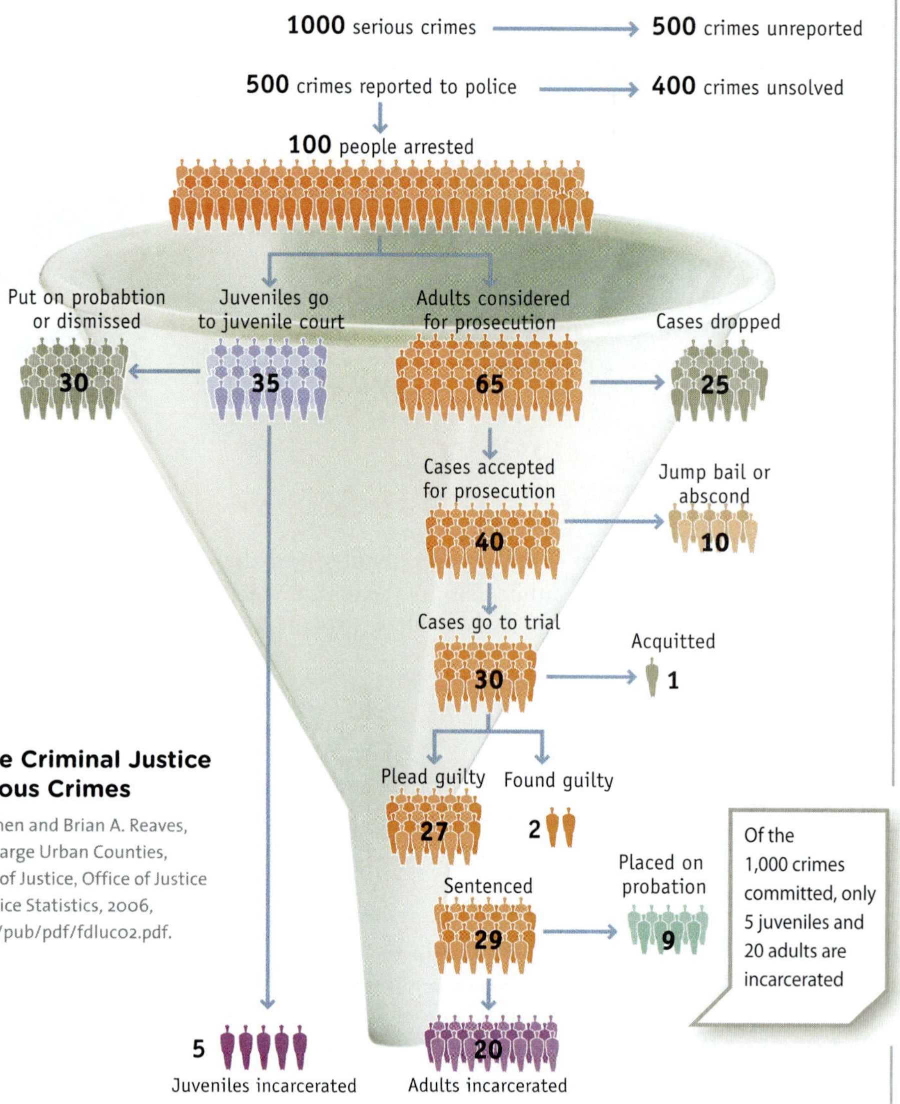

FIGURE 1-2 The Criminal Justice Funnel and Serious Crimes

SOURCE: Thomas H. Cohen and Brian A. Reaves, "Felony Defendants in Large Urban Counties, 2002." US. Department of Justice, Office of Justice Progress, Bureau of Justice Statistics, 2006, www.ojp.usdoj.gov/bis/pub/pdf/fdluco2.pdf.

Source Connection

SERIAL KILLERS

www.nydailynews.com/news/us_world/2008/07/09/2008-07-09_dont_put_all_serial_killers_in_same_box.html

The article "Don't Put All Serial Killers in the Same Box" provides more information about serial killers, including Gary Ridgway.

crime control model
A model of the criminal justice system that emphasizes the efficient arrest and processing of alleged criminal offenders.

due process model
A model of the criminal justice system that emphasizes individual rights at all stages of the justice process.

victims who were strangers to their perpetrators. The criminal justice system regards all of these situations as serious, and they are more likely to result in trials than the cases in either Layers 4 or 3.

The top of the cake, Layer 1, includes the very few cases that are considered celebrated cases, such as serial killings. They garner the most media attention. They may or may not involve celebrities, but the defendant in the case generally becomes a household name. These cases almost always involve a long trial, unless the defendant strikes a plea bargain. For example, Gary Ridgway, known as the Green River Killer, spared himself the risk of the death penalty by pleading guilty to killing 48 women in Washington state. Law enforcement believes he killed many more women, and Ridgway himself claims to have killed 90 or more.

The wedding cake model reminds us that most cases do not get the attention or resources spent on them that the high profile cases do. The system does not really work as TV shows like *Law and Order* would have viewers believe. Justice is usually not swift, and some worry that it is not deliberate enough. People who see the criminal justice system that way categorize the process as an "assembly line" with little consideration for the unique characteristics of a case. Of course, criminal justice professionals defend their actions by arguing that the system cannot handle thorough deliberation of all the cases.

Now that we have a better understanding of how the system actually works in practice, we can focus on debates regarding how it *should* work. Two models, crime control and due process, represent distinct value systems that compete for priority in a democratic society.[16]

Crime Control Model

The **crime control model** emphasizes the efficient arrest and processing of alleged criminal offenders. The value system underlying this model considers repression of criminal conduct as the most important function of criminal justice. In other words, what matters most is to reduce, quickly respond to, and punish criminal behavior. According to this model, the failure to bring criminal conduct under control leads to the breakdown of public order, a vital condition of human freedom. Because the emphasis here is placed on quick conviction and sentencing, advocates resist strong procedural protections that others would say help society ensure that only the guilty are punished.

As you will see in many parts of this book, the crime control model has dominated the public debate over how the criminal justice system should work since the 1980s. It has led to a tough-on-crime stance that doubts if perpetrators can be rehabilitated and feels that offenders have historically been treated too leniently by the criminal justice system. Proponents of the crime control model are satisfied with assembly-line justice because it speeds up the justice system and treats similar offenses and offenders in a consistent way. They worry more about threats to people's safety from crime than the constitutional protections of suspects.

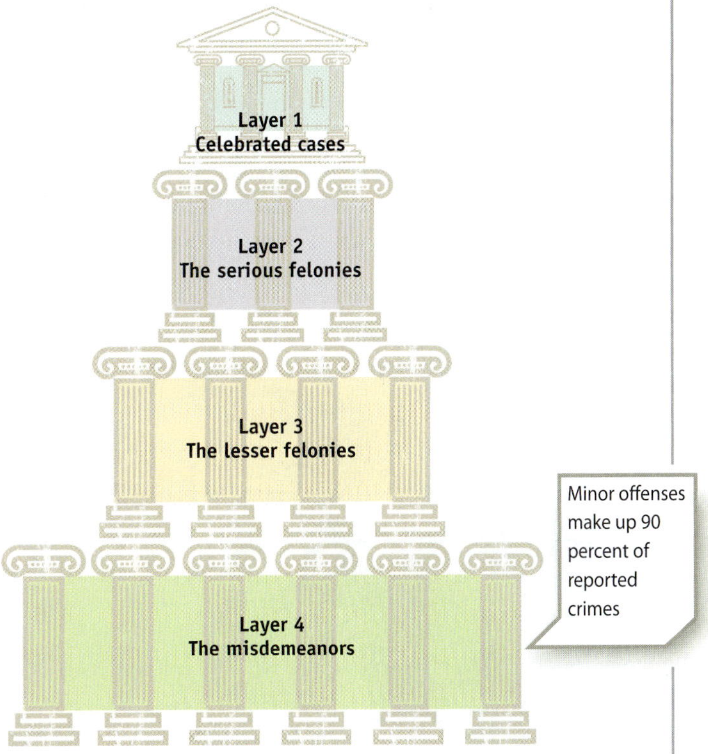

FIGURE 1-3 The Wedding Cake Model

SOURCE: Samuel Walker, *Sense and Nonsense about Crime and Drugs* (Belmont, CA: Wadsworth, Cengage Learning, 2001).

Due Process Model

The **due process model** emphasizes individual rights at all stages of the justice process. This model is more concerned with the threat to procedural rights of the offenders than with the general public's right to be free of crime. Advocates of the due process model argue that it is better to let guilty people go free than to convict the innocent.

"Due process" is the term used in the Constitution to describe procedural protections for the accused. Under the due process model, the police would recognize all the constitutional rights guaranteed to persons suspected of criminal conduct. Prosecutors and judicial authorities would actively support the same constitutional provisions before, during, and after any criminal proceeding. If the crime control model is more akin to an assembly line, then the due process model looks more like a maze with a variety of barriers to ensure that those punished are truly guilty.

The due process model likely saw its height in the 1960s when the Supreme Court was extending constitutional due process requirements to local and state criminal justice agents as well as federal ones. The law enforcement requirement to notify suspects of their rights, first introduced in 1966 in the famous case of *Miranda v. Arizona*, is consistent with the values of the due process model.

Although these two models seem to work as a dichotomy—one on each end of a value continuum—values of both models can be found at work in the criminal justice system today. In fact, the continued debate between these two positions helps us to evaluate from day to day how we want our criminal justice system to work.

▲ Serial Killer Gary Ridgway

Ridgway was convicted and sentenced to life for killing more than 40 women. *Should Ridgway have been allowed to plead guilty to avoid execution?*

INFLUENCES ON CRIMINAL JUSTICE

In an ideal society, the criminal justice system protects, defends, and upholds laws in an equitable way for all citizens. In the real world, however, people bring genuine fears and prejudices to the courtroom, the media can stoke those fears and prejudices, and lawmakers hold the purse strings to criminal justice initiatives. Thus, the criminal justice system does not operate in isolation; it is subject to many outside influences that can change the course of justice, either knowingly or unknowingly.

Real Careers

RACHEL DREIFUS

Work location: Redmond, WA

College(s): Bellevue College, tentative 2009

Major(s): Criminal Justice (AA)

Job title: Assistant Investigator, Securitas Security Services USA

Salary range for jobs like this: $40,000–$48,000

Time in job: 5 years

Work Responsibilities

Securitas Security is a vendor company contracted by Microsoft Corporation to provide investigative services. My job consists of reviewing and investigating cases requiring follow-up, such as ones involving theft, threats of violence, and assault. I am assigned between 5 and 25 cases per month, and I manage them by interviewing witnesses, communicating with police departments, and maintaining physical evidence in our secure climate-controlled evidence room. Some of the tools that make my investigations possible are video cameras, audio recorders, phone logs, and covert cameras that are as small as a pin! Every day I make sure all of my case notes are recorded in our database, which can be accessed by other Securitas Security investigators.

Why Criminal Justice?

I returned to college as an adult after having spent 5 years raising my children. When my youngest daughter became old enough to enter kindergarten, I decided to pursue the career that I always wanted: U.S. Marshal. After researching the qualifications to enter the U.S. Marshals Service, I found that an AA in Criminal Justice along with at least 3 years in private security was recommended. Although at times it has been a juggling act to balance family, work, and school, my classes were a purely rewarding experience. I am now proficient in all aspects of investigations, including gathering data, collecting evidence, analyzing crime scenes, and interviewing subjects. After 5 enjoyable years in corporate security, I no longer plan to pursue employment as a U.S. Marshal. My current job allows me to practice criminal justice without the dangers associated with police investigations.

Expectations and Realities of the Job

The realities of the job are a little bit different than I originally expected. First, I thought my deadlines would be more long term, but as it turns out, I am challenged on a daily basis to meet business objectives, such as resolve a certain number of cases and follow through with a report to our legal department. Also, before taking this job, I thought serving several years in the same position could get boring. But after 5 years on the job, I am pleased that I have never gotten tired of what I do. I make my work more interesting and rewarding by striving to go above and beyond the expectations of my supervisors.

My Advice to Students

Textbooks provide the knowledge you need for your job, but they cannot prepare you for the emotional aspects of starting a new job, particularly the nervousness. Taking responsibility for managing cases and any mistakes that might happen during the investigation put a lot of pressure on me. By speaking with experienced colleagues, I learned that these feelings are normal. Remind yourself that your employer thinks you are qualified for the job and, therefore, so should you. After a few months of getting settled in your new job, your confidence will grow.

MYTH/REALITY

MYTH: People fear strangers as being very likely to victimize them.

REALITY: Individuals are more likely to be victimized by someone they know.[17]

▲ Boarded Up Shops

Some people may regard a neighborhood in disrepair as a sign that the area is unsafe.

Fear of Crime

In general, U.S. residents believe there is much more crime than there actually is, and their fears are often misplaced. For example, women are consistently told not to walk alone at night, and they hear a variety of messages about how they should fear male strangers. Being cautious about one's surroundings is wise, but women are much more likely to be harmed by someone they know than by a stranger. It is uncomfortable to think about, but given the statistics on women's victimization, women should fear the men they know more than the men they do not know.[18] Fear of crime, specifically of crimes by strangers, influences where and when women are comfortable in public spaces and how they behave in those spaces. In other words, fear of stranger crime actually works to control women's choices.[19]

While the public's fear of crime continues to be significant, it has been lessening over the last decade or so. One measure of our fear of crime is the Gallup survey's question "Is there any area near where you live—that is, within a mile—where you would be afraid to walk alone at night?" In October 2004, 32 percent responded "yes."[20] That response was down from the 1989 level of 43 percent, which may reflect the reduction in crime during that time period. For example, in 2004, 42 percent of Americans responded that the nation's crime problem today was either "extremely serious" or "serious," down from 54 percent in 2003 and 60 percent in 2000. Furthermore, on a list of the most important problems facing the United States in December 2004, "crime/violence" ranked 20th and "drugs" ranked 14th among noneconomic concerns.

The level of fear we experience can be affected by a number of factors, such as our gender, age, past experiences with crime, ethnicity, income and educational levels, and the area in which we live. Criminologists point out that some of the most fearful groups are those less likely to be victimized.[21] For example, older people and women tend to have higher levels of fear than do young men, yet, as a group, young men are most likely to be victims of crime.[22] Women may have a greater fear of crime than males because their fear of sexual assault generalizes into an overall fear of crime.[23] Older people may be influenced in their fears by media exaggerations of crime in the streets, attention given to fraud and nursing home abuse, and heightened feelings of vulnerabilities that come with age.[24]

Those who have experienced crime tend to have elevated fears of crime. Victims of robbery, the unlawful taking of property by force or threat of force, tend to have high levels of fear afterward due to the sudden, unexpected, and personal nature of the crime. Victims of burglary, the act of entering a building or car for the purposes of theft, likewise tend to become more fearful due to the invasion of their home and loss of significant money or property.[25]

A moderate level of fear might serve citizens in a positive way, making them less vulnerable to victimization. Some people might purchase alarms or security systems designed to keep them safe. Some might avoid situations they perceive as dangerous. Locking an automobile or a home is a prudent action. However, when the public's unreasonable or unwarranted fear of crime influences public policy, it results in crime policies that are based on irrational fears rather than sound reason. The fear of crime also can have a major economic and social impact on society. How we spend money, go out to dinner, buy our houses, shop, travel, and spend leisure time can all be affected by our fear of crime.

Media Coverage

moral panic
The reaction by a group of people based on exaggerated or false perceptions about crime and criminal behavior.

Media coverage of crime inflates levels of fear. It produces a **moral panic**, the reaction by a group of people based on exaggerated or false perceptions about crime and criminal behavior. Individuals who watch local television news are more likely to be fearful of crime than those who watch national television news, listen to radio news, or access their news from the Internet.[26] The old adage "if it bleeds, it leads" appears to be especially true for local television news. Viewing sensational television news fuels fear of crime and results in support for the death penalty and handgun ownership, indicating that media coverage of crime can affect people's policy positions.[27]

Most criminal behaviors are not crimes against persons and are nonconfrontational. However, media reports focus heavily on violent crime. For example, homicides make up more than one-fourth of the crime stories reported on the evening news, but murder is actually a very rare event.[28] Further, in 2008 the incidence of violent crime in the United States was 454 per 100,000 population, as contrasted with an incidence of 3,215.5 property crimes per 100,000 population in the same year.[29] Media focus on these incidents via television, radio, newspapers, magazines, books, billboards, and the Internet leads people to believe violent crime occurs very frequently.

The media usually report or portray perpetrators of crime as minorities. White people are shown as victims out of proportion to their actual rates of victimization.[30] The image of the African American male, especially, as the victimizer of White people has a long historical legacy. Following the Civil War many African American males were lynched because there were often unsubstantiated claims that they had made sexual advances toward or sexually assaulted White women.[31] In actuality, most crime is intraracial—individuals most often victimize people of their own race.[32]

A significant downside to the "if it bleeds, it leads" mentality is the superficiality of reporting that results. This thinness is demonstrated by recent research from the City University of New York. A systematic analysis of 12 school shootings that took place between 1997 and 2002 revealed a high incidence of dating violence and sexual harassment as precursors to the shootings, but those incidents went unreported in the news. In five incidents, boys targeted and shot girls who had just rejected them. In three cases, boys' motivation to kill sprang from general unhappiness related to difficulties with girls. In three other cases, boys felt they "protected" their girlfriends by shooting other boys who threatened the relationships.[33]

The media have a public responsibility to report the news, but they are also in the business of making money for their shareholders. If the public chose sources that relayed a more accurate view of crime, media might change the way they cover the news. As we have seen, the media can affect people's fear of crime. Such fear can be translated into political positions and policy preferences.

Politics

The criminal justice system works within the larger U.S. political system, and politics influences the administration of justice in many ways. The legal system controls what actions are legitimate for criminal justice professionals. Legislators also decide how much money the country will spend on prisons, policing, the court system, and victim services. Federal policies influence the priorities that local justice agencies establish. For example, the Violent Crime and Law Enforcement Act of 1994 established the COPS office in the Department of Justice to provide grants for hiring community police officers. At the time, this was a new way to approach policing and required a high level of contact and cooperation between police officers and members of communities.

The U.S. Congress does not always require change by passing new laws. Instead, lawmakers can make access to federal funds dependent on states' compliance with certain

standards. For example, in 1984 Congress passed the National Minimum Drinking Age Act. The law did not mandate that states make their drinking age 21, but it specified that states that did not raise their minimum drinking age to 21 would not receive highway transportation funds. Even though some states objected to the higher drinking age, they agreed to it so they could access federal monies. Federal agents (such as the attorney general) can also choose to prosecute individuals under federal laws if they disagree with changes in state laws. For example, after California voters approved a proposition in 1996 allowing use of marijuana for medicinal purposes, federal prosecutors charged medicinal marijuana growers with federal offenses.

Political positions toward crime and justice have changed over time. Beginning in the 1920s, some political leaders held that criminals could be rehabilitated, and criminal justice policies for the most part reflected that belief. However, by the 1980s, the political mood had shifted to a tough-on-crime approach. At that point, the "war on crime" and the "war on drugs" were in full swing, and politicians of both parties pushed for more punitive criminal justice policies, such as stricter sentencing guidelines. Still, there is much debate about whether tougher sentences have reduced crime in the last few years or whether the decline is due to other factors. The Race, Class, Gender box shows how politically motivated mandatory sentences sometimes can have different effects on Whites and Blacks.

Some individuals who seek to influence the administration of justice band together in interest groups. They focus either on the overall administration of justice or on one particular aspect of the system or law to forward their interests. A particularly effective victim interest group is Mothers against Drunk Driving (MADD), which was instrumental in passing the National Minimum Drinking Age Act. Other organizations focus on broader issues such as reducing sentences for offenders. The Sentencing Project, Families against Mandatory Minimums, and the Drug Policy Alliance often argue that the tough-on-crime approach is not effective in reducing criminal behavior but does increase racial disparity. Crime Victims United, on the other hand, advocates more punitive sentences for offenders.

Many interest groups are intent on moving the criminal justice system back to its focus on rehabilitation rather than being solely focused on punishment. Often that issue is related to concerns about racial disparities found in criminal law and punishment, which we review next.

Discrimination

Individuals in jail or prison or on probation are disproportionately people of color.[34] This fact has raised a variety of questions regarding fairness in the administration of justice. The serious disparity can be seen in the imprisonment rates; per 100,000 U.S. residents, 410 White males, 3,188 Black males, and 1,419 Latinos are imprisoned.[35] In fact, nearly one-third of Black males aged 20–29 are under some form of criminal justice supervision on any given day.[36]

The conflict perspective would explain racial disparities in the criminal justice system as an extension of social divisions in U.S. society.[37] Historically, some definitions of what is criminal were clearly discriminatory. For example, in early America, when slavery was legal, it was a crime for antislavery activists to harbor African Americans seeking freedom. A patchwork of discriminatory laws against African Americans—generally called Jim Crow laws—were enforced from the years following the Civil War until the late 1960s. In the late nineteenth century, at a time when the White population considered Chinese immigrants a threat to their jobs, opium smoking, a fairly common habit in China, was criminalized in the United States.[38]

Today some argue that drug laws are discriminatory in their impact. Young Blacks report less alcohol and drug use than White youth,[39] yet Blacks are much more likely to be arrested for possession of illicit substances. The "war on drugs" has also had a significant disparate impact on women. Women's incarceration rates have increased steeply in the last few decades, most often for drug possession.[40]

Race, Class, Gender

Disparate Sentencing Guidelines for Crack and Powder Cocaine

Sentencing guidelines essentially tell the judge what penalty he or she must impose, sometimes within a range. They were meant to reduce disparities in sentencing, to ensure that judges were not treating defendants too leniently (as legislators defined leniency), and to create more uniformity in sentencing.

The U.S. Sentencing Commission's original guidelines, created in 1989, included sentences for crack and powder cocaine that resulted in a penalty ratio of 100:1. In federal court, possession of 5 grams of crack cocaine yields a mandatory felony sentence of five years in prison without the possibility of parole, but it takes 500 grams or more of powder cocaine to yield the same sentence (500 grams to 5 grams yields the ratio of 100:1).

Blacks constitute the majority of those arrested for crack cocaine, and Whites make up the majority of those arrested for the powdered variety. This difference in the races (and hence the arrest rates) is usually explained by the fact that crack cocaine is cheaper than powder cocaine. Because Whites as a group are better off economically than Blacks, they tend to be more able to purchase powder cocaine.

After years of review and evaluation, the Sentencing Commission advised Congress in 1995 that the sentencing guidelines were racially discriminatory. The two drugs are pharmacologically identical, but the sentencing was so disparate that minority offenders ended up serving much longer sentences. The Sentencing Commission recommended that the disparity be reduced. Congress, however, rejected the recommendation—the first rejection in the Sentencing Commission's 25-year history.

In 2007 changes were made to the sentencing guidelines to reduce the racial disparity (see Chapter 10). It is important to note that racial discrimination was a matter of sentencing law for decades with the approval of members of Congress. In the tough-on-crime climate, it was difficult for legislators to defend any vote that would result in reducing even overly harsh penalties. Therefore, the politics of the day influenced Congress so much that they even rejected the recommendation of their own commission.

Observe Investigate Understand

- **What is the rationale for sentencing guidelines?**
- **What do you think accounts for the huge disparity in the amounts of crack and powder cocaine used to determine sentencing?**
- **What political interests might be served by keeping the disparity in place?**

CHALLENGES TO CRIMINAL JUSTICE TODAY

Any discussion about the criminal justice system must also consider how it must adapt to the changing needs of the twenty-first century. The challenges confronting criminal justice today and into the foreseeable future may be categorized as global and domestic (or homegrown). These emergent challenges are putting significant strain on the resources of the criminal justice system. Just how adaptable the system and its practitioners can be is more crucial than ever before.

Global Challenges

The freeing of markets, the ease of transportation, and the phenomenal growth of the Internet have combined to enable crime to go global. Pornographic materials and gambling activities proliferate on the Internet. Counterfeit products are increasingly distributed worldwide via the Internet; the World Health Organization, for example, alleges that 50 percent of medicines sold online are counterfeit.[41] Many view identity theft as the defining crime of the information age—with an estimated 9 million incidents annually.[42] These illegal transactions are increasingly embedded among the myriad electronic messages transmitted daily.

Another area of global crime is trafficking of illegal goods. Drugs and weapons trafficking have capitalized on the lowered costs of freight and the increased number of transportation routes. After drugs and weapons, human trafficking is the third largest international illicit trade activity. It is estimated that more than 27 million individuals around the world are being held as slaves for sexual or labor purposes.[43]

Perhaps the most potentially virulent danger confronting the United States, and the world, is bioviolence. Various bacterial agents (such as plague, flu, polio, measles, or smallpox) could be altered to increase their lethality or to resist antibiotic treatments and then released as bioweapons. While technically far more difficult to create than conventional explosives, bioweapons have one unique and insidious quality: their ability to replicate and spread. As a device of terrorism, bioviolence can generate waves of extreme panic and wreak economic and political havoc. Not a single country admits to having a bioweapons program, but U.S. intelligence reports assert that as many as 10 nations might currently have active programs.[44]

When criminal justice agents tackle cases of cybercrime and terrorism, the government's need to gather information to prevent a catastrophe sometimes clashes with the individual's constitutional rights. Governmental surveillance, interception of communications, and detention of individuals for indefinite periods of time without formal charges continue to be significant points of tension and debate within the criminal justice system. To what extent, if any, do cybersecurity and antiterrorism efforts rub against privacy protections and civil liberties? What degree or type of governmental "intrusion" is tolerable in the interest of national security? How these questions play out will influence the orientation of the criminal justice system.

Domestic Challenges

While dealing with global challenges, we must not lose sight of the challenges generated within the United States. One major concern is the burgeoning prison population. Imprisonment within the United States is a lightning rod for divergence of opinion on crime and punishment along philosophical, sociological, psychological, and economic lines. During 2007, the prison population increased more rapidly than the U.S. resident population. At the end of 2007, federal and state prisons and local jails held just under 2.3 million inmates. Nineteen states and the federal system were operating at more than 100 percent of capacity. Another 19 states were operating between 90 and 99 percent of capacity.[45] Whatever the cause—for example, mandatory sentencing terms for repeat offenders or enhanced sentencing for drug offenses—the fact remains that prisons are bursting at their seams.[46] Moreover, the alarming rate of recidivism (67 percent[47]) and the lack of reentry policies and programs do not bode well for slowing either the rate or incidence of incarceration.

One particular portion of the prison population gives cause for concern: the mentally ill. A researcher who has studied this population states:

> On any given day, it is estimated that about 70,000 inmates in U.S. prisons are psychotic. Prisons hold three times more people with mental illness than do psychiatric hospitals, and U.S. prisoners have rates of mental illness that are up to four times greater than rates for the general population. Over the last several decades, states have emptied their psychiatric hospitals without moving sufficient resources into community-based programs.[48]

There is some good news. Many jurisdictions have established specialized mental health courts to reverse the overrepresentation of mentally ill individuals in incarceration.

a Case in Point

The Right to DNA Testing after Conviction

The due process clauses of the Fifth and Fourteenth Amendments of the United States Constitution protect individuals from unfair treatment by federal, state, or local government. If an individual can prove that he or she was unjustly convicted of a crime, fairness seems to dictate that the individual should be exonerated. The right for a review *after* a conviction, however, is not automatic everywhere in the United States. In some states the prosecutor must grant permission for this review. If a state does not have a law granting prisoner access to DNA testing, the prosecutor can deny the request without even giving a reason.

Such is the case in Alaska, one of three states that do not have a DNA testing law. Alaska has steadfastly refused to turn over DNA evidence to William G. Osborne, who was convicted in 1994 of kidnapping, sexual assault, and assault. Osborne claims the DNA evidence could prove his innocence. He also offered to pay the costs of a newer sophisticated test of the DNA, a procedure not available at the time of his original trial.

On June 19, 2009, the United States Supreme Court ruled in a 5–4 decision that convicted prisoners do not have a constitutional right to DNA testing to challenge their convictions. The court ruled that the due process clause of the Constitution does not apply in this situation. While acknowledging that DNA can positively identify the guilty while exonerating the wrongly convicted, the Court held that a defendant found guilty after a fair trial does not have the same rights as a free man. It is important, the Court argued, that the certainty of convictions be final and not undermined. The Court also said that access to DNA evidence for convicted individuals should be left up to the states, most of which have already enacted such laws. As noted, however, Alaska has no such laws and no prisoner in Alaska has ever been granted permission to obtain DNA evidence after conviction. Until Alaska changes this policy, William Osborne will not be able to introduce DNA evidence in his appeals.

Observe Investigate Understand

- **How and why would a defendant's rights be different before trial and after conviction?**
- **Why would Alaska not want to retest Osborne?**
- **Do you think the Supreme Court was correct in its decision? State your reasons.**

SOURCES: District Attorney's Office for the *Third Judicial District v. Osborne*, 129 S. Ct. 2308 (2009); Adam Liptak, "Justices Reject Inmate Right to DNA Tests," *The New York Times*, June 19, 2009; Jess Bravin and Jennifer S. Forsyth, "Court Upholds States in DNA Testing of Convicts," *The Wall Street Journal*, June 19, 2009; "The Supreme Court's DNA Ruling: Wrong on Rights," *Los Angeles Times*, Editorial, June 19, 2009; "DNA Testing: Supreme Court's Ruling Put Procedure before Justice," *The Star-Ledger Editorial Page*, http://blog.nj,com/njv_editorial_page/2009/06/dna_testing_supreme-courts-rul.html (retrieved July 3, 2009)

These courts connect participants to individualized treatment services in the community and provide for a team of criminal justice and mental health staff to facilitate ongoing treatment and support. But sustaining (much less expanding) mental health courts amid the competition for governmental funding constitutes a formidable challenge.[49]

Another aspect of progress in meeting domestic challenges is the use of DNA profiling, which has revolutionized forensic science and enabled law enforcement to match perpetrators to crimes. DNA testing of biological evidence not only helps to convict but also serves to remove the cloak of suspicion from the innocent and to free those wrongly convicted. According to the Innocence Project, which represents prisoners seeking reversal of convictions, 240 convicted persons in the United States have been exonerated by DNA evidence between 1989 and June 2009; 17 of them were on death row. Those exonerated had spent an average of 12 years in prison, some up to 27 years; the majority were Black. In 104 cases, the DNA evidence also led to the identification of the true offenders.[50] The A Case in Point box addresses a recent U.S. Supreme Court decision that will affect access to DNA for people who have been convicted.

The usefulness of DNA profiling, however, raises another challenge: the substantial backlog of DNA samples awaiting analysis. The backlog is caused by an increasing demand for analysis without a corresponding increase in laboratory capacity. This situation is exacerbated by a backlog of samples from convicted offenders awaiting analysis. Moreover, it is estimated that between 500,000 and 1 million convicted persons' samples are owed but not yet collected.[51]

A critical area for application of technology is in the use of force by law enforcement and correctional officers. Less-lethal technologies commonly in use include tasers, beanbag rounds, and pepper spray. The challenge is to understand the human health effects of less-lethal technologies to maximize safety for users and reduce the possibility of injury or death to those against whom such devices are deployed.[52]

SUMMARY

The criminal justice system is based in law. But laws are just what societies agree should be the norm for behavior. What works or is acceptable or is normal in one society, in one place, or in one time period may be considered deviant in another society, place, or period of time. When a law, or formal norm, is broken, the criminal justice system goes into motion.

The main parts of the criminal justice system are law enforcement, courts, corrections, and victim services. The actors in these different sectors interact in various ways with the offender and victim in the process of protecting society, providing a fair trial, and carrying out punishment and rehabilitation.

The challenge is to administer justice consistently, to balance efficiency with fairness, to keep the system up to date, and to avoid undue influence from outside sources, such as the media and interest groups.

OBSERVE
Investigate
Understand

Review

Illustrate how social norms help us define crime.

- A norm is a rule that makes clear what behavior is appropriate and expected in a particular situation. The term *abnormal* connotes deviance, the violation of a norm.
- Whether we consider a behavior deviant always depends on the context in which it occurs.
- Formal social norms, also called legal norms, are formally written, such as laws that result from a legislative process.
- Violation of formal norms, or laws, sets the criminal justice system in motion.

Define crime and explain how it is classified.

- Society defines crime in the same way it defines deviance—by labeling specific behaviors as such. Thus, behaviors considered criminal in one country (or place or time) may not only be legal in another country (or place or time) but the norm.
- One way of classifying crimes is as *mala in se* (an "evil unto itself," a behavior that is considered morally wrong). But no act or behavior is an inherently criminal act; society only labels it as criminal.
- Crimes can also be classified as *mala prohibita* (acts that are criminal because they are prohibited by law). *Mala prohibita* crimes reflect public opinion at a moment in time.
- The consensus perspective of crime views laws defining crime as the product of social agreement or consensus about what criminal behavior is. The conflict perspective of crime views the definition of crime as one outcome of a struggle among different groups competing for resources in their society.

Describe the consequences of crime for the offender and the victim.

- Those who break the law must face sanctions, which are used to reinforce people's conformity to norms. Sanctions can be positive or negative, and they can be formal or informal.
- Victims generally suffer some sort of loss or injury or even death. When victims are neglected or abused by the criminal justice system, their suffering worsens.

Outline the basic structure of the criminal justice system.

- The three major institutions of the criminal justice system are law enforcement, the courts, and corrections, with victim services additionally involved in these major components.

- The police are called upon to do far more than protect and arrest. Law enforcement officers are expected to correct many of society's problems and are entrusted to use force when necessary.
- The judiciary in the United States consists of a dual court system made up of state courts (trial and appellate courts) and federal courts (district courts, appellate courts or circuit courts where appeals are heard, and the Supreme Court).
- Corrections is the systematic, organized effort by society to punish offenders, protect the public, and change an offender's behavior. Correctional efforts include incarceration, probation, parole, treatment, and community service.
- Victim services offer a broad array of services within and outside government agencies to help the victim, including shelters and transitional housing programs, counseling services, 24-hour hotlines, and appointment of a victim advocate to assist the victim with legal needs.

Describe key models for the workings of the criminal justice system.

- Criminal justice professionals have discretion, which results in a filtering of cases, so that not all of them end up in court.
- The wedding cake model helps explain what cases make it through the funnel. The bottom layer (4) represents the vast majority of cases (largely misdemeanor and infraction cases), which are dispatched rather quickly. Each of the three layers on top represent more and more serious cases, with the most celebrated ones in the top layer (1) getting the most attention and resources.
- The crime control model emphasizes the efficient arrest and processing of alleged criminal offenders.
- The due process model values individual rights and procedural protections for the accused at all stages of the justice process.

Review the challenges to the criminal justice system today.

- Crime, such as cybercrime and terrorism, has become globalized.
- The continually increasing prison population has created problems of overpopulation.
- DNA testing has greatly affected the administration of justice, but there is a large backlog of evidence that has not been analyzed and questions about who should have access to DNA evidence and at what stage of the criminal justice process.

Describe how criminal justice is influenced by public opinion, the media, politics, and policy.

- Public fears of crime are often inflated and misplaced. The level of fear we experience can be affected by a number of factors, such as our gender, age, past experiences with crime, ethnicity, income and educational levels, and the area in which we live.
- Media coverage of crime inflates levels of fear by presenting exaggerated or false perceptions about crime and criminal behavior. Media reports disproportionately focus on violent and sensational crime.
- Politics influences the administration of justice in many ways. Legislators define crimes, determine what actions are legitimate for agents of criminal justice, and decide how much money to allocate to the criminal justice system. Some individuals who seek to influence the administration of justice band together in interest groups.

Key Terms

Study Questions

1. Norms can
   a. inform us as to what behaviors are acceptable.
   b. clarify what behaviors are unacceptable.
   c. vary according to culture.
   d. all of the above
2. Which of the following is not a formal negative sanction delivered in response to criminal behavior?
   a. Incarceration
   b. Court requirement of drug treatment
   c. Dirty looks
   d. Probation

3. Which of the following is a true statement about victims in the American criminal justice system?
   a. Most of the time victims and criminals are of the same race, class, and age.
   b. Historically, victims were neglected and abused by the criminal justice system.
   c. Today victims participate more in the criminal justice process and can receive money for their injuries and losses.
   d. all of the above
4. Which of the following models illustrates that most criminal cases do not go through the trial process?
   a. Crime control model
   b. Due process model
   c. Wedding cake model
   d. Conflict model
5. A person who believes that the focus of the criminal justice system should be on protecting individual rights and freedoms is a believer in which model?
   a. Due process model
   b. Crime control model
   c. United Nations model
   d. Criminology model
6. Which of the following has *not* given substantial support to the victim rights movement?
   a. Drug and alcohol movements
   b. Law-and-order movements
   c. Women's movements
   d. Victim-oriented coalitions
7. Laws are examples of
   a. statistical norms.
   b. informal social norms.
   c. cultural norms.
   d. formal norms.
8. Which perspective sees laws defining crime as the product of social agreement about criminal behavior?
   a. Conflict perspective
   b. Consensus perspective
   c. Wedding cake model
   d. Crime control model
9. Based on who, in reality, is most likely to be victimized, which group should be most fearful of crime?
   a. Women
   b. Older individuals
   c. Young men
   d. Children
10. Which of the following is *not* true of media coverage of crime?
    a. Is sensational
    b. Accurately represents criminal behavior
    c. Affects people's fear of crime
    d. Focuses on violent crimes

Critical Thinking Questions

1. What is considered a crime in one place may not be a crime in another place. How, then, is justice possible?
2. Do you believe the basis of most U.S. criminal laws is consensus or conflict?
3. How do you think media coverage of crime affects decisions about policies and the workings of the criminal justice system?

Internet Sites

The Office for Victims of Crime
www.ojp.usdoj.gov/ovc
Information about crime victims in the United States, victim rights, and victim services.

The Rise and Fall of Jim Crow
www.pbs.org/wnet/jimcrow/
Information about the history and impact of Jim Crow Laws.

Suggested Readings

Katheryn Russell-Brown, *The Color of Crime*, 2nd ed. (New York: New York University Press, 2008).
The book includes discussions of recent cases that raise issues about race and the administration of justice. The author explores reasons Blacks and Whites view the police differently and the consequences of those opinions. It is helpful for explaining the ways in which discriminatory beliefs and actions exist in the criminal justice system.

Ray Surette, *Media, Crime, and Criminal Justice: Images, Realities and Policies* (Wadsworth, Cengage Learning, Contemporary Issues in Crime and Justice, 2006).
This book helps readers become better consumers of media reporting about crime and the criminal justice system. The author dispels common myths that people have about the media and crime due to sensational media coverage.

Murray Lee and Stephen Farrall, eds., *Fear of Crime: Critical Voices in an Age of Anxiety* (New York: Routledge, 2008).
This book has an extensive discussion of the issues that affect people's fear of crime. It is a collection of essays that encourages the reader to think about "fear of crime" differently.

CHAPTER 2

Types of Crime

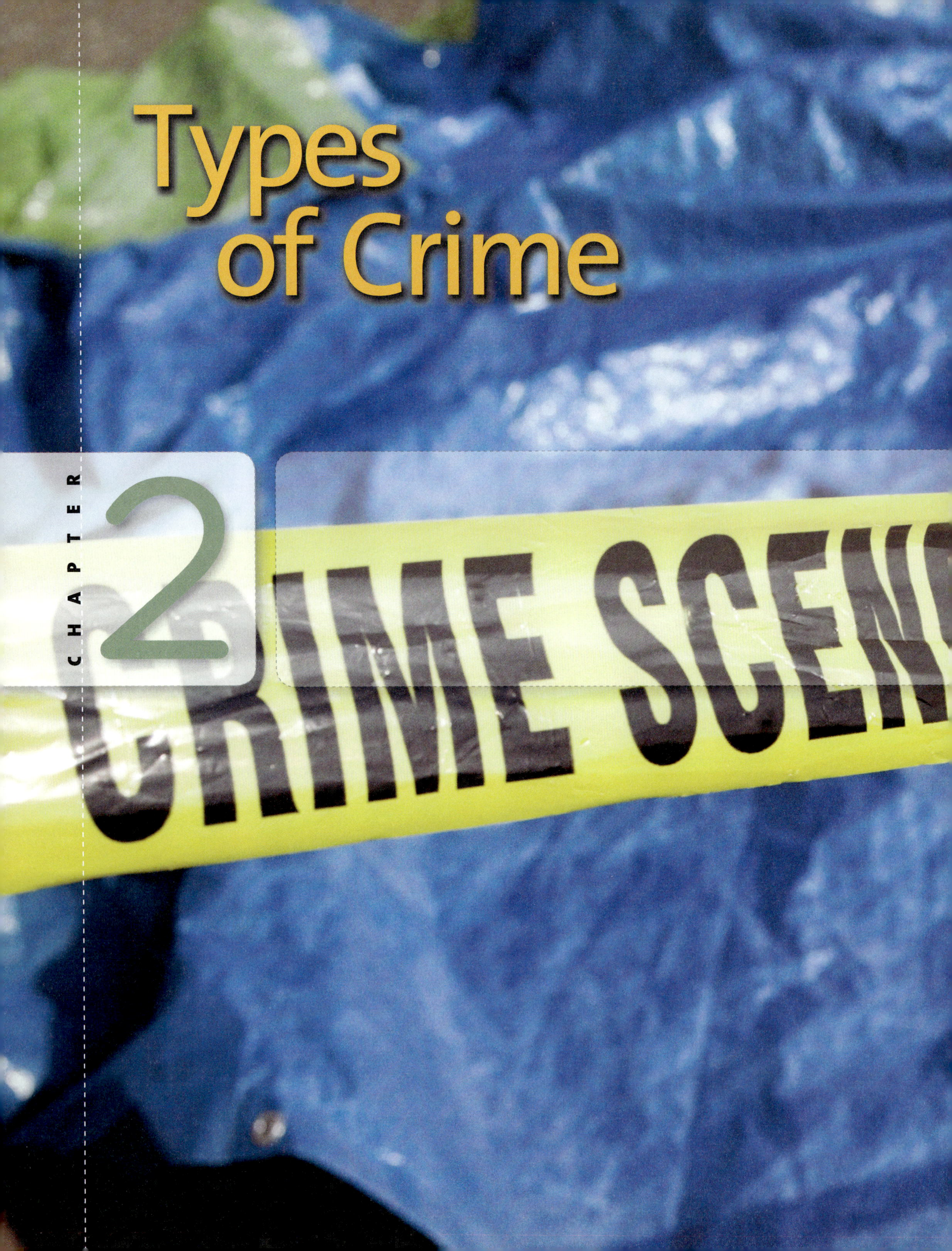

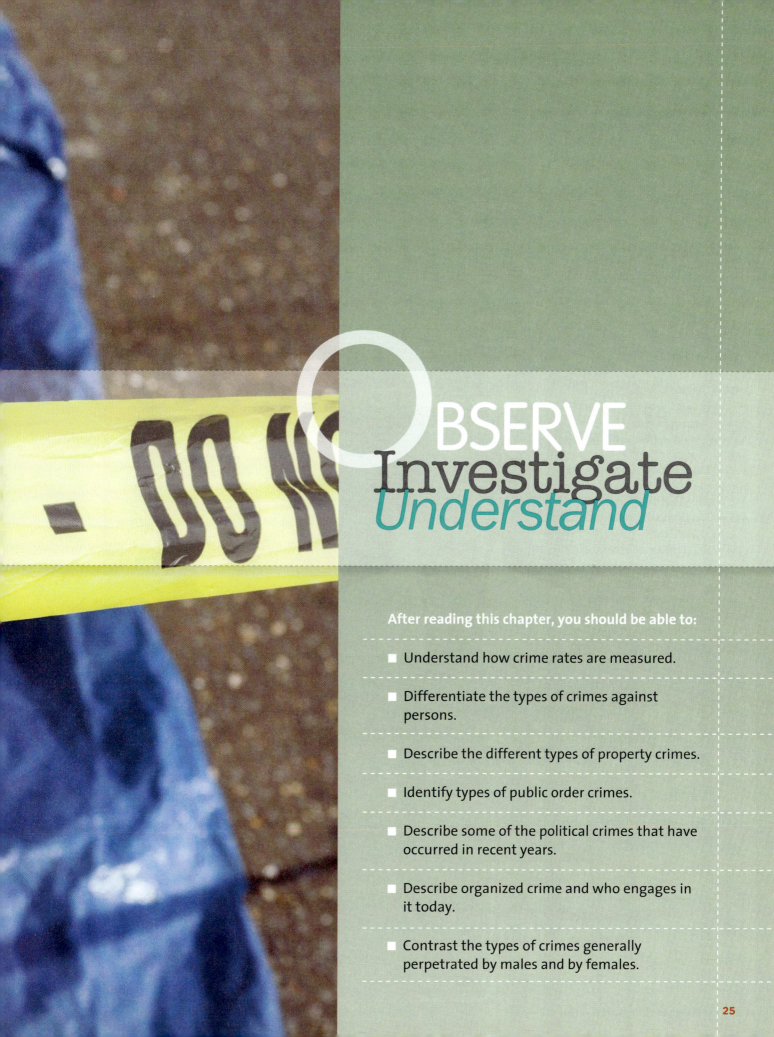

OBSERVE Investigate Understand

After reading this chapter, you should be able to:

- Understand how crime rates are measured.
- Differentiate the types of crimes against persons.
- Describe the different types of property crimes.
- Identify types of public order crimes.
- Describe some of the political crimes that have occurred in recent years.
- Describe organized crime and who engages in it today.
- Contrast the types of crimes generally perpetrated by males and by females.

Realities and Challenges

Can There Be a Crime but No Victim?

On June 11, 2007, according to the plainclothes police officer on duty, U.S. Senator Larry Craig (R-Idaho) entered a men's room at the Minneapolis–St. Paul airport, peered into a stall occupied (as it happened) by the officer, and entered the adjacent stall. The senator locked his stall, placed his luggage at the door to block anyone from seeing in, and tapped his foot under the officer's stall, allegedly communicating that he might be seeking sex. The officer arrested Craig for disorderly conduct, the crime with which the senator was eventually charged.

Two months later, Craig pled guilty to the charge. When the incident became public at a later date, Craig said that the police misconstrued his actions. Now asserting his innocence, he said that he regretted the plea, and he unsuccessfully attempted to withdraw it retroactively.[1] The Senate Ethics Committee found this attempt improper in that Craig was guilty of the charge against him and entered his plea "knowingly, voluntarily and intelligently."[2]

This case raises several issues, not least of which are What was the crime? Who, if anyone, was injured? and Who was the victim? Incidents like this one are classified as "crimes against morality," under the broad category of public order crimes, which have also been labeled "victimless," "consensual," or "fringe" crimes.[3]

▲ U.S. Senator Larry Craig

On June 11, 2007, U.S. Senator Larry Craig (R-Idaho) was arrested for disorderly conduct by a plainclothes police officer, and the senator was eventually charged with that crime. *Do you think the Larry Craig case represents a crime against morality?*

In Chapter 1, we asked how society determines what behaviors are crimes. We begin Chapter 2 by looking at how the incidence of crime is measured. Next, we consider how crimes are categorized in the United States today. Finally, we consider the effects different kinds of offenses have on victims and communities.

MEASURING CRIME

Information about crime and criminals is assembled by government agencies, private groups, and scholars. Four of the most frequently used data sources for estimating crime are the Uniform Crime Reports (UCR), the National Incident-Based Reporting System (NIBRS), the National Crime Victimization Survey (NCVS), and self-report studies. Each has advantages and disadvantages. Together, however, they yield a comprehensive picture of the extent and nature of crime.

Uniform Crime Reports

In the 1920s, the International Association of Chiefs of Police saw the need for national crime statistics. They formed the Committee on Uniform Crime Records to create a system for uniformly measuring crime. The most serious of these crimes, defined as Part I offenses, constituted the **Crime Index**. This index served as a gauge of the state of crime in the United States. Seven felonies constituted the Part I offenses: murder and nonnegligent manslaughter, forcible rape, robbery, aggravated assault, burglary, larceny, and motor vehicle theft.[4] Uniform definitions of crimes were created to provide standardization across jurisdictions. As an example, for reporting purposes the crime of "rape" required that it be forcible. Similarly, "aggravated assault" required that an attack be for the purpose of inflicting severe bodily harm, usually accompanied by use of a weapon—not, for example, a hand slap.

In 1930, the Federal Bureau of Investigation (FBI) was given the task of annually collecting, publishing, and archiving crime statistics from all the states' law enforcement agencies in the form of the **Uniform Crime Reports (UCR)**. In 1978, Congress mandated that arson be added to the Part I offenses.[5] Since 1996, the UCR also requires authorities to provide additional information when a crime appears to have been motivated by hate. Under a 1990 federal law, other felonies can be designated as hate crimes if they are motivated by the perpetrator's hatred of the victim's "race, color, religion, national origin, ethnicity, gender, or sexual orientation."[6] Racism motivates about half of all hate-crime convictions; most of the rest involve hatred for the victim's religion, sexual orientation, or ethnicity.[7] A notorious example of a hate crime is the 1999 murder of James Byrd Jr., a Black man killed by three Whites who chained him to their pickup truck and dragged him for 3 miles; Byrd's head and many other body parts were scattered along the road. Two of the killers belonged to a White supremacist gang and were sentenced to death (their sentences are still being appealed); the third got life imprisonment without parole.[8]

Preview

Crime Index
An officially compiled statistical measure of the incidence of crime in the United States.

Uniform Crime Reports (UCR)
An annual series of U.S. statistical measures of the incidence of selected crimes reported by police departments and compiled by the FBI.

MYTH/REALITY

MYTH: The UCR (the FBI's annual tally of serious crimes) accurately reflects the nature and level of crime in the United States.

REALITY: The UCR contains only crimes reported by police, which does not cover all crimes committed. As a result, the greater volume of property crimes overshadows occurrence of more serious but less frequently committed crimes.

Use of the Crime Index as an indicator of criminality was discontinued in 2004 because it was skewed toward property crimes. The Crime Index had been calculated by adding the total of Part I offenses. Offenses such as larceny, which accounts for a majority of reported crimes, distorted the crime total by overshadowing the incidence of more serious but less frequently committed offenses. Until a more viable index is created, crime statistics are now categorized and published as "Violent Crimes" and "Property Crimes."[9]

The UCR data can be confusing. For example, UCR definitions of crimes may differ from a state's definitions. In California, breaking into a locked car constitutes a burglary (entering with the objective of stealing), but the UCR classifies it as theft (defined simply as stealing). As mentioned, the UCR definition of rape encompasses only forcible rape and not other types of sexual assault. Another problem with the UCR system of data collection is that it undercounts offenses. Police have to report only the most serious offense when multiple offenses are committed in one incident. For example, a home invasion robbery that includes a rape and auto theft would yield only one offense for UCR reporting purposes. Most likely the rape will be the offense counted because it is considered the most serious offense.

The UCR also includes a schematic presentation of Index offenses—a "crime clock" designed to convey the relative frequency of crimes, such as one burglary every 14.9 seconds. However, by omitting such variables as time of day, day of week, location, and any relationship between offender and victim, it shows crimes occurring with a regularity (and implied randomness) that is not realistic.

UCR data are not the final word when it comes to assessing the level of crime in a given jurisdiction. Many other variables should be considered. Accurate assessments are possible only with careful study and analysis of the various unique conditions affecting each jurisdiction such as the strength of law enforcement agencies, stability of the population, family cohesiveness, local highway system, percentage of youth, and economic conditions.[10]

National Incident-Based Reporting System

National Incident-Based Reporting System (NIBRS)
A U.S. crime index (not yet fully national in scope) compiled by the FBI and the Department of Justice that tracks detailed information about 22 categories of crime incidents and arrests.

For more than five decades, the UCR program remained unchanged. Then, in response to the need for more informative data, the Department of Justice's Bureau of Crime Statistics and the FBI collaborated to formulate the **National Incident-Based Reporting System (NIBRS)**. This enhancement to the UCR program collects detailed information about criminal incidents and arrests in 22 offense categories made up of 46 specific crimes. NIBRS can provide information about type of premises involved, method of entry, type of property loss, weapon/force used, relationship of victim to offender, alcohol/drug use by offender, and many other details.[11] Data on when and where crime takes place and the characteristics of victims and perpetrators provide leads for follow-up investigations and strategies to prevent crime.

As valuable as NIBRS is, not every law enforcement agency has all the resources necessary for collecting, processing, and reporting the required array of data. As of 2008, 39 percent of the nation's law enforcement agencies participating in the UCR program submitted their data via the NIBRS. This rate of participation covered 25 percent of the nation's population.[12] NIBRS can provide information on nearly every major crime issue confronting society today, including terrorism, computer crime, drug/narcotics offenses, elder abuse, white-collar crime, organized crime, intimate partner violence, and driving under the influence. When NIBRS is fully implemented, individual states and the nation will have markedly upgraded investigative capabilities.[13]

National Crime Victimization Survey

Some criminologists and, more recently, victimologists—researchers who study victims and victimization—criticize the UCR as an inaccurate barometer of society's well-being. For a variety of reasons, many victims do not report the crimes perpetrated against them. Consequently, a large number of crimes remain unknown to police and never get into a database.

victim surveys
Interviews with individuals (including but not limited to actual victims) who have been personally affected by specific crimes.

Criminal justice professionals ultimately realized the only way to accurately measure the true extent of crime was to go directly to citizens and avoid the "filter" of the criminal justice system. The method that emerged was **victim surveys**, a phrase not entirely accurate because the persons interviewed were not always victims. However, the idea was well conceived, and in 1966 a presidential commission prompted the carrying out of the first national crime survey, based on a random sample of 10,000 households. The results confirmed that significant numbers of persons did not report their victimization to the police.[14]

National Crime Victimization Survey (NCVS)
A statistical sampling of households and individuals who have been personally victimized by specific crimes.

From 1972 to 1977, the Department of Justice (DOJ) undertook an annual victimization survey of residences and businesses in 26 large cities and published its reports annually. In 1973, the DOJ's Bureau of Crime Statistics and the Bureau of the Census launched the National Crime Surveys (NCS), and these have continued to the present. In 1992, the name was changed to **National Crime Victimization Survey (NCVS)** to more accurately reflect the central focus of this research: the extent of victimization among the general population.

The survey questionnaire for the NCVS has three sections: Personal Characteristics, Household Screen, and Individual Screen. If someone has been victimized, the survey asks a series of further questions about the victimization(s). The current sample size is about 76,000 households and encompasses 135,300 persons over the age of 12. These households remain in the sample for 3 years and are interviewed every 6 months.[15]

The NCVS differs substantially from the UCR. It does not include homicide, kidnapping, so-called victimless crimes, commercial crimes, or victimizations of children under the age of 12. It does include both reported and nonreported crimes, and it counts each crime separately, whereas the UCR counts only the most serious crime in an incident. (The NIBRS remedies that flaw.) The NCVS includes details about the victims as well as about the crime and its consequences. Perhaps most important for victimologists, the NVCS focuses mainly on victims and their victimizations, whereas the UCR is primarily oriented toward criminals and their crimes.

A comparison of data from both the NCVS and the UCR revealed that most crimes in the categories of rape/sexual assault, simple assault, and theft were not recorded by law enforcement. The actual number of persons victimized by violent crimes is almost double the reported figure. The actual number of victims of property crimes is almost two-thirds more than reported to the police. In the 2004–2005 time period, only 48.7 percent of all violent victimizations and 39.3 percent of all property crimes were reported. Since 1992 the trend for reporting crimes has been increasing steadily.[16] This group of unreported and unrecorded crimes is called the **dark figure of crime**.

dark figure of crime
The group of unreported and unrecorded crimes as revealed by crime victim surveys.

The NCVS has made a major contribution to the way we understand the crime problem and how we respond to victims, especially those who choose not to report their victimizations. We now have a much better understanding of victims of crime and the differences between those who report and those who do not. For example, the NCVS results suggest that some victims do not report victimization if the perpetrator is known to them. This finding has major implications for prosecuting sexual crimes and crimes within the family.

The NCVS has also helped to clarify how the criminal justice system, especially the police, influences victim reporting and cooperation with law enforcement. Victimologists are particularly concerned about **secondary victimization**, in which the victim who reports the crime is victimized again—this time, by the police, by the courts, or even by friends who judge his or her actions at the time of the offense. NCVS data show that victims take into consideration the way they think police will react to their report of victimization. Today, police know that treating victims with greater respect and taking victims seriously greatly improves their willingness to report and encourages them to be more cooperative witnesses. The result is that the efficiency of the criminal justice system significantly improves and the victims take a more meaningful role in that process. A Global View discusses victim surveys on an international scale.

secondary victimization
The suffering of a crime victim caused by his subsequent treatment by the police, the courts, or personal acquaintances.

Self-Report Data

In 1946, criminologist Austin Porterfield experimented with a method called "self-disclosure" in a small research project comparing college students to juvenile delinquents.[17] Porterfield's method was simple: he asked respondents to reveal the crimes they had committed. He found that the actual numbers of crimes disclosed was far greater than expected. This surprising result challenged the view, commonly held by criminologists and laypeople alike, that people are either criminal or not. Porterfield's findings suggest a very different and much more likely scenario: that criminality exists on a continuum in which some people commit few crimes, most people commit some crimes, and a very few people commit many crimes.

Self-report studies are an important source of information about offenders and their offenses. Academic and clinical researchers can choose from a wide range of methods to collect and analyze the information they get from offenders. They may engage a sample of burglars in personal interviews and learn that they have a human face and do not spend all their time plotting or engaging in crime. Or researchers can give a written questionnaire to a class of college students and learn, as Porterfield did, that more than 90 percent of us commit a crime during our adolescence for which we could have been incarcerated had we been caught and prosecuted. Telephone and mail surveys allow researchers to pose a series

self-report
Surveys in which individuals (who are guaranteed confidentiality) reveal offenses that they have committed but may or may not have been arrested and held accountable for their crimes. These surveys uncover another part of the dark figure of crime.

A Global View

Measuring Crime around the World

Measuring crime is a difficult undertaking in all corners of the globe, not just the United States. One of the most extensive crime victimization surveys is the International Crime Victim Survey (ICVS), which began in 1987 with funding from the Ministry of Justice of the Netherlands. The ICVS seeks to standardize the measurement of crime rates in different nations and to create a crime index independent of police statistics.

The ICVS contacts household members over 16 years of age by telephone in each of a country's largest cities. In recent survey distributions, some countries also provided an additional sample from rural areas. Respondents are asked to report on both household and individual crimes over the past 12 months. Household crimes consist of any property crime against any member of the household (for example, car theft, joyriding, theft from a car, motorcycle theft, bicycle theft, burglary, and attempted burglary) and crimes against persons. The latter category requires individuals to determine their experience with crime, the police, crime prevention, and safety concerns. Respondents are specifically asked if they were a victim of theft, vandalism, robbery, pickpocketing, sexual harassment, violence, or assault.

Survey participants also are asked about the frequency of the crime, the victim–offender relationship, physical violence, the extent of injuries, the use of social/victim services, preferred legal sanctions, punishment of the offender, and offender's detention status. The respondents also give information about their personal behavior including frequency of leaving the home and safety precautions they took in the home (for example, installing a burglar alarm, taking out insurance, or possessing a gun). The initial results of the ICVS were reported in 1989, with subsequent studies in 1992, 1996–97, 2000, and 2004–05. To date, more than 320,000 citizens representing 78 countries have participated in the ICVS.

OBSERVE Investigate Understand

- **What aspects of the ICVS can be used to improve the methods of the U.S National Crime Victimization Survey (NCVS)?**
- **How reliable a picture of crime do you think the ICVS provides?**
- **How likely is it that persons contacted by the ICVS will give honest answers, and why?**

SOURCES: National Archive of Criminal Justice. "International Crime Victimization Survey," *National Archive of Criminal Justice*, www.icpsr.umich.edu/cocoon/NACJD/SERIES/00175.xml (retrieved December 22, 2008); M. Planck, "International Crime Survey in the EU: Highlights and Policy Implications," *European Commission*, 2005, www.europeansafetyobservatory.eu/ (retrieved December 22, 2008).

of prepared questions to a sample of people representative of a larger population. If we wish to learn more about serial rapists, for example, we could conduct a survey of incarcerated serial rapists and compare their results with responses from a control group of men of the same age and socioeconomic background who lack a criminal background. Case studies, examining the experiences of an individual offender at length and in detail, can suggest useful hypotheses to test later with a larger sample of the same kind of offender.

Self-reports tell us about crimes committed by people who were never caught—even about crimes unknown to the police because the victims did not report them but about which the offenders are willing to talk. Researchers minimize concerns about the honesty of respondents and the reliability of their information by assuring them of anonymity. To maximize their confidence in the information, researchers can use a test–retest method to expose inconsistent responses to the same questions administered on different occasions. Thus, we can learn much from the offenders themselves—even when they choose to lie.

These various sources of information—police, victims, and offenders—complement one another by both offering overlapping data and filling in missing information. When we consider them together, they provide a more comprehensive picture of crime than we can glean from any one approach on its own.

CRIMES AGAINST PERSONS

Attacks or threats of an attack on a person's body constitute **crimes against persons**. The most serious of these offenses are murder and manslaughter (both mean wrongfully taking a life), sexual assault, kidnapping, robbery (theft with force or the threat of force), and battery (the intentional unwanted touching of one person by another with intent to injure).

crimes against persons
Attack or threats of an attack to a person's body, including murder and manslaughter (both mean taking a life), sexual assault, kidnapping, robbery (theft with force or the threat of force), and battery (the intentional unwanted touching of one person by another).

In 1973, the UCR cited 715,900 police reports for these violent offenses, but during the same period more than 1.8 million cases of violent crimes were reported in the NCVS about individuals' experiences with crime. The UCR and NCVS numbers steadily rose each year, fluctuating during the 1970s and 1980s. As you can see from Figure 2-1, UCR data peaked in 1992 at more than 1.6 million reported cases, and the next year the NCVS survey peaked above 2.2 million cases. Both measures began to steadily decline after these peaks, continuing their downward trend through the last year for which data are available, 2003, when the UCR reported more than 1.1 million serious violent crimes and the NCVS noted 1 million serious violent crimes. For years after its inception, the NCVS reported higher levels of crime than the UCR, but in 2000–03 this trend reversed, with the UCR noting more reported crimes than the NCVS.[18] It is unclear why this trend occurred, but possible explanations include an increase in stranger-related crimes (which are more likely to be reported to the police than nonstranger crimes) or that people are increasingly willing to call the police for all crimes.

Laws defining crimes against persons are probably the oldest rules in human societies. This continuity demonstrates both the enduring nature of human violence and the heavy toll violent acts take on individuals and communities.

Fortunately, crimes against persons constitute a relatively small proportion of all crime. For example, in 2003, FBI data show that about 1.4 million violent crimes were reported to the police in the United States compared to 10.4 million property crimes.[19] If we consider that many more property crimes than violent crimes probably go unreported, the disparity becomes even greater. Furthermore, contrary to popular belief, the rate of violent crimes committed in the United States has declined considerably since 1993.[20]

More than any other act, crimes against persons have the potential for causing greater damage to individuals, including economic losses, psychological and emotional trauma, physical pain and injury, disability, and death. These crimes generally rank as law enforcement agencies' highest priorities, and offenders usually receive the harshest penalties. Investigating the crime scene, interviewing victims and witnesses, and obtaining confessions are important steps to solving such crimes. A Case in Point shows that *false* confessions can traumatize both the victim and those accused of a crime they never committed.

Who are the "persons" against whom crimes against persons are committed? Anyone, of course, can be a victim. However, gender, health, intelligence, social associations, location, mental state, and age often determine an individual's likelihood of becoming a victim of particular types of crimes. In general, men are more likely than women to become victims of reported violent crimes. For example, the FBI reported that 78 percent of murder victims in 2004 were male.[21]

FIGURE 2-1 Serious Violent Crime Rates, 1973–2003
Given the dramatic drop in total violent crime from 1993 to 2003, consider what conditions might be responsible for the change.

SOURCE: Bureau of Justice Statistics, "Four Measures of Serious Violent Crime," September 2006, www.ojp.usdoj.gov/bjs/glance/tables/4meastab.htm (retrieved December 13, 2007).

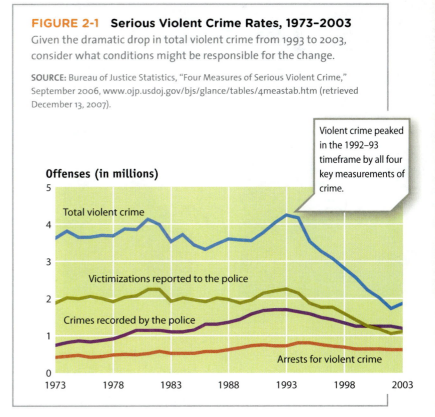

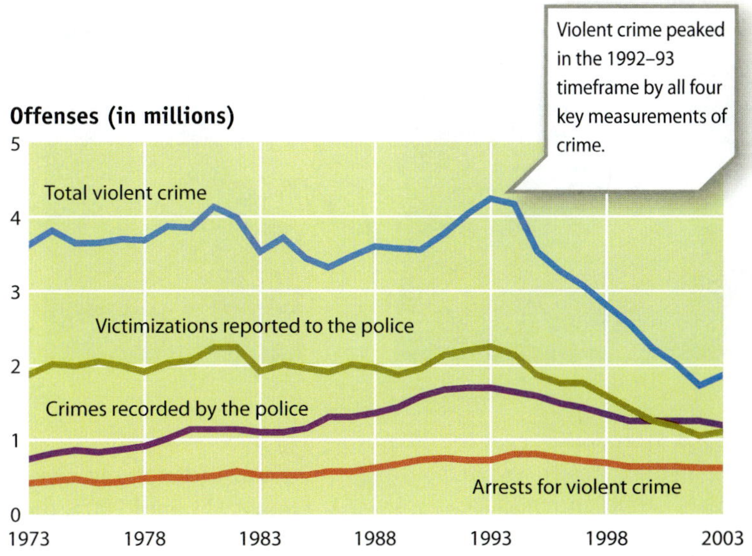

a Case in Point

False Confessions

The case looked easy. On June 13, 1987, an elderly woman was sexually assaulted and brutally murdered in her home in Tyler, Texas. On October 27, Robert Bush, a young man with a history of mental illness and drug abuse, wrote a lengthy confession to the murder, rich with details only the killer—and the police—could have known. Bush was taken into custody and charges were filed.

There was just one problem. An investigation by Bush's defense attorney revealed that between May and July 1987, Bush was locked up in a mental hospital in California, 1,200 miles from the murder scene. Clearly, the police had supplied him with some of the details of the crime he included in his "confession." Eventually the charges against Bush were dismissed, but he had spent more than a year in jail awaiting trial for a crime he could not have committed.

Police and prosecutors typically regard confessions as valuable evidence. Juries tend to weigh them heavily when determining guilt. Yet it turns out that cases like Robert Bush's are not as rare as we might think: people often confess to crimes they did not commit. In fact, according to the Innocence Project (a national organization dedicated to exonerating wrongfully convicted people through DNA testing and reforming the criminal justice system), false confessions are the second most common cause of wrongful convictions—the first being mistaken identification.[a] In one infamous case, after a jogger in New York's Central Park was severely beaten and raped, five teenagers confessed. All were convicted. Only after they had all served several years of their 6- to 11-year sentences did DNA evidence prove that another man, previously convicted of similar crimes, had actually attacked the woman.

Why would an innocent person confess to a crime? Researchers have many explanations: trained interrogators may easily manipulate suspects, especially if they are young, mentally ill, mentally impaired by drugs or alcohol, or a person with a developmental disabilitiy. Suspects may become exhausted after long interrogation sessions, or they may come to believe their fate will ultimately be better if they confess than if they continue to deny guilt. Or police may use a variety of tactics—even outright lies—to pressure suspects.[b] As the Supreme Court pointed out in its *Miranda* decision, even if the police do not overtly harm or threaten a suspect, just being in police custody is inherently coercive. Although we cannot know exactly what prompted Robert Bush's false confession or those of the defendants in the Central Park jogger case, it is probably significant that Bush had a mental illness. The defendants in the Central Park jogger case were all in their teens.

In response to increasing concerns about the reliability of confessions, some jurisdictions now require videotaping all custodial interrogation sessions, and some police departments have a policy of videotaping interrogations. Still, most interrogations go unrecorded.

Observe Investigate Understand

- **What is the most likely reason that Robert Bush "confessed?"**
- **Why did all five teenagers confess to the rape of the Central Park jogger when they knew that they had not committed it?**
- **Why do you think most interrogations still are not recorded?**

SOURCE: [a]The Innocence Project, www.innocence.org (retrieved February 22, 2007); Gisli Gudjonsson, *The Psychology of Interrogations and Confessions: A Handbook* (Hoboken, NJ: Wiley, 2003).

[b]See, for example, Saul Kassin and Gisli Gudjonsson, "The Psychology of Confessions: A Review of the Literature and Issues," *Psychological Science in the Public Interest* 5 (2004): 33; Richard Leo and Richard Ofshe, "Coerced Confessions: The Decision to Confess Falsely, Rational Choice and Irrational Action," *Denver University Law Review* 74 (1997): 979; Saul Kassin, "On the Psychology of Confessions: Does Innocence Put Innocents at Risk?" *American Psychologist* 60 (2005): 215–228.

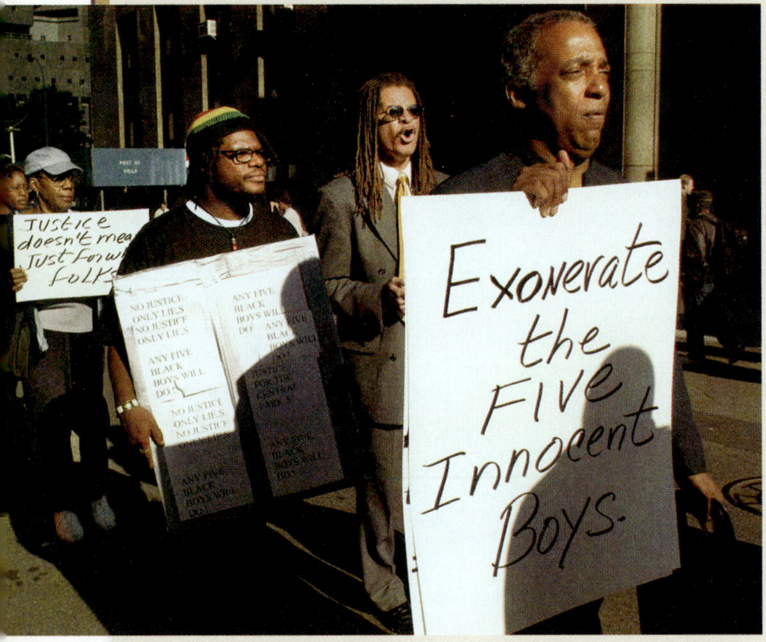

▲ Protestors demand the release of the convicted boys in the "Central Park Jogger Case."

An earlier study concluded that 60 percent of violent crime victims were male.[22] From 1973 until 2005, the NCVS has provided data about violent crime rates by gender for individuals 12 years old and older. As you can see from 30 years of collected data in Figure 2-2, males are consistently victimized at a higher rate than females. It is also apparent, however, that the overall violent crime rate has been decreasing since 1994, and the rates for male victims have fallen more than rates for females. Thus the disparity of victimization rates between males and females has narrowed considerably. However, women may be less likely than men to report a violent crime, so the official reported crime rates may be somewhat deceptive. Women are less likely to report victimization because they fear that the known perpetrator will retaliate if the police are contacted.

Men and women have different patterns of violent crime victimization. Most women are attacked by someone they know, whereas about half of the attacks on men are perpetrated by strangers.[23] Women are more likely to be attacked in the home; men, in public places. Most intimate partner violence and sexual assault victims are female. In fact, 85 percent of violent crimes committed by intimates (people in a romantic relationship) have female victims.[24] The number one cause of assault and murder of women in the United States is intimate partner violence.[25]

Age is also an important factor in victimization. In general, younger people are more likely than older people to be victims of violent crime. Children are vulnerable to abuse by parents and other caregivers. In 2004, there were nearly 3 million reports of child abuse and neglect in the United States, 28 percent of which were later substantiated.[26] Very young children are at particular risk of being abused and are especially likely to suffer severe injuries or death as a consequence. Of course, much child abuse goes unreported.

▲ Women may be less likely than men to report a violent crime.

MYTH/REALITY

MYTH: Older adults are more likely to be victimized than people in any other age group.

REALITY: Older adults have higher levels of *fear* of crime than other age groups. The reality is that most crime victims are under 25 years of age. According to the 2005 NCVS, children ages 12 to 15 were victims of violent crimes (rape or sexual assault, robbery, aggravated assault, and simple assault) at a rate of 46.9 per 1,000. Those ages 16 to 19 experienced victimization at a rate of 45.0 per 1,000, and 20- to 24-year-olds at a rate of 45.0 per 1,000. Those 65 years old and older experienced victimization at a rate of 2.3 per 1,000.[27]

Older people are significantly less likely than young people to be victims of violent crime. Like children, some older persons may have a heightened potential for being abused, both physically and emotionally. Research on elder abuse is relatively new, and law enforcement needs to learn more about it. The vulnerability of older people is unique, and law enforcement personnel must understand it as a separate phenomenon, whether they are dealing with crime prevention or victim assistance. Elder abuse is likely to increase significantly as the population shifts with baby boomers entering their senior years. It is estimated that half a million elderly people in the United States are abused each year.[28] This troubling statistic notwithstanding, of all age groups, it is teenagers who are most likely to be victims of violent crime.[29]

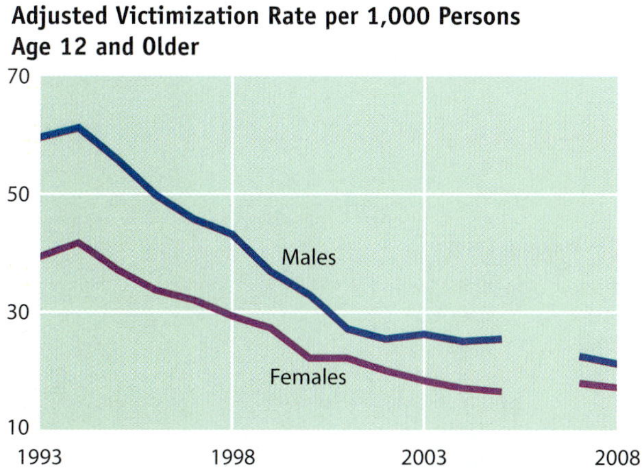

FIGURE 2-2 Rates by Gender of Victims

Rates for both males and females are well below rates of previous years.

SOURCE: Bureau of Justice Statistics, "Violent Crime rates for both males and females are well below rates of previous years," www.ojp.usdoj.gov/bjs/glance/vsx2.htm (retrieved October 7, 2009).

Homicide

Homicide occurs when someone unjustifiably causes the death of another human being. The different types of homicide are distinguished primarily by the culpability of the offender.

Source Connection
VICTIM CHARACTERISTICS

www.ojp.usdoj.gov/bjs/cvict.htm

For a comprehensive list of victim characteristics, go to the U.S. Department of Justice, Bureau of Justice Statistics, and examine the most recent National Crime Victimization Survey data.

first-degree murder
The most serious kind of murder. To be convicted of first-degree murder, an offender must have purposely killed the victim and must have planned the killing at least a short time in advance.

manslaughter
A killing in which the offender is less blameworthy than for murder; it usually carries a less severe penalty than murder.

voluntary manslaughter
Killing in the heat of passion.

Most intentional homicides are classified as murders. Different jurisdictions classify murders in different ways, but usually the most serious kind is **first-degree murder**. To be convicted of first-degree murder, an offender must have purposely killed his or her victim and must have planned to do so at least a short time in advance. In some states, people may receive the death penalty for first-degree murder. In most states, second-degree murder is an intentional killing not planned ahead of time.

Manslaughter is a killing in which the offender is less blameworthy, and it usually carries a less severe penalty. There are several types of manslaughter as well: **voluntary manslaughter**, when an offender is provoked and loses control, killing his victim in the heat of passion; and **involuntary manslaughter**, when the killing results from an offender's careless actions. For example, 20-year-old Collin Viens was playing with his hunting rifle and shot at a tractor he believed was empty. In fact, Rejean Lussier was sitting in the tractor and was killed. Viens was convicted of involuntary manslaughter and given a sentence of 1 to 5 years.[30] In some states, deaths resulting from careless driving are classified as involuntary manslaughter. Other states, such as California, classify such deaths as **vehicular manslaughter**.

According to the UCR, the U.S. murder and voluntary manslaughter rate is approximately 5.7 per 100,000 inhabitants, but it varies by geographical areas.[31] Homicide rates are highest in the South and lowest in New England and the Rocky Mountain West.[32] Internationally, the United States has some of the world's highest homicide rates (see Figure 2-3). Some nations with higher murder rates than the United States are Estonia, Lithuania, Russia, and South Africa; among the lowest are Japan, Spain, Greece, and Switzerland.[33]

The most grievous of crimes, homicide takes away a person's most prized possession—life. As the only form of victimization from which the victim cannot recover, it therefore

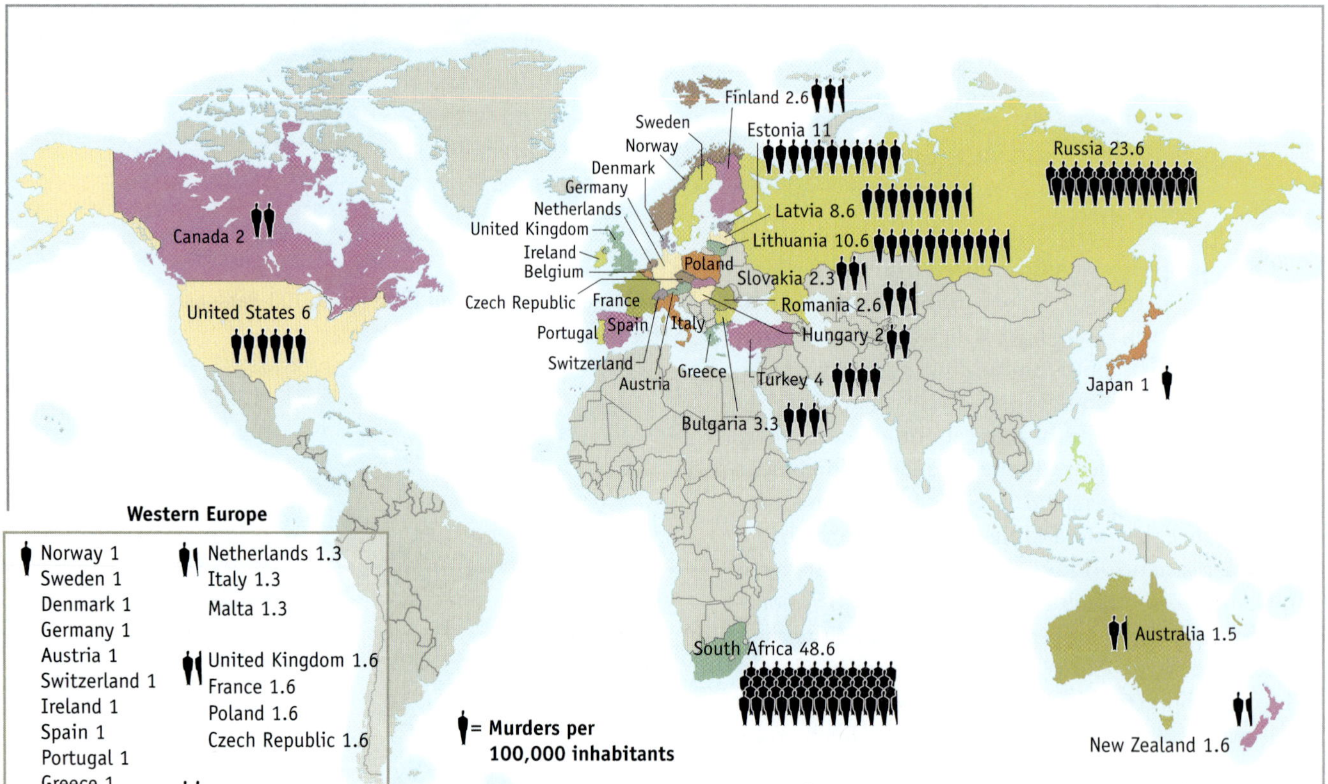

Figures are an average of 1999–2006: 1999–2001 Interpol; 2002 World Health Organization (WHO); and 2004–2006 European Union (EU). (EU figures for Australia, Canada, Czech Republic, Japan, and South Africa are for 2006 only.)

FIGURE 2-3 Homicide Rates around the World

SOURCE: Data from Andrew Karmen, *Crime Victims: An Introduction to Victimology*, 7th ed. (Belmont, CA: Wadsworth, Cengage Learning, 2010), 82.

◀ ▲ Wayne Gacy: The Jekyll-and-Hyde Serial Killer

John Wayne Gacy was a known and trusted member in his community, who sometimes entertained neighborhood children in full costume as "Pogo the Clown." (The photo above is Gacy's self-portrait as Pogo.) But Gacy also raped and murdered 33 boys and young men between 1972 and 1978, usually burying their corpses in a crawl space under his house.

incurs the severest penalties. Depending on the kind of homicide committed, an offender might receive anything from probation or a short time in prison to, in many states, a death sentence. The *survivor victims* (the deceased person's loved ones) are asked to cooperate with a system that they often perceive as being demanding, at times uncaring, and sometimes even abusive. The impact of the crime and criminal justice proceedings on grieving survivor victims is usually traumatic and long lasting. For victim service providers, this is the most challenging form of victimization.[34]

One of the most intriguing areas in the study of crime is multiple murder, in which perpetrators kill many victims. Serial murder, mass murder, and spree murder are each a type of multiple murder, differentiated by time. **Serial murder** is the killing of three or more people over an extended period. **Mass murders** are multiple murders that occur at one place and time. In **spree murder**, victims are killed within a fairly narrow time span, from several hours to a few days.[35]

People in mainstream society, and certainly students of criminology, are fascinated with *serial killers*—their lives, their motivations, their methods or modus operandi (MO), and their selection of victims. The media fuel this interest through sensational movies, television shows, and stories filled with gory details but short on facts. The stereotype of a serial killer is a "ruthless, blood-thirsty sex monster who lives a Jekyll-and-Hyde existence—probably next door to you."[36] In fact, not all serial murders are motivated by sex, and not all serial killers sexually violate their victims. That they live a Jekyll-and-Hyde existence is true to the extent that they present themselves in society as at least minimally acceptable individuals, not revealing their darker nature. They are not so much "taken over by strange forces" that change their fundamental identity; rather, they succeed in hiding their criminality from others. Some do this with more success than others.

Stereotypes often have some validity, but serial murderers are not homogeneous. Most exhibit particular patterns or have a specific modus operandi, but some are less consistent in the commission of their crimes, using, for example, a variety of weapons. Some seek a specific type of victim, and others are more opportunistic and kill because a victim is an easy target. Most known serial killers are male and use weapons or other means of physical violence to kill. Other serial killers, usually female, kill with relatively passive means,

Source Connection

JOHN WAYNE GACY

www.time.com/time/2007/crimes/13.html

Read the article "Top 25 Crimes of the Century—John Wayne Gacy" about this serial killer's life and crimes.

involuntary manslaughter
A killing that results from an offender's careless actions.

vehicular manslaughter
Death that results from careless driving.

serial murder
Killing three or more people over an extended period of time.

mass murder
Multiple murders that occur at one place and at one time.

spree murder
Killing several people within a fairly narrow period, such as several hours or days.

KEY CONCEPTS
Types of Homicide

Type	Definition
First-degree murder	An offender must have purposely killed his victim and must have planned to do so at least a short time in advance.
Second-degree murder	An intentional killing not planned ahead of time.
Manslaughter	The offender is less blameworthy, and it usually carries a less severe penalty.
Voluntary manslaughter	An offender is provoked and loses control, killing his victim in the heat of passion.
Involuntary manslaughter	The killing results from an offender's careless actions.
Vehicular manslaughter	Death resulting from careless driving.
Serial murder	The killing of three or more people over an extended period.
Mass murder	Multiple murders that occur at one place and time.
Spree murder	Victims are killed within a fairly narrow time span, from several hours to a few days.

such as poison or suffocation. For many male serial murderers, motivation includes sexual gratification; for many female offenders, the killings bring them attention or money from victims' insurance policies. Serial killers can murder within a specific location such as a home or known neighborhood, or be mobile, murdering throughout a city, state, or even across the country. Some victims know their assailant, perhaps through an intimate or familial relationship, or as a passing acquaintance; others are total strangers.[37]

Mass murders occur when several individuals are killed within moments or after being held hostage together. Some have occurred in workplaces or other public locales, such as post offices and, more recently, schools. However, in some intimate partner violence or family abuse cases, one person will take an entire family hostage within the home, kill each person, and then commit suicide.[38]

In the third category of multiple murder, *spree killing*, the offender is usually mobile and often acts in erratic, frenzied, and bold ways, making little effort to hide the murders from authorities. The spree murderer may kill several victims in a single location before moving on.[39] Andrew Cunanan killed five men over a 3-month period in 1997. He has been called both a spree killer (because he killed people in more than one location) and a serial murderer (because of his multiple murders). Such cases illustrate how even professionals may classify the same multiple murderer differently and how the complexities of serial murder are difficult to define simply.

Assault and Battery

assault and battery
A harmful or offensive physical attack by one person upon another.

Another type of crime against persons is **assault and battery**, a harmful or offensive physical attack by one person upon another. The UCR reported that in 2008 there were approximately 275 aggravated assaults in the United States per 100,000 population.[40] (The crime of aggravated assault means attacking another person with the intent to commit another felony, or using a deadly weapon.)

Like homicide, assault usually starts with interpersonal conflict and escalates to violence. When a victim and assaulter are married or partnered and charges are filed, the victim must come to terms with the prosecution of the offender. The criminal justice system offers both parties input in deciding whether to stay in or leave the relationship. Many relationships that include assault victimizations are not easy to leave, and those that include children, intrafamilial relationships, and employment may be complicated, even binding. If the relationship continues and the interpersonal problem cannot be resolved, the same conflict or similar ones are highly likely to erupt again and, over time, escalate into serious violence. Victims who cooperate with the criminal justice system thus may require special protections.

Sexual Violence

Sexual assault is one of the most sensationalized of all victimizations and has characteristics of both physical and sexual violence. **Sexual violence** encompasses a range of crimes, including sexual intercourse by force with vaginal, anal, or oral penetration and the use of weapons and foreign objects as sexual devices to torture and terrorize the victim. **Sexual victimization** means "forced or coerced sexual intimacy."[41]

sexual violence A range of crimes including vaginal, anal, and oral penetration that can include the use of weapons and foreign objects to torture and terrorize the victim.

sexual victimization Forced or coerced sexual intimacy.

Sexual assault is a devastating experience for victims, depriving them of their dignity and traumatizing them for a significant time. Anyone, regardless of age, sex, race, or other characteristics, may be sexually victimized.

Victims are likely to know their assailant; three-fourths of reported rape victims 18 and older named as the rapist their current or former husband or unmarried partner, or someone they had been dating.[42] The most common types of sexual assault perpetrated by a known assailant are marital rape and date rape. Another example is acquaintance rape; here, the victim knows or has at least seen the perpetrator prior to the assault, but they are not dating or in an intimate relationship. In all these cases, perpetrators can be of the opposite or the same sex as the victim.

Between 1992 and 2002, the NCVS received reports from 141,000 people ages 12 and older who said they were victims of attempted or completed rape. Slightly more than half of all women who reported being raped at some point in their lives said that the rape happened when they were 17 years old or younger, and almost a quarter said they were under the age of 12. Female victims accounted for 91 percent of attempted and 94 percent of completed rapes. Of all the female rape victims, 40 percent sustained physical injuries beyond the sexual assault, although only 32 percent sought treatment for them.[43]

Victimization research based on individuals and their experiences of crime, however, suggests that only one in four sexual assaults is reported to the police.[44] The remaining victims do not report assaults for a number of reasons. They may view it as a personal matter (25 percent) or fear retaliation (17 percent). Sometimes the crime was reported to a different official (13 percent), the victim wished to protect the offender (10 percent), or the victim believed the criminal justice system would be biased against her (6 percent).[45] Victimization survey data also show that victims do not report for various reasons, among them are self-blame (especially if the victim was under the influence of alcohol), an expectation of being judged negatively, a fear of retaliation (especially when the victim and offender know each other), a preference for dealing with the assault privately, a desire to avoid shame, and a wish to protect family from embarrassment.[46] Ethnic and cultural background seems to play a role in determining the willingness of women to report sexual attacks.

▲ **Rape Survivors** "Take Back the Night" demonstrations increase awareness of rape and sexual assault.

The closer the relationship between offender and victim, the less likely it is that the victim will contact police. Some reasons are fear of retaliation, fear that family or friends will side with the perpetrator, and fear that the crime will be perceived as "no big deal." One-fourth of victims reported the sexual assault when the offender was a current or former intimate partner, compared to 18 percent when it was an acquaintance or friend. In contrast, 66 percent of victims reported the crime to the police when the assailant was a stranger.[47] Ultimately, nonreporting of sexual assault ensures that the offender goes unpunished and keeps the crime a secret. Some call this a conspiracy of silence, which encourages victims (and witnesses) to accept victimization as not serious enough to report. Some victims develop a sense of helplessness, which lasts long after the initial victimization.[48]

Many rapes occur when the perpetrator and/or the victim use alcohol or other substances. In recent years, any substance used to facilitate a rape has been referred to as a *date rape drug.* Among the most common of these odorless and tasteless drugs are Rohypnol (also known as ruffies), gamma hydroxy butyrate (GHB), ketamine (also known as K or Special K), and Ecstasy (or E). The would-be rapist slips the drug into a beverage that a potential victim consumes. Within minutes of drinking it, the victim is likely to feel dizzy and nauseous, and very soon she will lose consciousness. Depending on the drug or combination of drugs used, the victim may not regain consciousness for several hours, sometimes even for days. Date rape drugs are also called "mind erasers" because once the victim awakens she typically has no memory of the preceding 24 to 48 hours. She may not remember being unconscious, what she drank, or even who she was with. This makes prosecution of these cases especially difficult.[49] Despite the availability of date rape drugs, the most commonly used substance in committing a sexual assault is still alcohol, the age-old means of lowering perpetrators' inhibitions and intoxicating or otherwise incapacitating victims.[50]

Once a rape has been committed, it is very important for the victim to receive medical attention, specifically, a sexual assault forensic exam. This exam allows for the collection of DNA evidence, which is vital when there is an unknown assailant. The components of this examination and its specific procedures are discussed in What about the Victim?

Although each victim responds differently to sexual victimization, many experience a number of symptoms collectively known as **rape trauma syndrome**, which has three phases. The *acute phase* occurs immediately after the crisis, and the symptoms usually linger for several weeks. During this phase, victims' reactions may include fear, anxiety, agitation, and crying; but other victims may appear in control, calm, and emotionless. Service providers may inaccurately assume this lack of emotion means the sexual assault was not serious or did not happen at all. The reality is that some individuals respond in a controlled manner initially, only to experience an emotional breakdown several days or even months after the attack. Some victims first express shock, disbelief, and disorientation. They may have difficulty concentrating, making deci-

What about the Victim?

The Sexual Assault Forensic Exam

The sexual assault forensic exam, also known as a rape kit, is an invasive and multistage testing process to collect evidence from the victim's body after a sexual assault. Testing with a rape kit includes removing all the victim's clothing to collect any hair, fibers, skin, and other materials (like sand, grass, or leaves) that may shake loose and indicate who committed the rape and where it occurred. Swabs are taken to obtain samples of semen, blood, and saliva—body fluids that may contain evidence of a sexual assault. A small comblike pick is used to comb the victim's relevant body parts to remove any skin, hairs, fibers, or bodily fluids left by the rapist.

Often hair is trimmed from the victim's head and genitals to provide samples for analysis. Fingernail clippings are obtained, and blood samples are collected for DNA. Toxicology tests determine what types of drugs—particularly date rape drugs—or alcohol may be in the victim's system. The victim is tested for sexually transmitted diseases (STDs) and AIDS. If the victim is a female, a full gynecological exam is performed, which may include the use of a colposcope, which detects microlacerations, bruises, and other victim injuries. A camera attached to this instrument documents any detected injuries.

Some rape kit programs also use toluidine blue, a dye that can reveal genital trauma, thereby enhancing the ability of the sexual assault nurse examiner (SANE) to detect microlacerations. Throughout this process, the SANE must take extreme caution to ensure that the evidence is properly collected, without being either contaminated or destroyed.

Collected evidence is sent to a crime lab for processing, and the results are forwarded to the district attorney's office. If the case is prosecuted, the SANE may be called to testify as a factual witness who verifies the evidence collected and injuries documented or as an expert witness who draws opinions and conclusions from the evidence.

Although these steps might seem invasive and insensitive, a victim advocate can be present to ensure the victim is treated with respect. The goal of these exams is to help the sexual assault survivor seek justice—not to cause further trauma.

OBSERVE Investigate Understand

- **How do you think the typical rape kit could be made more sensitive to the victim's needs while still preserving needed evidence?**
- **Many states require that the SANE call the police if a forensic exam is completed, even if the victim does not want to report the crime. Do you think the SANE should be required to call the police against the victim's wishes?**
- **Do you think that knowing what a forensic exam entails may deter some rape victims from reporting the attack? If so, what might be done in advance to counter such fears?**

SOURCE: Rebecca Campbell, Debra Patterson, and Lauren F. Lichty, "The Effectiveness of Sexual Assault Nurse Examiner (SANE) Programs: A Review of Psychological, Medical, Legal, and Community Outcomes." *Trauma, Violence, and Abuse* 6, no. 4 (October 2005).

sions, or answering questions. Service providers may misinterpret these normal reactions as uncooperativeness.[51]

In the second or *outward adjustment phase*, there is a seeming return to normal life but an inward struggle to cope with the assault. Some victims suppress the event and refuse to talk about what happened or what they are currently feeling. They try to live as if the rape never occurred. Others completely alter their lives to begin anew, moving to a new city or home, switching jobs, breaking off relationships, or changing their appearance. Some victims minimize the situation, saying that things could have been worse or that everything is fine. Others in this phase cannot stop talking about the crime; it becomes the focal point of their lives. Regardless of the coping technique used, behaviors associated with this phase include fear, helplessness, anxiety, flashbacks, difficulty concentrating, depression, severe mood swings, rage, eating and sleeping difficulties, sexual and relationship problems, and isolation from loved ones and familiar activities. The presence, intensity, and duration of these symptoms differ for each victim and can last anywhere from a few months to years.[52]

rape trauma syndrome
The three phases (acute phase, outward adjustment phase, and resolution phase) of symptoms that many victims experience after a sexual assault.

Finally comes the *resolution phase*, marked by the victim shifting focus from the crisis and the intensity of the attack to coping or resolution and moving on with life. This does not mean the victim has forgotten about the sexual assault; rather, she has placed the rape in perspective as a part, but not the totality, of her life. The victim does not feel the intensity or range of emotions that followed the assault or were the hallmarks of the outward adjustment phase. Instead, she may briefly experience a range of emotions, but the feelings subside and the pain lessens with time. Resolution occurs through a strong support system, counseling, and sometimes the ending of her involvement with the criminal justice system.[53]

Robbery

In 1999, the FBI reported that, on average, one **robbery** occurred every minute.[54] According to the UCR, in 2006 approximately 149 robberies were committed in the United States per 100,000 population.[55]

robbery
A crime against persons in which the offender takes personal property from the victim by either using or threatening force.

Robbery is always a crime against persons because, while taking personal property from the victim, the robber either uses or threatens to use force. In 41 percent of all robberies, the perpetrator instills fear with a handgun. Some victims were robbed of their cars while stopped at a traffic light; some, while walking the streets; some while at work. Many believe robbery is the victimization most people fear, thinking that they could be killed. Despite this fear, the likelihood of murder during a robbery is low. Since 1980, 99.8 percent of all robbery victims have survived their victimizations.[56] Primarily because of the intense fear and sense of helplessness it causes, some robbery victims suffer severe and lasting psychological trauma.

Crimes against Children

A crime against persons that is particularly difficult for most people to understand occurs when children are the targets of violence. Children are the most vulnerable of all groups, which is why **child abuse** victims are of great concern to society. Child abuse refers, for the most part, to neglect of or violence against children. Although it has been a major social concern only since the 1950s, throughout history adults have victimized children. From 1998 to 2002, among the 3.5 million victims of family violence, 10.5 percent of them, or 367,600, were children harmed by their parents.[57] The major forms of child

child abuse
Neglect of and/or violence against children.

◀ Emotional maltreatment and neglect are forms of child abuse.

abuse are physical, sexual, emotional maltreatment, and neglect. Each is unique and requires different responses by society and victim services providers.

physical abuse
The condition whereby an individual suffers serious physical injury, including intentionally assaulting, beating, biting, burning, strangulation, hitting, kicking, shaking, or pushing a victim.

Physical abuse, which includes corporal punishment (such as spanking), has been in the forefront of child abuse literature and research since the 1960s when the term *battered child syndrome* was coined. This phrase describes the condition whereby a child suffers serious physical injury, usually inflicted by parents.[58] Physical abuse includes intentionally beating, biting, burning, strangling, hitting, kicking, shaking, or pushing a child. Indeed, many argue there is a very fine line—if there is one at all—between spanking and abuse. One of the foremost advocates against corporal punishment has researched this topic for more than 30 years and concludes that children who are physically attacked by their parents (no matter how it is justified) risk suffering significant long-term psychological harm.[59]

Most people find the sexual abuse of children particularly disturbing, as it serves primarily not to control or correct a child's behavior but to gratify the perpetrator. With the exception of murder, sexual assault is the least commonly reported form of family violence (it constitutes just 0.9 percent of all such cases).[60] For the most part, child sex abusers are family members, friends, and neighbors of the victim. In one large survey, roughly 43 percent of sexual abusers were family members with whom victims had a long-lasting, trusting relationship. The psychological trauma is generally surmountable, although recovery becomes more difficult when the offender used coercive force or the child was older.[61]

MYTH/REALITY

MYTH: All child sexual abuse victims are girls.

REALITY: Recent large studies in the United States indicate that girls are at least twice—and in some studies four times—as frequently abused sexually as are boys.[62]

emotional abuse
A form of victimization by means of power or control that harms the victim's sense of self and is sometimes referred to as psychological abuse, including verbal threats, social isolation, intimidation, exploitation, or routinely making unreasonable demands, terrorizing, shaming, and putting the victim down.

A more subtle type of abuse against children is **emotional abuse**. In this form of victimization, sometimes called psychological abuse, power or control is used to harm the victim's sense of self. Emotional abuse often includes such acts as "verbal threats, social isolation, intimidation, exploitation, or routinely making unreasonable demands, terrorizing a child, or exposing [him] to family violence."[63] Other examples of emotional abuse are shaming and putting down a child.[64] Such abuse often results in impaired psychological growth, health, and development. Emotional abuse also can occur when a parent does not notice or seek help for a child's emotional problems. Due to vague and conflicting definitions of emotional abuse, and the difficulties in measuring it, the extent of this crime is unknown.

child neglect
Chronic and repetitive failure to provide children with food, clothing, shelter, cleanliness, medical care, or protection from harm.

Some forms of child abuse are acts of omission. **Child neglect** is the chronic and repetitive failure to provide children with "food, clothing, shelter, cleanliness, medical care or protection from harm." It constitutes the largest category of child abuse offenses; 52 percent of all child abuse cases in the United States (and roughly 40 percent in Canada) involve neglect.[65] Researchers once assumed the negative outcomes of neglect were relatively minor. Recent research indicates that child neglect, especially at an early age, causes substantial problems. In fact, some forms of early neglect lead to "severe, chronic, and irreversible damage."[66]

The more common forms of child abuse are usually committed by adults. However, other forms of abuse are committed by other children, which can also be traumatic and leave long-lasting effects.

MYTH/REALITY

MYTH: Bullying at school is a normal process that teaches children about life and helps them to mature.

REALITY: Bullying is not a necessary rite of passage that all children must endure to mature. It is an unnecessary experience that can and often does cause trauma and severe psychological injury if not properly treated, and it can result in life-long disability to the victims.[67]

One of the more disconcerting problems in schools around the country is **student bullying**. This form of victimization occurs when, over a span of time, a student repeatedly experiences harmful acts from other students.[68]

Bullying is especially disturbing for school administrators and teachers because most of it takes place in and around school grounds and often seriously disrupts learning. Ironically, bullying originates within the bully's home. The act of bullying—throughout the bully's life—seems to be highly correlated with the physical abuse the child suffered at the hands of his parents. For some children, being a bully is an early indication of later criminal behavior. For other children, victimization appears to be an early indicator of further, even life-long victimization. Fortunately, research indicates that child abuse interventions (see Chapter 14) can have beneficial effects in the homes of both offenders and victims.[69]

student bullying
A form of victimization in which a student is repeatedly exposed to harmful acts from other students over a period of time.

Source Connection

MISSING PERSONS

www.prisonpotpourri.com/MISSING_PERSONS/KTVU_com%20-%20KTVU%20-%20The%20Kevin%20Collins%20Case%20Turns%2020.html

Read "The Kevin Collins Case Turns 20," about the disappearance of Kevin Collins, who has been missing since 1984.

MYTH/REALITY

MYTH: Children kidnapped by one of their own parents do not suffer significantly because their kidnapper is usually known to them.

REALITY: Children who are taken by one of their own parents suffer more than we generally realize. The damage to the child's psyche from being trapped between warring parents and sometimes living on the run, using false names, and missing school and appropriate medical attention is enormous.[70]

One of the most ignored child victim types today is **missing children**. These are children who are not accounted for by their next of kin because they have been kidnapped (and perhaps killed), who have wandered away on their own due to a developmental disability or mental illness, or who have intentionally gone missing to escape violence at home. On December 31, 2006, there were 110,484 active missing person records in the National Crime Information Center's (NCIC) Missing Person File. About half the people in these files were under 18.[71]

missing children
Children not accounted for by their next of kin because they were kidnapped, killed, wandered away due to a developmental disability, or are intentionally missing in order to escape violence at home.

One response of families and friends of missing children is to offer special monetary rewards to help locate their loved ones. One of the more elaborate efforts was established

KEY CONCEPTS

Types of Child Abuse

Type	Definition
Physical abuse	Intentionally beating, biting, burning, strangling, hitting, kicking, shaking, or pushing a child.
Sexual abuse	The forced or coerced touching of a child through vaginal, anal, oral, digital fondling and/or penetration, sometimes with the use of foreign objects. Also includes forced masturbation, prostitution, pornography, and voyeurism.
Neglect	Chronic and repetitive failure to provide food, clothing, shelter, cleanliness, medical care, or protection from harm.
Emotional abuse	Verbal threats, social isolation, intimidation, exploitation, unreasonable demands, terrorizing, or exposure to family violence.
Bullying	Repeatedly experiencing harmful acts from other children.
Missing children	Children not accounted for by their next of kin because they have been kidnapped (and perhaps killed), have wandered away on their own due to a disability, or have intentionally escaped home violence.
Abandonment	The child has been intentionally left in circumstances in which the child might suffer serious harm, the parent or guardian's identity or whereabouts are unknown, or the parent or guardian has failed to maintain reasonable contact with the child or to provide reasonable support for a specified period of time with the intent of never resuming his or her interest or claim over the child. Sometimes also called foundling or throwaway.
Homicide	The intentional illegal taking of a child's life, in some cases caused by the use of physical abuse that results in the child's death.

by the parents of a California kidnapping victim. The reward ultimately led to finding the remains of their daughter, their granddaughter, and her friend, and it contributed to the successful prosecution of their killer. Subsequently these parents established a foundation that today provides these same services—in many cases successfully—across the United States.[72]

PROPERTY CRIMES

property crimes
Taking money and/or material goods *without* the use of force.

Although society clearly recognizes the seriousness of violent crimes, property offenses also can have a major impact on victims' lives. **Property crimes** include the taking of money or goods *without the use of force*. They consist of any act of *burglary* (entering another's property with the intent to commit a felony such as theft), *theft* or *larceny* (taking another's property without permission), and *motor vehicle theft*.

About three-quarters of all crimes committed in the United States in any given year are property crimes. According to the UCR, in 2008 approximately 3,212 property crimes were committed in the United States per 100,000 population.[73] As you can see from Figure 2-4, property crimes peaked in 1974, with a high of 551.5 victimizations per 1,000 households. Burglary also peaked that year, at 111.8 victimizations per 1,000 households. Crimes of theft peaked in 1995, with 424.1 victimizations. In contrast, motor vehicle thefts did not peak until 1991, with 22.2 victimizations per 1,000 households. In general, beginning in the mid-1970s all categories of property crimes have decreased steadily. In 2004, approximately 16 million households, or 12 percent of the U.S. total, experienced one or more property crimes—a 9 percent decrease from a high of 21 percent in 1994.[74] It is unclear why this decrease occurred. One possible explanation may be that people have taken more security measures to protect their homes, decreasing their vulnerability to property crimes.

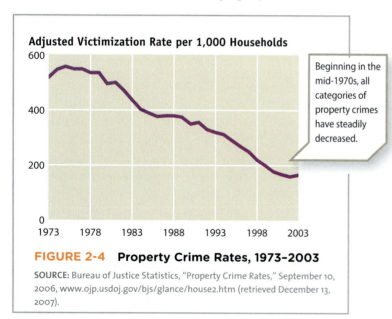

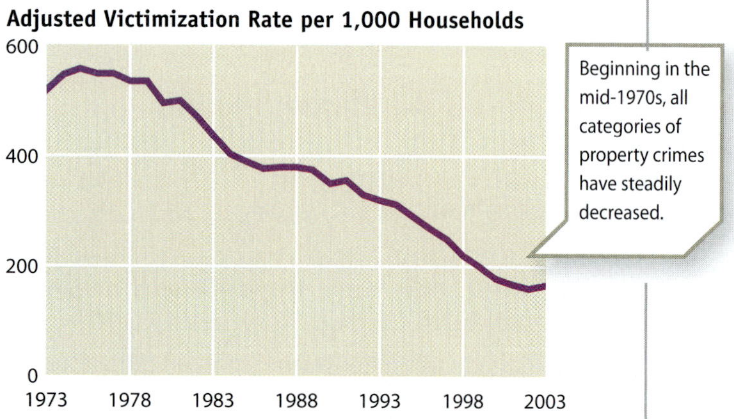

FIGURE 2-4 Property Crime Rates, 1973-2003

SOURCE: Bureau of Justice Statistics, "Property Crime Rates," September 10, 2006, www.ojp.usdoj.gov/bjs/glance/house2.htm (retrieved December 13, 2007).

People over the age of 65 experience more property crimes than other age group. Between 1993 and 2002, 9 of 10 crimes reported by the elderly were property crimes, compared to 4 of 10 reported by persons between 12 and 24 years old. Latinos were more likely to be victimized by property crimes (204 per 1,000 households) than African Americans (191 per 1,000) or Caucasians (157 per 1,000 households). The same trend holds true for motor vehicle thefts, with Latinos (19 per 1,000 households) victimized more frequently than African Americans (16 per 1,000 households) or Caucasians (8 per 1,000 households). Finally, people (including teens and unemployed persons) with annual incomes under $7,500 are victimized at a higher rate than those with higher incomes.[75]

Although property crime can happen anywhere, it is more common in urban than in rural areas, and in the western region of the United States. It is unclear why there are more property crimes in the West, but urban population densities and the resulting anonymity do contribute to the ease of stealing. The pervasiveness of property crimes suggests that many people who would never consider physically attacking others as the sole criminal act are willing to take others' belongings, sometimes even using violence. It may be tempting to let property crime take a distant second to violent crime in our attention, but we should not underrate it. Victims of theft, for example, can be devastated financially and psychologically, and the fear and stress of victimization can contribute to physical ailments.[76] Corporate crimes of theft, in particular, take an

◀ Motor Vehicle Theft

Breaking into a car can happen within minutes.

enormous financial toll on the economy as well as on public trust. Much property crime also occurs in conjunction with violent criminal acts, making it worthy of every effort to understand and control it.

Burglary

With the exception of larceny, **burglary**—entering another's property with the intent to commit a felony such as larceny—is the most common serious victimization perpetrated on those living in the United States. UCR statistics show that in 2007 approximately 723 burglaries per 100,000 population were committed in the United States.[77] Household burglary victimization produces a strong emotional reaction because it invades the victim's privacy and security, even though confrontations between burglars and victims are rare. A U.S. study in the early 1970s found that 92 percent of those who reported being burglarized stated there was no confrontation.[78] However, in a Canadian study 44 percent of burglary victims reported being at home when the burglary took place.[79]

burglary
Entering another's property with the intent to commit a felony such as larceny.

Regardless of the value of the property that is stolen, and even if the victims are not at home, burglary may have a particularly adverse impact on victims because of the psychological trauma involved in having strangers enter one's home and disturb private belongings.

Larceny

The most common form of victimization in the United States is **larceny**, a type of theft that includes both completed and attempted taking of cash or property from a location *without* attacking or threatening the victim and without obtaining permission. (If property is taken with force or the threat of force, the crime is considered robbery.) The larceny rate in the United States is close to 2,207 per 100,000 population.[80] In 2005 there were 15,605,590 thefts, or 116 victims per 1,000 persons.[81]

larceny
A type of theft that includes both completed and attempted taking of cash or property from a location *without* attacking or threatening the victim and without obtaining permission.

Theft victimization usually has the fewest physical and emotional effects. The most significant loss is the value of the object or cash taken. Victims of larceny are among the least likely victims to seek victim services because the crime normally does not result in significant fear or trauma. When they do request help, it is usually for administrative information to facilitate their cooperation with the criminal justice system's prosecution, to learn about applying for restitution or compensation, and to help prevent future victimization.

Motor Vehicle Theft

Another property crime that usually does not include contact with the offender and accompanying fear or trauma is **motor vehicle theft**. It is less common than household

motor vehicle theft
A property crime that usually does not include contact with the offender and accompanying fear or trauma. It is less common than household burglary or larceny.

Source Connection
BERNARD L. MADOFF

www.businessweek.com/blogs/recession_in_america/archives/2008/12/the_rise_and_fall.html

Read this article about "The Rise and Fall of Bernard L. Madoff."

burglary or larceny. According to the UCR, in 2008 approximately 315 motor vehicle thefts were committed in the United States per 100,000 population.[82]

The physical impact of motor vehicle theft is relatively minor. However, because the financial loss is high, victims often experience significant anger and a sense of major loss. Like other kinds of theft victims, they rarely see victim service providers. Their primary needs are for information about their role in the prosecution of the offender. Moreover, they want to find out how to obtain either restitution or compensation and how to avoid becoming a victim of future auto thefts.

White-Collar Crime

white-collar crime
Illegal or unethical acts that violate fiduciary responsibility or public trust, committed by an individual or organization, usually during the course of legitimate occupational activity, by persons of high or respectable social status for personal or organizational gain.

Because it is nonconfrontational, **white-collar crime** is frequently classified as property crime. Certainly, pain and suffering result from the victim's realization of loss, but violence has not been threatened or inflicted to accomplish the unlawful taking of money or goods. It can range in scope from a lowly employee embezzling a few thousand dollars from a Main Street business to the gigantic frauds perpetrated by Enron Corporation executives or financier Bernard Madoff. Defining white-collar crime has proved so problematic that some criminologists avoid it, favoring instead the broader concept of "occupational crime." In 1996, the National White-Collar Crime Center held a conference of researchers on the subject from across the United States and defined white-collar crime as "illegal or unethical acts that violate fiduciary responsibility or public trust, committed by an individual or organization, usually during the course of legitimate occupational activity, by persons of high or respectable social status for personal or organizational gain."[83]

MYTH/REALITY

MYTH: More people in the United States are affected by "street crime" than by white-collar crime.

REALITY: Although it is difficult to measure precisely the financial losses attributable to white-collar crime, criminologists generally agree that white-collar crime dwarfs street-crime losses.[84]

▼ Bernard Madoff

Bernard Madoff, former chairman of the NASDAQ stock exchange, perpetrated the largest investor fraud—estimated to be as much as $60 billion in cash and securities—ever attributed to a single individual. In 2009, he was sentenced to 150 years in prison, the maximum possible for his crimes.

White-collar crimes include such offenses as corporate fraud, health care fraud, environmental crime, and money laundering. The actual extent and costs of white-collar crimes are unknown. However, a 2005 survey by the National White-Collar Crime Center revealed that nearly 1 in 2 households surveyed reported experiencing at least one form of white-collar crime victimization within the previous year.[85]

"Criminologists generally agree that white-collar crime exacts a cost that dwarfs losses from street crime. Certified fraud examiners estimate that six percent of business revenues are lost to occupational fraud and abuse." "That six percent, when extrapolated over the U.S. gross domestic product, translates to annual losses of approximately $600 billion."[86] During the 1990s, the exponential growth of the securities and commodities markets, and the erosion of government regulations, led to great numbers of individuals involved in intentional corporate fraud. Using deceptive accounting practices, officers of Enron Corporation misled investors and regulators by falsifying its true financial condition.[87] Enron's collapse cost $60 billion in market value on Wall Street, almost $2.1 billion to pension plans, and 5,600 jobs.[88]

Despite increased public scrutiny, an enormous gap remains between the number of white-collar crimes committed and those actually brought to the attention of law enforcement. Only 14 percent of the crimes uncovered in the 2005 survey by the White-Collar Crime Center were reported to a crime control agency empowered to provide investigative or prosecutory action.[89] Moreover, federal attorneys have declined to prosecute almost two-thirds of the cases referred to them by the Securities and Exchange Commission (SEC). Two principal reasons for this are the difficulty of proving criminal intent and the complexity of the crimes. In the time it takes to conduct a white-collar crime trial, the prosecutor's office (which is an elected office) could have navigated eight less complicated cases through the criminal justice system—with, in all likelihood, a far greater political impact. Even among those prosecuted and convicted, 40 percent of white-collar criminals spent no time in prison.[90] These offenses (which often involve conspiracies) can be very hard to prove to juries of ordinary citizens, especially when accused white-collar offenders are wealthy business figures who can afford the best defense attorneys.

Many criminologists contend that the greatest damage done by white-collar crime lies not in its financial costs but in the corruption of U.S. society by those who occupy key roles in the economic and political systems.[91] The integrity of the financial markets and the public's resulting willingness to invest in them are crucial components of a capitalist economy. Widespread false reports of a company's robustness or other means of causing its shares to sell at inflated prices could cause people to lose trust in corporate reports altogether. The fallout to the economy could be devastating in terms of actual losses sustained directly by victims and the reluctance of others to invest in corporations.

PUBLIC ORDER CRIMES

Society considers as criminal a number of acts that, unlike property crimes, seemingly do not directly harm other people. Rather, the public believes **public order crimes** are harmful to society in general or to the person who commits the crime.

public order crimes
A wide variety of offenses considered immoral or public nuisances, including disorderly conduct, disturbing the peace, loitering, public intoxication, panhandling, bigamy, drunk driving, weapons violations, prostitution, obscenity, gambling, and possession of controlled substances.

Public order crimes encompass a wide variety of offenses, including disorderly conduct, disturbing the peace, loitering, public intoxication, panhandling, bigamy, drunk driving, weapons violations, prostitution, obscenity, gambling, and possession of controlled substances. In general, these are considered immoral acts or public nuisances. Crimes against public order often are called **victimless crimes** because, unlike property crimes or crimes against persons, they usually have no identifiable victim. However, the expression *victimless crime* may be misleading in that crimes against public order often do indirectly harm others.

victimless crimes
Often called crimes against public order and considered victimless because they usually have no identifiable victim.

For example, a storeowner may lose sales if panhandlers or prostitutes loitering outside drive away customers. On a larger scale, some argue that rampant obscenity, gambling, and drug use harm society itself. Arguably the most compelling case against such public order crimes as prostitution, money laundering, weapons offenses, and drug offenses is their link to organized crime and even terrorism. Some proponents of laws against public order crimes argue that such laws serve to protect people from themselves: If people face potential criminal sanctions, they may be less tempted to harm themselves through substance abuse or excessive gambling.

Data on public order offenses are not collected by the FBI and are not part of the Uniform Crime Reports. A great many public order laws are local ordinances rather than state statutes, and few of them are regularly or systematically enforced. It is therefore difficult to accurately determine who commits public order crimes and how often.

Crimes against Morality

Loud calls to enact specific laws against particular public order crimes, called **crimes against morality**, frequently dominate legislative agendas. Some see these laws as necessary to a civil and moral society. However, the morals they invoke may be questionable, if not unconstitutional. For example, at one time many states had antimiscegenation laws, making it a crime for people of different races to marry. These laws were declared unconstitutional in 1967 in *Loving v. Virginia*. Likewise, in *Lawrence v. Texas* in 2003 the Supreme Court struck down state laws forbidding couples to engage in acts of sodomy (oral or anal sex).[92]

crimes against morality
Specific laws against public order crimes.

Critics of morality laws have long argued that it is both wrong and impractical for society to "legislate morality." What business is it of the state, they ask, to punish acts between consenting adults that harm nobody (except maybe the people willingly engaging in them)? Many public order laws that are still on the books—against gambling,

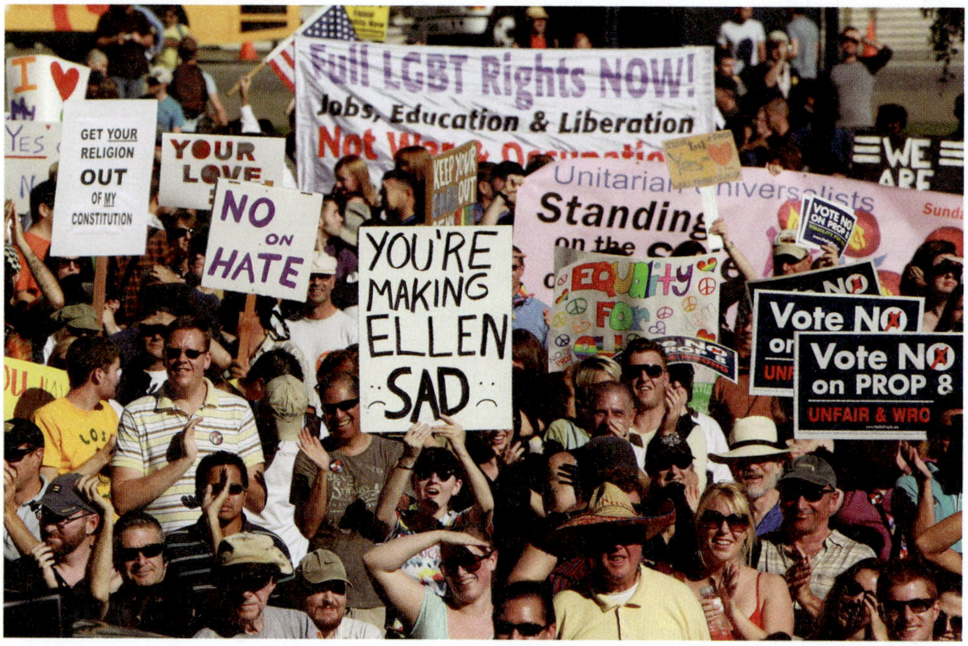

▶ People protesting Proposition 8, that established that only marriage between a man and a woman is valid or recognized in California.

Source Connection

RNC CONVENTION PROTEST

www.nytimes.com/2006/07/31/nyregion/31protest.html?_r=1

Read "In Court Papers, a Political Note on '04 Protests" about the protests and arrests at the 2004 Republican National Convention in New York City.

fornication (sex outside marriage), and adultery, for example—are ignored so frequently and universally as to make them virtually meaningless. Proponents of public order laws counter, however, that these acts do harm to others, indirectly if not directly, and that even if the laws are difficult to enforce, they have a symbolic purpose in signifying that certain behaviors are wrong.

Another argument used against public order laws is that they are often vague and broad and can easily lead to abuse of discretion by police and other public officials. Laws against disorderly conduct, for instance, often are used to arrest peaceful protesters. Public nuisance laws serve as a pretext for raids on gay bars and bathhouses. Riot laws are invoked to quash strikes. Under antilewdness laws, women who acted independently of their fathers' or husbands' control have been imprisoned, and laws against panhandling and sleeping in public are used in attempts to rid cities of homeless people. In fact, critics have noted that those in power use public order laws as a way of keeping relatively powerless people—minorities, women, and the poor—"in their place."

In 2004 almost 70 percent of prostitution arrests were of women. Yet not only must there be male customers in order for prostitutes to engage in sex work, but female prostitutes are often controlled by a pimp, a male who monitors their work and takes a percentage of their pay. Pimps, too, are arrested much less frequently than are prostitutes. The disparity between female and male arrests for the sale of sex has led to cries of "foul" by those who view the criminalization of sexual behaviors of women as a means of controlling women's sexuality.[93] Female runaways, 73 percent of whom were victims of sexual abuse, often turn to sex work to survive. Drug-addicted women are more likely to use sex to obtain drugs than are male drug users.[94] Other women are forced into prostitution through human trafficking.

Recent examples of problematic public order laws are the antigang laws passed in some locales. These laws allow the police to arrest people for such acts as talking with known gang members, wearing clothing with gang-related colors or symbols, blocking sidewalks, or approaching vehicles. Some argue these laws are an effective way to protect communities from gang-related violence, but opponents contend police use them to harass and intimidate youths, especially young people of color.[95]

drug offenses Public order crimes that include the unlawful possession, use, manufacturing, selling, growing, making, or distributing of drugs classified as having potential for abuse.

Drug Offenses

Public order crimes include such **drug offenses** as the unlawful possession, use, manufacturing, selling, growing, making, or distributing of drugs classified as having potential

TYPES OF ABUSED DRUGS

Drug	Examples
Stimulants	Cocaine, crack, Benzedrine, Dexedrine, methedrine, methamphetamines
Depressants	Seconal, Nembutal, Amytal, meprobamate, methaqualone, Librium, valium, thorazine, inhalants, alcohol
Opioids	Heroin, morphine, codeine, fentanyl
Hallucinogens	LSD, PCP, mescaline, psilocybin, ecstacy or MDMA, DPT
Marijuana	Cannabis, hashish
Performance-enhancing drugs	Ethylestrenol, methandriol, methenolone, methandrostenolone

for abuse. Illicit drugs may include (but are not limited to) heroin, cocaine, marijuana, barbiturates, amphetamines, hallucinogens, inhalants, and anabolic steroids. As you can see from the table "Types of Abused Drugs," there is a wide variety of illicit drugs.

The history of drug regulation in the United States begins in 1791, when Congress passed a tax on whiskey that led to the so-called Whiskey Rebellion. Refusing to pay the tax, Appalachian farmers tarred and feathered the federal revenue agents sent into the region by the government to collect the fees. In the end, the federal government won the confrontation, an outcome that established the U.S. government's power to enforce federal laws perceived to be in the national interest. Since then, numerous federal laws have imposed and increased punishments for drug offenses.

During the nineteenth and twentieth centuries, the negative effects of drug abuse by U.S. citizens grew into a major issue. Morphine and cocaine dependency became problems after the hypodermic syringe was invented in 1856. Opium smoking by Chinese immigrants and the widespread use of patent medicines containing opiates escalated during the late nineteenth and early twentieth centuries. Among major twentieth-century federal laws regulating narcotics, dangerous drugs, and controlled substances were the Pure Food and Drugs Act (1906), the Harrison Act (1914), the Eighteenth (or Prohibition) Amendment (1919–1933), the Jones-Miller Act (1922), the Drug Abuse and Control Amendments (1965), the Comprehensive Drug Abuse and Prevention and Control Act (1970), and the Omnibus Drug Act (1988), which created a U.S. "drug czar" with responsibility to develop a national drug-control strategy and a budget for federal agencies involved in drug enforcement. Each of these acts signifies increasing federal control and involvement in the "war on drugs."

The 1906 Pure Food and Drug Act required manufacturers of products containing drugs to clearly label the type of drug and to state how much of it was in the product. At the turn of the twentieth century, problematic drugs included alcohol, opium, morphine, cocaine, and marijuana. However, as long as the product containing the drug was not mislabeled, citizens could buy, sell, and use it freely, without prescriptions. The 1914 Harrison Act required those who sold or dispensed opiates and cocaine to register annually, pay a fee, and file a federal tax form. Users of these drugs could still do so without fear of penalty as long as they received the drugs from a registered physician who prescribed them for medical treatment. The 1922 Jones-Miller Act established the Federal Narcotics Control Board to deal with the illicit drug market. This law imposed a $5,000 fine and 10 years in prison for those convicted of illegally importing narcotics. The Jones-Miller Act also made addicted persons criminals if they had illegally obtained drugs in their possession. Between

▼ Ad for "Cocaine Toothache Drops"

During the late nineteenth and early twentieth centuries, cocaine was a common pain medication.

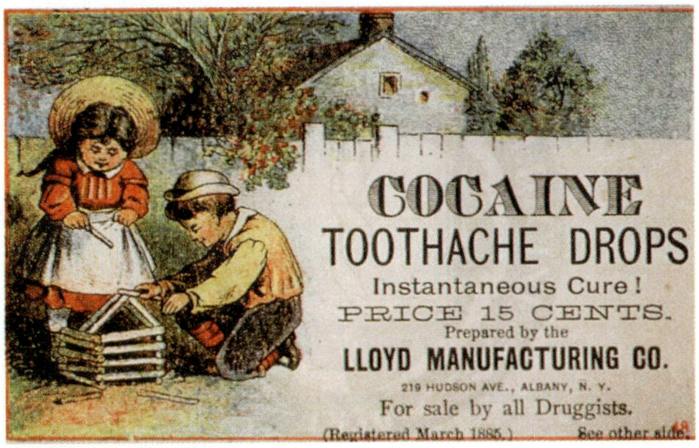

1919 and 1933 the Eighteenth Amendment authorized federal legislation (the Volstead Act) making the manufacture, sale, and use of alcohol illegal.

Responding to an increase in the use of illegal drugs and to a change in the type of drugs used by U.S. citizens during the 1960s, the 1965 Drug Abuse Control Amendments classified hallucinogens, barbiturates, and amphetamines as dangerous drugs and established the Bureau of Narcotics and Dangerous Drugs. In 1970 the Comprehensive Drug Abuse Prevention and Control Act (often called the Controlled Substance Act) replaced or updated earlier laws dealing with narcotics and dangerous drugs. This act created five different schedules of controlled substances (see "Controlled Substances Schedules" table). It also funded drug prevention and treatment, moved drug enforcement from the Treasury Department to the Drug Enforcement Administration (DEA), made the attorney general responsible for drug enforcement laws, and empowered the secretary of Health and

CONTROLLED SUBSTANCES SCHEDULES

Type	Use	Examples
Schedule I	The drug or other substance has a high potential for abuse. The drug or other substance has no currently accepted medical use in treatment in the United States. There is a lack of accepted safety for use of the drug or other substance under medical supervision.	Heroin, lysergic acid diethylamide (LSD), marijuana, and methaqualone
Schedule II	The drug or other substance has a high potential for abuse. The drug or other substance has a currently accepted medical use in treatment in the United States or a currently accepted medical use with severe restrictions. Abuse of the drug or other substance may lead to severe psychological or physical dependence.	Morphine, phencyclidine (PCP), cocaine, methadone, and methamphetamine
Schedule III	The drug or other substance has less potential for abuse than the drugs or other substances in schedules I and II. The drug or other substance has a currently accepted medical use in treatment in the United States. Abuse of the drug or other substance may lead to moderate or low physical dependence or high psychological dependence.	Anabolic steroids, codeine and hydrocodone with aspirin or Tylenol, and some barbiturates
Schedule IV	The drug or other substance has a low potential for abuse relative to the drugs or other substances in Schedule III. The drug or other substance has a currently accepted medical use in treatment in the United States. Abuse of the drug or other substance may lead to limited physical dependence or psychological dependence relative to the drugs or other substances in Schedule III.	Darvon, Talwin, Equanil, Valium, and Xanax
Schedule V	The drug or other substance has a low potential for abuse relative to the drugs or other substances in Schedule IV. The drug or other substance has a currently accepted medical use in treatment in the United States. Abuse of the drug or other substances may lead to limited physical dependence or psychological dependence relative to the drugs or other substances in Schedule IV.	Cough medicines with codeine

SOURCE: U.S. Drug Enforcement Administration, www.usdoj.gov/dea/pubs/abuse/1-csa.htm#Top.

Human Services to decide—on the basis of medical research—which substances should be controlled. The act also established penalties for drug possession and sales. The 1988 Omnibus Drug Act toughened approaches that dealt with drug users. For example, under this law those who use illegal marijuana face a civil fine up to $10,000, loss of federal benefits, forfeiture of airplanes, cars, and boats used to transport drugs, and removal from public housing for a family if any member of it engages in drug-related behavior on or near the housing project. One part of this act makes it possible for a person who murders someone or orders the killing of someone in conjunction with a drug-related felony to receive the death penalty.[96] Despite these efforts, people in the United States continue to use illegal drugs, and enforcement remains a serious, difficult, and costly problem.

Not all countries' approaches to regulating drugs are similar. There are cultural differences in attitudes toward drug use, addiction, and punishment. For example, the Netherlands takes a distinctive approach to regulating certain types of drug use. Marijuana was decriminalized in 1976 and now is sold, publicly and without penalty, in many of Amsterdam's licensed coffee houses. In the United States, the dominant approach centers on the idea that strict penalties are the best way to deter use. A comprehensive study comparing marijuana use in San Francisco and Amsterdam concluded that there were no differences between the two cities in age at onset of use, age at first regular use, or age at the start of maximum use.[97] Although the Dutch are concerned with illicit drugs and enforcement, they embrace the idea that addiction is a disease and are committed to treatment instead of punishment. These views influence Dutch drug policy.

Great Britain is another country that has taken a different approach than the United States to regulate heroin. In the 1960s and 1970s, registered British heroin addicts were given legal prescriptions that allowed them to obtain the drug in medical clinics to prevent withdrawal symptoms and to reduce heroin habits. In the 1980s the U.K. replaced prescription heroin with a narcotic antagonist, methadone—another very highly addictive substance.

Source Connection

DRUG ENFORCEMENT

www.usdoj.gov/dea/statistics.html

For more information on drug enforcement in the United States, check out the Drug Enforcement Administration's Web page.

MYTH/REALITY

MYTH: If law enforcement would destroy drugs at the source, we could eliminate the drug problem or reduce the supply of drugs entering the United States.

REALITY: Seizing drugs at the source does not solve the drug problem because many drugs are easy to produce, demand persists, and profits are high.[98]

Many illicit drugs are easy to produce. Marijuana, coca (the main ingredient of cocaine), and poppies (the main ingredient of heroin) thrive in many locales and climates.

◀ Poppy Farmers

Poppy cultivation is a lucrative business. *Do you think the United States can or should encourage other countries not to grow crops used in making drugs?*

DIS Con nects

Facts about Drugs and Crime

Today the prison population in the United States tops 2.2 million, and every week 1,000 new prisoners are incarcerated.[a] The war on drugs is primarily responsible for the exploding prison and jail populations. One in 10 children in the United States has a parent in jail, in prison, on probation, or on parole for drug-related offenses.[b] As you read the facts below, consider the effectiveness of incarceration as a punishment for nonviolent drug offenders.

- Most violent crimes are not committed to obtain drugs. About a quarter of convicted property and drug offenders committed crimes to obtain money for drugs in 2002, compared to 5 percent of violent and public order offenders who committed crimes to get money for drugs.[c]
- Homicides rarely happen during narcotics felonies. Only 3.9 percent of the 14,121 homicides in the United States in 2002 were narcotics related in that they occurred during a narcotics felony, such as drug trafficking or manufacturing.[d]
- A large percentage of prison inmates use drugs when they commit their crimes; however, the majority of these crimes are not violent. Thirty-three percent of inmates in state prisons and 22 percent of inmates in federal prisons say they committed their current offense while under the influence of drugs. Also, drug offenders (42 percent) and property offenders (37 percent) report the highest incidence of drug use at the time of the offense.[e]
- Offenders say marijuana and cocaine were the drugs most commonly used at the time of the offense.[f]
- Jail inmates are more likely to report using drugs while committing a violent crime such as robbery, weapons violations, burglary, and motor vehicle theft. Over half of jail inmates convicted of robbery (56 percent), weapons violations (56 percent), burglary (55 percent), or motor vehicle theft (55 percent) in 2002 were likely to report using drugs at the time of their offense.[g]

OBSERVE Investigate Understand

- **Looking at these facts, how effective is incarceration in curbing nonviolent drug abuse?**
- **What alternatives to incarceration might be considered for nonviolent drug offenders?**
- **Considering these facts, what effect do you think the legalization of drugs would have on the incidence of drug-related crimes?**

SOURCES: [a]Nell Bernstein, "Alone in the World: It's Time for Families of Prisoners to Let Their Voices Be Heard," *The Fresno Bee*, June 18, 2006, sec. J, and "Number of People Behind Bars in America Increasing By More Than a Thousand a Week," *Drug War Chronicle*, June 26, 2006, http://stopthedrugwar.org/chronicle-old/437/overathousand.shtml (accessed December 9, 2008).

[b]Nell Bernstein, "Alone in the World: It's Time for Families of Prisoners to Let Their Voices Be Heard," *The Fresno Bee*, June 18, 2006, sec. J, and Cynthia Seymour, "Children with Parents in Prison: Child Welfare Program, Practice, and Practice Issues," in *Children with Parents in Prison: Child Welfare Program, Practice, and Practice Issues*, eds. Cynthia Seymour and Creasie Finney Hairston (New Brunswick, NY: Transaction, 2001), 1.

[c]Bureau of Justice Statistics, *Substance Dependence, Abuse, and Treatment of Jail Inmates, 2002*, NCJ 209588, July 2005, www.ojp.usdoj.gov/bjs/dcf/duc.htm (retrieved April 30, 2006).

[d]Ibid.

[e]Bureau of Justice Statistics, *Substance Abuse and Treatment, State and Federal Prisoners, 1997*, NCJ 172871, January 1999, www.ojp.usdoj.gov/bjs/dcf/duc.htm (retrieved April 30, 2006).

[f]Bureau of Justice Statistics, "Substance Dependence, Abuse, and Treatment of Jail Inmates, 2002," July 2005, NCJ 209588, www.ojp.usdoj.gov/bjs/dcf/duc.htm (retrieved April 30, 2006).

[g]Ibid.

Specialized training is not required to harvest these crops and produce the drugs, and poor people in remote locations make profitable, easily replaced labor forces.[99] As a result, and because demand in rich countries persists and profits are high, the drug trade continues even when major drug busts occur. When production is stopped or interrupted in one place, it continues in another.[100] Latin American countries such as Colombia and Mexico have replaced Asia as the largest suppliers of heroin to the United States.[101] As you can see from the Disconnects box, a number of criminal justice problems are related to the drug war and crime in the United States.

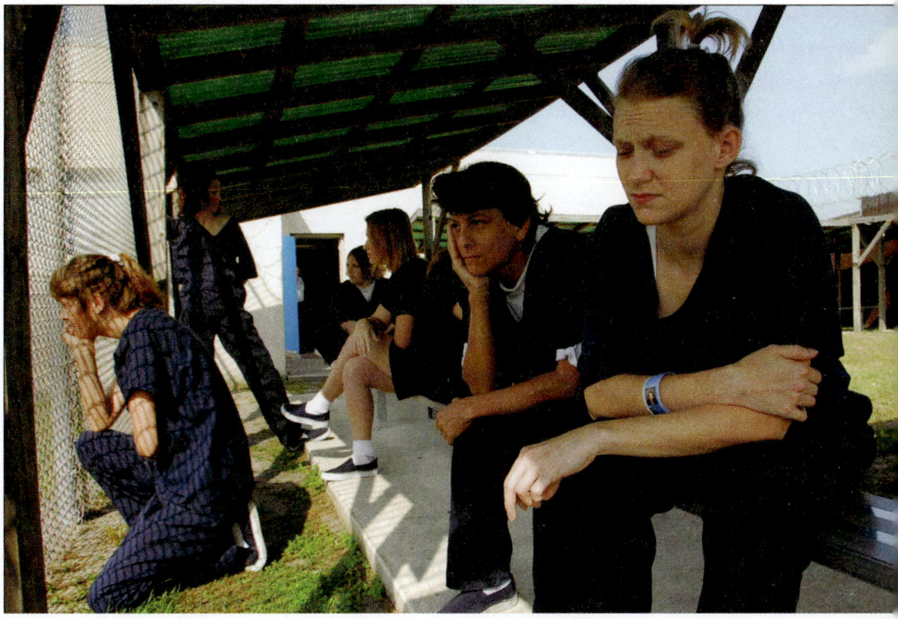

▲ **Women in Prison**

Incarcerated women have a great deal of time to think about their freedom.

We usually think of drugs as positive when they are used medically, in appropriately prescribed ways. On the other hand, when they are misused and people become addicted to them, we view drugs negatively. Drug addiction is frequently considered a public order offense because the user has lost control over taking drugs and faces harmful physical, personal, social, and legal consequences as a result.

Many experts today view substance abuse as a progressive disease (not a character defect or the result of willful choice) that changes the user for the worse until treatment occurs. It is a common misconception that people will turn to crime as a primary means of supporting their habit once they are addicted. With treatment, however, they can replace drug-using attitudes and behaviors with conventional ones and are often able to resume drug- and crime-free lifestyles. Regular recreational use of drugs, even heroin, does not mean addiction will automatically follow. Many veterans who used heroin during the Vietnam War (when it was pure, cheap, and readily available) stopped using it after returning home.[102]

Drug use, however, has several connections to crime. Many criminals are addicted to or abuse alcohol or other drugs and follow a drug-using lifestyle. Although addicted offenders typically have a drug of choice, many will use any available and convenient drug. Criminal and violent behaviors can result from effects of the ingested drug on the user's central nervous system. Certain drugs lower inhibitions, paving the way for behaviors that an individual would normally avoid, like initiating a fight. Moreover, the addict's need for the drug—to prevent agonizing withdrawal symptoms—motivates such crimes as burglary or robbery to obtain money to buy the drug. On a broader scale, manufacturing and trafficking in drugs can be so profitable that they command the power to corrupt and intimidate entire police agencies and high officials.

When we look at the results of U.S. drug laws and their enforcement, we find that although 72 percent of illicit drug users are White, 15 percent African American, and 10 percent Latino, most prison inmates serving time for drug offenses are not White (see Figure 2-5). In 2002, among all state inmates serving time for drug offenses, 43 percent were African American, 24 percent were White, and 23 percent were Latino.[103]

When we look at those convicted of drug felonies in federal courts, Whites are also less likely to be sent to prison. Thirty-three percent of convicted White defendants received prison sentences, as opposed to 51 percent of African American defendants.[104] Critics argue that racial discrimination exists in the prosecution of African Americans for drug violations based on the fact that African Americans are imprisoned for drug offenses at rates far exceeding their representation in the general population.

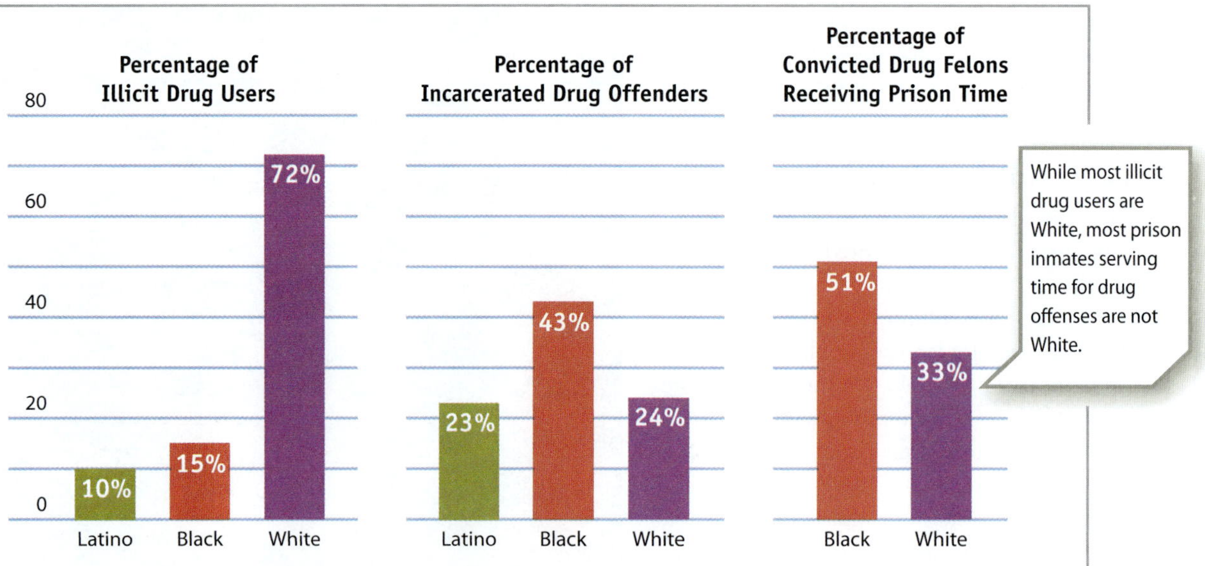

FIGURE 2-5 Racial Breakdown of Drug Abusers

Social, economic, and cultural factors contribute to the disparity in the ethnicity of illicit drug users and those incarcerated for drug-related crimes.

SOURCE: Paige M. Harrison and Allen J. Beck, "Prison and Jail Inmates at Midyear 2004," *Bureau of Justice Statistics* (Washington, DC: U.S. Department of Justice, April 2005), 11.

MYTH/REALITY

MYTH: U.S. drug laws are color and gender blind.

REALITY: Of those arrested for drug law violations, a disproportionate number belong to racial minorities. Further, the laws prohibiting use of specific drugs have resulted in the disproportionate incarceration of women of color.[105]

Women represent the fastest-growing and least violent segment of jail and prison populations. About 85 percent of female jail inmates, 65 percent of female federal prison inmates, and 31.5 percent of female state prison inmates are behind bars for nonviolent drug offenses.[106] New York's statistics also reflect this trend. In 2007, 84 percent of women sent to prison were convicted of nonviolent offenses, including drug possession only[107] (see Figure 2-6). Between 1986 and 1996, the number of women sentenced to state prison for drug-related crimes increased 10-fold, and drug convictions are primarily responsible for the explosion in the number of women behind bars.[108]

The number of women convicted for simple possession increased 41 percent, and the number of women convicted of drug felonies increased 37 percent between 1990 and 1996.[109] African American and Latino women tend to be imprisoned for drug offenses at higher rates than do White women, although their rates of illicit drug use are comparable.[110]

Critics contend that drug enforcement does disproportionate harm to women—generally minor players in the world of illegal drugs. For example, non–drug using women may become implicated if they fail to notify authorities of a partner's drug use. They typically have little or no exposure to the criminal justice system and lack knowledge about how to do such things as bargain for reduced sentences. Many feel powerless and dependent, do not assume responsibility for their lives, and are dominated by partners who are male offenders. In some cases, nonviolent women with no criminal history are given sentences on a par with those of drug kingpins when, in fact, they are minimally involved or are low-level users or dealers. The disruption of family and the impact on minor children is devastating; 60 to 80 percent of incarcerated women are mothers with dependent children.[111]

MYTH/REALITY

MYTH: Intensive law enforcement efforts at the street level will lead to the control of illicit drug use and abuse.

REALITY: Law enforcement efforts at the street level generally do not target those most directly engaged in drug trafficking. The main targets of arrest are low-level dealers and users.[112]

It is easy to get the wrong impression about drugs and their relationship to income level. When statisticians compose reports, they combine drug sales with drug use and assume that poor minority neighborhoods are the center of drug use. In fact, drug use in minority neighborhoods is only slightly higher than in more affluent nonminority areas.[113] Residents of disadvantaged neighborhoods—with high population densities and high concentrations of minorities—have only slightly higher levels of drug use and somewhat higher levels of drug dependency than do residents of more affluent nonminority neighborhoods. On the other hand, residents living in poor minority neighborhoods have much higher levels of visible drug sales. Also in poor minority neighborhoods, a major drug distribution market serves all segments of society (including purchases from those outside the minority community). Drug dealing plays a large role in the economies of poor urban neighborhoods.[114] Those who deal in drugs tend to have little formal education and few job skills, making it difficult to find well-paying lawful employment.

Consider Figure 2-7, showing that arrests for drug abuse violations have increased steadily for adults since 1970. Adult arrests for drug violations peaked in 2003 with over 1.4 million cases. Over the same period, juvenile arrests for drug violations indicate neither as sharp an increase nor as large a spike. By 1997, the number of juvenile arrests had reached an all-time high of 213,200 arrests.[115] Competing explanations for why drug abuse violations have increased vary from weak drug laws to a poor economy.

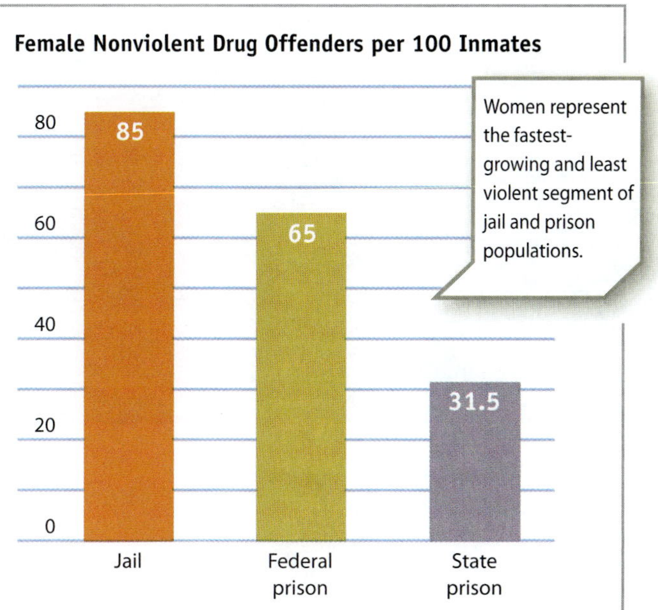

FIGURE 2-6 Incarceration of Women for Nonviolent Drug Offenses

SOURCES: John Irwin, Vincent Schiraldi, and Jason Ziedenberg, "America's One Million Nonviolent Prisoners" (Washington, DC: Justice Policy Institute, March 1999), 6–7; Paige Harrison and Allen Beck, "Prisoners in 2005" (Washington, DC: Bureau of Justice Statistics, 2007), 5; Natalie Sokoloff, "Women Prisoners at the Dawn of the 21st Century, *Women and Criminal Justice* 16, no. 1-2 (2005): 127–137; Allison T. Chappell and Scott R. Maggard, "Applying Black's Theory of Law to Crack and Cocaine Dispositions," *International Journal of Offender Therapy and Comparative Criminology* 51, no. 3 (2007): 264–278.

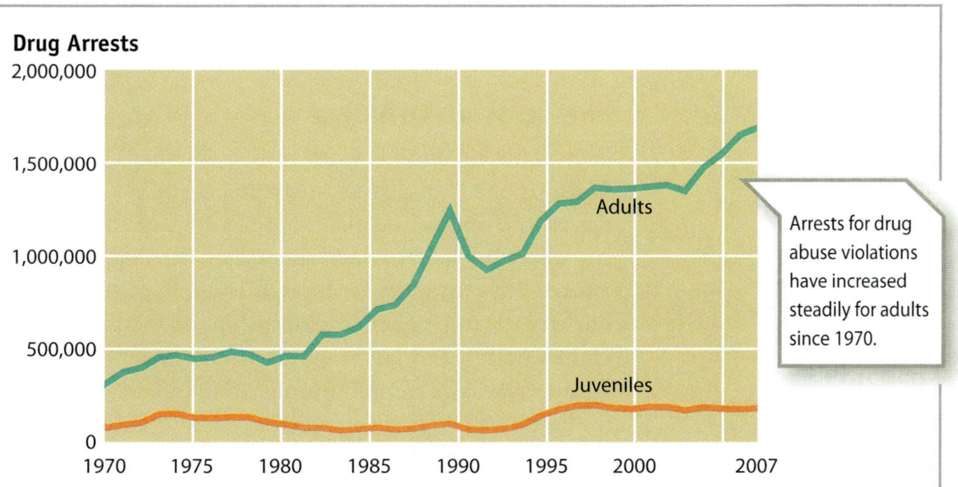

FIGURE 2-7 Drug Arrests by Age, 1970–2007

SOURCE: Federal Bureau of Investigation, *Crime in the United States, 2008.* (Washington DC: DOJ, 2008) Retrived (Oct .6, 2009), from http://www.ojp.usdoj.gov/bjs/def/enforce.htm.

Real Crime Tech

EMERGING DRUG TESTING TECHNOLOGIES

Once, drug tests involved taking urine, blood, or hair samples and required weeks of laboratory analysis. In recent years, drug tests provide results in less invasive ways, including sweat patches, saliva swabs, and breathalyzers. The sweat patch is a gauzelike patch in the middle of sticking tape, placed on a visually accessible part of the body such as the upper arm, which is cleansed with rubbing alcohol before the patch is attached. The patch is worn for up to 14 days, then removed and sent to a laboratory for analysis. This process can take several weeks—not always ideal for those in the criminal justice system.[a] The saliva swab provides a faster type of drug analysis. This handheld device allows for testing saliva, and results are available in less than 90 seconds, which is ideal when the criminal justice system needs instantaneous results. The latest rendition of the breathalyzer is the iBreath, which plugs into the base of an iPod and acts as a field sobriety test. The person being tested exhales into the breath wand, and the sensor automatically measures the results within seconds. A reading over .08 (the legal limit for being under the influence of a substance) sounds an alarm, indicating legal intoxication.[b]

All drug-testing systems can be tampered with and can provide false-positive results. The development of newer, more accurate, and more advanced devices will continue to be a real technology need for the criminal justice system well into the future.

SOURCES: [a]Drug Policy Alliance Network, "Drugs, Police, and the Law," www.drugpolicy.org/law/drugtesting/sweatpatch_/ (retrieved January 2, 2009).

[b]"Philips and Concateno Announce Revolutionary Drugs-of-Abuse Testing System," Marywn, November 21, 2008, www.marwyn.com/index.stm?article_id=73 (retrieved January 2, 2009); Dawn C. Chmielewski, "Blow into the iBreath and Your iPod Plays a Blood Alcohol Alert," *Los Angeles Times,* December 19, 2008, www.latimes.com/business/la-fi-idrunk19-2008dec19,0,3073178.storyn (retrieved January 1, 2008).

Cultural attitudes, politics, economics, and perceived harm to individuals drive proposals to solve the drug problem. Some strategies include harsher punishments for drug offenders, decriminalizing drug use and abuse, legalizing certain types of illegal drugs, enhancing law enforcement control efforts, and focusing on medical solutions to drug problems.

All these solutions have been attempted, but none has worked. Lack of resources limits law enforcement efforts—but even with unlimited resources it is impossible for law enforcement to prevent all illicit drugs from entering the country. Asset forfeiture laws have been passed to deter drug offenses, and are frequently criticized as unfair and overly harsh, but the enormous profits derived from the cultivation of poppies, coca, and marijuana means that crop control efforts meet resistance. Finally, addicts need to be highly motivated to find success in drug treatment because addiction is a relapsing disease, and victory is often incremental, transient, and temporary.

POLITICAL CRIMES

Acts, whether violent or nonviolent, that society perceives as threats to a government's survival constitute **political crimes**. At one extreme of severity are crimes such as terrorism and treason, which directly challenge the state (see Chapter 16). At the other end of the spectrum are the relatively minor offenses of immigration law violations and unlawful demonstrations. These offenses, while not intended as confrontational, may still threaten the established order and the state's political authority. They may also focus government resources on a perceived threat: for example, stationing the National Guard along the United States–Mexico border to counter illegal immigration. Choosing to fund National Guard troops at the border reduces money available for other priorities and, therefore, affects all U.S. residents.

Immigration Offenses

Federal immigration law determines whether a person is an "alien" (not a U.S. citizen) and stipulates all the legal rights, duties, and obligations aliens have in the United States. The law also establishes when aliens can become naturalized citizens (that is, citizens through law rather than through birth) with full rights of citizenship, who may enter the United States, and how long they may stay.[116] Those who violate these laws commit **immigration offenses**. According to the Bureau of Justice Statistics, in 2000 most immigration offenses involved entering the United States illegally (50 percent), making improper entry (25 percent), smuggling aliens (20 percent), and misusing visas or other immigration offenses (5 percent). By 2000, the official number of men and women referred to the U.S. Attorney General's

KEY CONCEPTS

Crimes Committed Due to Drugs

Crime Category	Types of Crime
Crimes against persons	First-degree murder, voluntary and involuntary manslaughter, vehicular manslaughter, serial murder, spree murder, assault, battery, sexual assault, robbery, child abuse, child neglect, child abandonment, bullying, kidnapping
Crimes against property	Burglary, larceny/theft, motor vehicle theft, white-collar crimes such as embezzlement, fraud, corporate fraud, environmental crime, money laundering, manufacturing, trafficking, distributing drugs, and selling drugs
Crimes against public order and morality	Disorderly conduct, disturbing the peace, panhandling, prostitution, pimping, public intoxication, loitering, drunk driving, weapons violations, gambling, obscenity, fornication, bigamy, adultery

Office for suspected immigration offenses had increased to 16,495. The majority were Mexican citizens (57 percent), but a few were U.S. (7 percent) and Chinese citizens (3 percent). In the same year, 14,540 individuals were charged with immigration offenses. These defendants were typically male (92 percent), Latino (87 percent), and between 21 and 40 years of age (80 percent). Of those charged with smuggling aliens, 64 percent were U.S. citizens. More than two-thirds of defendants charged with an immigration offense had a prior arrest history, and 36 percent had five or more prior arrests. In general, 96 percent of individuals charged with immigration offenses were convicted when prosecuted in federal courts. Over a 15-year period from 1985 to 2000, incarcerations in federal prisons for immigration offenses increased from 1,593 to 13,676 adult male and female inmates.[117]

political crimes
Violent or nonviolent acts that society perceives as threats to a government's survival.

immigration offenses
Violation of federal immigration law, which determines whether a person is an alien and stipulates all the legal rights, duties, and obligations aliens have in the United States.

U.S. immigration policy has become a divisive political issue over the past four decades. Until the late 1970s, Republicans and Democrats alike expressed concern for families separated by immigration, as well as for people displaced by wars, famine, and political oppression. The focus was humanitarian, emphasizing the need for family unification and assimilation. However, in the 1980s, as concerns mounted nationwide over the costs of health care for the uninsured, once bipartisan support evaporated, and many

Americans began demanding changes.[118] Citing the high cost of extending public benefits to illegal immigrants and reluctant to grant them amnesty, the federal government called for immigration reform with a focus on the criminality of immigration offenses. After September 11, fear of terrorism perpetrated by aliens made immigration a topic of great concern. The federal government focused intensely on illegal immigration, aiming to enforce and strengthen existing laws.[119]

Immigrants—legal and illegal—are vital to the U.S. economy. They make up 12 percent of the U.S. population and 14 percent of its workers. From 1994 to 2004, the

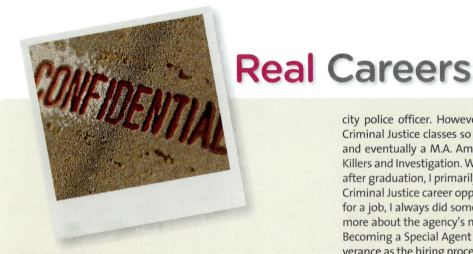

Real Careers

AMY NYE

Work location: (Cannot disclose)

College(s): Wayne State University, Detroit, IL

Major(s): Criminal Justice (B.S.), Near Eastern Studies (M.A.)

Job title: Special Agent with Immigration and Customs Enforcement

Salary range for jobs like this: $29,000-$37,000

Time in job: 1 year

Work Responsibilities

I conduct criminal investigations on a wide range of matters, such as visa security, illegal arms trafficking, document and identity fraud, drug trafficking, gang activity, child pornography and sex tourism, immigration and customs fraud, and intellectual property rights violations.

As a Special Agent, I enjoy a balance between working at the office and working in the field. Some of my more exciting field experiences include conducting surveillance on targets, working undercover operations, and executing search and arrest warrants. But being a special agent is certainly not a 9 to 5 job: very early mornings and late nights are often required.

Why Criminal Justice?

I had been interested in Criminal Justice since high school. My history teacher, a retired police officer, often told stories about his experience in that profession. Wanting to learn more about law enforcement, I took an independent study course with him and researched the challenges currently facing law enforcement agents, especially females in a traditionally male-dominated career path.

I entered college originally with the intention of obtaining an Associates Degree in Criminal Justice in order to become a city police officer. However, once I began college I loved my Criminal Justice classes so much that I decided to pursue a B.S. and eventually a M.A. Among my favorite courses were Serial Killers and Investigation. When I began looking for employment after graduation, I primarily used Wayne State's website to find Criminal Justice career opportunities. However, before applying for a job, I always did some of my own online research to learn more about the agency's mission and the requisites for the job. Becoming a Special Agent requires a lot of patience and perseverance as the hiring process can take a few years.

Expectations and Realities of the Job

Working in law enforcement is vastly different from the way it is portrayed in novels and TV shows. Criminals do not always confess and investigations can carry over for weeks, months, or even years. For example, a lot of intelligence gathering and database mining must be performed before an agent can even begin questioning a subject. Post-enforcement procedures can be just as lengthy: agents are required to report and update databases so that the most current Intel is available for future cases.

But regardless of the separation between reality and fiction, I love having a job that makes a difference. I don't just talk about making my country and my community safer, I am actually doing something about it.

My Advice to Students

The entire process of getting hired as a special agent can take a couple of years, so if you are interested in becoming an agent, apply as soon as possible. I waited a year and a half to be hired and had to work a part-time job in the meantime. To increase your chances of finding employment, I suggest you apply to a variety of agencies, which specialize in different areas of investigation. Your strengths and abilities might be better suited for one agency over another. But no matter which agency you apply to, federal agents must keep a clean criminal record. Keep in mind that background checks are always a component of the application process.

Try to get involved in extracurricular activities related to the field you want to enter. For example, during college I rode with local police agencies, which gave me a great feel for the career path I was choosing. I also took classes at the local gun range on firearm safety, weapon retention, and carrying a concealed weapon. Beginning my career training with prior firearm knowledge was quite valuable. Finally, keep yourself in great physical condition. Any type of martial arts training will also be beneficial.

◀ Day Laborers Waiting to Work

Day laborers, who are frequently in the United States illegally, are eager to find work.

number of foreign-born workers grew from 13 million to 21 million, accounting for more than half the growth of the U.S. labor force in that period. According to the American Immigration Lawyers Association, illegal immigrants hold 40 percent of farming, fishing, and forestry jobs in the United States, 33 percent of jobs in building and grounds maintenance, 22 percent of food preparation jobs, and 22 percent of construction jobs. Opinions differ as to what impact immigration reform will have on the United States and its economy, particularly in states like California that earn much of their revenue from immigrant farm workers, agriculture, and tourism.[120]

ORGANIZED CRIME

Groups can also commit crimes. **Organized crime** is an ongoing criminal conspiracy that exists to profit from providing illicit goods and services. It uses or threatens violence to further its criminal enterprises and to maintain monopoly control of specific markets.[121]

organized crime
An ongoing criminal conspiracy that exists to profit from providing illicit goods and services, using or threatening violence to facilitate its criminal enterprise and to maintain monopoly control of illicit markets.

Organized crime, much like serial murder, fascinates the American public. Mainstream society loves fiction and films about mob bosses, their families, and their associates (for example, *The Godfather* and *The Sopranos*). Indeed, much of what people believe they know about the underworld comes from the mass media, which has focused almost exclusively on the Italian community and is not necessarily based on reality.

Historically, Italians' involvement in U.S. organized crime was preceded by that of Irish and German Jewish immigrants. Most members of each ethnic group attempted to enter the mainstream of American life and attain financial security in law-abiding ways, but some pursued illicit shortcuts.[122] In the United States, organized crime groups originally drawn from successive waves of immigrants have yielded to a range of diverse criminal associations such as urban street gangs, outlaw motorcycle gangs, and prison gangs. A few large organizations once controlled an illicit market, but now an expanded number of small organizations operate autonomously.[123] Other organized crime groups have gained considerable influence in the United States; some are based on foreign soil, including the Colombian drug cartels and the Russian Mafia.[124]

Crimes perpetrated or controlled by criminal enterprises include gambling, prostitution, auto theft, and drug trafficking. Organized crime groups use legitimate business ventures as a cover and as a way to launder illegal profits. They may employ or contract with specialists, such as corrupt governmental officials or individuals in the private sector, who are in a position to ignore violations, conceal or move assets, or otherwise assist illegal activities.[125]

Members of the criminal organization may comprise a crime "family," a gang, a cartel, or a criminal network. Membership is restricted to those who have been formally accepted after demonstrating loyalty to the group's principles and its members. Most crime groups are local in scope and without cooperative relationships with other organized crime groups.[126]

By the late twentieth century, organized crime groups could exploit the same open borders and technological advances that have enabled multinational corporations to prosper. In fact, transnational crime groups may have profited more from globalization than legitimate business enterprises, which are subject to domestic and host country laws and regulations. Interestingly, despite their scope, transnational criminal operations are almost always compartmentalized. Most transnational activities, such as heroin trafficking and human smuggling, require numerous independent groups operating in source, transit, and destination countries.[127]

CRIMES BY GENDER

stalking
Willfully, maliciously, and repeatedly following or harassing another person and making a credible threat with the intent to place that person in reasonable fear for his or her safety, or for the safety of his or her family.

Anyone can commit a particular crime, but strong trends differentiate by gender the types of crimes committed and the frequency of offending.[128] **Stalking** today is a crime dominated by one sex: for the most part, men stalk women.

Stalking has existed since the beginning of human history, and through the ages has been depicted in music, poetry, novels, paintings, and films as part of romantic behavior. In the last decade, stalking has been criminalized throughout the United States.[129] Although definitions vary from state to state, a 1990 California statute defines as a stalker anyone who "willfully, maliciously, and repeatedly follow[s] or willfully and maliciously harass[es] another person and . . . makes a credible threat with the intent to place that person in reasonable fear for his or her safety, or of the safety of his or her family."[130]

A national survey of American women revealed that 1 in 12 survey participants had been stalked. (One man in 45 also had been followed or harassed at some point in his life.)[131] The victim's obvious reaction to stalking is fear, and stalkers eventually assault 81 percent of targeted individuals. It is ironic that the notoriety of stalking results from cases of celebrities stalked by strangers but rarely endangered. In reality, in the overwhelming majority of cases, intimate partners or former partners stalk women who are not celebrities and whose lives are often at considerable risk. As illustrated in Figure 2-8, stalking occurs in six types of relationships. Note the differences in gender between victims. Males often

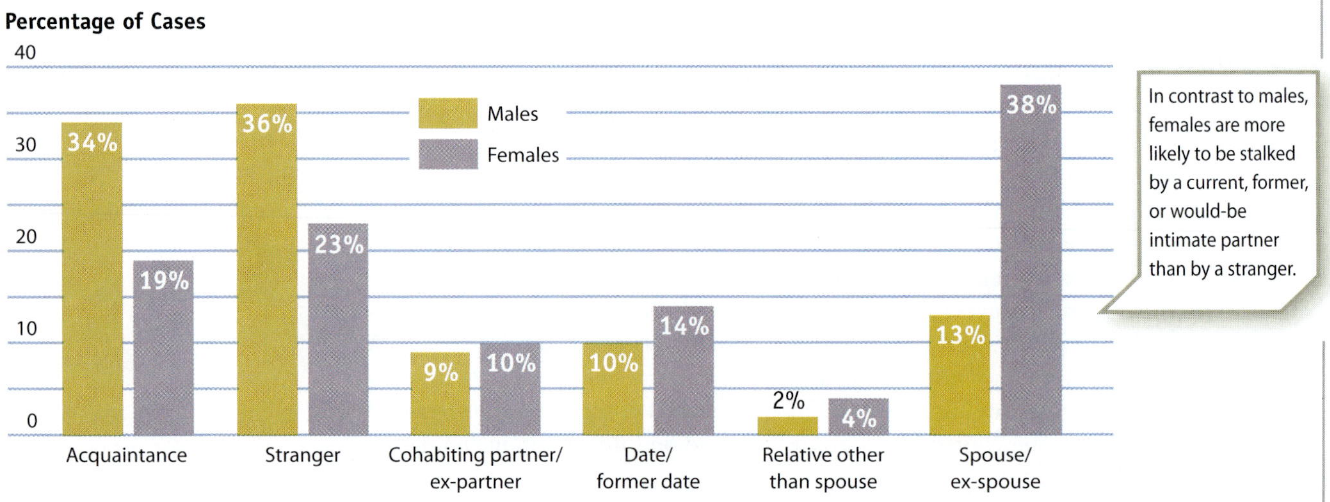

FIGURE 2-8 Gender Differences between Stalking Victims

SOURCE: Patricia Tjaden and Nancy Thoennes, *Stalking in America: Findings from the National Violence against Women Survey* (Washington, DC: NIJCDC, 1998), 6.

Race, Class, Gender

Gender and Crime

Females represent a small but increasing percentage of the offending population. On December 31, 2000, state or federal institutions incarcerated 93,234 women. Within seven years, out of a total prison population of 1.5 million, 114,420 were women—an annual increase of 3.2 percent, compared to a 1.9 percent increase for males.[a] Although males represent the largest percentage of prison inmates, female inmates present with more mental health problems than males. A 2006 study of the mental health of those incarcerated found that 23 percent of females both in state facilities and in local jails were diagnosed with a mental health problem, compared to 8 and 9 percent of male inmates, respectively.[b]

However, males offend with significantly greater frequency than do females. In general, male offenders are more likely than are female offenders to be violent. Women are much less likely than men to commit assault or murder, and the rate of murders committed by women has declined since 1980.[c] Despite the fact that women commit fewer violent crimes, data show that women increasingly do engage in that kind of criminality. A study that examined the gender of violent felons in the 75 largest counties from 1990 to 2002 found that males were responsible for 91 percent of all violent felonies and females for 9 percent.[d] The most recent data, from 2005, support previous statistics: women were incarcerated in state institutions for violent offenses (35.4 percent), property offenses (28.6 percent), drug offenses (28.7 percent), public order offenses (6.1 percent), and "other/unspecified offenses" (1.2 percent). During the same period, males were incarcerated in state facilities for violent offenses (54.3 percent), drug offenses (18.9 percent), property offenses (18.5 percent), public order offenses (7.7 percent), and "other/unspecified offenses" (0.6 percent). As these data indicate, women are committing more property, drug, and public order offenses than are males. Males continue to commit more violent offenses than females, but the gap is decreasing as women commit more violent crimes.[e] According to 2005 National Crime Victimization data of juvenile victims (ages 12–17), males were the perpetrator of 76 percent of violent crimes and females accounted for 22 percent (with 2 percent unaccounted for).[f] Despite the increase in female violence, males continue to commit certain violent crimes with greater frequency than do women, including intimate partner violence, stalking, aggravated assault, forcible rape, robbery, and murder.

OBSERVE Investigate Understand

- **What might explain why a larger proportion of incarcerated women than men present with mental health problems?**
- **Why do you think the rate of murders committed by women has declined since 1980?**
- **The statistics indicate that females are becoming more violent than ever before, but not for murder. Why?**

SOURCES: [a]Heather C. West, "Prisoners in 2007," *Bureau of Justice Statistics*, December 2008, www.ojp.usdoj.gov/bjs/pub/pdf/p07.pdf (retrieved December 28, 2008).

[b]Doris J. James and Lauren E. Glaze, "Mental Health Problems of Jail and Prison Inmates," *Bureau of Justice Statistics Special Report*, September 2006, NCJ 213600, www.ojp.usdoj.gov/bjs/pub/pdf/mhppji.pdf (retrieved December 20, 2008).

[c]Lawrence Greenfield and Tracy Snell, "Women Offenders," *Bureau of Justice Statistics Special Report* (Washington, DC: U.S. Department of Justice, December 1999).

[d]Brian. A. Reaves, "State Court Processing Statistics, 1990–2002: Violent Felons in Large Urban Counties," *Bureau of Justice Statistics*, July 2006, www.ojp.usdoj.gov/bjs/pub/pdf/vfluc.pdf (retrieved December 28, 2008).

[e]West, "Prisoners in 2007."

[f]Katrina Baum, "Juvenile Victimization and Offending," August 2005, Bureau of Justice Statistics, NCJ 209468, www.ojp.usdoj.gov/bjs/pub/pdf/jvo03.pdf (retrieved December 20, 2008).

are stalked by an acquaintance or stranger, but females are more likely to be stalked by a current, former, or would-be intimate partner. In these cases, the stalking is another form of abuse, used to control the victim.[132]

There are other differences in the incarceration rates and types of crimes committed by males and females. The Race, Class, Gender box highlights these patterns based on gender.

SUMMARY

For 20 years after the FBI began compiling its Uniform Crime Reports in 1973, the incidence of serious violent crimes increased. After peaking in the early 1990s, the number of both violent and property crimes reported to police has been declining, and rates of victim-reported and police-reported crime have been converging, for reasons not entirely understood.

Other important trends also stand out. On a global scale, the United States has a high murder rate, and within this country, murder rates are highest in the South. Males are more frequently victimized by all categories of violent crime except rape and intimate partner violence. Women are less likely to report a violent attack—especially rape, a crime in which perpetrator and victim very often know each other. Children are more frequently victimized by violent crime than are older people. Despite the great fear that crimes against people evoke, almost 10 times as many crimes against property are reported. Property crimes account for about three-fourths of all crimes reported in the United States, but like violent crime the rate has been falling since the 1990s. Property crimes are usually less traumatizing, although white-collar crime can inflict devastating economic losses.

A common characteristic of public order crimes is that they are offenses against morality. Although they often are called "victimless crimes," in fact many of them have negative consequences for the perpetrator as well as for others. Less is known about the incidence of these offenses because systematic statistics are not compiled. Drug offenses have been a great source of concern in the United States for a century. Although most crime is not drug related, drugs are a factor in both violent crimes (homicide, assault, and robbery) and nonviolent crimes (burglary and theft). Abusers can be physically and psychologically devastated by drug use. Unfortunately, enforcing drug laws and controlling drug-related crime has not been very successful. One significant impact of the U.S. "war on drugs" is an ever-rising proportion of persons incarcerated for drug-related offenses, including disproportionate numbers of women and racial minorities. A second major impact is the corrupting effect on the police and public officials that stems from organized crime's domination of the drug trade.

Political crimes directly challenge government authority. They run the gamut from such relatively minor offenses as immigration law violations to major crimes against the state—espionage, treason, and terrorism.

Organized crime is a serious problem in modern societies, and in the United States it was once largely associated with immigrant ethnic groups. It involves violence, exploits and profits from such public order offenses as prostitution, gambling, and drug trafficking, and frequently is implicated in the corruption of public authorities.

OBSERVE
Investigate
Understand

Review

Understand how crime rates are measured.

- The Uniform Crime Reports (UCR) is compiled annually by the FBI from data reported by local police departments. Today, the UCR covers murder and nonnegligent manslaughter, forcible rape, robbery, aggravated assault, burglary, larceny, motor vehicle theft, arson, and hate crimes.
- The National Incident-Based Reporting System (NIBRS), compiled by the FBI and the Department of Justice, is an index that tracks detailed information about 22 specific categories of crime incidents and arrests. Data are submitted by state authorities, and not all states are as yet able to take part in the system.
- The National Crime Victimization Survey (NCVS) is an annual national survey of selected households and

individuals to discover who has been victimized by crime, whether or not the crimes were reported to the police. Through this survey, the so-called dark figure of crime can be estimated—the gap between reported crime and crime that goes unreported and is therefore unrecorded. It can also reveal the extent of "secondary victimization:" that is, the negative experiences of crime victims based on their treatment by the police, the courts, and personal acquaintances.

Differentiate the types of crimes against persons.

- Crimes against persons involve attacks upon or threats to a person's body. The most serious crimes against persons are murder and manslaughter (both mean taking a life), sexual assault, kidnapping, robbery (theft with force or the threat of force), and battery (the intentional unwanted touching of one person by another).
- Homicide occurs when someone unjustifiably causes the death of another human being. Different types of homicide include first-degree murder (purposely planning to kill the victim), manslaughter (the offender is less blameworthy than for murder; it usually carries a less severe penalty than murder), voluntary manslaughter (the offender is provoked and loses control, killing his victim in the heat of passion), involuntary manslaughter (killing that results from an offender's careless actions) and vehicular manslaughter (the careless use of one's vehicle that results in a victim's death).
- Serial murder means killing three or more people over an extended period; mass murders are multiple killings that occur at one place and at one time; spree murder refers to multiple victims killed within a fairly narrow time span, such as several hours or days.
- Sexual violence encompasses nonconsensual vaginal, anal, and oral penetration and can include the use of weapons and foreign objects to torture and terrorize the victim.

Describe the different types of property crimes.

- Property crimes include taking money or material goods without using force. They consist of any act of burglary (entering another's property with the intent to commit a felony such as theft), theft (or larceny, both of which mean taking another's property without permission), motor vehicle theft (taking one's car or contents within the car), and white-collar crime (theft or other nonviolent offenses in a business setting).

Identify types of public order crimes.

- Public order crimes encompass a wide variety of offenses, including disorderly conduct, disturbing the peace, loitering, public intoxication, panhandling, bigamy, drunk driving, weapons violations, prostitution, obscenity, gambling, and possession of controlled substances.
- Public order crimes are characterized as immoral or public nuisances.
- Crimes against public order often are called victimless crimes because, unlike property crimes or crimes against persons, it is hard to find an identifiable victim.

Describe some of the political crimes that have occurred in recent years.

- Political crimes include acts, violent and nonviolent, that threaten a government's survival.
- Terrorism and treason are two extreme forms of political crimes, which represent a direct challenge to the government.
- Less extreme examples of political crimes include violations of immigration laws and unlawful demonstrations. These offenses, although not intended to be confrontational, may still represent a threat to the established order and to political authority.
- Political crimes may serve to turn government resources toward a perceived threat, such as having National Guard troops at the United States–Mexico border as a force to counter illegal immigration. The choice to use money to fund National Guard troops at the border reduces money available for other priorities and, therefore, affects all U.S. residents.

Describe organized crime and who engages in it today.

- Organized crime is an ongoing criminal conspiracy that exists to profit from providing illicit goods and services. By its nature, organized crime uses or threatens violence to facilitate its criminal enterprises and maintain monopoly control of illicit markets.
- Crimes committed or controlled by criminal enterprises includes gambling, prostitution, auto theft, and drug trafficking. Organized crime groups engage in many legitimate business ventures as a cover and as a way to launder monies from their criminal activities. They may employ or contract with specialists such as corrupt government officials or members of the private sector who can ignore violations, conceal or move assets, or otherwise assist the network of illegal activities.
- Members of the criminal organization may form a crime "family," a gang, a cartel, or some other kind of criminal network. Membership is restricted to those who have been formally accepted after demonstrating loyalty to the group's criminal principles and its members.
- By the late twentieth century, organized crime had exploited the same open borders and technological advances that have enabled multinational corporations to prosper. In fact, transnational crime groups may have profited more from globalization than legitimate business enterprises, which are subject to domestic and host country laws and regulations.

Contrast the types of crimes generally perpetrated by males and by females.

- In general, male offenders are more likely to be violent than female offenders. Despite that, data show that women are increasingly participating in violent crimes.
- Women are committing more property, drug, and public order offenses than are males. Males continue to commit more violent offenses than females, but the gap is decreasing.
- Women are much less likely than men to commit assault or murder.
- Despite the increase in female violence, males continue to commit certain violent crimes with greater frequency than women, including intimate partner violence, stalking, aggravated assault, sexual assault, robbery, and murder.

Key Terms

assault and battery 36
burglary 43
child abuse 39
child neglect 40
Crime Index 27
crimes against morality 45
crimes against persons 31
dark figure of crime 29
drug offenses 46
emotional abuse 40
first-degree murder 34
immigration offenses 55
involuntary manslaughter 35
larceny 43
manslaughter 34
mass murder 35
missing children 41
motor vehicle theft 43
National Crime Victimization Survey (NCVS) 28
National Incident-Based Reporting System (NIBRS) 28
organized crime 57
physical abuse 40
political crimes 55
property crimes 42
public order crimes 45
rape trauma syndrome 39
robbery 39
secondary victimization 29
self-report 29
serial murder 35
sexual victimization 37
sexual violence 37
spree murder 35
stalking 58
student bullying 41
Uniform Crime Reports (UCR) 27
vehicular manslaughter 35
victim surveys 28
victimless crimes 45
voluntary manslaughter 34
white-collar crime 44

Study Questions

1. The Uniform Crime Reports (UCR) are annual surveys that
   a. track the most serious crimes as reported by victims.
   b. track the most serious crimes as reported by police departments.
   c. provide detailed information about criminal incidents and arrests in 22 categories.
   d. are compiled by telephoning individuals in different countries about crimes against household members during the previous 12 months.
2. Which of the following is the number one cause of injuries and death to women in the United States?
   a. Traffic collisions
   b. Suicide
   c. Drug abuse
   d. Intimate partner violence
3. __________ are offenses against another person's belongings.
   a. Victimless crimes
   b. Property crimes
   c. Attempted crimes
   d. Infractions
4. Crimes against public order often are referred to as which of the following?
   a. Inchoate offenses
   b. Victimless crimes
   c. Property crimes
   d. Attempted crimes
5. Which of the following is *not* characteristic of organized crime?
   a. Part-time participation by the perpetrators
   b. Provision of illicit goods and services
   c. Use of violence or the threat of violence
   d. Corruption of public officials
6. Which of the following is *not* an example of a public order crime?
   a. Disorderly conduct
   b. Disturbing the peace
   c. Loitering
   d. Immigration offenses
7. Which of the following is *not* an example of an immigration offense?
   a. Entering the United States illegally
   b. Improper entry into the United States
   c. Alien smuggling
   d. White-collar crimes
8. Which age group is most vulnerable to crime?
   a. Young people
   b. Middle-aged people
   c. Older adults
   d. All age ranges are equally likely to be victimized.

9. Although property crime can happen everywhere, it is more common in urban than in rural areas, and in the ______ region of the United States.
   a. eastern
   b. northern
   c. southern
   d. western
10. In 1967, the Supreme Court's decision in the case ___________ declared antimiscegenation laws unconstitutional.
    a. *Loving v. Virginia*
    b. *Lawrence v. Texas*
    c. *Brown v. Board of Education*
    d. *Gideon v. Wainwright*
11. Which of the following is *not* based on NCVS data?
    a. Males are victimized more than females.
    b. There are 5 million victims of violent crimes each year.
    c. Between 1992 and 2002, 141,000 people ages 12 and older reported being victims of attempted or completed rape.
    d. None of the above.

Critical Thinking Questions

1. Do you think crimes can truly be victimless?
2. If white-collar crime is so costly, why doesn't the criminal justice system do more to prosecute these types of offenses?
3. How should we deal with the drug problem in the United States?

Internet Sites

Bureau of Justice Statistics
http://ojp.usdoj.gov/bjs/
A federal organization dedicated to collecting, analyzing, publishing, and disseminating information on crime, criminal offenders, victims of crime, and the operation of justice systems at all levels of government. These data are critical to federal, state, and local policymakers in combating crime and ensuring that justice is both efficient and evenhanded.

City Rating.com
www.cityrating.com/crimestatistics.asp
Crime statistics on your city and others can be found at the Web site.

The Innocence Project
www.innocenceproject.org
The Innocence Project is a national litigation and public policy organization dedicated to exonerating wrongfully convicted people through DNA testing and reforming the criminal justice system to prevent future injustice.

Rape, Abuse, and Incest National Network
www.rainn.org
The Rape, Abuse, and Incest National Network is the nation's largest anti–sexual assault organization. RAINN operates the National Sexual Assault Hotline and carries out programs to prevent sexual assault, help victims, and ensure that rapists are brought to justice.

Suggested Readings

John Jung, *Psychology of Alcohol and Other Drugs: A Research Perspective* (Newbury Park, CA: Sage, 2001).
This book provides students with a comprehensive understanding of alcohol, over-the-counter drugs, and illegal drugs, including the effects of each on one's development and body. Jung discusses how addiction influences someone based on age, gender, ethnic background, personality, family dynamics, and interpersonal relationships. Finally, theories of addiction are introduced, and treatment and recovery are discussed.

Lisa Maher, *Sexed Work: Gender, Race, and Resistance in a Brooklyn Drug Market* (Oxford: Clarendon Press, 1997).
This book uses criminological, anthropological, and sociological perspectives to provide a foundational understanding to the problems of race, class, and gender as they pertain to the divisions of labor in the street-level drug economy. The research is based on a 3-year ethnography of the experiences of drug-abusing women in New York City.

Dave Pelzer, *A Child Called "It:" One Child's Courage to Survive* (Deerfield Beach, FL: Health Communications, 1995).
This is an autobiographical account by Dave Pelzer, whose personal story about his childhood in the 1970s was one of the worst cases of child abuse in California history. The book provides readers with an insight into the thoughts and feelings of a child who was victimized by an abusive and alcoholic mother, a neglectful and alcoholic father, and siblings who were bullies. The book chronicles the daily abuse, the dynamics of an abusive family, and the school and law enforcement's response to this case.

CHAPTER 3

Causes of Crime

OBSERVE Investigate *Understand*

After reading this chapter, you should be able to:

- Understand the roles of biological (including genetic) and environmental factors on brain function and criminal behavior.
- Explain the key aspects of mental disorders and understand how they are classified.
- Recognize the cognitive factors of intelligence and moral reasoning as brain functions that influence criminal behavior.
- Understand how economic, class, and social inequalities can be linked to the causes of crime.
- Describe factors that cause some people to become victims of crime.

Realities and Challenges

A Mother, A Murderer

Andrea Yates waited for her husband, Rusty, to leave for work. She gathered their five young children—ages 6 months to 7 years—around the kitchen table for breakfast. The four boys enjoyed corn puffs cereal while Andrea fed milk to their infant sister, Mary. Rusty said good-bye at about 9 a.m. and left their suburban Houston home for work. The morning of June 20, 2001, seemed like any other in this thriving neighborhood of tree-lined streets and middle-class families.

As Rusty drove away, Andrea carried baby Mary to the bathroom, placed her in a bassinet, and filled the bathtub nearly full of water. She then called her four boys to the bathroom one by one and methodically drowned her children by holding them face down in the tub. Andrea would later say that her oldest son, Noah, put up the biggest fight, and she had to drag the boy back to the tub repeatedly until he succumbed. As he fought against his mother, Noah's last words were, "I'm sorry." He was then held down in the water while around him floated vomit and feces from the siblings who had died before him.[1]

After murdering her children, Andrea neatly arranged their bodies on her bed. She called 911 to report what she had done. Yates then called Rusty to tell him that he needed to come home.

Explaining Andrea Yates's crime is not easy. Her mental history included bouts of postpartum psychosis. Throughout most of her eight-year marriage she was either pregnant or breast-feeding. After the birth of her first child, she began to have visions of a knife stabbing her babies and claimed that Satan was speaking to her. Andrea attempted to kill herself on more than one occasion. Soon after the birth of their fourth child, Andrea overdosed on her mother's antidepressant pills; a month later Rusty found Andrea holding a knife to her own throat.

In the years leading up to her crime, Andrea also became increasingly isolated from the people and community around her. Not long after she married Rusty, Andrea gave up her career as a registered nurse to raise their family. For several years, before moving into their house, the couple lived with their children in a 20-year-old, 350-square foot Greyhound bus converted to living quarters. Two of the children slept with their parents in the main cabin of the bus, and the other two slept in the luggage compartment. She homeschooled her children and tended to her father who had Alzheimer's disease. Further complicating the situation, a friend of Rusty's from college held particular influence over Andrea with his "repent-or-burn" preaching in which he characterized women as being forever linked to the sin of Eve and that "bad mothers" created "bad children."[2]

After her suicide attempts Andrea was hospitalized. A psychiatrist prescribed medication for severe mental illness and advised the Yates not to have more children because having another baby could trigger more episodes of bizarre behavior.

When their youngest child was two and half, Andrea discontinued her medication at Rusty's urging and became pregnant again. After the birth of their fifth child, her psychiatrist told Rusty that Andrea should not be left alone with the children. The morning of the killings, Rusty left for work before his mother arrived to help Andrea with the children. That is when Andrea acted upon the tragic plan that she had been contemplating for many months.

Prosecuting the crime of Andrea Yates was as challenging as trying to understand why she did it. Under Texas law, Andrea was charged with capital murder: "intentionally and knowingly" causing the deaths of her children. Although she knew that killing her children was wrong, she had done so believing that it was the only way that she could save them from damnation. She willingly submitted herself to the judgment of the criminal justice system so that she could be punished for her "personal weaknesses."[3]

Originally found guilty of murder and sentenced to life in prison, an appeal led to a verdict of not guilty by reason of insanity.[4] Andrea was then sent to a psychiatric hospital where she remains in treatment as a psychiatric patient.

The case of Andrea Yates shows that many factors may contribute to the commission of a crime. These range from psychological and biological factors such as mental disorders, cognitions, and neurological conditions to the sociological influences on a person's life. Yates's crime was unusual, the result of a perfect storm of mental, medical, and sociological stresses. But her case nonetheless illustrates that the extraordinarily complex nature of human behavior continually challenges the efforts of criminal justice experts to understand the causes of crime.

Much research has been devoted to understanding why people commit crimes. Knowing the causes of crime—its etiology—is an important key to preventing criminal acts and changing the behavior of offenders. Being able to explain crime also influences the decisions of the courts. In the Yates case, understanding the causes of her crime ultimately led the court to find her "not guilty by reason of insanity." This chapter looks at the causes of crime from several different angles—biology, psychology, and sociology—and explores why some people are victimized, even repeatedly, and others are not.

Preview

SEEKING THE CAUSES OF CRIME: EARLY SCHOOLS OF THOUGHT

The causes of crime have been the subject of research in the disciplines of biology, psychology, sociology, and victimology for years. Criminologists recognize two major schools of thought or belief systems as among the first attempts to organize a view of crime causation. They are known as the classical and the positivist schools of criminology.

The Classical School: Choosing to Be a Criminal

The **classical school of criminology** viewed the criminal as having free will, the freedom of individual choice to deliberately choose a criminal path. The Italian economist and jurist Cesare Beccaria (1738–1794) articulated this position in *On Crimes and Punishments* (1764), the cornerstone of the classical school of criminology.[5] Jeremy Bentham (1748–1832), an English philosopher, also contributed to the classical school's view of crime causation with his *Introduction to the Principles of Morals and Legislation* (1789).[6] Both Beccaria and Bentham believed that criminal behavior resulted from a person's rational

classical school of criminology
A system of thought that views the criminal as having free will to choose a criminal path.

◀ The classical school of criminology believes that the criminal has a free will and should be punished as dictated by law.

and conscious choices—that is, criminals were responsible for their behavior—and that appropriate punishments would deter further criminal actions.

According to Beccaria, if punishment was to deter offenders, it must be dictated by law, proportionate to the crime committed (not too harsh or too easy), certain, swiftly imposed, and dispensed in public.[7] Bentham proposed that people acted in a way that brought them the greatest pleasure and the least pain and that they would not commit crime if the pain of punishment was greater than what might be gained from carrying out the crime. This idea was known as Bentham's "hedonistic calculus." Bentham also developed the philosophy of utilitarianism, an ethical philosophy of social control that focused on imposing punishments that were believed best for the majority of people in society.[8]

neoclassical school of criminology
Recognizes differences in criminal circumstances and assumes that some people, such as children, the insane, and the intellectually deficient, cannot reason. In such cases the criminal justice system must look at the needs of the offender in determining appropriate punishments.

Like the classical school from which it is derived, the **neoclassical school of criminology** is based on the principle of free will, the concept that people are responsible for their actions, and the idea that punishment can prevent crime. However, the neoclassical school incorporates some practical modifications necessary for the equitable administration of criminal law and justice. For example, the neoclassical school recognizes differences in criminal circumstances and assumes that some people, such as children, the insane, and the intellectually deficient, cannot reason. In such cases, the criminal justice system must consider the needs of the offender in determining appropriate punishments. Proponents of the classical and neoclassical schools frequently support the crime control model discussed in Chapters 1 and 11.

rational choice theory
Criminals choose to commit crime because they believe the benefits they will derive will overshadow the risks of getting caught.

A present-day derivative of the classical and neoclassical schools of criminology is **rational choice theory**. This theory assumes that criminals choose to commit crime because they believe the benefits they will derive will overshadow the risks of getting caught.[9] The benefits of crime may be economic, physiological, or both. For example, one offender may commit a crime because she thinks she will obtain a great deal of money; another offender might receive an adrenaline high or a boost in self-esteem from committing the crime. In both cases, the offender considers her crime and victims carefully before proceeding and comes to the conclusion that there is little chance of getting caught or of being punished.

The Positivist School: Criminal Behavior Is Predetermined

positivist school of criminology
Views criminal behavior as a product of biological, psychological, and social forces beyond a person's control.

The **positivist school of criminology**, which emerged after 1850, replaced the classical school concepts of free will and rational choice with the concept of determinism—the idea that criminal behavior is a product of biological, psychological, and social forces that are beyond a person's control. Moreover, the positivist school de-emphasized punishment as a deterrent to crime and emphasized instead the need to treat the offender. To treat offenders successfully, they had to be scientifically studied to determine what factors caused them to commit crime.

atavism
The belief that criminals are evolutionally primitive or subhuman people characterized by certain "inferior" identifiable physical and mental characteristics.

The positivist school is associated with Cesare Lombroso (1835–1909), who is known as the father of modern criminology. Lombroso was one of the first researchers to apply the scientific method to his study of offenders. He spent much of his life measuring the skulls of criminals and recording his findings. As a biological determinist, he believed that biology and genetics were the main determinants of criminal behavior. Lombroso proposed that criminals were born with criminal traits, and he espoused the concept of **atavism**—the idea that, viewed from an evolutionary perspective, criminals were primitive, subhuman, biological throwbacks characterized by certain "inferior" identifiable physical and mental characteristics.[10] For example, Lombroso described criminals as having small glassy eyes, big ears, and excessive amounts of hair. Proponents of the positivist school of criminology are frequently supporters of the rehabilitation model discussed in Chapter 11. The major tenets of the classical and positivist schools of criminology are compared in Key Concepts.

The classical and positivist schools of thought are starting points from which to view crime and criminal behavior, but their ability to predict who will engage in criminal behavior and who will be victimized by crime is limited. Although free will and biological determinism continue to be useful explanations of crime, today we recognize that crime is caused by multiple factors. Research focusing on biological, psychological, sociological, and victimological factors contributes further to our understanding of what causes crime and victimization.

KEY CONCEPTS
Principles of the Classical and Positivist Schools of Criminology

Classical School	Positivist School
Criminal behavior is motivated by free will.	Criminal behavior is a result of determinism.
Punishment prevents crime.	Treatment prevents crime.

BIOLOGICAL FACTORS

Social forces can lead people to behave in criminal and violent ways, yet most people who experience poverty, racism, and the like do not become criminals. Differences in the biological and psychological makeup of individuals largely account for this fact. The ways each person thinks and feels—and thus behaves—are largely the result of brain structure and function. Understanding the psychology of an offender's mind requires first knowing something about the biology of the brain.

Criminologists have benefited greatly from new technologies that permit the study of brain activity and function. Today's technologies enable researchers to see various structures of the brain as well as to observe the brain in action. Although much of human behavior is largely influenced by the thought processes associated with making choices (individual free will), biological factors are also involved.

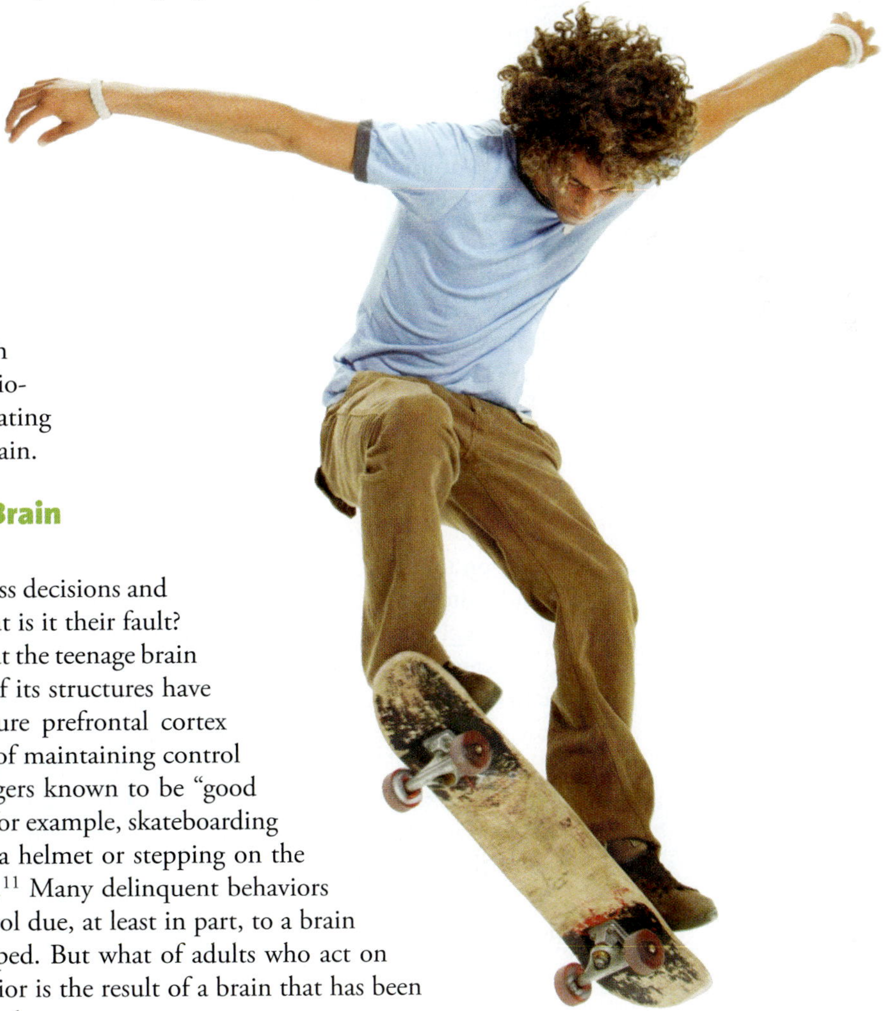

Advances in science and medicine, and their respective technologies, are making it possible to identify and measure a variety of biological factors related to the expression and suppression of criminal and violent behaviors. For this reason, much current research on criminal and violent behavior is turning to investigating the structure and function of the brain.

Neurobiological Factors of Brain Function

Teenagers are known to make careless decisions and to engage in high-risk behaviors, but is it their fault? Neurological studies have shown that the teenage brain is still a work in progress. Not all of its structures have matured. In teenagers, the immature prefrontal cortex area of the brain is not yet capable of maintaining control over a teen's impulses. Thus, teenagers known to be "good kids" sometimes behave recklessly: for example, skateboarding down some steps without wearing a helmet or stepping on the gas to speed away from a stoplight.[11] Many delinquent behaviors are the result of poor impulse control due, at least in part, to a brain that has not yet completely developed. But what of adults who act on impulse? In many cases their behavior is the result of a brain that has been injured or has developed in abnormal ways.

Brain functioning may be affected by disease, injury, or the effects of such chemical agents as alcohol and drugs. There is no scale for predicting the degree to which any of these factors might induce criminal behavior, but these abnormalities are widely recognized as factors contributing to aberrant and violent behavior. How a person's behavior may change after a head injury depends largely on the site and extent of the trauma. Forensics expert Gail Anderson examined a variety of studies of violent offenders in which their violent and criminal behaviors (for example, spousal battery, murder) were linked to brain damage.[12] Other studies have linked head injury to violent behavior in juveniles who grow up in a home where there is violence and where the juvenile has a mental disorder (most often depression, often undiagnosed at the time).[13] Although it is not clear how these three factors—trauma to the brain, violence in the home, and psychological disorder—specifically relate to each other (that is, whether depressed children are more prone to head injury or whether head injury results in depression), their combined result can be chronic violent behavior.

A simple explanation of brain function shows that behavior results from interactions between the rational prefrontal cortex and the emotional limbic system. When an individual has an urge to act in a particular way (to yell at someone for cutting in line at the movie theater, for example), that person's prefrontal cortex will judge whether that behavior is the best response. If the person cutting in line is a large and imposing stranger, yelling at him may provoke him to become violent. The prefrontal cortex may then decide that no action is the best course of action. For some individuals, however, the urge to yell at the stranger is uninhibited by rational thought. Because their prefrontal cortex is not functioning normally, they yell without thinking about the possible consequences of doing so.

Source Connection

ADHD AND CRIME

www.mental-health-matters.com/articles/article.php?artID=682

To understand more about ADHD and crime, read "ADHD and Implications for the Criminal Justice System," by Sam Goldstein, a clinical instructor at the University of Utah School of Medicine in Salt Lake City.

Impulsive behaviors are characteristic of individuals with attention deficit hyperactivity disorder (ADHD), a syndrome with many symptoms, including poor impulse control, restlessness, and an inability to concentrate. Considering the structure of the brain, we can understand how a stimulant medication such as Ritalin works to calm the behavior of someone with ADHD. Normally, such a drug would stimulate a person; however, in those with ADHD, the drug acts to stimulate the underaroused prefrontal cortex, prompting it to do its job of dampening impulses that come from the limbic system—the part of the brain responsible for the experience of emotions (such as rage) and basic drives (such as sex).

Using scanning imagery, we can identify the activity in the brain as people under the same experimental conditions are given a task (such as counting backwards by multiples of 7) to stimulate the prefrontal cortex. During such an experiment, activated regions of the brain appear as red areas on the scan. The brain scan of a control subject with no psychiatric or criminal history results in an image in which much of the prefrontal cortex is red, indicating its activation as the brain concentrates and performs the task. The scan for an impulsive murderer, however, appears decidedly different. Shades of blue and green in the prefrontal cortex reflect reduced activity in this region of the brain. Such a scan is consistent with what we would expect in people who tend to behave on impulse. It is the type of image seen on the scan of an impulsive murderer—an individual who killed out of his feelings of rage at that moment. A scan with such reduced activity is different from a normal scan, in which the prefrontal cortex is highly active when the brain performs tasks involving concentration. Even more interesting, the brain scans of individuals who kill in the heat of the moment appear to differ from those of predatory murderers. The brain scans of individuals who plan their series of killings reveal higher than normal levels of activity in the prefrontal cortex during such cognitive tasks. The elevated level of activity in this region of the brain could explain, in part, why serial murderers manage to be successful in committing a number of killings. Their behavior may be under better self-control and less susceptible to impulse.

The human brain contains some 100 billion neurons, the basic nerve cells that process and respond to incoming signals from the outside world through the five senses: vision, hearing, touch, taste, and smell. **Neurotransmitters** are chemicals secreted by neurons that facilitate the transmission of information from one neuron to another. These chemicals operate much like switches, turning neurons off and on—terminating the impulse or passing along the information. The neurotransmitter serotonin has been linked to impulsive and aggressive behaviors. A person whose serotonin levels in particular regions of the

neurotransmitter
A chemical secreted by neurons that facilitates the transmission of information from one neuron to another.

brain are too low will be significantly more likely to act on impulse and behave aggressively.[14] Another neurotransmitter, dopamine, appears to play a major role in the disordered thinking of schizophrenics.[15]

Like neurotransmitters, hormones are also chemical messengers, except that they are released into the bloodstream and so circulate throughout the body. The male sex hormone testosterone has long been associated with aggressive behavioral tendencies such as competitiveness and dominance. Increasing the level of testosterone (for example, by injecting it into the bloodstream) can result in higher levels of aggression.[16] Although being aggressive does not necessarily involve violence, the probability of a violent outcome increases when an individual is highly aggressive in interactions with others.

The adrenal gland secretes the stress hormone cortisol in response to a threatening situation. Extremely violent boys tend to have abnormally low levels of cortisol, suggesting they would be less physiologically responsive to situations most others would experience as threatening.[17] This "no fear" state in the face of potential threat could serve a criminal well. For most of us, our stress level alone would deter us from committing a serious crime. If we tried to rob a bank, we would probably bail out by the time we got to the front of the teller line, sweating profusely and with our heart beating out of our chest. An individual whose body does not register the situation as threatening is much more likely to successfully execute the crime in a calm and controlled manner.

MYTH/REALITY

MYTH: A specific gene, when inherited, results in criminal behavior.

REALITY: More likely, some individuals inherit particular combinations of genes that make them more likely to act on impulse or respond with aggression to certain situations.[18]

Genetic Factors: The Inheritance of Criminal Tendencies

Do criminals inherit their criminality? The basic unit of heredity is the gene—a segment of an individual's DNA that contains the information for making specific proteins that, in turn, contribute to particular biological or behavioral traits. The field of behavioral genetics explores the roles of genes in behavior. Of the approximately 25,000 genes that humans have, no single gene codes for any particular behavior. There is no "crime gene" per se. Rather, a variety of genetic and environmental factors interact to produce specific traits. Fetal exposure to toxins and viruses, stress and emotional trauma in childhood, and nutritional status are just a few of the factors that affect the way genes are expressed.

Criminal behavior tends to run in families.[19] Some families produce successive generations of criminals largely because of the way those families raise their children. In other cases, genes that predispose individuals to behave in aggressive and impulsive ways are carried along family lines. Dutch geneticist Han Brunner discovered a mutation in a specific gene that affects, among other things, serotonin levels. Every male in the family he studied who had the mutated gene also had a history of violent behavior.[20] This particular mutation is so rare, however, that it cannot explain violent behavior in general. Future researchers will no doubt identify other contributing genes, along with the kinds of environments in which they come to be expressed as criminal behaviors.

What are the respective contributions of genes and the environment? Studies of twin siblings offer substantial evidence of the role genes play in criminal behavior.[21] Identical twins have identical genes, and they tend to behave more similarly than do

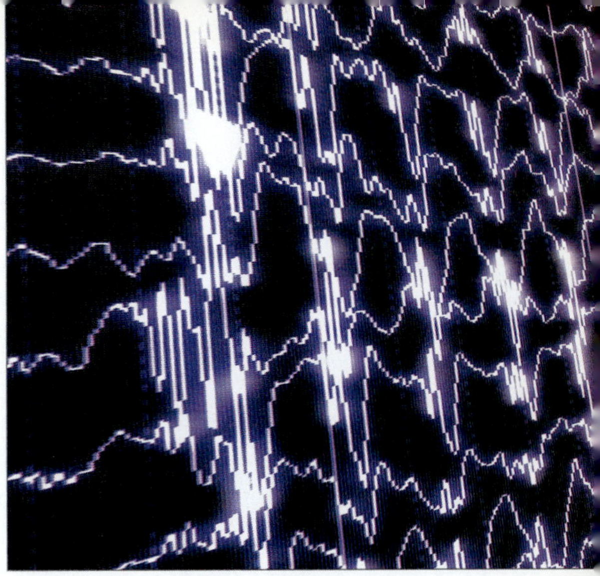

Real Crime Tech

LIE DETECTION BY BRAINWAVE ANALYSIS

The electroencephalogram (EEG), long used to detect abnormal brain function, has been adapted to indicate when a person is lying. Electrodes are placed at specific points on the surface of an individual's head to pick up the electrical fields generated by impulses as they are transmitted between systems of neurons. The "brain finger-printing" technique examines the brain's response to crime scene–related images. When the brain recognizes a familiar image, EEG waves are different from those that are observed when the brain is presented with a novel stimulus. Thus, if a criminal suspect lies about committing a burglary, his brain may "say" otherwise when it recognizes images from the burglarized house. In 2008, this technology was accepted as evidence against Aditi Sharma in an Indian court for the poisoning murder of her fiancé. The defendant was convicted and sentenced to life imprisonment—this was before the scientific community had assessed the validity and reliability of using EEGs in this way. Because science and the law are not always in sync with each other, such cases pose serious challenges to the quest for justice.

SOURCE: Anand Giridharadas, "India's Novel Use of Brain Scans in Courts Is Debated," *The New York Times*, September 15, 2008.

▲ **Identical Twins**

When one identical twin is criminal, the twin sibling is more likely to be criminal as well. This occurs more frequently in identical twins than in other siblings.

other brothers and sisters. With regard to criminal behavior, when one identical twin is criminal, the other twin is more likely to be criminal as well—this occurs more frequently than with other siblings. In research on adoptees, the genetic influences of biological parents who themselves were criminal were found to outweigh the influence of the parents who raised the children, whether these parents were criminal or not. Thus, although both the rearing environment and genetic makeup have a role in a child's (and later an adult's) behavior, genes appear to carry more weight.[22]

The recognition that, except for identical twins, individual humans have stretches of DNA that uniquely identify them has broad application in criminal investigations. DNA can be extracted from bone tissue to identify skeletal remains of victims of crime. Offenders leave samples of their DNA (for example, from semen) at the scenes of their crimes. Just as current research strives to link specific genes and combinations of genes to physical and mental illnesses, genetic "profiles" are being sought for behavioral traits such as violence.

Many people, researchers and the general public included, believe that linking criminal behavior to biological factors unjustly frees offenders from responsibility for their crimes. However, the complexity of criminal behavior makes it both difficult to understand and difficult to control. Perhaps the most admirable goal would be to identify what we are capable of changing and recognizing what we are not, at least not with current knowledge.

PSYCHOLOGICAL FACTORS

All aspects of our psychological makeup have biological underpinnings. The question is not whether mental illnesses have a genetic component but how combinations of genes work to increase an individual's vulnerability to mental disorder. When an individual's brain does not work properly, the person's psychological responses may lead to deviant behavior and crime. Some people commit crimes because there is something psychologically wrong with them. Some have mental disorders that affect their ability to function in accordance with society's laws. Others may have psychological problems even if they do not suffer from a recognized mental illness.

MYTH/REALITY

MYTH: People with mental disorders are more likely than other people to commit crimes.

REALITY: In general, mentally disordered people are no more likely than others to commit crimes. There is, however, a relationship between some kinds of mental disorder and criminal behavior. The way a particular mental disorder affects an individual's thinking and feeling will affect that person's behavior.[23]

Mental Disorders and Criminal Behavior

psychoses
Serious mental disorders that cause individuals to be out of touch with reality and unable to cope with the demands of everyday living.

A mental illness or mental disorder is a medical condition that interferes with a person's ability to function on a day-to-day basis. The most serious disorders—**psychoses**—leave individuals out of touch with reality and unable to cope with their surroundings. A person suffering from a psychotic disorder may experience hallucinations, which are sensory experiences in the absence of actual stimuli, such as hearing voices or seeing things that are not there. They may also have delusions, false and sometimes preposterous beliefs about the world, such as believing that people are out to get them.

Criminals depicted in television and movies are often stereotyped as having mental problems.[24] The truth is that mentally disordered individuals are generally not violent, nor are they criminal.[25] The best predictor of future criminal behavior—for those with and without mental disorders—is a history of past criminal behavior.[26] No particular mental disorder indicates that a person will behave violently or break the law. Some mental disorders do, however, make certain individuals more susceptible to acting in criminal or violent ways. This is especially true when a person's mental state is further altered by the abuse of drugs or alcohol or when a person has gone without prescribed medication for such a disorder.[27]

A Global View

Christianity Criminalized

The new constitution of Afghanistan proclaims that "no law can be contrary to the sacred religion of Islam." Under current Islamic Shariah law, apostasy—the formal renunciation of one's religion—is a crime punishable by death.

In 1990, Abdul Rahman, a 25-year-old Afghan, converted to Christianity while serving as a medical worker with an international Christian aid group helping Afghan refugees in Pakistan. Following the fall of the Taliban in 2002, Rahman returned to Afghanistan to rejoin his wife and two daughters. Because he had converted to Christianity, Rahman's wife divorced him and his parents disowned him. But it was not until the divorced Rahman sought custody of his two daughters that his parents reported their son's religious conversion to the police. He was arrested when the police found that he possessed a Bible. Rahman was charged with apostasy in February 2006. The prosecution contended that Rahman's conversion to Christianity amounted to an act of treason, warranting the death penalty. The prosecutor offered to drop the charges if Rahman would convert back to Islam. He refused and was slated to go on trial before a Shariah court of Islamic law. If found guilty, he would likely be hanged.

Out of the public's eye, moderate Afghan leaders negotiated asylum for Rahman with the Italian government. On March 26, 2006, the Afghan Supreme Court dropped its case after a medical team examining Rahman said it suspected mental illness had caused him to reject Islam. Nonetheless, extremists demanded "God's justice" and threatened to kill Rahman if he were set free. For his safety, Rahman was released from a Kabul jail into the custody of the Afghan Independent Human Rights Commission and the United Nations mission in Afghanistan, whereupon he was taken to Italy.

A man's life was spared and a sensitive political situation resolved by claiming that Rahman was mentally ill. In the view of the Afghan judicial system, Rahman's religious conversion—the crime—was the result of mental illness. This case illustrates the arbitrariness with which mental disorders are defined.

Observe Investigate Understand

- **What factors make it difficult to define mental disorders?**
- **Should it be possible to manipulate the assessment of a person's mental state for political reasons?**
- **What other examples can you think of in which religions define crimes or in which religious beliefs have been criminalized?**

SOURCES: Information about Rahman's case comes from The Institute on Religion and Democracy: www.irdrenew.org/site/apps/nl/content2.asp?c=fvKVLfMVIsG&b=401661&t=2095483 (retrieved May 2, 2007); Amnesty International USA, "Afghanistan: Case of Abdul Rahman Underlines Urgent Need for Judicial Reform," March 26, 2006, www.amnesty-usa.org/document.php?lang=e&id=ENGASA110082006.

Classifying Mental Disorders

The American Psychiatric Association publishes the ***Diagnostic and Statistical Manual of Mental Disorders*** **(DSM)**, the standard classification reference used by mental health professionals in the United States. The DSM describes the approximately 400 mental disorders currently recognized by the psychiatric community, along with their identifying symptoms.[28] The criminal justice system regularly calls upon mental health professionals to assist in making a wide range of decisions, and these professionals rely on the DSM, which describes mental disorders largely based on their effects on an individual's ability to meet the demands of everyday life. The A Global View box (above) illustrates how what is defined as mental illness can vary from culture to culture.

Diagnostic and Statistical Manual of Mental Disorders (DSM) The standard classification reference used by mental health professionals in the United States.

The current edition of the DSM lists four categories of serious mental disorders: schizophrenic disorders, paranoid disorders, mood disorders, and psychotic disorders not classified elsewhere.[29] A number of criminal cases making the news involve schizophrenic disorders or some form of major mood disorder. We discuss both of these types of disorders in the following sections to illustrate the influence of serious mental disorders on human and criminal behavior.

Schizophrenic Disorders

schizophrenia
A mental illness characterized by an individual's split from reality.

The term **schizophrenia** comes from the Latin *schizo* (meaning "split") and *phrenia* (meaning "mind"). This may explain why so many people wrongly believe schizophrenia means split personality. In fact, schizophrenia refers to the individual's split from reality. Schizophrenics typically suffer from both delusions and hallucinations. Approximately one percent of U.S. adults have a form of this debilitating mental disorder.[30] The majority of schizophrenics are not violent, but the odds of them being so increase if they have the paranoid type of the disorder[31] or also have certain other mental disorders. Schizophrenics who are substance abusers also are more likely to be violent.[32]

Andrei Chikatilo, executed for murdering 52 fellow Russian citizens over a 12-year period beginning in 1978, likely suffered from paranoid schizophrenia. He mutilated most of his victims, removing or wounding their eyes because he believed the image of a killer could be retrieved from his victim's eyes. He cannibalized some victims. Chikatilo seemed quite normal on the outside. He was married with two children and was able to hold down a steady job as a clerk for a factory. The bizarre nature of his crimes, however, betrayed his serious mental illness.

The search for the causes of schizophrenia focuses on a number of factors. Because the disorder tends to run in families, genetic studies are a logical area of research. Multiple genes that affect brain structure and function appear to be involved. A particularly productive line of research is focusing on abnormalities in different neurotransmitter systems. As the biochemistry of schizophrenia becomes better understood, medications to more effectively manage its symptoms will undoubtedly follow.[33]

Major Mood Disorders

Major mood disorders involve extreme and prolonged emotional states that render the individual incapable of coping with the demands of everyday life. Approximately 6 percent of the adult population has a major depressive disorder marked by feelings of guilt and worthlessness, loss of appetite for food and sexual activity, sleep disturbance, and thoughts of suicide.[34] The severity of these symptoms distinguishes the person with major depressive disorder from someone who is only mildly depressed. In the same way that medications can treat the symptoms of schizophrenia, drugs can affect the biochemistry of the brain in ways that alleviate serious depression.

▼ Aftermath of the James Oliver Huberty Massacre

James Oliver Huberty was killed by a police sharpshooter after killing 21 people and wounding 19 in a McDonald's restaurant.

People suffering serious depression may be inclined to harm themselves, and they may also present a risk to others. There are highly publicized cases of individuals with serious depression who murder others before taking their own lives ("angry suicides") or who position themselves to be killed by police after they have murdered others ("suicide-by-cop"). On a July morning in 1984, 41-year-old James Oliver Huberty told his wife that "society had its chance." Later that afternoon, as he was leaving home dressed in military-style camouflage clothes, he told her: "I'm going hunting. Hunting humans." Seventy-seven minutes after Huberty entered the McDonald's restaurant close to their home in San Ysidro, California, 21 people were dead and 19 wounded. A police sharpshooter killed Huberty, making him the 22nd fatality, ending the incident—and aiding Huberty in his apparent suicidal quest.

The day before, Huberty had called a local mental health center seeking help. Since he did not say it was an emergency situation, his name was apparently put on a waiting list. Huberty's wife later told the media that her husband appeared to be delusional around this time, indicating a major depressive disorder. The autopsy revealed extremely high levels of lead and cadmium in his body, perhaps from his years of work as a welder. Both are toxic elements known to significantly affect brain function. Thus, in Huberty's case, brain function may have been compromised by toxic elements. Altered brain function coupled with major depression proved a fatal mix, resulting in a mass murder.

Another form of major mood disorder is **bipolar affective disorder**. Formerly known as manic-depression, this mood disorder is characterized by periods of severe depression that alternate with periods of mania, whose symptoms include extreme elation and exaggerated self-importance. Persons suffering from major depression may become suicidal, whereas individuals in the manic phase of bipolar disorder are often irritable and hostile and can become violent. Hallucinations or delusions may contribute to their aggression.

bipolar affective disorder
A major mood disorder manifested by bouts of serious depression alternating with periods of extreme elation and exaggerated self-importance.

postpartum psychosis
A serious mental illness characterized by hallucinations, delusions, and obsessive thoughts about the baby.

A woman who has bipolar affective disorder is at higher risk to experience **postpartum psychosis** after having a baby. Symptoms of this disorder, which include delusions, hallucinations, and obsessive thoughts about the baby, generally start within the first 6 weeks after the baby's birth but may not appear for as long as a year. It is not surprising that some of these mothers kill their babies.[35] Postpartum psychosis, combined with a number of other factors, likely led Andrea Yates to a mental state in which she decided killing her five children was the only way to save them from eternal damnation (see the chapter-opening story). As her grip on reality faded, the influence of extremist religious views took hold, and her increasing isolation increased her vulnerability. Andrea's family also had a history of mental illness: one brother had bipolar affective disorder and another brother and sister had long-standing histories of depression, as did their mother.[36] This family history of mood disorder suggests Yates's psychological problems, as is true of most others with serious mental illness, had genetic roots.[37]

Psychopathy

Most mental disorders are not as debilitating as the psychoses previously described. Yet many of the most serious and brutal crimes are the product of these so-called less serious mental disorders.

Antisocial personality disorder is diagnosed by the presence of a pattern of behavioral problems before age 15 that include truancy, theft, and compulsive lying, and the continuation of such a pattern into adulthood. In fact, repeated lawbreaking is considered a core symptom of antisocial personality disorder, and most prison inmates would qualify for this diagnosis.[38] Beyond confirming that these individuals have a pattern of antisocial behavior, this diagnosis offers little to distinguish among offenders or to explain their behavior. An alternative approach, particularly in the forensic arena, relies on the concept of psychopathy.

psychopathy
A personality disorder exhibited by a lifelong pattern of antisocial behavior about which the individual has no remorse.

Psychopathy is a disorder of personality revealed by a lifelong pattern of antisocial behavior about which the individual has no remorse. Although it is not currently listed in the DSM, variants of it have appeared in previous editions. Most people have heard of psychopathy but do not fully understand what it is. A common mistake is to confuse the word "psycho," a slang term for psychotic, with the term "psychopath." Whereas psychotics typically experience distorted thoughts and perceptions, psychopaths are in touch with reality and appear to be quite normal on the surface. Typically, psychopaths are manipulative, superficial, and self-centered. They lack empathy and do not experience remorse for their antisocial behavior. They tend to act on impulse and are, by and large, irresponsible. Their behavior is thus like people with antisocial personality disorder; but the nature of their behavior is more complex in that psychopaths have specific cognitive and emotional deficits as well. Taking this definition to its logical conclusion, psychologist Robert Hare noted, "[i]f crime is the job description, the psychopath is the perfect applicant."[39] Many criminals who commit serial offenses, from burglary to confidence schemes to serial murder, are psychopaths. The kinds of feelings and associations that stop us from engaging in antisocial acts are notably absent in psychopaths. They do not care about others or the harm that their antisocial behaviors—criminal and otherwise—do to them. This is one reason criminal psychopaths are significantly more likely to reoffend than are nonpsychopathic offenders.[40] Moreover, while most psychopaths are not criminal or violent, criminal psychopaths as a group commit more than half the violent crimes in society.[41]

Other nonpsychotic disorders have been linked to criminal behavior. Individuals suffering from posttraumatic stress disorder (PTSD), for example, have been reported to perpetrate serious crimes. The woman who kills her long-abusive husband or the war veteran who engages in violence following his return from active duty are two examples. In both cases, prior experience with a situation perceived to be life threatening has serious and long-term psychological consequences. In fact, virtually any mental disorder can contribute to, if not be the basis for, criminal behavior.

Intelligence and Morality—The Cognitive Brain

The way in which the brain processes information is another factor related to the causes of crime. Two areas of cognitive research that warrant discussion in relation to crime are intelligence and moral reasoning.

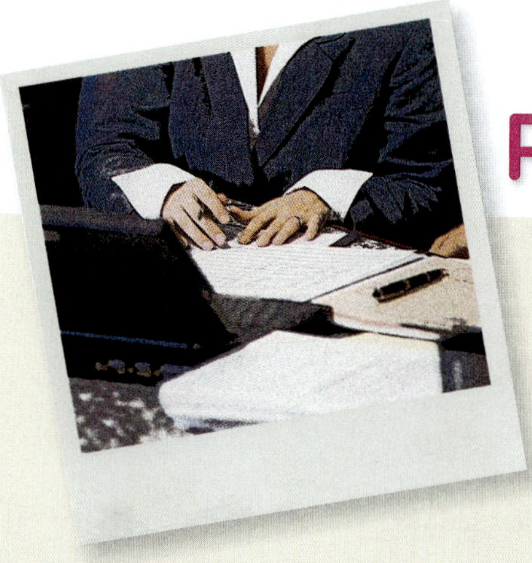

Real Careers

JESSICA DUBNOFF

Work location: New York City, New York

College(s): Northeastern University (2008)

Major(s): Criminal Justice with a minor in Political Science (BS)

Job title: Contracted Area Coordinator in the Department of Probation, Special Offenders Unit

Salary range for jobs like this: $30,000–$35,000

Time in job: 1.5 years

Work Responsibilities

As area coordinator for a mental health treatment program for sex offenders, I act as a liaison between the probation officers, probationers, and mental health clinicians. My responsibilities include gathering information for new referrals, explaining the program to probationers, and scheduling appointments for probationers with one of our mental health clinicians. I also make sure all the relevant monthly paperwork, such as progress reports, monthly updates, sign-in sheets, session notes, and billings, is distributed to the proper probation officer and a copy is filed at our office. My favorite part of this job is when I oversee containment meetings with the sex offender and probation officer and serve as a moderator, an integral part of this multidisciplinary team. Through my current employment, I have found myself becoming much more interested in the social work aspects of supervising and monitoring a case than in the department administration and law enforcement aspects.

Why Criminal Justice?

Since high school I knew I wanted to work in the criminal justice field. However, I was unsure which career was right for me—criminal defense attorney, police officer, forensic psychologist, and prosecutor all seemed like excellent choices. I decided to attend Northeastern University for guidance in making this difficult decision. Northeastern is well known for its co-op program, which allows students to work full-time for 6 months per year for class credit in a hands-on environment. By the time I was a senior, I had participated in three co-ops. In fact, I landed the job I have now because my co-op experience led me to a successful internship with the same company.

Expectations and Realities of the Job

From my co-ops, academics, and employment I gained a wealth of knowledge about the field, and I knew what to expect in terms of financial compensation and work hours. However, my education did not fully prepare me for the negative effects that my job would have on my personal life. For example, when riding the subway, I found myself questioning whether everyday unavoidable brush-ups were intentional (a crime called frotteurism). Similarly, if I passed a car with tinted windows, I would wonder if a sexual crime was being committed within. It took some time before I was able to go about my everyday life without thinking about sexually related crimes.

My Advice to Students

If you want to work in a setting that deals with the rehabilitation of offenders, you need to be able to separate the person from the crime. There are many other facets of a person's character and personality that need to be considered apart from the crime he or she committed. Offenders need solid, unbiased counseling to improve their lives and avoid future arrests. It can be tough to do this at first, but experienced colleagues or supervisors can be supportive and offer advice.

◀ **Posttraumatic Stress Disorder Sufferer**

Those who suffer from posttraumatic stress disorder (PTSD) have been reported to perpetrate serious crimes.

Intelligence

Intelligence is the capacity to learn or comprehend, shown through the ability to solve problems and adapt to life's everyday experiences.[42] Intelligence tests such as IQ tests provide a standardized measure of cognitive ability (as demonstrated by, for example, solving problems or engaging in abstract reasoning). The Wechsler Adult Intelligent Scale is commonly used in clinical and forensic settings.[43] In addition to providing measures of capacities such as verbal comprehension and motor coordination, scores on particular subtests can indicate brain damage and other deficits. Incarcerated offenders tend to score lower on average than nonoffenders on such intelligence tests.[44]

intelligence
The capacity to learn or comprehend, manifested by the ability to solve problems and adapt to life's everyday experiences.

The relationship between intelligence and criminal behavior is complex. Complicating this discussion is the fact that there are different kinds of intelligence. People with high emotional intelligence accurately perceive others' emotions, understand emotional meanings, and can manage their own emotions.[45] The behavior of serial murderers would indicate, however, that they are low in emotional intelligence, as they appear to lack the ability or the capacity to understand emotional information or to reason with emotions. Psychopaths, in particular, lack these abilities.

With an IQ in the genius range, serial murderer Edmund Emil Kemper III is unusual as a person and as a serial killer. Yet there is reason to believe that his high cognitive abilities came with significant emotional deficits. After he had picked up a young woman hitchhiker, Kemper saw that as he drove her around she began to get anxious because they did not seem to be going to her destination. "So I pulled out the gun to calm her down."[46] Kemper knew, intellectually, that pulling out his gun would have an effect on the hitchhiker, but it was evident that—even with his superior IQ—he could not identify with the terror she felt when she saw the gun. Brain imaging studies and other research show that the brains of violent psychopaths work differently from people who do not suffer from mental disorders and from those who do not commit violent crimes.[47]

▼ Edmund Emil Kemper III was a serial killer with an IQ in the genius range.

Moral Reasoning

Moral reasoning involves the application of a set of ethical principles based on what society views as good versus bad behavior. For most people, the ability to discern right from wrong develops and is internalized in childhood. Young children tend to see things as right or wrong, black or white. We do not begin to identify "shades of gray" until we are about 7 years of age.[48]

moral reasoning
Application of a set of ethical principles based on what society views as good versus bad behavior.

Like children, many criminals appear to have immature moral reasoning. Damage to the prefrontal cortex (the part of the brain responsible for making decisions and judgments, planning, and self-control) from stroke, injury, or infection can result in a pattern of reckless, antisocial, and violent behavior about which the individual has no remorse.[49] This knowledge offers a model with which to understand how some offenders can repeatedly violate the rights of others and not feel guilty about it. The biology that sets the moral compass for their behavior is undeveloped or defective.

Learning Criminal Behavior from Others: Social Learning Theory

social learning theory
Behavior is learned and is maintained or extinguished based on the rewards or punishments associated with it.

Behavioral psychologists argue that we learn behavior, which is then maintained or extinguished by the rewards or punishments we associate with it.[50] This is known as **social learning theory.** How a person behaves is also influenced by his experiences with the behavior of others. Thus, social learning can entail watching others and noting the consequences of their behaviors. This type of social learning may explain the boy who grows up to batter his wife. For years he observed his own father gain the compliance of his mother through acts of violence and intimidation. Similarly, children can learn to behave violently by seeing violent behavior rewarded in movies or through the instant rewards of killing the enemy in video games.[51] A major aspect of the socialization of every individual involves internalizing the rules for appropriate behavior. Anticipating punishment for bad behavior facilitates learning these rules.

Psychodynamic Factors

Sigmund Freud, the father of psychoanalysis, believed humans have primitive urges and drives that exist below the level of conscious awareness.[52] A main principle of Freudian thinking—also known as psychodynamic psychology—is that an individual's personality and behavior traits develop early in life.

Freud posited that there are three parts to personality:

- The id consists of unconscious drives that demand instant gratification, always seeking pleasure and avoiding pain. Sexual urges or the cry of a baby to be fed are expressions of the id. We are born with an id; it helps us to survive during a stage in life when we cannot communicate with language.
- The ego incorporates conscious thoughts that cope with the demands of reality and tries to satisfy the id by bringing the individual pleasure within accepted norms of society. The ego develops early in childhood and can be adversely affected by abuse and neglect.
- The superego constitutes the moral aspect of personality, or conscience, and internally judges one's actions based on principles of right and wrong. The superego regulates behavior so that the impulses of the id can be satisfied within acceptable moral terms.

The id, the ego, and the superego work together in a psychologically healthy individual to regulate behavior. Others have used Freud's conception of the three-part personality to explain aspects of criminal behavior. For example, some theorists have proposed that the personality of offenders often suffers from an imbalance in the roles played by id, ego, and superego. A person with a damaged ego (say, from child abuse) may be prone to act on impulses because the urges that come from the id go unchecked by what otherwise would be the rational judgment offered by a healthy ego. A person with a weak superego might be less able to control his violent or sexual impulses. Conversely, a person with an overactive superego might experience overwhelming feelings of guilt, persecution, and worthlessness, factors that can lead her to commit crimes—so she will get the punishment she deserves.

The Key Concepts table on the next page illustrates the biological and psychological factors involved in criminal and delinquent behavior.

KEY CONCEPTS

Biological and Psychological Factors Involved in Criminal and Delinquent Behavior

Mental Disorders
- Psychoses
- Schizophrenia
- Depression
- Mania
- Bipolar affective disorder
- Postpartum psychosis

Psychodynamic Factors
- Id
- Ego
- Superego

Situational Variables
- Life circumstances
- Defense mechanisms
- Guilt

Genetic Factors
- Genes

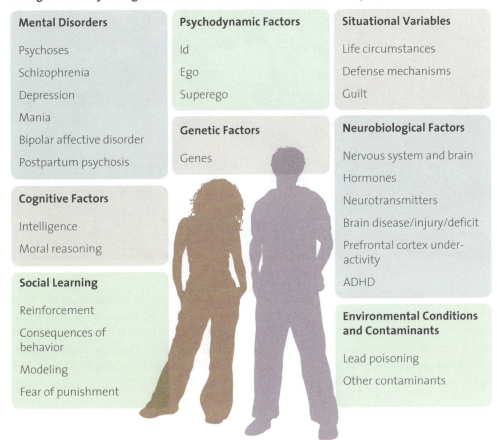

Neurobiological Factors
- Nervous system and brain
- Hormones
- Neurotransmitters
- Brain disease/injury/deficit
- Prefrontal cortex under-activity
- ADHD

Cognitive Factors
- Intelligence
- Moral reasoning

Social Learning
- Reinforcement
- Consequences of behavior
- Modeling
- Fear of punishment

Environmental Conditions and Contaminants
- Lead poisoning
- Other contaminants

SOCIOLOGICAL FACTORS

Sociology is the study of human beings within their social environments and includes looking carefully at how people behave and interact in societies. Sociological factors that relate to the study of crime and its causes include income, racism, sexism, capitalism, education, religion, ethnicity, neighborhood, subculture values, geography, family, occupation, politics, media, gang membership, health status, socialization, and the presence of weapons.

For most of the twentieth century U.S. criminologists embraced sociological explanations of crime causation more fervently than biological and psychological theories. However, with advances in science, biological and psychological theories are gaining more interest among U.S. criminologists. Nevertheless, many researchers and theorists still look closely at the role of sociological factors in explaining crime and criminal behavior.

When Adversity Leads to Crime: Strain Factors

Strain theory proposes that extraordinary pressures make a person more likely to commit crime. Strain factors can come from a variety of sources—individuals, groups, and social institutions. For example, a teenager can experience strain when parents do not provide a safe home life, when he does not make a football team, and when he has to pass through a crime-prone neighborhood while walking home from school. Most people encounter pressures and hardships in life, but very few turn to a life of crime.

strain theory
Extraordinary pressures make people more likely to commit crime.

▶ Arab and African Youth Riot

In 2005, French Arab and African young people rioted in the streets in Paris suburbs.

Unfortunately, strain factors make some people more likely to engage in crime. General strain theory proposes that experiencing repetitive negative emotions and thoughts might dispose some people to crime and delinquency.[53] The experiences of the death of a loved one, abuse, divorce, poverty, hunger, dysfunctional home lives, and loss of significant relationships can produce negative emotions such as anger, fear, rejection, hurt, and even mental illness such as depression.

Feelings of Alienation

anomie
A feeling of alienation or a condition that leaves people feeling hopeless, rootless, cut off, alienated, isolated, disillusioned, and frustrated.

The French sociologist Émile Durkheim (1858–1917) introduced the term **anomie** to describe a feeling of alienation or a condition that renders a person hopeless, rootless, cut off, alienated, isolated, disillusioned, and frustrated.[54] A person who experiences anomie cares very little about society's rules and norms and instead feels intense strain or pressure. In some cases, anomie can result in criminal behavior. For example, in November 2005, France's young Arabic and African immigrant communities staged angry street protests in Paris as a number of jobless immigrants took the law into their own hands.[55]

Inability to Achieve Desired Life Goals

Sociologist Robert Merton introduced the concept of goals–means dysjunction—a disconnection between legitimate goals that society values and the way we attain them.[56] He recognized that U.S. culture values wealth, prestige, and power but not all people achieve these goals.

The desire to achieve these goals without the means to acquire them produces pressure, frustration, and anomie for many. Merton suggested that crime is more prevalent in the lower classes because those with lower economic status are less likely to succeed, a situation that results in extraordinary stress—or strain—on some individuals. If the pressure is great enough on some individuals, they may feel pressured into breaking the law. People have different kinds of responses when they cannot reach their desired goals (see Merton's Adaptations to the Goals–Means Dysjunction table). Not all people choose to commit a crime just because they lack opportunity to achieve society's desired goals. Most people conform, some innovate to achieve success, some retreat or drop out of the race, some basically accept their fate (ritualism), and others rebel, often turning to crime.

Other strain factors that contribute to criminal behavior are lack of available opportunities coupled with pressure to be part of a gang. One of the major reasons boys—primarily from working-class neighborhoods—join gangs is their discomfort with unfamiliar middle-class values that are expected of them while attending school. They temporarily

MERTON'S ADAPTATIONS TO THE GOALS-MEANS DYSJUNCTION

Cultural Goals	Institutionalized Means	Modes of Adaptation
+	+	Conformity
+	−	Innovation
−	+	Ritualism
−	−	Retreatism
±	±	Rebellion

resolve their anxiety and discomfort by finding others who feel the same way and hanging out together in a gang.

The gang experience provides members with a heightened sense of social status, respect, fellowship, and relief from strain by opposing middle-class values. Committing delinquent acts is gang members' way of saying that middle-class values are unimportant.[57] The Race, Class, Gender box examines why so many poor kids often become members of a gang and what can be done to combat the problem.

Race, Class, Gender

Why Join Gangs?

In the United States today and throughout the nation's history, a variety of groups have joined gangs. In early U.S. history, Irish gangs were common. Today there are Southeast Asian gangs, Russian gangs, and Mexican American gangs as well as others. The race or ethnicity of gangs varies, but their class rarely does. Individuals who join gangs are poor. There is very little economic diversity among those—both male and female—who choose to be members of gangs or associates of gang members.

Few professionals have reached out to understand why poor young males often turn to gang life. Jesuit priest Father Gregory Boyle in Los Angeles is an exception. He has worked with thousands of former gang members, many of whom have backgrounds that include psychological, emotional, and physical abuse, poverty, and neglect. He finds a set of characteristics common to them all: lack of opportunity, social alienation, and economic vulnerability—any of which may lead to criminal behavior. He concludes, quite simply, that people join gangs in order to feel connected to something, to feel included and loved, and to give meaning to their lives.[58]

To combat factors that lead to gang membership, Boyle created a more positive organization for them to join, Homeboy and Homegirl Industries. The organization provides a means by which to feel connected to others, and it helps former gang members find jobs so they are not as economically vulnerable. Homeboy Industries offers tattoo removal, counseling, and job training, among other things. Boyle likes to say, "if you want to get someone out of a gang, offer him a job."

Father Boyle's work is important for many reasons. Not only does he help many to leave the life of gangs, but he also teaches the rest of us who do not have firsthand experiences with gang members that they are just like us—they are people who want to be loved and to be successful. Boyle does not say their actions should be excused, but rather that they should be given a chance to do right in the world. That is the same opportunity we all want. We need to be mindful, however, that some of us were born into situations that made it easy for us to live a life absent of crime. For others it is much more difficult.

OBSERVE Investigate Understand

- **Why is it important to understand why people join gangs?**
- **Why are jobs important for people who want to get out of gangs?**
- **Can gang membership ever be a positive experience?**

SOURCES: Celeste Fremon, *G-Dog and the Homeboys* (Albuquerque: University of New Mexico Press, 2004), and Homeboy Industries, www.homeboy-industries.org/.

On a Path to Crime: The Life Course Delinquency Perspective

Juvenile delinquency refers to illegal acts committed by minors. According to the life course delinquency perspective, delinquency follows identifiable trends from birth to old age. When a person is very young, delinquency is rare but becomes more frequent during a person's early adolescence. Delinquency is most common during the late teens and early adulthood and then declines during old age.[59]

Dual taxonomic theory, a contemporary offshoot of strain theory of criminal behavior that combines biological and psychological elements with social factors, asserts that because of brain damage, chemical imbalances, and other neuropsychological deficits, as well as factors such as poverty and dysfunctional families, some individuals get into trouble and engage in delinquency at young ages and continue their criminal behavior throughout the course of their lives.[60] These offenders are referred to as **life course persistent offenders**. By contrast, **adolescence-limited offenders** tend to participate in antisocial behavior during limited periods of time during adolescence, while maintaining school performance and respectful relationships with adults such as parents and teachers. Adolescence-limited offenders frequently give up criminal behaviors when they get older and begin to realize the problems they will bring on themselves if their offending behavior continues. Offending behavior tends to peak around age 17 to 18 and then declines as offenders mature. Many take up a conventional law-abiding lifestyle by age 35.[61]

life course persistent offenders
Those who engage in delinquency at young ages and continue their criminal behavior throughout their lives.

adolescence-limited offenders
Young people who participate in antisocial behavior for a limited period of time during adolescence while maintaining school performance and respectful relationships with parents and teachers.

Social Bonds and Crime: Social Control Factors

Social control theory focuses primarily on belief systems—not laws or formal rules—that hold people to society's standards by putting limits on their actions. According to this theory, what keeps people from wrongdoing most of the time is their belief system. Whether on the street, at home, at parties, at school, at church, with friends, or in prison, beliefs regulate behavior. Control factors exist at several different levels in society.

social control theory
An individual's belief system, the police, and parental supervision are important in preventing individuals from getting into trouble.

Control by the Community

Small and large communities control the behavior of their citizens in different ways. Small communities whose inhabitants live closely together frequently have tight bonds to one another. Citizens know what their neighbors do and are able to quickly identify and report anything out of the ordinary. In small communities, most citizens share the same norms, traditions are similar, people tend to think similarly, and those who do not follow norms are dealt with swiftly. Deviance tends to be rare in this type of community.

In contrast, people living in larger communities are not as tightly bonded with others in their community. Citizens do not get involved with many of their neighbors or their comings and goings and are less likely to identify and report unusual happenings. In these large and diverse communities, norms and traditions vary across different subcultures. People are accustomed to being among those who are different and tend to tolerate many types of deviance.[62]

Beyond One's Control—Avoiding Responsibility

Some criminologists argue that for people to break the law they must accept rationalizations that allow them to overcome feelings of responsibility. This perspective, known as **neutralization theory**, was developed by Gresham Sykes and David Matza.[63] When caught and arrested, many offenders point to others, not themselves, as the sources of their problems with the law. The justifications used to avoid taking responsibility are called techniques of neutralization because they neutralize the feelings of responsibility that would otherwise prevent a person from committing crime. Types of neutralization techniques include the following:

neutralization theory
If people break the law, they overcome their feelings of responsibility through rationalizations.

- Denial of responsibility: "It wasn't my fault; I was a victim of circumstances."
- Denial of injury: "No one was hurt, and they have insurance, so what's the problem?"
- Denial of victim: "Anyone would have done the same thing in my position; I did what I had to do given the situation."

- Condemnation of the condemners: "I bet the judge and everyone else on the jury has done much worse than what I was arrested for."
- Appeal to higher loyalties: "My friends were depending on me and I see them every day. What was I supposed to do?"[64]

There are other ways to justify or neutralize unlawful behavior. For instance, a person may protest that the law itself is unjust. Offenders sometimes claim that since everyone else is doing something illegal, such as speeding, they should be able to do it too. When people use neutralizations to excuse their actions and overcome their guilt, their beliefs may not prevent them from committing crime.

Personal Bonds to Society

The types of bonds people have to society also are factors that control behavior and keep them from committing crime. One type of bond essential in controlling or containing delinquency is the "good boy" concept—the perception boys have of themselves as good, law-abiding people. These ideas are the basis of Walter Reckless's **containment theory**, which argues that some factors that keep behavior in check are personal, such as self-concept, self-control, goal-directedness, conscience, tolerance for frustration, sense of responsibility, realistic levels of aspiration, and identification with lawful norms. When these control mechanisms fail to restrain or check behavior, delinquency is likely to occur.[65]

containment theory
Factors that keep behavior in check are personal, such as self-concept, self-control, goal-directedness, conscience, tolerance for frustration, sense of responsibility, realistic levels of aspiration, and identification with lawful norms.

Travis Hirschi's **social bond theory** focuses on four facets of the social bond people have with society:

social bond theory
The social bond people have with society consists of attachment, commitment, involvement, and belief.

- Attachment: development of an emotional connection with and affection for people and institutions that make up society
- Commitment: the act of pledging and promising to people and institutions
- Involvement: the time spent engaged in conventional activities with others
- Belief: holding society's values and beliefs as true for oneself[66]

When all these aspects of the social bond are present, a person is unlikely to commit crime. Social bonds in the form of strong ties to work and family can also move youthful offenders away from crime, and a secure marriage and job can be turning points in a young offender's life course.[67]

Another social bond that keeps people from engaging in crime is self-control, or the ability to control one's impulses, emotions, desires, and behaviors.[68] Gottfredson and Hirschi propose that individuals with low or limited self-control exhibit certain characteristics that make them more likely to engage in crime. People who are impulsive, narcissistic, risk-taking, physical, and active are more likely to commit crime. Those who do not derive pleasure from hard work and mastering tasks and who are insensitive to how others feel are more likely to take the chance of committing crime.[69]

Self-esteem, the feelings of self-worth that stem from positive or negative beliefs about being valuable and capable, is another facet of the social bond with society.[70] In some cases, low self-esteem appears to contribute to delinquency, whereas in others delinquent behavior might serve to enhance low self-esteem.[71] Low self-esteem is frequently cited as a cause of crime and delinquency,[72] and being successful in crime can raise self-esteem.[73] Low self-esteem is related to problems in school achievement, drug and alcohol abuse, hostility, conflicts with others, frustration, attraction to gangs, and engaging in violence.

Power and Inequality: Crime and Social Conflict Theory

Social conflict theory emerged in the United States following the turbulent 1960s, a period characterized by a variety of social movements that sought to improve the civil rights of various subgroups in American society. Economic gains made by corporate America stood in stark contrast to the large number of people living in abject poverty in the great industrial centers of the nation. The women's movement called for women's greater equality with the economic standing of men. African Americans exposed racial and class discrimination and demanded change, and the gay rights movement gained momentum. These

social conflict theory
Crime is the result of conflict between the wealthy and powerful and the poor and powerless in society.

circumstances demanded new theories to explain problems threatening social stability in the United States. Social conflict theories view criminal behavior as the product of the conflict between the wealthy and powerful and the poor and powerless.

critical theory
A branch of social conflict theory concerned with the way in which structural conditions and social inequalities influence crime.

Critical theory is a branch of social conflict theory concerned with the way in which structural conditions and social inequalities influence crime. Structural conditions refer to factors rooted in corporate, political, and environmental conditions that block and exploit the less powerful in society. In this view, those in power strive to maintain their social status by dictating laws and policies to reinforce their control over people of lesser advantage. Critical theorists attribute criminal activity to the social and economic institutions that adversely affect the lower socioeconomic classes.[74] The social and economic gap between rich and poor who live close together can also influence crime. When impoverished people observe the extravagant lifestyles of the wealthy, they may experience a sense of deprivation that leads to anger, resentment, and jealousy. These negative feelings can bring about behavior that can ultimately result in crime.[75]

Social conflict criminologists view crime from a broad perspective and are highly critical of the criminal justice system, lawmakers, corporations, and others in privileged positions who set policy in society. A Case in Point describes the case of a large drug company accused of exploiting the poor and powerless in Nigeria.

a Case in Point

Nigerians Sue Pfizer over Test Deaths

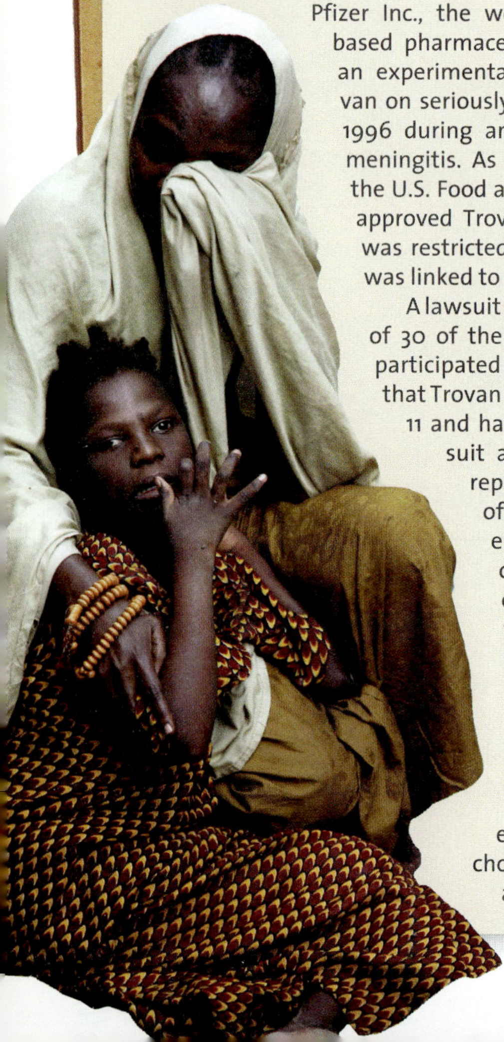

Pfizer Inc., the world's largest research-based pharmaceutical company, tested an experimental antibiotic called Trovan on seriously ill Nigerian children in 1996 during an epidemic of bacterial meningitis. As a result of these tests, the U.S. Food and Drug Administration approved Trovan in 1997, but its use was restricted in 1999 after the drug was linked to liver failure.

A lawsuit on behalf of the families of 30 of the Nigerian children who participated in clinical trials claimed that Trovan resulted in the deaths of 11 and harmed many others. The suit also alleged that Pfizer representatives visited one of Nigeria's most impoverished regions specifically to find subjects for clinical testing, that the company did not explain to the families that Trovan was experimental and known to have life-threatening side effects, and that it did not tell parents they could instead choose an internationally approved treatment for their children—offered free by a charitable medical group. Pfizer denied the accusations, stating it was proud of the way the study had been conducted and that both the Nigerian government and the families had given approval to test the drug.

Social conflict criminologists argue that incidents like the Trovan trials, which would not be allowed in the United States or any other affluent country, are an example of how large corporations driven to make profits no matter what the cost exploit the poor and powerless in developing countries. Critical criminologists point out that corporate acts such as this are not viewed as crimes but should be. The case was settled in 2009 when Pfizer agreed to pay an undisclosed amount in the millions of dollars to the children and families involved as well as to the Nigerian government.

Observe Investigate Understand

- **How do social conflict and critical criminologists redefine crime?**
- **Can you think of other examples in which corporations were charged with crimes? How would critical criminology explain these crimes?**
- **What would be appropriate punishments for corporations found guilty of crime?**

SOURCES: BBC News, "Nigerians Sue Pfizer over Test Deaths," August 30, 2001, http://news.bbc.co.uk/1/hi/business/1517171.stm (retrieved May 13, 2006); Joe Stephens, "Pfizer Reaches Settlement in Nigerian Drug-Trial Case," *Washington Post*, April 4, 2009, www.washingtonpost.com/wp-dyn/content/article/2009/04/03/AR2009040301877.html.

Feminist criminology applies feminist thought to the study of crime. Feminist criminologists argue that women's inequality is partly explained by the power differences between men and women and social expectations of both.[76] Most studies conducted prior to the 1970s assumed that women were like men and, therefore, what was learned about men's behavior would also apply to women.[77] Studies of women's criminality relied on gender stereotypes and assumptions about healthy and unhealthy sexuality. Theorists often explained female criminality by pointing to what was said to be women's sexual misbehavior.[78]

feminist criminology
The application of feminist thought and analysis to the study of crime.

By 1975, some theorists believed that the success of the women's movement would result in a corresponding increase in crimes committed by women.[79] They argued that as women gained equality with men, women would also begin to act more like men, even committing crimes with the same frequency as men. Evidence has not supported this hypothesis, and today we see that women's criminal patterns are still significantly different from men's (see Chapter 2).[80] After gaining a foothold in the 1970s, feminist criminologists have continued to explain not only women's criminality but also how female suspects and offenders are treated by criminal justice institutions.

Feminist criminologists draw our attention to a number of criminology's sexist practices and point out that women and men experience the world differently. As a result, it is essential that women researchers and activists be involved in interpreting crime as perpetrated by and against women. As women have entered the field of criminology, they have made a variety of contributions, including a fuller understanding of the complexity of women's offending and victimization.

Feminist criminologists find the roots of crime in economic and political conditions that contribute to the exploitation of women. Most recently, their research has examined the ways in which women's experiences with crime, victimization, and the criminal justice system differ based on race, class, and gender.[81] Not all women are treated the same by the criminal justice system, nor do they experience or commit crimes in exactly the same ways. In other words, female victims and offenders should not be treated as homogenous groups. They have important differences, just as there are differences among men.[82]

A contemporary theme stemming from critical criminology is **peacemaking criminology**. This perspective of criminology represents a departure from mainstream criminology and urges us to think of crime causation from a different point of view.[83] Peacemaking criminologists point out that crime is a form of violence and criminology should advocate a nonviolent, peaceful society.[84] They argue that widespread social justice would eliminate crime and that new forms of punishment should replace coercive ones.[85] Peacemaking criminology urges a transformation of policies in the criminal justice system to achieve a more just, peaceful, and crime-free world where the needs of offenders, communities, and victims are balanced.[86] Peacemaking criminology is the cornerstone of the humanistic restorative justice approaches discussed in Chapter 13.

peacemaking criminology
A branch of criminology that views crime as a form of violence and urges criminology to advocate a nonviolent, peaceful society.

A Different Set of Values: Cultural Deviance Factors

Cultural deviance theory focuses on how the social traditions with which people live and the subcultures with which they identify contribute to the values that guide their behaviors. Criminologists who subscribe to this perspective believe that adoption of negative and antisocial values learned in neighborhoods and subcultures produces criminal behavior.

cultural deviance theory
Adoption of negative and antisocial values learned in neighborhoods and subcultures produces criminal behavior.

Social Disorganization: Factors Related to Where We Live

Social disorganization theory attributes crime to the failure of social institutions and organizations, such as police, church, and welfare services, to meet the needs of a community or neighborhood. Social disorganization factors are typically found in high-crime areas that have been subject to rapid change due to industrialization, immigration, and urbanization. Social disorganization theorists examine neighborhood characteristics to find explanations of high crime rates among urban immigrants from other countries and communities.

social disorganization theory
Explains crime rates by examining city neighborhood characteristics.

▶ Migration to Chicago in the Early Twentieth Century

People from the rural South and immigrants began moving into large northern U.S. cities during the early twentieth century, resulting in rapid social disorganization.

During the early twentieth century, large numbers of immigrants and people from the rural South began moving into large northern U.S. cities. Researchers from the University of Chicago began studying the social disorganization and other problems that resulted from these population shifts, and they became known as the Chicago School of Social Ecology.[87] Chicago School researchers Robert Ezra Park and Ernest Burgess examined Chicago's disorganized neighborhoods by analyzing ecological (geographical) areas. This research led Burgess to develop a model of Chicago that consisted of concentric zones (see Figure 3-1).

Social disorganization theory claims that crime, delinquency, health problems, truancy, and unemployment are greater in areas near the city center.

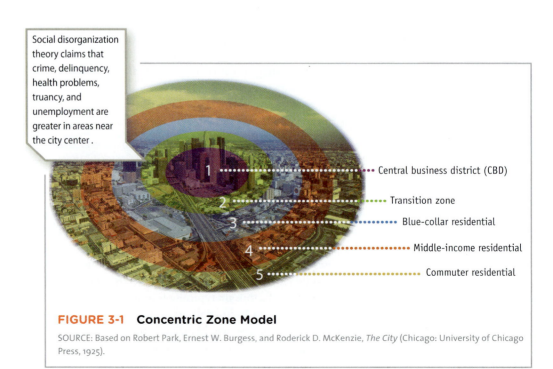

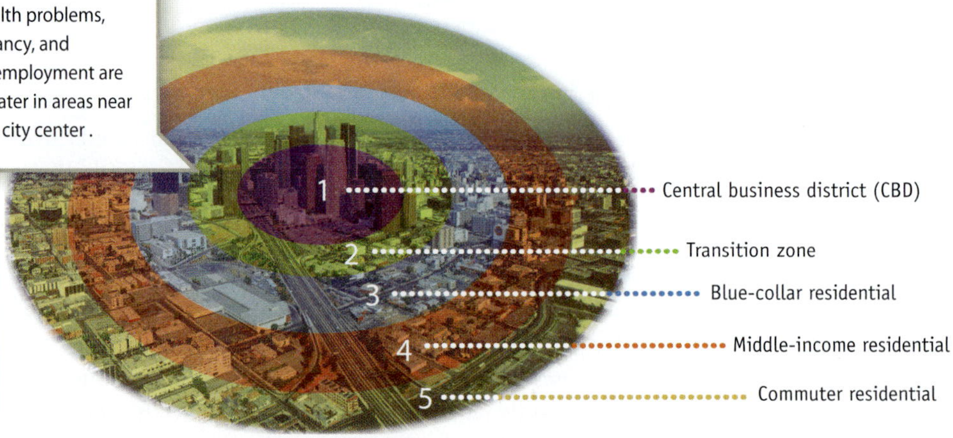

FIGURE 3-1 Concentric Zone Model

SOURCE: Based on Robert Park, Ernest W. Burgess, and Roderick D. McKenzie, *The City* (Chicago: University of Chicago Press, 1925).

Each zone has its own structure, organization, culture, and unique people. According to Clifford Shaw and Henry McKay (sociologists who in later decades expanded the research of Park and Burgess), the city center and Zone II are the zones of transition—home to the city's poor, unskilled, and disadvantaged living in dilapidated housing, frequently near factories. Moving away from this region, neighborhoods exhibit signs of greater social organization. For example, in Zone III, more working-class people own homes than rent, and in Zone IV the affluent purchase homes that reflect their status. Crime, delinquency, health problems, truancy, and unemployment are greater in areas near the city center than in neighborhoods farther away from the center. Social institutions and organizations have a difficult time responding to the needs of residents in areas where people are transient and not invested in the community.[88]

The concentric circle theory has changed over the years as residential patterns in cities have changed. As affluent suburbanites move back into city centers, many poor inner city residents are forced to relocate to find affordable housing and jobs. Future geographical studies of crime and delinquency are likely to yield results different from those found by Shaw and McKay.

Various crimes arise from social disorganization. For example, neighborhoods that do not discourage vandalism of homes and buildings seem to encourage or at least tolerate crime. How society is structured, largely in relation to the distribution of its wealth, affects the behavior of its residents. In response to the social disorganization brought on by economic disparities, people cope with whatever is their lot in life by forming groups of common interests and values.

Subcultures and Crime

A **subculture** is a group that has some of the same norms, values, and beliefs as members of the dominant, mainstream culture, but also other norms, values, and beliefs *not* held by society at large. A subculture is not necessarily bad or violent. For example, college students or animal lovers can be considered subcultures. However, a juvenile gang is also an example of a subculture. Its members could be said to value loyalty (like members of the dominant culture do), but they hold other values not consistent with mainstream culture (such as graffiti tagging buildings). Marvin Wolfgang and Franco Ferracuti formulated the theory that an independent subculture of violence exists in some extremely poor and disorganized areas.[89] In these areas, people are socialized to resolve conflicts via the use of violence. In fact, violence is the expected and valued response.[90]

subculture
A group that has some of the same norms, values, and beliefs as members of the dominant, mainstream culture but also other norms, values, and beliefs *not* held by society at large.

When the norms of conduct for one group conflict with conduct norms of another group, the result is **culture conflict**.[91] Crime may occur when there is culture conflict, but not all culture conflict results in law violation. The What about the Victim? box on page 88 illustrates one case in which culture conflict resulted in sexual abuse of underage women.

culture conflict
When the norms of conduct for one group conflict with conduct norms of another group.

Acting-Out Expectations: Social Process Factors

Assuming that criminality results from a sequence of successive interactions with others and society's institutions, **social process theory** seeks to explain the developmental stages leading to delinquent or criminal behavior. Proponents of social process theory minimize factors such as poverty, social institutions, and mental disorders, emphasizing instead factors such as interaction with others, socialization, imitation, reinforcement, role-modeling, stereotyping, and reaction of others to our behavior. Key concepts in social process theory include the looking-glass self, labeling, tagging, and differential association.

social process theory
Criminal behavior results from successive interactions with others and with society's institutions.

Charles H. Cooley developed the idea of the **looking-glass self** in 1902 based on his belief that we come to define ourselves by the way others see us.[92] If we perceive that others see us as good, bad, smart, dumb, responsible, flakey, manipulative, or criminal, we learn to see ourselves in those ways. How we see ourselves, in turn, will affect who we become and what we do in life. A person who sees himself as a crook is more likely to commit criminal acts; a person who sees himself as a law abider is less likely to commit criminal acts.

looking-glass self
The idea that if we perceive that others see us in certain ways, we learn to see ourselves in those ways.

What about the Victim?

Victims of Culture Conflict

Warren Jeffs had been one of the FBI's 10 most wanted fugitives for years when he was finally arrested in a routine traffic stop near Las Vegas, Nevada, on September 4, 2006. Jeffs was the leader of a fundamentalist branch of the Mormon Church located near the Arizona-Utah border. Fundamentalist Mormons had practiced polygamy in this area for more than 70 years, in opposition to the law and mainstream Mormon beliefs. Some of the beliefs of this sect are that men must have at least three wives to reach the highest levels of heaven, and that women can go to heaven only if their husbands bring them along.

In Utah sexual contact with 16- or 17-year-olds is illegal for people who are 10 years older, unless the couples are legally married. In polygamous unions, only first marriages are legal (Utah law bans plural marriages). In addition to being a polygamist with an estimated 14 wives, Jeffs kidnapped an underage Mormon girl and had sexual relations with her. The girl was 17 years old when she conceived Jeffs's baby. The first substantial evidence of criminal behavior by Jeffs was the baby's July 2000 birth certificate, which showed that Jeffs had had illegal sexual conduct with a minor.

Jeffs underwent trial for his role in arranging "spiritual" marriages of underage girls to older polygamist men. He was convicted on September 25, 2007, of being an accomplice to the rape of a 14-year-old girl, and on September 27, 2007, he was himself charged with committing rape. Jeffs, 51, faces life in prison. Officials estimate that hundreds of young teenage girls were victims of Jeffs and other sexual predators in the Utah sect.

Observe Investigate Understand

- **Compare the Jeffs case with the case of Abdul Rahman, the 25-year-old Afghan who converted to Christianity (page 73). Is the Jeffs case an example of culture conflict or of criminalizing religious beliefs?**
- **Who is the victim of culture conflict in the Jeffs case?**
- **Can you think of other cases in which culture conflict results in law violation?**

SOURCES: John Dougherty, "Fornicating for God," *Phoenix New Times,* March 20, 2003, www.polygamyinfo.com/plygmedia%2003%2032newti.htm (retrieved May 13, 2006); Kirk Johnson, "Man Charged in Rape of Teenager in Fundamentalist Sect," *The New York Times,* September 27, 2007, www.nytimes.com/2007/09/27/us/27jeffs.html (retrieved September 29, 2007); John Dougherty and Kirk Johnson, "Sect Leader Is Convicted as an Accomplice to Rape," *The New York Times,* September 27, 2007, www.nytimes.com/2007/09/26/us/26jeffs.html?_r=1 (retrieved September 29, 2007).

Labeling theory, associated primarily with Howard Becker,[93] is related to the theory of the looking-glass self. Labeling theory attempts to explain the complicated route a person takes in becoming criminal, progressing through gradual stages of criminality, and the role that society plays in defining a person as a criminal. According to this theory, the social process a person experiences has the potential to define him or her as "bad" or "good," and some people become bad because others do not believe them to be good. The label is powerful and defines a person as criminal in his or her own eyes as well as in the eyes of others. Once an individual accepts and internalizes a label, negative behavior can follow. Criminals often act in accordance with these labels, and it is hard for them to reject and change their labels, making reformation difficult.[94]

As people progress through the criminal justice system, they are marked each step of the way in a process known as tagging. Tagging reinforces offenders' negative traits. During tagging, offenders shift from perceiving their acts as bad to seeing themselves as bad or evil. Opportunities for offenders to change this view decline over time.[95]

Differential association theory, developed by Edwin Sutherland,[96] suggests that criminal behavior is learned during normal social interactions and that the same learning principles are involved in reinforcing criminal and law-abiding behavior. A person who is exposed to and learns a large number of criminal attitudes and values is more likely to commit criminal acts than a person who is exposed to and learns very few criminal attitudes and values. Perhaps most important, differential association theory emphasizes that learning criminal behavior occurs in intimate groups and assumes that anyone can become criminal if placed in a situation that fosters such behavior.

Social process theories attempt to explain how we become who we are and how changing our identity is a monumentally difficult job. Figure 3-2 shows how a sociological theory about working-class delinquency organizes information about specific sociological factors.

It is extremely difficult for the criminal justice system to deal with all the biological, psychological, and sociological factors that affect criminal behavior. The Disconnects box on page 90 highlights the difficulty in connecting the factors that produce crime and criminality with the ability of criminal justice professionals to consider those factors in the administration of justice.

The table titled "Internal and External Factors Leading to Criminal Behavior" synthesizes the biological, psychological, and sociological factors that interact with one another to produce criminal behavior. In the next section we consider factors related to victims: their characteristics, their behavior, and their responses to being victimized.

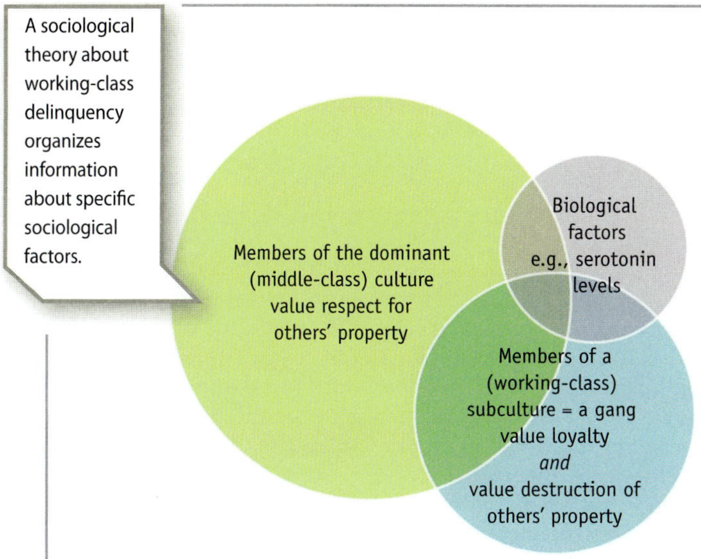
A sociological theory about working-class delinquency organizes information about specific sociological factors.
Members of the dominant (middle-class) culture value respect for others' property
Biological factors e.g., serotonin levels
Members of a (working-class) subculture = a gang value loyalty *and* value destruction of others' property

FIGURE 3-2 A "Factors" Approach to Explaining Criminal Behavior
Working-class youth experience strain from being seen as "a nobody" in the eyes of the dominant middle class, driving them to form their own subculture, a gang, with its own rules.

VICTIMIZATION FACTORS

The U.S. population is much more aware of efforts to apprehend criminals and prevent crime than it is aware of the plight of crime victims. This lack of concern for the victim even extends to criminal justice practitioners.[97] One of the major themes of the victim rights' movement, which began in the early 1900s in England, was recognizing and correcting the way crime victims had been neglected. Trying to provide victims with some form of reparation and compensation was one of the first types of assistance.[98] California was the first U.S. state to respond to the financial needs of crime victims. In 1965 the state established a victim compensation program, which repaid crime victims for damages and injuries resulting from a crime.[99]

Most of the pioneers in **victimology**, the scientific study of victims, were criminologists who were intrigued with the role that victims played in crime causation.[100] To appreciate the role of victims in the study of crime and criminal justice, criminologists and victimologists need to understand victims without judging them. They must know the factors that shaped victims' development, especially any factors during childhood that might have influenced their behaviors before their adult victimization. For example, some victims of intimate partner violence contribute to the violence that ultimately injures them.[101] Some of those factors have to do with coping behaviors victims have learned for dealing with conflicts, the kinds of victimizing situations they are unable to avoid, and the circumstances that put them at risk.

The Risk of Becoming a Victim

Offenders tend to target individuals who display a variety of attributes that make them easy prey. These attributes can be behavioral, physical, social, or attitudinal and may change over time.[102]

Vulnerability factors are human characteristics that can be exploited by criminals and can result in victimization. Examples include having been previously victimized[103] or having a disability (for example, being blind, deaf, or mute).[104] Demographic factors also

labeling theory
The belief that the social process individuals experience has the potential to define them as "bad" or "good" and that some people become bad because others do not believe them to be good.

differential association theory
Criminal behavior is learned during normal social interactions, and the same learning principles are involved in reinforcing criminal and law-abiding behavior.

victimology
The scientific study of victims, which includes their behaviors, injuries, assistance, legal rights, and recovery.

INTERNAL AND EXTERNAL FACTORS LEADING TO CRIMINAL BEHAVIOR

Internal Factors	External Factors
Genetics	Toxins
Intelligence	Nutrition and diet
Mental disorders	Socioeconomic status
Hormones	Cultural values
Neurotransmitters	Geographic conditions
Brain disease and injury	Environmental change

DIS Connects

Causes of Crime and the Administration of Justice

The criminal justice system rarely considers the psychological, biological, or sociological factors associated with criminal behavior. As a criminal case proceeds, criminal justice professionals have little opportunity to take into account how specific factors associated with the offender's behavior might inform an appropriate response. In other words, there is a disconnection between the causes of crime and the administration of justice. For example, the criminal justice system has struggled with how to treat women who have killed their abusers.

For a long time, victims of domestic violence who killed their abusers were unable to offer the evidence of abuse or well-researched psychological theories to explain why they resorted to killing. In recent years, this has begun to change. For example, a 2001 California law allows victims of domestic violence who have been convicted of killing their abusers to "challenge convictions with evidence of the abuse and its psychological effects." [a] Research on the effects of domestic violence has accumulated to such a degree that it is difficult to ignore the impacts of abuse on victims and why they resort to the ultimate act of self-defense. The first woman to successfully use the 2001 law for a retrial was acquitted in 2006 after having served 21 years in prison for killing her husband, who had abused her for years.[b] Other states, however, deal with this issue differently, and the ability to introduce evidence of abuse and theories that seek to explain why a victim might resort to violence herself varies greatly from state to state.

Observe Investigate Understand

- **How should criminal justice professionals consider various theories of criminal behavior during the process of doling out justice?**
- **Do theories of criminal behavior absolve offenders from responsibility for their behavior?**
- **How do theories of criminal behavior explain—or justify—an abuse victim's use of violence against the abuser?**

SOURCES: [a]Merrill Balassone, "Retrial acquits wife who killed husband," *Sacramento Bee*, June 2, 2006, p. A20.
[b] Ibid.

may increase vulnerability and the likelihood of being victimized. Demographic factors include being female,[105] working in a high-risk profession,[106] being in a new country,[107] or belonging to a discriminated group.[108] The risk of victimization can increase when vulnerabilities are combined. For example, an individual may have multiple conditions such as physical disability, diminished intellectual capacity, and mental impairment that, when combined with being in a dangerous environment like a bar where high-risk activities take place, can further increase the risk of victimization.

Obtrusive vulnerabilities are visible, obvious, and recognizable. For example, a person who is very drunk does not have the mental awareness or ability to think clearly and avoid a criminal attack. Unobtrusive vulnerabilities are not easily observed. For example, a child who has been victimized in the past by a classmate might develop a sense of helplessness. Persons in a state of helplessness are convinced that they cannot protect themselves and consequently are more likely to give up when attacked.[109] When threatened again, they are likely to put up little resistance. When offenders know the vulnerabilities of potential victims, and especially when they live in close proximity to them, the probability of harm significantly increases.[110] In general, most crimes against persons occur between acquaintances largely because there are more opportunities for conflict and the offender has greater awareness of the victim's vulnerabilities.[111]

Persons with high levels of both obtrusive and unobtrusive vulnerabilities are often victimized repeatedly. Thus, they are **recidivist victims**. The children of battered women, for example, often live in situations of high stress, often observe violence in their homes, are usually not properly protected from family abuse, do not receive proper guidance from their parents, and do not experience consistent child rearing and positive disciplinary practices. As a consequence, these children lack many important social skills, do not know how to cope well with conflicts within the family, and thus are more vulnerable to repeat victimization than children who come from nonviolent families.[112]

recidivist victims
Persons who are victimized repeatedly.

MYTH/REALITY

MYTH: People who want to avoid being victimized can—if they put their mind to it.

REALITY: A large part of what causes people to become victims is mostly out of their control. An example of how different settings, different behaviors, and different lifestyles result in different levels of victimization can be seen in the differences between the rates of victimization in public and private schools. In public schools, 71 percent of children in grades 6 to 12 reported knowing about events of bullying, physical attacks, or robberies; in the same grades in private schools, only 45 percent knew about these incidents of violence.[113]

routine activities theory
Some individuals' daily activities make them more vulnerable to being crime victims.

Another type of victim vulnerability is the result of an individual's daily **routine activities.** Examples include leaving and returning home at the same time each day, taking the same route to school or work, and going to the same hangouts on the weekends. Offenders learn to recognize the victim's predictable and patterned behaviors. Some lifestyles, such as bar-hopping and getting drunk with friends every weekend, or some occupations, such as those requiring late night work shifts, provide greater opportunities for criminals than do others.[114] While these behaviors may make some individuals more vulnerable to potential offenders, it is the actions of the offenders (as determined by the law) that *cause* the victimizations.

Victim Behavior during the Crime

During the commission of most personal crimes, some level of communication generally occurs between the offender and the victim.[115] During a property crime, the interaction between offender and victim starts when the offender makes contact with an object that belongs to the victim. The outcome of this interaction will determine whether victimization will occur and the degree of injury or damage that will result. For example, in a first encounter with an unknown victim, an offender will start a conversation with someone the offender identifies as vulnerable. The victim's response depends on his or her perception of threat. The offender will then test the victim's vulnerability; either the vulnerability is confirmed as a weakness or the offender realizes he or she made a mistake in judgment.

A male offender may be physically aggressive with a female victim. In such a case, the victim will test defenses she assumes are effective. If she perceives the threat as significant, she may attempt to fight back. If the victim feels that she is too vulnerable, she may attempt to flee the scene as quickly as possible. In one study comparing victims' and nonvictims' responses to hypothetical scenarios, victims tended to be confrontational or abusive to an initial approach by the perpetrator. In contrast, nonvictims were more likely to withdraw quietly and say or do nothing.[116] A confrontational or abusive response in an offensive situation increases a person's chances of becoming a victim. A person who withdraws from an offensive situation will likely not become a victim. Some offenders will commit their crimes regardless of the victim's response to the initial confrontation, but the way a potential victim responds may convince the offender not to continue.

A Typology of Victimology

The "father of victimology," Beniamin Mendelsohn, was a Romanian defense attorney who, in preparing for his cases, interviewed both victims and offenders in an effort to understand who contributed more to the criminal act. Mendelsohn coined the term *victimology* and created a typology (that is, a logical classification of types) of crime victims based on the degree to which they contributed to the criminal act (see the table on page 93 for a list of Mendelsohn's victim categories).

Mendelsohn's typology focused attention on the notion that victims' actions play a significant role in the outcome of a criminal act. With this typology and his later proposals for victim clinics, victim studies, a victim journal, an international victimology organization, and victim institutes—all of which have been realized—Mendelsohn started a movement that today spans the globe and has had a major impact on the way victims are understood and treated. (See the table on page 92 for a list of factors associated with criminal and delinquent behavior.)

FACTORS ASSOCIATED WITH CRIMINAL AND DELINQUENT BEHAVIOR

Psychological and Biological Factors	Sociological Factors	Victim Factors
Mental Disorders Psychoses Schizophrenia Depression Mania Bipolar disorder Postpartum psychosis	*Strain Factors* Life pressures Feelings of alienation Anomie Inability to achieve desired life goals Lack of opportunity and gang membership Maturation during the life course	*Previctimization Factors* Behavior Attitudes Physical attributes Vulnerability Routine activities
Cognitive Factors Intelligence and IQ Moral reasoning	*Control Factors* Communities Taking responsibility Rationalization Bonds to society Self-control Self-esteem	*Victim Behavior during the Crime* Aggressiveness Passivity Weakness Confrontation
Social Learning Factors Reinforcement Consequences of behavior Modeling Fear of punishment	*Critical Factors* Capitalism Racism Sexism Discrimination Poverty Power Inequality	*Victimology Theory* Victim's role in a crime
Situational Variables Life circumstances Defense mechanisms Guilt	*Cultural Deviance Factors* Neighborhoods Social disorganization Subcultures Culture conflict	
Psychodynamic Factors Id Ego Superego development	*Social Process Factors* Looking-glass self Labeling Tagging Differential association	
Neurobiological Factors Nervous system and the brain Hormones Neurotransmitters Brain disease, injury, or deficit Prefrontal cortex underactivity ADHD		
Environmental Conditions and Contaminants Lead poisoning Other contaminants		
Genetic Factors Genes		

MENDELSOHN'S TYPOLOGY OF CRIME VICTIMS

Victim	Example
Completely innocent victim or ideal victim	Children and those who are unconscious during the crime
Ignorant victim with minor culpability	A woman who induces a miscarriage and dies herself
Victim who is as guilty as the offender and the voluntary victim	Suicides
Victim who is guiltier than the offender	A victim who provokes an attack against which the "offender" defends him- or herself
Guiltiest victim	An aggressive "victim" who is alone guilty or an attacker who is killed by another in self-defense
Simulating and the imaginary victim, who tries to mislead justice and have the accused punished	Paranoids, hysterical persons, senile persons, and some children

SOURCES: Beniamin Mendelsohn, "The Victimology," *Etudes Internationale de Psycho-sociologie Criminelle* (July–September, 1956): 23–26; Stephen Schafer, *The Victim and His Criminal: A Study in Functional Responsibility* (New York: Random House, 1968).

SUMMARY

Traditional approaches to the study of the causes of criminal behavior tended to focus separately on psychological, biological, or sociological theories. Theories represent different ways of organizing information about factors. In reality, a person's behavior is the product of the interactions among many psychological, biological, and sociological factors. Different factors interact with each other in complex ways.

Most crimes are the product of the interactions between victim and offender, and one area of the focus on victims involves understanding how victim behavior interacts with offender behavior to produce a crime. Victimologists are interested in victims' perception of their victimization, their contributions to their own victimization, the extent of their injuries, and their responses to the experience of victimization. Many of the same biological, psychological, and sociological factors that produce criminal behavior are related to why people become victims.

OBSERVE
Investigate
Understand

Review

Understand the roles of biological (including genetic) and environmental factors on brain function and criminal behavior.

- Biological factors associated with brain function influence behavior and the thought processes associated with making choices.
- Biological factors related to the expression and suppression of criminal and violent behaviors can be identified and measured.

Explain the key aspects of mental disorders and understand how they are classified.

- Mental disorders are medical conditions that interfere with a person's ability to function on a day-to-day basis.

- The *Diagnostic and Statistical Manual of Mental Disorders* (DSM) classifies mental disorders as psychoses and nonpsychotic disorders, which include mood disorders and personality disorders.

Recognize the cognitive factors of intelligence and moral reasoning as brain functions that influence criminal behavior.

- On average, incarcerated offenders tend to score lower than nonoffenders on standardized intelligence tests. Offenders may have lower emotional intelligence, which can influence criminal behavior.
- Damage to the prefrontal cortex area of the brain can affect moral reasoning and lead to criminal behavior.

Understand how economic, class, and social inequalities can be linked to the causes of crime.

- When people need and want to make money and are not able to, they may experience extraordinary strain and feel pressured to breaking the law to obtain the things they need and want.
- Social and economic differences among the classes adversely affect the lower socioeconomic classes, resulting in crime.

Describe factors that cause some people to become victims of crime.

- Many of the same biological, psychological, and social factors that influence why crime is committed are related to why people become victims.
- A variety of behavioral, physical, social, and attitudinal factors can cause people to become victims of crime.

Key Terms

adolescence-limited offenders 82
anomie 80
atavism 68
bipolar affective disorder 75
classical school of criminology 67
containment theory 83
critical theory 84
cultural deviance theory 85
culture conflict 87
Diagnostic and Statistical Manual of Mental Disorders (DSM) 73
differential association theory 89
feminist criminology 85
intelligence 77
labeling theory 89
life course persistent offenders 82
looking-glass self 87
moral reasoning 78
neoclassical school of criminology 68
neurotransmitter 70
neutralization theory 82
peacemaking criminology 85
positivist school of criminology 68
postpartum psychosis 75
psychopathy 75
psychoses 72
rational choice theory 68
recidivist victims 91
routine activities theory 91
schizophrenia 74
social bond theory 83
social conflict theory 83
social control theory 82
social disorganization theory 85
social learning theory 78
social process theory 87
strain theory 79
subculture 87
victimology 89

Study Questions

1. Psychoses are
   a. false beliefs.
   b. false perceptions.
   c. serious mental disorders.
   d. all of the above.
2. According to psychoanalysts, criminals are dominated by their _____, which resulted from a damaged ____ during childhood.

a.	ego	id
b.	superego	ego
c.	ego	superego
d.	id	ego

3. Which of the following is *not* true of psychopaths?
   a. They tend to experience hallucinations and delusions.
   b. They exhibit a lifelong pattern of antisocial behavior.
   c. They have no guilt for their antisocial behaviors.
   d. All the above are true statements.
4. The chapter discusses several major categories of thought regarding sociological factors. Which of the following is *not* one of them?
   a. Social conflict
   b. Social process
   c. Techniques of neutralization
   d. Control
5. Which of the following concepts is considered a social process factor?
   a. Looking-glass self
   b. Anomie
   c. Socioeconomic status
   d. Techniques of neutralization

6. The attributes of potential victims that are visible, obvious, and recognized are called
   a. obtrusive vulnerabilities.
   b. routine activities.
   c. victim susceptibilities.
   d. precipitating clues.
7. Which of the following strain factors can lead to criminal behavior?
   a. Feelings of alienation
   b. Inability to achieve desired life goals
   c. Frustration
   d. All of the above
8. Offenders who begin their criminal activities when young and continue them throughout their lives are called
   a. adolescence-limited offenders.
   b. delinquent recidivist offenders.
   c. life course persistent offenders.
   d. all of the above.
9. Which of the following factors is not a control factor?
   a. Feelings of alienation
   b. Community responses
   c. Taking responsibility
   d. Bonds to society
10. Which of the following statements describes feminist criminology?
   a. Feminist criminology is an outgrowth of social conflict theories of crime causation.
   b. Feminist criminology was developed in the 1990s.
   c. Feminist criminology points out that men and women experience the world in similar ways.
   d. All of the above.

Critical Thinking Questions

1. Why are we so quick to embrace the research that has found specific genes associated with breast cancer but so reluctant to accept a genetic basis for criminal behavior?
2. What are some of the factors that contribute to anomie in modern life? What are some of the things that can be done to prevent anomie from occurring?
3. Why is it important to understand that victims are not all 100 percent innocent and offenders are not all 100 percent guilty?

Internet Sites

Brain Fingerprinting Laboratories
www.brainwavescience.com/HarringtonForensicReport.php
Advances in technology are providing us with tools to better understand brain structure and function. This site details the use of electroencephalograph (EEG) recordings—recordings of brainwave activity—to reveal whether a suspect committed a crime, or whether his alibi is true. The technique is called brain fingerprinting.

Homeboy Industries
www.homeboy-industries.org/index.php
You can find out more about Homeboy Industries, the organization that helps individuals abandon their gang membership, at their Web site.

Understanding Victim Behavior
www.ncvc.org/ncvc/main.aspx?dbName=DocumentViewer&DocumentID=38393
Explore this Web site to get a brief understanding of the psychobiology of trauma as it relates to all forms of victimization.

Suggested Readings

Christopher Berry-Dee, *Talking with Serial Killers* (London: John Blake, 2003).
Based on interviews with the 10 serial murderers presented in this book, criminologist Christopher Berry-Dee offers information about each that gives us the opportunity to speculate about the psychological makeup of these offenders.

Celeste Fremon, *G-Dog and the Homeboys* (Albuquerque: University of New Mexico Press, 2004).
This book is based on Father Gregory Boyle's gang intervention work with Pico/Aliso East L.A. gang members.

John P. J. Dussich, "Social Coping: A Theoretical Model for Understanding Victimization and Recovery," in *Victimology: International Action and Study of Victims*, ed. Zvonimir Paul _eparovi (Zagreb: Somobar, 1988).
The social coping model places all types of victims at the center of its focus and provides definitions and postulates that have explanatory and heuristic power for the study of victimology. Core features of the model include the use of personal resources to explain why victimization occurs and how to help victims recover, concepts that are behavioral rather than legal, and the use of a systems approach to psychosocial coping.

Criminal Law and Defenses

CHAPTER 4

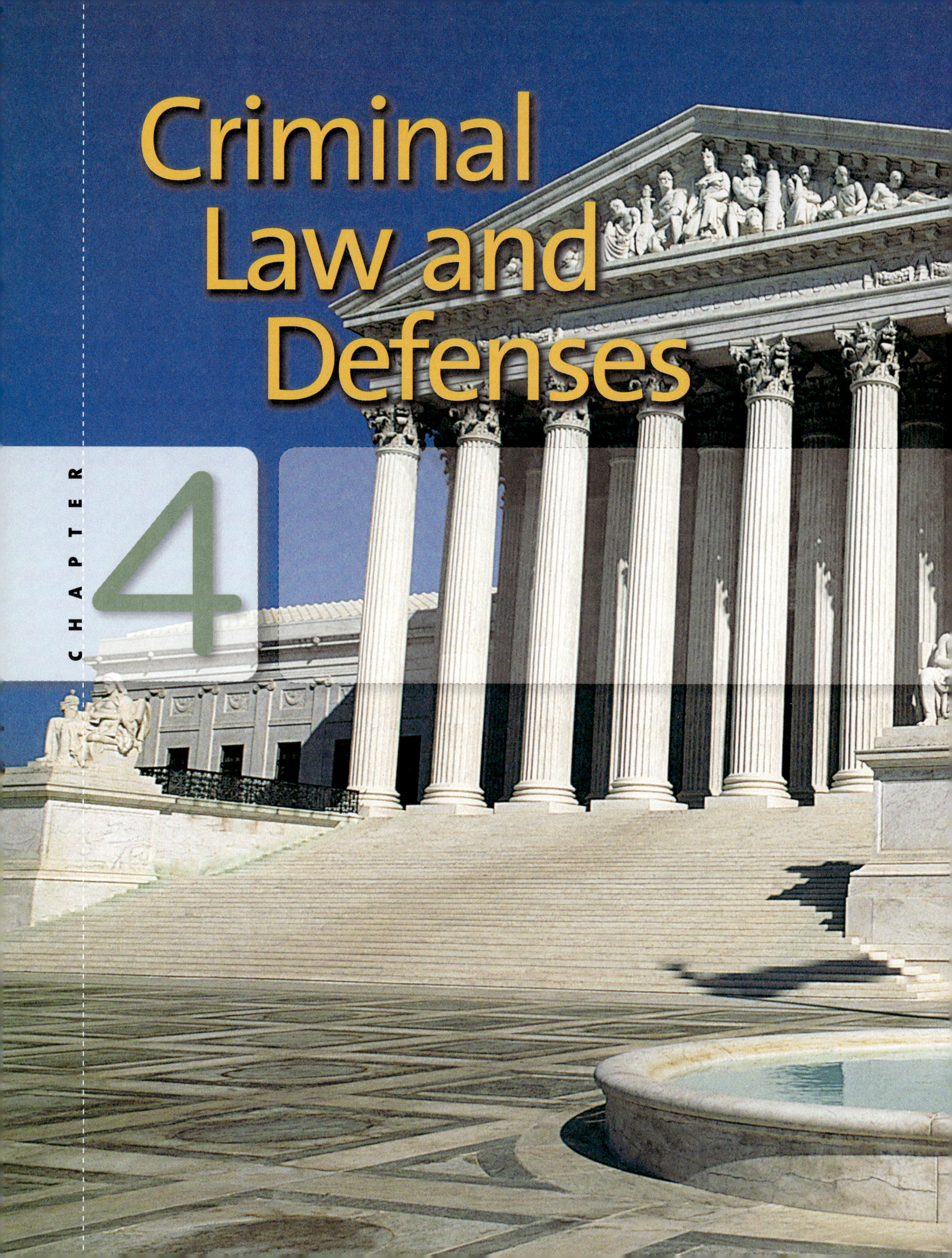

OBSERVE Investigate *Understand*

After reading this chapter, you should be able to:

- Explain the rule of law.
- Provide a short history of lawmaking.
- Identify modern sources of laws in the United States.
- Examine the key elements of civil and criminal law.
- Define the three types of criminal offenses.
- Describe the legal elements of a crime.
- Explain common criminal defenses allowed by the court.
- Explore aspects of the insanity defense.

Realities and Challenges

What Kind of a Crime Is Hazing?

Twenty-one-year-old Matthew Carrington wanted to join a fraternity at California State University, Chico. In February 2005, he rushed and pledged Chi Tau. As part of his initiation, Carrington was made to drink an excessive amount of water and exercise in a cold, damp basement. Tragically, he died of water intoxication and hypothermia, an abnormally low body temperature.

After Carrington's death, criminal charges were filed against the hosting fraternity and three of its members. If convicted of manslaughter, Gabriel Maestretti, Jerry Lim, and John Fickes faced up to four years in prison. Instead, the students were sentenced to three months to a year in jail after pleading guilty to misdemeanor hazing and felony manslaughter charges. As a part of their sentence, the students were required to educate others about the dangers of hazing.

Interviewed from jail, the convicted students described living in a large cell with 48 other inmates who shared four toilets, three shower heads, six sinks, and some picnic tables. Although the conditions of their imprisonment were not as bad as they had anticipated, Lim and Fickes questioned whether they deserved to be put behind bars for their offense. Fickes went even further, claiming that it was stupidity that killed Carrington; how were they to know that simply taking in too much water could kill someone? Lim and Maestretti were more remorseful, shouldering responsibility for the fact that their actions had contributed to the death of the pledge.[1]

Matthew Carrington's death inspired a new law in California, Matt's Law. Enacted in 2006, this law makes it a felony for people to participate in hazing activities that result in death or serious injury.[2]

The sad case of Matthew Carrington illustrates that criminal law is not always easy to interpret. Sometimes it is a challenge to determine what crimes were committed. Attorneys and judges often are pressed to define the meaningful legal elements of a case and to spell out an appropriate judicial outcome for such offenders. Fortunately, the foundation of law underlying the criminal justice system may be interpreted and tailored to meet the needs of a wide variety of cases.

In this chapter we explore the basic elements of criminal law and common criminal defenses, including the insanity plea. As Matthew Carrington's case demonstrates, the specific nature and meaning of laws may change over time to address specific problems that arise. However, the basic roots of criminal laws can be traced back almost 4,000 years.

WHAT IS LAW?

Imagine a system in which a king could punish his subjects whenever he wished, for whatever acts he wished, and using whatever kinds of punishment he desired. People would have no idea what they could or could not do. The king could wield his power to punish anyone to whom he took a dislike. Most of us would find this brand of "justice" intolerably unfair.

Unlike such a kingdom, the justice system in the United States relies on the **rule of law**. The government can punish people only when there are written laws, created by established procedures, prohibiting specific activities. Furthermore, under the rule of law no government official, no matter how powerful, is above the law.

Preview

rule of law
The guiding principle of our legal system, which states that no single person is more powerful than the law.

Purpose and Function of the Law

Laws have governed human conduct for thousands of years, and today the criminal laws of just a single state are complex enough to fill hundreds of pages. Why do we have all these laws?

Criminal laws serve a number of functions. By providing penalties for certain behaviors, they protect people and property from harm. By designating which behaviors are forbidden, they provide clear standards of behavior, warning people about acts that will or will not be punished. They also limit the government's power to penalize people unfairly or arbitrarily. On a broader scale, criminal laws regulate and sometimes maintain social order. Criminal laws also serve a symbolic function, sending a message that a society disapproves of particular acts.

History of Criminal Laws

Long before recorded history began, human behavior was governed by unwritten social norms, and these norms continue to shape daily life. Norms evolve slowly through social consensus, but some of them have been imposed by those in power. As people began living in larger communities—in cities and kingdoms—the first formal rules of conduct were devised, and eventually put in writing, by heads of state and their representatives. Not only did these rules require or prohibit certain behaviors, but they also specified sanctions for violations. Sanctions could include fines, enslavement, banishment, physical punishments such as whipping or maiming, and execution. These rules of state became the earliest **laws**.

laws
Formal rules of conduct sanctioned by the state.

One of the earliest known records of written laws dates from the time of Babylonian King Hammurabi (reigned 1792–1750 BCE). The laws known as **Hammurabi's Code** established high standards of behavior, setting forth 252 written rules and designating punishments for violators. The core of Hammurabi's Code was the principle that violators should suffer punishment equal to their offense. Hammurabi had his code carved in stone and set up for all to see; it still survives and today is displayed at the Louvre Museum in Paris. The entire text of the code has been translated into English and is available online.[3]

Hammurabi's Code
The earliest known written laws, which were set down by Babylonian King Hammurabi (1792–1750 BCE). The core of the code was the principle that violators should suffer punishment equal to their offense.

◀ **Hammurabi's Code**
The Code of Hammurabi was one of the earliest known records of written laws.

Another early system of written laws was Mosaic Law, which like Hammurabi's Code rested on the principle of "an eye for an eye." Because these laws

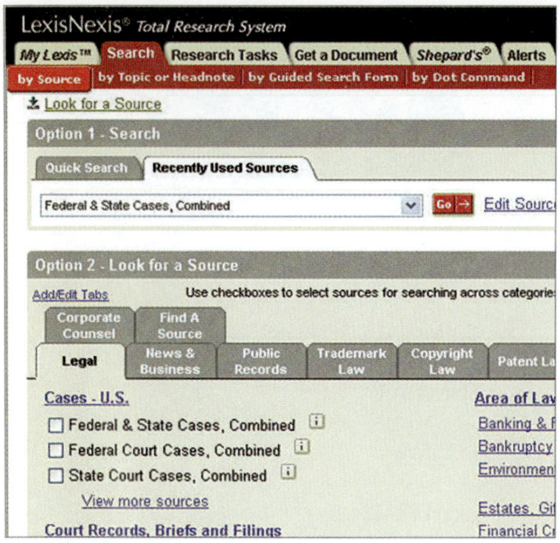

Real Crime Tech

LEXISNEXIS

The ability to conduct legal research, to search for legal codes, court cases, and across different types of laws (to name a few examples, administrative law, corporate law, criminal law, and tax law) has been revolutionized courtesy of the Internet and Web-based legal search programs. One of the most widely used programs is LexisNexis (www.lexisnexis.com). LexisNexis began in 1973 when Lexis and the National Automated Accounting Research Service (NAARS) provided full text of Ohio and New York codes and cases, the U.S. Code, and some federal case law. Within a year, Lexis provided a searchable legal database for attorneys to search case law. The Nexis, or news, database began in 1979 with access to full articles from a variety of national news journals, Reuters, and the Associated Press. By 1997, LexisNexis began the first Web-based service for legal professionals, and within one year worldwide Internet usage exceeded 50 million customers. Since 2000, LexisNexis has expanded to include Risk & Information Analytics Group, which addresses law enforcement and homeland security concerns; CourtLink, which provides access to the litigation history of companies, attorney experience, and trends in federal litigation; and TotalPatent, which focuses on major patents and intellectual property information issues internationally.

SOURCE: LexisNexis, "History," 2009, www.lexisnexis.com/about-us/history.aspx (retrieved February 24, 2009).

are included in the books of Exodus, Leviticus, and Deuteronomy in the Bible, they became the basis for Judaism and, to some extent, Christianity. The Ten Commandments are part of Mosaic Law.

Both the ancient Greeks and the Romans relied heavily on written laws. In the sixth century CE, the Roman Emperor Justinian created a series of law books that eventually served as the basis of the legal system implemented across most of Europe. Those books were called the *Corpus Iuris Civilis* (Body of the Civil Law). Justinian's Code was one of the first systematic collections of laws. Countries with systems based upon the *Corpus Iuris Civilis* have *civil* or Roman law systems; these countries include most of continental Europe and many other countries throughout the world.

Prior to the Norman Conquest of England in 1066, laws in England varied a great deal from place to place. England had previously consisted of several smaller kingdoms, which traced their roots to many different countries and cultures.

As late as the twelfth century, England had no uniform system of laws or courts. But King Henry II, who ruled from 1154 to 1189, created, under his own control, a single system of laws for the entire kingdom. Henry dispatched royal judges to "ride circuit"—that is, to travel around the country hearing cases, assisted by locally chosen juries. Royal judges carried with them a consistent set of rules that became known as **common law**, so called because it was uniform, or common, throughout England.

Common law relies on judges' interpretations of previous cases. A previous case that guides decisions in later cases is known as **precedent**. In contrast, civil (Roman) law systems do *not* rely on precedent. The fact that courts rely on precedent to shape their decisions—a concept known as *stare decisis*, or "to stand on the decision"—means that courts themselves become a significant source of laws and law interpretation. The use of precedent also helps ensure uniformity and predictability of legal decisions.

When the first British colonists arrived in North America in the seventeenth century, they brought from their homeland many traditions and practices, including the common law system. English law was not the only law in colonial America. Other European colonizers, such as the Dutch, Spanish, and French, brought with them civil law–based legal systems, and Native American societies had their own (unwritten) laws. In the end, the English system prevailed. As the colonies grew, however, the settlers encountered a number of conditions and challenges that had not existed in England and that required new laws. Two obvious examples arose from the colonists' desire to subdue the American Indians and to control their slaves. Common law made no provision for slavery. Then, after the Revolutionary War, the new United States faced the opportunity to create a legal system virtually from scratch rather than relying on bits and pieces cobbled together over several hundred years. Still, common law remains the foundation of the legal system of the United States, as well as in England, Canada, Australia, India, and other countries that were once British colonies.

As the government of the United States evolved, common law remained one source of law. Over time, other vital sources were added to the body of laws that govern the country. These include the federal and state constitutions, case law, regulations, and statutes (the laws enacted by Congress and the state legislatures). All these sources of law are discussed in the next section.

Modern Sources of Law in the United States

Today, the average citizen of the United States is governed by a large number of laws from a variety of sources. These laws and regulations emanate from federal, state, and local administrative agencies and affect everything from getting a dog license to serious criminal acts. Some acts are illegal throughout the United States, but wide variation continues to exist from place to place in the way we enforce laws and define and punish crime. The Key Concepts feature on page 102 illustrates the different sources of law that govern our behavior.

A **constitution** specifies the components of a government, the duties of each component, and the limits of their power. The U.S. Constitution is the supreme law of the United States, which means all laws within all jurisdictions in the United States must conform to its requirements. The U.S. Constitution regulates the federal government, and each state has its own constitution as well.

The U.S. Constitution contains sections specifying the powers and responsibilities of the three branches of the federal government (Congress, the executive, and the courts) and the qualifications for holding various federal offices. It also contains 27 amendments, many of which specify certain rights that are afforded to individuals in the United States, and with which the government cannot interfere without good cause. Freedom of speech, which is guaranteed in the First Amendment, is one of these rights. Many of these rights are discussed in later chapters of this book.

Statutes are written laws enacted either by legislatures or (in states that allow for this procedure) by the citizens themselves through the voting process. Federal statutes form a multivolume set known as the United States Code. Each state also has its own set of statutes. Thousands of statutes cover everything from business licenses to water use. Both federal and state statutes include laws that specify punishments for certain kinds of acts, but because most crimes are considered primarily to be matters of local concern, there are many more of these criminal laws in state codes than in the federal code. Cities and counties also create their own written laws. These are usually called **ordinances**.

In 1962 the American Law Institute (ALI)—a board of judges, lawyers, and legal scholars—published the first version of its **Model Penal Code**. It was most recently updated in 1981. The MPC is not a set of laws but a suggested prototype for criminal laws, intended to guide states in bringing their systems of criminal law up-to-date and making them more uniform. In some places, the MPC offers states several options, among which they are invited to choose. No state uses the entire MPC, but four have adopted it almost whole, and two-thirds have used it extensively in modernizing their criminal laws. Many definitions of crimes and of criminal responsibility used in this book reflect usages suggested in the Model Penal Code.

FIGURE 4-1 History of Law Timeline
What factors impelled societies to begin writing down formal laws?

common law
The legal system created in England after the Norman Conquest and still used in the United States today.

precedent
Previous court decisions that have binding authority on subsequent cases.

constitution
A document that specifies the components of a government, the duties of each component, and the limits of their power.

statutes
Laws enacted by state legislatures or by Congress.

ordinances
Laws enacted by local governments such as cities and counties.

Model Penal Code
A suggested code of criminal law drafted by the American Law Institute and used to guide the states in modernizing their laws.

case law
Decisions judges have made in previous court cases.

KEY CONCEPTS

Sources of Law

International	Federal	State	Local
Compacts and treaties	U.S. Constitution U.S. Code (consists of U.S. statutes) Federal case law Federal administrative regulations	State constitutions State statutes State case law State administrative regulations	Local ordinances Local administrative regulations

Another major source of law in the United States is **case law**, which consists of decisions judges have made in court cases. Federal, state, and local judges cannot actually write or pass laws, but they interpret them in the course of formulating their court decisions. Other judges generally follow these interpretations in later cases.

Administrative agencies provide still another source of law in the United States. The hundreds of agencies at the federal, state, and local levels include the Department of Motor Vehicles, the Board of Education, and the Environmental Protection Agency. Many of these agencies can create rules that carry the force of law. These rules are usually called regulations. The body of law that concerns the content and use of these regulations is known as administrative law, and it is quite extensive.

A final source of law in the United States that few of us think about is international law. It consists of the rules that operate between nations, and between citizens of different nations. International law generally resides in treaties and compacts that countries enter into with each other; these are agreements between two or more nations. International law also includes regulations created by organizations such as the United Nations. In the United States, the Constitution grants Congress the power to make and sign international treaties. A Global View illustrates that it can be extremely difficult to enforce laws across international borders.

Civil and Criminal Laws

The system of laws in the United States is large, complicated, and diverse. We can understand it more easily when we separate American laws into broad categories. Two of the most important of these are civil law and criminal law. The term *civil law*, as used here, differs from the meaning of civil law in the legal tradition deriving from ancient Roman law.

civil law
(1) The system of laws, sometimes known as the Roman system, used in many countries that do not use the common law system; or (2) noncriminal law, or law that concerns disputes between individual parties.

plaintiff
The party who initiates the lawsuit in a civil case.

defendant
The person against whom criminal charges or a civil lawsuit are filed.

▶ **U.S. Constitution**

The Constitution is the supreme law of the United States; it establishes the powers of the federal government and limits those powers .

A Global View

Intellectual Property Piracy in the Twenty-First Century

The piracy of copyrighted works is a serious problem in the twenty-first century. Creative works such as books, music, movies, software, and video games are protected internationally under copyright laws. These laws are meant to ensure that for a specified period of years nobody profits from protected works without their creators' permission. When someone downloads a copyrighted song or makes a copy of a copyrighted DVD, that person has deprived the creative artist of income and has broken the law. These actions are now commonly known as piracy.

Piracy is big business, and it affects many forms of mass media. In 2005, the Motion Picture Association of America estimated that film producers lost $18.2 billion in revenue to pirated copies of films. According to the International Federation of Phonographic Industries, one of every three CDs sold worldwide in 2005 was an illegal copy. When the book *Harry Potter and the Deathly Hallows* was published in 2007, it was almost immediately accompanied by illegally posted scans of the novel and unauthorized translations into other languages. In China, unauthorized Chinese translations of the *Potter* book were sold for the equivalent of about $2.50—about 10 percent of the novel's retail value if purchased through legitimate booksellers. A 2008 study concluded that, if software piracy in the United States were reduced by only 10 percent, more than 30,000 new jobs would be created and $7 billion in additional tax revenues would be collected. Although much piracy is committed by individuals who make illegal copies for their personal use, organized crime rings also are active participants in piracy and profit from it.

Content producers make numerous attempts to reduce piracy, many aimed at college students. They file lawsuits against individuals, lobby for stricter copyright protection laws, and encourage law enforcement agencies to vigorously pursue pirates. Producers also employ high-tech methods of piracy prevention, such as embedding invisible codes in movies that enable them to trace illegal copies to their source.

Despite these ongoing efforts, billions of dollars worth of works are pirated each year. Some countries—including China, Paraguay, Pakistan, and Russia—are notoriously lax in policing copyright violations. Although there are international treaties prohibiting piracy, not all countries have signed these treaties, and those that have don't always enforce them well. Some have promised to do better; in 2007, for example, Russian authorities promised stricter adherence to copyright protections. Even in countries such as the United States where there is strong enforcement, piracy flourishes because it is difficult to prevent illegal copying. Many individuals who download unauthorized music or make illegal photocopies do not view their own activities as immoral or criminal. As one Lehigh University student put it, "I was just downloading some Bruce Springsteen. What's the big deal?"

Observe Investigate Understand

- **Evaluate this statement: It is wrong to prosecute people for downloading pirated materials.**
- **What measures can be taken to reduce the piracy of music, books, and movies?**
- **Why do you think China and Russia are among the leading offenders in permitting piracy?**

SOURCES: Business Software Alliance, "The Economic Benefits of Lowering PC Software Piracy," January 2008, www.bsa.org/sitecore/shell/Controls/Rich percent20Text percent20Editor/~/media/Files/idc_studies/bsa_idc_us_final percent20pdf.ashx (retrieved January 22, 2008); John Healey and Chuck Philips, "Piracy Spins a Global Web," *Los Angeles Times*, October 9, 2005, www.latimes.com/business/la-fi-piracy9oct09m1m641553.story (retrieved October 24, 2005); Motion Picture Association of America, "Who Piracy Hurts," www.mpaa.org/piracy_WhoPiracyHurts.asp (retrieved January 16, 2008); BBC News, "Pirate Chinese Potter Book Sold," August 1, 2005, news.bbc.co.uk/2/hi/entertainment/4734161.stm (retrieved October 17, 2005); Kristen Blake, "Download Crackdown: File-Sharing Problems May Cause Computer, Legal Headaches for Students," *The Brown and White*, September 26, 2004, www.bw.lehigh.edu/story.asp?ID=17818 (retrieved October 17, 2005); James Niccolae, "Russia Pledges Piracy Clampdown," *PC World*, March 15, 2007, www.pcworld.com/article/129860-1/article.html?tk=nl_dnxnws (retrieved February 22, 2009).

Civil law governs relationships between individuals. In civil law, a party who is injured financially or physically by another person or organization can bring a lawsuit against that entity. Civil proceedings focus on the injuries of the victim. The party who initiates the lawsuit is the **plaintiff**, and the other party is the **defendant**. For example, if a person is trimming a tree on her own property and a branch falls onto her neighbor's car, damaging it, the owner of the car could bring a civil lawsuit against the person trimming the tree. Lawsuits of this kind are called **torts**. If a pedestrian is struck by a car and wins a lawsuit against the driver, the latter may have to pay for the pedestrian's medical bills, lost wages, pain and suffering, and any other losses experienced as a result of the accident. These payments are known as **damages**. Other kinds of civil law include contract law (disputes

torts
Civil disputes in which one party sues another for the damages the defendant's actions have caused.

damages
Payments a defendant must make to a winning plaintiff in a civil lawsuit to compensate the plaintiff for the injuries or costs the defendant's actions have caused.

arising from legal agreements between parties) and property law (disputes related to land ownership and use).

criminal law
A body of laws in which people are punished by the government for specific prohibited actions.

Criminal law is distinguished from civil law in a number of important ways:

- Criminal law operates under the assumption that *society*—rather than an individual—has been injured by the defendant's actions.
- Only the government may bring criminal cases. Although many people believe that the victim must press charges, the prosecutor alone decides whether to pursue criminal cases. Furthermore, prosecutors are not bound by the wishes of the victim. Prosecutors will pursue a criminal case based on the merits of the case, regardless of what the victim may want. In civil proceedings, however, the victim, not the government, brings the case to court.
- Defendants who lose criminal cases may pay fines to the government, but they also may be incarcerated in a jail or prison and, in some jurisdictions, even be put to death. Civil defendants who lose are not incarcerated or executed; instead, they pay damages to the victim.
- Criminal defendants are found *guilty*; civil defendants are found *liable.*
- A criminal conviction tends to bring greater moral condemnation from society than does losing a civil lawsuit.
- Criminal defendants are entitled to a number of legal protections, such as access to a government-paid attorney if they are too poor to afford one, the presumption of innocence, and a speedy trial. Civil defendants do not automatically have such government protections.
- In the U.S. criminal justice system, the state, not the victim, charges the defendant. Therefore, victims have little or no influence on how a criminal case proceeds. Victims have more control in the civil justice system because they, not the government, make the decision to begin the court process. They also hire their own attorneys, and they have the right to be present during the entire proceeding.
- The standard of proof in criminal cases is high: guilt must be proven beyond a reasonable doubt. In civil cases, the party that proves its case by a preponderance of the evidence (a lower legal threshold) can win. (Standards of proof are discussed in more detail in Chapter 9.)

The differences between criminal and civil law are summarized in the Key Concepts feature.

MYTH/REALITY

MYTH: Double jeopardy occurs when someone is sued in civil court and tried in criminal court for the same act.

REALITY: According to the U.S. Constitution, double jeopardy protection does not apply to civil cases.

double jeopardy
The Fifth Amendment right that protects anyone from being tried twice for the same offense.

The Fifth Amendment's protection against **double jeopardy** prohibits a defendant from being tried twice for the same crime. However, many acts can result in both civil and criminal cases and double jeopardy protection does not prohibit the victim from filing a civil lawsuit. In 1995, former football star O. J. Simpson was tried in a criminal case by the State of California for the murders of his ex-wife Nicole Brown Simpson and her friend Ronald Goldman. Simpson was tried but acquitted (found not guilty) of the criminal charges. After the acquittal, the victims' families brought a civil lawsuit against Simpson for "wrongful death." In the civil case, the jury found Simpson responsible for the deaths, and he was ordered to pay the families $33.5 million. Contrary to what many people believe, the civil trial did not violate Simpson's constitutional protection against double jeopardy because that protection only prohibits trying someone more than once on *criminal* charges for the same offense. If a man is criminally

KEY CONCEPTS

Criminal versus Civil Law

	Criminal Law	Civil Law
Harm	To society	To individual
Case brought by	Government	Injured party
Sanctions	Fines, incarceration, death	Damages
Terminology	Guilty	Liable
Brings moral condemnation	Usually yes	Usually no
Special legal protections	Yes	No
Control by victim	Very little	Very much
Standard of proof	Beyond a reasonable doubt	Preponderance of the evidence

convicted and then a civil lawsuit is brought, that conviction can be used against him in the civil trial.

Not only may a single act result in both criminal and civil trials, but those trials will bear many similarities. Both may take place in the same courtroom, although not at the same time and not in front of the same judge or jury. The outcomes also may share similarities. Defendants who lose civil cases may be required to pay punitive damages if their behaviors are held to be especially unconscionable or malicious. Similarly, criminal defendants may be required to pay their victims **restitution**, which is reparation for their losses.

Many people think victims use the civil justice system as a way to obtain huge monetary settlements. In fact, many victims do not go through the civil justice system at all because they cannot afford to hire an attorney. Others use the civil justice system in an attempt to bring about policy changes that can occur when civil juries grant large monetary settlements. Sometimes a multimillion-dollar judgment is granted, but others are for undisclosed amounts, and still others are for a few hundred or a thousand dollars. What about the Victim? on the next page describes a case that led to victim-initiated policy changes.

restitution
In a criminal case, money a defendant must pay a victim to compensate the victim for damages.

Criminal Laws: Misdemeanors, Felonies, and Infractions

A useful way to categorize criminal laws is according to the seriousness of the offense. In the United States, most crimes are felonies, misdemeanors, or infractions. This classification scheme dates back more than a thousand years, to the Norman Conquest of England in 1066. Prior to the Conquest, early medieval English kings punished only a small number of crimes. Usually victims were expected to deal with wrongdoers themselves, either by taking compensation or (more commonly) through private vengeance. However, those who committed serious acts such as murder could be executed by the king's representatives, and their property could be seized by the crown. These serious acts were called **felonies**.

Following the Norman Conquest, and especially after Henry II established his system of royal courts in the late twelfth century, the number of acts defined as felonies increased, and people faced execution or property forfeiture for a variety of acts, many of which we would not consider very serious today. But juries often were hesitant to find defendants guilty of relatively minor offenses if the judge's sentence would be death. Consequently, some less serious crimes came to be classified as **misdemeanors** and carried relatively mild punishments. The procedures for prosecuting misdemeanors were considerably less complex than those for felonies.[4]

felony
A serious criminal offense that brings a potential punishment of a year or more in state or federal prison.

misdemeanor
A criminal offense that is punished by fines or a maximum of a year in a county or city jail.

What about the Victim?

Civil Damages in Action: Creating the Jeanne Clery Act

Jeanne Clery was a 19-year-old freshman at Lehigh University, located in a quiet community outside Philadelphia. On the evening of April 5, 1986, another student entered Jeanne's dorm room and brutally raped and killed her. Access to the dormitory was easy because other students had propped open the outside doors.

Jeanne's parents were outraged, not only by the rape and murder of their daughter but also by the fact that the university had provided inadequate protection for its students. As the Clerys wrote on their Web site, Security On Campus:

> We learned that institutional response to such tragedies could involve callousness, cover-ups and stonewalling. Lehigh officials publicly passed off Jeanne's torture/murder as an "aberration." The college, in an ill-conceived attempt to protect its "image," produced a self-serving "report," written by one of its trustees, K.P. Pendleton, which concluded that there was no negligence on the part of the university and that "our present safety policies were complete;" this, despite the administration's knowledge of prior violent crimes on the campus and that there had been 181 reports of propped-open doors in Jeanne's dormitory in the four months prior to her death.

Jeanne's parents also discovered that students had not been informed about 38 violent crimes at Lehigh University in the three years prior to her murder.

As a result, the Clerys filed a civil lawsuit against the university for negligent failure of security and for failure to warn of foreseeable dangers on campus. They received an undisclosed financial settlement. They used the money to create Security On Campus, Inc., a grassroots, nonprofit organization devoted to creating safe campuses for college and university students. The organization also lobbies for state and federal laws for campus security.

In the late 1980s, Pennsylvania enacted a law requiring all postsecondary education institutions receiving federal aid to collect crime statistics. Institutions must publish and disseminate these statistics in a campus security report that is updated each year by October 1. These statistics must cover all campus and non-campus properties, including those controlled by student organizations and recognized by the institution (such as officially sanctioned Greek housing), and all public areas in close geographic proximity to university property that are accessed by students for school-related activities. Each year, all students, faculty, staff, and administrators must be informed that the statistics are available, and the institution must inform the campus community whenever a crime is committed and the alleged offender remains at large, posing a continued threat to those on campus.

The Pennsylvania law and comparable legislation in nine other states gave the Clerys the momentum they needed to persuade Congress to enact the Crime Awareness and Campus Security Act of 1990. The law later was amended twice, and in 1998 it was renamed the Jeanne Clery Act. Collectively, these amendments provide for campus victims' rights, expanded reporting requirements, and the disclosure of results from disciplinary hearings to victims. The Clery Act is just one example of the ways in which victims use the civil justice system, not for personal monetary gain but to bring about policy changes in an attempt to prevent future victimizations.

OBSERVE Investigate Understand

- **In what ways did the Clery Act pave the way for victim awareness?**
- **Has your college taken appropriate steps to ensure your on-campus safety, and, if so, do you think it did so in response to the concerns the Clery Act highlighted?**
- **Could the objectives of the Clery Act have been achieved without the Clery family resorting to a civil suit?**

SOURCE: Security on Campus, www.securityoncampus.org/index.php?option=com_content&view=article&id=52:jeanne-clearys-victim-blog&catid=34:victim-blog-category&Itemid=54 (retrieved July 3, 2009).

Today, the most serious crimes are still classified as felonies; less serious offenses constitute misdemeanors and infractions. Jurisdictions differ in how they classify specific offenses, although very serious crimes such as murder and rape are always felonies. But in Florida, for example, stealing something worth $350 is grand theft, a felony, whereas in California it is petty theft, a misdemeanor. **Infractions** include minor traffic offenses such as speeding, as well as violations of local laws, such as failure to properly license a dog.

infraction
A minor violation of a local ordinance or state law that brings a potential punishment of fines.

People convicted of felonies can be punished by incarceration in state or federal prisons, usually for terms of more than one year. *Capital felonies* are those that in some states

a Case in Point

Jailed for a Seat Belt Violation

In March 1997, Gail Atwater was driving her two young children home from soccer practice in Lago Vista, Texas. One of the children lost a toy, so she allowed them to unlock their seat belts to search for it. She was driving her pickup on a rural dirt road at approximately 15 mph.

But Lago Vista police officer Bart Turek saw Atwater and pulled her over. He had caught her once before because he thought, incorrectly, that her son was not wearing his seat belt. This time, Turek immediately started yelling at Atwater, telling her, "You're going to jail!" Atwater could not produce her driver's license because her purse had recently been stolen.

As the children looked on, frightened and crying, Turek handcuffed Atwater. He refused to let her take her children to a neighbor's house and threatened to take them into custody as well. However, the neighbor noticed what was going on and took the children to her house, whereupon Turek drove Atwater to the police station. There she was forced to remove her jewelry, shoes, and glasses, and to empty her pockets. Her mug shot was taken and she was locked in a jail cell. An hour later, she was released on $310 bond. In the meantime, her truck had been towed.

Atwater eventually pleaded no contest to seat belt offenses and was fined $50. She then sued the City of Lago Vista, claiming her constitutional rights were violated when she was locked in jail for an offense that brought, at most, a small monetary fine. Her case eventually reached the U.S. Supreme Court in 2001.

In a 5–4 decision, the Court held that police may arrest suspects and take them into custody without warrants, even for minor offenses, and even when those offenses can be punished only by fines. The majority opinion found no constitutional impediment to such arrests. The dissenting Justices pointed out that the decision in this case would permit the police to search a minor offender's car and belongings, conduct a body search of the suspect, and lock the suspect up for as long as 48 hours, even in the same cell with violent criminals.

You can read the Supreme Court opinion in this case at http://straylight.law.cornell.edu/supct/html/99-1408.ZS.html.

OBSERVE Investigate Understand

- **What are the pros and cons of strictly enforcing even the most minor of laws?**
- **Why do you think the police officer was so quick to arrest Ms. Atwater?**
- **Do you think the U.S. Supreme Court decided the Atwater case correctly? Why?**

SOURCE: *Atwater v. Lago Vista*, 532 U.S. 318 (2001).

might result in a death sentence. In contrast, people who commit misdemeanors usually face sentences of fines, probation, or incarceration in local jails, usually for less than one year. In states that have "three-strikes" laws (which punish repeat offenders with harsher penalties), felonies may count as "strikes" but misdemeanors usually do not. There are also procedural differences between the two categories of crimes. Felony defendants in some places may be entitled to a grand jury (see Chapter 8), but misdemeanor defendants are not. In some states, misdemeanor cases are heard by different courts than those that try felonies.

In many states, certain crimes are known as *wobblers*, which may be charged either as misdemeanors or as felonies, usually at the discretion of the judge or prosecutor. For example, in Florida certain kinds of vandalism are wobblers.

MYTH/REALITY

MYTH: Speeding tickets and other infractions are not criminal offenses.

REALITY: All infractions, even minor ones, are criminal.

▲ **John George Haigh**

John George Haigh was a notorious English serial killer during the 1940s. *How should the U.S. criminal justice system deal with serial killers?*

Depending on the jurisdiction, some minor offenses are categorized as violations or infractions. For example, common traffic offenses such as illegal parking and speeding are only punished with fines. Although those found guilty of violations or infractions do not incur a criminal record, the U.S. Supreme Court has held that people may be placed under arrest and taken into custody even for such relatively minor matters as speeding or seat belt violations (see A Case in Point, page 107).

LEGAL ELEMENTS OF A CRIME

Whether a crime is a felony, a misdemeanor, or an infraction, before an individual can be convicted, the state must prove a crime has actually occurred. Although this may seem obvious, the legal requirements for identifying a criminal action are quite precise. These requirements are known as the corpus delicti of a crime.

Corpus Delicti—Proof That a Crime Has Been Committed

The **corpus delicti** of a crime (literally "the body of the offense") refers to the particular elements required in order for prosecutors to establish that a crime was indeed committed.[5] To meet the corpus delicti requirement, the prosecutor must show that a defendant's criminal action (*actus reus*) was the product of his **criminal intent** (*mens rea*) and that this intended action (or failure to act) resulted in some manner of harm or injury to the victim. Collectively, these three elements—action, intent, and harm—constitute the essence of a crime. Each crime requires a specific actus reus and a specific mens rea. All three are generally required to convict a criminal defendant. In some cases, however, a defendant can be found guilty of a crime even though one or more of the key elements is absent. The Latin terms *corpus delicti, actus reus,* and *mens rea* come from ancient and medieval law.

The term corpus delicti is often mistakenly taken to mean the corpse of a victim. But in a homicide case the body of the murdered victim is only one of the elements constituting the corpus delicti. In some cases, if circumstantial evidence is compelling enough, the actual body of an alleged murder victim need not be found for the killer to be convicted. British serial murderer John George Haigh used acid to decompose the bodies of people he killed for financial gain, under the mistaken belief that without a corpse murder could not be proven because there was no corpus delicti. "No bodies. No crime. No punishment."[6] Haigh made the common error of misunderstanding the word *corpus.* That was his undoing. The evidence against him, albeit circumstantial, was substantial. Haigh was found guilty of nine murders and executed in 1949.[7]

corpus delicti
"The body of the crime"; the specific elements that must be proved to convict someone of a specific offense.

criminal intent
The degree to which a defendant must have intended his or her actions or the consequences of those actions.

actus reus
The specific act required to convict a person for a specific crime.

Actus Reus—The Criminal Act

Each kind of crime has a specific **actus reus**, literally the "evil" or "guilty act." For example, the actus reus for the crime of perjury in Florida is making a false statement under oath during a public proceeding (such as a trial).[8]

To be found guilty of murder, you must cause another person's death. Usually this means that you, the defendant, must have used the murder weapon yourself. There are, however, exceptions to this requirement. If a person hires or compels somebody else to do the actual killing, he can still be found guilty of murder by having caused the crime. This would obviously be the case if a person were to hire a hit man to kill his spouse. (Of course, the hit man would also be guilty of murder.) The murder conviction of cult leader Charles Manson is another example of how a person can be found guilty of a crime without meeting the usual requirement of actus reus.[9] In 1971, Manson was convicted of the murders of seven people in 1969, even though he was not present during the killings. In fact, it was a small group of his followers who actually committed the murders. Manson and four members of his "family" were all sentenced to death, though these were reduced to life sentences when the U.S. Supreme Court temporarily abolished capital punishment in 1972. They are still imprisoned.

Mens Rea—The Defendant's Mental State

> *Actus non facit reum nisi mens sit rea.*
> (An act does not make a man guilty unless his mind be also guilty.)
>
> —Sir Edward Coke (1644)[10]

To say that a person *committed* a criminal act is not the same as saying that he is *criminally responsible* (or *criminally liable*) for the crime. What makes the difference is the perpetrator's **mens rea**, or state of mind at the time of the crime.

mens rea
The level of criminal intent, or the mental state, required to convict a person of a specific crime.

Different crimes represent different levels of mens rea, or criminal intent. To be convicted of first-degree murder, the offender usually must commit the crime with "premeditation and malice aforethought;" that is, having planned and intended ahead of time to kill the victim. First-degree murder carries the heaviest penalty—usually long-term sentences, life imprisonment, or death. Other levels of mens rea required for different offenses include *purposefully* (intending the offense and its consequences), *knowingly* (being certain in the result of the actions, regardless of whether the offender wants them to happen), *recklessly* (knowing that there's a substantial risk of the consequences), and *negligently* (behaving differently from the way a reasonable person would have).

For a deed to be criminal, intent and act must concur. In other words, if you intend to do one kind of harm to someone (for example, rob him) and attempt to carry out that actus reus, but accidentally do unrelated, unplanned harm to that person (such as run over and kill him while driving to his house), then the concurrence of act and intent for murder has not been established.

Source Connection
PUNISHMENT OF PEOPLE WITH MENTAL DISABILITIES

www.law.cornell.edu/supct/html/00-8452.ZS.html

To learn more about how the courts interpret mens rea, read the U.S. Supreme Court decision *Atkins v. Virginia* (2002), a case involving the punishment of a person with a mental disability.

Some offenses do not require that the offender actually intended to commit the actus reus or cause the victim harm. Reckless or very careless behavior may be sufficient. For example, Michael Derderian owned a nightclub in Rhode Island. He knew that the cheap soundproofing material around the stage was highly flammable, and he also frequently allowed the nightclub to become crowded beyond capacity. On one such packed evening in 2003, he permitted the band Great White to use pyrotechnics during their performance. The pyrotechnics set the soundproofing material on fire, and many of the club's patrons were unable to escape. One hundred people died in the inferno. Derderian was convicted of involuntary manslaughter and sentenced to four years in prison.

The general idea behind the mens rea requirement is that people should usually not be held criminally liable if they didn't intend to commit certain acts or to cause certain consequences. Furthermore, the law often assumes that people should receive more severe criminal sanctions when they intended to harm others, as opposed to when the harm was careless or accidental.

In some instances, the perpetrator may not understand the consequences of his injurious act. For example, a child might know that an act is wrong but not truly comprehend how the crime affects others. A chilling example is the beating death of 4-year-old Derrick Robie in Savona, New York in 1993. The murderer in this case was another child, 13-year-old Eric Smith. Smith lured Robie into the woods and there beat him to death with a large rock. Although Smith was aware that his act was criminal, he did not fully comprehend how the murder would affect others. In a televised interview a year after the crime, when Smith was asked how the parents of the murdered child might feel about the killing, Smith replied, "I guess they're mad at me and stuff."[11] He still did not "get it." A jury convicted the juvenile of second-degree murder. He has been in prison ever since.

▲ **Derrick Robie**

Four-year-old Derrick was beaten to death by a 13-year-old. *Do you think a 13-year-old can understand how his crime will affect others?*

Whenever a defendant lacks the required mens rea or intent for a particular crime, he cannot be held criminally responsible for that crime. To establish mens rea, the judge or jury makes a judgment of the individual's capability of forming it. Assuming the person is capable of forming mens rea, the judge or jury must then establish whether the person actually did form the requisite mens rea prior to committing the actus reus. In most states, a defendant with an extraordinarily low IQ would not be considered able to form mens rea.[12]

It is often difficult to determine whether a person had the required mens rea. This is particularly true when the person is a child or has a mental disability. Criminal law attaches culpability to criminal intent, yet mens rea cannot be measured in any objective way.

EXAMPLES OF ELEMENTS OF CRIME

Offense	Actus Reus	Mens Rea
Silent or abusive calls to 911 service (Texas Pen. Code § 42.061)	A person makes a phone call to 911 when there is not an emergency and remains silent or makes abusive or harassing statements	Knowingly or intentionally
Kidnapping (Texas Pen. Code § 20.03)	A person abducts another person	Knowingly or intentionally
Criminally negligent homicide (Texas Pen. Code § 19.05)	A person causes the death of an individual	Criminal negligence

The same requirements of proving actus reus and mens rea apply when it comes to accomplices to a crime. The prosecution must establish beyond a reasonable doubt that someone who supplied a weapon, served as a lookout, drove a getaway car, or sheltered a fugitive did so with the conscious intent of aiding and abetting the crime. Sometimes this can be difficult to prove. Suppose, for example, that Mary sells a gun to John, who uses it to commit a holdup or a murder. If it can be proven that Mary had foreknowledge of the use to which John would put the weapon, or if she knowingly accepted from John some of the proceeds of the robbery or murder, then she is liable as an accomplice. She might also face criminal consequences if she supplied the weapon to John in reckless or negligent disregard of the consequences—for example, knowing that he was a violent lawbreaker.

strict liability offenses
Crimes that have no mens rea requirement; a person who commits the requisite actus reus may be convicted of the offense regardless of intent.

Some specific acts constitute crimes regardless of the presence or absence of criminal intent. These **strict liability offenses** are generally associated with less harsh punishments than if they were accompanied by mens rea. Statutory rape is one controversial example. By law, an adult who has sex with a minor is committing a crime, regardless of whether it was consensual or whether the adult had a good-faith belief that the minor was older. In most states, the age of consent is 16, but in some it is 17 or 18. If sexual relations occur, the law dictates that the adult be held criminally responsible. But because mens rea is not an element of the offense, the punishment is typically less severe than for the crime of forcible rape.

MYTH/REALITY

MYTH: The law excuses children from criminal responsibility.

REALITY: Even young children may be found criminally responsible for their criminal behaviors and can be tried as adults in some states.

Inchoate Offenses

inchoate crimes
Crimes that have been begun but not completed.

Sometimes a person has the mens rea to commit a crime, and even takes some steps to commit the actus reus, but for various reasons is unable to complete the offense. He may still face criminal liability, however. These incomplete acts are called **inchoate crimes.**

One common inchoate crime is attempt. For example, suppose a person decides to rob a liquor store. She obtains a gun, drives to the store, enters, points the gun at the clerk, and demands the money in the till. Before the clerk can respond, however, an off-duty police officer tackles the would-be robber to the ground, disarms her, and places her under arrest. Should she escape criminal liability merely because she was unable to complete the actus reus for robbery, which is taking another person's property through force or threats? That would seem unjust. Because she clearly intended to commit robbery and had taken substantial steps to commit it, she could be charged with attempted robbery. Attempt usually carries the same penalties as the completed offense.

Other inchoate crimes include conspiracy (an agreement with other people to commit a criminal act) and solicitation (persuading or inducing someone else to commit a crime). In general, the idea behind all inchoate offenses is that someone who tries to commit a crime, but who is unsuccessful, is as dangerous and as culpable as someone who succeeds.

CRIMINAL DEFENSES

The law views human beings as conscious, rational, and intentional agents of behavior. In the U.S. judicial system, criminal defendants have the opportunity to claim a variety of circumstances and conditions that may serve as defenses if they are accused of committing crimes. What all these defenses have in common is the argument that mens rea was lacking or diminished at the time of the crime.

Although the courts determine criminal responsibility, criminal defenses are set by statute and are heavily influenced by common law. We look next at the criminal defenses allowed in courts in the United States.

Real Careers

CHRISTOPHER GOWEN

Work location: Washington D.C.

College(s): Villanova University (2000); University of Miami School of Law (2005)

Major(s): Business Administration (B.S.); Juris Doctorate (J.D.)

Job title: Senior Staff Attorney, American Bar Association (ABA)

Salary range for job like this: $60,000–$80,000

Time in job: 1 year

Work Responsibilities

As the Senior Staff Attorney for the Criminal Justice Section of the American Bar Association (ABA), I am responsible for overseeing and developing new policy on pertinent criminal justice issues with our attorney members. Once our section has decided on a policy, it goes for a vote by the ABA House of Delegates. If the policy passes, the ABA will then take it to the United States Congress and lobby the legislators to make it law. I am currently developing policy that would not allow schools and employers to deny opportunities to applicants based on their contact with the criminal justice system as juveniles.

My section also follows criminal cases before the Supreme Court and reports on them to our members. When a criminal case is going to be heard by the Supreme Court that has a legal issue that the ABA has developed policy on, we will write an Amicus brief for the court in favor of the side our policy supports.

I also develop programs to train attorneys on different aspects of the law around the country in such areas as evidence, criminal procedure, and public corruption.

Last but not least, the ABA allows me to practice law on a pro bono basis. I can represent indigent children in criminal cases for free and the ABA will allow me to work on the cases during normal work hours.

Why Criminal Justice?

After Law School I worked for the Miami Dade Public Defenders Office where I learned how important the role of a public defender is to society—the only hope to protect people falsely accused by the police or whose rights have been violated by the government.

After my second year as a public defender, I worked in Iowa in a senior position for the Hillary Clinton for President Campaign. Following the campaign, I moved to Washington, D.C., married, and took a job with the ABA. If I could still afford to be a public defender I would return in a heartbeat. Unfortunately, Public Defender offices around the country are facing serious budget problems and can't afford to pay their attorneys reasonable salaries.

Expectations and Realities of the Job

I had expected things to move a little faster in Washington, D.C. The reality is it takes a very long time to get new law passed. But the pace at which a new Public Defender or Prosecutor works is incredible—you get thrown right into the fire and are representing clients on day one. In two years I tried over 40 cases as a Public Defender. Many trial lawyers do not try that many cases in a life time.

My Advice to Students

Get some real life experience (bill paying, working 9–5) before you go to graduate school, especially law school. In law school you learn about cases that shaped and developed law, each of which is based on facts that occurred in someone's life. The more you have experienced in life, the better you will understand the consequences of the law and the cases you are learning about.

DIS Connects

Rape and Intoxication Laws

Public outrage led to a change in Canadian law with regard to the mens rea requirement in a case that involved intoxication and rape. In 1989, Henri Daviault raped a 65-year-old woman who was partially paralyzed and wheelchair-bound. Although he did not deny raping her, he had no memory of it (apart from awakening naked in her bed). He was found not guilty because, as he argued, he was too drunk at the time to have known what he was doing. A pharmacologist called by the defense testified to what Daviault's likely alcohol level was. Under conditions of such extreme intoxication, an individual's consciousness may be so impaired that he has no awareness of his actions and no memory of them the next day. The trial judge found that although the defendant had committed the act, there was reasonable doubt as to whether he possessed the minimal intent required for culpability under the Canadian Charter of Rights and Freedoms (the national constitution).

When the prosecution appealed the case, the Quebec Court of Appeal found Daviault guilty and sentenced him to a year in jail. Daviault then took his case to the Supreme Court of Canada. In September 1994, the Supreme Court acquitted him of the rape he never denied committing, holding it is possible for a person to become so intoxicated that he lacks the necessary mental capacity to form the intent to commit sexual assault.

Outrage from defenders of women's rights forced legislators to propose a bill limiting the use of drunkenness as a defense in rape cases. Parliament responded in 1995 by barring the use of extreme (self-induced) intoxication as a defense for violent crimes, including sexual assault.

The laws in the United States focus not so much on the offender's level of intoxication as a defense but on the victim's level of intoxication as to whether she was able to consent. If the victim is unable to consent, then a rape occurred. In a 2008 Massachusetts case, *Massachusetts v. Blanche*, the court ruled that in a rape trial the jury must be instructed about the victim's capacity to consent to sexual intercourse. Specifically, if the state proves beyond a reasonable doubt that there is evidence to support that the victim was so impaired due to alcohol or drugs or was incapacitated (for example, sleeping, unconscious, developmentally disabled, or helpless), then the victim was incapable of giving consent. Once the state meets the burden of proof that the victim was unable to give consent, the prosecution need only prove the amount of force used during intercourse. The court also ruled that the defendant knew or should have known that the victim was incapable of consenting for the above mentioned reasons and, therefore, it is rape.

Observe Investigate Understand

- **How do rape and intoxication laws differ in the United States and Canada?**
- **Should intoxication, no matter what its degree, be abolished as a criminal defense?**
- **If a person is so completely addicted to drugs or alcohol that he or she cannot control becoming intoxicated, should that fact be considered a criminal defense?**

SOURCES: *Regina v. Daviault* [1994] 3 SCR 63; *Commonwealth of Massachusetts v. Blanche* 450 Mass. 583 (Feb. 8, 2008) http://masscases.com/cases/sjc/450/450mass583.html (retrieved February 26, 2009).

Source Connection

INTOXICATION AS A DEFENSE

http://masscases.com/cases/sjc/450/450mass583.html

Read more about using intoxication as a defense and the court ruling in this rape trial case in Massachusetts.

Mistake

We are generally presumed to know the law, but its enormity and its changing nature make it impossible for everyone to know all the laws all the time. Nonetheless, ignorance of the law is not an acceptable defense. If it were, it is easy to imagine how flooded the courts would be with defendants claiming "I didn't know there was a law against that!" The defense of mistake argues that a mistake related to a *fact of the crime* may have affected the state of mind of the defendant in such a way as to cause her to commit the crime, but without mens rea.

Generally, people can use mistake as a defense if they were mistaken about a fact, but not if they were mistaken about a law. For example, imagine a woman whose husband disappears overboard while they are on a cruise ship together. Ten years later, believing him to be dead, she remarries. If her first husband then suddenly reappears, alive and well, is the woman guilty of bigamy? Most likely not, as she reasonably (although mistakenly) believed her husband was dead.

But now imagine a woman who is married, who knows her husband is alive, but who (mistakenly, she says) believes her state permits people to have multiple spouses. If she marries a second time before divorcing her first husband, she will be guilty of bigamy because she is mistaken about the law. Cases involving mistake of fact or law are uncommon.

Intoxication

In most cases, people who become intoxicated by alcohol or other drugs cannot use intoxication as a defense. However, if a person becomes so intoxicated that he cannot form the mens rea required for a particular crime, he may have a successful intoxication defense. For example, if a man was so impaired that he did not realize what he was doing when he killed his friend, he would probably not be convicted of first-degree murder, which requires that the crime be premeditated. He would probably be convicted of a lesser offense, such as involuntary manslaughter.

In the United States, states vary as to whether they will accept intoxication as a defense at all, and if so, when. Montana, for example, never allows voluntarily intoxicated people to use the defense, whereas New York accepts voluntary intoxication as a defense in cases not involving extremely reckless behavior.[13]

However, the intoxication defense can be used when someone becomes intoxicated involuntarily. For example, if someone slipped a drug into a woman's soft drink without her being aware of it and she committed a crime while under the drug's influence, she would be able to claim intoxication as a defense.

The Justification Defenses

Duress: Being Coerced into Committing a Crime

Situations may occur in which a person is literally forced into committing a crime because failure to commit it would result in more serious harm. As long as the crime is not murder (owing to the principle that one person's life is no more valuable than another's), the defendant may make the claim of **duress**.

duress
A defense in which the defendant claims he or she was forced or coerced into committing a crime.

Consider this example: A man forces his way into a home and holds a handgun to the wife's head. Because he is convinced that mind-controlling waves are emanating from the neighbor's television set, he directs the husband to break into the neighbor's house and destroy the set. The husband is given 10 minutes to complete the deed and return with the remote control for the television, or his wife will be killed. Even though the husband realizes the man has a serious mental illness, he does as he is told and returns (with the remote control) to report the television destroyed. Although the husband indeed committed more than one crime (burglary, destruction of property, and theft), it would be clear to any reasonable person that to not have done so could have resulted in a much more serious outcome: the killing of his wife by this deranged man. Should the husband ultimately be charged with the crimes? Under the circumstances, a plea of duress may be appropriate.

A defense of duress would not be accepted, however, if the husband was directed to murder his neighbor's wife instead of destroying the television. The law would not recognize that the life of his own wife was more valuable than that of his neighbor's wife.

Necessity: When Circumstances Require an Illegal Act

Sometimes under extreme circumstances a person cannot avoid taking criminal action to resolve a situation. A case such as this might use the defense of **necessity**. Such was thought to be the case when, in 1884, a ship capsized off the coast of Africa. For a week, four crewmembers survived in a lifeboat by sharing two cans of turnips and the carcass of a sea turtle. During the second week, the youngest member of the crew, Richard Parker, was approaching death from starvation. At one point the ship's captain, Dudley, and first mate Stephens decided that if help did not arrive by the following morning, they would kill Parker and consume his remains. (The other crewmember refused to participate in the plan.) The help did not come. The two stabbed Parker and ate from his remains over the next four days, until a German ship rescued them. On their return to England, Dudley and Stephens were put on trial for Parker's death.

necessity
A defense in which the defendant must demonstrate that he or she had to commit the crime to avoid more severe consequences.

Courtroom debate examined questions of how to measure and compare the value of lives. "Is it to be strength, or intellect, or what? . . . In this case the weakest, the youngest,

▲ A person may claim that he acted in self-defense if he can show that use of force was absolutely necessary to protect himself or his property.

the most unresisting was chosen. Was it more necessary to kill him than one of the grown men? The answer must be, "No." A panel of five judges found Dudley and Stephens guilty of murder and sentenced them to die. However, public outrage about the trial's outcome prompted Queen Victoria to commute the death sentences to six months in prison.[14]

Subsequent cases have, however, etched out exceptions whereby killing is deemed a necessity. If, for example, the death of the victim was imminent and the continuation of the victim's life threatens the life of others, the defendant can make a case for necessity. This is the kind of determination made in cases where the life of one conjoined twin is taken in order to save the other. Necessity would also have applied as a defense on September 11, 2001, if military jets had managed to shoot down any of the hijacked planes, together with the kidnapped passengers, before the terrorists' mission was accomplished.

In general, to successfully use the necessity defense, the defendant must demonstrate that he had to commit the crime in order to avoid more severe consequences. For this reason, it is sometimes called the "lesser of two evils" defense. In the nineteenth century, many states prohibited people from doing business on Sundays. Courts permitted the necessity defense in the cases of shipping companies, which had set sail on Sundays to avoid storms, and in the case of telegraph companies, which transmitted telegrams concerning emergencies.[15]

In 1976, four inmates of a jail in Washington, D.C. escaped by removing a bar from a window and sliding down a knotted bed sheet. When they were eventually caught and charged with escape, they claimed that there were frequent fires in the jail, the guards had beaten them, and one of them wasn't receiving adequate care for his medical conditions. They said they had to leave the jail to protect their health and lives.[16] A majority of the U.S. Supreme Court eventually upheld their convictions.

Self-Defense: Protecting Yourself or Your Property

When someone is threatened by another, the threatened person may be compelled to defend herself with the use of force. A person may claim that she acted in self-defense if she can show that the use of force was absolutely necessary to protect herself or her property.

Three requirements must be satisfied to justify the use of the self-defense claim. The first is that the action against the perceived threat must be necessary; no other less harmful means of dealing with the threat can be reasonably available. For example, in considering available "fight or flight" options, flight must not be possible. Most states used to require a person who was attacked to flee, rather than fight back, if flight was possible. Recently, however, several states have passed "Stand Your Ground" laws that eliminated this requirement.

The second requirement for an act of self-defense is that it be proportionate to the threat. To defend against the threat, force used by the defendant cannot be significantly greater than the unlawful force threatened or used against her. Running onto the street in pursuit of someone who has just burglarized your house and then shooting him does not constitute self-defense. The fact that the perpetrator was fleeing removed the imminence of any threat he may have posed inside the house.

The third requirement is that the threat against which you are defending yourself must be imminent, or immediate. This requirement has prompted much debate. Consider the wife who for years has been battered by her abusive husband and finds the level of his violence increasing. He may, for example, threaten her with a knife—something he has never done before. Is it self-defense when she kills him later that night as he sleeps? Traditionally, the answer was no, and the wife would be convicted of murder. In recent years, however, some courts have retreated from the imminence requirement in some cases (see the Race, Class, Gender box).

entrapment
Law enforcement officers or agents trap or trick a person into committing a crime that the person would not otherwise have committed.

Entrapment: Being Deceived into Committing a Crime

When law enforcement officers or agents trap or trick a person into committing a crime that she would not otherwise have committed, **entrapment** occurs. The standards for entrapment vary, but generally the defense exists when the defendant had no predisposition

Race, Class, Gender

Battered Person Syndrome and Self-Defense

Frances Headley and Brian Evans were cohabitating partners living together in Parkersburg, West Virginia, and sharing a history of intimate partner violence. Court, police, and hospital records documented four instances of violence in the months before Evans was stabbed and later died. On April 5, 1998, the Parkersburg police found Headley bruised from punches to her face, but she declined to press charges. Within two weeks, Headley shoved Evans and pled guilty to domestic battery. On May 26, 1998, Evans knocked Headley to the ground, kicking her repeatedly, and within a month he hit Headley in a convenience store. On both occasions, Evans was charged with domestic battery. Finally on October 6, 1998, before those cases went to court, Evans wrestled Headley to the ground and broke her nose. She attempted to escape, but, finding herself unable to get out of the house, she went to the kitchen and grabbed a knife to defend herself. Evans came at her again, and she stabbed him. She tried to call the police, but Evans yanked the telephone cord out of the wall and, before falling to the ground, threw the phone at her.

When the case went to trial, the trial court ruled that Headley was not allowed to present her theory of self-defense. Headley was later sentenced to one year in county jail and a restitution fine of nearly $188,000. In *West Virginia v. Headley*, Headley appealed the case to the Circuit Court of Wood County, which supported her right to present the theory of self-defense to the jury. Based on the circuit court's ruling, Headley's conviction and sentence for involuntary manslaughter were vacated and the case was remanded for an entry of a judgment of acquittal.

Until recently, abused women who killed their abuser usually could not claim self-defense because killings rarely occurred while the batterer was actually attacking his victim. Typically they happened later, often when the batterer was asleep or unarmed. Because the battered victim faced no "imminent" threat, the prevailing legal view was that she did not have to resort to violence to save her own life.

By the early 1980s, however, some courts began to reconsider this view. Spurred by research on the psychological effects of being battered, some jurisdictions began to permit abused women to present expert testimony on intimate partner violence. Experts testified that people who suffer from repeated incidents of intimate partner violence become unable to leave the abusive situation. In fact, battered person syndrome (BPS) is recognized by psychologists as a mental disorder. Although an outsider might believe that a victim can simply leave the abuser, people with BPS may believe that leaving is impossible and that killing their abuser is necessary to save their own lives or the lives of their loved ones. Today, not all states permit testimony on BPS or permit abused victims to use it as a defense to murder, as the Frances Headley case shows.

Observe Investigate Understand

- **Considering the circumstances described here, do you think Frances Headley was justified in killing her partner?**
- **Should BPS be recognized as a mental disorder?**
- **What are the pros and cons of allowing testimony on BPS?**

SOURCES: *West Virginia v. Headley*, 210 W. Va. 524, 558 S.E.2d 324 (2001); Linda L. Ammons, "Why Do You Do the Things You Do? Clemency for Battered Incarcerated Women, A Decade's Review," *American University Journal of Gender, Social Policy, & the Law* 11 (2003): 533–565; Lenore E. Walker, *Terrifying Love: Why Battered Women Kill and How Society Responds* (New York: HarperCollins, 1990).

to commit the crime—that is, when it seems clear that she had no preexisting desire to commit the offense until the police persuaded her to do so.

When entrapment is alleged, the state has the burden of proving beyond a reasonable doubt that the defendant was not entrapped. Today, the entrapment defense is often viewed as an effort to deter police misconduct.

Entrapment cases typically concern individuals authorities already suspect are involved in criminal activity. For example, an undercover police officer may be sitting at a bar to see who will attempt to purchase alcohol as a minor. Once the officer sees someone walk up to the bar, order a drink, show a fake ID, and pay for the drink, he is able to offer to buy that person a drink without risking a claim of entrapment. It becomes entrapment if the police officer is in the same bar, sees someone who appears to be under 21 years old, offers to purchase that person an alcoholic beverage, and then, after the person has said yes and consumed the drink, arrests the person for underage drinking. In this case, there is no clear determination that the minor would have purchased or consumed alcohol if the police officer had not offered to purchase it.

Insanity

insanity
A defense in which the defendant admits committing the criminal act but claims not to be culpable due to mental illness.

Although the term's meaning has changed in everyday usage, the legal definition of **insanity** as a defense refers to an individual whose mind was disordered because of defective mental processes at the time of committing a crime. The legal definition of insanity is unrelated to the medical community's understanding of mental disorder. Although experts in psychiatry and psychology often contribute their opinions about a defendant's mental status and behavior, the judge or jury ultimately determines whether a defendant was insane at the time of a crime.

Like other criminal defenses, insanity implies diminished or no criminal responsibility based on a lack of mens rea. The underlying principle of the insanity defense has been well established in Anglo-American law for centuries. British courts developed the "wild beast" test in the eighteenth century, which held a defendant innocent if he was "so bereft of sanity" that he could not understand the consequences of his behavior, "no more than . . . an infant, a brute, or a wild beast."[17]

not guilty by reason of insanity (NGRI)
A verdict in which the jury determines that the defendant is not criminally culpable due to mental illness.

When a defendant is found **not guilty by reason of insanity (NGRI)**, he is acquitted of the criminal charges against him and discharged from the criminal justice system. Instead of being punished, he is generally viewed as needing psychiatric treatment. A well-established body of civil mental health laws for involuntary commitment dictates the terms of the defendant's incarceration in a psychiatric facility. As a patient there, he can be held against his will until such time as he is found to present no danger to himself or to others.

MYTH/REALITY

MYTH: Insanity is a common verdict in criminal courts in the United States.

REALITY: An insanity plea is put forward in less than 1 percent of all felony trials, and of those only 25 percent succeed with a not guilty by reason of insanity verdict. Thus, in 1,000 felony cases, only 10 defendants plead insanity and, of those, fewer than 3 succeed.[18]

Definitions of Insanity

The legal system has a long history of considering a person's impaired mental state as part of his defense. In contrast, a popular view outside the judicial system is that a plea of NGRI is little more than a legal dodge for getting away with murder. To facilitate the judicious application of the insanity defense, the courts have developed a system of definitions, guidelines, and practices that enables them to assess the mental state of a defendant. To

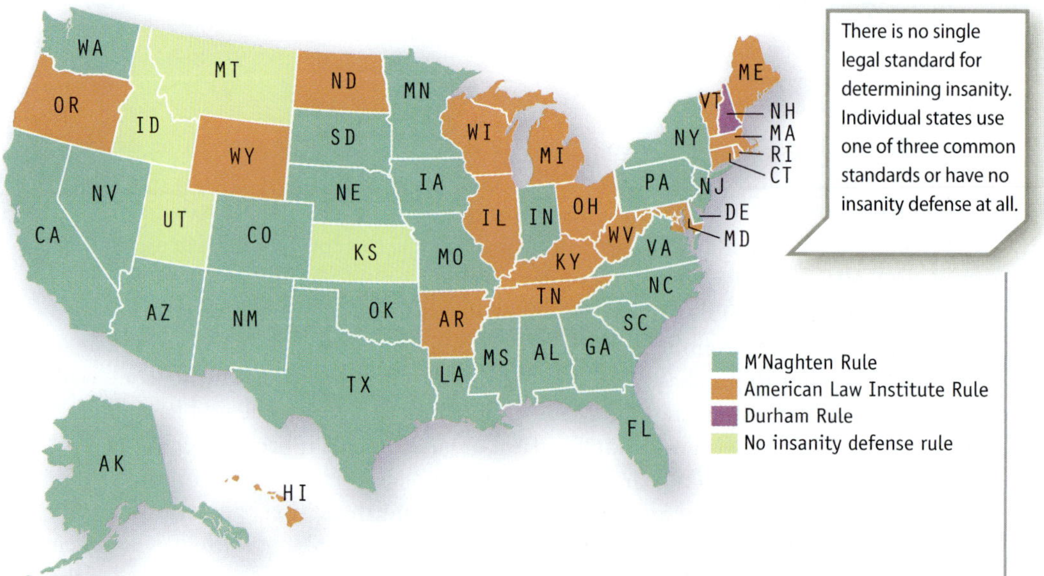

FIGURE 4-2 Insanity Defenses by State

evaluate insanity, courts seek to determine whether the defendant has some kind of mental disease or mental defect that was directly involved in commission of the crime.

There is no single legal standard for determining insanity. Three primary rules form the basis of an insanity defense in the United States: the M'Naghten Rule, the Durham Rule, and the American Law Institute Rule (see Figure 4-2). The legal standards that define insanity, and that therefore determine criminal responsibility, vary across courts in state and federal jurisdictions and in the military. None of these rules and standards makes reference to any specific mental disorder. Even though a defendant has a specific, serious mental disorder, it does not necessarily mean that the defendant will qualify for a verdict of insanity.

▲ **John Hinckley Jr.**

Hinckley (in back seat of car), who shot President Ronald Reagan in 1982, was found not guilty by reason of insanity; he is still confined to a psychiatric facility.

The M'Naghten Rule

By far the most commonly used standard for insanity is the **M'Naghten Rule,** or some variation of it. This test was established in 1843 in England, following the acquittal of Daniel M'Naghten for the assassination of the secretary of Sir Robert Peel, the prime minister. M'Naghten was delusional, believing the government was plotting to kill him, and he displayed symptoms consistent with what today we would call paranoid schizophrenia. In response to public outcry denouncing the court's acquittal "by reason of insanity," Queen Victoria convinced the House of Lords to establish standards for the insanity defense. As for M'Naghten, he was transferred to the psychiatric institution popularly known as Bedlam where he remained incarcerated as a psychiatric patient until his death 20 years later.[19]

M'Naghten Rule
A standard for insanity that asks whether the defendant was unable to understand the nature of his actions or to distinguish right from wrong.

The M'Naghten Rule is known as the "right or wrong" test. To be found insane, the defendant must have had, at the time of the crime, a "defect of reason, from disease of the mind" that rendered him unable to know what he was doing or, if he did know what he was doing, that it was wrong.[20] Some states have broadened their application of the M'Naghten Rule by including an **irresistible impulse test** to help ascertain whether the defendant's mental disorder rendered her incapable of controlling urges to behave in particular ways. Being *unable* to resist an impulse is, of course, different from merely *not* resisting an impulse. An irresistible impulse is not a matter of choice. The irresistible impulse test thus broadens M'Naghten from being solely a cognitive test of insanity to one that considers behavioral control.

irresistible impulse test
A standard for insanity that asks whether the defendant had a mental disease or defect, as a result of which the defendant was unable to control his or her behavior.

The Durham Rule

From the time he was 17, Monte Durham had been incarcerated in mental and penal institutions many times. As he exhibited signs of a serious mental disorder, the hospitalizations generally followed his arrests. In 1953, the 25-year-old Durham was convicted of housebreaking in Washington, D.C. His unsuccessful defense had been that he was of "unsound mind." On appeal to the District of Columbia Federal Court of Appeals in 1954, Durham's conviction was overturned. The court argued that the M'Naghten standard was outdated in view of the growing body of psychiatric knowledge about mental disorders and disease.

Under the **Durham Rule**, "an accused is not criminally responsible if his unlawful act was the product of mental disease or mental defect." The Durham Rule recognized mental illness as a disease that could be treated, if not cured.[21] But it quickly fell from favor due to its vagueness in defining mental disease. Many feared that the rule would be used to exonerate criminals who could cite their "mental diseases" of alcoholism, drug addiction, and compulsive gambling as the underlying cause of their criminal behavior. There also was discomfort with the amount of influence the Durham Rule gave psychiatrists and psychologists in the courtroom. Eventually the federal courts rejected the Durham Rule

Durham Rule
A standard for insanity that asks whether the defendant's conduct was the product of a mental disease or defect.

as too broad a standard. Nonetheless, today, one state (New Hampshire) continues to use it to determine insanity.

The American Law Institute Rule: The Substantial Capacity Test

American Law Institute Rule
A standard for insanity that asks whether the defendant lacked the substantial capacity to appreciate the criminality of the act or conform to the law.

In 1962, the American Law Institute (ALI) offered a new rule for measuring insanity in its Model Penal Code. The **American Law Institute Rule** required that the defendant have a mental disease or defect that causes him to lack "substantial capacity either to appreciate the criminality of his conduct or to conform his conduct to the requirements of the law."[22] Some scholars considered this test an improvement over the M'Naghten Rule because it permitted the defense for those who were severely affected by mental illness, and yet still able to understand what they were doing when they committed the crime to a limited extent. However, it was not nearly as broad a rule as Durham.

In 1992, serial murderer Jeffrey Dahmer was tried in Wisconsin using the ALI Rule as the standard for insanity. Although Dahmer stated, unhesitatingly, that he knew what he had done was wrong—killing 17 men, dismembering and sexually violating their corpses, and even cannibalizing some—the basis of his defense was that his mental disorders rendered him incapable of controlling his sexually deviant urges. His plea was "guilty but insane," essentially the same as a plea of not guilty by reason of insanity. Although Dahmer was found guilty and thus sane, his trial generated heated controversy about how a person could have done what he admitted doing to his victims and not have been insane at the time. Sentenced to life imprisonment and put into the general prison population, in 1994 Dahmer was beaten to death by another inmate.

Currently most states use the M'Naghten Rule or some variation of it; about half of these include an "irresistible test" as part of their standard. The ALI Rule or a variation of it defines insanity in the courts of 19 states, as well as in federal and military courts.

Four states no longer provide a court definition of insanity. This was a direct result of the acquittal of John Hinckley Jr. in 1982 for the attempted assassination of President Ronald Reagan. In the shooting, Reagan was seriously wounded and his press secretary received a head wound that resulted in permanent brain damage. Hinckley was found not guilty by reason of insanity, a verdict that outraged many and caused a series of reforms to insanity laws around the country. Yet even with a decision of not guilty by reason of insanity, Hinckley has been under federal supervision for a very long time and is still confined to a Washington, D.C. psychiatric facility. Because his mental illness has been found to be in remission, a federal court recently has allowed him limited supervised and unsupervised release time.[23]

In addition to the passage of the Insanity Defense Reform Act in 1984, which made it more difficult to prove insanity in federal cases, many individual states changed their rules to make it more difficult to do the same. Some states went so far as to abolish the insanity defense altogether. Currently, Utah, Montana, Idaho, and Kansas have no legal provision for an insanity defense. In these states, unlike those where the defense has the burden of

KEY CONCEPTS
Definitions of Insanity

Standard	Definition
M'Naghten	Unable to know the nature and quality of the act as being wrong, or unable to distinguish right from wrong
Irresistible impulse	Unable to control impulses
Durham	Behavior is a product of mental disease or defect
American Law Institute (ALI)	Unable to substantially appreciate criminality of act or conform to the law

proving insanity, the prosecution bears the burden of proving the defendant had mens rea at the time of the crime. Recently, the Nevada Supreme Court ruled that the state's abolition of the insanity defense is unconstitutional.

The movement toward eliminating the insanity defense or requiring adherence to stricter standards for measuring insanity marks a trend in the courts to hold individuals more fully accountable for their criminal actions. Still, a growing body of scientific evidence reveals that many mental disorders have a biological rather than a behavioral cause. It will be interesting to monitor the clash of these opposing points of view as the post-Hinckley debate over the insanity defense continues to develop.

guilty but mentally ill (GBMI) Verdict for a person recognized to be mentally ill but still considered criminally responsible for the crime.

consent A defense against criminal liability because the victim actually gave the defendant permission to engage in the prohibited acts.

infancy A defense that sometimes protects very young offenders from criminal liability because they do not understand the consequences of their actions.

Guilty but Mentally Ill

The **guilty but mentally ill (GBMI)** verdict, introduced in 1976, was intended as a compromise between acquitting a defendant who is mentally disordered as NGRI and finding him guilty. A person found GBMI is recognized to be mentally ill but is still considered criminally responsible for his crime. His mental illness grants him the right to psychiatric treatment during his incarceration. Should the mental disorder be effectively treated prior to the end of the term of his sentence, he will nonetheless be required to complete whatever time remains in a regular correctional institution.

In courts that provide the option of a GBMI verdict, the jury has the power to decide if a defendant is mentally ill but not insane, making him responsible for his crime. This alternative might appear to dispel concerns that a defendant "got away with" his crime, notwithstanding his mental illness. But how can a person be found guilty of a crime for which he lacks the requisite mens rea? The availability of a GBMI verdict has not reduced the number of insanity acquittals, nor has it resulted in longer periods of confinement of offenders who are determined to be mentally ill and dangerous.[24] Currently, 23 states have enacted laws providing for the GBMI verdict.

Although the insanity defense is hardly a recent invention, it continues to be a matter of frequent and lively debate. The trend in the 1950s and 1960s was to make the defense more widely available, but that trend sharply reversed in the 1980s and 1990s. It remains to be seen what will become of the defense in the twenty-first century.

Other Defenses

In addition to the defenses we've discussed, most jurisdictions recognize a variety of others. For example, under some circumstances a defendant may escape criminal liability if the victim actually gave the defendant permission to engage in the prohibited acts. This defense is called **consent**. For example, a boxer who hits his opponent during a match or a football player who tackles another will normally not be convicted of battery. However, if the scope of the attack exceeds what is considered acceptable within the rules of the game, a jury might conclude that the victim did not consent to the violence, and the attacking player might still be convicted. National Hockey League players Marty McSorley, Todd Bertuzzi, and Dino Ciccarelli all received criminal convictions for such attacks on opposing players.[25]

Another commonly recognized defense is that of **infancy** (the name dates back to medieval England). This defense sometimes protects very young offenders (those under the age of 7) from criminal consequences. Traditionally, those between 7 and 14 were presumed incapable of forming the mens rea necessary for criminal liability. This presumption could be overcome by evidence that a particular child knew what he was doing. The premise was that children should not be held responsible for acts when they cannot fully comprehend the nature or consequences of them. Chapter 14 discusses the infancy defense in more detail.

SUMMARY

The rule of law means that the state must exercise its power to coerce and punish within strict bounds. Laws must be written according to established procedures, and no government official is supposed to be above the law. These basic concepts have defined law-abiding societies for thousands of years, ever since ancient Babylonia. Roman law is the basis of the legal codes of contemporary continental Europe and many other countries, and medieval England's common law is the foundation of modern English and American law. Other sources of law in the United States are the federal and state constitutions, the body of case law (judges' decisions in prior cases), administrative regulations, and international treaties.

Most legal systems differentiate between civil and criminal law. In the United States, society (that is, the state) and not the individual is considered to be injured by criminal acts, and a government prosecutor alone decides whether to bring a criminal case. Criminal defendants can be found "guilty" or "not guilty" (rather than liable for civil damages); they are afforded certain rights not granted to civil litigants; they can be fined, imprisoned, or executed if found guilty; and the standards of proof are higher in criminal than in civil cases.

Depending on their seriousness, criminal law offenses in the United States are classified as felonies, misdemeanors, and infractions. To be convicted of any of these, the state must show that actus reus (guilty act) and mens rea (criminal intent) coincided. Different "degrees" of mens rea affect the severity with which an offense is punished. Some acts—so-called strict liability offenses—are defined as criminal regardless of intent (for example, having sex with a minor), and some acts that are intended but not completed (such as conspiracy to commit an illegal action) can also incur criminal consequences.

For those accused of breaking the criminal law, a number of valid defenses are available in the U.S. These are mistake (about the facts of the case, not about the law itself), severe intoxication, duress, necessity, self-defense, entrapment (by a law enforcement officer), and insanity. The common element in all these defenses is the absence of mens rea, or criminal intent.

OBSERVE
Investigate
Understand

Review

Explain the rule of law.

- Offenders can be punished only by written laws.
- The laws must be created through an established process.
- Nobody is supposed to be above the law.

Provide a short history of lawmaking.

- Early societies relied on unwritten social norms.
- One of the earliest known records of written laws dates from the rule of Babylonian King Hammurabi (reigned 1792–1750 BCE).
- England created the common law system after 1066.
- American colonists borrowed from the English system but made many changes and adaptations.

Identify modern sources of laws in the United States.

- Federal and state constitutions
- Federal and state statutes
- Local ordinances
- Federal and state case law
- Administrative regulations
- International treaties and compacts

Examine the key elements of civil and criminal law.

- Civil law deals with issues between individuals.
- An injured party can bring a civil lawsuit against another person or organization.
- In civil cases, the losing party pays damages directly to the injured parties.

- Civil defendants are found "liable."
- Victims have more rights in civil cases than in criminal cases.
- Criminal law focuses on injuries to society as a whole rather than to individuals.
- Criminal cases can only be brought by the government.
- A criminal defendant may be ordered to pay fines, may be incarcerated, or sometimes could even be put to death.
- Criminal defendants have more rights than civil defendants.
- The standard of proof is higher in criminal cases than in civil cases.

Define the three types of criminal offenses.

- Felonies can be punished by state or federal prison for more than a year and, sometimes, by death.
- Misdemeanors can be punished by probation, fines and/or up to a year in local jail.
- Infractions or violations can be punished only by fines or community service.

Describe the legal elements of a crime.

- The corpus delicti of a crime (literally "the body of the offense") refers to the particular elements required in order for prosecutors to establish that a crime was indeed committed.
- Actus reus is the guilty or illegal act of a crime; it is the first of the two key elements required for determining criminal liability.
- Mens rea is the criminal intent or mental state of the defendant at the time of a crime; it is the second of the two key elements required for determining criminal liability.

Explain common criminal defenses allowed by the court.

- The mistake defense argues that a mistake related to a fact of the crime may have affected the state of mind of the defendant who otherwise had no criminal intent.
- The intoxication defense argues that a person was so intoxicated that he could not control the mental state required for a particular crime.
- The duress defense argues that a person was forced to commit a crime because failure to do so would result in more serious harm.
- The necessity defense is used when under extreme circumstances a person cannot avoid committing a criminal act.
- Self-defense can be argued when a person is threatened by another and is compelled to protect herself or her property.
- The entrapment defense is used when a person is deceived by law enforcement officials into committing a crime that he would not otherwise have committed.
- The insanity defense refers to an individual whose behavior was affected by defective mental processes at the time of committing a crime.

Explore aspects of the insanity defense.

- Successful insanity defenses require defendants to have had a mental disease or defect that affected their behavior at the time of the crime.
- The M'Naghten Rule is a cognitive test that requires defendants to have known right from wrong when they committed their crimes.
- The Durham Rule defines insanity broadly as the product of a mental disease or defect that affected the defendant's behavior at the time of the crime.
- The American Law Institute (ALI) Rule requires that the defendant lacked substantial mental capacity for the wrongfulness of his behavior or could not stop himself because of the mental problem.

Key Terms

Study Questions

1. Hammurabi's Code was
   a. one of the earliest written systems of laws.
   b. a famous case involving shipwrecked sailors.
   c. a law intended to reduce copyright piracy.
   d. a standard for proving insanity.
2. Which of the following is *not* a source of law in the United States?
   a. Constitutions
   b. Presidential decree
   c. Statutes
   d. Case law
3. One important distinction between civil and criminal cases is that
   a. only criminal cases involve injuries to a victim.
   b. only criminal cases use juries.
   c. only in civil cases must the losing party pay money.
   d. only in criminal cases can the losing party be incarcerated.
4. A criminal offense that may result in incarceration in prison for more than a year is called a(n)
   a. felony.
   b. misdemeanor.
   c. infraction.
   d. offense.
5. The specific unlawful act that must be proven to convict someone of a crime is called the
   a. mens rea.
   b. actus reus.
   c. corpus delicti.
   d. final straw.
6. An inchoate offense is
   a. a crime that is punishable only by fines.
   b. a crime committed by a juvenile.
   c. an act illegal only under common law.
   d. a crime that was begun but not completed.
7. The main purpose of a criminal trial is to
   a. establish whether the defendant was insane.
   b. determine criminal responsibility.
   c. establish whether the defendant committed a crime.
   d. establish justice.
8. A person who would not otherwise have committed a crime, but who was persuaded to do so by a police officer, would best use which defense?
   a. Insanity
   b. Entrapment
   c. Necessity
   d. Mistake
9. About what percentage of felony criminal cases involve an insanity plea?
   a. 1 percent
   b. 25 percent
   c. 50 percent
   d. 75 percent
10. In legal terms, insanity is considered a serious mental disorder.
    a. True
    b. False

Critical Thinking Questions

1. What are the advantages and disadvantages of having a formal, written system of laws, as opposed to relying on unwritten social and cultural norms?
2. Under what circumstances should a person who commits an unlawful act be excused from criminal responsibility for that act?
3. How do you think a prosecutor should go about proving mens rea in a case?

Internet Sites

FindLaw
http://criminal.findlaw.com/
There are several places on the Internet where you can browse information about federal, state, and local laws. One of the most comprehensive of these sites is FindLaw. Among other things, at FindLaw you can read the definitions of many common crimes and find links to your state's laws concerning these crimes.

Legal Information Institute
www.law.cornell.edu/supct/
U.S. Supreme Court decisions since 1990 as well as historic decisions can be found here.

Suggested Readings

Randall G. Shelden, *Controlling the Dangerous Classes: A Critical Introduction to the History of Criminal Justice* (Boston: Allyn & Bacon, 2001).
This book provides a thought-provoking analysis of the evolution of the criminal justice system. Shelden argues that throughout history the primary goal of criminal justice has been to protect the people in power from those who were deemed to be "dangerous."

Henry J. Steadman, Margaret A. McGreevey, Joseph P. Morrissey, and Lisa A. Callahan, *Before and After Hinckley: Evaluating Insanity Defense Reform* (New York: Guilford Press, 1993).
This book provides a history of the insanity defense and discusses the chilling effects that John Hinckley Jr.'s verdict had on laws related to insanity.

Overview of Policing

CHAPTER 5

OBSERVE
Investigate
Understand

After reading this chapter, you should be able to:

- Identify the distinguishing characteristics of policing.
- Trace the evolution of policing in the United States.
- Describe the structure of law enforcement.
- Recognize how recruitment, selection, and training affect quality of service.
- Describe the dynamics of the police subculture.
- Contrast the positives and negatives in the use of police discretion.
- Distinguish between corruption and misuse of authority.
- Examine the extent and functions of private security agencies.

Realities and Challenges

From Celebration to Confrontation at Kent State

▲ May 14, 1970 Kent State incident.

On April 25, 2009, two to three thousand students at Kent State University in Ohio were celebrating College Fest, an annual spring ritual (though not an authorized university event) marking the end of the school year with drinking and general partying. When police arrested one young woman for underage drinking, the celebrating turned violent. Students began taunting the police and throwing rocks, bottles, and bricks at them. Ordered to disperse by the police, the students responded by setting fires, tossing couches, chairs, street signs, tree branches, and other debris on the flames, which reached 25 to 30 feet high.[1]

A total of 125 officers, including Kent City Police, the city's SWAT (special weapons and tactics) team, and officers from other area law enforcement agencies, responded to the incident. Officers, dressed in riot gear, used pepper balls (marble-sized pellets that release a nonlethal gas), stinger grenades, rubber balls, and tear gas to try to break up the crowd. The state highway patrol provided a helicopter to light the street.[2] According to Kent City Police Chief James Peach, at least 50 people (half of whom were students) were arrested, most on minor charges of failure to disperse. Several officers suffered minor injuries. One officer who had responded to the scene suffered a heart attack later that evening at his home and died.[3]

Chief Peach publicly stated that he thought the law enforcement response was appropriate and commendable, but others questioned the officers' actions. Ben Wolford, editor of the Kent State newspaper, commenting on the police response, noted, "I think if they just blocked off the street, let kids have that road to party on for that night, it would've just been a party and people would've gone home."[4] Use of force issues are particularly sensitive at Kent State given the incident of May 4, 1970, when members of the Ohio State National Guard shot into a crowd of unarmed students who were protesting. Four students were killed and nine others were wounded.[5]

As we note in this chapter, the use of force by the police raises many questions: Did the police need to use force? Was the level of force they used appropriate for the situation? Did the officers follow department policy and legal requirements and restrictions? Police often have to make decisions about use of force in split seconds, and their decisions affect both their own safety and the safety of others. Decisions about the use of force also can affect officers' psychological well-being.

This chapter introduces the realities of policing. We first address how society defines policing, then briefly trace the history of policing. We describe the structure of U.S. policing at the local, state, and federal levels and review the consequences for the public of that fragmentation of authority. We explain how officers are recruited, selected, and trained and describe how the police subculture can influence them while on the job. Finally, we discuss the great degree of discretion officers have and what happens when they abuse their power.

DEFINING POLICING

Since the mid-1900s, the term *law enforcement* has been used synonymously with policing. Most people would say the police are those given the task of enforcing the law, and the most common image of police is as crime fighters.

Most of what police officers do on a daily basis, however, has little to do with directly enforcing the law. We call on the police to perform a variety of tasks even when no law has been broken. For example, police direct drivers when traffic lights are out, respond to calls about neighbors' disagreements over property lines, and deal with individuals who are mentally ill and are bothering people. The way we define policing influences both how the public views the police and how officers view their own jobs.

Individuals granted policing powers were not always charged with enforcing the law. In the past, for example, police officers were expected to enforce not the law but the will of those with political power. Today, the rise of private police forces such as Triple Canopy, provider of security for U.S. forces in Iraq, has led some to question whether these private forces should be included under the umbrella of law enforcement. What distinguishes the police from others? In other words, what makes the police the police? If we consider everything police do and all the reasons citizens call upon them for assistance, the best definition is that police officers are individuals to whom society has granted the power to use physical force when they deem it necessary or appropriate.[6]

Why *do* people call the police? Only 19 percent of calls to police relate to a crime of any kind,[7] and an officer typically spends only 10 to 15 percent of patrol time on crime-related activities.[8] Clearly this percentage of time is much less than that portrayed on television series. Society has identified local police officers as the people residents should call when they need immediate assistance. We often call them because we do not know where else to turn, and we believe officers can make other people do what should be done. That power comes from officers' authority to use force.[9]

Police officers and criminal justice professionals are a product of their environment, and the ethnic and racial tensions and alliances found in society at large exist in policing as well. Consider, for example, the emigrants from Ireland who came to the United States in the mid-nineteenth century. Those in power often regarded the Irish immigrants as violent troublemakers. Hence, they frequently came into conflict with the police, who were responding to what individuals in power wanted them to do.[10] In time, however, the Irish gained political power and served in public positions—including in the police force. As the evolving relationship between the police and the Irish demonstrates, police reflect the broader society.

Preview

HISTORY OF POLICING

One way to understand the present is to learn about the past. Knowing something about the history of policing helps us appreciate its present challenges and understand why some groups of people distrust law enforcement officers.

Vigilantism: Policing by Self-Appointed Committees

A great deal of police activity existed before the development of well-organized, big city police departments. If we think of the police as individuals authorized by a community to use force, then we can consider vigilantism as very much a part of the history of policing

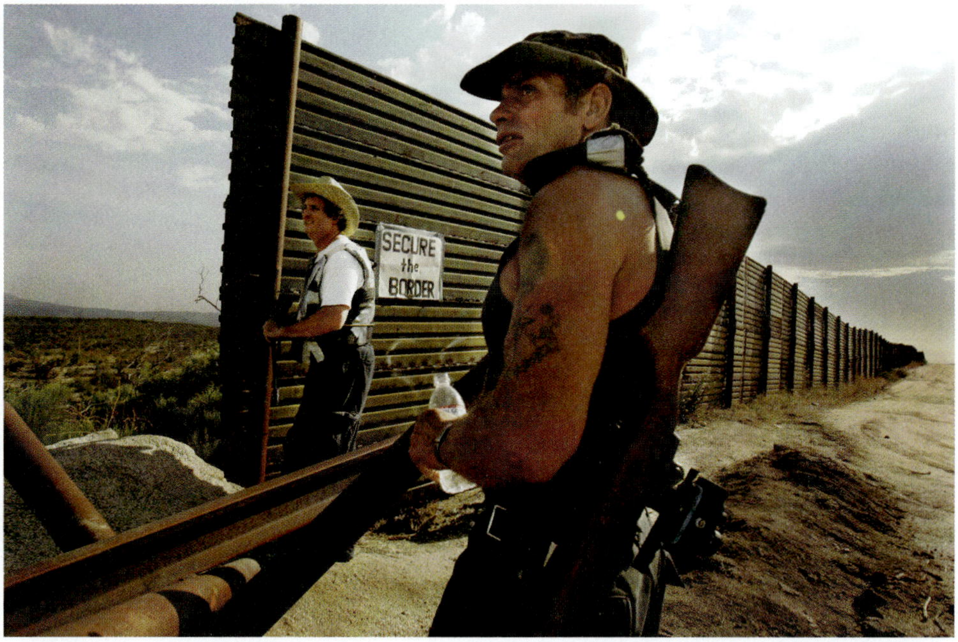

▶ Today's Minutemen

Anti-immigration activists have taken to patrolling the borders themselves to reduce illegal immigration.

vigilantism
Use of volunteer, self-appointed committees organized to suppress crime and punish criminals.

in the United States. **Vigilantism** is the use of volunteer, self-appointed committees organized to suppress crime and punish criminals. Vigilantes were local residents who organized themselves to apprehend and punish those they considered outlaws. Vigilantism flourished from the mid-1700s to about 1900, years when the rapid spread of settlement throughout the country outpaced the establishment of formal law enforcement in new communities. Although vigilantism started in the East, it became much more common in the West as a means of regulating behavior and enforcing U.S. society's developing cultural norms.[11]

Our modern image of vigilantes is that of a group of people outraged by some heinous offense who spontaneously spring into action to catch and punish the offender. Vigilante movements of the past, however, were quite different. They were well organized, quasi-military groups of 100 or more participants who were the elites of the community. Many vigilante groups even had constitutions or manifestos to explain their rules and means of operation. Vigilantes often hanged those they apprehended, and between 1767 and 1900 they killed more than 700 people. Suspects' crimes included horse theft, counterfeiting, and offenses against the newly established private property system, which created haves and have-nots in the developing West. Vigilantism is an example of how the police (in this case, self-appointed police) historically enforced the norms of society rather than the laws.[12]

The West was not, however, without formal law enforcement. One of the most effective and ethical law enforcement officers of the Old West was Bass Reeves, who was appointed U.S. Deputy Marshal in 1875 to curb lawlessness in the "Indian Territory" (the eastern portion of present-day Oklahoma). You can read a brief summary of Reeves's highly successful career in the Race, Class, Gender box.

Slave Patrols: Capturing Fugitives

The first publicly funded city police departments were slave patrols created to keep slaves from rebelling or running away.[13] In South Carolina, for example, mounted daytime slave patrols were formed in the 1740s.[14] One of the primary duties of the Texas Rangers, the forerunner of organized state police forces, was retrieving runaway slaves.[15] Slave patrols were also created out of fear the state militia would be unable to control slave rebellions.[16]

Slavery was not just an accepted practice; it was a legally protected one. Local governments passed a variety of laws giving Whites the power to control African Americans. These slave codes varied from place to place, but they generally required slaves to have passes any time they left their owner's land, forbade more than a few slaves to congregate at any one time, prohibited their education, and required the return of slaves to their "owners."[17] Those choosing to work as police were required to uphold these laws, whether or

Race, Class, Gender

Bass Reeves: African American Deputy Marshal of the Old West

Bass Reeves was born in 1834 in Paris, Texas, to parents who were enslaved. After a fight with the individual who "owned" him, Reeves escaped and lived with American Indian tribes until 1863. He then became a successful stockman and farmer in Arkansas and Oklahoma. In 1875, a new judge appointed to the Federal Western District Court at Fort Smith, Arkansas, was given the responsibility of curbing lawlessness by White settlers in the "Indian Territory." The judge responded by appointing African American deputies to round up White outlaws and work with the tribes. Reeves, who could speak some tribal languages and knew the land, was an especially good candidate for the job.

Due to his childhood as a slave, Reeves was never taught to read or write (teaching slaves to read and write was against the law) and had to rely on others to read arrest warrants to him. In his 32 years as a deputy, Reeves earned a reputation as being able to capture any criminal. He once even served a warrant of arrest on his own son after pursuing him for two weeks. The son was convicted of killing his wife but was eventually issued a full pardon. Over the course of his career, Reeves killed 14 men. He claimed to have fired his weapon only in self-defense and was found to have acted properly each time.

In 1907, at the age of 69, Reeves became a city police officer in Muskogee, Oklahoma, and served until 1909. He died the following year. His obituary in the *Muskogee Phoenix* noted, "Reeves had many narrow escapes. At different times his belt was shot in two, a button shot off his coat, his hat brim shot off and the bridle reins which he held in his hands cut by a bullet."

The story of Bass Reeves reveals a history less often told: that the faces of those who tamed the "wild West" were not all White. In fact, the federal judge who hired Reeves hired several other African American deputies. African American men like Reeves paved the way for others like them to pursue a career in law enforcement.

Observe Investigate Understand

- **What reasons might the judge who appointed Reeves have had for appointing African American deputies to pursue White outlaws in the Indian Territory?**
- **What challenges would Reeves, as an African American man, have faced in pursuing and apprehending White criminals?**
- **How do the history of the taming of the West and the actions of men like Reeves affect policing today?**

SOURCES: For more information see Art Burton, *Black Gun, Silver Star: The Life and Legend of Frontier Marshall Bass Reeves* (Lincoln, NE: University of Nebraska Press, 2006). See also Gary Paulsen, *The Legend of Bass Reeves* (New York: Bantam Doubleday Dell, 2008).

not they agreed with them. Even if a Texas Ranger, for example, was opposed to slavery, a primary responsibility of his job was to retrieve runaway slaves. After the Civil War, the former Confederate states enacted black codes to ensure that the former slaves remained under the control of the White majority. The black codes required that individuals could marry only someone of their own racial background, outlined who could hold property (Whites), and included laws against vagrancy to force freed African Americans to work on White-owned farms.[18]

Early vigilantism and slave patrols demonstrate that police-type agencies were created to protect individuals in power by controlling those without it.[19] This historical development sowed resentment toward the police among some groups.

The English Model

Rapid settlement of the West and the institution of slavery influenced the development of policing in the United States, but so too did events in England, especially the innovations of the London Metropolitan Police Department. Policing in England featured a decentralized or local patrol force, limited authority, the mission of preventing crime, and a quasimilitary organizational structure.

frankpledge
Peacekeeping system in early England in which a group of 10 local families agreed to maintain the peace and make sure lawbreakers were taken into custody and brought to court.

watch system
System in which particular men were assigned the job of watchman and became responsible for patrolling the streets, lighting lanterns, serving as a lookout for fires, and generally keeping order.

preventive patrol
Officers maintaining a visible presence in communities to serve as a deterrant to a variety of street-level crimes.

Initially, keeping peace in England occurred at the local level. In the **frankpledge** system, which developed in England before the eighteenth century, 10 families in a community agreed to maintain the peace in their area and make sure lawbreakers were taken into custody and brought to court. In time the frankpledge system gave way to a **watch system** in which particular men were assigned to be watchmen and were responsible for patrolling the streets, lighting lanterns, serving as a lookout for fires, and generally keeping order. Maintaining peace, then, was first seen as a local affair. As policing developed in England and then in the United States, police departments continued to be controlled by local government. This decentralized system had both positive and negative consequences, as we'll see later in this chapter.

Sir Robert Peel's tireless efforts to create a disciplined and organized police force to battle the turmoil and crime in London led to the creation of the London Metropolitan Police Department in 1829. Peel structured the London Metropolitan Police on a quasi-military arrangement with clear hierarchical ranks of command. For example, there were sergeants, lieutenants, and captains. "Bobbies," named for Sir Robert, also wore uniforms that made them easily identifiable. As in the military, lower ranks were required to follow the orders of their superiors. Because of public concern about potential threats to civil liberties, police in London were given limited authority, meaning that their powers and duties were specified in law.

Police departments in the United States adopted the same mission as the London police: to stop crime through **preventive patrol**. To accomplish this goal, officers patrolled the streets, maintaining a visible presence in the community.[20] Preventive patrol remains a large part of police activities today.

Yet the United States of the 1800s was very different from England of that era, and the police forces of the two countries differed in some significant ways. New York City police, for example, tended to gain their legitimacy—the public's trust in them—by being *of* the people. In other words, they were usually of the same ethnic background as those they policed, so they were able to develop more personal relationships with the public. Because there was little ethnic diversity in London, matching the ethnic backgrounds of police to citizens was not a concern. English bobbies established their authority as members of an impersonal independent agency, whereas New York City officers got their legitimacy from their personal relationships with residents and the political connections they made.[21]

Political Era: Patronage-based Policing

The political era of policing in the United States began with the creation of organized police departments in the nation's major cities in the 1840s and lasted until the early 1920s. During this period, local political bosses selected members of their party to be police officers as a reward for party loyalty. In this patronage system, it was *whom* the police knew, rather than *what* they knew, that was important. In fact, there wasn't much police officers were actually expected to know. During this era, police were not thought of primarily as law enforcers. Instead, their role was to control undesirable immigrants, maintain order, and provide a variety of social services not otherwise available to the poor or needy, such as housing the homeless.[22]

Officers received little if any training, and the use of force was fairly common. Holding facilities were generally located far from where an officer was likely to confront a suspect. Rather than bringing a suspect to department headquarters, officers often practiced "street justice" by physically punishing the suspect on the spot.

Professional Era: The Police as Law Enforcers

The professional (or reform) era of policing, which emerged in the late 1920s and lasted through the late 1970s, began in response to the many problems of the political era. During the 1920s, major reforms swept all levels of government. Progressive reformers created formalized hierarchical government agencies, or bureaucracies, to increase specialization, reward merit, and decrease corruption. Progressives wanted government bureaucrats, including the police, to be free of political influence. Critical of the partisan politics that characterized police departments, they advocated hiring people for government positions on the basis of merit and thoroughly training them. Progressives also embraced science and believed research could increase the efficiency of government operations, including law enforcement. Changing technology, such as the increased availability of telephone service, also had an impact on everyday policing. The early reformers believed change would fundamentally improve policing and its effectiveness. But like all reforms, the professional era had both positive and negative outcomes.

August Vollmer (1876–1955), the first police chief of Berkeley, California, was appointed to that position in 1909 and held it until 1932. An early reformer who had a great impact on the history of policing, Vollmer believed in hiring individuals with a broad-based education. He advocated using science to solve crimes and created modus operandi ("modes of operation") files to systematically connect offenses of similar types—a key element in modern investigative profiling. Perhaps his greatest innovation came in 1908 when he created a police school to train officers. In 1914, Vollmer oversaw the first completely mobile force, in which all officers used automobiles for transportation. Vollmer's ideas about policing and the innovations he instituted in Berkeley served as an example to other departments across the country.[23]

▲ **August Vollmer**

In the early twentieth century, Vollmer was a leading innovator in law enforcement.

During the professional era, law enforcement emerged as the primary function of police officers. The Uniform Crime Reports (UCR) discussed in Chapter 1, which began in this era, assessed police departments based on reported crimes in their jurisdictions and their rates of solving them. Such developments focused departments' efforts on law enforcement, as police chiefs knew they would be judged on their ability to catch criminals. The development of the 911 system during this era is also indicative of the emphasis on law enforcement. The idea behind the system was that citizens would report crimes by calling 911, and officers would quickly respond and perhaps even catch perpetrators in the act.

The professional era of policing had many positive outcomes. Political control over the hiring and firing of officers was eliminated, and entrance to the force was based on merit. Officers were expected to police all residents evenly without political favoritism. Training for new officers became much more systematic. Pay for officers and resources for departments increased, both because the mission of the police became more professionalized and articulated and because newly created police unions successfully pressed for salary increases.

The professional era had some negative outcomes as well. By the time of the civil rights movement and anti-Vietnam war protests of the 1960s, officers had grown distant from their communities. Protesters and police clashed, sometimes violently. The confrontations of the 1960s also exposed the troubled relationship between Blacks and the police. The definition of police officers as primarily law enforcers created an atmosphere in which some people saw the police as an occupying force in their neighborhood rather than as public servants. A Case in Point on the next page illustrates that some of these problems of strained relations still exist today.

Changes in technology also increased the distance between officers and citizens. Instead of patrolling on foot, police rode in department automobiles, dispatched through a central radio call system. The telephone also changed the way the public contacted police. By the mid-1970s, residents were being advised to call the police only on crime-related matters, and patrol officers and the public interacted only when residents had problems to report.

MYTH/REALITY

MYTH: Putting police officers in radio-equipped vehicles proved to be of substantial benefit in helping the police get a finger on the public's pulse.

REALITY: Patrolling the streets from within the isolating confines of a radio-equipped car distanced the police from the people they served.[24]

Another negative consequence of professionalization was the decrease in the number of minority officers hired as departments implemented educational and test requirements. People of color who had been making steady progress in entering police forces were less likely to have the education required, partly because they were often denied

a Case in Point

Conflict with Antiwar Protestors

On April 7, 2003, approximately 500 demonstrators protesting the Iraq War gathered at a port in Oakland, California, from which ocean carriers transported military supplies. Oakland police officers fired nonlethal weapons on the crowd. Fifty-eight people, including nine dockworkers who were not protesting, were hurt by wooden bullets, sting ball grenades, and shot-filled bean bags. Injuries included bloody noses, welts and bruises, and broken bones.

Police contended that they had ordered the protestors to disperse and that they had not complied. Demonstrators claimed they were never told to disperse. Nationwide reaction to the incident was swift and largely negative. A longshoremen's spokesperson who had observed the protest said of the demonstrators, "They were just standing around. It was the police who were the aggressors." The mayor of Oakland, however, said at the time, "That's what happens when you don't get out of the way."

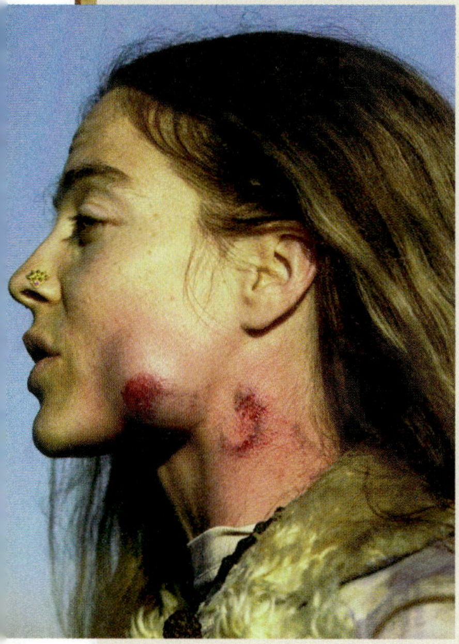

Fifty-two people filed a class action suit against the City of Oakland, contending their First Amendment right to free speech had been violated. In a negotiated settlement, the Oakland Police Department adopted a policy not to use weapons as a means of crowd control. Instead, they would use force against protestors only if they threatened police, other individuals, or property. Furthermore, in those instances, police would *specifically* target the individuals who were threatening, rather than the crowd as a whole or individuals indiscriminately.

High-profile clashes between the police and demonstrators during the 1960s led to a concerted effort to balance people's First Amendment rights with public safety. The incident in Oakland, however, illustrates that confrontations continue between demonstrators and the police.

The Oakland case also shows that police departments can learn from their mistakes. The City of Oakland could have continued fighting the case in the courts. Instead, it negotiated a settlement that changed the police department's crowd control strategy.

Observe Investigate Understand

- **What does the Oakland incident suggest about the relationship between the police and protestors?**
- **In what circumstances, if any, are police justified in using force against protestors or demonstrators?**
- **How does the negotiated settlement in the Oakland case protect the rights of both the protestors and the police?**

SOURCES: Bill Mongelluzzo, "Dockworkers Hurt in Oakland War Protest," *The Journal of Commerce Online*, April 7, 2003; Herbert A. Sample, "Oakland Bans Several Crowd Control Devices: An Accord Stemming from a 2003 Protest Is Hailed by Police and Civil Rights Groups," *Sacramento Bee*, November 10, 2004.

access to education for much of this time period. As a result, the police forces that policed multicultural urban centers were largely White, male, and suburban.[25]

Despite the reforms of the professional era, crime increased. Individuals within and outside the profession of policing began to ask why the changes had not resulted in a decrease in crime. The realization that many policing strategies were proving to be ineffective led to the development of community policing, which focuses on developing positive relationships between the police and the public they serve.

Community Policing Era: Working for—and with—the Public

During the 1970s, reformers came to believe that if the police were to have any impact on crime they would need the full cooperation of the people in the communities they served. Reformers also recognized that the relationship between the police and the public was strained. Because of these dual realizations, reformers advocated fundamental changes in the way police interact with members of their communities. Policing in the professional era focused solely on solving crimes; **community policing** emphasizes crime prevention and focuses on developing positive relationships between the police and the public (see Chapter 6). Community policing uses the strategies of officers on foot patrol in the community and engaging residents in the work of policing in the effort to prevent crimes before they occur.

community policing
Philosophy of policing that emphasizes crime prevention and focuses on developing positive relations between the police and the public.

sworn personnel
Police department employees entrusted with arrest powers; usually referred to as "peace officers."

The most fundamental change in the era of community policing, which began in the late 1970s and continues today, concerns the way the police view the public and the relationship between the police and the public. Officers are now expected to cultivate positive relationships with individuals in the communities they serve, and with neighborhood organizations such as the Boys & Girls Club and Neighborhood Watch, in order to include the public in crime prevention and enforcement. Officers attend local meetings and ask residents what they would like to have happen in their communities. Are there particular areas they would like police resources to focus on? What problems would they like to see addressed? In community policing, officers are given greater discretion to address these problems.

Increased communication is the key to improving relations between police and the public. If police are to rely on residents to help them solve crimes and problems, community members must feel positively about their local officers. Indeed, one of the strongest factors in solving a crime is the ability and willingness of a victim, complainant, or witness to work with police to identify a suspect.[26] Community policing increases the demands of time on officers—time to interact with residents, time to attend community meetings, and time to investigate neighborhood problems. Because the public still expects police to answer calls for service, some officers are designated exclusively as community policing officers and are either relieved of responding to calls for service or respond only to those in their assigned neighborhood.

Another major change during the community policing era was the shift toward proactive rather than reactive police work. Proactive policing aims to prevent crime not just through the threat of capture but also through elimination of the presumed causes of crime, such as disorder in a community. To accomplish this goal, police officers are expected to deal with lifestyle issues such as public drunkenness, vandalism, loitering, and other minor offenses that reduce the quality of life.

The community policing era continues today. We discuss community policing as a policing strategy in greater detail in Chapter 6. We also assess the effectiveness of community policing and review critiques of this policing strategy in that chapter.

History often is presented as falling into neatly defined, distinct categories, but change takes place gradually. Characteristics of any one era may overlap with the next. The Key Concepts feature summarizes the different policing eras and illustrates that overlap.

STRUCTURE OF THE LAW ENFORCEMENT SYSTEM

Policing in the United States has adopted many aspects of the London model: a focus on crime prevention, visible patrol, and a quasimilitary organization. In addition, a division in staffing is characteristic of U.S. policing, with police departments employing both sworn and nonsworn personnel. **Sworn personnel** are those entrusted with arrest powers and are usually referred to as *peace officers* in the statutes conferring such powers. In the language of policing, nonsworn personnel are *civilians.*

The independence of local government is deeply rooted in U.S. culture, as is the fear of a national police force and the tyranny that could accompany it.[27] Thus policing in the United States has always been highly localized.[28] Yet despite the localized nature of policing, law enforcement agencies in the United States exist at the federal, state, and local levels.

Real Crime Tech

PUBLIC SURVEILLANCE TECHNOLOGY

Although the public has largely accepted the presence of security cameras in public places and U.S. courts have long held that there is no expectation of privacy in such places, many people do not trust the police with regard to the use of surveillance systems. In community policing, police departments work closely with community and business leaders and Neighborhood Watch groups in developing guidelines for the use of surveillance technology and building trust that the technology will not be abused.

Just as the public may distrust the police use of surveillance technology, many police officers are concerned about the public's use of cameras and other devices to record and distribute images of police activities. Despite these concerns, nearly all law enforcement professionals believe that more good than harm results when members of the public use cameras, recorders, and other instruments to capture images of police officers on the job because these images may help the public gain a better understanding of and appreciation for the work of the police.

SOURCES: James Cannon, "Winning Framework to Implement Surveillance Technologies to Enhance the Police and Community Partnership," *The Journal of California Law Enforcement* 42, no. 2 (2008): 20; Mary Erpenbach, "The Whole World Is Watching," *Law Enforcement Technology* 35, no. 2 (2008): 44–47.

KEY CONCEPTS

The History of Policing in the United States

Policing Era	Time Period	Defining Characteristics
Vigilantism	Mid-1700–1900	Residents organized to punish people deemed outlaws.
Slave patrols	1740–1840	Residents organized to enforce laws meant to control slaves.
English model	1700–1800	Local patrol force had limited authority and quasimilitary organizational structure. Police departments in U.S. cities developed similarly.
Political era	1840–1920	Police received jobs because of political affiliation and enforced the priorities of the political party in power.
Professional era	1920–1970	Focus was on enforcing the law, hiring qualified officers, using technology, and improving police training.
Community policing era	1970–present day	Focus is on crime prevention with the assistance of improved relations with community members.

Local Law Enforcement Agencies

We can divide local law enforcement agencies into two broad categories: sheriffs' offices and police departments. Sheriffs' offices tend to serve larger areas with fewer people, whereas police departments serve smaller, urban areas with more people.

Sheriffs' Offices

Sheriffs' offices typically police counties in which no city provides law enforcement services. Sheriffs respond to violations of criminal statutes (usually defined by state-level penal codes) as well as to violations of city or county ordinances. In addition, they provide jail facilities for both accused and convicted persons and transportation services for all incarcerated persons within counties. In their court-related functions, most sheriffs' offices serve summonses (which direct persons accused of crimes to appear in court) and subpoenas (which direct individuals to appear in court to present evidence), provide court security, serve eviction notices, and enforce child support orders.

Police Departments

Police departments outnumber sheriffs' offices by four to one, operate mostly in urban areas, and perform most law enforcement duties. They respond to violations of state penal codes and local ordinances and generally provide only temporary housing of arrested persons. Usually, arrested persons remain in police custody only until their initial appearance in court.[29]

State Law Enforcement Agencies

The Texas Rangers, organized by Stephen Austin in 1823 to protect his fledgling colony from American Indians, was the forerunner of state law enforcement agencies.[30] Other states later created their own state-level police agencies.

Because the roles and missions of state law enforcement agencies are defined by state law, they vary considerably and include motor vehicle law violation investigation, lottery oversight, alcoholic beverage control, and narcotics enforcement. About half of all state agencies also offer crime lab services for local police departments.[31] State agencies make up only about 8 percent of the law enforcement community.[32] The number of state and local

LOCAL AND STATE LAW ENFORCEMENT AGENCIES AND EMPLOYEES IN THE UNITED STATES, 2004

Type of Agency	Number of Agencies	Sworn Employees*
Local police department	12,766	446,974
Sheriff's office	3,067	175,018
State	49**	58,190
Total	15,882	680,182

*Sworn employees are those with general arrest powers.

**Hawaii is the only state without a state law enforcement agency.

SOURCE: Bureau of Justice Statistics, "Census of State and Local Law Enforcement Agencies, 2004," June 2007, Bulletin NCJ 212749.

law enforcement agencies in the United States and their respective numbers of employees are shown in the table above.

Federal Law Enforcement Agencies

Federal law enforcement agencies deal with violations of federal statutes. The most prominent employers of sworn law enforcement officers at the federal level are the Federal Bureau of Investigation (FBI), the U.S. Secret Service, and the Drug Enforcement Administration (DEA), but peace officer positions are found in many other federal agencies as well, including the U.S. Railroad Retirement Board, the Federal Deposit Insurance Corporation, and the Bureau of Engraving and Printing.

Department of Justice

The Department of Justice (DOJ) is the chief federal law enforcement department. Headed by the attorney general, who is a member of the president's cabinet, the DOJ provides federal leadership in preventing and controlling crime. The DOJ also has responsibility for enforcing the law and defending the interests of the United States according to the law, and ensuring public safety against foreign and domestic threats. Several agencies within the DOJ provide law enforcement services:

- Federal Bureau of Investigation (FBI)
- Drug Enforcement Administration (DEA)
- Bureau of Alcohol, Tobacco, Firearms, and Explosives (ATF), formerly the Bureau of Alcohol, Tobacco, and Firearms
- U.S. Marshals Service

The FBI, created in 1908, employs more than 30,000 people, of whom just over 13,000 are special agents. Support personnel, numbering nearly 19,000 persons, include information analysts, language specialists, scientists, and information technology specialists. The mission of the FBI is to protect and defend the United States against terrorism and foreign intelligence threats and to uphold and enforce the nation's criminal laws. The FBI provides criminal justice services, such as fingerprint identification, laboratory examinations, and police training, to federal, state, and local law enforcement agencies.

The DEA was established in 1973 to combat the "war on drugs." Its mission today remains the same: to enforce the nation's laws and regulations governing controlled substances. The DEA investigates and prepares for the prosecution of those charged with violating controlled substance laws at both the interstate and international levels.

Passage of the Homeland Security Act in 2003 transferred ATF from the Department of the Treasury to the Department of Justice. ATF responsibilities include enforcing federal laws, regulating the firearms and explosives industries, and investigating and reducing crimes involving firearms and explosives, acts of arson, and the illegal trafficking of alcohol and tobacco products.

The U.S. Marshals Service, which has operated since 1789, is the nation's oldest federal law enforcement agency. Duties of the deputy U.S. marshals and criminal investigators, who form the backbone of the agency, are to apprehend federal fugitives, protect the federal judiciary, operate the Witness Security Program, transport federal prisoners, and seize property acquired by criminals through illegal activities.

Department of Homeland Security

The newest cabinet department of the federal government is the Department of Homeland Security (DHS), which was created following the terrorist attacks of September 11, 2001. The DHS mission is to lead the unified national effort to protect the American people and their homeland, to prevent and deter terrorist attacks, to protect against and respond to threats against the nation, and to prepare for and respond to all hazards and disasters. In order to prevent duplication of effort, DHS groups 22 federal agencies into one cabinet department. There are seven major DHS agencies:

- Transportation Security Administration (TSA)
- U.S. Customs and Border Protection (CBP)
- U.S. Citizenship and Immigration Services

Real Careers

JOHN TORRES

Work location: Los Angeles, California

College(s): Sacramento State University (1982, 1986)

Major(s): Criminal Justice (BA), Criminal Justice (MA)

Job title: Alcohol, Tobacco, Firearms (ATF) Agent

Salary range for job like this: $45,000–$65,000

Time in job: 25 years

Work Responsibilities

As the Special Agent in Charge of ATF in Los Angeles, I enforce federal firearms, explosives, and arson laws. We conduct criminal investigations, regulate the firearms and explosives industries, and assist other law enforcement agencies. We also work to prevent terrorism, reduce violent crime, and protect the public in a manner that is faithful to the Constitution and the laws of the United States. One of my most memorable moments on the job was when I was Incident Commander for the takedown of an outlaw motorcycle organization, the Mongols Motorcycle Club. We arrested more than 80 club members and seized over 100 motorcycles. We also seized their trademark, the first time this was ever done.

Why Criminal Justice?

Ever since I was a teenager, I knew that I wanted to be in law enforcement in some capacity. While I was still a student at Sacramento State, I saw a small ad in the Criminal Justice building that ATF recruiters would be at the school. I applied, and the rest, as they say, is history.

Expectations and Realities of the Job

My job has changed significantly from when I started. The early years of my career were spent investigating career criminals, using the expertise within ATF. The middle years were spent developing my skills as an ATF supervisor and providing direction to less experienced agents. Most recently, I have been the leader within my agency. I admit that when it came time for me to become a supervisor, I expected leadership to come naturally. However, I quickly realized that anyone can "manage" an agency, but to be truly successful you need to have compassion and vision and let those around you know that you care about them as people. The relationships I have formed during my career have nurtured my love of the job.

My Advice to Students

It is so important to set your goals and stay the course. Your journey may not be an easy one or what you expected, but if you continue to pursue your goals with conviction and effort, you will achieve what you set out to do.

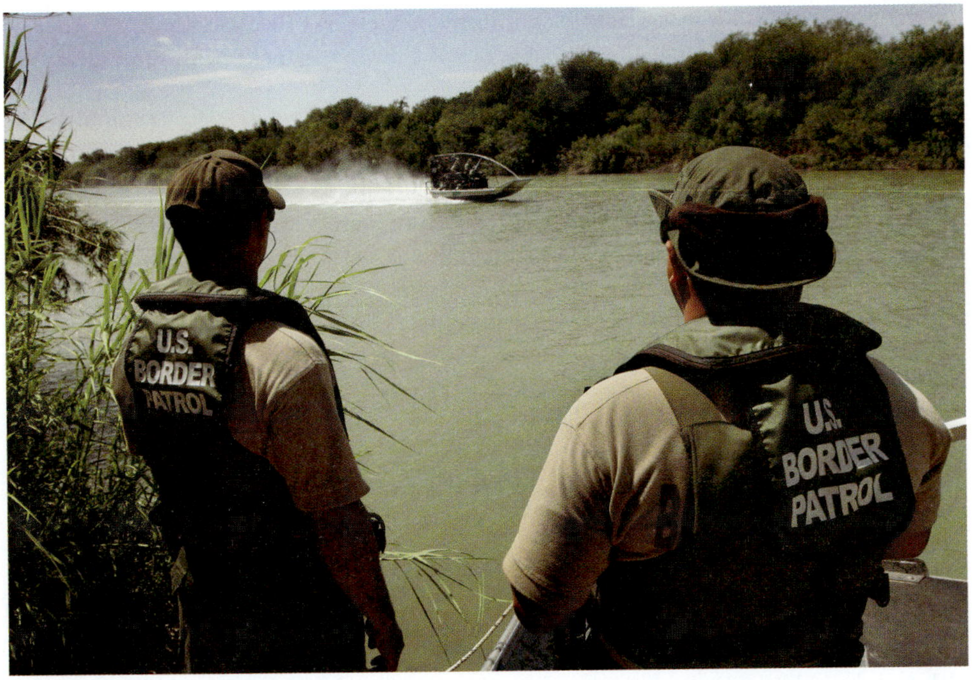

◀ U.S. Customs and Border Protection Officers

U.S. Customs and Border Protection is a federal law enforcement agency.

- U.S. Immigration and Customs Enforcement
- U.S. Secret Service
- Federal Emergency Management Agency (FEMA)
- U.S. Coast Guard

The two major law enforcement components of DHS are the U.S. Customs and Border Protection (CBP) and the U.S. Immigration and Customs Enforcement (ICE). CBP, which guards 7,000 miles of U.S. land borders and 2,000 miles of coastal waters, is charged with protecting the nation's borders from terrorism, human and drug smuggling, illegal immigration, and importation of agricultural pests. ICE enforces the nation's customs and immigration laws. Both agencies were significantly larger by 2004 than their pre-DHS predecessors eight years earlier. CBP's U.S. Border Patrol, formerly part of the Immigration and Naturalization Service, roughly doubled in size in eight years.[33]

While DOJ and DHS are the chief law enforcement departments of the federal government, perhaps the most complex arrangement for law enforcement services in the country belongs to the federal Bureau of Indian Affairs (BIA), which is part of the Department of the Interior. American Indian tribes may provide for policing services in several ways:

- They may contract with the BIA for funding of their own tribal police departments. Officers in such arrangements are tribal employees.
- They may elect to have federal employees of BIA provide policing services.
- They may rely on state and local authorities for policing services.
- They may fund policing exclusively with tribal funds.

The type of policing occurring in much American Indian land is of particular concern because law enforcement activities often clash with tribal values and norms. For example, a police officer on a Tohono O'odham reservation who aggressively confronts a suspect will offend tribal norms. Conversely, an officer on a reservation of the Turtle Mountain Band of Chippewa Indians who fails to confront a suspect will be guilty of a misstep. Law enforcement officers need to incorporate tribal values in their policing mission to create workable, tribe-specific policing institutions and approaches informed by traditional customs.[34]

Many people work in federal law enforcement agencies. To understand the scope of federal law enforcement, refer to the table below showing agencies with more than 500 full-time officers.

The Problem of Fragmentation

fragmentation
The lack of coordination among law enforcement agencies in the same geographic region due to the existence of many small departments.

Localized policing allows local values to inform police practices and better positions officers to use their judgment in resolving local community problems. This historic approach, however, has led to the problem of **fragmentation**, a lack of coordination among law enforcement agencies in the same geographic region due to the existence of many small departments. Suppose, for example, that criminals commit crimes in several different police jurisdictions. Investigators in one police department may have information that could help a neighboring agency, but the two agencies do not routinely communicate. (This situation can exist even within a single agency—usually a large, urban agency—where the bureaucratized division of responsibilities hinders or prevents information sharing and cooperation among different units.) If one community enforces certain laws more strictly than others, criminals may take their criminal activities to a neighboring jurisdiction that takes a less aggressive approach. Duplication of services is another frequent result of fragmentation. For example, separate agencies generally operate their own call dispatch and crime laboratory units and bear the expenses individually.[35]

Problems resulting from fragmentation are not easily solved. Law enforcement officials and the public are accustomed to the independence of their local police departments. Nevertheless, as problems linked to drug trafficking and terrorism cross jurisdictions, the disadvantages of fragmentation may reduce support for this approach to policing.[36]

Consolidation is one option for dealing with the problem of fragmentation. For example, in Florida in 1968, the Duval County Sheriff's Department and the Jacksonville

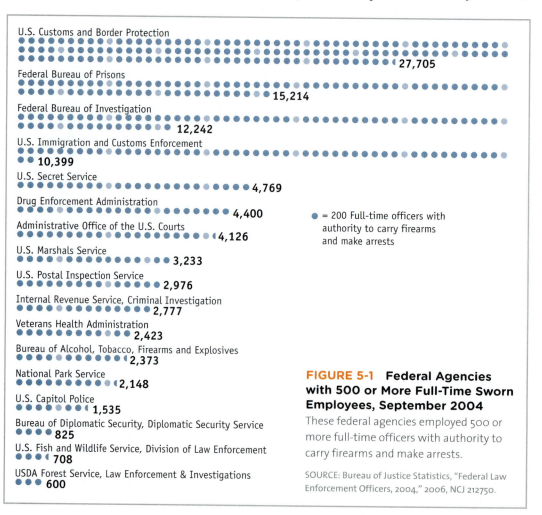

FIGURE 5-1 Federal Agencies with 500 or More Full-Time Sworn Employees, September 2004

These federal agencies employed 500 or more full-time officers with authority to carry firearms and make arrests.

SOURCE: Bureau of Justice Statistics, "Federal Law Enforcement Officers, 2004," 2006, NCJ 212750.

Police Department conducted one of the earliest consolidation efforts in the United States. More than four decades later, the Office of the Sheriff–Jacksonville Police (commonly referred to as the "Jacksonville Sheriff's Office") has significantly enhanced its quality of service. Its Continuous Improvement Unit is specifically dedicated to perfecting the agency's capability to add value to the services provided to the community. Its quality of service has been formally recognized through its status as a "triple crown accredited law enforcement agency," meaning that it has been accredited by the national Commission on Accreditation for Law Enforcement Agencies, the American Correctional Association, and the National Commission on Correctional Health Care.[37]

Instead of consolidating, smaller agencies can contract with larger agencies for specific services. This arrangement has been especially efficient for detention facilities and communications systems.[38] Contracting for specific services may also make sense for emergency planning. A city, for example, can contract to have the county's SWAT unit available in the event of a major riot, invasion by an outlaw motorcycle gang, or a hostage situation at a school.[39]

RECRUITMENT, SELECTION, AND TRAINING

Effective policing in a community requires a force of high-quality, well-trained peace officers who are responsive to the community's needs. The processes of recruitment, selection, and training are critical to developing such a force. Many police departments have made efforts to develop a diversified police force that includes representative numbers of minorities and women.

Recruitment

"The most fundamental human resource process in a law enforcement organization is the recruitment of a sufficient number of qualified applicants to meet the staffing needs of an agency."[40] At a minimum, "qualified" applicants possess good oral and written communications skills, are fit both physically and psychologically, have a solid employment history, and are free of convictions for criminal offenses. Agencies face significant challenges in recruiting, which include the following:

- Better-paying jobs outside law enforcement
- Unusually high attrition as older generations retire
- Negative publicity over matters such as alleged discrimination in arrests and excessive use of force[41]

Difficulties in recruitment also may result from the nature of the contemporary workforce. Fewer individuals are interested in public service work today than was true of previous generations. Potential recruits know only good economic times and have come to expect such; if an employer doesn't meet their needs, they are likely to leave. Police officers today want balanced lives that allow them time for family, leisure activities, and other priorities. Officers may resist extending a work shift to handle a late-breaking homicide or traffic accident.[42]

Demand for Officers

A study of law enforcement agencies conducted by the National Institute of Justice in 2002 to examine the "cop crunch"—the shortfall in the ranks—revealed that state agencies and those employing more than 500 officers had significant problems attracting enough qualified candidates.[43] Reasons cited for these problems included the view of many people that government careers are uninteresting or that the federal workplace is in need of reform. These perceptions make it difficult for law enforcement agencies to attract and retain talent.[44]

Competition for workers is another problem. The State of California projects that by 2014 it will need to increase the number of law enforcement workers to 139,100, a jump of almost 14 percent. However, the state also is projected to create approximately 2.6 million new state jobs between 2004 and 2014.[45]

Methods of Recruitment

Newspaper ads, career fairs, and the Internet are some common means agencies use to recruit candidates. Some agencies also use their own programs to recruit young people, including college internships, explorer programs (worksite-based program for adolescents interested in law enforcement careers), and school resource officers. The most commonly targeted groups are those with previous police experience, followed by college graduates, racial and ethnic minorities, and women.[46]

Selection

Once an agency has attracted a sufficient number of applicants, the next step is selecting the best-qualified individuals to fill sworn positions. A peace officer's work is complex, potentially dangerous, and emotionally stressful, and it requires above-average intelligence to apply an ever-changing body of laws and police regulations to the solution of problems created by crime.[47]

Selection Process

The selection of police recruits has become decidedly more professional, thanks to the recommendations of several law enforcement commissions.[48] For example, psychological testing of recruits originated from a government recommendation in 1931.[49] The 1973 National Advisory Commission on Criminal Justice Standards and Goals recommended that all police agencies institute a formal selection process that would include "a written test of mental ability, an oral interview, a physical examination, a psychological examination, and an in-depth background investigation."[50] Affirmative action goals set by the Equal Employment Opportunity Commission have helped eliminate standards or testing that could adversely affect a particular group of candidates.[51]

siege mentality
Police view of themselves as a "band of brothers"—or "sisters"—against everyone else in society.

Even with these recommendations, some police departments still hire officers who are attracted by the adventure of the job rather than by its service functions. An emphasis on adventure and an attitude of derring-do distance police from the community and produce a **siege mentality** that sets the police up as a "band of brothers"—or "sisters"—against everyone else. In contrast, a service-oriented police department balances enforcement activities and basic police work with sensitivity to community needs and believes that developing trust with the community will go far to solve its problems and control crime.[52]

Background checks are a vital element in the hiring process. Typically, background investigators seek evidence of good moral character, solid work habits, interpersonal skills, stress tolerance, and decision-making ability. However, background checks have not been reliable indicators of which individuals will become good officers. Background investigators can be subjective and may use past criminal records as a means to eliminate candidates, without regard to how recent a conviction was or to the facts surrounding the particular criminal event. Improperly conducted background investigations are common, especially in cases involving Black and Latino applicants being assessed by White investigators who may be unfamiliar with the culture and lifestyle of the candidates' communities.[53]

Demographics of Candidates

Over the past few decades, law enforcement agencies have increased their efforts to attract qualified minority and female candidates. Although they have unquestionably made strides, much remains to be accomplished. As you can see from examining the table, the percentages for minorities and women in law enforcement have increased, but they are still low.

BLACKS, LATINOS, AND WOMEN IN LOCAL LAW ENFORCEMENT AGENCIES
Law enforcement agencies have increased efforts to attract qualified minority and female candidates. Although strides have been made, much remains to be accomplished.

Demographic	1987 (percent)	2000 (percent)	2003 (percent)
Black	9.3	11.7	11.7
Latino	4.5	8.3	9.1
Women	7.6	10.6	11.3

SOURCE: Bureau of Justice Statistics, *Local Police Departments, 2003* (Washington, DC: Bureau of Justice Statistics, 2006), iii.

MYTH/REALITY

MYTH: Women are underrepresented in police departments today chiefly because they have only recently been permitted to become police officers.

REALITY: Marie Owens was appointed as an officer with the Chicago Police Department in 1893. Several other women were appointed soon thereafter; however, the nature of their duties was long limited to juvenile and custodial activities.[54]

The greatest disparity, by far, is in gender when measuring the percentage of women police against the percentage of women in the general population. Women have been employed by police departments in the United States since 1893, when the Chicago City Council passed an ordinance giving Marie Owens the title and pay of "patrolman." Although Owens received the title, she was given neither a uniform nor the authority to arrest. Instead, she was assigned to assist detectives with cases involving women and children and to conduct follow-up interviews of witnesses or victims.[55]

The number of female police officers has increased, and women officers now perform all law enforcement activities. Still, women are unlikely to achieve equal representation with men for several generations—if ever.[56] See the Disconnects box for some reasons why.

▼ Women are increasing their numbers in law enforcement agencies.

MYTH/REALITY

MYTH: Women are not strong enough to perform police work.

REALITY: Most police work does not require physical strength. In fact, the federal government is encouraging police departments to hire more women because females are less likely to use force inappropriately. Departments with a greater number of female officers face fewer lawsuits.[57]

Some departments are reluctant to hire women because they believe women lack the physical strength needed for police work. Yet physical strength has not been shown to correlate with either general police effectiveness or the ability to handle dangerous situations. Furthermore, female officers not only tend to exhibit more reasoned caution than their male counterparts, but the presence of female officers also encourages their male partners to proceed more cautiously.[58]

African Americans wanting to become police officers also faced discrimination. In the late 1860s, some southern cities began to hire African American males as police officers, but members of the White public strongly objected. After the end of Reconstruction (the political process designed to unify the North and South after the Civil War) in 1877, southern police departments expelled their African American officers. By 1910 there were no African American officers on southern police forces.[59]

Like the White public who objected to African American policemen, White officers also deeply resented and fought the hiring of African American officers. Departments forced to hire African Americans set aside specific positions for them

DIS Con nects

Where Are the Women?

Female police officers rely on minimal use of physical force and are typically better than men at defusing potentially violent confrontations. Women officers also often respond more effectively to incidents of violence against women—crimes that represent a large category of calls for service. They have better communication skills than their male counterparts and are better able to win the trust that motivates citizens to cooperate with community policing. All these factors work to the advantage of the police and the communities they serve.

Despite their demonstrated competence and superiority in certain functions, and despite the fact that chief executives of law enforcement agencies overwhelmingly endorse their hire, women make up a disappointingly small percentage of the law enforcement workforce. Where are the women?

A serious image problem may lie at the heart of the answer. Stereotypical images of police as macho crime fighters who spend most of their time engaged in combat and high-speed pursuits discourage women from considering careers in law enforcement. In addition, job descriptions continue to emphasize physical attributes over skills in communication and mediation. Most police academies in the United States still use a boot camp approach to training, which emphasizes tearing down individuality and rebuilding recruits in the military model. The entire setting is a subculture decidedly foreign to most women.

Given the many challenges facing modern police agencies, the need for more women in the ranks is clear. However, at the current rate of hiring, women will continue to be represented in disproportionately low numbers unless the practices that discourage them are eliminated. The police departments of Albuquerque, New Mexico, and Tucson, Arizona, have both experienced significant increases in recruitment and retention of women by implementing initiatives that emphasize the importance of interpersonal and communications skills. At the same time, initiatives have accommodated needs for child care and customized uniforms and equipment.

Observe Investigate Understand

- **Why should police departments hire women police officers—or should they?**
- **What hiring accommodations—if any—should police departments make in order to hire more women for the force?**
- **What are the benefits of having women as police officers?**

SOURCES: David Burlingame and Agnes L. Baro, "Women's Representation and Status in Law Enforcement: Does CALEA Involvement Make a Difference?" *Criminal Justice Policy Review*, 16 (2005): 391–411; National Center for Women and Policing, *Hiring and Retaining More Women: The Advantages to Law Enforcement Agencies* (Arlington, VA: National Center for Women and Policing, 2003), 1–16.

so that African American job candidates were not competing with White candidates.[60] During the 1970s, Black males began to enter police departments at meaningful levels, and their numbers continue to rise. Between 1987 and 2003, the percentage of Black local police officers increased from 9.3 percent to 11.7 percent.[61]

Black and Latino candidates are more likely to be hired as police officers in cities with substantial minority populations and Latino or Black mayors or police chiefs.[62] The number of Latino police officers increased from 4.5 percent in 1987 to 9.1 percent in 2003.[63]

Some police departments have begun recruiting gay and lesbian candidates to improve the quality of services provided to gay, lesbian, bisexual, and transgender individuals. For example, the District of Columbia's Metropolitan Police Department created a Gay and Lesbian Liaison Unit in June 2000. Other cities, including Atlanta, Georgia, and Missoula, Montana, are following this example.[64] Job opening announcements on the Web site of California's Golden State Peace Officers Association include information tailored for gay candidates. A typical example is "A current leader in gay recruitment, the Los Angeles County Sheriff's Department currently serves the City of West Hollywood, a city that embraces diversity and the gay community."[65]

Training

Training has evolved in step with policing. In the political era of policing, there was no formal training, and officers often learned how to police by serving as apprentices to senior personnel.[66] They focused on developing competence in the technical aspects of policing

◀ **GLBT Police Group in Parade**

GLBT officers have created groups to support one another.

and learning the laws of arrest, penal code provisions, patrol tactics, firearms proficiency, and interview and interrogation techniques.

Systematic basic training in police academies was one of the reforms instituted in the twentieth century. Basic training in a formal classroom environment enables uniform coverage of standard curricula designed to equip "student-officers" with the fundamental skills and knowledge necessary to perform essential policing activities. The transition from reactive policing to the more proactive orientation of community policing has meant a shift to problem solving, conflict resolution, crime prevention, and service.[67] A college education is often the best preparation for the knowledge and skills officers are asked to exercise in community policing.[68]

Training Facilities

States typically train their recruits in special academies, and each state determines its own training requirements. Some large law enforcement agencies (for example, large municipal police departments or state or federal agencies) operate their own academies. Most often, however, training centers work with institutions of higher education, especially community colleges. Prospective officers usually pay for their own training in anticipation of being recruited after they graduate.[69]

◀ **Police Recruits Training**

Law enforcement training includes a wide variety of physical and intellectual tasks.

Training Curricula

Upon completion of basic recruit training, rookie officers receive training in the field under the supervision of a senior officer. During this probationary period, supervisors scrutinize the new officer's work, actions, and attitude on a daily basis. After probation ends, the new officer is deemed competent to work alone or without close supervision. Beyond field training, all officers complete continuing professional training at specified intervals throughout the rest of their careers. This continuing training ensures refreshment of skills such as arrest and control tactics and pursuit driving and coverage of any changes in laws or agency procedures.

adult learning
Method of learning that emphasizes engaging the learner by incorporating the learner's experiences in the curriculum.

Community-oriented policing required change not only in academies' curricula but also in their teaching methods. **Adult learning**, with its emphasis on engaging the learner and incorporating his or her experiences, is rapidly replacing the traditional lecture form of academy instruction.[70] Contemporary curricula include topics such as human diversity, special populations, ethics and integrity, and community building. The State of California requires that each topic in a police academy's curriculum includes the themes of ethics and

Real Careers

RANDALL D. WATKINS

Work location: San Marcos, Texas

College(s): Texas State University–San Marcos, 2006

Major(s): Criminal Justice (BS); Military and Law Enforcement Certifications

Job title: Tactical Logistics Coordinator/Tactical Instructor, Advanced Law Enforcement Rapid Response Training Center (ALERRT)

Salary range for job like this: $50,000–$75,000

Time in job: 2 years

Work Responsibilities

I help accomplish ALERRT's mission to provide first-response officers and military personnel with the training and tools they need to perform their duties in a hostile environment. For example, I ship and receive roughly $3 million worth of training equipment all over the United States. I also teach courses in Responding to an Active Shooter, Breaching, Rural Operations, Low-Light Operations, and Tactical Rifle/ Pistol.

Why Criminal Justice?

I served 5 years on active duty in the Marine Corps Infantry and was a part of Operation Iraqi Freedom in 2003. After completing my enlistment, I went to Texas State University to finish my degree and pursue a career as a Marine Officer. In late 2004, the unit that I had just left took very heavy casualties in Iraq, so I decided to leave school and volunteer for another deployment. While conducting a raid in Iraq in May of 2005, my platoon was ambushed; we lost four Marines, and eight were severely wounded including me. After a year and a half in the hospital, I returned to Texas State and completed my degree. Being medically retired from the Marine Corps, I knew my options as an officer in the field would be limited. The ALERRT program was the answer to my prayers. I am able to use my experience and knowledge to train members of the military and law enforcement to learn from the mistakes that I made and to help them become the best officer, Marine, or soldier that they can be.

Expectations and Realities of the Job

I have been struck by the similarities and transferability of skills between military and law enforcement. For example, although the military is designed as a fighting force, the mission and role of the military in Operation Iraqi Freedom and Operation Enduring Freedom evolved to be more law enforcement in nature. And much like in the military, I have seen that law enforcement agencies must tailor their tactics according to the specific criminal.

My Advice to Students

I cannot emphasize enough how important it is to go to college. College gave me analytical and research skills that I never had before. It bridged the gap of being strictly an operator in the field to having the skill set to look at the big picture and plan for accomplishing the mission while jumping the necessary hurdles.

community policing.[71] Training for special areas such as domestic violence also serves the interests of community policing and its focus on the victims of such crimes.

Classroom training has obvious limitations, especially for critical incident training (which deals with barricaded suspects or crimes in progress), and live-scenario exercises are both expensive and potentially dangerous. **Simulation-based training** relies on computers, media players, interactive screens, and authentic-looking replicas of police firearms and vehicles to simulate field conditions.[72]

simulation-based training
Use of computers, media players, interactive screens, and authentic-looking replicas of police firearms and vehicles to simulate field conditions.

Training in Legal Issues

Training in legal issues is designed to help officers perform well; it also serves to shield officers and their employers from liability in lawsuits. This type of training ranges broadly, from the mandate to ensure the safety of a child left behind when a parent or guardian is arrested through the latest court decisions regarding warrantless searches of premises or vehicles. A prime example is the 1984 case of Eleanor Bumpurs described in the What about the Victim? box on the next page. As a result of this case, the New York City Police Department and the New York City Department of Mental Health developed an intensive week-long training program designed to educate officers about emotionally disturbed persons and how to deal with them.

Standardized training also establishes customary practices. Plaintiffs have a more difficult task of attributing bad outcomes to errors or omissions if officers are properly trained.[73] For example, if an officer frequently applied a particular control measure but on one occasion application of this measure resulted in injury to a suspect, the concerned agency (and officer) would be much better protected against liability than if the officer had not been so conscientious.

POLICE SUBCULTURE

Along with the training that new police recruits receive in police academies and in the field, they also absorb the police subculture—the attitudes, values, and beliefs—that permeates the law enforcement agency. Although U.S. police agencies are organized in formal hierarchies and have clear policies and intensive training, the police subculture may influence officer behavior more than any formal rules and orders. There are two types of police subculture.

Police occupational subculture is a set of norms and beliefs held by most officers in a given country. Police occupational subculture in the United States is influenced by the perception of the danger and irregularity of police work, the need for officers to support one another, and the necessity for them to demonstrate and maintain their authority.[74]

police occupational subculture
Norms and beliefs embraced by most officers in a given country.

A **police organizational subculture** is particular to an individual department.[75] For example, one department may value community policing, whereas another stresses maintaining law and order. One agency's subculture may rate diversity among the rank and file as a worthy goal, whereas another department feels the value of diversity is overemphasized.

police organizational subculture
Norms and beliefs particular to an individual department.

MYTH/REALITY

MYTH: Police demonstrate virtually blind obedience to the mandates of superiors and top management.

REALITY: Police occupational subculture is frequently in conflict with management's orders and directives, as illustrated by this often-cited warning from a training officer to his new charge: "Forget everything you were taught at the academy. Just keep your mouth shut and your ears open."[76]

There is no doubt that compared to most occupations, policing is dangerous. Beginning during academy training, police cadets are reminded daily of the possibility of danger. They are trained to make sure they can always see exits and entrances, even when

What about the Victim?

Eleanor Bumpurs: Shot by Cop during Eviction

On October 29, 1984, Eleanor Bumpurs, a 275-pound mentally ill Black woman, was shot and killed by New York City police officer Stephen Sullivan while being evicted from her apartment in a city housing project in the Bronx.

Bumpurs, who had been in and out of psychiatric treatment for years, had not paid her rent for three months because she complained that her toilet and stove were not working. Efforts to respond to her complaints were unsuccessful, and the Housing Authority began eviction procedures. When Bumpurs was found to be hostile, a social worker was assigned to her case. During interactions with the social worker, other workers, and a psychiatrist, Bumpurs held a large knife in her hand, but no one felt threatened by her. The psychiatrist concluded that she was psychotic, hallucinatory, and delusional and should be hospitalized.

The Social Services supervisor decided Bumpurs should first be evicted, and then hospitalized. A group of officials was sent to remove her from the apartment. When Bumpurs refused to leave, the city police and the police department's Emergency Services Unit (ESU), a squad specially trained in subduing emotionally disturbed people, were called. Two officers made a hole in the door and saw Bumpurs standing nearby wielding a knife. They called for backup personnel and additional equipment.

Three more ESU officers and a supervising sergeant arrived. One of the officers was Stephen Sullivan, who had 14 years of distinguished service in the ESU, including 18 commendations. Through the hole in the door the officers saw a hazy cloud and smelled a strong odor they thought was lye or another caustic liquid and realized that Bumpurs was standing behind the door with a long knife. The sergeant in charge decided Eleanor Bumpurs had to be subdued. The first officer who went in carried a Y-shaped bar used to restrain EDPs (in police language, Emotionally Disturbed Persons). Next came two officers carrying plastic shields to protect themselves. Sullivan, whose assignment was to protect his fellow officers, entered next, followed by the sergeant. One last officer remained at the door.

What happened next lasted only a few seconds. The ESU officers could not get Bumpurs to drop the knife and one lost his balance in the process. As he lay on the floor, Bumpurs moved toward him, making stabbing motions with the knife. Sullivan shouted for her to drop the knife. When she did not, he fired his shotgun twice. Later analyses showed that the first shot destroyed Bumper's hand and shattered the knife. The second shot killed her. The issue was raised: Why did Sullivan shoot a second time?

Officer Sullivan was acquitted of manslaughter charges in 1987. Bumpurs's family sued the City of New York and the Housing Authority for $10 million and in 1990 was paid $200,000 by the City of New York for loss of companionship, care, and assistance.

The Bumpurs case revealed the need for better training for those interacting with emotionally disturbed persons. As a result, the New York City Police Department created an "Emergency Psychology Technician" program, consisting of a week of intensive training. When law enforcement officers are properly trained to work with the emotionally disturbed, police departments are less likely to be subject to lawsuits.

Observe Investigate Understand

- **How might the situation with Eleanor Bumpurs have been handled before it escalated into a violent confrontation?**
- **How would better training in dealing with emotionally disturbed persons prevent tragic outcomes in similar cases?**
- **Are the police too quick to fire their weapons?**

SOURCES: Mario Merola, *Big City D.A.* (New York: Random House, 1988), http://bronxblotter.home.mindspring.com/merola/p009.html (retrieved March 15, 2007); "New York City to Pay Heirs in Bumpurs Case," *The New York Times*, March 29, 1991.

eating lunch in a restaurant. They are told to remember that any person with whom they come in contact could pose a physical threat. The belief that their job includes daily risks of danger is a strong component of the police subculture and creates solidarity among officers, despite the fact that most of them will never need to discharge their firearm.

At the core of police occupational subculture is the belief that officers must support one another, not only in physical confrontations but also if and when questions are raised about their actions. By and large, officers resist reporting the misbehavior of their fellows.[77] This **blue code of silence** places loyalty to fellow officers above all other values and tacitly assures all officers that they can count on a back-up to any story they tell, regardless of the truth.[78]

blue code of silence
Adherence to a code of conduct that places loyalty to fellow officers above all other values.

Officers often work under extremely tense conditions, with little information, and generally in ways that will leave someone unhappy with the outcome.[79] The public is not always sensitive to these fundamental constraints. Therefore, police officers often feel that only other officers really understand them and the conditions under which they work.

The need to maintain authority is another major component of police occupational subculture. Officers expect the individuals with whom they come in contact will be both deferential and respectful. They realize that even though they may have the power to resort to force, their greatest tool is communication. By and large, they believe if they do not maintain their authority, they will not be able to accomplish their job. Individuals who challenge police authority are likely to experience unpleasant consequences.[80]

Because officers regularly deal with people who are not honest with them and because they feel members of the public are often quick to second-guess their decisions, an "us versus them" mentality develops as a common element of police occupational subculture. Public opinion of police is generally high, but officers may have difficulty believing that. Everywhere they go in uniform, people stare at them. A sign greeting officers driving their police cars out of the garage at Calgary Police Services headquarters in Alberta, Canada, reminds them: "Drive like everyone is watching you, because they are."

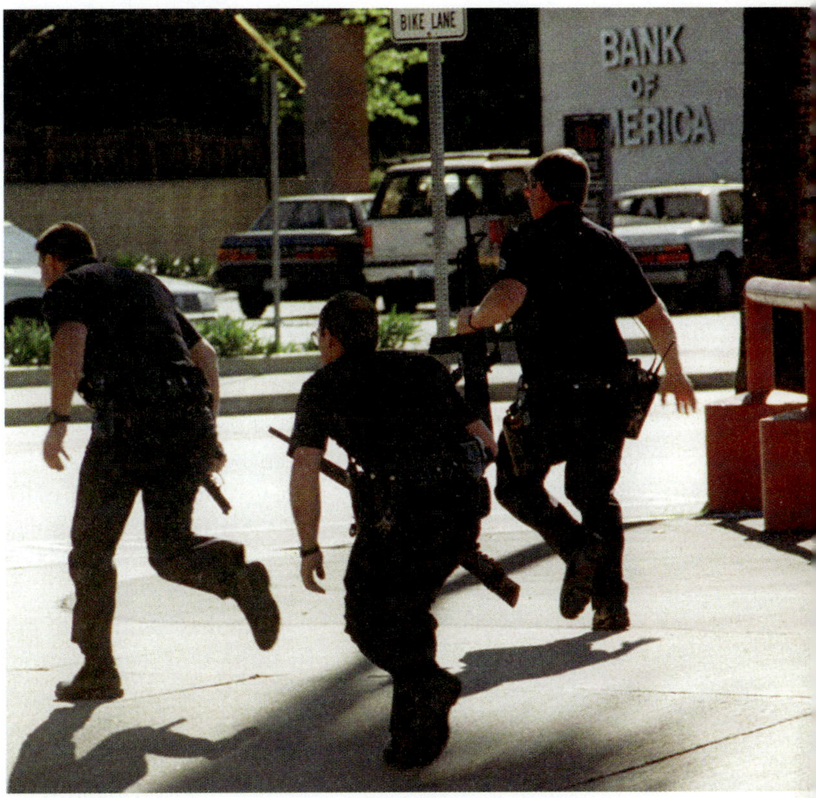

▲ **Police Charging a Bank**

Such images reinforce the idea that officers' jobs are constantly fraught with danger and excitement.

The media reinforces the message that the real work of policing is crime fighting. There is not a single major television show about the daily tasks of a community policing officer. Patrol officers also learn that crime fighting is what administrators value because police effectiveness is often assessed on measures such as numbers of citations issued, numbers of traffic stops made, numbers of arrests made, and the like. The focus on crime fighting is so deeply ingrained that even community policing officers believe those traditional police responsibilities are their most valuable work.[81]

There are merits to a strong police occupational subculture. For example, it creates a high level of group solidarity. But officers who value its main tenets are found to engage in more coercive actions, from verbal threats to physical force, than officers who do not.[82] Both within and across departments, however, there are variations in the police subculture and the degree to which officers support the subculture. The relative strength of each component and the way it influences individual officers also varies somewhat by agency.

POLICE DISCRETION

Most members of the public believe all or most actions of the police are dictated by law. Officers, however, have a high degree of **discretion** in their everyday activities that enables them to act in the manner they judge most appropriate in a given situation. When officers use discretion, the choices they make are largely up to them; they use their own judgment. Discretion is necessary because there are too many laws for all to be enforced, so police must choose which ones are most important in the particular incident. Furthermore, laws and policies are often vague and can be interpreted in many ways. The legislators who write laws and the police administrators who develop policies understand that any given situation will require officers to make the best choice for those involved.

discretion
Authority to act in a manner that officers judge most appropriate for a given situation.

There are, however, definite limits on police discretion. For example, a number of Supreme Court decisions and police policies have reduced officers' discretion regarding the use of force—especially lethal force. The discretion to initiate and continue vehicular pursuits when a driver does not comply with a police request to pull over often comes under the microscope, largely because innocent bystanders can be injured or killed during these pursuits. Some state legislatures have passed laws requiring police departments to develop or revise their policies in order to give patrol officers clear directions concerning pursuits.

As we've noted, most police work does not involve dealing with crimes. But those who call the police rarely want to hear, "No crime has been committed, so there is nothing I can do," as the officer leaves the scene. The outcomes of calls for service, which make up the vast majority of requests for police assistance, depend on how the responding officer uses discretion. Suppose a father and son are having an argument, but the dispute has not turned physical. One officer called to the scene may spend half an hour counseling the parties on conflict management. Another may simply advise the family members to make sure they do not assault each other and be gone in five minutes.

Positives and Negatives of Police Discretion

One of the greatest benefits of police discretion is that it allows officers to act in the most just manner in a given situation. Consider the following. An officer observes a driver roll through a stop sign and pulls the vehicle over. The driver is clearly upset and crying and tells the officer he was just notified that a family member has died. The officer decides there is no need to give the driver a citation and instead advises him to call someone to pick him up or perhaps talk to someone on the phone until he is calm enough to drive, for his own safety and that of others. Most people would agree the officer acted in the most just manner in that situation. Officers' discretionary decisions can sometimes fulfill the spirit of the law by not following the letter of the law.

Another benefit of police discretion is that it allows officers to decide where to focus their energies. The criminal justice system cannot manage the burden of fully enforcing all aspects of the penal and traffic codes at all times. Serious crimes occur more rarely than people think, but minor crimes are pervasive. Jaywalking, hanging objects from a car's rearview mirror, loitering, not wearing a seat belt, and underage drinking are all common occurrences. If law enforcement resources were spent on these and all the other minor offenses, police would be stretched too thin, leaving little time to devote to serious crimes.

Police discretion has many benefits, but there are disadvantages as well (see the Key Concepts feature). All professionals who exert discretion are susceptible to the temptation to abuse that authority. Discretion allows for the possibility that decisions could be influenced by race, ethnicity, class, gender, or sexuality. The Fourteenth Amendment to the Constitution, as well as state laws guaranteeing all persons equal protection under the law, should lead officers to treat all individuals equally—even when exercising discretion. But the influences of racism, sexism, and other discriminatory attitudes are widespread throughout the United States and may be found even among law enforcement personnel.

Influences on the Use of Discretion

The discretionary decisions to stop a vehicle and to make an arrest are the subject of much research. Both the seriousness of the offense and the quality of the evidence influence an officer's decision to arrest. Suspects who are male or juvenile are more likely to be arrested than are females or adults. Black suspects are significantly more likely to be arrested than White suspects. Intoxicated suspects are more likely to be arrested than those who are sober. Those who exhibit a negative attitude to police are much more likely to be arrested.[83] Finally, with all other variables held constant, White officers are more likely to

KEY CONCEPTS
Positives and Negatives of Police Discretion

Positives	Negatives
Results in increased justice	Increases the possibility for discrimination
Relieves the criminal justice system of the need to handle all cases it otherwise would receive	Allows some people who deserve punishment to avoid it

arrest than are Black officers. If the suspect is a Black male, however, a Black officer is more likely to arrest than is a White officer.[84]

Officers generally have "working rules" that influence whom they deem suspicious and, therefore, how they use their discretion when deciding whether to stop someone. If an individual seems like a person who is not usually in a neighborhood or is in a business district late at night, for instance, an officer may become suspicious.[85]

MYTH/REALITY

MYTH: Police treat all individuals the same regardless of race, class, and gender.

REALITY: A variety of characteristics of officers, citizens, victims, and suspected perpetrators influence police behavior.[86]

An officer's decision to stop a vehicle, for which the traffic code affords many possible reasons, is also a discretionary matter. The extent of **racial profiling**—police contact with an individual initiated because of the person's skin color or ethnicity—is widely debated in the United States. Although many say claims of racial profiling are divisive and unsubstantiated, numerous studies, some conducted by police departments themselves, show that drivers who are Black are disproportionately stopped by police.

racial profiling
Police contact with an individual initiated because of the person's skin color or ethnicity.

Some defenders of racial profiling say officers are merely responding to the fact that people of color are more likely to commit crime, and that police often use traffic stops as a means to uncover criminal behavior beyond violation of the traffic code. The incidence of illegal drug use, however, does not support these explanations. Based on self-reports of illegal drug use, Whites use drugs at rates about equal to Blacks. If racial profiling were good police work, then motorists of color who are stopped by police should be more likely than Whites to be engaging in criminal activity. However, data from a recent national study revealed that Black and Latino males were at an increased risk of citations, searches, arrests, and use of force, but minority drivers were *not* more likely than White drivers to be in possession of anything illegal.[87] Another defense of the higher rate of traffic stops of people of color is that they are more likely to drive recklessly. That claim has also been disproved.[88] Racial profiling is not only discriminatory, it is ineffective police work.

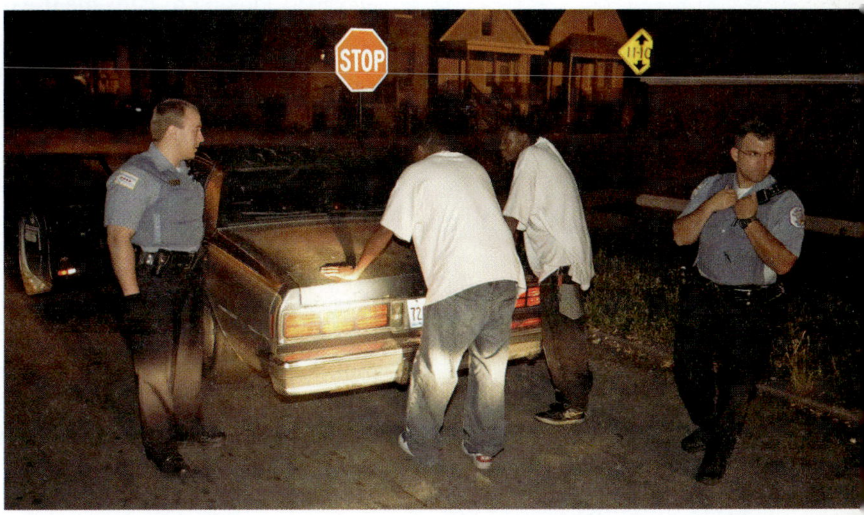

▲ Numerous studies have shown that racial profiling does occur.

Victims and the Use of Discretion

People generally assume arrest decisions are based on whether there is sufficient evidence to indicate a crime occurred. In fact, police arrest in only about half the cases in which evidence of a crime is present; the greatest influence on the decision to arrest is the victim's or complainant's preference for arrest. The public, therefore, influences how officers exercise discretion.[89]

The degree of relationship between the victim and perpetrator—whether they are family, friends, acquaintances, or strangers—also influences arrest decisions. The closer the relationship between victim and perpetrator, the less likely an arrest will be made. An arrest is more likely when two strangers are in a physical altercation than when one family member assaults another.[90] Unfortunately, this practice puts those who are the most vulnerable in greatest jeopardy. Individuals who perpetrate violence against a stranger, in a bar fight, for instance, usually never see their victim again, so the likelihood of another conflict is minimal. Victims who know their perpetrators have a much greater chance of continued interaction with them and, therefore, are at greater risk of being victimized again. Yet in situations in which the victim needs the most protection from future assaults, retaliation, and threats, an arrest is less likely to be made.

ABUSE OF AUTHORITY

Probably nothing is more harmful to a law enforcement agency than the abuse of authority. Abuse of authority damages both public confidence in the police and the ability of law enforcement administrators to control and direct the workforce. Police officers are uniquely entrusted to protect the safety and rights of all citizens. Moreover, police officers are given special powers and prerogatives—the authority to investigate people, to deny them freedom to move about, and to use force if warranted. If police departments feel their operations are placed under intense scrutiny by the media following accusations of corruption or unlawful use of force, they are quite correct. "If you can't trust the police, whom can you trust?"[91]

Two types of abuse of authority by the police are corruption and misuse of authority. The possibility of personal gain is what distinguishes the two.

Misuse of Authority

misuse of authority
Police disregard for policies, rules, or laws in the performance of their duty.

noble cause
Justification for wrongdoing committed by an officer based on the premise that the end justifies the means.

Misuse of authority occurs when police disregard policies, rules, or laws in the performance of their duty. Generally those who commit such misuse believe in a **noble cause** that they claim excuses their wrongdoing because "the end justifies the means."[92] Noble cause is present, for instance, when officers frame individuals they believe are "dirty," and who would be imprisoned but for lack of evidence. Police may also seek to administer their own "street justice" through brutal means. The police often believe that their concern for the victim justifies their behavior in such incidents. Officers may recall the brutality suffered by victims of past gang violence or drug dealing when they encounter persons trying to commit similar crimes. The police may believe any extralegal actions they take to remove perpetrators from the streets pale in comparison to the harm the next victim will suffer.[93] Many critics and reformers looking to curb the use of violence by the police fail to recognize that the use of violence against perpetrators often stems from police officers' concern for the victims.[94]

Officers who misuse their authority may face criminal prosecutions for violations of state and federal laws. However, civil lawsuits against the police for misuse of authority are more common than criminal prosecutions.[95] It is easier for victims to prevail in civil court, where the standard of proof is a preponderance of evidence, than in criminal court, which requires proof beyond a reasonable doubt. Claims charging misuse of authority often cite use of excessive force and false arrest.

Police departments and cities can be civilly liable for failures to act that result in denial of equal protection as set forth in the Fourteenth Amendment, as was demonstrated in the landmark case of *Thurman v. City of Torrington*.[96] Tracey Thurman was awarded a $1.9 million judgment as a result of the local police department's chronic failure to arrest her former husband for the violent acts he committed upon her. The large settlement made this case a catalyst for the development of mandatory arrest laws (see Chapter 7).

Source Connection

CIVIL LIABILITY FOR DEPRIVATION OF RIGHTS

www4.law.cornell.edu/uscode/42/1983.html

Title 42, United States Code, Section 1983: Civil Liability for Deprivation of Rights provides for an action at law when a citizen alleges that he has been deprived of his constitutional protected rights under color of authority.

MYTH/REALITY

MYTH: Most changes in police behavior have resulted from police efforts to serve citizens better.

REALITY: Changes in police behavior are often forced by legislative action or court cases such as *Thurman v. City of Torrington*, which gave notice to police departments across the country to treat domestic violence as they would a crime in which the perpetrator and victim do not know each other.[97]

Misuse of authority may occur in police vehicular pursuits. Police officers are charged with protecting the public, and placing the public at unnecessary risk by engaging in a high-speed chase is counter to established police protocol. In any decision to engage in a vehicular pursuit, officers must weigh the need to apprehend the suspect against the need to avoid endangering other parties. Police chases have prompted many claims of negligence and liability.[98]

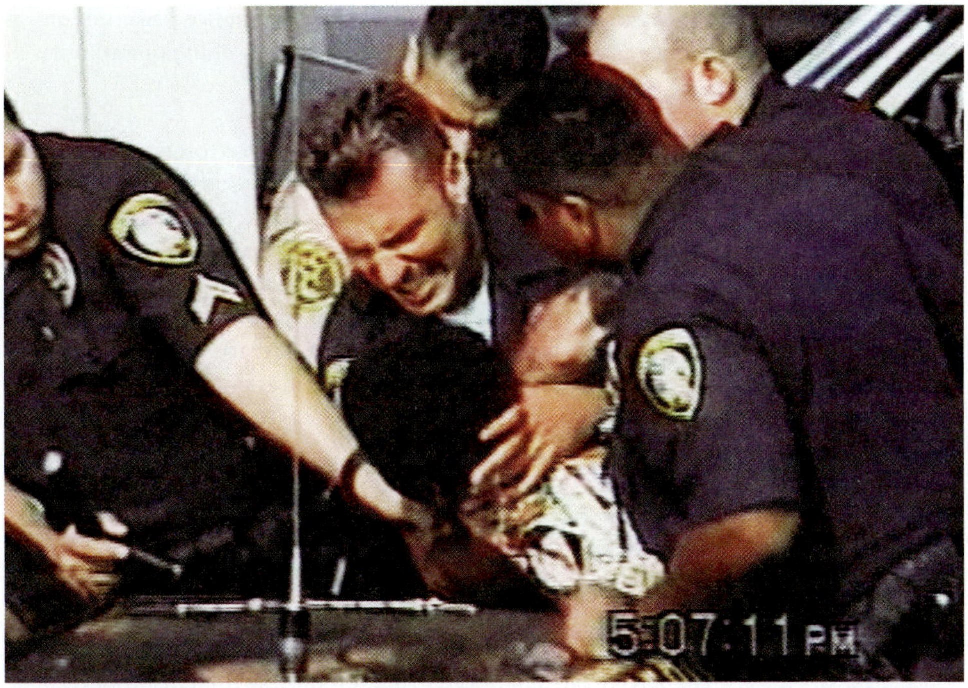

◀ **Excessive Force**

There are a variety of explanations for police use of excessive force. *What explanations, if any, justify the use of excessive force?*

Police Corruption

corruption
Misuse of authority for personal gain, such as skimming seized narcotics monies.

Corruption is generally defined as the misuse of authority for personal gain, such as skimming seized narcotics monies.[99] Motives are not limited to money, however. Personal gain may take the form of services rendered or political influence gained. A police officer may let a tavern remain open after the required closing time because a local politician is part owner and the officer believes that "looking the other way" will lead to a promotion or a better assignment through the politician's influence. Two schools of thought have developed to explain police corruption: the first focuses on the police organization, and the second on the individual.[100]

Organizational Explanations for Police Corruption

Organizational explanations of corruption often attribute it to the police occupational subculture, especially the "code of silence." The code of silence operates not only in police organizations but also exists as a mechanism of worker self-protection in virtually every group that finds itself vulnerable to discipline.[101] Officers who adhere to the code of silence are motivated by fear of being labeled a "rat" and being ostracized for snitching—and, conceivably, even being left without timely aid when endangered in a street situation.[102]

Individual Explanations for Police Corruption

Police occupational subculture helps explain why corruption exists among the rank and file. It does not, however, explain why some officers are corrupt and others are not. Individual factors also come into play.

Even the best screening protocol provides only a snapshot of an officer's psychological qualifications at the beginning of his or her career.[103] Some corrupt individuals may manage to slip through the selection screening process. Other recruits may be impulsive, harbor a sense of entitlement, lack empathy, or have difficulty following the rules. Individuals react differently to the normal day-to-day events police officers confront, and some turn to misconduct. Training police leaders to recognize and address operational stress before it leads to problems is crucial.[104]

Attaining Integrity

integrity
Adherence to moral principles and professional standards.

The opposite of abuse of authority is **integrity**, which in the context of policing refers to moral principles and professional standards that help officers resist the temptation to abuse their rights and privileges. Integrity can be an attribute of police organizations as well as of individuals.[105] Strategies to enhance integrity help reduce abuse of authority.

Management's Leading Role

Management is responsible for reducing vulnerability in the police force. For example, management must create tight protocols for handling narcotics evidence so no one can remove or skim either money or drugs. Perhaps most important, however, is management's role in setting the tone by condemning abuse. The way managers detect, investigate, and discipline misconduct shows officers how serious they consider it to be. Managers must also demonstrate their own integrity. If rank-and-file officers do not see their managers or supervisors practicing what is expected of them, integrity will be shelved in that spacious cabinet labeled "forget everything you learned in training—this is how we do it on the street."[106]

Early Warning Systems

early warning systems
Data-driven programs that identify police whose behavior suggests misconduct.

Early warning systems are data-driven programs that identify police officers whose behavior is beginning to suggest problems. By automatically recording each employee's role in all incidents including uses of force, vehicular pursuits, formal complaints, and informal counseling, the programs reveal patterns that indicate an inclination toward or potential for misconduct. Early warning systems came into use after evidence showed that in most police departments a small percentage of employees are responsible for a disproportionate share of instances of abuse of authority.[107] Only about one-third of agencies have early warning systems. Among those that do, more than 95 percent of survey respondents rate them as "effective."[108]

Targeted Integrity Testing

targeted integrity testing
Strategy of using controlled opportunities to test for unlawful or unethical behavior.

One strategy for uncovering serious, systemic corruption within a department is **targeted integrity testing** in which investigators create controlled opportunities to test for unlawful or unethical behavior. For example, they may place wallets or other valuables at crime scenes where police would be expected to find them. They then monitor officers who are suspect to see whether they "take the bait." Courts have upheld the legality of targeted integrity testing and similar covert practices as a contractual right of employers.[109]

Formal Mechanisms for Detecting and Investigating Misconduct

All large law enforcement agencies have internal affairs units to handle real and reported misconduct. Sworn personnel from within the agency staff these units. Citizen review boards also are common. These boards, which frequently include members from the community's minority groups, can review and make recommendations regarding complaints of police misconduct. They also may have authority to investigate complaints and even adjudicate claims. The presence of a Black mayor in a city increases the likelihood that a citizen review board will be created there.[110]

Independent auditors who evaluate citizen complaints generally work at high levels within law enforcement agencies or in outside government entities. They often have law degrees and are dedicated to ensuring a fair and thorough investigation.

Regardless of the mechanism, the key to a successful investigation is the ease with which people can register complaints. The intake process must be "color-blind" and accessible via many channels, including mail, anonymous phone numbers, and in-person opportunities at police stations.[111] The other crucial component is a speedy and fair resolution of complaints.

privatization
The transfer of government programs and functions to the private sector.

private security
Any individual, organization, or service—other than public law enforcement and regulatory agencies—engaged primarily in the prevention and investigation of crime, loss, or harm to specific individuals, organizations, or facilities.

UNDERSTANDING PRIVATE SECURITY

Privatization is the transfer of government programs and functions to the private sector.[112] **Private security** consists of any individual, organization, or service—other than public law enforcement and regulatory agencies—engaged primarily in the prevention and investigation of crime, loss, or harm to specific individuals, organizations, or facilities.[113] Private security agencies provide for the safety and security of private individuals and organizations and prevent and detect criminal activity on private property. They help companies enforce corporate policy and respond to natural and other disasters. Private security is indispensable as extra "eyes and ears" for matters related to homeland security.[114]

Growth

There are now at least twice as many private security officers in the United States as public law enforcement officers. One reason for this dramatic growth is the expanded service offered by private security organizations. In addition to providing security guards, these organizations install and monitor alarms, manufacture security equipment, and conduct polygraph tests, background investigations, and drug screening.[115] In addition, private security companies often augment the workforce employed by the Transportation Security Administration (TSA).

Quality Concerns

In the early days of private security services, untrained and poorly disciplined staff committed many abuses (such as use of excessive force or sleeping while on duty). No licensing standards applied, and training was superficial. Many of those hired were unfamiliar with citizens' basic constitutional protections. In fact, many security workers could have been arrested for battery had citizens known the criminal statutes and complained to police. The private security industry is slowly professionalizing, partly in response to concerns about liability. To ensure at least a minimal degree of competence among private security workers, a number of states now require a licensing process.[116]

Private Security/Law Enforcement Cooperation

Some forms of economic crime are beyond the scope or jurisdiction of local police, and some police departments are ill equipped to investigate corporate cases. System complexities make it particularly difficult for public law enforcement agencies to prevent and investigate high-tech crimes. In addition, many private enterprises—financial institutions, for example—are reluctant to have monetary losses or service interruptions due to criminal conduct (for example, via hacking) brought to the attention of their shareholders and the general public. Police are thus finding liaisons with private security agencies a useful way to increase the effectiveness of investigating and preventing crime. Collaboration is likely to help both private and public agencies prevent losses and interruption of vital services due to crime.[117] Private security firms are not always better than public law enforcement agencies, but neither are public agencies "automatically superior in every respect" to private organizations.[118] A Global View on the next page reports on the dilemma now facing the private sector in Russia as the government takes over more tasks formerly provided by private security agencies.

SUMMARY

The popular view of policing, one that is reinforced by the media, sees the police primarily as crime fighters and law enforcers. In fact, most tasks that police perform involve neither fighting crime nor enforcing the law. But when the occasion demands, the police are those who are entrusted with the authority to use force. The community policing strategy in vogue today

A Global View

The Decline of the Russian Private Security Industry

Following the collapse of the Soviet Union in 1991, the private security industry in Russia had been growing by more than 20 percent a year. Observers attributed this dramatic boom to problems with the transition to a market economy and the government's inability to provide physical and economic protection to individual and corporate citizens.

Private security companies and investigators must be licensed by the local police, but this process rarely includes more than a cursory check against criminal records. An estimated 70 percent of former KGB (the Soviet Union secret police and security agency) officers who left the service before retirement age found work in the private security sector. By the late 1990s, industry sources were claiming the industry employed three times as many people as the public police force.

In 2005, however, the government established "Okhrana," a "Unitary Federal State Enterprise," to bring an array of the state's own pseudo-private security forces (comprised of local police commands' "moonlighting" officers) together within the Ministry of Internal Affairs and essentially nationalize them. (The term *Okhrana* is derived from the internal security department that was formed in 1880 by the Russian police to combat political terrorism; it was dissolved in 1917 after the February Revolution of 1917.)[a] In 2006 a new law granted officers of Okhrana significantly wider powers, apparently to squeeze out as much of the private sector as possible. The bona fide Russian private security industry now faces the threat of being dramatically downsized—or eliminated. Disappearance of the private security industry would be particularly troublesome in light of the fact that Russia houses some of the world's most creative hackers, and public law enforcement has not given cybercrime priority status. In fact, a recent study by the Moscow-based Kaspersky Lab revealed that Russia is the world's number one spam distributor and leading innovator in virus technology.[b]

OBSERVE Investigate Understand

- **How might further expansion of Okhrana affect security, protection, and crime fighting in Russia?**
- **Why would the Russian government seek to eliminate private security agencies within the state?**
- **What are the advantages of a country's having both public law enforcement agencies and private security forces? What are the dangers of having two forces?**

SOURCES: John Barham, "Russia's Cyber Crime Haven," *Security Management* 52, no. 11 (2008): 36; Mark Galeotti, "The Rise of the Russian Private Security Industry," *Crime & Justice International* 22, no. 95 (2006): 10–12.

[a]"Okhrana," The National Archives Learning Curve, sss.sparticus.schoolnet.co.uk/RUSokhrana.htm (retrieved March 15, 2009).

[b]http://readrussia.com/blog.blah-blah/00066/ (retrieved June 26, 2009).

emphasizes crime prevention and developing a positive relationship between the police and the public. Even though policing in the United States has always been highly localized—a reflection of the high value placed on independence—law enforcement agencies exist at the federal, state, and local levels. The proliferation of agencies can afford greater protection for all citizens but can also result in the problem of fragmentation when agencies fail to communicate critical information to one another or provide duplicate services.

Law enforcement agencies recruit widely and screen recruits through a careful selection process. Selected candidates receive classroom training in police academies and one-on-one field training under the direction of a senior officer. Despite the training recruits receive, police occupational subculture may influence officer behavior more than the agency's rules and policies. Police are given wide discretion to act in the manner they deem most fitting in the particular circumstance. Still, there are some limits on their discretion, especially with the use of force and in vehicular pursuits. An element of police subculture is the need to maintain authority, but police can misuse their authority when they disregard rules, orders, and laws in the performance of their duty. Officers sometimes try to justify such misconduct by claiming adherence to a "noble cause." Police who abuse their authority for personal gain are guilty of corruption. To maintain the integrity of a department and its officers, management must investigate any suspicion of misconduct and root out those who are guilty.

OBSERVE
Investigate
Understand

Review

Identify the distinguishing characteristics of policing.

- Most of what police officers do on a daily basis has little to do with enforcing laws.
- Less than one-fifth of calls to police relate to a crime, and even less patrol time is spent on crime-related activities.
- The primary distinguishing feature of police is society's grant of authority to use physical force as necessary.

Trace the evolution of policing in the United States.

- Vigilantism was an early method for enforcing group norms.
- The first publicly funded city police departments were slave patrols.
- The innovations of the London model of policing, such as preventive patrol and hierarchical organization, had a significant influence on early urban policing in the United States.
- During the political era of policing, most police jobs were filled through political patronage.
- Changes in technology, a focus on crime control, and hiring based on merit characterized the professional era of policing.
- The present-day community policing era emphasizes a police–community partnership and proactive policing.

Describe the structure of law enforcement.

- From its inception, U.S. policing has been highly localized.
- Law enforcement agencies exist at the local (municipal and county), state, and federal levels.
- Problems resulting from fragmentation—that is, the lack of coordination among neighboring local agencies—include duplication of services and the failure to share critical information.

Recognize how recruitment, selection, and training affect quality of service.

- Law enforcement agencies are challenged to recruit for an unprecedented number of vacancies and to ensure diversity in the force.
- The selection process typically includes a test of mental ability, an interview, physical and psychological examinations, and a background check.
- Police officers today need to be service-oriented and proactive problem solvers.
- Systematic training of police officers includes classroom study at a police academy, field training under the supervision of a senior officer, continuing professional training, and training for special areas.

Describe the dynamics of the police subculture.

- Police subculture may influence officer behavior more than formal rules and orders.
- Police subculture stresses the danger and irregularity of the work, the need for officers to support one another, and the necessity of maintaining authority.
- The blue code of silence is a code of loyalty among many officers that supersedes all other values and assures support regardless of the circumstances—including misconduct.

Contrast the positives and negatives in the use of police discretion.

- Discretion enables officers to enforce the spirit rather than the letter of the law.
- Police must exercise vigilance to ensure that discretion does not become discrimination.

Distinguish between corruption and misuse of authority.

- Misuse of authority occurs when police disregard policies, rules, or laws to attain what they perceive to be a worthy outcome.
- Corruption includes taking advantage of the opportunity for personal gain.
- Management is responsible for establishing and maintaining integrity among officers and must incorporate mechanisms to facilitate reporting, detecting, and investigating allegations of abuse of authority.

Examine the extent and functions of private security agencies.

- Private security agencies direct most of their attention to the safety and security of private individuals and organizations, and to the prevention and detection of criminal activity on private property.
- Police are finding liaisons with the private sector and the business community a particularly fruitful way to increase effectiveness in attaining mutual goals of loss prevention and prevention of interruption of vital services.

Key Terms

adult learning 144
blue code of silence 146
community policing 132
corruption 151
discretion 147
early warning systems 152
fragmentation 138
frankpledge 130
integrity 151
misuse of authority 150
noble cause 150
police occupational subculture 145
police organizational subculture 145
preventive patrol 130
private security 152
privatization 152
racial profiling 149
siege mentality 140
simulation-based training 145
sworn personnel 132
targeted integrity testing 152
vigilantism 128
watch system 130

Study Questions

1. How should we define police officers?
   a. Individuals granted the power to use force
   b. Crime fighters
   c. Order maintenance providers
   d. Emergency management personnel

2. Vigilantes
   a. operated as well-organized groups.
   b. were often poor people.
   c. were paid by local governments.
   d. were mostly harmless.

3. The policing era strongly influenced by Progressive era reforms was the
   a. vigilante era.
   b. political era.
   c. professional era.
   d. community policing era.

4. A problem resulting from the structure of policing in the United States is
   a. over policing.
   b. centralization.
   c. fragmentation.
   d. under policing.

5. A preferred characteristic in police recruits is
   a. political acumen.
   b. a service orientation.
   c. adventurousness.
   d. militarism.

6. A major component of police occupational subculture is
   a. stress.
   b. individuality.
   c. blind obedience to superiors.
   d. perception of omnipresent danger.

7. Which of the following, by itself, is *least* likely to result in an arrest?
   a. Suspected narcotics dealer's negative attitude
   b. First-time, female adult shoplifter
   c. Black male hit-and-run drunk driver
   d. Felony arrest warrant

8. Which of the following is an essential component of a sound police disciplinary system?
   a. Having an early warning system
   b. Prolonging the adjudication of complaints
   c. Restricting the filing of complaints to in-person appearances at local precincts
   d. Limiting the acceptance of complaints to within a year of their reported occurrence

9. Which of the following is a reason for giving police officers a relatively high degree of discretion?
   a. Enables an increased use of racial profiling
   b. Broadens the situations in which lethal force can be employed
   c. Vagueness of many laws
   d. Noble cause

10. Which of the following describes officers acting wrongfully on the grounds that inappropriate means are justified by the outcome?
   a. Siege mentality
   b. Bounded lawlessness
   c. virtuous misconduct
   d. Noble cause

Critical Thinking Questions

1. Does the image of police as crime fighters make recruitment easier or more difficult? Why?
2. How did events in the professional era affect recruitment of Blacks to policing?
3. What accounts for the widespread police occupational subculture when neither police management nor the public condones an "us versus them" attitude?

Internet Sites

National Center for Women and Policing
www.feminist.org/police/ncwp.html
The National Center for Women and Policing promotes increasing the number of women in all ranks of law enforcement as a strategy to reduce police excessive force, strengthen community policing reforms, and improve police response to violence against women.

Bureau of Justice Statistics
www.ojp.usdoj.gov/bjs/pub/pdf/lpo3.pdf
The Bureau of Justice Statistics publishes the results of an annual survey of local police departments. The survey report presents data descriptive of local police departments' personnel, expenditures and pay, operations, community policing initiatives, written policies and procedures, information systems, and equipment.

Internal Affairs News
www.officer.com/article.jsp?id
Officer.Com provides full text articles on incidents of corruption and misuse of authority and reports on the breadth of incidents of serious misconduct occurring nationwide.

Suggested Readings

Egon Bittner, *Aspects of Police Work* (Boston: Northeastern University Press, 1990).
This classic work on policing reveals what makes the police the police. It describes the fundamental characteristics of policing and explains why the power to use force is so essential in understanding the relationship between law enforcement officers and the public.

Samuel Walker and Charles M. Katz, *Police in America: An Introduction* (New York: McGraw-Hill, 2008).
This excellent textbook on policing in the United States incorporates scholarship on policing in a readable, student-friendly style.

Robert Worden, "The 'Causes' of Police Brutality: Theory and Evidence on Police Use of Force," in *The Police in America: Classic and Contemporary Readings*, eds. Steven G. Brandl and David S. Barlow (Belmont, CA: Wadsworth, Cengage Learning, 2004): 128–173.
This work explains the factors that affect police officers' legitimate and illegitimate use of force.

Policing Operations

CHAPTER 6

OBSERVE Investigate Understand

After reading this chapter, you should be able to:

- Identify the principal policing roles.
- Compare the various policing strategies.
- Describe the different jobs in policing.
- Explain how police departments strive to maximize their resources.
- Identify the factors that shape public opinion about the police.
- Compare the service needs of diverse populations.

Realities and Challenges

A Rescue Turned Tragic

In 2008, New York City police received a call regarding a Brooklyn resident who was acting strangely and screaming in his third-floor apartment. Members of the Emergency Service Unit of the New York City Police Department (NYPD) were soon on the scene. The man, 35-year-old Iman Morales, suffered from mental illness and was apparently threatening to kill himself. When officers arrived at his apartment, Morales was naked and uncooperative. They chased him around his apartment as Morales jabbed wildly at them with an eight-foot fluorescent light bulb. Morales led the chase out to his fire escape. When officers followed, Morales jumped from the fire escape to the narrow ledge on top of a security door. There he stood, just out of reach of the officers, naked, ranting, and erratically swinging the light tube.

Police repeatedly asked Morales to come down. This continued for about 30 minutes until a police lieutenant gave the order for another officer to fire a Taser stun gun (Conducted Energy Device, or CED) at Morales. When Morales was hit with the Taser, he fell headlong to the sidewalk 10 feet below and died shortly after from serious head trauma.[1]

The tragic story spread rapidly across the media in New York City. Amateur photos and videos of the incident surfaced almost immediately. Newspapers and blogs were quick to brand the NYPD as the heavies in this case, using such vivid headlines as "Cops in Nude Taser Slay."[2] The NYPD released a formal statement the same day as the incident indicating that the use of the Taser in this situation was a direct violation of department policy, indicating that "when possible, the CED should not be used . . . in situations where the subject may fall from an elevated surface."[3]

The NYPD dealt swiftly with this case of a rescue attempt gone terribly wrong. The lieutenant who gave the order and the officer who fired the weapon were both immediately reassigned to administrative duties. All 400 officers in the Emergency Service Unit were ordered to take a refresher course on how to deal with those suffering mental illness. The lieutenant, a 21-year veteran of the force, was so emotionally distraught by the outcome that he committed suicide just days after Morales's death.[4]

This terribly tragic case that resulted in the loss of both a civilian's and an officer's life illustrates the complexity of situations that the police face every day. Policing operations are continually challenged to adapt their strategies, organization, and know-how to a broad and almost unimaginable range of possible situations in need of their expertise. Further complicating things are the special skills and approaches needed to work effectively with the many kinds of populations found in a police jurisdiction, including the elderly, people with disabilities, homeless individuals, and persons suffering mental illness.

In this chapter you will examine the functions and services that make up policing operations. As we review proven strategies for fighting crime and the key duties assigned to police officers, you will also see differences between the popular image of policing operations and the reality of a typical officer's day-to-day activities. Police work encompasses a variety of roles and tasks. Within a week's tour of duty, a single officer might respond to calls relating to found property, injured person, shots fired, abandoned car, traffic collision, barking dog, and landlord-tenant dispute. These calls, and any number of others, constitute the essential fabric of police work.[5]

POLICING ROLES

Preview

The popular image of a law enforcement officer is that of a heroic crime fighter who puts his or her life on the line every day. In the movies and on television, police officers spend most of their time combating criminals and rescuing victims from the grip of gun-toting, drug-sniffing thieves, killers, and psychopaths. Reality is a far less dramatic vision of law enforcement. About half of all calls to police result in the dispatch of a police officer, but often upon interviewing the caller, it becomes apparent that dispatch of an officer may not be necessary. For example, questioning the caller may reveal that the crime occurred some days earlier and does not now require an on-scene investigation. In such a case the victim could have a police report prepared at the police station. Contrary to popular belief, most calls do not involve in-progress violent crimes or criminal activities requiring arrest. Between 70 and 80 percent of dispatches are based upon requests to maintain order in the community or to provide a certain service.[6] Only 19 percent of citizen calls for police service involve a crime, and only 2 percent involve a violent crime.[7] In fact, only 39 percent of crimes are even reported to the police.[8] Still, whether or not a crime is reported, police are also responsible for enforcing the law. Thus three principal policing roles are maintaining order, enforcing the law, and providing services.

Maintaining Order—Keeping the Peace

MYTH/REALITY

MYTH: Police work primarily entails responding to crimes in progress or crimes that have just occurred.

REALITY: The vast majority of calls to police relate to neither violent confrontations nor criminal activities requiring arrest, but rather to minor disputes such as a landlord-tenant disagreement or requests for service such as a vehicle blocking a driveway.[9]

The first of the three major policing roles is **maintaining order**, or keeping the peace. The goal of maintaining order is to reinforce informal control mechanisms already operating in the community.[10] Sometimes this role involves enforcement of local statutes and laws, such as when the police respond to complaints about someone disturbing the peace. At other times the peacekeeping role involves activities undertaken to maintain the civility of life in the community. For example, the police may be called to investigate and deal with an abandoned car. Police officers deal with many incidents not by enforcing the law but rather by handling the situation.[11] Typical examples of maintaining order, or the peacekeeping function, include traffic control and managing crowds during sporting events, concerts, and parades. Officers engaged in maintaining order typically use informal sanctions such as warnings far more than formal sanctions such as citations or arrests.

maintaining order
Peace-keeping activities, including enforcement of quality of life laws such as no loitering.

law enforcement
The police agency's application of the criminal code to specific situations.

Enforcing the Law—When Arrest Is Needed

The primary function of **law enforcement** is the application of the criminal code to specific, developing situations. But the process of enforcing laws is not as clear cut as you might expect. There are more laws in the criminal codes than police can routinely enforce, so they enforce laws based on their department's priorities, which are determined by such factors as the seriousness of a crime and the availability of police resources. These priorities are conveyed through departmental directives, training, peer interactions,

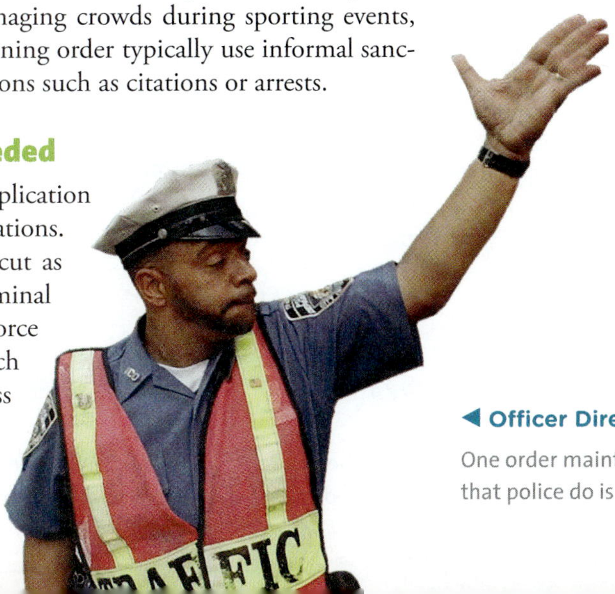

◀ **Officer Directing Traffic**

One order maintenance activity that police do is traffic control.

KEY CONCEPTS
Policing Roles

Function	Definition	Example
Maintaining order	Keeping the peace	Managing crowds
Enforcing the law	Applying criminal laws	Making an arrest
Providing service	Non–law enforcement activities provided to residents	Giving someone directions

and the preferences of supervisors. Some laws are minor offenses, such as jaywalking, while others have a more serious impact on the community, such as toxic waste dumping. Police often tailor enforcement actions to community norms. For example, they may routinely arrest shoplifters if that is what local retailers desire.

Apprehending suspects lies at the heart of the law enforcement function. The degree to which patrol officers and follow-up investigators work cooperatively will, in many cases, determine the quality of crime scene investigations and thus their outcome—that is, whether or not officers apprehend suspects.

Providing Service—Nonemergency Police Work

service activities
Non-law enforcement activities performed by officers on an as-needed basis.

Service activities are non–law enforcement duties performed by police officers on an as-needed basis. Such activities include giving directions, arranging for tows of disabled vehicles, assisting disoriented elder adults, and arranging for barricade placement at dangerous spots along public roads. These duties fall to the police primarily because of their round-the-clock availability.

The meaning of "service" in U.S. policing has significantly developed from its early politically based form. A new service orientation evolved in the later twentieth century as criminal justice scholars and policing practitioners recognized the value of community outreach both to reduce crime and address community needs on a broad scale.

POLICING STRATEGIES

Reducing and responding to crime remains a key focus of police work. Police departments have developed several approaches to preventing and addressing criminal activity. These strategies are tailored to different types of crime situations.

Preventive Patrol

preventive patrol
The practice of assigning an officer to random patrol of a neighborhood to serve as a deterrent to a variety of street-level crimes.

The assumption behind the strategy of **preventive patrol**, in which officers randomly patrol a neighborhood, is that the visible presence of an officer serves as a deterrent to a variety of street-level crimes, including prostitution, drug dealing, burglaries, and robbery. Preventive patrol is most often conducted by patrol car, but police may also patrol on foot or by bicycle. The common feature of preventive patrol is the clearly identifiable presence of a uniformed police officer. Preventive patrol focuses on reducing street crime rather than offenses committed in the privacy of people's homes.

MYTH/REALITY

MYTH: Police presence reduces crime.

REALITY: Police presence alone does not reduce crime.[12]

The Kansas City Preventive Patrol Project, a police study conducted in 1974, was designed to test the degree to which preventive patrol affected a variety of factors, including offense rates, response time, the number of traffic accidents, level of public fear, and public satisfaction with the police. To measure the influence of preventive patrols on crime levels, the researchers created three different kinds of districts in Kansas City. One type of district maintained the same number of patrols as before the study. A second type eliminated preventive patrol units altogether and required officers to leave the district immediately after responding to a call for service. In the third type of district, the number of patrol officers was increased.

The results of the study shocked police administrators and academics. The level of patrol in a neighborhood had no effect on any of the factors under study. There was no significant relationship between the number of officers patrolling a district and the number of crimes committed, number of vehicle accidents, level of fear, level of support for the police, or response time to calls for service.[13]

▲ Police Officer Conducting Preventive Patrol

A typical police strategy is random patrol of neighborhoods.

Perhaps we should not be so surprised by the findings of the study. The assumption that preventive patrol reduces crime also presumes that offenders are acting rationally, but criminal behavior is influenced by a variety of factors that limit rational decision making. Offenders may find themselves in situations that lead to criminality or suffer from maladies that affect their mental capacity.[14]

Problem-Oriented Policing

A strategy proposed by Herman Goldstein in the late 1970s, **problem-oriented policing** focuses on discovering the underlying causes of problems. Goldstein encouraged police departments to consider the complexity of problems rather than narrowly focusing on crimes—a change from previous policing strategies. For example, suppose there have been several arsons in an area. Some were the work of teenagers burning down buildings, while others occurred when homeowners set fire to their homes to collect insurance monies. Both would be considered crimes of arson, but the underlying causes would be completely different and would call for different police responses. To identify the underlying causes of problems and then appropriately respond to them, Goldstein recommended that police take specific sequential steps.[15]

problem-oriented policing A policing strategy based on conducting specific and detailed research on a community's problems to discover the underlying dynamics of crime.

The first step in a problem-oriented policing strategy is conducting specific and detailed research on a community's problems to reveal the underlying dynamics of crime.[16] For example, suppose police discovered that burglaries in a college town largely victimized students and increased when the college was on break and most students had gone home. They noticed that the pattern of these crimes differed from that of other residential crimes and commercial burglaries. The crimes tended to victimize a specific population (college students), occur at particular times of year (during the breaks), and take place in a specific area of town (near the college). Once departments identify characteristics of burglaries, they can more effectively respond to and prevent these crimes.

The second step in problem-oriented policing is to examine the ways in which the police department currently deals with a particular problem in order to identify the most effective responses. In the case of campus burglaries, the department would examine how it has dealt with such criminal patterns before and what strategies were most successful in preventing burglaries and apprehending perpetrators. Problem-oriented policing strategies also include learning from other departments' successful practices and published studies on policing. The key concept in this second step is that departments are reviewing both their own responses and other relevant research as well.[17]

Once the department has identified the problem and researched ways to deal with it, the third step is devising strategies to address the problem. Police officials must consider how they might relay needed information to residents, develop new skills in their officers, and enhance community resources.[18] New skills might include learning how to adapt campus patrols while college students are out on break or introducing surveillance cameras to watch over the dormitories.

Many police departments engage in some version of problem-oriented policing. The way problem-oriented policing is practiced in any individual department is influenced by both its priorities and resources. In one approach, departments assign problem-oriented policing officers to a particular geographic area that suffers from a variety of specific problems. Another approach is to assign these officers to specific problems that cross neighborhood boundaries. For example, police departments have used problem-oriented policing to tackle crimes involving both domestic violence and gang activity. In the case of domestic violence (DV), departments have created DV units to follow up with individuals who have made calls for police help in such cases. With gangs, teams of officers may successfully reduce some crimes by maintaining close contact with area youths known to have gang associations.

One model of problem-oriented policing is called SARA (Scanning, Analysis, Response, and Assessment). In the *scanning* step, the police department identifies the problem, its consequences, the frequency with which it occurs, and any other information relevant to understanding it. The next step, *analysis,* identifies anything that may be causing or influencing the problem. During the analysis step, police department researchers gather information on the problem to better understand how the department is currently handling it. While conducting analysis, the department will also learn what resources are already available to help solve the problem. In the third step, *response,* participants think creatively about ways to solve the problem. As part of the response step, a department will most likely learn how other jurisdictions have dealt with the same problem. The department then creates an implementation plan with clear objectives that will allow for measurable results. The final step is *assessment,* during which officers determine whether the program was put into effect as intended and whether the goals were met. A plan for continuing assessment of the chosen strategy may also be a part of the assessment stage. Figure 6-1 illustrates the SARA process.

community-oriented policing
A policing strategy that depends on getting community members to address the problems that plague their neighborhoods.

police–community reciprocity
A policing practice that relies on collaboration between police and community members to solve and prevent crime.

decentralization of command
The fanning out of substations in various areas so the police maintain a physical presence throughout the city.

proactive foot patrol
A component of community policing that leads to increased interactions between the police and community members to improve relationships.

Community-Oriented Policing

A policing strategy that focuses on reducing crime and disorder, such as loitering and graffiti, by involving residents in the job of policing is **community-oriented policing**. It has four components: police–community reciprocity, decentralization of police units, proactive policing using foot patrols, and the civilianization of the police force.[19] These four components result in policing that is focused more on maintaining positive police–community relations than on crime rates.

Police-community reciprocity requires collaboration between police and community members to solve and prevent crime. The success of community policing relies on a mutually beneficial bond between the police and the public. Community policing contends that policing is the responsibility of *all* members of a neighborhood and that the public is a partner in the effort to fight crime, disorder, and other community problems.[20]

A second component of community policing is **decentralization of command**, the creation of substations or police buildings in various areas so the police maintain a physical presence throughout the community. Decentralization gives individual patrol officers more discretion to come up with ways to solve neighborhood problems. The belief is that because patrol officers interact daily with people in the neighborhood, they are better positioned than police managers to know what that community needs.

A third component of community policing is **proactive foot patrol**. Walking beats allows officers to learn more about the people in the neighborhoods they patrol and to develop relationships

Notice that problem-oriented policing calls for specific sequential steps.

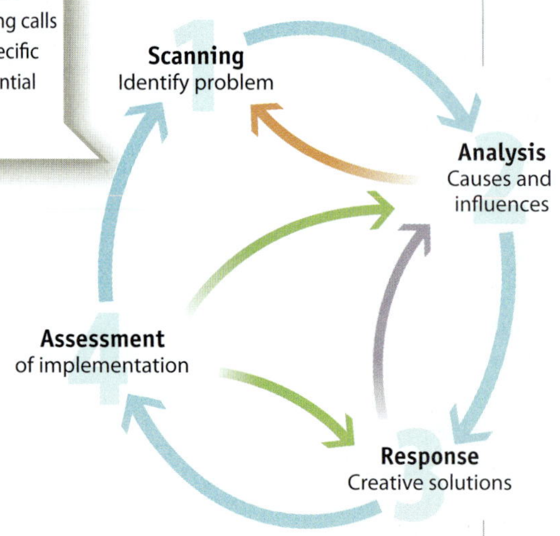

FIGURE 6-1 The SARA Process
SOURCE: Center for Problem-Oriented Policing

with them. Officers assigned to foot patrols generally report higher levels of satisfaction in their jobs.[21] Perhaps the greater satisfaction occurs because officers on foot patrol have more opportunities to interact with a wide variety of people rather than dealing almost exclusively with suspects and victims.

Civilianization of the police force, the fourth component of community policing, involves assigning to civilians tasks previously performed by police officers. The goal of civilianization is to increase the number of community residents actively involved in

civilianization
A component of community policing that increases the number of community residents active in the profession of policing by assigning to civilians tasks previously performed by sworn officers.

Real Careers

STACY SHAMBLIN

Work location: Reno, NV

College(s): University of Nevada, Reno, 2007

Major(s): Criminal Justice (BS)

Job title: Methamphetamine Program Coordinator, Reno Police Department

Salary range for jobs like this: $35,000–$50,000

Time in job: 1.5 years

Work Responsibilities

I coordinate drug education and prevention activities for the Reno Police Department. We educate citizens about the drugs commonly abused in their area, the effects and paraphernalia associated with those drugs, and drug prevention strategies. In general, the program serves middle and high school students, parents, and professionals who work with teens and young adults. My role in the program is to fulfill requests for instructional materials and presentations and to provide drug awareness training targeted for the specific audience. Trends in substance abuse often change, and I adapt our curriculum to provide the most accurate information possible.

In addition to managing the program, I am responsible for monitoring and reporting quarterly progress to the federal office that funds our activities—COPS, or Community Oriented Policing Services (part of the U.S. Department of Justice). Although writing reports is not as exciting as planning presentations, it is certainly an important aspect of my job because these reports determine whether our program will continue to receive federal funding.

Why Criminal Justice?

When I was a teenager, I wanted to pursue a career as a criminal prosecutor. As I prepared for college, I realized I wanted to have a more direct impact on crime and public safety through a career in civilian law enforcement. I did not know what careers were possible in law enforcement other than Police Officer, so I consulted my professors and worked two internships while in college.

During my junior year, I applied for the FBI Scholastic Honors Internship Program and was selected to intern in the Economic Crimes Unit at FBI Headquarters in Washington, D.C. My summer with the FBI proved to be a valuable work experience and was certainly a great asset to my resume, but the internship that was most instrumental to my current career was at the Crime Analysis Unit of the Reno Police Department. Shortly after I graduated, my former supervisor, who was impressed with my work as an intern, notified me that the position of Methamphetamine Program Coordinator had become available.

Expectations and Realities of the Job

I have been somewhat surprised by my influence in making key decisions for the program. Even though I am an entry-level employee, I have been encouraged to suggest and even implement new strategies to improve the success of the program. I am impressed with the effectiveness of the COPS approach to tackling drug problems, which utilizes cooperation and partnerships with outside agencies. I frequently work with schools and community organizations, such as Join Together Northern Nevada, Nevada Prevention Resource Center, and Boys & Girls Club.

My Advice to Students

Apply for internships. My internship experiences gave me a competitive edge in the employment marketplace. They allowed me to explore potential career opportunities, including some nontraditional criminal justice careers that I previously had not known about. In addition, my internships provided me with opportunities to build my project management and professional communication skills, which are applicable to any career in law enforcement. Internship experiences definitely helped me begin my new role as Methamphetamine Program Coordinator with confidence in myself and my abilities.

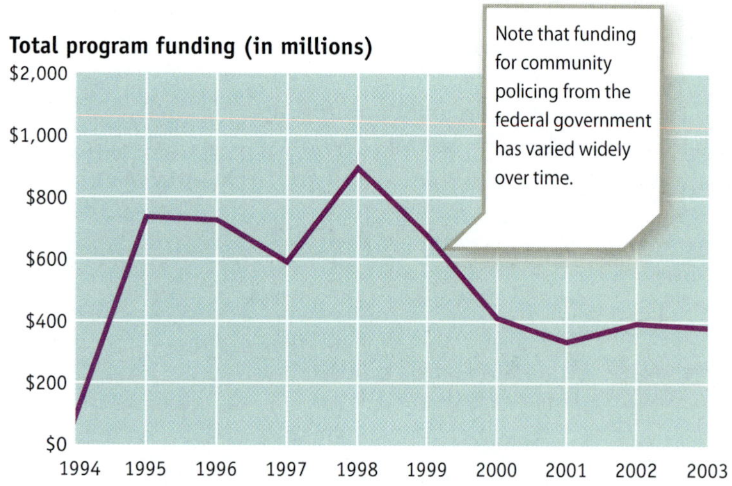

FIGURE 6-2 Community-Oriented Policing Funds Granted to Police Departments

policing. Civilian Community Service Officers (CSOs) might help with gathering nonemergency reports or addressing community problems that are not of a serious criminal nature. CSOs typically perform tasks that involve no inherent danger or risk. For example, if a resident reports that her house was burglarized while she was on vacation, a police department may send a CSO to take the report because the crime occurred several days before the call for service, and no one is in imminent danger.

Although the goals of community policing are laudable, this policing strategy has come in for some criticism. For example, scholars have raised questions about what constitutes a community and how different groups—the police, other city employees, or residents—define geographic areas as a community. In other words, what the police define as a community, the residents may not.[22] Some critics point out that police do not communicate equally with all members of a community. Often individuals with greater resources are also more likely to have opportunities to interact positively with police. Other critics observe that all members of the community do not always agree on identified problems and solutions.[23] Some critics view community policing as the latest strategy in the overpolicing of Blacks, as police take advantage of the high number of police–resident contacts that are part of community policing to keep surveillance over this group of people.[24]

Implementing Community Policing

Because community-oriented policing is a relatively new and different policing strategy, there have been difficulties in implementing its various components. Some police departments have received federal grants to encourage them to implement community policing programs. In 2008, the U.S. Department of Justice's Community Oriented Policing Services (COPS) office granted funds to 308 police departments.[25] In 2006, COPS spent over $200 million to fund community policing projects for state and local agencies nationwide.[26] Figure 6-2 illustrates how COPS funding has varied over time. Despite this federal financial assistance, questions remain about the degree to which departments have adopted community policing.

One measure of the implementation of community policing strategies is the way in which a department deploys its officers. A 1999 survey of local police administrators across the country revealed the following:

- 64 percent reported they employed full-time officers as community resource or community relations officers.
- 63 percent responded that their officers used foot or bicycle patrol on a "routine" basis.
- 79 percent of the agencies had met with community groups in the previous year.[27]

Although these statistics indicate that not all departments have adopted all aspects of community policing, the data clearly show that many law enforcement agencies are incorporating at least some of the components of community-oriented policing, such as foot patrol and police–community consultations.

Another way to measure whether a department has implemented community policing is to examine its organizational structure. Community policing reformers argue that community policing allows police to change their relationship with the public, partly by reducing the number of ranks in a department. Then, there are not as many different levels

Source Connection

OFFICE OF COMMUNITY ORIENTED POLICING SERVICES

http://www.cops.usdoj.gov/

The U.S. Department of Justice's Office of Community Oriented Policing Services (COPS) offers a variety of resources on community policing.

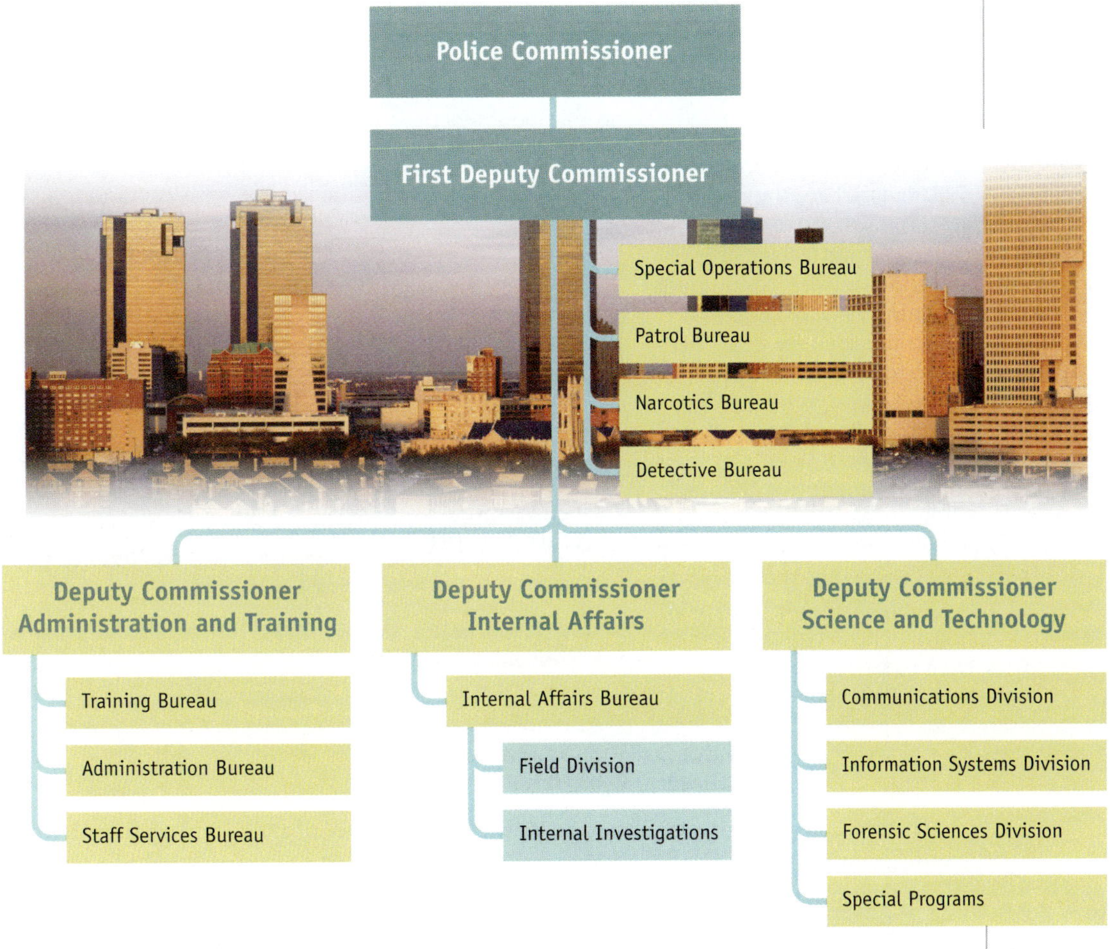

FIGURE 6-3 Hierarchical Structure of a Traditional Police Department

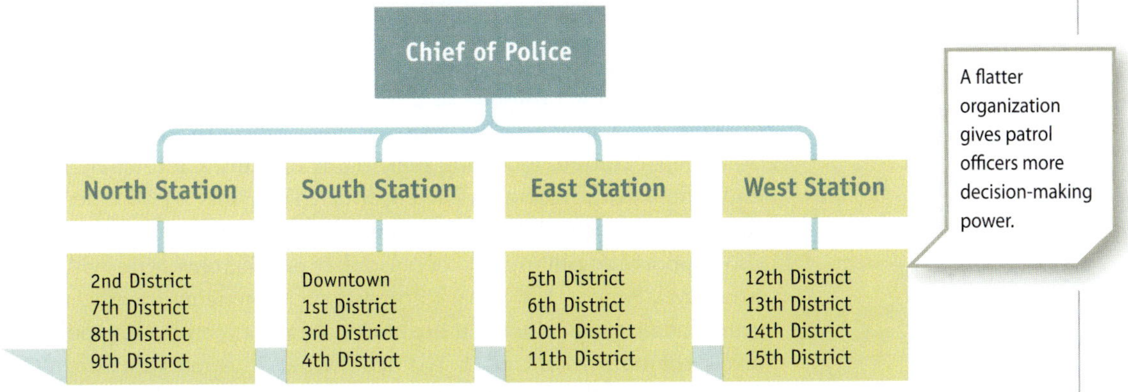

FIGURE 6-4 Structure of a Community-Oriented Policing Department: Fewer Ranks and Sections

of officers from the patrol level to the chief's level. Because community policing emphasizes that officers should be generalists and deal with all the problems of a community, some police departments have reduced the number of department sections that focus on a particular task or crime. There is, however, no significant difference in organizational structure between departments that claim to be using community policing and those that do not, which means that departments who say they are implementing community policing have not reduced either the number of ranks in the department or the number of sections focused on a particular task or crime.[28] As shown in Figures 6-3 and 6-4, the

Race, Class, Gender

Community Policing as "Women's Work"

Criminal justice professor Susan Miller studied the adoption of community-oriented policing in a major U.S. city. The first officers willing to become neighborhood police officers, or NPOs, were mainly women, men of color, and gay and lesbian officers. White male heterosexual officers tended to see community policing as social work and, hence, "women's work."

A crime-fighting ethos and a masculine identity, regardless of an officer's sex, are highly valued in the police subculture. In Miller's study, male heterosexual officers who worked as NPOs tended to emphasize traditionally masculine aspects of the job. They would, for example, work with the residents of their assigned neighborhoods by organizing competitive children's sports such as a soccer or baseball team. Men who interacted with children in these ways were highly praised, while female officers who interacted with children in activities such as working with Girl Scouts were not acknowledged. (In the same way, when someone sees a man changing a diaper a typical response is, "What a good father!" But when a woman changes a diaper no one notices.) Because men who do "women's work" often expect their sexuality to be questioned, male NPOs made sure no one doubted their heterosexual status. For example, in a variety of conversations they often made sure to mention their female significant others or their children.

Miller's research illustrates how the police subculture can influence a department's ability to implement new strategies. If community policing is not seen as "real" police work, officers will not value it and there will continue to be barriers to its implementation. Miller argues that for officers to truly value community policing strategies their departments need to encourage them to do so by providing job incentives such as promotions.

OBSERVE Investigate Understand

- **Is community policing real police work, or is it social work?**
- **What obstacles hinder the implementation of a community policing strategy?**
- **How could police leaders make community policing tasks more appealing to all officers?**

SOURCE: Susan Miller, *Gender and Community Policing: Walking the Talk* (Boston: Northeastern University Press, 1999).

structure of a department that has reduced the number of ranks and sections looks very different from that of a traditional department. A department structured like that shown in Figure 6-4 is more likely to give patrol officers increased discretion, which is a central tenet of community policing. Thus, a department like that pictured in Figure 6-4 is likely implementing a community-oriented policing strategy.

Implementing community-oriented policing requires change not only in organizational structure but also in police culture. Because of these two requirements, implementation of community policing across the nation is occurring slowly.[29]

Traditional police culture regards the tasks of crime prevention and law enforcement as the sole responsibility of the police. In community policing, crime prevention is considered a joint responsibility of police officers and community members. This notion is a fundamental change in the understanding of what makes up police work. Changing any professional culture, including policing, is difficult. Cultural changes often start with the leadership of organizations. There is little chance that a police department will implement community policing if the chief is not fully committed to the strategy.[30] Patrol officers must also support the philosophy, because they are the ones who will put it into effect at the street level. Support for such a cultural change among police officers, however, is uneven. In general, officers of color are more likely to support community policing.[31] The story in the box "Community Policing as 'Women's Work'" illustrates the difficulties in changing police culture. Some officers are more likely to volunteer to work as community policing officers, and leaders need to offer incentives to officers to obtain the necessary changes.

The Impact of Community Policing

During the early 1990s, when community policing became the model for departments, the crime rate declined, but community-oriented policing was not necessarily the reason.[32] If community policing does not reduce crime, why is the strategy so popular with federal, state, and local governments?

Crime reduction is not the only way to assess the impact of community policing. Another significant measure is the community's confidence in the police and the development of a positive relationship between the police and the public—a central goal of community-oriented policing. Volunteers in community policing programs within their local police departments generally report high confidence in the police. Furthermore, law-abiding individuals who have a greater number of contacts with the police department are more likely to have a higher level of support for their police.[33]

Aggressive Order Maintenance

Disorder is frequently a major contributor to residents' discontent with their neighborhoods, especially in urban communities. Residents often fear and disapprove of vagrants, drunks, addicts, loud teenagers, and others who may frequent the streets.[34] For some, the presence of such people means that the neighborhood is experiencing disorder.

One strategy for fighting disorder is **aggressive order maintenance**, or zero-tolerance policing. Aggressive order maintenance entails police focusing on minor public order offenses that affect residents' quality of life. For example, they target abandoned cars, graffiti, public urination, and loitering by identifiable gang members with "stop and frisk" actions and field interrogations. Aggressive order maintenance results in an increase in arrests for minor offenses.

aggressive order maintenance Policing activities that address noncriminal or minor offenses that affect residents' quality of life.

One influential perspective on aggressive order maintenance goes by the name of the **broken windows theory**. Proposed by social scientists James Q. Wilson and George Kelling, the broken windows theory argues that there is a relationship between the deterioration of a neighborhood and higher crime rates. In their view, disorder leads to crime because criminals assume that a neighborhood that tolerates disorder—in the form of broken windows, graffiti, and the like—will also ignore more serious criminal acts.[35] In this view, minor crimes lead to more serious crimes. The broken windows theory also holds that having officers focus on minor offenses will reduce serious offenses. This point of view seems logical, but showing a relationship between disorder and crime is not always easy.

broken windows theory Theory proposing that disorder leads to crime because criminals assume a neighborhood that tolerates disorder will also ignore criminal acts.

The broken windows theory has had a major impact on how criminal justice professionals and members of the public think about crime and how they believe police departments should use their resources. The idea that disorder leads to more serious crimes suggests that police officers should focus more of their time on addressing minor nuisance-type enforcement that previously was unlikely to get much notice from patrol officers. Wilson and Kelling also contend that a police focus on reducing disorder would ease public fear. Hence, if police could reduce disorder, they could also reduce more serious crimes and fear of crime.

Although the broken windows theory is politically popular, the relationship between disorder and crime is more complicated. The link between disorder and crime has not been proven, with the exception of the crime of robbery.[36] The lack of community efficacy, or the feeling among community members that they can do something about their neighborhood, leads to both disorder and crime. When people in a neighborhood are bound together by common values about public disorder and crime, they create a common community culture and a sense of community efficacy. Community efficacy is more common in affluent communities, which means that poor communities are more likely to have neighborhoods characterized by disorder.

Many of the ideas behind the broken windows theory remain popular. For example, some metropolitan law enforcement agencies, such as the New York City Police Department, see aggressive order maintenance as a successful policing strategy. They believe that strict enforcement of minor offenses increases the quality of life in neighborhoods that were previously considered blighted. Supporters of aggressive order maintenance argue that it reduces crime and residents' fear of crime. Opponents of the strategy argue that aggressive order maintenance results in targeted policing in poor neighborhoods and focuses mainly on people of color. One community's efforts, described in "Broken Windows Theory in the Real World: A Plan for Success in White Plains, New York," illustrate how aggressive enforcement can be applied as part of a broader community-oriented policing approach for reducing street crime.

a Case in Point

Broken Windows Theory in the Real World: A Plan for Success in White Plains, New York

All law enforcement agencies do not apply the practice of community policing equally. In some jurisdictions, community policing becomes little more than a program of community relations. The broken windows approach is often watered down to mean nothing more than maintaining zero tolerance for the physical deterioration of the neighborhood without regard for the concerns of residents. The inherent value of broken windows, however, is that the police are called on to address social disorder and incivility to prevent more serious crime while engaging residents to exert their own control over their neighborhood.

One police department that made a serious commitment to community policing is that of White Plains, New York. After only a few years, they achieved remarkable success in applying the principles of community policing to curtail a rise in street violence and cultivate a strong, mutually beneficial partnership between the police and the community.

In 2006, a series of violent crimes sprang up in downtown White Plains and in the neighborhood of city public housing facilities. The offenses were generally gang related. The White Plains Police Department responded by stepping up quality-of-life enforcement within crime hot spots. The intelligence unit identified the whereabouts of high-risk offenders and their "crews." Detectives closely surveilled and arrested gang members. These enforcement efforts were accompanied by an outreach program conducted jointly by the police department and the White Plains Youth Bureau. The outreach program consisted of discussion sessions held with young men and women of these neighborhoods to explore nonviolent ways of resolving conflicts and disputes. These sessions between the youth and the police were intentionally held outdoors within the public housing complexes so the residents could see them occurring. The very public demonstration of police–youth interaction, which included role playing, drew favorable responses from residents.

The Youth Bureau worked intensively with at-risk and gang-involved young men and women. Once engaged, the youths were exposed to services that address issues such as unemployment, poor school performance, parenthood, and drug and alcohol addiction.

Another innovative program developed at White Plains is a prisoner reentry program that assists former inmates in rejoining the community. The city team in charge of this program comprised a diverse group of workers from social services, religious, and not-for-profit agencies led by the police department. The team met with inmates before their release, conveying a message that the community would work with them in leading productive lives. As of this writing, the program boasts a recidivism rate of only 8 percent.

In 2008 the crime rate in White Plains had declined to its lowest level in 42 years, despite a significant recent increase in the city's racially diverse population. Thus the White Plains Police Department confirmed the power of a concurrent, multipronged approach—measured, focused enforcement, interagency cooperation, and community building—for preventing crime.

Observe Investigate Understand

- **What key aspects of the White Plains program led to its success?**
- **What does the White Plains program demonstrate about the relationship between aggressive order maintenance and community policing programs?**
- **Could the techniques used by the White Plains police work in your community? Why or why not?**

SOURCE: Community Oriented Policing Services, "Achieving Results through Innovation: Policing in White Plains, New York," *Community Policing Dispatch* 1, no. 12 (2008), http://www.cops.usdoj.gov/html/ dispatch/December_2008/police_innovation.htm.

◀ **Dispatcher at Work**

Dispatchers are essential in helping police officers do their job.

POLICE OFFICERS ON THE JOB

The principal activities performed by law enforcement officers are patrol, follow-up investigation by detectives, and traffic operations. These are customarily referred to as **line activities**. Additional activities that support line activities are referred to as **support activities**.[37] These may include communications, custody, and forensics. Law enforcement agency employees who are sworn officers usually fill line positions, while civilian employees usually occupy the support positions.

line activities
The principal activities performed by law enforcement officers, including patrol, follow-up investigation, and traffic operations.

support activities
Additional policing activities that support line activities, such as communications, custody, and forensics.

The Rookie Officer—Meeting the Real World

The first day of work for the average police academy graduate working in a city is often overwhelming. The role-playing scenarios practiced at the academy suddenly become real as the rookie officer is immersed in the daily functions of policing: maintaining order, enforcing the law, and providing service. The rookie learns the rhythm of the patrol officer while working under the watchful and often hypercritical eye of a training officer. The vehicle pull-overs are now real as are the tickets issued to motorists. To the rookie's surprise, every action takes much longer to complete than expected.

As radio calls arrive from the dispatcher, the rookie gains a sense of the call load queue. The "queue" is the array of calls for service awaiting handling. Depending on the communications equipment installed in police vehicles, the queue of calls may or may not be visible to the officer. Already on the way to a "landlord-tenant dispute," the officer must turn the squad car around in the hope of catching the perpetrator of a "burglary in progress." As the new call receives priority, the officer wonders what might be waiting at the scene. The training officer and other senior officers will scrutinize the rookie officer's performance closely; so the new officer must act carefully, know when to call for backup, and not make any serious rookie mistakes such as exposing the gun side of the hip (a position of tactical disadvantage) while interviewing a suspicious person.

Patrol Officers—The Backbone of Policing

Uniformed personnel (patrol officers) assigned to patrol specific regions of a city or county perform the bulk of police work. The majority of patrol officer contacts with the public are responses to calls for service.

Patrol officers are the first individuals to respond to a call for service. They are in many ways the backbone of the law enforcement organization. The patrol officer is the most visible face of the agency and the initial responder to virtually any incident requiring a police response. The patrol force is the component around which a police department is constructed; without the patrol component, there would be no law enforcement capability. Patrol officers do not merely wait around the precinct station for a call; they are out and about in the geographic region that makes up their jurisdiction, always on the lookout for any suspicious activity. They keep a watchful eye on the streets they patrol, noting such variables as time and place, appearance, and behavior of an individual to determine whether the scenarios they observe might be considered suspicious activity.[38]

MYTH/REALITY

MYTH: Detectives are most responsible for preserving the integrity of a crime scene.

REALITY: The quality of the patrol officer's preliminary investigation is the key determinant in solving crimes. If the description obtained at the scene of the crime is accurate, there is a reasonable likelihood of solving the case.[39]

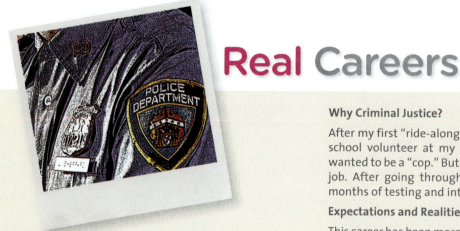

Real Careers

MARK DEMMER

Work Location: Washington County, OR

College(s): California State University, Chico (2008)

Major(s): Criminal Justice (B.S.)

Job title: Patrol Officer

Salary range for jobs like this: $45,000 to $50,000

Time in job: 1 year

Work Responsibilities

A usual day consists of making traffic stops and writing reports for any number of things, from thefts to automobile crashes. There is really no such thing as a typical week. One week I might write five reports and make 40 traffic stops; the next I might write 15 reports and only make five traffic stops. The work week is dynamic and keeps me energized. It doesn't even feel like a chore for me to go work. Every day I feel proud to be helping people and making a difference in their lives and the community. What makes the job even more of a pleasure are the new friendships I have developed with my co-workers since starting one year ago.

Why Criminal Justice?

After my first "ride-along" in Great Falls, Montana, as a high school volunteer at my local police department, I knew I wanted to be a "cop." But I had to work hard to get my dream job. After going through four years of college and seven months of testing and interviewing, I landed the position.

Expectations and Realities of the Job

This career has been more difficult than I expected. For example, while I learned how to write in college, I had to learn how to write detailed police reports after I got hired. These are important because they are used in court and can make the difference in what the verdict in a case might be.

Multi-tasking has also been an unwritten requirement of the job. For example, while I'm driving the police vehicle, I have to operate the communications equipment. During vehicle pull-overs or when I arrive at the location of a call for service, I have to tactically position the police vehicle for maximum safety and efficiency. Shift rotations (e.g., moving from the daytime shift to the "graveyard" shift and having to stay awake at 3:00 A.M. and then going to bed at 10:00 A.M.) take some getting used to as well. Thank goodness for aluminum foil, which does do the trick in terms of shutting out the daylight. Extended shifts, often resulting from a court appearance or overtime for an arrest or a search for a suspect or missing child, are another challenge. But with a few months of work experience under my belt, I became more confident in my abilities.

My Advice to Students

Once you leave college for the real world, it is important to set achievable goals. For me it was work hard and get hired. And even if you reach your goal, don't think it can't be taken away. I've realized it's hard to get hired, but even harder to stay hired. Try learning from the veterans and consider their advice.

◀ **Myth or Reality? Nothing happens at the crime scene until a detective arrives.**
Detectives work strategically on cases by prioritizing those that are most likely to be solved.

The patrol officer has a crucial role at crime scenes. As the first responder on the scene, she must be alert for any fleeing suspects and assess the scene for the safety of other officers or emergency medical technicians who are on the way. At the crime scene, the patrol officer must locate key parties (victims, suspects, or witnesses), control them, and identify and preserve any physical evidence. Once the patrol officer musters sufficient resources to secure the crime scene and identify or control persons of interest, she must document all she observed.[40] In large agencies, the officer's reports and notes are provided to detectives for their follow-up investigation. In small agencies, the first responding officer may also handle the follow-up.

A 1975 study revealed that the bulk of the cases solved by detectives hinged on information obtained by patrol officers during their preliminary investigation, with a witness's or victim's at-scene description of a suspect a crucial factor.[41] A second and larger 2001 study reaffirmed the importance of patrol officers in the investigative process, with 72 percent of surveyed agencies reporting efforts to enhance patrol officers' investigative role.[42]

Follow-up Investigation

A follow-up investigation occurs after a patrol officer documents the facts of the crime. For serious crimes (e.g., homicides or home invasion robberies), the detective may be called directly to the scene and receive a briefing from the first responder. In most cases, however, the detective receives the patrol officer's report the next day, after physical evidence and suspects have already been secured.

Because resources are limited, priorities among criminal incidents requiring investigation are determined by the seriousness of the crime and its **solvability**, that is, the likelihood the crime will be solved. Solvability depends upon the presence of clues or evidence that makes apprehension of a suspect more likely. Several factors affect solvability: the quality of the patrol officer's preliminary investigation, the availability of witnesses, a suspect's name or identifying information, significant physical evidence, and identification of a unique method of operation, or MO, by the perpetrator.

solvability
The likelihood that a crime will be solved.

Although television shows often focus on detectives as the ones who make the arrest, in fact, patrol officers make about 80 percent of arrests.[43] Solving crimes, however, can be very difficult. For example, "nationwide in 2007, law enforcement cleared 44.5 percent of violent crimes and 16.5 percent of property crimes by arrest or exceptional means. Examples of exceptional clearances include, but are not limited to, the death of the offender (e.g., suicide or justifiably killed by police or citizen); the victim's refusal to cooperate with the prosecution after the offender has been identified; or the denial of extradition because the offender committed a crime in another jurisdiction and is being prosecuted for that offense.[44]" This low solvability rate can be partly explained by the fact that solving crimes when the suspect is not identified by a witness or victim is very difficult.

A detective's follow-up investigation plan typically includes visiting the crime scene and documenting everything related to the case. When all the evidence and information have been obtained, and a suspect apprehended, the detective prepares the case for presentation to the prosecutor, who reviews its worthiness for a court's scrutiny.[45]

Enforcing Traffic Laws

Police are the primary public safety agency in charge of the enforcement of traffic laws. Law enforcement officers have this responsibility for several reasons. One reason is the relationship between crime and traffic incidents. Automobiles are frequently used in the commission of crimes, and police are equipped to find and capture suspects on the run. Police are also equipped and trained to handle situations that might result from traffic stops, such as belligerent drunk drivers, aggravated traffic violators, and persons with outstanding warrants. Finally, police use their investigative skills to elicit statements and document facts relating to traffic collisions.[46]

Until recently, the police alone were responsible for enforcing traffic laws. The nature of so-called traffic services functions has now begun to extend beyond the law enforcement agency. In many communities, the police partner with community agencies that draft and implement transportation policy, such as the local department of transportation. These partnerships effectively identify existing traffic-related problems and develop solutions that benefit the whole community. For example, the accident reports taken by police feed into local and statewide computerized databases that may be accessed by city, county, and state government transportation entities. Sharing this database helps them identify problems that may be mitigated through engineering solutions such as roadway alterations or the placement of traffic lights. Police may use these databases to identify locations that are particularly prone to traffic accidents and increase their patrols accordingly. Direct interaction with citizens enables police to learn about the specific concerns of the community while providing a forum to educate the public on evolving traffic safety practices such as speed bumps and roundabouts that restrict speed and increase pedestrian safety. Law enforcement also relies on devices such as photo radar cameras and electronic message signs to prevent collisions and provide advisories of traffic conditions.[47]

Communications Technology—The Central Nervous System of Policing

Law enforcement activities require support services for maximum efficiency and effectiveness. Patrol vehicles must be maintained in top running condition. Criminal history records must be stored yet readily retrievable. Communications, custody, and forensics all demand current technologies to keep pace with never-ending needs.

Just as the patrol function is often considered the backbone of policing, communications might be thought of as the central nervous system that coordinates the performance of law enforcement activities. Computer-aided dispatch supplements radio communication and allows patrol officers to remotely search databases for warrants for individuals or vehicles without having to go through the central dispatch center.

RealCrime Tech

CAMERAS IN PUBLIC SPACES

Law enforcement agencies are increasingly turning to video cameras to catch law breakers. The most well known are the video cameras on top of traffic lights to catch people who run red lights. They have also been used to monitor protesters and to catch anyone committing crimes in locations like subways. Some individuals support the idea of the police using new technologies, while others worry about individuals enjoying less privacy.

communications interoperability
The ability of police and other public safety agencies from different jurisdictions to talk and share data.

DISConnects

A Literal Disconnect: Agencies' Inabilities to Communicate

The United States has no national strategy for funding public safety radio. As a result, while some jurisdictions migrate to higher frequency bands and digital channels, some rural fire departments, for example, use radio technologies more than 50 years old—making it impossible for two departments to talk directly with each other. When a large-scale incident requires agencies from different jurisdictions to respond in a coordinated fashion, the inability to communicate can become life endangering. Ironically, as technology has advanced, communications interoperability has diminished. With more different types of radios and more frequencies, it is less likely than ever that any two agencies will have compatible systems and use common frequencies.

Although uniformity is too expensive for many agencies, equipment that receives a radio transmission on one frequency and automatically retransmits it on another can achieve limited interoperability. The National Institute of Justice created the CommTech Program to bridge the gap in emergency communications and enable multiple parties to exchange voice, data, image, and video communications "on the spot"—no matter where that "spot" happens to be.

Since public safety agencies will likely continue to broadcast in different frequency bands for some time, interagency planning and cooperation are critical. Agency representatives must agree on who can authorize a link between agencies, under what circumstances, and with what radio protocol, and they must conduct multiagency training and regularly test equipment and its capabilities to help reduce the technological incompatibilities that prevent interagency communication.

Although technology contributes to a lack of interoperability, technology can also contribute to potential solutions, as examples from Danville, Virginia, and Newberry County, South Carolina, illustrate. The city of Danville capitalized on a public-private partnership to explore the possibilities of using the "Voice over Internet Protocol" (the digital routing of voice conversations over the Internet) to connect five dispatch centers within the Danville environs and provide instant regional communication among them. The National Institute of Justice provided technology support to the public safety agencies, and two vendors donated equipment and services. In rural Newberry County, local law enforcement used a grant to create a multifaceted approach that includes laptops, WiFi "hot spots" in the county's schools, and a shared records management system that enables real-time sharing of information.

OBSERVE Investigate Understand

- **What are the consequences of public safety agencies' inability to communicate across different jurisdictions?**
- **What problems stand in the way of enabling public safety agencies to communicate with one another across jurisdictions?**
- **Should government take the lead in making sure agencies can communicate with one another in a large-scale emergency? If so, what level of government?**

SOURCES: National Institute of Justice, *Communications Interoperability: Basics for Practitioners* (Washington, DC: National Institute of Justice, 2006), 1–2.

National Law Enforcement and Corrections Technology Center, *First Step to Interoperability: Cooperation* (Washington, DC: National Institute of Justice, 2008), 1–3.

National Institute of Justice, *Communicating across State and County Lines: The Piedmont Regional Voice over Internet Protocol Project* (Washington, DC: National Institute of Justice, 2008), 1.

Mobile video systems consist of vehicle-mounted cameras that capture audio and video information, providing evidence of crimes such as drunk driving while monitoring officers' conduct.[48] Before the widespread use of in-car video systems, evidence of alleged offenses or of misconduct by an officer was sorely lacking. The availability of video greatly reduced the burden of producing evidence for both the alleged offender and the officer. Accused parties may introduce portions of the video to refute police allegations, just as police officers may introduce video evidence to refute allegations of misconduct.

Communications interoperability is the ability of police agencies (and other public safety entities such as fire departments or emergency management agencies) from different jurisdictions to talk and share data in real time. Such communication is often a challenge, because different jurisdictions operate on different frequency bands (see the Disconnects box above). Precious time is lost while dispatchers manually relay emergency communications between radio systems. Technology that facilitates communication among different bands is being developed, but interoperability challenges extend beyond technical issues. For instance, which codes will officers employ?[49]

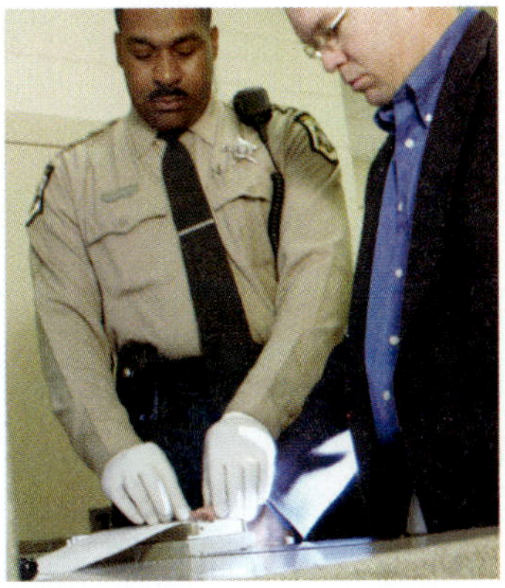

▲ **Suspect Processing**

The police officer is transferring custody of a suspect to a sheriff department's jail facility.

▶ Forensic Chemist/Anthropologist with Bones

Technology has helped solve crimes, but getting evidence analyzed is sometimes difficult given limited resources.

Custody—Booking and Holding Offenders

custody
The incarceration of persons either accused or convicted of a crime.

Custody is the incarceration of persons either accused or convicted of a crime. The length of time a law enforcement agency keeps an arrested person in custody varies. In general, police departments maintain only temporary holding facilities for arrested persons. They may be booked into the police station for a few days before being taken before a judge, who then evaluates the grounds for arrest and determines whether the person can be detained longer. A suspect in police custody may be questioned by the detective assigned to the follow-up investigation, and the police may run a fingerprint identification on the suspect.

Custody is usually a core function of a sheriff's department. As county entities, sheriff's departments maintain a central jail for persons awaiting trial and for those who have been convicted and are serving a period of incarceration up to a year. Newly appointed deputy sheriffs commonly serve a stint in the county's jail facility before being assigned to patrol, traffic, or investigative details.

Forensics—Applying Science to Investigations

forensics
The application of scientific knowledge and methods to criminal and civil investigations and legal procedures, including criminal trials.

forensic science laboratories
Facilities using scientific or technical methods to process and analyze evidence.

criminalistics
The application of scientific techniques to recognizing, identifying, individualizing, and evaluating physical evidence in legal proceedings.

Forensics is the application of scientific knowledge and methods to criminal and civil investigations and legal procedures, including criminal trials. Facilities using scientific or technical methods to process and analyze evidence are called **forensic science laboratories**. **Criminalistics** is the use of scientific techniques in recognizing, identifying, individualizing, and evaluating physical evidence.[50] In the past, scientific analysis of evidence occurred near the end of a criminal investigation—when a case was being prepared for trial. Today, scientific analysis begins with the first responder to the crime.

MYTH/REALITY

MYTH: Forensics results are available quickly and reliably to most major police departments.

REALITY: Even when forensics tests are available, results can take days, weeks, or even months. And, due to evidence contamination or other problems, the results are not always reliable.[51]

The prominent role of forensics in criminal investigations rests on two factors: increased awareness of its value in identifying and protecting evidence, and advances in technology. Popular television shows highlighting forensic techniques have had a profound influence on public expectations in terms of evidence collection, analysis, and presentation in court. On television, the forensic laboratory returns results to police

CAREERS IN FORENSICS

Listed here are some of the careers available in forensics, as well as the educational requirements for each.

Title	Job Description	Minimum Education Usually Required
Forensic accountant	Analyzes financial transactions	Bachelor's degree in accounting to determine fraud
Computer forensics investigator	Finds and analyzes computer evidence	Education and experience in computer science
Evidence technician	Receives, processes, and stores physical evidence	Some coursework in forensics
Ballistics and firearms expert	Matches projectiles to particular weapons	Experience in firearms and determining trajectories
Fingerprint examiner	Collects and analyzes latent print evidence	Bachelor's degree in science
Criminalist	Analyzes physical evidence through use of scientific techniques, usually in a laboratory	Bachelor's degree in biology, chemistry, physics, or criminalistics
Forensic pathologist	Determines cause and time of death	MD
Forensic entomologist	Uses insect evidence to determine time, place, and cause of death	PhD in biology
Forensic anthropologist	Helps determine identity of human remains as well as cause of death	PhD in anthropology
Forensic psychologist	Uses psychology to help make decisions relevant to the law (determining competency to stand trial, assisting attorneys in juror selection)	PhD in psychology

within hours of evidence collection. In real life, forensic testing analysis can take days, weeks, or even months.[52]

The backlog of evidence awaiting DNA analysis is enormous. This problem is especially acute in Los Angeles. A rape kit is one type of instrument used for collecting DNA evidence. It includes a set of tools used by medical personnel for gathering DNA following a sexual assault. Once used, the rape kit contains the set of physical evidence for a particular sexual assault, including DNA samples. The kit is saved for future use. At the end of 2008 the Los Angeles city comptroller indicated that at least 7,000 rape kits had been untouched by the police department's forensic laboratory. California is not alone; the West Virginia State Police's DNA case backlog grew to 697 cases at the beginning of 2008.[53] Because of this huge backlog, the National Institute of Justice in 2008 released a solicitation seeking applications for funding a Forensic DNA Backlog Reduction Program to increase the capacities of forensic laboratories to analyze DNA samples more efficiently.[54]

Scientific analysis is applied to a wide range of evidence, including DNA, controlled substances, fire debris, explosive residues, hairs, fibers, glass, soil, paint, fingerprints, tire tracks, footwear, tool marks, and firearms.[55] Included too are the complex analyses that involve computer-stored information and insects that inhabit corpses (to determine time and location of death). The table above lists the types of careers in forensics.

THE POLICE ORGANIZATION

Most agencies that deploy uniformed personnel have certain characteristics in common, such as a hierarchical organization and a degree of centralization. Embedded within these characteristics are the concepts of chain of command, unity of command, and span of control. **Chain of command** is the line of authority that extends throughout the organization.

chain of command
The line of authority that extends throughout a police organization.

unity of command
The requirement that each individual within an organization reports directly to a single individual higher in the chain of command.

span of control
The extent of an individual's authority, or the number of individuals that one person is responsible for overseeing.

Unity of command requires that each individual within the organization reports directly to a single individual higher in the chain of command. **Span of control** is the extent of an individual's authority, or the number of individuals that one person is responsible for overseeing. The general behavior of all officers is embodied by the will of the chief, whose actions represent a consistency of conduct that assures citizens that the law is applied in an equitable manner.[56]

Most police departments are hierarchically organized, with several layers of personnel and a rigid chain of command, but the move to community policing during the latter decades of the twentieth century sparked calls for changes in police organization. Community policing requires a more decentralized approach in order to give rank-and-file officers the flexibility and autonomy needed to develop closer ties with the community and to involve the public in solving community problems. Community policing empowers field officers to exercise increased amounts of discretion in solving problems, while management acts as coach.

The 9/11 terrorist attacks led to another organizational change. Police departments created units or assigned personnel (e.g., "terrorism liaison officers") responsible for gathering information that could be linked to possible terrorist activity. At the same time, agencies increasingly shared information with one another. Before the 9/11 attacks, police organizations had been relatively insular, relying on adjoining agencies only in the case of acute emergencies. Review of the events leading up to 9/11 highlighted the importance of sharing intelligence information proactively to help prevent such emergencies from happening. As illustrated in Chapter 16, piecing together a terrorist plot often requires the gathering of information possessed by different jurisdictions. Networks of policing agencies equipped to share information across regional jurisdictions are critical to the success of antiterrorist intelligence gathering. These networks are made up of all agencies within regions and effectively cross the borders of jurisdictional authority that have been characteristic of American policing since its inception.[57]

DEPLOYMENT OF POLICE RESOURCES

A police operation needs a strategy for allocation of police resources to ensure that those resources are being used appropriately. As is the case in almost all organizations, a police department's most important resources are money and people. Financial resources for law enforcement agencies come primarily from government agencies. For example, municipal policing agencies receive most of their funds from city governments. The resources of people include sworn police officers and nonsworn civilian employees. Police departments have other resources as well, such as police vehicles and technological equipment.

Factors Affecting Resource Allocation

Many factors influence how police resources are allocated, including demands of the citizens, administrative requirements of the police agency, and agendas of local government leaders. Decisions about how many police officers to have on the streets versus assigned to other tasks are resource choices that often come under scrutiny. If, on the one hand, the local population prefers a community-oriented policing strategy, the number of police officers assigned to patrol can be relatively high. If, on the other hand, the community prefers a policing strategy focused primarily on rapid response to crime-related calls for service and apprehension of offenders, fewer officers are assigned to foot patrol in the community.

The policing strategy in practice also affects a police organization's administrative and support needs. Agencies emphasizing community policing strategies need additional staff to support substations in the community and to conduct special programs operating from main stations.

Local politics also plays a role in the deployment of police resources. A recent national survey found that 65 percent of large-department and 48 percent of small-department police executives believed local elected officials had at least some influence on increases in police staffing.[58]

MYTH/REALITY

MYTH: Police are almost always deployed in greatest numbers where there is the highest percentage of minority populations.

REALITY: Police deployment is often the result of political influence. A cohesive minority bloc can wield significant political clout in the competition for policing resources.[59]

Insistent pressure from a particular group that more police should be deployed to their neighborhood is most likely to be effective in cities with traditional political structures and operations, such as a mayor-council form of government, partisan elections, and district-based city councils. In these cases local elected officials tend to be sensitive to political pressure.[60]

Technological Resources

In addition to money and personnel, equipment is an important resource for law enforcement agencies. More and more, police departments are using new technological equipment, such as geographic information systems, computerized statistical systems, and crime analysis, to increase their efficiency.

Geographic Information Systems (GIS)

Crime mapping is the process of pinpointing the locations and times of crimes. The potential of crime mapping to help solve crimes is greatly enhanced by **geographic information systems (GIS)** technology, which uses a computerized mapping system to produce detailed descriptions of crime occurrences and analyze the relationships between variables such as location and time. GIS technology reveals areas of concentrated crime or higher risk of victimization, commonly called **hot spots.**[61] This information enables police to concentrate their resources and problem-solving activities on the hot spots.

crime mapping
A technique used by police to pinpoint the locations and times of crimes.

geographic information systems (GIS)
A technology that uses a computerized mapping system to produce descriptions of crime occurrence and analyzes the relationships between variables such as location and time.

hot spot
Areas of concentrated crime or higher risk of victimization.

CompStat
A computerized statistical program that integrates information from crime maps across the city for department leaders' review.

Computerized Statistics

GIS technology has been augmented by **CompStat** (COMPuterized STATistics), a program developed by the New York City Police Department in 1994. CompStat integrates information from crime maps across the city for department leaders' review. It increases the flow of information between agency executives and commanders of operational units, allowing executives to monitor commanders' success in dealing with emerging crime patterns and allocating resources. CompStat has proven to be highly useful as an accountability tool, helping ensure that resources are being used effectively.[62]

The Department of Justice identifies six aspects of CompStat that improve the ability of police departments to understand and cope with public safety problems: mission clarification, internal accountability, geographic organization of command, organizational flexibility, data-driven problem identification and assessment, and innovative problem solving. One reason for the success of CompStat is that it can be readily adapted by existing policing operations without making radical organizational changes.[63]

Crime Analysis

The assessment of crime-related information to help prevent crime, deploy law enforcement resources, apprehend suspects, and support crime investigations is termed **crime analysis.** Crime analysis techniques have greatly improved the way agencies deploy their resources. Before modern crime analysis practices became widespread, the task of allocating resources was jokingly referred to as the "Bud-Shell Method": a police administrator sitting with a six-pack of Budweiser and a Shell gas station road map used a marker to draw lines down major arteries and create policing districts on the basis of geography.[64] Although these districts were uniform in terms of size, the incidence of crime did not

crime analysis
The application of processes designed to analyze information pertinent to crimes and develop correlations useful in crime prevention, resource deployment, investigations, and suspect apprehension.

▶ Geographic Information Systems (GIS)

Geographic information systems (GIS) help police departments identify high crime areas, or hot spots.

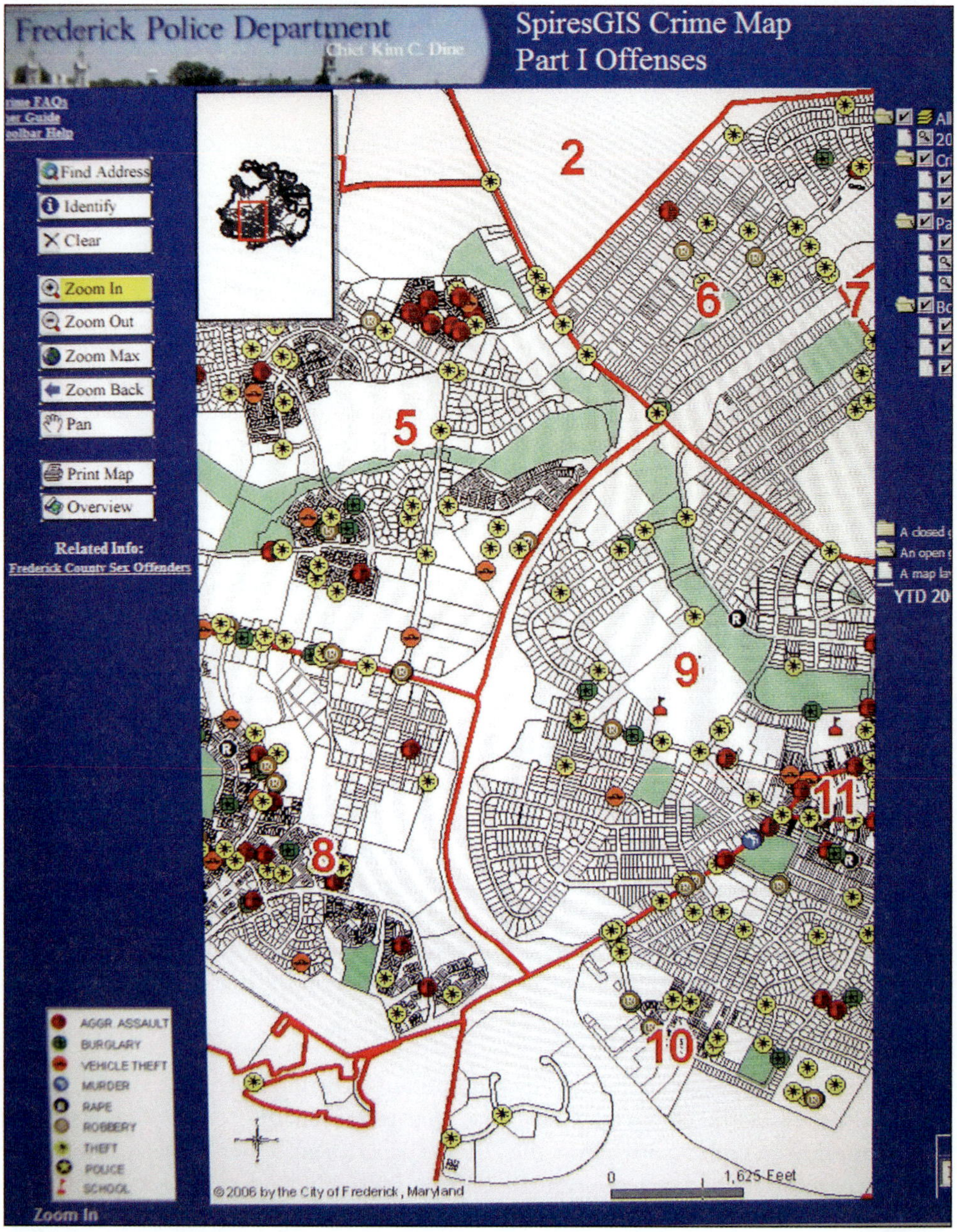

distribute itself accordingly. Yet, administrators in the past had little in the way of current crime statistics to help them with the task of allocating resources. Today, using computerized methods, resources may be allocated based on analysis of the incidence of crime by type of offense, time of commission, and a complex mix of other variables. Combining computer-aided dispatch with automatic vehicle locator systems, commanders now may reposition resources at will via real-time views of crime occurrence.

Crime analysis is useful in follow-up investigations through examination of a crime scene in the context of an offender's behaviors. Knowing the *how* of a crime—what the perpetrator did and did not do—can help illuminate the *why*—the offender's likely motivation for the crime as well as his personality. For example, an offender who uses a surprise approach (lying in wait or attacking a sleeping victim) reflects a lack of confidence, or inadequacy. Crime analysis can thus identify correlations that can reduce the pool of possible suspects. At the same time, crime analysis can reveal links among crimes, suggesting they may have been committed by the same individual(s).[65]

THE POLICE AND PUBLIC OPINION

Overall, the U.S. public is supportive of the police. Fifty-eight percent have a "great deal" or "quite a lot" of confidence in the police, rating the police second only to the military and higher than churches or organized religions, banks, the U.S. Supreme Court, the medical system, and public schools. The age group with the greatest confidence in police are individuals 65 years and older.[66] Fifty-four percent of people also rate police "very high" or "high" on honesty and ethical standards, almost as high as clergy and much better than members of Congress, state governors, lawyers, journalists, business executives, and psychiatrists.[67] See Figure 6-5 for an overview on public support for the police.

In contrast to public opinion about the police, the criminal justice system as a whole fails to garner as much public support. Only 25 percent had a "great deal" or "quite a lot" of confidence in the criminal justice system.[68]

Despite the generally high levels of support for the police, the media often highlight cases of police brutality and racial profiling. Yet only 31 percent of adults polled said that they believe police brutality occurs in their area.[69] Statistics seem to support the public's view. In data from large law enforcement agencies in 2002, there were 6.6 complaints about use of force per 100 officers, and 8 percent of those complaints were sustained or determined to be valid.[70] Public opinion is influenced by high-profile cases about the police use of force. For example, after the widely publicized 1991 incident in which Los Angeles Police Department (LAPD) officers kicked, hit, and used their batons on motorist Rodney King, who was stopped for a traffic violation following a pursuit, public opinion of the LAPD dropped sharply. A couple of years later opinion returned to its pre–Rodney King levels.[71]

The public generally believes that racial profiling is more common than police brutality. For example, 53 percent of U.S. residents believe racial profiling is widespread in traffic stops.[72] Numerous studies have found evidence of racial profiling or at least evidence that Whites and Blacks are stopped at different levels, which supports the belief of many U.S. residents.[73]

Although overall, U.S. residents are supportive of the police, there are fairly large differences in opinion between Whites and people of color. Among Whites, 57 percent have a great deal or quite a lot of confidence in the police, whereas 40 percent of nonWhites and 32 percent of Blacks have that same level of confidence.[74]

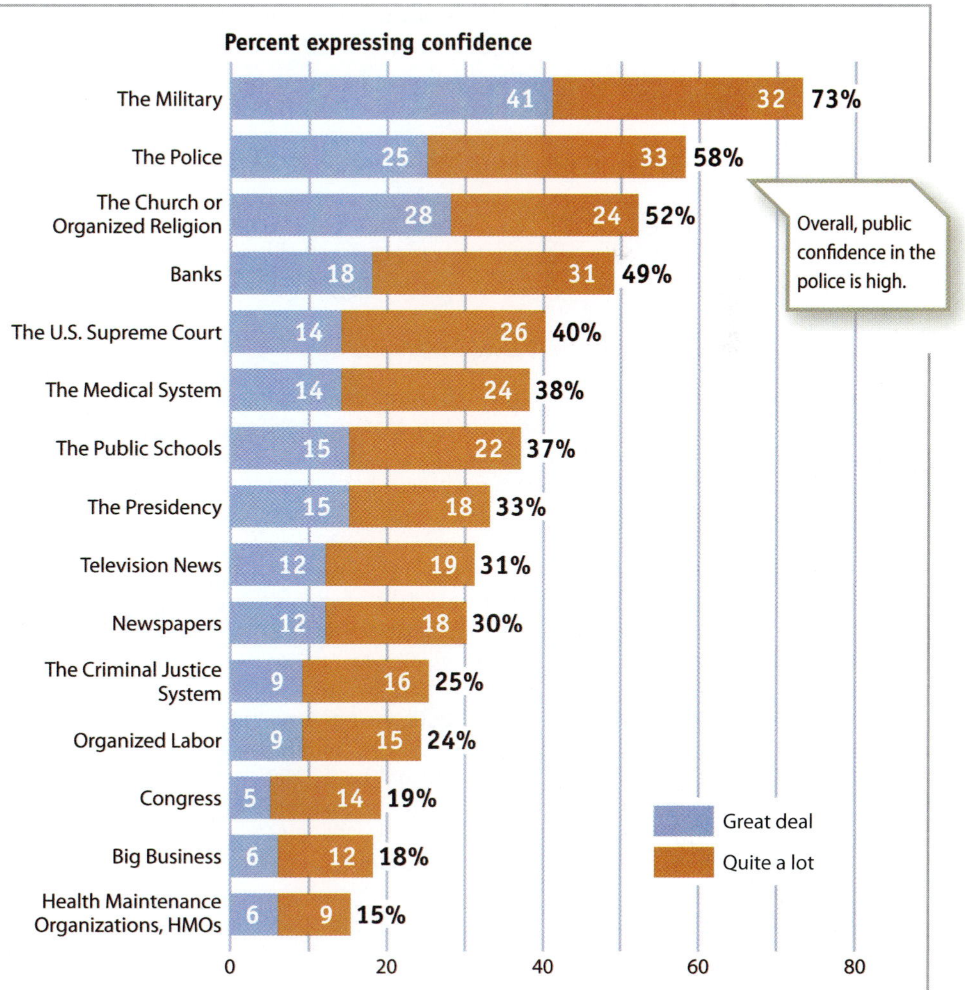

FIGURE 6-5 Police and Public Support

One explanation for this difference in opinion is the fact that Blacks have a different relationship with the police than do Whites. For example, 72.7 percent of Black men between the ages of 18 and 24 report being victimized by racial profiling at least once, whereas 10.9 percent of White males in that age group make a similar claim. Race and personal experience with racial profiling appear to have the greatest influence on opinions of the police.[75] Both Black and White communities believe that police treat the two communities differently, although for different reasons. Whites tend to believe that differential treatment is warranted because Blacks are more likely to commit crimes. Blacks see differential treatment as discriminatory.[76]

In September 2005, during the Hurricane Katrina crisis and in the weeks that followed, media coverage of the New Orleans Police Department was almost entirely negative. There were reports of officers abandoning their posts, committing violence against residents, shoplifting, and looting. A poll conducted in March 2006 assessed New Orleans residents' views about how government leaders and institutions had responded to the effects of the hurricane. Given that in general Whites' and Blacks' views of the police differ and that Black residents of New Orleans were more seriously affected by Hurricane Katrina, the poll results are not surprising. The percentage that approved of the way the New Orleans police responded to the effects of the hurricane was 57 percent among Whites, 40 percent among Blacks.[77]

In general, Blacks' views of the police vary by class and level of education. Blacks living in middle-class Black neighborhoods report their relationship with police as more similar to that of White communities than that of lower-class Black communities.[78] Whites' opinions of the police and views on racial profiling do not vary by class. Better-educated Blacks, however, are more likely than less-educated Blacks to have a negative view of profiling, to report having experienced it, and to think it is widely practiced.[79]

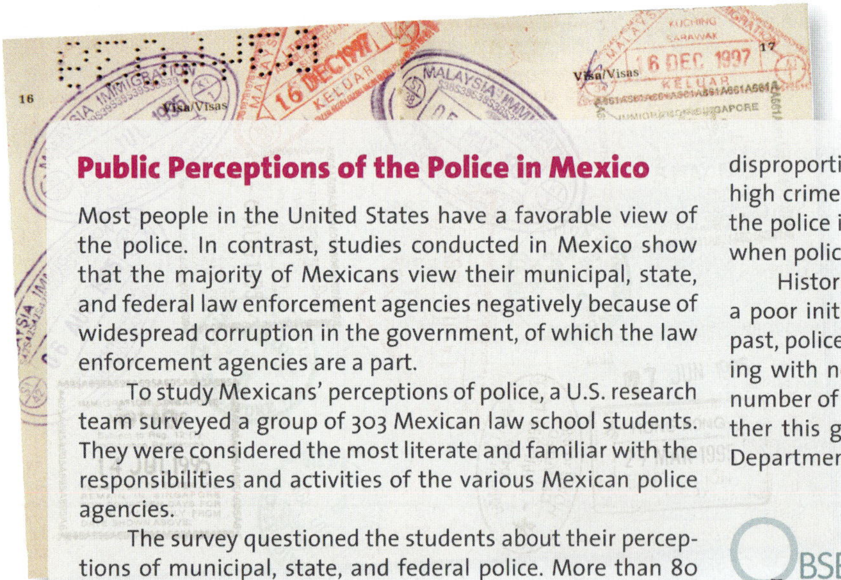

A Global View

Public Perceptions of the Police in Mexico

Most people in the United States have a favorable view of the police. In contrast, studies conducted in Mexico show that the majority of Mexicans view their municipal, state, and federal law enforcement agencies negatively because of widespread corruption in the government, of which the law enforcement agencies are a part.

To study Mexicans' perceptions of police, a U.S. research team surveyed a group of 303 Mexican law school students. They were considered the most literate and familiar with the responsibilities and activities of the various Mexican police agencies.

The survey questioned the students about their perceptions of municipal, state, and federal police. More than 80 percent of the students believed the municipal police did an inadequate job of controlling crime and treating people fairly. More than 70 percent believed the state police performed inadequately in the same tasks, and more than 60 percent rated federal police inadequate on these measures. The study reinforced a widespread impression that the country needs to reform its policing agencies.

The study also had implications for Mexican immigrants in the United States. Some recent Mexican immigrants speak limited English (which is historically true of most immigrants when they first come to the United States), and disproportionate numbers live in urban neighborhoods with high crime rates. But because of negative experiences with the police in Mexico, they may be hesitant to contact police when police services are needed.

Historically, new immigrant groups commonly have a poor initial relationship with law enforcement. As in the past, police agencies today must devise methods of connecting with new immigrant groups to ensure public safety. A number of agencies have already launched programs to further this goal. For example, the Brownsville (Texas) Police Department offers a citizen academy taught in Spanish.

Observe Investigate Understand

- **Why is public opinion of the police in Mexico so much more negative than public opinion of the police in the United States?**
- **How do the views of Mexican immigrants about the Mexican police affect their views of police in the United States?**
- **What should the police do to make sure that all individuals feel safe contacting them?**

SOURCE: Ben Brown, William Reed Benedict, and William V. Wilkinson, "Public Perceptions of the Police in Mexico: A Case Study," *Policing: An International Journal of Police Strategies & Management* 29 (2006): 158–171.

Blacks are not the only group that perceives the police differently than do Whites. Although Latinos' views are not as negative as those of Blacks, neither are they as favorable as those of Whites. For example, Latinos are more likely than Whites to believe racial profiling is widespread.[80] Among both Latinos and Blacks, men are more likely than women to believe racial profiling is widespread.[81] This difference is likely related to the relationship between personal experience and opinions of the police, since men of color generally have more contact with the police than do women of color. After the 9/11 terrorist acts, Arab Americans reported fearing the police because of what they viewed as increased surveillance and racial profiling of Arab Americans.[82] Historically, new Chinese and Vietnamese immigrants have also reported perceiving the police as prejudiced.[83]

Although public opinion of the police varies by group, most of the U.S. public has a fairly positive view of the police. That is not true in all countries, as illustrated in the Global View box.

elder abuse
Any knowing, intentional, or negligent act by a caregiver or other person that causes harm or serious risk of harm to a vulnerable adult 60 years of age or older.

adult protective services (APS)
Services provided to older people and dependent adults who are in danger of being mistreated or neglected, are unable to protect themselves, and have no one to assist them.

RESPONDING TO DIVERSE POPULATIONS

The public generally expects the police to serve all people fairly and equitably, keeping everyone safe. These expectations are challenging, as the police are called upon to serve a wide variety of people, with different needs, problems, and experiences.

Elder Adults

In the United States the issue of mistreatment of elder adults garners attention as more people are living longer. The Census Bureau projects that more than 62 million Americans will be age 65 or older in 2025.[84] **Elder abuse** is any knowing, intentional, or negligent act by a caregiver or other person that causes harm or a serious risk of harm to a vulnerable elder. The harm may be physical abuse, emotional abuse, sexual abuse, exploitation (the taking, misuse, or concealment of funds), neglect, or abandonment.[85]

Elder abuse is still a relatively new area of criminal justice intervention. It was first formally addressed in the United States in the mid-1970s, with the creation of Adult Protective Services funding under Title XX of the Social Security Act. **Adult protective services (APS)** are services provided to older people and dependent adults who are in danger of being mistreated or neglected, are unable to protect themselves, and have no one to assist them.[86]

Although the investigation of suspected cases of elder abuse does not vary greatly from other criminal investigations, investigators need to be particularly alert to the physical condition of the home environment and the elder's accommodations and apparent health. They will treat skeptically any attempts by a caregiver or relative to answer for the elder or keep the elder from providing information. They also need to be aware that a victim's recall may be clouded by complications of the aging process, disorientation or nervousness, or medication.[87] In the event of the death of an elder adult due to possible abuse or neglect, investigators must first determine whether the death was expected and consistent with the appearance of natural causes and whether there was a delay in notifying authorities.[88]

Police dispatchers are an integral part of the law enforcement team approach to dealing with elder abuse. Many elderly people have difficulty articulating their problems or clearly describing their situations. Dispatchers are trained to be patient and diligent in seeking information that may point toward instances of abuse. They must also know how to refer callers to appropriate agencies if the facts do not warrant law enforcement involvement.[89]

▲ Police Aiding a Senior Woman

Today police are often called upon to investigate cases of elder abuse.

Determining the incidence of criminal offenses of elder abuse presents some special problems. Victims may be cognitively impaired and unable to recognize or report offenses. Those who have been exploited financially may not be aware that they have been so victimized.[90] The National Center on Elder Abuse, the major source of statistical information on elder abuse in the United States, collects and analyzes national data on cases referred to and investigated by APS. A national study of state-level APS data conducted in 2004 revealed that "self-neglect" made up approximately one-third of substantiated reports of abuse, closely followed by neglect by caregivers and exploitation of finances. Over 65 percent of victims were women, and over 40 percent of victims were 80 years of age or older. Perpetrators were divided evenly among men and women. The largest category of perpetrators was between 30 and 50 years of age. Most alleged perpetrators were adult children of the victim or other family members. The study collected data nationwide, but states vary widely on the type of statistics they maintain. For example, only 40 percent of the states maintain a database of alleged perpetrators, and only 25 percent were able to provide data on racial composition of victims and perpetrators.[91]

Many law enforcement agencies have established partnerships with the elder adult population and the support agencies that serve them. The intent of these relationships, often organized under a program called TRIAD, is to create trust between law enforcement and the elder adult population. (TRIAD is not an acronym; it simply represents a union of police, sheriff, and retired persons associations.) Elder action programs use problem solving and community policing strategies to meet the concerns of the elderly.[92] A volunteer council called SALT (Seniors and Lawmen Together) guides local TRIADs. Each SALT council decides what services the TRIAD will offer, recruits volunteers, and oversees the results. The Texas state TRIAD program, offered through the state office of the attorney general, includes consumer protection, crime prevention, and health and safety oversight. It also provides toll-free hot lines for seniors who have complaints about consumer goods, nursing homes, and Medicaid provider fraud, as well as a legal services center hot line and a 24-hour abuse hot line.[93]

People with Disabilities

Individuals with physical or developmental disabilities are at higher risk of being victimized, according to the National Organization for Victim Assistance. Because the perpetrators are frequently their caretakers, reporting the crime puts them at further risk, and few cases come to the attention of police. Individuals with disabilities may not be able to report a crime because of constraints on their mobility or difficulties communicating. Recognizing these issues, the National Organization for Victim Assistance offers a number of recommendations on how criminal justice agencies, including police departments, can protect people with disabilities and respond when they have been victimized. Recommendations include ensuring access to buildings for people of all abilities, training officers about disabilities and the subcultures of people with disabilities, and encouraging police departments to work with victim services providers and disability support services organizations.[94]

The Mentally Ill

Providing services and protection for people with mental disabilities is another police priority requiring special attention. Police became more involved with people with mental disabilities in the 1980s, when a large number of institutions for the mentally ill closed because of cuts made to federal mental health funding. (See Chapter 12 for a discussion of the mentally ill in jails and prisons.) Officers generally encounter individuals suffering from mental illness as a result of complaint calls from members of the public. Most police academies do not include specific training to identify individuals who may be mentally ill or information on how to use community resources to address problems that may result from mentally disturbed individuals.

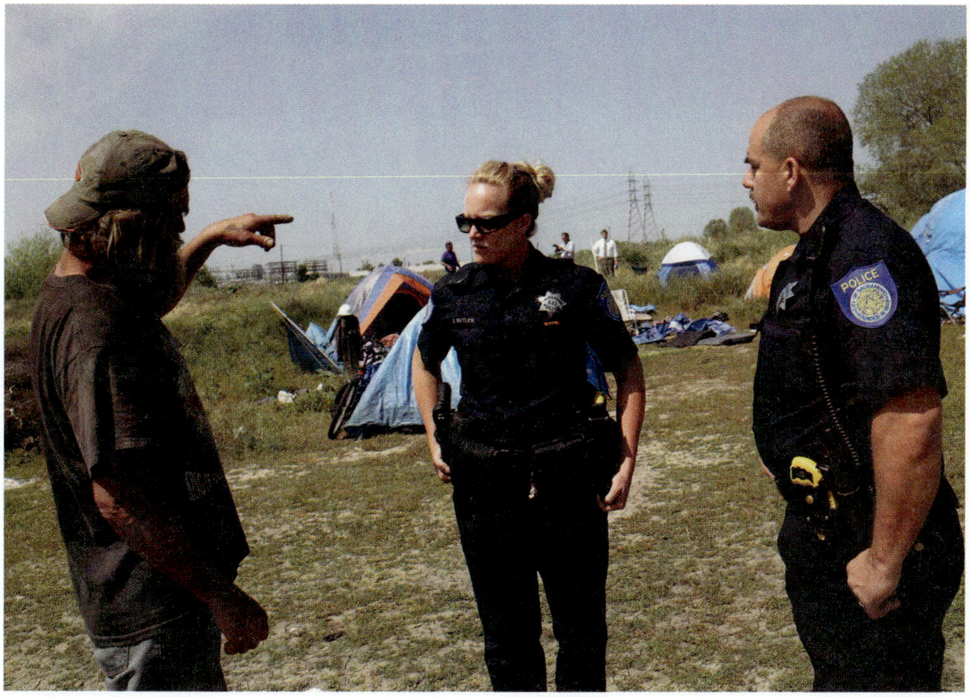

◀ **Police and the Homeless**

Police are often asked to move homeless people out of a particular neighborhood.

Officers encountering a person whose behavior appears irrational generally respond in one of three ways. The first is to transport the individual to a facility that provides psychiatric care if she is a danger to herself or others, although in some locations hospitals refuse anyone they deem "dangerous." Regardless, a physician on site has sole authority whether to admit the person.[95]

The second choice is to arrest a mentally ill person for an offense such as disorderly conduct. This option is most often used when a hospital refuses admission and the individual cannot be left in the situation in which she was found. An officer makes an arrest because he believes the individual will continue to cause problems.[96]

The third option is to resolve the situation informally if the mentally ill individual is a "neighborhood character," a "troublemaker," or a "quiet mental." Neighborhood characters are individuals the police know well because of their visibility in the community, and they are not a threat to public safety. For example, individuals seen muttering to themselves and walking aimlessly might cause some people concern, but they aren't a danger to anyone. Police are also likely to ignore troublemakers, or those who have created problems for officers in the past. In some instances, if police were unsuccessful in previous attempts to have someone admitted to the hospital, an officer may avoid dealing with that individual. Dealing with such troublemakers requires a lot of energy—and paperwork—that officers are not necessarily willing to expend. Police are also not likely to intervene with "quiet mentals"—individuals who seem detached from reality but do not present a nuisance to themselves or the public.[97]

Although police use all these options, the probability of being arrested is 67 percent greater for those who appear mentally ill than for those who do not. Some mental health professionals argue that this high arrest rate constitutes criminalization of mentally disordered behavior. Taking mentally ill individuals to jail is, however, often the only option for police if hospitals and service agencies turn them away.[98]

There is a relationship between psychiatric admission rates and crime and arrest rates. When rates of admission to psychiatric hospitals decrease, crime and arrest rates increase, because those who are unable to function in society are not cared for in institutions best equipped to do so. Psychiatric hospitalizations are also related to levels of homelessness. When hospital admissions decrease, the number of people who are homeless increases.[99] People who are severely mentally ill and are homeless or drug and alcohol abusers are both more likely to be victims of crime and more likely to be arrested for committing crime.[100]

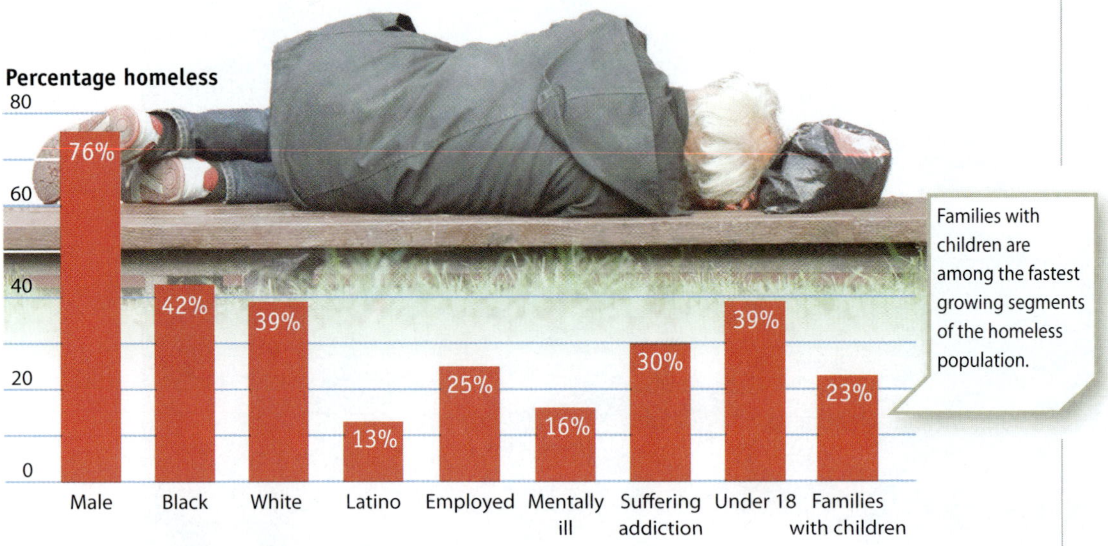

FIGURE 6-6 Who Are the Homeless?

SOURCE: National Coalition for the Homeless, June 2008, http://www.nationalhomeless.org/publications/facts/who.html.

The Homeless

Large and small communities across the United States have homeless persons. Homelessness is defined as the state of having no fixed, reliable, or adequate night-time residence. Nationwide estimates of the homeless population (measured as the number of individuals experiencing homelessness in a year) vary from 400,000 to over 3.5 million.[101] At 23 percent of the homeless population, families are the fastest growing segment of the homeless. See Figure 6-6 for an overview of who is homeless.

Residents of communities with visible homeless populations often call the police to "do something" about them. Individuals complain that homeless people affect the quality of life in their communities, making some locations, such as city parks, undesirable to visit. Perhaps because of these demands, over 70 percent of police departments report that homelessness is a problem in their communities.[102]

Pressure from community members has led some police officers to transport homeless individuals out of their jurisdiction to another locale. Police may put problematic individuals on a bus or some other form of transportation to move them out of the area. Although media reports from a number of cities have lamented this practice of "dumping," it continues to be one way of dealing with the homeless.[103]

Homeless persons are often victims of crime.[104] Sexual victimization of homeless individuals is one of many serious concerns. In-depth interviews with homeless teenagers reveal that some trade sex for items they need to survive, such as food, shelter, money, or drugs. Others are forced to have sex.[105] Sixteen percent of single adult homeless persons suffer from some form of mental illness.[106] The discussion in "The Homeless: Among the Most Vulnerable" illustrates how the homeless often fall prey to victimization.

Cultural Differences and Language Barriers

In the 1800s and early 1900s, police officers were the only government employees who interacted with new immigrants.[107] Both in the past and today, many new immigrants are not proficient in English, so reporting crimes to the police is difficult. Cultural practices in immigrants' native countries may be prohibited in the United States. In such a situation police may be called upon to educate immigrants on the norms of their new country. Immigrants' lack of proficiency in English and different cultural practices can create challenges to police to ensure that all residents—newcomers and the native born—are equally protected and served.

Immigrants have come in waves from a large number of countries at different periods in U.S. history and to different states and regions. In recent years, about 15,000 Hmong people from Southeast Asia emigrated to the United States. Severely persecuted in Laos because they or their ancestors aided the U.S. military during the Vietnam War, they received safe haven in the United States.[108]

The United States is an increasingly diverse country. Police officers must know how to interact with all people in culturally sensitive ways (see Figure 6-7).

Some police departments respond to demographic changes in their communities by recruiting from among the newcomers, who may be better prepared to respond to problems in ethnic neighborhoods in culturally sensitive ways. For example, in some countries if an individual is told to kneel and put his hands behind his head, he knows he is about to be executed. When an officer asks an individual from that cultural background to assume such a position, he should not be surprised if the immigrant responds as if in fear of his life. Today, police academies include cultural diversity training to help officers respond to problems in diverse communities. In some departments, task forces engage in outreach programs to different immigrant and cultural groups to foster a positive relationship.

Another major issue in immigrant communities is the language barrier. Most officers speak only English, but the communities they serve are often multilingual. Many departments offer pay incentives to bilingual officers who can serve as interpreters. Doing so can create tension, however, because most bilingual officers applied to be police officers, not interpreters. They may begin to resent the amount of time they spend on interpreter services, rather than on other aspects of their job.[109]

An example from 1980 illustrates the danger posed by the language barrier. Police were called to a supermarket in Brooklyn, New York. The security guard at the store was a Korean man, and with a gun in his hand, he shouted to the officers in Korean. The two officers thought the security guard was the suspect and shot and killed him.[110] In addition to this tragic loss of life, the man's family, the Korean community, and the police officers themselves all suffered. Although the officers were not criminally charged, they still had to face the realization that they had accidently killed an innocent man.

Because the language barrier presents risks for the safety of both the police and community members, some police departments have instituted "crash" language skill training. Officers are taught a few key phrases in the language or languages most common in the neighborhoods they work in. For example, they may be taught how to say, "drop your weapon," "you're under arrest," or "please show me some identification."

Rural Communities

Almost half of all policing agencies in the United States have fewer than 10 sworn officers. Nearly 90 percent of police departments nationwide serve communities of 25,000 people or fewer.[111]

What about the Victim?

The Homeless: Among the Most Vulnerable

According to the National Coalition for the Homeless, between 1999 and 2004, homeless people were victims of 156 murders and 386 acts of violence. The victims of these crimes—many characterized as hate crimes—were as young as 4 months and as old as 73.

Attacks on the homeless are often vicious and usually include more than one perpetrator. In San Francisco in 2007, a homeless woman died after being splashed with gasoline and set on fire. In 2006, a 15-year-old boy was arrested for beating a homeless man in Redlands, California, and videotaping the scene with his friends. The boy was arrested after adults heard him bragging about the incident.

Even hospitals are accused of mistreating homeless patients. In February 2007, several hospitals in Los Angeles were accused of dumping 55 patients on the city's skid row, where a large number of homeless individuals live on the streets. One ambulance driver left a disabled man, unable to walk and still in a hospital gown, in a gutter outside a skid row park. The police were summoned, and after the case became public, calls to criminalize such dumping behavior followed. Crimes against the homeless occur much more frequently than most people realize and get widespread media attention only when the incidents are particularly heinous. Such incidents raise questions about society's treatment of the less fortunate.

OBSERVE Investigate Understand

- **Why are homeless persons often the victims of crime?**
- **Can "dumping" as a way of dealing with the homeless ever be justified?**
- **Do homeless persons deserve the same quality of police protection as the rest of us?**

SOURCE: Richard Winton, "Patient Dumping May Be Criminal but . . . ," *Los Angeles Times*, February 25, 2007, retrieved March, 20, 2007, from http://www.latimes.com/news/local/la-me dumping25feb25,1,1900583.story?ctrack=1&cset=true.

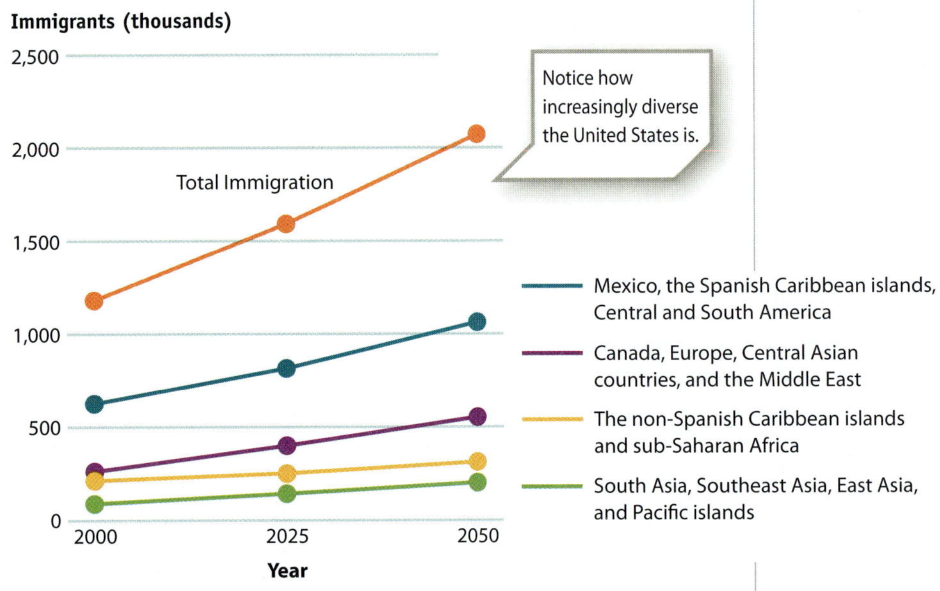

FIGURE 6-7 U.S. Immigration Trends

SOURCE: U.S. Census Bureau, Population Division.

The attitudes of rural officers toward their work often differ from those of officers in big cities. Rural officers are much more supportive of community policing strategies than their urban counterparts.[112] Indeed, rural and small-city police administrators reported that while community policing was considered a reform in large cities, it was already a standard practice for them. These smaller police departments always have closer relationships with members of their communities.[113]

Crime is not as prevalent in rural communities as it is in urban ones. In rural areas there are 16.4 crimes of violence per 1,000 people, while the rate in urban areas is 29.8 violent crimes per 1,000 people.[114] In 2008, however, large cities saw a decline in the murder rate of between 4 and 8 percent, while small towns of fewer than 10,000 residents saw their murder rate increase by 4.4 percent.[115] Some problems previously found only in urban areas, such as gang activity and drugs, are creeping into rural communities. These relatively new problems seriously challenge rural police agencies to adapt their crime-fighting strategies to more proactive, targeted enforcement. In sum, rural police departments support community policing and deal with less crime than urban departments. Nevertheless, rural departments are starting to see historically urban problems such as gang activity and drugs come to their communities.

SUMMARY

The popular image of the police officer—reinforced by the media—is that of a heroic crime fighter engaged in fighting violent crimes and apprehending dangerous suspects. In reality, police officers spend most of their time on the job responding to calls to maintain order or to provide service. Of course, police do also respond to crimes in progress, and apprehending suspects is part of the policing role of enforcing the law. Yet the police cannot routinely enforce all the laws in criminal codes. They tend, therefore, to enforce laws based on their department's priorities and community norms.

Maintaining order, enforcing the law, and providing service are policing roles common across agencies, but police departments employ different strategies to perform these roles. Preventive patrol involves police randomly cruising a neighborhood to maintain a visible police presence in the area, the idea being that maintaining a visible police presence will reduce street crime. However, research experiments failed to validate the claim that random patrols prevent crime. Problem-oriented policing focuses on identifying the causes of problems in an area and then implementing appropriate, sequential steps to alleviate those problems. In community-oriented policing, police and residents work together to reduce crime and disorder. The principle underlying community policing—that crime prevention is a joint responsibility of police and community members—requires a change in the police culture that sees crime prevention and law enforcement as the responsibility of the police alone. Police departments that follow a strategy of aggressive order maintenance, or zero-tolerance policing, target minor public order offenses that affect residents' quality of life. Zero-tolerance policing may reduce crime but can have negative effects on police–community relations.

Most police departments are organized hierarchically, with several ranks of officers and a clear and rigid chain of command. Community policing calls for organizational change, with fewer ranks and fewer special departments, thereby allowing patrol officers greater discretion in deciding how to respond to community needs and problems. The communications function within a police department coordinates the performance of law enforcement activities, but the difficulty or impossibility of communication across jurisdictions presents serious problems, particularly in large-scale emergencies. Local government plays a large and influential role in determining how and where police resources of money, equipment, and personnel are allocated. Local politicians must be sensitive to citizens' demands for police resources.

Even though the media regularly highlight incidents of police brutality or racial profiling, the public generally supports the police, with the level of support higher among Whites than among people of color. Most people expect that the police will keep everyone safe, but, in fact, most violent crimes occur among persons who know each other. Expecting the police to prevent violent acts by one family member against another or friend against friend is a tall—and unrealistic—expectation.

OBSERVE
Investigate
Understand

Review

Identify the principal policing roles.

- A major part of the workload of police is maintaining order.
- Police engage in law enforcement when they enforce criminal law and apprehend law breakers.
- Service activities are nonenforcement actions performed on an as-needed basis.

Compare the various policing strategies.

- In preventive patrol, officers are assigned to randomly drive or walk around an area.
- Problem-oriented policing focuses on discovering the underlying causes of problems and encouraging police to find innovative solutions to solve those problems.
- Community-oriented policing focuses on reducing crime and disorder by involving residents in the job of policing.
- Aggressive order maintenance entails police focusing on minor public order offenses that affect residents' quality of life.

Describe the different jobs in policing.

- The rookie police officer quickly learns the realities of police work while working under the guidance of a training officer.
- Patrol officers are the first individuals to respond to a call for service.
- A follow-up investigation occurs after a patrol officer documents the facts of the crime.
- Police are the primary public safety agency in charge of enforcing traffic laws.
- Communications coordinates the performance of law enforcement activities.
- Custody is the incarceration of parties either accused or convicted of a crime.
- Forensics is the application of scientific knowledge and methods to criminal and civil investigations and legal procedures, including criminal trials.

Explain how police departments strive to maximize their resources.

- Departments use geographic information systems (GIS) technology to produce detailed descriptions of crime occurrences and analyze the relationships between variables such as location and time. This information helps police know how to respond to an incident.
- CompStat is a computerized information system that integrates information from crime maps across the city for department leaders' review. This information helps police administrators decide how to allocate their resources.
- Crime analysis can be helpful in reducing the pool of possible suspects, thereby making investigation more efficient.

Identify the factors that shape public opinion about the police.

- High-profile incidents of police brutality affect public opinion about the police.
- Because their experiences with police have not been as positive, racial and ethnic minorities tend to have lower opinions of the police than do Whites.

Compare the service needs of diverse populations.

- Police aid elder adults in protecting them from and solving crimes of elder abuse.
- Individuals with physical or developmental disabilities are at higher risk of being victimized and, therefore, are in need of police protection.
- Police generally deal with apparently mentally ill persons in one of three ways: transporting them to a facility for psychiatric care, arresting them, or leaving them alone if they don't appear to present a threat or danger.
- The homeless are a vulnerable population that is increasingly subjected to violence.
- Rural communities experience less crime, but are starting to see an increasing amount of gang activity.

Key Terms

adult protective services (APS) 183
aggressive order maintenance 169
broken windows theory 169
chain of command 177
civilianization 165
communications interoperability 174
community-oriented policing 164
CompStat 179
crime analysis 179
crime mapping 179
criminalistics 176
custody 176
decentralization of command 164
elder abuse 183
forensic science laboratories 176
forensics 176
geographic information systems (GIS) 179
hot spot 179
law enforcement 161
line activities 171
maintaining order 161
police–community reciprocity 164
preventive patrol 162
proactive foot patrol 164
problem-oriented policing 163
service activities 162
solvability 173
span of control 178
support activities 171
unity of command 178

Study Questions

1. Three major policing roles are enforcing the law, providing service, and
   a. crime mapping.
   b. custody.
   c. maintaining order.
   d. forensics.

2. The policing strategy that incorporates the SARA process is
   a. random patrol.
   b. split-force.
   c. problem-oriented policing.
   d. directed patrol.

3. The policing strategy that has a police-public partnership as a central feature is
   a. problem-oriented policing.
   b. random patrol.
   c. community policing.
   d. split-force.

4. Communicating across jurisdictions is called
   a. synchronous telephony.
   b. asynchronous telephony.
   c. interoperability.
   d. frequency incompatibility.

5. Which of the following integrates information from crime maps with an exchange of information among an agency's leaders?
   a. CompStat
   b. SARA
   c. Abrasion
   d. NCIC

6. Which of the following examines a crime scene from a behavioral perspective?
   a. Broken windows theory
   b. Crime analysis
   c. SARA
   d. Order maintenance

7. Which of the following presents an efficient means for use of limited policing resources?
   a. Team policing
   b. Air support to ground operations
   c. Crime mapping
   d. DNA analysis

8. A forensics specialist who employs insect evidence to determine time and place of death is known as a
   a. forensic pathologist.
   b. forensic anthropologist.
   c. phrenologist.
   d. forensic entomologist.

9. Which of the following affects police-community relations?
   a. Officers' use of force
   b. Crime rate
   c. Use of forensic scientists
   d. Crime mapping

10. Police departments in rural areas claim they have always practiced
   a. team policing.
   b. preventive patrol.
   c. community-oriented policing.
   d. gang enforcement.

Critical Thinking Questions

1. Is community-oriented policing practical for every community? Why or why not?
2. What is the basis for differing opinions about the police among people of different races?
3. Are the persons suffering mental illness and the homeless really law enforcement problems, or should social services assume an expanded role?

Internet Sites

National Emergency Communications Plan
http://www.dhs.gov/xlibrary/assets/national_emergency_communications_plan.pdf
The Department of Homeland Security prepared, in 2008, the National Emergency Communications Plan to enhance the ability of emergency responders to communicate among jurisdictions, disciplines, and levels of government using a variety of frequency bands.

National Institute of Justice—Mapping Crime: Principle and Practice
http://www.ojp.usdoj.gov/nij/pubs-sum/178919.htm
The National Institute of Justice website introduces the reader to the science of crime mapping and discusses what types of questions crime mapping can help answer.

Office of Community Oriented Policing Services
www.cops.usdoj.gov
The COPS office was created as a result of the Violent Crime Control and Law Enforcement Act of 1994. As a component of the U.S. Justice Department, the mission of the COPS office is to advance community policing in jurisdictions of all sizes across the country.

Suggested Readings

Herman Goldstein, "Improving Policing: A Problem-Oriented Approach," *Crime & Delinquency* 25 (1979).
In this work Goldstein presents his proposal for a new way of policing—problem-oriented policing. The article defines problem-oriented policing and outlines the steps departments need to make to implement it.

Robert Trojanowicz and Bonnie Bucqueroux, *Community Policing: How to Get Started* (Cincinnati, OH: Anderson, 1998).
This book explains community policing as a new way for police departments to do business and outlines how police departments can take the steps necessary to implement community policing.

James Q. Wilson and George Kelling, "Broken Windows: Police and Neighborhood Safety," *Atlantic Monthly* 249 (March 1982).
This is one of the most famous police-related articles published. The main premise is that disorder in neighborhoods leads to more serious crime.

Legal and Special Issues in Policing

CHAPTER 7

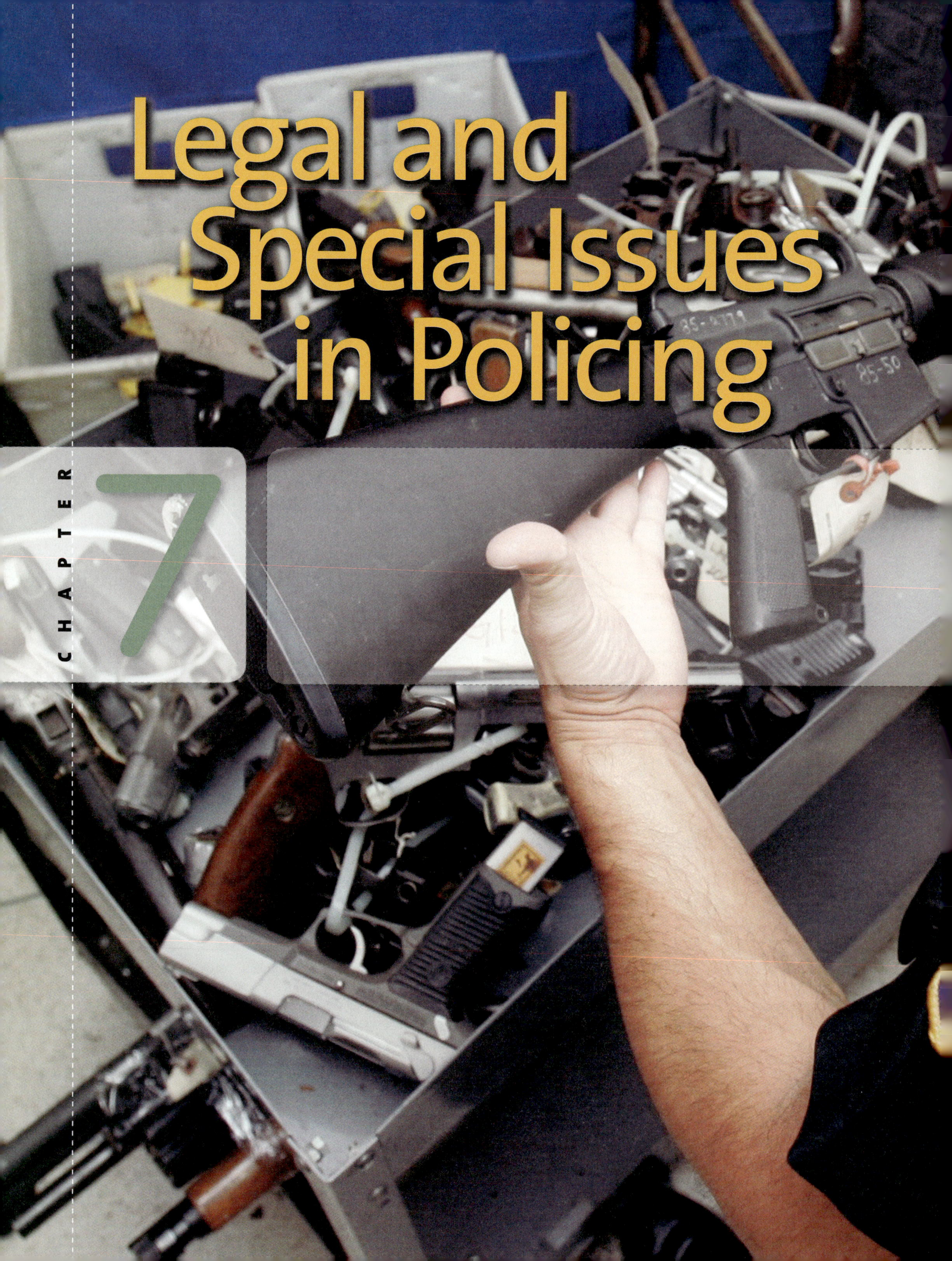

OBSERVE Investigate Understand

After reading this chapter, you should be able to:

- Identify the limitations on law enforcement activities imposed by the Fourth, Fifth, and Sixth Amendments to the U.S. Constitution.
- Identify the situations most likely to entail use of force by the police, and explain how the police use of force is regulated.
- Analyze the impact of the use of force on community relations.
- Describe the major legal and policy issues raised in police pursuits.
- Contrast the strategies of enforcement and prevention used to curb illegal drug use.
- Explain how police departments have responded to gangs.
- Describe how the police response to intimate partner violence has changed over time and explain why.
- Describe the factors that create stress for police officers and efforts to deal with these pressures.

Realities and Challenges

A Shooting in Cincinnati

In April 2001, riots broke out in the city of Cincinnati, Ohio, following the shooting of Timothy Thomas, an unarmed 19-year-old Black male, by White police officer Stephen Roach. Thomas had 14 outstanding misdemeanor warrants and had run from the police when stopped for questioning. He became the 15th Black male since 1995 to be killed by Cincinnati police, during a period in which police killed no White males in the city.[1] The rioting lasted three nights, and the mayor declared a state of emergency and imposed a curfew.[2]

The City of Cincinnati charged Officer Roach with negligent homicide and obstructing official business. He was found not guilty of both charges; the judge criticized the city for bringing the charges at all. "The reasonableness of an officer's actions should be judged from the officers on the scene," he said. "If an officer mistakenly believed that a suspect was likely to fight back, the officer might be justified in using more force than was actually necessary."[3]

Roach left the Cincinnati police department after his acquittal and became an officer in Evendale, a suburb of the same city. Five years after the shooting, in 2006, the Justice Department reported that federal civil rights charges would not be filed against him either. The federal investigation acknowledged that Roach repeatedly changed his story when explaining why he shot Thomas, but the inconsistencies were not enough to conclude he had unconstitutionally denied Thomas his right to be free from excessive force.[4]

Timothy Thomas's mother filed a wrongful death suit against Cincinnati for the killing of her son. Fifteen other unrelated plaintiffs also sued the city, claiming their civil rights had been abused by the police in a number of ways, including unlawful searches and the use of excessive force. In May 2003, Cincinnati settled 16 suits for $4.5 million to be divided among the plaintiffs, by far the largest legal settlement ever paid by the city.[5] Also, partly as a result of the Thomas shooting, the city and citizen groups drafted a collaborative agreement that brought a problem-oriented approach to policing in Cincinnati. The agreement acknowledges that "different groups within the community with different experiences and perspectives share much more in common than not, and can work together on common goals and solve problems together."[6]

The Thomas shooting and the events that followed highlight many issues that arise in police use of force. First, use of force greatly affects how the community views the police. Second, some individuals, particularly young Black males, are more often subjected to use of force than are others. Third, the criminal justice system generally supports officers when they use force. Roach, for example, was acquitted in a criminal court, and the federal government chose not to file charges. Fourth, police use of force can be costly for cities. Beyond the financial losses from lawsuits related to these incidents, the harm done to community relations can be substantial. Finally, police use of force may result in changes to departmental policies or strategies, as illustrated by Cincinnati's collaborative agreement.

In this chapter we examine the legal limitations on law enforcement activities and explore some special issues that prove especially challenging for law enforcement officers. We begin with a discussion of the constitutional limitations on police behavior. In our consideration of special issues with the police use of force, we describe how the use of force has been regulated and how communities have responded to the use of force. Next we discuss some of the major problems in police pursuits. Our discussion of the use of and trafficking in illegal drugs focuses on enforcement, prevention, and rehabilitation efforts. Gangs—particularly in urban areas—pose special problems, and we examine ways in which the police respond to gang activity. A particularly troubling problem is that of intimate partner violence, and we will see how police response to this issue has changed over time. The topics discussed in this chapter contribute greatly to police officer stress. In the last section of the chapter, we discuss the causes of officer stress and some strategies to cope with the particular stresses of being a police officer.

Most of us would like to live in a safe community. Nearly everyone would agree that police ought to be given the authority and tools to catch criminals. But nearly everyone also would agree that police powers should have limits. We would not want to allow law enforcement officers to do anything they want, to anyone they want, any time they want. Several sections of the Constitution, especially the Fourth, Fifth, and Sixth Amendments, place important restraints on what the police may do.

Preview

THE FOURTH AMENDMENT

The Fourth Amendment to the U.S. Constitution protects residents from "unreasonable searches and seizures." This clause raises two basic questions: What is a search or seizure? And what is unreasonable? In other words, first we must determine whether particular actions by the police constitute searches or seizures. If they are, we then must determine whether those searches or seizures are permissible under the Constitution.

Searches and Seizures

Although the language of the Fourth Amendment is succinct, the Supreme Court has interpreted its meaning in a number of cases that define a search or seizure. First, these limitations apply only to actions taken by a government agent; that is, a local, state, or federal law enforcement officer, or someone working for or on behalf of government. The Fourth Amendment does not limit the actions of private individuals and companies unless they are acting at the request or demand of the government. Many employers, for instance, require job applicants to submit to drug testing, a procedure that would likely be unconstitutional for most government agencies because it would be considered an unreasonable search.

MYTH/REALITY

MYTH: The actions of any individual or company can be unconstitutional.

REALITY: Only actions taken by government agencies or those working for those agencies can be in violation of the Constitution.

Second, in order for an act to be a search or seizure, the target of the act must have a reasonable expectation of privacy. If a man is standing on a sidewalk talking loudly into his cell phone to his friend with whom he is planning to rob a bank, a police officer who overhears him has *not* conducted a search or seizure. It would be unreasonable for the man to expect a loud conversation in a public place to be private. However, if he plans the robbery while in his home, it *is* reasonable for him to expect privacy. If the officer places a wiretap on the man's phone so she can listen in on the conversation, she is conducting a search.

In its rulings on the issue of privacy, the Supreme Court has found that people possess the expectation of privacy regarding the contents of their postal mail, phone conversations held in a closed phone booth, most activities in and contents of a home, and the contents of suitcases and other containers.[7] On the other hand, the Court has held there was *no* expectation of privacy, and therefore no search occurred, when police rummaged through a suspect's trash bags after the garbage was placed outside for collection, when police used an electronic device to keep track of which phone numbers a suspect was calling, when police hovered 400 feet above a suspect's home in a helicopter, or when DEA agents used a narcotics detection dog to sniff the outside of a suspect's luggage.[8]

Recent technological advances make it particularly challenging to determine the scope of the Fourth Amendment. To what extent does the amendment protect electronic information such as e-mail, computerized databases (including, for instance, medical records), and records of Internet surfing? The USA PATRIOT Act, enacted after the 9/11 terrorist attacks, gave the government wide authority to engage in various kinds of electronic

DIS Connects

Busted—or Not?

Danny Lee Kyllo lived in the small town of Florence, on Oregon's central coast. Members of a federal drug task force were investigating another man, Sam Shook, for illegal drug activity, and they began to suspect Kyllo was involved. Kyllo lived next door to Shook's daughter, and his sister was the roommate of Shook's daughter. Informants had implicated Kyllo in growing and selling marijuana, and Kyllo's wife had recently been arrested for possession of a controlled substance. A member of the task force obtained Kyllo's utility records and found his electricity use was unusually high. Circumstantial evidence suggested Kyllo was engaged in illegal activities, but there was not enough evidence to obtain a warrant to search Kyllo's house.

At 3:20 a.m. on January 16, 1992, and without first obtaining a search warrant, law enforcement agents parked outside Kyllo's house and used an "Agema Thermovision 210 thermal imager" to scan the house for infrared radiation (heat energy not visible to the naked eye). The officers found parts of the house were unusually hot and concluded Kyllo was using halide lights to grow marijuana.

Based on the results of the heat scan as well as the corroborating evidence, the agents requested and received a warrant to search the home. Once inside, they discovered over 100 marijuana plants and charged Kyllo with manufacturing marijuana in violation of federal law. When his case went to trial, he argued that his Fourth Amendment rights had been violated when the agents used the thermal imager without first obtaining a search warrant.

The government argued that no Fourth Amendment search occurred, because the scan revealed only the heat emanating from the house and not any private activities occurring within. Kyllo was convicted but appealed the decision. His appeal eventually reached the U.S. Supreme Court. In a 5–4 decision (written, surprisingly, by conservative Justice Antonin Scalia), the Supreme Court agreed with Kyllo and concluded:

> Where, as here, the Government uses a device that is not in general public use, to explore details of the home that would previously have been unknowable without physical intrusion, the surveillance is a "search" and is presumptively unreasonable without a warrant.

Eventually, Kyllo's conviction was overturned because there was not sufficient admissible evidence against him.

OBSERVE Investigate Understand

- **How would you justify the Fourth Amendment's limitations on unreasonable searches and seizures if they allow guilty parties to escape punishment?**
- **Does the Fourth Amendment impose unreasonable and unfair limitations on the police?**
- **If law enforcement officers were to access a private unencrypted wireless computer network, would they be in violation of the Fourth Amendment's restriction on unreasonable searches and seizures? Why or why not?**

SOURCE: *Kyllo v. United States*, 533 U.S. 27 (2001).

surveillance. Many critics claim that portions of the act violate the Fourth Amendment's protection of privacy. (The USA PATRIOT Act is discussed in more detail in Chapter 16.) A related question is the extent to which the government may use technology to assist law enforcement activities, especially when the technology is not widely available to the general public. The Disconnects box illustrates the differences between what police see as good detective work and what the Supreme Court views as unconstitutional.

The courts have accorded certain groups less expectation of privacy than other people, making it easier for government agents to justify searches of these individuals. These classes include schoolchildren, prisoners, parolees, and probationers.

If government agents undertake actions, and these actions infringe on reasonable expectations of privacy, the actions are searches or seizures within the meaning of the Fourth Amendment. The subjects of those searches and seizures may be people—an arrest of a person is a seizure—or things. If actions constitute a search or seizure, they must be reasonable to be permissible. But what is reasonable?

Reasonableness

The Fourth Amendment offers a few clues on what constitutes a reasonable search or seizure. The amendment states, "[N]o warrants shall issue, but upon probable cause, supported by oath or affirmation, and particularly describing the place to be searched, and the persons or things to be seized." The courts interpret this passage to mean that ordinarily the government must obtain a **warrant** before its agents can conduct a search or seizure. The agent must collect enough evidence to lead a reasonable person to believe there is a good likelihood—**probable cause**—a crime was committed or that evidence or illicit materials are present. The agent describes the evidence in a sworn written or oral statement and presents it to a neutral party, usually a judge or magistrate. If the judge determines probable cause exists, she authorizes a warrant. The warrant must be specific about what or who is to be searched or seized. Only then can the agent conduct the search or make the seizure. The purpose of this somewhat unwieldy process is to protect people from abuses of police authority and from unjustified or mistaken intrusions into their privacy and freedom.

warrant
A legal document, based on probable cause, permitting police to conduct a search or seizure, or to arrest someone.

probable cause
The amount of evidence necessary to obtain a warrant or conduct most searches and seizures.

stop-and-frisk
Police action allowing the police, with reasonable suspicion, to briefly detain a person, question him about his activities, require him to show identification, and frisk him, or pat him down for weapons; also known as a *Terry* stop.

***Terry* stop**
Another name for stop-and-frisk, in which the police, with reasonable suspicion, briefly detain a person, question him about his activities, require him to show identification, and frisk him, or pat him down for weapons.

Government agents are not required to obtain a warrant before every search or seizure if doing so would endanger public safety by obstructing the agents' ability to do their jobs. For example, few of us would want a firefighter to pause to secure a search warrant before dashing into a burning house to save a trapped child. Consequently, the Supreme Court recognizes a large number of exceptions to the warrant requirement. Of course, to comply with the Fourth Amendment, even warrantless searches and seizures must be reasonable.

Felony arrests may always be made without a warrant—as long as the officer has probable cause to believe the suspect committed a felony. Nevertheless, police sometimes choose to obtain an arrest warrant for practical reasons. First, doing so allows them to enter a home to make the arrest. Entry would usually not be allowed without a warrant if much time had passed since the crime was committed. Second, by having a neutral party confirm that probable cause exists, the warrant protects the police so the arrest is less likely to be declared invalid later. To be considered reasonable seizures, felony arrests always require probable cause—with or without a warrant.

At one time, police could make warrantless arrests for misdemeanors only when suspects committed a breach of the peace in their presence. However, the Supreme Court rejected the breach of the peace requirement in *Atwater v. Lago Vista* (2001) and hinted that it might also reject the requirement for an agent to be present. Like felony arrests, misdemeanor arrests—with or without a warrant—require probable cause.

The Court also authorizes other types of warrantless seizures. One of the most common is called a **stop-and-frisk** or ***Terry* stop** (after *Terry v. Ohio*, 1968, the case in which the Court first made the ruling). A *Terry* stop is permitted

▼ Police Entering a Residence

In most cases, officers need a warrant to search a person's home. *Under what circumstances are search warrants not required?*

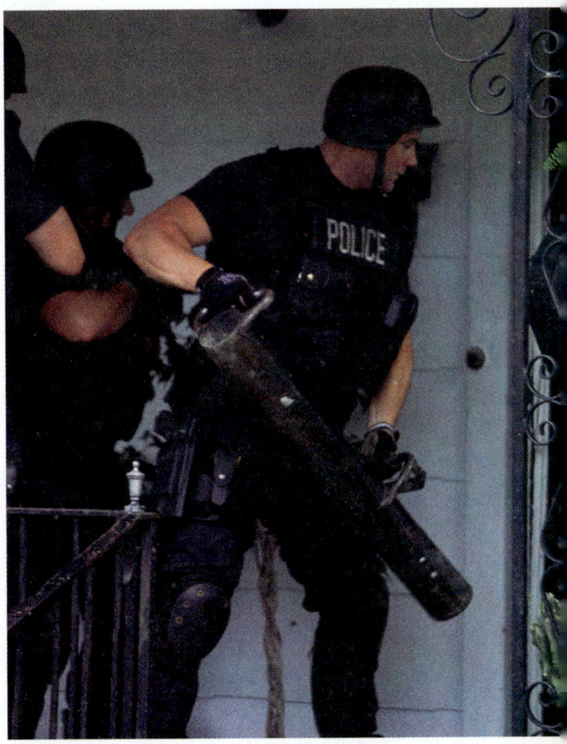

reasonable suspicion
Amount of evidence necessary for officers to conduct a stop-and-frisk, or *Terry* stop.

when police have **reasonable suspicion** to believe a person is engaged in criminal activity. Reasonable suspicion is less certain than probable cause, but more than just a hunch. In the *Terry* case, for example, Terry and another man were pacing back and forth in front of a store, periodically peering in the store windows. An experienced police officer concluded they might be preparing to rob the store. Reasonable suspicion is the amount of evidence required before officers may conduct a stop-and-frisk, which allows a police officer to briefly detain a person, question him about his activities, require him to show identification, and frisk him, or pat him down for weapons. Although this action is a seizure, it does not amount to a full arrest.[9] A full arrest means taking a suspect into police custody for a longer period of time.

automobile exception
An exception to the warrant requirement holding that police do not need warrants to search automobiles, just probable cause.

Like seizures, reasonable searches may be conducted without a warrant. Figure 7-1 lists a number of exceptions to the warrant requirement. One of the most common is the **automobile exception**, first articulated by the Supreme Court in 1925 in *Carroll v. United States*.[10] The Court held it impractical to require police officers to obtain search warrants for cars because, while the officer was obtaining the warrant, the suspect could simply drive away. Furthermore, because it is easy to see into cars, and because their use is already heavily regulated, people have a reduced expectation of privacy in the contents of their

Over time, the U.S. Supreme Court has extended the reach of warrantless searches and seizures and in so doing expanded the powers of police. Warrants are not required for:

- *Terry* stops (stop-and-frisk)
- Automobile searches
- Searches incident to arrest
- Searches at international borders
- Searches at airports
- Stops at sobriety checkpoints
- Inventory searches (when police make inventory lists) of items impounded by police, such as the contents of a car when the car is impounded
- Searches of buildings when police are in hot pursuit of a fleeing felon
- Searches under exigent circumstances such as when someone's life is in immediate danger; for example, when a house is on fire or when a victim is being held hostage
- Protective sweeps—quick searches of a home to ensure no other people are present
- Searches when the items are in plain view
- Searches in open fields and outside the "curtilage" or area immediately surrounding a home
- Consent searches—when the suspect allows the officer to search
- Regulatory searches such as by health inspectors and building inspectors
- Searches where "special government needs" exist, such as in random drug testing of student athletes, customs inspectors, and railway employees involved in accidents

FIGURE 7-1 Exceptions to the Warrant Requirement
Some people argue that this long list of exceptions has essentially gutted the warrant requirement; others assert that the exceptions are necessary for law enforcement officers to do an effective job. *Which argument do you find more persuasive, and why?*

automobiles. The Court, therefore, allows searches of motor vehicles based on probable cause, with no warrant necessary. In subsequent rulings, the Court expanded the automobile exception to include all packages and containers inside a car, even in the trunk. The automobile exception also encompasses vehicles other than cars. In *California v. Carney* (1985), for example, the Court upheld the warrantless search of a motor home.[11]

Another major exception to the warrant requirement is a **search incident to arrest.** When a person is placed under arrest, police may search her body, clothing, and any packages she is carrying. Such searches protect police from any weapons suspects may be carrying, prevent suspects from carrying contraband into a jail, and reduce the chances that evidence will be destroyed. If a suspect is arrested in her home, police may search any areas within her "wingspan"—that is, her approximate reach—even if she is handcuffed. If she is arrested in a car, or shortly after exiting a car, police may search the car's passenger compartment. If her car is impounded and taken into police custody, they may search the entire vehicle. Officers need neither probable cause nor reasonable suspicion to conduct a search incident to arrest. If a person is arrested (as opposed to simply being issued a ticket) for not wearing a seat belt, for example, police could legally search the person's car, purse or backpack, clothing, and body.

search incident to arrest
A warrantless search of a person and the area around that person, conducted shortly after the person is arrested.

After the 9/11 terrorist attacks in 2001, national debates emerged over how much leeway government officials should be allowed in conducting warrantless searches for the protection of national security. In late 2005, newspapers reported that the National Security Agency (NSA) was electronically eavesdropping on hundreds of thousands of domestic and international phone calls and e-mails without search warrants or notification. Only a handful of the thousands of people thus monitored—fewer than 10 a year—were actually found to be acting suspiciously. While critics lambasted the program as a constitutional violation and a severe infringement on privacy, federal authorities defended it as necessary in the "war on terrorism."[12] Also since 9/11, more intrusive searches are being made of people and luggage at airports, and some cities have begun random searches of subway passengers' belongings.[13] In early 2008, Amtrak announced that it would begin random searches of luggage for explosives.

The Exclusionary Rule

Government agents who conduct an unreasonable search or seizure are violating someone's Fourth Amendment rights. But what could the person do about it? Certainly she could sue the police for violating her civil rights. But lawsuits charging unreasonable searches yield little in monetary damages and could even be damaging if the person could be convicted in a trial that used unconstitutionally obtained evidence against her. Nor would lawsuits do much to deter the police from infringing on people's rights in the future, especially if they thought they might obtain valuable evidence.

The Supreme Court recognized this problem in its ruling in *Weeks v. United States* (1914):

> If letters and private documents can thus be seized and held and used in evidence against a citizen accused of an offense, the protection of the 4th Amendment, declaring his right to be secure against such searches and seizures, is of no value, and, so far as those thus placed are concerned, might as well be stricken from the Constitution. The efforts of the courts and their officials to bring the guilty to punishment, praiseworthy as they are, are not to be aided by the sacrifice of those great principles established by years of endeavor and suffering which have resulted in their embodiment in the fundamental law of the land.[14]

In *Weeks*, the Court first articulated the **exclusionary rule**, which says evidence obtained in violation of an individual's Fourth Amendment rights cannot be used against her in a criminal trial. The rule originally applied only to cases in which searches or seizures were conducted by federal officials, but when Dollree Mapp's case reached the U.S. Supreme Court in 1961, the Court extended the rule to state and local officials. Mapp's

exclusionary rule
Illegally obtained evidence cannot be used against a criminal defendant at trial.

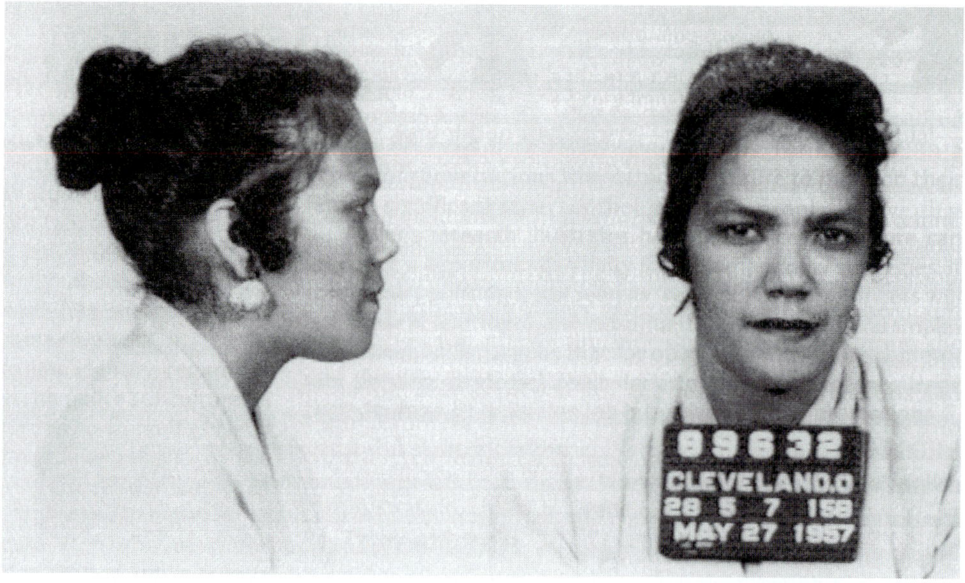

▶ Dollree Mapp

Mapp's case resulted in the extension of the exclusionary rule to the actions of state and local law enforcement officials.

case was based on the following facts. At 3 a.m., a bomb went off outside the home of a small-time bookie in Cleveland, Ohio. The bookie told police the bomb might have been planted by a man to whom he owed money. A few days later police showed up at the home of Dollree Mapp, who ran a boarding house where they suspected the man responsible for the bomb may have spent time.

When the police arrived, Mapp called her lawyer and, on his advice, refused to let the police in without a search warrant. Three hours later more officers as well as Mapp's attorney arrived at the house. The police barred the lawyer from entering the house, broke down Mapp's front door, and went inside. Mapp demanded to see a warrant. One officer claimed he had a warrant and waved a piece of paper in her face. She grabbed it and shoved it down the front of her shirt, but the officer pulled the paper out again. Mapp was then forcibly placed in handcuffs.

The police looked through dressers, closets, suitcases, and photo albums throughout the house. In a trunk in the basement police found pictures of nudes as well as booklets containing lewd stories that apparently belonged to a former boarder who had left them when he moved. Mapp was charged with possession of obscene materials. At her trial, even though no evidence was produced of the existence of a search warrant, Dollree Mapp was convicted and sentenced to a maximum of 7 years in prison.[15]

Dollree Mapp's conviction was overturned, and *Mapp v. Ohio* became a landmark case in the protection of constitutional rights.[16]

MYTH/REALITY

MYTH: The exclusionary rule is a technicality that lets many guilty people go free.

REALITY: The exclusionary rule is the only effective way to protect important constitutional rights from government intrusion. Furthermore, in most cases in which evidence is excluded from a trial under the rule, the defendant is convicted based on other evidence.[17]

How to apply the Constitution to law enforcement is a subject of considerable and lively debate. On one hand, people argue that to require police to follow strict rules in criminal investigation is both unrealistic and dangerous. Furthermore, the argument goes, criminals should not get away with their crimes merely because police make mistakes.

Other people contend that protecting people from infringements on their basic constitutional rights is more important than catching criminals. According to this argument, excluding illegally obtained evidence effectively deters police misconduct. Moreover, if the courts set out clear rules for police, rather than muddying the waters with more and more exceptions, police will be able to do their jobs without having to worry about whether evidence might be excluded.

The exclusionary rule is a strict rule. If evidence that was illegally seized is the only evidence—or even the primary evidence—against a defendant, and that evidence is excluded from trial under the exclusionary rule, the defendant may go free. Thus the exclusionary rule may allow people *known* to have broken the law—sometimes even dangerous and violent people—to escape punishment for their actions. Many government officials complain that the exclusionary rule makes criminals harder to catch and leaves guilty people free to commit more crimes. Many would argue that the danger a suspect presents to the community should outweigh Fourth Amendment rights against illegal searches and seizures. Victims often find it difficult to see those who harm them go unpunished. The public tends to view those who are released on Fourth Amendment grounds as having "gotten off on a technicality." Because we usually hear about Fourth Amendment violations in the context of someone having broken the law (if no illegal evidence is found, the case never goes to court, and nobody hears about the violations), many people view the amendment and the exclusionary rule as granting "special rights" to guilty people. After all, the argument goes, if I have nothing to hide, why should I care whether the police search my belongings?

In reality, however, the Fourth Amendment protects everyone, guilty and innocent alike. Even completely law-abiding people may not want to give the government unrestricted authority to rummage through their private affairs and belongings any time some government employee feels like it. Defenders of the exclusionary rule, including justices of the Supreme Court, contend that the rule makes constitutional rights meaningful and effectively deters government officials from violating the Constitution. Most criminals can eventually be successfully prosecuted without infringing on Fourth Amendment rights, and if a few guilty people do go free, perhaps that is a reasonable price to pay for protecting everyone's freedom and privacy.[18]

Even the Supreme Court, however, has had difficulty applying the exclusionary rule when doing so allows an obviously guilty person to go unpunished. After *Mapp*, the Court held the rule does not apply to proceedings other than criminal trials. Therefore, illegally obtained evidence can be used in deportation proceedings, civil tax proceedings, and grand jury hearings. Such evidence also can be used in criminal cases to *impeach* a defendant or other witness (that is, to prove the defendant gave false testimony or is an untrustworthy person). This is one reason criminal defendants sometimes do not take the stand to testify in their own defense. If they do testify, evidence that would otherwise be inadmissible can be brought in to impeach them. If they refrain from testifying, the jury will never hear that evidence.

The Derivative Evidence Rule

The **derivative evidence rule**, also known as the **fruit of the poisonous tree doctrine**, further extends the exclusionary rule. The derivative evidence rule provides that any evidence *derived from* something that is illegally seized is itself inadmissible. For example, suppose police illegally record a phone conversation in which a suspect reveals the location of stolen goods. The police then obtain a warrant based on the content of that conversation, and they find the stolen goods. Not only would the taped conversation be suppressed as evidence under the exclusionary rule, but so would the stolen goods. Even though police had a warrant to search for the goods, that warrant was the "fruit" of the "poisonous" phone tap.

The derivative evidence rule extended the scope of the exclusionary rule, but the Supreme Court has carved out a number of exceptions to the exclusionary rule. These exceptions permit illegally obtained evidence to be used against a defendant at trial.

derivative evidence rule
An extension to the exclusionary rule holding that evidence derived from something that is illegally searched or seized is itself inadmissible; also known as the fruit of the poisonous tree doctrine.

fruit of the poisonous tree doctrine
Another name for the derivative evidence rule, which excludes evidence derived from an illegal search or seizure.

The Good Faith Exception to the Exclusionary Rule

Articulated by the Supreme Court in *United States v. Leon* in 1984,[19] the **good faith exception** applies when police officers act in good faith on a warrant or law that is later declared invalid. If police reasonably believe the warrant or law authorizing a search or seizure is

good faith exception
Exception to the exclusionary rule allowing illegally obtained evidence to be used if officers relied in good faith on an invalid warrant.

legitimate, but it later turns out it is not, the evidence will not be suppressed. In *Arizona v. Evans* (1995), for example, an officer stopped Evans for a traffic violation. The officer made a computer check for outstanding warrants and discovered a misdemeanor warrant, so he placed Evans under arrest. When he searched Evans incident to the arrest, he discovered marijuana. Later it turned out the warrant had been declared invalid 17 days earlier, but the court clerk's office had mistakenly left it in the system. Because the officer was acting in good faith reliance on the computer check, the Supreme Court upheld Evans's conviction for marijuana possession.[20]

Other Exceptions to the Exclusionary Rule

inevitable discovery
Exception to the exclusionary rule allowing illegally obtained evidence to be admissible if it would inevitably have been discovered through legal means.

independent source
Exception to the exclusionary rule permitting the use of evidence discovered independent of any improper search or seizure.

attenuation
An exception to the exclusionary rule that applies when the link between the unconstitutional acts and the evidence becomes weak due to intervening time or events.

standing
The legal ability to assert a particular constitutional claim.

Other exceptions to the exclusionary rule include **inevitable discovery**, in which illegally obtained evidence is admissible if police officers would have discovered it anyway had they used proper procedures. The **independent source** exception allows evidence to be admissible if its discovery was independent of any improper search or seizure. **Attenuation** is the exception that applies when the link between the unconstitutional acts and the evidence becomes weak due to intervening time or events. For example, if a defendant was wrongly arrested but then released and, after consultation with his attorney, returns to the police station several weeks later to confess, his confession will almost certainly be admissible even though the original arrest was unlawful.[21]

The exclusionary rule does not apply when the defendant does not have **standing**; that is, if it was not the defendant's own rights that were violated by the unreasonable search or seizure. For example, if police improperly search a home and find evidence implicating a person who does not live in the home, that evidence can be used against the visitor.

The Supreme Court recently created another exception to the exclusionary rule, this one involving "no-knock warrants." The Court had previously ruled that unless police have obtained a no-knock warrant, when they execute a search warrant at a house, they must knock before entering, announce their presence, and give the resident a reasonable amount of time to voluntarily comply with the warrant.[22] The Court's decision in *Hudson v. Michigan* (2006) did not overturn the knock and announce rule, but it did hold that if police violate the rule, the exclusionary rule does not apply. Justice Scalia wrote,

> [T]he social costs of applying the exclusionary rule to knock-and-announce violations are considerable; the incentive to such violations is minimal to begin with, and the extant deterrences against them are substantial—incomparably greater than the factors deterring warrantless entries when *Mapp* was decided. Resort to the massive remedy of suppressing evidence of guilt is unjustified.[23]

Therefore, even though violation of the knock-and-announce rule violates a suspect's constitutional rights, any evidence that is found will be admissible. Critics have argued that this ruling makes the knock-and-announce rule meaningless.

Opponents of the exclusionary rule support its long list of exceptions, saying those exceptions make it easier for police to do their jobs and let fewer obviously guilty people go free. Others argue that exceptions have essentially gutted the rule, leaving little incentive for police to comply with the Constitution and little recourse for individuals when they don't. Because many cases from which exceptions arose were prosecutions for drug possession, some commentators believe the exclusionary rule, and to a large extent the Bill of Rights itself, is the biggest casualty of the war on drugs.[24]

THE FIFTH AMENDMENT

The Fifth Amendment states that no person "shall be compelled in any criminal case to be a witness against himself." This amendment gives criminal defendants the right to refuse to testify—to "take the Fifth." But these words also affect the manner in which police may question suspects.

Voluntariness

In the spring of 1934, a White man named Raymond Stewart was found beaten to death at his home near Meridian, Mississippi. Soon after, sheriff's deputies, accompanied by other men, took three young African American men from their houses and demanded they confess to the murder. All three men were viciously beaten and whipped; one of them twice had a rope tied around his neck and was suspended from a tree. Threatened with death, all three eventually confessed to the murder. At trial (which occurred only a few days later), even though the police admitted to hanging and whipping the defendants, the confessions were admitted as evidence. All three defendants denied having anything to do with Stewart's death. After brief deliberation, the all-White jury found the defendants guilty and sentenced them to death.

When the Supreme Court finally heard the case (*Brown v. Mississippi*) two years later, it held that the Constitution prohibits the use of coerced confessions as evidence, ruling that such confessions violated the due process clause of the Fourteenth Amendment. Chief Justice Charles Evans Hughes wrote, "It would be difficult to conceive of methods

Real Careers

BRIAN HILSINGER

Work location: Cincinnati, Ohio

College(s): University of Cincinnati, 2001

Major(s): Criminal Justice (BS)

Job title: Deputy United States Marshal, Southern District of Ohio

Salary range for job like this: $30,000–$35,000

Time in job: 7 years

Work Responsibilities

I am primarily responsible for the security of all parties in the courtroom. That includes helping to transport federal inmates to their court appearances and protecting all courtroom personnel from the inmate and any witnesses or family members who may become belligerent. One duty that is unique to U.S. Marshals is protecting federal judges. In fact, I once went to Oklahoma City as part of a week-long protection detail of Supreme Court Justice Sandra Day O'Connor.

A new function that the U.S. Marshals have assumed in the last two years is enforcing the Adam Walsh Act. This act requires a person who has been convicted of a sex offense to register as a sex offender. When an offender fails to comply with this act, and crosses interstate commerce or state lines, the violation becomes federal, and a U.S. Marshal becomes responsible for making the arrest. But I should point out that Marshals are unique because they can make arrests on both federal and local warrants.

Why Criminal Justice?

I majored in criminal justice because I knew that this was the first step on the road to working in law enforcement. While I was a student at the University of Cincinnati, I was an intern with the U.S. Marshals. My first job in the field was with the Ohio Adult Parole Authority as a parole officer. Having a positive first encounter with the profession, I knew I wanted to pursue a career with the U.S. Marshals Service.

Expectations and Realities of the Job

I did not expect the job to entail so much precision and attention to detail. For instance, I now see that part of being an effective U.S. Marshal, and investigator, is making sure I am working with the most current information. This means taking comprehensive notes when in the field, and documenting the casework carefully. Other than this aspect of the work, the expectations that I had prior to becoming a U.S. Marshal met the realities of the job. In addition to my internship, I did a lot of research on my own to learn about the training and responsibilities of U.S. Marshals.

My Advice to Students

No matter what career track you have in mind, just get a foot in the door with any CJ-related job. You will mostly likely need that valuable field experience to pursue a career in CJ. Also, networking with colleagues, professors, and classmates is one of the best ways to learn about potential career paths and job openings. Finally, regardless of the job you choose, keep your criminal record clean as that can affect your eligibility to be hired.

voluntariness test
Rule that confessions are inadmissible unless made willingly.

more revolting to the sense of justice than those taken to procure the confessions of these petitioners, and the use of the confessions thus obtained as the basis for conviction and sentence was a clear denial of due process."[25] In overturning the defendants' convictions, the Court established the **voluntariness test**, the rule that confessions are inadmissible unless made willingly.

▲ **Ernesto Miranda**

His case resulted in the famous requirement of the *Miranda* warnings.

Miranda v. Arizona

At the time that *Brown v. Mississippi* was decided and for the next 30 years, the Fifth Amendment applied only to actions taken by federal government agents. In 1964, in *Malloy v. Hogan*, the Supreme Court held that the self-incrimination clause of the Fifth Amendment applied to actions taken by state, local, and federal governments.[26] This ruling set the scene for one of the Court's most famous cases, *Miranda v. Arizona*.

The *Miranda* case actually arose out of several unrelated criminal cases in which suspects were taken into custody and interrogated without being informed of their constitutional rights, after which they confessed. Twenty-two-year-old Ernesto Miranda was suspected of committing a series of kidnappings and rapes in Phoenix, Arizona. After police questioned him for two hours, he confessed to one of the rapes and, based in part on his confession, was convicted and sentenced to 20 to 30 years.

Unlike the situation in *Brown*, there was no evidence Miranda was beaten, threatened, or otherwise compelled to confess. Nevertheless, the Supreme Court held that even without the use of threats or physical force, custodial interrogation is inherently coercive. The conditions of being held against one's will in an unfamiliar place, separated from family and allies, and questioned by investigators often trained in psychological techniques to obtain incriminating statements all lead to a situation in which a suspect cannot truly exercise free will. Without prohibiting police interrogations altogether, how can we ensure a suspect is not compelled to confess in violation of the Fifth Amendment?

The Court's solution was the ruling that before people in police custody may be questioned, they must be informed of their constitutional rights. This instruction is, of course, the famous ***Miranda* warnings**, and anyone who has ever watched a crime show on TV can probably recite them:

***Miranda* warnings**
Notifications that police must give suspects about their rights prior to beginning custodial interrogation.

- You have the right to remain silent.
- Anything you say may be used in court.
- You have the right to consult a lawyer and have a lawyer present during questioning.
- If indigent, you may have a lawyer provided at no cost.
- You have the right to end questioning or consult with a lawyer at any time.

Informing suspects of their rights was seen as the only effective way to safeguard their privilege against self-incrimination.[27]

The *Miranda* decision was controversial. Critics claimed that reading suspects their rights would result in significantly fewer confessions and, therefore, significantly fewer convictions—thus hobbling effective law enforcement. In reality, however, approximately 75 percent of suspects waive their *Miranda* rights and choose to speak to police rather than remaining silent or consulting a lawyer.[28] Clearly, the criminal justice system has not come to a grinding halt since *Miranda*. In 2000, in *Dickerson v. United States*, the Court reaffirmed the *Miranda* requirements.[29] If a person is in custody and is questioned without first being informed of his rights, the exclusionary rule applies and any statements he makes will be inadmissible.

MYTH/REALITY

MYTH: Police must *always* read suspects their *Miranda* rights.

REALITY: Suspects do not have to be read their rights if they are not in custody or if police do not plan to interrogate them.[30]

The *Miranda* rule is limited in several ways. First, it applies only to *custodial* interrogations. A suspect who is not actually under arrest need not be warned. If a suspect is under arrest, police must read her the warnings only if they want to question her. Just talking to a suspect or asking for identification does not constitute an interrogation. In *Rhode Island v. Innis* (1980), the Supreme Court defined interrogation as "words or actions . . . that the police should know are reasonably likely to elicit an incriminating response."[31]

Second, *Miranda* applies only to **testimonial evidence**—statements made by the suspect. *Miranda* does not apply to nontestimonial evidence such as fingerprints, DNA samples, and so on, even if that evidence may link the suspect to a crime.

testimonial evidence
Words or statements made by a person.

In *Miranda*, the Court was specific about what information police must give to suspects when they warn them. Many police departments ask officers to read from prepared cards that contain language virtually identical to that in the *Miranda* opinion—although the Supreme Court later held that the content of the warnings does not need to be exactly the same. Police may use different words as long as the correct basic information is given and the officers are not overly coercive. In fact, even if proper *Miranda* warnings are given, a suspect's statements may be suppressed if the police use too much intimidation. For example, if a suspect was read her rights and then police pointed a gun at her head and told her to confess, the confession would not be admissible.

Exceptions to the *Miranda* Rule

Just as there are exceptions to the Fourth Amendment's prohibitions against unreasonable searches and seizures, there are also exceptions to the *Miranda* rule. The **public safety exception** allows police to dispense with the warnings if they believe there is an immediate threat to public safety. For example, police may question a person suspected of kidnapping a child about the child's location if they think the child is in danger. Even though the suspect is not "Mirandized," any statements he makes in this situation will still be admissible against him at trial. All the exclusionary rule exceptions to the Fourth Amendment apply as well to the Fifth Amendment. For instance, the statements of suspects who are not properly Mirandized may be used to impeach them (to prove they are lying) at trial.

public safety exception
Exception to *Miranda* requiring police to interrogate suspects without first warning them of their rights if there is a significant threat to public safety.

Suspects may waive their Fifth Amendment rights and choose to speak to police without an attorney present, and suspects who waive their rights may change their minds later. The only requirements for waiver are that it be knowing—that is, the suspects must be aware of what their rights are and voluntarily decide to waive them. Social scientists question whether certain people, such as teenagers and the developmentally disabled, can really understand their rights enough to knowingly waive them, but the courts refuse to impose blanket prohibitions of waivers for any group of people.[32]

Innocent people are more likely than guilty ones to waive their rights, perhaps in the naïve belief that by cooperating with police they will talk their way out of trouble.[33] Perhaps this explains why, according to the Innocence Project, false confessions are the second leading cause of wrongful convictions.[34]

THE SIXTH AMENDMENT

The Sixth Amendment affords accused persons several constitutional protections, but one guaranteed right is of particular significance to law enforcement: "In all criminal prosecutions, the accused shall enjoy the right . . . to have assistance of counsel for his defense." This statement means that criminal defendants are entitled to the help of an attorney at trial. However, the rights protected by the Sixth Amendment apply well before trial. In fact, they apply as soon as formal charges are filed against a defendant. A defendant who has been charged is in more peril than a suspect who is merely being questioned (and who could still be released without being charged with any crime). Therefore, the Sixth Amendment right to counsel is broader and more powerful than the Fifth Amendment rights under *Miranda.*

The Supreme Court articulated the general rule about questioning defendants outside the presence of counsel in *Massiah v. United States* (1964).[35] Winston Massiah was indicted for transporting cocaine. He obtained a lawyer, and while he was out on bail, federal agents convinced his codefendant (a friend who was accused of committing the crime with him) to have a conversation with Massiah in the presence of a hidden radio transmitter. The codefendant purposely got Massiah to make incriminating statements while an agent listened to the conversation. The statements Massiah made during that conversation were later used against him at trial. In a 6–3 decision, however, the Supreme Court held that Massiah's Sixth Amendment rights had been violated. To question a defendant without his lawyer present, whether secretly, as in this case, or openly, interferes with the lawyer's ability to effectively represent her client. Therefore, once a person has been formally charged with a crime, any questioning must take place in the presence of an attorney. If statements are obtained in violation of the *Massiah* rule, the exclusionary rule applies.

The *Massiah* decision was less controversial than the *Miranda* ruling, in part because *Massiah* usually applies only after police have had the opportunity to conduct a fair amount of investigation. Nonetheless, some were concerned that *Massiah* might interfere with the ability to put wrongdoers behind bars. A more conservative Supreme Court later limited the *Massiah* ruling somewhat by finding that *Massiah* rights, like *Miranda* rights, may be waived. Thus a defendant who has been charged with a crime and has a lawyer may still be questioned without her lawyer being present as long as she is adequately notified of her rights and expressly and voluntarily chooses to waive them. In addition, a defendant who "lawyers up" on one charge—invokes his Sixth Amendment rights and obtains an attorney—may be interrogated by police about a different crime.[36]

All the exceptions to the exclusionary rule apply to the Sixth Amendment just as they do to the Fourth and Fifth Amendments. A famous example is the "Christian Burial Speech" case. Robert Williams was the suspect in the kidnapping and probable murder of a 10-year-old girl in Des Moines, Iowa. The body had not yet been found, although a major search was under way. Williams turned himself in to authorities in Davenport, 160 miles away, was arraigned, and hired an attorney who was in Des Moines. Police officers from Des Moines picked Williams up in Davenport. On the drive back to Des Moines, one of the officers had a conversation with Williams and said how sad it was that the girl's parents would be unable to give her a Christian burial. Williams, who the officers knew was religious and who had a history of mental illness, eventually led them to the girl's body.

The Supreme Court held that the officer had violated Williams's Sixth Amendment rights by questioning him, and therefore the statements Williams made to the officers were inadmissible. However, the Court also eventually ruled that the body's location and condition could be admitted as evidence because, the Court said, the search party was nearby and the body would have been discovered even without Williams's incriminating statements. Therefore, the evidence was admissible under the inevitable discovery exception.[37]

Police officers need to balance their responsibilities to uphold individuals' liberties with securing public safety. A Global View illustrates how difficult that balancing act can be, especially when policing international events.

Constitutional restrictions and guarantees place legal limitations on what police in the United States may and may not do. In addition, police face a number of special issues and situations that affect both police performance and the way communities interact with law enforcement.

USE OF FORCE

A number of cases of excessive police use of force have galvanized public concern.[38] The term *use of force* encompasses an array of coercive actions, from control holds (for example,

A Global View

Policing and Civil Liberties

In the summer of 2006, Germany hosted the international soccer World Cup, an event expected to draw about 3 million foreign tourists. Eager to portray their country in a positive light, German leaders instituted security measures designed to protect against any terrorist action, large-scale protests against governments, and fan altercations that could provoke rioting.

Fans deemed to be "hooligans" and, therefore, security risks were banned from attending.[a] Ticket buyers had to supply personal information, including their home address. The tickets could be electronically read to identify who bought them and where the buyer was seated in the stadium. Germany redesigned its stadiums and installed video cameras to allow more efficient surveillance of the crowds. A "fan zone" near the major stadium in Berlin was monitored with heavy electronic surveillance and a major police presence. Tens of thousands of police and private security guards were employed to ensure security.

All went off without a major incident, but the combination of a major police presence, the banning of some fans, and the greatly increased public surveillance raised criticisms from some that the extensive security measures greatly outstripped individuals' rights to privacy.

The policing of the World Cup in 2006 and other major international events sparked much discussion about compromising civil liberties in the name of security needs. These arguments surfaced again as the Chinese government prepared for the Summer 2008 Olympic Games. Human rights activists documented that the Chinese government rounded up political dissenters and imprisoned them. The activists were then imprisoned themselves.[b]

The Bill of Rights and other legal protections limit what U.S. law enforcement can do in the name of public safety. But balancing security and civil liberties can be difficult, and different countries clearly choose to balance them in different ways.

Observe Investigate Understand

- **Which, if any, of the security measures enacted by Germany in connection with the 2006 World Cup would be constitutionally prohibited in the United States?**
- **What crowd control measures are used in the United States?**
- **How can protection of individual civil liberties be balanced against the need for public safety?**

SOURCES: [a]Clifford Scott and Geoff Pearson, "Football Banning Orders, Proportionality, and Public Order Policing," *The Howard Journal of Criminal Justice* 45 (July 2006): 241.

[b]Hu Jia and Teng Biao, "The Real China and the Olympics," *The Washington Post*, Saturday, April 5, 2008, A15.

"wrist-locks" and "twist-locks") to deadly force. Because it is now so easy to record the use of force in public places, it is being illuminated as never before. Video recording devices are increasingly ubiquitous, from on-board video cameras in law enforcement vehicles to citizens' handheld video recording devices. The omnipresence of video recordings was underscored in a 2008 incident in New York City, in which a citizen videotaped a police officer inappropriately shoving a bicyclist to the pavement. Besides becoming a featured news story on New York media, the video was widely distributed via YouTube.[39]

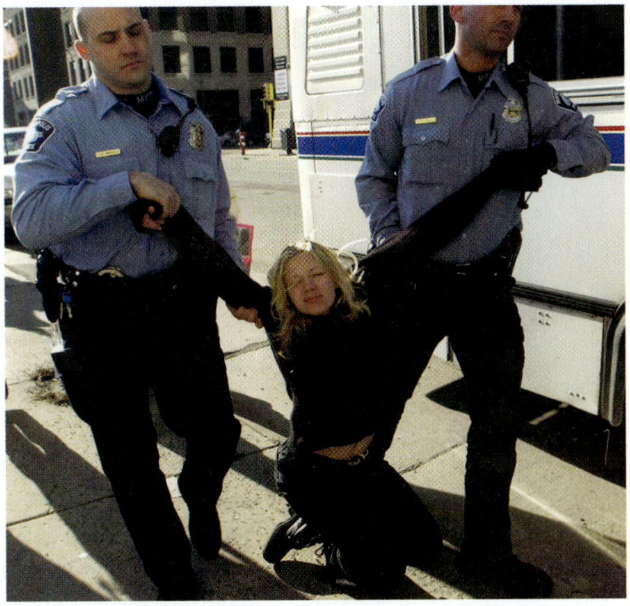

▲ **Police Use of Force**

Officers' use of force is heavily regulated.

Regulating Use of Force

No aspect of the exercise of law enforcement powers poses greater potential for harm than the misuse of force. Therefore, the laws and policies concerning police use of force are particularly important.

Case Law

The facts of three key cases define lawful use of force: *Tennessee v. Garner*, *Graham v. Connor*, and *Saucier v. Katz*. In *Tennessee v. Garner* (1985), the U.S. Supreme Court held that the use of deadly force was not reasonable unless the suspect committed a crime that inflicted serious harm and his or her escape posed a significant risk of further serious harm to persons at large. The *Garner* decision reversed the common law authorization to use deadly force against any fleeing felon.[40]

KEY CONCEPTS
Constitutional Provisions that Limit Police Actions

Amendment	Provisions
Fourth Amendment	
Searches and seizures	Applies only to actions undertaken by government agents
	Applies only when there is a reasonable expectation of privacy
Reasonableness	Many searches require valid search warrants based on probable cause
	There are numerous exceptions to the warrant requirement
Exclusionary rule	Evidence seized in violation of the Fourth Amendment is excluded at trial
	There are numerous exceptions to the exclusionary rule
Fifth Amendment	Prohibits compelled confessions
	Originally, confessions were permitted as evidence as long as they were voluntary
	In *Miranda v. Arizona*, the U.S. Supreme Court required that defendants must be informed of certain rights prior to custodial interrogation
	There are exceptions to the *Miranda* rule
Sixth Amendment	Guarantees criminal defendants the assistance of counsel
	Once formal charges have been filed, a defendant cannot be questioned outside the presence of the defense attorney
	Exceptions apply as they do to Fourth and Fifth Amendment rights

The Court's decision in *Graham v. Connor* (1989) established the "objective reasonableness" standard. Recognizing that police officers are often forced to make split-second decisions about the amount of force necessary in a particular situation, the Court ruled that the reasonableness of a particular use of force incident must be judged from the perspective of a reasonable officer on the scene. Other factors determining whether the use of force meets the objective reasonableness standard include severity of the crime, immediacy of the threat to the safety of officers or others, and whether the suspect is resisting arrest or attempting to evade arrest by flight.[41]

qualified immunity
The inability of officers to be sued for their actions under certain circumstances.

In *Saucier v. Katz* (2001), the Court recognized that on occasion police officers apply force that may eventually be determined unconstitutional yet remains protected by **qualified immunity**—meaning that the officers, under specific circumstances, cannot be sued for their actions. In the words of the Court, "qualified immunity operates to protect officers from the sometimes 'hazy border' between excessive and acceptable force."[42]

A number of cases following *Saucier* more closely examined the "hazy border" between excessive and acceptable use of force. In *Brosseau v. Haugen* (2004), the Court established the pivotal factor in determining whether qualified immunity would be warranted: whether the officer had fair notice that use of force in that situation was unlawful. "The contours of the right must be sufficiently clear that a reasonable official would understand that what he is doing violates that right."[43] The "contours" test translates to an objective evaluation of whether an officer should know whether her conduct was unlawful. If the officer was aware of how similar situations had been handled and then evaluated in legal proceedings in the past, then qualified immunity likely would not operate to excuse her inappropriate actions. Commonly, an officer's training records are accessed to determine exposure to knowledge.

Court decisions have made it clear that we must judge the need for and appropriateness of any level of force objectively on the facts in a given situation. Law enforcement officers must use only non-deadly force options when deadly force is not appropriate, and they may use only a level of force that is objectively reasonable to bring an incident under control.

Use of Force Continuum

The **use of force continuum** is a guideline depicting the appropriate amount of force a law enforcement officer may use in particular kinds of situations. As Figure 7-2 illustrates, the continuum includes strategies for escalating force when a subject does not comply with officers, as well as strategies for de-escalating force when a subject *is* compliant. The underlying principle of a force continuum is that force should be applied proportionately and increased or decreased in increments.[44]

use of force continuum Guideline depicting the appropriate amount of force a law enforcement officer may use in particular kinds of situations.

Policy

Clear guidelines and consistent punishments for misconduct reduce the incidence of excessive force.[45] Requiring officers to report incidents in which they use force allows the agency to monitor them and their behavior. The influence of police leadership on officer behavior and use of force may be substantial. As in other areas, the agency chief is the main architect of police officers' street behavior.[46]

Training translates policy and procedure into real-world scenarios.[47] In new recruit training at the Los Angeles Police Department, for example, recruits role-play immediate intervention if they believe another officer is using inappropriate force.[48]

Community Response to Police Use of Force

Excessive use of force by police is probably infrequent. National surveys reveal that fewer than 2 percent of police–citizen contacts include use of force by the police, and in the majority of these, absent a complaint from the subject of the force, one has to presume the degree of force was appropriate to the situation.[49]

When police do use excessive force, however, the harm done extends far beyond the individuals directly involved in an incident. Many urban riots of the late twentieth century—such as those that occurred in Los Angeles, Miami, and New York—resulted from public perceptions of misuse of force by law enforcement. Excessive force reduces public confidence in the police, depresses officer morale, and generates conflict between police and residents. Police violation of the spirit of the law blurs the line between totalitarian and democratic governance.[50]

Critics of the police assume that use of any force, including excessive force, primarily occurs when White officers deal with minority citizens. Use of force appears, however, to be more closely related to the dynamics of the situation than to a citizen's personal characteristics such as age, gender, and ethnicity. Calls for service most likely to result in use of force relate to interpersonal disturbances, intoxicated persons, fleeing suspects, and suspects resisting arrest.[51] For example, force is more likely if the incident includes a suspect in a violent crime or occurs after a vehicle pursuit or includes more than four bystanders or more than one officer in an encounter.[52]

Officers are actually most likely to use force against individuals of the same ethnic background. For example, Latino officers are most likely to use force against other

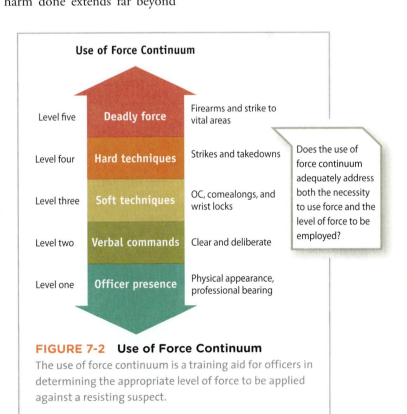

Does the use of force continuum adequately address both the necessity to use force and the level of force to be employed?

FIGURE 7-2 Use of Force Continuum
The use of force continuum is a training aid for officers in determining the appropriate level of force to be applied against a resisting suspect.

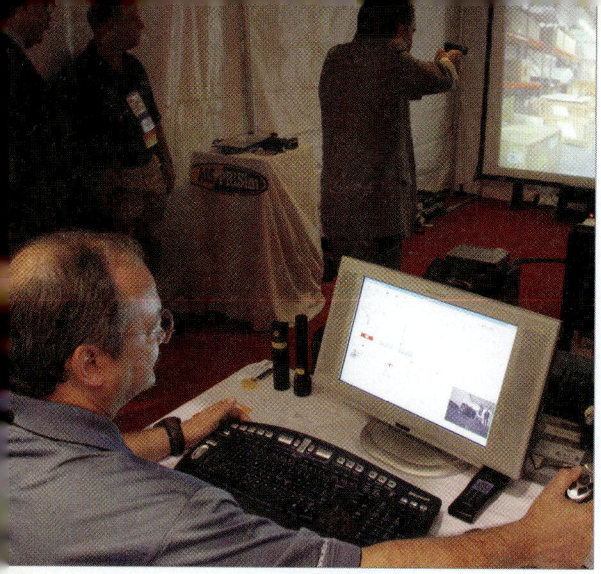

RealCrime Tech

TAKING SIMULATION TRAINING IN USE OF FORCE TO THE NEXT LEVEL

Most people are familiar with the concept of virtual reality, which is an *artificial environment* "entered" when one is outfitted with special head gear and full-body wiring. A step beyond this is the concept of "augmented reality." Augmented reality inserts simulated humans into an actual physical environment. The simulated humans, known as "avatars," can hide, move about, or crawl within the environment at hand. The avatars can be encircled, be given voice commands, and engage in a variety of intelligent behaviors. The only thing they cannot be subjected to is handcuffing—because these "beings" do not exist.

Officers undergoing augmented reality training carry a computer mouse customized as a weapon. Pulling (that is, "clicking") the weapon's trigger activates the mouse. The helmet a player wears includes a camera that records what the participant is seeing and his reaction. This enables a glimpse into decision making and sets the stage for a comprehensive review of actions taken—or omitted. The augmented reality simulation permits participants to act within the type of environment (such as kitchen chairs and a table) that might typically be encountered and enables multiple players to be involved.

SOURCE: National Law Enforcement and Corrections Technology Center, *TECH Beat: A Different Reality* (Washington, DC: National Law Enforcement and Corrections Technology Center, 2007), 1–2.

Latinos. However, force other than use of officers' hands is most likely to be used on Black suspects regardless of the officer's ethnicity. Officers with less than 5 years on the force are more likely to use force than are their more experienced peers.[53]

The role that race of a suspect plays in police use of force is complicated.[54] In the end, however, it may not matter what the evidence indicates if people believe what they witness in the media—that police violence is primarily directed at Black males. Highly publicized incidents such as the beating of Rodney King in Los Angeles in 1991 and the 2006 shooting of Sean Bell in New York City the night before his wedding led U.S. residents, especially those of color, to believe police are more likely to use force against Black males.

Because their feelings about police develop, in part, from highly publicized incidents of violence in their communities, Blacks may hesitate to call the police for help, fearing the result. That distrust can have devastating consequences for both police and residents. In December 1998, a 19-year-old Black woman, Tyisha Miller, waited alone in her car in Riverside, California, while her friend went to ask family members for assistance with a bad tire. When the friend returned with Miller's cousin, they found Miller in the locked car, unconscious and foaming at the mouth with a gun on her lap. Her cousin called police and described the situation. The police arrived, broke the window of the vehicle, and shot inside, hitting Miller in the head and back 12 times. Initially, police said Miller shot at them first, but they later retracted the claim, and no evidence ever indicated Miller fired her gun. After her death, her loved ones blamed her cousin for calling the police.[55] The focus of the blame in this case suggests the police are viewed as a threat to the Black community. In May 1999, the four officers were cleared of any criminal wrongdoing by the county district attorney. Nonetheless, the Riverside Police Department fired them.

In 1994, Congress ordered the U.S. Department of Justice (DOJ) to acquire data about the use of excessive force by police officers and publish an annual summary. The DOJ has, however, had difficulty collecting this information, as official records of excessive use of force by the police are rarely kept. To comply with the mandate, the DOJ instead publishes statistics related to the general use of force by police, acknowledging that "current indicators of excessive force . . . are all critically flawed." The available data suggest that criminal and civil liability for excessive force has little effect on police behavior.[56] At the end of the day, the best checks on excessive use of force appear to evolve from a police administration that sets a tone of "zero tolerance" for such transgressions.

PURSUITS

Like instances of excessive force, police vehicle pursuits that result in the loss of innocent lives can be particularly problematic for law enforcement. A pursuit begins when a law enforcement officer signals a driver to stop his automobile and the driver refuses to do so. Police and many members of the public believe that allowing officers to pursue someone who fails to yield is an absolute necessity. If offenders know they can drive away and the officer will not pursue, many believe a serious hazard to public safety is created. Others argue that officers should make decisions to pursue based on a variety of relevant factors, such as the seriousness of the suspected activity or the potential danger to bystanders. Driving 10 miles over the speed limit might not be an offense worthy of pursuit. Officers need to quickly weigh competing safety issues—the possible risk to public safety of not apprehending the suspect—against the risk of pursuit and the possibility of an accident.

Risks of an accident increase when more officers participate in a chase. As noted earlier, an officer is also more likely to use force in events that follow a pursuit.[57] Suspects who flee from police not only put themselves at risk of an accident, they also increase the likelihood of police use of force when they are apprehended.

Pursuits are dangerous for suspects, bystanders, and police. A good deal of controversy surrounds the data about how many innocent bystanders a year are killed because of police pursuits. Some estimates suggest as many as 40 percent of pursuits end in accidents, and approximately 300 deaths of suspects, bystanders, and police occur each year.[58] In 2005, 9 percent of the officers feloniously killed on duty lost their lives as the result of a pursuit. In July 2006, an officer in his vehicle was struck and killed by the driver of a van who was trying to elude police.

There are few legal limits on when and under what conditions police may pursue a suspect. In several cases, someone who was harmed as a result of a police pursuit sued the officer and the department. Generally, courts have ruled that qualified immunity shields these officers from civil suits.

The U.S. Supreme Court recently ruled on officer liability in *Scott v. Harris* (2007). Victor Harris was driving 73 miles per hour in a 55-mile-per-hour zone. When Officer Timothy Scott tried to pull him over, Harris failed to yield and attempted to flee. Six minutes and 10 miles into the pursuit, Scott rammed his bumper into the rear of Harris's vehicle. Harris lost control of his automobile, and the resulting crash left him a quadriplegic. Harris sued Scott, claiming Scott had violated his constitutional rights by subjecting him to excessive force. The Court ruled Scott had not violated Harris's constitutional rights because his actions were reasonable in that Harris's driving was causing a threat to public safety. Scott was not therefore liable under the doctrine of qualified immunity. In the majority opinion, Justice Antonin Scalia wrote, "A police officer's attempt to terminate a dangerous high-speed car chase that threatens the lives of innocent bystanders does not violate the Fourth Amendment, even when it places the fleeing motorist at risk of serious injury."[59]

Although the courts have largely supported police in their efforts to apprehend fleeing suspects, the risk of lawsuits and the need to ensure the safety of the public and officers have led many law enforcement agencies to review and revise their pursuit policies. A 2005 suit against the Millbrae, California, city police department shows why. An officer was pursuing a pickup truck when the fleeing suspect hit an innocent bystander. The bystander was severely injured and subsequently sued the police department, which had been revising its pursuit policy in order to qualify for immunity. (Under California state law, police agencies are generally immune from liability in police pursuits if they adopt a standard policy.) Millbrae settled the suit for $3.15 million, and the Millbrae police department revised its pursuit policy so that such a pursuit would not occur the same way today.[60]

In 1996 the International Association of Chiefs of Police created a model pursuit policy to aid law enforcement agencies in developing their own. Some states have begun mandating that agencies develop a pursuit policy if they do not yet have one and regularly review their policies if they do. Most law enforcement departments have policies, but a high percentage of them have not reviewed their policies for many years.[61] Citizen advocates like Candy Priano, the mother of a young woman who was an innocent bystander killed during a police pursuit, want departments not only to develop their own policies but to hold officers accountable when they do not follow departmental policies.[62] Currently, laws and courts have not *required* officers to follow their own department policies.

DRUG ENFORCEMENT

The use and sale of illegal drugs is another issue that challenges law enforcement. Illegal drug use is widespread in the United States. According to a 2005 national survey, 19.7 million people reported using an illicit drug in the previous month. About 54 percent had used marijuana and no other illicit drugs, almost 20 percent had used marijuana and

▶ Methamphetamine Lab

Methamphetamine labs are extremely toxic for both people and the environment.

another illicit drug, and more than 25 percent said they used another illicit drug only. About 53 percent of men and 42 percent of women reported using an illicit drug in their lifetimes.[63]

Marijuana appears to be the clear drug of choice for illicit users, but methamphetamine use tends to be associated with a variety of other criminal behaviors not necessarily found with other drugs. For example, methamphetamine use has been found to predict violent behavior in parolees.[64] Furthermore, the labs in which methamphetamine is made are particularly dangerous. About 15 percent of the methamphetamine labs discovered in California are uncovered because unsafe handling of the highly combustible chemicals required often results in explosions, fires, toxic fumes, and other environmental hazards.[65] Perhaps most troubling are the risks to children who live in homes where methamphetamine is manufactured.[66]

As we learned in Chapter 1, enforcement of drug laws has varied over time. Enforcement strategies today are aimed at preventing drugs from entering the United States, stopping drug sales, and arresting individual users in possession of illicit drugs. The federal budget for drug enforcement, prevention, and rehabilitation illustrates where most of the government's efforts are focused. In the $2.77 trillion budget proposed by the White House in 2007, $187 million was earmarked for prevention efforts, $209 million for rehabilitation efforts (including $69.2 million for drug courts), and almost $1.8 *billion* for enforcement efforts. While some might assume that a change to a Democratic presidential administration in 2009 would lead to greater prevention rather than enforcement strategies, President Obama's 2010 budget proposal calls for an increase in funds for enforcement and a reduction in funds for prevention.[67]

Although the focus of a good deal of taxpayer money, enforcement strategies have been largely ineffective in reducing the use or sale of illegal drugs.[68] However, measuring the effect of police interventions is difficult because there is little data on their long-term results. Still, drug use in the United States has not declined in recent years.[69]

Differential enforcement of drug laws is also a concern. Whites and Blacks report about the same level of drug use, but Blacks are much more likely to be arrested for a drug offense.[70] In fact, 75 percent of incarcerated drug offenders are people of color, even though 72 percent of drug users are White, 13 percent are Black, and 11 percent are Latino.[71] The Race, Class, Gender box illustrates how aggressive drug enforcement can encourage increased rates of searches that may cross the line of constitutionality.

Police also engage in drug prevention efforts. In the Drug Abuse Resistance Education (DARE) program, the best known of these strategies, officers talk to students in classrooms about illegal drugs and the negative effects of drugs on users' lives. The preventive orientation is appealing to communities, and many have implemented the program

Race, Class, Gender

Searches and the War on Drugs

Stephen Mastrofski and Jon Gould systematically studied police searches (via ride-alongs with patrol officers) to assess their constitutionality. One-third of the 115 police searches observed were unconstitutional. Only a handful of these searches were ever reviewed by a court because the officers did not cite the suspects or take them into custody. Searches were most likely to be unconstitutional when the officers were looking for drugs, and pat-down searches were more likely to be unconstitutional than more intrusive searches. The researchers also noted that police searched Blacks at almost twice the rate of Whites.

None of the small number of officers responsible for conducting a high percentage of the illegal searches appeared to be the stereotype of an aggressive, angry cop. Instead, they were all considered high-performing, all-around good officers who strongly supported community policing and its focus on reducing drug crime and violence in neighborhoods. Because pat-downs were the most common unconstitutional search, the intrusiveness of the searches appeared to influence officers' comfort level with potential unconstitutionality.

Police officers are taxed with cleaning up the streets by getting rid of drugs and are encouraged to maintain a high level of surveillance of and contact with those suspected of drug use in order to do so. After all, how can police make an arrest for drugs unless they know an individual is in possession of narcotics? Searches are central to drug enforcement. As a part of the war on drugs, many police departments have created proactive drug units that conduct stop-and-frisks and vehicle stops in areas with high levels of drug trafficking. Such tactics are influenced by race and class, with young Black men largely the targets of drug enforcement.

Critics contend that the war on drugs has resulted in many unforeseen problems, including overly aggressive actions on the part of some police. They argue that stop-and-frisks and vehicle stops cross the line of professional law enforcement and enter the zone of unethical, if not unconstitutional, behavior. Mastrofski and Gould's research supports those contentions.

Policymakers and the public might reasonably question whether the war on drugs is worth the consequences.

Observe Investigate Understand

- **If police actions risk individuals' constitutional rights but fail to stem the trafficking in and use of illegal drugs, how should the drug problem be addressed?**
- **Do constitutional restrictions on police actions unnecessarily hamper police efforts to deal with illicit drug use and sale?**
- **How do race and class affect police decisions to conduct stop-and-frisks and vehicular stops? Are the influences of race and class on such decisions justifiable?**

SOURCES: Jon Gould and Stephen Mastrofski, "Suspect Searches: Assessing Police Behavior under the U.S. Constitution," *Criminology and Public Policy* 3, no. 3 (2004): 315–362; William Chambliss, "Policing the Ghetto Underclass: The Politics of Law and Law Enforcement," *Social Problems* 41 (1994): 177–194.

in their public schools. But individuals who receive DARE programming are not any less likely to use illegal drugs.[72] Unfortunately, neither enforcement-oriented nor prevention-oriented policing strategies appear to have a notable impact on illegal drug use.

The challenge to police of dealing with illegal drugs and drug enforcement policy often overlaps with police confrontations with gangs and gang members, the topic we take up in the next section.

GANG ENFORCEMENT

There is no single accepted definition of gangs, and their characteristics and the behavior of members vary from place to place. Classifying crimes as gang-related is equally difficult. So we cannot be as confident in our knowledge of gang involvement in criminal events as we are in other areas of criminology.[73]

We define gangs as "any identifiable group of youngsters who (a) are generally perceived as a distinct aggregation by others in their neighborhood, (b) recognize themselves as a denotable group (almost invariably with a group name), and (c) have been involved in a sufficient number of delinquent incidents to call forth a consistent negative response from neighborhood residents and/or law enforcement agencies."[74] In other words, gangs are groups, recognized as such by themselves and others, that have a history of trouble with neighbors and police.

Patterns of Gang Activity

Gang membership and violence was, and still to a large degree is, a major urban area problem.[75] Rural areas and small towns lack the necessary population base to sustain gangs, and any disruption such as an arrest or members leaving can severely weaken the gang. Gang problems reported by most rural agencies are occasional and minor.[76]

Eighty-five percent of gang members live in large cities and suburban counties. News media frequently report about gang members moving into communities from other places. However, gangs are not as mobile as these reports might lead some to believe, and membership in gangs has been fairly stable. For the most part, gang problems develop within a community rather than being imported into it.[77] Gangs are the primary distributors of illicit drugs throughout the United States and often use drug trafficking as their primary means of financial gain.[78]

Gangs are also associated with organized crime entities. Criminal alliances exist between Mexican organized crime groups and U.S. gangs, and Asian criminal enterprises also work with street gangs in the United States. In addition to illegal drugs, Asian organized crime groups are often engaged in credit card fraud, illegal gaming, and money laundering. In California, Russian organized crime groups have been associated with the Crips (a well-known gang) for the purpose of fencing stolen goods.[79]

Gangs have kept pace with technology and use it extensively. For example, gangs use cell phones as much as does the public at large. Gangs also monitor police communications with scanners and use surveillance equipment to detect hidden microphones or "bugs." They track legal proceedings online and use computers to identify witnesses for intimidation, steal information, and perpetrate fraud.[80]

Police Response to Gangs

To deal with the gang problem, police departments have created task forces or gang units and offered specialized training in gang signs, colors, tattoos, and codes. Gang units, like drug units, generally use proactive police strategies and maintain a high degree of contact with known gang members or gang affiliates for intelligence purposes. Operation Ceasefire, an innovative problem-oriented policing program in Boston, successfully reduced gang violence. The program identified young gang members who were especially active in crime and focused enforcement efforts on them. When members of a gang committed violence, the police would flood the area and indicate they would strictly enforce any law broken. Community organizations also offered gang members a variety of social services such as health care, substance abuse assistance, and food and shelter.[81]

In February 2007, Los Angeles began offering $50,000 rewards to anyone providing information that led to the arrest and conviction of any of the city's "10 Most Wanted" gang members. Despite fears that advertising gangs would increase their attractiveness, the LAPD focused its resources on the 11 gangs it considered the most dangerous. Los Angeles also has recruited former gang members to work with the police to reduce gang violence. The program has been viewed as particularly successful.

Some critics contend that police and politicians have become overzealous in their desire to protect society from the criminal behavior of gang members. For example, some cities have imposed juvenile curfews that have been challenged as unconstitutional or illegal.[82] Given their training, officers report they can identify gang members by their clothing, the people they associate with, their tattoos, and the hand signals they flash. Some agencies document names and identities of those they believe to be gang members.

Critics, however, say these lists cast a shadow of suspicion on all young men of color, some of whom can find their names listed, though there is little supporting evidence. According to law enforcement agencies, gang membership by race is divided in the following manner: 35 percent of gang members are Black, 49 percent Latino, 9 percent White, and 7 percent some other race or ethnicity.[83]

Success in eliminating problems and crime associated with gangs demands a coordinated response that includes suppression, community mobilization, and social opportunities for youth.[84] Of course, all such efforts must be clearly defined, constitutional, and nondiscriminatory.[85]

INTIMATE PARTNER VIOLENCE

Domestic violence is the traditional term for an assault on a person with whom the attacker is intimately involved. Today the preferred term is **intimate partner violence**, which encompasses the variety of couples who experience this violence—dating couples, same-sex couples, life partners, married couples, and couples recently separated (the aftermath of separation is an extremely dangerous time for this kind of victimization). Intimate partner disputes occur in all social classes and make up a large percentage of calls to the police. Yet only half of female victims call the police, with lower-class women reporting their victimization at the highest rates.[86]

intimate partner violence
An assault on a person with whom the attacker is intimately involved.

One of the reasons victims may be hesitant to contact the police is that for years police officers treated violence between intimates as a private problem, a family matter not appropriate for police intervention. Hence, officers rarely made arrests even when there was clear evidence an assault had occurred.[87] Police response to the crime of intimate partner violence has, however, changed for a number of reasons.

First, in the 1970s victim advocates and women's rights advocates began to raise public awareness of police unresponsiveness to victims of intimate partner violence. That publicity put pressure on departments to change the way they handled these calls for service. A second force for change was that local governments were successfully sued for failing to protect female victims. In the pivotal case discussed in A Case in Point on the next page, a Connecticut city awarded $2.3 million to a victim for violating her right to equal protection. This case illustrated to police and government officials that if they failed to protect victims, they would be held responsible, at least financially.[88] A third reason the police response changed so significantly was the Minneapolis Domestic Violence Experiment, a study that revealed that offenders were less likely to reoffend if officers arrested the offender instead of suggesting mediation or separation.[89]

Police officers still tend to dislike intimate partner calls, in part because they believe such incidents pose the greatest risk to their own safety. There is little evidence to support that belief, however. The situations that pose the greatest threat to officer safety are traffic stops and pursuits.[90]

Today **mandatory arrest policies** dictate that officers must make an arrest when there is evidence of an assault. These policies were created to reduce police discretion in incidents of intimate partner violence because evidence showed that when police had discretion, they chose not to make an arrest. Critics of the policies say arrests have not consistently been shown to reduce violence and have unintended negative impacts on poor women and women of color.

mandatory arrest policy
Requires officers to make an arrest when there is evidence of an assault.

Mandatory arrest policies have resulted in an increase in dual arrests. **Dual arrests** occur when an officer arrests *both* parties in a physical altercation instead of identifying and arresting only the primary aggressor. Dual arrests are troubling because in at least 85 percent of cases men are the perpetrators.[91] Some jurisdictions discourage dual arrests and instead expect officers to identify the primary aggressor.

dual arrest
The arrest of *both* parties in a physical altercation instead of identifying and arresting only the primary aggressor.

Women who are illegal immigrants are particularly vulnerable victims of intimate partner violence. Although they can call police for assistance without fear of being deported, most are likely unaware of this rule or may not believe authorities will respect it.

a Case in Point

Thurman v. City of Torrington (1984)

Tracey Thurman did everything she could to prevent the continued violence her husband, Charles Thurman, inflicted upon her. Unfortunately, the Torrington, Connecticut, police department would not help her. From October 1982 to June 1983, Tracey Thurman and family members repeatedly attempted to persuade Torrington police officers to protect her from Charles. When Charles attacked Tracey at a friend's home in October 1982, Tracey's friends filed a complaint with the police. The next month he attacked her at the same friend's home again. Tracey and her friend went to the police department again, but the officers refused to take a complaint—even of trespassing. A few days later, as a police officer looked on, Charles Thurman screamed threats at Tracey while she was in her vehicle. The officer took no action until Charles broke the windshield, at which point he was arrested. Charles Thurman was then convicted of breach of peace, sentenced to probation, and instructed to stay away from his wife.

Between December 1982 and May 1983 Tracey Thurman repeatedly called the police to report threats by Charles. At the beginning of May, she requested an arrest warrant be served because Charles was making death threats against her. The officer would not take the complaint and instead told her to return in three weeks. Tracey turned to the court and obtained a restraining order against Charles Thurman. The police were notified of the order.

At the end of May, Tracey told police Charles had violated the restraining order and again requested an arrest warrant. An officer told her no one could help her until after Memorial Day when a particular officer would return from vacation. Calls to police from Tracey's brother-in-law to protest their behavior were also ignored.

Finally, on June 10, 1983, Charles Thurman went to where Tracey was staying and demanded she come out to talk to him. Instead, she called the police. After 15 minutes she finally went outside to convince Charles to leave without taking their son as he had done before. As soon as she was outside the home, Charles stabbed her with a kitchen knife 15 times in the chest, neck, and throat. The police arrived 25 minutes after they were called but did not immediately take Charles into custody, even though he twice kicked Tracey in the head in their presence. Officers finally arrested Charles after he charged at Tracey for the third time while she lay on a stretcher. Tracey Thurman is disfigured and paralyzed from the neck down as a result of the violence Charles Thurman inflicted on her.

The court ruled that the police department violated Tracey Thurman's right to equal protection by failing to protect her. The court also said that police departments cannot treat women abused by someone with whom they have a domestic relationship any differently than they would victims of any other violent crime.

OBSERVE
Investigate
Understand

- **How did Tracey Thurman's case affect the way police respond to calls involving intimate partner violence?**
- **How should police respond when faced with evidence of intimate partner violence?**
- **Is violence between intimate partners a private matter, or is police intervention appropriate in such cases?**

SOURCE: *Thurman et al. v. City of Torrington*, 595 F. Supp. 1521 (D. Conn., 1984).

MYTH/REALITY

MYTH: A victim of domestic violence who is in the United States illegally cannot call the police for assistance because she will automatically be deported to her country of origin.

REALITY: It is against federal law to deport someone who is a victim of domestic violence. All victims of domestic violence can access law enforcement assistance, as well as emergency shelters, without fear of deportation.[92]

On January 6, 2006, President George W. Bush signed into law the Violence Against Women and Department of Justice Reauthorization Act of 2005 (H.R. 3402). This federal law, also known as VAWA for Violence Against Women Act, was first authorized in 1994. The original act removed the obstacles of "immigration laws that prevent immigrant victims from safely fleeing domestic violence and prosecuting their abusers."[93] VAWA was reauthorized in 2000 and extended assistance to immigrants who are victims of sexual assault, human trafficking, and other violent crimes, so long as the victim cooperates with law enforcement and prosecution. The goal of this legislation is to protect victims from abusers and traffickers who seek to control the victims by threatening them with deportation. VAWA 2005 extends the legal provisions set forth by earlier VAWA legislation and further allows immigrant victims to seek legal assistance, victims of child abuse to petition on their own behalf for citizenship until they are 25 years old, and victims of elder abuse to receive assistance.[94]

Source Connection

H.R. 3402

www.govtrack.us/congress/bill.xpd?bill=h109-3402

Established by statute following the passage of VAWA (and its reauthorization in 2000 and 2005), the Office of Violence Against Women has the authority to administer the grants authorized under VAWA, as well as develop federal policy related to intimate partner violence, sexual assault, and stalking.

STRESS

The constitutional and legal limitations imposed on police officers as well as the special issues discussed in the preceding sections greatly affect officers' levels of stress. Officers

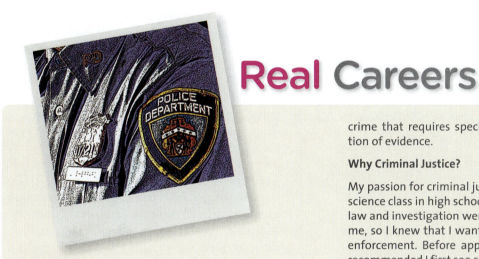

Real Careers

RYAN BAL

Work location: Roseville, California

College(s): California State University–Sacramento, 2004

Major(s): Criminal Justice (BS)

Job title: Patrol Officer, Roseville Police Department

Salary range for job like this: $56,000–$76,000

Time in job: 4 years

Work Responsibilities

As a patrol officer, I respond to emergency calls, like automobile accidents, and nonemergency calls, such as noise complaints and fallen trees. But I also partake in proactive law enforcement, which means I do traffic stops, locate subjects, and conduct searches.

I work on a 3/11, 4/11 schedule, which means every other week I work 3 days for 11 hours or 4 days for 11 hours. On top of that, I recently received special training in evidence collection techniques and became a CSI (Crime Scene Investigator). Now I am always on call for homicides or any other crime that requires specialized documentation and collection of evidence.

Why Criminal Justice?

My passion for criminal justice began when I took a forensic science class in high school. When I entered college, criminal law and investigation were the only subjects that interested me, so I knew that I wanted a career in some aspect of law enforcement. Before applying for any jobs, my professors recommended I first see criminal justice in the field by taking an internship or part-time job. My internship with the City of Roseville as a Cadet Officer not only confirmed for me that I wanted a career that let me serve my community but also let me prove to myself that I could handle a heavy workload and dangerous situations.

Expectations and Realities of the Job

A career in law enforcement is definitely a stressful lifestyle. I often work an 11-hour shift, go home to sleep for a couple hours, and wake up to start the next shift. Transitioning to this type of schedule was especially difficult for me because only two weeks after graduating from college, I began the police academy. I went from only afternoon classes to a 10-hour day of both physical and academic classes beginning at 7:00 a.m.

My Advice to Students

My best piece of advice is to get an internship before deciding on a career. This is the only opportunity you will really have to explore a career path before taking a full-time job. If you have a successful internship, the department might call you back for a full-time position.

routinely deal with emotionally charged situations knowing there is always a potential for danger, yet they report that agency-related matters create the greatest job stress.[95] A major complaint among patrol officers is lack of support from their superiors.[96] Veterans express less job satisfaction than rookie officers.[97]

Experiencing Stress

Stress from the job affects life at home.[98] Police officers often work irregular hours, reducing the amount of time they can spend with their families. The transition from dealing with traumatizing events on the job, such as multiple deaths in a traffic accident, to attending to family needs at home can be difficult.

Female officers and officers of color tend to experience higher levels of stress than their White male colleagues, much of it the result of discrimination from fellow officers.[99] Officers who identify as gay or lesbian also report increased levels of stress. Lesbian officers report that their gender is a greater barrier in policing than their sexuality.[100] Gay male officers, on the other hand, experience clear hostility from straight male officers.[101]

Although only about 14 percent of police–citizen interactions involve citizen resistance,[102] police often find it hardest to forget these are incidents, and they greatly affect the level of occupational stress. Of course, even when residents are cooperative, the police are dealing with trauma. They confront social problems most people hope never to witness, such as sexual assault, child abuse, intimate partner violence, runaways, and drug addiction. These emotionally difficult problems can take their toll on officers' psychological and emotional well-being.

Sometimes the police themselves are victims, as discussed in What About the Victim? Such cases affect not only the individual officers who are victimized but other officers who feel as though an assault on one officer is an assault on them all.

Strategies for Dealing with Stress

Some officers may rely on alcohol to "deal with" stress.[103] Unfortunately, alcohol use is likely to create additional problems in family relationships and on the job. Officers can turn to one another for support or utilize services offered by departments to help them deal with stress and the effects of handling traumatizing events.

There are many types of stress prevention and treatment programs, some that individuals can pursue on their own and some the department must provide. Individual coping strategies include participating in a support system, maintaining a healthy

What about the Victim?

When the Police Are the Victims

September 11, 2001, was the kind of day public safety officers dread: a major terrorist attack on a heavily occupied building in the middle of one of the most densely populated cities in the world and on a major governmental building several hundred miles away. The police and firefighters behaved as expected—they saved lives as best they could. In the aftermath, officers on the scene of the destruction of the World Trade Center and Pentagon suffered high levels of stress.

The collapse of the World Trade Center's Twin Towers killed 50 police officers ranging from 26 to 63 years of age. As explained in Chapter 5, police feel a great deal of solidarity and, therefore, suffer terribly from the loss of their colleagues. The deaths of fellow officers cannot help but remind them of the danger and unpredictability of their job.

One-third of the officers who were first responders at the Pentagon attack have been found to suffer high levels of posttraumatic stress disorder (PTSD), an anxiety disorder that can occur after a critical or life-threatening incident. PTSD, whose symptoms include nightmares, flashbacks, anxiety, and emotional detachment, can last for years after the triggering event. The need for officers always to appear in control may have prevented many other officers from reporting that they also experienced the symptoms associated with PTSD. Officers reported wanting to make sure they helped in whatever way they could and needing to stay out of their sense of duty. The average length of time officers spent at the Pentagon after the plane struck was 136 hours, and the longer the period of time officers spent at the Pentagon site, the more likely they were to suffer PTSD.

The terrorist events of September 11, 2001, at the World Trade Center and the Pentagon cost many officers their lives, but the resulting stress of the events also created many surviving victims.

OBSERVE Investigate Understand

- **Are police officers better prepared than ordinary citizens to deal with unusual levels of job stress? Why or why not?**
- **Why would police officers be reluctant to admit to experiencing PTSD?**
- **Should police officers suffering PTSD remain on the job?**

SOURCES: "September 11, 2001 Victims," http://www.september11victims.com/september11victims/ (retrieved March 21, 2007); Monica Robbers and Jonathan Mark Jenkins, "Symptomatology of Post-Traumatic Stress Disorder among First Responders to the Pentagon on 9/11: A Preliminary Analysis of Arlington County Police First Responders," *Police Practice and Research* 6, no. 3 (July 2005): 235–249.

diet and exercise regimen, venting feelings appropriately, and seeking out a change of focus and positive feedback. The single most important factor is having a dependable support group. Generally, from the perspective of police officers, no one is better equipped to understand the pressures of law enforcement than a peer. Officers who serve as peer counselors should, however, be trained by mental health professionals.[104]

Organizational strategies for addressing stress include training for supervisors on sound supervisory techniques, constructive feedback on job performance, open communication channels, opportunities for input into organizational decisions whenever possible, and active support of stress management programs.[105] Although the vast majority of police departments aggressively equip their personnel with weapons, communications equipment, and bullet-proof vests, they may not always undertake adequate measures to "bullet-proof the mind." Supervisors are not always trained to recognize the symptoms of stress or take appropriate action to deal with it. If secondary problems such as alcohol abuse or marital conflict are allowed to fester, depression, intimate partner violence, and attempts at suicide may result.[106] The organization can play a central role in minimizing the potential for harm not only from criminal assailants but also from unattended stress.

The Cleveland Police Department's program to help reduce on-the-job stress included equipping patrol officers with laminated cards identifying the symptoms of stress in themselves and others and providing information on how to deal with and recover from stress. The program also involved training police supervisors on how to recognize the symptoms of stress and how to assist officers suffering from stress. To encourage participation in the program, the department awards participants bronze medals in the shape of dog tags and engraved with the words "One for All" and "Strengthening the Chain."[107]

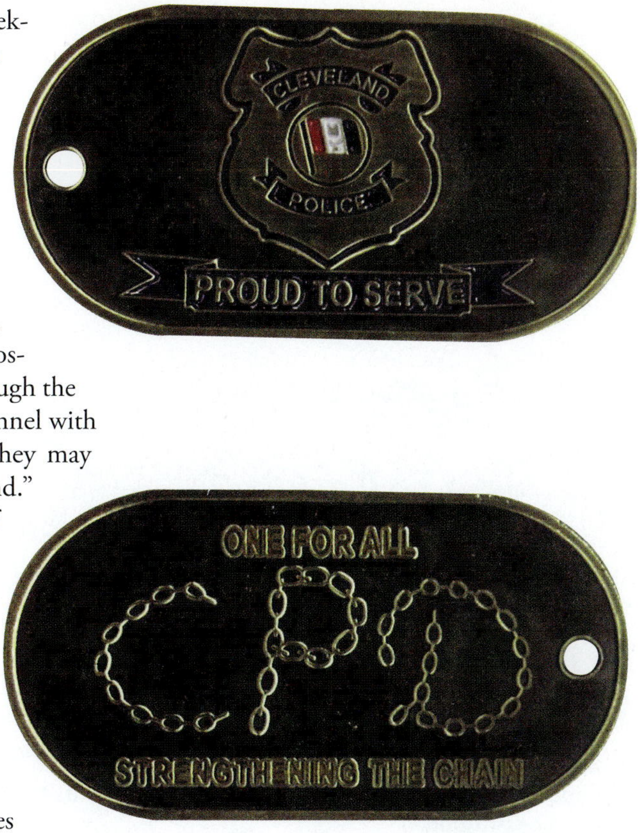

▲ **Cleveland Police Department Dog Tags**

The Cleveland Police Department awarded these tags to officers who participated in the department's innovative program on how to deal with on-the-job stress.

SUMMARY

Police officers must balance their authority to enforce the law with citizens' constitutional guarantees of civil liberties and the right to due process. Constitutional provisions, especially those of the Fourth, Fifth, and Sixth Amendments, protect the civil liberties and rights of the criminally accused and legally limit what the police may do when interrogating, detaining, or arresting persons suspected of committing a crime.

Officers must sometimes exercise force to enforce the law and maintain order, but the use of force must be lawful, according to Supreme Court guidelines. Police decisions to use force or to pursue fleeing suspects should be based on the particular situation at hand. Factors to consider include the seriousness of the situation, the potential risk to innocent bystanders, and the effect on police–community relations.

Police efforts to curtail the sale of and trafficking in illegal drugs encompass both enforcement and prevention strategies. To deal with gangs, many police departments have created gang units or specialized task forces. Success in dealing with gangs and eliminating gang violence requires community involvement and support. The police response to incidents of intimate partner violence has changed over time, with police now more likely to respond and intervene promptly. Nevertheless, police still tend to dislike calls involving such incidents, in part because they mistakenly believe these calls present the greatest threat to their own safety.

The nature of police work creates stress for many officers, and legal restrictions on police actions can compound that stress. So, too, can dealing with the special issues discussed in this chapter—the use of force, pursuits, illegal drugs, gangs, and intimate partner violence. Specialized training in recognizing and relieving stress can be helpful, but the most important factor is having a dependable support group. For many officers, that means a support group of fellow officers.

Observe Investigate Understand

Review

Identify the limitations on law enforcement activities imposed by the Fourth, Fifth, and Sixth Amendments to the U.S. Constitution.

- The Fourth Amendment requires that police conduct searches and seizures that are reasonable.
- The Fifth Amendment prohibits police from coercing confessions.
- The Sixth Amendment prohibits police from questioning defendants outside the presence of their attorneys.

Identify the situations most likely to entail use of force by the police, and explain how the police use of force is regulated.

- Situations most likely to entail use of force are those involving interpersonal disturbances, intoxicated persons, fleeing suspects, or suspects resisting arrest.
- Use of force rules are derived largely from case law and agency guidelines.

Analyze the impact of the use of force on community relations.

- The police use of force, especially excessive force, usually has a negative effect on community relations.

Describe the major legal and policy issues raised in police pursuits.

- Officers must consider the risks to public safety when deciding to pursue a suspect.
- Officers are generally protected from liability when engaging in pursuits, but pursuits can be dangerous to the officers themselves and can result in lawsuits.

Contrast the strategies of enforcement and prevention used to curb illegal drug use.

- Enforcement strategies include attempting to stop drugs from entering the United States, targeting drug sales, and arresting individual users who are in possession of illicit drugs.
- The best-known police department drug prevention effort is the DARE program.

Explain how police departments have responded to gangs.

- Departments have created special task forces or gang units to deal with the gang problem.
- Gang units, like drug units, generally use proactive police strategies.

Describe how the police response to intimate partner violence has changed over time and explain why.

- Police historically did not provide victims of domestic violence the protection they deserved.
- Victim rights advocates, women's rights advocates, and civil suits put pressure on police departments to change the way they responded to intimate partner violence.
- Today mandatory arrest policies and dual arrests are common.

Describe the factors that create stress for police officers and efforts to deal with these pressures.

- Police officers report that agency-related matters create the greatest stress.
- Female officers and officers of color tend to experience higher levels of stress due to bias within police departments.
- Strategies for dealing with stress include individual efforts and department programs.

Key Terms

attenuation 202
automobile exception 198
derivative evidence rule 201
dual arrest 215
exclusionary rule 199
fruit of the poisonous tree doctrine 201
good faith exception 201
independent source 202
inevitable discovery 202
intimate partner violence 215
mandatory arrest policy 215
Miranda warnings 204
probable cause 197
public safety exception 205
qualified immunity 208
reasonable suspicion 198
search incident to arrest 199
standing 202
stop-and-frisk 197
Terry stop 197
testimonial evidence 205
use of force continuum 209
voluntariness test 204
warrant 197

Study Questions

1. To obtain a search warrant, police officers must
   a. place the target of the warrant under arrest.
   b. permit the suspect to consult with an attorney.
   c. demonstrate to a judge that probable cause exists to search for evidence or contraband.
   d. prove the suspect's guilt beyond a reasonable doubt.
2. According to the exclusionary rule, evidence will be excluded at a defendant's trial if
   a. police obtained the evidence through illegal means.
   b. there is sufficient other evidence to obtain a guilty conviction.
   c. the defendant has no standing.
   d. the police did not have a valid search warrant.
3. Which of the following statements about the *Miranda* warnings is most accurate?
   a. Police must recite them before asking suspects any questions.
   b. They are meant to protect suspect's rights against self-incrimination.
   c. They have resulted in significantly fewer confessions.
   d. They include the right to a jury and a speedy trial.
4. Which of the following means a police officer who pursues a fleeing suspect will likely not be held financially responsible for any harm that comes to a suspect or other individual?
   a. Qualified immunity
   b. Qualified liability
   c. Limited suability
   d. Total vulnerability
5. What is one of the major effects of a police officer's excessive use of force?
   a. The public's confidence in the police is reduced.
   b. Officer morale remains static.
   c. Interdepartmental cohesion ends.
   d. The police officer could get promoted.
6. What is one of the most important stressors police officers deal with, regardless of their ethnicity, gender, race, or sexuality?
   a. General societal problems
   b. Hostile situations while on duty
   c. Agency-related stress
   d. Occupational stress
7. Which of the following factors explain why differential enforcement of drug laws is a concern?
   a. People of color use drugs at a higher rate than Whites, yet both groups are arrested at proportional rates.
   b. One-fourth of incarcerated drug offenders are people of color.
   c. There should be no concern because differential enforcement of drug laws does not exist.
   d. Whites and Blacks report about the same level of drug use, but Blacks are much more likely to be arrested for a drug offense.
8. How have police departments responded to gang problems in their areas?
   a. Depended on faceless-oriented policing that utilized reactive police strategies
   b. Established special task forces or units that utilized proactive police strategies
   c. Created intradepartmental alliances that depended on proactive policing strategies
   d. Relied on problem-oriented policing and reactive police strategies

9. What is the main reason many female victims do not call the police about intimate partner violence?
   a. Intimate partner violence continues to be a private matter that should not be dealt with outside the home.
   b. Female victims are emotionally strong enough to handle intimate partner violence without the help of law enforcement agencies.
   c. Historically, the police response to intimate partner violence was victim-centered and scared women away from making the call.
   d. Historically, the police response to intimate partner violence was not victim-centered.

10. How does the Sixth Amendment limit police behavior?
   a. It protects people from unreasonable searches.
   b. It protects people from coerced confessions.
   c. Once a defendant has been charged, police cannot question him without his attorney present.
   d. It protects people from unwarranted police pursuits.

Critical Thinking Questions

1. Where should we draw the line between freedom and safety? What are some specific situations in which we might want to emphasize safety over freedom? When might we emphasize freedom over safety?
2. How do you think race is or is not related to police use of force?
3. How should police respond to the crime of intimate partner violence?

Internet Sites

Voices Insisting On Pursuit Safety
www.pursuitsafety.org
This is a citizen organization interested in reforming police pursuit policies.

National Black Police Association
www.blackpolice.org

Hispanic National Law Enforcement Association
http://www.angelfire.com/md2/hnlea/
Minority officers usually experience a higher level of stress. Organizations such as the National Black Police Association and the Hispanic National Law Enforcement Association provide a unified voice for minority officers, which can reduce officers' levels of stress.

National Coalition Against Domestic Violence
http://www.ncadv.org/
This organization focuses on making changes in society that reduce violence against women and children.

Suggested Readings

Anthony Lewis, *Gideon's Trumpet* (New York: Vintage, 1989).
An extensive history of the landmark case of *Gideon v. Wainwright* (1963), in which the U.S. Supreme Court acknowledged poor defendants' rights to have the government provide attorneys for them.

Geoffrey Alpert and Roger Dunham, *Understanding Police Use of Force: Officers, Suspects, and Reciprocity* (New York: Cambridge University Press, 2004).
Answers to the questions why, how, and when police officers resort to the use of force; includes original data as well as a brief survey of prior research on police use of force.

Albert Roberts, *Handbook of Domestic Violence Intervention Strategies* (New York: Oxford University Press, 2002).
A guide to the latest research, public policies, and legal criminal justice responses covering federal and state legislation and trends in police and court responses to domestic violence.

CHAPTER 8

The Courts

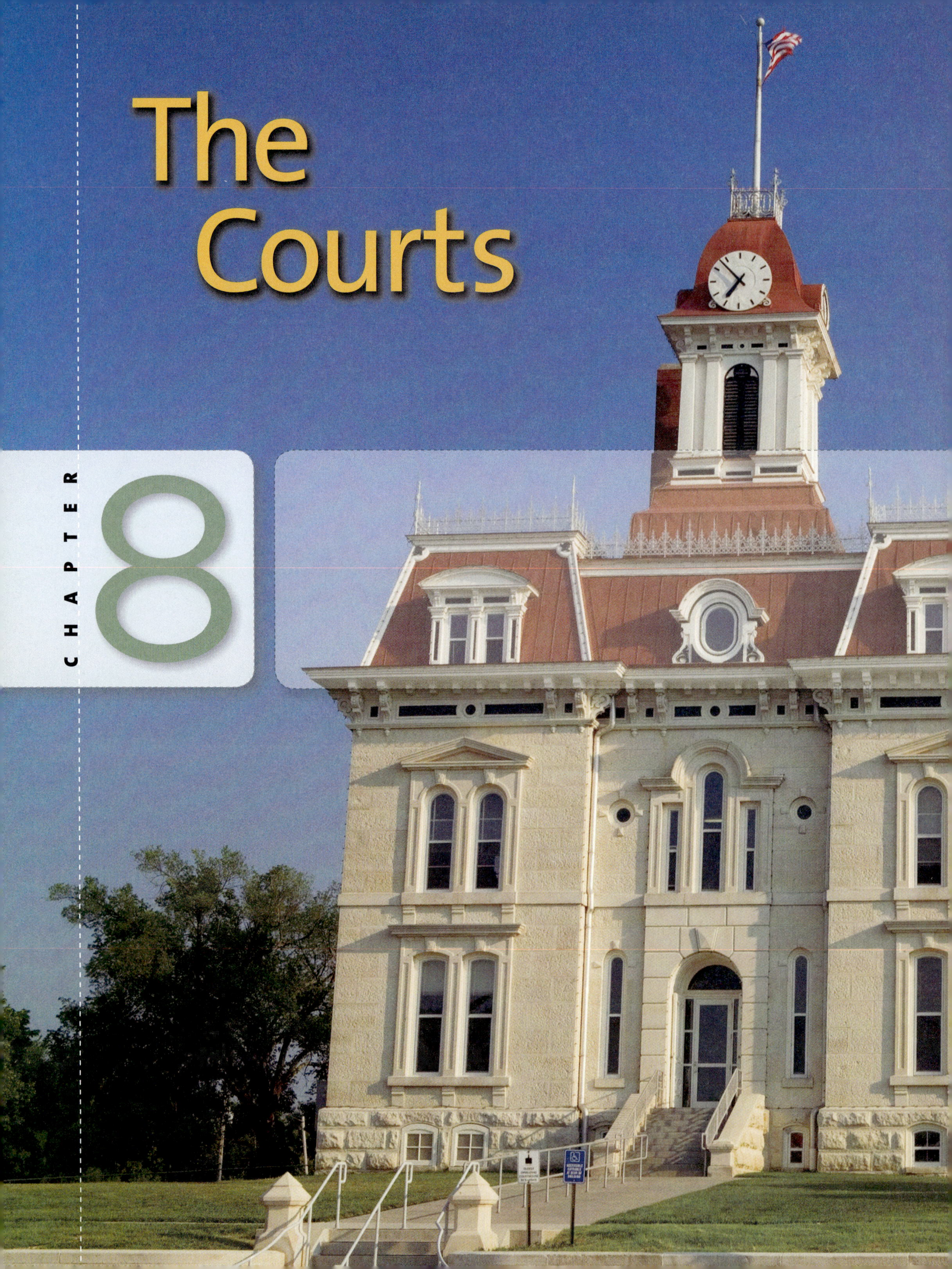

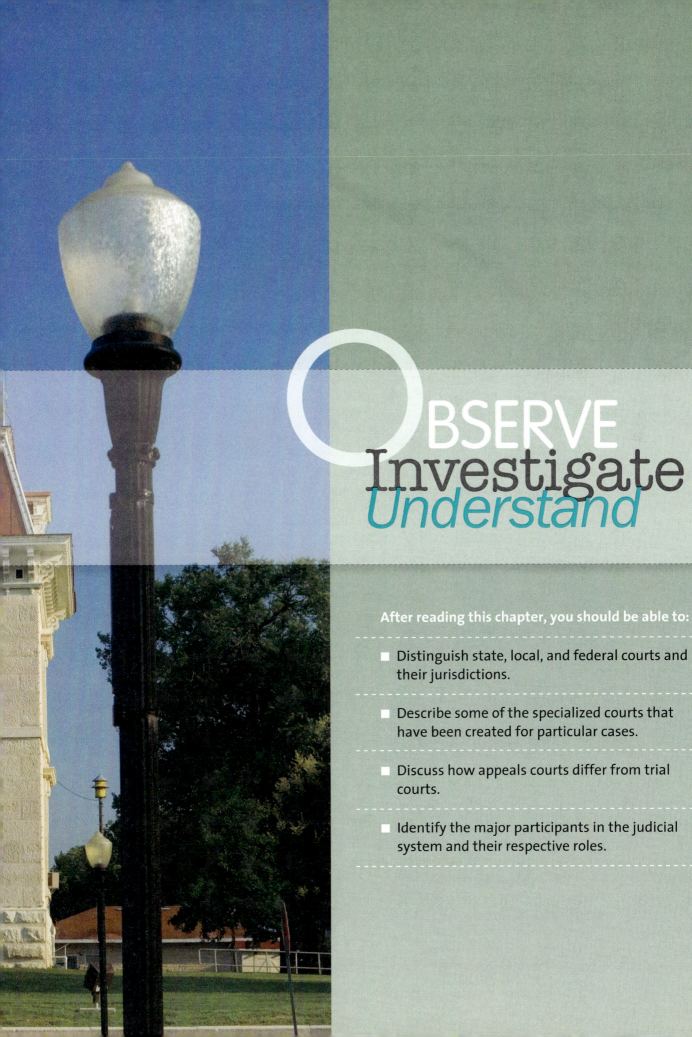

OBSERVE Investigate *Understand*

After reading this chapter, you should be able to:

- Distinguish state, local, and federal courts and their jurisdictions.
- Describe some of the specialized courts that have been created for particular cases.
- Discuss how appeals courts differ from trial courts.
- Identify the major participants in the judicial system and their respective roles.

Realities and Challenges

Three Terrorists Face American Courts

By 9 a.m. on the morning of April 19, 1995, most employees were already at their desks, and many children had been dropped off at the day care center located inside the Alfred P. Murrah Federal Office Building in Oklahoma City. Parked outside stood a rented Ryder truck. At 9:02 a.m., the 6,200 pounds of bomb-making materials packed in the truck detonated with a blinding flash. The explosion was powerful enough to cause the north face of the Murrah building to collapse into dust. Hundreds of buildings in a 16-block radius were damaged or destroyed. In this unspeakable crime, more than 800 people were injured, and a nation was left traumatized. It took weeks of searching through the rubble before it was confirmed that 168 people had died, including 19 children. The victims ranged in age from 3 months to 73 years old. Until the attacks on September 11, 2001, this was the worst act of terrorism ever to occur on U.S. soil.

Approximately 90 minutes after the explosion, 26-year-old Timothy McVeigh was pulled over for driving without a license plate on his pickup. After making that routine traffic stop, the highway patrol officer found that McVeigh had an unregistered gun. McVeigh was arrested immediately on a firearms charge. While McVeigh was in jail, the news broke that he was tied directly to the bombing of the Murrah building. Upon further investigation, almost all the purchases of materials used to make the bomb, as well as the truck rental agreement, were linked to McVeigh. It quickly became clear that he was the mastermind behind the plot, but evidence turned up that others also seemed to be involved. A few days after the bombing, Terry Nichols was questioned and then arrested for his role in assisting McVeigh with his plan.

Terry Nichols was tried twice for his crimes in both federal and state courts. In 1997 the federal court tried Nichols and found him guilty of conspiring to build a weapon of mass destruction and of eight counts of involuntary manslaughter of federal officers. For these federal crimes, Nichols was sentenced to life imprisonment without the possibility of parole. In 2000, the state of Oklahoma tried and convicted Nichols of 161 counts of first-degree murder, for which he is now serving 161 consecutive life sentences without the possibility of parole. A third accomplice, Michael Fortier, testified against McVeigh and Nichols and received a $200,000 fine and a 12-year prison sentence.

McVeigh was originally scheduled to be tried in Oklahoma City, but in 1997 a request for a change of venue was granted and the trial was moved to Denver. In an attempt to reduce leaks, the judge issued a gag order prohibiting the prosecution and defense from talking with the media. After the jury deliberated for 23 hours, Timothy McVeigh was found guilty of 11 counts of murder and conspiracy. McVeigh was given the death penalty for his crimes. In 2001, President George W. Bush approved the execution, as required in federal death penalty cases, and Timothy McVeigh died by lethal injection.[1]

As the McVeigh case demonstrates, specific types of courts in the United States have differing jurisdictions. In complicated cases—such as that of the Oklahoma City bombing—more than one court may be involved in the legal process that manages offenders and their cases. Running this complicated system requires an equally daunting network of workers within the court system, ranging from clerks to judges, each with a dedicated role in moving the stages of justice forward. This chapter focuses on various types of criminal courts and the roles and responsibilities of those who work within the court system.

COURT STRUCTURE AND JURISDICTION

Like other components of the justice system, U.S. courts are complex. There are federal courts, state courts, and sometimes municipal or local courts. There are **courts of general jurisdiction**, which can hear almost any kind of case, and specialty courts, often called **courts of limited jurisdiction**, which hear only cases of a certain type. Most criminal trials occur in courts of general jurisdiction; an example of a limited jurisdiction court is a juvenile court. There are trial courts and appellate courts. Each kind of court is organized differently, and different states have different ways of structuring their court systems.

Preview

State Courts

The basic structure of most state courts is similar, but their names vary. Figure 8-1 illustrates typical state court organization. Most criminal cases begin in trial courts, usually called district courts or superior courts or even, as in New York State, supreme courts. In most states, each county has at least one of these trial courts.

Appeals are usually heard in the state court of appeals, sometimes known as the intermediary appeals court. Cases in intermediary appeals courts are heard by a panel of judges rather than a jury. Most states have only one appeals court, but some have several. Appeals courts may be divided geographically into circuits, much like the federal circuits only smaller, or by subject matter into civil and criminal courts. Some states with small populations, such as Montana and North Dakota, do not have an intermediary appeals court. The next level is the state's highest court, usually called the state supreme court. Some states, such as Texas and Oklahoma, have a special high court just for criminal cases. In most states, high courts have discretionary appeals, meaning that the justices can refuse to hear a case. However, defendants in death penalty cases often are entitled to automatic, nondiscretionary appeals to the high court. The number of justices on state high courts varies between five and nine; most states have seven.

court of general jurisdiction
A court that can hear nearly any type of case.

courts of limited jurisdiction
A specialty court that can hear only cases of a certain type.

FIGURE 8-1 A Typical State Court
State court systems are complicated bureaucracies.

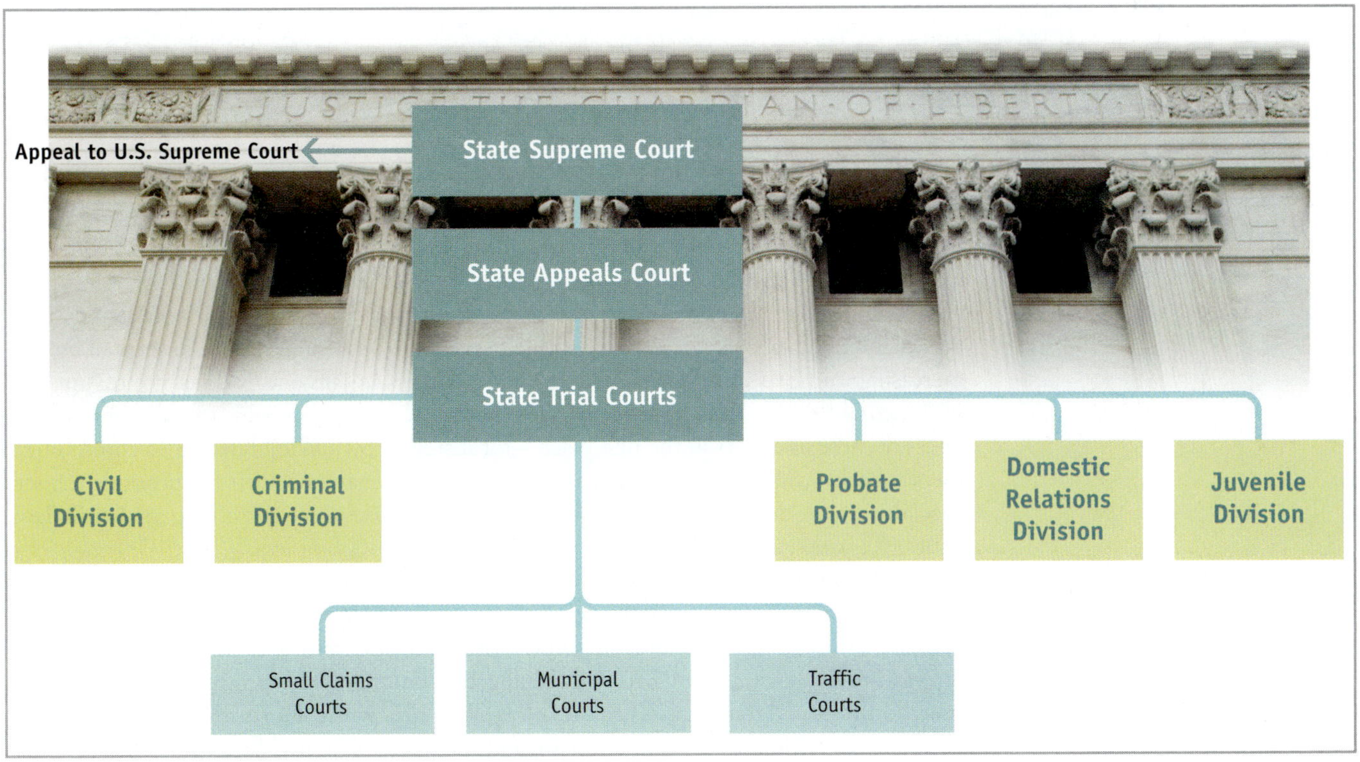

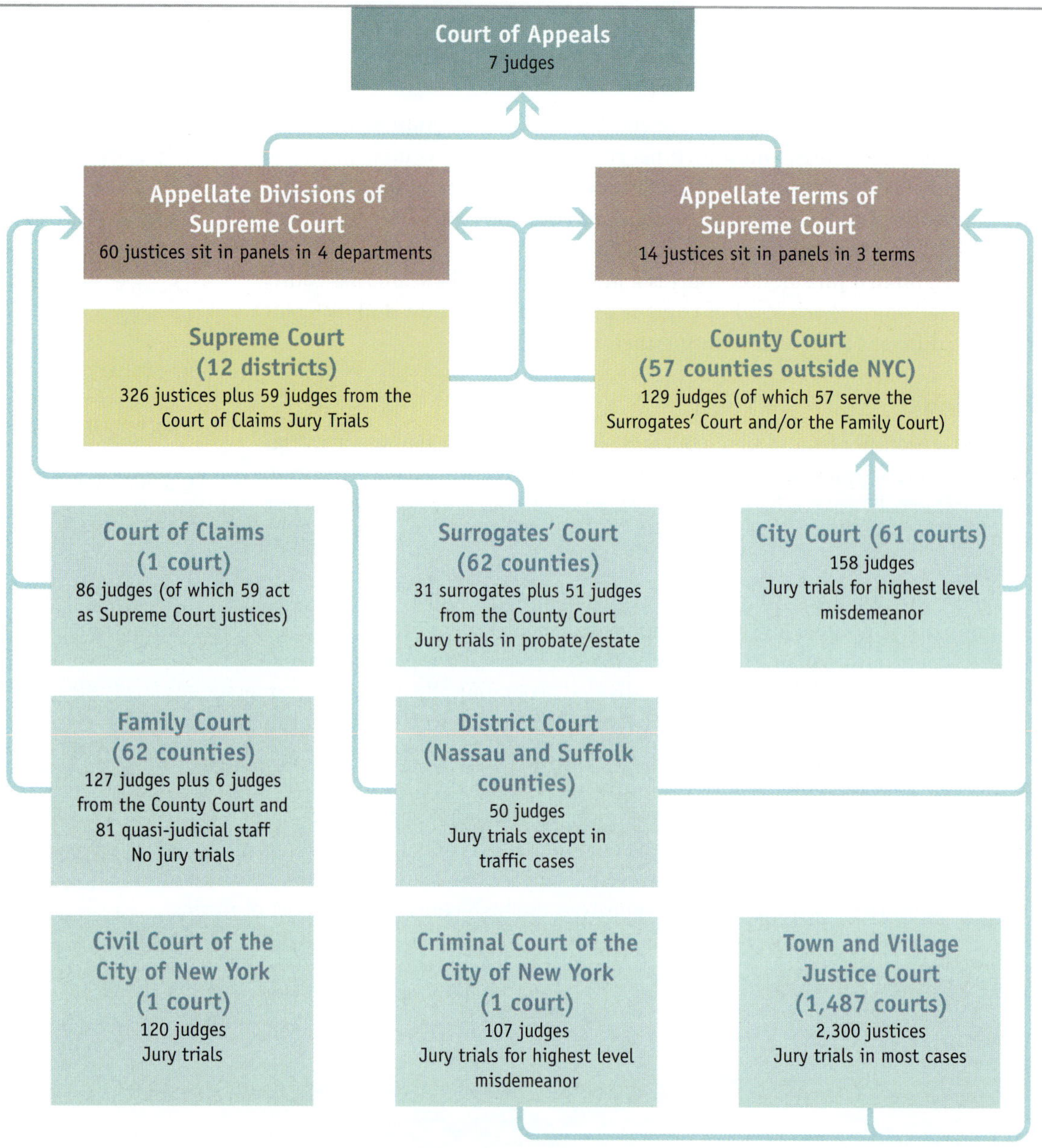

FIGURE 8-2 New York's Court System

Most states have other courts as well. Some have many—New York has 13 different kinds of courts (see Figure 8-2). Typically, local courts, run by cities or counties, hear minor civil and criminal matters, but they also may conduct some early stages of more serious civil and criminal cases. Most states have specialty courts as well. Since 2000, prompted by the increasing numbers of offenders with mental disorders in jails and prisons, approximately 100 mental health courts have been established. Their primary goal is to help prevent the arrest of these offenders in the first place—for instance, by making referrals to community mental health centers to ensure that at-risk individuals maintain their medications. Other specialty courts deal with traffic infractions, drug offenses, juvenile offenders, family law issues, tax issues, and civil "small claims," typically of $1,000 or less.

Trial courts do not have to be administered locally; they could be administered by the state. On one hand, centralization can mean a more streamlined bureaucracy, greater consistency in procedures and outcomes within a state, and less vulnerability to local political pressures. California recently changed from county-administered trial courts to state-administered trial courts. On the other hand, locally run courts might be more sensitive to local needs and face less competition for the state's limited funding.

Federal Courts

The federal courts have **jurisdiction**—that is, the power—to hear only limited types of cases. In general, a federal case must involve federal law or the federal Constitution, or it must either involve citizens of different states and at least $75,000 in controversy or have as a party the United States itself.

jurisdiction
A court's legal power to hear a particular case.

Thus the only criminal cases that go to federal courts are those that charge someone with violating a federal law or those in which a defendant claims a state has violated her constitutional rights. Very few criminal cases are prosecuted in federal courts. In 2003, for example, there were fewer than 95,000 federal criminal prosecutions—less than 0.05 percent of the number of total prosecutions in the United States. Only 4 percent of federal criminal trials were for violent crimes,[2] and less than one in five cases appealed in the federal court system is a criminal, as opposed to civil cases.

Figure 8-3 illustrates the federal court system. There are three basic types of federal courts. Trials are held in one of the 94 U.S. district courts. States with large populations have more than one district court. Pennsylvania, for example, has three—the Western, Middle, and Eastern districts. Each district court employs several judges, who hear federal civil and criminal cases.

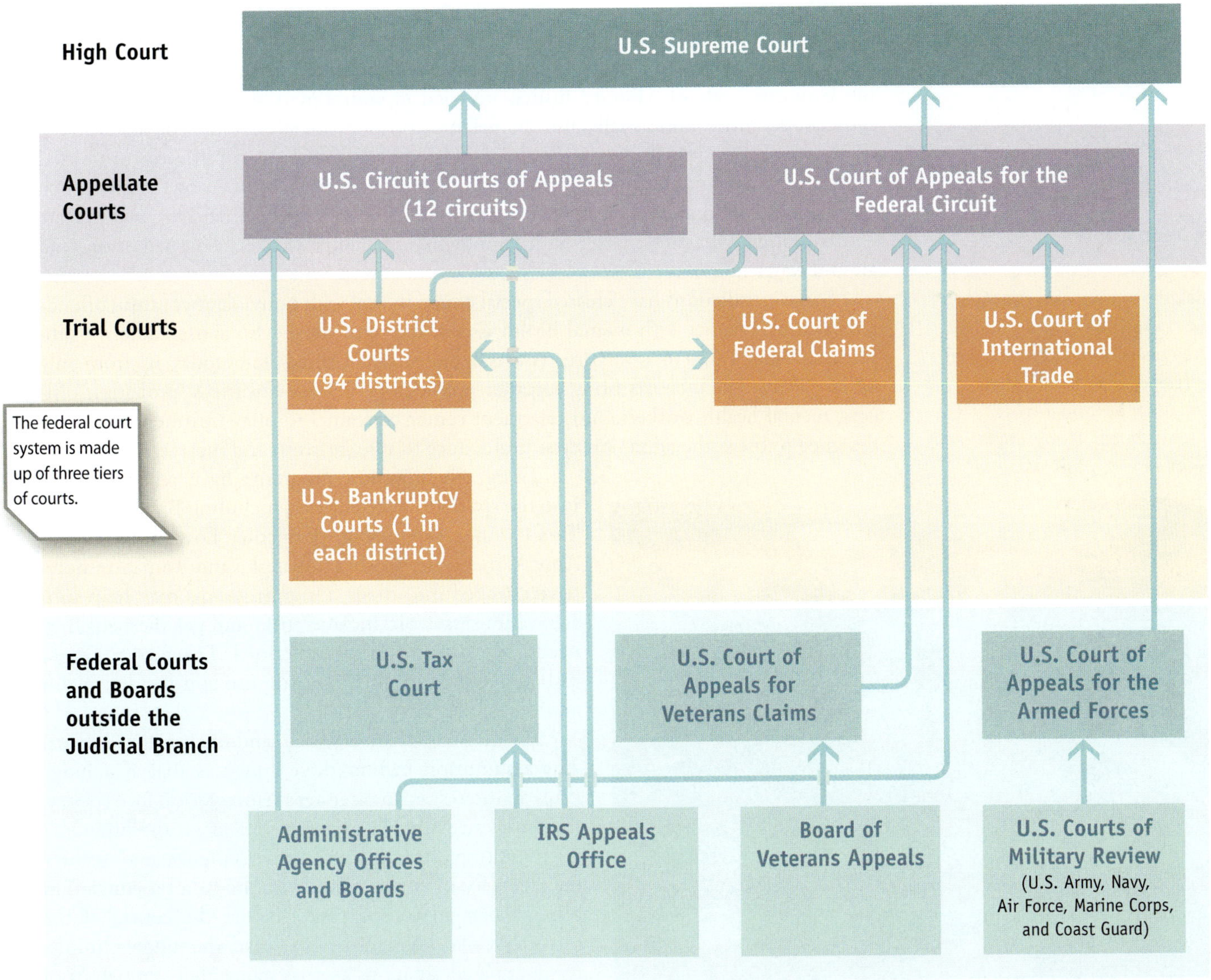

FIGURE 8-3 The Federal Court System

An appeal from a federal district court's decision is heard by a U.S. circuit court of appeals. Eleven federal circuits each cover several states, but the Twelfth Circuit is for the District of Columbia alone. The Thirteenth Circuit Court of Appeals handles cases from the entire nation involving patent rights, as well as cases in which the United States itself is the defendant. Each circuit employs many judges—the Ninth Circuit, for example, currently has 28—and hears cases in a few locations within the circuit. The Ninth Circuit hears cases from 11 western states and territories. Several recent proposals call for splitting this circuit into two or more smaller jurisdictions to reduce case processing time and make the circuits more equal in size.

en banc
An appeals case presided over by a larger than usual panel of judges (more than three judges).

A case before a U.S. court of appeals is usually heard by a panel of three judges, although occasionally cases will be heard **en banc**. Literally that means by the whole court, but in practice the case is simply heard by a larger group than three judges. Appeals from the courts of appeal (including cases that originated in military and tribal courts) go to the United States Supreme Court.

Federal specialty courts hear specific kinds of cases. For example, each district has a bankruptcy court. The United States sometimes also uses special military courts to try those accused of being enemy combatants. In 2006, the U.S. Supreme Court held that special military courts could not try suspected terrorists being held at Guantánamo Bay.[3]

Other Courts

The vast majority of criminal cases are tried in state or federal courts. A few cases, however, go to other types of courts. Members of the U.S. armed forces accused of violating the Uniform Code of Military Justice are tried in courts-martial, in which the judges, prosecutors, juries, and usually also the defense attorneys are all members of the military. Members of American Indian tribes may be tried by tribal courts for crimes committed on tribal land. Many state and federal administrative agencies have their own courts, such as the U.S. Immigration Court and the National Labor Relations Board, as well as state courts dealing with such matters as unemployment benefits, workers' compensation, and air and water resources.

Some jurisdictions have created special courts to deal with nonviolent youthful offenders, with defendants with mental health issues, and with those who abuse addictive substances. About 1,200 to 1,800 drug courts operate in the United States today, up from only 12 in 1994.[4] These courts bring together prosecutors, defense attorneys, probation officers, mental health workers, and treatment center personnel to offer treatment programs designed to break the addiction cycle and reduce relapse, rearrest, and incarceration.

▼ Teen Court

Teen courts are based on the idea that young defendants are more likely to be influenced by their peers. *What are the benefits of teen courts for defendants and other participants? What disadvantages, if any, might teen court defendants experience?*

Drug rehabilitation programs have recently come into the spotlight as celebrities, including Britney Spears, Tara Conner, Boy George, Courtney Love, Leif Garrett, Amy Winehouse, Rush Limbaugh, and Tom Sizemore, have checked into them. Drug programs may help substance abusers avoid incarceration and get the help they need to overcome their addictions. Drug courts tend to be effective for reducing drug use and recidivism for adults and youth.[5]

Reentry courts are another kind of specialized court. The assumption behind these courts is that if a judge takes an interest in an offender's reintegration into society, that concern will have a positive effect on the offender's rehabilitation. Judges thus act as sentence and reentry managers for offenders, who live at home after conviction but make regular appearances before the court.[6] If the offender violates the terms of release, the judge administers graduated sanctions and assistance that stops short of returning the offender to prison and fosters reintegration instead. Reentry court staff workers ensure that offenders fulfill the education, work, counseling, and community service requirements that the judge has imposed. Offenders, their family members, and other support agencies all are responsible directly to the court.[7]

Teen courts are another kind of specialized court, focused on first-time, nonviolent youthful offenders. On the assumption that teenagers may be more likely to listen to their peers, the juries consist of teenagers, and the "prosecutor" and "defense attorney" are frequently teens as well. The judge is generally a professional judge or attorney. To participate, the defendant usually must first admit guilt. The jury can set a variety of sentences, including community service, counseling, and letters of apology. In the hope that active participation in the justice system itself can deter future offenses, defendants usually also are required to serve as jurors in a specific number of future cases. Today there are more than 600 teen courts in the United States.[8]

Criminal Appeals

If a criminal defendant in the United States is acquitted of a crime, that acquittal automatically ends the case. The Fifth Amendment's protection against double jeopardy prohibits a defendant from being tried twice for the same crime. Double jeopardy protection does not, however, prohibit the victim from filing a civil lawsuit. Because the burden of proof in civil cases is lighter than in criminal cases, it is not unusual for a person to be acquitted on criminal charges and still be found civilly liable for the same acts—for example, former football star O. J. Simpson in 1997 was found responsible in civil court for the wrongful deaths of his ex-wife, Nicole Simpson, and her friend, Ronald Goldman. Similarly, actor Robert Blake was held responsible in 2001 for the wrongful death of his wife.

If the defendant is convicted, however, he or she may appeal to a higher court. In a capital case, a convicted person's appeal is usually automatic. As we have seen, all state and federal jurisdictions have at least one appellate court. Appellate courts are very different from trial courts in terms of both their structure and function.

▲ Oral Arguments in an Appellate Court

Appellate courts determine whether legal errors were made at trial.

Unlike trial courts, appellate courts do not decide on the facts of a particular case, and they do not decide whether the defendant is guilty. Instead, they determine whether legal errors were made at the trial and, if so, whether those errors were important enough to invalidate the conviction. Therefore, courts of appeals provide direct oversight of trial judges.

To appeal a conviction, the defendant, or, more often, the defendant's lawyer, files a document called an **appellate brief** with the appeals court. The name is misleading. This document is not at all brief, but is a lengthy text in which the defendant, now called the "appellant," describes all the legal errors alleged to have been made at her trial and provides legal precedents—that is, earlier court decisions that support her arguments. The appellant cannot dispute any of the findings of fact made at trial, although errors might include evidence that should have been excluded or admitted but that the judge did not allow. Appeals also examine allegations of faulty jury instructions by the judge and impermissible statements by the prosecutor. In addition, the appellant may claim the jury was improperly chosen, that the law under which she was prosecuted was unconstitutional, or that her sentence was not appropriate.

appellate brief
Written document containing legal arguments in an appellate case, submitted to a court by attorneys for one party.

Once the appellant files her brief, the prosecutor will respond with a brief in which he argues that no legal errors were made. These arguments also must be supported by precedent.

There is no jury in appellate courts, no evidence is presented, and no witnesses testify. Instead, a panel of judges reads the briefs. Usually, oral arguments are held in which each side highlights the arguments made in the briefs and answers questions posed by the judges. Oral arguments are usually quite short—generally 15 to 60 minutes per side—and the appellant herself is generally not present.

Also unlike trial courts, the decisions of appellate courts are rarely issued right away. After hearing the oral arguments, the judges meet to discuss the case. Eventually—sometimes months later—they give a written opinion, which may be read aloud in court. Opinions vary from a few sentences to hundreds of pages, depending on the number and complexity of the issues. Opinions not only state the judges' decisions but also elaborate the reasons for the decisions. Often they become precedents for future cases.

Appellate judges need not be unanimous in their judgment; a simple majority suffices. It often happens that some judges on the appellate court disagree with the majority decision and therefore may write dissenting opinions.

If the appellate court finds that legal errors were made at trial and that they were significant enough to affect the outcome of the case, they will vacate, or invalidate, the conviction. Usually, they will then **remand** the case—send it back to the trial court. The prosecution may choose to try the case again, sometimes several times. Alternatively, the prosecution may appeal the appellate court's decision to a higher appellate court.

If the court finds no significant legal errors, it will uphold the conviction. The defendant may then appeal to a higher court, if she chooses. Higher courts frequently overturn lower courts' decisions. If a party loses the appeal at the **court of last resort**—usually the state supreme court but sometimes the U.S. Supreme Court—there is nowhere left to go except to seek habeas corpus relief (see Chapter 10).

The U.S. Supreme Court sometimes hears appeals from state high courts, but these tend to be limited to matters of constitutional law. Unlike the U.S. circuit courts of appeal, the Supreme Court chooses whether to hear a case. If at least four justices agree that a case merits the Supreme Court's attention, then a **writ of certiorari** is issued, ordering the lower court to deliver all relevant records of the case for the Court's examination. If, however, the Supreme Court refuses to hear an appeal—and in fact it refuses about 99 percent of the cases appealed to it—then the parties have no further recourse and the previous judgment stands. The Court hears only about 100 cases a year, usually on matters it deems particularly important from the standpoint of constitutional law or about which the lower courts widely disagree.

remand
The act by which an appellate court sends a case back to a lower court for further proceedings.

court of last resort
The highest court to which a case may be appealed.

writ of certiorari
A request that a case be heard by an appellate court such as the U.S. Supreme Court.

in chambers
Meeting that occurs between attorneys and a judge in the judge's office rather than in the courtroom.

recusal
The act by which a judge removes herself from a case because she may be biased, or may have the appearance of being biased.

▼ Judge in Her Courtroom

Judges must make many kinds of decisions. *How might a judge's personal beliefs affect the decisions she makes on matters of law?*

THE COURTROOM WORKGROUP

The U.S. court system has many different participants, each with a unique role to play. Their relationships, everyday interactions, and job performance can influence the administration of justice.

Judges

The judge, seated at the front of the courtroom, is often the most distinctive participant in a criminal case. By traditions that go back centuries, she is treated with certain respectful formalities and addressed as "Your Honor." Everyone in the courtroom rises when she enters. Attorneys must ask her permission to approach "the bench"—that is, the judge—to discuss a point of law. The opposing attorneys hold conferences with the judge **in chambers**—that is, in her private office, closed to outsiders. Of course, if a case comes before the judge in which she has an economic or personal interest—for example, involving some property in which she has invested or individuals whom she knows—she must exercise **recusal** by turning the case over to another judge who can act with total impartiality. Such a degree of disinterestedness is not routinely expected of members of legislative bodies. The judge, in short, symbolizes the majesty, the power, and the impartiality of the law, serving as a referee to ensure that the trial proceeds according to the rules of **due process.**

due process
The right, guaranteed by the Fifth and Fourteenth Amendments, that laws and processes be fair.

In the U.S. criminal justice system, judges decide whether to issue search and arrest warrants. Once suspects have been arrested, the judge determines whether probable cause exists to believe they committed a crime. Decisions about whether to release suspects from custody while trials are pending and about the amount of bail that the defendant must provide are also within the purview of judges.

During a trial, it is a judge's job to decide all matters of law—as opposed to matters of fact, which the jury usually decides. Thus the judge decides what evidence may be admitted, rules on various motions the attorneys make, and gives the jurors their instructions. But it is the jurors who determine the guilt of the defendant based on their interpretation of the evidence. Of course, if it is a bench trial rather than a jury trial, the judge makes the determination of guilt. (For more on bench trials, see Chapter 9.) When a defendant is convicted, it is usually the judge's job to sentence her as well. In most states that have the death penalty, however, the jury decides whether to give the defendant death or some other sentence, usually life in prison, with or without the possibility of parole.

If a defendant appeals his conviction, the appeals court judges will decide whether errors were made at trial or whether any of his constitutional rights were violated. Furthermore, because the meaning of written laws is often unclear or contradictory, especially as they apply to specific activities, appellate judges interpret statutes and constitutions. For example, in 2001 a motorist named Robert Lee Coggin gestured with his middle finger at another driver whom he felt was driving too slowly. The other driver, offended, called 911. Coggin was subsequently pulled over and charged with disorderly conduct. He was convicted, fined $250, and appealed to the Texas Court of Appeals. Although a Texas statute defines as disorderly conduct gestures that "tend to incite an immediate breach of the peace," it was up to the court to determine whether "shooting the bird" incites an immediate breach of the peace. The majority of the court held that it did not, and Coggin's conviction was overturned. As A Case in Point explains, the courts' power to interpret laws and the Constitution was established in 1803 in one of the most important rulings of the U.S. Supreme Court.

MYTH/REALITY

MYTH: Judges "pass" laws.

REALITY: Legislators pass laws. Judges interpret those laws, and their interpretations carry legal authority.

There are several kinds of judges. Today, **magistrates** and **justices of the peace** generally handle minor matters such as warrants—legal documents giving government agents authority to conduct searches, seizures, and arrests—and infractions. They may also preside over some of the early steps in criminal cases such as arraignments (see Chapter 9). In a few cases, a special magistrate is appointed to preside over a case that requires particular technical expertise or that cannot be heard by any ordinary judge due to potential conflicts of interest. Court **commissioners** or **referees** also may preside over early stages, and some perform all the duties of regular judges in specialty courts such as family or juvenile courts. The men and women who hear felony trials and many misdemeanors are called judges, as are those who hear most appeals. The judges of the U.S. Supreme Court, as well as of most states' highest courts, are called justices.

magistrate
A judge who handles matters such as warrants, infractions, and the early stages of a criminal case.

justice of the peace
A judge who handles matters such as warrants, infractions, and the early stages of a criminal case.

commissioners
People who preside over the early stages of some criminal trials, or serve as judges in specialized courts.

referees
People who preside over the early stages of some criminal trials, or serve as judges in specialized courts.

There are generally no absolute qualifications for becoming a state or local judge, and none are specified by the U.S. Constitution for federal judges or Supreme Court justices. At one time, many justices of the peace and juvenile court judges did not have any law training at all. Today, however, nearly all judges have law degrees, and most have had extensive experience in practicing law, or sometimes in legal scholarship and teaching.

Most federal judges are nominated by the president of the United States. The Senate, however, must confirm these nominations. Once federal judges have been confirmed, they hold office for life. Unless they retire or resign, they may be removed from office only by

a Case in Point

Marbury v. Madison (1803)

The U.S. Constitution is fairly detailed about the roles and responsibilities of the executive and legislative branches, but it says little about the powers of the courts. The Supreme Court, in a clever decision, therefore gave the federal courts authority to interpret the meaning of laws and constitutions.

The year was 1801. Congress had just created several dozen new federal judgeships, and outgoing Federalist President John Adams appointed members of his own political party to fill these positions. They were called "midnight judges" because Adams was still signing their hastily bestowed commissions on the eve of his departure from the White House. However, when President Thomas Jefferson of the opposition Democratic Republican Party took office a few days later, he ordered his Secretary of State, James Madison, to ignore any new commissions that Adams had failed to sign. Thus a Federalist named William Marbury never received his commission to become a federal Justice of the Peace, and so he filed a lawsuit against Madison that went directly to the U.S. Supreme Court. A federal law, the Judiciary Act of 1789, had provided that this kind of lawsuit must originate in the Supreme Court rather than in a lower federal court.

The Supreme Court faced some tough choices. If it held for Marbury, there was a good chance that Jefferson would simply ignore the ruling, thus reducing the Court's power almost to zero. If it held against Marbury, the Court would be viewed as too tightly controlled by the president. To further complicate matters, Chief Justice John Marshall had also served as Adams's secretary of state and was Jefferson's political enemy (and also his distant cousin). Worse, Jefferson and his Democratic Republican supporters in Congress seemed determined to strip the Federalist-dominated U.S. court system of power. A few years later, they would impeach a highly unpopular Supreme Court justice, Samuel Chase. Marshall himself might well be a target for impeachment.

Marshall found an ingenious way around these problems. He wrote an opinion in which the Court held that the Judiciary Act of 1789 was unconstitutional and, therefore, that Marbury's case could not be brought directly before the Court. President Jefferson was unlikely to dispute that ruling because it meant that Marbury and other last-minute Adams appointees would not become judges. At the same time, however, the Court declared for itself the right of judicial review—that is, the right to interpret laws and constitutions. Since then, the right has been extended to all state and federal appellate courts, expanding the role of the judiciary far beyond its original scope.

The case of *Marbury v. Madison* remains a great milestone in shaping the role of courts in the U.S. justice system. It is the foundation of the modern federal courts' power to "make law" through judicial review and under their authority to interpret the law.

OBSERVE Investigate Understand

- **What types of factors determine whether something should be considered unconstitutional?**
- **In what other ways might the Marshall Court have decided *Marbury v. Madison*, and what would have been the impact of a different decision?**
- **In his *Marbury v. Madison* ruling, was John Marshall being an "activist" judge, "legislating from the bench" and failing to follow the "original intent" of the authors of the U.S. Constitution?**

SOURCE: *Marbury v. Madison*, 5 U.S. 137 (1803).

impeachment—essentially, a special kind of trial—although this rarely happens. Since 1789, only 13 federal judges have been impeached, and 4 of those, including Samuel Chase, were found not guilty.

Depending on the jurisdiction and position, state court judges may be either appointed, usually by the governor, or elected by voters, and they hold office for life or for a set number of years.

Both methods of judicial selection—appointment and election—have their critics. Some claim appointment can lead to judges being chosen not because of their qualifications but because of their personal views or their political beliefs and connections. Since the 1980s, the confirmation process for Supreme Court Justices, in particular, has repeatedly polarized the nation and resulted in bitter battles between the two political parties and between the Senate and the White House. On the other hand, some argue that the voting public is ill equipped to decide on the qualifications of state and local judges who are running for election, sometimes on blatantly political platforms, and that judges' concerns about raising campaign contributions and winning reelection may affect their decisions. In 2009, the U.S. Supreme Court ruled that judges must recuse themselves from deciding cases involving parties who have given them significant campaign contributions.[9]

In an attempt to ensure the accountability of state judges to voters while avoiding the worst problems of partisan politics, Missouri in 1940 introduced a system of appointment that has subsequently been adopted in other states. Under the "Missouri Plan," a nonpartisan board suggests candidates for judgeships, and from this slate the governor makes appointments. After several years, the appointed judges must submit to a "retention election" in which voters decide whether they have performed well enough to warrant staying on the bench.

Other controversies pertain to the lack of diversity among judges. Only about 10 percent of state judges and 19 percent of federal judges are people of color.[10] Considering that about 24 percent of the U.S. population are people of color, those relatively low percentages reveal the degree of racial disparity on our benches. Women, who are 51 percent of the national population, are also underrepresented—only 23 percent of federal judges and 29 percent of state high court justices are female.[11] In the entire history of the United States, there have been only two African American U.S. Supreme Court Justices and only three women Justices. The judiciary lacks not only ethnic and gender diversity but social class and age diversity, for most judges come from relatively privileged backgrounds and are well into middle age when appointed or elected.

Judges' attitudes, values, and beliefs directly affect the decisions they make and, therefore, the precedents they leave in their wake—although some people argue that this is

▼ New U.S. Supreme Court Justice Sonia Sotomayor

Justice Sotomayor is the first female Latin Justice to serve on the Supreme Court.

not the case and claim that judges can separate their ideology from their decision making, resolving cases based on the requirements of the law.[12] During his 2005 confirmation hearings, U.S. Supreme Court nominee John Roberts repeatedly refused to answer senators' questions about his personal views on such subjects as abortion, civil rights, and women's rights, claiming his views would not influence his decisions. Asked about the separation of church and state, Roberts replied, "[M]y faith and my religious beliefs do not play a role in judging. When it comes to judging, I look to the law books and always have."[13] Roberts was confirmed, and today he serves as Chief Justice.

However, both the political left and the political right have repeatedly accused judges with whom they disagree of "judicial activism"—using the courts to further their own personal or social agendas. As one scholar wrote, "Studies demonstrate that the ideology of a Supreme Court Justice is one of the most powerful predictors of his decisions."[14] Even a quick look at Supreme Court decisions over the past several decades reveals that although all nine Justices are using the same "law books," they are frequently sharply divided in their decisions, and those divisions are nearly always along ideological lines. Lower court judges are no better at preventing their attitudes from influencing their decisions. In fact, some scholars have argued that judges' beliefs not only must be an important basis of their decisions but also should be. For example, when the meaning of laws is unclear, judges should use their beliefs as a guide to interpreting those laws.[15]

▲ **Prosecutors at Work**

Attorneys work on cases outside the courtroom.

Prosecutors

MYTH/REALITY

MYTH: With some crimes, such as intimate partner violence, the victim has to agree to press charges.

REALITY: Only a prosecutor has the power to decide whether a suspect is charged with a crime.

In the U. S. criminal justice system, the prosecutor (and usually only the prosecutor) has the power to bring formal criminal charges against someone. If a prosecutor declines to bring charges, a victim has little legal recourse, aside perhaps from a civil lawsuit against the alleged offender. Conversely, if a prosecutor chooses to initiate charges, even a victim who does not want the offender to be tried can do little about it. This is in contrast to many other countries, such as England, where victims may hire private (nonpublic) attorneys to prosecute their cases.

Prosecutors in the United States go by different names, depending on the jurisdiction. Each of the federal districts has a U.S Attorney, an employee of the Department of Justice. Federal prosecutors are appointed by the president. Each U.S. Attorney oversees several assistant attorneys who actually conduct most of the prosecutions. Occasionally Congress insists that the president and attorney general appoint a **special prosecutor**, armed with independent authority to investigate and bring charges in very high-profile political scandals.

Most states have an **attorney general**, the state's head law enforcement officer. Among other duties, the attorney general and his deputies prosecute criminal appeals. They also may prosecute criminal cases at trial level when the cases are large and complex or have attracted great public attention. At the state level, the attorney general is usually an elected official.

Most criminal prosecutions, however, are conducted at the local level. The people who prosecute cases are called—depending on the jurisdiction—**district attorneys** (DAs), state's attorneys, commonwealth's attorneys, or county prosecutors. This is most often an elected position, although in some jurisdictions prosecutors are appointed by a governor or other official. They oversee deputies or assistants, who do most of the actual prosecuting.

special prosecutor
A prosecutor who is appointed specifically for one particular case, usually because of his specialized knowledge or experience.

attorney general
A state's head law enforcement officer; also the head of the U.S. Department of Justice.

district attorney
The lawyer who prosecutes criminal cases at the local level.

In large prosecutors' offices, deputies and assistants are charged with handling specialized kinds of cases: white-collar criminals, repeat offenders, perpetrators of sexual offenses, and so on.

Whatever the jurisdiction and title, prosecutors have the duty to prove all elements of a criminal charge beyond a reasonable doubt. Not only do prosecutors argue the state's case at trials and appeals; they also conduct investigations, make bail recommendations, do plea bargaining, and make sentencing recommendations. A prosecutor must have a law degree and pass the bar exam for that jurisdiction.

Prosecutors are invested with an enormous amount of discretion. We've seen that it's their choice whether or not to pursue a case. Prosecutors make this decision based on the amount and the quality of the evidence, which in turn means whether they think they can win a conviction. If the prosecutor decides to go ahead with a case, he also usually decides whether to offer the defendant a plea bargain. If the defendant either accepts a plea bargain or is convicted, the prosecutor usually recommends a sentence to the judge. In a capital case, only the prosecutor can decide whether to seek the death penalty.

There are few constraints on **prosecutorial discretion**. Unfortunately, this means prosecutors may, intentionally or not, perpetuate racial, ethnic, social, and gender inequalities within the justice system. Ultimately, the prosecutor is the embodiment of the law: if a prosecutor chooses not to enforce a law, or enforces it badly, the law has little value.

prosecutorial discretion
The prosecutor's power to determine when to bring criminal charges and which charges to bring.

Whether prosecutors should be elected or appointed is much debated. On one hand, prosecutors literally represent "the people" in a criminal prosecution, so perhaps the people—that is, the voters—ought to choose their representative. On the other hand, a prosecutor concerned about being reelected may base her choices about who to prosecute on what she thinks may be popular among the electorate rather than what is fair or good policy. She may decide not to charge a suspect who is wealthy or powerful and who she believes can help reelect her. Because prosecutors routinely decline to bring cases unless they are fairly certain they will win, poor suspects who cannot afford the best attorneys are more likely to be charged. And because some cases, such as intimate partner violence, hate crimes, and sexual assaults, tend to be more difficult to prove, prosecutors may be particularly unlikely to pursue them.

Another controversy focuses on prosecutors' place within the justice system. Are they agents of law enforcement or of the courts? Their duties and responsibilities differ depending on the role they play. For example, should a DA be more concerned with locking up a dangerous person or with avoiding injustice?

Defense Attorneys

Defendants usually have the right to argue their own cases, if they wish and if the judge rules that they are mentally competent to conduct their own defense. Most, however, choose to have a lawyer represent them. In addition to arguing the case in court, this **defense attorney** may conduct pretrial investigations, be present during some police questioning, bargain with the prosecution and the judge over bail amounts, engage in plea bargaining, determine defense strategy, argue about the sentence, and represent the defendant in appeals.

defense attorney
The lawyer who represents the defendant in a criminal case.

American law recognizes as a fundamental right the principle of **attorney–client privilege**—that is, the confidentiality of oral and written communications between the accused and his attorney. After all, if what is said between a criminal defendant and his attorney were known to the prosecution and the judge and thus could be used against the defendant at the trial, the Fifth Amendment protection against self-incrimination could be violated. What then would remain of an accused person's right to defend himself in court? However, the Supreme Court has ruled that if a defense attorney learns from her client that another crime is going to be committed, the principle of attorney–client privilege cannot serve as an excuse for her failing to report such future criminal actions. By failing to report, the attorney herself would become an accessory to another crime.[16]

attorney–client privilege
The right of a person to prevent the government from asking his lawyer to provide evidence of the content of discussions between the person and his attorney.

Defendants who can afford their own attorneys must pay for them, even if they are found not guilty. These fees will not be reimbursed. For many middle-class people, this may mean taking out a second mortgage or other loans. Indigent (poor) defendants, however, are entitled to have the government appoint and pay for a defense attorney (see Chapter 9). Public defenders often carry extremely heavy caseloads. In Minnesota in 1999, for example, about 500 public defenders handled more than 178,000 cases, or more than 350 cases each.[17]

There are three methods by which indigents' defense attorneys may be assigned. Some jurisdictions, mostly larger cities, have public defenders. These attorneys work only for the government to defend indigents. A second method is the assigned counsel system. Here, individual lawyers in private law firms take indigent clients on a case-by-case basis and are paid according to a set fee schedule. Finally, some jurisdictions use a contract method, in which law firms or nonprofit agencies accept indigent cases for a set fee. Whatever the method, indigent defendants do not get to choose their own attorneys.

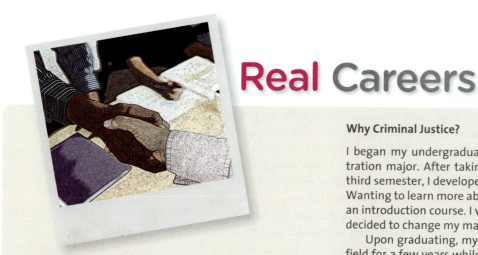

Real Careers

ALMA VALENCIA

Work location: Redwood City, California

College(s): California State University, Chico, 2007

Major(s): Criminal Justice (BS)

Job title: Fee Arbitration Coordinator, San Mateo County Bar Association

Salary range for job like this: $40,000–$45,000

Time in job: 2 years

Work Responsibilities

My work primarily involves assigning arbitrators to cases that involve fee disputes between clients and their attorneys. The goal of an arbitrator is to examine the facts of the disagreement and assist the parties in arriving at a fair solution. In addition to assigning cases, I coordinate events, such as Community Law Night and Judges Night, hosted for the judges and bar members in San Mateo County. I even design the invitations and pamphlets for the events.

As part of my professional training, I was required to attend a presentation on the rules and procedures of fee arbitration by the State Bar of California. I also learned strategies for speaking assertively and confidently with attorneys and their clients. Such training has certainly helped me develop more successful professional relationships.

Why Criminal Justice?

I began my undergraduate studies as a business administration major. After taking a business law class during my third semester, I developed an interest in the justice system. Wanting to learn more about the criminal justice field, I took an introduction course. I was captivated by the material and decided to change my major to criminal justice.

Upon graduating, my plan was to work in a law-related field for a few years while preparing to take the LSAT exam. I was fortunate enough to have a friend working at the San Mateo County Bar Association who informed me of a job opening and suggested that I apply. Having the bachelor's in criminal justice gave me the competitive edge I needed to land my current position as Fee Arbitration Coordinator. Working closely with lawyers over the past 2 years has confirmed for me my original goal of attending law school.

Expectations and Realities of the Job

I had expected my academic courses to prepare me for work. But working in the real world has taught me the importance of developing certain practical career skills that are best mastered outside of the classroom. For example, after 6 months, my supervisor noticed that my communication and leadership skills improved and offered me a salary raise. I strive to continue developing these skills because they allow me to do my job more effectively: I have more productive conversations with clients, and I better coordinate meetings and activities.

My Advice to Students

Take advantage of the career development resources your school offers. I revised my resume many times with a Career Center counselor, discussed career paths with the Criminal Justice Department adviser, and sought course information from the Educational Opportunity Program. All of these resources were available to me free of charge and provided me the assistance I needed to interview and land my current position at San Mateo County Bar Association.

Most felony suspects in the United States are poor, and thus most—approximately 80 percent—are represented by appointed counsel.[18] Almost invariably, appointed attorneys have many fewer resources available than do either prosecutors or privately paid defense lawyers. Critics argue that this fosters inequalities: rich or celebrity defendants such as O. J. Simpson can afford top-notch teams of attorneys, whereas poor defendants must accept lawyers who are overworked, underpaid, often inexperienced, and sometimes poorly motivated. People who are poor and have to depend on less than stellar legal counsel may be convicted more often and receive harsher sentences. According to one study, defendants with public defenders were convicted at about the same rate as those represented by private counsel but were more likely to be incarcerated.[19] This unfairness is likely to fall hardest on people of color, whose incomes tend to be lower than those of Whites.

Although there are a few extremely highly paid and famous criminal lawyers, who for the most part defend wealthy or celebrity clients, the typical defense attorney usually earns less than a prosecutor. In general, within the legal profession defense work carries less prestige than prosecution. Consequently, prosecutors' offices are more likely than public defenders' offices to attract top law school graduates. Again, this means poor defendants are likely to receive second-rate legal assistance.

Judges, prosecutors, and defense attorneys are members of courtroom workgroups that interact on a regular basis. Especially in smaller locales, the numbers of participants in this group can be small and static over time. Such relationships among the three parties could result in the creation of a **local legal culture**—that is, a shared understanding of how cases should be processed. Most seriously, a local legal culture could include a going rate for each crime. A **going rate** is a generally agreed-upon sentence for a defendant based on the crime and prior record.[20] For example, in Butte County, California, almost every individual arrested for minor possession of alcohol receives a sentence that includes a 1-year revocation of his driver's license. Such a harsh sentence is rare in other California counties. The likely explanation is that Butte County takes alcohol offenses comparatively seriously because California State University, Chico resides in the county and is perceived as a university that hard-drinking students attend.

local legal culture
A shared understanding of how cases should be processed.

going rate
A generally agreed-upon sentence for a defendant based on the crime and prior record.

OTHER COURTROOM PARTICIPANTS

People without formal legal training play important roles in the courtroom. In fact, nearly any U.S. citizen may be called upon to serve as a juror, and anyone—whether a citizen or not—who has knowledge about a crime or sees it being committed might be required to testify as a witness.

Juries

In one form or another, juries have been used for thousands of years. Most countries with civil law systems don't use them any longer, but in common law countries such as the United States, England, and Canada juries are invested with unique powers. There are two kinds of U.S. juries: the **grand jury** and the **petit jury** (*petit* is French for "small" and in Anglo-American legal usage is pronounced "petty"). Grand juries sometimes investigate crimes and determine whether there is sufficient evidence to prosecute a particular suspect. Petit juries decide whether defendants are guilty of the crimes with which they are charged. We can trace our jury system back to eleventh-century England, and, as discussed in A Global View, the United States makes more extensive use of juries than any other country in the world.

grand jury
Panel of citizens who may investigate certain crimes and determine whether sufficient evidence exists to bring a defendant to trial.

petit jury
Small groups of citizens who determine whether a criminal defendant is guilty of the crimes with which he is charged.

A jury is composed of citizens who reside in the trial court's jurisdiction and are typically picked at random from lists of registered voters and licensed drivers. To make juries more representative of their communities and to increase the jury pool, some states recently began choosing citizens using utility bills, telephone bills, or property taxes. In the United States, jurors must be citizens over the age of 18 who can understand English and

A Global View

Juries around the World

That a jury trial is guaranteed by the U.S. Constitution speaks to its importance to us. In the rest of the world, however, juries are used sparingly, if at all.

Other countries that share the common law tradition, such as Canada and England, generally limit juries to a small number of serious criminal cases. Even when defendants are allowed to choose a jury trial, they are less likely to do so than in the United States. Today in England, for example, jury trials are chosen by only about 5 percent of eligible defendants, whereas about 40 percent of U.S. felony cases are tried by juries.

Most countries with civil law or other legal systems use juries rarely, if at all, and in an advisory rather than a decision-making role. Some countries have experimented with juries. Japan, for example, used them between 1923 and 1943. Under a recently enacted law, beginning in 2009 some Japanese criminal cases will be tried by panels of three judges and six citizens. More typical of civil law countries is the Netherlands, which uses a three-judge tribunal with no jury.

Is a jury-based system better than one that uses only judges? Juries enable citizens to participate directly in the justice process. On one hand, they are more representative of their communities than are judges and, perhaps, better able to empathize with defendants or, conversely, with victims. Juries can refuse to convict when they feel a conviction would be unjust. On the other hand, jurors may be more easily swayed than judges by bias, pretrial publicity, and emotion. Some critics question how well juries understand and follow the instructions they are given, and how well they understand the evidence in complex or highly technical cases.

OBSERVE
Investigate
Understand

- **What are some of the reasons the United States has retained the jury-based system that it inherited from England centuries ago?**
- **Should jury trials be abolished in the United States and all criminal cases be tried before a three-judge panel, as in the Netherlands?**
- **Can the new Japanese system of trying criminal cases before a three-judge and six-citizen panel be fairly described as a compromise between jury trials and judge-only trials? Why or why not?**

SOURCES: Richard Terrell, *World Criminal Justice Systems*, 5th ed. (Cincinnati: Anderson, 2003), 46; Bureau of Justice Statistics, *Felony Defendants in Large Urban Counties, 2002* (Washington, DC: U.S. Department of Justice, 2006).

who are physically capable of sitting through the trial. Vision- and hearing-impaired individuals and those with significant mobility problems are usually excused. In some places, a criminal record may permanently disqualify a person from jury service, and other factors such as the person's profession may also prevent jury service. When a person is called for jury duty, she has a legal obligation to serve unless she can convince the judge that doing so would impose undue hardship, either on her dependents or on herself. Professionals associated with law enforcement and the justice system, such as police officers and lawyers, are sometimes automatically excused.

In some jurisdictions, a pool of potential jurors is chosen for one particular case, whereas in other jurisdictions the pool may be for whatever trials arise during a particular time frame. In that case, people designated as potential jurors typically have to present themselves for jury duty for several weeks or until they are selected for a trial. In either case, this pool is called the **venire** (pronounced "ven-eer"). The goal is to obtain a venire as representative of the community as possible. In practice, this is difficult; some groups of people may be less likely to register to vote or may have personal or financial needs that keep them from serving. Depending on how lenient local judges are about requests to be excused, a venire might be disproportionately made up of middle-class and retired people. The problem was worse in the past, however. Until well into the 1960s, non-Whites and women were routinely excluded from juries.

venire
A group of people called to be prospective jurors.

Jury duty is necessary under the U.S. system of justice, but many people regard it as a burden. The amount of time jurors must commit varies enormously across jurisdictions, but being called for jury duty can mean days or even weeks of waiting in the courthouse before being put on a jury, and some trials can last for weeks or even months. Although employers are forbidden by law to penalize employees for work time lost while doing jury duty, the compensation paid to jurors is usually only a few dollars per day. Self-employed individuals, part-time workers, day laborers, and students, for all of whom the loss of work time can spell a significant burden, are seldom able to persuade judges to excuse them entirely from service. In addition, serving on a criminal jury can be emotionally wrenching, especially in a violent murder or rape case or when a difficult verdict must be rendered or a decision made about inflicting the death penalty.

Once a venire has been formed, the judge or attorneys may ask members about their personal background and history, profession, education, and criminal record, whether they have knowledge of the case or the individuals involved, and their opinions about matters relevant to it. For example, in states that employ capital punishment, potential jurors in a murder trial may be asked whether they would categorically refuse to recommend a death sentence should the defendant be found guilty. This process is called **voir dire** ("vwar deer"). Anyone biased against the prosecution or the defendant—for example, a relative of the victim—is excused from the pool. These are called **challenges for cause**. The prosecutor and defense attorney may use **peremptory challenges** to release some people they think will not be sympathetic to their case. In federal capital trials—that is, for crimes punishable by death—both the prosecution and the defense are allowed 20 peremptory challenges, and 3 in noncapital trials; state rules for peremptory challenges vary. By law, these challenges are not supposed to be used to exclude jurors on the basis of race, ethnicity, or gender. In fact, however, lawyers often do consider potential jurors' race and gender in trying to build a persuadable jury.[21]

voir dire
The process of questioning prospective jurors about their background, opinions, and knowledge relevant to a particular case.

challenges for cause
Excusing potential jurors from a jury because they might be biased in that case.

peremptory challenges
An attorney removes a prospective juror she feels will not be sympathetic to her side of the case.

jury nullification
The power of juries to refuse to apply criminal laws when they feel applying them would be unjust.

Some lawyers use jury consultants to help them choose jurors. These consultants, usually people with graduate training in psychology or other social sciences, conduct mock trials, surveys, and other exercises to try to determine the characteristics of those jurors most—and least—likely to be sympathetic to the clients' cases. Some critics argue that jury consultants help lawyers unfairly stack the deck in favor of their clients. Others say they affect trial decisions in only some cases.[22]

Once voir dire is complete, the venire will be narrowed down to an actual jury, typically of 12, although the Supreme Court has allowed juries as small as 6 members. The jury's role is to be the finder of facts. When all the evidence has been presented and both sides have completed their arguments, the jurors withdraw to a closed room to deliberate together and reach a verdict. A defendant who is found guilty may appeal, but higher courts will not overturn that verdict unless it was completely unreasonable or the judge made legal errors during the trial. A verdict of not guilty is final. No matter how obvious it may seem that the defendant committed the crime, double jeopardy prohibitions prevent the prosecutor from appealing or retrying a defendant found innocent. (See Chapter 9 for more on double jeopardy.)

Even though judges instruct juries to follow the law, if they refuse and acquit an obviously guilty individual, there is no recourse. Therefore, juries may sometimes choose not to apply criminal laws when they feel doing so would be unjust. This power—**jury nullification**—has been recognized in U.S. law for more than 200 years. An early example occurred in 1735, when a jury in New York refused to convict John Peter Zenger of seditious libel for

▼ The Courtroom at Work

Many different parties participate in trials.

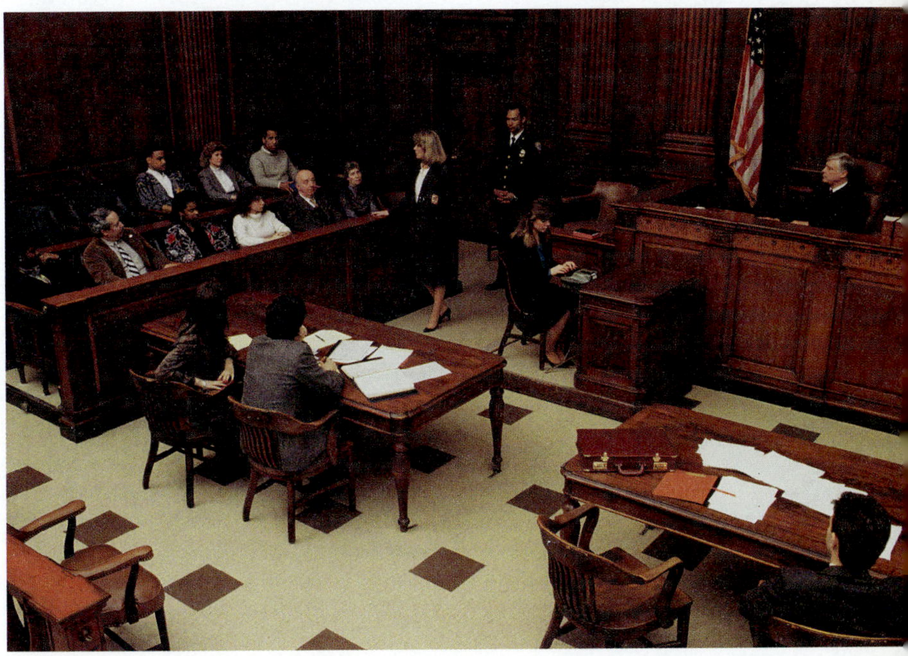

lay witness
A person who has personally seen or heard information relevant to the case at hand; also called a fact witness or eyewitness.

expert witnesses
People who have specialized knowledge of some scientific or technical matter that may help in the decision of a case.

subpoena
A legal document ordering a person to appear in court.

contempt of court
Violation of a court's order, punishable by fine, jail time, or both.

printing newspapers that criticized the colony's governor. In the Jim Crow South before the 1970s, all-White juries routinely refused to convict Whites for committing crimes against Black people and almost invariably found Blacks guilty when they were accused of raping, assaulting, or killing Whites, regardless of the facts of the case.

MYTH/REALITY

MYTH: Juries administer equal justice.

REALITY: Jurors are influenced by many extralegal considerations including racism, sexism, and heterosexism.[23]

Race, Class, Gender

Race and Jury Decision Making

Racism infects every component of the criminal justice system, perhaps nowhere more so than in death penalty cases. In 1972, the U.S. Supreme Court in *Furman v. Georgia* struck down most death penalty statutes as "arbitrary and capricious." New laws that followed in the wake of *Furman* were intended to address these shortfalls. Yet in 1990 the U.S. General Accounting Office reported to Congress that its review of the empirical studies on racism and capital punishment since 1972 revealed "a pattern of evidence indicating racial disparities in the charging, sentencing, and imposition of the death penalty."

As of 2006, among more than 3,300 condemned inmates in the United States, over 40 percent were Black, even though Blacks make up only 12 percent of the U.S. population. Prosecutors decide in which cases to seek the death penalty and ultimately choose only about 1 percent of all eligible cases. Thus the vast majority of cases that could be pursued as capital cases in fact are not. What determines whether a particular crime will result in a capital case? According to the American Civil Liberties Union, in the 38 states having the death penalty, approximately 98 percent of prosecutors are White. The race of the prosecutor may be a factor in this trend—White prosecutors choosing to prosecute as capital cases those with African American defendants—but it is not the only one.

According to a 1990 report to Congress by the General Accounting Office (GAO), for murders committed under otherwise similar circumstances by defendants with comparable criminal histories, if the victim was White, the defendant was several times more likely to be given the death penalty than if the victim was Black. Approximately half of all murder victims are White, but in death penalty cases about 80 percent of victims are White. In fact, the single factor that most reliably predicts whether someone will be sentenced to death is the race of the victim. Across the United States, cases involving a White victim and a defendant of color are statistically most likely to result in a death sentence.

OBSERVE Investigate Understand

- **What measures can be implemented to better ensure that race is not a factor in sentencing a person to death?**
- **Do you believe that infliction of the death penalty in the United States can still be accurately described as "arbitrary and capricious"?**
- **Do racial disparities in death sentences prove that the death penalty in contemporary America has become "cruel and unusual punishment"?**

SOURCES: U.S. Census, "The Black Population: 2000," www.census.gov/prod/2001pubs/c2kbr01-5.pdf (retrieved February 23, 2007); The American Civil Liberties Union, "Race and the Death Penalty," February 26, 2003, www.aclu.org/capital/unequal/10389pub20030226.html (retrieved February 2, 2007); Criminal Justice Project of the NAACP Legal Defense Fund, Inc., "Death Row U.S.A.," *Quarterly Report* (Winter 2006); United States General Accounting Office, "Death Penalty Sentencing: Research Indicated Pattern of Racial Disparities," *Report to Senate and House Committee on the Judiciary* (February 1990), 5.

Of course, any power brings with it the possibility of abuse. No one but a juror is permitted to be present during jury deliberations. And because jurors need not discuss their deliberations with others after the fact, no one knows how often their decisions are affected by factors that are not supposed to be considered in criminal cases, such as the defendant's race, gender, social class—and even physical attractiveness. See the Race, Class, Gender box for a discussion of how race can affect jury decisions.

Witnesses

Some evidence in criminal trials is physical evidence—things we can actually see and touch, such as weapons, bloodstains, surveillance videos, and letters. Most evidence, however, comes from witnesses—individuals who have some information pertinent to the trial. There are two kinds of witnesses. **Lay witnesses**, also referred to as fact witnesses or eyewitnesses, are people who heard or saw firsthand something directly related to the crime. **Expert witnesses** are people who have some special knowledge—scientific, technical, and the like—that can help the triers of fact decide a case.

Lay Witnesses

The prosecution and the defense may call as witnesses anyone who personally heard or saw things related to the case, including the crime itself. Even if no one actually saw the crime occur, the prosecution could still call upon witnesses to establish the defendant's motive for or knowledge of the case. When there are victims, there will nearly always be witnesses. The defense, on the other hand, might call people who can testify that the defendant was somewhere else when the crime was committed—that is, they establish an alibi—people who provide evidence that someone else committed the crime, or even those who can claim that the alleged crime never occurred at all.

The Sixth Amendment to the U.S. Constitution guarantees criminal defendants the right to confront and cross-examine their accusers and to have witnesses testify in their defense. The attorneys can therefore request the judge issue a **subpoena**, a legal document ordering a witness to appear in court even if unwilling. A person who disobeys a subpoena may be found in **contempt of court** and punished.

Eyewitness testimony is powerful evidence that tends to carry considerable weight with jurors. Unfortunately, it is not as reliable as many people assume. In criminal cases the witnesses themselves often are facing criminal charges; by testifying against the defendant, they hope to absolve themselves or at least receive a lighter sentence. Prosecutors frequently offer one suspect a plea bargain, recommending a relatively light charge or sentence in exchange for testimony against someone else. See, for example, the case of Michael Fortier, the accomplice who testified against Timothy McVeigh and Terry Nichols in the Oklahoma City bombing trial, described at the beginning of this chapter. Of course, witnesses in these situations have a strong incentive to provide damaging evidence against the defendant and may be less than honest in their testimony.

Real Crime Tech

FREEING WRONGFULLY CONVICTED PERSONS

The partnership between law and forensics, especially DNA analysis, is helping to free wrongfully convicted persons and ensure greater constitutional protection. In cases of wrongful conviction, the leading responsible factor (77 percent of the time) has been eyewitness misidentification. Because of new technology for DNA testing and an innovative program called the Innocence Project, large numbers of convictions of innocent persons are being overturned. Thanks to the pioneering work of Peter Neufeld and of attorney Barry Scheck (a member of the successful O. J. Simpson criminal trial defense team), the Innocence Project was established in 1992 at the Cardozo School of Law, Yeshiva University, in New York City. The term that has come to identify this type of technological legal work is DNA exonerations. As of October 21, 2009, there have been 244 such exonerations in the USA; the first exoneration occurred in 1989. Among all those exonerated, 17 were serving time on death row, the average time served was 12 years and the average age was 26. The majority (59.5 percent) of these wrongful convictions were Blacks. As of this writing, there are 74 such projects around the world: 43 U.S. states and the District of Columbia have them, as well as four other countries (Canada, the United Kingdom, New Zealand, and Australia). This innovative use of DNA technology in partnership with law reformers is being used to provide unquestionable substantiation that wrongful convictions from systemic flaws in the legal process can be corrected and can help free those that are innocent.

SOURCES: Innocence Project, www.innocenceproject.org/ (retrieved February 22, 2009); Paul C. Roberts, "The Causes of Wrongful Conviction," *Reflections*, www.independent.org/pdf/tir/tir_07_4_roberts.pdf (retrieved February 22, 2009).

MYTH/REALITY

MYTH: Eyewitness testimony is reliable evidence.

REALITY: Eyewitness testimony is often unreliable, even when witnesses are positive they are testifying accurately.[24]

Most people, including jurors, are skeptical of testimony from coconspirators and police informants. What many do not realize, however, is that *all* eyewitness testimony is suspect. Research demonstrates that even witnesses who have no incentive to lie and are trying to be as truthful as possible perceive and remember events with little accuracy. The brain does not operate like a video camera, accurately recording what it sees and reproducing it later. Environmental conditions such as lighting and physical obstructions and the trauma associated with the crime all compromise eyewitness identification. According to the Innocence Project, out of 183 cases in which defendants were later proven to have been wrongfully convicted, mistaken eyewitness identification was a factor in about 75 percent.[25]

Mistaken eyewitness identification is the foremost cause of wrongful convictions. Social scientists and legal scholars have made recommendations for reducing these errors, such as using identification procedures that are less suggestive. Evidence suggests that at least some of these solutions work, but few jurisdictions follow them.[26]

Expert Witnesses

Lay witnesses testify about what they observed or what they know as fact. Expert witnesses, on the other hand, can express *opinions* based on their specialized knowledge, research, and experience, as long as the judge is satisfied that their testimony will help the jury discover the facts about the case. Most often, expert witnesses help jurors understand particular evidence about, for example, the insanity defense, eyewitness identification, child custody matters, intimate partner violence, and class action suits.

Ideally, expert witnesses are impartial and educate the court. The adversarial nature of judicial proceedings, however, often puts them under considerable pressure to give their loyalty to the winning of the case rather than to their discipline. They could, for instance, fail to mention contradictory findings or exaggerate or even falsify claims. Such behavior is especially troubling because it is very difficult to prosecute expert witnesses for perjury as they are ostensibly giving an opinion rather than presenting a fact. At worst, an unethical expert witness will be deemed incompetent.

In one homicide case, the fingerprint expert for the prosecution noted two fingerprints—both matching the defendant's—on an item admitted into evidence.[27] A third print—not the defendant's—was later discovered on the object, but not before the defendant had been convicted and sentenced to death. Whether the expert in this case was dishonest or incompetent is difficult to establish, and when there is doubt, the expert is given the benefit of that doubt. Some expert witnesses are certainly sincere in their testimony but nonetheless hold opinions not grounded in science (see the Disconnects box for a discussion of "junk science").

Victims in Courts

In the criminal justice system, victims serve as witnesses because technically they are not a party to the court case. Instead, the case is brought by the state against a defendant. As such, the state is legally the "victim" of the crime; the actual person who was victimized is merely a witness to the crime. The distinction is a difficult one for many victims to understand because they are the ones who suffered as a result of the crime.

Victims feel they should play a larger role in the court process than merely serving as a witness when called by the state. Instead, the prosecutor representing the state determines whether there is enough evidence to bring a case forward—a decision that is often made without consulting the victim. If the prosecutor feels that there is enough evidence, she will bring charges against the defendant. If the case goes to a plea bargain, the prosecutor

DIS Connects

Junk Science in the Courtroom

Do jurors and judges understand the language used by expert witnesses? Do they know what an expert means when he uses terms such as "consistent with" or "statistically significant"? Do they understand the science that underlies an expert's testimony? The answers to these questions are generally no. How, then, can the triers of fact recognize when expert witnesses present unreliable information based on unscientific methods and analyses? The adversarial nature of judicial proceedings should serve to expose such "junk science" as well as outright fraud in the courtroom. Expert witnesses from the other side should catch it. Even when faulty science is exposed, however, it might not make a difference to jury members.

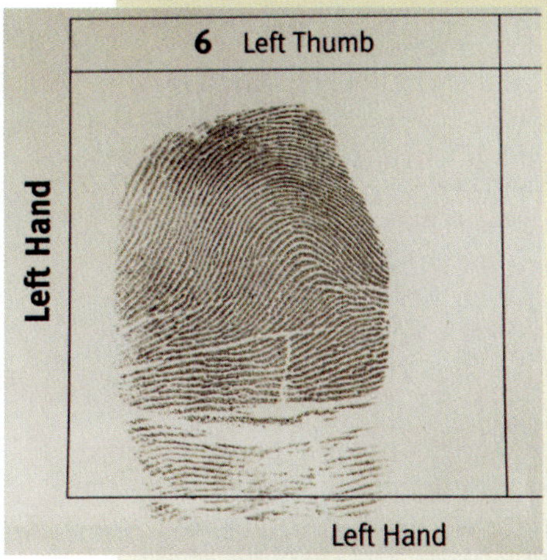

Unfounded scientific opinions may be shrouded by the charismatic presentation of the expert. Huber, for example, discussed the civil case of a woman whose claim of losing her psychic powers after having a CAT scan was supported by expert testimony from a doctor. A Philadelphia jury awarded her $1 million. Although the trial judge threw out that verdict, jurors had been persuaded of an unverifiable claim by an effective courtroom presentation that overruled their common sense.

Sometimes the science itself is good but the person who uses it is mistaken, incompetent, or fraudulent. Despite having flunked organic chemistry in college, Fred Zain became a forensics expert for West Virginia and Texas and testified against defendants in hundreds of cases. Zain was ultimately charged with lying and fabricating evidence, leading to as many as 134 wrongful convictions.

Sometimes the science itself is suspect. Polygraph (lie detector) evidence is generally not admissible because it is considered scientifically unreliable. Even fingerprint evidence has been called into question in recent years. Of course, as scientific techniques advance, what was once considered unreliable may eventually grow strong enough to become acceptable in court.

Observe Investigate Understand

- **Is it necessary for jurors to understand the science that underlies the testimony of expert witnesses?**
- **Why are jurors so willing to believe junk science in a courtroom?**
- **Is the problem of jurors sometimes accepting junk science in criminal trials a valid argument against continuing to use the jury system in American criminal justice?**

SOURCES: P. Huber, "Junk Science in the Courtroom," *Forbes* (July 8, 1991), 68; Supreme Court of Appeals of West Virginia, *Renewed Investigation of the West Virginia State Police Crime Laboratory, Serology Division*, January 2006, www.state.wv.us/wvsca/docs/spring06/32885.htm (retrieved February 23, 2007); Michael Specter, "Do Fingerprints Lie?" *The New Yorker* (May 27, 2002).

will negotiate a plea with the opposing defense attorney and the defendant. The victim in the case is not present when the plea bargain is negotiated, might not approve of the plea bargain process, and may not be notified that the defendant entered into the agreement or that a plea agreement was reached. If a plea agreement is not reached or the defendant wants the case to go to trial, the case will proceed to trial even if the victim does not want to press charges, denies that the crime ever occurred, or does not want to participate in the court process. The victim does not have a voice in any of these stages and the case will proceed, often without his knowledge or approval. At this point, the case is in the prosecutor's hands and she can subpoena or compel the victim to testify as a witness. If the victim does not participate, he can be found in contempt of court, which is punishable by a fine, incarceration, or both.

The final stage of victim participation occurs during sentencing, when the victim is given an opportunity to describe how the crime has influenced his life—also known as giving a victim impact statement. Because many victims are unfamiliar with the criminal justice system or may find it overwhelming or intimidating to deal with, in some places they may be offered the help of victim advocates (see What about the Victim?).

What about the Victim?

The Role of the Victim Advocate

Susan is a 21-year-old college student in a serious relationship with Jake, her high school sweetheart. Each claims to love the other very much, but Jake has become increasingly controlling—wanting to know where Susan is, what she is doing, and who she is with. Jake says that he does this because he loves Susan, but she feels pressured and uncomfortable. The couple fights more, and Jake often says Susan is "stupid" when she expresses opinions different from his.

Susan lives off campus with two roommates. One night Jake visits, and they get into a heated argument. He pushes her, and Susan screams, "You have no right to do that!" He responds by slapping Susan across the face so hard that she falls against a coffee table, striking her mouth and breaking open her lip. As she lies bleeding on the floor, Jake yells, "Don't ever tell me what to do, ever! Next time, I'll make sure your mouth is shut for good." Susan is scared and calls the police.

Once the police arrive, they interview Susan about the incident. They inquire about her level of safety in the apartment and determine whether she needs alternate housing, such as a shelter for battered women. In all 50 states, the police are supposed to give a person in Susan's position a business card with an abuse hotline number and the services available for victims of intimate partner violence and their children. In some states, the hotline worker will refer the victim to a local service provider, which will assign a victim advocate to the case. The victim advocate typically works for a local intimate partner violence or rape crisis center, with law enforcement, or in the district attorney's office.

The victim advocate will work with Susan throughout the criminal justice process. Depending on the severity of the violence, the police may contact the victim advocate at the crime scene and relate that Susan is being transported to the hospital. The victim advocate will go to the hospital and immediately begin working with Susan to ensure her safety, determine her needs, and explain what happens next. Victim advocates can assist with further police investigations by obtaining a restraining or protective order, working with the district attorney's office, and preparing Susan to testify against Jake. The victim advocate also will notify Susan about all court proceedings, accompany her to court, and help her write a victim impact statement. If Jake is incarcerated, the victim advocate will work with the county jail to determine whether or when he will be released and will inform Susan of his status. The victim advocate can help Susan with any paperwork for victim compensation, which helps offset the costs to her of her victimization, including her participation in the criminal justice system.

OBSERVE
Investigate
Understand

- **In the fictional case presented here, do you think that Susan was justified in calling the police after Jake struck her? Assume that this is the first time such an incident has occurred involving this couple.**
- **What kind of personal characteristics do successful victim advocates need to possess?**
- **Why do so many intimate partner violence victims refuse to press charges against their assailants?**

SOURCE: Julie Tomz Esselman and Daniel McGillis, *Serving Crime Victims and Witnesses*, 2nd ed. (Washington, DC: U.S. Department of Justice, February 1997).

Other Participants

The defendant, judge, attorneys, jury, and witnesses are the most obvious and visible participants in a trial. A body of other individuals may provide services to the court, attorneys, defendant, and victim. Figure 8-4 provides a brief summary of some of the other trial participants.

SUMMARY

The essence of the Anglo-American system of justice is its adversarial nature, in which the state must prove the defendant's guilt beyond a reasonable doubt. The defendant is entitled to a vigorous, professional defense that need only prove the existence of real doubt about the defendant's guilt. As the two sides contend in the courtroom, the judge serves as referee, ensuring due process and the correct application of the law, and the jury weighs the evidence

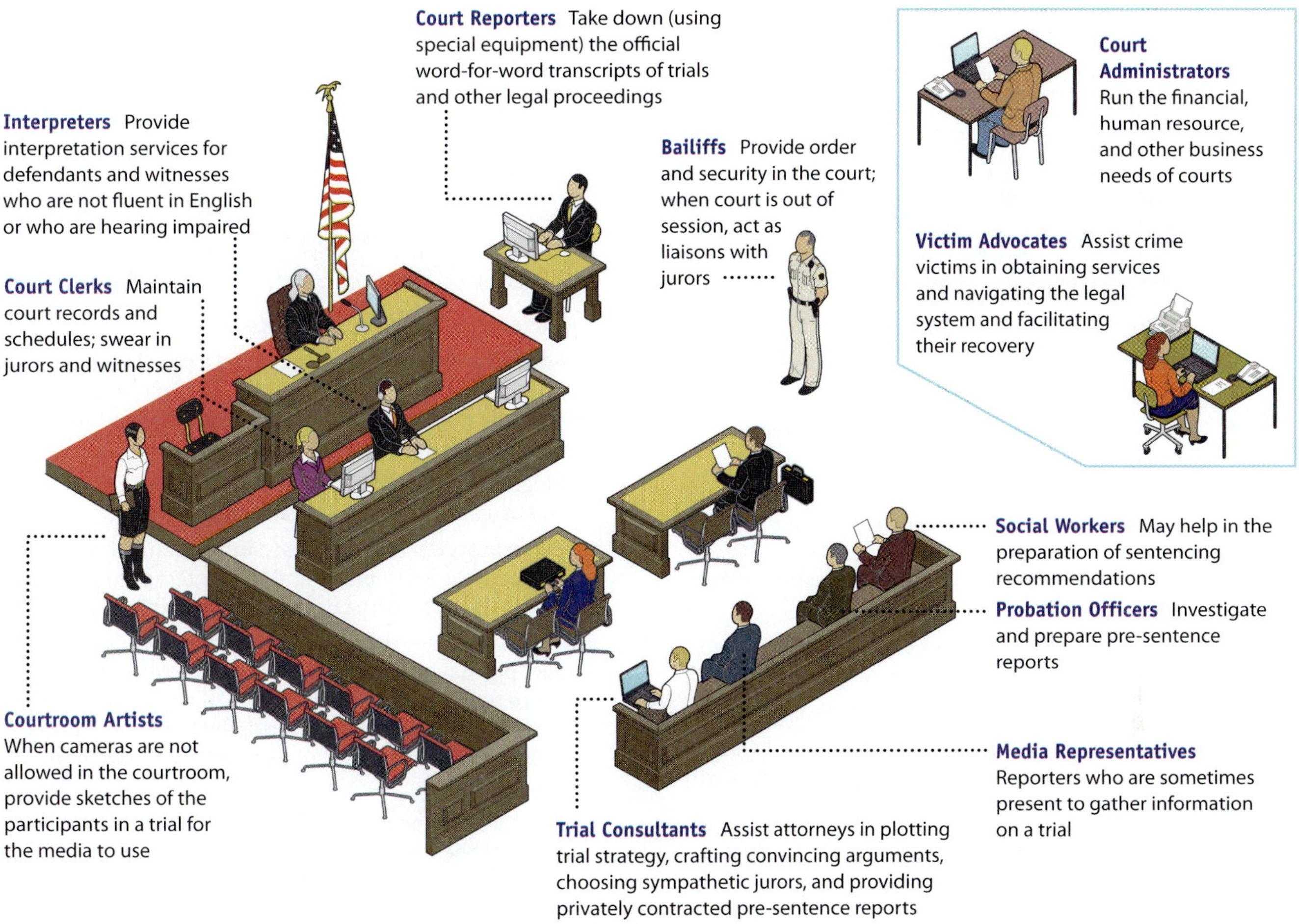

Court Reporters Take down (using special equipment) the official word-for-word transcripts of trials and other legal proceedings
Interpreters Provide interpretation services for defendants and witnesses who are not fluent in English or who are hearing impaired
Bailiffs Provide order and security in the court; when court is out of session, act as liaisons with jurors
Court Administrators Run the financial, human resource, and other business needs of courts
Victim Advocates Assist crime victims in obtaining services and navigating the legal system and facilitating their recovery
Court Clerks Maintain court records and schedules; swear in jurors and witnesses
Social Workers May help in the preparation of sentencing recommendations
Probation Officers Investigate and prepare pre-sentence reports
Courtroom Artists When cameras are not allowed in the courtroom, provide sketches of the participants in a trial for the media to use
Media Representatives Reporters who are sometimes present to gather information on a trial
Trial Consultants Assist attorneys in plotting trial strategy, crafting convincing arguments, choosing sympathetic jurors, and providing privately contracted pre-sentence reports

FIGURE 8-4 Other Participants in a Criminal Trial

and decides the question of guilt. A "not guilty" finding means that the constitutional protection against double jeopardy ensures that the defendant will not be tried again for the same offense (though this does not protect an acquitted defendant against a civil trial for damages, in which the standard of proof is lower).

In the United States, federal cases—those subject to federal law—are tried in federal district courts. Appeals from district courts go to federal appellate courts, which determine not guilt or innocence but rather ensure that mistakes were not made at the trial court level. The Supreme Court of the United States hears a limited number of further appeals. States maintain a parallel track of trial courts, appellate courts, and a state supreme court. There also are special courts of limited jurisdiction to handle a variety of special cases.

Serious problems still affect the U.S. court system. Courts often are overwhelmed with more cases than can be handled efficiently. Prosecutors enjoy (and occasionally abuse) enormous discretionary powers, including the right to decide which cases are prosecuted. Apart from a few highly paid celebrities, defense attorneys are typically overworked and not well compensated. Jury service is regarded by most Americans as an unpleasant duty, and juries occasionally make serious mistakes. Victims are sometimes badly treated. Members of racial and ethnic minorities are underrepresented among prosecutors and judges, and a disproportionate share of death sentences are given to people of color. Judges and jurors often rely on expert witnesses to understand evidence, but not all expert testimony is reliable.

OBSERVE
Investigate
Understand

Review

Distinguish state, local, and federal courts and their jurisdictions.

- State courts hear most criminal cases.
- Local courts generally hear minor criminal or civil cases, or conduct the early stages of a criminal trial.
- Federal courts have limited jurisdiction and can hear only cases involving federal law or certain civil cases.

Describe some of the specialized courts that have been created for particular cases.

- Mental health courts involve cases with defendants with mental health issues.
- Drug courts involve cases with defendants with substance abuse problems.
- Reentry courts focus on reintegrating offenders with society.
- Teen courts focus on youthful offenders, and their juries consist of other teenagers.

Discuss how appeals courts differ from trial courts.

- The purpose of appeals courts is not to decide the facts of the case but to determine whether legal errors were made at trial.
- The attorneys in appeals cases file lengthy documents known as appellate briefs.
- There is no jury in an appeals case.
- Appeals cases are usually heard by a panel of judges.

Identify the major participants in the judicial system and their respective roles.

- Judges interpret the law, decide appropriate legal issues, and usually determine the sentence.
- Prosecutors decide whether to bring criminal charges and which ones to bring, and they attempt to prove all elements of the crime beyond a reasonable doubt.
- Defense attorneys represent the defendant; they conduct pretrial investigations, are present during some police questioning, argue about bail amounts, engage in plea bargaining, determine defense strategy, argue about the sentence, and represent the defendant in appeals.
- Juries determine the facts of the case and, ultimately, whether the defendant is guilty or innocent.
- Lay witnesses testify about things they heard or saw that are relevant to the case.
- Expert witnesses testify about scientific or technical matters that are helpful in determining the facts of a case.
- Victims may serve as witnesses and may also testify during the sentencing process.

Key Terms

appellate brief 231
attorney–client privilege 237
attorney general 236
challenges for cause 241
commissioners 233
contempt of court 242
court of last resort 232
courts of general jurisdiction 227
courts of limited jurisdiction 227
defense attorney 237
district attorney 236
due process 233
en banc 230
expert witnesses 242
going rate 239
grand jury 239
in chambers 232
jurisdiction 229
jury nullification 241
justice of the peace 233
lay witness 242
local legal culture 239
magistrate 233
peremptory challenges 241
petit jury 239
prosecutorial discretion 237
recusal 232
referees 233
remand 232
special prosecutor 236
subpoena 242
venire 240
voir dire 241
writ of certiorari 232

Study Questions

1. Which is *not* an example of a specialty court?
   a. Mental health court
   b. Drug court
   c. Reentry court
   d. Appeals court

2. Appellate courts
   a. are triers of fact.
   b. decide whether legal errors were made at trial.
   c. often let guilty people go free.
   d. are speedy in providing justice.

3. When a case is heard en banc, it means that
   a. one judge resides over the case.
   b. a panel of three judges reside over the case.
   c. more than three judges reside over the case.
   d. None of the above.
4. Which of the following is not typically the job of a trial court judge?
   a. Determine matters of fact
   b. Determine matters of law
   c. Interpret laws
   d. Determine the sentence
5. A state's chief law enforcement officer is known as a/an
   a. district attorney.
   b. attorney general.
   c. sheriff.
   d. police chief.
6. If a prosecutor refuses to try someone for a crime, the victim may
   a. sue the prosecutor.
   b. press charges and require the prosecutor to act.
   c. hire an attorney to prosecute the accused.
   d. bring a civil lawsuit.
7. The pool of people called to serve as potential jurors in a case is called the
   a. habeas corpus.
   b. voir dire.
   c. venire.
   d. grand jury.
8. A lay witness is
   a. someone who has information directly pertinent to the case.
   b. someone who is an expert in a scientific or technical area.
   c. someone who has a personal relationship with the defendant.
   d. rarely allowed to testify.
9. The foremost cause of wrongful convictions is
   a. mistaken eyewitness testimony.
   b. jury tampering.
   c. attorney malpractice.
   d. poor scientific evidence.
10. A person with specialized knowledge that may be helpful in a particular case is known as a/an
   a. district attorney.
   b. expert witness.
   c. voir dire.
   d. accomplice.

Critical Thinking Questions

1. Which do you think is more likely to result in a fair decision: a trial by jury or a bench trial? What do you see as the potential risks and benefits of each? Why do you think the United States relies so much more on juries than does the rest of the world?
2. How should district attorneys be chosen: by political appointment or election? What difference does it make?
3. What are some ways to ensure the accuracy of scientific testimony in the courtroom?

Internet Sites

What Jennifer Saw
www.pbs.org/wgbh/pages/frontline/shows/dna/
This site accompanies the Frontline film *What Jennifer Saw* and has much information on mistaken eyewitness identification.

National Center for State Courts
www.ncsconline.org/D_Research/Ct_Struct/Index.html
This site contains charts of state courts for each state.

Alliance for Justice
www.independentjudiciary.com/
This organization supports the nomination of fair federal judges. Among other things, the organization provides information on the judicial selection process, as well as on specific federal judicial nominees.

Suggested Readings

Scott Christianson, *Innocent: Inside Wrongful Conviction Cases* (New York: New York University Press, 2005).
The author reviews 42 cases in which individuals were convicted of crimes they did not commit.

Paul Wice, *Public Defenders and the American Justice System* (Santa Barbara, CA: Praeger, 2005).
This book offers an inside look into the work of public defenders.

Pretrial and Trial

CHAPTER 9

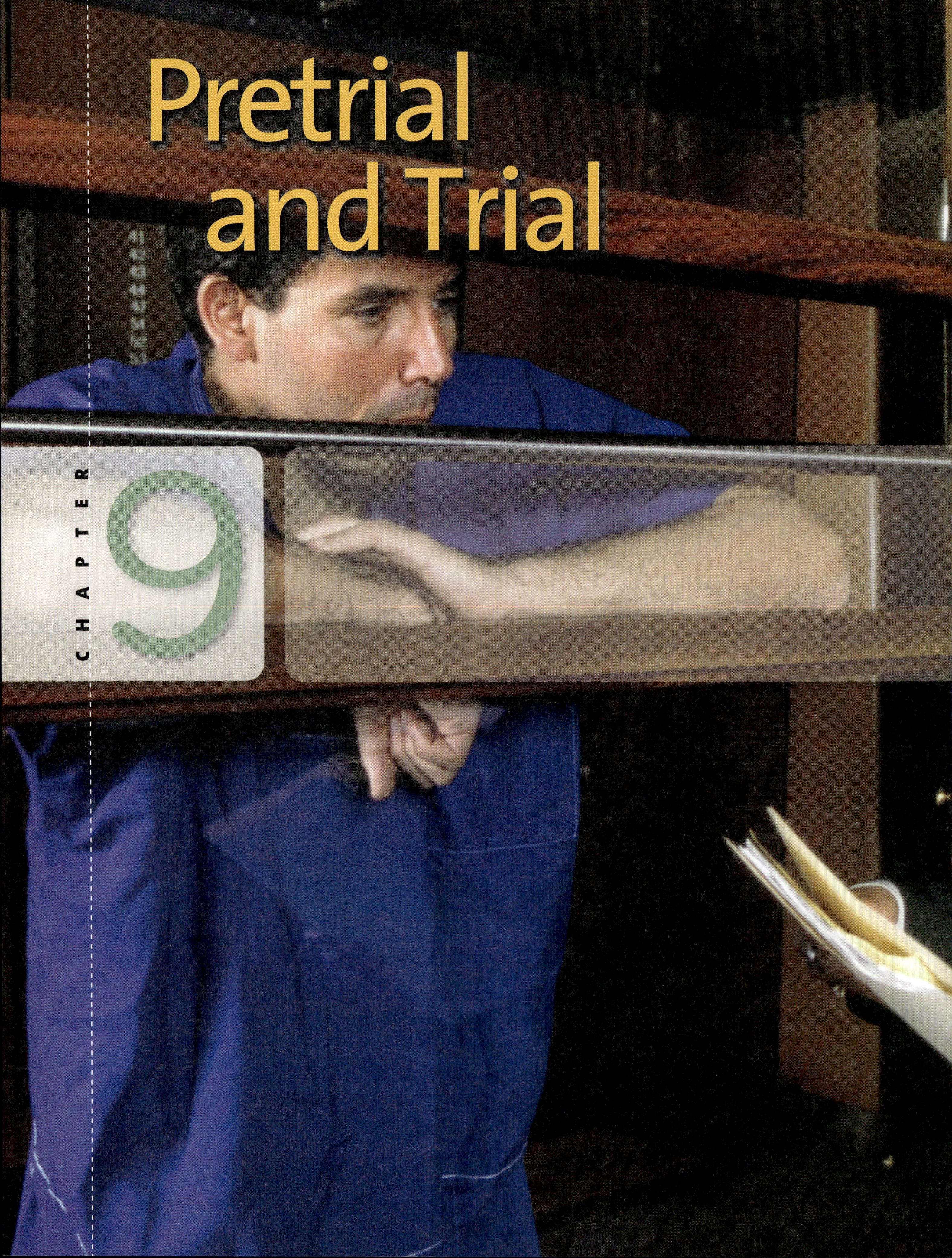

Observe Investigate Understand

After reading this chapter, you should be able to:

- Describe the Eighth Amendment right to bail.
- List the rights afforded to criminal defendants by the Sixth Amendment.
- Describe the scope and limitations of the right against double jeopardy.
- Identify the steps of the pretrial process.
- Analyze the meaning of the due process clause.
- Distinguish the differing standards of proof used by the U.S. legal system.
- Identify the stages of a criminal trial.

Realities and Challenges

Innocent—and Twelve Years on Death Row

On February 25, 1983, 10-year-old Jeanine Nicarico was abducted from her home near Chicago, sexually assaulted, and beaten to death. Her body was discovered a few days later. Amid much public outcry, and only 2 weeks before the local prosecutor came up for reelection, two 19-year-olds, Rolando Cruz and Alejandro Hernandez, were arrested and charged with the crime. Both had several previous arrests for burglary. There was no physical evidence to link them to the crime, and both had alibis placing them away from the murder scene. At their trial, however, several police informants testified that Cruz and Hernandez had admitted to committing the crime. Police officers also testified that Cruz had confessed to having "visions" containing details of the crime that only the true assailant would know. Cruz and Hernandez were convicted and sentenced to death.

Soon afterward, a convicted rapist and murderer named Brian Dugan claimed he had killed Jeanine Nicarico. Cruz's and Hernandez's convictions were overturned by the Illinois Supreme Court, but prosecutors again tried them for Nicarico's murder. Retrials for convicted defendants are not violations of double jeopardy protections. The jury in the second trial never heard about Dugan's confession, and Cruz and Hernandez were again sentenced to death. Again, their convictions were overturned. Newly available DNA testing then revealed that sperm found at the crime scene likely came from Brian Dugan and could not have come from Cruz and Hernandez. Incredibly, however, prosecutors tried the men a third and then a fourth time. Only when a police officer admitted lying about Cruz's alleged "visions" were the cases finally dismissed.

Cruz and Hernandez each served nearly 12 years on death row. Several police officers and prosecutors in the case were charged with perjury (lying under oath) and obstruction of justice, but they were found not guilty.

Brian Dugan was charged with Jeanine Nicarico's murder in January 2006, and he pleaded guilty n July 2009. He is already serving two life terms for earlier crimes.[1]

In any given year, more than 20 million criminal cases are referred to state courts in the United States.[2] About one-quarter of these cases are felonies; the rest are misdemeanors. More than 95 percent of them never go to trial but instead are settled by plea bargains, in which the defendants plead guilty (either to the original charge or to a lesser charge) in exchange for reduced sentences. Still, approximately 1 million cases do go to court.

As Jeanine Nicarico's murder case demonstrates, the criminal justice process is long and complicated—and it does not always result in justice being served. In this chapter, we explore the rights of criminal defendants, how the court system works, and how criminal trials proceed.

DEFENDANT RIGHTS

Constitutional protections do not end with the actions of legislatures or police. They also extend to the processes and procedures that occur after a suspect has been arrested and formally charged with a crime.

The Eighth Amendment: Bail

bail
A sum of money deposited by a defendant with a court to ensure the defendant's appearance at trial.

Frequently, those who are charged with crimes are permitted to remain free while they wait for their case to be tried or otherwise settled. In many cases, these defendants deposit a sum of money with the court to ensure their appearance in court. This money is called **bail**. The Eighth Amendment to the U.S. Constitution clearly states: "Excessive bail shall not be required." Interestingly, this is one of the few sections of the Bill of Rights that does not apply to the states. This privilege only applies to federal cases. If states want to set high bail amounts—or even do away with bail altogether—the Eighth Amendment will not prohibit them from doing so. Even in federal cases, the scope of the excessive bail clause is limited.

The purpose of bail is to ensure that a defendant appears at trial. Those who fail to appear forfeit the bail money they have put up for their release. Generally speaking, the Supreme Court has given few guidelines about what constitutes "excessive" bail, and judges have wide latitude with respect to the amount of bail they set. Essentially, the courts have held that "excessive" means bail that is too high relative to the severity of the offense, not to the defendant's ability to pay. Judges or legislatures also may deny bail altogether when the risk of flight is very high, such as when the charges are extremely serious. In addition, the Supreme Court held that suspects can be held without bail if they pose a potential danger to the community. This is known as **preventive detention**.

Generally the amount of bail is determined by the severity of the offense. In many states, each court sets particular bail amounts for specific crimes. Amounts vary widely. In Los Angeles, for example, a person charged with writing a bad check will probably be released on $5,000 bail, whereas someone charged with selling very large amounts of drugs may have bail set at $5 million.[3]

Most defendants who are granted bail do not pay the full amount themselves but instead hire a bail bonding service. For a fee charged to the defendant, the bail bonding company guarantees the court that the defendant will appear at trial. Bail bonding is a profitable business, conducted mainly in the poorer parts of town and around court houses, jails, and police headquarters. The professionals who run bail bonding offices charge high interest for their services, as much as 10 to 15 percent. To insure themselves against defendants who may be tempted to flee, they employ bounty hunters—usually former police officers, retired military personnel, and even ex-convicts—who must be prepared to use very rough tactics to hunt down and catch bail-jumping fugitives.

Being free on bail gives an accused person a chance to put his personal affairs in order before facing trial, to work more closely with defense counsel, to search out evidence and witnesses who can help establish innocence—and, above all, to avoid jail. Most jails are badly overcrowded, and sometimes they are dilapidated and poorly maintained for lack of funding. The disparities in granting bail mean that the inmates are overwhelmingly poor, and they include as well a disproportionate number of violent offenders. Almost invariably, confinement in a county jail is extremely unpleasant, and often it can be dangerous.

The Sixth Amendment: The Right to Counsel and a Speedy Trial

The Sixth Amendment to the Constitution affords several rights, including the right to counsel, the right to a speedy trial, the right to a jury, and the right to confront and cross-examine witnesses. The Sixth Amendment "attaches," or takes effect, as soon as formal charges are filed, so some of its provisions may affect the actions of law enforcement. The amendment is, however, of greater significance later in the criminal justice process because it contains several provisions that concern criminal trials.

The Right to Counsel

During the Great Depression, many people hopped freight trains as they traveled from one town to the next in a desperate search for work. In Alabama in March 1931, a fight broke out on one of these trains between a group of young Black men and a group of young White men. Shortly after the fight, two White women, who were also on the train, claimed they had been raped by several of the Black men, nine of whom were ultimately charged with rape. The atmosphere before and during the trial was so rife with potential violence that military guards were called in to protect the defendants from the hostile public; even so, a lynching was only narrowly averted. The defendants were all poor and

preventive detention
The practice of holding a suspect without bail because he is believed to pose a potential danger to the community or at risk of fleeing the jurisdiction.

▶ **The Scottsboro Boys**

This case raised many questions about whether justice had been served. *Should individuals who have been wrongfully convicted receive compensation from the state? What should the criminal justice system do if it is discovered that someone who has been convicted is innocent?*

uneducated, and none had friends or family in Alabama. None was given a lawyer prior to the beginning of his trial, and after the trials—each lasting only one day—all were convicted by an all-White jury. Eight were sentenced to death.

When the convictions were appealed, the International Labor Defense, a left-wing organization that often handled civil rights cases, represented the defendants pro bono, meaning without charging the defendants for their services. The defendants lost their appeal to the Alabama Supreme Court and then appealed to the U.S. Supreme Court.

When the case reached the U.S. Supreme Court, the Justices held that the defendants' due process rights had been violated because they were not given effective assistance of counsel. The Court, however, stopped short of holding that the Sixth Amendment right to counsel applies to state prosecutions. The defendants, who became known as the Scottsboro Boys, were later retried. Even though one of the alleged victims testified at the retrial that the rapes never happened, the men were once again convicted. Most were later paroled or pardoned, but only after serving many years in prison.[4]

The right to counsel had its own day in court when, in 1963, the Supreme Court ruled in *Gideon v. Wainwright* that the Sixth Amendment gives all defendants—whether tried by the state or by the federal government—the right to counsel.[5] The Court wrote: "[I]n our adversary system of criminal justice, any person hauled into court, who is too poor to hire a lawyer, cannot be assured a fair trial unless counsel is provided for him."[6] This means that defendants who cannot afford an attorney must be provided with one at government expense and that the assistance provided must be effective.

The Sixth Amendment right to counsel comes into play well before a case goes to trial. A defendant has the right to an attorney at any critical stage that could influence the right of the accused to a fair trial. These stages include preliminary hearings, plea bargaining, police interrogations, and lineups that occur after a defendant has been charged. It does not include photographic lineups, lineups, or field showups that occur before charges are filed. A showup occurs shortly after a crime has been reported, and usually consists of a police officer showing a single suspect to a witness or victim in the field. A Case in Point discusses one example of a situation in which the right to counsel applies before trial.

Once a defendant has been convicted, she has the right to counsel at her sentencing hearing and at any "appeal of right"; usually, this means just her first appeal. However, she does not have the right to have appointed counsel at discretionary hearings, where the court can refuse to hear the case, at habeas corpus proceedings, or at hearings to revoke probation or parole.

a Case in Point

Supreme Court Reaffirms Right to Counsel at Initial Appearance

When he arrived at the Texas RV park he was to manage, Walter Rothgery's new job instantly evaporated. He lost not only the job he had relocated to take but also the space at the RV park where he and his wife were to reside. The next day, June 15, 2002, things went from bad to worse. Texas police officers arrested Rothgery on the charge of carrying a gun as a convicted felon. (Unknown to the officers, the computer used to query Rothgery's criminal history accessed inaccurate data showing he had a prior felony conviction—when in fact he did not.) The officers brought Rothgery before a Gillespie County magistrate for a hearing to determine probable cause for further detention. The magistrate determined that probable cause existed for the arrest and committed Rothgery to jail. Rothgery subsequently posted a bond and was released on the condition that he appear in court for any subsequent proceedings. Rothgery lacked the funds to retain an attorney and made several requests for appointed counsel, which went unheeded. This denial of counsel was based on the Texas county's policy of denying appointed counsel to defendants out on bond until at least the filing of an information or an indictment. In short, the perspective was that the right to assistance of counsel did not attach until a prosecution had commenced. In Rothgery's case, the prosecutor was alleged not even to have been aware of Rothgery's initial appearance before the magistrate.

Rothgery spent the next months in a legal limbo, unable to get a full-time job because of the report of a firearms conviction hanging over him. Six months after the appearance before the magistrate, he was indicted, re-arrested, had his bail tripled, and held in a county jail more than 100 miles from where he resided. Eventually, a sympathetic warden helped him find a lawyer who obtained documentation proving he had no felony record. The indictment was then dismissed.

Years later, Rothgery brought a federal lawsuit against Gillespie County, alleging that the county's policy of denying appointed counsel until an indictment had been entered violated his Sixth Amendment right to counsel. The case went all the way to the U.S. Supreme Court. Finally, on June 23, 2008, the Supreme Court decided that the Sixth Amendment right does attach at the time of a defendant's initial appearance before a magistrate where he learns of the charges against him and his liberty is subject to restriction. Moreover, the Court stated that the attachment of the right does not require that a prosecutor be aware of the initial proceeding or be involved in it.

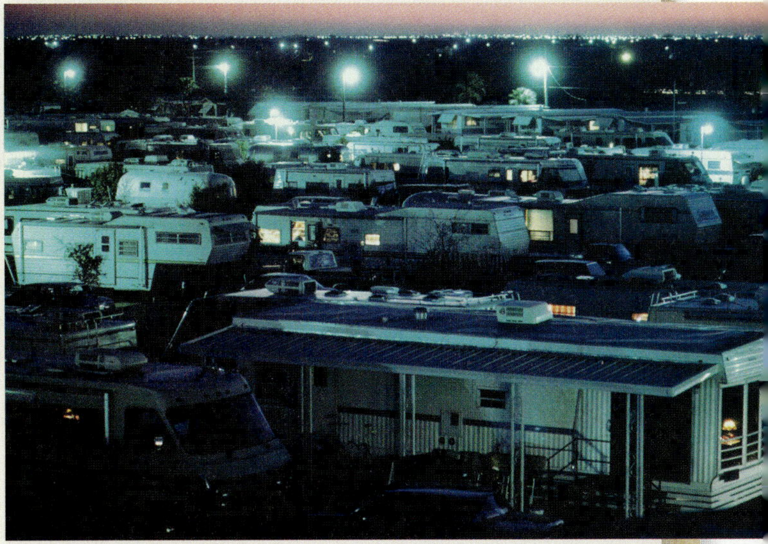

Perhaps what is most startling about this case is the fact that in the year 2008 the U.S. Supreme Court would actually need to promulgate what a vast majority of U.S. jurisdictions had already accepted as a given. Of course, this case had not gone straight to the Supreme Court. It had been heard in both the respective federal district court and the Fifth Circuit appellate court, both of which rejected Rothgery's claim.

Observe Investigate Understand

- **Gillespie County is a rural, agricultural area with a population of less than 21,000. Is it possible that preservation of county funds for indigent defense might enter into the county's policy of not appointing legal representation at initial appearance before a magistrate?**
- **What can and should be done to prevent abuses such as Walter Rothgery's case reveals?**
- **Why did it take so long for Rothgery to obtain justice?**

SOURCES: FBI Academy Legal Instruction Unit, "Supreme Court Cases: 2007–2008 Term," *FBI Law Enforcement Bulletin* 77, no. 11 (2008): 26–27; Michael Graczyk, "High Court Hears Case of Texan Denied a Lawyer," *Laredo Morning Times*, March 16, 2008; *Rothgery v. Gillespie County, Texas*, 128 S. Ct. 2578 (2008).

MYTH/REALITY

MYTH: Poor defendants have a right to legal representation until they have fulfilled their sentence.

REALITY: Defendants need to be facing the threat of incarceration, have the right to legal representation only for their first appeals, and don't have the right to a lawyer for some postconviction hearings.[7]

There are exceptions to the right to counsel based on the severity of the offense. Defendants facing only fines or probation are not entitled to a lawyer, although they can have one if they can afford the legal fees. Only defendants who face the possibility of incarceration have the constitutional right to an attorney, regardless of whether the offense is a felony or a misdemeanor. The Supreme Court also holds that the Sixth Amendment includes the right to have the assistance of certain expert witnesses; most notably, defendants pleading insanity are entitled to the assistance of psychiatrists.

Like other rights, the right to counsel may be waived by the defendant. This leads to problems when the prosecution or the judge fears a particular defendant will use his criminal trial as a soapbox. The example of convicted terrorist Zacarias Moussaoui is a case in point. Prosecuted for his involvement in the September 11, 2001, terrorist attacks, Moussaoui defended himself and used court proceedings to make inflammatory speeches calling for the destruction of several nations, including the United States. Nevertheless, the Supreme Court has held that defendants have the right to represent themselves, so long as their waiver of their Sixth Amendment rights is voluntary, knowing, intelligent, and expressed.

A Speedy Trial

The Sixth Amendment states that defendants have the right to a "speedy" trial. Thus they do not have to defend themselves years after an alleged crime has occurred, which could be long after evidence has disappeared, witnesses have forgotten the circumstances, or principals in a case have died. The amendment also ensures that defendants who cannot make bail do not sit in jail for years without ever facing trial. Even for those defendants who are freed on bail, a speedy trial avoids having the weight of possible conviction hanging over their heads indefinitely. Crime victims also may benefit; some experience closure only after the trial is complete. However, if a defendant wishes to waive his right to a speedy trial in order to have more time to prepare his defense, victims have no right to force an earlier trial.

▲ Men in Jail Awaiting Closure of Their Cases

Accused individuals have a right to a speedy trial. *What do you think is the maximum amount of time the state can leave an accused person in jail before trial? In other words, how much time has to pass before a person's right to a speedy trial has been violated?*

The right to a speedy trial does not come without cost. If the right is violated, a defendant will go free, even if he obviously broke the law. Furthermore, this right means that most trial courts give preferential scheduling to criminal cases. Litigants in civil cases, who do not have similar Sixth Amendment rights, may face delays—sometimes extended delays—before their cases are heard.

When prosecutors are unnecessarily slow in initiating a trial, the Federal Speedy Trial Act of 1974 allows for the dismissal of charges. The Supreme Court has refused to set a hard-and-fast deadline for how quickly a prosecution must move because some cases are more complicated than others or, like capital cases, carry greater weight and so require more time for preparation. Judges are given broad authority to weigh the reasons for the delay versus the potential costs to the defendant. In addition, defendants cannot claim their right to a speedy trial was violated if the delays were due to the defense's own requests to delay the trial. In large urban areas in 2002, 87 percent of felony defendants had their cases decided within a year of their arrest.[8] Some people believe that defendants aren't the only ones who deserve the right to a speedy trial. Victim advocates argue that victims, too, ought to be accorded this right (see the What about the Victim? box).

Jury Trials

Another important privilege protected by the Sixth Amendment is the right to be tried by an impartial jury. Although the Sixth Amendment originally was intended to apply only

What about the Victim?

Balancing Victims' and Offenders' Rights to a Speedy Trial

As of July 1, 2005, victims of crime in Florida were granted rights similar to those of the accused in requesting a speedy trial. Traditionally, defendants were the only ones in the court process to have a right to a speedy trial as protected by the Sixth Amendment of the U.S. Constitution. Under a new Florida law, any person charged with a felony must be brought to trial within 175 days. If the trial does not occur, the defendant or his representative may file papers to force a trial by the 190th day.

Despite this new law and others like it elsewhere in the United States, the right to a speedy trial has often meant that the defendant also has the right to stall the court process. Prosecutors have long expressed anger about the willingness of defense attorneys and their clients to retard court proceedings, thereby delaying justice, further harming victims and other witnesses, and ultimately costing taxpayers millions of dollars. Prosecutors point out that delaying the court process can be particularly problematic for older victims, whose health and ability to participate in the court process may deteriorate over extended periods of time. Victim advocates have echoed these sentiments by asking, "Where is the victim's right to a speedy trial?"

The Florida legislature addressed these concerns and answered this question by passing a law that sailed through the Florida State House and Senate with only one dissenting vote. On May 24, 2005, then-Governor Jeb Bush signed the Florida law, the first of its kind in the United States, to authorize state attorneys to act on behalf of victims by filing a demand for a speedy trial. The state attorney can make the demand for a speedy trial only after 125 days have passed from the time that the defendant was arrested and formal charges were filed. In addition, a court must have granted at least three continuances (that is, delays) over the prosecutor's objections before a demand for a speedy trial can be made on behalf of the victim. Once the state files a demand for a speedy trial, the law stipulates that the judge must put the trial date on the docket within 5 days. At that point, the trial must begin with the next 45 days unless there are necessary or good legal causes that merit further reasonable delay. Opponents of this law claimed that forcing a speedy trial was a violation of the defendant's Fourteenth Amendment right to due process. The Florida law accounts for this concern with language that enables judges to grant further extensions to ensure that defendant's due process rights are secured.

OBSERVE Investigate Understand

- **The Florida law has several stipulations that allow for continuances even after the state attorney has filed a demand for a speedy trial on the victim's behalf. Do you think there is a way to ensure that the rights of both victim and defendant are not violated?**
- **How speedy should a "speedy" trial be?**
- **Why might opponents of the Florida law raise questions about the law's impact on the defendant's right to due process?**

SOURCE: Dan Christensen, "In Florida, Speedy Trials for All, Not Only the Accused," *Daily Business Review*, June 21, 2005, www.law.com/jsp/article.jsp?id=1102709494 (retrieved December 12, 2008).

to federal cases, the Supreme Court in 1968 extended the application of the amendment to state cases as well.[9]

This right has several components. First, the right to a jury trial—as opposed to a **bench trial**, in which the judge determines guilt—applies only in criminal cases in which the defendant faces 6 months or more of incarceration. Therefore, individuals who are charged with most petty offenses will not get juries. This saves the state significant time and expense and reduces the number of citizens who must do jury duty.

bench trial
A trial in which guilt is determined by a judge rather than by a jury.

Second, the jury must be impartial. This means any potential jurors who have personal knowledge about the case or who express their belief that the defendant is guilty before the trial even begins may be excluded from the jury. Further, if pretrial publicity in an area makes it very difficult for the defendant to secure an impartial jury, the defendant

change of venue
Relocation of a case to another court because the case has received too much publicity in the original jurisdiction for the defendant to receive a fair trial.

may seek a **change of venue**—that is, the trial may be moved to another location where there is less publicity. We saw in Chapter 8 how this consideration was invoked in moving Oklahoma City bomber Timothy McVeigh's trial to Denver.

Third, although the tradition of 12-person juries and the requirement of unanimous verdicts can be traced all the way back to England in 1215 and the Magna Carta, the Supreme Court holds that neither of these is a requirement of the Sixth Amendment. In fact, the Court holds that states may have juries of any size they choose, so long as there are at least 6 jurors.[10]

Finally, unlike most other constitutional rights, the right to a jury is not fully waivable. In federal cases the defendant cannot have a bench trial if the prosecutor wishes to have a jury. Some states follow this rule as well. Even when a defendant is permitted to waive a jury, the accused must express that he understands what waiving the right to a jury means and must verbalize that understanding.

A Global View describes the way juries are organized in Japan today.

Confrontation and Cross-Examination

The Sixth Amendment gives criminal defendants the right to confront witnesses—that is, to have witnesses actually present at trial—and to examine or question them. This gives the defendant or, more precisely, his attorney the chance to ask a witness about possible inconsistencies, inaccuracies, or biases; it also makes it less likely that a witness—who will be positioned to look the accused in the eye—will be dishonest. In practice, these rights

A Global View

Japan's Quasi-Jury System, with Lay Judges

The Japanese judicial system had been criticized by the United Nations, the Council of Europe, and human rights groups for its presumption of guilt, forced confessions, and 99.9 percent conviction rate. On May 21, 2004, Japan enacted into law a bold change and implemented it 5 years later on May 21, 2009. Japan started a new reform criminal trial procedure allowing six ordinary citizens, called lay judges (*saibanin*), to participate with three professionally trained judges to deliver verdicts and hand down sentences.

Japan's previous system of criminal trials involved hearing cases by only one judge or a panel of three judges. This new system, which combines elements from the United States and Europe, involves felony cases for arson, rape, and murder. The challenge in this new procedure is to stimulate a sense of civic responsibility in a top-down society that usually grants deference to experts, males, older persons, the more educated, and the more experienced. The lay judges are picked at random from voter lists and serve for only one trial. The challenge was to overcome the traditional dynamics for Japanese group behavior. Although cultural habits are taking a while to function exactly as hoped, the government's wish to be more democratic in criminal trial procedures was implemented and is being tested.

OBSERVE Investigate Understand

- **In a felony trial system that ensured very high conviction rates, why would Japan want to go to such lengths to change?**
- **Would the Japanese system work in the United States?**
- **Do the patterns of deference that are characteristic of Japanese society operate in the United States, and on what evidence do you base your answer?**

SOURCES: S. Kamiya, "Mansfield Center Eyes Lay Judge Debut," *The Japan Times*, 2006, http://search.japantimes.co.jp/print/nn20061229fl.html (retrieved February 28, 2009); Kyodo News, "Lay Judge Law to Start May 21 Next Year," *The Japan Times*, 2008, http://search.japantimes.co.jp/cgi-bin/nn20080409a2.html (retrieved February 28, 2009).

mean that hearsay evidence usually is excluded, and defendants nearly always are entitled to be present during their own trials.

Hearsay evidence is any statement made by a witness that is not based on that witness's personal knowledge. For example, it would be hearsay if a witness testified to the following: "My wife told me that she heard the defendant say that he killed his wife." Any such statement is considered an "out of court" statement. Such statements are normally considered inadmissible because they infringe on the defendant's Sixth Amendment right to confront witnesses and because they tend to be unreliable. To be admitted as evidence, the witness's wife herself would have to appear on the witness stand, testify to what she herself claimed to have heard, and then be subjected to cross-examination. Out of court statements also include such evidence as recorded 911 emergency calls; the operator who took the call would have to be the witness to testify to what she heard. There are a number of exceptions to the hearsay rule, including statements made while a person is dying.

hearsay evidence
Any statement made by a witness that is not based on that witness's personal knowledge.

There are times when a prosecutor can show that a witness may be vulnerable to harm if forced to testify in the presence of the defendant.[11] This is often the case in trials involving possible child abuse by the accused. In these cases, the Supreme Court has ruled that the witnesses may be permitted to testify via one-way closed-circuit television rather than being called to testify in the actual courtroom.

Double Jeopardy: Protection from Repeated Trials for the Same Crime

The Fifth Amendment prohibits subjecting anyone twice to "jeopardy of life or limb" for the same offense. This is known as the **double jeopardy** clause. The Supreme Court has held that the right against double jeopardy applies in state as well as federal cases.[12] This clause prevents a person from being prosecuted again and again for the same crime. If it were not for the protection against double jeopardy, a prosecutor could use his power to torment an innocent person by repeatedly dragging him into court for the same charges. As the Supreme Court wrote, "[T]he State . . . should not be allowed to make repeated attempts to convict an alleged criminal . . . thereby subjecting him to embarrassment, expense and ordeal and compelling him to live in a continued state of anxiety."[13]

double jeopardy
The Fifth Amendment prohibition against subjecting anyone twice to "jeopardy of life or limb" for the same offense.

The right against double jeopardy has several aspects. It means once a person has been tried for a crime, he cannot be tried again on the same charges, even if new evidence appears. It also means that once a person has completed the punishment for an offense, he cannot be punished again for that same offense.

MYTH/REALITY

MYTH: Double jeopardy means that once a person has gone through a criminal trial for a particular act, the prosecutor can never bring that person to trial again.

REALITY: It is not a violation of double jeopardy if the defendant is charged with a different offense.[14]

There are several limitations to the right against double jeopardy. First, it does not prohibit a person from being tried for a crime by more than one state, or by the state and the federal governments. For example, a person who kidnaps another person in Texas and transports his victim to Oklahoma might be tried and convicted in the courts of both Texas and Oklahoma, as well as in federal court. Second, the right does not keep a person from being tried on different charges. If a person accused of robbing a store and killing the cashier is found not guilty of murder, he still may be tried for robbery. Third, the right does not prohibit a victim from bringing a civil lawsuit against a person who was acquitted in a criminal trial, as happened in the O. J. Simpson and Robert Blake murder cases (see Chapter 8). Fourth, the right does not apply if a defendant is convicted and appeals, and then the appeals court remands the case for a new trial due to errors in the original trial. Finally, the right usually does not prevent a retrial if the jury in the original trial fails to reach a verdict, or if a mistrial is declared for some other reason.

PRETRIAL PROCESS

booking
The process of photographing and fingerprinting a suspect and creating the police record of personal information and the crime(s) with which the suspect is initially being charged when taken into custody.

complaint
The document containing the initial crimes with which a defendant is charged.

A criminal case typically begins with an arrest, although sometimes an arrest warrant is issued first. In either case, a suspect is generally taken into custody and booked, most often at a local police station or jail. During **booking**, the suspect is photographed (this photo is known as a mug shot) and fingerprinted, and the police record her personal information and the crimes with which she is initially being charged. Unless the crime is very minor and she is released, the suspect is normally confined in a local jail.

The police then refer the case to the prosecutor, who will make an initial decision about whether to bring charges, and what they will be. These charges, outlined in official paperwork called the **complaint**, are not necessarily the ones for which the suspect was initially arrested. As an investigation proceeds and reveals new evidence, the prosecutor may drop or change some charges or add new ones. Specific charges later may be dropped as part of a plea bargain, so the charges that are filed can give the prosecutor negotiating leverage. Once the prosecutor has filed a complaint, a suspect officially becomes a defendant.

▲ **Britney Spears**

After a suspect is arrested, she is taken to the police station to be booked and photographed.

A defendant in custody is entitled to a speedy **arraignment**, or a hearing before a judge or magistrate. During this hearing, the complaint is formally read. Arraignments often take place within a day of the arrest, although they may be delayed if the arrest takes place on a weekend or a holiday. The arraignment may be the first time the defendant learns which charges he is facing. If he has not already retained an attorney, he is informed of his right to counsel. If he is indigent, he is assigned a defense attorney. The defendant is also formally read his other rights. Finally, the defendant enters an initial **plea**, or answer, to the charges. Generally, he may plead guilty, meaning he admits to all the charges; not guilty, meaning he denies the charges; or **no contest**, also called **nolo contendere**, meaning he does not admit to the charges but will not dispute them in criminal court. This last plea may help him avoid civil liability for the acts of which he is accused. Convictions and guilty pleas can be used as evidence of a defendant's liability in a related civil lawsuit, but no contest pleas cannot be used in civil suits.

arraignment
A hearing before a judge or magistrate during which the complaint is formally read.

plea
A defendant's formal denial or admission of guilt.

no contest (nolo contendere)
A plea in which a defendant admits that sufficient evidence exists to convict him, but he does not actually admit his guilt.

In many minor misdemeanor cases, defendants simply plead guilty and the arraigning judge sentences them, usually to time already served in jail and perhaps also to fines or probation. Some have argued that for minor offenses the criminal process itself is designed to be so unpleasant that it serves as punishment.[15] In felony cases, defendants usually plead not guilty at the arraignment. The judge will then determine whether they are entitled to be released on bail, and if so, how much the bail will be. The purpose of bail is to guarantee that defendants will appear for trial. If defendants do not appear, they will forfeit their bail money and the court will issue a warrant for their arrest.

The next step is a hearing to determine whether there is probable cause to believe the suspect committed the offenses in the complaint. There are two major kinds of probable cause hearings: grand juries and preliminary hearings. All defendants in federal felony cases are entitled to a grand jury under the Fifth Amendment. Some states also require grand juries to be seated in some circumstances; others give the prosecutor the choice of whether to use one or not. A grand jury is composed of 12 to 23 local citizens, who may serve for a particular length of time or for a specific case. They are usually selected in the same way as members of petit juries, such as from voter lists.

Grand juries do not determine whether the suspect is guilty. Instead, they decide whether sufficient evidence exists for a prosecution to proceed. The stated purpose of the grand jury is to protect people against unjust or overzealous prosecutors. Critics claim, however, that grand juries usually go along with whatever the prosecutor asks them to do.[16] During a grand jury hearing, the prosecutor presents evidence against the defendant. The grand jury may subpoena witnesses or conduct investigations on its own, but it rarely does so independently of the prosecutor. Grand jury hearings are closed to the press, and defendants have few rights during the process. For example, they are not entitled to counsel and cannot call their own witnesses. However, defendants and witnesses may invoke their Fifth Amendment right against self-incrimination during grand jury proceedings.

If a grand jury finds probable cause exists, it issues an **indictment**, which formally sets out the charges against the defendant. Again, these are not necessarily the charges that were in the original complaint. On the rare occasion that a grand jury fails to find probable cause, the case is dismissed. The prosecutor can, however, bring another complaint against the accused containing different charges, or he can later bring the same charges with new evidence. This does not constitute double jeopardy because that protection does not begin until a trial begins.

indictment
A document issued by a grand jury after if finds probable cause, formally listing the charges against the defendant.

In most state cases, instead of a grand jury hearing, a **preliminary hearing** is held. The purpose is the same—to determine whether probable cause exists—but the preliminary hearing, often called the prelim, is held before a judge instead of a grand jury. It must occur 10 to 30 days after the complaint is filed, depending on whether the defendant is in jail or free on bail. As at a grand jury hearing, the prosecutor presents most, or often all, the evidence; during the prelim the defense usually presents no evidence at all. The prosecutor does not have to offer all the evidence available to him—just enough to ensure the defendant is put on trial. Unlike the case of grand jury proceedings, however, prelims are held in public and defendants are entitled to representation by counsel. A defendant can waive her right to a preliminary hearing, but doing so often is not in her interest.

preliminary hearing
A proceeding in which a judge determines whether probable cause exists to bring the defendant to court to face trial for the crimes with which he has been charged.

The prelim serves several important functions. For example, it helps avoid the prosecution of people against whom evidence is scanty. It also gives the defense an opportunity to preview the strength of the case against them. If the case appears strong, the defendant will be more willing to plea bargain instead of taking his chances at trial. During the prelim, the defense may object to the inclusion of certain pieces of evidence at trial. If the judge rules important evidence inadmissible, perhaps because of the exclusionary rule (see Chapter 7), the prosecutor may drop the charges. In short, prelims decrease the number of unnecessary trials, lessen the risk that a defendant will be tried unfairly, and reduce courts' caseloads.

If the judge fails to find probable cause at the prelim, the case is dismissed. As in the grand jury process, however, the prosecutor can try again with new charges or new evidence. If the judge does find there is probable cause to try the defendant, the case is held over for trial. The prosecutor then produces the **information**, a formal document that lists the charges for which the defendant will be tried. The defendant is entitled to a second arraignment on the information because the charges in the information may be different from those on which he was initially arraigned, although he may waive it. A trial date is then set by the court.

information
A document filed by a prosecutor after a preliminary hearing, formally listing the charges against the defendant.

Before the trial begins, the attorneys on both sides are especially busy. They continue to investigate, working to uncover evidence to support their cases. Each attorney may request that opposing counsel or other parties give them certain evidence or information. This process is called **discovery**. In a criminal case, the prosecution frequently has the advantage of greater resources and greater access to evidence because prosecutors' offices usually have bigger budgets than public defenders. Moreover, prosecutors have police departments and their own investigators at their disposal. Discovery is intended to level the playing field by allowing the defense to obtain some of this evidence, but critics claim the process is cumbersome and inadequate. The prosecutor is forbidden to intentionally hide or destroy evidence that might exculpate the defendant or clear her of blame. In 2009, for example, the conviction of Ted Stevens, a U.S. Senator from Alaska, for failing to report gifts properly, was thrown out because the prosecutors had deliberately withheld

discovery
The process in which an attorney requests that opposing counsel or other parties provide certain evidence or information.

evidence from the defense. However, a prosecutor's ethical and legal duties to inform the defense about the existence of such evidence are often unclear. Overworked and underfunded public defenders are often accused of doing a poor job of investigating their cases, which may result in an inadequate defense.

Pretrial motions are specific requests that lawyers file with the judge. A common request is to suppress evidence. At both the federal and the state level, the procedural rules governing what evidence is permissible are detailed and explicit. A defense attorney who believes a particular piece of evidence is not admissible because, for instance, it was illegally obtained, can ask the judge to rule that the prosecution cannot use it at trial. Successful motions to suppress evidence can leave the prosecution without enough evidence to obtain a conviction, leading the prosecutor to request that the case be dismissed.

Another motion is a request for a change of venue. If a case receives so much publicity where the crime allegedly happened that potential jurors have already formed opinions about the defendant's guilt and it would be virtually impossible to hold a fair trial, the defendant, almost never the prosecution, may ask that the case be moved to another location where there has been less publicity. The venue was changed in the sensational 2005 trial of Scott Peterson for killing his wife and unborn child in California, and in the equally sensational 2003 trials of the "Beltway Snipers," John Allen Muhammad and Boyd Lee Malvo. See the Race, Class, Gender box for a discussion of some controversies concerning change of venue motions.

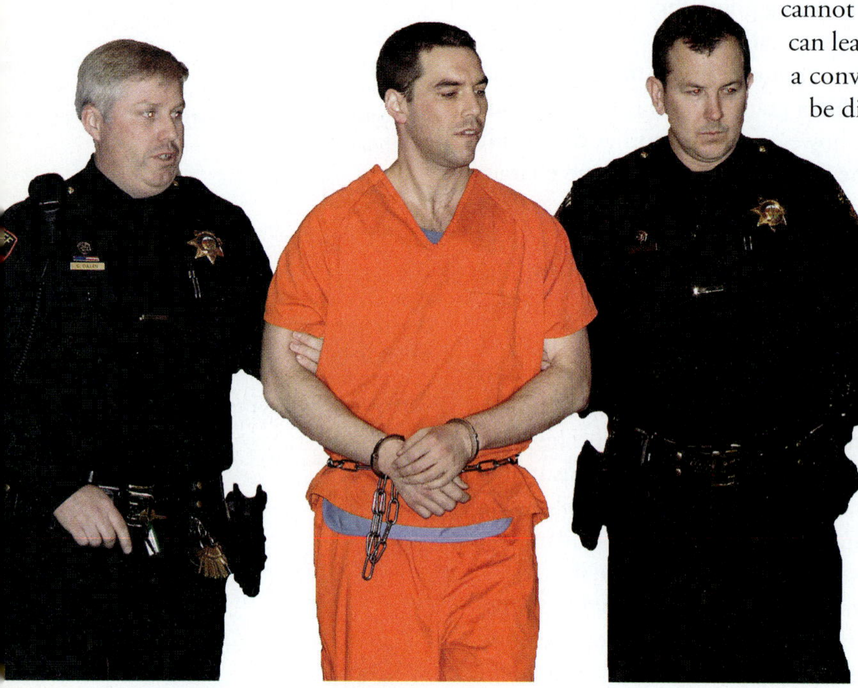

▲ Scott Peterson Was Arrested for Killing His Wife

The Peterson case received so much media attention that his lawyers were successful in changing the venue of the trial. *Should defendants or prosecutors be able to change the location of the trial? Why or why not?*

plea bargains
Agreements between defendants and prosecutors, in which defendants plead guilty to the original or reduced charges in exchange for reduced sentences.

Plea Bargaining

Occasionally, prosecutors drop the charges. More often, however, the prosecutor and the defense strike a deal in which the defendant agrees to plead guilty in exchange for reduced charges or a reduced sentence. This is called a **plea bargain**. In cases involving multiple defendants, such as the Oklahoma City bombing case discussed in Chapter 8, prosecutors often offer one or more of the defendants reduced charges in exchange for their testimony against other defendants. Judges are required to approve plea bargains, and it is the judge's duty to make sure that the bargain is voluntary—that the defendant realizes what rights she is surrendering and what other implications are entailed when she agrees to a plea bargain. And only with the judge's consent may the defendant withdraw a guilty plea that she has made under a plea bargain.

Plea bargaining can occur at any time before or during the trial, right down to the moment before the jury delivers a verdict. In most cases, however, it occurs before trial.

The U.S. criminal justice system encourages plea bargains because they are an efficient means of disposing of a great many of the 20 million criminal cases that arise each year. Plea bargains also allow prosecutors to pursue more cases and to pursue them more thoroughly. Today, about 97 percent of criminal convictions result from plea bargains rather than completed trials.[17] Alaska banned plea bargaining in 1975, and in some other jurisdictions attempts have been made to restrict its use. But, in general, plea bargaining has become indispensible to the efficient functioning of the U.S. system of criminal justice.

Plea bargaining is not without controversy; the Disconnects box on page 264 discusses one of these controversies. Defendants face a high-stakes gamble: If they go to trial, they may be acquitted, or they may be found guilty and receive a harsher sentence than they were offered through the plea bargain. This is a difficult choice for anyone to make,

Race, Class, Gender

Concerns about Change of Venue

Some believe that the consequences of a change in venue for a case may be a different outcome. In other words, a person might be found guilty in one community but not guilty in another. The explanation for that difference might be a result of the racial and/or class demographics of a community. The argument follows that different groups of people will understand evidence differently and come to different conclusions based on that evidence.

The 1992 trial of four White Los Angeles police officers for using excessive force against Rodney King, an African American, following a car pursuit is one example of a high-profile case that has been criticized because a change of venue motion was granted. Despite video evidence of a severe beating being inflicted, the officers were found not guilty by an all-White jury from Simi Valley, a suburb in the northern part of Los Angeles. Sadly, news of this verdict led to riots in Los Angeles. A federal trial followed, charging the officers with violating King's civil rights. Two officers were convicted and two acquitted. The jury for the federal trial was more racially balanced.

Many issues rose out of this complex case. One significant issue was the consequence of change of venue motions when the result is to have juries look very different depending on location. Questions also were raised concerning what it means to be heard by a jury of your peers. Does that mean a case should be tried in the community where the crime was committed? Following the King trials, states began to consider legislation that would require judges to consider the racial makeup of communities when considering change of venue motions.

It is not only racial demographics that should be considered when judges are deciding change of venue motions. Another consideration might be the differences between urban and suburban communities. Another high-profile case that involved police use of force and a Black victim was the killing of Amadou Diallo by four New York City officers in 1999. In this case the defendants successfully changed the venue to Albany, which was not only largely White, but also culturally very different in terms of urbanization. In 2000, the jury found the officers not guilty. Some argued that a jury consisting of residents of the Bronx, where the crime had occurred, would have found the officers guilty.

These examples illustrate that there is much to consider in change of venue cases. The racial and class demographics of communities, as well as the type of community (urban, rural, or suburban), could all possibly affect the outcome of criminal trials.

Observe Investigate Understand

- **Should defendants be allowed to change the location of their trials? If so, what should judges consider?**
- **Do the facts surrounding the trials of the assailants of Rodney King and Amadou Diallo justify or not justify the changes in venue that were ordered?**
- **Do you think that the verdicts in the two trials described here would have been different had there not been changes of venue? Why or why not?**

SOURCES: Mark Hansen, "Different Jury Different Verdict? A Rehearing on Change of Venue," *American Bar Association Journal* (1992;Omar Williams, "When Change in Venue Means Change in Verdict: A Critical Analysis of Venue and Its Impact on the *Diallo* Trial," *University of Connecticut Law Journal* 2, no. 1 (2002): 65–97.

but it is especially so for a person who really is innocent. Of course, all defendants must be presumed innocent at this point. How can defendants make a good choice? They must consider many factors. What is the conviction rate for the offenses with which they are charged? Felony conviction rates range from 41 percent for assault to 80 percent for murder.[18] Will the jury be sympathetic to them? How strong is the prosecution's evidence?

A defendant's choice is also likely to be heavily influenced by who his lawyer is. A public defender might be eager to unload a case quickly to reduce her workload; a private attorney will earn more if the case goes to trial. Public defenders are often less experienced than private attorneys and typically have heavier caseloads with fewer resources at their disposal. Defendants with public defenders are more likely to accept a plea bargain than are defendants with private attorneys.[19] This is yet another way in which the process of justice is different for the poor.

Plea bargaining also provides a reason for opposition to capital punishment. Prosecutors may use the threat of the death penalty to compel innocent people to plead guilty. Even if you know you are innocent, you will likely be tempted to plead guilty to, say, second-degree murder and a sentence of 15 years rather than face a trial for first-degree murder in which you could receive a death sentence.

DISConnects

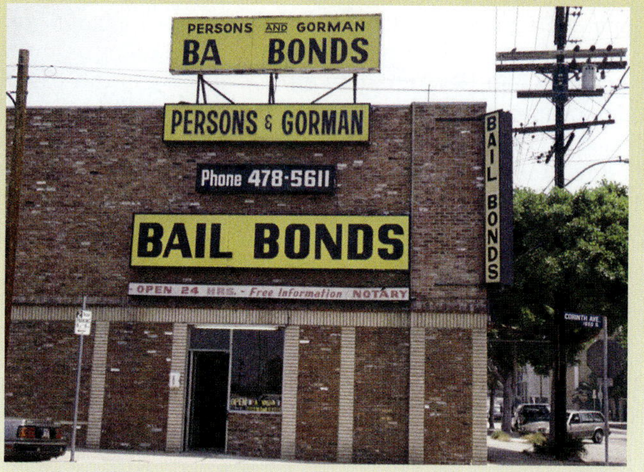

Bargain Justice

The ability to obtain bail can be a critical factor in whether or not defendants are convicted and, if convicted, how they are sentenced. When defendants are released on bail, they are able to participate in their own defense. They can meet with their attorneys and are less likely to accept a harsh plea bargain. If they remain in jail until their trial, often the first time they get to see their public defender is in court.

Courts often deal more harshly with non-Whites than with Whites in setting bail. The Joint Center for Political and Economic Studies reported that a study in Connecticut uncovered the fact that African American males and Latino males were charged twice the bail of White men accused of the same crimes. Most of these cases do not go to trial; they are settled by the defendant pleading guilty and in return getting a lighter sentence. Those who can make bail have a better chance of striking a better deal.

In a study dealing with sentencing disparities, researchers found that defendants represented by public defenders were at a great disadvantage compared to those with private attorneys. The study argues that overworked public defenders often push defendants, regardless of their guilt or innocence, into pleading guilty to avoid trials that would result in longer sentences. In effect, a defendant is being penalized for exercising a constitutional right: namely, the right to a trial. A person who has grown up with little faith in "the system" could not be blamed for taking the safe way out and pleading guilty even if innocent.

OBSERVE Investigate Understand

- **Can we really consider it justice if defendants are pushed into pleading guilty to avoid trials that would result in longer sentences?**
- **Should plea bargaining be abolished?**
- **Would the system be fairer for rich and poor alike if the right to be released on bail were abolished for all?**

SOURCES: Joseph S. Hall, "Guided to Injustice? The Effect of the Sentencing Guidelines on Indigent Defendants and Public Defense," *American Criminal Law Review* 36 (1999); Eric Lotke, "Racial Disparity in the Justice System: More than the Sum of Its Parts," *Joint Center for Political and Economic Studies,* Focus 3 (May/June 2004); www.jointcenter.org/index.php/publications_recent_publications/focus_magazine/2004/january_february_2004/bias_infects_system_from_investigation_to_incarceration.

It is not only advocates for defendants who criticize plea bargains. Victims and their advocates may be deeply displeased as well, believing that the people who hurt them are not getting as much punishment as they deserve. Some states require that prosecutors confer with victims before completing a plea agreement, either to ask for their input on the deal or simply to notify them of it. Some states allow victims to make a statement in court when the plea is entered. In no state, however, does a victim have the power to veto a plea agreement. To many victims, it must seem that expedience is valued more than justice. One noteworthy example is the case of Gary Ridgeway, the "Green River Killer." In 2003, Ridgeway pleaded guilty to 48 murders. In return for giving police enough information to locate the victims' bodies and close these cases, he was given 48 life sentences instead of the death penalty.

In general, the prosecutor may decide what sort of plea bargain to offer the defendant. Specific rules differ by jurisdiction. For example, in federal cases the proposed sentence will usually comply with federal sentencing guidelines. In most cases, once a defendant has entered a guilty plea as part of a plea bargain, she cannot withdraw it, and prosecutors are usually bound to carry out the deals they have struck as well. However, a judge may set aside a plea bargain, which might require that a new plea bargain be struck or that the case go to trial. Jurisdictions generally develop a local legal culture as a result of the same actors working together over a long period of time. Defense attorneys, judges, and prosecutors develop similar ways of looking at cases and concluding what justice calls for in particular offenses.[20] For example, in many jurisdictions a "going rate" will exist for common crimes such as possession of a small amount of narcotics, intimate partner violence, or possession of alcohol while a minor. In one jurisdiction, the major actors might all agree that an individual cited for having a fake driver's license in order to purchase alcohol should have his license revoked. Another jurisdiction, however, might require the offender simply to take responsible-drinking classes. The adversarial system of criminal justice is more theory than reality in such cases.

Real Careers

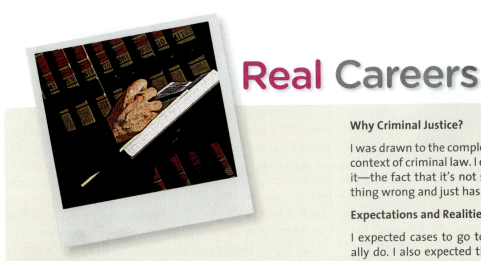

SARAH CORY

Work location: St. Paul, Minnesota

College(s): University of Minnesota, 1998; William Mitchell College of Law, 2001

Major(s): Sociology (emphasis in criminology) and Philosophy (BS); Juris Doctorate (JD); Minnesota Bar Certified (2001)

Job title: Assistant County Attorney III, Ramsey County Attorney's Office

Salary range for job like this: \$80,000–\$120,000

Time in job: 7 years

Work Responsibilities

During my 7 years as assistant county attorney, I have worked in three different divisions in the office: child support enforcement, juvenile prosecution, and adult felony prosecution. But jury trial work is my primary responsibility. A typical workweek involves meeting with witnesses, talking with police officers, preparing cases for trial, and appearing in court for motion hearings, sentencing hearings, and jury trials.

Why Criminal Justice?

I was drawn to the complexities of what justice means in the context of criminal law. I enjoy the problem solving aspect of it—the fact that it's not so simple that someone did something wrong and just has to pay for it.

Expectations and Realities of the Job

I expected cases to go to trial more often than they actually do. I also expected that it would be obvious to victims that I am working to help them. But sometimes it feels as a criminal prosecutor that I'm not really helping them at all. Victims can find seeking justice to be a bit of a burden or punishment—first the crime, then the interruptions to meet with law enforcement, meet with attorneys, and testify in court. But this doesn't at all change how satisfying I find the work to be. I am working to bring about justice.

My Advice to Students

Be resourceful and try to understand as much as you can about how things work—whether it's the technology you use or the day in the life of a probation officer. This will help you build relationships with people that can help you figure things out in your job and make you self-sufficient when there isn't anyone around to help. Be naturally inquisitive and genuinely interested in how things work, and you will learn things you didn't think to ask about. And while you are in school, take advantage of the opportunity to learn whatever you can about the practice of law. If you're not at the top of your class (which I wasn't), it's all the more important to seek a part-time job or internship with a law firm. From this experience not only will you learn firsthand how to practice law, but you will have an opportunity to show your employer just how irreplaceable you are.

▲ **Melissa Huckaby**

Melissa Huckaby was indicted on charges of kidnapping, raping, and murdering her eight-year-old neighbor.

THE CRIMINAL TRIAL

As we've seen, only a small percentage of criminal cases actually make it to trial. But the criminal trial, with all its ceremony and drama, is what most people have in mind when they think about criminal cases. Most people believe they have an accurate idea of what happens during a trial, in large part because of television and movies. In reality, though, trials are much more complex—and usually much less dramatic—than the ones seen on *Law & Order.*

Due Process: Providing Fair and Equitable Treatment

The **due process clause** is arguably the most important phrase in the Constitution. Simply stated, due process stands for the proposition that government laws and proceedings must be fair.

The due process clause appears twice in the Constitution: once in the Fifth Amendment and again in the Fourteenth. In both places it reads: "No person shall be . . . deprived of life, liberty, or property, without due process of law." The difference is that the clause in the Fifth Amendment, part of the original Bill of Rights and ratified in 1791, applies only to the federal government, whereas the Fourteenth Amendment, ratified in 1868 after the Civil War, applies specifically to the states. Because the words within the Fifth and the Fourteenth Amendments themselves give no specifics about what is and isn't permissible, the Supreme Court has often struggled with the precise meaning of the due process clause. In general, the Supreme Court has discussed two kinds of due process: procedural and substantive due process.

Procedural due process stands for the idea that the processes and methods used to try people for crimes cannot be arbitrary or unfair. For instance, if a person were to be put on trial without first being adequately notified of the specific charges against him, it would be very difficult for that person to adequately defend himself. Substantive due process means that the government cannot unfairly, or without just cause, deprive people of certain fundamental liberties. An example of this is an individual's right to privacy, which the government cannot invade unless it has a good enough reason, such as strong evidence that the person has committed a serious crime.

due process clause
A clause of the U.S. Constitution that represents the proposition that government laws and proceedings must be fair.

Due process is, perhaps, the core of the criminal justice system. Unless that system is administered fairly, it is of little value. Due process protections can help ensure that individuals aren't discriminated against or persecuted by government officials, and that people's rights are respected. Some critics of the criminal justice system complain that its procedures are often time consuming, complicated, and expensive. Other critics say that those in the system sometimes make mistakes or act in ways that are arbitrary or biased. The due process clause demands that we find a reasonable balance between these competing concerns, but actually finding that balance is often a challenge.

Burden of Proof and Standards of Proof

Many procedures are built into the U.S. criminal justice system to minimize mistakes. We also make a value judgment: As a society, we have decided it is better to risk letting some guilty people go free than to risk convicting the innocent. Accordingly, we place heavy burdens on the prosecution in criminal cases.

All criminal cases begin with the presumption of innocence—the legal assumption that the defendant did not commit any crimes. To overcome this presumption and gain a conviction, the prosecution has the burden of proving every element of each crime. This means that even if the defense presents no evidence at all, the defendant may still be acquitted if the prosecution does not carry its burden.

In some cases, the defense may also have a **burden of proof**. For example, if the defendant claims she was acting in self-defense or that she was insane, in most cases she must prove her claim, as opposed to the prosecution's having to prove she was not defending herself or was not insane.

burden of proof
The burden falls on the party that must prove a particular thing in court.

MYTH/REALITY

MYTH: In a criminal trial when a defendant is found not guilty, this means the trier of fact believes the defendant is innocent of the crime for which he was charged.

REALITY: A judge or jury may find a criminal defendant not guilty even if they believe he is probably guilty. A not guilty verdict means the trier of fact believes the prosecutor has failed to establish the defendant's guilt beyond a reasonable doubt.

The burden of proof falls on the party who must prove a particular thing in court; in contrast, "standard of proof" describes how convincing the proof must be. In most civil cases, the plaintiff, the person who brings the suit, must prove his case by a **preponderance of the evidence**, meaning simply that his case must be slightly stronger than the other side's. This is a relatively light burden. In criminal cases, the prosecutor must meet a more difficult standard—he must prove his case **beyond a reasonable doubt**. In other words, the jurors must have no real uncertainties about the defendant's guilt. Even if the jury is fairly sure that the defendant has committed the crime, it must acquit him if the jurors can conceive of another plausible explanation for the evidence. In our criminal justice system, therefore, people are not found innocent but rather are found not guilty, meaning the prosecution has not carried its burden. When the prosecution has given sufficient proof of all elements of the crime, defendants are, of course, found guilty.

preponderance of the evidence
The standard of proof required to win a civil lawsuit.

beyond a reasonable doubt
The standard of proof required to criminally convict a person.

clear and convincing evidence
An intermediate standard of proof, sometimes required for certain defenses such as the insanity defense.

Other standards of proof appear in criminal cases as well. Sometimes defenses must be proved or disproved by a preponderance of evidence. Other defenses might require **clear and convincing evidence**, which lies somewhere between a preponderance and beyond a reasonable doubt. The standard of proof depends on the jurisdiction and on the particular defense. For example, in Delaware a defendant must prove insanity by a preponderance of the evidence, whereas in Florida he must prove it with clear and convincing evidence. Whether jurors are really able and willing to understand such subtle nuances of proof is not clear, but our system does expect them to.

▲ O. J. Simpson Embracing His Lawyer Johnnie Cochran
Simpson celebrates the not guilty decision in his criminal trial, but he lost in his subsequent civil trial when he was found liable for the deaths of Nicole Brown Simpson and Ronald Goldman. *What do the differing verdicts in the two trials indicate about the U.S. system of justice?*

A party may meet the burden of proof through direct evidence, circumstantial evidence, or a combination of both. Direct evidence is evidence that tends to directly prove something without any inferences required. For example, a defendant's statement to an informant that the defendant is willing to sell the defendant a gram of methamphetamine is direct evidence that the defendant is selling illegal narcotics. In contrast, circumstantial evidence requires some assumptions in order to prove something. A defendant's fingerprints on a murder weapon are circumstantial evidence that the defendant committed the murder. To convict the defendant based on this evidence would require the assumption that the defendant did not handle the weapon before or after the true murderer. A person may be convicted solely on circumstantial evidence, but it is often more difficult for the prosecution to meet its burden of proof without direct evidence.

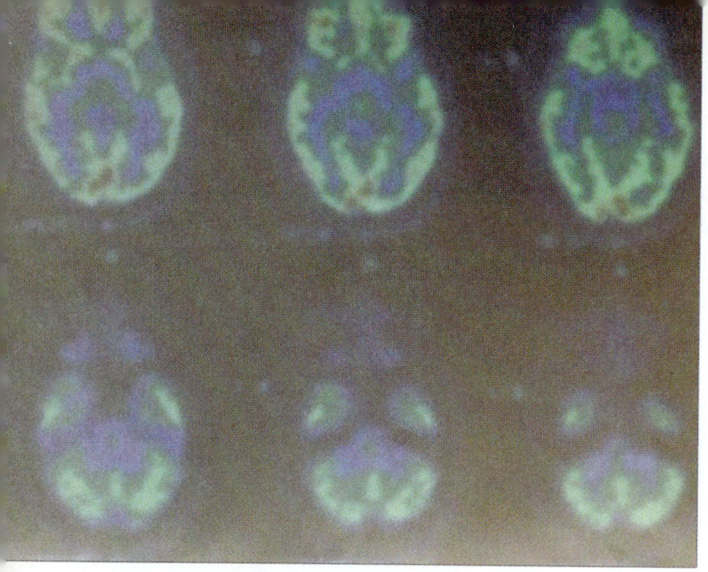

Real Crime Tech

BRAIN SCANS ON TRIAL

As a general rule, criminal courts find defendants criminally responsible—that is, guilty—for their crimes when their criminal actions were the product of a so-called criminal mind. In other words, when the offender committed the crime, he had mens rea (see Chapter 4). Unfortunately, mens rea cannot be measured by a blood or urine test. Brain scan technology can, however, reveal abnormalities in the brain that may affect a person's ability to know that what he is doing is wrong or to truly understand the consequences of that behavior. An MRI scan can reveal a tumor that may put pressure on nearby brain structures that affects, for example, the individual's ability to control his emotions. Another kind of scan, the PET scan, shows actual brain activity and can reveal abnormalities of function in different parts of the brain.

In 1992, a New York court was first to allow PET scans into evidence at trial to support an insanity plea. The 65-year-old defendant, Herbert Weinstein, had strangled his wife and thrown her body from a 12th floor window to make it appear a suicide. Apparently concerned about the influence brain scan images would have on the jury, once the judge ruled the scans were admissible the prosecutors agreed to the lesser plea of manslaughter. Even when admitted as evidence, however, abnormal brain scans do not always lead juries to reach a finding of no guilt or lesser guilt on the part of the defendant. Some court experts go so far as to see this technology as "junk science." In fact, the "jury"—that is, the scientific community—is still out on this issue.

SOURCE: J. Rojas-Burke, "PET Scans Advance as Tool in Insanity Defense," *The Journal of Nuclear Medicine* 3, no. 1 (January 1993), http://jnm.snmjournals.org/cgi/content/citation/34/1/13N (retrieved July 13, 2009).

Stages of the Trial

The first thing that typically happens when a case comes to trial is that a jury is chosen and the bailiff swears the jurors in. Contrary to popular belief, it is only in a few very high-profile cases that jurors are **sequestered**—that is, kept isolated from outside contact. As the trial begins, however, the judge will usually give jurors some general instructions and warn them not to discuss the case with anyone outside the jury until the case is complete.

The trial begins with the opposing attorneys' **opening statements** to the jury. The lawyers introduce the case from their perspective and summarize the main evidence or main arguments they intend to put forward. Lawyers will attempt to establish an emotional connection with the jurors at the outset of the trial. In fact, opening statements can carry much influence and affect how the jury views the evidence that follows.[21] As a district attorney recently told one of this book's authors, "If I haven't convinced the jury by the end of my opening statement, I've lost the case." The prosecutor always makes the first opening statement. The defense may then choose to make its opening statement right away or wait until the prosecution's **case-in-chief**, or main body of evidence, is complete.

The prosecution's case-in-chief begins when the first witness is sworn in. The prosecution has already decided on a trial strategy that includes the order in which witnesses will appear, the questions they will be asked, and the evidence the attorney will attempt to include through their testimony. The prosecutor will ask the witness a series of questions. This is called **direct examination**. The defense attorney may object to questions that are improper, for example, if the prosecutor is leading the witness—suggesting to the witness what her answers should be—or if the evidence is inadmissible hearsay. The judge will immediately overrule the objection—allowing the question—or sustain the objection, in which case the prosecutor must rephrase the question or pursue a different line of inquiry.

Once the prosecutor finishes the direct examination, the defense may choose to question, or **cross-examine**, the witness. Now the prosecution may object to particular questions. The defense will often try to impeach the witness—that is, make the witness himself or his testimony appear unreliable. When the defense is finished, the prosecutor may choose to redirect, after which the defense may recross, and so on until both sides have finished with that particular witness. In some trials, this may take many days. The witness is then excused, and the prosecutor calls the next one. Unlike what we see in movies and on TV or read in whodunits, surprise witnesses are rarely allowed. Through the discovery process, the defense almost always knows well in advance of the trial who the prosecution will be calling to testify; springing a last-minute witness can be grounds for dismissing a case.

Eventually, the prosecutor will conclude, or "rest," his case. At this point, the defense attorney will almost always move to have the case dismissed; this is called a motion for a **directed verdict**. The judge now must determine whether the prosecution has carried its burden of proof—that is, whether it has proven every element of the criminal charges beyond a reasonable doubt. If not, the judge will dismiss the case without the defense ever having to make arguments of its own. Because of the protections against double jeopardy, the prosecution would be forbidden to try the defendant again on the same charges. In practice, few defense motions for dismissal are granted at this point.

The defense then begins its own case-in-chief by making opening statements, if it did not already do so at the start of the trial. This proceeds very much like the prosecution's case, only this time it is the defense that conducts direct examination and the prosecution that cross-examines. Then the defense rests.

Whether or not to put the defendant on the stand to testify is a crucial decision that the defense must make. Certainly a defendant who can make a convincing and truthful case for her innocence on the stand can greatly increase her chances for being found not guilty. However, the Fifth Amendment guarantees the defendant's right not to be compelled to testify against herself—and self-incrimination is exactly what could happen if she takes the stand only to be subjected to a withering cross-examination by the prosecutor. Giving false testimony under such cross-examination would, in addition, constitute the crime of perjury, and it would be highly unethical for a defense attorney knowingly to encourage or allow his client to perjure herself. Furthermore, if a defendant does take the stand, evidence that would otherwise not be admissible may be used to impeach her or attempt to prove that she is a liar.

On the other hand, the Fifth Amendment rule against self-incrimination forbids the prosecutor from drawing the jury's attention to the defendant's failure to testify, and the judge must enforce this rule, both as the case proceeds and in his instructions to the jury. Since the defense is not required to prove the defendant's innocence, but only needs to create a reasonable doubt about her guilt, it is quite possible for the defendant to be found not guilty even though she never testified in her own defense.

The next step is called rebuttal. Here the prosecution may call new witnesses or recall old ones in an attempt to refute the defense evidence. And, of course, the defense can rebut as well, which is called the surrebuttal. The whole process once again continues until both sides are satisfied.

Finally, it is time for closing statements. The attorneys cannot bring new evidence during this phase; they summarize and highlight what they have already presented to the jury. In some jurisdictions, the defense gives closing statements first, and then the prosecutor. In other places, the prosecutor goes first, followed by the defense. Finally, the prosecutor may speak once more. Some critics feel this order gives the prosecution an unfair

sequestered
A jury that is kept separate from outside contact during a trial.

opening statements
Initial statements made by attorneys to a jury outlining the case they will present during the trial.

case-in-chief
A stage in a criminal trial during which a party presents the main body of evidence.

direct examination
A stage in a trial when an attorney questions his own witness.

cross-examine
A stage in a trial when an attorney questions the opposing side's witness.

directed verdict
A motion made by a defense attorney after the prosecution has rested its case; the motion asks for the judge to direct the jury to find the defendant not guilty due to the prosecution's failure to meet its burden of proof.

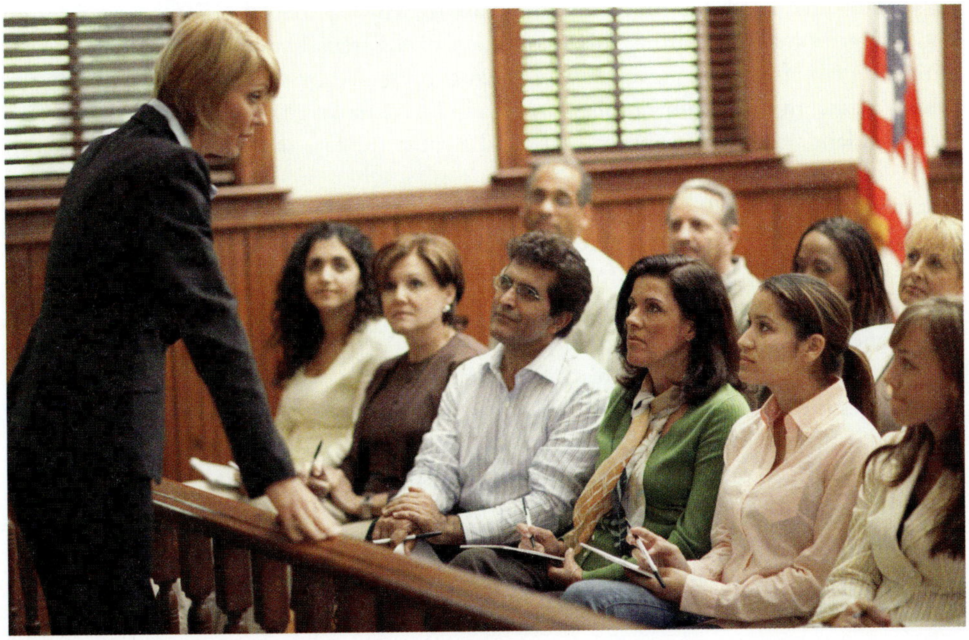

◀ Lawyer Making Closing Statement

During closing statements, attorneys summarize what they have presented to the jury.

advantage because jurors' decisions are likely to be heavily influenced by the first and last words they hear. Others maintain that the heavy burden of proof the prosecution carries in criminal cases requires this particular order.

Next, the judge gives the jury directions, including descriptions of exactly what facts they must find to convict the defendant on each count. Although most states have collections of jury instructions that judges may use, the attorneys may suggest or object to particular instructions, and sometimes these objections result in the jury being recalled to hear new instructions. Defense attorneys' challenges to the judge's instructions can become the basis of appeals. Once the jury goes off to deliberate, its deliberations are always in secret. Deliberations may take minutes or days, depending on the complexity of the case and the evidence. In most jurisdictions, the jury must reach a unanimous decision, although some jurisdictions permit convictions based on 10–2 or 9–3 votes. (See Chapter 8 for more details about juries.) If the jurors report that they are unable to reach a verdict, the judge will urge them to keep trying. If, however, a verdict is still impossible—if there is a **hung jury** in which one or more jurors absolutely refuse to vote for conviction—the judge will declare a **mistrial**. The prosecutor can then choose to try the case again. If she does, the whole process begins anew—an expensive and time-consuming course of action, to be sure. Often prosecutors decide not to retry such cases, taking the mistrial as a sign that the evidence is not strong enough to produce a conviction.

hung jury
A jury that is unable, after concerted effort, to reach a verdict.

mistrial
A judge's ruling that declares a trial invalid, often because of a hung jury.

If the jury does reach a verdict, as it does in most cases, the jurors return to the courtroom and the judge or the jury foreman reads the verdict. If the defendant is found not guilty of all charges, he is released from custody. If he is convicted, the judge may sentence him immediately or set a later date for a hearing to determine the sentence. Many jurisdictions allow victims or their families to speak during the sentencing hearing about how the crimes affected them. The effect of these statements on sentencing decisions has not been clearly established. See Chapter 11 for more on victim impact statements. Figure 9-1 illustrates how the criminal justice process works from arrest through trial.

Bifurcated Trials

bifurcated trial
A two-part trial in which the first part decides guilt and the second decides the penalty whether the defendant was insane.

capital crime
An offense punishable by execution.

In a **bifurcated trial**, different issues of the case are decided in separate hearings or trials. Since capital punishment was reinstated in the United States in 1976, capital cases have had to proceed in two separate phases—effectively, two separate trials.[22] In the guilt phase, the jury determines whether the prosecution proved, beyond a reasonable doubt, that the defendant committed a **capital crime**, an offense that is punishable by death. If so, the case then proceeds to a separate penalty phase. During this sentencing phase, the jury will determine whether the capital defendant should be given the death penalty or life without the possibility of parole. Jurors are to arrive at their decision by considering evidence presented only during this second part of the trial. They are instructed to weigh mitigating factors against the aggravating factors presented by the prosecution during the penalty phase. In their deliberations, jurors might have to weigh, for example, the fact that the defendant was severely abused as a child against the fact that he tortured his victim before killing her.

In approximately 20 percent of states, when sanity is an issue, it is determined in separate proceedings after the jury has resolved the issue of guilt. In California and most other states, insanity trials proceed as follows. First, the defendant is put on trial to determine his guilt. If he is found guilty, then in a second, separate phase the jury decides whether he was insane at the time he committed the crime.

By the time a criminal case reaches its final outcome, several years may have passed since the crime was committed. Dozens of people will be involved in dealing with the case, and it may go through multiple courts. Many people criticize the size and complexity of the judicial component of the criminal justice system, and the time and money it takes to settle cases. Critics of jury trials, in particular, criticize the institution for the occasional instances when jurors apparently cannot render impartial verdicts, overcome racial or other prejudices, or fail to understand complex cases, particularly those involving conspiracies, sophisticated economic crimes, or scientific evidence such as DNA tests.

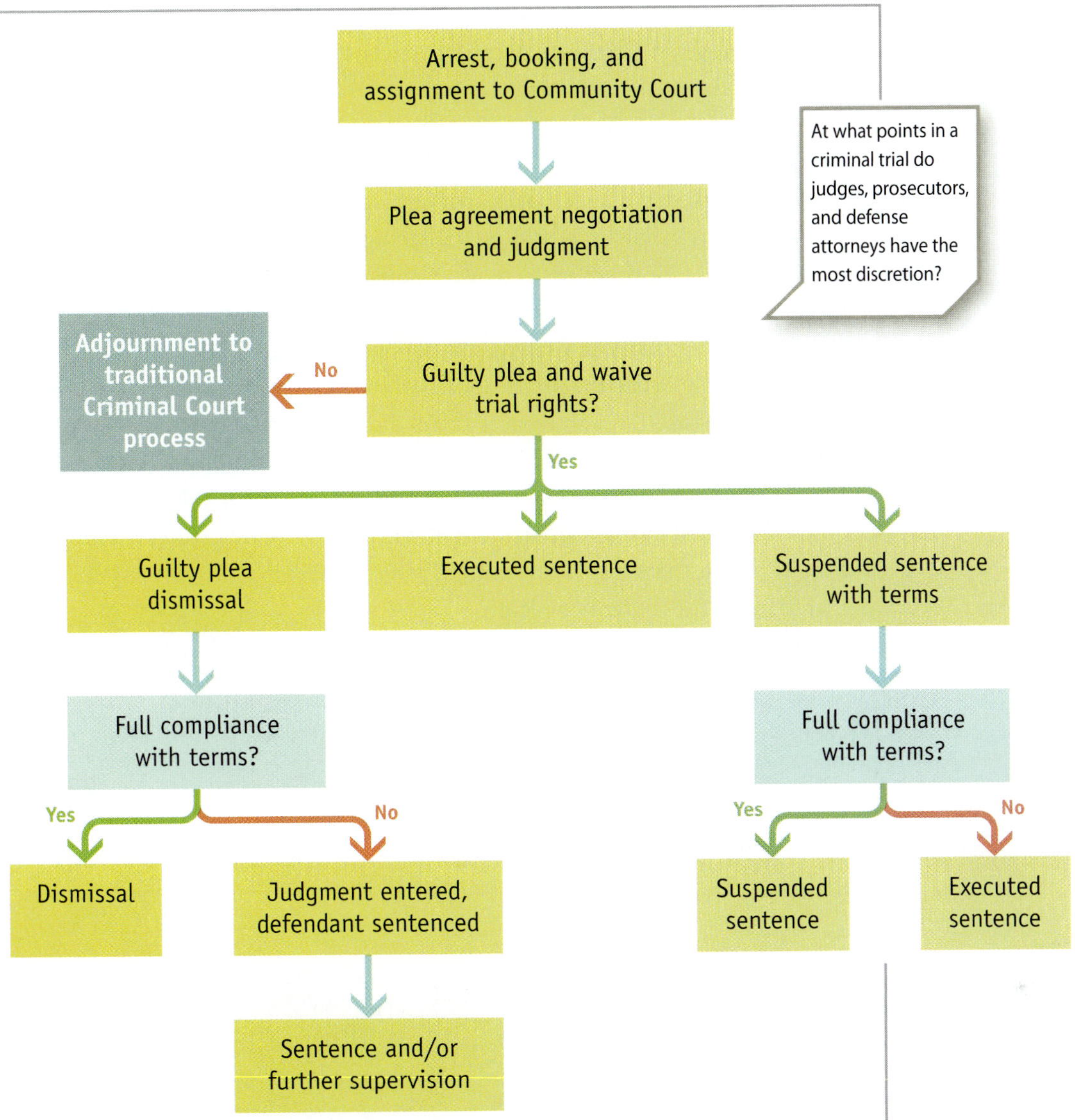

FIGURE 9-1 The Criminal Justice Process

At what points in a criminal trial do judges, prosecutors, and defense attorneys have the most discretion?

Proposals are frequently made to streamline the system and reduce the number and kinds of resources involved.

However, human beings are fallible and the law is intricate. Any reduction in procedures, appeals, or resources will likely mean that more errors are made and that more innocent people will be subjected to criminal prosecution and punishment. What price are we willing to pay to ensure that justice is done?

SUMMARY

Any criminal justice system involves the state bringing to bear on an individual its immense coercive power—its ability to deprive the accused of liberty and even of life. For that reason, the U.S. system of justice insists that due process and high standards of proof be observed in order legitimately to convict people of crimes and punish them.

The U.S. Constitution and the other laws and rules governing the U.S. justice system afford criminal defendants significant safeguards, but there are still limitations. For example, the Constitution's ban on excessive bail applies only to federal offenders (the states are under no obligation even to grant bail), and "excessive" means disproportionate to the gravity of the offense and the risk of the defendant fleeing, not to the defendant's ability to pay. The right to counsel does not mean that poor defendants (who constitute the vast majority of those who must face the criminal justice system) will receive more than perfunctory assistance from an overworked and underpaid public defender. Rules providing for a speedy trial by jury, excluding hearsay evidence, and guaranteeing against double jeopardy are sometimes surrounded by qualifications when they are put into practice in a specific case.

The rules of criminal process are very precise in order to protect the defendant's rights at every stage. These rules apply at arraignment during the determination of probable cause to proceed toward a trial, while the prosecution and the defense are gathering and sharing information about the case through what is called discovery, and during negotiations over possible changes in venue and plea bargains. Most criminal cases culminate not in a trial but in a plea bargain. If the defendant pleads not guilty and goes to trial, the courtroom procedures are also surrounded by many guarantees of due process. Finally, if a defendant is convicted of a capital crime, there must be a separate penalty phase in which the jury deliberates over whether to inflict the sentence of death.

OBSERVE
Investigate
Understand

Review

Describe the Eighth Amendment right to bail.

- The Eighth Amendment states that bail cannot be excessive.
- The right does not apply to states, only to the federal government.
- Courts may deny bail altogether in some cases.

List the rights afforded to criminal defendants by the Sixth Amendment.

- Criminal defendants have a right to counsel—to be represented by an attorney.
- Criminal defendants have a right to speedy trial—to be brought to trial within a reasonable amount of time.
- Criminal defendants have a right to a jury—to be tried by an impartial jury of their peers.
- Criminal defendants have a right to confront and cross-examine witnesses.

Describe the scope and limitations of the right against double jeopardy.

- Generally, this right prohibits trying the same person more than once on the same charges.
- It does not apply in cases where a person is tried by multiple states, or by a state and by the federal government.
- It does not apply when a person is tried on charges different from the original charge.

- It does not prohibit a victim from filing a civil lawsuit after a person has been criminally tried.
- It does not apply in most cases when the jury fails to reach a verdict, or when there is a mistrial.

Identify the steps of the pretrial process.

- The suspect is placed under arrest.
- The suspect is booked.
- The prosecutor files a criminal complaint.
- The defendant is arraigned.
- A grand jury hearing or preliminary hearing is held.
- The grand jury files an indictment or the prosecutor files an information.
- Attorneys make pretrial motions.

Analyze the meaning of the due process clause.

- Generally, the due process clause means laws and procedures must be fair.
- Procedural due process means that the process itself, and the components of that process, must be fair.
- Substantive due process means that the government cannot arbitrarily interfere with certain liberties.

Distinguish the differing standards of proof used by the U.S. legal system.

- Beyond a reasonable doubt means that there is no reasonable conclusion other than that the defendant is guilty of the crimes with which he is charged. It is the amount of proof needed to convict a person of a crime.
- Clear and convincing evidence is the amount of evidence required for some defenses. It lies between preponderance of the evidence and beyond a reasonable doubt.
- Preponderance of the evidence is the amount of evidence needed to win a civil lawsuit. It means that there is at least slightly more evidence in that person's favor than against it.

Identify the stages of a criminal trial.

- A jury is sworn in.
- The attorneys make opening statements.
- The prosecutor presents the case-in-chief.
- The defense presents the case-in-chief.
- The attorneys conduct rebuttals and surrebuttals.
- The attorneys make their closing statements.
- The judge instructs the jury.
- The jury deliberates.
- The jury issues a verdict.
- The defendant is sentenced.

Key Terms

arraignment 260
bail 252
bench trial 257
beyond a reasonable doubt 267
bifurcated trial 270
booking 260
burden of proof 267
capital crime 270
case-in-chief 269
change of venue 258
clear and convincing evidence 267
complaint 260
cross-examine 269
direct examination 269
directed verdict 269
discovery 261
double jeopardy 259
due process clause 266
hearsay evidence 259
hung jury 270
indictment 261
information 261
mistrial 270
no contest (nolo contendere) 260
opening statements 269
plea 260
plea bargains 262
preliminary hearing 261
preponderance of the evidence 267
preventive detention 253
sequestered 269

Study Questions

1. The Eighth Amendment protects the right to
   a. bail.
   b. a jury trial.
   c. an attorney.
   d. confront witnesses.
2. Which of the following rights is *not* guaranteed by the Sixth Amendment?
   a. Jury trial
   b. Counsel
   c. Speedy trial
   d. Due process
3. Sam was tried and acquitted of theft in the state of New Jersey. Which of the following would the right against double jeopardy prohibit?
   a. The victim of the alleged theft sues Sam for damages.
   b. Sam is tried for theft by the state of New York.
   c. Sam is tried for the same theft by New Jersey when new evidence is found.
   d. Sam is tried for murder by New Jersey.
4. Which of the following accurately gives the usual sequence of events prior to a trial?
   a. Complaint, arraignment, preliminary hearing, information
   b. Information, complaint, arraignment, preliminary hearing
   c. Preliminary hearing, information, complaint, arraignment
   d. Preliminary hearing, complaint, arraignment, information
5. If there has been so much publicity about a case that a defendant believes she cannot receive a fair trial, her attorney will
   a. file a motion for a change of venue.
   b. try to create more positive publicity about the case.
   c. request that all charges be dropped.
   d. sequester the jury.
6. Due process basically means that government procedures and laws must be
   a. swift.
   b. expedient.
   c. fair.
   d. inexpensive.
7. Plea bargaining
   a. rarely occurs.
   b. can occur only until the trial begins.
   c. settles the vast majority of criminal cases.
   d. results in increased court workloads.
8. A prosecutor must always prove every element of a criminal case
   a. within 1 week.
   b. by clear and convincing evidence.
   c. beyond a reasonable doubt.
   d. beyond all doubt.
9. The part of a trial in which the prosecutor presents the evidence against the defendant is called the
   a. rebuttal.
   b. case-in-chief.
   c. surrebuttal.
   d. deliberations.
10. A bifurcated trial is one in which
   a. the judge acts as trier of fact.
   b. the defendant is found not guilty.
   c. the jury first determines guilt, and then determines insanity or whether to impose a death sentence.
   d. there are two defendants.

Critical Thinking Questions

1. Describe the struggle that often exists to have a justice system that is fair yet workable. What are some ways that you would advocate balancing these goals?
2. Of the rights granted to criminal defendants by the Sixth, Eighth, and Fourteenth Amendments, which do you see as essential? Discuss whether there are other rights that you believe should be protected as well.
3. List as many points as you can in support of plea bargaining, and as many points as you can against it. Then evaluate the totality of these lists to decide whether plea bargaining is a "necessary evil."

Internet Sites

Scottsboro Boys Case
www.law.umkc.edu/faculty/projects/FTrials/scottsboro/scottsb.htm
Douglas O. Linder, a professor at the University of Missouri-Kansas City School of Law, has created a website with detailed information about the Scottsboro Boys case.

Jurors' Handbook
www.wawd.uscourts.gov/JuryService/HandbookforTrialJurors.htm
The jurors' handbook from the U.S. District Court for Western Washington has detailed information on jurors' tasks, as well as on the stages of a trial.

Suggested Readings

Anthony Lewis, *Gideon's Trumpet* (New York: Vintage Books, 1989). This classic book tells in detail the story of James Earl Gideon, the man whose case recognized the Sixth Amendment right to counsel for poor defendants.

Joel Seidemann, *In the Interests of Justice: Great Opening and Closing Arguments of the Last 100 Years* (New York: Harper, 2005). This book collects attorneys' opening and closing arguments from a number of well-known cases, including the Scopes trial and the trials of Adolph Eichmann, Timothy McVeigh, and Zacarias Moussaoui.

Sentencing

CHAPTER 10

OBSERVE Investigate *Understand*

After reading this chapter, you should be able to:

- Describe the constitutional protections that affect sentencing.
- Describe the various goals of sentencing.
- Compare the different sentencing models.
- Review how a capital punishment trial proceeds.
- Outline controversies surrounding the death penalty.

Realities and Challenges

A Web of Sentencing Complexities

In April 2006, Sergeant Patrick Lett found himself in front of U.S. District Judge William Steele on the federal charge of trafficking crack cocaine. Lett pled guilty. He had served 17 years in the army, including two tours of duty in Iraq, and that day he wore his army uniform as he stood in front of Judge Steele. Lett testified that he had had difficulty since returning from Iraq to Alabama in April 2004. He was dealing both with family struggles and the effects of seeing peers and friends killed in Iraq.[1]

In the spring of 2004, when Lett's car needed work, he turned to his cousin for assistance. The cousin offered to fix the car if Lett made seven deliveries of crack cocaine worth a total of $2,100. Lett agreed. Unfortunately, he sold some of the cocaine to an undercover federal agent. He was arrested shortly after he had reenlisted in October 2004 and just before he was about to redeploy to Iraq.[2]

Lett's luck turned around, though, when his old friend and law student Matthew Sinor attended his sentencing hearing. Judge Steele sentenced Lett to 5 years in prison. Sinor believed that there was a legal "safety valve" that was relevant to the case. It would allow a shorter sentence for defendants who had no prior record, played a minor role in the offense, and admitted their crime. Sinor wrote a letter to the judge pointing out that this safety valve applied to Lett's case. Judge Steele agreed and entered a new sentence of 11 days, which was the time served. Lett would be free. The prosecutor, however, appealed the revised sentence.[3]

The state won the initial appeal. A three-judge panel of the Eleventh U.S. Circuit Court of Appeals ruled that a district judge did not have the authority to change his sentence once it had been imposed. In essence, Steele had failed to recognize his power to apply the safety valve and could not do so retroactively. In the years since the original sentence, however, the sentencing context had changed. The U.S. Supreme Court ruled in *U.S. v. Booker* (2005) that the U.S. Sentencing Guidelines were merely advisory and that judges were not bound to follow them. Therefore, on February 27, 2009, when the case came back to Judge Steele's court after the Eleventh Circuit decision and the U.S. Supreme Court's denial of certiorari, Steele agreed with the defense that he was now afforded the discretion to reinstate the 11-day time-served sentence.[4]

In this one case we can see several factors that are related to ensuring justice in the sentencing process. First, Lett would surely have been stuck with the 5-year prison sentence had not his friend Sinor been aware of the safety valve provision. Lett's original defense attorney thought Lett should be happy with the 5-year sentence and found Sinor's interference "insulting." The intricacies of sentencing law affect justice substantially in individual cases. Second, the severity of federal crack cocaine offenses is apparent in this case, with a first-time offender eligible for 5 years in prison. Third, we can see how for decades the U.S. Sentencing Guidelines firmly constrained what judges could do and that recent changes in the law have restored judicial discretion.

This chapter focuses on the stage after a defendant has been found guilty but before he begins his punishment—sentencing. We review the constitutional context of sentencing, the various goals and models of sentencing, and the ultimate sentence—the death penalty. Both the historical and contemporary effects on sentencing are discussed.

CONTEXT FOR SENTENCING

When a judge in the United States sentences a defendant, she does so within a constitutional context. In the following section we review the Eighth Amendment's protection against cruel and unusual punishments and Article I, Section 9's prohibition of wrongful conviction—that is, habeas corpus. These constitutional provisions confine sentencing behavior and provide a context for sentencing. We also review the presentence sentence investigation because it provides guidance for the judge when sentencing.

Preview

Eighth Amendment Protection against Cruel and Unusual Punishment

As discussed in Chapter 9, the Eighth Amendment includes the bail requirement in federal cases. The remainder of the Eighth Amendment comprises the cruel and unusual punishments clause, which applies to all criminal cases. A **cruel and unusual punishment** can be defined as a sentence or conditions of confinement that in the time period of sentencing or confinement goes beyond what is acceptable to society.

cruel and unusual punishment A sentence or conditions of confinement that at that time period goes beyond what is acceptable to society.

MYTH/REALITY

MYTH: What constitutes cruel and unusual punishment is objective and obvious.

REALITY: A practice considered cruel and unusual at one point in time might not be considered so in another.[5]

In interpreting the Eighth Amendment, the Supreme Court deems certain types of punishments to be unconstitutional. This includes penalties that were considered cruel at the time the Eighth Amendment was ratified in 1791, but also those that "evolving standards of decency" have rejected.[6]

Even if a particular type of penalty is not cruel and unusual in and of itself, it may be cruel and unusual in terms of its application. Punishments that are excessive compared to the seriousness of the offense may be unconstitutional, as may be punishments that outweigh the defendant's culpability. For example, the Supreme Court ruled that it would violate the Eighth Amendment to execute an offender with mental retardation, or one who was under age 18 when he committed his offense.[7] Even though the Court refuses to prohibit capital punishment altogether, it has found that the death penalty is unconstitutional for the offense of rape.[8] The Court also holds that it is cruel and unusual to punish a person for a status or a characteristic, such as being a drug addict, as opposed to a behavior such as possessing illegal drugs.[9]

The Eighth Amendment also prohibits certain conditions of confinement when a person is sent to prison. For instance, prisoners may challenge extended use of solitary confinement, restricted diets, and conditions of prison overcrowding.

In general, the Court is hesitant to consider Eighth Amendment violations to the cruel and unusual punishments clause. The Court has, at least under certain circumstances, allowed executions to continue and allowed life sentences for minor crimes, such as stealing $150 worth of videotapes (see A Case in Point), to stand under the three strikes and other habitual offender laws discussed later in this chapter. Many prisoners are kept in solitary confinement for years, especially in "supermax" facilities (see Chapter 12).

Habeas Corpus: Protection against Illegal Detainment

Article I, Section 9 of the Constitution provides a safeguard against illegal detainment. The writ of **habeas corpus** consists of a written judicial order requiring that a prisoner's case be reviewed in court to determine if he is being held unconstitutionally. The concept of habeas corpus (Latin for "you have the body") was created to prevent the government

habeas corpus A written judicial order requiring that a prisoner's case be reviewed in court to determine if he is being held unconstitutionally.

a Case in Point

Is Three Strikes Cruel and Unusual Punishment?

Leandro Andrade was an army veteran and a father of three. He had spent 13 years in and out of state and federal prisons for petty theft, burglary, and transporting marijuana. His main problem seemed to be an addiction to heroin he had acquired while in the army; he often stole to buy drugs. In 1995, after Andrade stole $153.54 worth of videotapes from two K-Marts in California, he was charged with two counts of petty theft. Normally, this offense would be considered a misdemeanor, and the punishment would be quite minor—at most, a few years in prison. However, California law allowed the court to prosecute the thefts as felonies instead of misdemeanors because Andrade had previous theft convictions. Furthermore, because two of his previous convictions were for the felony offenses of burglary and drug possession, Andrade was also subject to California's three strikes law, which permits much more severe punishments for repeat offenders who previously were convicted of two felonies, whether they were violent or nonviolent. The third offense makes the individual eligible for a long prison sentence. Andrade was sentenced to two consecutive prison terms of 25 years to life.

Andrade's appeal eventually reached the U.S. Supreme Court. He argued that it was cruel and unusual punishment to receive such a severe sentence for such a minor offense. The Court analyzed whether the sentence was "grossly disproportionate" to the crime he had committed, and the majority determined it was not. Andrade's sentence was upheld. He will not be eligible for parole until he is 87 years old. As of 2004, there were 359 other people in California serving 25-year to life sentences for shoplifting.

OBSERVE Investigate Understand

- **Is it just to incarcerate individuals for life when their most recent offense was nonviolent?**
- **Is it cost-effective to incarcerate repeat offenders whose offenses are relatively minor?**
- **Why do states enact three strikes laws, and should they be declared unconstitutional?**

SOURCES: *Lockyer v. Andrade*, 538 U.S. 63 (2003); Erwin Chemerinsky, "Cruel and Unusual: The Story of Leandro Andrade," *Drake Law Review* 52 (2003): 1–24; Erwin Cheminsky, "Life in Prison for Shoplifting: Cruel and Unusual Punishment," *Human Rights Magazine* 31 (2004), www.abanet.org/irr/hr/winter04/ (retrieved December 17, 2007).

from illegally detaining and punishing people. Although the phrase and the general legal concept behind it date back to medieval England, over 700 years ago, modern habeas law in the United States has evolved well past its original meaning.

Habeas cases may take place in state or federal courts. There are no juries. The offender cannot argue that he is innocent of the crime, nor unlike an ordinary appeal can he raise ordinary procedural errors that he believes were made at trial. Instead, he must claim that some aspect of the trial itself, or of the sentence he received, violates one or more of his constitutional rights. For example, many people who are sentenced to death argue that the death penalty itself, or the method in which it is carried out, is cruel and unusual punishment, violating the Eighth Amendment. Defendants usually may bring a habeas case only after they have exhausted, or completed, all their other remedies in a case.

Habeas cases have several advantages. They may help avoid injustice to those who are accused or convicted of crimes. They may permit a person who has been tried on state criminal charges and whose case so far has been heard only by state courts to get into federal court. In some cases, federal courts may be seen as more sympathetic to certain legal arguments. And they may allow those who are detained for lengthy amounts of time without a trial, such as those people who were suspected of terrorism after 9/11, to finally obtain their day in court.

Habeas corpus has been blamed by some for the often lengthy delays in implementing criminal sentences, especially the sentence of death. Among the most vocal critics was the late Chief Justice William Rehnquist, who denounced the "abuse" of habeas corpus

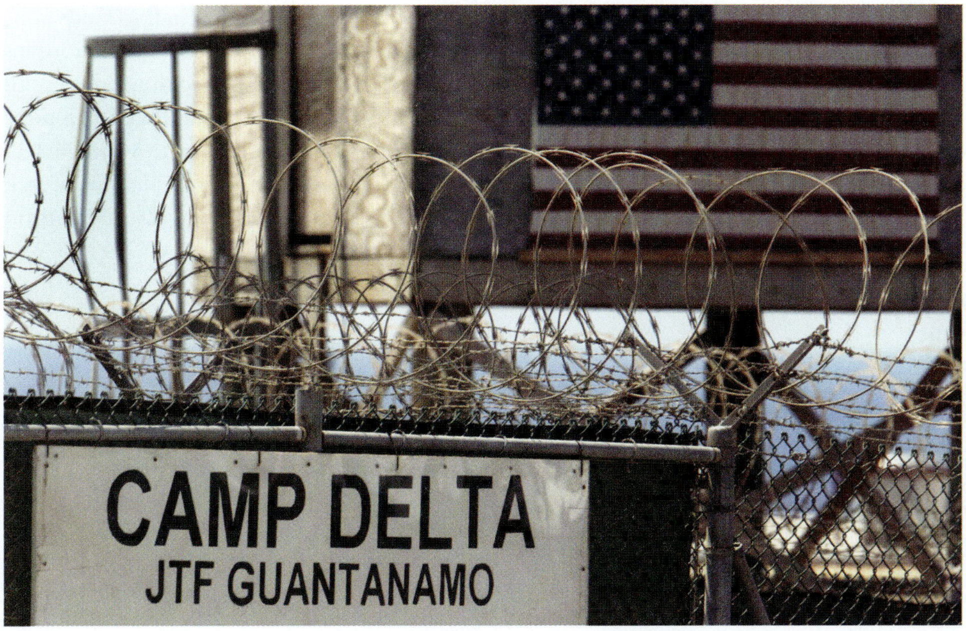

◀ **Guantánamo Bay Prison**

The imprisonment of enemy combatants at Guantánamo Bay raises habeas corpus concerns. *Should the U.S. government be able to hold individuals they consider enemy combatants without telling them why they have been imprisoned? Why or why not?*

petitions by death row inmates. Following the Court's ruling in *McCleskey v. Zant* (1991), Rehnquist led an increasingly conservative Court in imposing limits on further appeals. Later Court rulings have required even tighter limits. In 1996 Congress passed the Antiterrorism and Effective Death Penalty Act, which, among other things, required that habeas cases be brought within 1 year after a defendant exhausts his regular appeals. Some prisoners who have valid claims may be unable to pursue habeas relief quickly enough, especially because the Sixth Amendment right to an attorney does not apply to habeas cases, and inmates may therefore be forced to represent themselves. Few inmates have the ability to complete the extensive filing requirements in a timely manner without the help of an attorney.

Currently, approximately 20,000 habeas cases a year are filed in federal courts. About 1 percent of these are cases in which the defendant had been sentenced to death.[10]

There have been a few attempts to suspend the right to habeas corpus. During and shortly after the Civil War, Presidents Lincoln and Grant suspended it in selected locations. In Grant's case, the suspension was part of a federal effort to crush the Ku Klux Klan, a southern terrorist organization resisting the empowerment of the newly freed slaves. The courts declared portions of these suspensions unconstitutional. More recently, Congress and President George W. Bush tried to deny habeas to suspected enemy combatants held at a U.S. military detention camp in Guantánamo Bay, Cuba. For the most part, the U.S. Supreme Court has held that denial of habeas rights to these suspected enemy combatants violates the Constitution. If an offender wins his habeas case, he does not go free. Usually he will get a new trial or a new sentence.

A variety of factors influence how a judge determines a sentence. The judge is expected to weigh the severity of the individual's offense, the prior record of the offender, any relevant statutory minimums, and any sentencing guidelines meant to guide judicial discretion. To provide information about the offender to the judge and to provide victim input, the probation department prepares a presentencing report.

Presentence Investigation Reports

A trial judge is supplied information for making a sentencing decision in **Presentence Investigation Reports (PSI)**, or Presentence Reports (PSR). These documents contain a personal history of the offender, often a victim impact statement, and a sentencing recommendation. Personal data include the defendant's marital history, prior record (including juvenile and adult arrest history), family background, educational history, employment history, physical and mental health issues, military service, and financial situation. The

Presentence Investigation Reports (PSI)
Reports that provide the court with a basis for making a sentencing decision by including a personal history of the offender, often a victim impact statement, and a recommendation for sentencing.

report covers the state's and the defendant's versions of the offense. The final sections contain an evaluation, sentencing information or guidelines, and finally a recommendation to the court. Originally, the purpose of the PSI was to assist the judge in deciding whether to grant probation. With the shift in philosophy in many states from rehabilitation to punishment, the personal aspects of the offender became less important than the crime itself. Where specific sentencing guidelines are used, the PSI focuses on the guidelines within which the crime belongs and information that will be used to sentence the offender within the guidelines.[11]

Real Careers

SEAN BERNHARD

Work location: Oklahoma City, Oklahoma

College(s): Southern Nazarene University, 2006; University of Central Oklahoma, 2008

Major(s): Sociology with emphasis in Criminal Justice (BS); Criminal Justice Management and Administration (MA)

Job title: Probation Officer Assistant, U.S. Probation and Pretrial Services Office

Salary range for job like this: $35,000–$40,000

Time in job: 1.5 years

Work Responsibilities

The U.S. Probation and Pretrial Services Office in Oklahoma City has three main divisions: Presentence Investigations, Pretrial Services, and Supervision. I am currently in the Presentence Investigation Unit, which means that I write presentence reports that are used to assist the court in sentencing defendants. When writing these reports, I review investigative documents, apply sentencing guidelines, and interview defendants and family members to obtain and verify information, such as family history, education, and employment.

My other duties include completing misdemeanor reports for crimes committed on federal land, such as in national parks and military bases, and helping probation officers write collateral reports. Collateral reports, or "collaterals" for short, are background checks for offenders that have committed a crime in my district but will be sentenced elsewhere in the United States. To write this report, I gather records and any supporting documentation that the officer needs. Usually I am assigned between two and eight collaterals a week.

But what makes my work especially exciting, and meaningful, is that the federal district judges rely on my reports to sentence defendants. On multiple occasions I have been called into judges' chambers to discuss a case and be recognized for my work.

Why Criminal Justice?

Wanting to understand the techniques psychologists use to analyze criminals, I eagerly declared my major in criminal justice, with the hope of becoming an FBI agent. However, I later learned that being color-blind disqualifies me from that job. Before graduation, my professors told me that the U.S. Probation Office was hiring Probation Officer Assistants. I applied for my current position and was hired. There are tremendous opportunities for advancement and promotion within the U.S. Probation Office. For example, I started as a probation officer assistant and was recently promoted to probation officer. U.S. probation officers can continue to be promoted within the agency to positions such as drug specialist, supervisor, deputy chief, or chief probation officer. Of course, along with promotions come higher salaries, which can range from the government pay scale equivalent of GS-12 to GS-17.

Expectations and Realities of the Job

I did not expect that being a probation officer assistant at the U.S. Probation Office would also mean I have to help defendants cope with the emotional stress of undergoing trial and probation. For many defendants and their families, this is their first experience with the criminal justice system, and they do now know what to expect from the process. Therefore, it is also my responsibility to serve as a resource and provide my knowledge of the pretrial and sentencing systems to those who need it. Helping others in this way has turned out to be one of the most rewarding aspects of my job.

My Advice to Students

Keep an open mind when seeking your first job. Apply for as many positions as possible. After several years in the field, you will find that it is possible to move to other careers within criminal justice. For instance, a career as a U.S. probation officer not only allows for promotion within the agency, but it also gives officers the tools and knowledge to transfer to other federal law enforcement agencies.

What about the Victim?

Victim Impact Statements

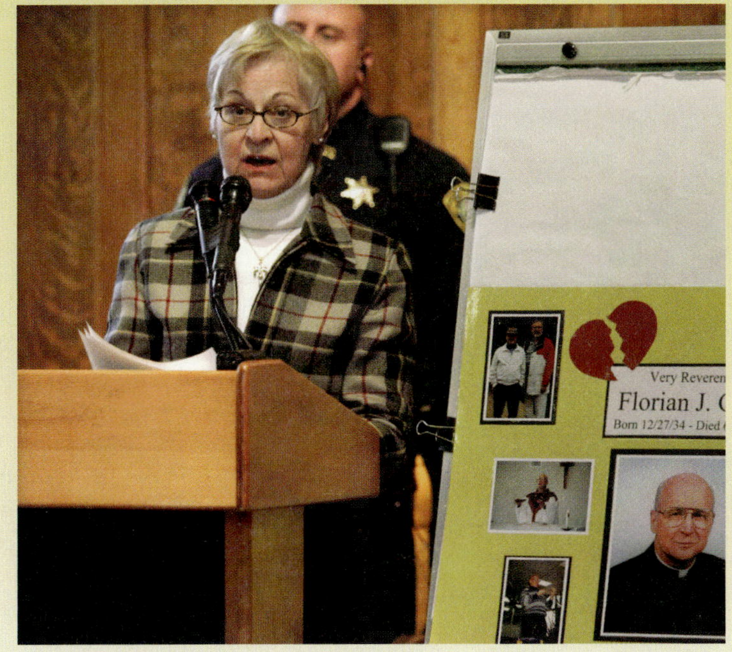

Traditionally, victims of crime played only a small role in the process of trying and sentencing defendants. In fact, unless they were called as witnesses, victims would not get a chance to speak at all during a trial. If they did testify, they were limited as to what they could speak about. Victim impact statements are intended to give victims the opportunity to talk about the harms the defendant caused them and to allow these harms to be considered when the defendant is sentenced. The first victim impact statement in the United States was introduced in Fresno, California, in 1976. Today most jurisdictions allow these statements.

Typically, victim statements are made during a sentencing hearing. For example, after Zacarias Moussaoui was convicted for his participation in the September 11 terrorist attacks, 45 people whose family members died in the attacks made statements to the jury during the penalty phase of the trial.

The use of victim impact statements is controversial. Those who support their use argue that they give victims a voice in the criminal justice system, help provide closure to victims, and help ensure that sentences are proportionate to the harm caused by the criminal acts. Opponents, however, claim that victim impact statements can result in unfair and unequal treatment of some defendants and that use of the statements is therefore unconstitutional.

In 1991, the U.S. Supreme Court ruled on the constitutionality of victim impact statements. Pervis Payne brutally murdered a woman and her 2-year-old daughter and seriously injured her 3-year-old son. During the penalty phase of his trial, the murdered woman's mother testified about the effects of the attacks on the surviving child, and the jury sentenced Payne to death. The Supreme Court held that the use of victim impact testimony does not constitute cruel and unusual punishment. Although some research exists on the topic, it is still unclear what effect victim statements have on sentencing decisions.

OBSERVE Investigate Understand

- **Victim impact statements are supposed to help the victims of a crime achieve closure. Do you think they actually have this effect?**
- **What effect do you think victim impact statements have on sentences? Should they continue to be used?**

SOURCES: Ellen K. Alexander and Janice Harris Lord, "Impact Statements: A Victim's Right to Speak, A Nation's Responsibility to Listen," 1994, www.ojp.usdoj.gov/ovc/publications/infores/impact/welcome.html (retrieved December 31, 2007); *Payne v. Tennessee*, 501 U.S. 808 (1991).

Another document that the judge will consider when deciding on the appropriate sentence is the victim impact statement, which is described in What about the Victim?

GOALS AND MODELS OF SENTENCING

Having pled guilty or been convicted through a trial, the defendant is sentenced by the court. The four goals of sentencing parallel the goals of punishment (see Chapter 11). The primary goal in sentencing often varies by time period and crime. For example, one goal of sentencing may get the most focus in the 1950s, but a different sentencing goal may be most common in the 1990s. In addition, violent offenses may call for different sentencing goals than property crimes.

retribution
A sentencing goal focused on punishing the convicted for the crime.

Retribution is focused on punishing the convicted for the crime. A judge takes this focus when saying, "Because of the severity of your crime, you deserve to be punished with a year of incarceration." Because this goal is primarily punitive, there is little focus on whether or not the sentence will result in future criminal behavior. When society wishes retribution, it wants to punish or retaliate against a perceived harm. Often this sentencing goal is evidenced by language that the offender "deserved" the harsh sentence because of the severity of the crime. Retribution is a common goal when the crime is violent or in some other way particularly troubling to a community.

The various sentencing goals can be compared based on the time frame they address. For example, one sentencing goal may be primarily concerned with preventing crime in the future; another might be most interested in the crime itself or in the offender's past behavior. In the case of the sentencing goal of retribution, society is less interested in the degree to which the sentence will prevent future crime and more determined to make sure the sentence affords society "just deserts" or that the punishment fits the crime.

deterrence
A sentencing goal focused on convincing the offender or others not to commit crime.

A second goal is **deterrence**, which means the sentence is meant to serve as a lesson that such behavior will not be tolerated in society and that those actions will be punished. Deterrence can have either a specific or a general focus. Specific deterrence is meant to convince the particular person being sentenced not to offend again. General deterrence focuses on convincing other members of society that they should not commit crimes either. A goal of specific deterrence is clear when a judge says, "I am sentencing you to 2 years in prison so that you understand the severity of your crime and will not do it again." Some supporters of the death penalty use the idea of general deterrence to argue that if people know they can be executed for committing murder, they will be less likely to kill someone.

Deterrence is most focused on the future. The concern for affecting future behavior means that research can test whether sentences are effective in deterring future crimes. Supporters of the goal of using sentences to determine future criminal behavior note that punishment must be swift, certain, and severe to have the desired impact. Of course, for general deterrence to work, people need to be aware of the harsh sentence that has been imposed and that will also fall on them if they commit the same crime. Hence, deterrence relies on the public being fairly well educated about the workings of the criminal justice system and sentencing policy. Research has generally been unable to find that tough sentencing results in general deterrence, although concentrated campaigns to raise awareness of strict sentences for certain types of crimes may be effective. For example, Project Safe Neighborhoods, a major initiative during the presidency of George W. Bush, was found to be effective at reducing gun crimes largely because it used a public campaign to educate people about the harsher prosecution of gun crimes.[12]

incapacitation
A sentencing goal that aims to make it impossible for the offender to commit a future crime because he is imprisoned.

The third goal of sentencing, **incapacitation**, aims to make it impossible for the offender to commit a future crime because he is imprisoned. The assumption is that the offender will reoffend if he is not kept from doing so. Hence, like deterrence, incapacitation is a goal focused on affecting future behavior. Unlike deterrence, though, there is a resignation that perhaps the only way to keep the offender from committing future crimes is to "lock him up and throw away the key." Habitual offender policies, explained in detail later in this chapter, which focus on imprisoning individuals who have broken the law repeatedly, are based on a sentencing goal of incapacitation. The 1990s saw the rise of popularity of incapacitation as a sentencing goal as the "tough on crime" philosophy gained steam and the public began to feel that the only way to stop crime was to lock up offenders and throw away the key. A judge is exercising the goal of incapacitation when she says, "Your past behavior illustrates that you are unwilling to end your life of crime; therefore, the best way to keep society safe from you is to sentence you to life in prison."

rehabilitation
A sentencing goal focused on aiding offenders in changing their lives.

A final goal of sentencing is **rehabilitation**. This goal focuses on aiding offenders in changing their lives. It is assumed that an offender can change with assistance, and help is built into the sentence. For example, a sentence of probation with required attendance at drug counseling sessions allows for the possibility of rehabilitation. This sentencing goal was to some extent popular in the United States from the 1950s through the 1970s. In that era, however, crime continued to rise, and the public began to lose faith in rehabilitation. Today sentencing policy tends to reserve the goal of rehabilitation for specific crimes and perpetrators, and even then only in some jurisdictions. Thus in some states, such as California, first offenses for drug possession result in rehabilitation-oriented sentences, including probation and drug counseling. In terms of specific perpetrators, even though we now treat juvenile offenders more like adult offenders in many ways, the criminal justice system still generally views young people as being able to be rehabilitated. As with most criminal justice policies, these rehabilitation-oriented sentencing commitments vary by state.

A sentence rarely encompasses only one goal. For example, if a judge wishes to both punish an offender for her actions and make sure she will not be able to commit a future crime for a certain period of time, her sentence of 5 years in prison likely embodies the judge's dual goals of retribution and incapacitation. See the Key Concepts on the next page for a comparison of the goals of sentencing.

Related to the goals of sentencing are different sentencing models.

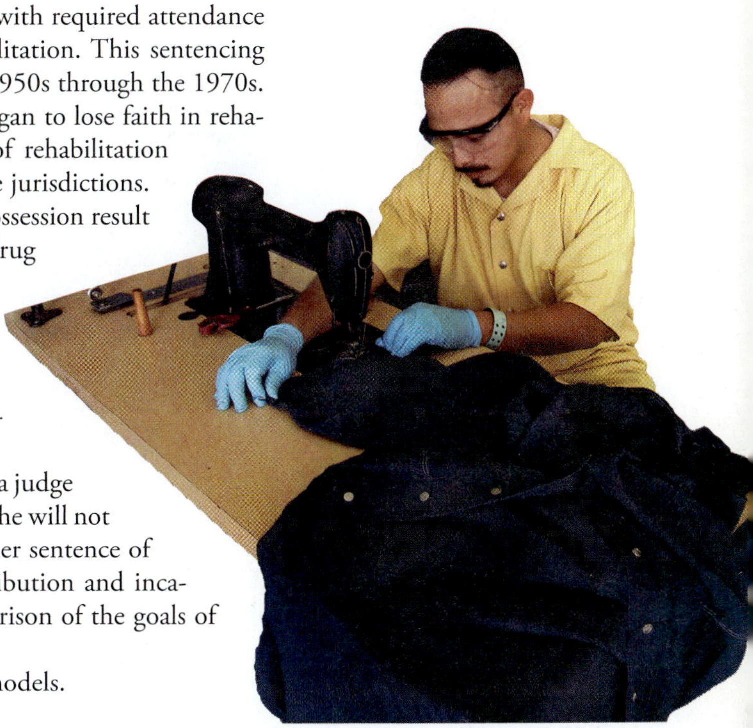

▲ **Prisoner Sewing**

Some inmates receive vocational training in prison. *What goal of sentencing would encourage vocational training in prisons?*

Indeterminate Sentences

With an **indeterminate sentence**, the offender is given a range of time he can serve, such as 5 to 7 years, which is dependent on how he behaves while in prison. The assumption is that during that time rehabilitation will occur and the offender will be motivated to change if by doing so he can reduce his sentence. Indeterminate sentences were much more common in the 1960s when the primary goal of the criminal justice system was rehabilitation. Since the 1980s, the dominant philosophy of the criminal justice system has been punishment, and indeterminate sentences have seriously declined because they came to be seen as too lenient.

indeterminate sentence
The offender is given a range of time he can serve, such as 5 to 7 years, dependent on how he behaves while in prison.

Determinate Sentences

A **determinate sentence** indicates a precise period of time that the offender must serve. For example, a sentence of 7 years in prison is a determinate sentence. However, that does not mean the offender will serve the entire 7 years. Prisoners often receive good-time credits that ultimately reduce their stay in prison. Also, beginning in the 1980s, questions were raised about how judges determine sentences. In particular, studies found that Blacks received harsher sentences than their White counterparts for similar crimes. There were also complaints that judges' use of discretion resulted in too-lenient sentences. A variety of legislative interventions resulted to limit judges' discretion. Determinate sentences are more common today, as are statutory minimums, mandatory sentences, and sentencing guidelines.

determinate sentence
Specifies a precise period of time that the offender needs to serve.

Sentencing Guidelines and Mandatory Sentences

Presumptive sentencing models assume that judges should sentence within sentencing guidelines, or ranges specified for particular charges. Legislatures enacted statutory minimums to reduce both judicial discretion and sentencing disparity. A **statutory minimum** occurs when a legislature sets a minimum sentence that must be imposed for a particular crime. For example, a statutory minimum might state that an individual convicted of aggravated assault must be sentenced to at least 1 year in prison. Another name for statutory minimum is mandatory minimums.

presumptive sentencing models
A sentencing model assuming that judges should sentence within sentencing guidelines, or within ranges specified for particular charges.

statutory minimum
The minimum sentence set by a legislature that must be imposed for a particular crime.

There has been a backlash against mandatory minimums. For example, Families Against Mandatory Minimums maintains that many drug offenses result in mandatory minimum sentences because judges are no longer allowed to adjust the sentence to fit the

KEY CONCEPTS

Goals of Sentencing

What are the positives and negatives of each of the sentencing goals?

Retribution	Focused on punishment that matches the crime
Deterrence	Focused on preventing future crime from occurring by convincing the offender (specific) and others (general) that punishment will be swift, severe, and certain
Incapacitation	Focused on preventing future offenses by imprisoning offender for long periods of time
Rehabilitation	Focused on preventing future crime by helping the offender change his life

offender's particular role in a crime. Instead, they must impose the minimum with little regard for the specific circumstances.

Both the states and the federal government have established sentencing guidelines. The motives for establishing sentencing guidelines included wanting to ensure equal treatment, reduce racial disparity, and reduce a perceived leniency of federal judges. Sentencing guidelines have now been in place for decades, and researchers are beginning to get a clear picture of the degree to which sentencing guidelines have produced the desired results. In the area of racial disparity, sentencing differentials have not been eliminated. In fact, similarly situated federal drug offenders of different races continue to receive different sentences. White offenders still receive lighter sentences than their Black and Latino counterparts, with Latino offenders receiving the harshest sentences of all.[13] Sentencing guidelines do not appear to reduce sex disparities in sentences either. Recent research in Pennsylvania comparing sentences in time periods with and without sentencing guidelines found that female offenders were still receiving more lenient sentences than similar male offenders.[14]

MYTH/REALITY

MYTH: Drug offenders are treated leniently by the criminal justice system.

REALITY: Sentences for drug offenses increased greatly with the move to legislative mandatory minimums and sentencing guidelines that reduced judicial discretion.[15]

Congress established the U.S. Sentencing Commission (USSC) to create sentencing guidelines for federal offenses in 1984. These guidelines went into effect in January 1989, and as of 2007, more than 700,000 defendants had been sentenced under the guidelines. Each federal judge is given a USSC table that classifies all federal crimes into 43 offense categories and classifies the past behavior of the defendant into six criminal history categories. The judge is expected to sentence the offender within the guideline indicated where the two relevant categories intersect.[16] Consult Figure 10-1, the USSC Sentencing Guidelines Table, to see how this process works.

A variety of constitutional challenges have been levied against the guidelines. The U.S. Supreme Court, however, has repeatedly found the guidelines constitutional. The first significant high court challenge came in January 2005 with the ruling in *U.S. v. Booker*. Beginning in 2000, the Supreme Court had decided a series of cases that affect how sentencing guidelines can be used. The Court held that whenever a judge relies on certain facts to give a defendant a sentence longer than the guidelines' maximum, those facts must be determined by the jury to be true beyond a reasonable doubt. If the judge, rather than the jury, decided those facts to be true, it would violate the defendant's Sixth Amendment rights. This rule applies in both state and federal cases. In *U.S. v. Booker* (2005), the Court held that this rule means that the federal sentencing guidelines are no longer mandatory and that appeals courts can review sentences to determine whether they are reasonable.[17] The guidelines are still important, however, because a sentence that falls within the guidelines will usually be considered reasonable.

Source Connection

FULL TEXT OF SUPREME COURT CASES

www.law.cornell.edu/

The Legal Information Institute of Cornell University Law School provides full text of U.S. Supreme Court cases, including *U.S. v. Booker* (2005).

USSC Sentencing Table in Months

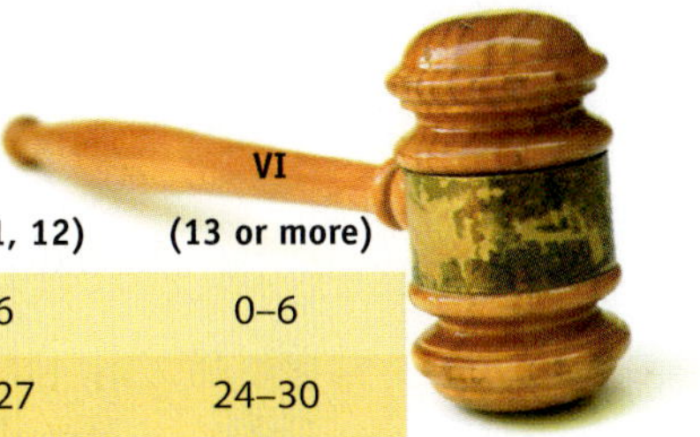

Offense Level	Criminal History Category (Criminal History Points)					
	I (0 or 1)	II (2 or 3)	III (4, 5, 6)	IV (7, 8, 9)	V (10, 11, 12)	VI (13 or more)
1	0–6	0–6	0–6	0–6	0–6	0–6
10	6–12	8–14	10–16	15–21	21–27	24–30
20	33–41	37–46	41–51	51–63	63–78	70–87
30	97–121	108–135	121–151	135–168	151–188	168–210
40	292–365	324–405	360–Life	360–Life	360–Life	360–Life
43	Life	Life	Life	Life	Life	Life

FIGURE 10-1 **USSC Sentencing Guidelines Table**

Although a stated objective of the USSC sentencing guidelines was to ensure that like offenders were treated similarly, questions were quickly raised about sentences for possession of powder cocaine and "crack" cocaine. The original guidelines recommended a sentence 100 times harsher for crack cocaine than for powder cocaine. In other words, possession of 5 grams of crack cocaine resulted in the same sentence as possession of 500 grams of powder cocaine. Concerns resulted from the fact that African Americans were much more likely to possess crack than powdered cocaine, and vice versa for Whites. Supporters of these guidelines and of Congress's harsh mandatory minimum sentence argued that longer sentences for crack cocaine were warranted because both the use of crack cocaine and dealing in that drug resulted in more violence than did use of and dealing in powder cocaine. Recently, however, such claims have been invalidated. For example, surveys of prison inmates show that offenders under the influence of alcohol when they committed their crimes were more likely to be incarcerated for violent offenses than were prisoners using crack or powder cocaine. Furthermore, prisoners under the influence of crack were no more likely to be incarcerated for a violent offense than were those under the influence of powder cocaine at the time of the offense.[18]

In November 2007 the USSC recommended the sentencing disparity be reduced, changing the average sentences for crack offenders from 121 months to 106 months.[19] In December 2007, the USSC voted unanimously to make sentenced crack cocaine offenders eligible for reduced sentences. This decision could affect 19,500 prison inmates who will be able to petition judges to be resentenced under the revised November 2007 guidelines and, therefore, be released from prison earlier than they had expected.[20]

The Supreme Court also seems to have become increasingly troubled by the racial disparity so often found in cocaine sentencing. The Supreme Court ruled in December 2007 that to address this problem federal district judges can use their discretion to sentence a crack cocaine offender to less than the recommended guidelines. Taking the recent cases together, the Supreme Court is clearly indicating that federal judges should consult the USSC guidelines but are not strictly bound by them.[21]

Preventive Detention

In recent decades there has been a move to identify offenders who the government has determined are most dangerous and to use laws that allow the system to prevent these individuals from committing future crimes by imposing lengthy incarceration or placing them in mental health facilities. These laws have been collectively called **preventive detention laws**. The individuals the laws focus on have been convicted a number of times, thus demonstrating a tendency to relapse into criminal activity after they have been punished. By the early 1900s, most states had enacted some form of **habitual offender statute**, authorizing

preventive detention laws
Legislation that allows the criminal justice system to prevent offenders from committing future crimes by lengthy incarceration or placement in mental health facilities.

habitual offender statutes
Laws that create enhanced penalties for repeat offenders.

recidivists
Offenders who have been previously convicted of crimes.

enhanced sentences for repeat offenders, called **recidivists**, who had been previously convicted of certain offenses. California's 1994 "three strikes, you're out" law, for example, doubles the sentence of felons who have previously been convicted of a serious crime and calls for a 25-years to life sentence for felons with two previous violent felony convictions—even if the third crime is not violent. As outlined in A Case in Point, page 280, Leandro Andrade ran afoul of this law.

These laws are based on the premise that a three-time offender has demonstrated an inability or unwillingness to conform to the laws of society and should be incarcerated for a long time, perhaps for life, for the better protection of the public. Rehabilitation of recidivists is not their goal.[22] Washington and Georgia have even passed "two strikes" laws, which mandate life sentences for certain offenders on their second conviction. California's three strikes law, though, is the broadest, the most frequently used, and generally considered the toughest sentencing policy. For example, the third "strike" need not be a violent crime. California's tougher three strikes policy, however, has not been found to affect crime rates to any greater degree than do other states' more limited laws.[23] Research shows that habitual offender laws are more often applied to racial and ethnic minorities and, therefore, increase sentencing disparity.[24]

DIS Connects

Sexually Violent Predator Laws

Earl Shriner had a 24-year history of violent sexual assaults against children. He had been repeatedly incarcerated for the same crimes and then released. In 1989, he sexually violated a 7-year-old Tacoma, Washington, boy. Although he had been convicted numerous times, once Shriner had served his sentence, authorities had to release him. Under sexually violent predator laws, however, once such recidivists complete their prison sentence, they may be declared sexually violent predators if in a formal hearing the court decides they meet specific criteria.

Sexually violent predators are confined in the mental health system. Their civil commitment is predicated on their need for psychiatric treatment—these individuals are considered mad, not bad—as well as on society's need for protection from them. Their release from the secure psychiatric facility is contingent on subsequent evaluations of their perceived dangerousness.

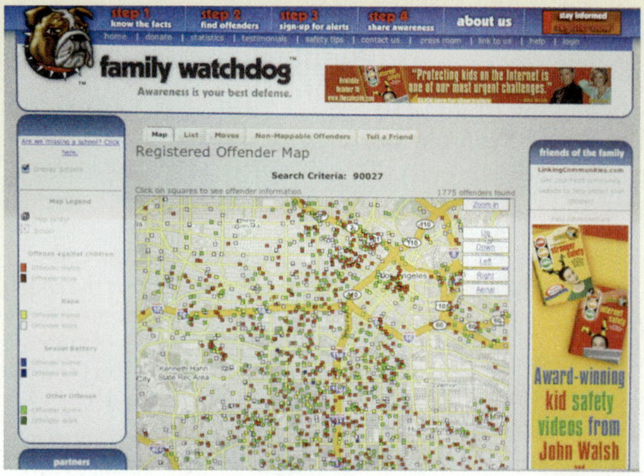

Although most people appear to favor the extended civil commitment of sexually violent predators, this practice is at odds with the general view of the medical community that such offenders are not treatable.

Costa Rica takes a different approach to such offenders. The Costa Rican criminal justice system has created a penal institution specifically for older offenders who were convicted of committing violent crimes of a sexual or domestic nature. The correctional professionals are concerned with ensuring the rehabilitation of these largely senior citizen inmates, while at the same time working to assist their transition back to their family upon their release.

Observe Investigate Understand

- **How should society deal with people who are prone to violent criminal behavior but whom the medical community says are untreatable?**
- **Should violent sexual offenders simply be confined to the general prison population? Why or why not?**
- **Should the United States emulate Costa Rica in creating special, rehabilitation-oriented penal institutions for older sexual or domestic abuse offenders?**

SOURCES: Roxanne Lieb, "Washington's Sexually Violent Predator Law: Legislative History and Comparisons with Other States" (Olympia, WA: Washington State Institute for Public Policy, December 1996); "Involuntary Commitment of Sexually Violent Predators: Comparing State Laws," Document No. 05-03-1101 (Olympia, WA: Washington State Institute for Public Policy, March 2005).

Repeat sex offenders have been targeted by special sentencing provisions that began with the so-called sexual psychopath laws, first enacted in 1937 in Michigan. By 1975, more than half the states had mentally disordered sex offender (MDSO) laws. These laws allowed the state to confine sex offenders with a mental disease or defect for indefinite periods of time, dependent on treatment needs, in a secure psychiatric facility rather than a prison. The popularity of these laws declined as fixed-term sentencing gained acceptance. More recently, however, calls for a return to indeterminate periods of incarceration have arisen due to the results of our experience with fixed sentences. Many violent sex offenders with fixed sentences are released back into the community, and many of those reoffend.

Today, through a new wave of sex offender statutes, most states allow the period of incarceration to be extended beyond that of the original court-mandated sentence because of fear that these criminals, once released, will reoffend. Under preventive detention laws, incarceration in a secure psychiatric facility can follow completion of a sentence in prison, or incarceration in prison can be extended beyond what would have been given for a particular crime had it been the offender's first or second offense. The individual is confined not for what he did but rather to prevent what he is believed likely to do in the future.

The Washington state legislature was first to enact this kind of law. In 1990, the Sexually Violent Predator (SVP) Law was passed in response to a number of highly publicized sex crimes.[25] As of 2007, 19 states have provisions for civilly committing dangerous sex offenders.[26] The Disconnects box illustrates the problems these offenders present to society, first in their recidivism and, second, in our apparent inability to effectively treat many, if not most, of them.

Even though preventive detention laws are popular with the general public, their future is uncertain. Under existing law, sexual predators can be freed only after they have been effectively "cured." But most psychiatrists consider sexual predation to be an antisocial behavior rather than a mental illness and therefore argue that it cannot be cured. The Washington State Psychiatric Association, for example, has called for the repeal of that state's sexual predator law. The association has gone on record to assert that "[s]exual predation in and of itself does not define a mental illness. It defines criminal conduct."[27] Except when a person is mentally ill and poses a danger to self or others, preventive detention is unconstitutional. Washington's psychiatrists have raised the claim that sexually violent predator (SVP) laws give offenders what is tantamount to a sentence of life imprisonment. Thus far, however, these statutes have managed to withstand judicial challenges to their constitutionality.

Another problematic issue is that if we use chronic recidivism as the basis for defining a mental abnormality, such as SVP, the public may well call for the preventive detention of

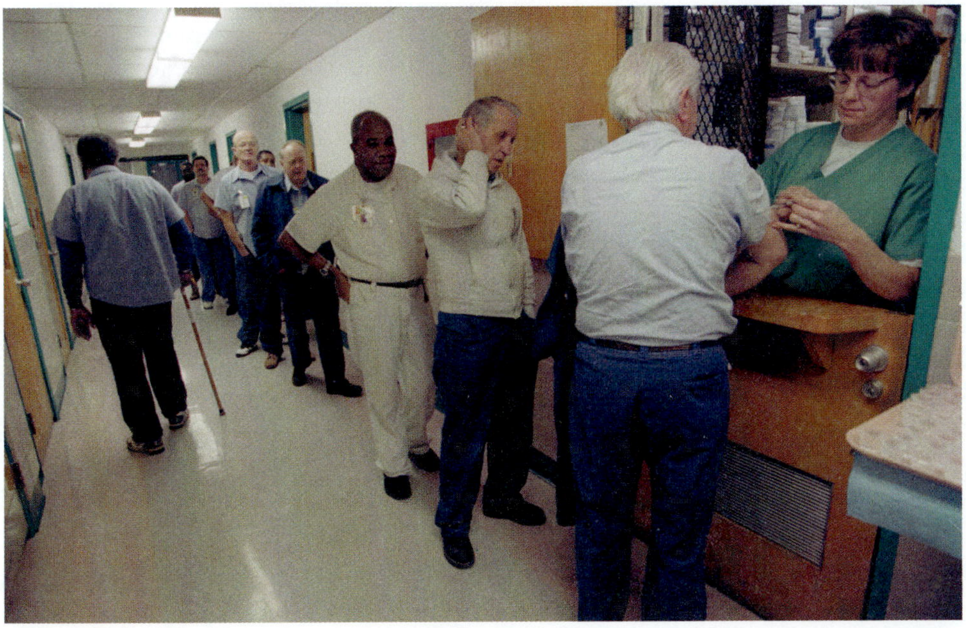

◀ **Older Prison Inmates Receiving Health Care**

Habitual predator laws contribute to the increase in older prisoners. *Do you think it is worth the high medical costs to keep older prisoners incarcerated?*

those who perpetrate other repeated felonies as well. Men who repeatedly batter their partners might then qualify for terms of civil commitment beyond the length of their criminal penalties. If an SVP is considered mentally ill, why is a batterer or, for that matter, a professional thief not given the same status? These are matters future courts are likely to face.

Even though such issues may prompt us to question the fairness of preventive detention laws, current legislatures seem inclined toward accepting them. In 1994, the California legislature passed a "one strike rape bill," assigning a penalty of 25 years to life for sexual assaults involving torture, kidnapping, or burglary with intent to commit rape. Repeat offender laws are controversial, but they remain popular. The public considers them the remedy for the persistent problem of offenders who have not been, and as some suggest cannot be, cured.

capital crime
An offense punishable by execution.

Habitual offender laws and preventive detention contain the threat of crime by incapacitating criminals for extended periods of time. They come, however, at high financial cost. It remains to be seen how long the public will be able to bear the costs of putting more criminals in prison for longer terms. To illustrate, older inmates have the same needs as older people in the general population. Health care needs alone raise annual inmate costs threefold over those for younger inmates. The RAND Corporation studied costs associated with "three strikes you're out" legislation in California and concluded that unless there are changes to its implementation, the result for the state will be "three strikes and we're broke."[28] On top of these troubling facts, a 2002 evaluation of the effects of this law concluded that it had played only a minimal role in the state's declining crime rate.[29] Nonetheless, this law continues to enjoy the support of the majority of California voters—another sign that what we are learning about crime is not being translated into the laws designed to control it.

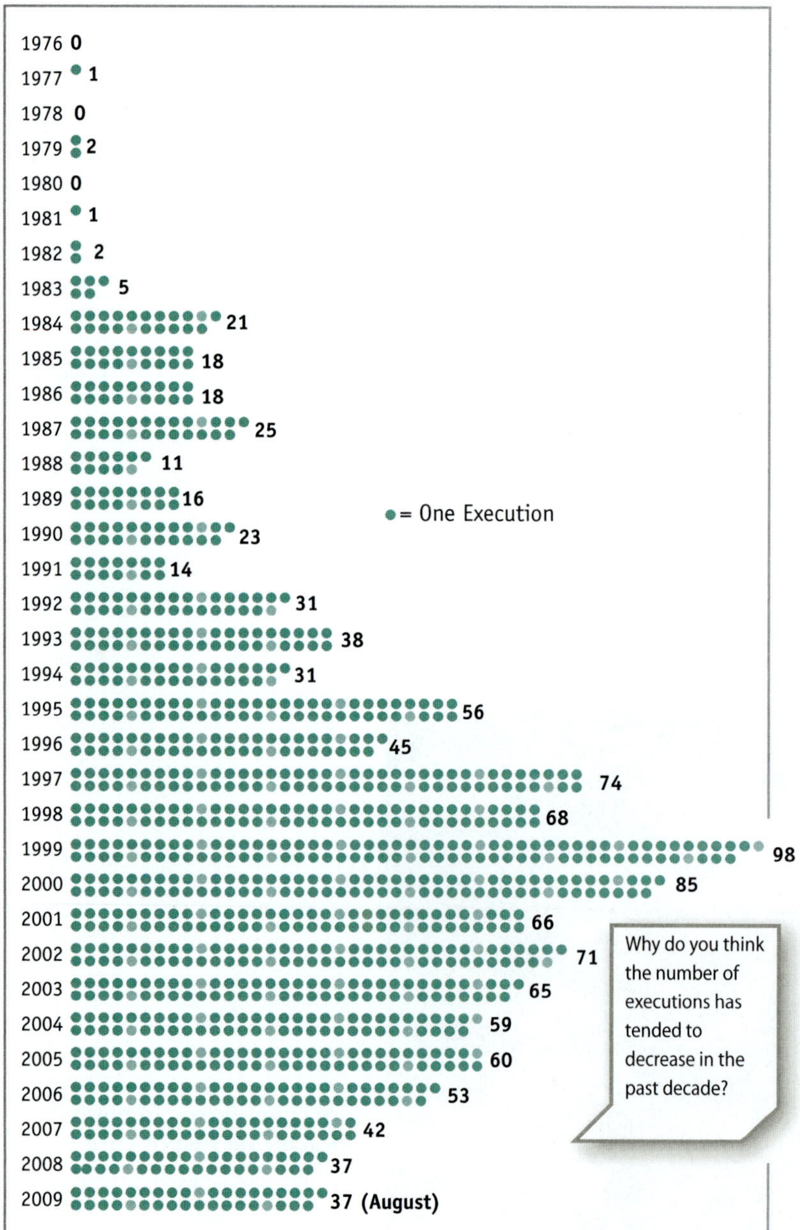

FIGURE 10-2 Number of Executions in the United States over Time

CAPITAL PUNISHMENT

A **capital crime** is an offense punishable by execution. The U.S. military, the federal government, and 36 states currently provide for capital punishment, but the offenses that constitute capital crimes vary. Most state laws specify that first-degree murder with special circumstances is a capital crime, but the specific circumstances vary by state.[30] Special circumstances are features of the crime that include torturing victims, lying in wait for them, and killing for financial gain. Jurors consider whether these special circumstances were present when deciding if death is an appropriate sentence for the offender.

◀ **The Last Public Hanging in the United States**

More than 15,000 people witnessed this execution in 1936.

MYTH/REALITY

MYTH: Most death row inmates will be executed eventually.

REALITY: On average, fewer than 2 percent of condemned inmates are executed in any given year. The vast majority will never be executed.[31]

Today, very few people convicted of homicide find their way onto death row.[32] Over the last 30 years, fewer than 3 percent of those convicted of murder in the United States received the death penalty.[33] We might assume that this 3 percent of murderers represent the "worst of the worst," but that is not necessarily true. For example, fewer than half of the 11 serial murderers convicted in 2004 were sentenced to death.[34] In 2008, 37 people were executed in the United States for committing capital crimes (Figure 10-2). Fifty-six percent of offenders put to death were White, 35 percent were Black, and 7 percent were Latino. As for the race of the murder victims, almost 80 percent of the victims were White, whereas they are only 50 percent of all murder victims nationally.[35] This has led some to argue that capital punishment trials are most likely to occur when the victim is White.[36] There are regional differences in the administration of capital punishment as well (see Mapping Capital Punishment on the next page). By far, the South has executed the most individuals (949) and the Northeast has executed the least (4).[37] In 2007, there were 3,233 people on death row in the United States;[38] only 51 of them were women.

Rather than having their death sentences carried out, death row inmates tend to die in prison of natural causes, to commit suicide, to have their cases overturned, or to have their sentences reduced to life imprisonment.[39] Even though the majority of states have a death penalty statute, most have not executed anyone in decades. These variations across states have caused many to question the fairness of laws that define capital crimes and apply capital sentences differently. Still, in 2008, across the United States, only two men were on death row for crimes that did not include killing someone; both were in the Louisiana penal system. One of those men, Patrick Kennedy, had his death sentence overruled by the U.S. Supreme Court in June 2008. In *Kennedy v. Louisiana* (2008), the Court ruled that Louisiana's law making the rape of a child a crime punishable by death was unconstitutional and indicated that the death penalty would be unconstitutional in any instance that the offender did not kill the victim.[40]

The Supreme Court and Capital Punishment

European settlers, particularly those from England, brought the death penalty with them to the new colonies. Early U.S. Supreme Court decisions upheld different methods of

Mapping Capital Punishment in the U.S.

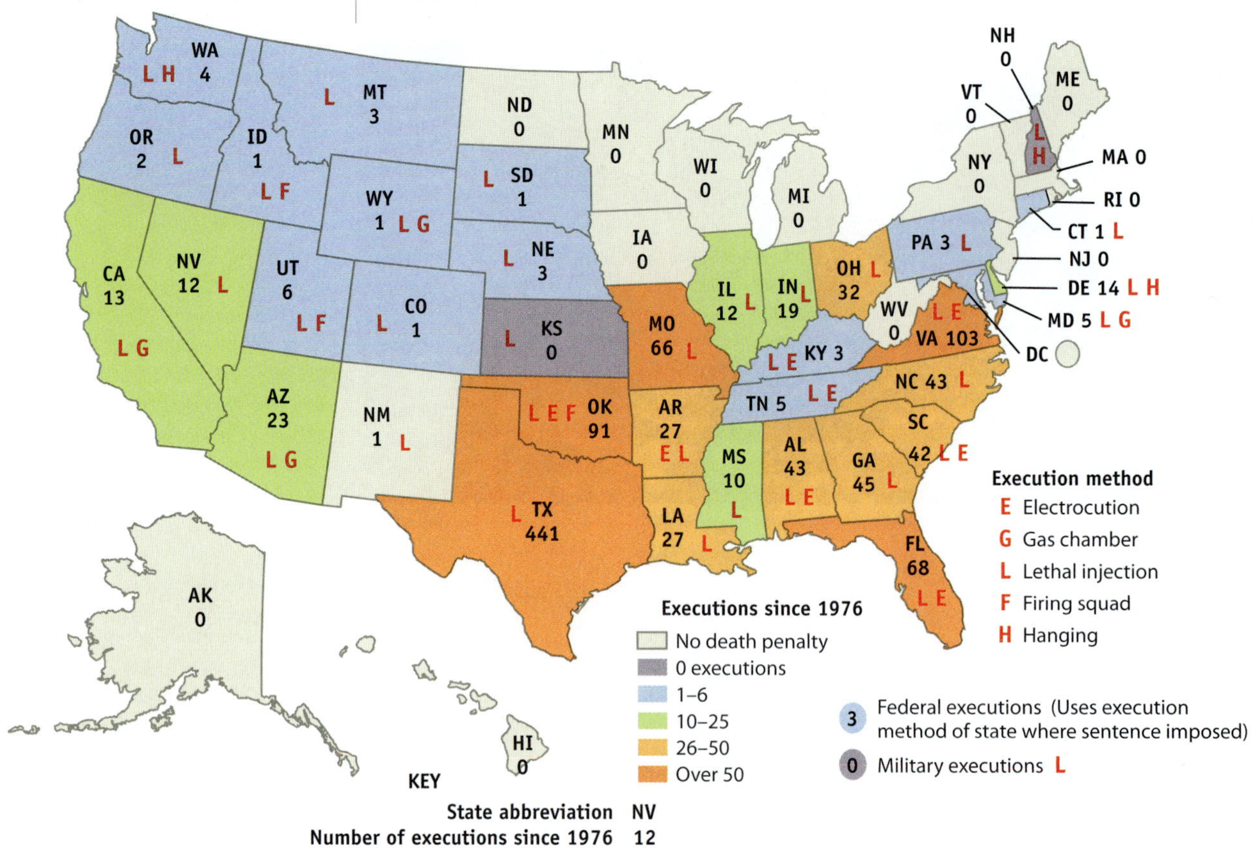

execution. In *Wilkerson v. Utah* (1878), the Court rejected the claim that firing squads constituted cruel and unusual punishment, and in *In re Kemmler* (1890), the Court ruled similarly on electrocution. Not until the early 1970s did the U.S. Supreme Court rule against any state for its administration of capital punishment.

The "arbitrary and capricious" manner in which death sentences were imposed prior to 1972 led the U.S. Supreme Court to strike down state and federal capital punishment laws in effect at the time.[41] An immediate consequence of this decision, *Furman v. Georgia* (1972), was that the death sentences of more than 600 condemned inmates were commuted to life imprisonment. In *Furman,* the Court required that states must have a two-stage trial. Guilt or innocence must be decided first, and only then must the penalty phase be conducted. Because the Court did not rule that the death penalty itself was unconstitutional, but rather that the specific laws determining how the penalty would be administered were, states were permitted to redraft their laws to make them constitutionally acceptable. In *Gregg v. Georgia* (1976), the U.S. Supreme Court upheld a series of new death penalty laws that included the new two-stage procedure. The following year, under these new laws, Utah became the first state to resume executing condemned inmates.

Another important capital punishment case involved Georgia yet again. In *McClesskey v. Kemp* (1987), death penalty opponents argued that Georgia's capital punishment law was racially discriminatory. Attorneys for McClesky, an African American man convicted of killing a White police officer, presented a wide variety of systematic evidence illustrating racial disparity concerning how defendants were treated. In particular, the attorneys pointed out that defendants who killed White people were 11 times more likely to receive the death penalty. The Court agreed that the evidence was supportive of their overall claims but ruled that for McCleskey to win on the question of whether his equal protection rights were violated, he would have to prove that there was racial discrimination in his individual case. In other words, it was not enough to show overall racial disparities. Instead, he needed to illustrate that he personally was subjected to racial discrimination.[42]

In recent years, the Supreme Court has primarily dealt with issues of who should and should not be eligible for capital punishment. For example, the Court has ruled that individuals with mental retardation—those with an IQ lower than 70—cannot be executed.[43] The Court has also ruled that juveniles cannot be executed. In *Roper v. Simmons* (2005), the Court held that individuals who were under 18 years of age when they killed someone could not be sentenced to the death penalty.

The mostly widely used method of execution—lethal injection—has also come under scrutiny of the courts. Lethal injection is used by 30 of the 36 states that allow capital punishment, and they all generally use what is referred to as a "three drug cocktail." The first drug is administered to make the process painless, and then the other two drugs kill the individual. Arguing that despite claims to the contrary, the process was painful and that it also was administered improperly, prisoners in Kentucky sought to have lethal injection deemed an unconstitutional violation of the Eighth Amendment. In *Baze v. Rees* (2008), the Kentucky prisoners lost and the Court upheld lethal injection as constitutionally permissible.

The Capital Punishment Trial

As we saw in Chapter 9, ever since capital punishment was reinstated in 1976, bifurcated trials have been used in capital cases—one trial to determine guilt, and if the verdict is guilty, a second trial to establish the penalty, which might be death or life imprisonment without the possibility of parole. In making this determination, jurors are instructed to weigh mitigating factors against the aggravating factors presented by the prosecution during the penalty phase.

Mitigating factors are presented to provide a larger context on the life of the now-convicted offender. Defense attorneys highlight these factors to argue that the defendant does not deserve to be executed. Mitigating factors might include evidence that the offender himself had been a victim of abuse, that he suffers from mental illness, or that he previously led a very respectable life. When presenting these mitigating factors, defense attorneys hope that the jury will decide that life imprisonment would be more appropriate for the defendant.

Aggravating factors, which are presented by the prosecutor, generally need to be proved to be present in order to make execution an appropriate penalty. For example, in many states capital punishment is appropriate if the murder was especially heinous, atrocious, cruel, or involved torture. Alabama defines as an aggravating factor any murder committed in order to avoid arrest.[44] The prosecutor in the case during the penalty phase would want to produce evidence that illustrates any relevant aggravating factors were present in the commission of the crime so that the jury returns a sentence of death. Ultimately, in their deliberations jurors weigh the mitigating and aggravating factors presented. In 2007, juries in 115 cases decided the offender should be executed.[45]

Controversies

To those who support the death penalty, there is the absolute assurance that no further crimes will be committed by the individual scheduled for execution. Although research does not support this claim, advocates also believe that there may be some degree of deterrence through the state-sanctioned taking of a life. Those who oppose this ultimate

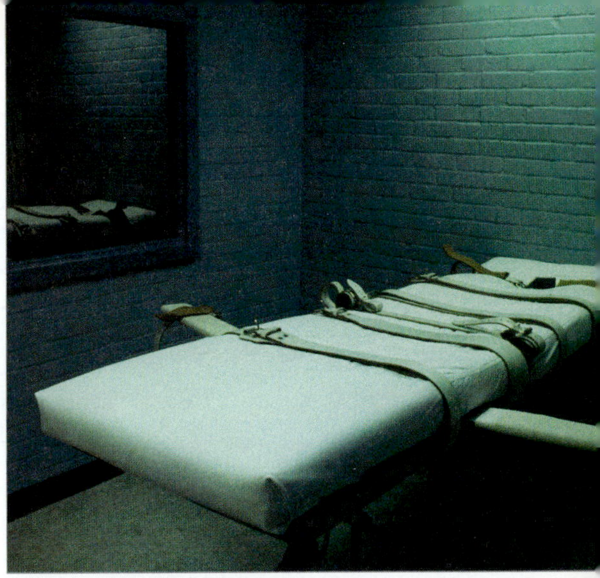

Real Crime Tech

TECHNOLOGY CHANGES THE DEATH PENALTY

How the death penalty is administered has changed over time, partly because of technological changes. Public hangings did not require technological sophistication, although the knot had to be tied skillfully to ensure a swift death rather than slow strangulation, but use of the electric chair required the creation of electricity and the death device itself. The first execution by electrocution occurred in 1890. In 1924 cyanide gas began to be used, and the first gas chamber was constructed. The new death technology of lethal injection was largely adopted as a cost-saving measure. It was first adopted as an option in Oklahoma in 1977, but was not actually used until 1982 in Texas.

SOURCES: Phillip English Mackey, *Voices against Death: American Opposition to Capital Punishment, 1787–1975* (New York: Burt Franklin, 1976); Hugo Adam Bedau, *The Death Penalty in America* (New York: Oxford University Press, 1982); R. Bohm, *Deathquest: An Introduction to the Theory and Practice of Capital Punishment in the United States* (Cincinnati, OH: Anderson, 1999).

sanction argue that the death penalty per se violates human rights through its inhumane and degrading treatment of an offender. Capital punishment is controversial not just in the United States but throughout the world. A Global View examines the concept from the perspective of the United Nations.

The table on page 295 depicts how U.N. member countries weighed in on a groundbreaking resolution calling for a moratorium on the use of the death penalty.

Public opinion in the United States has slowly been shifting away from support of capital punishment. In 2006, the death penalty was favored by 65 percent of the adults in the United States, down from the 77 percent who supported it in 1999. Perhaps even more

A Global View

United Nations Resolution on a Death Penalty Moratorium

Capital punishment continues to be one of the most controversial justice-related issues in the world. Besides the fundamental ethical advocacy for the value of a human life and the possibility of executing innocent persons, debates focus on cost, deterrence, social class, race, age, and gender. Within the global context, the United States remains the only western industrialized nation where capital punishment is employed. Moreover, it is one of only six countries known to have executed juveniles since 1995. Remember, however, that the U.S. Supreme Court ended such executions in 2005. The other five countries known to have executed juveniles are China, the Democratic Republic of Congo, Iran, Nigeria, and Pakistan.

In 2007, at least 1,252 individuals were executed in 24 countries. In descending order, the top 5 countries were China, Iran, Saudi Arabia, Pakistan, and the United States. The year 2007 proved significant for a reason other than the number of executions. It marked the adoption of United Nations General Assembly Resolution 62/149. This groundbreaking resolution, adopted by an overwhelming majority of 104 U.N. member countries, called for a worldwide moratorium on the use of the death penalty, with a view to abolishing the death penalty altogether, and it called upon countries that had already abolished the death penalty to not reintroduce it. It was further resolved that the matter would continue to be discussed at the United Nations' 63rd session.

The 63rd session of the United Nations convened in 2008. On the General Assembly's agenda, Resolution 63/168 provided for further discussion of the moratorium. The resolution elicited protests from countries with death penalty statutes. The spirit of protest was that nations used the death penalty to protect their citizens and that it was not a human rights matter; rather, it was a criminal justice issue. Given such a classification, the death penalty would fall outside the purview of the United Nations, which does not have authority to intervene in matters that are within the jurisdiction of the countries. Despite their protests, those countries opposing the death penalty remained in the minority. In fact, the data reflect an undeniable trend toward abolition of the death penalty throughout the world: In 1977, only 16 countries had abolished the death penalty; by 2008, the abolitionist countries tallied 91.

OBSERVE Investigate Understand

- **What do you believe to be the motivation for the U.S. advocacy for retention of the death penalty?**
- **Do you think international disapproval will sooner or later oblige the United States to abolish capital punishment?**
- **In what ways does retention of the death penalty damage the global reputation of the United States, and should this make any difference in whether this nation retains capital punishment?**

SOURCE: Amnesty International, *UN General Assembly 2008: Implementing a Moratorium on Executions*, September 2008, ACT 50/016/2008; United Nations, *Moratorium on the Use of the Death Penalty*, 63rd General Assembly Session, 2008, Resolution 63/168; Bijou Yang and David Lester, "The Deterrent Effect of Executions: A Meta-Analysis Thirty Years after Ehrlich," *Journal of Criminal Justice* 36, no. 5 (2008): 453–459.

U.N. GENERAL ASSEMBLY RESOLUTION 62/149: COUNTRY VOTES

On December 18, 2007, the United Nations General Assembly adopted a groundbreaking resolution calling for a moratorium on the use of the death penalty. The resolution was adopted by an overwhelming majority of 104 U.N. member states in favor, 54 countries against, and 29 abstentions. Check how countries voted on this resolution.

In Favor	Against	Abstain
Albania, Algeria, Andorra, Angola, Argentina, Australia, Austria, Azerbaijan, Belgium, Benin, Bolivia, Bosnia and Herzegovina, Brazil, Bulgaria, Burkina Faso, Burundi, Cambodia, Canada, Cape Verde, Chile, Colombia, Congo, Costa Rica, Cote d'Ivoire, Croatia, Cyprus, Czech Republic, Denmark, Dominican Republic, Ecuador, El Salvador, Estonia, Finland, France, Gabon, Georgia, Germany, Greece, Guatemala, Haiti, Honduras, Hungary, Iceland, Ireland, Israel, Italy, Kazakhstan, Kiribati, Kyrgyzstan, Latvia, Liechtenstein, Lithuania, Luxembourg, Macedonia (former Yugoslav Republic of), Madagascar, Mali, Malta, Marshall Islands, Mauritius, Mexico, Micronesia (Federated States of), Moldova, Monaco, Montenegro, Mozambique, Namibia, Nauru, Nepal, Netherlands, New Zealand, Nicaragua, Norway, Palau, Panama, Paraguay, Philippines, Poland, Portugal, Romania, Russian Federation, Rwanda, Samoa, San Marino, Sao Tome and Principe, Serbia, Slovakia, Slovenia, South Africa, Spain, Sri Lanka, Sweden, Switzerland, Tajikistan, Timor-L' Este, Turkey, Turkmenistan, Tuvalu, Ukraine, United Kingdom, Uruguay, Uzbekistan, Vanuatu, Venezuela	Afghanistan, Antigua and Barbuda, Bahamas, Bahrain, Bangladesh, Barbados, Belize, Botswana, Brunei, Chad, China, Comoros, Dar es Salaam, Democratic People's Republic of Korea, Dominica, Egypt, Ethiopia, Grenada, Guyana, India, Indonesia, Iran, Iraq, Jamaica, Japan, Jordan, Kuwait, Libya, Malaysia, Maldives, Mauritania, Mongolia, Myanmar, Nigeria, Oman, Pakistan, Papua New Guinea, Qatar, Saint Kitts and Nevis, Saint Lucia, Saint Vincent and the Grenadines, Saudi Arabia, Singapore, Solomon Islands, Somalia, Sudan, Suriname, Syria, Thailand, Tonga, Trinidad and Tobago, Uganda, United States, Yemen, Zimbabwe	Belarus, Bhutan, Cameroon, Central African Republic, Cuba, Democratic Republic of Congo, Djibouti, Equatorial Guinea, Eritrea, Fiji, Gambia, Ghana, Guinea, Kenya, Lao People's Democratic Republic, Lebanon, Lesotho, Liberia, Malawi, Morocco, Niger, Republic of Korea, Sierra Leone, Swaziland, Togo, United Arab Emirates, United Republic of Tanzania, Vietnam, Zambia

SOURCE: www.amnesty.org/en/death-penalty/international-law/moratorium/voting-records (retrieved November 18, 2008).

important, the public is evenly divided when it comes to supporting the death penalty (48 percent) versus life in prison (47 percent).[46]

Opposition to capital punishment is based on several concerns. Many people believe that the death penalty is applied unfairly. The *Furman* ruling did not put to rest concerns regarding racial bias in the administration of death penalty cases. Data continue to show disparities along racial lines. Blacks are disproportionately represented on death row. They make up 35 percent of death row inmates but only 13 percent of the U.S. population. Furthermore, those of any race who murder Whites are more likely to receive a death sentence than those who murder people of color. Hence both the race of the perpetrator and the race of the victim are related to death sentences. Some have concluded that racial disparities in the administration of the death penalty are evidence of racial discrimination in the criminal justice system. There is also a relationship between the economic class of the victim and the sentence of the offender. If the victim was of a higher social status, a death penalty sentence is more likely than if the victim was poor or of lower social status.[47]

Another reason for questioning the fairness of the death penalty is that a surprising number of death row inmates are later proven innocent. Since 1973, 130 people have been exonerated and released from death row as a result of evidence of their innocence.[48] The Race, Class, Gender box on the next page reviews how one organization, the Innocence Project, has been very successful in exonerating individuals who had not committed the crimes of which they were accused. Perhaps because of concerns about mistakes in the criminal justice system and the risk of executing an innocent person, death sentences dropped 50 percent between 1999 and 2004.[49]

A third concern about using the death penalty focuses on whether it serves as an effective crime deterrent. Studies that have compared use of the death penalty to violent crime rates have found that threat of execution does not deter violent offenses. The FBI's 2004 Uniform Crime Reports indicate that the South has the highest murder rate, but that region also accounts for 60 percent of executions in the United States. On the other hand, the Northeast has the lowest murder rate of any region and accounts for just 1 percent of total executions.[50] Although deterrence is definitely not the only argument for the death penalty, current research is undermining the degree to which we can believe that the likelihood of execution deters murder.

Another area of controversy concerning capital punishment is its cost. Proponents argue it is cheaper to execute than to pay the costs of imprisoning someone for life. In fact, this is not true. Because of the expense of the extraordinary judicial processes required

Race, Class, Gender

Exonerating the Innocent

The Innocence Project was founded by Barry Scheck and Peter Neufeld at the Benjamin N. Cardoza School of Law at Yeshiva University in 1992. Their goal was to help prisoners who could be proven innocent with DNA analysis. As of March 1, 2009, the Innocence Project had exonerated 232 people. Seventeen of those individuals were at some point on death row. The Innocence Project's clients tend not to see justice done soon after their wrongful conviction. In fact, the average amount of time that Innocence Project's exonerated clients serve is 12 years.

Many who are exonerated of the crimes for which they were convicted had relied on public defenders because they were poor. Public defenders may have the best of intentions, but they are often overworked and given less than adequate resources. The Innocence Project contends that to reduce the number of wrongful convictions, national standards must be established for the indigent defense system, which currently varies greatly from state to state.

People on death row are typically not just poor; they also are largely uneducated. Fifty-one percent of death row inmates are educated at the eleventh-grade level or lower. More than half have never been married.

It is also illustrative to consider the profiles of jurors who decide whether defendants deserve the death penalty. For a citizen to become a member of a capital punishment trial jury, he must be willing to vote for the death penalty. If his feelings generally tend toward an anti–death penalty position, they can't be so strong as to "prevent or substantially impair the performance of his duties as a juror." As a result, the people who are eligible to serve on capital punishment juries tend to be politically conservative, male, White, and either Catholic or Protestant. A recent study found that people who qualified to serve on a death penalty jury had higher levels of homophobia, racism, and sexism.

The combination of all this information is that we have a largely disadvantaged group of individuals who are on death row and jurors who are unlikely to either think or look like them.

Observe Investigate Understand

- **What do you think best explains why so many people have been wrongfully convicted in the United States?**
- **What explains the finding that more than half of those on death row in the United States have less than an eleventh-grade education and have never been married, and why is that significant?**
- **Will the wider application of DNA testing significantly reduce the number of persons who receive the death penalty in the United States and who are actually executed?**

SOURCES: Brooke Butler, "Death Qualification and Prejudice: The Effect of Implicit Racism, Sexism, and Homophobia on Capital Defendants' Right to Due Process," *Behavioral Sciences and the Law* 25 (2007): 857–867; "Capital Punishment," Bureau of Justice Statistics, www.ojp.usdoj.gov/bjs/cp.htm (retrieved March 1, 2009); *Wainwright v. Witt* 469 U.S. 412 (1985).

in capital cases, the costs associated with capital cases typically far exceed those of life imprisonment.

As noted earlier, there are some indications that public and legal support for the death penalty is eroding. In 2000, the Republican governor of Illinois, George Ryan, suspended all use of capital punishment in Illinois because he felt the system was flawed and too many innocent people were being sentenced to death.[51]

SUMMARY

The U.S. Constitution bans "cruel and unusual punishments," but exactly what this means has changed greatly between the time the Constitution was written in the late eighteenth century and the present day. Whether or not that constitutional language now makes it appropriate to ban the death penalty is a contentious issue.

Another important constitutional guarantee—the right to seek a writ of habeas corpus—affects the kind of punishment that the criminal justice system can impose. Habeas corpus proceedings involve challenging the justice of a convicted person's trial or sentence, particularly if the sentence is death. Today, the parameters within which convicts may institute habeas corpus proceedings are narrowing.

Sentences are determined by the trial judge on the basis of Presentence Investigation Reports (PSIs) and victim impact statements, which help the judge determine whether there are aggravating or mitigating circumstances that would affect the severity of the sentence. Various goals and principles of sentencing have been identified: retribution for the crime that has been committed; deterrence, to discourage others from committing the offense; incapacitation, to remove the offender from the rest of society; and rehabilitation, to encourage the offender to change his or her future behavior. Of these principles, rehabilitation is less frequently invoked today than it was a generation ago. Sentences of imprisonment can be either indeterminate (dependent on the convicted person's behavior while imprisoned and on the likelihood of rehabilitation) or determinate (for a more or less precise term of years). Legislation often requires judges to impose mandatory sentences.

Capital punishment has become extremely controversial in the United States, in part because it retains strong popular support despite equally strong disapproval in other industrial democracies. Disparities of race and class in the implementation of capital punishment remain significant.

OBSERVE Investigate Understand

Review

Describe the constitutional protections that affect sentencing.

- According to the Eighth Amendment, sentences cannot be cruel and unusual.
- Habeas corpus protections allow offenders to challenge their detainment.

Describe the various goals of sentencing.

- Retribution is a sentencing goal focused on appropriately punishing the offender in a manner equal to his crime.
- Deterrence is a sentencing goal focused on convincing the offender herself and society at large that criminal actions will be punished and therefore should not be committed.
- Incapacitation is a sentencing goal focused on detaining the offender so it is impossible for him to commit any future crimes.
- Rehabilitation is a sentencing goal focused on helping the offender change her behavior.

Compare the different sentencing models.

- Indeterminate sentencing models include sentences with ranges rather than a specific amount of time.
- Determinate sentencing models include sentences that enumerate a specific amount of time that should be served.
- Presumptive sentencing models assume judges should sentence within sentencing guidelines, or within ranges specified for particular charges.

Review how a capital punishment trial proceeds.

- A capital punishment trial is bifurcated.
- The first stage of a capital punishment trial decides guilt or innocence.
- In the second stage the jury weighs both mitigating and aggravating factors to decide whether the defendant should be sentenced to death.

Outline controversies surrounding the death penalty.

- There is a growing global sentiment that the death penalty should be abolished in all countries.
- There are questions about whether capital punishment is applied fairly.
- Research indicates that the death penalty does not deter murder.
- Sentencing a person to death ultimately costs more than sentencing him to life imprisonment because of the associated costs of appeals.

Key Terms

capital crime 290
cruel and unusual punishment 279
determinate sentence 285
deterrence 284
habeas corpus 279
habitual offender statutes 287
incapacitation 284
indeterminate sentence 285
Presentence Investigation Reports (PSI) 281
presumptive sentencing models 285
preventive detention laws 287
recidivists 288
rehabilitation 284
retribution 284
statutory minimum 285

Study Questions

1. Which of the following is *not* a goal of sentencing?
   a. Retribution
   b. Rehabilitation
   c. Victim advocacy
   d. Incapacitation
2. A sentence that is a range of time served such as 2 to 3.5 years is what kind of sentence?
   a. Indeterminate
   b. Determinate
   c. Presumptive
   d. Mandatory minimum
3. What is a judicial order that says someone has been wrongfully imprisoned?
   a. Cruel and unusual punishment
   b. Preventive detention
   c. Capital offense
   d. Habeas corpus
4. Preventive detention laws generally target what types of offenders?
   a. Recidivists
   b. Sex offenders
   c. Neither a nor b
   d. Both a and b
5. A punishment is cruel and unusual if
   a. it inflicts any pain on the defendant.
   b. the defendant is under the age of 18.
   c. it is rejected by the "evolving standards of decency."
   d. it does not fit the crime.
6. How many stages are there in a capital punishment trial?
   a. One
   b. Two
   c. Three
   d. Four

7. Which U.S. Supreme Court case established the stages of a capital punishment trial?
   a. *Furman v. Georgia*
   b. *Gregg v. Georgia*
   c. *McClesky v. Kemp*
   d. *U.S. v. Booker*

8. A state that uses sentencing guidelines and mandatory minimum sentences likely has a/an
   a. indeterminate sentencing model.
   b. determinate sentencing model.
   c. presumptive sentencing model.
   d. preventive detention sentencing model.

9. Which of the following is *not* typically found in a Presentence Investigation Report?
   a. Statements from the defendants' family members
   b. An overview of any past crimes the offender has been convicted of
   c. A sentencing recommendation
   d. A victim impact statement

10. Which group of people did the U.S. Supreme Court recently rule was ineligible for the death penalty?
   a. People with mental retardation
   b. Individuals who were 18 years of age or younger when they committed their crimes
   c. Both a and b
   d. Neither a nor b

Critical Thinking Questions

1. What goal of sentencing do you think should be the most important and why?
2. Which sentencing model should be used for violent crimes? Property crimes? Drug crimes?
3. There are many arguments both for and against the death penalty. Which arguments do you find most persuasive and why?

Internet Sites

Families Against Mandatory Minimums
www.famm.org/
The Families Against Mandatory Minimums holds that laws requiring judges to impose mandatory minimum sentences are unjust and bad policy.

Pro-Death Penalty.com
www.prodeathpenalty.com
This organization provides information and resources that support the death penalty.

The Innocence Project
www.innocenceproject.org/
This nonprofit legal clinic and criminal justice resource center includes different kinds of information related to wrongful convictions. For example, you can learn about eyewitness identification—the single largest source of information contributing to wrongful convictions. Visit the Web site to see if your state engaged in any projects dedicated to the release of wrongfully convicted inmates.

Suggested Readings

Andrew Ashworth, Julian Roberts, and Andrew Von Hirsh, eds., *Principled Sentencing: Readings on Theory and Policy*, 3rd ed. (Oxford: Hart, 2009).
This collection of essays covers the variety of moral, ethical, and policy issues surrounding sentencing.

Hugo Adam Bedau and Paul G. Cassell, eds., *Debating the Death Penalty: The Experts from Both Sides Make Their Best Case* (New York: Oxford University Press, 2004).
This collection of essays presents the main issues of contention that surround the death penalty along with evidence to support both sides of the argument.

Andrew Welsh-Huggins, *No Winners Here Tonight: Race, Politics, and Geography in One of the Country's Busiest Death Penalty States* (Athens OH: Ohio University Press, 2009).
This book provides a history of the death penalty in the state of Ohio. In reviewing the development of the death penalty the author also raises questions of its fairness.

CHAPTER 11

Overview of Corrections

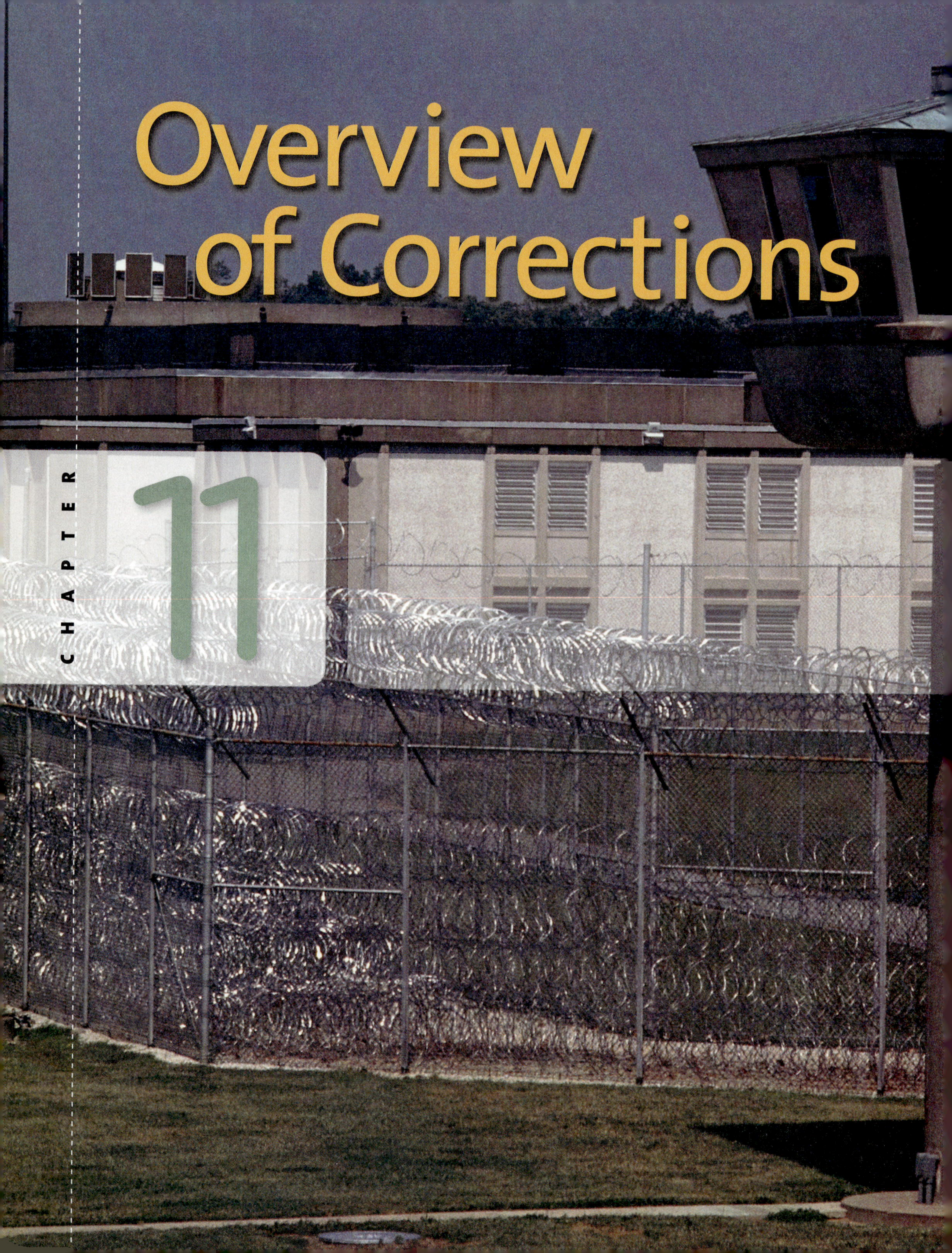

OBSERVE Investigate *Understand*

After reading this chapter, you should be able to:

- Define corrections and describe its role in society.
- Identify precursors to the U.S. prison.
- Contrast the features of the Pennsylvania system with the Auburn system.
- Identify the defining features of reformatories and therapeutic prisons.
- Trace the defining features of industrial prisons.
- Describe and evaluate each of the four major models of corrections.
- Describe the populations found in correctional institutions today.
- Identify the types of victim services found in corrections.
- Examine the extent and nature of privatization of prisons.

Realities and Challenges

Flaws in the System Overwhelm Corrections

Wayne Boatwright Jr., an 18-year-old inmate at a state prison in Georgia, feared being raped by fellow inmates and wrote his grandmother a four-page letter pleading with her to contact prison officials. He said it was the only way the administration would listen to him. Both his grandmother and his father contacted the officials, but in vain.[1] In 2004, Wayne was jumped by three inmates, raped, and strangled to death. Two hours passed before correctional officers even found Boatwright and attempted CPR. In another case, Jay Write, an inmate in California, died in prison of medical neglect because he did not receive necessary heart medication.

These are just two of many documented cases highlighted by the Commission on Safety and Abuse in America's Prisons. The commission's report alleged that violence, overcrowding, and inappropriate use of segregation took place in prisons and that the prisons were releasing inmates who were more violent after serving time than when they were first incarcerated.[2] In the words of Michael Buie, an inmate in a Kansas prison: "I know prison is for punishment, but would you put a pit bull in a cage and poke him with a stick and let him out in a classroom full of kids? . . . That's the same thing you're doing to inmates."[3]

The reality of the U.S. corrections system is that it is huge, expensive to run, and laden with problems. Some of these problems are violence, inadequate medical and mental health care, overcrowding, lack of meaningful and productive inmate activities, inappropriate segregation, and dehumanization.[4] Moreover, what happens behind bars does not stay behind bars. About 95 percent of inmates get sent back into the community, and these offenders bring their prison experiences to the streets when they are released.[5] The challenge for the corrections system is to institute the right blend of punishment and rehabilitation that will, in fact, "correct" offenders and safely return them to society.

This chapter discusses a range of options for correcting inmates. We begin by defining corrections and then examining the origins of corrections. We trace the major stages in prison development in the United States and explore the major models of corrections. We then turn our attention to the populations who are under the supervision of corrections. We take a close look at the victim's involvement in corrections and end the chapter by discussing the development of privately owned and operated prisons.

institutional corrections
Incarceration in jails and prisons.

community corrections
Court-imposed programs and sanctions that allow offenders to serve their sentences within the community instead of in jail or prison.

rehabilitation
Changing an individual from an offender into someone who is law-abiding.

DEFINING CORRECTIONS

The term *corrections*, as used today, denotes society's efforts to punish and treat those who break the law and thereby protect the public. These efforts take the form of programs, services, and facilities that deal with offenders after they enter the criminal justice system. Local, state, federal, and private agencies manage the custody and treatment of convicted adult and juvenile offenders in the system. Correctional programs are divided into two categories. **Institutional corrections** refers to incarceration in jails and prisons, and other types of secure confinement programs; **community corrections** refers to probation, parole, and other programs that supervise offenders within the community. The roots of today's institutional programs date back to ancient times. Practices we now associate with community corrections are a relatively recent departure from the traditional reliance on incarceration as the only means to correct offenders. (Chapters 12 and 13 address institutional and community corrections, respectively.)

Depending on the context, "to correct" means to make right, rectify, make amends for, chastise, compensate, or treat a defect. As it relates to criminals, the term *corrections* came into use in the United States around the turn of the twentieth century, reflecting a widely held belief that the corrections system would transform offenders into law-abiding citizens. This has never been a universally accepted belief. For centuries, society dealt with crime and criminal activity by punishment alone. Punishment was seen as both a form of retribution (or revenge) and a deterrent to scare people into not committing crimes. Severe punishments and fear of being caught were thought to be the only way to control crime. The field of corrections subsequently moved from the philosophy of punishment to the philosophy of **rehabilitation**, changing an individual from an offender into someone who is law-abiding. However, in recent decades there has once again been an increased reliance on incarceration and punishment.[6]

Punishment and rehabilitation are two very different methods of dealing with offenders, and each is based on a different philosophy. The punishment philosophy holds that offenders must pay for their crimes and serve as a deterrent for other would-be criminals. The rehabilitation philosophy holds that offenders can and should be helped to change and become productive members of the community. Some people question whether these two approaches are compatible within the same institution.[7]

Punishment was long thought to be a deterrent to crime. For example, prior to 1808, the penalty for pickpocketing in England was death by hanging. The harsh penalty seemed to be necessary to curtail this very prevalent activity. It was a common belief that the harsher the penalty, the greater the chance of reducing the crime. To make certain that the hanging would have the desired deterrent effect, the hangings were held as a public event, usually in the town square.[8] These gatherings were huge affairs, with a festive atmosphere and townsfolk coming from all the surrounding villages to witness the spectacle. The irony is that the highest rates of pickpocketing activity occurred at these crowded public events. It was not the degree of harshness of the punishment that determined the criminal activity but the fact that the probability of getting caught was low.

If we are to believe that harsh penalties reduce crime, we must assume that potential criminals weigh the benefit and cost before committing a crime. But criminals usually act impulsively and seem unconcerned with the future or the threat of possible future punishment.[9] A very high percentage of active criminals do not perceive any risk of being caught and therefore give no thought to the punishments for their crimes.[10]

MYTH/REALITY

MYTH: If correctional sanctions are severe enough, people will think twice about committing crimes.

REALITY: Increasingly harsh correctional sanctions do not necessarily reduce crime or recidivism.[11]

Preview

▼ Medieval Punishments

Devices used to torture and extract confessions from accused offenders were sometimes very elaborate.

▲ Guards in prison towers are armed with deadly weapons they can use to prevent inmates from escaping.

recidivism
The habitual relapse into criminal behavior.

Source Connection
REHABILITATION IN AMERICA'S PRISONS

http://media.www.thepenn.org/media/storage/paper930/news/2007/02/16/Opinion/Is.Rehabilitation.Possible.In.Americas.Prisons-2725710.shtml

For one view on rehabilitation, read "Is Rehabilitation Possible in America's Prisons?" by Robert L. Hulbrook.

workhouse
An institution that held jobless vagrants, debtors, and sometimes serious criminals.

Harsher sanctions do not necessarily deter crime and **recidivism** (habitual relapse into criminal behavior), they actually may have the opposite effect of encouraging recidivism.[12] A 2006 Canadian bill introduced in Parliament noted that in Canada harsher penalties do not reduce crime.[13] A 2003 study of more than 2,300 adolescents found that those prosecuted in harsh criminal courts were more likely to be rearrested more quickly and more frequently for violent, property, and weapons offenses than the juveniles prosecuted in more lenient juvenile courts. Adolescents prosecuted in juvenile courts were more likely to be rearrested for drug offenses.[14] Overall, harsher punishments did not result in improved public safety.[15] Researchers who have studied punishment believe that the motive for harsh punishment is not deterrence but retribution.[16]

ORIGINS OF CORRECTIONS

The practices of contemporary corrections have deep roots in early forms of punishment throughout the world. Before the use of imprisonment, early punishments were not only harsh but often gruesome. The most common punishments were execution and public corporal punishments such as flogging, branding, and mutilation.

Early Forms of Confinement

An early form of imprisonment was practiced in England during the reign of William the Conqueror (1027–1087). Before the establishment of the jail as an institution, those who broke laws were sometimes confined in dedicated sections of estates of private landowners until it was time to impose the punishment. As time passed, offenders, the mentally ill, and other people deemed undesirable by the government were confined in mines, ships, sulfur pits, stone quarries, ship ruins ("hulks"), and dungeons.[17] In the thirteenth century, the church throughout Europe confined offenders in cells within monasteries to serve years of solitary penance, foreshadowing the use of isolation to "correct" disobedience.

A corrections solution known as the "plague town" arose in Europe during the fourteenth century. Originally intended as a means to confine people in communities infected by the bubonic plague, the organization of these towns anticipated the defining features of later prisons: isolation, organized surveillance, custodial maintenance, regimentation, prayer, and penance.[18] Another punishment option for those who were not sentenced to immediate death or torture during the late 1400s and 1500s, a time when explorers needed laborers to row their ships, was confinement of condemned criminals on galleys. This practice was known as galley slavery. The offenders were chained to their oars on ships, often without protection from the elements, with minimal food and water, and forced to work until their deaths.[19]

The Workhouse

Another stage in the development of the modern prison system began in the sixteenth century when Holland and England developed the first workhouses, also known as houses of correction and houses of compulsory reformation.[20] The **workhouse** held a mixture of people: jobless vagrants, debtors, and sometimes serious criminals. The first workhouse was established in 1552 by King Edward VI of England in Bridewell Castle, London.

Being admitted to a workhouse was a mortifying and humiliating experience. Men, women, and children were often segregated, causing families to be split up, and some were never brought back together again. When people entered a workhouse, their personal possessions were taken away. They were stripped, searched, cleaned, shorn, issued workhouse clothing, closely confined with others, and forced to work. They were counted regularly, fed poorly, and required to get up early and go to bed early.[21] Paupers were confined until they could pay off their debts.

The workhouses did take vagrants off the streets and offer employment to those who did not have jobs. They were an approach to reform that quickly spread throughout

Britain and other European countries. By the late seventeenth century, workhouses were used to house a broader range of criminals and became widespread in England.[22]

Transportation

Workhouses provided a long-term strategy for detaining the poor and homeless, but European nations were faced with another problem: the growing ranks of criminals throughout society. One solution that quickly became institutionalized was **transportation**, the export of criminals to other lands. In the eighteenth century, the British practice of banishing criminals led to the establishment of foreign penal colonies.[23] Transportation was popular because of growing opposition to the death penalty for all but the most serious offenses, lack of local facilities to imprison offenders, and the need for a labor force to colonize new lands. Convicts were shipped to the British colonies of America, Australia, Tasmania (currently the southernmost island state of Australia), and New Zealand.[24]

transportation
The export of criminals to other lands to complete their sentences.

By 1776, as many as 2,000 criminals per year were being transported from Britain to the American colonies. These criminals were not placed in penal colonies but were sold as servants to private individuals, a practice known as **indentured servitude**. Indentured servants worked for their masters until the term of servitude was complete. The masters had control over every aspect of the servants' lives. Many of the transported convicts were guilty of only minor offenses, such as robbery or shoplifting.[25]

indentured servitude
The practice of selling criminals as servants to private individuals instead of sentencing them to penal colonies.

Between 1787 and 1867, approximately 160,000 convicts were transported to Australia and New South Wales from Britain and Ireland.[26] The French transported more than 100,000 offenders to penal colonies in French Guiana and New Caledonia beginning in 1852 and continuing doing so well into the twentieth century.[27]

Life in penal colonies was brutal. Gallows were prominently displayed; criminals ate, slept, and worked in irons; the whip, gag, solitary confinement, and other forms of torture were used regularly; and subservience was required of all criminals all the time.[28] For example, Charles Anderson, age 18, was sentenced to 7 years transportation to a penal colony in Australia for breaking into some shops in England. The following provides an illustration of what happened after he tried to escape:

> Recaptured, he received 100 lashes and, on being returned to Goat Island, another 100, and was ordered to wear irons for twelve months. During that twelve months he received in all 1,200 lashes for the most trivial offences, such as looking up from his work. He escaped again, and this time was sentenced to 200 lashes, to which 100 more lashes were added by a sentence which directed as well that he be chained to a rock for two years. He was put in irons, and attached to the rock by a chain twenty-one feet long. A hollow in the rock served him for a bed, and at night a wooden lid, perforated with holes for air, was put over him and locked into position. His food was pushed into his eating vessel on a pole. Other prisoners were forbidden to speak or approach him under penalty of 100 lashes. His wounds became maggot-infested but he was refused water with which to bathe them.[29]

hulks
Abandoned ships that functioned as enormous holding blocks within which offenders were chained.

A Global View on the next page provides a look at the practice of transportation today and the evolution of penal colonies. Isla Maria is a contemporary Mexican penal colony that embodies the correctional goals of rehabilitation and reform.

Hulks

With the coming of the American Revolution, England could no longer export its convicted criminals to the American colonies. Instead, they used abandoned ships, docked in British harbors, to house prisoners. These abandoned ships, called **hulks**, were reconfigured as enormous holding blocks in which offenders were chained. These floating dungeons perpetually stank, and a gallows was often found at the front of the

▼ Prison Hulk

In England during the 1700s persons convicted of crimes were incarcerated on the abandoned hulks of ships.

A Global View

The Legacy of Penal Transportation and Isla Maria

For the most part, penal colonies are a thing of past. One exception to the rule is the unique modern-day prison on Isla Maria in the Pacific Ocean, off Mexico's coast. In the early 1900s, it held the Mexican prisoners who were sentenced to a life of hard labor in the colony. In sharp contrast to those times, the corrections philosophy behind today's Isla Maria seeks to keep families and loved ones together during an inmate's period of incarceration.

Of the 3,000 male prison inmates on Isla Maria today, most have been sentenced for drug trafficking. The prison is humane and has no cells or bars; the 36 correctional officers carry no guns, and inmates, who are called "colonists," wear regular clothing. While prisoners complete their sentences—which are often lengthy—their families can choose to live with them in houses and communities similar to those in many small Mexican towns. There are about 600 children on the island, and they go to public schools. Some prisoners' families believe that their prison homes are safer and more comfortable than the homes they left behind.

The correctional philosophy of Isla Maria is one of humane rehabilitation and reform. To this end, the Mexican government provides a setting that closely approximates a normal community. In comparison to a typical prison, Isla Maria is expensive to operate. The cost of incarcerating a prisoner at Isla Maria is about three times higher than that in other Mexican prisons. This is largely due to the cost of transporting goods to and from the island and the need to provide services for both prisoners and their families. The experiences of the inmates are poles apart from the experiences of those who were transported to Australia, the American colonies, and French Guiana. The Isla Maria prisoners are closely connected to their families throughout their incarceration, a support necessary for successful rehabilitation.

Observe Investigate Understand

- **Do you think the United States would benefit from exploring the use of prison colonies such as Isla Maria? What factors would contribute to its success or failure?**
- **How does Isla Maria contrast with what you know of the U.S. military penal colony at Guantánamo Bay in Cuba?**
- **What are the pros and cons of including family members in the penal colony? Do the benefits outweigh the disadvantages?**

SOURCES: Stephen A. Toth, *Beyond Papillon: The French Overseas Penal Colonies, 1854–1952* (Lincoln: University of Nebraska Press, 2006); Mary Jordan, "Convicts Are Condemned to a Paradise in Mexico," *Washington Post Foreign Service*, February 3, 2002, sec. A22; American Correctional Association, *The Mexican Penal Colony at Islas Maria* (College Park, MD: American Correctional Association, 1981).

Source Connection
PRISON HULKS

www.portcities.org.uk/london/server/show/ConNarrative.56/chapterId/418/Prison-hulks-on-the-River-Thames.html

Read "Prison Hulks on the River Thames" to learn more about early confinement of prisoners.

vessel.[30] Food was scarce and frequently contaminated with mold and insects. Unsanitary conditions promoted the spread of disease. The life expectancy of prisoners held in such conditions was short. This practice continued for approximately 15 years until Britain began transporting convicts to Australia. Even though viewed at the time as a desperate stopgap measure, the confinement of prisoners to hulks was a forerunner of the modern prison in the use of incarceration as punishment.

Colonial Jails

Historically, the term *jail* comes from the old English term *gaol*—a place of imprisonment. We can trace jails as a local form of institutional corrections back to at least 1166 in England. Henry II ordered the construction of facilities to detain offenders awaiting trial or to carry out their sentence—typically torture, mutilation, or execution.

Prior to the development of prisons in the United States, most local jail facilities were ordinary houses—literally, jail-houses—without cells where suspects were given rooms while awaiting trial. Early jail keepers were civilian citizens or sheriffs. Many were abusive and often took bribes from inmates and their families for extra money to feed, clothe, and care for prisoners' needs. All prisoners were confined together, regardless of sex, age, or the nature of the crimes of which they were accused. As the number of offenders grew, overcrowding, poor sanitation, disease, and escape attempts were commonplace.

By the time of the American Revolution, local jails in the colonies were largely used as holding pens for suspected thieves, debtors, and murderers. Most of those confined could anticipate some form of physical, or corporal, punishment, such as whipping or being held in wooden stocks in public arenas, or execution (capital punishment). English common law (the basis for the U.S. legal system) specified that hundreds of crimes be punished in these ways.[31]

Debtors who were confined in jail were freed during the day so they could work to pay off their debts, but they had to return at night. Once convicted, debtors had difficulty regaining their freedom because their forced labor was needed in the workforce. In 1785, half the persons sentenced to jail in Philadelphia were debtors. Although most debts were small, even those found not guilty were required to pay court fees before being released. This was often more than they could afford, and release from custody was not possible until all debts and fees were paid.[32]

In the American colony of Pennsylvania, the Quakers were dominant. They did not believe in harsh punishment, torture, or, in most cases, death for wrongdoers. Instead, they believed in reform. In 1682, under the leadership of William Penn, the Quakers developed a new penal code based on advanced European ideas and humanitarian thought. Penn's code, known as the "Great Law," used imprisonment as the major penalty for offenses previously punished by torture, mutilation, and death.[33] In the next section, we turn our attention to how the Quakers in Pennsylvania influenced the way prisoners were confined in the first U.S. prisons.

▲ Punishments during colonial times were public spectacles.

HISTORY OF CORRECTIONS IN THE UNITED STATES

Following the Revolution, some prisons were built solely as confinement facilities. Philosophically, these prisons were rooted in the punishment model. Prison administrators did not believe they could change the behavior of a criminal in any way, so they made no pretense of reforming or rehabilitating offenders. The prisons were intended only as alternatives to capital punishment and to deter offenders and others from committing future crimes. One such institution was the Newgate Prison in Connecticut, basically a large hole in the ground where inmates lived like lepers without any supervision or care.[34] The hole was a remnant of an old copper mine that became a prison in 1773.[35]

The Pennsylvania System and the Penitentiary

As a reaction to the harsh and dehumanizing conditions of prisons in the New World, the Quakers in Pennsylvania wanted to reform the system. They believed in the rehabilitation model: in the right circumstances, offenders could be changed. Pennsylvania was established by the Quakers as a colony with a constitution that guaranteed freedom of religion and a new penal code. They were reformers and opposed corporal and capital punishment.[36] In 1787 a group of Quakers formed the Philadelphia Society for the Alleviation of the Miseries of the Public Prisons. The Society sought to remove cruelty from the institutional process. The Quakers believed that criminals could be reformed if they were isolated and segregated in complete silence, giving them time to reflect on their crimes and repent.

Walnut Street Jail
The first public institution to specifically use imprisonment as the primary method of reforming offenders.

As a result of pressure from the Quakers and the Society, the **Walnut Street Jail** in Philadelphia opened a special wing in 1790.[37] This wing was the first public institution to

▲ The first U.S. prisons were harsh, monolithic environments.

penitentiary
Term the Quakers coined from the word *penitent*—referring to a residence where offenders could be sorrowful for their wrongdoings.

Pennsylvania system
A system of prison administration in which inmates lived in solitary confinement, total silence, and religious penitence as the way to prevent future criminal behavior.

use imprisonment as the primary method of reforming offenders.[38] A crude attempt to classify prisoners tried to ensure that women, vagrants, capital offenders, and debtors did not intermingle.[39] Many consider the Walnut Street Jail to be the first **penitentiary**, a term the Quakers coined from the word "penitent"—meaning sorrowful for one's sins or wrongdoings. Labor was seen as necessary, not for reform or training but as a way for the state to be reimbursed for the cost of operating the jail. Isolation and solitude, it was thought, led to offender reform. Although the Walnut Street Jail seemed successful in its first decade, this experiment failed primarily due to overcrowding. In 1817 the Philadelphia Society began to plan to build a new prison system in Pennsylvania.[40]

A penitentiary was specifically designed to reform inmates according to the principles of absolute solitary segregation, resulting in the Western Penitentiary in the outskirts of Pittsburgh, built in 1826. This was followed in 1829 by the Eastern State Penitentiary in Philadelphia (also called the Cherry Hill Penitentiary). The architecture of these facilities called for small, self-contained solitary cells in which inmates slept, worked, and ate. New inmates were taken blindfolded to their cells and given a Bible. They saw only their keepers and were not allowed to communicate with one another. Nor could they leave their cells, except under unusual circumstances, until their entire sentences were completed. This system is now called the **Pennsylvania system**, the Philadelphia system, or the solitary system.

The psychological toll of this near-total isolation, however, caused mental disorder in some of the prisoners. In his 1842 visit to the United States, English novelist Charles Dickens described the Pennsylvania system and the effects of using solitary confinement on the mind and spirit of inmates. Although he believed the prisons he visited were originally developed to reform criminals into law-abiding citizens, he saw the system as going astray:

> I am persuaded that those who devised this system of Prison Discipline, and those benevolent gentlemen who carry it into execution do not know what they are doing. I believe that very few men are capable of estimating the immense amount of torture and agony which this dreadful punishment, prolonged for years, inflicts upon the sufferers; . . . [and] I am only the more convinced that there is a depth of terrible endurance in it which none but the sufferers themselves can fathom, and which no man has a right to inflict upon his fellow-creature. I hold this slow and daily tampering with the mysteries of the brain to be immeasurably worse than any torture of the body.[41]

Contemporary research bears out Dickens's concerns and criticisms. Damage to prisoners held in solitary confinement has been well documented (see Chapter 12).[42]

The Auburn System

Auburn system
A system of prison administration in which prisoners were isolated in cells at night but allowed to congregate during the day for work duty and meals, but in total silence.

In New York City's Newgate Prison, which opened in 1797, inmates worked in groups and were confined in apartment-like spaces during the night. This prison became so severely overcrowded that by 1809 the governor was forced to pardon prisoners just to make room for new inmates. The legislature authorized the building of a new prison in the interior of New York State. Auburn State Prison, established in 1816, became the model of the **Auburn system** of prison administration.[43]

Both the Pennsylvania and the Auburn systems were based on reformation, and both relied on completely separate confinement of inmates.[44] The basic philosophy of each system was noncommunication.[45] This practice was said to reduce "contamination" from other inmates.[46] But the Auburn system differed from the Pennsylvania system in one key way. Once the Pennsylvania inmates were taken to their cells, they never encountered another human being other than the official who brought them their food until the day they were released. They were totally and completely isolated. In the Auburn prison system, although isolated in cells at night, the prisoners were allowed to congregate, in silence, during the day for work duty and meals. Accordingly, the Auburn system came to be known as the congregate, or silent, system.

Prisoners at the State Prison at Auburn.

◀ Auburn Prison

Prisoners move in lockstep at Auburn Prison.

The buildings in Auburn featured blocks of small individual cells placed back to back and reaching five tiers high, a design cheaper to build than the Pennsylvania prisons. Auburn also was more efficient in guarding and administrating congregate labor.[47] The officials believed severe discipline would reform the inmates under their care. When they were out of their cells and working together, inmates were forbidden to exchange words or even glances with one another. Prisoners wore striped suits, walked in lockstep to allow guards tight control while moving groups of inmates, and were frequently subjected to corporal punishment such as beatings and floggings.[48] Although Pennsylvania had done away with corporal punishment, in Auburn it became the method to maintain strict discipline.[49]

Between 1830 and 1850 there was much debate over which was the better system. During this period, prison development and the need for reform received a great deal of attention, both in the United Stated and in Europe. Many European prisons came to adopt the solitary Pennsylvania system, believing it to be more humane. The Auburn system seemed too harsh and impersonal. The Europeans also objected to the increasing use of corporal punishment in the Auburn system.

Most prisons in the United States, on the other hand, came to be modeled on the congregate Auburn system—not because of its correctional philosophy but for economic reasons. The Pennsylvania system needed cells large enough to accommodate an inmate 24 hours a day. Such cells were expensive to build and maintain, compared with the Auburn system cells, used only at night for sleeping. Furthermore, the small amount of money from the sale of handicrafts made by prisoners in their cells in Pennsylvania did not yield enough income to support the prison. By contrast, the Auburn architecture with back-to-back cells was more cost-effective, and the inmates who congregated for work generated considerable income for the prison.

An important aspect of life in the Auburn system was the work system. Essentially, a factory within the prison used convict labor to make goods for the private sector. An outside business person paid the prison—not the working inmate—a daily rate in accordance with the number of inmates doing work. A convict leasing system evolved, and soon other prisons in New York adopted the Auburn model.[50] Revenues for the prison were a foremost concern; the welfare and reformation of the prisoner was of secondary importance. The Auburn model dominated the U.S. prison system until the early 1900s.

In reality, neither the Auburn nor the Pennsylvania system met the hopes of those who initially attempted to reform the correctional system. Prisons soon became overcrowded, and correctional officers had increasing difficulty maintaining control over inmates, leaving early reformation ideals to fall by the wayside.

The Reformatory System

By the 1860s every state but Pennsylvania had adopted the congregate system. By that time, overcrowding, cruel treatment, and corruption undermined the effectiveness of many established penitentiaries in the United States. Two and three prisoners were housed in cells designed for one, and brutal punishments were again a feature of incarceration. Money earned by inmates would often end up in the pockets of administrators. The original philosophy of these prisons—noncommunication—faded away, and the prisons degenerated into institutions that used cruel regulations to maximize the productivity of their prison industries.[51]

Life at Auburn, for example, was a living hell. "Within an atmosphere of repression, humiliation and gloomy silence, the Auburn convict performed an incessantly monotonous round of activity."[52] Sing-Sing Prison, in New York, modeled after Auburn, was even worse. Legislative investigations found that some guards had wrapped their whips with wire; others had used them on the genitals of inmates, often without reason.[53] From such abuses a movement for reform emerged.

In 1870, the New York Prison Association issued a highly critical report on penal methods and recommended specific reforms. In the belief that the purpose of a prison should be to reform not to punish, the association argued that an inmate's sentence should be based on how well reform is progressing. Thus, a primary recommendation was a call for indeterminate sentences—effectively telling prisons that rehabilitation was to be at the forefront of their mission, and that the sentence was in the hands of the individual prisoner. Good behavior would bring early release.

Elmira Reformatory
A New York reformatory that emphasized rehabilitation rather than punishment.

New York's **Elmira Reformatory**, built in 1876 and guided by Zebulon Brockway as its superintendent, was based on principles of rehabilitation. Elmira called itself a reformatory to underscore its emphasis on reform rather than punishment. Reformatories rejected the nineteenth-century philosophies of silence, obedience, and labor. Instead they called for rehabilitation through education, indeterminate sentences with maximum terms, and the opportunity for parole. Elmira's philosophy was so popular many believed it would become the dominant model for prisons in the United States. Education, central to the reform program, would include "general subjects, sports, religion and military drill."[54]

While former prisons focused on punishment, the new model would emphasize reformation through education; while correctional officers in the old prisons just needed to be tough and firm, the new system called for specific training; while old-style prison cells were small, the reformatory called for larger cells, state inspections, and preparations for release. In addition, all physical punishments were to be banned.[55] These ideas became so popular that the principles of the reformatory movement soon spread throughout the country, but without many of the practices necessary to make them work. For example, every state adopted the practice of classifying prisons and inmates to fit them to individualized programs, but most institutions did little to differentiate these inmates and put them into specific rehabilitation programs.[56]

By the early twentieth century, many states had built institutions they called reformatories, although some were reformatories in name only.[57] Most U.S. prisons, including those associated with the reformatory approach, were no more than "custodial warehouse[s] for social refuse."[58] Ultimately, the reformatory model fell from grace. Trained personnel to implement the educational and classification systems were scarce,[59] and the programs that were offered affected only a small portion of the prison population.[60]

The reformatory movement had greater impact in Europe. In 1897 Sir Evelyn Ruggles-Brise came to the United States to study the Elmira reformatory and to obtain ideas about reforming the English prison system. On his return to England he established the Borstal system, incorporating the principles of the reformatory model and targeting offenders ages 16 to 21.[61] Ultimately, the Borstal system had a greater impact on corrections and the treatment of juveniles than the reformatory movement that inspired it.[62]

Back in America, however, reformatories did not meet with lasting success, primarily due to overcrowding. Within two decades of its construction, Elmira had more than twice the number of inmates it was designed to house, making effective rehabilitation programs

◀ **Prison Metal Shop**

Inmates produce license plates and other items in prison metal shops.

impractical. Moreover, Elmira's program was intended for youthful, first-time offenders, but the institution incarcerated many older and hardened offenders—one-third of whom were repeat offenders. The reformatory movement did not live up to its billing.[63]

The Industrial Prison System

In the course of correctional history there is a pendulum effect. Over time the pendulum swings back and forth between rehabilitation and punishment. Following the failure of the reformatory movement, the pendulum swung back to punishment and away from treatment and rehabilitation.

The phenomenon of prison industry returned at the beginning of the twentieth century. Using strict discipline and regimentation, prison administrators capitalized on the availability of free inmate labor to subsidize the cost of running the institution. Goods made by prisoners were sold on the open market, outside the walls of the penitentiary.[64] In these **industrial prisons**, or prison factories, attention was focused on creating a productive work environment rather than rehabilitating prisoners. The need to create order to maximize productivity made conditions in prisons more oppressive and violent.[65] Much of the rationale for the industrial prison system was to use inmate labor to reduce the prison's costs.[66]

industrial prisons
Prison factories where the focus was on creating a productive work environment rather than the rehabilitation or reform of prisoners.

In the southern states, where Blacks made up more than 75 percent of the convicts, the practice of the industrial prison became little more than institutionalized slavery. States leased prisoners to private parties outside the prison who frequently misused them. Prisoners were organized into chain gangs to work on roads and used as a labor force on large farms and plantations. The buildings that housed prisoners were little more than small cages.[67] What about the Victim? on the next page illustrates how the criminal justice system was manipulated after the emancipation of slaves to try to maintain control over Black inmates.

Prison labor served to meet the institution's needs and gave little back to the inmate other than the most rudimentary vocational training. Eventually, the output of prison factories was so successful that labor unions complained about unfair competition. Federal legislation brought the widespread use of prison labor to an end in the 1930s.[68] In 1979 Congress relaxed these restrictions somewhat through the Percy Amendment. This act allowed private companies to employ prisoners under specific conditions.[69]

The Therapeutic Prison

With the popularity of psychology and psychoanalysis growing in the United States during the twentieth century, the concept of treatment caught the attention of prison reformers.

What about the Victim?

The Criminal Justice System, Slaves, and "Free" Blacks in the South

Laws in southern slave states offered protection—though minimal—to slaves before the Civil War. Slaves were not to be killed or cruelly treated, but these laws were usually ineffective. When cruelty occurred, a slave had virtually no legal recourse. No slave in the United States could testify against his master. In fact, no slave was allowed to testify against any White person. Because most witnesses of such cruelty were likely to be Black, the criminal justice system was clearly stacked against any such prosecution.

Only when the crimes were egregious and so public they could not be concealed would a case of cruelty or murder of a Black come to a court's attention. Although the murder of a Black slave was nowhere near on par with the murder of a White person, killing a slave in North Carolina could yield 1 year imprisonment and also require that the murderer pay the owner for the value of that slave. There were a few instances when a White accused of the murder of a Black resulted in a conviction. In these cases, the accused was from the poorest class. Although rare, such cases reinforced the southern slaveholders' belief that they were dispensing equal justice.

After the Civil War, laws in southern states specifically targeted Blacks to keep the slave culture alive. Blacks in the South could be arrested on arbitrary grounds (usually vagrancy), fined, and when they could not pay, sold as forced labor to anyone willing to pay the fine. The Black Codes, as they were known, were thus used to bind Black workers to the land as (underpaid) contract workers. The laws also protected southern landowners who compelled Blacks into unpaid and involuntary servitude. These criminal codes served to enforce the low status of Blacks, resulting in practices not much better than slavery. Forced labor was used for farming or for heavy labor such as mining, railroad work, building river levees, and lumber camps.

It was also a crime for a Black to quit his job if he was "under contract." Leaving a job led to additional fines, forced return, and harsh physical punishments. The laborers were often beaten and physically abused. Basically this was a system of years of forced involuntary servitude for these victims, from which many could not escape by any means other than death. As contract convict labor became less common, forced labor in the form of chain gangs emerged as its replacement. Chain gang life was brutal and the mortality rate high. Not surprisingly, the majority of convicts on chain gangs were Blacks.

The Black Codes and chain gangs enabled the White population in the South to continue to control Black labor after slavery was abolished. Using the corrections system to victimize former slaves in this way largely mimicked the slavery that had existed earlier.

Observe Investigate Understand

- **How were laws stacked against the prosecution of Whites for offenses against Blacks?**
- **Describe the process by which the Black Codes led to involuntary servitude for Blacks.**
- **Why do you think the majority of convicts on chain gangs were Black?**

SOURCES: Lawrence M. Friedman, *Crime and Punishment in American History* (New York: Basic Books, 1993); Douglas A. Blackmon, *Slavery by Another Name: The Re-Enslavement of Black Americans from the Civil War to World War II* (New York: Doubleday, 2008).

medical model
A viewpoint focusing on mental illness and behavioral problems, such as committing a crime, as diseases.

In corrections, treatment is based on the **medical model**. According to this perspective, people, if not healthy, are ill. This model was gradually popularized in the nineteenth century, when mental illness and behavioral problems began to be viewed as diseases. However, this view was not implemented in the corrections field until the late 1920s, when inmates came to be viewed as mostly "sick" individuals in need of treatment. Accordingly,

◀ Attica Prison Riot

Prison riots frequently result in violence.

criminals were "mad," as in mentally ill, rather than "bad." The "symptoms" of their disorders were their crimes, and it was believed that their condition was treatable.

The therapeutic prison gained momentum in the 1930s, giving rise to a widespread practice of diagnosing and classifying inmates. This practice established a place for psychologists and psychiatrists in U.S. prisons. Group therapy (dealing with offenders in groups rather than individually), behavior therapy (using rewards and punishments to change behavior), and aversion therapy (using noxious or painful stimuli to remove unacceptable behaviors) were just a few of the many treatment approaches to grow out of the therapeutic movement. By the mid-1960s, therapeutic programs had reached the height of their popularity in U.S. prisons.

As the 1960s came to a close, however, doubts were raised about the effectiveness of treatment programs to treat and "cure" offenders. The rehabilitative ideal lost favor with both the public and correctional administrators. At the same time, the rapidly growing prison population diverted existing resources to institutional management, and funding for treatment programs faded from prison budgets.[70] Following several disturbing and brutal prison riots in the United States during the 1970s and 1980s, public opinion turned further away from the plight of prisoners, and calls for more punitive policies came to replace what had been widespread support for treatment programs.

The death knell to the rehabilitative ideal in U.S. prisons came with the **1974 Martinson report**. Sociologist Robert Martinson, along with colleagues Douglas Lipton and Judith Wilks, analyzed published studies on the therapeutic effectiveness of more than 200 treatment programs. In looking at this broad picture, Martinson concluded, "with few and isolated exceptions, the rehabilitative efforts that have been reported so far have had no appreciable effect on recidivism." He found that some treatments were effective for some kinds of inmates. His conclusions, however, came to be summarily reduced to "nothing works"—although Martinson himself never wrote this.[71]

1974 Martinson report
Indicated that rehabilitative efforts, for the most part, have had little to no effect on recidivism.

The unfortunate mantra of "nothing works" gave support once again to those who argued that what criminals needed was not treatment but punishment. The enormous amount of negative spin around the Martinson report dealt a severe blow to funding for correctional treatment programs. Many researchers, including Martinson himself, attempted to correct the misunderstandings surrounding the 1974 study, but the damage was done.[72] Correctional rehabilitation programming has not recovered. It is estimated that less than $100 a year is spent on rehabilitation programs for each U.S. prisoner. Furthermore, less than 5 percent of the inmate population has access to any treatment

a Case in Point

Drug Treatment versus Incarceration

Overcrowding is a major problem in managing jails and prisons. Sometimes new laws can contribute to prison overcrowding by creating a new zeal for arresting and jailing certain kinds of offenders. For example, the federal government launched its "war on drugs" in 1982. This expanded law enforcement effort shifted emphasis away from treatment for drug offenders to punishing them. The war on drugs resulted in new and harsher statutes and mandatory sentencing for many offenders accused of using—not even selling—drugs. As a result, incarceration rates of drug offenders rose sharply in the United States. Criminologists and addiction specialists suggested that mandating treatment programs instead of incarceration would reduce jail and prison populations. California voters agreed in 2000 when they passed Proposition 36, allowing nonviolent drug offenders to receive treatment instead of incarceration.

Addicted individuals frequently use drugs during and after drug treatment. Relapse is a characteristic of the disease of addiction and is expected with all drug treatment programs. The California Society of Addiction Medicine concluded in a 2007 report, however, that Proposition 36 successfully reduced drug incarceration rates. This study also reported that flash incarceration, or short-term incarceration of offenders who relapse, does not work and should not be used. The California Medical Association supported this position, arguing that punishment is ineffective and inappropriate for relapses. Nonetheless, the California legislature approved flash incarceration in 2006 to be coupled with drug treatment Proposition 36 programs.

In 2008, California's Nonviolent Offender Rehabilitation Act (NORA) attempted to further alleviate the state's prison overcrowding crisis by introducing Proposition 5 to the voters. Proposition 5 would significantly increase individualized treatment and rehabilitation programs for nonviolent offenders, provide for more rehabilitation and less incarceration, increase accountability for treatment programs, and shorten parole for drug offenses. The impact would be to increase the costs of treatment but reduce the costs of prison. Opponents labeled Proposition 5 a drug dealer's bill of rights, and one that would allow addicted people to continue to use drugs while in treatment. Proponents of Proposition 5 viewed its defeat as the end of one of the boldest prison and sentencing reforms in the United States.

Drug treatment diversion programs might be controversial, but they provide a number of benefits to the criminal justice system. A study by the Justice Policy Institute, a Washington, D.C. prison reform think tank, stated that diversions to treatment programs have substantially reduced incarceration in jails and prisons. The report asserted treatment programs lower crime rates and reduce the need for prison expansion, while reducing overcrowding. It concluded that treatment programs were cost-effective and much less expensive than incarceration in California.

Observe Investigate Understand

- **What do you think of when you hear the term "war on drugs"? Is there a benefit to jailing convicted drug users as well as sellers?**
- **Do you think prison time for nonviolent drug offenders serves as a deterrent to continued drug use?**
- **What are the benefits of drug treatment and rehabilitation programs for the criminal justice system?**

SOURCES: J. Michael Kennedy, "Drug Treatment Program Lowers Jail Population," *Los Angeles Times*, April 13, 2006; "Drug Policy and the Criminal Justice System," The Sentencing Project, 2001, www.sentencingproject.org/Admin/Documents/publications/dp_drugpolicy_cjsystem.pdf (retrieved May 31, 2008); Jason Ziedenberg, "Beyond Bars: Jail Sanctions for Drug-related Offenders Are Harmful and Counterproductive," Justice Policy Institute, August 1, 2007, www.lhc.ca.gov/lhcdir/AOD_Review/ZiedenbergAug07.pdf (retrieved May 31, 2008); "Drug Use Rearrests Up After Prop. 36," *Addiction and Recovery News*, www.dawfarm.org/2007/04/drug-use-rearrests-up-after-prop-36-los.html (retrieved May 31, 2008); Peter Banys, "Recommendations for Improvements to Proposition 36," California Society of Addiction Medicine (CSAM), www.csam-asam.org/pdf/misc/Prop36-2007.pdf (retrieved May 31, 2008); "Proposition 5—In Depth Nonpartisan Analysis: Nonviolent Offender Rehabilitation Act of 2008," League of Women Voters of California Education Fund, November 4, 2008, http://ca.lwv.org/lwvc/edfund/elections/2008nov/id/prop5.html, (retrieved-January 2, 2009); "Prop 5—Nonviolent Drug Offenses: Sentencing,Parole and Rehabilitation, Initiative Statute," *California General Election Official Voter Information Guide*, November 4, 2008, www.voterguide.sos.ca.gov/argu-rebut/argu-rebutt5.htm (retrieved January 3, 2009).

programs.[73] For example, California spends $43,000 on each prisoner annually but only $2,053 on rehabilitation programs. The majority of the remaining money is spent on custody.[74] As you can see from the controversies presented in A Case in Point, California's Proposition 36 drug rehabilitation program legislation has given rise to additional debate about the effectiveness of rehabilitation and punishment.

This brief history of corrections has shown how rehabilitation and punishment have seesawed in prominence over the years in the development of the U.S. corrections system. A brief chronology of selected events in this history is displayed in the table. In the section that follows we look at how prisons today make use of the various historical models of correction we have discussed.

punishment model
A viewpoint that assumes the offender is inherently a bad person and deserves to be placed under correctional authority for punishment.

MODELS OF CORRECTIONS TODAY

The responsibility for administering institutional and community corrections today rests at local, state, and federal levels of government and sometimes in the private sector, as illustrated in Figure 11-1. Jails are local facilities used to hold those awaiting trial and punishment and to incarcerate those convicted of misdemeanor crimes. Prisons are funded by and responsible to the state or federal government and hold those who are sentenced to longer terms. Government entities also contract with private companies to operate private jails.

Whatever the type of facility, corrections has the responsibility of keeping society—and convicted offenders—safe until the offender is, ideally, transformed from a law-violating to a law-abiding member of society. People in the United States also expect corrections to punish, deliver retribution, incapacitate, and rehabilitate offenders, and then integrate them back into society. In recent years, the goal of compensating victims has been added to this list.

Accomplishment of any one of these goals, let alone all, is a monumental challenge. In large measure they represent conflicting philosophies of corrections. In response to these goals, four different operational models have developed for correctional facilities. The punishment model developed first, followed by the crime control model, then the rehabilitation model, and finally the reintegration model. In practice, today's institutions draw from all of these models to achieve results.

Punishment Model

At the core of the **punishment model** of corrections is the assumption that the offender is inherently a bad person and deserves to be placed under correctional authority for punishment. From this perspective, offenders are not seen as individuals with particular problems in need of treatment. For the most part, they are viewed as people who choose to commit crime and should thus be punished. Rehabilitation is irrelevant, except to the extent punishment has rehabilitative potential by instilling fear in an offender, deterring the offender from committing future crimes. Treatment programs are viewed as a waste of resources. Appropriate and timely punishment is thought to be more cost-effective.

Advocates of this model lean toward severe sanctions for offenders. They charge that the criminal justice system is too soft on criminals, compromising true justice, and that retribution should be the primary goal of corrections. They oppose many of the amenities provided by prisons such as television and special recreation programs. These advocates also criticize the use of probation and parole to eliminate or reduce an inmate's sentence of incarceration.

The punishment model uses negative reinforcement such as fines, incarceration, confiscation of property, use of heavy body chain constraints, and isolation cells to mold behavior. This model falls short of its goal, however, because recidivism rates under this system remain high. Research indicates that punishment can temporarily change behavior and make people comply, but these changes are not long-lasting.[75] Furthermore, the punishment model may eventually release antisocial offenders back into society without having had any positive or permanent impact on their behavior. The punishment model is most likely to be found in correctional institutions with high security levels.

RealCrime Tech

ELECTRONIC LOGBOOKS REDUCE METH LABS

Methamphetamine (known as meth) is a highly potent stimulant. It is highly addictive and can produce convulsions, violent behavior, brain aneurysms, and even death. Meth use has become a major problem in the United States. Illegal meth labs can produce the drug from common products found in some cold medications readily available at local pharmacies. The ingredients used to produce another substance are called "precursors." Many states now have laws limiting the quantities of meth precursors that a person can purchase. However, those who want them can easily purchase a large enough supply by going to different pharmacies and acquiring the maximum amount at each.

To combat this practice, some states have begun requiring the use of electronic logbooks. The shopkeeper keeps a record of who buys precursor drugs and how much and requires an ID. The ID is entered on a special Web site by the store clerk, and information comes up to determine whether the cold medication can be sold to the buyer. The state of Arkansas claims meth labs have declined since this system came into use.

SOURCE: Chad Vander Veen, "Halting Meth Abuse," *Government Technology* 21, no. 12 (December 2008): 44–45.

SELECTED EVENTS IN CORRECTIONAL HISTORY

Trends and patterns in the history of corrections.

1000 CE–1300 CE	Secular and church law ordaining harsh punishments for criminals evolved during the Middle Ages.
1556	Bridewell opened for vagrants and the homeless.
1619	Transportation of British convicts to the colonies in North America begins.
1790	Walnut Street Jail—first penitentiary wing is opened.
1816	Auburn Prison is built in New York State.
1826	Western Penitentiary is built in Pittsburgh, Pennsylvania.
1829	Eastern State Penitentiary opens in Philadelphia.
1873	First women's prison, the Indiana Reformatory Institution, opens.
1876–1900	The reformatory movement is strong.
1876	Elmira Reformatory opens.
1900–1930	Industrial prison movement is strong.
1930–1960	The therapeutic prison movement dominates U.S. corrections systems.
1960–1980	The community-based corrections movement is strong.
1980–present	Incarceration movement dominates U.S. corrections systems.

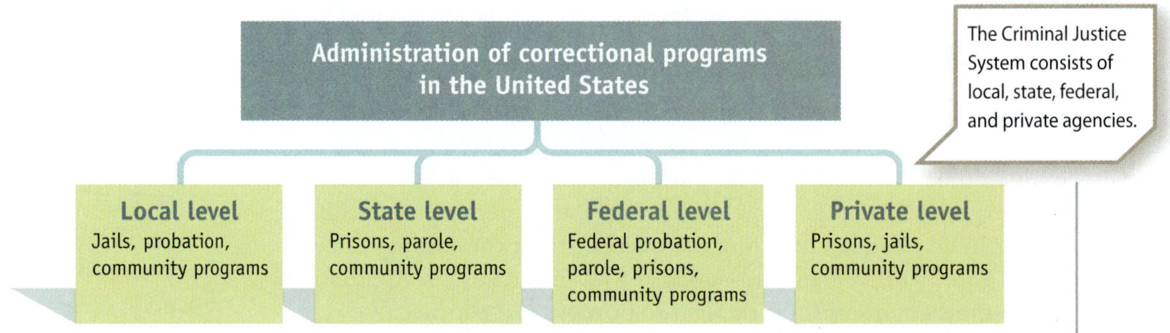

FIGURE 11-1 Administration of Correctional Programs in the United States

Crime Control Model

crime control model
A corrections model that has as its primary goal suppression and containment of the behavior of criminals.

The **crime control model**, an extension of the punishment model, gained momentum in the United States during the early 1980s when prison building surged. Under this model, infliction of harsh punishments on wrongdoers is not the major goal; the primary goal is to suppress and contain the behavior of criminals through incarceration.

This model is used today in medium-, maximum-, and supermaximum-security prisons, where the primary correctional goals are to contain and control inmates. There is little attempt to change prisoners' behaviors, short of making them comply within the walls. Rehabilitation and reform are not the goals. A drawback of the crime control model, like that of the punishment model, is that when prisons release nonrehabilitated offenders back into the community, the streets are often less safe because offenders have not learned prosocial behaviors while incarcerated. Some prisoners even learn more sophisticated crime techniques while being locked up with other offenders. The benefit of this model is that offenders are not on the streets committing crimes during their time of confinement.

The means by which offenders can be incapacitated are many. In the past, these methods included such questionable practices as overmedicating violent criminals to suppress assertive behavior, castrating sex offenders, and execution. However, the most widely accepted and least controversial method of incapacitation is incarceration, the hallmark of the crime control model. As crime rates rose in the 1970s, there were calls to increase the number of correctional facilities and maximize the number of inmates they house; hire more correctional officers and give them greater power over prisoners; reduce the rights of criminals; and push for more punitive sanctions for all kinds of offenders. The clear demand was to remove offenders from the streets so they could no longer victimize

▲ Prisoners are often seen working on highways in chain gangs.

Real Careers

ISAAC TORRES

Work location: Fresno, California

College(s): California State University, Fresno, 2009

Major(s): Criminology with Corrections Option (BS)

Job title: Correctional Officer, Population Management Unit, and Gang Officer, Fresno County Jail

Salary range for job like this: $60,000–$80,000

Time in job: 4 years

Work Responsibilities

My work responsibilities entail monitoring the inflow and outflow of inmates at the jail and ensuring that each inmate is appropriately housed within the facility. My workweek includes three to four 12-hour shifts that begin at 6 p.m. and end at 6 a.m. During each shift I ensure that our inmate count is in compliance with federal guidelines to avoid overcrowding.

My unit is responsible for interviewing all newly processed inmates and assigning them a classification score by points. To do this I review the inmates' criminal history, behavior during any previous stays in the facility, nature of current charges, and any information gathered from them that would affect their safety in the facility. In addition, I respond to any institutional disturbances and investigate the need for housing changes after an incident occurs. As the designated Gang Officer in my unit, I am responsible for the collection of gang information, current trends, institutional gang-related conflicts, and possible threats to the safety and security of staff, inmates, or the facility.

Why Criminal Justice?

I chose to major in criminology because I have been interested in law enforcement since my childhood. Law enforcement gives me the opportunity to have a positive impact on the lives of people who are in need. In addition, law enforcement is a well-respected and relatively stable career track that allows me to provide for my family.

Expectations and Realities of the Job

Before I started this job I was unaware that the population I would be working with had such prevalent mental health issues. The majority of the population I deal with has some sort of mental illness and/or substance abuse issue that directly affects their behavior, posing many challenges to me and my coworkers as well as threats to our safety and the safety of other inmates. It is difficult to find appropriate housing for inmates with mental health issues and to provide mental health care in a safe manner.

My Advice to Students

Enter your career with the spirit of being a team player. Sometimes collaborating with your coworker is the only way you can get the job done.

innocent citizens. By the late 1970s, the crime control model had become the dominant philosophy of corrections. It continues to guide current practices as a component of the tough-on-crime criminal justice response of recent decades.

Rehabilitation Model

rehabilitation model
A viewpoint that assumes the offender is inherently a good person and focuses on changing an offender's behavior.

As we saw earlier in this chapter, the **rehabilitation model** developed late in the nineteenth century in response to the harshness of the punishment model. At the core of the rehabilitation model is an effort to change an offender's behavior, often using medical approaches. Thus in the nineteenth century many forms of deviance, such as alcoholism and crime, came to be seen as treatable conditions. Rehabilitation can be helpful for a wide variety of crimes against persons and property precipitated by substance abuse, poverty, lack of job skills, and many types of mental illness. Intervention in the form of rehabilitation also is especially important to prevent juvenile offenders from becoming adult offenders. Rehabilitation models support programs that provide therapy, job training, and education for offenders.

By the 1930s, correctional institutions were being developed around the medical model. Their primary mission was to treat offenders, make them better, and then return them to society as law-abiding citizens. Correctional professionals studied offenders, attempted to make accurate diagnoses, and developed treatment plans that included counseling, education, and vocational training.[76] The medical model is still used today in therapeutic community treatment programs dealing with alcohol and drug addictions. The medical model is also used to treat offenders who suffer from attention deficit disorder, other types of biologically based brain dysfunctions, and learning disabilities. It is the model of choice to treat offenders who have physical or mental illnesses. By utilizing medical model strategies and protocols, prison administrators hope to change (and perhaps cure) the offenders.

An important part of the rehabilitation model is the indeterminate sentence, which ensures an inmate will stay incarcerated for as long as necessary to be cured. The indeterminate sentence recognizes that the length of time needed to successfully treat and reform offenders varies from individual to individual.

In addition to indeterminate sentences, a comprehensive system of classifying inmates is considered essential for effective rehabilitation. Classification is based on both the nature and the degree of risk inmates pose for an institution and an evaluation of their specific treatment needs. This classification enables prisoners to be matched with appropriate programs designed to assist them in the reformation process.

Reintegration Model

reintegration model
A viewpoint that assumes that offenders must be helped to readjust and fit successfully back into the community.

The **reintegration model** developed gradually as a logical extension of the rehabilitation model. Its goal is to help offenders readjust and successfully fit back into the community. This end is accomplished through supervised, structured programs that reinforce preexisting positive ties as well as establish new ones with people and institutions in the community.[77] Most offenders return to their community after being released from prison.[78]

halfway house
A loosely structured prerelease, community-based residence that helps prisoners adjust to the community after total incarceration.

restorative justice
A perspective that focuses on the offender's responsibility to repair the hurt, damage, and injustice the crime victim experienced by making restitution and doing community service.

In corrections, reintegration programs give offenders increased freedom and responsibility before they are released into the community without supervision. Parole is an example of a reintegration program. Another example is the **halfway house**, a structured, prerelease, community-based residence that helps prisoners adjust to the community after total incarceration. Most prisons have programs that attempt to prepare offenders for release back into the community as their sentence comes to a close. Reintegration programs also are emphasized in institutions where large numbers of prisoners serve shorter sentences. Not surprisingly, many who support the reintegration model align themselves with the goals of the rehabilitation model.[79]

The reintegration model is based on the principles of **restorative justice**, a subject enjoying a great deal of attention today. Restorative justice focuses on the offender's responsibility to repair the hurt, damage, and injustice the crime victim experienced by making restitution and doing community service.[80]

KEY CONCEPTS

Principles of the Punishment, Crime Control, Rehabilitation, and Reintegration Models of Corrections

Each model approaches corrections from a different perspective and emphasizes different aspects.

	Punishment	Crime Control	Rehabilitation	Reintegration
Purpose of corrections	Retribution	Incapacitation	Behavior change	Accountability to community
Perception of offender's nature	Offender is bad	Offender is bad	Offender is human, makes mistakes, and is capable of guidance	Offender is human, makes mistakes, and is capable of guidance
Cause of offender's behavior	Free will	Free will	Social determinism	Social determinism
Treatment's role	No treatment	No treatment	Treatment needed and helpful	Treatment needed and helpful
View of offender's behavior change	Change questionable	Change questionable	Change possible	Change possible
Best practices for behavior change	Fear-producing sanctions	Incarceration	Programs	Programs

The reintegration model holds offenders accountable to the people and communities they have injured. It seeks to return the rehabilitated offender back into society as a productive, reformed citizen who accepts responsibility for her actions, has prosocial attitudes, and no longer commits crime. See the Key Concepts feature for a comparison of the principles of the punishment, crime control, rehabilitation, and reintegration models of corrections.

▲ **Overcrowding in Prison**

When cells are not available, prisoners are double- and triple-bunked in public areas of the prison. *How does overcrowding lead to prison violence?*

PRISON POPULATIONS—WHO IS BEHIND BARS?

The number of adults in the United States under some form of correctional supervision—probation, jail, prison, or parole—reached 7.2 million persons in 2006. This means 1 in 31 adults, or 3.2 percent of the adult population, was under some form of correctional control that year.[81] More than 4 million U.S. adults were on probation, approximately 1.5 million were confined in a state or federal prison, more than 798,000 were on parole in the community, and almost that number were in jails.[82] More specifically, 1 of every 136 adults was incarcerated in a jail or prison, making the U.S. incarceration rate the highest in the world (738 per 100,000 population). The United States incarcerates about half the world's prisoners held in penal institutions. Other countries with high incarceration rates are the Cayman Islands (453 per 100,000 population) and Russia (611 per 100,000 population). Among the countries with low incarceration rates are Japan (62 per 100,000 population) and Iceland (40 per 100,000 population).[83] (See Figure 11-2.)

The number of jail inmates varies widely from state to state. As of 2005, one-third of all U.S. inmates incarcerated in jails were held in a facility in California, Texas, Florida, or Georgia. This is in sharp contrast to 10 other states that, combined, held just over 3 percent of the nation's jail inmates. The implications of such differences for local budgets are major. In 2005, jails in Maine held a total of 1,545 inmates; jails in California held more than 82,000.[84]

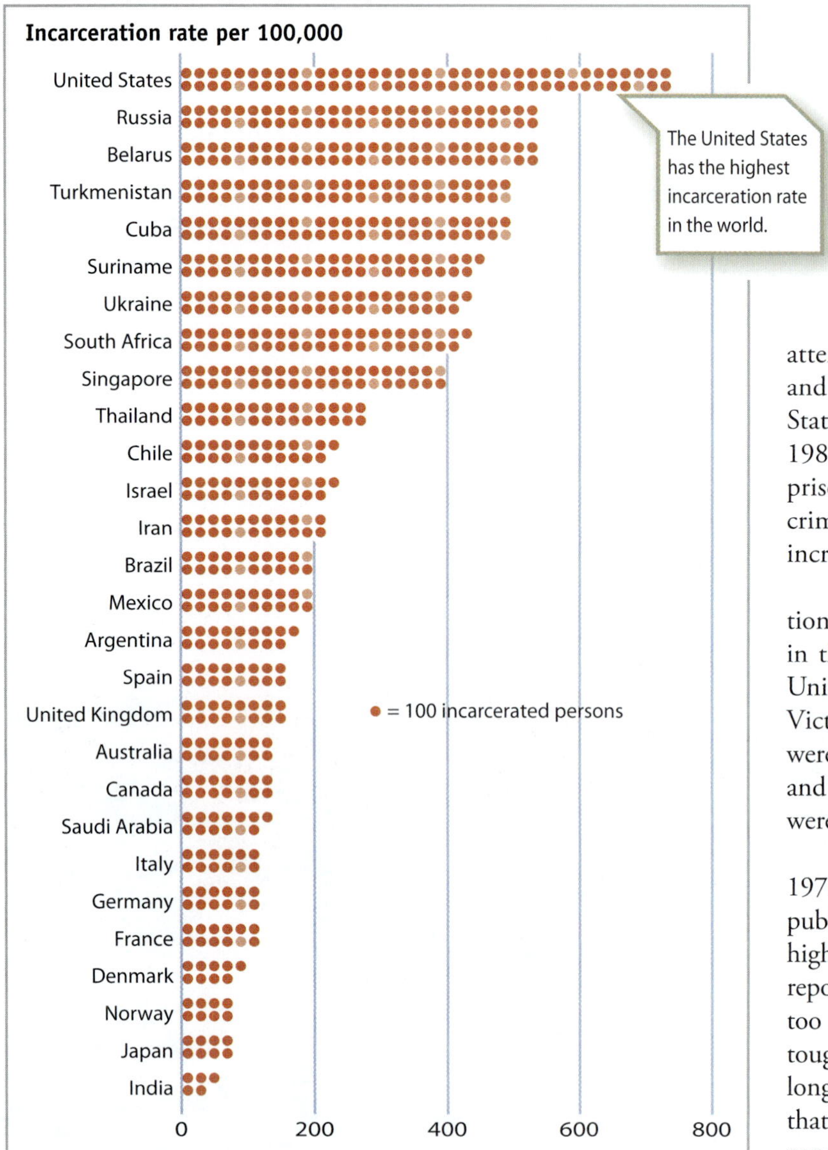

FIGURE 11-2 Incarceration Rates for Selected Countries, 2001-2005

SOURCE: Roy Wolmsley, *Findings:World Prison Population List*, 7th Ed. (London: Research, Development and Statistical Directorate, 2006).

MYTH/REALITY

MYTH: Prisons are overcrowded because more people are committing violent crimes.

REALITY: The exploding prison population is due to changes in public policies that increase the use of prison as a sanction and lengthen the prison sentences imposed by the courts.[85]

Over the years overcrowding has doomed every attempt at humane prison reform. Between 1970 and 1980 the prison population in the United States doubled. It more than doubled again from 1981 to 1985, overwhelming both federal and state prison systems.[86] Even during periods of decreasing crime rates, prison populations have continued to increase.

For example, in the 1990s the prison population increased even though there were no increases in the rates of crimes reported either by the FBI's Uniform Crime Reports or by the National Crime Victimization Survey. In 1995, 1.75 million persons were confined in prison or jail in the United States, and by midyear 2008 more than 2.3 million inmates were confined in these institutions.[87]

The increase in prison population from the 1970s to the present was largely due to changes in public policy—driven by public fear. The media highlighted sensational cases of violent crimes. News reporting portrayed judges and parole authorities as too lenient. Both the media and politicians took a tough-on-crime stand, calling for more punitive and longer sentences, reinforcing the widespread belief that harsh punishment would reduce crime. One consequence of this changing public attitude was that judges and parole boards felt pressured to increase jail terms as a way of assuring the public that the criminal justice system was responsive. Many state legislatures and the federal government adopted fixed mandatory minimum sentences. Such sentencing "reforms" left little discretion to the courts and curtailed parole release by severely reducing choice in parole decisions. The bottom line for prisons: overcrowding increased.[88]

Source Connection

PRISON OVERCROWDING

www.nytimes.com/2008/12/08/us/08calif.html?_r=1&scp=9&sq=prisons&st=cse.

Read this article from *The New York Times* on whether overcrowding in California prisons is unconstitutional.

Differences by Gender and Race

There are vast and continuing differences in jail incarceration by gender, as Figure 11-3 illustrates. The same holds true for prisons: males accounted for 93 percent of all inmates in 2005—making them 14 times more likely to be imprisoned in a state or federal facility than females.[89] But increasing numbers of women are going to jail. Between 1990 and 2007, the number of women in jails increased an average of 6.2 percent per year. This compared to an average annual increase of 3.7 percent in the male jail population.[90]

The fact that there have always been more males than females within the criminal justice system has given rise to the "chivalry hypothesis"—the belief that women offenders are treated differently from male offenders by law enforcement, the courts, corrections, and victim services. The assumption behind this hypothesis is that women are either good and in need of male guidance and gentle protection, or bad and in need of extreme punishment.

Examples of male chivalry may be a greater tendency for male police officers not to arrest women, and a greater tendency for male judges to give females release on bail, to dismiss cases, and to grant lighter sentences.[91] See the Race, Class, Gender box for a discussion of the development of U.S. women's prisons.

Not only are males disproportionately represented in U.S. jails and prisons, so are people of color (see Figure 11-4). Blacks are almost three times more likely than Hispanics and five times more likely than Whites to be incarcerated in a jail or prison. For example, by midyear 2007, almost 4.6 percent of Black males in the general population were in prison or jail, compared to 1.7 percent of Latino males and 0.7 percent of White males.[92] Furthermore, even though incarceration rates typically drop with increasing age, Black males over age 55 continued to have higher rates of incarceration than did Latino and White males over 55—although the differences are not as marked. For males of any age, incarceration rates for Blacks were between five and seven times greater than those for Whites. The same overall pattern held true for Black and White females, regardless of age group.[93]

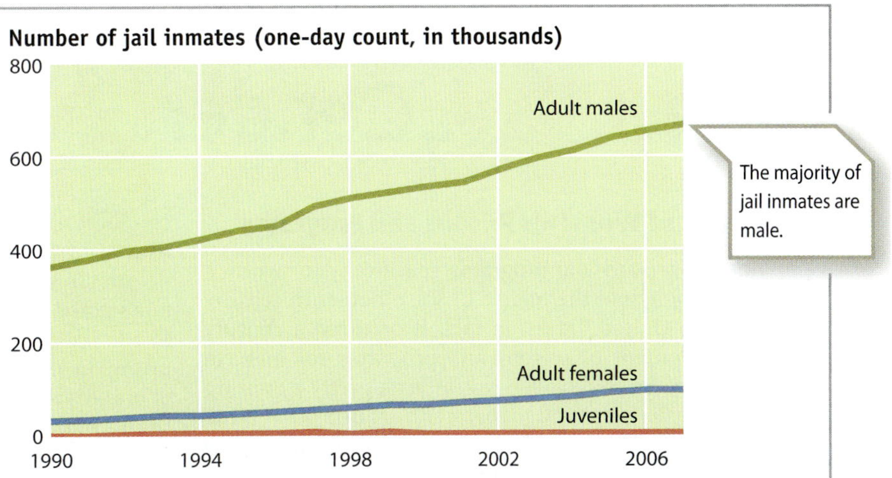

FIGURE 11-3 Jail Population by Age and Gender, 1990–2007

SOURCE: Bureau of Justice Statistics Correctional Surveys, "The Annual Survey of Jails and Census of Jail Inmates," in *Correctional Populations in the United States, 1997*; "Prison and Jail Inmates at Midyear Series, 1998–2006"; "Jail Inmates at Midyear 2007."

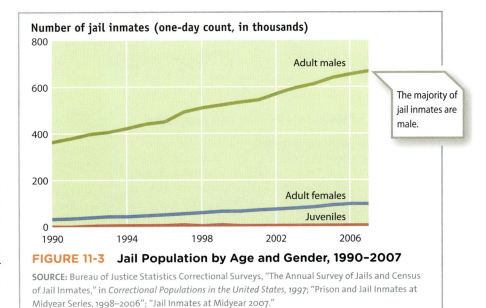

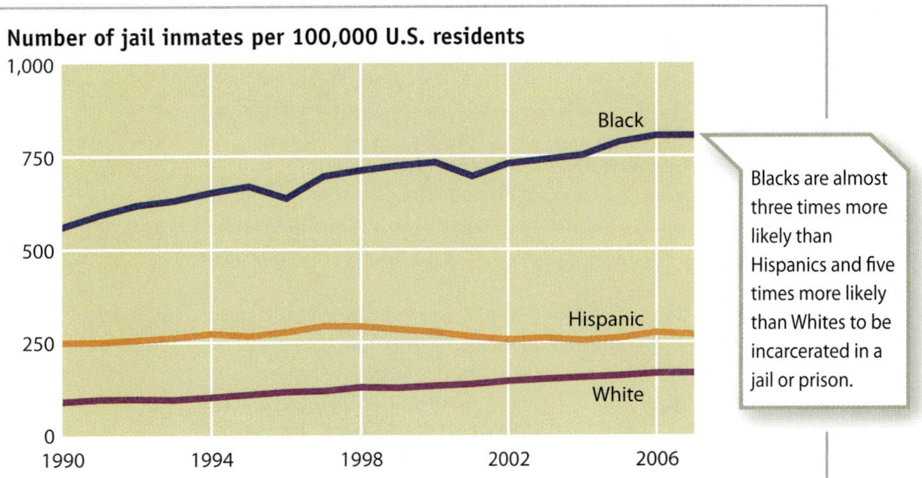

FIGURE 11-4 Jail Incarceration Rates by Race and Ethnicity, 1990–2007

SOURCE: Bureau of Justice Statistics Correctional Surveys, "The Annual Survey of Jails and Census of Jail Inmates," in *Correctional Populations in the United States, 1997*; "Prison and Jail Inmates at Midyear Series, 1998–2006"; "Jail Inmates at Midyear 2007."

Types of Offenders

MYTH/REALITY

MYTH: Prisons in the United States are full of violent offenders.

REALITY: More inmates are serving life sentences for drug possession than for all major violent crimes combined, such as second-degree murder.[94]

Almost half (48 percent) of those confined in our nation's state and federal prisons in 2003 were serving time for nonviolent crimes, including drug, property, and crimes against the public order (also called public order crimes). Among federal inmates, those sentenced for drug offenses constituted the largest number of prisoners (55 percent) that year.[95]

Variations of chronic offender laws have clouded this picture for a number of states. For example, a growing proportion of California prisoners are being sentenced under that state's "three strikes, you're out" legislation. According to this law, if a person receives two or more felony convictions, any subsequent felony conviction—violent or nonviolent—can result in an automatic sentence of life imprisonment.[96]

MYTH/REALITY

MYTH: Third-strike convictions are always for violent offenses.

REALITY: In many cases, third strikes are for nonviolent crimes.[97]

Race, Class, Gender

Development of Women's Prisons and Programs

Development of prisons and programs specifically for women was not a priority before the middle of the nineteenth century in Europe or the United States. In fact, it occurred a century after the development of prisons and programs for men. In the United States, we can explain this at least partly by noting the relatively few females brought before the courts prior to the Civil War and the fact that judges were hesitant to convict any but the most habitual female offenders.

The few women who were imprisoned were typically confined together with men or kept in separate sections of men's prisons where they were exposed to the same conditions as men—overcrowding, filth, violence, and disease. In addition, male correctional officers and male prisoners sexually abused female inmates, often resulting in pregnancy.

Women imprisoned in male prisons lived a highly restricted existence compared to their male counterparts. They typically had limited access to clergy, doctors, exercise, fresh air, and light. Early in the nineteenth century, following her visit to an English prison where women were imprisoned, Elizabeth Gurney Fry, the Quaker wife of a wealthy London merchant, fought for the development of separate women's facilities run by women and staffed by women, and with adequate provisions for religious and secular instruction. In 1818, such reforms began in England.

Early in the history of U.S. prisons, women did not have the benefit of matrons (female correctional officers) to look after them or programs to deal with their special needs. The need for separate women's prisons became apparent during the Civil War period when the conviction rate of both Black and White women dramatically increased. In the absence of men, who were away at war, women were left to provide for their families. At the same time, many of the manual labor jobs women could do were being eliminated because of the Industrial Revolution. The confluence of these factors led some women to commit crime to survive. Crime rates for women soared, regardless of race.

An 1869 campaign to end the sexual abuse of women in Indiana's state prison, led by two Quaker women, Sarah Smith and Rhoda Coffin, instigated the decision to build the first women's prison. In 1873 the Indiana Reformatory Institution opened its doors. Prison life for females in early women's prisons mimicked the life of their male counterparts. Practices derived from slavery were applied to prison work. Women worked on state-owned penal plantations and were leased out to work on private farms, in mines, and on the railroad. Women were also placed on chain gangs.

Female prisoners in the United States are no longer housed in prisons for men, nor do they normally work in chain gangs. Female prisoners have issues that differ from male prisoners, and women's prisons are being challenged to respond to their unique needs (see Chapter 12).

OBSERVE Investigate Understand

- **Why do you think so few women committed crimes early in our country's history? What role does economics play in crime statistics, particularly as it relates to women?**
- **Give some reasons for the mistreatment of women in the early years of the U.S. prison system.**
- **Why do women need separate prisons from men? What needs do female inmates have that males do not?**

SOURCES: Todd R. Clear and George F. Cole, *American Corrections*, 3rd ed. (Belmont, CA: Wadsworth, 1994); E. R. Pitman, *Elizabeth Fry* (New York: Greenwood, 1969); Nancy Kurshan, "Women and Imprisonment in the U.S.: History and Current Reality," Prison Activist Resource Center, www.prisonactivist.org/women/women-and-imprisonment.html (retrieved August 12, 2006).

Of the offenders sentenced under this law, more are likely to be serving time for nonviolent than for violent crimes. To illustrate, about 65 percent of California's second- and third-strike inmates were serving time for nonviolent crimes in 2003. In fact, there were more third-strikers serving time for drug offenses than for second-degree murder, assault with a deadly weapon, and rape combined.[98]

Federal Prison Inmates

Since 1999, the number of inmates in the federal prison system has been steadily increasing, at a rate more than twice that for state inmates. This increase outpaces the number of inmates released, explaining, in part, why federal prisons report operating at 40 percent above their capacity. A major reason for the increase in the federal prison population was the transfer of responsibility in 2001 from local jails to federal prisons for housing the District of Columbia's felons sentenced by superior courts. Problems with overcrowding have led the Federal Bureau of Prisons to assign many of the inmates under its authority to do their time in privately operated facilities. By 2005, more than 27,000 federal inmates were held in such facilities—a 74.2 percent increase since 2000.[99]

The population of federal prison inmates is about 93 percent male. Most are White (57 percent). Blacks constitute about 40 percent of the population, and Latinos about 32 percent. Native Americans and Asians together comprise 3.5 percent of federal inmates. The average age of federal inmates is 38.[100]

Individuals sentenced for drug offenses constituted the largest number of federal inmates (55 percent) in 2003. That same year, 10 percent of federal inmates were immigration violators, but their actual numbers marked a significant increase over the previous decade. Between 1995 and 2003, the number of federal inmates held for public order offenses increased 170 percent. Most of these convictions were for immigration offenses. By 2005, 39 percent of all noncitizen prisoners were held in a federal prison; together these inmates accounted for 19 percent of the inmates in federal custody.[101]

▲ Federal prisons are secure environments, and prisoners cannot move around at will. *Why do people believe federal prisons are country club environments?*

State Prison Inmates

Each of the 50 U.S. states operates a prison system. The number of prisons each state runs is determined by the number of prisoners sentenced by the courts to state institutions. There is wide variation among the states in the number of state prisons and prisoners. For example, California (176,059), Texas (172,626), Florida (95,078), and New York (63,536) operate large prison systems; North Dakota (1,435), Vermont (2,165), and Maine (2,185) operate small prison systems.[102] More prisoners are held in state prisons than federal prisons, but the increase in federal prisoners is rising faster than the rise of state prisoners. For example, between the end of 2000 and the middle of 2007, the state prisoner population increased 1.7 percent compared to the 4.8 percent increase of the federal prisoner population.[103]

Between 2000 and 2007, the states with the highest average annual increase in percentage of sentenced prisoners were West Virginia (7.1 percent), Arizona (6.6 percent), and Minnesota (6.5 percent). During this time period, New York experienced a decrease in sentenced prisoners (–1.8 percent) as did New Jersey (–1.4 percent).[104] (See Figure 11-5.) During the same time frame, male state prisoners increased 1.6 percent, and female state prisoners increased 3.1 percent.[105] As of June 2007, the state prison incarceration rate for U.S. males was 846 per 100,000 population and for females 62 per 100,000 population.[106] The number of sentenced state prisoners who were admitted (2.9 percent) and released (2.6 percent) during the 5-year period remained about the same.[107]

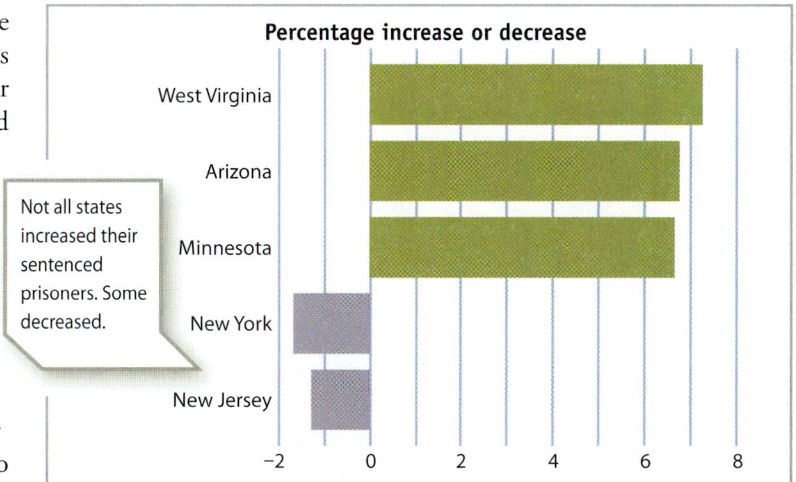

FIGURE 11-5 States with Highest and Lowest Percentage Increase or Decrease of Sentenced Prisoners, 1990–2007

SOURCE: William J. Sabol and Heather Couture, "Inmates at Midyear 2007," *Bureau of Justice Statistics Bulletin* (Washington, DC: Department of Justice, June 2008), 14.

Noninstitutional or Community Corrections

Chapter 13 addresses the role community corrections plays in the broader system of corrections. Here we describe the population under supervision of community corrections programs to distinguish it from institutional populations.

Correctional programs administered in the community include probation and parole. In 2006, more than 5 million adults were under the authority of federal, state, or local probation or parole

▶ Parole Officer and Parolee

Parole officers are responsible for protecting society by making sure parolees do not reoffend.

agencies; 84.7 percent of these were on probation and 15.9 percent on parole. Among probationers, 77 percent were male; of parolees, 88 percent were male. The majority (55 percent) of those on probation were White; 29 percent were Black, and 13 percent Latino. Percentages of White and Black parolees, on the other hand, were effectively equal (at 41 percent and 39 percent, respectively), with Latinos constituting 18 percent of this population.[108] Even though the number of individuals in correctional programs in the community is considerably larger than the number of inmates in U.S. jails and prisons, demographic characteristics of these populations are similar. The main exception is that there are more females and Whites under community supervision than are incarcerated in jails and prisons.

VICTIM INVOLVEMENT IN CORRECTIONS

Traditionally, correctional institutions have focused solely on the offender to the exclusion of the victim. Victim services is a fairly recent concept in the context of corrections, beginning in 1984 with a victim-witness notification program within the federal prisons system. This program requires corrections personnel to contact or notify victims and witnesses when there is a change in an inmate's status. By 1987, the American Correctional Association (ACA) had created a task force to address issues, concerns, and rights of victims. Within 10 years, some state correctional institutions had created specific offices to work with victims.

These offices represent the rights and interests of victims in relation to offenders in the correctional system and before parole boards. For example, they notify victims about inmates' location and movement within the system, changes in their status (movement from a maximum- to a medium-security facility, death while incarcerated, or escape), their release into the community, and the status of pardons or executions. Victims also are notified about parole hearings and educated about their rights to attend and to participate by discussing the impact of the crime on their life. When victims participate in parole hearings, they can request that specific conditions be implemented, such as preventing a parolee from living in the same county as the one in which the victim resides, and ask that a protection order be issued upon the offender's release.

Victim Services within Institutions

Victim services offices work with individuals victimized within a correctional institution, including correctional officers, staff, and administrators. For example, if a correctional officer is assaulted on the job, victim services can assist with crisis intervention and referrals for long-term counseling. If a visitor has a face-to-face contact visit with an inmate and is not protected by a barrier (for example, glass) and is emotionally or physically abused during a visit, that person is eligible for victim services. Corrections also protects victims and witnesses from inmate contact by monitoring phone and mail correspondence.

In addition, victim services may work with correctional personnel in discussing a traumatic event after it occurs, to ensure that those affected receive appropriate services and to prevent future violent incidents (also known as critical incident debriefing). For example, if a riot occurs within a correctional institution, victim services may be called on to work with those correctional officers who were involved.

Victim services offices can help inmates who are physically or sexually abused by staff or inmates while incarcerated. These offices can help victims identify safe and appropriate services in the institution and in the community postrelease. The offices also play a role in helping inmates file grievances with a third party such as an ombudsman about the victimization and the postvictimization response to the incident. Some inmate grievances might include lack of access to medical or mental health care, improper service provision, or failure to respond to the incident in a timely manner.[109]

Victim Impact Panels and Classes

Victim impact panels and classes provide an opportunity for crime victims to tell a group of offenders about the impact of the crime on their lives and on the lives of their families, friends, and neighbors. The latter is important if the crime affected the whole community such as the death or kidnapping of a child or young person. These panels typically include three or four speakers who are victims: they spend about 15 minutes each telling their story in a nonjudgmental, nonblaming manner. The specific offenders of the crime presented normally are not present. Some time is usually dedicated to questions and answers, but the main purpose of the panel is for the victims to speak to offenders, rather than for victims and offenders to engage in a dialogue.

Victim impact panels were initiated in 1982 as a method of changing the attitudes of first-time drunk drivers after their conviction in traffic court and of repeat drunk drivers serving time in prison. Because of the devastating consequences of drunk driving on its victims and on society, MADD (Mothers Against Drunk Driving) considered it critical to change the generally accepted attitude that these incidents were "accidents" rather than crimes. In 2002, 41 percent of the 42,815 traffic deaths in the United States were alcohol-related.[110] MADD contends that an effective way to change attitudes is to confront drunk drivers with firsthand testimony from the victims of drunk-driving crashes.

The results are mixed on victim impact panels because early research indicates that there is no difference in the recidivism rates of either DWI (Driving While Intoxicated) offenders who go to a DWI school or those who attend victim impact panels.[111] Despite the paucity of data on the effectiveness of these panels, in March 2008 the National Highway Transportation Safety Administration (NHTSA) called for the continued use and expansion of victim impact panels for first-time and repeat DUI offenders.[112]

The positive feedback from both victims and offenders who have participated have led courts to order victim impact panels for those who commit other crimes such as property crimes, physical assault, intimate partner violence, child abuse, elder abuse, and homicide. Survivors or family members of victims often serve as panelists in prison and jail settings, with parolees, and in treatment programs, as well as in defensive driving schools, youth education programs, and training forums for juvenile and criminal justice professionals to help them better understand the scope and trauma caused by these victimizations.

Viewing Executions

Once an offender has been sentenced, it can be many years before an execution actually takes place (see Disconnects box on the next page). Legislators and corrections departments

DIS Connects

Gridlock on Death Row

One of the major arguments in favor of the death penalty is that it can serve as a deterrent, especially for those at risk of committing heinous crimes. But for such a penalty even to begin to be effective, it must be both sure and swift. In California it is neither.

A prisoner on death row in California waits an average of more than 17 years for execution. Four hundred eight prisoners have been waiting on death row for more than 10 years, 119 prisoners for more than 20 years, and 30 prisoners for more than 25 years. California's system of criminal justice is bogged down. Nor does the current process provide inmates with a speedy or an efficient appeal process.

This gridlock will likely get worse rather than better. California's situation is so serious that its decades-long delays could be ruled cruel and unusual punishment. If so, the death penalty could be declared unconstitutional.

A respected U.S appeals court judge, Arthur L. Alarcon, believes the problem is due not to delays by defense attorneys or lenient judges but to the shortage of available attorneys to represent death row inmates during the appeal process. Judge Alarcon also blames California's procedures, which require the state Supreme Court to review all death penalty appeals. The judge recommends that these appeals be handled at the appellate court level. This is unlikely to occur, however, because such a change in California would require a constitutional amendment.

The U.S. Department of Justice may add another twist to this issue. A provision of the USA PATRIOT Act gives the U.S. Attorney General the power to decide whether a state is providing adequate counsel during the early critical review process. If it is, that state's death row appeal process could be placed on a fast track. As of 2007 Arizona was the only state to request that its appeal process be placed on this fast track; however, like California, Arizona also lacks a sufficient number of attorneys to handle the appellate workload.

California, under protest, may be required to meet the fast-track criteria. If this occurs, it would speed the early process when petitions, such as those for habeas corpus, must be filed within a specified period. Many inmates are forced to file these complex petitions themselves. There is clearly a disconnect between the urgent need for California to speed the appeals process and the rights of a condemned prisoner to be represented competently and fairly at all stages of this same process.

OBSERVE Investigate Understand

- **What is a compelling argument for *not* fast-tracking death sentences?**
- **Do you think long delays in executions should be considered cruel and unusual punishment? Why or why not?**
- **Does a state have a responsibility to provide lawyers to death row inmates seeking appeal? Why or why not?**

SOURCES: Henry Weinstein, "Judge Takes on Death Row Gridlock," *The New York Times*, August 30, 2007, http://latimes.com.news/local/la-me-death30aug30,1,6927212.story (retrieved September 9, 2007); "Dysfunctional Death Row," *The New York Times*, August 31, 2007, http://latimes.com.news/opinion/la-ed-counsel3aug31,1,1,113963. story (retrieved September 9, 2007); Richard B. Schmitt, "Gonzales Could Get Say in States' Executions," *The New York Times*, August 14, 2007, www.latimes.com/news/local/la-na-penalty,14,1,3604537.story (retrieved September 9, 2007); Erwin Chemerinsky, "Don't Rush to Execution," *The New York Times*, August 16, 2007, http://latimes.com/news/opinion/commentary/la-oe-chemeerinsky116aug16.16,1,5884838.story (retrieved September 9, 2007).

in a number of the states that have capital punishment must decide whether members of a victim's family should be permitted to attend the execution of their loved one's murderer. Witnessing the execution helps bring closure for some but may not be right for everyone. States that permit such attendance allow survivors to make that choice for themselves.[113]

In general, state offices that provide services to victims will assist them with the process of viewing an execution. For example, in Texas, the victim witnesses generally meet with a representative of the Texas Department of Criminal Justice, Victim Services Division, on the afternoon of the execution at a designated location in Huntsville, Texas. The execution protocol is discussed, and witnesses view a video that includes footage of the execution chamber and the witness viewing room. The witnesses are then advised what to expect from the time they arrive at the prison until their departure.[114]

UNDERSTANDING PRIVATE PRISONS

privatization
Transfer of government programs and functions to the private sector.

Privatization is the transfer of government programs and functions to the private sector.[115] The recent movement to privatize the operation of government prisons and security has come about because of overcrowded prisons and an aggressive prison industry, which took advantage of the political climate favoring privatization. As the number of protective resources available through the public sector has declined, private security has experienced rapid growth. The privatization of prisons and security presents a number of issues and challenges to the criminal justice system.

Private Prisons

The belief that private enterprise could build and run prisons more cheaply and efficiently than the government sparked the shift toward privatization of prisons, which began in the 1980s. This idea was especially attractive to federal and state governments struggling to curtail skyrocketing costs.[116]

Growth of Privatization in Corrections

In 1983, private, for-profit, prison-building corporations began competing for contracts with local, state, and federal governments, mostly in southern states with high crime rates, large prison populations, weak labor unions, and strong right-to-work laws restricting union activity. Now almost every state contracts with private firms to manage the incarceration of juvenile and adult inmates. The number of private jail and prison beds increased from 20,687 in 1992 to 143,021 by mid-2001. In 2004, there were almost 99,000 inmates in private institutions in the United States. Texas and Oklahoma lead the nation with the largest number of inmates in private prisons.[117] In 2005 about 100,000 state and federal prisoners were housed in private prisons.[118]

Costs of Privatization

Although the original rationale for use of private prisons was financial savings, private prisons are, in fact, no less expensive to operate than government-run prisons.[119] To realize savings, some private prisons cut back on spending for prisoner health, provide lower salaries for personnel, and reduce staff training. One analysis of 24 independent studies concluded that private prisons were no more cost-effective than public prisons.[120]

In 2001, at least $628 million in tax-free bonds and other public subsidies went to private prisons, with almost 75 percent of these private institutions receiving public subsidies.[121] The receipt of tax dollars allowed these private institutions to operate profitably. By lobbying the public and politicians for longer sentences for inmates and more prisons, private companies looked to further increase their profits.[122]

Quality

The evidence on quality in private prisons is mixed. Some studies in New Mexico and West Virginia indicated that privately operated prisons provide higher quality services than publicly operated prisons, but others did not.[123] Services included food preparation, medical and dental care, education, job training, religious services, and other rehabilitative programming. Other studies also reported that hiring less costly workers in private prisons negatively affects public safety and inmate care.[124] One Florida study found lower rates of recidivism among inmates released from privately operated prisons than among those released from public facilities.[125] Many researchers contend that most comparisons of outcomes use flawed methods, making it impossible to be certain whether private prisons are better or worse than public ones.[126]

Legal Issues

In *Richardson v. McKnight* (1997), the U.S. Supreme Court held that an employee of a private firm who is sued cannot invoke the qualified immunity defense available to state government employees (see Chapter 7).[127] The Court noted that because private firms seek to maximize profits and minimize costs, they must be subject to liability rules to prevent them from engaging in harmful activities for the sake of realizing cost benefits. Private firms do not have all the same protections against lawsuits that government entities do; thus, a government entity using a private prison may be at risk of lawsuits. If a state uses a private corporation to run a prison and someone sues the private company over prison conditions, the state also may be vulnerable unless it can clearly show it had no knowledge of the problem.

An important—and as yet unsettled—issue is the use of force, including deadly force, by guards and officers. Private prisons could face civil liability and criminal lawsuits for violating the rights of inmates.[128]

Faith-based Prisons

faith-based prison programs
Services provided when a private prison corporation builds or operates a prison under contract with a government agency and invites religious organizations to offer rehabilitation services to the inmates.

Faith-based prison programs are rehabilitation and other services offered by religious organizations to inmates in private prisons. Community volunteers from different religious groups act as personal mentors to inmates both during incarceration and after release. Inmates' belief in God is said not to be a requirement, and volunteers are not allowed to persuade inmates to change their beliefs. Religious instruction is supposed to accompany, rather than supplant, other services such as psychological counseling and treatment for addiction.

In 2001 President George W. Bush signed executive orders creating the White House Office of Faith-Based and Community Initiatives and Centers for Faith-Based and Community Initiatives in five cabinet departments: Justice, Education, Labor, Health and Human Services, and Housing and Urban Development. According to Bush, "The indispensable and transforming work of faith-based and other charitable service groups must be encouraged . . . whether run by Methodists, Muslims, Mormons, or good people of no faith at all."[129] Although President Obama has expressed some support for faith-based initiatives, he has not yet dealt with the issue of faith-based prisons.

Some faith-based programs are housed in separate dormitories within a prison; in other cases, the entire prison is faith-based. The first faith-based prison opened in Florida in 2003. A year later 10 states had faith-based prison programs, and the number was expected to increase dramatically as the Corrections Corporation of America, the largest private prison corporation in the United States, planned to introduce more.[130] Theoretically, faith-based programs are to offer instruction in all faiths equally. However, in Florida, more than 90 percent of inmates are Christian, 5 percent are Muslim, and less than 1 percent are Jewish. Atheists and members of pagan religions, such as Wicca and Odinism, are on waiting lists for housing in faith-based prisons.[131]

Florida opened its third faith-based prison in November 2005.[132] A 2007 report of Florida's faith-based prisons concluded that these institutions seem to be effective with some inmates, but questions remain about the effectiveness of faith-based prisons in terms of recidivism rates, employment outcomes, increased civic involvement, and improved family relationships. There is debate as well over whether the model is effective for all inmate types.[133]

Faith-based facilities are not supposed to attempt to convert inmates; however, a pending lawsuit charges at least one program with pressuring inmates to convert to Christianity. On June 2, 2006, a federal judge in Iowa ruled that a state-financed evangelical Christian program was "pervasively sectarian." The facts, he said, "leave no room to doubt that the state of Iowa is excessively entangled with religion." In other words, since public (tax) funds were used for religious purposes (conversion), Iowa had violated the constitutional protections regarding the separation of church and state.[134] The court ordered the Iowa Department of Corrections to disband the program within 60 days and directed the program to pay back at least $1.5 million it had received from the state. The judge criticized what he saw as the lack of real choice on the part of inmates who wanted a similar nonsectarian option, with the same treatment privileges, incentives, and visitation rights afforded to inmates who participated in the faith-based program.[135] He stated, "Though an inmate could, theoretically, graduate from InnerChange [the name of the faith-based program] without converting to Christianity, the coercive nature of the program demands obedience to its dogmas and doctrine."[136]

The case was appealed, and a final ruling would set precedent about faith-based initiatives and might clarify issues regarding the separation of church and state.[137] On

December 3, 2007, the judge's decision was upheld. A federal appeals panel ruled that the program did violate the constitutional separation of church and state and fostered religious indoctrination. The appeals court, however, ruled that the InnerChange program would not have to repay the $1.5 million it had received from the state of Iowa.[138]

MYTH/REALITY

MYTH: Faith-based prisons are more effective in reducing recidivism than traditional prisons.

REALITY: Research findings on the efficacy of faith-based prisons are not clear.[139]

Advocates of faith-based prison programs claim the approach cuts recidivism rates more than traditional prison rehabilitation and job training programs and results in fewer disciplinary actions. Critics argue there is as yet no valid study supporting any of these claims.[140]

A 2-year study conducted between 2000 and 2003 examined a faith-based prison program run by the evangelical InnerChange Freedom Initiative in Texas. The InnerChange group said the study illustrated that in-prison Bible education, community service, and aftercare had a positive effect on reducing recidivism because graduates of the program had lower rearrest and reimprisonment rates than inmates in a matched control group. In fact, however, InnerChange participants did less well than the control group of prisoners who did not participate in the faith-based program.

The study's author, Byron Johnson, noted that when compared to prisoners who did not participate in the program, InnerChange participants overall did not have lower recidivism rates. Supporters of faith-based prisons, however, simply ignored the data about the 102 participants who started the InnerChange program but did not "graduate" and claimed success for the program based on the results of the 75 graduates.[141]

The Future of Private Prisons

Private prisons in the United States are big business, and the industry expects continued growth.[142] Faith-based prison programs are also predicted to multiply.[143] Supporters of private prisons argue that having stockholders to whom they must report imposes "market accountability" on corporations, which want to prevent their stock prices from dropping.[144] The potential for economic gain for private prison companies is great, but the real benefits to the government and for inmates are as yet unclear.

SUMMARY

U.S. correctional facilities today are under tremendous pressure because of the huge number of convictions being churned out of the criminal justice system. Many governing bodies are wrestling with the consequences. Should they build more prisons? Or should they try to reduce the correctional population through mandating shortened sentences, parole, and treatment programs that attempt to prepare the inmate for return to the community? In some ways this dilemma reflects the historical swings from punishment to rehabilitation to punishment and back again.

The philosophy that governs a particular correctional institution depends to some extent on the degree of overcrowding and on the severity of the crimes of the inmates. Those with long sentences tend to be strictly regulated (under the punishment model) or incapacitated through incarceration (the crime control model). Those who are classified as ill generally are offered treatment (under the rehabilitation model), and those who serve shorter sentences may be prepared for return to the community (under the reintegration model). Public opinion, media coverage of crime, and sympathy for victims may sway which direction governing and correctional officials lean in sentencing and treating offenders.

Observe Investigate Understand

Review

Define corrections and describe its role in society.

- Corrections is one of the components of the criminal justice system, including but not limited to probation, parole, prisons, and jails.
- It is responsible for managing and treating offenders after they enter the criminal justice system.
- It refers to the social control and punishment of offenders through a system of imprisonment and rehabilitation programs.

Identify the precursors to the U.S. prison.

- Corporal punishment, such as flogging, branding, and mutilation, was used readily throughout the early history of punishment.
- Torture as punishment was commonplace prior to incarceration.
- Church confinement, in which offenders were held in cells within monasteries to serve years of solitary penance, substituted for immediate death and corporal punishment during the early years of penology.
- Transportation and banishment led to the establishment of foreign penal colonies.
- Galley slavery confined condemned criminals to a life sentence rowing ships prior to the use of incarceration as punishment.
- The confinement of prisoners in hulks of abandoned ships led to the development of contemporary prisons on land.
- Workhouses held a mixture of people including jobless vagrants, debtors, and sometimes serious criminals, paving the way for the development of prisons.
- Primitive jails sometimes took the form of confining lawbreakers in dedicated sections of estates of private landowners until it was time to impose the punishment.

Contrast the features of the Pennsylvania system with the Auburn system.

- The Pennsylvania system called for solitary confinement of offenders and forced silence and isolation on offenders; offenders only saw their keepers; all work and meals took place in offenders' individual cells.
- The Auburn system included severe discipline and corporal punishment for offenders; work and meals took place with other offenders outside of their cells but in silence; offenders did not live in solitary confinement cells but rather had cell block living arrangements; movement of offenders took place in lockstep.

Identify the defining features of reformatories and therapeutic prisons.

- Indeterminate sentences—that is, releasing offenders when they had been reformed—was instituted to promote rehabilitation in the prison system.
- Rehabilitation and treatment of offenders became a popular concept at Elmira and during the reformatory movement.
- The goal of reformation was to enable an offender to be released into society and not offend again.
- Parole is early and conditional release from custody.
- Classification systems for prisons and inmates should make it easier for custodial programs to better meet the needs of the inmates.

Trace the defining features of industrial prisons.

- Prisoner labor was used to pay for the cost of operating prisons.
- Prisons were modeled after factories.
- Industrial prisons used oppressive and violent discipline and regimentation.

Describe and evaluate each of the four major models of corrections.

- The punishment model assumes that offenders are inherently bad people and must be punished. After correctional punishment, many offenders become more antisocial than before.
- The crime control model uses incarceration to suppress the behavior of criminals and keep them off the streets. Most offenders are eventually released back to the streets where they committed crimes.

- The rehabilitation model seeks to change an offender's behavior; it views offenders as sick and capable of being cured. Most U.S. prisons do not emphasize rehabilitation.
- The reintegration model seeks to help offenders readjust successfully back into the community. For reintegration to work, correctional programs must help offenders learn to take responsibility for their crimes.

Describe the populations found in correctional institutions today.

- Overcrowding is due not to higher crime rates but to changes in policy that imprison more offenders for longer terms.
- Prison populations are overwhelmingly male and disproportionately Black.
- Most offenses are not violent but are nonviolent drug offenses.
- The number of federal prison inmates is increasing at a greater rate than the populations of state prisons.
- The number of individuals in community or noninstitutional programs (such as probation and parole) outnumbers those in prisons and jails but represents the same demographics.

Identify the types of victim services found in corrections.

- Correctional institutions are responsible for the facilitation and mediation of inmate–victim interactions.
- Correctional institutions organize victim impact panels and classes for inmates to learn about the effects crime has on the victim's life.
- Correctional institutions are responsible for assisting victims in the process of viewing executions.

Examine the extent and nature of privatization of prisons.

- Private prisons are based on the rationale that private enterprise can run prisons cheaper and more efficiently than government can.
- Faith-based prison programs are developed when a private prison corporation builds or operates a prison under contract with a government agency and invites religious organizations to offer rehabilitation services to the inmates.

Key Terms

Study Questions

1. The term *corrections* refers to
   a. probation and parole.
   b. jails and prisons.
   c. juvenile detention facilities.
   d all of the above.
2. Which model of corrections assumes most offenders will remain in the community and society will benefit if offenders have connections to institutions in free society?
   a. Punishment
   b. Rehabilitation and treatment
   c. Crime control
   d. Reintegration
3. Which of the following groups is most disproportionately represented in the U.S. prison population?
   a. African Americans
   b. Latinos
   c. Whites
   d. Asian Americans
4. The function of the practice of transportation was to
   a. eliminate convicts from Britain.
   b. colonize new British territories.
   c. circumvent the death penalty.
   d. all of the above.
5. The _____ system's major characteristic was absolute solitary confinement.
   a. Pennsylvania
   b. Auburn
   c. reformatory
   d. industrial
6. Very harsh punishments
   a. tend to decrease criminal activity.
   b. tend to increase criminal activity.
   c. do not make a difference in criminal activity.
   d. are justified by the research.
7. The first prison in the United States was
   a. Bridewell.
   b. the Walnut Street Jail.
   c. the Western Penitentiary.
   d. Cherry Hill.
8. The indeterminate sentence was a part of the history of the ____________ model.
   a. rehabilitation
   b. crime control
   c. punishment
   d. reintegration
9. Most of the inmates in U.S. prisons are serving time for
   a. murder.
   b. burglary.
   c. drug offenses.
   d. car theft.
10. The crime control model is a way to
    a. teach control to inmates.
    b. control crime in the inner city.
    c. control crime by using harsh punishments.
    d. control crime by imprisoning and incapacitating offenders.

Critical Thinking Questions

1. How have U.S. correctional practices changed since the colonial period?
2. Describe some of the punishments that were precursors to prison, and explain how they changed to become contemporary correctional practices.
3. Which of the models of corrections do you think has been most successful in accomplishing the goal of correcting an offender's unlawful behavior? Why?
4. Compare and contrast the Pennsylvania and Auburn systems. Why was Auburn more successful?

Internet Sites

Federal Bureau of Prisons
http://bop.gov/
This site contains statistical information on federal prison populations by gender, race, ethnicity, age, and other demographic characteristics.

Bureau of Justice Statistics
www.ojp.usdoj.gov/bjs/
This site contains useful statistical information and reports on correctional topics.

Center on Juvenile and Criminal Justice
www.cjcj.org/
This site contains information on juvenile and adult correctional policy. It also offers model programs, public education, and policy research concerning alternatives to incarceration, sentencing and reentry issues, drug policy reform.

Suggested Readings

Robert Johnson, *Hard Time: Understanding and Reforming the Prison*, 2nd ed. (Belmont, CA: Wadsworth, 1996).
This book takes a broad look at imprisonment and its history and examines the role of inmates and correctional officers. The author suggests that the pains of imprisonment that inmates experience can be used in a positive way.

Thomas Mathiesen, *Prison on Trial*, 3rd ed. (Newbury Park, CA: Sage, 2005).
This book focuses on the arguments for and against imprisonment in a post–September 11 world.

Jeffrey Reiman, The *Rich Get Richer and the Poor Get Prison: Ideology, Crime, and Criminal Justice*, 6th ed. (Needham Heights, MA: Allyn & Bacon, 2000).
This book argues that the criminal justice system is biased against the poor and does not reduce crime.

CHAPTER 12

Jails and Prisons

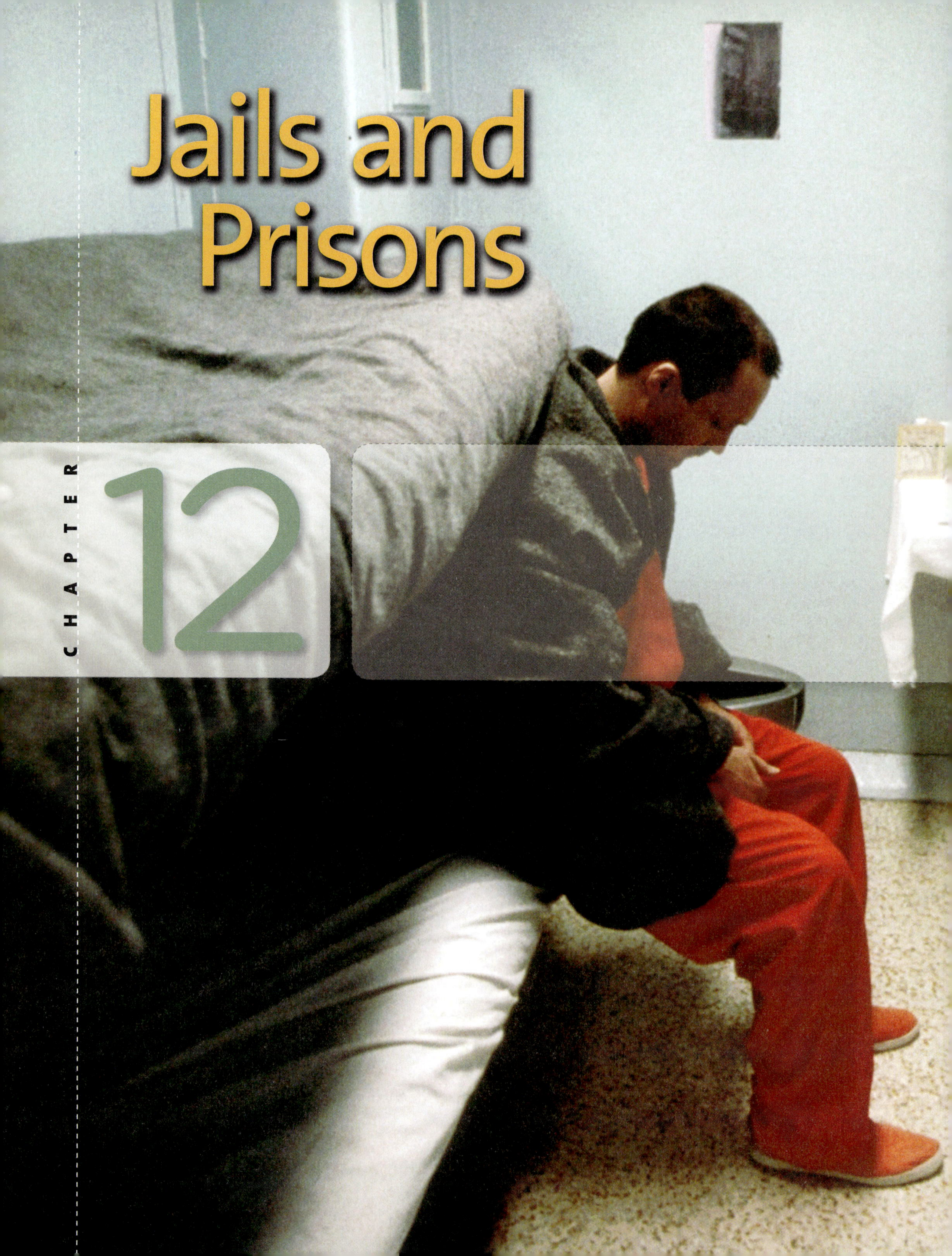

OBSERVE Investigate *Understand*

After reading this chapter, you should be able to:

- Distinguish between jails and prisons.
- Differentiate between minimum, medium, maximum, and supermax prisons.
- Apply the concept of professionalization to the role of correctional officers.
- Describe the rights of prisoners.
- Describe the inmate subculture.
- Outline the differences between male and female prison life.
- Describe methods of treatment and rehabilitation in prisons.
- Describe the ways incarceration affects the prisoner's family life.

Realities and Challenges

The Psychology of Imprisonment

In the makeshift prison, it took the guards no time to become aggressive, abusive, and even sadistic to the prisoners, and the prisoners rapidly became passive, hopeless, depressed, and dehumanized. Sound like the plot of an action film set in a war zone? In fact, this was the result of an experiment conducted at Stanford University in 1971 by social psychologist Philip Zimbardo, using students as the participants.

This classic study, known as the Stanford Prison Experiment (sometimes called the Zimbardo Prison Experiment), was designed to explore the psychological effects of being a "prisoner" and a "guard" in a simulated environment.[1] The 24 subjects, all students, were middle-class male volunteers; none had prior exposure to the criminal justice system. The "prisoners"—decided by a coin toss—were held in a mock prison-type environment in a basement on the Stanford University campus.

The experiment, designed to last 2 weeks, had to be cut short after 6 days because the "guards" and "prisoners" behaved in such unexpected and disturbing ways. Some students were so troubled by their actions that they needed professional counseling afterward.

Zimbardo and his team of researchers concluded that the prison social structure powerfully determines human behavior, leading individuals to suspend or abandon their personal values. The experiment raises questions about how the social environment of jails and prisons can influence the effectiveness of the corrections system.

Society has a vested interest in how incarceration affects inmates because the vast majority of inmates one day return to the community. This chapter provides an overview of incarceration in the criminal justice system. In this chapter, we explore the realities of the corrections system, the culture of prison life, and the challenges of making these elements work to the benefit of both prisoners and society.

THE STRUCTURE OF CORRECTIONS

MYTH/REALITY

MYTH: Incarcerating criminals reduces crime in society.

REALITY: Jails and prisons do not deter criminal behavior.[2] Crime rates and recidivism rates remain high in the United States despite high rates of incarceration.[3]

The most common formal sanction for criminal behavior today is **incarceration**, or imprisonment. Indeed, legislative initiatives to put more criminals behind bars have wide popular support, even though shutting more people in jails and prisons has not stemmed the tide of crime or recidivism.[4] What increasing the number of inmates has done is create major problems for both inmates and correctional employees.

incarceration
Imprisonment in the criminal justice system.

jail
Municipal or regional facilities that house pretrial individuals believed to present a risk of danger or flight, those awaiting probation or parole revocation, and those sentenced to less than 1 year incarceration.

Jails

Jails are local facilities operated by municipal and regional governments such as cities, counties, and parishes. Some local governments contract with private agencies to provide jail services. Jails house pretrial individuals believed to present a risk of danger or flight and those serving short-term sentences of incarceration. Jails also hold those awaiting probation or parole revocation hearings, and people with mental disorders who await transfer to psychiatric facilities. Increasingly, with public and political pressure to control illegal immigration, jails have become a way station for suspects en route to deportation.[5]

Most large cities and many towns throughout the United States have a jail. There are about 3,300 local jails in the United States, operating at an estimated cost of $3 billion per year, about $2.3 billion of it for adult facilities. Juvenile jails, known as juvenile halls, are discussed in Chapter 15.

Jails reported an annual average cost of $13,803 per inmate, or $37.82 a day in the late 1980s.[6] In recent years costs have increased substantially due to cost shifting of mental health care to the jails.[7] The total cost-per-inmate figure includes such things as institutional security, health services, food, accommodation, and salaries of personnel. Jails are normally less expensive to operate than prisons because they offer fewer programs and services to inmates.

Preview

Problems in Jails

Jail overcrowding is a major problem nationwide. In Los Angeles in 2004, the problem became so severe that a U.S. district judge ordered the county to develop a plan to improve conditions. Because jails are used to hold suspected offenders until trial, one obvious solution to overcrowding is to simplify and expedite pretrial activities, such as using a credit card program to facilitate processing of bail bonds. Another solution is to reduce the time sentenced inmates spend in jail. Some counties substitute labor for jail time for inmates sentenced to 30 days or more, thus freeing space while saving money.

Using local jails to incarcerate people with mental illnesses overtaxes the jail system. In 2000, more than 16 percent of jail inmates had a mental illness, and almost three-quarters of these were incarcerated for nonviolent offenses.[8] Some counties cope with the large numbers of people with mental illness who end up in their jails by bypassing the jail system altogether. They send offenders diagnosed with serious mental illness and deemed treatable to community health facilities.[9] Many communities, however, do not have resources, other than jail, to handle the mentally ill criminal population—a problem not only for the individuals who commit crimes but also for the communities to which most will soon return.

Another problem in the jails stems from the concept of **preventive detention**: holding persons who have not yet been found guilty of a crime but are considered at risk of fleeing jurisdiction. A judge can deny bail and order the defendant held in jail until trial. The judge also may set bail so high that the defendant cannot possibly be released until the end of the trial. Pretrial preventive detention has been held constitutional to date,[10] but debate continues on the legality of incarcerating persons not on the basis of what they have done but of what we fear they will do. This was the argument used to hold enemy combatants indefinitely in Guantánamo Bay Detention Camp.

preventive detention
Holding persons who have not yet been found guilty of a crime but are considered at risk of fleeing the jurisdiction.

The Jail Population

In 2005, the U.S. jail population was approximately 820,000, of whom more than 87 percent were men. Figure 12-1 illustrates the racial makeup of jail inmates: Whites made up 44.3 percent of jail inmates; Blacks, 38.9 percent; Latinos, 15.0 percent; and other races, 1.7 percent. The majority of jail inmates (62 percent) had not yet been sentenced but were awaiting court action.[11]

Of the 820,000 offenders under jail supervision in 2005, only 9 percent were in alternative programs, such as home detention or electronic monitoring, that permitted them to remain out of jail. Similar programs

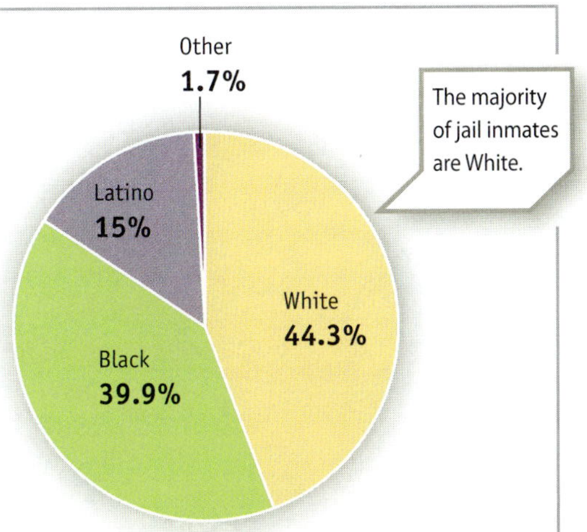

FIGURE 12-1 Race of Jail Inmates, 2005

SOURCE: Paige M. Harrison and Allen J. Beck, *Prison and Jail Inmates at Midyear 2005* (Washington, DC: Department of Justice, 2006).

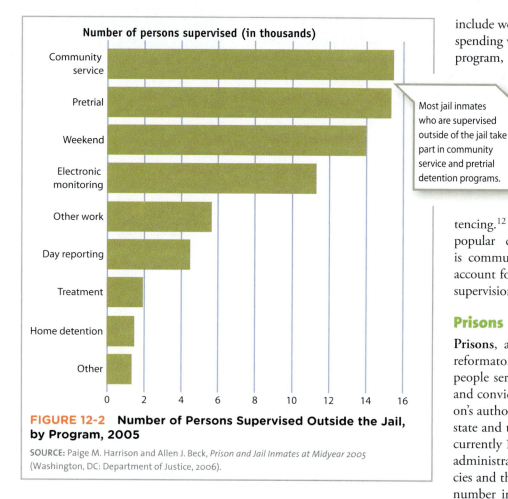

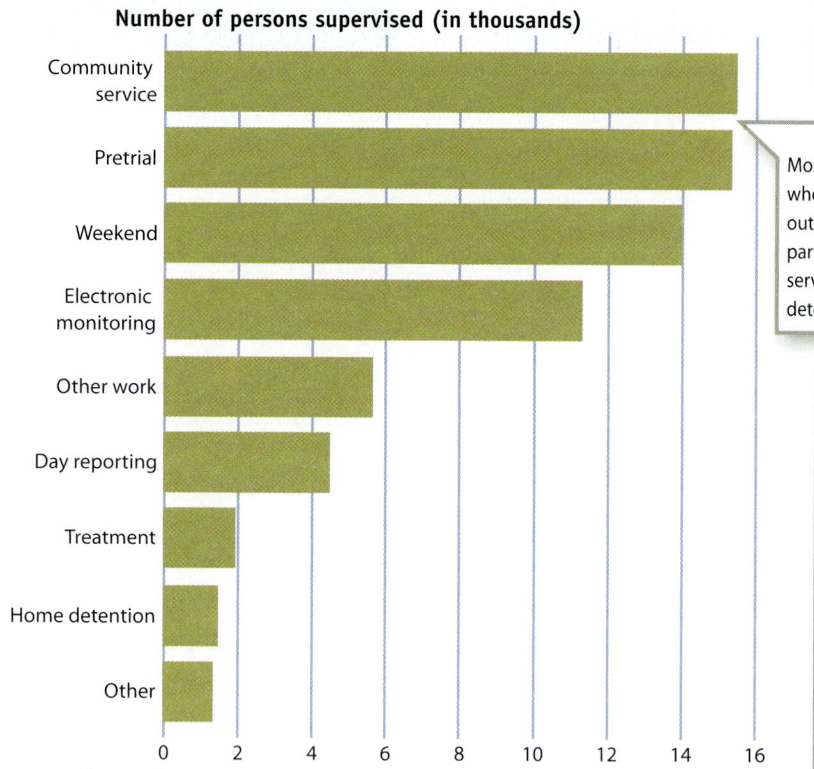

FIGURE 12-2 Number of Persons Supervised Outside the Jail, by Program, 2005

SOURCE: Paige M. Harrison and Allen J. Beck, *Prison and Jail Inmates at Midyear 2005* (Washington, DC: Department of Justice, 2006).

include work release and community service, spending weekends in jail, reporting to a day program, and participating in mandatory drug, alcohol, or mental health programs. Approximately one in five jail inmates was under pretrial supervision. These people have not yet been sentenced, and some not even convicted, but they are held in jail while waiting for arraignment, trial, or sentencing.[12] As shown in Figure 12-2, the most popular community corrections program is community service. Treatment programs account for a mere 3 percent of those under supervision outside of jail.[13]

Prisons

prisons
State or federal facilities that hold offenders sentenced to 1 year or more incarceration.

Prisons, also known as penitentiaries and reformatories, are secure facilities where people serve a year or more after their trial and conviction. In the United States, a prison's authority over violators comes from the state and the federal government. There are currently 1,400 adult U.S. prisons under the administration of state correctional agencies and the Federal Bureau of Prisons. This number includes privately contracted prisons, which are also responsible to a state or the federal government. In addition, prisons include specialized facilities for confining parolees and shock incarceration facilities (boot camps).[14] The U.S. military operates its own prisons, which house those in the military convicted of major crimes and those who are national security risks, such as prisoners of war or enemy combatants.

More than 100 federal prisons—not including military prisons—fall under the jurisdiction of the Federal Bureau of Prisons. The map on the adjacent page shows the locations of the different Federal Bureau of Prisons' facilities. Generally they hold offenders who violate federal laws; state prisons hold those who violate state laws. In 2005, about 176,000 prisoners were confined in federal institutions, far fewer than the 1.26 million in state prisons across the country at the time.[15]

Rising Prison Costs

The average cost of incarcerating prisoners is high and rising. In 2007 in California, it cost $43,287 per year or $119 per person per day, to house an inmate—twice the national average. In 1997, the annual cost for California state prisons was $21,000 per inmate. The cost more than doubled in a decade—largely due to rising staffing costs and health care expenditures.[16] Costs of housing special-needs prisoners, such as older adults, juveniles, and offenders who are mentally or physically impaired, are also high. Figure 12-3 on page 340 illustrates the increase between 1986 and 2001, when state prison costs rose dramatically.

Rising Prison Populations

The U.S. prison population continues to increase. In California, inmates are double- and triple-bunked in gymnasiums and other communal areas. Overcrowded conditions create stress for both inmates and staff and make it difficult to operate viable rehabilitation programs. In 2006, California tried to send 8,000 medium-security inmates to prisons in other states to relieve overcrowding, but the plan was blocked in court.[17]

Mapping Prisons in the U.S.

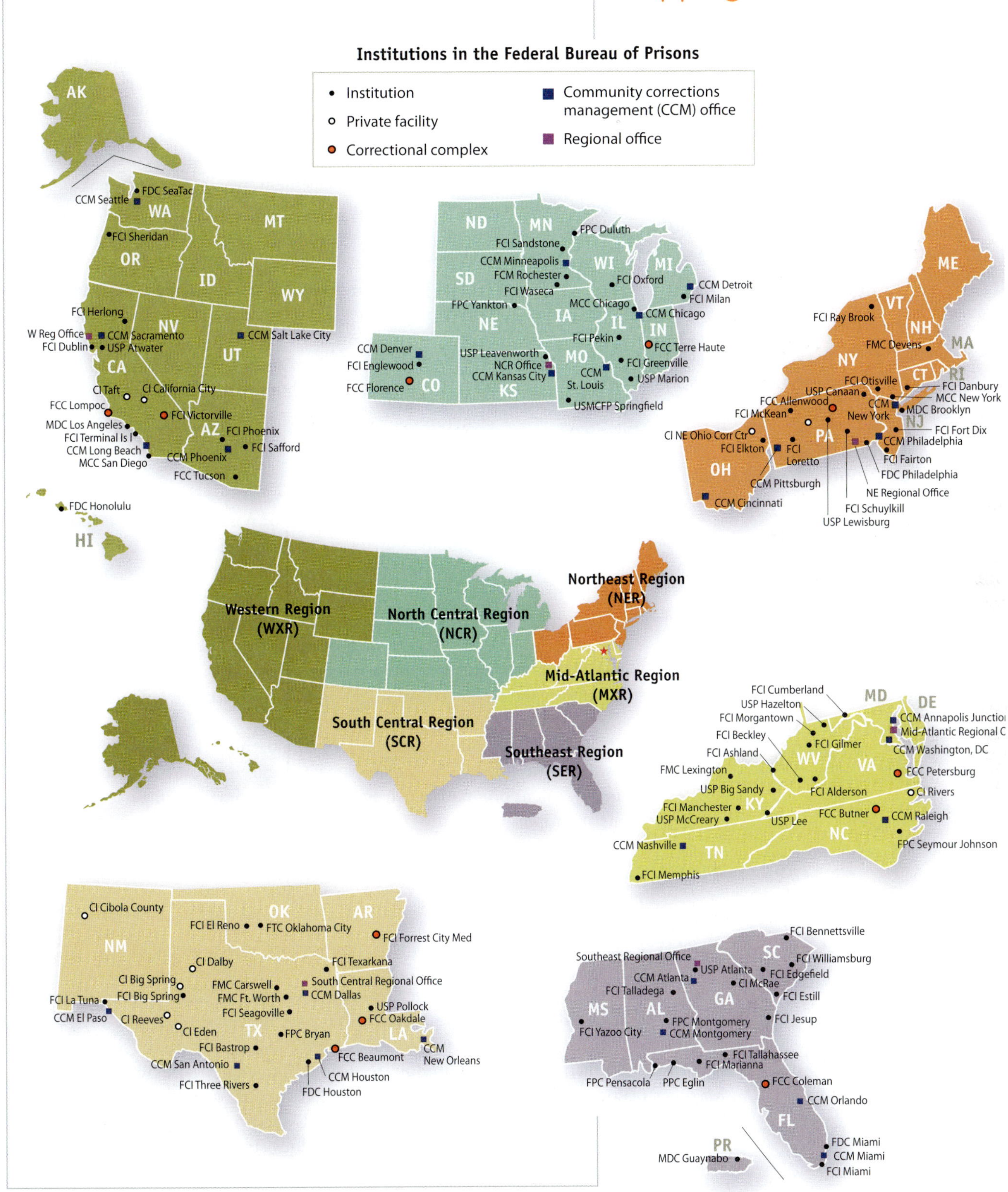

"Get tough" sentencing policies and practices are largely responsible for the increase in the prison population. Reduced use of parole keeps inmates in prison longer, and increases in parole revocations—often for minor violations—return large numbers of parolees to prison. Finally, many judges are required to impose long sentences on substance abusers arrested for drug violations, creating high rates of imprisonment for nonviolent offenders. In fact, nearly 75 percent of current admissions are for nonviolent crimes.[18] Of those sentenced to federal prisons in 2005, 11 percent had committed violent crimes, whereas

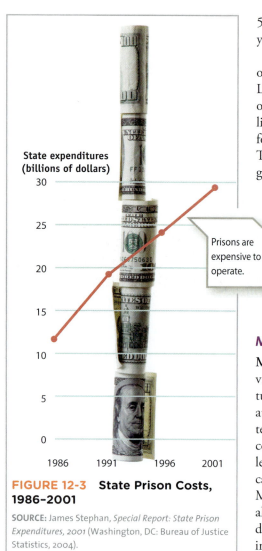

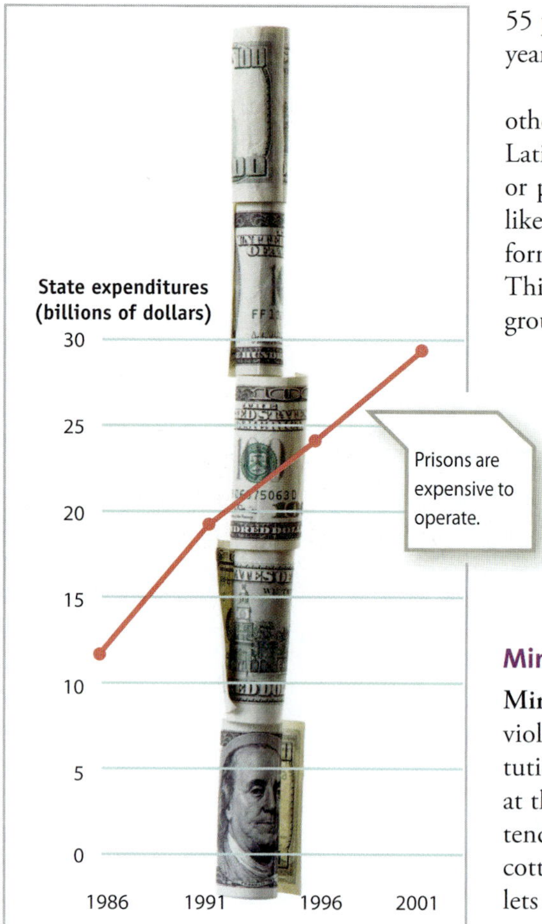

FIGURE 12-3 State Prison Costs, 1986–2001

SOURCE: James Stephan, *Special Report: State Prison Expenditures, 2001* (Washington, DC: Bureau of Justice Statistics, 2004).

55 percent were nonviolent offenders doing time for drug offenses—and that year federal prisons operated at 134 percent of their authorized capacity.[19]

In Chapter 11 we discussed the disproportionate rate at which Blacks and other people of color are incarcerated. In 2005, 1 in 8 Black males, 1 in 26 Latinos, and 1 in 59 White males ages 25–29 were incarcerated in a U.S. jail or prison.[20] Prisoners, like people in general, gravitate toward those who are like them racially, ethnically, and culturally. Male prisoners, and the gangs they form, segregate themselves largely by race for safety, support, and protection. This creates problems for prison management, which, in the face of organized groups of inmates, literally cannot let its guard down.

Types of Prisons

State and federal prisons are classified as minimum-, medium-, maximum-, or supermaximum-security facilities. These facilities are often referred to by levels, beginning with Level 1 for minimum-security prisons, Levels 2 and 3 for medium-security prisons, Level 4 for a maximum-security prison, and advancing to Level 5 for a supermaximum-security prison.

Minimum-Security Prisons

minimum-security prisons
Institutions that hold offenders who have short sentences, are nonviolent, and are unlikely to attempt escape or pose risks to others in the institution.

Minimum-security prisons hold offenders who have short sentences, are nonviolent, and are unlikely to attempt escape or pose risks to others in the institution. Sometimes offenders are transferred to minimum-security institutions at the end of long sentences to better prepare them for release. Such facilities tend to be smaller and may resemble a campus, with buildings arranged in a cottage style. Inmate housing units are dormitory-style with communal toilets and showers, although some have individual sleeping quarters. In either case, this arrangement represents a significant departure from locked cells. Minimum-security facilities might not have perimeter fencing, and generally no armed correctional officers patrol the grounds. Prisoners have a great deal of freedom of movement and may be permitted to wear civilian clothes instead of uniforms. The inmates are encouraged to pursue education, work, and treatment programs when available. Approximately 20 percent of all prisons are minimum-security institutions.

MYTH/REALITY

MYTH: Minimum-security prisons are country club environments.

REALITY: In general, prisons have a harsh, undesirable environment.[21]

Minimum-security prisons are often referred to as "country clubs" because their atmosphere can be casual and rules appear relaxed. But even though it is a low-security setting, a minimum-security prison is populated with felons, and violent outbursts can occur at any time. Although inmates in minimum-security facilities have more freedom than those in other prisons, they may not leave, and their activities are greatly restricted. They are allowed few personal possessions, visits are restricted, and privacy nonexistent. The loss of personal freedoms causes some individuals tremendous stress. Living conditions may be cramped and unsanitary. There may be little opportunity for work, education, or treatment, and personal safety is never assured.

Medium-Security Prisons

medium-security prisons
Institutions in which inmates are under greater control than in minimum-security prisons, and their freedom of movement is restricted to areas that are under close surveillance.

Approximately 25 percent of all state and federal U.S. prisons are **medium-security** institutions.[22] Inmates are under greater control than in minimum-security prisons, and their movement is restricted to areas that have close surveillance. Gun towers hold armed correctional officers who carefully watch barbed- or razor-wire perimeters. Sally ports—secure entrances with a series of gates or doors—control movement between closed zones. Closed-circuit monitoring and other security mechanisms are positioned virtually everywhere. Prisoners may take part in limited educational, vocational, and therapeutic programs, but the inmates are subject to lockdown (confinement to their cells) at any time. The numerous prisoner counts each day shut down all activities and require inmates to report to a designated area for the count.

Inmates usually share cells in a medium-security prison. Typically the buildings have several wings and two tiers, with each tier housing about 150 to 200 inmates in double bunk cells. Some prisons have open dorm sections that contain about 12 double bunks. Public bathroom areas are heavily used. There is a communal area for inmates to interact with others. Officer stations are located so they can view the entire housing unit at any given time.[23]

Privileges include mail, limited and monitored visitation, radio, television, work release, and furlough. However, few prisoners are able to take part in vocational and educational programs.

▲ A Minimum-Security Prison

Minimum-security institutions do not allow inmates access to life beyond the prison perimeters. *How does life in a minimum-security prison differ from life outside the prison?*

Maximum-Security Prisons

Inmates in **maximum-security prisons** are subject to high levels of control. Physical barriers severely restrict the mobility of prisoners. Inmates are shackled when they are moved. These prison facilities are often constructed of massive concrete walls with armed guards on patrols and in towers. Lethal electrical fences, infrared and motion-sensing devices, and electronic locking systems to keep inmates in confinement are features of maximum-security prisons. Inmate counts typically take place four times a day. Depending on prison policies, inmates are either locked in their cells or are expected to stand outside their cells during counts. Recounts are done immediately if numbers do not tabulate. Inmates know they are subject to daily inspections, constant surveillance, and random searches.[24]

maximum-security prisons Institutions subject to high levels of control in which the mobility of prisoners is severely restricted by physical barriers.

In a maximum-security prison, cells are set back-to-back in tiers in the center of a secure building, making escape more difficult. Prisoner living quarters are arranged in separate units or sections known as cell blocks, each having its own security system and correctional officers. Individual cells have sliding doors with locks operated by remote control. Toilet facilities are in the cells because prisoners are often confined there so many hours each day. When allowed out, they must remain in the cell block or in a specially caged area. When leaving their cell block, inmates are shackled and accompanied by correctional officers. These inmates may be allowed visitors but only under highly secure conditions. Death rows are normally in maximum-security prisons.

Approximately 15 percent of all U.S. prisons are maximum-security institutions. Fewer than 0.1 percent of prisoners housed in all types of prisons escape.[25] The probability that a prisoner in a maximum-security level prison will escape is even lower.

▼ Different Prison Designs

Prison architecture varies greatly.

▶ Inside a Cell Block

Cell blocks are secure, and prisoners are watched around the clock. *In what ways does lack of privacy affect prisoners?*

Supermaximum-Security Prisons

supermaximum-security (supermax) prisons
Facilities that provide the highest level of security possible—solitary confinement—using the latest correctional technology.

Supermaximum-security (supermax) prisons provide the highest level of security possible—solitary confinement—using the latest correctional technology. Most inmates are isolated because their level of violence poses a risk of serious harm to other inmates and to the correctional staff. Some have gang affiliations that would give them inordinate power in the prison or make them targets of other gangs. Others possess an antagonistic temperament or antisocial disposition. Inmates deemed high escape risks are also housed here.

Judges do not usually sentence offenders to supermax prisons. Offenders are sent there because of extreme misbehavior in other prisons, such as killing or attempting to kill other inmates or staff. Supermax prisons are said to confine "the worst of the worst." Prisoners contained in supermax prisons are not controllable in the traditional types of segregation units available in other prisons.

A whole institution can be designated supermax, but so can a single wing within a maximum-security institution, usually a housing unit or cell block. As of 2007, there were 31 supermax institutions or housing units in state and federal prisons. Fewer than 2 percent of U.S. prison inmates—approximately 20,000—are confined in supermax prisons or wings.[26] Reliance on these facilities is increasing in the United States despite criticisms that they are expensive to build and operate, violate constitutional guarantees against cruel and unusual punishment, and damage the mental health of those who live and work within them.

Supermax conditions are severe. Inmates spend 23 hours in their cells and 1 hour in a solid-walled secure recreation area only slightly larger than a cell. In the typical supermax facility, prisoners live within featureless concrete and steel enclosures and are under constant electronic surveillance. Mattresses on concrete slabs serve as beds. When windows to the outside world are present, they are typically no wider than 4 inches, and there may be small, security-reinforced skylights in some cells. Food is provided through locked food ports in cell doors. Cells are soundproof and designed to minimize social contact; inmates are not permitted even eye contact with other inmates or staff. All incoming mail is read and censored before delivery. Prisoners are subject to strip searches whenever they leave their cells and are typically accompanied by at least two correctional officers. Treatment and vocational programs are rare. When they do exist, they tend to be confined to the inmate's cell and consist of televised programming.[27]

KEY CONCEPTS

Types of Prisons

Minimum-, medium-, maximum-, and supermaximum-security institutions are difficult places to do time.

Minimum-Security Prisons	Medium-Security Prisons	Maximum-Security Prisons	Supermaximum-Security Prisons
Hold those with short sentences who are nonviolent and not likely to escape	Hold those with longer sentences and both violent and property offenders	High levels of control	Solitary confinement
Smaller facilities	Larger facilities	Houses violent prisoners	Total isolation from other prisoners
Dormitory-style housing units	Cell confinement and sometimes dorm confinement	Severe restriction of prisoner mobility	Houses antisocial violent prisoners with antagonistic temperaments
Communal toilet facilities	Daily activity dominated by counts	Shackled movement	High escape risk prisoners
May or may not have perimeter fencing	Prisoner movement is restricted	Gun towers	Twenty-three hours a day cell confinement in a soundproof cell
Normally no gun towers	High surveillance of public social areas	Lethal electrical fencing	One hour of recreation alone in walled recreation area slightly larger than a cell
More casual atmosphere	Officer stations in each housing unit	Infrared and motion-sensing devices	Twenty-fours hour electronic surveillance
Minimal restriction of movement and dress	Sally ports	Electronic locking systems	No interaction or eye contact with inmates or staff
Rehabilitation programs are encouraged	Closed zones	Daily life dominated by counts and random searches	Strip searches whenever a prisoner leaves a cell
	Close surveillance	Daily inspections	At least two correctional officers must accompany the prisoner when moved
	Gun towers	Constant surveillance	Rehabilitation programs are rare and televised into cells
	Barbed- and razor-wire perimeter fencing	Cell block living units	
	Limited rehabilitation programs	Cell confinement	
		Toilets in cells	

These isolating features take on particular importance when we consider that most of the inmates released from supermax prisons go directly into the community, with little or no "decompression" to ease them back into the mainstream.[28] Because this kind of confinement denies the basic human need to interact with others, such institutions are often accused of "manufacturing madness."[29] A Case in Point on the next page describes the U.S. military prison at Guantánamo Bay, which used supermax facilities for detainees, most of whom were not even charged with crimes.

Prisoner Classification Systems

The **classification** of inmates is a crucial area of prison management. Classification determines which inmates go to which institutions and the specific conditions under which they will be confined. Prisons are classified into different **security levels** depending on the danger level associated with the inmates being housed. Inmates, on the other hand, are classified according to **custody levels**—the risk of danger they pose to other prisoners and to correctional staff. Classification differs in men's and women's prisons. Women's prisons tend to confine all custody levels within the same facility, whereas in men's facilities custody levels may be spread among prisons.[30]

Custody levels are determined by criteria such as the crime committed, sentence length, record of past violence, prior institutional behavior, and social and medical factors such as substance abuse. An inmate may be placed in a high-security prison yet be a low (custody) risk in that institution, with privileges denied to other higher (custody) risk

classification
Determination of which inmates go to which institutions and the specific conditions under which they will be confined.

security level
The degree of danger associated with the inmates being housed in a prison.

custody level
The degree of danger an inmate poses to other prisoners and to correctional staff.

a Case in Point

Doing Time at Guantánamo Bay

Until 2009 the U.S. government's Guantánamo Bay Naval Base military prison in southeastern Cuba held about 400 male prisoners with suspected links to terrorist organizations. Detainees being held there were alleged to be unlawful enemy combatants. From the time it opened in 2002, only a handful of detainees at Guantánamo were formally charged with a crime.

The prison had six camps or compounds, ranging from low-level security to supermax. The two supermax camps were reserved for "high value" detainees, some of whom were alleged to be close associates of Osama bin Laden.

The supermax prisoners spent 23 hours a day isolated in their cells. They were not permitted to congregate. Their hour of recreation took place in a concrete courtyard encircled by high walls. When the prisoners needed to be moved, military guards handcuffed them through slots in steel doors and covered their eyes and ears. There were concerns that their minimal exposure to sunlight and lack of human interaction would cause some of these prisoners to develop serious psychological problems during their confinement.

Upon capture, none of the 400 individuals was charged with an offense. The George W. Bush administration supported this practice because "all of its detainees at Guantánamo are enemy combatants in the war against terrorism and therefore properly detained until terrorism is vanquished." In January 2009, President Barack Obama signed an executive order to close Guantánamo Bay Detention Camp. At the same time, he signed other executive orders to ban torture in interrogation and to establish a task force to review all detention policies and procedures as well as individual cases. The task force is responsible for determining whether the detainees will be sent to U.S. military and civil courts and jails, or to international tribunals. Congress is engaged in a major debate about closing Guantánamo. One of the issues is where to house the prisoners if Guantánamo is closed. The city of Hardin, Montana, has offered to provide incarceration for the Guantánamo detainees as a way of boosting economic development. The city has a brand new maximum-security facility that is fully stocked with prisoner supplies and is prisoner ready. Approximately 100 jobs would be created if Guantánamo inmates were transferred to the facility at Hardin.

OBSERVE Investigate Understand

- **What are conditions like at Guantánamo Bay?**
- **How are human rights being violated, if at all, at the prison camp?**
- **Does the kind of treatment the Guantánamo Bay prisoners received improve or worsen the chances for rehabilitating prisoners? Why or why not?**

SOURCES: "Obama Signs Order to Close Guantanamo Bay Facility," CNN, January 22, 2009, www.cnn.com/2009/POLITICS/01/22/guantanamo.order/ (retrieved February 8, 2009); "United States: Guantanamo Two Years On: U.S. Detentions Undermine the Rule of Law," *Human Rights Watch*, January 9, 2004, http://hrw.org/english/docs/2004/01/09/usdom6917.htm (retrieved April 24, 2007); Thomas Andrews et al., "Self-Mutilation and Malingering among Cuban Migrants Detained at Guantanamo Bay," *New England Journal of Medicine* 336, no. 17 (1997): 1251–1253; Marco Sassoli, "The Status of Persons Held in Guantanamo Under International Humanitarian Law," *Journal of International Criminal Justice* 2, no. 1 (2004): 96–106; George Fletcher, "Black Hole in Guantanamo Bay," *Journal of International Criminal Justice* 2, no. 1 (2004): 121–132; James Stewart, "Rethinking Guantánamo: Unlawful Confinement as Applied in International Criminal Law," *Journal of International Criminal Justice* 4, no. 1 (2006): 12–30; Ben Fox, "Life Harsher in New Guantanamo Unit," Associated Press, February 3, 2007, www.salon.com/wire/ap/archive.html?wire=D8N2DPV01.html (retrieved February 4, 2007); Josh White and Robin Wright, "Guantanamo Splits Administration: Arguments Center on How to Handle Remaining Detainees," *Washington Post*, June 22, 2007, www.washingtonpost.com/wp-dyn/content/article/2007/06/21/AR2007062102341.html (retrieved April 27, 2008); International Committee of the Red Cross, *ICRC Report on the Treatment of Fourteen "High Value" Detainees in CIA Custody* (Washington, DC: International Committee of the Red Cross, 2007); Bob Reynolds, Aljazeera.net, "Smalltown USA's Guantanamo's Hopes," May 17, 2009, http://english.aljazeera.net/news/americas/2009/05/2009515211913607892.html (retrieved May 23, 2009).

risk classification
An assessment of the level and kind of risk an individual presents to correctional staff and other inmates.

inmates. These decisions are based on **risk classification**, an assessment of the level and kind of risk an individual presents to correctional staff and other inmates.

Risk classification follows a complex protocol. An offender sentenced to prison first goes to a centralized classification facility where a team of experts conducts a battery of tests to evaluate security risk and program needs. Offenders generally stay there fewer than 90 days. While there, they are subject to high-security practices and isolation from others.

Correctional Staff

Correctional officers—otherwise known as prison guards—describe their job as the most difficult job in the world, even more difficult than police and firefighters, because stress and risks to officers' personal safety are constant. They are expected to occupy many roles. They do their jobs while trying to maintain order and discipline in a population that, for the most part, has little regard for authority.[31] Officers often see themselves as "forgotten people in a hostile social system made up of politicians, the public, prison administrators, and inmates."[32] Many officers say that they feel alienated and resent the negative stereotypes that portray them as brutal, unfeeling, rigid, authoritarian individuals who enjoy the power they can wield over the inmates. Although the Stanford Prison Experiment lends some support to these stereotypes, they are, for the most part, overstated and inaccurate.[33]

▲ Correctional officers are watching whenever prisoners gather.

Who Are Correctional Officers?

In a study of officers at Auburn Prison, a maximum-security facility in Auburn, New York, Lucien X. Lombardo painted a more sympathetic picture of correctional officers. Lombardo saw the officers as having been attracted to these careers primarily for job security, but then they are left basically alone in a hostile, dangerous, and ambiguous environment.[34] Even those who begin their careers wanting to be helpful to inmates and assist in their rehabilitation process are thwarted. New officers are thrown into their jobs with little help, forcing them to fend for themselves or rely on more seasoned officers to show them the ropes. Inmates, correctional administration, and even fellow officers are often hostile to these naïve newcomers.[35]

Lombardo found that each assignment puts different demands on the officer. For example, a yard officer must be seen as an aloof figure who watches, listens, and controls the inmates, whereas a housing block officer must deal with security, housekeeping, supervision, and human services. Officers must discretely enforce rules and use their authority wisely and humanely to cultivate inmates' cooperation.[36] Job satisfaction is greater among officers working in more service-oriented prisons than in traditional custody-oriented institutions.[37] In Real Careers on the next page, Angela Solorzano describes her job in a juvenile facility focusing on rehabilitation.

Studies of police officers have shown that those who attended college tend to be more flexible and less authoritarian than those who did not.[38] In the case of correctional officers, entry-level education standards have not increased in more than 40 years. Only 22 states require a college degree, and in others, a high-school diploma or a high school equivalency (GED) is sufficient for a candidate to qualify for employment. Only 24 percent of states screen candidates using psychological testing.[39] Thus three-quarters of the states may not know whether correctional officers in their employ are psychologically a good fit for work with offenders.

Negative attitudes and perceptions of inmates held by correctional officers create a barrier that distances them from inmates. In the extreme, some correctional staff may view inmates as less than human.[40] For example, in the 1990s, correctional officers in California were charged with staging gladiator-style fights among prisoners and shooting unarmed prisoners for sport.[41] In the Stanford Prison Experiment, Zimbardo attributed the behavior of both prisoners and correctional officers to factors in the situation, not to individuals' personalities. He believed the prison social structure was an inherently unhealthy environment that produced the aberrant, antisocial behavior of "guards" and "prisoners." The abuse Iraqi prisoners suffered at the hands of some U.S. soldiers assigned to guard them at the military prison at Abu Ghraib (see What about the Victim? on page 347) was what Zimbardo might have predicted.[42]

Professionalization

The 1990s marked a turning point for the field of corrections. To combat a negative image and gain the confidence of the public, correctional agencies followed a plan that had proven successful for the law enforcement community—professionalization of its officers. Professionalism requires a commitment to a clearly articulated set of ideals and standards that instill pride in and raise the public's view of the profession. Members of a profession acquire specialized knowledge and develop skills consistent with these ideals. They abide by an established code of ethics policed by other members of the profession.

hands-off doctrine
An approach that made courts reluctant to interfere with prison management or prisoner rights.

The key to this professionalization was education. In 1991 a joint task force of correctional administrators and academics endorsed a standardized curriculum consisting of 18 semester hours of higher education course work in corrections.[43] The conversion from an occupation to a profession required, among other changes, raising the educational minimum for entry-level positions, providing incentives for continuing education, and increasing entry-level salaries.[44]

New standards of recruitment and training for correctional officers better equip the prison staff to handle the high level of stress on the job. A new regimen of practices creates a

Real Careers

ANGELA SOLORZANO

Work location: Downey, California

College(s): East Los Angeles City College, 2004; California State University, Los Angeles, 2007

Major(s): Administration of Justice (Associate's); Criminal Justice (BS)

Job title: Detention Services Officer, Los Padrinos Juvenile Hall

Salary range for job like this: $46,000–$55,000

Time in job: 3 years

Work Responsibilities

I am a deputized peace officer who supervises detained juveniles during their activities within the living unit. I am primarily responsible for their safety and security, which means controlling and restraining combative or emotionally disturbed juveniles and providing them with situational counseling to help them perform their daily routines.

A typical workweek for me is 40 hours with 2 days off. Detention Services Officers at Los Padrinos Juvenile Hall can work any of three shifts: 6 a.m. to 2 p.m.; 2 p.m. to 10 p.m.; or 10 p.m. to 6 a.m. I have worked all three shifts, and each one involves facilitating a different routine.

6 a.m.–2 p.m.: Awaken the juveniles, make sure that they groom for school, eat breakfast and lunch, attend scheduled court hearings, and receive medical care or counseling, as needed.
2 p.m.–10 p.m.: Pick up detainees from school and conduct recreational programs. Ensure that detainees eat dinner, shower, and receive medical attention or counseling, as needed.
10 p.m.–6 a.m.: Supervise detainees during sleeping hours. Make sure that they receive medical attention, as needed. Assist them with getting up for court appearances or being transported to a facility to serve their sentence.

Regardless of which shift I work, I always need to chart the behavior of the detainees and report it to the probation officer and the court. The juvenile system is focused on rehabilitation, and we as a department hope that our services and guidance will help these young adults return to society and become productive individuals.

Why Criminal Justice?

Ever since I was a child, I enjoyed watching crime-solving TV shows like *Matlock*; *Murder, She Wrote*; *Columbo*; and *People's Court*. But it was not until high school that I realized how much I wanted to break the barrier into law enforcement, which has traditionally been a male profession. Ultimately, I would like to be a judge, and working as a detention services officer is a steppingstone toward reaching this goal.

Expectations and Realities of the Job

Before I started this job, I thought I would make a difference in the lives of all the juveniles at the facility. As it turns out, not all detainees are as open to rehabilitation and services as I had expected. To be an effective detention officer, I always have to be willing to dedicate additional time and effort to those who require it. I am disappointed that the system does not rehabilitate all of the detainees, but when a juvenile does emerge from the facility a changed citizen, I know that my job is worthwhile.

My Advice to Students

To be a successful detention services officer you have to be willing to serve and respect the juveniles with whom you work. This can mean being patient with someone who suffers mental illness, or being accepting of someone who comes from a different social or cultural background. You must put aside your own opinions, emotions, and beliefs and not judge the juveniles for the crimes they have been accused of committing.

supportive subculture that reinforces professional attitudes and competencies. Formal education alone is not sufficient. Pre- and in-service training are the most important ways correctional agencies can increase the professionalism of their officers and help set the tone and shape the attitudes of an institution.[45]

PRISONER RIGHTS

MYTH/REALITY

MYTH: Once an inmate has served time, the debt owed to society is paid and life as usual can resume.

REALITY: Many rights are taken away from offenders during and after they serve time in prison. In some states, ex-offenders lose civil rights such as the right to vote, hold public office, serve on a jury, have occupational licenses, or own a firearm. Incarceration may affect the life of the ex-convict long after release.[46]

Civil Rights

Until the 1960s, convicted offenders had no civil rights other than those granted by specific laws. Under the **hands-off doctrine**, courts were reluctant to interfere with prison management, and an inmate had little legal recourse if subjected to abuse and neglect while in custody. Convicted prisoners were considered civilly "dead." In 1964, however, the U.S. Supreme Court ruling in *Cooper v. Pate* gave prisoners access to the courts by granting them the right to bring civil actions against prison authorities for violations of civil rights.[47] Inmates could now sue for officer brutality, inhumane conditions, and inadequate nutrition and medical care. Also in *Cooper v. Pate*, the Court specifically held that Muslim inmates had the right to challenge prison officials for acts of religious discrimination under the Civil Rights Act of 1871.

An individual serving time for a crime today still loses certain rights. For example, she cannot hold public office. In many states even after serving her sentence she still loses the right to vote, to serve on a jury, to be a witness, or to own a firearm. She also may lose rights of employment forever by being stripped of or barred from holding occupational licenses, such as therapist, doctor, nurse, dental hygienist, or bartender.

Due Process Rights

In 1974, in *Wolff v. McDonnell*, the Supreme Court applied Fourteenth Amendment procedural rights to prison inmates, guaranteeing them not only access to the courts but also due process in disciplinary

What about the Victim?

Implications of Abu Ghraib Prisoner Abuse in Iraq

Shocking reports of the abuse of prisoners by some U.S. soldiers assigned to the Abu Ghraib prison facility in Iraq were brought to the public's attention in 2004 by the television news program *60 Minutes* and *The New Yorker* magazine. Photographs depicted guards humiliating naked Iraqi inmates and intimidating them with snarling attack dogs. Subsequent inquiry documented a number of other abuses that included guards urinating on detainees.

In Abu Ghraib, as well as other institutions where officers have total control over prisoners, abuses of power can take place. In such situations, unless clear leadership prohibits the misuse of power, it appears inevitable that abuses like those in Zimbardo's Stanford Prison Experiment will occur. Also relevant is social psychologist Stanley Milgram's 1960s series of experiments on obedience to authority. Two-thirds of Milgram's subjects, when directed by a researcher in a white lab coat, obediently increased the level of shock they gave another individual, despite screams and pleas from the "victim"—actually an unharmed confederate—in the next room. Some 45 years later, in 2006, social psychologist Jerry Burger obtained similar outcomes in his partial replication of Milgram's experiment.

Such studies help us understand how ordinary people can use the rationalization of "just obeying orders" to free themselves of inhibitions to do harm to others. To the extent they believed they were acting on orders from a legitimate authority, the military officers in Abu Ghraib could justify to themselves the abuses they inflicted on the inmates. Without institutional checks on that exercise of power, and without proper training, oversight, and supervision, such behavior, Zimbardo believes, is inevitable.

OBSERVE Investigate Understand

- **In your own everyday experience, have you ever seen an ordinary person act questionably when put into a position of unsupervised authority or power?**
- **What causes people to act questionably in these positions?**
- **How can a situation such as this be mediated or resolved?**

SOURCES: Phillip G. Zimbardo, *The Lucifer Effect: Understanding How Good People Turn Evil* (New York: Random House, 2007); Seymour M. Hersh, "Torture at Abu Ghraib," *The New Yorker*, May 10, 2004, www.newyorker.com/archive/2004/05/10/040510fa_fact (retrieved March 22, 2007); Salon.com, "Salon Exclusive: The Abu Ghraib Files," www.salon.com/news/feature/2006/02/16/abu_ghraib/ (retrieved March 22, 2007); APA Online, "How Psychology Can Help Explain the Iraqi Prisoner Abuse," American Psychological Association, May, 2004, www.apa.org/topics/iraqiabuse.html (retrieved March 22, 2007); Jerry Burger, "Replicating Milgram: Would People Still Obey Today?" *American Psychologist* 64, no. 1 (January 2009), 1–11; Phillip Zimbardo, *The Psychological Power and Pathology of Imprisonment* (San Francisco, CA: U.S. House of Representatives, Committee on the Judiciary, 1971).

hearings.[48] Prisoners must be notified of charges, be able to call witnesses, have the right to assistance in a defense, and have the right to an impartial hearing before any administrative decisions are made that could deprive inmates of their rights or freedom. The protection is particularly important when disciplinary action could take away **good time** credits (earned for satisfactory behavior), thus jeopardizing early release, or when an administrative decision places an inmate into solitary confinement. The Court also declared racial discrimination intolerable except where "prison security and discipline" necessitated a particular action, such as assigning an inmate to a certain cell block because of imminent racist threats.

good time
Time taken off a prison sentence for satisfactory behavior or for participating in a prison program.

Rights guaranteed by the Eighth Amendment prohibiting cruel and unusual punishment were addressed in *Estelle v. Gamble* (1976).[49] The ruling in this case required that "deliberate indifference" to an inmate's alleged plight be proved in order for that inmate's challenge to succeed. This standard is, however, difficult to meet. In 1986, in

A Global View

Executed Chinese Prisoners Become Organ Donors

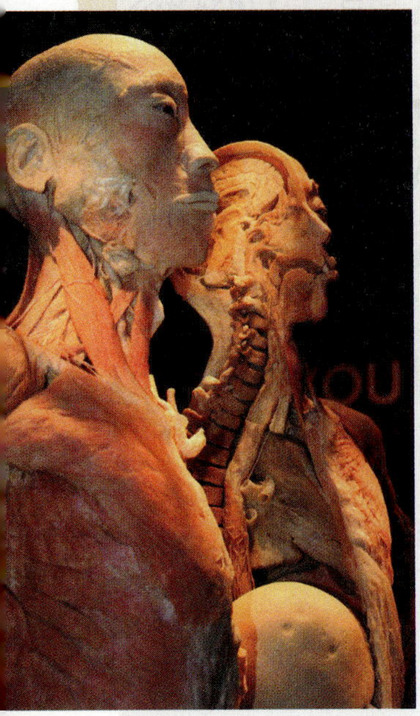

Prisoners in China are routinely stripped of their legal rights when they are charged with offenses. Those who are executed for their crimes are routinely stripped of their organs. Throughout the 1990s the United States pressed for changes to this practice of involuntary organ harvesting, which the World Medical Association and the World Health Organization both regard as unethical.

China, which uses the death penalty for 68 crimes, is responsible for a large percentage of the world's executed prisoners. According to human rights groups, these prisoners are used as a source of organ donation throughout the world. Human rights advocates allege that many of the organs are transplanted into wealthy Asian and other foreign patients who can afford to pay top dollar. Chinese doctors who have participated in or witnessed organ transplants attest that some 99 percent of the organs came from executed prisoners. Some critics charge that organs are removed from still-living prisoners and that executions are scheduled to meet the need for particular organs. The time between arrest and execution may only be days or even hours.

Do these condemned inmates give permission for their organs to be used after death? If so, do they give it freely? The fact that China has strong cultural prohibitions against organ removal before burial suggests that voluntary organ donation in China is not common. Critics argue that, in any case, condemned inmates are not capable of giving truly voluntary consent in the conditions of their incarceration.

The Chinese government contends that organ donation by condemned prisoners is regulated and occurs only in extraordinary cases following strict rules. Condemned prisoners must voluntarily express the wish to donate their organs, or their families must give consent. Nevertheless, China is feeling strong international pressure to eliminate secrecy and make organ transplant policies transparent, so it is clear that condemned prisoners are truly volunteering to donate their organs after execution. An additional concern is that bodies of Chinese prisoners have been exported for traveling "Bodies" exhibits in the United States.

Observe Investigate Understand

- **What are the arguments for and against China's use of organs from executed prisoners?**
- **Even if the organ donation is involuntary, should China be allowed to continue the program as it benefits those who receive the transplants?**
- **What if somebody proposed an organ donation program for death row inmates in the United States? In what circumstances would such a program succeed or fail?**

SOURCES: Fu-Jin Shih, Ming-Kuen Lai, Min-Heuy Lin, Hui-Ying Lin, Chuan-I Tsao, Bau-Ruei Duh, and Shu-Hsun Chu, "The Dilemma of 'To-Be or Not-To-Be': Needs and Expectations of the Taiwanese Cadaveric Organ Donor Families During the Pre-Donation Transition," *Psychosomatic Medicine* 63 (2001): 69–78; Brian Ross, Rhonda Schwartz, and Anna Schecter, "Exclusive Secret Trade in Chinese Bodies," ABC News, February 14, 2008, http://abcnews.go.com/Blotter/story?id=4291334 (retrieved February 8, 2009); Amnesty International, "China, The Death Penalty, A Failure of Justice," http://asiapacific.amnesty.org/apro/APROweb.nsf/pages/appeals_adpan_china (retrieved April 15, 2007); Associated Press, "China: Use of Prisoners' Organs Regulated," Forbes.com, March 14, 2007, www.forbes.com/feeds/ap/2007/03/14/ap3514172.html (retrieved March 16, 2007); Joshua Pantesco, "China Court Official Insists Organ Donation by Executed Prisoners Strictly Regulated," *Jurist: Legal News and Research*, March 14, 2007, http://jurist.law.pitt.edu/paperchase/2007/03/china-court-official-insists-organ.php (retrieved March 16, 2007); Michael Parmly, "Sale of Human Organs in China," U.S. State Department, June 27, 2001, www.state.gov/g/drl/rls/rm/2001/3792.htm (retrieved March 16, 2007).

the case of *Daniels v. Williams*, the Supreme Court held that neglect or unintentional acts causing injury are insufficient grounds, on their own, to assign culpability to corrections officials.[50] For prison officials to be held responsible for an injury, the inmate must show that the officials had knowledge of a situation and deliberately allowed it to occur. Merely being careless in their duties is not a constitutional violation. Limited though this protection might be, A Global View explains that not all countries have due process for prisoners.

During the so-called Prisoner Rights Era (1970–1991), the Supreme Court tended to support rights of prisoners in accordance with the Constitution. This era came to a close in 1991 when the composition of the Supreme Court changed and the majority of justices began to support prison administrators. In close 5–4 decisions, changing just one justice on the Court can change the entire philosophy of its decisions.

This happened when the Supreme Court decided in 1991 that prison conditions such as overcrowding do not violate the Constitution because the intent of overcrowding is not malicious nor are overcrowded conditions the result of "deliberate indifference."[51] The Court also ruled that the prohibition against cruel and unusual punishment is not applicable to overcrowding because this standard implies intent on the part of the perpetrator. Yet in 1993 the Court held that exposing a prisoner to secondhand smoke with deliberate indifference would violate the prisoner's Eighth Amendment rights regarding cruel and unusual punishment.[52] Many gray areas thus await future judicial determinations.

First Amendment Rights

The First Amendment of the U.S. Constitution guarantees freedom of speech and freedom of religion. In 1974 California inmates in *Procunier v. Martinez* asserted that state regulations censoring a prisoner's mail were unconstitutional because they violated freedom of speech and expression.[53] One regulation banned letters that criticized prison conditions. Another banned the use of law students and other legal paraprofessionals to conduct attorney–client interviews with inmates. The U.S. Supreme Court struck down these state regulations as unconstitutional. When prison authorities restrict an inmate's religious practice, they usually justify it by claiming a need for institutional security. Sometimes questions are raised about the legitimacy of a prisoner's stated religion. In one case thrown out by a federal appeals court, inmates claimed they were members of the "Church of the New Song" (CONS) and were required to eat steak and drink Harvey's Bristol Cream sherry as part of their religious practice. For religions considered more mainstream and whose strictures do not interfere with the security of the institution, inmates have the right to practice their faith. For example, in 1972 the Supreme Court affirmed the right of an inmate to practice Buddhism in the case of *Cruz v. Beto.*[54]

In 1987, the Supreme Court held in *O'Lone v. Estate of Shabazz* that prison officials were not required to alter a Black Muslim's work schedule to enable him to attend Friday afternoon services, as long as they had a rational reason for the restriction.[55] In 2005 the U.S. District Court in Colorado ruled that a Muslim inmate did not have to register as Jewish to receive kosher meals, in order to meet his religious dietary requirements.[56] More recently, in response to a lawsuit, the Wyoming State Penitentiary agreed to adjust the mealtimes of Muslim prisoners that interfered with their required prayers.[57] In 2005, in *Cutter v. Wilkinson*, the Supreme Court unanimously upheld the constitutionality of the Religious Land Use and Institutionalized Persons Act of 2000 (RLUIPA), which protects the religious freedom of prison inmates.[58]

LIFE IN PRISONS AND JAILS

Institutional life for inmates and staff is centered on custody and security. The result for prisoners is monotony and regimentation, yet the climate can turn to violence in an instant as individuals and gangs compete for scarce resources in the prison.

The Inmate Subculture

total institutions
Facilities responsible for, and in control of, every aspect of life for those who live and work within them, including food, shelter, medical assistance, clothing, and safety.

institutionalization
The state of being dependent on an institution to meet basic needs, such as for food, shelter, and friends, to the point of being unwilling—or unable—to function in the outside world.

Prisons are one type of **total institution**, a facility responsible for, and in control of, virtually every aspect of life for those who live and work within them, including food, shelter, medical assistance, clothing, and safety. These total institutions exist within the broader society yet are isolated from it. Contacts with outsiders are limited and tightly controlled.

When people depend on an institution to meet their basic needs, such as for food, shelter, and friends, to the point of being unwilling—or unable—to function in the outside world, we say they are a product of **institutionalization**. The more time offenders spend incarcerated, the more likely that institutionalization will occur. "State-raised convicts" are those who spend more of their lives in confinement—in juvenile halls, detention centers, training schools, jails, or prisons—than in free society. There are ex-convicts who, not long after their release, commit new crimes in order to be sent back to prison where they know what is expected of them. Their friends are there, and the institution meets their most basic needs of food and shelter.

Having all needs provided by a single institution, however, comes at a price. Unique subcultures develop that establish values, roles, and communication patterns and largely determine how inmates relate to one another. The behaviors of the "guards" and "prisoners" in the famous Stanford Prison Experiment demonstrate how these roles affect behavior. Correctional officers and prisoners are frequently suspicious of and hostile toward one another. The prisoners see the officers who enforce the rules of the institution as their adversaries. The officers, in turn, see prisoners as untrustworthy and manipulative.[59] Each group behaves according to an "us versus them" mentality. In such an environment, it is not surprising Zimbardo found he had to terminate his experiment prematurely.

prisonization
A process of socialization whereby individuals adopt the norms, values, and beliefs of the inmate subculture as their own.

inmate subculture
The norms, values, and beliefs that develop among prisoners.

deprivation model
The perspective that the hardships prisoners endure lead to the development of a distinctive way of behaving in prison.

importation model
The perspective assuming that inmate subculture does not develop as a result of prison circumstances but rather is brought in, or imported, from the outside when offenders enter.

pains of imprisonment
The deprivations inmates experience such as liberty, autonomy, security, personal goods and services, and heterosexual relations.

inmate code
Rules of behavior that inmates follow.

Prisonization is the process of socialization whereby individuals adopt the norms, values, and beliefs of the **inmate subculture** as their own. The longer offenders spend in prison, the more they become prisonized. Inmates become decidedly opposed to authority, for instance, and resist those in authority.[60] They learn not to share information with their keepers and not to portray themselves as needy, weak, or vulnerable. They are suspicious of the motives of others. An inmate who firmly accepts these values becomes increasingly difficult to rehabilitate to life outside of prison.

How Subcultures Are Formed

The inmate subculture has its own norms, language, and roles (see Key Concept table on the next page).[61] How this subculture arises in a prison has long been the subject of two competing schools of thought: the **deprivation model** and the **importation model**.

The deprivation model proposes that the **pains of imprisonment**—the deprivation of liberty, autonomy, security, personal goods and services, and heterosexual relations—lead to the development of a distinctive inmate subculture to cope with the pain of these losses. The subculture forms its own **inmate code**, or rules of behavior. Inmates are not to exploit one another. They are to be strong in confronting the pains of imprisonment. And they are to oppose prison authority. In short, "don't rat on others," "don't lose your cool," and "don't trust the guards." The inmate subculture provides solidarity and the means by which inmates, collectively, cope with incarceration.[62]

The importation model holds that the inmate subculture does not arise from prison circumstances but rather is imported from the outside when offenders enter.[63] For example, aspects of the drug subculture of the streets become part of the inmate subculture.[64]

In truth, both inside and outside factors contribute to the development of the inmate subculture.[65] Adherence to the inmate code does not necessarily lead to solidarity (or less violence). Male inmates divide themselves primarily along racial lines. The tensions between racially diverse inmates—not between inmates and correctional officers—account for most of the instability in prisons today.[66] (For female inmates, prison is by and large a different world, as we will see later in the chapter).

PRISON SLANG TERMS
Prisoners have their own language.

Slang Term	What It Means
Beef	A crime
Bullet	1-year period of time
CO or hack	Correctional officer
Dorm	Security housing unit
Fish	A new arrival, first-timer to a prison, or anyone not wise to prison life
Gated out	Released from prison
Ink	Tattoo
Mule	Someone who smuggles drugs into an institution
Rolled up	Arrested
Shank	Prison-made knife
Turned out	Being forced into homosexual acts
Bootie flu The ninja	AIDS/HIV
The hole	Solitary confinement
Tipped up	Gang affiliated
Yolked	Muscular

Racial Concerns

During the 1970s, a number of court decisions held as unconstitutional prison practices that assigned inmates to cells or programs on the basis of their race. Prison officials expressed concern that forced integration would fuel already strong tensions among inmates and lead to significantly more violence. Some violence did occur in response to integration, but not as much as predicted. Still, much of the violence in men's prisons today occurs between gangs of different racial affiliations.[67]

Racial and ethnic tensions are a significant feature of male prison life. Unlike the world outside, male prisons tend to be dominated by people of color. Some have argued that as a result, the minority White males have greater difficulty adjusting to the prison environment than do men of color.[68] Whites also tend to be victimized more frequently and severely. Evidence suggests that Whites are raped more than any other racial group.[69]

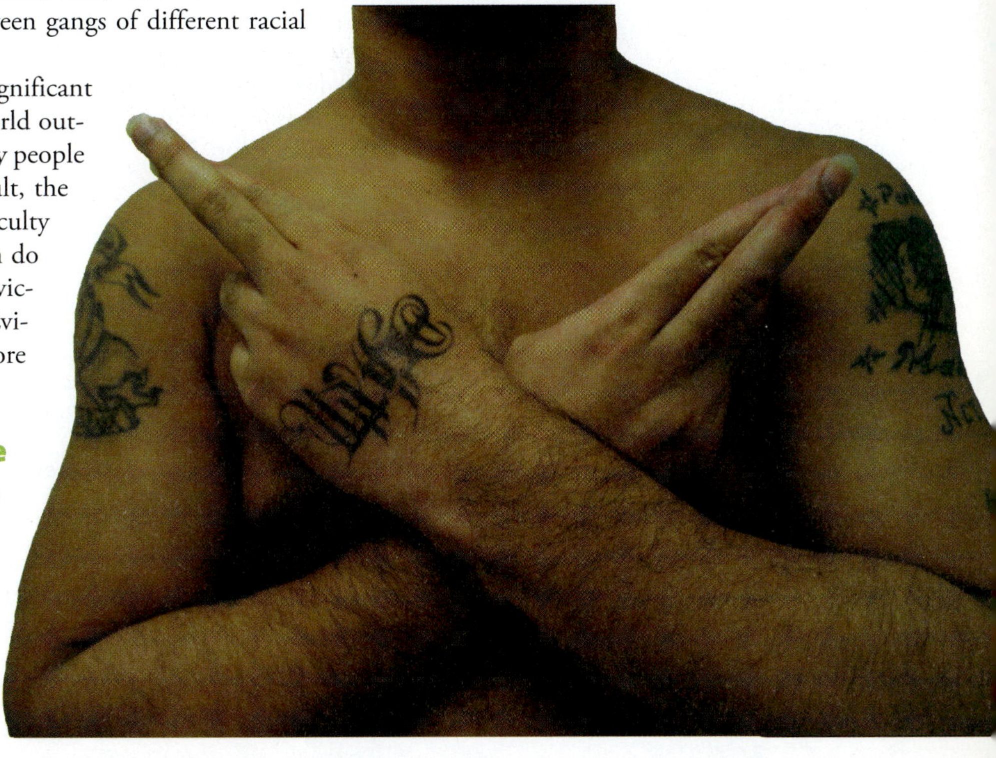

▼ Prison gang members show their affiliations by their tattoos and gestures.

Institutional Gangs and Violence

Prison gangs are a major aspect of prison life, providing support for and protection of their members. As prisons in the United States became increasingly overcrowded, the prison subculture became more fragmented and disorganized. Inmates saw life in prison as more dangerous. Belonging to a gang provides the member with a sense of stability as well as protection.[70] Most gangs are racially segregated, with members coming from the same city—and often the same neighborhood.[71]

Gangs manage drug trafficking, not only within the prison but often also on the streets, through associates in the community with whom they communicate. They also control the availability of many illegal goods and services in prisons. In fact, the tension and violence between rival prison gangs involve protecting "business interests" in the black market.[72]

Gangs operate in the prisons in at least 40 states as well as in federal prisons.[73] The rise of violent racist prison gangs began, in part, as a result of the desegregation of the U.S. prison populations in the 1960s. Racist rhetoric and animosity increase tension within prisons and undermine security.[74] The Aryan Brotherhood, one of the first and best-known racist prison gangs, began at San Quentin Prison in California. There are other White supremacist gangs with neo-Nazi identification in prisons. Because gangs tend to identify themselves along racial lines, Black, Latino, and Asian gangs also formed. Visitors carry messages back and forth between gang members in prison and street gangs.

Control of Gang Violence

security threat group (STG) Inmates who, when they collaborate, can jeopardize the institution's security.

Strategies to control gang activity begin by identifying **security threat groups (STGs)**—inmates who, when they collaborate, can jeopardize the institution's security. Typically, inmates in an STG are members of White supremacy groups, street gangs, cults, or outlaw motorcycle gangs who use intimidation and violence to control drug trafficking, gambling, and extortion in prison. Many build loyalty by appealing to inmates' existing racial hatred and their need for protection from other inmates.[75] Most prison gangs have a paramilitary organization with rules and regulations. While in prison, gang members tend to associate with other members in their gang.

Gang affiliations are sometimes difficult to identify. Gang-related tattoos, self-admission, possession of gang-related literature, as well as monitoring correspondence with outside known gang members are some of the ways officials identify gang affiliations.[76] Most experts believe that prison gangs will never be completely eliminated. Once a member joins a gang, it is extremely difficult to leave.[77]

Some allege that correctional officers encourage—or do not discourage—racial violence to minimize the possibility that inmates will organize themselves against the officers.[78] Others point to STG policies as the source of many tensions that result in violence. For example, it is not uncommon for state corrections departments to separate gang members from the general population and different gangs from one another. Many states have special lockdown units or "gang blocks" specifically for housing STG inmates. Some critics charge that prison administrations arbitrarily classify prisoners as members of STGs based on racial stereotyping.[79]

Prison Riots

MYTH/REALITY

MYTH: Prison riots are evidence that inmates are violent and dangerous.

REALITY: Prison riots are often the result of administrative policies that inmates resist. When offenders feel their needs are dismissed by correctional administrators and perceive that other avenues to express grievances are exhausted, riots can occur.[80] Since the 1930s, psychologists have linked frustration with aggression.[81] Incarceration can produce frustrations that can to lead to violence.[82]

Riots are only one form of prison violence. When they occur, however, they generate media attention because they frequently harm both inmates and staff. Prison riots are not new. Since 1855, it is estimated that there have been 500 prison riots in the United States, most at maximum- or medium-security facilities.[83]

Prison riots arise from a variety of factors: the authoritarian and demeaning behavior of some correctional officers, conflict between gangs, the subculture of violence, deprivations associated with imprisonment, racial tensions, boredom, overcrowding, and poor prison management. Yet some riots appear to happen randomly, making them impossible to predict.[84]

Two of the most infamous riots were at New York's Attica Prison in 1971 and at Santa Fe's New Mexico State Prison in 1980. These two riots were very different in nature. In Attica the rioters attempted to force reforms such as more exercise and better food and programs. It was reported that correctional officers who were hostages were protected by inmates from violence. Nonetheless, in overtaking the rioters, 43 deaths of inmates and hostages occurred. The abuses that occurred took place after the riots, when officers retaliated with violence against the prisoners. In Santa Fe there were no demands for reforms, just violence on the part of inmates against other inmates and against officers. This riot occurred as a result of harassment and abuse of inmates. The underlying driving forces were revenge and counterrevenge.[85] It appears that some riots can be prevented if prison policies provide inmates with accessible means to voice their complaints, such as surveys or inmate councils that relay concerns to prison officials.[86]

Sex and Sexual Assault in Prison

Sexual assault is physically and emotionally devastating, and its scars can last a lifetime.[87] In 2005, according to the Department of Justice, there were 6,241 reports of sexual violence in jails and prisons, including allegations of sexual assault by correctional staff.[88] The general opinion is that this figure is much lower than the actual number of such incidents.[89] Many men who are victims of male rape in prison are reluctant to report these incidents due to either embarrassment or fear of retaliation.[90] One study of the federal prison system estimates about half of the rape victims interviewed had not told anyone about their experience. Another factor in underreporting is that some prison officers simply do not report the assaults to the authorities. They may consider rape a price the offender must pay for the crime he committed.[91]

The community outside prison generally views sexual assaults by males on other males as homosexual acts. Inmates, however, do not see this in the same way. The aggressor sees himself as a masculine heterosexual and views the passive individual as effeminate and homosexual. Thus inmates tend to see physically stronger aggressors who force sex on a "weaker" inmate not as rapists but as dominant males asserting their manhood.[92]

MYTH/REALITY

MYTH: Sexual violence against and exploitation of inmates of the same gender are primarily the result of a lack of heterosexual opportunities.

REALITY: Sexual violence and exploitation in prisons are mostly centered on power, status, and control—not on sexual needs.[93]

Male prisoners with certain characteristics, such as youth, attractive looks, small stature, and naiveté, who enter a correctional facility as first-time offenders are immediately identified by other prisoners and targeted by some for sexual assault.[94] Twenty-two percent of male inmates claim to have been raped or forced into sex while incarcerated. Only 29 percent of these victims reported their rape to the authorities. These figures mask the much larger scope of sexual assault, the many instances—technically not rape—in which inmates consent to being sexually exploited after being threatened with rape or other types of violence.[95] Often staff members ignore sexual assaults, but they also can contribute to

RealCrime Tech

BLOCKING CELL PHONE USE TO ENHANCE PRISON SECURITY

Prison officials in several states have requested the Federal Communications Commission (FCC) to allow them to test new phone jamming equipment that would block illegal cell phone use by prison inmates. Riots, intimidation of public officials, smuggling of drugs and weapons, and credit card and tax fraud have been traced to the illegal use of cell phones. There have also been charges that inmates ordered murders outside the prison by means of cell phones.

The cell phone companies are fighting use of or even testing of this new jamming technology. They say that jamming cell signals could interfere with other communications, a claim disputed by prison officials.

SOURCES: www.cellantenna.com/pressreleases/CA_TRtechnologystory_11.21.08.htm (retrieved January 14, 2009); http://online.wsj.com/article/SB122722803428046289.html (retrieved January 14, 2009); www.keyetv.com/content/news/topnews/story/Test-to-jam-prison-cell-phones-nixed-FCC-says-it/kWRTk8zleUCpdGXj8MBYow.cspx.

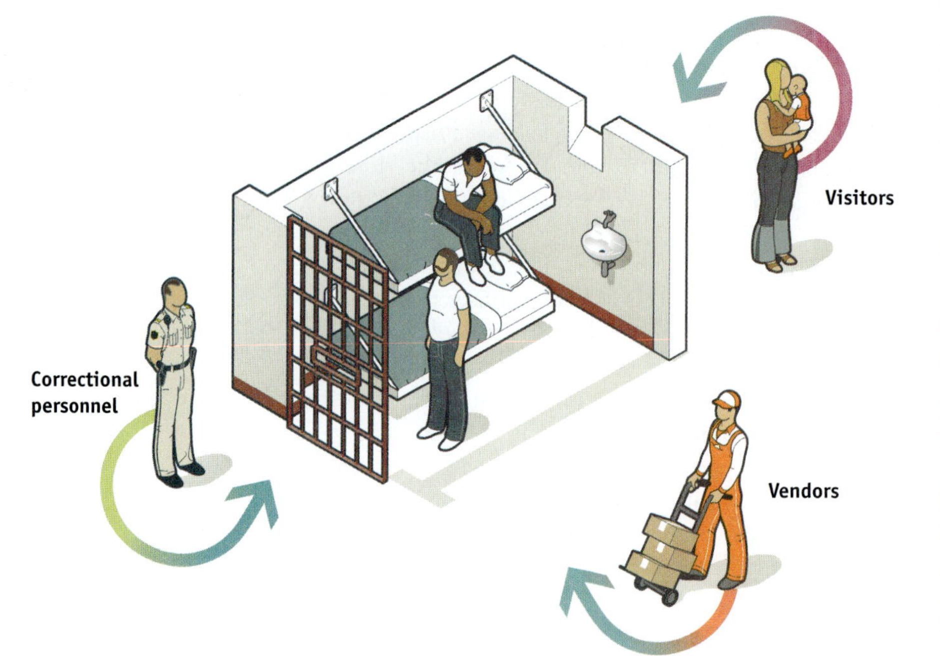

FIGURE 12-4 Illegal Drug Traffic in Prison
Inmates obtain drugs in a variety of creative ways.

them. In one notorious case in California's Corcoran Prison, correctional officers were accused of placing inmates in cells with known prison rapists as punishment.[96]

Illegal Drugs

Illegal drugs are pervasive within jails and prisons even though these substances are strictly prohibited. In spite of aggressive prison search practices, drugs are continually smuggled into institutions by visitors as well as by correctional personnel (see Figure 12-4).[97] Also, with some yeast, sugar, and water, inmates can easily make a form of alcohol (called pruno).[98]

Although the majority of drug offenders are convicted of nonviolent crimes, inmates under the influence of prohibited substances may become aggressive and pose a risk to themselves, other inmates, or staff. Drug use then becomes not only a problem for the inmate but also a concern for the institution. Some inmates, however, claim that use of drugs such as cannabis and tranquilizers have a calming effect on them, improve their ability to deal with the prison environment, and improve their psychological health.[99]

Solitary Confinement

solitary confinement
Isolation that denies the basic human need to interact with others.

While supermax institutions specialize in providing **solitary confinement**, all prisons have the ability to place inmates in solitary when necessary, physically segregating them from other inmates and severely restricting their interactions, generally limited to correctional staff. Solitary confinement cells are bare and austere, providing virtually no sensory stimulation. Inmates often become disoriented and may emerge with mental disorders that did not exist before their isolation.[100]

punitive segregation
A special area in a prison that provides additional supervision and control of inmates for disciplinary reasons.

administrative segregation
A special area in a prison in which inmates are deprived of the services available to the general population.

An inmate may be placed in solitary for disciplinary reasons, which is called **punitive segregation**. Prisoners can be assigned to punitive segregation for violent behavior, setting fires, and possession of contraband such as illegal drugs, among other causes. Prison authorities must follow a legal process before taking such actions because prisoners do have legally protected liberties, though not all the rights of defendants in criminal court. Inmates also may be placed in solitary to provide supervision and control beyond that given to the general prison population; this is called **administrative segregation**. So-called ad seg inmates are considered likely targets of physical (including sexual) harm by other inmates because of the nature of their crimes (such as sex crimes against children), the notoriety of their crimes, or their gang affiliation. Or they may pose a threat to others or to themselves.

The United States holds more prisoners in solitary confinement than any other country in the world. Some 25,000 inmates are isolated in supermax facilities, and 50,000 to 80,000 more are held in some form of isolation for varying amounts of time in maximum-security prisons. The use of prolonged solitary confinement is relatively recent in U.S. prisons. The first supermax prison opened in 1983; by the end of the 1990s, 60 supermax facilities had opened and nearly all maximum-security prisons had established units for solitary confinement.[101]

Solitary confinement does a good job of protecting a prison population by isolating those prone to violence and harm to others. But many of those who are isolated are not in that category, and their isolation only feeds a tendency to irrational behavior, anger, and violence. Studies have found that prolonged isolation from human contact leads to brooding, retaliation fantasies, hallucinations, panic attacks, withdrawal, and, in some cases, a catatonic state. Moreover, being deprived of human contact does a poor job of preparing inmates who are freed the ability to adjust to the outside community.[102]

What are the alternatives to solitary confinement? Some groups have suggested limiting isolation to 90 days. Some favor abolishing the system altogether. Beginning in the 1980s, Britain gradually moved away from using solitary confinement because correctional officials found it did not diminish violence in the prisons, it was costly, and the public did not support it. The British corrections system developed a strategy to prevent violence instead of heaping punishments on violent behavior. Noting that prisoners who act violently in one kind of environment will behave reasonably in another setting, the British began to give the prisoners more, rather than less, control; provided them more opportunities for work, education, and mental health treatment; and allowed them to earn rights for privileges. This preventive approach has had good results, and the use of isolation in British prisons is now minimal.[103]

WOMEN IN PRISON

As we learned in Chapter 11, women's prisons were largely ignored in the United States until the mid-1800s. Attention to women's prisons and the incarceration of women, however, gained gradual momentum in the twentieth century.

The Female Prison Population

Women make up approximately 7 percent of state and federal prison inmates.[104] Although there are fewer women than men incarcerated in U.S. prisons, the female population is rapidly growing. Between 2005 and 2006, the growth rate of women in prison (4.5 percent) was much faster than the growth rate of men in prison (2.7 percent). Furthermore, in 2006 the growth rate for incarcerated women rose faster than in the preceding 5 years.[105] Moreover, the three largest U.S. prison systems combined—California, Texas, and the Federal Bureau of Prisons—held more than one-third of the nation's incarcerated women.[106] Some reasons for the rapid increase in the population of female prisoners include the increase in the crime rate among women, the "get tough" movement and policies dealing with crime, the drug epidemic, and mandatory sentencing that went into effect in the mid-1980s that no longer permitted judges to consider family and gender factors in sentencing. This ended the role that chivalry (judicial courtesy) played in sentencing women during earlier years.[107]

Of all female inmates in U.S. prisons during 2006, 48 percent were White, 28 percent Black, and 17 percent Latina. Between 2000 and 2006, the percentage of White sentenced female inmates increased, the percentage of Black female inmates decreased, and the number of sentenced Latina inmates remained about the same. Still, women of color in U.S. prisons have significantly higher incarceration rates than White women.[108]

▲ When prisons are overcrowded, public spaces are used as dormitories.

Most women incarcerated in U.S. prisons are not young. The 35 to 39 age group represents approximately 19 percent of all incarcerated women.[109]

Characteristics of Women's Prisons

Women are imprisoned in various types of facilities. They may be housed in prisons only for females, or they may be imprisoned in a separate wing of a men's institution. Rarely women may be held in "coed" prisons in which the females are housed separately from the males but share programs for both sexes. Institutions for women are primarily run according to a custodial model and have few rehabilitation programs.

With the increasing number of women being sentenced to prison, overcrowding is becoming a problem. For example, California's prisons for women are 171 to 200 percent over capacity.[110] Federal women's facilities are also over capacity. The era of designing small cottage-style women's prisons is fading. Many jurisdictions are likely to follow California's lead in building large women's prisons. One women's prison complex in California incarcerates more than 7,000 women and is the largest prison complex for women in the world.

How Women Do Time in Prison

Male and female prisoners respond differently to custody and supervision and have different needs. Yet the policies, procedures, and practices developed for male inmates have traditionally been superimposed on female prisoners. Frequently they do not work well. Many women are subject to difficulties and complications not experienced by male prisoners. They might be the primary caretaker of children, have female-related medical and mental health needs, or have experienced more physical and sexual abuse than typical male offenders.[111] A gender-specific model for programs in women's prisons is essential for effective treatment of incarcerated women.[112]

The social structure that develops in prisons for women is different than in prisons for men. Some evidence suggests that women have greater social support needs than men while incarcerated.[113] Women in prison tend to develop closer and more personal relationships than men. Although men may bond with each other (for example, as members of a gang), they avoid emotional entanglements that could be problematic. In marked contrast, women tend to create pseudo or "play" families with kinship alliances that mimic the family structure of the wider society. Within these surrogate families, they take on roles such as mother, father, sister, aunt, and uncle and develop emotional and sometimes sexual relationships with other incarcerated women. These family-type units provide a support network for dealing with prison life and separation from their true families.

Incarceration takes an enormous toll on women who are mothers and primary caregivers for children. Those who are pregnant when they enter prison, or who become pregnant while there, present special management challenges such as prenatal and obstetric care, gynecologic care, and proper nutrition.[114] The amount of time an inmate mother is allowed to spend with her newborn before separation varies with jurisdiction—but all jurisdictions impose a limit. Separation is particularly painful, especially if the infant must be placed in foster care or given up for adoption.[115] The Race, Class, Gender box describes an innovative pregnant inmate program of the Washington Corrections Center for Women's Residential Parenting.

Overall, the atmosphere of a women's prison differs significantly from that of a men's institution. There is far less violent behavior, sexual aggression is almost nonexistent, and homosexual activity is generally consensual.[116] A study of the racial climate in women's institutions found no evidence of serious racial conflicts among female inmates.[117] In fact, many pseudo family structures are interracial, in marked contrast to most men's prisons in which interracial tensions run high. Although women tend to do their time using less physical aggression than men, incarceration for women is not without problems.

Race, Class, Gender

A Pregnant Inmate Program

Pregnant inmate programs are the exception and not the norm. The Washington Corrections Center for Women—one of the exceptions—developed a program in 1999 called "Her Hand Rocks the Cradle" that combines a residential parenting program with Early Head Start. Her Hand Rocks the Cradle allows eligible pregnant inmates, classified as minimum-security level and serving sentences of less than 3 years, to remain with their babies during their sentence. They live in a designated unit and are given support and education and have time to bond with their infants and develop trust.

Each mother has a room with a bed, a crib or toddler bed for the child, and a dresser. The unit contains a communal playroom with toys, a children's bathing room, clothes washing facilities, a place to prepare snacks, and enclosed outside play areas. Pediatricians and counselors are available on a regular basis. Caregivers—volunteer inmates trained to take care of and be responsible for the children while their inmate mothers are working, attending school, going to therapy, and attending to other institutional requirements—are essential to the success of the program.

The program provides an alternative to foster care, adoption, or abortion. Advocates say it encourages mothers to participate in rehabilitation programs because they are motivated to provide the best they can for their children when they return to the community.

At the heart of the program is the Children of Incarcerated Parents Bill of Rights:

> I have the right to be kept safe and informed at the time of my parent's arrest.
> I have the right to be heard when decisions are made about me.
> I have the right to be considered when decisions are made about my parent.
> I have the right to be well cared for in my parent's absence.
> I have the right to speak with, see, and touch my parent.
> I have the right to support as I struggle with my parent's incarceration.
> I have the right not to be judged, blamed, or labeled because of my parent's incarceration.
> I have the right to a lifelong relationship with my parent.

The education and bonding experiences provided by the program are intended to strengthen family ties—with the hope that those who participate will not reoffend.

Observe Investigate Understand

- **What are the rights of pregnant prison inmates? What are the rights of children whose mothers are in prison?**
- **What obligations, if any, do prisons have for caring for pregnant prisoners?**
- **How do both mothers and children benefit from special programs like Her Hand Rocks the Cradle?**

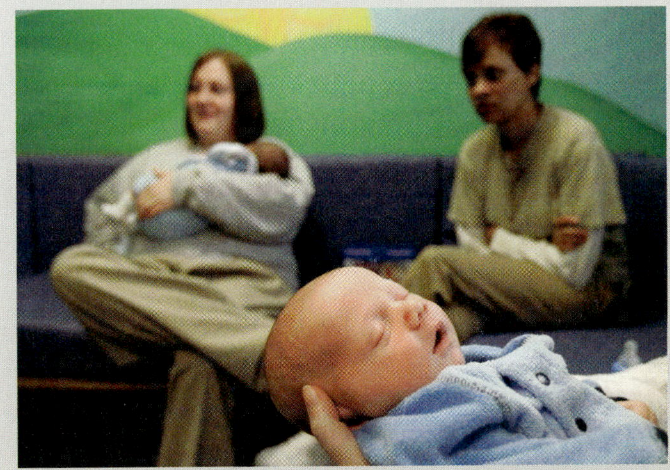

SOURCES: Cheryl Hanna-Truscott and Inmates and Staff of the Washington Corrections Center for Women, "A Photodocumentary Project at the WCCW," *Her Hand Rocks the Cradle*, www.residentialparenting.com/index.htm (retrieved April 25, 2007); Nell Bernstein, *Children of Incarcerated Parents Bill of Rights* (San Francisco, CA: Northern California Service League), www.norcalserviceleague.org/billrite.htm (retrieved April 25, 2007).

Problems of Incarcerated Women

Women in prison experience many difficulties. Problems are related to drug abuse, separation from children and other family members, physical and mental health issues, educational inadequacies and vocational unpreparedness, a history of abuse, and sexual abuse in prison.

Drug Abuse

Most women in prison are incarcerated for nonviolent crimes that involve drugs.[118] About 80 percent of women in jail and prison have substance abuse problems. Between 1986 and 1996, drug offenses accounted for half the increase in the number of women incarcerated in state prisons, compared to one-third of the increase for men.[119]

The needs of incarcerated women with drug problems differ from those of their male counterparts.[120] Women drug users are more likely to call in sick for work assignments, have more reproductive-related medical problems, be HIV-positive, have children living with them at the time of incarceration, and have incomes less than $600 per month prior to arrest.[121] Drug treatment programs need to focus on gender-related mental health, employment, education, economic, social, relationship, family, medical, and housing issues.[122]

Separation from Family and Children

Most incarcerated women (more than 65 percent) have minor children.[123] The importance of children to women is one of the major differences between incarcerated women and men.[124] Prison is painful because it cuts women off from their families and friends. Maintaining relationships with children and other family members while in prison is difficult at best. Prisons are rarely located near where children and other family members live, making regular visits unlikely. If children are not placed with family members who have the means and desire to facilitate visits, women will not see their children. More than 50 percent of incarcerated women report that they never had personal visits with their children while incarcerated.[125] Loss of parental rights is also a concern for incarcerated women.

Physical and Mental Health Issues

Women in prison face a number of health issues. In addition to HIV, incarcerated women may have infectious diseases such as hepatitis, tuberculosis, and other sexually transmitted diseases. Their mental health problems involve guilt, depression, fear, anxiety, and substance abuse, mood, personality, and psychotic disorders. Many female inmates experience posttraumatic stress disorder (PTSD) in connection with their incarceration.[126] Destructive behaviors, frequently viewed as psychological in origin, result in self-injury such as cutting, head-banging, and burning.[127] Suicidal behavior is yet another serious problem for incarcerated women.[128]

Many female inmates come from unstable family backgrounds that might contribute to the development of emotional and behavioral difficulties. For example, approximately 67 percent of women in prison have one or more family members who had been incarcerated.[129] Also, many incarcerated women come from homes with only one parent.[130]

Another problem facing incarcerated women with mental disorders is that they tend to have difficulty negotiating their lives in prison. They frequently break rules and engage in assaultive acts that affect other inmates and staff. As a result, they are often penalized by being segregated from others in the general population, a practice that can exacerbate their mental illness.[131]

Educational Inadequacies and Vocational Unpreparedness

Women in prison have educational obstacles and achieve very low levels of formal education. Approximately 64 percent of women in prison do not have a high school diploma, yet only 16 percent of them achieve a GED while imprisoned.[132]

These women also have limited job skills and so are poorly prepared for work. They have a difficult time supporting themselves and their families. When they do find work, it is usually minimum wage and typically does not pay enough to support their needs. Women gravitate to jobs that pay less rather than to higher-paying jobs that attract men, such as auto mechanics, welding, truck driving, and electrical work.

History of Abuse

Many incarcerated women report histories of physical and sexual abuse. Many of them were raised strictly and had childhoods characterized by severe physical child abuse in which regular spanking and violent beatings were the norm. These women also report that the abuse tended to blindside them, coming without any warning.[133] A study of women incarcerated in a large southern prison system found that 68.4 percent of the women reported lifetime sexual victimization, 17.2 percent reported in-prison sexual victimization, and 3 percent reported being a victim of a completed rape.[134]

Sexual Abuse in Prison

Women usually commit few violent crimes during incarceration.[135] Women's prisons have lower rates of sexual violence than men's prisons, and the violence takes different forms, from sexual pressure, intimidation, and coercion to sexual assault.[136] Like male prisoners, female inmates underreport sexual coercion and assaults for fear of possible repercussions.[137] They may lose privileges, be subject to disciplinary action themselves, or be shunned or attacked by other inmates.

The most common form of sexual abuse of female inmates is forced sex with male staff. Men comprise over 50 percent of the custody force in women's prisons.[138] They may conduct unwarranted pat-downs and strip searches, address female prisoners in humiliating ways, use inappropriate language, and observe women unnecessarily under the pretext of surveillance. For victims of past sexual abuse, these intrusions can be especially traumatic. Such abuse is difficult to avoid because female prisoners cannot remove themselves from being in prison, grievance procedures may be inadequate, employees do not take responsibility for their actions, and the public does not take an interest in the problem.[139]

In general, however, female inmates, like their male counterparts, complain that reports of sexual abuse are not formally investigated.[140] Of investigated and substantiated reports of sexual violence and harassment, approximately half implicate correctional staff.[141] Regardless of the employee's gender, under federal law all sexual relations between staff and inmates constitute abuse—even when an inmate consents to sexual relations—because of the power correctional employees have over inmates.[142] Consent is never a legal defense. One measure that can reduce abuse of female prisoners by male staff is to increase the penalties for staff sexual abuse of inmates.[143]

In response to documented abuse of male and female inmates, the **Prison Rape Elimination Act (PREA)** was unanimously passed by Congress and signed into law by President George W. Bush in September 2003.[144] The legislation established the National Prison Rape Elimination Commission (NPREC) to develop national standards for detecting and preventing prison rape, as well as for punishing perpetrators. NPREC provides grants to states to implement policies and practices that reduce or prevent rapes in prison and gives the commission authority to collect data on a broad range of sexual misconduct.[145] NPREC's authority covers not only adult prisons and jails but juvenile and community correctional facilities as well.

Prison Rape Elimination Act (PREA)
Legislation that established the National Prison Rape Elimination Commission to develop national standards for detecting and preventing prison rape, as well as for punishing perpetrators.

REHABILITATION AND TREATMENT IN PRISON

Prisons today are under increasing pressure to move from simply being custodial to being therapeutic—offering programs to equip inmates for life after prison and providing treatment for various needs, including the needs of special populations such as the disabled, seniors, and those who are ill.

Inmate Labor

Chapter 11 outlined the development of the industrial prison movement, labor unions' objections to what they felt was unfair competition, and their pursuit of legal means to restrict the sale of goods made with inmate labor. As a result, when prisoners were sentenced to incarceration with "hard labor," the labor was hard, but largely useless.[146] Moreover, the routine inmate work assignments, such as sweeping or washing dishes, rarely provide meaningful experience for future jobs in the community. They neither foster pride nor the hope of supporting families after prison. It is one thing to keep individuals busy with work while they are incarcerated; it is another to provide them with meaningful work they will be motivated to continue and that will pay a living wage.

▲ Some prison programs put inmates to work training dogs.

Meaningful Work Assignments

Today's prison officials agree that useful, productive work is important for rehabilitation. Private companies are beginning to take advantage of the prison labor force, engaging inmates in more meaningful work and helping prepare them for reentry into the community. When there was low unemployment in the general population coupled with high incarceration rates, new job opportunities for U.S. inmates were actively developed, such as telemarketing, call centers, arranging business meetings, and manufacturing computer circuit boards.

In 2000, more than 80,000 inmates in 36 states were employed in private sector jobs and earned between 25 cents and $7 an hour.[147] Felon labor programs range from building car parts in Virginia to battling mudslides and fires in California. Female inmates in Tennessee train dogs to make them more adoptable. In Missouri, they train service dogs to assist people with disabilities. Prison officials agree these programs benefit both inmates and the community.[148] For private business, it is a way of cutting costs by employing cheap labor without having to outsource these jobs outside the United States. During bad economic times, the use of prison labor as a cost-saving measure might increase. On the downside, an increase in the use of prison labor might hurt outside businesses that cannot compete with this cheaper labor source.

Benefits of Prison Work Programs

In 2001 Florida published a study of academic, vocational, and substance abuse programs offered by its Department of Corrections to determine whether they were effective in reducing recidivism. Seventy percent of those who completed the Graduate Equivalency Diploma (GED) had not been rearrested during a 24-month follow-up period after their release. Inmates who received a GED and participated in work release for at least 60 days were 10.1 percent less likely to reoffend than inmates who completed their GED but had no work experience. Inmates who earned a vocational certificate were 14.6 percent less likely to reoffend than those who did not complete such programs, and inmates who completed substance abuse programs were 6.2 percent less likely to commit new crimes than those who did not.[149] In short, inmates in work programs are less likely to reoffend than those without that experience.[150]

Another benefit of prison work programs is the economic gain for the states that have them. California prisons generate more than $150 million in direct annual sales of products made with inmate labor. In California, prison products can be sold only to government agencies; however, in other states such as Nevada, inmates make cars sold on the open market. In Oregon, jeans are produced and sold to the public under the label "Prison Blues."[151] The Disconnects box describes a work program that teaches inmates deep sea diving skills, directly helping them change their lives upon release.

Treatment Programs

Treatment programs are designed to help inmates change illegal or destructive behavior that resulted in the prison sentence. Many treatment programs focus on anger management and drug and alcohol abuse.[152] Others focus on education, vocational skills, and parenting. Some inmates require medications to manage impulsivity, depression, and anxiety before they can benefit from behavioral approaches or psychotherapies. Treatment tailored

DISConnects

Vocational Program's Success

The idea of inmates donning wetsuits and oxygen tanks for a deep sea dive might seem unusual. But beginning in 1970 the California Prison Industry Authority developed a very successful commercial deep sea diving program at a minimum-security facility in Chino.

There are only about 600 commercial deep sea divers worldwide, so the need for qualified workers is great. The trained inmates in Chino's Marine Technology Training Center are virtually assured good paying jobs ranging from $50,000 to $100,000 annually in areas such as underwater construction, offshore oil drilling, and dam repair. The program accommodates about 100 inmates, lasts approximately 11 months, and follows a curriculum of diving physics, navigation, report writing, air systems, welding, seamanship, blueprint reading, diesel engines, and marine construction. It also fosters the development of professional attitudes, confidence, pride, determination, perseverance, initiative, and courage. The low rates of recidivism for these offenders suggest such skills and attitudes go far toward their successful reentry into society.

Overcrowding and budgetary problems in California prisons forced closure of this program in 2003, but the California Department of Corrections and Rehabilitation restarted it in 2006. Program administrators report recidivism rates among the inmate graduates are as low as 6 percent.

This program illustrates the disconnect between the need to prepare inmates to make a comfortable living that prevents the need to commit crime to survive and the many work programs (when available) that prepare prisoners only for low-paying jobs. The Chino program is an exception.

OBSERVE Investigate Understand

- **What does deep sea diving prepare prisoners for?**
- **What is the best way to set up a rehabilitation program like the deep sea diving skills?**
- **What aspects of this deep sea diving training program do you think make it a successful form of rehabilitation?**

SOURCES: Kevin Johnson, "California Diving Program Helps Anchor Ex-Inmates," USA TODAY.com, July 14, 2008, www.usatoday.com/news/nation/2008-07-13-Reentry-inmates_N.htm (retrieved February 10, 2009); "PIA Re-Establishes Commercial Diving Center: Training Touted as Effective Tool in Reducing Recidivism," *California Department of Corrections Staff News*, December 15, 2006, www.cdcr.ca.gov/AboutCDCR/staffNews/sn20061215.pdf (retrieved February 1, 2007).

to the specific needs of individual inmates is most likely to have an impact and, it is estimated, could cut recidivism by as much as 50 percent.[153]

Today's treatment programs expect offenders to take responsibility for their crimes. When counseling is provided to inmates who have no desire to change or participate, the results are poor, reinforcing the "nothing works" mentality.[154]

Drug treatment programs in prison have the advantage of operating in a controlled residential environment over a long period of time. One popular drug treatment strategy makes use of a therapeutic community.[155] First used in England in the 1940s, therapeutic communities (or milieu therapy) separate inmates with particular problems such as substance abuse from the general prison population. The assumption is that the social climate within which inmates live in prison will affect their behavior upon release. Thus every effort is made to create an environment in which inmates will take responsibility for their actions. Staff, including correctional officers, counselors, and administrators, are recruited in this effort. Therapeutic communities engage inmates in productive experiences that include education, group therapy, peer pressure, and town hall–style decision making.[156]

Whatever the mode of treatment, the most effective prison programs dedicate specific funds to drug treatment, are operated by specialists contracted by the prison, and employ treatment specialists—as opposed to relying on prison personnel to deliver treatment.[157] Unfortunately, such programs tend to be few. Furthermore, the plight of inmates with drug problems is often compounded by other factors, such as mental illness. In fact, a growing proportion of inmates have special needs to which our jails and prisons are expected to respond.

The Needs of Special Populations

Inmates in U.S. jails and prisons are diverse, and many have special needs. Offenders who fall within these categories pose unique problems. They are highly vulnerable to

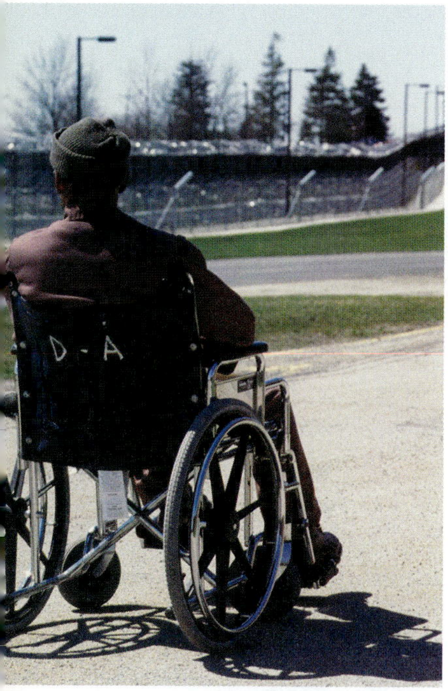

▲ **"Senior Citizens" Inmates**

Senior inmates are a growing population in today's prisons.

exploitation by the general inmate population, must be closely monitored for their safety, and require special accommodations while incarcerated. Some of the most frequently encountered special populations are discussed in this section.

Older Adult Inmates

The prison population is aging. The number of older inmates, defined as age 55 and over, has increased more than 200 percent since the 1990s. They now constitute 1 of every 23 prisoners, making them the fastest growing population in state prisons.[158] A major reason for the increase is that inmates are serving more time than in previous decades. For example, between 1992 and 2004, the number of prisoners serving life sentences increased 83 percent.[159]

The cost of confining inmate seniors is high—approximately $2.1 billion annually.[160] Most of the expense is attributable to the costs of health care. Many jails and prisons are not prepared to deal with the medical problems, physical disabilities, and chronic and terminal illnesses that come with aging. Seniors require special accommodations such as hearing aids, bath rails, wheelchairs, and walkers. Those with age-related dementia and senility require constant supervision. These factors require correctional institutions to take on many of the functions of nursing homes. As another sign of the times, prison programs that give hospice care to dying inmates are becoming more common in U.S. correctional institutions.[161]

Older inmates are generally given lighter-duty work assignments in the institution. Such practices can create resentment among younger inmates, presenting management problems for the administration. For all these reasons, a case could be made for establishing prisons exclusively for geriatric inmates as well as for granting parole to more nonviolent, low-risk inmate seniors.[162]

State policies that provide for early release on humanitarian or compassionate grounds are rarely applied. Because of the serious nature of their crimes and the lengthy sentences they were given, few elder adult inmates receive early release.[163] Most, however, pose a low risk of recidivism.[164]

Inmates with Mental Disorders

An inmate with a mental disorder is one who has impaired cognitive, emotional, or behavioral functioning. Impairment may have stemmed from social, psychological, biochemical, or genetic factors, or from purely physical factors such as head trauma and infection.

Unfortunately, those who are mentally disordered or intellectually challenged (with an IQ below 70) far too often end up in U.S. jails and prisons and not in the care of the mental health system where they belong. The number of inmates with psychological disorders who are in correctional institutions is four times greater than in the general population.[165] Recent estimates put the number of individuals with mental disorders in jails and prisons between 200,000 and 400,000—or more.[166] As noted in other chapters, this situation is one long-term outcome of the large-scale release of patients from psychiatric facilities to the community—part of the deinstitutionalization of mental hospitals that began in the mid-1950s.[167]

Inmates with mental disorders clearly present significant challenges for correctional institutions. Psychotic, personality, mood, and substance abuse disorders are common problems found in inmate populations. Because the symptoms may include hallucinations, bizarre behavior and beliefs, paranoia, depression, mania, self-mutilation, anxiety, and poor self-care, these inmates are easy prey for institutional predators on the lookout to take advantage of others, sexually and otherwise. Another problem for management is whether to remove afflicted inmates from the general population and how much support to provide. Correctional staff must monitor inmates with mental disorders more closely (for instance, to assess their risk of suicidal or violent behavior) and be prepared to administer psychotropic medications when needed. Some inmates require disciplinary segregation because of their threatening behavior; others require administrative segregation because of their vulnerability. Either way, segregating them is akin to punishing them for their symptoms.[168]

MYTH/REALITY

MYTH: Inmates with mental disorders are housed in hospitals, not jails and prisons, and given treatment.

REALITY: The population of inmates with mental disorders in jails and prisons is surging. Treatment is spotty where it exists at all and may consist of tranquilizing drugs administered more for control than for treatment.[169]

Treatment for mental disorders in jails and prisons is mostly driven by the institution's management resources rather than by the needs of the inmate. Few psychologists and psychiatrists are available on staff, and mental health services tend to be exhausted by calls for crisis intervention (for instance, an inmate attempting to hang himself in his cell) and the need to manage problematic symptoms (such as a delusional inmate screaming at 3 a.m. about satellites trying to control his mind). Psychotropic medications—essentially used as "chemical straitjackets"—have become the treatment of choice; with few exceptions, other methods such as intensive psychotherapy are not available. Most facilities lack enough sufficiently trained staff to properly diagnose and treat inmates with the wide range of mental disorders they bring with them or develop during their incarceration.[170]

Sex Offenders

As a group, sex offenders commit a wide range of offenses including voyeurism, exhibitionism, child molestation, Internet child pornography, and rape. Sex offenders are predominantly male. A Canadian study found that females perpetrated only 4 to 5 percent of all sex offenses.[171]

Of special concern to prison and jail administrators are sex offenders who victimize children. Inmates and correctional staff alike consider child molesters the "lowest of the low" in the status hierarchy of prison society. These offenders routinely experience threats, hostility, and beatings from other inmates. As a result, they are frequently placed in protective custody or in special institutions.

A growing trend in the United States is to incarcerate sex offenders beyond their prison terms under **civil commitment** programs. Civil commitment is a process in which a judge decides a person is mentally ill and a danger to himself or others, and incarcerates that person indefinitely in a mental hospital rather than a prison. An individual convicted of a crime and sent to prison is released once his sentence has been served. But an individual deemed mentally ill and a danger can be incarcerated in an institution indefinitely, or at least until he is "cured." This type of commitment has been used for sexual offenders throughout the United States. Once a sex offender completes his prison term, he may be subject to a state judicial hearing to ascertain whether he should continue to be incarcerated in a secure psychiatric facility. If the state rules that such an offender is eligible for civil commitment, he can be confined in such a facility until such time as he is no longer deemed dangerous.

civil commitment
A process in which a judge decides a person is mentally ill and is a danger to himself or others, and incarcerates that person indefinitely in a mental hospital rather than a prison.

Civil commitment programs are popular with the public but expensive to operate. The cost of housing a sex offender for a year can average more than $100,000.[172] There are a number of other troubling aspects. First and foremost is the legality of extending an individual's incarceration, not for what he did in the past but for what he *may* do in the future. Another is that available treatments have had little effectiveness with this population.[173]

Inmates with Physical Disabilities

Prisons are required by federal law to make accommodations for the small number of inmates with physical disabilities. These inmates number less than 1 percent of the total in state prisons.[174] However, every prison system has offenders with physical disabilities to manage. Correctional institutions are required to follow the Americans with Disabilities Act (ADA) of 1990, which mandates reasonable access and accommodation to most prison programs. Most jails and prisons, however, remain limited in their facilities and programs for inmates with physical disabilities.[175]

In a 1997 case, inmates with disabilities in California brought a class action suit charging, among other things, that prisons did not provide them equal access to vocational education and work opportunities, thus keeping them from earning credits to reduce their sentences.[176] In 1998, the Supreme Court deliberated whether convicted offenders with disabilities have the same rights as those who are not disabled.[177] The offender in the case was disabled by hypertension and was thus considered ineligible for a camp program for juveniles that would have reduced his time in prison. In both cases, the Court gave those incarcerated the same ADA rights as nonincarcerated people.

Prisons respond to the needs of inmates with physical disabilities in a number of ways. Personnel are trained to be sensitive to inmates' needs for safety and to assist medical personnel. Procedures are developed to protect them from being exploited by the general prison population and to be evacuated in case of a fire or other catastrophe. Also, correctional personnel are trained to do specialized wheelchair, prostheses, and strip searches and to safely use restraints such as handcuffs and leg and body chains on paralyzed inmates or inmates who might use crutches. Prison work opportunities are provided so that inmates with disabilities can have the opportunity to reduce their sentences by acquiring work credits. Special accommodations are made for inmates who need assistance with eating their meals.[178]

There are also housing accommodations for inmates with physical disabilities, who need more space than other inmates because of wheelchair requirements. Also, these inmates may not be physically able to clean their cells as inmates in the general population are required to do. In such cases, other arrangements are made.[179]

Foreign-Born Offenders

Foreign-born offenders are offenders who may lack U.S. citizenship. Many foreign-born offenders find their way into the corrections system simply by residing in this country without lawful documentation. If they do not commit other criminal acts, they are normally referred to as "resident aliens." If, however, they commit additional crimes they become criminal aliens. Federal and state prisons in New York, Texas, California, Florida, and Illinois have substantial populations of criminal aliens. These states attract immigrant populations because of their vitality, climate, variety, and promise of jobs.[180] The responsibility of federal and state prisons is to incarcerate inmates—regardless of citizenship. It is the responsibility of the U.S. Bureau of Immigration and Customs Enforcement (ICE) to undertake legal action to deport criminal aliens from the United States.

Both criminal and resident aliens pose a number of problems for jails and prisons. Many foreign-born offenders do not speak English. They may have cultural needs that are difficult to accommodate, such as dietary restrictions or daily prayers to perform at specific times. Security concerns and institutional procedures may make it difficult to meet inmates' daily prayer needs. Often family members are miles—or countries—away, contributing to their isolation. Institutions may also face diseases rarely seen in the United States such as polio, plague, and malaria.[181] Many prisons are screening and treating foreign-born inmates for tuberculosis infection and disease. The incidence of TB is high within this population; providing treatment may prevent the spread of the disease within prisons and throughout the United States.[182]

AIDS and Ill Inmates

The presence of disease in the prison environment poses two serious problems for administrators of jails and prisons. On one hand, they want to prevent the spread of communicable diseases such as tuberculosis, hepatitis, and AIDS to otherwise healthy inmates and staff. On the other hand, inmates with serious illness require special handling because of their weakened physical state, medical needs, lack of privacy, stigma attached to their illness, and fear of dying in prison.

The prevalence of HIV/AIDS in inmate populations is approximately two and one-half times greater than in the general U.S. population. Although AIDS-related deaths

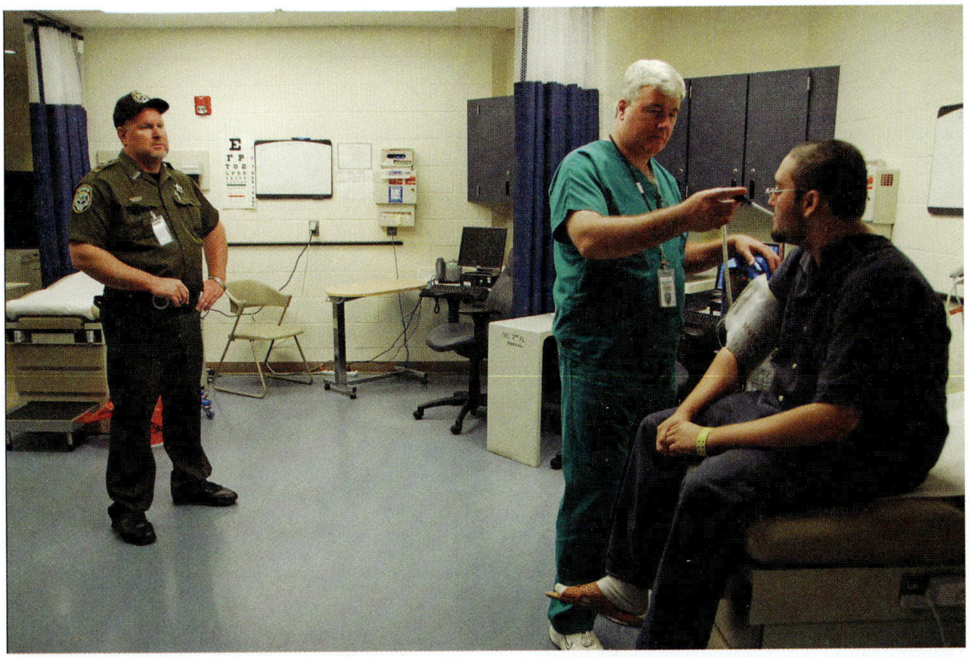

◀ **Prison Health Facility**

Even when prisoners get sick, correctional officers guard them.

in state prisons have declined in recent years, AIDS-related deaths among Black inmates account for approximately three-quarters of all AIDS deaths (see Figure 12-5).[183]

AIDS and AIDS-related conditions account for approximately 29 percent of all inmate deaths.[184] The spread of sexually transmitted diseases (STDs), including the AIDS virus, is common in prisons. Because all sexual activity outside conjugal visits is prohibited in U.S. prisons, distributing condoms to inmates could be seen as condoning and, indeed, facilitating illegal activity. On the other hand, not distributing them facilitates the transmission of the AIDS virus and other STDs throughout the prison and beyond. Most inmates will be released, many will be infected—and most of them will have sexual relations with members of the community.

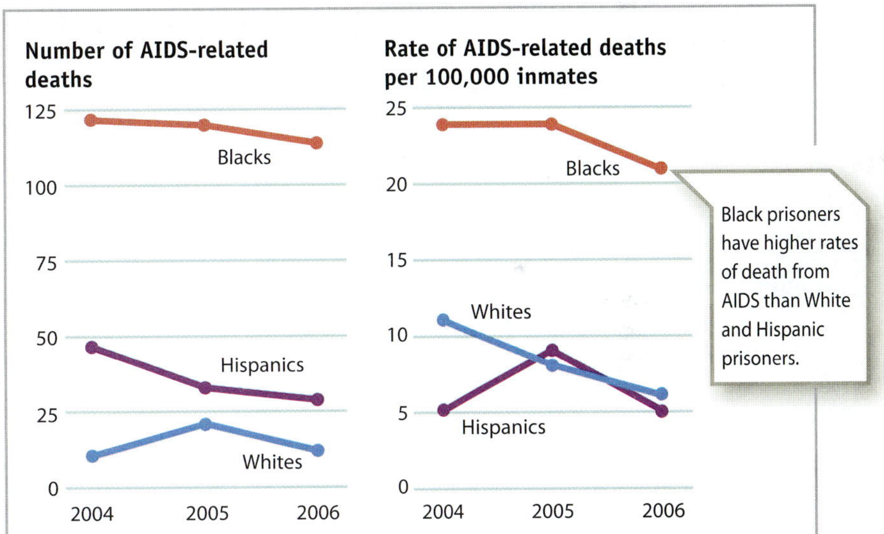

FIGURE 12-5 AIDS-Related Deaths in State Prisons by Race

SOURCE: Laura Maruschak, *HIV in Prisons, 2006* (Washington, DC: Bureau of Justice Statistics, 2008).

Identifying HIV/AIDS inmates can be difficult because testing policies in jails and prisons vary in different jurisdictions. Some institutions test inmates upon entry, others upon their return to the community, and others only when it becomes medically necessary or an inmate specifically requests it.[185] Mandatory testing has been very controversial among researchers and public policy advocates.[186] Although there are many good reasons for testing, especially getting the infected inmates early treatment and safeguarding prison personnel, there are some serious drawbacks also, including confidentiality of prison records and segregation and discrimination.[187] The extremely high direct and indirect costs have also been cited. Once an inmate has been diagnosed, the prison has the moral and legal obligation to provide treatment.[188]

Not knowing who may spread a communicable disease raises anxiety levels of both inmates and staff. In fact, professional organizations advise correctional personnel to assume that all inmates are potential carriers of communicable diseases.[189]

THE IMPACT OF PRISON ON FAMILY LIFE

Separation places major stresses on family relationships. Male and female inmates are removed from daily interactions in the family. Mothers and fathers are not available to participate in making decisions for their children. Also, children may come to know their caregivers as parents. Male and female inmates in committed relationships before incarceration may worry that their partners will engage in sexual relationships with others during their absence.

Some programs encourage parent–child contact in correctional settings. Girl Scouts Behind Bars is an enhanced visitation program in which incarcerated mothers and their daughters meet twice per month. Some state and federal programs for pregnant inmates allow inmates to have their children with them in a community-based corrections facility. Some prisons provide an opportunity for conjugal visits.[190]

Approximately 60 to 80 percent of all incarcerated female offenders have minor children, usually at least two.[191] Being identified as a prisoner—a disgraced group—is particularly difficult for inmates with families. Although more than half of male inmates also have at least one minor child, incarceration tends to be more painful for women because it cuts them off not only from friends and family but especially from their children.[192] Many female inmates are single, divorced, or separated and have typically assumed sole physical, financial, and emotional responsibility for their children. It is not surprising that with incarceration comes guilt over the breakup of the family, worry about the care of their children, and fear of losing custody rights during their absence.[193]

conjugal visit program Allows an inmate a private extended visit with a partner or spouse.

▼ Prisoners look forward to rare visits with their families.

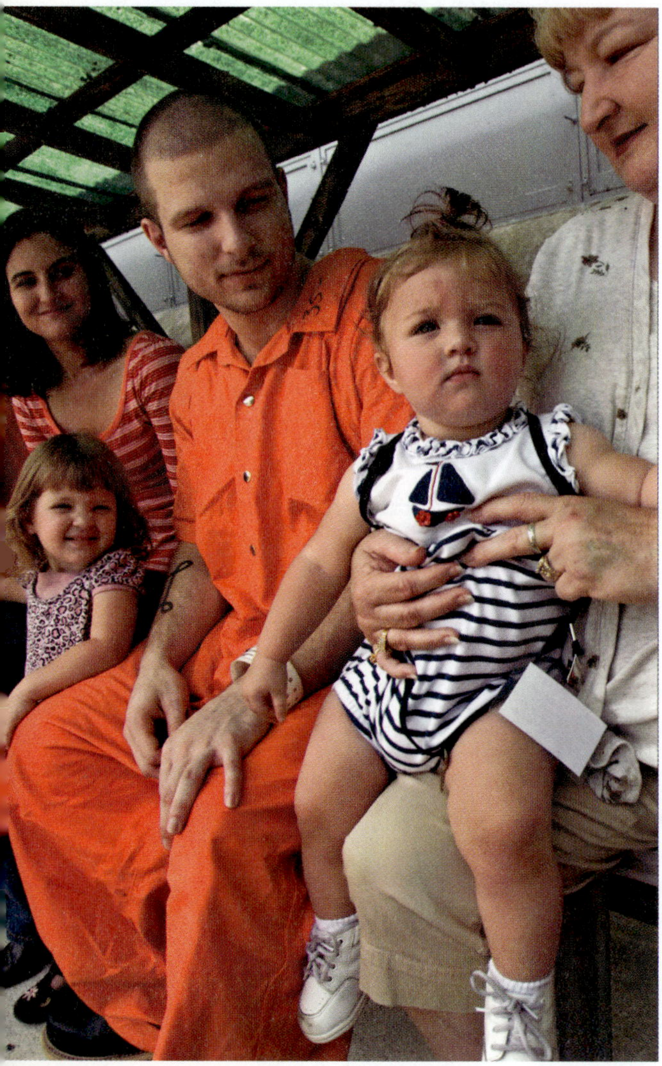

Among the many problems of incarcerated mothers, one of the most stressful is the inability to maintain regular contact with their children and their children's caregivers. Many times children are afraid of going into prison.[194] Incarcerated men tend to have more contact with their partners than do female inmates. Because female partners are more likely to bring the children with them on visits, male prisoners have more opportunity to see their children than do most female inmates.

Further complicating matters is that imprisoned mothers have difficulty explaining to their children why they are not with them—and why they are in prison. If they face long prison terms, children may learn to see their caregivers as parents, making the transfer of care to the biological mother upon release difficult for all.[195]

Conjugal visit programs offer an inmate a private extended visit with a partner or spouse. In some states the inmate is given a small apartment or trailer inside the prison grounds for the visit. These programs provide inmates with private meetings, perhaps over a weekend, with their spouses and families and accommodate the possibility of sexual contact. The primary purpose is to facilitate keeping the marriage or family intact, thus increasing the probability of rehabilitation.[196]

Federal prisons do not permit conjugal visits, and just six states allow them: California, Connecticut, Mississippi, New Mexico, New York, and Washington.[197] Even when permitted, conjugal visits may be restricted. Inmates at risk of transmitting diseases and unmarried inmates may be barred from having conjugal visits.[198] California has approved conjugal visits for domestic partners of gays and lesbians.[199]

Despite the presumed importance of visitation, the Supreme Court has held that conjugal visiting in prison is not a right and therefore is not protected under the due process clause of the Constitution.[200]

SUMMARY

Social psychologist Philip Zimbardo, who conducted the Stanford Prison Experiment, attributed the antisocial behavior of the "guards" and "prisoners" participating in the experiment to the inherently unhealthy social environment of the prison. The experiment raised questions about how the social environment of jails and prisons can influence the effectiveness of the corrections system.

Despite high rates of incarceration, crime rates remain high, challenging the notion that imprisonment is an effective punishment for and deterrent to crime. Rising costs, whether for jails or prisons, create problems for the authorities with jurisdiction over the facilities. For inmates and correctional employees, a major problem is overcrowding. Correctional staff work in a hostile and dangerous environment, overseeing and controlling large numbers of inmates, many of them angry, resentful, and with little regard for authority. Inmates contend with near-constant surveillance, lack of privacy, and cramped living conditions—even in minimum-security prisons. Problems escalate in higher-level security prisons that house more dangerous and violent offenders and where levels of control are more restrictive. For both correctional staff and inmates, personal safety—at any level prison—is always at risk.

Just as for men in prison, overcrowding is a problem for women inmates as more and more women are being sentenced to prison. The policies, procedures, and practices developed for male inmates have traditionally been superimposed on female prisoners, even though female prisoners have different needs and face some additional problems not experienced by male inmates. However, women in prison tend to develop closer and more personal relationships than men.

In addition to providing custodial care of inmates, prisons are coming under increased pressure to provide rehabilitative and therapeutic programs to prepare inmates for reintegration into society. Prisons are charged with developing meaningful and productive work training and experience for inmates as well as effective treatment for mental disorders, behavioral problems, and drug use—tall orders for institutions already facing a great many challenges.

OBSERVE
Investigate
Understand

Review

Distinguish between jails and prisons.

- Jails are operated by municipal and regional governments; prisons are operated by states or the federal government.
- Jails house pretrial detainees, those awaiting parole or deportation, and those serving short-term sentences; prisons hold offenders sentenced to more than 1 year.

Differentiate between minimum, medium, maximum, and supermax prisons.

- Minimum-security prisons are intended to hold offenders who have short sentences, are nonviolent, and are unlikely to attempt escape or pose risks to the general public.
- Medium-security prisons are intended for inmates needing greater oversight and supervision than prisoners in minimum-security prisons. Prisoners are allowed freedom of movement only within secured areas.
- Maximum-security prisons use high levels of control on prisoners, and prisoners have limited freedom of movement within the facility.
- Supermax-security prisons offer the highest level of prison security possible—solitary confinement—using the latest advancements in correctional technology.

Apply the concept of professionalization to the role of correctional officers.

- Professionalization is the commitment to a set of ideals and standards that raise the view of the occupation and instill pride in the profession itself.
- Professionalization requires standards of education, recruitment, and entry-level salaries.
- Correctional officers need a professional infrastructure on which they can rely and develop professional attitudes and competencies.

Describe the rights of prisoners.

- A prisoner may not hold public office, vote, serve on a jury, be a witness, or own a firearm.
- A prisoner may lose the right of employment by being stripped of an occupational license.
- Until the 1960s, courts were reluctant to interfere with prison management and adopted a hands-off doctrine in protecting prisoner rights. In the Prisoner Rights Era (1970–1991), the courts tended to support the rights of prisoners, but the pendulum swung back again toward less protection in the 1990s with changes in the composition of courts.

Describe inmate subculture.

- Institutionalization refers to a prisoner's excessive dependency on prison as a way of life.
- Prisonization refers to the inmate's internalization of the inmate subculture's norms, values, and beliefs as the inmate's own.
- Total institutions can foster institutionalization, prisonization, and an environment that can cause inmates to lose their sense of identity.

Outline the differences between male and female prison life.

- Men tend to bond together in prison gangs and resort to violence; women tend to bond together in surrogate families that provide a support network with which to deal with prison life and separation from their true families.
- Male inmates are subject to high numbers of sexual assaults, including male rape; sexual aggression is almost nonexistent and homosexual activity is generally consensual in women's prisons.
- Women who are pregnant have special challenges such as medical care during pregnancy; women who give birth while in prison face infant separation issues.

Describe methods of treatment and rehabilitation in prisons.

- Prison officials today agree that useful, productive work is important for rehabilitation. Meaningful work programs lead to lower rates of recidivism for those who take part in them.
- Treatment programs help inmates change illegal or destructive behavior, such as violence, anger, and alcohol and drug abuse. When treatment programs are tailored to individual inmates and professionally staffed, recidivism declines by as much as 50 percent.
- Prisons must meet the special needs of certain populations, such as the elderly, the mentally ill, sex offenders, the physically disabled, the foreign-born, and those who are HIV-positive or have AIDS.

Describe the ways incarceration affects the prisoner's family life.

- Incarceration causes an inmate to be identified with a disgraced group.
- Incarceration causes prisoners to be cut off from their family, friends, and children.
- Incarceration takes inmates away from physical, financial, and emotional responsibility and from their children.
- Incarceration causes inmates to worry about their children and the possible loss of custody rights during their absence.

Key Terms

administrative segregation 354
civil commitment 363
classification 343
conjugal visit program 366
custody level 343
deprivation model 350
good time 348
hands-off doctrine 346
importation model 350
incarceration 336
inmate code 350
inmate subculture 350
institutionalization 350
jail 336
maximum-security prisons 341
medium-security prisons 340
minimum-security prisons 340
pains of imprisonment 350
preventive detention 337
Prison Rape Elimination Act (PREA) 359
prisons 338
prisonization 350
punitive segregation 354
risk classification 344
security level 343
security threat group (STG) 352
solitary confinement 354
supermaximum-security prisons (supermax) 342
total institutions 350

Study Questions

1. U.S. prisons are normally operated at _______________ levels.
   a. county and city
   b. state and federal
   c. federal and county
   d. state and city

2. After conviction, a felon in many states is deprived of
   a. the right to serve on a jury.
   b. the right to hold public office and vote.
   c. the right to carry a firearm.
   d. all of the above.
3. Which of the following statements is true?
   a. Women and men experience prison life in the same ways.
   b. Policies, procedures, and practices imposed on male and female prisoners should not differentiate according to gender.
   c. Male prisoners have more physical and sexual abuse in their preincarceration histories than women prisoners.
   d. Incarceration tends to be especially painful for women because it cuts them off from friends, family, and children.
4. Prisonization refers to
   a. dependency on the institution.
   b. the acquisition of the convict code.
   c. the prison providing for all of the offender's needs.
   d. the internalization of the norms, values, and beliefs of the inmate subculture as the inmate's own.
5. The importation model refers to
   a. importing slaves into the United States.
   b. importing the inmate subculture into prisons.
   c. ways sexually transmitted diseases are imported into the prisons.
   d. methods by which drugs are imported into the prisons.
6. STG stands for
   a. sexually transmitted gene.
   b. secretive transsexual group.
   c. security threat group.
   d. scientific technology group.
7. Which of the following is/are a cause(s) of riots in prisons?
   a. Attitudes of correctional officers
   b. Prison management
   c. Racial tensions
   d. All of the above
8. Which of the following inmate special populations is likely to pose problems for prison management?
   a. Pregnant inmates
   b. Elderly inmates
   c. Mentally challenged inmates
   d. All of the above
9. PREA stands for
   a. Prison Reduction Economic Activity.
   b. Prison Rehabilitation Educational Activities.
   c. Prison Rape Elimination Act.
   d. Penal Responsibility Educational Act.
10. Conjugal visit programs in the United States allow inmates who have behaved well to spend time with
   a. their significant other.
   b. their lawfully married spouse or registered domestic partner.
   c. their common law wife or husband.
   d. all of the above.

Critical Thinking Questions

1. What is the difference between prison security levels and prisoner custody levels? Why do some maximum-security prisons classify inmates as having minimum, medium, and maximum custody levels? Explain.
2. What are the similarities and differences in the ways female and male inmates do time?
3. Identify the reasons for prison and jail overcrowding. What do you see as some solutions to this problem?

Internet Sites

The Sentencing Project
www.sentencingproject.org/IssueAreaHome.aspx?IssueID=2
This site contains information about a number issues related to incarceration.

Prisonwall.org
http://dictionary.prisonwall.org/
This site contains a comprehensive listing of prison slang.

Human Rights Watch
www.hrw.org/
This site contains information on human rights issues and advocacy in prisons.

Stop Prisoner Rape
www.spr.org/
This site contains information about prisoner rapes and other types of sexual assault in prisons.

Suggested Readings

Erving Goffman, *Asylums* (Garden City, NY: Anchor, 1961).
This book is about total institutions such as prisons and mental hospitals, and the ways these institutions affect those who live and work in them.

John Irwin, *The Felon* (Englewood Cliffs, NJ: Prentice-Hall, 1970).
This book contains discussions about the acquisition of criminal identities and how inmates experience prison from the inside looking out. Inmate classification and social organization are also dealt with.

Victor Hassine, *Life without Parole: Living in Prison Today* (Los Angeles, CA: Roxbury, 1996).
This is the author's account of his life as an inmate in a Pennsylvania prison. It provides insight into how inmates manipulate and reveals wrongdoing on the part of inmates and staff.

CHAPTER 13

Community Corrections

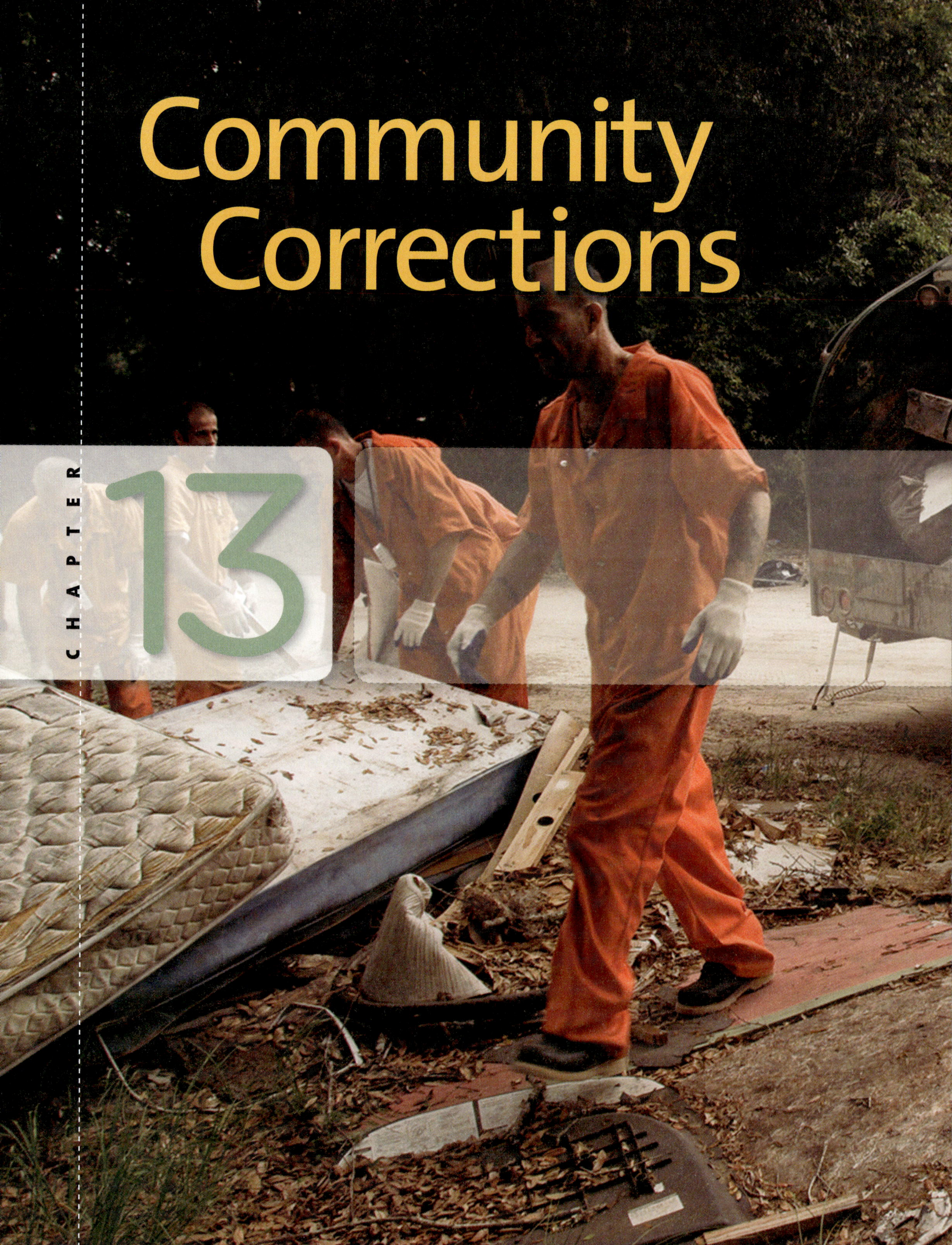

OBSERVE Investigate *Understand*

After reading this chapter, you should be able to:

- Identify distinctive features of probation.
- Contrast intensive and traditional supervision probation.
- Assess the success of probation.
- Identify the distinctive features of parole.
- Assess the success of parole.
- Describe the role of intermediate sanctions.
- Identify various types of intermediate sanctions.
- Describe private sector and risk-based community corrections.

Realities and Challenges

Mel Gibson Enters Community Corrections

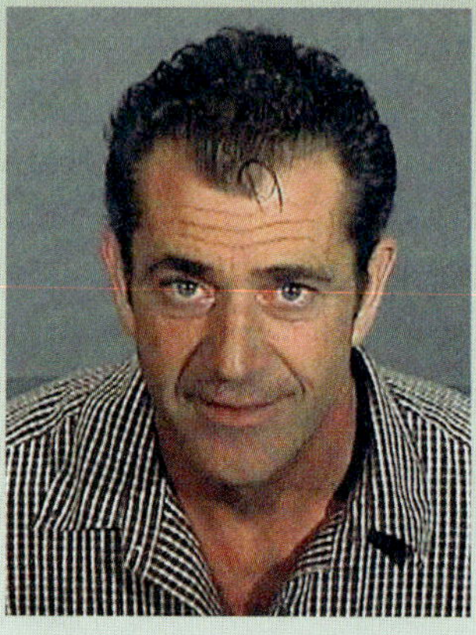

Mel Gibson, the Hollywood star, was arrested at approximately 2:30 a.m. on July 28, 2006, in Malibu, California, for speeding and on suspicion of driving under the influence. He had an open container of tequila at his side in his car. His blood alcohol level measured 0.12 percent, higher than California's legal limit of 0.08 percent. Gibson attempted to leave the scene and, when arrested, angrily shouted "Are you a Jew?" to the officer who made the arrest. During his ensuing tirade, Gibson claimed Jews were responsible for all the wars in the world, and he made belligerent and antisocial remarks to the other officers. He was released on $5,000 bail later in the morning amid almost instant worldwide coverage.

Gibson made a plea bargain in which he plead guilty to misdemeanor drunk driving in exchange for no jail time. He volunteered to make public service announcements about drinking and driving, paid a $1,300 fine, was placed on 3 years of supervised probation, and the presiding judge ordered him to attend 6 to 12 months of Alcoholics Anonymous meetings. By the time of sentencing, Gibson had already checked himself into a treatment center for alcoholism.

Mel Gibson's celebrity status subjected his case to worldwide scrutiny. Many people could not forgive him for his hateful remarks. And many were concerned that his drunk driving set a very bad example for his fans, young and old. Some people felt strongly that he should serve time behind bars. But because this was Gibson's first drunk driving conviction and because he sought treatment for his alcoholism immediately after the incident, many believe it was appropriate for his sentence to include no jail time.[1] He was given the opportunity to work out his penalty in the community and in treatment programs through the process of community corrections.

Public opinion tends to question the wisdom and efficacy of allowing offenders to serve their sentences out of institutions and in the community. People generally feel incarceration protects public safety and that community corrections too often "coddles" criminals. But being behind bars does not help the offender get adjusted to society and prepare for reintegration and may just socialize the offender to a criminal lifestyle. As we will see, these cross currents are playing out in the political and legal arenas today.

This chapter provides an overview of community corrections, or non-jail sentencing, beginning with its purpose and goals. We also address the practices of the two major forms of community corrections in the United States: probation and parole. Finally, we discuss intermediate sanctions that provide offenders with alternative avenues for reintegration into the community.

DEFINING COMMUNITY CORRECTIONS

community corrections
Court-imposed programs and sanctions that allow offenders to serve their sentences within the community instead of in jail or prison.

probation
An alternative to jail or prison in which the offender remains in the community under court supervision, usually within the caseload of a probation officer who is an officer of the court.

Community corrections includes a diverse array of programs and sanctions that allow offenders to serve their sentences within the community instead of in jail or prison. Most offenders supervised in community corrections programs are considered nonviolent and low risk and therefore pose a minimal threat to the public.

As we learned in Chapter 11, society expects corrections to punish, rehabilitate, and reintegrate the offender and control crime at the same time. A community corrections sentence can accomplish these goals by allowing the offender to stay in the community, remain employed, maintain family connections, pay taxes, and make restitution to victims. A further benefit is that offenders who can remain in the community do not become institutionalized, or socialized to the prison environment and to its subculture of violence. Some evidence suggests that correctly managed community corrections programs can reduce recidivism.[2]

The most common community corrections are probation and parole. Community corrections also includes strategies such as community service, mediation, sex registers, house arrest, and work release. Both public and private agencies provide programs for community corrections, including halfway houses and drug treatment centers. These community-centered practices and programs are available at each stage of the justice system: before trial, during trial, and after trial.

Preview

PROBATION

Probation is an alternative to jail or prison in which the offender remains in the community under court supervision, usually within the caseload of a probation officer who is an officer of the court. (This chapter focuses on adult probation; Chapter 15 discusses juvenile probation.) Although the U.S. criminal justice system incarcerates more people than ever before, probation, not imprisonment, is the most frequent criminal sanction.

Purpose and Goals of Probation

The basic purpose of probation is to allow the probationer an opportunity to be rehabilitated without having to be incarcerated. Probation diverts the offender from jail or prison. Probation (from the Latin, meaning "to prove") gives offenders the chance to prove themselves to be law-abiding in the community and not to be incarcerated.[3]

The goal of probation is to both protect society and rehabilitate the offender. Thus, probation encompasses rehabilitation, reintegration, punishment, and deterrence, as well as crime control. The reasoning behind probation is the idea that human beings are capable of change and that with proper supervision, resources, and services, offenders can be rehabilitated at the same time public safety is protected.

Figure 13-1 shows the number of people who were under adult correctional supervision in 2006. Fifty-eight percent of those offenders were on probation, more than on parole and in jail and prison combined.[4]

Probation is a privilege, not a right.[5] Some people today view probation as a lenient practice. When it was originally conceived, however, probation was considered to be another serious form of punishment, albeit one that was served in the community. The earliest form of what we now know as probation existed in English criminal laws of the Middle Ages. Royal pardons, judicial reprieve, and sanctuary in the church where fugitives were immune to arrest offered some degree of protection from the severe sanctions of the era. In the fourteenth century, English courts also began to practice "binding over for good behavior"—a form of temporary release to allow the offender time to secure a pardon or to try to obtain a lesser sentence.[6]

Both England and the American colonies recognized the court's power to suspend a sentence and the accused person's right of **recognizance**, or "an obligation to the court." Usually this obligation required the accused, if released on his own recognizance (or his own word), to perform some act such as appearing at trial instead of being incarcerated. With a little help from a Boston shoemaker named John Augustus, these early

recognizance
Literally, "an obligation to the court" that usually requires the accused, if released on his own recognizance, to perform some act such as appearing at trial instead of being incarcerated.

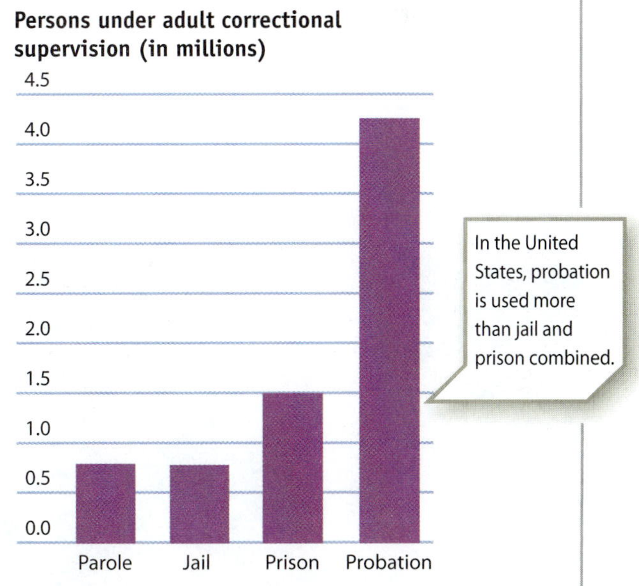

FIGURE 13-1 Persons under Adult Correctional Supervision in the United States, 2006

SOURCE: Lauren E. Glaze and Thomas P. Bonczar, "Probation and Parole in the United States, 2006," *Bureau of Justice Statistics Bulletin* (Washington, DC: U.S. Department of Justice, July 2008), www.ojp.usdoj.gov/bjs/pub/pdf/ppus06.pdf.

practices eventually evolved into the practice of probation.[7] In 1841 Augustus attended a Boston police court and bailed out a "common drunkard." He returned to court 3 weeks later with the offender in tow, now sober and apparently changed for the better. Thus was launched Augustus's 18-year career as a forerunner of the probation officer. Although a volunteer, he was asked by the court to evaluate whether various offenders were good prospects for probation. Today the background investigation that grew from his efforts is considered a cornerstone of modern probation practice.

Not until after Augustus's death in 1859 was the first probation statute passed in Massachusetts. The concept of probation eventually spread throughout the United States, especially with the growth of the juvenile court movement. Today, all states and the federal government offer both juvenile and adult probation services.[8]

Traditional Conditions of Probation

MYTH/REALITY

MYTH: Probation is a lenient sanction.

REALITY: Probation can have hefty consequences. Limits often are placed on behavior, along with fees and other costs, and the stigma attached to being on probation can make it difficult for a probationer to obtain a job. Monetary costs, in addition to restitution, could include fines and fees for services such as drug testing, counseling, and anger management classes.[9]

The standard (also called traditional) conditions imposed on all probationers, regardless of the crime, require that the offender must do the following:

- Report on a regular basis to the probation department.
- Obtain and maintain employment or attend school or training.
- Allow the probation officer to visit the probationer's home or place of employment.

The offender must not do the following:

- Commit any additional crimes while on probation.
- Change residence without first notifying the probation officer.
- Associate with persons with criminal records.

Probationers are required to report to their probation officer on a predetermined schedule, perhaps as often as once a week. The frequency depends on the type of crime committed, prior criminal record, and perceived risk to the community. Failure to appear can result in revocation of probation. The court may set other special conditions, such as regular drug or alcohol testing, attendance at an Alcoholics Anonymous group, or active participation in a treatment plan or anger management program. The court can combine conditions, such as restitution with community service. Other sanctions might include a suspended jail sentence, fines, and random searches. Although the probation officer will usually make a recommendation, the length of probation is set by the court, and only the court can modify or revoke the term or the conditions.

▼ Probation Officer with Probationer

Probation officers are required to make sure probationers understand the conditions of their probation. *How can probation officers be sure that probationers understand the conditions of their probation?*

Probationers can expect unannounced visits at home or at work at any time, especially if the probation officer suspects something might be wrong. These visits, along with the stigma attached to being a convicted offender, can make it difficult for the probationer to find and keep employment. The probationer may be prevented from using alcoholic beverages or be required to undergo medical, psychiatric, or psychological treatment; reside in an institution or community corrections facility for a specified period; or participate in a designated treatment program. The offender may be required to remain at home during certain nonworking hours and be monitored by an electronic device. A violation of any one of these conditions could result in revocation of probation.

Intensive-Supervision Probation

Some probation programs target high-risk offenders who have been convicted of serious crimes and would ordinarily be prison-bound; they require a high level of supervision and surveillance and strict probation conditions. **Intensive-supervision probation (ISP)** describes a variety of programs characterized by smaller officer caseloads and closer surveillance. The premise behind ISP is that smaller caseloads enhance rehabilitation and public safety by creating greater contact between the probation officer and the offender. These programs also enable offenders to remain employed while serving their sentences.

intensive-supervision probation (ISP)
A variety of probation programs characterized by smaller officer caseloads and closer surveillance.

ISP programs vary greatly. In addition to increased supervision, they may include house arrest, curfews, mandated restitution, specific restrictions on where the offender may live, drug or alcohol testing and treatment programs, and the use of electronic devices for monitoring the offender's whereabouts.[10] Offenders who enter the ISP program are screened and assessed thoroughly.

Evaluations of ISP programs have been inconclusive. An early review of an ISP program in Georgia found it to be effective.[11] It relied on teams of two probation officers with small caseloads. However, Georgia traditionally sends a higher proportion of offenders to prison than other states, so those diverted from prison may already have been less of a threat than those diverted elsewhere. The program, in effect, sorted out those offenders who were easier to deal with and more amenable to supervision. Thus the participants may have done well regardless of the program.[12]

Other studies question whether ISP programs were responsible for reported successful outcomes. A study by the RAND Corporation concluded that judges used extra caution in sentencing offenders to ISP programs, perhaps biasing study results.[13] Another study of 14 California counties found no significant differences between the recidivism of juvenile probationers in a special program and those in traditional probation.[14] Although smaller caseloads seem to provide greater protection to the community, studies do not clearly show them to enhance rehabilitation or decrease recidivism.[15]

The State of New York ISP program makes finding employment for high-risk ISP offenders one of its major goals. It limits caseloads to 21 probationers per officer, and in 2005 it began helping offenders learn new skills and change their behaviors. That year 61 percent of probationers were successfully discharged from the program, with 32 percent unsuccessful and 7 percent in the "neutral" category (probationers who died or were transferred to another jurisdiction).[16]

The cost of probation services of all types ranges from $710 to $3,526 per probationer per year. Costs vary widely although traditional probation supervision is far less costly than intensive probation supervision.[17] The cost of even the most expensive probation services, however, is substantially lower than the $23,205 needed to incarcerate an offender in the federal system for a year.[18]

Who Serves Probation?

During 2006 the adult probation population grew 1.7 percent, the largest increase since 2002. Five states (California, Minnesota, Alabama, Colorado, and Pennsylvania) accounted for over half (57 percent) of that growth. About 49 percent of all probationers had been convicted of felonies, 49 percent had been convicted of misdemeanors, and 2 percent had been convicted of other minor violations, such as infractions, parking violations, or violations of a city ordinance. Of all the offenders on probation, almost three-quarters (73 percent) of them in 2006 were sentenced for nonviolent offenses.[19]

At the end of 2006, 4,166,757 U.S. adults were on probation, or 1 of every 53 people. Of these probationers, 7 of 10 were being actively supervised.[20] "Active supervision" means probationers are required to report regularly either in person, by mail, or by telephone to a probation officer. Probationers on "inactive supervision" are generally

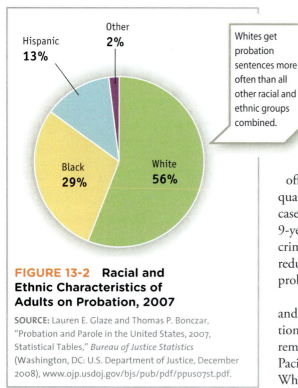

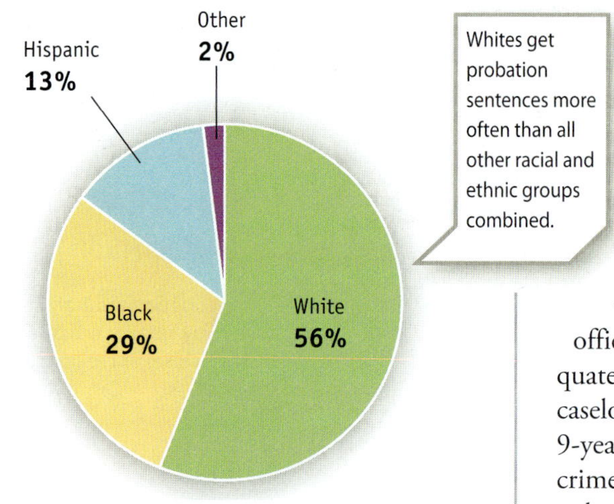

FIGURE 13-2 Racial and Ethnic Characteristics of Adults on Probation, 2007

SOURCE: Lauren E. Glaze and Thomas P. Bonczar, "Probation and Parole in the United States, 2007, Statistical Tables," *Bureau of Justice Statistics* (Washington, DC: U.S. Department of Justice, December 2008), www.ojp.usdoj.gov/bjs/pub/pdf/ppus07st.pdf.

convicted of misdemeanors or less serious felonies and have little, if any, contact with the probation officer, whose large caseload is called a "banked or bank" caseload, meaning the probationers are on probation in name only. These probationers just have to fill out forms each month to report any changes in address, employment, school, and so forth.

A survey of California's adult probation systems found that county probation departments are increasingly using banked caseloads rather than traditional supervision. The survey also indicated that banked caseloads can reach as high as 3,000 probationers per officer due to scarce resources, increased offender population, and inadequate numbers of staff.[21] Another study addressed the relationship between caseloads and property crime rates for every county in California over a 9-year period. Researchers found that as probation caseloads increased, crime increased too. They concluded that smaller caseloads can and do reduce crime: as probation supervision decreases, the opportunities for a probationer to reoffend increase.[22]

Of adults on probation nationwide in 2007, 77 percent were male and 23 percent were female. Furthermore, 55 percent of those on probation were White, 29 percent were Black, 13 percent were Latino, and the remaining 2 percent were Native American, Asian, Native Hawaiian, or Pacific Islander. In 2007, proportionate to the offender population, more White offenders received probation than Blacks and Latinos, who received more prison sentences.[23] Figure 13-2 shows the racial and ethnic breakdown of U.S. adults on probation in 2007. See the Race, Class, Gender box for a report on bias in the probation system.

Roles and Tasks of the Probation Officer

Probation officers are often referred to as "arms of the court." That means the probation officer is responsible for making recommendations to the court as to sentencing, supervising offenders placed on probation by the court, and seeing that court orders are carried out. Probably the most important task of a probation officer is to help the court determine who should be placed on probation by providing the Presentence Investigation Report (see Chapter 10).

For probation officers to make a proper recommendation to the court, they must investigate the events and obtain a solid history of the offender. In effect, the probation officer is the fact-finder for the court. The officer gathers information about the offender's family, education, employment, mental and physical health, motivations, attitudes, and skills. It is also important to assess the risk that an offender's release might have on the community. In addition to making a recommendation regarding probation, the probation officer recommends a plan and conditions for release.[24]

The role of probation officer is not just that of investigator and court enforcer. The officer is also expected to assist offenders in solving everyday problems so they can develop a constructive and law-abiding pattern of living. The following scenario presents a typical day in the life of a probation officer:

> Joe, a probation officer in a small rural county, gets to work about 8 a.m. Already there are four calls from the wife of one of his probationers. Her husband, Ted, on probation for a minor drug offense, has been clean for the last 5 months since he was arrested. Last night he made the mistake of going out with some of his buddies, getting drunk, getting into a fight, and getting arrested. He is now in jail, and she is afraid he will lose his job and go to prison because he violated his probation. Joe may have to write a report and recommend to the court that Ted's probation be revoked. Before he can call Ted's wife back, he must see two probationers in the waiting room. One is seeing him to discuss the results of a positive drug test, and Joe might have

Race, Class, Gender

Police, Probation, and Racial Discrimination

Nassau County's Probation Department in New York State has suffered many discrimination problems. In 2001 serious accusations were made about the tactics employed by a special joint police and probation department program called Operation Nightwatch. This program paired members of the police and probation departments in groups of 5 to 10 officers who paid unscheduled evening visits to the homes of probationers and searched their premises.

Critics claimed that, through Nightwatch, the police department improperly used the probation department to conduct raids without warrants. (Such raids are unconstitutional unless a probation officer is present.) Critics also asserted that the police department's law enforcement practices clashed with the probation department's rehabilitative goals.

Lawsuits alleged the program used racial profiling. In other words, the police chose the homes they searched based on probationers' ethnicities. Black and Latino homes were primarily targeted. There also were numerous complaints about police and probation officers "ransacking" homes and confiscating items that were not contraband.

A spokesman for Black officers in New York explained the problem with Nightwatch this way: "When you have two different agencies such as police and probation, whose jobs and goals are different—one is enforcement, the other rehabilitative—you have different rules of search and seizure." Some probation officers felt strongly that because of police department bias, their participation in Nightwatch interfered with their goal of helping rehabilitate offenders. Another stated that he saw the program as a misuse of power. Some probation officers refused to engage in what they referred to as "street sweeps."

Since these complaints, Nassau County's Probation Department has made changes in the department's guidelines and replaced the officer in charge of the program. The director of the department, however, defended the Nightwatch program, saying that it had been successful in removing drugs and guns from the community.

OBSERVE Investigate Understand

- **How do the goals of a police department clash with those of a probation department?**
- **Do you think the participants in the "street sweeps" engaged in racial profiling? Why or why not?**
- **How can the police and probation departments work together in ways that don't compromise their individual goals?**

SOURCES: Colleen Callan, "Insiders Assail Nassau Probation Department," *The New York Times*, February 4, 2001, http://select.nytimes.com/search/restricted/article?res=F30F16FC3C5A0C778CDDAB0894D9404482,(retrieved April 19, 2007); Colleen Callan, "In Brief; Nassau Makes Changes in Probation Guidelines," *The New York Times*, March 11, 2001, http://query.nytimes.com/gst/fullpage.html?res=9D00E3DE143AF932A25750C0A9679C8B63, (retrieved April 19, 2007).

to arrest him. In the afternoon Joe needs to pay a home visit to a probationer who did not show up for his appointment last week. He may need to have the police standing by because the probationer has been known to be violent. Later in the day, Joe has an appointment with an employment agency that might be interested in hiring some of Joe's clients.

Probation officers are frequently expected to accomplish the dual roles of protecting society by supervising offenders in the community (which may mean arresting and incarcerating them) and treating offenders by counseling them and assisting them with other services. Successfully carrying out these sometimes conflicting roles can be taxing.

How Successful Is Probation?

Success rates for probation programs are usually measured by recidivism—specifically, whether or not the offender has been rearrested. If the term of probation is completed without a new arrest, the individual is deemed a success. This method of measuring success was questioned as early as 1937 by Bennet Mead, whose article was reprinted in 2005. Mead criticizes the field for defining success only as the absence of failure.[25] The concept of success must recognize other possible forms of achievement, such as improving work skills and employment, remaining clean and sober, establishing or maintaining family and relationship ties, and fiscal responsibility. All of these factors may truly indicate success, but they are not easily measured or quantified. Recidivism is still the variable that is universally used to measure success.

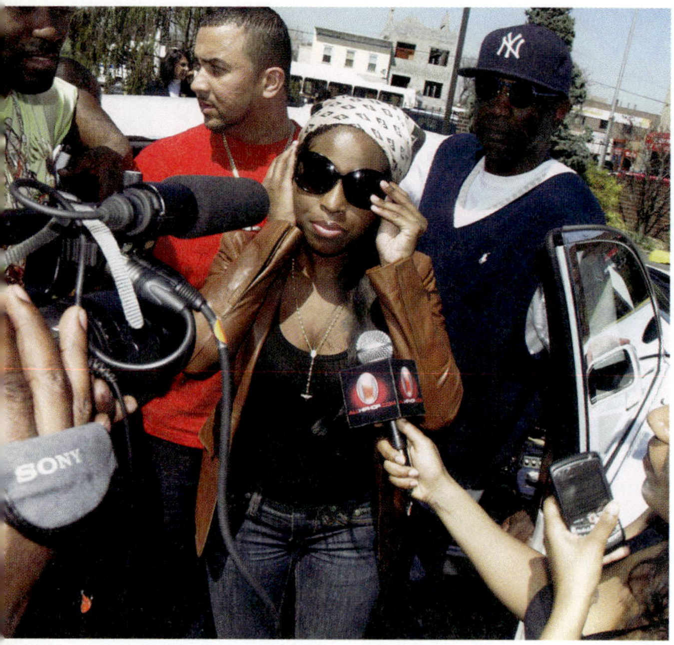

▲ **Foxy Brown's Probation Violation**

Rapper Foxy Brown was incarcerated for 8 months in the New York City Riker's Island jail facility for violating conditions of her probation.

The number of persons successfully completing probation has remained relatively constant since 1995, although it has declined somewhat, from 60 percent in 2000 to 57 percent in 2006. In 2006, 18 percent of probationers were incarcerated: 9 percent were incarcerated for a probation rule violation, and 4 percent were incarcerated because of new offenses. The rest of the probationers were incarcerated for reasons unknown or unreported.[26]

A probationer who violates one or more of the conditions of probation—called a technical violation—may be taken back to court. The judge may then revoke probation and send the offender to jail, even though the offender has committed no new crime. Rates of revocation for technical violations can vary greatly from place to place because the court has complete discretion over whether to revoke. An offender in one jurisdiction may be sent back to prison for a technical violation, whereas an offender in the next county may just get a slap on the wrist and be sent home. In some jurisdictions the majority of probation revocations are for technical violations.[27] A study in Ohio found smaller rural counties had more technical violations than larger urban ones.[28]

Revocation of probation also can occur if the offender is found to possess any controlled substances or firearms or fails to submit to drug testing ordered by the court or the probation officer. The probationer who violates these conditions often has to pay fines as well as risk revocation.

In 1973 the U.S. Supreme Court ruled that probationers are entitled to certain due process rights if the court is to revoke probation.[29] Probationers must be allowed to present evidence on their behalf, receive written notice of the hearing and the charges against them, and be allowed to challenge and confront the evidence and witnesses. In addition, probationers might have the right to legal counsel if the case warrants the advice and services of an attorney.

The Future of Probation

At the end of 2007, the total number of incarcerated persons in the United States exceeded 2.4 million, and 19 states and the federal system operated facilities over 100 percent of capacity.[30] Because states and the federal government are facing extreme economic pressures, alternatives to incarceration are being considered more seriously than ever before.[31] Arizona, for example, is integrating its surveillance with law enforcement and expanding automation to give officers more time for supervision and to increase the use of community service.[32]

Increasing trends in probation include electronic monitoring of offenders, more automation in the workplace, and more use of alternative sanctions and restitution for victims. With these directions and the increase in high-risk caseloads, Isiah Brown, a researcher in Florida, warns that officers are moving toward control of probationers and away from traditional concepts of casework.[33]

The American Probation and Parole Association in 2001, endorsed an approach called "Transform Probation through Leadership." The proposal calls for reengineering probation practices by building on community partnerships and placing public safety first. It also advocates doing supervision not in the office but in the field. The emphasis, the report states, should be on crime prevention and reduction.[34]

PAROLE

Parole is the early conditional release of a prisoner from incarceration after the person successfully serves a portion of the sentence in prison. In this section, we discuss adult parole, its meaning and philosophy, and issues related to this type of community corrections. Juvenile parole is discussed in Chapter 15.

parole
Early conditional release of a prisoner from incarceration after the offender successfully serves a portion of the sentence.

◀ **Parole Board Meeting**

Parole board members make decisions about a prisoner's eligibility requirements and suitability for parole. *What types of release conditions do parole boards set?*

Purpose and Goals of Parole

The purpose of parole is to reward inmates who follow prison rules and behave positively while incarcerated and to provide citizens with a more cost-effective form of supervision than incarceration without sacrificing protection of society. Parole aims to provide inmates who no longer need imprisonment with close supervision and appropriate programs in the community that will help them rehabilitate and reintegrate. Offenders who are paroled from prison promise to follow specific rules. (The French word *parole* means "word" or "promise.") Parole officers provide the supervision, aftercare, and support services to help offenders reintegrate into the community. Like probationers, parolees can be sent back and incarcerated if they violate their conditions of parole. They are granted the *privilege* (not a right) of completing their sentence in the community.

MYTH/REALITY

MYTH: Probation and parole are the same thing.

REALITY: Typically probation is a judicial sanction used in place of incarceration. Parole, on the other hand, is an administrative procedure for early release after an offender has served time in prison. Both are conducted in the community, with conditions and under supervision, and revocation of either usually leads to imprisonment.

Although parole and probation officers both supervise offenders in the community and use similar casework techniques, parole is an administrative function, whereas probation is a judicial function (see Key Concepts on the next page). This means that **parole boards**, not judges, grant permission for selected offenders (who have served a portion of time in prison) to serve their remaining sentence in the community. Members of parole boards are citizens with experience in criminal justice or related fields who are normally appointed to the board by a state's governor, although this can vary from state to state. In most states, victims are given the right to provide a victim impact statement to the parole board requesting any special conditions on the release (for example, not to be released to the county where the victim lives, granting a restraining order, and the like).

parole boards
Groups of persons authorized by law to grant permission for selected offenders—after serving a portion of time in prison—to serve their remaining sentence in the community.

Parolees tend to have more serious prior criminal records than probationers, which is why they have been in prison rather than in jail or on probation. Reintegration is often more difficult for parolees because those who serve time in prison tend to become institutionalized; that is, they adjust to prison life and have difficulty readjusting to the outside world.[35] Parolees' options are limited, and a number of their rights are restricted. They are unable to vote in many states, to hold political office, to work in certain professions, or to enter into contracts. The label "ex-con" frequently becomes their primary identity and overshadows all aspects of their life. Frustration over how nonoffenders view them can lead to defeatist attitudes and actions.[36]

KEY CONCEPTS
Comparison of Probation and Parole

Probation	Parole
A judicial function	An administrative function
Judges grant probation	Parole boards grant parole
Takes place in the community	Takes place in the community
Requires conditions	Requires conditions
Can be revoked	Can be revoked
Supervision is by a probation officer	Supervision is by a parole officer
Probationers typically are not prisoners	Parolees are released from prisons
Criminal records normally less serious	Criminal records more serious
No "ex-con" stigma	Parolees carry "ex-con" stigma
Reintegration is less of an adjustment	Reintegration is a major adjustment
Offenders are on a caseload	Offenders are on a caseload
Restitution may be ordered by a judge	Restitution may be ordered by a parole board

mandatory release
Early release mandated by law after an offender has served a specified time in prison.

discretionary release
A procedure by which a parole board decides whether the offender meets eligibility requirements and is ready to be released from prison.

There are two major ways offenders can be released on parole. In **mandatory release**, the law requires early release after an offender has served a specified time in prison. In **discretionary release**, a parole board decides whether the offender meets eligibility requirements and is ready. In either type of release, parole boards are responsible for setting the conditions for release and have the authority to return offenders to prison when they violate rules. Parole officers report directly to parole boards (not courts) and have the main responsibility for supervising parolees.

Discretionary release gives parole boards a great deal of power. Release depends on a state's sentencing structure and on the parole board's assessment of whether the prison has prepared the offender enough to reenter the community, whether continued incarceration might be harmful to the offender's eventual reintegration, whether the offender's mindset is positive toward reentry, and whether the offender has a viable parole plan. A parole plan is a proposed course of action the parolee will follow upon release to ensure success on parole.

Modern parole is typically administered at two levels of government—state and federal—depending on whether offenders violate state or federal criminal codes. State systems vary, but normally parole and probation are separate functions at the state level. The federal system is centralized, standardized, and uniform and employs officers who work in both probation and parole to assist offenders. Most states hire parole officers who work exclusively with either adult or juvenile populations. Federal probation and parole officers supervise both parolees and probationers simultaneously and work with offenders of all ages.

Who Is Paroled?

By the end of 2007, approximately 824,365 adults were on parole from federal and state prisons. This means 360 adults per 100,000 people in the United States were under parole supervision.[37] In 2007 alone, the parole population in the United States increased almost 3.2 percent.[38] Of the total estimated U.S. adult correctional population, approximately 11 percent were on parole.

Most prison inmates—and therefore most parolees—are male, poor, undereducated, unskilled, people of color, young, and convicted of property or drug offenses. Thirty-seven percent of parolees in 2007 were on parole for drug offenses. Approximately 24 percent were supervised for property offense violations, 26 percent for violent offenses, and the rest for public order and other unclassified offenses.[39]

At the end of 2007, about 12 percent of adults on parole were female.[40] Although their numbers are on the rise, women parolees are released to the community with limited help to secure employment, housing, health care, mental health and substance abuse services, transportation, and child care.[41] Many have entered the prison system with—and bring to parole—such problems as homelessness, unemployment, separation from their children, sexual and physical abuse, and mental health and addiction issues.[42]

In 2007, approximately 42 percent of those on parole were White, 37 percent were Black, 19 percent Latino, and 2 percent of other races and ethnicities.[43] Blacks made up approximately 13 percent of the U.S. population and almost half of the prison population, but under the new tough-on-crime policies they were not being granted parole as frequently as Whites.[44] Incarceration custody rates for Black males were higher than for any other race.[45] The average age of state parolees is rising because inmates are being sentenced to, and staying in prison for, longer periods of time. In 1990 the median age of a parolee was 31, and in 1999 it was 34. About 26 percent of all those entering parole were age 40 or older.[46]

All these data suggest that the profile of those reentering the community on parole is changing. The number of drug offenders is increasing as is the number of older parolees.[47] Because of the higher incarceration rates of women, the number of women on parole is also on the increase.[48] As you can see from Figure 13-3, growth in the probation, parole, jail, and prison populations shows no indications of slowing down.

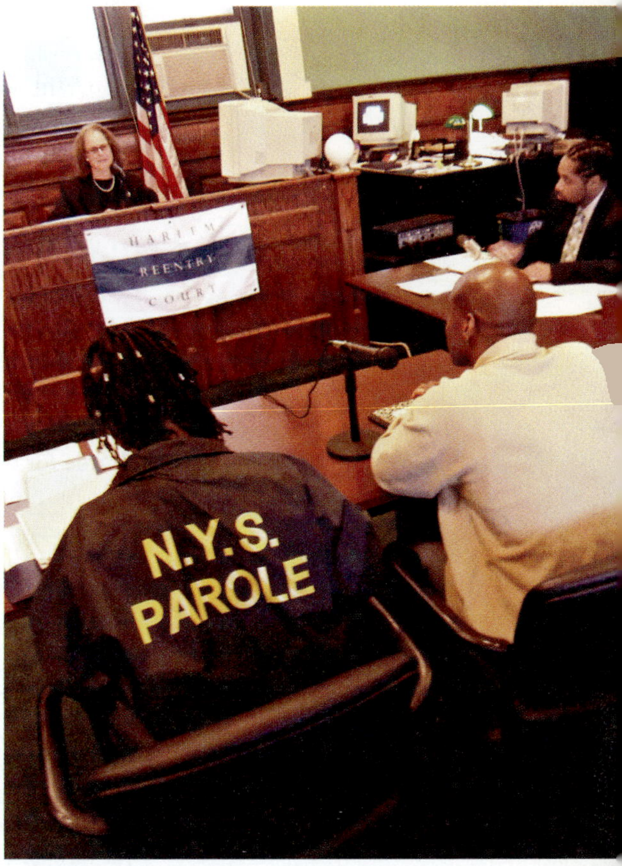

▲ **Parolee in Court**

A parolee arrested for a crime committed while on parole will frequently go to trial on the charges.

Roles and Tasks of the Parole Officer

Parole officers are charged with helping offenders readjust to the community and preventing new crimes from occurring. In their *assistance role*, officers operate as resource brokers and advocates by developing parole plans that specify what inmates must have in place before they are released. After release, parole officers operate as social workers, counselors, and life coaches, making arrangements for housing, employment, education, counseling, medical care, referrals to other agencies, and the like.

In their *supervision role*, parole officers conduct surveillance, supervise drug tests, enforce conditions of parole, conduct investigations, initiate revocation hearings, do parole searches, seize evidence, make arrests, and place parolees in custody. Parolees are

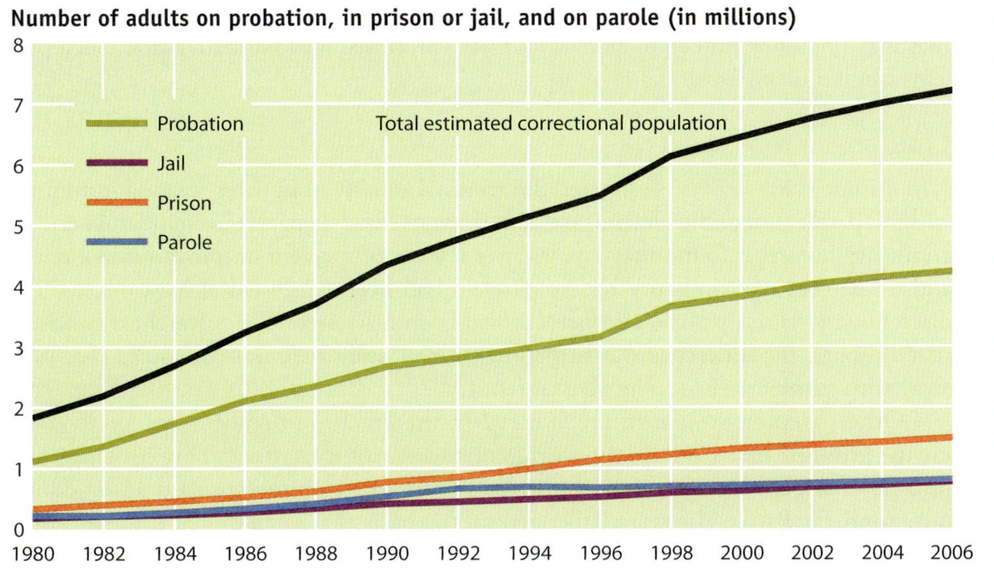

FIGURE 13-3 Population Comparison of Adults on Probation, on Parole, in Jail, and in Prison

subject to surprise searches on their bodies and their premises, and even arrest, by their supervising officers without a search warrant at any time.

Without a parole officer who is proactive and intervenes to protect society if necessary, offenders are more likely to fail upon their return to the community. The argument that abolishing parole is somehow consistent with being tough on crime and a benefit to public safety may be misguided.[49]

How Successful Is Parole?

More prisoners begin a term of parole than successfully complete it.[50] Successfully completing parole means the parolee did not have a violation serious enough to be returned to custody and was not rearrested for a new offense.[51] In 2007, approximately 45 percent of those discharged from parole had successfully completed their supervision, approximately 38 percent had their parole revoked and were returned to prison, and 17 percent had left parole for other reasons such as death, escape, or out-of-state supervision.[52]

As more drug offenders, older inmates, and women are released on parole, more offenders will be subject to parole violations. Some 70 percent of parolees who were returned to prison had committed a technical violation.[53] These violations can include moving to a new residence without the permission of a parole officer, taking a shopping trip without permission to a city not in the parolee's county of residence, or leaving the state without permission. Driving a car, failing a drug test, or taking a sip of champagne to toast a bride and groom during a wedding reception can result in revocation if those acts were specified as violations of parole.

A parolee accused of a new crime while on parole normally faces more severe consequences and will likely be held in jail until the new charges are resolved. If convicted, the parolee will have a revocation hearing to determine how much extra prison time will be required. The number of parole violators returned to prison has increased steadily since 1977, requiring prisons to develop new strategies to deal with enormous numbers of returning inmates as well as new court commitments.[54] The rate of parole violations varies greatly from state to state. California is at the top of the list with approximately 67 percent of parolees returning to prison; in Alabama and Indiana fewer than 10 percent of parolees return. Most states fall somewhere between these extremes.[55]

It is not surprising that most parole failures occur within the first 6 to 12 months.[56] For many parolees released after a long incarceration, life outside prison is distressing and even overwhelming. Most leave with limited resources—the clothes on their backs, few job skills, low literacy, no reliable means of transportation, and only a little money. They may have physical and mental problems or addiction. They must report to parole officers they may not know, and employment they were promised may not materialize. Such problems would quickly stress many of us.

Challenges to Parole

unconditional release
Releasing inmates from prison without parole.

A multistate study in 2005 compared the criminal activity of inmates released from prison without parole (**unconditional release**) and those released on parole by mandatory and discretionary release. It found that 2 years after release, 62 percent of unconditional releases and 61 percent of mandatory release parolees had been rearrested at least once. Of the discretionary release parolees, 54 percent had been rearrested. The researchers concluded that although the difference was surprisingly small, they were not convinced that doing away with parole was in society's best interest.[57]

Others are not so sure. In the late 1970s, the practice of parole came under attack on the grounds that rehabilitation programs were not effective.[58] This conclusion fed into popular beliefs that prisons and rehabilitation programs were pampering dangerous criminals. Parole also was challenged on the basis that open-ended (indeterminate) sentences were "cruel and unusual punishment" because they were uncertain, or that they gave too much discretion to parole boards.[59]

Responding to these challenges, the Sentencing Reform Act of 1984 abolished parole for offenders sentenced under federal guidelines. Instead they had to complete their full

A Global View

An International Perspective on Community Corrections

In 1998, the Correctional Services of Canada conducted a survey comparing the Canadian conditional release system (or parole) to equivalent systems in the United States, Denmark, Norway, Sweden, France, the United Kingdom, the Netherlands, and Australia.

Most of the countries surveyed expressed some desire to increase their use of noncustodial measures (what we would call community corrections), either as an alternative to jail or as part of a supervised conditional release program. In the United States, use of incarceration and parole varied from state to state, but most states emphasized incarceration.

All parole agencies in all the countries studied described their primary purposes as crime prevention or public protection; they also recognized the need to help offenders reintegrate into the community. Many European countries supported parole-type programs because they recognized that imprisonment makes reintegration more difficult. In the United States, the report states, the main objective of many community corrections programs seemed to be alleviating prison overcrowding and reducing costs.

In all countries in the study, public opinion held that incarceration is the only meaningful sentence and that community corrections are too lenient, even though treatments like drug or alcohol or psychiatric counseling are almost always part of such programs. For a conditional release program to be successful, community involvement and community support systems were seen as crucial ingredients. British, U.S., and Australian probation/parole services make little use of community volunteers, but the Scandinavian countries do. In Denmark, Norway, and Sweden, offenders may request to be supervised by a volunteer from the community. These lay supervisors are independent of the probation service but are expected to report to the government authorities regularly. Parole officers in these countries are required to coordinate contacts between offenders and various community health, labor, education, and housing support agencies.

Observe Investigate Understand

- **How are the objectives of U.S. community corrections similar to or different from the objectives of European countries?**
- **How might programs in the United States make use of volunteers in community corrections?**
- **Why do you think public opinion in the various countries studied was so similar?**

SOURCES: Correctional Service of Canada, *Human Rights in Community Corrections,* Report of the Working Group on Human Rights, May 1999, www.csc-scc.gc.ca/text/pblet/rights/wgroup/toce-eng.shtml, chap. 3 (retrieved March 26, 2007), chap. 1 (retrieved March 7, 2009), executive summary (retrieved June 19, 2008); "Government of Canada Proposes Amendments to the *Corrections and Conditional Release Act* and New Measures to Benefit Victims" (Ottawa, Canada: Department of Justice, April 20, 2005), www.justice.gc.ca/eng/news-nouv/nr-cp/2005/doc_31456.html (retrieved March 7, 2009).

sentences—minus time for good behavior—within federal prison. Unlike parole such determinate sentences do not offer offenders the support needed to reintegrate. They may even put the community at greater risk because the offender is not supervised upon release.

The U.S. Parole Commission, which still exists, is responsible for eligible federal offenders who committed offenses before November 1, 1987, as well as for paroling eligible offenders sentenced under the Uniform Code of Military Justice, transfer treaty cases, and state probationers and parolees in federal witness protection programs.

Several landmark U.S. Supreme Court cases in the 1970s changed the way parole was revoked. In 1972, parolees were granted limited due process rights when a process of revocation is initiated.[60] As noted earlier, in 1973 probationers were granted limited rights to counsel in revocation hearings, and the Court left it to the hearing body to decide on a case-by-case basis whether counsel should be provided.[61] The ruling in this case also applied to parolees. In 1979, however, the Court ruled that parole was a privilege, and states are still determining what privileges parolees may have during revocation hearings.[62]

Some critics are calling for parole to protect society by becoming more involved in the community, developing more community collaboration, placing protection of society before treatment of offenders, and enforcing the punishment of parole violations.[63] This approach has its roots in both the crime control and punishment models of corrections discussed in Chapter 11. A Global View illustrates how the approach to community corrections varies by country.

INTERMEDIATE SANCTIONS

intermediate sanctions
Judicial punishments that do not require incarceration but stop short of allowing offenders to remain in the community on probation with minimal supervision.

Intermediate sanctions are judicial punishments that do not require long terms of incarceration but stop short of allowing offenders to remain in the community on probation with minimal supervision. Hence, these sanctions are not quite prison and not quite traditional probation. Some require offenders to live in a communal residence (such as community centers and halfway houses) while participating in work and rehabilitation programs; others allow offenders to live at home but under close supervision (such as with electronic monitoring devices). Intermediate sanctions reinforce the need for offenders to take responsibility for their actions while providing more structure than traditional probation provides. They also broaden the range of alternatives available to deal with offenders' different needs. A Case in Point illustrates what can happen when inmates are allowed to take part in community corrections programs such as weekend furloughs.

diversion
An intermediate sanction that is used in place of incarceration.

Intermediate sanctions are also called **diversion** because they divert the offender from prison. They sometimes occur at the end of incarceration to give the offender more freedom and control in preparation for release. There are many different types

a Case in Point

The Willie Horton Case

William R. Horton, an African American male, and two other men robbed Joseph Fournier, a 17-year-old White attendant at a gas station, in Lawrence, Massachusetts, in 1974. Fournier was stabbed 19 times and left in a trash can to die. Horton was convicted of murder and sentenced to life in prison without possibility of parole at the Concord Correctional Facility in Massachusetts.

In 1986, Horton was released on an unguarded weekend furlough program for which he was eligible under state law because of his good institutional record. He never returned to the prison. In 1987, while at large in Maryland, he raped a White woman twice and pistol-whipped, bound, and gagged her fiancé. Afterward he stole the fiancé's car but was captured by police after a chase. In October, Horton was sentenced to two consecutive life terms plus 85 years in prison by a Maryland judge who refused to return him to Massachusetts for fear he might be furloughed again.

In 1976 the governor of Massachusetts, Michael Dukakis, had vetoed a bill that would have made offenders convicted of first-degree murder ineligible for furloughs. Dukakis supported the furlough program on the grounds that it was a method of rehabilitation and a management tool for prison personnel, as well as 99 percent effective.[64] Such furloughs were outlawed in Massachusetts in 1988 after a grassroots petition drive allowed the people of the state to vote on the issue. When Dukakis ran for president in 1988, opposition ads featured mug shots of Willie Horton. Many people attribute Dukakis's loss to that ad.

Although work furloughs are not technically the same as parole, Horton's case raised questions about the feasibility of community corrections, in general, and parole for violent offenders, in particular. The Horton case led to major debates about whether U.S. correctional systems are too lenient on prisoners. It also fueled fear of crime and racist stereotypes about offenders.

Observe Investigate Understand

- **Should offenders sentenced to life without parole be given furloughs from prison? Why or why not?**
- **How did the Willie Horton case get injected into U.S. politics?**
- **Does the Willie Horton case prove that U.S. correctional systems are too lenient on prisoners? State your reasons.**

SOURCES: Edward Latessa and Paula Smith, *Corrections in the Community*, 4th ed. (Cincinnati, OH: Anderson, 2007), 150–151; Terryl Arola and Richard Lawrence, "Broken Windows Probation," *Perspectives* 24, no. 1 (2000): 27–33.

and varieties of community corrections available in the criminal justice system today, and even more creative strategies will likely be developed as prison and jail populations continue to increase. One thing is very clear: community corrections are less expensive than sanctions that include incarceration.[65] The future appears to be ripe for the further development of community corrections. We describe some of the most common forms of intermediate sanctions next. See the Key Concepts to understand how they compare in their degree of supervision.

Community Service

Community service began in 1966 in Alameda County, California, as a punishment for traffic offenders. It then became popular as a condition of probation for a wide range of white-collar violations.[66] Community service requires the offender to provide a specific number of hours of unpaid labor in a public service activity, such as working for a non-profit agency, hospital, public park, or poverty program, picking up roadside litter, or removing graffiti. If a person does not complete community service, a judge can order more service hours or send the person to jail or prison.

Restorative Justice

restorative justice
A process that emphasizes the offender's responsibility to repair the harm criminal behavior causes by healing the victim's traumas and resuming a law-abiding life.

Restorative justice emphasizes the offender's responsibility to repair the harm criminal behavior causes by healing the victim's traumas and resuming a law-abiding life.[67] It is accomplished through a cooperative process among participants in victim–offender mediation, victim assistance providers, ex-offender assistance programs, restitution, and community service.[68]

Restorative justice is an alternative way of thinking about crime. It looks at crime as harm done to people and the community rather than just as a breach in the legal code. It elevates the role of crime victims and community members by actively engaging them in the justice process, and it holds offenders accountable to the people and communities they have injured. The goal is for healing and forgiveness to replace punishment and retribution. Restorative justice practices began in Native American cultures in the United States and Canada and in the Maori culture of New Zealand and were then adopted by faith-based organizations.[69] Faith-based organizations are religious affiliated groups that volunteer to run programs for offenders.

KEY CONCEPTS

Comparison of Intermediate Sanctions by Degree of Supervision

	High Supervision	Medium Supervision	Low Supervision
Community service		X	
Restorative justice		X	
Mediation		X	
Restitution			X
House arrest	X		
Shock programs	X		
Fines and forfeitures			X
Community centers		X	
Work release		X	

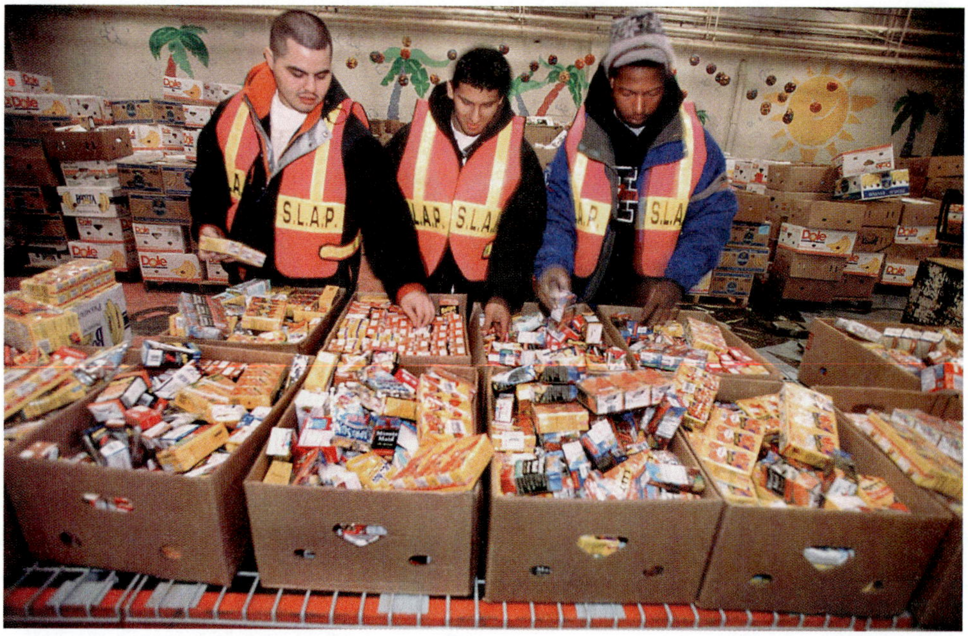

▶ Offenders Doing Community Service

When offenders do community service, agencies receive the benefit of their labor.

Restitution, Fines, and Forfeitures

restitution
Court ordered monetary repayment to the victim for losses, damages, or expenses suffered at the hands of the offender.

Court ordered monetary repayment to the victim for losses, damages, or expenses suffered at the hands of the offender is called **restitution**. It has a long history. The Code of Hammurabi (c. 1750 BCE) and the Hebrew Bible prescribed restitution to the victims of theft. In the Twelve Tables Roman law (c. 449 BCE) required convicted thieves to pay double the value of stolen goods. English medieval law contained a detailed restitution schedule. Following the Norman invasion of Britain in 1066, however, retributive justice began to replace the restitution system; crimes came to be viewed as offenses against the state that disturbed the "king's peace."

On the principle that crimes are, in fact, committed against individuals and not the state, we can view restitution as payment of a debt owed to the victim, not a state mandated punishment or fine paid to the state. In this way, restitution can be one part of restorative justice sanctions; it is, in fact, often ordered as a condition of probation.

The financial impact of crime on victims is staggering. Each year the costs of crime, as measured by medical bills, lost earnings, and the maintenance of victim assistance programs, are estimated to be $1.1 billion for violent crime, $15 billion for property crimes, $56.6 billion for identity fraud, $40 billion for insurance fraud, $94 billion for child abuse, and $16.8 billion for victim compensation for sexual assault crimes. These figures do not include pain, suffering, or reduced quality of life.[70]

Such statistics underscore the importance of restitution. However, for restitution to be truly meaningful, the offender must be strictly accountable to pay the prescribed amount. Similarly, the criminal justice system must be accountable for collecting and processing restitution, and for enforcing collection when offenders are delinquent.[71] In many cases courts ask for more restitution than is likely to be collected (only about 7 percent of ordered restitution is actually collected). When offenders are not able to afford restitution, little can be done to collect it.[72]

Because many victims never receive restitution monies, some states are taking innovative steps to investigate the convicted offender's assets, preserve them, and file paperwork to garnish any source of income including wages, lottery winnings, and awards in civil lawsuits. Kansas provides the victim with access to all the offender's financial assets and income until the restitution is paid. Pennsylvania allows the prosecutor to preserve the offender's assets at the time a criminal complaint is filed. In California, it is a misdemeanor and sometimes a felony for an offender to dispose of property to avoid paying restitution. The consequences of willfully failing to pay restitution can be revocation of probation or parole.[73]

Restitution can serve as an act of atonement or remorse and can help offenders take responsibility for their behavior. It can also greatly reduce recidivism when coupled with other rehabilitative processes such as mediation and negotiated sanctions between offenders and victims.[74] One argument against restitution, however, is that a financial penalty has little, if any, effect on a wealthy defendant. Conversely, such sanctions may be harsh for poor defendants who already have overwhelming financial burdens.[75]

A successful restitution program took place at the Los Angeles branch of Volunteers of America. Seventy-four offenders were residents, paying for their keep and paying restitution to their victims through their employment. Unfortunately, the State of California shut down the program in an effort to save money. The residents were sent back to prison without even having time to inform their employers.[76]

Fines, imposed by judges, constitute another form of monetary payment, but to the state, not the victim. Offenders must pay or forfeit a specific sum of money as a penalty for committing an offense. The fines may be in addition to or instead of incarceration or other sanctions and usually punish relatively minor misdemeanors and infractions. Different agencies of the criminal justice system are responsible for collecting them.

Fines are often criticized as being unfair. For someone as wealthy as Mel Gibson, for instance, the $1,300 fine mentioned in the introduction to this chapter might be a penalty without much clout. An alternative is **day fines**, also called structured fines. Day fines originated in Scandinavia and are relatively new in the United States. Instead of imposing the same penalty regardless of ability to pay, the day fines determine a fair fine for a specific offender, using formulas similar to those used to determine spousal and child support payments. The fines are based on a scale that ranks the severity of offense and the offender's daily income and number of dependents.[77]

Forfeiture includes the confiscation by law enforcement of profits made by committing a crime and property used to commit a crime. Asset forfeiture has been used in the prosecution of drug trafficking and organized and environmental crimes.

fines
Payments, imposed by judges, that require offenders to pay or forfeit a specific sum of money as a penalty for committing an offense.

day fines
Fines based on what is fair for a specific offender to pay, instead of the same penalty regardless of ability to pay. Also called structured fines.

forfeiture
Confiscation by law enforcement of profits made by committing a crime and property used to commit a crime.

victim–offender mediation
A process that brings victims and offenders face-to-face to work out a restitution and restorative strategy under the direction of a trained counselor or mediator.

house arrest (home confinement)
An intermediate sanction that restricts offenders to their homes during the time they are not working or attending treatment programs.

Mediation

Victim–offender mediation brings victims and offenders face-to-face to work out a restitution and restorative strategy under the direction of a trained counselor or mediator. The mediation may include family and community members who wish to take part.

During the mediation meeting, both the offender and the victim can reveal how the crime affected their lives. Victims may express their feelings about being victimized, and the offender can accept responsibility, express remorse, and perhaps even make an apology.[78] These programs have high participant satisfaction rates and reduce the criminal behavior of offenders who participate.[79] Mediation is not appropriate for all victims, however. In fact, for some it can reinforce the trauma associated with the crime.[80]

▼ Victim–Offender Mediation

The mediation process allows victims to tell offenders how the crimes affected their lives.

House Arrest

House arrest (or **home confinement**) restricts offenders to their home during the time they are not working or attending a treatment program. It may be either a condition of intensive-supervision probation or a stand-alone sanction. House arrest is a sentence given by a court, or a condition imposed when a defendant is awaiting trial at home rather than in jail. In some authoritarian countries such as China, Myanmar (Burma), and Sudan, house arrest is a way of silencing political dissenters without giving them a criminal trial that might bring negative publicity to the government in power.[81]

House arrest is not a new concept; it was used to confine England's King Richard II to Pontefract castle in 1399. In the seventeenth century, Galileo was placed under house arrest for his assertion that the

▲ **House Arrest**

Monitoring and supervising offenders in their homes is cost-effective.

earth revolved around the sun. He remained there for 9 years until his death in 1642.[82]

The basic goal of home confinement is to permit offenders to be employed and support themselves and their families while continuing their punishment. It has the advantage of reducing jail and prison overcrowding and incarceration costs while promoting reintegration into the community. Candidates for home confinement tend to be first offenders who have close family ties, are employed full time, and do not have drug or alcohol problems.[83] House arrest is often coupled with the use of an electronic sensor to monitor the offender's whereabouts.[84]

Electronic Monitoring

Electronic monitoring, sometimes called "technocorrections," uses technology to enforce house arrest or to keep track of an offender on intensive-supervision probation or specialized parole. Courts can order it for those awaiting trial who might not be able to make bail but for whom temporary incarceration is not appropriate.

Electronic monitoring uses a transmitter placed around the offender's ankle that sends a continuous signal. If the signal is broken by the offender leaving a designated area, a correctional employee checks to see whether the break was authorized. If not, the employee notifies the probation officer, the parole officer, or the court. Most home signal devices are waterproof, can report tampering, and cannot be removed without special tools.[85]

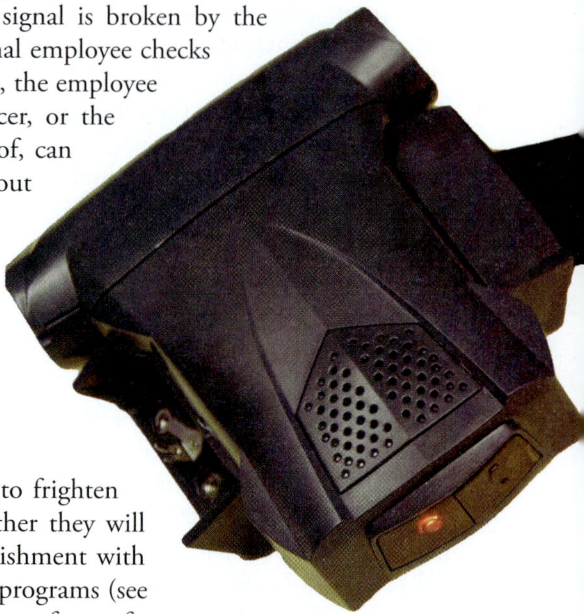

► **Electronic Monitoring**

Electronic monitoring devices give probation and parole officers greater flexibility for controlling an offender's whereabouts.

The effectiveness of electronic monitoring is in doubt. Some studies have touted their use, but studies measuring recidivism with and without electronic monitoring have shown no statistical differences.[86]

electronic monitoring
The use of technology to enforce house arrest or to monitor the whereabouts of an offender through electronic sensors, usually placed around the offender's ankle, that send a continuous signal.

shock programs
Short-term incarceration programs used to frighten the offender by instilling uncertainty about whether the offender will be released and, if so, when.

Shock Programs

Shock programs use short-term incarceration to frighten offenders by instilling uncertainty about whether they will be released and, if so, when. They merge punishment with leniency, generally at military-style boot camp programs (see Chapter 15). Technically, these programs are not a form of community corrections, but they are considered intermediate sanctions so we discuss them here.

Shock Probation

shock probation
A combination of probation with short-term incarceration.

probation kiosks
Automated reporting machines, resembling an ATM, that monitor low-risk nonviolent offenders.

Shock probation combines probation with short-term incarceration. This intermediate sanction requires that an offender serve a short time—normally 30 to 60 days—in prison or jail and then be resentenced to probation. Most of these programs target young offenders who are nonviolent substance abusers without previous incarcerations in adult facilities, and who do not have mental health problems.

The shock can occur on a couple of levels, one of which is the experience of being locked up itself. It is meant to be so vividly unpleasant that the offender fears returning to jail or prison and thus avoids further criminal behavior. After the incarceration, the offender may experience shock at being released on probation so swiftly. Shock programs may make offenders more receptive to probation supervision by showing them what awaits them if they violate their probation conditions.[87]

In spite of its popularity, there is little evidence that shock probation reduces recidivism or has a long-term positive effect on an offender's behavior.[88] Recidivism rates of those who successfully completed the shock incarceration programs were similar to those of comparable offenders who spent a longer time in prison without shock programs. In addition, the more intensely offenders were supervised in the community after they were released—that is, the more contact they had during aftercare—the better they adjusted.[89]

Shock probation programs are not without problems. They make offenders' needs for rehabilitation secondary to the smooth running of the institution. Another problem is that they tend to deliver drug treatment to all offenders in the same way.[90] In a study examining drug treatment in 43 state and 2 federal shock incarceration (boot camp) programs, offenders were rarely assessed to see whether they were receptive to treatment. Furthermore, most shock incarceration programs did a poor job preparing drug offenders for community release.[91]

Shock Parole

Shock parole is similar to shock probation, but it applies to those who have been sentenced to prison. The paroling authority—instead of the judge—makes the decision to release the prisoner after a short prison stay, in hopes that the incarceration experience has shocked her into law-abiding behavior. The unexpected release is expected to be an incentive to stay out of prison in the future.[92]

Sex Offender Registers and Tracking

MYTH/REALITY

MYTH: Strangers are more likely to molest children than family members.

REALITY: Only 10 percent of sex offenders are strangers. The other 90 percent are family, friends, and acquaintances.[93]

Laws that require sex offenders to register with law enforcement in the community where they reside and to be tracked were originally enacted to enable parents to protect the safety of their children. Unfortunately, most of the legislation related to policing sex offenders focuses on the "stranger perpetrator." Children are actually at much greater risk of molestation from family members than from strangers. The rhetoric around sex offenses perpetuates parents' fears of strangers rather than prompting an objective assessment of the people who are regular features in their children's lives.

Sex Offender Registers

The call for sex offender registration in the United States began in 1994, following a series of highly publicized acts by sex offenders who had prior records of sexual offenses. These crimes set off a perception that sex offenders are more likely to reoffend than other types of offenders. They led to federal and state legislation: The 1994 Violent Crime Control and Law Enforcement Act and the 1994 Jacob Wetterling Crimes Against Children and Sexually Violent Offenders Registration Act set guidelines for the establishment of sex offender registers. In 1996 Megan's Law refined the ways states could constitutionally notify the public about sex offenders, and the 1996 Pam Lychner Act set up a national sex offender database while providing assistance to states without sex offender

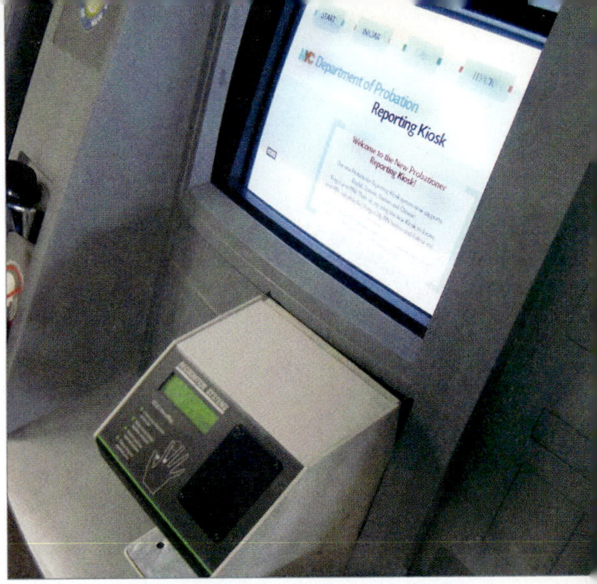

Real Crime Tech

PROBATION KIOSKS

Several agencies, including the New York City Department of Probation, are using automated reporting machines called **probation kiosks** to monitor low-risk nonviolent offenders. After an initial face-to-face meeting with a probation officer, the offender checks in regularly at a kiosk that resembles an ATM machine. After verifying his identity, the offender updates a profile with work information, change of address, and any arrests or new warrants since the last check-in. False information will generate a response from the probation department.

Probation kiosks can free probation officers to spend more time with high-risk offenders on a face-to-face basis. In Dallas, however, authorities were using kiosks to monitor high-risk probationers as well, reducing costs but eliminating valuable personal contact with probation officers. Concern heightened when it became known that about half the offenders in the program were on probation for having committed felonies, including drugs, robberies, and organized crime activities. As a result, the program was suspended.

SOURCES: "Tech Beat," National Law Enforcement and Corrections Technology Center, http://gritsforbreakfast.blogspot.com/2005/11/grits-best-practices-to-reduce-county.html (retrieved January 20, 2007); "Probation Kiosk Draws Concerns," *Dallas Morning News*, September 19, 2005, www.kioskmarketplace.com/article.php?id=14969&na=1 (retrieved January 20, 2007); Brooks Egerton, "Probation Kiosk Program Suspended," *Dallas Morning News*, November 9, 2007, www.dallasnews.com/sharedcontent/dws/news/longterm/stories/092905dnmetprobationkiosk.1f3eb626b.html (retrieved March 7, 2009).

programs of their own. The well-publicized crimes leading to the statutes named after three victims are described in What about the Victim?[94]

All states now have laws requiring convicted sex offenders to register with local police when placed on either probation or parole. Some states require the offender to remain registered while under supervision, some for a fixed number of years, and some for life. Some states assess the risk of individual sex offenders when they are released into society and set reporting requirements accordingly.[95]

Strong public support for registration laws can make it politically risky for an officeholder to vote against new and sometimes harsh laws. In 2006, California passed a sweeping law preventing registered sex offenders from living within 2,000 feet of a school or park, effectively keeping them from living in many residential areas. Like many other states, California makes no distinction between habitual offenders at high risk of reoffending and those who pose little or no threat.

Some studies show that sex offenders can experience harassment, threats, evictions, loss of jobs, family breakups, or loss of life as a result of registration laws. Two sex offenders were shot to death in Maine by a man who got their names from the state's online register.[96] One problem is that many states make no distinctions among different types of sex offenders. A person arrested for indecent exposure or a youth who engages in consensual sex with another youth may be treated the same as a rapist or sexual predator. In a 2-year study, Jamie Fellner of Human Rights Watch found that laws in California enacted to protect children often punished consensual sex between teenagers, the antics of streakers, and other nonviolent offenses.[97] See the case of one such teenager in the Disconnects box.

MYTH/REALITY

MYTH: Sex offender registers have been proven to protect the public from sexual predators.

REALITY: There is little evidence that these registers provide effective protection from or act as a deterrent to repeat sex offenders.[98]

Although sex offender registers are popular with the general public, there is little evidence they actually protect the public. A sex offender study that dealt with a sample of rapes in 10 states did not show that registration laws had any effect on the number of rapes committed, although there is some evidence that the laws motivate some sex offenders not to reoffend on release.[99] On the basis of his study of California's laws, Jamie Fellner contends that instead of reducing sexual offenses, registers force offenders underground and out of range of supervision. In his opinion, the registration laws do more harm than good.[100]

Sex offender notification and registration laws have been challenged in the courts on constitutional grounds. The issues include violations of due process, double jeopardy

What about the Victim?

Who Are Jacob Wetterling, Megan Kanka, and Pam Lychner?

The three major federal statutes dealing with crimes by sexual offenders are named after victims in cases that received national publicity.

In 1989, 10-year-old Jacob Wetterling and two of his friends rode their bicycles to a video store. As they left the store, they were accosted by a man wearing a mask and holding a gun. The man forced the boys to lie down in a ditch and then had Jacob's two friends get up and leave, one at a time. One of the boys saw the man grab Jacob, who was never seen again. The first U.S. sex offender registration law, passed in 1994, carries Jacob's name and mandates that states establish and maintain registers for law enforcement agencies. Because the identity of Jacob's abductor is unknown, there is no information about whether he was a previous sex offender, or whether a register would have prevented the crime.

Seven-year-old Megan Kanka was invited to play with a neighbor's new puppy in 1994. The neighbor, a twice-convicted pedophile, raped Megan and murdered her. Megan's Law, enacted in 1996, required that information in the registers be released as allowed by state laws. It effectively eliminated confidentiality of the registration data.

Pam Lychner was a real estate agent showing a house to a male client with a long history of sexual assaults. The client attempted to assault her, and she narrowly escaped when her husband arrived. The 1996 law named after her directs the FBI to establish a national database to track the movement of sex offenders.

Observe Investigate Understand

- **If Jacob Wetterling's abductor had been registered, do you think it would have prevented his kidnapping? What is your reasoning?**
- **Should register information be kept confidential? Why or why not?**
- **What effect did publicity have on the legislation that resulted from each of these cases?**

SOURCES: Sean Maddan and Paula Gray Stiz, *Sex Offender Registry Protocol Training Manual*, Arkansas Crime Information Center, www.acic.org/Registration/Sex%20Offender%20Manual%203rd%20edition.pdf (retrieved January 26, 2007); Bureau of Justice Assistance, U.S. Department of Justice, Office of Justice Programs, "Background Information on the Act and Its Amendments," www.ojp.usdoj.gov/BJA/what/2a2jwactbackground.html (retrieved April 20, 2008).

(prohibiting being punished twice for the same crime), ex post facto law (prohibiting a person from being charged for a crime committed before a law was enacted), and the "cruel and unusual punishment" protection in the Constitution. To date, the laws have withstood the challenges.

A major argument for sex offender registers is that they enable police to investigate sex crimes more easily, on the assumption that sex offenders are likely to repeat. But the Center for Sex Offender Management claims that this reasoning is a myth, and that recidivism rates for sex offenders are *lower* than for the general criminal population.[101]

Tracking Systems for Sex Offenders—Global Positioning Systems

The **global positioning system (GPS)** is a satellite-based system placed in orbit by the U.S. Department of Defense and made available for civilian use in the 1980s. Twenty-four satellites circle the globe and send microwave signals to receivers that can calculate users' exact locations, direction, and speed.

global positioning system (GPS) A satellite-based system that can calculate users' exact locations, direction, and speed. Many states use GPS systems to monitor sex offenders while they are on parole.

Twenty-three states have laws requiring GPS tracking devices to monitor convicted sex offenders in an effort to deter additional crimes. Some GPS units can be programmed with certain exclusion zones where an offender may not go. Many states use GPS systems to monitor sex offenders while they are on parole, and several monitor registrants permanently.

Research about the effectiveness of GPS devices is inconclusive. A major study funded by the U.S. Department of Justice found flaws in research designs trying to show the effectiveness of GPS monitoring.[102]

Community Centers

Day reporting centers and residential community centers offer additional structure and supervision for offenders.

Day Reporting Centers

Day reporting centers are places in the community, either public or private, where offenders report their daily activities, schedules, and plans to program staff.[103] Such centers offer offenders a daily contact point, with immediate access to people who can assist them if problems arise. Centers also provide additional supervision for high-risk offenders by monitoring employment and residence status and providing drug testing. Some offenders are required to report to centers daily to take part in specific activities. Others are required to call in on a regular basis. It is not unusual for offenders to be required to contact their centers 60 times a week.[104] Offenders remain in day reporting center programs until they are deemed successful or until they reoffend.

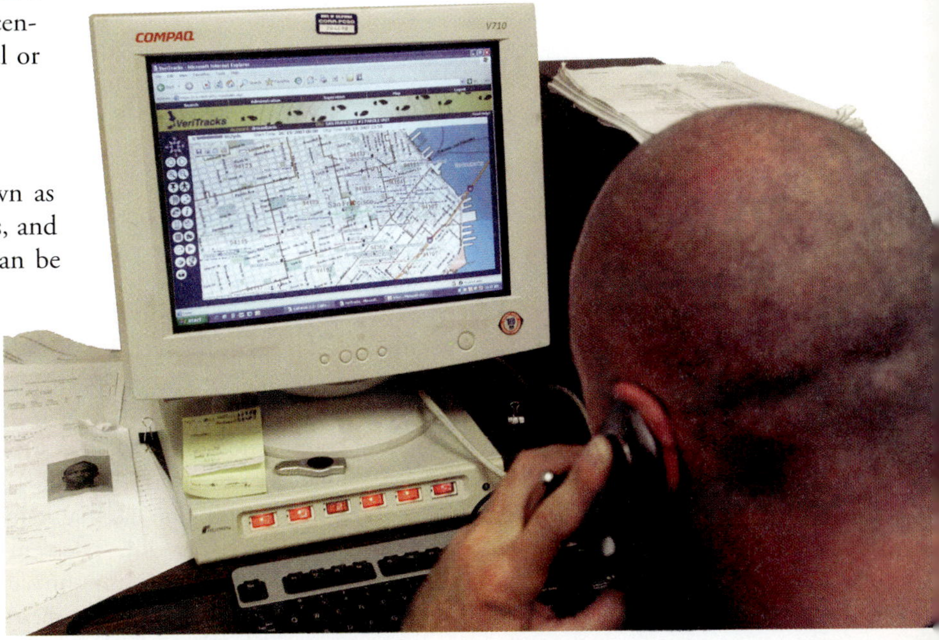

▼ Sex Offender Tracking

States now have laws requiring convicted sex offenders on probation or parole to register with local police so that the offenders can be tracked.

Residential Community Centers

Residential community centers are also known as halfway houses, community treatment centers, and community correctional centers. Offenders can be sentenced to serve time directly in a community treatment center, or they may be released from prison to a center as a "halfway" step between incarceration and freedom.

To ease adjustment, centers provide offenders with greater structure and control than probation or parole, but less than jails and prisons. They offer a variety of support services such as counseling, education, and job placement assistance. The

DISConnects

Blurred Legal Distinctions in Sex Offense Cases

Brad Totman, a resident of Mulberry, Kansas, is a registered sex offender. His crime, "lewd and lascivious behavior," was having consensual sex with his 15-year-old girlfriend when he was 19. Several years later, when the two had been married more than 3 years, Totman's name and picture were published in the local paper in an article identifying him as a sex offender. His neighbors became afraid of letting their children play with Totman's 3-year-old daughter.

Kansas, like many other states, paints people like Brad Totman with the same brush as child molesters, pedophiles, and rapists. Brad must register with the state twice a year and pay a $20 fee each time. In addition, he must verify his address every 90 days through the mail. Failure to do so is a major felony punishable by 3 years in prison.

Observe Investigate Understand

- **At what point, if any, should sex between teenagers be considered a sex offense? Does it depend on age? Consent?**
- **Should local media be allowed to publicize the presence of registered sex offenders?**
- **How can the criminal justice system distinguish between sex offenders and people like Brad Totman?**

SOURCES: Eric Westlander, "Critics Call Registry for Sex Offenders Vague, Unfair," *Lawrence Journal World and News*, August 27, 2006, http://www2.ljworld.com/news/2006/aug/27/critics_call_registry_sex_offenders_vague_unfair/?state_regional (retrieved May 15, 2007); Scott Rothschild, "Lawmakers Clash over Sex Offender Policy," *Lawrence Journal World and News*, March 23, 2008, http://www2.ljworld.com/news/2008/mar/23/lawmakers_clash_over_sex_offender_policy/ (retrieved April 19, 2008).

residents usually attend work or educational programs. Typically they must sign in and out of the house and abide by curfew rules, but they are generally free to come and go. Once they adjust to the demands of the community, offenders find residence elsewhere. Some community treatment centers specialize in dealing with either women or men. Some specialize in dealing with addicted offenders or other types of special needs offenders.

Work Release Programs

work release (furlough) Partial release of inmates to work for pay in the community and return to a correctional facility each night.

Work release (or **furlough**) programs were first used extensively in the 1950s. Selected inmates work for pay in the community and return to a correctional facility each night. Originally, work release participants were low-risk offenders (those convicted of a misdemeanor), but they now also include felons and youthful offenders. Variations of work release include weekend sentences, extended work release, and release for vocational or educational (study release) programs. Allowing inmates to work or study outside prison helps them establish and maintain links to the community.[105]

Many of these programs are situated in halfway houses.[106] Others are located in more restrictive facilities such as jails or prisons, which offenders are permitted to leave only to work or study.

Access to work release programs has decreased since 1994 because of political pressure to keep offenders out of the community. The public has often opposed halfway house programs as well, even for low-risk jail inmates. In 2000, residents in Orange County, California, became outraged at the approved opening of a work furlough program in their neighborhood.[107] Slightly over 2 months later the Orange County Board of Supervisors killed the proposal.[108] In 2006, residents in the mid-Mississippi valley forcefully opposed a plan for a halfway house for work release prisoners in their neighborhood.[109] These public fears seem counterproductive because studies show that these programs are effective and that few offenders commit crimes while working.[110]

The State of Washington has maintained its commitment to its work release program since its inception in 1967. Only 5 percent of the inmates on work release committed new crimes while working in the community, and 99 percent of those crimes were less serious property offenses, such as forgery or theft.[111] Other studies show positive but somewhat more tentative results.[112]

OTHER TYPES OF COMMUNITY CORRECTIONS

Not all community corrections take place in the public sphere. Just as there is a movement to privatize prisons (see Chapter 11), there also is a movement to privatize community corrections. Drug testing and treatment, electronic monitoring, and halfway houses are all activities in which private sector firms may take the place of government agencies.

At least 15 states have some form of private probation services. They justify the practice by its cost-effectiveness. Connecticut and Colorado privatized much of their community supervision of low-risk offenders in order to focus on higher-risk offenders in the community, thereby increasing public safety as they see it. Delaware contracts with a private group to supervise those awaiting trial. Florida, Mississippi, Missouri, Montana, New Mexico, North Dakota, Ohio, Oklahoma, Tennessee, Utah, Wisconsin, and Wyoming use private agencies to supervise a portion of their offenders who are on probation.[113]

Real Careers

MALISSA MINARD

Work location: Cincinnati, Ohio

College(s): University of Cincinnati, 2004; Northern Kentucky University, 2007

Major(s): Criminal Justice (BS) with a minor in Addictions; Public Administration (MA)

Job title: Probation Officer II, Hamilton County

Salary range for job like this: $30,000–$40,000

Time in job: 5 years

Work Responsibilities

A typical workweek for me consists of monitoring cases and clients by taking victim impact statements, interviewing arresting officers, and making service referrals to outside agencies. All of my findings must be well documented in reports, which are then shared with attorneys and judges and reviewed to determine sentencing for the offender.

Why Criminal Justice?

Working as a probation officer allows me to combine my interest in law enforcement with my desire to help people. I knew this was the field that I wanted to enter after taking an internship with federal probation during my senior year of college, and working full time during college at the Talbert House in the Pathways and Adapt program for female offenders. At the Talbert House, I began as an activity security monitor, which means I tracked behavior and movement of clients, including home and employment verifications. After about a year in that position, I was promoted to case manager. In my new role, I was responsible for completing assessments and intake evaluations and providing information for probation and parole officers. I worked at Talbert House until I landed my current job as probation officer for Hamilton County.

Eventually I would like to advance through the ranks to federal probation officer and finally federal chief, which will give me the opportunity to manage other probation officers. My 5 years of working as a probation officer will help qualify me for such promotions.

Expectations and Realities of the Job

Because I was exposed to the work of a probation officer during my internship and prior work experience, I understood the daily tasks and pressures of the job and knew what to expect in terms of pay and benefits. The only aspect of the job that I did not fully understand as an intern was the significance of a probation officer's work. I am responsible for helping offenders regain their livelihood through counseling, rehabilitation programs, and mentoring. My supervisors have emphasized the importance of always being fair, courteous, and professional with offenders in order to be an effective probation officer.

My Advice to Students

Try to get all the experience possible while still in school. Most agencies actively seek out student interns. Working in the field during my studies helped me make a seamless transition from school to work. Not only did I know what to anticipate as a working probation officer, but I was already used to the working lifestyle. And finally, practical work experience is required for most entry-level positions in the criminal justice field.

DPP - SUP - 10 (Revised 10-92)

STATE OF MARYLAND
DEPARTMENT OF PUBLIC SAFETY AND CORRECTIONAL SERVICES
DIVISION OF PAROLE AND PROBATION

P&P NO. ☐☐☐☐☐☐☐ OFFENDER'S NAME ______ LAST NAME ______ FIRST NAME

OTHER NO. ______

RISK ASSESSMENT

1. PRIORITY CASES (check all that apply. DDMP do not score): 1. ☐
   - Parole or Mandatory Supervision Case ______ ☐
   - Child Abuse related offense ______ ☐
   - Sex related offense ______ ☐
   - Other ______ ☐

   a. One or more checks ______ Enter 15
   b. None of the above ______ Enter 0

2. TOTAL LIFETIME FELONY CONVICTIONS: (including juvenile and current offense) 2. ☐
   a. Two or more ______ Enter 4
   b. One ______ Enter 2
   c. None ______ Enter 0

3. CONVICTION OR JUVENILE ADJUDICATION FOR (include current offense, add all categories and enter total): 3. ☐
   a. Domestic Violence related offense (current offense only) ______ Add 6
   b. 643B or felony drug or sex offense within last 5 years ______ Add 6
   c. 643B or felony drug or sex offense more than 5 years ago ______ Add 4
   d. Other assaultive offenses ______ Add 4
   e. Fraud, forgery, deceptive practices ______ Add 2
   f. Theft, auto theft, B&E ______ Add 1
   g. None of the above ______ Enter 0

4. TOTAL DWI/DUI CONVICTIONS (DWI/DUI cases only): 4. ☐
   a. Two or more ______ Enter 4
   b. One ______ Enter 2
   c. None ______ Enter 0

5. BAL (Blood Alcohol Level) AT TIME OF ARREST (DWI/DUI cases only): 5. ☐
   a. Refused/unknown ______ Enter 3
   b. 14 and above ______ Enter 3
   c. 10 to 13 ______ Enter 2
   d. 09 and below ______ Enter 1
   e. Not Applicable ______ Enter 0

6. AGE AT FIRST CONVICTION OR JUVENILE ADJUDICATION: 6. ☐
   a. 19 or younger ______ Enter 4
   b. 20 to 25 ______ Enter 2
   c. 27 or older ______ Enter 0

SEX OFFENDER: y☐yes n☐no

7. NUMBER OF PRIOR SUPERVISION PERIODS (Parole/Mandatory Supervision/Probation/Monitor/Juvenile): 7. ☐
   a. Two or more ______ Enter 4
   b. One ______ Enter 2
   c. None ______ Enter 0

8. NUMBER OF SUPERVISION PERIODS RESULTING IN UNSATISFACTORY CLOSINGS (Parole/Mandatory Supervision/Probation/Monitor) 8. ☐
   a. Two or more ______ Enter 4
   b. One ______ Enter 2
   c. None ______ Enter 0

9. IMPACT OF DRUG USE ON BEHAVIOR: 9. ☐
   a. High ______ Enter 4
   b. Low ______ Enter 2
   c. None ______ Enter 0

10. IMPACT OF ALCOHOL USE ON BEHAVIOR: 10. ☐
    a. High ______ Enter 4
    b. Low ______ Enter 2
    c. None ______ Enter 0

11. EMPLOYMENT HISTORY FOR PAST 12 MONTHS (Prior to incarceration, if applicable): 11. ☐
    a. Unemployed and virtually unemployable ______ Enter 2
    b. Part-time, seasonal, unstable employment or underemployed ______ Enter 1
    c. Full-time employment, no difficulties reported; homemaker; full-time student; retired; or disabled and unable to work ______ Enter 0

12. IMPRESSION OF OFFENDER RISK: 12. ☐
    a. High ______ Enter 5
    b. Average ______ Enter 3
    c. Low ______ Enter 0

☐ Total Score

DOMESTIC VIOLENCE OFFENDER: y☐yes n☐no

Instructions: Check appropriate block

SCORING AND OVERRIDE

SCORE BASED CLASSIFICATION: CRIMINAL ☐ DDMP ☐ INTENSIVE ☐ WEEKLY ☐ STANDARD ☐ BIWEEKLY ☐ ADMINISTRATIVE ☐ MONTHLY ☐

CHECK HERE IF THERE IS AN OVERRIDE ☐ OVERRIDE EXPLANATION IF NEEDED: ______

FINAL CATEGORY OF CLASSIFICATION: CRIMINAL ☐ DDMP ☐ INTENSIVE ☐ WEEKLY ☐ STANDARD ☐ BIWEEKLY ☐ ADMINISTRATIVE ☐ MONTHLY ☐ DATE ASSIGNED ☐

______ APPROVED ______ DATE

______ AGENT/MONITOR ______ LAST NAME ______ FIRST INITIAL ______ DATE

______ CHANGE AGENT/MONITOR ASSIGNMENT TO ______ LAST NAME ______ FIRST INITIAL

OPERATOR'S INITIALS: ______ DATE: ______

FIGURE 13-4 Maryland's Risk Assessment Scoring Form

Another type of community corrections makes use of risk-based treatment. It relies on risk assessment tools that evaluate data and assign a score to an offender that reflects the likelihood the offender will reoffend after release. The U.S. Parole Commission's salient factor score (SFS) is a statistical measure dependent on such factors as age of the offender, addiction history, history of violence, and conduct in prison. Figure 13-4 provides an example of a risk assessment scoring form. A score of 0 reflects a very good risk on parole or probation, and a score of 4 a poor risk.

Risk analysis also assists in determining the kind of supervision that probationers and parolees will need on the street. Potentially violent offenders are of particular concern. When correctional workers are able to identify those likely to reoffend, they can dedicate scarce resources to treatment that specifically meets the needs of these offenders and ultimately protects the community.

A major problem with risk-based assessment is that it is impossible to make accurate predictions all the time. Typically the assessment instruments overestimate the odds of reoffending, which may protect society but also punishes some offenders for future crimes they are not likely to commit.[114]

SUMMARY

Community corrections allows offenders to spend all or part of their sentence in the community through a wide range of programs and practices, including probation, parole, work release, community service, house arrest, registers and tracking, electronic monitoring, and vocational, educational, and drug treatment programs. Those who are allowed to take part in community corrections are generally nonviolent offenders or offenders judged to be low risk.

The advantages of community corrections are that offenders can maintain ties to family and the community while serving their sentence, and not become socialized to an institution. By reducing the prison and jail populations, community corrections saves costs for local, state, and federal governments. But public opinion resists the idea of releasing offenders, especially sex offenders, into the community. And politicians often follow the lead of public opinion in the legislation they write concerning corrections. Despite the lower recidivism rates obtained in community corrections, it appears likely that incarceration will continue to be the sentence of choice.

OBSERVE
Investigate
Understand

Review

Identify distinctive features of probation.

- The offender is sentenced by a judge and conditionally released into the community under court supervision to serve a sentence.
- A probation officer supervises the offender in the community.
- Probation is a privilege, not a right.
- Probation is the most frequently used form of correctional supervision in the United States.
- Whites get probation more often than Blacks and Latinos combined.

Contrast intensive and traditional supervision probation.

- Intensive-supervision probation programs are characterized by smaller officer caseloads, closer surveillance, and more contact between probation officer and offender than traditional probation.
- ISP programs were designed primarily to target high-risk offenders who would otherwise be prison-bound; traditional probation applies mainly to low-risk offenders.

Assess the success of probation.

- Probation is less expensive than incarceration.
- Success on probation is difficult to measure because recidivism is all that is usually measured, and revocation can vary enormously by jurisdiction and location.
- About half of those on probation completed their term satisfactorily.

Identify the distinctive features of parole.

- Parole is an administrative procedure that allows inmates to serve their remaining sentence in the community conditionally under the supervision of a parole officer.
- Social reintegration is the objective of parole.
- Revocation of parole is possible if an offender violates the terms of parole or reoffends.

Assess the success of parole.

- Parole is less expensive than incarceration.
- Parole rewards inmates who follow prison rules and behave positively while incarcerated.
- Parole provides inmates who no longer need imprisonment with supervision and appropriate programs in the community.

Describe the role of intermediate sanctions.

- Intermediate sanctions are judicial punishments that do not require long terms of incarceration but stop short of allowing offenders to remain in the community on probation with minimal supervision.

- Intermediate sanctions are not quite prison and not quite traditional probation; they encourage offenders to take responsibility for their actions but under closer supervision than traditional probation.
- Some intermediate sanctions require offenders to live in a communal residence.

Identify various types of intermediate sanctions.

- Community service is a practice whereby offenders are sentenced to activities that provide a benefit to the public.
- House arrest is a practice that requires offenders not to leave their residence.
- Electronic monitoring is a way to monitor offenders' whereabouts by using technology.
- Community centers offer halfway house residential and treatment options.
- Work release programs allow inmates to leave a correctional facility during the day to work in the community.

Describe private sector and risk-based community corrections.

- Private sector firms, instead of public agencies, run some community corrections programs, such as halfway houses and drug treatment.
- Some community corrections programs make use of risk assessment of offenders to determine who can participate and what treatment is appropriate.

Key Terms

community corrections 372
discretionary release 380
diversion 384
day fines 387
electronic monitoring 388
fines 387
forfeiture 387
global positioning system (GPS) 391
house arrest (home confinement) 387
intensive-supervision probation (ISP) 375
intermediate sanctions 384
mandatory release 380
parole 378
parole boards 379
probation 372
probation kiosks 388
recognizance 373
restitution 386
restorative justice 385
shock probation 388
shock programs 388
unconditional release 382
victim–offender mediation 387
work release (furlough) 392

Study Questions

1. The term *community corrections* refers to
   a. probation.
   b. supervision in communities.
   c. parole.
   d. all of the above.

2. Probation and parole are similar in that
   a. a judge sentences an offender to both probation and parole.
   b. a parole board grants probation and parole.
   c. both probation and parole officers supervise offenders in the community.
   d. both probationers and parolees have to deal with the label "ex-con."

3. Which of the following sanctions is *not* considered an intermediate community corrections sanction?
   a Jail
   b. Shock probation
   c. House arrest
   d. Restitution

4. Which of the following is considered a technical parole violation?
   a. Leaving the state without parole agent permission
   b. Moving into a new residence without parole agent permission
   c. Failing a drug test
   d. All of the above

5. _____refers to the technology to enforce house arrest or to monitor the location of the offender.
   a. Technocorrections
   b. Day reporting centers
   c. Day fines
   d. Norplant implant

6. Which statement is *not* true?
   a. Probation is a right that must be granted for certain crimes.
   b. Probation is a privilege.
   c. Probation officers do not make the ultimate decision as to who gets probation.
   d. Probation officers make recommendations as to who should get probation.

7. The term *recognizance* means
   a. recognition of the authority of the court.
   b. recognition of an inmate's rights.
   c. release of a prisoner on his word.
   d. the search for the truth in a hearing.

8. The term *diversion* means
   a. diverting a criminal away from crime.
   b. diverting an offender from jail before or during trial as an intermediate sanction.
   c. distracting an offender so she can adjust to incarceration.
   d. changing the method of treatment to improve the offender's behavior.

9. *ISP* stands for
   a. international subjective profiles.
   b. immediate suicidal precautions.
   c. inmate's substantial progress.
   d. intensive-supervision probation.

10. The decision to revoke an offender's probation is made by a
    a. probation officer.
    b. review board.
    c. judge.
    d. probation officer and a judge.

Critical Thinking Questions

1. What are the similarities and differences between probation and parole?
2. What are some pro and con arguments for the use of intermediate sanctions as alternatives to incarceration? Which arguments do you find more compelling?
3. Is victim–offender mediation really a type of punishment for the offender? Why or why not?

Internet Sites

Bureau of Justice Statistics Bulletin
www.ojp.usdoj.gov/bjs/pub/pdf/ppus05.pdf
This site contains information about probation and parole statistics.

Center for Program Evaluation and Performance Measurement
www.ojp.usdoj.gov/BJA/evaluation/psi_sops/sops2.htm
This site contains information about problems with sex offender registration laws.

Electronic Monitoring Resource Center
https://emresourcecenter.nlectc.du.edu/
This site contains information about electronic monitoring.

Suggested Readings

Julian V. Roberts, *The Virtual Prison: Community Custody and the Evolution of Imprisonment* (Cambridge: Cambridge University Press, 2004).
This book develops a compelling argument for working intensely with offenders in the community as opposed to imprisonment.

Edward Sieh, *Community Corrections and Human Dignity* (Boston: Jones & Bartlett, 2005).
This book examines a number of issues related to community corrections: supervision models, probation and parole, different kinds of probationers, offender treatment, and the importance of treating offenders respectfully. It also contains a number of street examples.

Jennifer Gonnerman, *Life on the Outside: The Prison Odyssey of Elaine Bartlett* (New York: Picador, 2004).
This book explains the U.S. reentry system and its problems.

Understanding and Helping Victims

CHAPTER 14

OBSERVE Investigate *Understand*

After reading this chapter, you should be able to:

- Differentiate between the various victims' responses to trauma.
- Identify the major historical milestones that have influenced the formation of victimology and the victims' rights movement.
- Identify the various types of victims and the roles and responsibilities of victim advocates.
- Describe the various types of crisis intervention programs that exist to work with crime victims.
- Differentiate between Adult Protective Services and TRIADs.
- Describe the various types of collaborative responses to victims.

Realities and Challenges

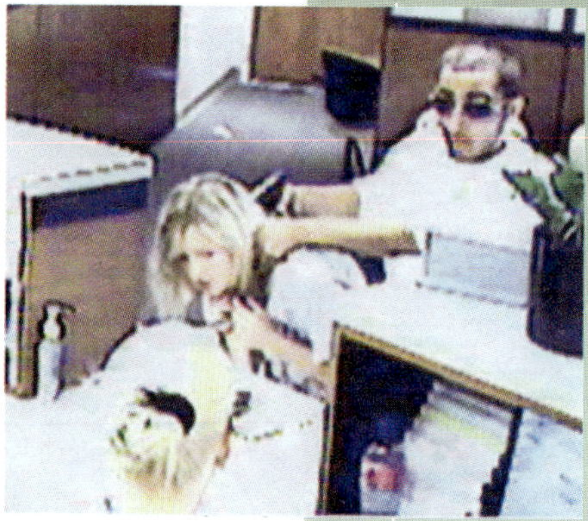

From the Victim's Perspective

It was 10 a.m. on Monday, April 3, 2006. Three men entered the Garden State Bank in a small New Jersey town. One man yanked a mask over his face and pointed a pistol at Steve Thoresen, a teller with 2 years' experience. Thoresen's stomach turned to jelly. The two others also put on masks and pulled out pistols. One went to the door to stop customers from leaving. The other jumped on the counter and yelled, "Everyone get on the floor or I'll start killing people!" Thoresen smelled urine and noticed a puddle at the feet of one of his colleagues.

The robbers ordered Thoresen to fill a large backpack with all the money in his drawer and the other drawers as well. At first he was paralyzed; then he began to move as if in a dream. Shock kept everyone speechless and motionless. In less than a minute the robbers were gone. There was complete silence until a customer went up to the guard and whispered, "You should call the police."

Five long minutes later, police officers arrived with weapons drawn. Thoresen tried to speak but couldn't, and then he started to cry. Two coworkers comforted him, but he couldn't stop. The bank's vice president seemed elated that no one was hurt—in fact, she was laughing nervously—and then told everyone, "Take the rest of the morning off. We'll close the bank until 1 p.m.; come back after lunch." Thoresen finally regained some composure, and then he called his wife at her job. As he told her the story of what had happened, he became fearful again.

In the week that followed, the bank tellers all had different experiences: flashbacks, anxiety, insomnia, and the urge to tell their stories of the robbery over and over again. They experienced a variety of symptoms into the second week, and for some the reaction lasted well beyond that. Then came the police investigators and hours of questioning. The police were angry because no one had sounded the alarm to give them a chance to catch the robbers. The bank president was relieved the stolen money was insured, so none of the bank's customers would lose their savings. Officially, the bank returned to "business as usual."

Steve Thoresen felt it was strange that everyone focused on the bank's money and the robbers, not on the tellers. Over the next 6 months, two tellers resigned, one started seeing a psychiatrist, and one began secretly carrying a gun in her purse.

In fact, everyone in the bank during the robbery was a victim. That no one in the investigation recognized the impact of this victimization clearly prolonged their suffering and delayed their recovery. Ultimately, Thoresen and three other valuable employees left the bank, and those who remained continued to experience a range of traumatic symptoms, which affected their job performance and their private lives.

In this chapter we introduce crime victims. We identify how many there are, discuss trends over the past 30 years, describe the main types of victims, and explain some of the major ways victims are affected by their victimization. We look at how society responds to all the different types of victims and describe the special services that are available to help ease victims' suffering, facilitate their recovery, and prepare them for their role in the criminal justice process. Finally, we consider how these services are supported by a wide range of laws, policies, programs, and research, which has resulted in a greatly improved status for crime victims in the United States.

RECOGNIZING VICTIMIZATION

About 40 years ago the U.S. government started collecting data about victims on a regular basis (see Chapter 3). Official statistics show that property victimization has been steadily declining over the past 30 years. So has the number of victims of crimes against persons, with an especially dramatic drop in the last 10 years. Despite these declines, however, tens of millions of people become crime victims every year. According to the National Crime Victim Survey (see Figure 14-1), in 2007 there were 17.5 million property crime victims, 5.2 million victims of crimes against persons, and 194,100 victims of personal theft (mostly pickpocketing and purse-snatching).

The experience of being victimized takes most people completely by surprise, especially if it has never happened to them before. The fear of dying or of being seriously injured is often accompanied, naturally enough, by terror. Under these circumstances, **psychic trauma**, which results from severe emotional stress, immobilizes the victim's mind and body and can result in long-lasting emotional injury.

Each person responds differently to stress. Even though all the tellers in that New Jersey bank were witnesses to the same event, each one of them brought to work that day a different history of coping with stress and crisis, and different coping strengths and weaknesses. These differences result in a variety of responses. Resilient people might show no effects and cope well. Others might show mild effects and recover within a few minutes or hours, but others may show extreme effects and take days, weeks, or months to heal. People are generally not familiar with the dynamics of psychic trauma and can easily misinterpret what they observe and the way victims cope. The president of that New Jersey bank might have assumed those who appeared calm were not in crisis. Other observers and the police could also easily dismiss the victims' plight and quickly shift their focus to the offenders and the lost money.

The New Jersey bank robbery demonstrates that society is slow to recognize who victims are, how they become victimized, how much they suffer, and how important it is to provide them with support. The reality is that all victims suffer to some degree, whether they've faced a crime or a traffic accident, a natural disaster, or a war. Many need some level of help or intervention to recover. As a society, we have lately come to understand the magnitude and the character of victimization. We now have the added tool of victimization surveys to provide us with a more accurate and complete picture.

This chapter describes who victims are, why society needs to be concerned about them, how victimologists have tried to explain victim behavior, how society influences victim services, and what methods and services are needed if we are to make victims whole again. One way to understand the impact on victims is to read their own words on the aftermath of their victimizations (see What about the Victim? on the next page).

Preview

psychic trauma
Severe emotional stress that immobilizes the victim's mind and body and can result in long-lasting emotional injury.

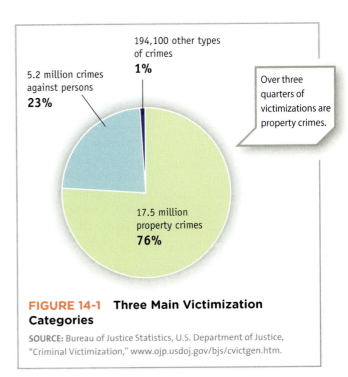

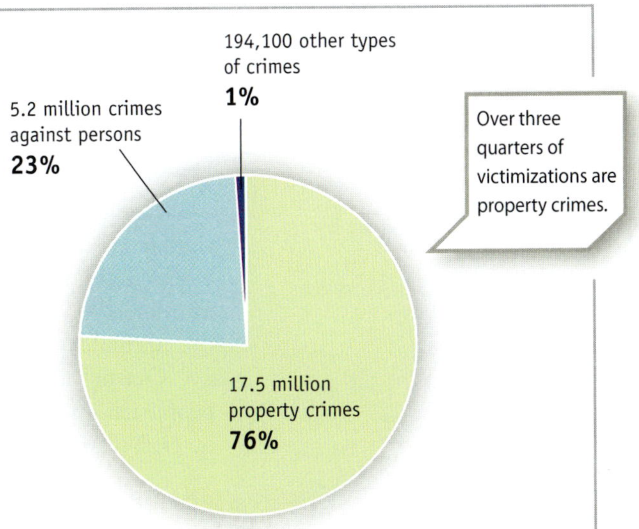

FIGURE 14-1 Three Main Victimization Categories

SOURCE: Bureau of Justice Statistics, U.S. Department of Justice, "Criminal Victimization," www.ojp.usdoj.gov/bjs/cvictgen.htm.

HISTORY OF VICTIM ADVOCACY

In preliterate societies, one of the main goals of law was to make the victim whole again. Most early cultures placed the victim at the center of their legal procedures, giving victims a dominant role in righting the wrongs committed against them. The Code of Hammurabi from ancient Babylon, for example, required equity to be restored between offender and victim.[1] Equity meant that whatever was taken from the victim was also equally taken from the offender—a principle enshrined in a famous phrase in Hammurabi's Code, "an eye for an eye and a tooth for a tooth."

This victim-centered approach reached its height during the European early Middle Ages, a period sometimes called the Golden Age of the Victim.[2] In this era, crime victims were the center of the justice process; they participated in responding to

What about the Victim?

The Words of Crime Victims

The following statements were taken from real victims soon after their victimization:

- "He said, 'Move or yell and I'll kill you.' I didn't doubt his word."
- "I didn't hear anything about the case for almost a year. Then all of a sudden they called me up at work and said, 'Come down to court right away, the trial is going to take place.' "
- "It is almost impossible to walk into a courtroom and describe in detail the thing you most want to forget. It is also devastating to have to face your assailant. Although you are surrounded by people and deputies of the court, the fear is still overwhelming."
- "Why didn't anyone consult me? I was the one who was kidnapped, not the Commonwealth of Virginia."
- "I'm a senior citizen, but I never considered myself old. I was active, independent. Now I live in a nursing home and sit in a wheelchair. The day I was mugged was the day I began to die."
- "What others see as an inconvenience is for the victim an endless nightmare."
- "I will never forget being raped, kidnapped, and robbed at gunpoint. However, my sense of disillusionment of the judicial system is many times more painful. I could not in good faith urge anyone to participate in this hellish process."

OBSERVE Investigate Understand

- **Why are there fewer thefts reported to the police than assaults?**
- **Why is the incidence of injury very low among victims of robbery?**
- **Why do people who experience the same traumatic event suffer in different ways?**

SOURCE: *President's Task Force on Victims of Crime: Final Report* (Washington, DC: Government Printing Office, 1982).

the crime and in determining the offender's punishment. A thousand years later, with the advent of the Industrial Revolution in the nineteenth century, societies rejected traditional models of community governance. Nations became more centralized, government functions became more focused on efficiency and specialization, and justice systems replaced the older focus on the victim with a focus on the witness.

The Romanian criminologist Beniamin Mendelsohn coined the word *victimology* in 1947, calling attention to the need to understand crime from the perspective of how people are victimized and how the criminal justice system treats them. The next year, in 1948, the well-known psychiatrist Frederick Wertham observed that in sensationalizing the murderer, society had forgotten the victim. He concluded that to thoroughly understand the murderer, we must also understand the victim, and thus "a science of victimology was needed."[3] Some years later, Wertham wrote *A Sign for Cain*, in which he presented what he saw as the negative impulses that exist in society; its title was a metaphor for the evildoer.[4] How interesting it is that he would use the Sign of Cain as a metaphor for his book, yet not recognize how the victim in that biblical story was ignored. One can only speculate how history would have been altered for victims had the opposite metaphor been created: the Mark of Abel.

The Mark of Abel

In the Judeo-Christian Bible, the fourth chapter of the Book of Genesis tells how Cain murdered his younger brother Abel. Thus in Judeo-Christian tradition, Cain is the first murderer. Today, the expression "the mark of Cain" means the stigmatization of someone as an evildoer, and we can view the label as a metaphor for the way some societies find the image of the offender more interesting than the image of the victim. Abel, as the Bible's first victim, was not immortalized. Other religious traditions have had similar accounts of early victimizations, which have mostly downplayed the role of the victim and emphasized the offender. Although societies have professed a desire to reject murderers for their violence and to help victims in their innocence and their need, often the cultural and legal support systems have done the opposite.[5]

One of the most significant outcomes of World War II was the shock and revulsion that people felt on learning about the Holocaust—the murder of just more than 6 million Jews by Nazi Germany. This horrific event helped refocus attention on the victims of crime.

Social Forces That Led to the Victims' Rights Movement

Influential social movements arose in the 1960s and 1970s that concentrated on civil rights, women's rights, children's rights, gay rights, and opposition to the Vietnam War. These movements popularized nonviolent protest, protection of the disadvantaged, equality of opportunity, and the right to be free of pain and suffering and to be treated with respect and dignity. Thus they paved the way for the victims' rights movement.

The study of victim assistance is relatively new, emerging only during the mid-1970s. Initially, victim assistance was provided largely by people who had themselves been victimized, for specific treatment of crime victims had not been developed. Victims were often stigmatized as being somehow partially to blame for their misfortunes, and assisting and comforting them was left mainly to the volunteer efforts of other victims, who understood their feelings and could help them recover through peer support groups. This tradition still exists today in many victim assistance programs across the United States.

Research on the benefits of peer support groups has been sparse. A recent study with victims of crime and traffic accidents has suggested, however, that sharing or having contact with other victims may not be helpful as a coping mechanism—and may actually be harmful. This research suggests that recovery is more likely when guided by a therapist skilled in the use of evidence-based supportive interventions.[6] Another common victim treatment method is psychological debriefing, originally proposed to help persons who have been traumatized in emergency situations (natural disasters, for example) either avoid posttraumatic stress or recover from it.[7] We do not yet have enough studies to know whether such treatment is effective. Although this form of victim treatment continues to be used, especially for mass victimizations, the support for its use has not been completely demonstrated through empirical research.

Another significant influence contributing to the rise of the new discipline of victimology were the first victimization surveys conducted in 1966 for the President's Commission on Law Enforcement and the Administration of Justice (see Chapter 3). These surveys made clear what types of victims there were and how many (at least twice as many as the Uniform Crime Reports showed), demonstrating the need to study victims and provide services for them.[8]

A rising level of crime, stretching from the mid-1960s until the early 1980s, produced a demand from concerned citizens for a national response. This crime wave was attributed to massive numbers of post–World War II baby boomers, disproportionate to other age groups, reaching their mid-teen years. It is in the mid-teen years that most young people begin to pull away from parental controls, experiment with relationships and with new identities and role models, and test the limits of acceptable behavior. Consequently, many got into trouble with the law. To cope with this crime wave, the Omnibus Crime Control and Safe Streets Act of 1968 created a federal agency called the Law Enforcement Assistance Administration (LEAA). This major national effort against crime poured vast amounts of federal funds into the fight against delinquency and crime and, ultimately, also into research and programs for victims.[9]

▲ Cain Killing Abel

Islam, Christianity, and Judaism all tell the story of Cain, the son of Adam and Eve, killing his brother Abel. Cain is considered the first murderer and Abel the first victim. *Explain the irony of how and why these two persons have been remembered throughout history. How does Abel symbolically reflect the image of victims today in the struggle to have equal status with offenders?*

◀ Protestors of the 1960s

At the Woodstock rock festival in New York in 1969, half a million people celebrated "three days of peace and music" with sex and drugs and rock 'n' roll instead of guns and war.

In the early 1970s the women's movement gave rise to the first rape crisis centers, including California's Bay Area Women Against Rape, Seattle Rape Relief, and the (Washington) D.C. Rape Crisis Center. Feminist activist Susan Brownmiller's influential book on the history of rape added credibility to the victims' rights movement in general and to efforts to combat violence against women in particular.[10] By the end of the 1970s, most large cities and many smaller ones had rape crisis centers, staffed mostly by feminists who lobbied on behalf of sexual assault victims and provided them with legal information, counseling, and training in defensive tactics. Eventually, these workers began to counsel battered women.

In his 1975 book *The Victims*, Frank Carrington argued that courts were too permissive and that excessive concerns about prisoners' rights, as well as a general weakening of law enforcement, were largely responsible for the 1960s crime surge. Carrington insisted that supporting victims was more important than protecting the rights of the accused.[11] Several influential victim-oriented groups arose during the 1970s, including the National Organization for Victim Assistance (NOVA) in 1976, Parents of Murdered Children in 1978, and Mothers Against Drunk Driving (MADD) in 1980.[12] Together, concern for victims and a widely shared public feeling that the criminal justice system had grown too permissive brought pressure on the criminal justice system to get tough on crime: for example, by lengthening sentences and otherwise imposing harsher punishments. In response to this pressure, many state legislatures passed minimum sentencing laws. The President's Task Force on Victims of Crime of 1982 and the Attorney General's Task Force on Violent Crime also launched a campaign to toughen penalties and to induce prosecutors to focus more on victims and their rights.[13]

LEAA no longer exists. Its place has been taken by such national sources of federal money as the 1984 Victims of Crime Act (VOCA). Under this law, fines collected from convicted federal criminals are redistributed to provide for victim compensation and victim assistance programs throughout the United States.[14]

In 1994 Congress passed the original Violence Against Women Act (VAWA). Its primary objective was to support the investigation and prosecution of violent crimes against women, but it also contained provisions designed to offer women better protection from those who had offended against them, especially in the period after the offender's arrest.[15]

Advocates for victims point out that although defendants are protected by the Bill of Rights and by major Supreme Court decisions, nowhere does the Constitution address the rights of victims. In the late twentieth century, repeated attempts were made to enact a "Victims' Rights Amendment." In 2004, however, these efforts collapsed amid Congress' concerns that such an amendment would undermine law enforcement and clash with long-established criminal defendants' rights. To replace this proposed amendment, in October 2004 Congress enacted and President George W. Bush signed into law the Crime Victims' Rights Act. It declares that victims of those who break federal laws will be "reasonably protected" against the accused, including being promptly notified if the alleged perpetrator escapes or is released from custody. The act also provides for the fair, dignified, respectful, and prompt treatment of victims by federal prosecutors, and the right to "full and timely restitution as provided by law."

Today, a vast array of service programs exist for a broad range of victims, and a large group of committed professionals work as victim advocates and victimologists. International, federal, and state rights have been enlarged to ensure that more victims are treated with dignity, fairness, and care. Public policies attend to victims' suffering, needs, and recovery, and innovative strategies are aimed at preventing victimization.

primary victim
A person injured or killed as a direct result of a criminal act.

secondary victim
Someone who experiences sympathetic pain as a result of a primary victim's suffering.

secondary victimization
Includes insensitivity and abuse of the primary victim by the police, prosecutors, and judges, manifested in the process of identifying, prosecuting, and punishing the offender.

WORKING WITH VICTIMS

American culture is crammed with distorted images of reality. Crime stories typically describe offenders, police, and lawyers, but rarely dwell on the victims, their suffering, or the services they need to recover. Even the television show *Law & Order, Special Victims*

Unit is largely about police investigators and the laboratory skills they use to identify offenders and not about victims.

When we think of crime victims, most of us imagine people who are targets of street crimes, to which the media devotes most of its attention. Victims of Uniform Crime Report Part II crimes such as fraud, vandalism, drug abuse violations, drunkenness, and vagrancy generally suffer less and get less attention. But victims of all crimes are affected to some degree, depending on the nature of the force used against them; their economic loss; the social, psychic, and physical resources available to them; and the setting in which the victimization takes place.

The **primary victim** is the person injured or killed as a direct result of a criminal act. A **secondary victim** is someone affected by the primary victim's suffering and who experiences sympathetic pain. A man who learns his sister has been raped and who consequently suffers emotional distress is a secondary victim of the attack. A closely related term, **secondary victimization**, encompasses the insensitivity and abuse that the primary victim may suffer at the hands of police, prosecutors, and judges as they identify, prosecute, and punish the offender. Sometimes people not in the criminal justice system—medical personnel, mental health workers, social workers, clergy, and even family and friends—also are responsible for secondary victimization.

When a victim is killed, his or her close relations are called **survivors**. Victims who cope well and are able to resume a normal life also consider themselves survivors, a term that helps them reject the hopelessness of the victim label and signify that they consider their suffering and sense of helplessness to be over.

Crime victimization means injuring or killing a human being in the course of a crime. It focuses on the victim rather than on the event. **Victim recidivism**, or repeat victimization, occurs when a person, household, or business is victimized more than once. For almost two decades, victim recidivism of a small number of victims has been known to account for a disproportionately large number of victimizations. This means that people who are victimized even once are at higher risk of further victimization than those who have not been victimized.[16] One British research study reported 4 percent of victims accounted for 44 percent of all victimizations in personal crimes.[17] For property offenses, another British study found a mere 2 percent of property crime victims experience 41 percent of all property crimes. According to this study, career burglars took advantage of information gained during successful burglaries to strike the same location more easily again.[18] These findings suggest that if we could stop repeat victimization, we might prevent a large proportion of all victimizations.

In the aftermath of victimization, we expect society to help victims cope with their misfortunes. **Victim services** are dedicated activities conducted to help reduce victims' suffering and facilitate their recovery.[19]

survivor
A relative or loved one of a person who has been killed; also, a crime victim who copes well and manages to resume a normal life.

crime victimization
Injuring or killing a human being in the course of a crime; the term focuses on the victim rather than on the event.

victim recidivism
Occurs when a person, household, or business is victimized more than once; also called repeat victimization.

victim services
Dedicated activities conducted to help reduce victims' suffering and facilitate their recovery so they can return to their previctimization status.

victim advocate
A direct provider of victim services who works in intimate partner violence programs, rape crisis centers, district attorneys' offices, police departments, Child Protective Services, and Adult Protective Services; other victim advocates are assigned to a specific justice system.

Victim Advocates

The direct providers of victim services are **victim advocates**, who work in intimate partner violence programs, rape crisis centers, district attorney's offices, police departments, Child Protective Services, and Adult Protective Services. Other victim advocates are assigned to a particular justice system—federal, judicial, military, juvenile, or tribal, for example. Victim advocates are not the only occupational group with direct contact with victims. Law enforcement and medical personnel also have direct contact, but their focus is on victims' immediate needs rather than the longer-term and wider concerns that victim advocates address.

The victim advocate assists the victim with obtaining community services such as health care, housing, education, and employment and

▼ Victim Advocate Meeting with Volunteers

Seema Singh, victim advocate for the state of New Jersey, meets with volunteer members of the Asian Women's Safety Net, a domestic violence task force. The 12 women of the task force support and guide women who are victims of intimate partner abuse.

supports victims in every phase of the criminal justice process to help them achieve recovery. Advocates provide crisis intervention and accompany the victim to the hospital and to court. They also support victims as they interact with social and legal agencies that may not understand or be sympathetic to the victimization.[20]

Victim advocates help victims navigate the confusing criminal justice system by explaining court procedures and ensuring victims' rights. In a 2-year study that followed victims of intimate partner violence, those who used advocacy services experienced greater safety and a better quality of life. Nearly a quarter of those who worked with an advocate experienced no further physical abuse, whereas of those who did not have an advocate, only 10 percent were free of abuse. Compared to women who did not have an advocate, those who had one obtained more of the resources they sought, showed fewer symptoms of depression, and were more effective at acquiring social services.[21]

During the 1980s and 1990s, specializations developed among advocates as they began working with specific kinds of victims: children, victims of intimate partner violence or sexual assault, older and dependent adults, homicide survivors (or those who had survived the homicide of a loved one), and victims of gang violence, human trafficking, and cybercrimes (also called Internet crimes). Few services yet exist to assist victims of

Real Careers

LIA CHACON

Work location: Orange County, California

College(s): California State University, Fresno, 2008

Major(s): Criminology (BS)

Job title: Legal Advocate

Salary range for job like this: $28,000–$35,000

Time in job: 1.5 years

Work Responsibilities

The mission of the intimate partner violence agency where I work is to help victims regain control of their lives through effective legal action. As a legal advocate in the agency, I assume two primary roles. First, I act as a resource of knowledge by informing victims of their rights and how the processes of the legal system work. Second, I serve as moral support by accompanying victims to their court appearances.

The victims who come to our agency are usually referred by law enforcement, the court house, or social services. My first encounter with clients is always emotional: They are discouraged and in desperate need of assistance. But as clients get closer to their goals, such as finding a safe place to live, I see their self-confidence increase. For example, I once helped a woman gather witness testimony to prove spousal abuse and secure a restraining order against her husband for herself and her children.

Why Criminal Justice?

Although I had been interested in criminal justice since high school, I did not discover victimology until I started college. When I took my first victimology class, I wanted to learn more. I got my first hands-on experience working with victims during my senior year of college, when I took an internship at the Victim Offender Reconciliation Program. In my role as mediator, I was able to see how some guidance can really make a difference in a person's life. In the future, I plan to teach so I can inspire people as my professors inspired me. Working as an advocate will help me to obtain experience in my field.

Expectations and Realities of the Job

I was pleasantly surprised to find that the agency I work for encourages me to attend workshops and take continuing education courses to better assist our clients. With this type of support from my employer, I expect to be able to help the agency expand by providing more services to our clients.

My Advice to Students

Dare to dream! Upon graduating from college, I knew I wanted to work as a victim advocate. However, I was unsure whether an entry-level employee could apply for such a position. So I went online and applied for the lowest job opening at one of the best-known intimate partner violence agencies in Fresno. To my surprise, although I applied for a lower position, I was offered employment as a victim advocate. Just by having the interview to present my skills and career goals, I was able to secure the job of my dreams.

Race, Class, Gender

The Juarez and Guatemala City Femicides

Unsolved serial victimizations targeting large numbers of women, called femicides, are occurring in at least two Latin American cities, Juarez in Mexico and Guatemala City in Guatemala.

In the border town of Juarez, a network of *maquiladoras*—factories manufacturing goods for U.S. markets—draws thousands of young girls from all over Mexico to earn money they cannot make in their own villages. The women lack protection from a largely corrupt police force. In Juarez, a city of approximately 1.5 million people, with a transient population of about 500,000 and one of Mexico's largest drug cartels, these women face a mostly ineffective criminal justice system. Over the past decade, at least 400 women reportedly have been raped, mutilated, and brutally murdered, and the fate of many others remains unknown. Due to the absence or the mishandling of credible evidence and official indifference, no one has been successfully prosecuted for these crimes. The killings have attracted international attention, but Juarez has yet to find a solution. Meanwhile relatives and friends of the victims have suffered extensive trauma. Many have been served by local victim advocates organized after these victimizations became known. Not only have these advocates provided direct services, but they have also served to coordinate lobbying efforts aimed at changing Mexican laws and generating funding to support community prevention programs.

There has been an even higher rate of femicide in the suburbs of Guatemala City, the capital of Guatemala—approximately two women per day over the past 8 years. Since 2000, about 4,000 women are said to have been killed. Amnesty International reported that 665 were killed in 2005. The Guatemalan Human Rights Commission placed the number of killings in 2006 at 672; in 2007, at 590; and in 2008, at 722.

About 70 percent of these cases have not been investigated, and in 97 percent of them no arrests have been made. Guatemala does have a national network of victim assistance offices, developed in the mid-1990s mostly for victims and witnesses, which operates under the auspices of the National Attorney General; another network of victim assistance centers was organized in the late 1990s within the Public Ministry, cooperating with the national police. These victim advocates are primarily psychologists, trained in victim advocacy.

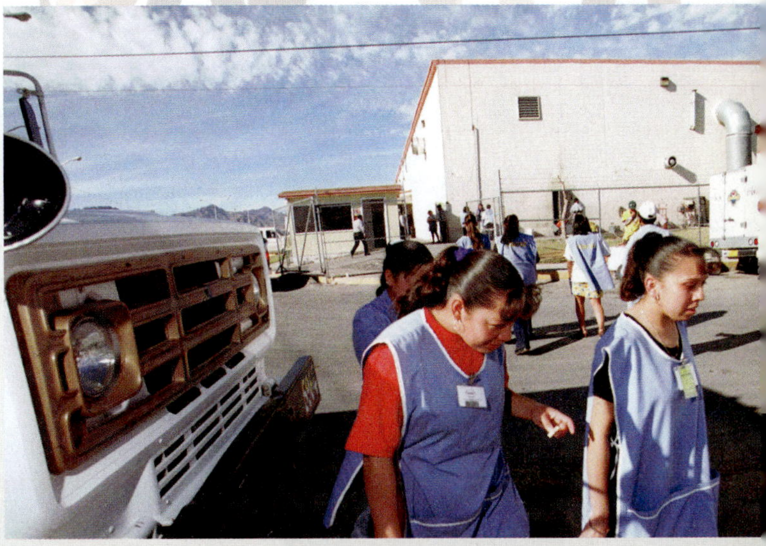

Observe Investigate Understand

- **What are the unique characteristics of the femicides that have been occurring in Juarez, Mexico, and in Guatemala City, Guatemala?**
- **How do victim advocates help victims navigate through the criminal justice system?**
- **How does the work of victim advocates help the prosecutorial process?**

SOURCES: National Organization for Women—2007, "Stop the Killings of the Women in Juarez," Femicides of Juarez Fact Sheet, 2007, www.now.org/issues/global/juarez/femicide.html (retrieved May 31, 2007); Billy Briggs, "The Price of Life," *Guernica Magazine* (2007), www.guernicamag.com/features/299/the_price_of_life_1/ (retrieved May 31, 2007); Theresa Braine, "Argentine Experts Study Juarez Murder Remains," April 16, 2006, www.womensenews.org/article.cfm/dyn/aid/2707/context/archive (retrieved March 21, 2009); Guatemalan Human Rights Commission/USA, May 2, 2008, Latin American Press, www.ghrc-usa.org/Resources/2008/FemicideLaw.htm (retrieved March 9, 2009); Ministerio Público, Biblioteca Virtual, www.mp.gob.gt/index.php?ID=5478&action=display&ID_LIBRARY=27822 (retrieved March 9, 2009); Prensa Latina, "First Femicide Trial in Guatemala," February 2, 2009, www.nisgua.org/themes_campaigns/index.asp?id=3302&mode=pf (retrieved March 21, 2009).

cybercrimes and economic crimes, such as white-collar offenses and identity theft. One reason for this is the limited funding available for services even for traditionally recognized victims of child abuse, intimate partner violence, sexual assault, and elder abuse.

Victim Advocates and Federal Crimes

Victim advocates in the federal system are known as "victim witness specialists" and work primarily for a U.S. Attorney's office or the FBI. They are responsible only for victims of federal crimes. More federal agencies, including the U.S. Postal Service, are now expanding their operations to include victim advocates.

▲ **Native American Women on a Reservation**

The Hopi live in northeastern Arizona on reservations set aside for their exclusive use by U.S. federal law.

The victim witness specialist is responsible for working with victims of terrorism, counterintelligence, cybercrime, public corruption, civil rights violations, organized crime, major theft, and violent crime. Sometimes victim witness specialists work in other countries with victims of trafficking in persons (TIP), also called human trafficking, or with victims such as those described in the Race, Class, Gender box. If a victim has been murdered, as in the case of the Juarez femicides, then the advocate will work with the survivors (usually family members and friends).[22]

Victim Advocates and Tribal Lands

Regardless of whether or not they live on tribal lands, Native Americans are victimized at much higher rates than other populations in the United States. According to the Bureau of Justice Statistics, between 1992 and 2002 Native Americans experienced violent victimization twice as often as Blacks, 2.5 times more often than Whites, and 4.2 times more often than Asian Americans.[23] During this period, Native American women were more than twice as likely to be victims of violent crime than were women of other races, and they were more likely to be victimized by a stranger than by an acquaintance or intimate partner. This means that a Native American woman is more likely to be targeted by—and more vulnerable to—an unknown assailant. It is unclear why this is the case, but the victim service providers working with Native Americans must specifically address the issue of stranger assaults, victim vulnerability, and ways in which a victim can reduce her vulnerability. These figures are especially high, considering that in 2000, Native Americans made up only 1.5 percent of the U.S. population.[24]

Responding to these high victimization rates among Native Americans, in 1987 the federal government created the Victim Assistance in Indian Country (VAIC) program. VAIC's 52 programs provide direct services, including crisis intervention, emergency shelter, crisis hotlines, counseling, emergency transportation of victims to a safe location, and court accompaniments.[25]

Victim Advocates and the Military

In 1994, the Department of Defense (DoD) mandated creation of victim and witness assistance programs for all branches of the military, with the aim of helping victims and witnesses deal with the investigation, prosecution, and punishment of crimes committed on military bases or by military personnel. The programs also provide victim services. Since 1994, the DoD has worked with the Office of Victims of Crime to create policies, programs, and training to promote victims' rights and to ensure that victim services are provided at military installations in the United States and around the world. When services are not available on a military base, the DoD enters into agreements with community victim service providers for service provision and referrals.

Death Notification

One of the most difficult tasks is to tell someone that a loved one has died. Death notifications are usually delivered in person by medical personnel, coroners or medical examiners, law enforcement officers, spiritual leaders, social service workers, or victim advocates. When doing this painful assignment, the notifier must identify herself and the organization she represents, ensure that she is speaking to the appropriate person, and identify the victim by name. Equally important is not to hide the harsh reality of death by using euphemisms such as "he has passed away," "she is no longer with us," or "he has gone to a better place." Such phrases can be very confusing, particularly if there is a language or cultural barrier. The survivor should be given enough details about the date of death, the time of day, and the location (such as a car, school, or apartment) to understand how it occurred, but a great deal of detail is not necessary, particularly in the case of a violent death. If the survivor asks for further details, however, the advocate should answer honestly. Finally, the advocate can assist the survivor with identifying the victim, contacting the appropriate spiritual leader (if any) for guidance, and making funeral arrangements.[26]

crime victim compensation
Programs administered at the state level to provide financial assistance to victims and their families.

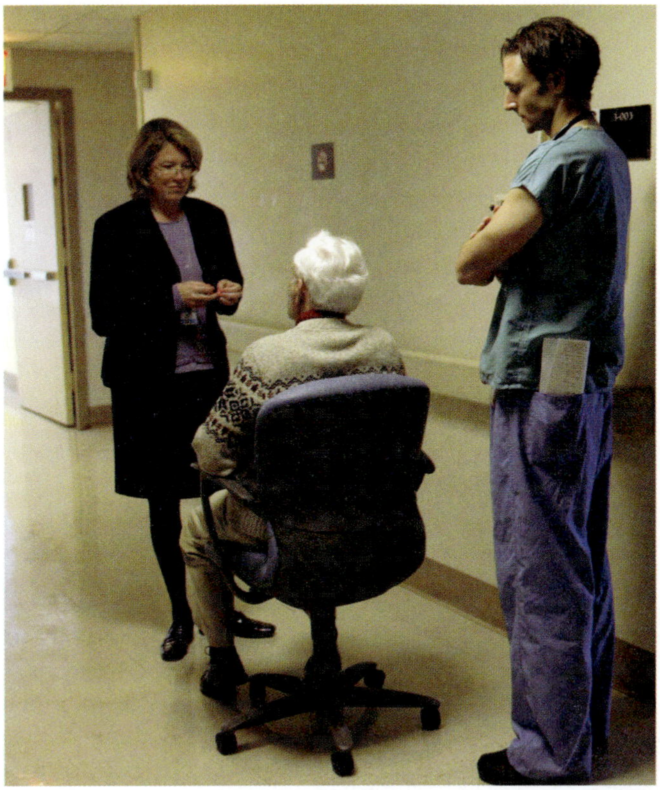

▶ Victim Advocate Speaking with a Victim

The work of victim advocates often requires them to visit victims in hospitals immediately after their victimization. During this time, a victim can be very confused and frightened; speaking with a victim advocate can help reduce this anxiety and excess worry.

Crime Victim Compensation

At the state level, **crime victim compensation** programs provide financial assistance to victims and their families throughout the 50 states, the District of Columbia, Puerto Rico, the Virgin Islands, and Guam. Any victim of violent or personal crime is eligible for compensation to help offset the costs of medical care, counseling, lost wages or support, and funerals. In most states, property crimes are not covered under compensation programs.

MYTH/REALITY

MYTH: Victims can make money as a result of the crime(s) committed against them.

REALITY: Victims must exhaust all sources of insurance, restitution, or other benefits before they can retain state compensation funds; and, the upper limit of compensation is different in each state.[27]

Victim compensation is not an opportunity for victims to make money from their circumstances. Each state sets a limit on compensation funds, usually $25,000 per victim.[28] To receive funding, the victim must report the crime promptly (usually within 30 days), cooperate with law enforcement and the prosecution, not have contributed to the victimization (say, by starting a brawl), not be in jail or on probation or parole, and exhaust all other insurance or benefits such as health insurance, worker's compensation, and lawsuits.[29] Crime victims apply for funding in the state where the crime was committed, not in the state where they live.

Under the USA PATRIOT Act, enacted in the wake of the 9/11 terrorist attacks, victims of international terrorism and their families are eligible for compensation through a special fund administered by the federal Office for Victims of Crime (OVC), part of the U.S. Department of Justice.[30]

Each year, about $450 million is distributed among about 200,000 victims in the United States. Across the states, the average allocation per victim is $2,000. Figure 14-2 shows how the funds were distributed in 2005. Of the 53 percent given for medical expenses, approximately $17 million was paid to victims when they had out-of-pocket expenses associated with completing a forensic sexual assault exam. Approximately 20 percent of all recipients of compensation funds are children, and 20 percent of all compensated adults are victims of intimate partner violence.[31] Compensation programs are funded from fees and fines collected from state and federal offenders and from the Victims of Crime Act (VOCA), the federal law that provides funding for victim services and compensation programs. State and federal taxes are not used for these funds. The Key Concepts table on the next page lists eligibility requirements for those receiving victim compensation.

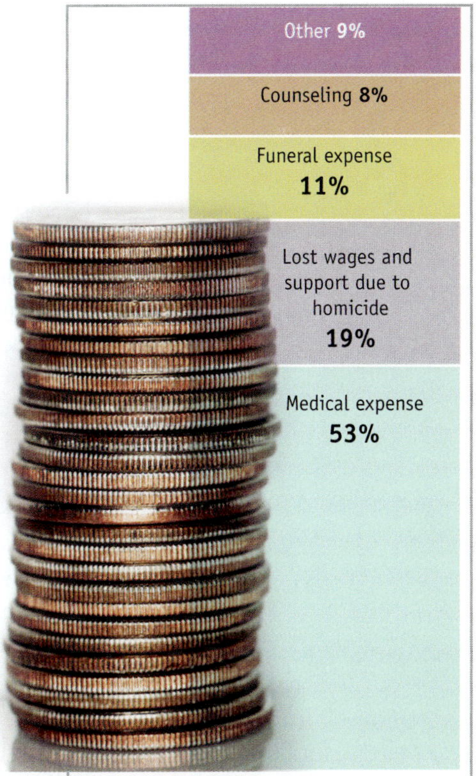

FIGURE 14-2 Victim Compensation Payments, 2005

SOURCE: National Association of Crime Victimization Compensation Boards, www.nacvcb.org/.

Victim Recovery

In the immediate aftermath of a victimization, the first official personnel to be notified are usually victim advocates. It is their responsibility to give victims at least

KEY CONCEPTS

Eligibility Requirements for Receiving Victim Compensation

Any victim of violent or personal crime is eligible for compensation to help offset the costs of the crime.

Victims of property crimes are not eligible to receive victim compensation.

Eligible costs include medical care, counseling, lost wages or support, and funerals.

Each state sets a limit on compensation funds, usually $25,000 per victim.

To receive funding, the victim must report the crime promptly (usually within 30 days), cooperate with law enforcement and the prosecution, not have contributed to the victimization (say, by starting a brawl), not be in jail or on probation or parole, and exhaust all other insurance or benefits such as health insurance, worker's compensation, and lawsuits.

Crime victims apply for funding in the state where the crime was committed, not in the state where they live.

three kinds of help: psychological first aid, survivor support, and recovery interventions. Most laypeople can provide psychological first aid with minimal training. It includes recognizing that someone has been victimized and ensuring he is removed from danger and placed in a safe environment. When there is physical injury, victims' workers must ensure that victims are first taken to a medical facility and given emergency attention and subsequently put in contact with a victim assistance agency. The challenge for all victim advocates is to know how to perform crisis intervention, to assess victims and to use that assessment to create a treatment plan to determine the victim's short- and long-term mental health needs, to refer the victim to appropriate community service providers, and to carry out the treatment plan to help the victim achieve recovery. Recovery is perhaps the most important goal of victim services. A recovered victim is one who has come to terms with having been victimized and acknowledges what was lost. Going through this process assists him in finding meaning from the experience and finally integrating what has been learned so he can resume a functional life.

Working with someone who has experienced a traumatic event can be difficult because victims have different reactions. Some victims experience shock and numbness, intense emotion, fear, distress, guilt, anger and resentment, depression and loneliness, and isolation. Others have more physical responses: anxiety, panic, headaches, gastrointestinal problems, sleeplessness, and loss of appetite.[32] Despite their different reactions, however, most victims go through a three-phase process of impact, recoil, and recovery.

The *impact stage* occurs in the immediate aftermath of a crime and is marked by shock, horror, and numbness. Some victims may be at further risk because they are vulnerable and unable to protect themselves, though others may think and act in a rational manner. Only about 10 percent of victims experience panic.[33] At the impact stage, the victim is primarily concerned with basic needs such as rescue, safety, warmth, and food. As soon as victim advocates and those working with victims identify appropriate interventions, referrals should be made for mental health services to assist the victim with long-term recovery. In this phase, therapy ideally should be offered to victims during the victim's first meeting with a victim advocate or other allied professionals, such as law enforcement and medical and mental health practitioners.

In the *recoil stage*, victims show more varied responses to the crime, including self-blame, fear, anxiety, helplessness, and impaired memory and decision making. These feelings can be all-consuming and can impair the victim's work, school, and social life. Insomnia, headaches, changes in appetite and libido, and lowered energy are all common physical and psychological responses to varying levels of preoccupation.[34]

Helping a victim recover requires specialists with more extensive training and experience, who can assess victims' needs and give appropriate support. Specific tasks at this stage include providing basic information about victims' situations, offering advocacy services, accompanying victims to various agencies to ensure that they receive needed services, and helping them, if they wish, to cooperate with the criminal justice system.

As advocates and allied professionals continue to work with victims through this phase, therapy should again be offered to help the victim recover. Victim therapy can be short or long term. **Short-term therapy** is usually administered by clinical psychologists, clinical social workers, and marriage and family counselors. It focuses on individual therapy, relationship therapy, peer support, and group therapy, and it assists victims who have minor phobias or fears, eating and sleeping disorders, and stress management and health issues. **Long-term therapy** usually focuses on the victim's responses to trauma, symptoms of PTSD, anxiety disorders, depression, terminal conditions, and dysfunctional behaviors that render victims vulnerable. In some cases it deals with major phobias or fears and other trauma-related symptoms. It also may include institutional care, where psychiatrists must administer psychotherapy, and it may include medication and close observation in a hospital setting. In any setting, the therapist's objective is to alleviate suffering and reduce trauma symptoms so the person can resume a functional life. Prosecutors are also interested in facilitating victim recovery because those who suffer trauma can become psychologically impaired and cannot cooperate in the prosecution of offenders.

short-term therapy
Usually administered by clinical psychologists, clinical social workers, and marriage and family counselors to address immediate mental health concerns.

long-term therapy
Focuses on the victim's responses to trauma, symptoms of PTSD, anxiety disorders, depression, terminal conditions, and dysfunctional behaviors that render victims vulnerable.

The *recovery stage* is an extended period of struggle in which the victim alternates between the effects of impact and recoil, but with less severe responses. Many also experience PTSD, which includes recurring memories of the traumatic event. Regardless, however, of what may seem like setbacks, triggered perhaps by a reminder or anniversary, the victim is usually moving forward, resuming normal activities, and coping with the crime's aftermath. The crime is a part of her life, but not—as in previous stages—the whole of it.[35] The stages of recovery are illustrated in the Key Concepts table below.

Victim advocates have many different responsibilities as they provide assistance to victims throughout the stages of recovery. The work of victim advocates in helping victims is highlighted in A Case in Point on the next page.

Vicarious Trauma

vicarious trauma
Psychological distress experienced by persons who know about a traumatic event experienced by another person and who feel the victim's pain.

The psychological distress experienced by persons who know about a traumatic event directly experienced by another person and who feel that person's pain is called **vicarious trauma**. Many individuals who come into direct contact with victims can experience

KEY CONCEPTS
Stages of Recovery and Mental Health Care Options

Stages of Recovery	Mental Health Options
The *impact stage* occurs in the immediate aftermath of a crime and is marked by shock, horror, and numbness.	*Short-term therapy* is usually administered by clinical psychologists, clinical social workers, and marriage and family counselors. It focuses on individual therapy, relationship therapy, peer support, and group therapy, and it assists victims who have minor phobias or fears, eating and sleeping disorders, and stress management and health issues.
In the *recoil stage*, victims show more varied responses to the crime, including self-blame, fear, anxiety, helplessness, and impaired memory and decision making.	*Long-term therapy* usually focuses on the victim's responses to trauma, symptoms of PTSD, anxiety disorders, depression, terminal conditions, and dysfunctional behaviors that render victims vulnerable.
The *recovery stage* is an extended period of struggle in which the victim alternates between the effects of impact and recoil, but with less severe responses.	To help achieve recovery, mental health professionals focus on reducing the symptoms of PTSD, helping victims understand themselves through self-examination, and restoring control over their lives to them.

a Case in Point

The Massacre at Virginia Tech

Seung-Hui Cho was a senior English major at Virginia Tech University in Blacksburg, Virginia. He had a history of stalking and harassing female students on campus and of writing stories about violent incidents in such graphic detail that he was removed from a creative writing class. A professor suggested he receive psychological counseling to address his violent tendencies and his expressed hatred of society in general and of women in particular, but apparently Cho did not follow through with this service.

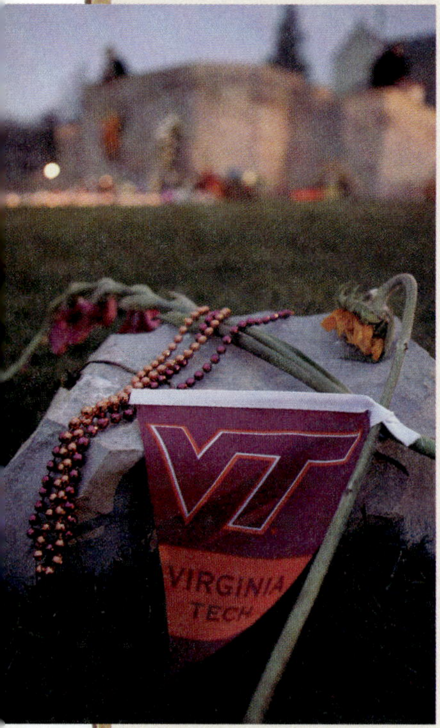

At 7 a.m. on April 16, 2007, Cho entered a campus dormitory. The first gunshots were heard at 7:15 a.m., leaving two students dead in their rooms. Approximately 1 hour later, Cho walked across the campus and entered a classroom building, where he fired 170 rounds of ammunition, apparently at random. Cho killed 32 people and wounded 26 more before committing suicide. It was the deadliest school shooting in U.S. history.

In the immediate aftermath, thousands of Virginia Tech students along with members of the university community met for a campus candlelight vigil to remember the many victims. Local community-based organizations as well as state and federal agencies went to the campus to offer support to university students, faculty, staff, administrators, and family members. The Inn at Virginia Tech served as the main gathering place for family members and organizations to disseminate information as it became available. Many family members arrived on campus not knowing the location or status of their loved ones, which added to the fear and uncertainty of the tragedy.

Given the students' experience of crisis, university officials allowed them to end their semester immediately and still receive a grade for completed course work. Two days after the shootings, a team of state victim service providers came to campus to provide assistance for family members. The services included informing victims and survivors of their rights; helping with funeral arrangements; talking with medical examiners on behalf of the families; and arranging child care, transportation, and referrals for support services in the community. Once family members left Virginia Tech, they did not have access to the same type and level of services, which proved problematic for some in addressing their immediate and long-term needs.

After the tragedy, the university created the Virginia Tech Office of Recovery and Support to help those affected by this tragedy in Blacksburg. This university-based office provided a central point of contact for students and families most directly affected by the tragedy. The office was responsible for streamlining communication with victims and their families, the university, and the larger community. Virginia Tech also established the Hokie Spirit Memorial Fund to cover the costs of counseling, memorials, and goods and services used by victims and survivors. In the days, weeks, and months that followed, with the help of victim advocates who brought comfort, assistance, and support, the students banded together to communicate a sense of unity and forgiveness.

Observe Investigate Understand

- **Have you ever known the victim of a violent crime? What do you wish you had known about how to help the person recover?**
- **Are you aware of any new policies or victim services offices that your school may have established in the wake of the Virginia Tech tragedy?**
- **If a major tragedy such as the Virginia Tech killings should ever occur at your school or in some other setting in which you might find yourself, would you be prepared to help assist victims? What might you do in advance to prepare yourself mentally for such a traumatic event?**

SOURCES: Larry Hincker, "University Announces Plans for Intermediate and Permanent Memorial to Honor Victims of April 16 Tragedy," *VT News*, June 7, 2008, www.vtnews.vt.edu/story.php?relyear=2007&itemno=333 (retrieved May 19, 2008); Elizabeth Schwinn, "Virginia Tech Creates Memorial Fund after Monday's Rampage," *The Chronicle of Philanthropy*. April 18, 2007, http://philanthropy.com/free/update/2007/04/2007041801.htm (retrieved May 19, 2008); "Immediate Aftermath and the Long Road to Recovery," *Report of the Virginia Tech Review Panel Mass Shootings at Virginia Tech* (August 2007), 135–147, www.governor.virginia.gov/TempContent/techPanelReport.cfm (retrieved May 19, 2008); "Tech Shooting Victims: Moving Forward," *Roanoke Times*, May 5, 2007, www.roanoke.com/vtvictims/wb/115937, (retrieved May 8, 2007); "Worst U.S. Shooting Ever Kills 33 on Va. Campus: 15 Others Wounded as Panic Grips Virginia Tech for 2 1/2 Hours," *MSNBC.com*, April 16, 2007, www.msnbc.msn.com/id/18134671/ (retrieved May 2, 2007).

vicarious trauma, including law enforcement officers, medical care providers, victim service providers, those providing mental health services, and even such secondary victims as family members or friends. Vicarious trauma may manifest itself as stress, burnout, fatigue, loss of empathy, or taking on the victim's suffering as one's own. Sometimes the practitioner may feel as if she has experienced the victim's reenactment of the crime. Others experience nightmares, avoidance and emotional numbing, hypersensitivity, and substance abuse.[36]

These experiences can be particularly problematic if the practitioner has intimate knowledge about the details of the crime or has experienced trauma in his own life. In either situation, the practitioner experiences difficulty learning more about the crime and working with the victim. This result is problematic on two levels—the victim is not receiving the best, most objective services, and the service provider is suffering along with the victim, with few outlets for personal thoughts, feelings, fears, and anxieties. This phenomenon is also called **compassion fatigue**.[37]

compassion fatigue
Occurs when a practitioner working with a victim experiences difficulty learning more about the crime and working with the victim.

It's not clear why some people are likely to experience vicarious trauma and others are not, or what affects the extent, severity, or duration of vicarious trauma. Organizations can assist practitioners who experience vicarious trauma by providing a quiet room for employees who work directly with victims to relax, by extending the number of personal days off, by allowing for shorter work days and workweeks, and by providing counseling. In combination, such practices can provide short- and long-term support.[38]

Source Connection

VICARIOUS TRAUMA

http://brief-treatment.oxfordjournals.org/cgi/content/full/6/1/1

You can learn more about vicarious trauma in this article.

TYPES OF VICTIM SERVICE ASSISTANCE

Being a crime victim is frightening and confusing. Victims may call the police, seek medical care, or even flee their homes with no clothes, no money, and crying children in tow. Many do not know where to go, what to do, or how to get help. Until the 1970s, there were few options other than law enforcement and medical personnel to help victims cope with the trauma and recover from the crime. Today, however, thousands of programs, services, and resources can help victims repair their lives and property, obtain rights while seeking justice, and try to heal.

Crisis Intervention

After a traumatic event, **crisis intervention** provides immediate assistance. Such intervention can assume a number of forms, including responding to a crime scene, transporting a person to a shelter, providing medical assistance, helping a victim locate a missing loved one, or simply providing a shoulder to cry on. During crisis intervention, victim services personnel must ask what victims want and need. Instead of making assumptions about what is in the victim's best interest, workers should provide options so victims can begin to make their own choices about the future.[39]

crisis intervention
Immediate assistance after a traumatic event.

Effective crisis intervention depends on accurately assessing the situation, working with the victim to determine immediate needs, and focusing treatment on those needs.[40] Referrals to other organizations address longer-term needs. From the victim service providers' perspective, work with victims is usually highly taxing. A provider often must be on call all hours, day and night. Often they must hear and see the results of extreme victimizations—stressful experiences that take a toll on the providers and require them to receive counseling. Good victim advocacy requires extensive training, personal maturity, experience with victims, and constant supervision. In some cases, supervisors must provide their employees with breaks away from field work and even insist on vacations and periodic counseling to avert burnout or compassion fatigue. A well-run victim service agency requires a balanced number of advocates to cover the existing workload, so victims receive referrals and adequate treatment in a timely manner that leads to the victim's recovery.

Hotlines

Most local and national victim services agencies provide a telephone crisis hotline 24 hours a day, 7 days a week, through which a victim and any secondary victims can discuss any type of victimization, get information and resources such as shelter or child care, and learn how to get a protective order. Hotlines are staffed by volunteers and professionals trained in crisis intervention techniques and victim services. They provide immediate short-term counseling to help victims through the crisis, but not ongoing, long-term counseling, therapy, or treatment. Instead, the hotline worker will provide information and referrals for these types of services.[41]

Shelters and Transitional Housing

MYTH/REALITY

MYTH: Victims of intimate partner violence are partially at fault for the situation in which they find themselves because they will not leave their abusers.

REALITY: Abusers often economically and psychologically distance their victims from the rest of society. Leaving the batterer is often financially difficult, especially if the victim has children.[42]

Real Careers

TINA FIGUEROA

Work location: Madera, California

College(s): California State University, Fresno, 2007

Major(s): Criminology (BS)

Job title: Victim Services Manager

Salary range for job like this: $40,000–$53,000

Time in job: 2 years

Work Responsibilities

I supervise daily operations of the rape crisis center, the victim/witness center, and the intimate partner violence program. I ensure that staff comply with policy standards, develop protocols for crisis response, and train staff on procedures for working with victims of crime. In practical terms, I monitor services at the battered women's shelter by selecting files at random and verifying that progress is being properly documented. I train our staff members by developing instructional materials and organizing training sessions. Our facility receives funding from state and federal grants to provide these services. I have been delegated the task of maintaining compliance with fund sources and researching new fund opportunities.

Why Criminal Justice?

I majored in criminology because the field is very broad and there are many professions from which to choose. Wanting to work with abused or at-risk youth, I researched potential career paths and came up with many possibilities, such as a correctional officer at juvenile hall, juvenile probation officer, and victim services advocate. To prepare myself for such a career, I earned a Victim Services Certificate from CSUF during the summer. For this certificate, I had to take courses in family violence, victim rights, intimate partner violence, and child abuse.

Expectations and Realities of the Job

I did not expect grant funding to be so readily available to crisis facilities. That is not to say the money is simply given out. First, a center needs to apply for a grant. Once a grant is awarded, the center must comply with the guidelines outlined by the fund source and update that source with regular progress reports. One way our center has benefited from grant money is with the installation of a modern child-friendly interview room for children who have been sexually assaulted. It is designed with creative art and playful colors, but at the same time hidden cameras and microphones aid investigators in their work.

My Advice to Students

Begin to develop your resume and start searching for jobs while you are still in college. The application process can take up to 1 year because employers typically administer some or all of the following: background check, physical assessments, interviews, and entry exams. Most agencies require personal references, so it is important to begin that process while you are still on campus and can readily meet with your professors. Depending on the job for which you are applying, you may need to acquire other certifications. For example, to work at a battered women's shelter, victim/witness agency, or rape crises center in California, you need to complete 60 hours of training. Again, the sooner you begin your employment search, the sooner you can identify the credentials you will need to obtain before applying for the job.

A major premise of victim services is that most victims are not to blame for the crime they experience. Thus victims of intimate partner violence are not responsible for the abuse they experience at home—the batterer is. Many times batterers will isolate the victim from her family and friends, use physical and sexual force to intimidate her, psychologically taunt her, and control the couple's finances. These factors leave the victim afraid for her safety yet with few resources to escape.

Some victims will flee to seek safety; some may be thrown out of their homes by their battering partner. When victims leave, typically going first to family and friends, batterers often follow, asking forgiveness, begging for a second chance, and promising never to be violent again. Many victims are encouraged to return by those who want to keep the family together, including children who want to be with their father. This pressure, coupled with the lack of financial resources to venture out on their own, means that many victims return to their batterer. The average victim will leave and return several times before finally terminating the relationship.

Shelters are a temporary housing option for battered women and their children. They offer a safe place to escape a violent relationship; provide an opportunity to determine options for legal, medical, social, housing, education, employment, and child care; and make it possible to rebuild a life free of violence.

The maximum time a person may stay in a shelter is set by state law and can range from 30 to 90 days. Most shelters offer 60 days.[43] If a victim contacts the police, they will often drive her and her children directly to the shelter. If she calls a hotline, the person answering the phone will usually contact the police for her. In most states, the shelter location is kept private to better ensure the safety of the residents; in California, it is a misdemeanor to disclose the shelter's location. Shelters usually are large, older homes in residential neighborhoods, unmarked but renovated to meet the residents' safety needs, including perimeter cameras and secure entries. Typically, shelters house approximately 25 women and children.[44]

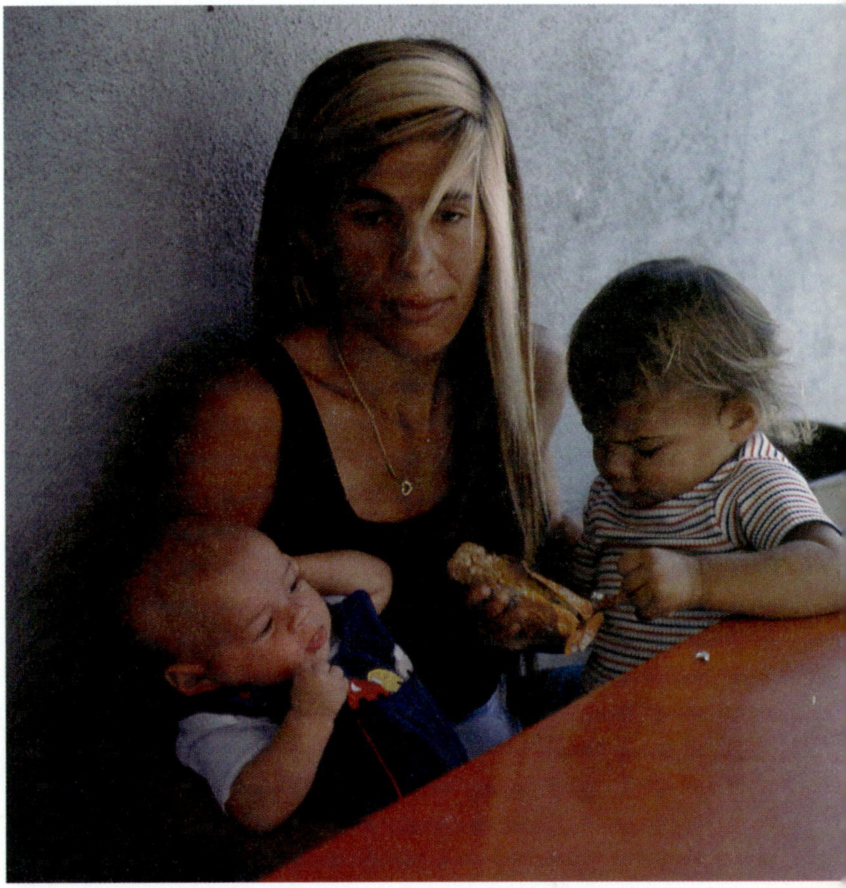

▲ Women and Children in an Intimate Partner Violence Shelter

All major U.S. cities have special protective places where women who are victims of abuse and violence by their partners can go for a brief time to escape the danger and stay in safety, often with their children.

MYTH/REALITY

MYTH: If there is space in an intimate partner violence shelter, victims are not turned away.

REALITY: Individuals can be denied entry if they are alcoholics or drug abusers. Some shelters cannot accommodate victims with a disability, and most deny housing to male children over 13.[45]

At the shelter, an advocate will determine the victim's needs and those of her children (if she has them) through an intake process. The intake is a questionnaire that is completed by a shelter employee with a victim as the prospective shelter resident. The intake is a means of screening clients to determine whether she and her children are eligible to enter the shelter. The intake will inquire about the extent of the violence and continued threat to the victim and her children, mental health status, suicidal tendencies, financial and social support resources, employment and school matters, and alcohol or drug use. If the shelter staff believes that the victim or her children will be a threat to themselves or other residents, they will not be permitted residence and will be given alternative housing options. Many shelters will not admit someone with a serious mental illness or who is under the influence of alcohol or drugs. Those who pose a threat to themselves or other residents will not be allowed to enter. Despite Americans with Disabilities Act (ADA) requirements that all public buildings be wheelchair-accessible, have elevators, and otherwise accommodate victims with a disability, some shelters are not in compliance and cannot accept such victims. Women who are in same-sex relationships may use shelter services, but male victims do not have access to intimate partner shelter services.[46] If male victims need shelter, they have to go to a homeless shelter—not an ideal setting because there is usually no intake screening process that precludes the batterer from entering the facility and further harming the victim. As such, a homeless shelter is not as safe as a shelter for battered women, with its perimeter cameras or fencing, secure access points, or extra patrol and security features.

People often wrongly believe that only the woman in a violent relationship is abused. In reality, a man abusing his partner is also likely abusing any children in the home. Returning children to a violent home is never advisable because the abuser is likely to hurt or sexually assault them to get back at the victim.[47]

Source Connection

EFFECT OF INTIMATE PARTNER VIOLENCE ON CHILDREN

www.nccev.org/pdfs/series_paper6.pdf

To learn more about the impact of intimate partner violence on children, read "Young Children's Exposure to Adult Domestic Violence: Toward a Developmental Risk and Resilience Framework for Research and Intervention" (2004).

Even if the child is not physically or sexually abused, growing up in a violent home has a long-term detrimental impact. Between 3 million and 10 million children in the United States are exposed to intimate partner violence each year.[48] Since the early 1990s, research has focused greater attention on the psychological effects on children of witnessing violence. Recent studies indicate that children suffer chronic symptoms of traumatic stress, anxiety, depression, and suicidal behaviors.[49] They are also at risk for substance abuse, medical and health issues, parental mental health issues and unemployment, poverty, and malnutrition.[50] Children who witness severe or chronic violence are more likely to have psychological problems at younger ages if the violence is frequent, and if it happens in close proximity—within the home versus in the community—and to a loved one versus to a stranger.[51] Some studies indicate that children who witness their mothers being abused may be as traumatized as if they were the direct victims of abuse.[52] As a result, it is important for children to be removed from a violent environment and not be returned to it.[53]

A limited number of studies have evaluated shelter programs. They suggest such services may be more helpful to battered women than traditional counseling services alone.[54] Those who stay in a shelter experience fewer and less intense incidents of new violence. After even a short stay of 14 days, women tend to experience less depression and feel a greater sense of hope.[55] In a 2005 statewide evaluation of shelter programs in Illinois, researchers found intimate partner violence victims feel safe while in a shelter and gain important information about violence. Increased support and the counseling programs offered contribute to their improved ability to make decisions and their greater self-esteem and coping skills.[56]

Sexual Assault Resource Centers

Direct victim support, including hospital and court accompaniments; individual counseling; hotline services; community education; and advocacy for political, social, and institutional change are offered at rape crisis centers.[57]

MYTH/REALITY

MYTH: Only young, pretty women are sexually assaulted.

REALITY: Any person can be the victim of a sexual assault.[58]

Sexual assault resource centers help educate the community to understand that no one "asks for" or wants to be sexually assaulted, that anyone can be a target, that rape is a violent act of power and dominance (not of sex), and that victims are far more likely to be raped by someone they know than by a stranger. These centers also focus prevention programs on school-age children, who are most at risk for sexual assault.

Traditionally, no services were available for secondary rape victims. Rape crisis centers and other victim service programs realized the impact of vicarious trauma and broadened their work to include services for loved ones. They now also place greater emphasis on outreach to underserved populations such as minority and immigrant groups for whom English is a second language. Recent government budget cuts have required some rape crisis centers to merge with other victim service providers such as intimate partner violence programs and to work with more diverse victim populations.

Sexual Assault Nurse Examiners

The first **sexual assault nurse examiner** (SANE) program was created in Minnesota in 1977. By the mid-1990s, many hospitals in the United States and around the world had sexual assault nurse examiners on staff. These nurses provide 24-hour, first-response medical care and crisis intervention for rape victims in hospitals and clinics.

sexual assault nurse examiner (SANE)
Nurse who provides 24-hour first-response medical care and crisis intervention for rape victims in hospital and clinics.

In a case of sexual assault, the victim's body is considered a crime scene. It is thus essential that she go to the hospital as quickly as possible and not eat, drink, shower, or urinate until after she has been seen by the SANE nurse, who will conduct a forensic exam known as a "rape kit" (with or without the presence of a victim advocate, depending on the victim's wishes). The nurse has received extensive training in evidence collection, use of specialized equipment such as a colposcope (a lighted magnifying instrument used during gynecological exams), chain-of-evidence requirements, expert testimony, injury detection and treatment, pregnancy and emergency contraception, STD/AIDS testing, rape trauma syndrome, and local victim services. By the mid-2000s, special pediatric examiners were also being trained to work with the youngest victims of sexual assault, those under two years old.[59]

Community Education and Outreach

One of a victim service provider's critical roles is to offer community education and outreach to victims who may not know about services. Education can be community-based through groups such as AARP (formerly known as the American Association of Retired Persons), Boy Scouts and Girl Scouts, and Rotary Club, or school-based through elementary, junior high, high school, and colleges and universities. Education enables the victim services organization to raise awareness about various types of victimization, provide an expanded definition of victimization, target specific populations most likely to be victimized, discuss specific services, and dispel misconceptions about crime and victims.

Lack of knowledge about available services can stem from a language barrier, immigrant status, or a culture that limits a victim's ability to seek protection against abusers. Other barriers include race, geography, disability, and sexual orientation. In the case of sexual orientation, the victim may perceive victim service providers as homophobic and unwilling to provide services. As such, some same-sex victims have individual barriers that prevent them from seeking services even though they may know of their availability. Victim service providers must use creative means of reaching these diverse populations and the public, including word-of-mouth from those who used the services in the past; advertisements in local and non-English newspapers, buses, train stations, and public restrooms; and billboards on streets and highways. Public service announcements on the radio, television, and Internet, including language-specific media, are critical tools for reaching those who may be illiterate or non-English speaking, or who have limited reading skills.[60]

▼ Victims' Rights Advocate Bret Vinocur

Bret Vinocur, holding a photo of Bruce Lower—a man who spent 16 years in prison for killing a 3-year-old girl—speaks to the Ohio Senate Criminal Justice Committee at the Ohio Statehouse in Columbus, Ohio.

VICTIM ASSISTANCE FOR OLDER ADULTS

Older adults, usually defined as those over 65 years old, have unique needs as victims compared to those in other age groups. Although older adults may seek services from victim service providers, some programs specifically serve older adult victims.

Adult Protective Services

Adult Protective Services
Safeguards older people and dependent adults with disabilities who are in danger of being mistreated or neglected, are unable to protect themselves, or have no one to assist them.

Elder abuse is a relatively new area of criminal justice intervention, but it is not a new phenomenon. Once viewed as a private matter, it was first formally addressed in the United States in the mid-1970s, with the creation of Adult Protective Services funding under Title XX of the Social Security Act. **Adult Protective Services** are provided to older people and to dependent adults with disabilities who are in danger of being mistreated or neglected, cannot protect themselves, or have no one to assist them. The mandatory reporting provision of Adult Protective Services in all states was motivated by the government's concern about an increase in reports of abuse and neglect among older and dependent adults.[61] In 2004, the National Committee for the Prevention of Elder Abuse and the National Adult Protective Services Association conducted a follow-up study of vulnerable adults over age 18. The findings indicate that Adult Protective Services had received 565,747 reports of elder abuse, almost 20 percent more than in the original 2000 study. Of reported cases, 81 percent were investigated and almost 42 percent were substantiated, 16 percent more than in 2000. In the victim services field, we are never certain whether an increase in reporting indicates there is more abuse or whether increased education about the issue brings more people to report abuse or to seek services.[62]

TRIADs

TRIAD
A collaborative effort between police departments, sheriff's offices, and senior groups (like AARP) to reduce crime and the victimization of older adults.

Police departments, sheriff's offices, and senior groups like AARP have joined in a collaborative effort called **TRIADs** to reduce crime and the victimization of older adults. The first TRIAD was created in 1987, and a cooperative agreement was signed the following year. Today, district attorneys' offices, fire departments, agencies and departments on aging, emergency social and medical services, and other organizations that work directly with older adults are members of TRIAD. At the local level, TRIAD works through a cooperative partnership to reduce and prevent crime, decrease fear of victimization, and improve services. It also informs older adults about such crimes as identity theft, teaches them ways to reduce their vulnerability, and increases their awareness of community resources.[63]

COLLABORATIVE RESPONSES TO VICTIMS

Although a wide range of 1960s social activism set the stage, the emergence of efforts in support of crime victims owes most to the women's movement, which put considerable pressure on the criminal justice system to do more to protect victims, ensure their rights, and help them seek justice. Responding to this pressure, the criminal justice system has created programs to address specific types of crimes, streamlined the investigation and prosecution of cases, experimented with alternative sanctions to deter criminal behavior, and worked to ensure victims' rights.

To accomplish its mission, the criminal justice system needs crime victims, and victims, in return for their cooperation, want to be treated fairly (see Disconnects box). They do not want to have to endure further victimizations at the hands of the criminal justice system itself. To help recover from their injuries and trauma and to rebuild their relationship with the community, victims need the assistance of many different professionals from different disciplines. Rarely does a single approach or a simple answer address all of a victim's problems. The need to provide victims with comprehensive services has inspired many organizations to form partnerships.

Intimate Partner Violence Councils

By the late 1980s, intimate partner violence service providers realized that there was a problem in the lack of coordination of health, social, and other services across the criminal justice system. Battered women who did not receive all the services they needed might fall through the social safety net or, even worse, return to their abusive partners. Thus intimate partner violence service partnerships were created.[64] In different places these have various

DIS Connects

Don't Bite the Hand That Feeds You

We're all familiar with the adage, "Don't bite the hand that feeds you." Yet the criminal justice system often does exactly that. For the criminal justice process to start, a victim must report the crime to the police, cooperate with investigators, and be willing to testify in open court. Although these processes are necessary, for many people they may be difficult. The justice system expects victims to cooperate, sometimes risking their safety and sometimes enduring secondary victimization at the hands of police, prosecutors, judges, and medical personnel. In return, victims' expectations are reasonable: to be believed, to be treated with respect, to be protected from the offender, to be kept informed of the status of their case, to be heard prior to the key decisions in the justice process, and ultimately to be helped toward their own recovery.

The law largely mandates how victims are treated by the criminal justice system and other government agencies after their victimization. Sometimes, however, police officers do not accept reports of victimization because they do not believe what victims tell them. Victims may then lose faith in law enforcement and feel betrayed. A national survey reported that from 1992 to 2000, 6 percent of victims said they did not report their victimization because they felt the police would not view it as important. During the investigation of a crime, police may ignore the victim's condition in their zeal to gather evidence, secure as much information as possible, and finish completing their reports. During the trial, victims must explain details of their victimization (sometimes including intimate details of sexual violations) in front of friends and relatives, the offender, and strangers. Not only are they intimidated, but they often suffer from having to retell the painful experiences they endured. This is especially true when children testify. Defense attorneys frequently challenge victims' and witnesses' testimony and may treat them as if they were dishonest. Prosecutors may mistreat them in an attempt to secure better testimony, perhaps grilling them beyond their endurance. Judges may scold victims for not being cautious enough to avoid victimization. Unfortunately, because victims usually know their offender, people often assume that if the assailant is "bad" there must be something wrong with the victim too. Blaming the victim can worsen and prolong a victim's suffering.

"Victims should be treated with compassion and respect for their dignity," announces the United Nations Declaration of Basic Principles of Justice for Victims of Crime and Abuse of Power. "They are entitled to access the mechanisms of justice and to prompt redress, as provided for by national legislation, for the harm that they have suffered." For the criminal justice system to achieve a high level of efficiency in its fight against crime, it is critical that victims cooperate. To ensure their cooperation and their recovery, victims must be treated with fairness, must be protected, and must be compensated for their expenses, time, and efforts. Without fair recompense for their expenses, victims are being revictimized by the criminal justice system, and they are not recovering from their suffering. In the final analysis, those who are innocently injured, robbed, or devastated by the murder of a family member or friend must be made whole again. This will require continuing to restructure the criminal justice system and laws, which (along with the victims' rights movement) began in the mid-1970s.

OBSERVE Investigate Understand

- **What is it about the U.N. Declaration of Basic Principles of Justice for Victims of Crime and Abuse of Power that makes it important?**
- **Can you list five reasons victims might not want to report their victimization?**
- **What is the negative impact on police operations caused by victims not reporting their victimizations?**

SOURCES: National Organization of Black Law Enforcement Executives, *Minority Community Victim Assistance: A Handbook*, 2007, www.ojp.usdoj.gov/ovc/publications/infores/minor/welcome.html (retrieved June 15, 2007); Amanda Konradi, "Pulling Strings Doesn't Work in Court: Moving Beyond Puppetry in the Relationship between Prosecutors and Rape Survivors," *Journal of Social Distress and the Homeless* 10, no. 1 (January 2001): 5–28; Gerald T. Hotaling and Eve S. Buzawa, "Victim Satisfaction with Criminal Justice Case Processing in a Model Court Setting," NCJRS (NCJ 195668); Andrew Karmen, *Crime Victims; An Introduction to Victimology*, 6th ed. (Belmont, CA: Wadsworth, 2007), 140; Timothy C. Hart and Callie Rennison, "Reporting Crime to the Police, 1992–2000," *Bureau of Justice Statistics Special Report* (Washington DC: Office of Justice Programs, March 2003); Beth Schwartz-Kenny, Margaret Wilson, and Gail S. Goodman, "An Examination of Child Witness Accuracy and the Emotional Effects on Children of Testifying in Court," in *Understanding and Managing Child Sexual Abuse*, ed. R. Kim Oates (Philadelphia, PA: W. B. Sanders, 1990), 293–311; United Nations Office for Drug Control and Crime Prevention, *Handbook on Justice for Victims* (New York: Office for Victims of Crime, 1999).

▲ Texas Council on Family Violence "Silent Witness" Campaign

Survivor Angela Catalina De Hoyos speaks at an intimate partner violence rally at the Texas State Capitol to remember the 115 women killed in 2004 by their intimate partners.

names, but most often they are called domestic violence councils, coordinating councils, response teams, or roundtables. Regardless of the name, their goals are the same: to work collaboratively to end intimate partner violence, increase survivor safety, and raise the accountability for batterers.

Despite the early efforts and widespread adoption of intimate partner violence councils, few of these programs have been evaluated. A 2006 evaluation in one mid-Western state with 44 intimate partner violence councils found that councils varied in size from 8 to 116 members and were in existence from 7 months to 16 years, with an average of about 5 years. Members were drawn from intimate partner violence programs (law enforcement, prosecutors and district courts, and legal services), batterer intervention programs, health and mental health care organizations, social service agencies, child protective services, faith-based organizations, educational institutions, and local businesses. Interestingly, however, only 29 percent of the councils included an intimate partner violence survivor.

The study found that leaders of these councils perceived the organization as an important step in creating a coordinated community response to intimate partner violence. On average, they rated their councils as moderately effective at accomplishing their goals.

The study concluded that councils can play a positive role in addressing intimate partner violence, but it recommended that they focus more on criminal justice than on health care or education. Although interagency cooperation contributes to increasing rates of identification and intervention and reducing violence, determining its overall effectiveness will require more research.[65]

Sexual Assault Response Team

sexual assault response team (SART)
Made up of local police officers, victim advocates, SANE practitioners, and prosecutors, who in many states work together to determine the most effective way to work on sexual assault cases.

Local police officers, victim advocates, SANE practitioners, and prosecutors make up the **sexual assault response team** (SART), which in many states works together to determine the most effective way to respond to sexual assault. SARTs investigate recent cases of sexual assault to determine how they were handled, whether mistakes were made, and when something was done well. They also examine the types of sexual assaults that occur, by whom, when and where, and what preventive measures can be taken and what services are needed. The goal is to improve reporting practices, to provide more effective services, and to remove barriers that prevent investigating and prosecuting rape.[66]

Source Connection

SENTINALS FOR INTIMATE PARTNER VIOLENCE

www.nytimes.com/2008/11/20/nyregion/20salons.html

Information on the role that hairdressers may play in identifying and ending intimate partner violence can be found in "Enlisting the Aid of Hairstylists as Sentinels for Domestic Abuse."

Specialized Units

Recognizing differences among victims and their responses to crimes, all levels of the government created units to provide specialized training for practitioners who work with a single type of victim with special needs. These units are primarily located in law enforcement agencies, district attorneys' offices, and government-run victim services agencies like Child Protective Services and Adult Protective Services.

Specialized units give practitioners knowledge, skills, and experience in working with assigned victims. Although every victim is different, there are similarities between victims of a particular crime, such as intimate partner violence, sexual crimes, child abuse, elder abuse, property crime, and homicide. In addition to providing direct victim services, specialized units develop interview strategies and training curricula for others who may work with these victims but are not housed in a specialized unit.[67]

One example of a specialized unit is a multidisciplinary interview center (MDIC), also known as a child advocacy center. Here, child victims of physical and sexual assault are interviewed by a trained specialist in a child-friendly environment. The MDIC staff coordinates the interviews of law enforcement, prosecutors, defense attorneys, and others who may have to talk with the child about the victimization. Before meeting the child, the interviewer collects questions from all participants in the process. Thus the victim has to retell her story about the crime only once to the trained specialist, without having to repeat it multiple times, in different locations, and to different people.[68]

Restorative Justice

A victim-centered process, restorative justice recognizes that the individual, not the state, is the true victim. It seeks to empower the victim to resolve the conflict, move beyond her vulnerabilities, and achieve closure. It also focuses on trying to have the offender make amends rather than on increasing the punishment.[69]

Restorative justice is a primary form of seeking redress in many parts of the world (see A Global View on the following page). In the late 1970s, the United States began to adopt restorative justice to rehabilitate juvenile offenders who committed property crimes, showing them the impact of their actions on victims. By the mid-2000s, restorative justice programs were being used for all types of offenses, including personal crimes, homicides, family violence, and even sexual assault.[70] Participants may be victim advocates, victim services providers, and persons trained to understand the dynamics of abusive relationships. As practiced in the United States, the restorative justice process takes place outside the formal criminal justice system. Recall that in the United States it is "the people," not the individual victim, who actually prosecutes accused offenders and, if they are found guilty, punishes them.

Restorative justice programs are controversial when they are attempted in cases of family violence and sexual assault due to the violent nature of these crimes, the relationship between victim and offender, and the power imbalances inherent in these situations. Critics point to the victim's safety; the potential for the offender to pressure, coerce, or manipulate the victim into accepting certain outcomes; and the possibility that the remedy will be too lenient and send the wrong message to the offender.[71] The emphasis on forgiveness can even serve to continue family violence: batterers often ask forgiveness, only to batter again.[72]

Proponents of restorative justice respond that the ideals of these programs neither minimize the victimization itself nor call for reconciliation.[73] They highlight as well the merits of justice alternatives and the availability of more options for women, offenders, and the community than the criminal justice system can provide. Critics, on the other hand, oppose diverting an offender from the criminal justice system because it gives the appearance of being lenient on crime.[74]

Clearly, restorative justice can benefit some victims, but there are limits to what it can achieve.

SUMMARY

A journey that began in 1947–48 with the pioneering work of Beniamin Mendelsohn and Frederick Wertham, which coincided with the United Nation's 1948 Universal Declaration of Human Rights, has grown into a worldwide movement on behalf of crime victims. In the mid-1960s the United States launched the National Crime Victimization Surveys, which for the first time measured the full scope of victimization and

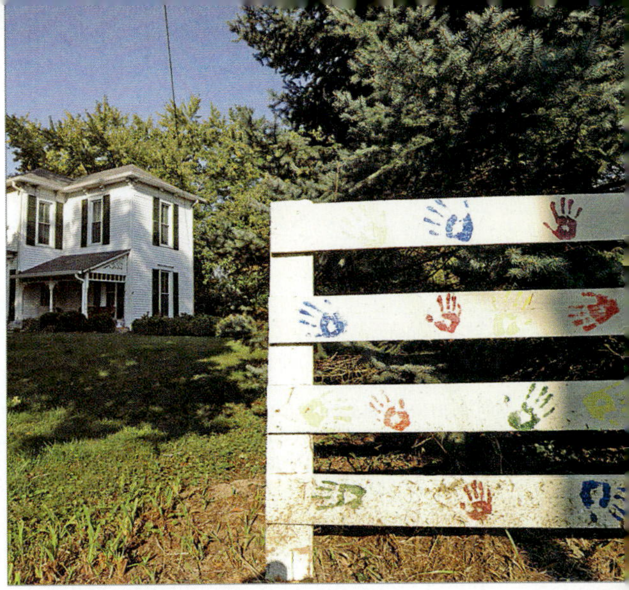

RealCrime Tech

USING iRECORD TO RECORD CHILD INTERVIEWS AT MDICs

iRecord is a digital recording and management system designed for interview and interrogation rooms, including recording interviews with children at multidisciplinary interview centers (MDICs). The iRecord was designed by law enforcement professionals to increase the efficiency, availability, and management of interviews. The iRecord allows interviewers to make and instantaneously store a recording on a DVD. This new technology is used at a handful of MDICs throughout the United States, including the Delaware County Child Advocacy Center, which adopted the iRecord in January 2007. The Delaware Center uses the iRecord in conjunction with a hidden camera in the interview room. The camera then projects the interview into a second room, where other interested parties (such as law enforcement officers and attorneys) can view the interview in real time. The child interviewer is provided with an earpiece so that those in the viewing room can feed additional questions to him. This system enables all parties to participate in a thorough and less intrusive investigation of a child at a single time in a child-friendly environment. The iRecord then saves the interview on a DVD, which may be viewed later or used as evidence in court. This type of technology helps to minimize the trauma of the interview process for child victims.

SOURCE: "iRecord Gives the Delaware County Child Advocacy Center Efficient Interview Process," www.irecord.tv/irecord-delawarecasestudy.pdf (retrieved February 12, 2009).

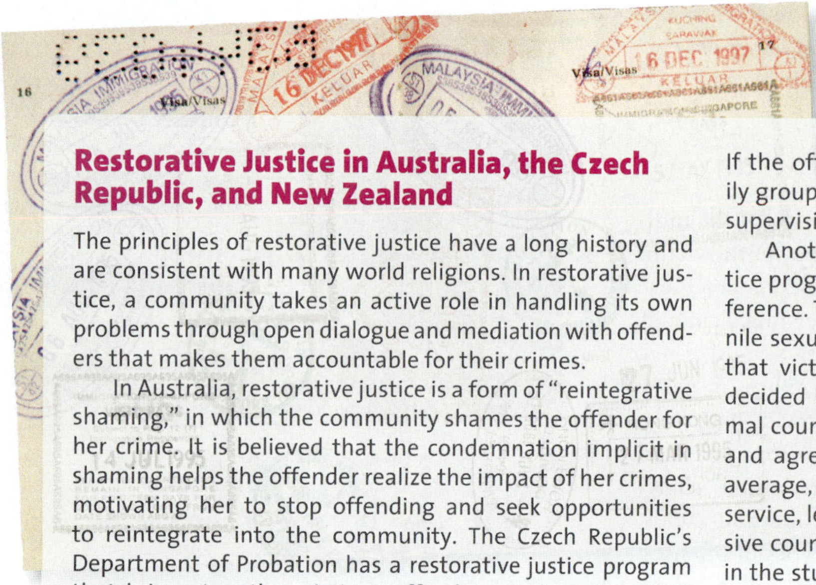

A Global View

Restorative Justice in Australia, the Czech Republic, and New Zealand

The principles of restorative justice have a long history and are consistent with many world religions. In restorative justice, a community takes an active role in handling its own problems through open dialogue and mediation with offenders that makes them accountable for their crimes.

In Australia, restorative justice is a form of "reintegrative shaming," in which the community shames the offender for her crime. It is believed that the condemnation implicit in shaming helps the offender realize the impact of her crimes, motivating her to stop offending and seek opportunities to reintegrate into the community. The Czech Republic's Department of Probation has a restorative justice program that brings together victims, offenders, and mediators to develop presentence reports and determine alternative sanctions for the crime. The mediator works with offenders specifically to improve interpersonal relationships, understand the implications of the crime for society, and address its consequences, as well as determine the type of rehabilitation—substance abuse treatment, anger management, education, or job training—needed to prevent reoffending.

Community and family group conferencing is another restorative justice model, launched in 1989 in New Zealand and also used in Australia, the United States, and South Africa. This program is based on the principles of sanctioning and dispute resolution common among the Maori, New Zealand's indigenous population. Managed by the police and used primarily with juvenile offenders, it outlines the consequences of the crime and encourages youth to reform rather than reoffend. The victim and the offender's family, friends, and community work together to determine appropriate sanctions and outcomes, to explore prevention, and to support the offender in meeting the conference's guidelines. If the offender does not comply, the community and family group reconvenes to determine whether more restrictive supervision or custody is needed.

Another, and more controversial, type of restorative justice program in New Zealand is called the Youth Justice Conference. These conferences are specifically designed for juvenile sexual offenders and their victims. A 2004 study found that victims felt they were better off if their cases were decided by restorative justice rather than through the formal court process because the offender admitted the crime and agreement was usually reached relatively quickly (on average, within 3 months) on a remedy, such as community service, legal orders to stay away from the victim, and intensive counseling. In contrast, only 51 percent of the 227 cases in the study ever went to court, a process that averaged 6.5 months; the rest were either dismissed or withdrawn.

- **Why do you think restorative justice is not more widely practiced in the United States?**
- **Should restorative justice be used as an alternative or addition to the U.S. criminal justice system? Why or why not?**
- **Are there some types of crimes in which restorative justice should not be used?**

SOURCES: Kathleen Daly, "A Tale of Two Studies: Restorative Justice from the Victim's Perspective," in *Restorative Justice: Emerging Issues in Practice and Evaluation*, eds. E. Elliott and R. Gordon (Collompton, UK: Willan, 2004); Yvon Dandurand and Curt T. Griffiths, *Handbook on Restorative Justice Programmes: Criminal Justice Handbook Series* (New York: United Nations Office on Drugs and Crime, 2006); Mark S. Umbreit, *The Handbook of Victim Offender Mediation: An Essential Guide to Research and Practice* (San Francisco, CA: Jossey-Bass, 2001).

paved the way for new insights about victims and their role in the crime problem. This new information helped create victim programs and enact needed laws.

Victim assistance programs began providing services to all types of victims, and in 1976 the National Organization for Victim Assistance was created to help forge a new profession of victim advocates, enabling them to share their knowledge and become a national voice on behalf of victims. In 1984 the U.S. Department of Justice established the Office for Victims of Crime and Congress enacted the Victims of Crime Act, which together serve as major resources for helping victims. In 1985 the United Nations adopted its Declaration of Basic Principles of Justice for Victims of Crime and Abuse of Power, in which all the nations of the world agreed victims should be treated with dignity and respect and should receive a wide range of rights.

All these events helped bring about many important innovations in laws, programs, research, and policies that have significantly improved the status of victims of crime in this country. What began as a lone voice in Europe has become a world movement that has significantly humanized the way victims are treated and that continues to move toward the challenges of tomorrow when all victims will be treated with the fairness, care, and respect they deserve.

OBSERVE
Investigate
Understand

Review

Differentiate between the various victims' responses to trauma.

- Psychic trauma, which results from severe emotional stress, immobilizes the victim's mind and body and can result in long-lasting emotional injury.
- Resilient persons might show no effects and cope well.
- Victims may show mild effects and recover in a few minutes or hours, but some might show extreme effects and need days, weeks, or months to recover.

Identify the major historical milestones that have influenced the formation of victimology and the victims' rights movement.

- Early human cultures placed victims at the center of their legal procedures, giving them a dominant role in righting the wrongs committed against them.
- The Code of Hammurabi called for restoring equity between the offender and the victim.
- In the 1960s and 1970s, social activists in such areas as civil rights, women's rights, children's rights, gay rights, and opposition to the Vietnam War paved the way for the rise of the victim rights movement.
- In 1966, the first victimization surveys were conducted for the President's Commission on Law Enforcement and the Administration of Justice.
- Under the Victims of Crime Act (VOCA) of 1984, funds were distributed throughout the United States for victim compensation and victim assistance program.
- In 1994, Congress enacted the Violence Against Women Act (VAWA) to support the investigation and prosecution of violent crimes against women.

Identify the various types of victims and the roles and responsibilities of victim advocates.

- A primary victim is the person injured or killed as a direct result of a criminal act.
- A secondary victim is someone who, experiencing sympathetic pain, is affected by the primary victim's suffering.
- Secondary victimization is a process whereby the primary victim is abused a second time, usually by members of the criminal justice system, when they use the victim to help arrest, prosecute, sentence, and punish the offender.
- A *Survivor* is a term used to describe a relative or loved one of someone who has been killed; also a crime victim who copes well and manages to resume a normal life.
- Victim advocates are direct providers of victim services.
- Other victim advocates are assigned to a particular justice system—federal, judicial, military, juvenile, or tribal.
- The role of the victim advocate is to help the victim to achieve recovery by providing assistance with such community services as health care, housing, education, and employment, as well as to support the victim in every phase of the criminal justice process.

Describe the various types of crisis intervention programs that exist to work with crime victims.

- Crisis intervention offers immediate assistance to victims.
- Crisis hotlines operate 24 hours a day, 7 days a week, and through them the primary victim and any secondary victims can discuss any type of victimization, get information and access resources such as a shelter or child care, and find out how to get a protective order.
- Shelters are short-term housing options for victims fleeing an abusive home.
- Rape crisis centers provide immediate assistance and accompany victims of a sexual assault to the hospital and to court.
- Sexual assault nurse examiners (SANEs) provide immediate assistance and conduct the rape exam for victims of a sexual assault.

Differentiate between Adult Protective Services and TRIADs.

- Adult Protective Services are provided to older people and dependent adults with disabilities who are in danger of being mistreated or neglected, are unable to protect themselves, or have no one to assist them.
- A TRIAD is a collaborative effort between police departments, sheriff's offices, those who work with senior citizens, and representatives of older adult groups (such as AARP or a local agency on aging, or AAA) to address issues of interest to the senior citizen community.

Describe the various types of collaborative responses to victims.

- Intimate partner violence councils work collaboratively to end intimate partner violence, increase survivor safety, and increase batterer accountability.
- The SART is made up of local police officers, victim advocates, SANE practitioners, and prosecutors, who work together to determine the best and most effective way to work on sexual assault cases.
- Restorative justice aims to empower the victim to resolve the conflict, to move beyond perceived vulnerabilities, and to achieve closure. Restorative justice focuses on having the offender make amends for his actions, rather than on increasing punishments.

Key Terms

Adult Protective Services 418
compassion fatigue 413
crime victim compensation 408
crime victimization 405
crisis intervention 413
long-term therapy 411
primary victim 404
psychic trauma 401
secondary victim 404
secondary victimization 404
sexual assault nurse examiner (SANE) 417
sexual assault response team (SART) 420
short-term therapy 411
survivor 405
TRIAD 418
vicarious trauma 411
victim advocate 405
victim recidivism 405
victim services 405

Study Questions

1. A mother mourning the loss of a child due to criminal behavior is a/an
   a. primary victim.
   b. secondary victim.
   c. secondary victimization.
   d. inconsequential victim.
2. _____________ has been a long-standing societal response in the United States.
   a. Victim ignoring
   b. Victim criticism
   c. Victim rights
   d. Victim concern
3. Which of the following did *not* influence the victim rights movement?
   a. President's Commission on Law Enforcement and the Administration of Justice
   b. Women's movement
   c. World War II movement
   d. Civil rights movement
4. __________ refers to the condition of being free of dysfunctional symptoms caused by victimization, such as difficulty working, sleeping, eating, and forming relationships.
   a. Victim recidivism
   b. Revictimization
   c. Victim services
   d. Victim recovery
5. ________ investigates allegations of abuse against older and dependent adults.
   a. Adult Protective Services
   b. Child Protective Services
   c. TRIAD
   d. Office for Older Victims of Crime
6. ________ provides immediate 24-hour, 7 days a week crisis intervention to all primary and secondary victims, as well as information, resources, and referrals for more long-term assistance.
   a. A sexual assault nurse examiner
   b. A hotline
   c. The Office for Victims of Crime
   d. Mandatory reporting
7. A/an _________ is a nurse who performs forensic exams for victims of sexual assault.
   a. SANE
   b. SART
   c. POMC
   d. OVC
8. Which of the following *cannot* be repaid by victim compensation programs?
   a. Medical expenses
   b. Counseling
   c. Pain and suffering
   d. Funeral expenses
9. Victim compensation programs set maximum limits on the amount a victim can receive. Most state maximums are
   a. $10,000.
   b. $25,000.
   c. $50,000.
   d. $75,000.

10. ________ are victimized at much higher rates than are other populations in the United States.
   a. Native Americans
   b. Blacks
   c. Whites
   d. Latinos

Critical Thinking Questions

1. Explain why it is important to understand the impact of victim blaming in victimology and victim services.
2. Should a person on probation or parole who is a victim of a crime be denied victim compensation?
3. Should restorative justice be used for intimate partner violence and sexual assault related crimes? Why or why not?

Internet Sites

International Victimology
www.victimology.nl/
A quick link to U.N. publications and declarations on victim rights, victimology, and other victimology-based resources.

National Coalition Against Domestic Violence (NCADV)
www.ncadv.org
This organization provides information on services, policies, publications, and resources regarding intimate partner violence.

Office for Victims of Crime (OVC)
www.ojp.usdoj.gov/ovc/
This government office provides information on grants, funding, training, statistics, victim assistance, research, and other resources for victims of crime.

Rape Abuse & Incest National Network (RAINN)
www.rainn.org
This organization provides information on services, policies, publications, and resources regarding sexual assault.

World Society of Victimology
www.worldsocietyofvictimology.org/
The society is open to members and nonmembers with links to many other international victimology organizations; fosters symposia, training courses, and publications on behalf of victim rights, victim assistance, and research.

Suggested Readings

Robert C. Davis, Arthur J. Lurigio, and Susan Herman, eds., *Victims of Crime,* 3rd ed. (Los Angeles, CA: Sage, 2007).
This book provides an overview of the various types of victims and their responses to crimes.

James E. Hendricks and Bryan D. Byers, eds., *Crisis Intervention in Criminal Justice/Social Service,* 3rd ed. (Springfield, IL: Charles C Thomas, 2002).
This book provides an overview of the various types of crisis intervention models that exist in the criminal justice and social service systems.

Albert L. Shostack, *Shelters for Battered Women and Their Children: A Comprehensive Guide to Planning and Operating Safe and Caring Residential Programs* (Springfield, IL: Charles C Thomas, 2001).
This book provides a comprehensive step-by-step approach to the operation and management of a shelter for battered victims and their children.

Thomas L. Underwood and Christine Edmunds, eds., *Victim Assistance: Exploring Individual Practice, Organizational Policy, and Societal Responses* (New York: Springer, 2003).
This book provides a comprehensive approach to understanding the various types of victim assistance that exist to intervene and assist crime victims with recovery.

CHAPTER 15

Juvenile Justice

OBSERVE Investigate Understand

After reading this chapter, you should be able to:

- Describe the early treatment of youthful offenders.
- Analyze current juvenile crime rates and trends.
- Evaluate the philosophy behind the creation of juvenile courts.
- Describe the breadth and limitations of juvenile court jurisdiction.
- Compare and contrast the constitutional rights of youthful offenders and adults.
- Characterize the types of juvenile correctional facilities in the United States.
- Analyze victimization of juveniles and the services to support them.

Realities and Challenges

Death at a Boot Camp

In the summer of 2005, 14-year-old Martin Lee Anderson and his cousins stole their grandmother's car from a church parking lot in Florida. They were arrested, charged, and put on probation. Anderson was later sent to a boot camp for juvenile offenders for violating his probation by trespassing at a school.

When Anderson arrived at the boot camp, he was sent to the training field with a group of boys to undergo a physical assessment test. Supervised by several camp guards, the boys were required to complete a rapid round of sit-ups and push-ups followed by a 16-lap (1.5 mile) run within the training yard. Anderson completed his sit-ups and push-ups, but by the 10th lap of the run something was clearly wrong with him. The boy fell to his knees and was immediately surrounded by camp guards.

Believing that Anderson was being uncooperative, the guards kicked and punched him in an effort to make him continue the workout. Since they thought he was faking, they tried to revive him by forcing him to inhale ammonia fumes five times, causing his vocal cords to spasm, blocking his airway. Anderson soon became unresponsive. He was taken to an emergency medical facility where he never regained consciousness and died 14 hours later. The incident marked the third time within a 3-year period that an African American male had died in one of Florida's boot camps.[1]

A medical examiner attributed Anderson's death to natural causes stemming from sickle cell anemia. However, a boot camp surveillance video came to light showing Anderson being kicked, kneed, and dragged by boot camp guards during the incident, leaving him limp and passive. He was not aggressive nor did he try to escape. Anderson's body was exhumed, and a second autopsy showed he died of suffocation from the ammonia inhalation after being severely beaten.[2]

Had Anderson been an adult, his story would have turned out very differently. It is unlikely he would have received more than a light jail sentence, if that, for his minor offenses. But because he was only 14, Anderson entered the juvenile justice system. The juvenile system was created to help children by addressing important distinctions between children and adults, and, as we will see, it differs from the adult criminal justice system in many respects. However, as this case illustrates, the U.S. juvenile justice system is sometimes flawed in troubling ways.

The roots of the Western criminal justice system go back centuries, but only within the last hundred years or so has it given special attention and treatment to offenders who are not yet adults. Throughout the twentieth century and into the twenty-first century, society has struggled with how to deal with children who commit crimes. Should we focus on rehabilitation or punishment? How can a juvenile justice system process delinquents and reduce delinquency, yet not deny juveniles fairness and justice? What kinds of incarceration and treatment programs should we provide, and how should these differ from those for adults? At what point should we treat a youthful offender as an adult?

This chapter describes youth crime today and interactions between law enforcement and youths. It discusses the evolution of juvenile courts and the Supreme Court cases that have significantly affected the rights of children accused of crimes. We explore the procedures in the juvenile judicial and correction systems and how they differ from those of the adult system, and we examine the growing trend to try juveniles as adults. Finally, we look at the support services for juveniles who are victims, not offenders.

A BRIEF HISTORY OF JUVENILE JUSTICE

Throughout most of recorded history, young offenders were tried by the same courts that tried adults and were subject to the same sanctions, including incarceration and execution. Even the concept of "adolescent" is itself recent.[3] Historically, parents had nearly absolute authority over their small children, whom the law treated as "chattel"—literally, property. Children took on the responsibilities of adulthood at a very young age. For example, they often were expected to work and help support their family at ages 4 or 5, and they usually married in their early teens.

Even so, some people understood that youthful criminals should not always be treated like adults. For example, English common law recognized the **infancy defense**, in which children under age 7 could not be criminally prosecuted because they were too young to form *mens rea*, or criminal intent. A child between the ages of 7 and 14 could be prosecuted, but only if the prosecutor could prove the child knew what he had done was wrong. After reaching age 14, a child was prosecuted like an adult. The American colonies adopted the infancy defense, and many states still recognize it in some form.[4]

Preview

Early Methods of Control

Changes in the European economy during the sixteenth and seventeenth centuries brought people from rural areas to the cities and increased the number living in poverty. Crime rates went up. The traditional method of controlling children—the family—no longer worked well because parents worked long hours away from home, often leaving children alone. Many impoverished parents were unable to provide for their children at all; children were abandoned or orphaned and left to beg, steal, or starve. Those in power, increasingly concerned about the threat they perceived from errant or unmanageable youths, created several methods to deal with them.

One option was **binding out** (sometimes called "placing out"), sending children to live with relatively wealthy families who provided food, shelter, and clothing, the basic necessities of life. In return the children were obligated to work for the families until adulthood, typically doing manual labor such as farming and domestic duties. Another option was to send the children to institutions that served as poorhouses and prisons for young and old alike. The first of these was Bridewell, which opened in London in 1556. Similar institutions were soon built throughout England, some with specific facilities for youths. Inmates were required to work long hours at tasks such as textile manufacturing.[5]

infancy defense
A defense holding that children under age 7 could not be criminally prosecuted because they were too young to form *mens rea*, or criminal intent.

binding out
Sending children to live with relatively wealthy families who provided the child with the basic necessities of life in return for labor.

The colonization of North America brought another solution for problem children in England: they were encouraged or required to immigrate to the colonies where they provided a ready source of labor. The distinction between this practice of indentured servitude and actual slavery was slight. In the colonies, children who committed crimes were controlled by their parents, their communities, and their churches. Parents had few restrictions on their authority over their children. Actions we would consider abusive today, such as beating children with rods, were not only permitted but often encouraged. Several colonies authorized capital punishment for children who disobeyed their parents, although it was seldom, if ever, carried out.[6]

As the Industrial Revolution began at the end of the eighteenth century, conditions for children in the United States were often appalling. Many lived in dire poverty, and those as young as 4 worked in factories and mines, under dangerous conditions and for very little pay. Initially, children who committed crimes and poor children were placed in adult jails and workhouses. In 1825 in New York, an organization called the Society for the Prevention of Pauperism opened the first institution specifically for youths, the House of Refuge. Other cities soon opened their own refuges to house criminal children as

▲ **Child Laborers**

Until well into the twentieth century, even young children often worked long hours at dangerous jobs.

well as orphans and the destitute. The philosophy was to keep the inmates from a life of poverty and crime by imposing strict discipline and order and requiring them to perform hard work such as making furniture or nails if they were boys, or sewing or doing laundry if they were girls. Conditions within the houses of refuge were often deplorable: racism and sexism were common, adults beat the children, and stronger children preyed upon the weak.[7]

The Child Saving Movement

By the middle of the nineteenth century, most child advocates recognized the need for separate correctional institutions for children. Some states, counties, and cities opened their own institutions for wayward youth. These were called **reform schools** or industrial schools, and they housed children who were delinquent (who committed crimes), disobedient, or otherwise wayward.[8] However, no special legal procedures for juveniles were available until the early twentieth century, when juvenile courts were created.

In the late 1800s, a number of middle-class and wealthy women became activists for better living conditions for children. Known as the **child savers**, these women lobbied for child labor regulations, laws against child abuse, and a specialized justice system that would focus on the needs of youths. Largely due to their efforts, the first juvenile court opened its doors in Chicago in 1899. By 1925, all but two states had specialized juvenile courts.[9]

Several factors made it logical to try young people in juvenile rather than adult court and not impose adult sanctions on them. First, adult correctional institutions were dangerous places for children. Not only were the young preyed upon by adult inmates, but they usually learned new criminal behaviors. Second, early intervention can lead to full rehabilitation of children. Third, because children do not yet have the cognitive ability to fully appreciate the consequences of their actions, they should not be held fully responsible for them as adults are. Finally, troubled children often live in troubled families. They have not yet had the opportunity to mature and move away from those influences.

Juvenile courts were intended to be less formal than adult courts. Instead of focusing on punishment, they were to use the treatment model (see Chapter 11) and emphasize solving children's problems and preventing crime. The legal doctrine of ***parens patriae***—literally, the parent of the country—gives the government authority to step in and make decisions about children, even against the wishes of their parents, when doing so is in the children's best interests. The juvenile court judge, who often did not even have a law degree, was given much more discretion than a criminal court judge and would sit down with the child and other interested parties, such as the parents, determine what the problems were, and devise a solution. The intention was that children would have many more placement options than adults, so a treatment plan could be tailored to each child's needs.

Unlike adult criminal cases, juvenile cases were not public, and children were often referred to by their initials rather than their names. Juvenile records were usually kept private and often erased once the child reached adulthood. The creators of juvenile courts even devised a new vocabulary to avoid the stigma of criminal corrections.

reform schools
Industrial schools that housed children who were delinquent, disobedient, or otherwise wayward.

child savers
Women in the 1800s who lobbied for child labor regulations, laws against child abuse, and a specialized justice system that would focus on the needs of youths.

parens patriae
A legal doctrine that gives the government authority to step in and make decisions about children, even against the wishes of their parents, when doing so is in the children's best interests.

MYTH/REALITY

MYTH: The problems faced by the juvenile justice system are recent because juveniles today are much more delinquent than they were 100 years ago.

REALITY: The problems the juvenile justice system faces are not related to changes in juvenile behavior. From its creation, the juvenile justice system encountered problems, such as large caseloads and an overwhelmed and undertrained staff.[10]

The promises of the juvenile court were never realized. Almost as soon as the courts opened, they found themselves with enormous caseloads that made it impossible for judges to give each child individualized attention. Courts were understaffed and poorly funded, and judges often had little or no experience or training in dealing with children. Cases were completed in as little as 10 minutes, and placement options remained few, especially for females. As the juvenile court system enters its second century, these problems remain even as new ones surface. Nevertheless, the juvenile court remains an important part of the justice system.[11]

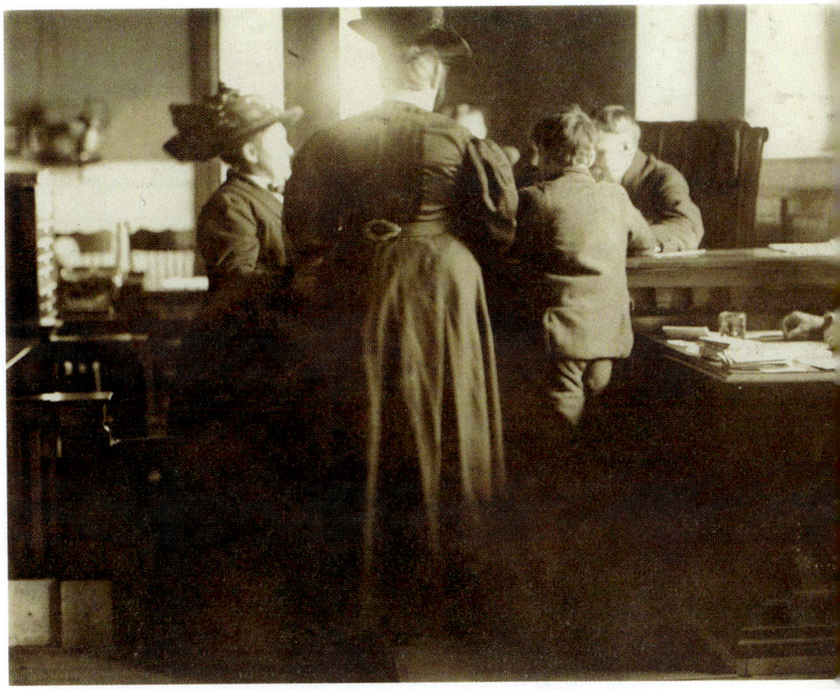

▲ **Early Juvenile Court**

Compared to adult courts, juvenile courts were intended to be less formal.

JUVENILE CRIME TODAY

The term **juvenile delinquency** is used to describe criminal acts that are committed by juveniles (also called minors). Depending on the state, a minor is anyone under either the age of 18 or 21. An additional category of misbehavior by children is the **status offense**, an act that would not be a crime if committed by an adult. Examples of such offenses are running away from home, curfew violations, and school truancy.

juvenile delinquency Criminal acts that are committed by juveniles.

status offense An offense that is illegal only because the defendant is a child, such as playing truant or running away.

Causes of Juvenile Delinquency

Over the years, biologists, sociologists, psychologists, and criminologists have proposed many different theories to explain the causes of juvenile delinquency. These theories cover a large range of explanations and include a host of biological, psychological, and sociological factors (see Chapter 3). Nonetheless, some specific social factors are particularly important in looking at delinquency.[12]

Many researchers have tied delinquency to family factors such as poor parenting. Parental rejection and lack of supervision and involvement are strong predictors of conduct problems and delinquency. Poor parenting skills are specifically linked to the seriousness of the delinquency.[13] Delinquent behavior is also connected to a juvenile's experiences at school.[14] Students who do not do well in school are more likely to become delinquent.[15]

◀ **Dilapidated Housing**

Youths who grow up in poor neighborhoods with a lot of crime seem to be more likely to engage in delinquent behavior. *How would you explain the relationship between poverty and delinquency?*

The connection of class differences among juveniles to the likelihood of delinquent acts has been studied extensively. Historically lower social class was tied to delinquency. The poor have always been seen as more criminal and more delinquent.[16] But those views were based on the use of arrest data. When self-report surveys gained popularity in the 1950s, they seemed to show that middle-class juveniles were committing more delinquent acts than was previously thought.[17] Early studies based on these surveys concluded there was little, if any, difference between social classes regarding delinquency. More recent research, however, has found that there is a difference in delinquency between lower-class and middle-class juvenile males; the significant factors seem to be growing up in poverty and in neighborhoods with high rates of delinquency.[18]

arrest rates
The number of arrests per 100,000 persons.

Race also influences delinquency statistics. Blacks have a higher arrest rate than Whites, although the difference has declined since the mid-1990s. But arrest rates do not tell the complete story here either. Which crimes come to the attention of the police and who gets arrested are the factors that determine the final arrest statistics. A Black youth growing up in a poor neighborhood will more likely attract the attention of the police than a White youth in a middle-class environment.[19]

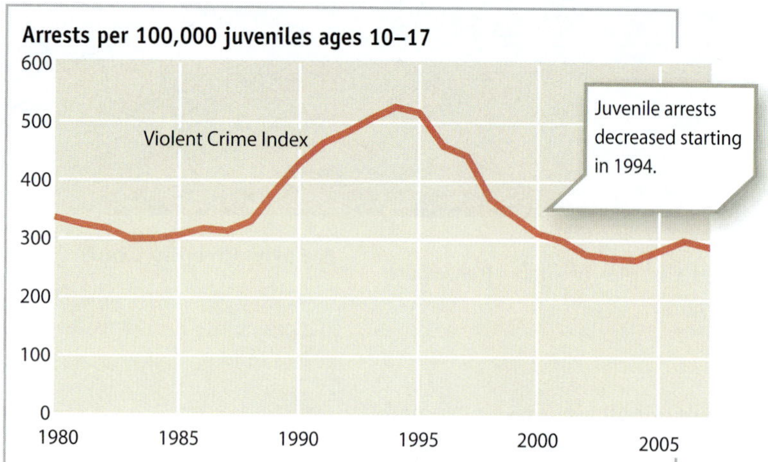

FIGURE 15-1 Juvenile Arrest Rate, 1980–2003

SOURCE: Howard N. Snyder and Melissa Sickmund, *Juvenile Offenders and Victims: 2006 National Report* (Washington, DC: U.S. Department of Justice, March 27, 2006), chap. 5, p. 132.

Measuring Juvenile Crime

MYTH/REALITY

MYTH: Juvenile crime rates are skyrocketing.

REALITY: Juvenile crime rates have been decreasing since 1994, especially for violent crimes.[20]

Despite the problems and the built-in bias of arrest data, the most common way to measure the amount of juvenile crime in the United States today is to look at **arrest rates**, the number of arrests per 100,000 persons.[21] Contrary to the picture presented by the media, since 1994 the rate of violent crime arrests for juveniles has consistently decreased. Figure 15-1 shows the juvenile arrest rate from 1980 to 2003. By the early 2000s, this rate had fallen to a level not seen since the 1970s. Although juvenile arrests increased slightly in 2005 and 2006, they decreased again in 2007, and were still far fewer than the peaks seen in the 1990s.[22] In 2007, for instance, 20 percent fewer arrests of juveniles occurred than in 1998.[23]

The exception to this decrease was a rise in the number of female juveniles arrested for violent crime. Remember, however, these are arrest rates and not offending rates. The media in recent years have highlighted isolated incidents of violent female youths and used them to argue that young women are becoming more violent. But with the possible exception of some property crime and drug offenses, female juvenile criminal behavior has remained relatively stable over the years, according to self-reports. The increase in the female juvenile arrest rate results instead from changes in criminal justice policies, including the tough-on-crime philosophy shared by some criminal justice professionals, parents, and school administrators.[24] Figure 15-2 shows the percentage of female juveniles arrested for violent crimes from 1980 to 2003.

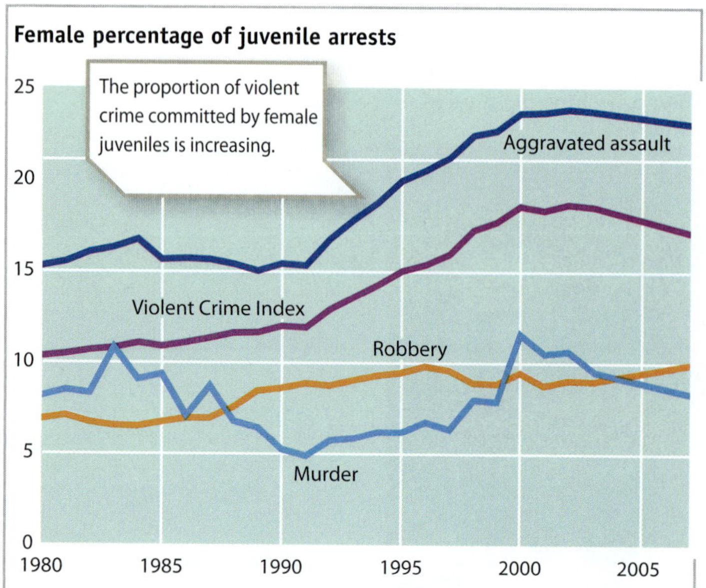

FIGURE 15-2 Percentage of Female Juvenile Violent Crime Arrests, 1980–2003

SOURCE: Howard N. Snyder and Melissa Sickmund, *Juvenile Offenders and Victims: 2006 National Report* (Washington, DC: U.S. Department of Justice, March 27, 2006), chap. 5, p. 128.

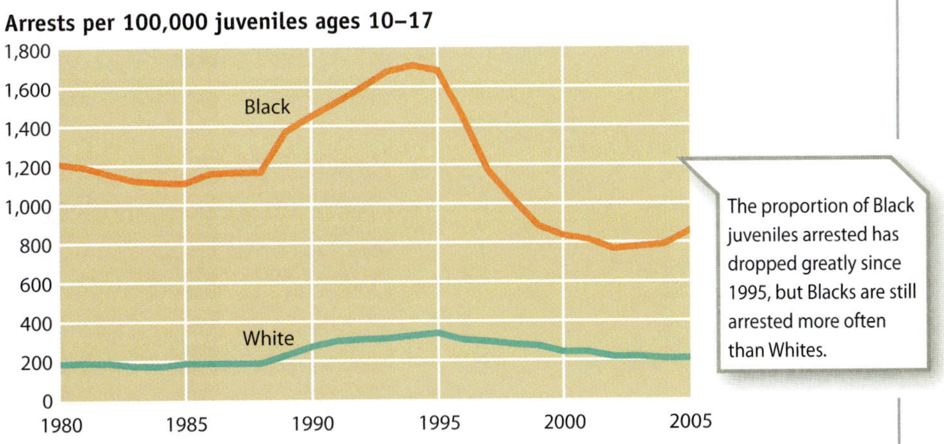

FIGURE 15-3 Arrest Rate for Black and White Juveniles, 1980–2005

SOURCE: Howard N. Snyder and Melissa Sickmund, *Juvenile Offenders and Victims: 2006 National Report* (Washington, DC: U.S. Department of Justice, March 27, 2006), chap. 5, p. 132.

One possible explanation for the increase of juvenile female arrests for aggravated assault is the heightened response by law enforcement to intimate partner violence disputes. More female juveniles than males were arrested for assaults against family members. Researchers say these arrests, coupled with the mandatory intimate partner violence arrest laws, rather than an actual increase in violent crimes committed by females, may be the reason for the increase in rates of females arrested for assault.[25]

The proportion of Black juveniles arrested for violent crimes has decreased. In the late 1980s the violent crime rate for Black juveniles was six times the rate for White juveniles, but by 2003 it was only four times the rate of Whites.[26] Although this is a major decrease, disproportionately more Black juveniles are still arrested in the United States than other groups. In 2002, Blacks were 16 percent of the population under age 18, but 29 percent of delinquency cases. In contrast, Whites made up 78 percent of the population under 18, but 67 percent of delinquency cases. Figure 15-3 shows the delinquency case rate from 1980 to 2005 by race. Note the decrease in the rate of violent crimes attributed to both White and Black juveniles and the disproportionate rate of Black juvenile arrests.

Murders by juveniles declined between the mid-1990s and 2002. In 2007 the rate of juvenile arrests for murder was 77 percent lower than its peak in 1993.[27] Experts attribute the decline to a decrease in the killing of minority males by other minority males. The rate of other violent and nonviolent offenses committed by juveniles also dropped. In 2003, the rate for juveniles arrested for burglary was one-third what it was in the 1980s, and the arrest rate for simple assault was less than half the 1980 rate.[28]

What explains these decreases? In searching for answers, we must remember that the official numbers underreport the actual extent of juvenile crime in the United States. Many delinquent acts are never reported, and many that are do not result in an arrest. Fewer than 50 percent of all violent crimes are reported to the police, and close to 35 percent of all U.S. police departments report their arrest data incompletely. The *Juvenile Offenders and Victims: 2006 National Report*, which is the most reliable national data we have, is used by practitioners throughout the field.[29] However, because of the underreporting, we also use methods other than arrest statistics to measure crime.

Self-report studies are one way to fill in the missing data. Self-report data may be inaccurate because self-reports rely on the memory and honesty of the person reporting, but they do show a large discrepancy from the official arrest data.[30] Victimization surveys are another method to determine the amount of crime. These surveys collect information directly from a representative sample of the general population rather than relying on police records.

POLICE AND YOUTH CRIME

A juvenile usually enters the justice system through the police. Police often try to handle trivial offenses such as curfew violations informally—by issuing a citation, meeting with the juvenile and parents, or some other informal arrangement or understanding. Handling a juvenile informally avoids formal arrest and a court proceeding that could result in

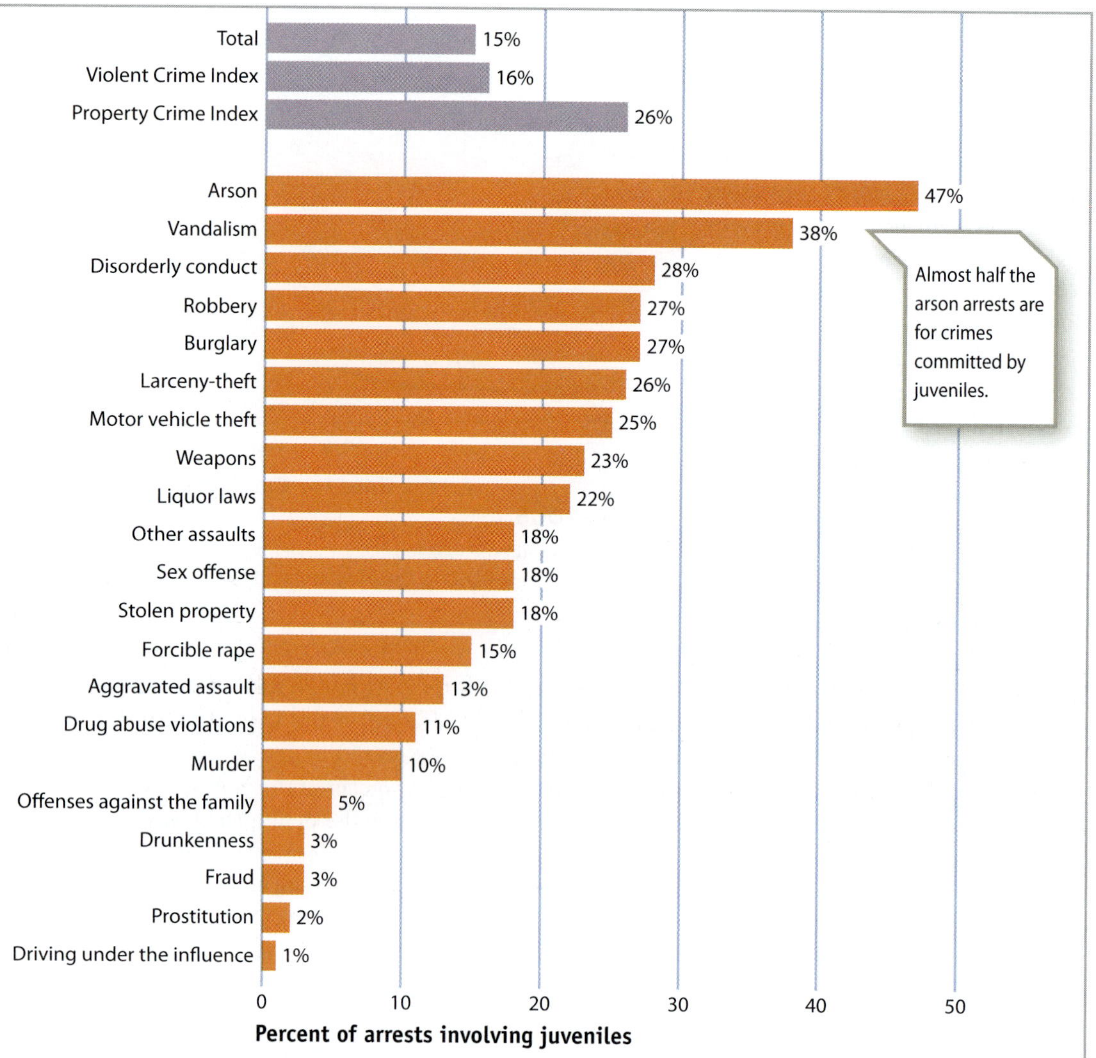

FIGURE 15-4 **Juvenile Proportion of Arrests by Offense, 2007**

NOTE: The Violent Crime Index includes the offenses of murder and non-negligent manslaughter, forcible rape, robbery, and aggravated assault. The Property Crime Index includes the offenses of burglary, larceny-theft, motor vehicle theft, and arson. Running away from home and curfew and loitering violations are not presented in this figure because, by definition, only juveniles can be arrested for these offenses.

SOURCE: U.S. Department of Justice, Office of Justice Programs, Office of Juvenile Justice and Delinquency Prevention, "Juvenile Arrests 2007," *Juvenile Justice Bulletin*, April 2009, www.ncjrs.gov/pdffiles1/ojjdp/225344.pdf.

juvenile justice system
The justice system that attempts to address important distinctions between children and adults and differs from the adult system in many respects.

incarceration and possibly a criminal record. A police decision to make an arrest—many jurisdictions use the term *detain*—automatically triggers an investigation by authorities of the **juvenile justice system**. If the court places the youth on probation, any violation of probation could bring further court action and possibly more serious charges.

In the United States police agencies arrest more than 2 million persons under 18 each year. In 2005, 1 of 11 arrests for murder was of a juvenile, and juveniles accounted for 1 of every 10 arrests for drug violations. Figure 15-4 shows the proportion of arrests of juveniles by type of crime. As you can see, in 2007 15 percent of all arrests, 16 percent of arrests for violent crime, and 26 percent of property crime arrests were of juvenile offenders.[31]

Police Discretion

Police have a large amount of latitude in how to handle juveniles. In other than serious cases, this latitude is necessary, and the police are called on to make judgments on whether to warn, handle a case informally, or detain. Not every juvenile offense ends in arrest, nor should it.

Many of the police officers' judgments are necessarily subjective and are based on factors other than the offense. One important factor is the attitude and demeanor of the juvenile. A polite juvenile stands a better chance than one who is hostile. There is some evidence that some police treat male and female juveniles differently.[32] Other biases can affect a police officer's decision as well. For example, some officers may treat juveniles who are from minority and disadvantaged communities more harshly.[33] Factors such as more frequent patrolling of Black and Latino neighborhoods and racial profiling by officers—whether conscious or unconscious—exacerbate the situation.[34]

If a juvenile case is handled informally, a citation or reprimand may be issued. This could require the juvenile and the parents to appear at the police station for a meeting with the officer. If the juvenile is detained, he or she is usually brought to a facility like a juvenile hall and is referred to the probation department. At this point the formal juvenile court procedures are set in motion.

▲ Police Officer Speaking to a Class

Many police programs aim to improve police interactions with youths.

Police in the Neighborhood and Schools

Police have long worked with juveniles in the community, providing positive role models. One common program is the Police Athletic League (PAL). Although a study evaluating these programs did not show strong positive changes in the youth who participated, most of the youth in these programs reported the experience as very positive.[35]

Across the United States, police–school liaison programs aim to change students' attitudes about the police, reduce school violence and crime in and around the school, and provide positive adult–youth connections.[36] A program, founded in 1983, that has gotten much attention in the use of police officers in the classroom is Drug Abuse Resistance Education (DARE). In this program, police officers teach students how to resist using illegal drugs. Police officers receive 80 hours of training to teach this curriculum.[37] However, there has not been much evidence-based research showing the DARE program is effective.[38] In addition, the U.S. Government Accountability Office (GAO) stated that DARE provided no long-term effect in preventing use of illegal drugs. The results just don't seem to last. Youth who participated in the DARE program did show some positive attitude changes after 1 year, but those results diminished over time.[39]

THE MODERN JUVENILE COURT SYSTEM

Juvenile courts were created with different goals from those of adult criminal courts. Rehabilitation rather than punishment was to be the focus, and the court's primary interest was to be in the child rather than on the offense. Although the process in juvenile courts has evolved to be quite similar to adult courts, some important distinctions remain, including differing terminology, narrower jurisdiction, and more restricted procedural rights for juvenile defendants.

Juvenile Court Jurisdiction

Juvenile courts are courts of limited jurisdiction, meaning they have the power to hear only certain kinds of cases defined by the child's behavior and age. Juvenile courts can hear delinquency cases, in which a minor is accused of committing a criminal act, as well as status offense cases, in which the offense is illegal only because the defendant is a child. In the past, status offenses were often too vaguely defined. Children could be sent before the court and, ultimately, placed in facilities for behavior that was considered "vicious," "immoral," "profane," "incorrigible," or "indecent." Other behaviors that could subject a child to the juvenile court included selling things, singing or playing an instrument in public, loitering, staying out at night, frequenting dancehalls, or being sexually promiscuous. Although juvenile courts have generally treated males more harshly for delinquency, females have generally experienced harsher treatment for status offenses such as breaking curfew. This bias may result from stereotypes that appear to support the need to "protect" females and to control their sexual behavior. Finally, juvenile courts may also hear dependency cases, in which a child's parents cannot or will not care for her properly.[40]

It might seem strange for a single court to have jurisdiction over a grade school truant, an armed teenage robber, and a preschooler abandoned by parents, but there is logic behind this plan. All three youths have a problem that needs fixing. They may even have the same problem: inadequate parental guidance and supervision. The system was devised under the assumption that curbing minor offenses today will help prevent criminal behavior later—that when a young person makes a mistake and undergoes some form of punishment or rehabilitation, he is more likely to avoid errant behavior in the future. As one early proponent wrote, "The problem for determination by the judge is not, 'Has this boy or girl committed a specific wrong,' but 'What is he, how has he become what he is, and what had best be done in his interest and in the interest of the state to save him from a downward career?'"[41]

▼ **Juvenile in Court**

All states have laws permitting juveniles to be tried in juvenile courts.

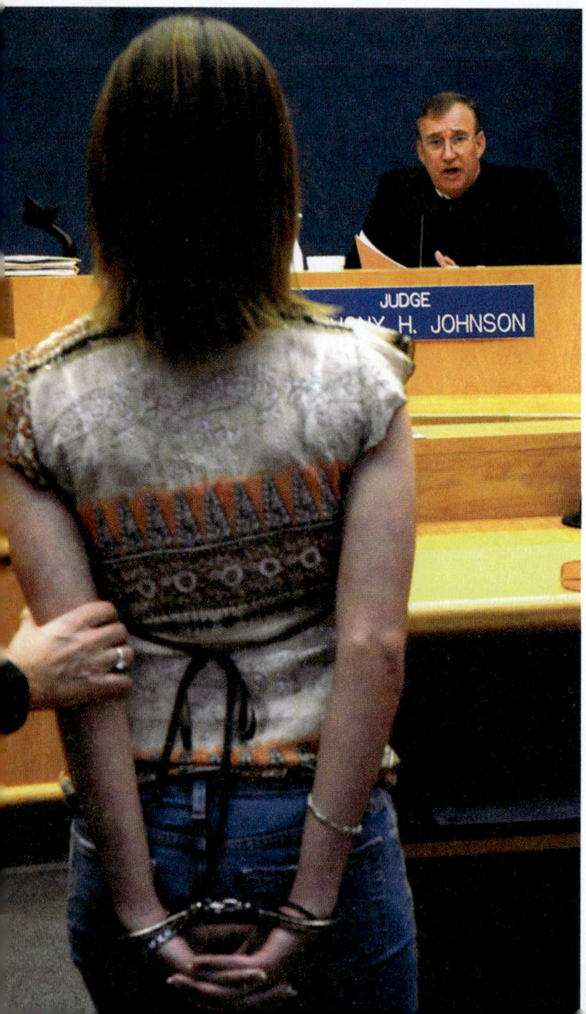

The upper and lower age limits for the legal definition of a child vary from state to state (see the table). In most states, an offender is eligible for juvenile court until turning 18. In 10 states, juvenile court jurisdiction expires on a person's 17th birthday, and in North Carolina, Connecticut, and New York, a 16-year-old who commits a crime must be tried as an adult.[42]

In most states, once the juvenile court has heard a case, its jurisdiction may extend beyond the offender's 18th birthday. For example, if a 15-year-old is judged delinquent in juvenile court, the juvenile justice system may confine her in juvenile facilities or monitor the delinquent through probation even after turning 18. The most common maximum age of a confined or monitored delinquent is 20, although it ranges between 18 and 24 depending on the state.[43] No matter how serious the crime, offenders tried in juvenile court must be released from custody on their 21st birthday (or 25th in a few states).

Some states also have a minimum age for juvenile court jurisdiction, a reflection of the common law idea that young children cannot form criminal intent. Children younger than the minimum who commit criminal acts cannot be tried either as juveniles or as adults; if their actions are serious, however, they and their families may be referred to counseling or other social services (see the Mapping Juvenile Court Jurisdiction maps on the facing page). This minimum age varies from 6 in North Carolina to 10 in 11 other states.[44]

Most states have no minimum age for juvenile court jurisdiction, and very young children who commit crimes may be brought before juvenile courts. In recent years, children as young as age 7 have been charged with crimes such as murder, attempted armed robbery, and arson.[45] In 1996, a 6-year-old boy in California kicked and beat a 1-month-old infant, causing the baby permanent brain damage. Despite his age and the fact that he was mildly mentally challenged, the boy was charged with attempted murder and held for several months in a juvenile detention facility. The prosecutor told reporters, "It doesn't matter whether you're 6 or you're 106. If you do something that hurts somebody else, with knowledge of the wrongfulness of it, you're responsible for it, period." Eventually, the judge ruled the boy incompetent to stand trial, and he was sent to live in a group home for troubled children.[46]

Mapping Juvenile Court Jurisdiction

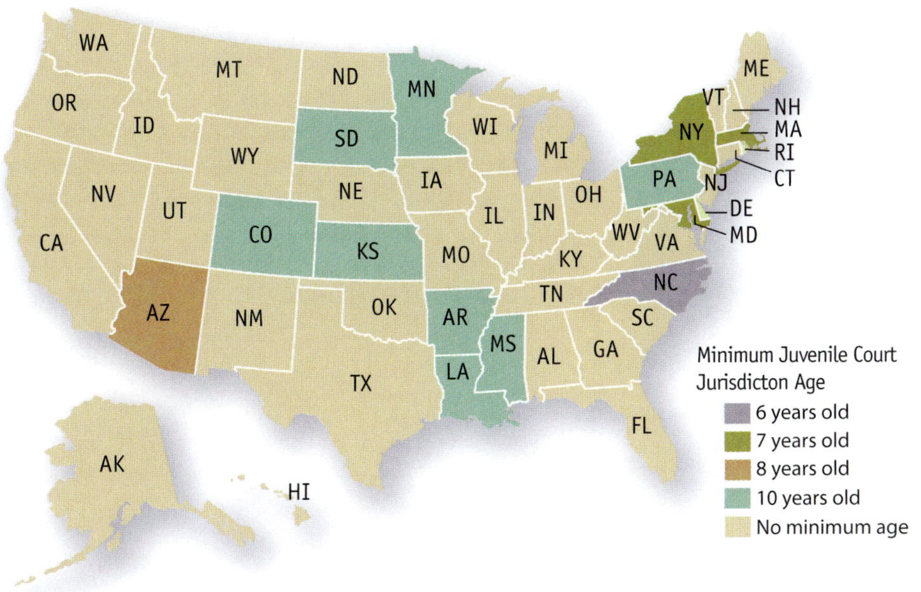

Minimum Age for Juvenile Court Jurisdiction in Each State

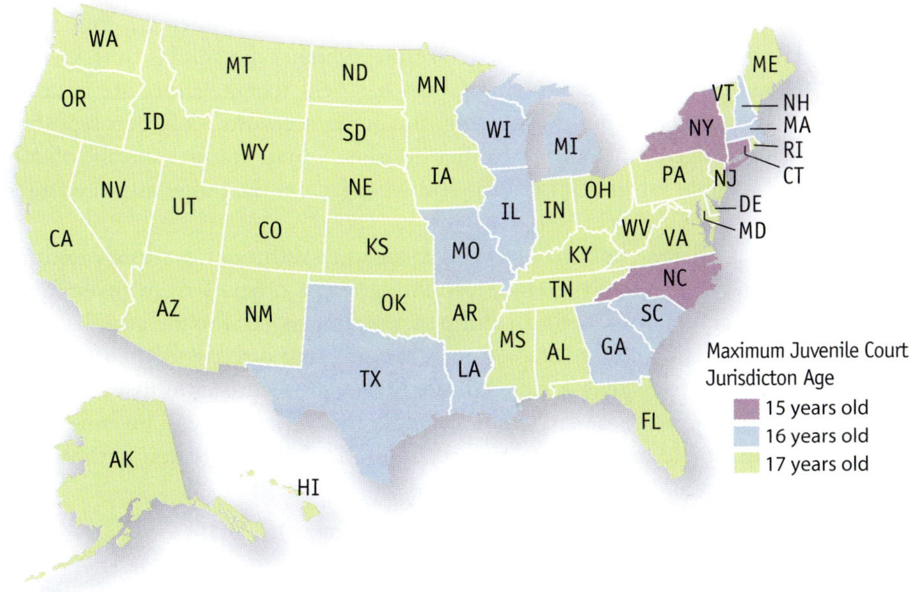

Maximum Age for Juvenile Court Jurisdiction in Each State

Juvenile Court Waivers

When the juvenile justice system was created, its founders recognized it would not be appropriate for all youthful offenders. The seriousness of their crimes, the complexity of their problems, or their relatively advanced age might make them less amenable for treatment within the juvenile system. Thus mechanisms exist to permit the juvenile court to waive jurisdiction and allow the transfer—or **waiver**—of these offenders to adult court. In the past 20 years, nearly every state has expanded the methods and circumstances under which juveniles may be waived, and most have lowered the minimum age for waiver.[47] Some states have no minimum at all; others specify minimums as young as 10 (see the map above and the table on the next page).

waiver
A mechanism to permit the transfer of some juvenile offenders to adult court.

MINIMUM AGE FOR WAIVER

Age for Waiver	States with Minimum Age
No minimum	Alaska, Arizona, Delaware, District of Columbia, Florida, Georgia, Hawaii, Idaho, Indiana, Maine, Maryland, Nebraska, Nevada, Oklahoma, Oregon, Pennsylvania, Rhode Island, South Carolina, South Dakota, Tennessee, Washington, West Virginia, Wisconsin
10	Kansas, Vermont
12	Colorado, Missouri, Montana
13	Illinois, Mississippi, New Hampshire, New York, North Carolina, Wyoming
14	Alabama, Arkansas, California, Connecticut, Iowa, Kentucky, Louisiana, Massachusetts, Michigan, Minnesota, New Jersey, North Dakota, Ohio, Texas, Utah, Virginia
15	New Mexico

SOURCE: Building Blocks for Youth, "Charts on Transferring Youth to Criminal Court," www.buildingblocksforyouth.org/issues/transfer/transchart.html.

Types of Waivers

judicial waiver
A means by which a juvenile is sent by a judge to be tried in adult court.

statutory exclusion
A state law categorically excluding certain ages and offenses from juvenile court jurisdiction.

direct file (prosecutorial waiver)
A method that allows the prosecutor to choose whether to bring the juvenile's case to juvenile or adult court.

Waiver laws vary from state to state. Almost all states use at least one of three major methods, and some use a combination of these. The first kind of waiver is called **judicial waiver.** Under this method, a prosecutor or probation officer recommends a child be tried as an adult. The juvenile court judge then determines whether the child is fit to be treated within the juvenile system. The Supreme Court has held that juveniles are entitled to certain due process rights during this hearing, including access to probation reports and a statement by the judge of the reasons for her decision.[48] State statutes specify what ages and offenses are eligible for judicial waiver, and what factors the judge must consider in the decision.

The second way that a child may be tried as an adult is through **statutory exclusion,** in which state laws categorically exclude certain ages and offenses from juvenile court jurisdiction. For example, in Wisconsin children as young as 10 who are accused of first- or second-degree intentional homicide are automatically sent directly to adult court.

The third method for waiver is called **direct file,** or **prosecutorial waiver.** For certain ages and offenses, the prosecutor can choose whether to bring the case to juvenile or adult court. No hearing is held and no legal criteria apply. The decision is left entirely to the prosecutor's discretion and cannot be appealed.

▼ Juveniles Tried as Adults

In recent years, juveniles increasingly have been tried in adult courts.

Problems with Waivers

The use of waivers has increased and often enjoys popular or political appeal as part of a tough-on-crime approach. However, critics and scholars raise several objections to waiving children to be tried in adult courts. One is that waivers perpetuate racial and ethnic biases. There is evidence that minority youths are disproportionately likely to be tried as adults.[49] The Race, Class, Gender box describes one case of a very young Black offender who was given a life sentence.

MYTH/REALITY

MYTH: Only the most violent juveniles are tried as adults.

REALITY: A large proportion of juveniles tried as adults are accused of nonviolent crimes.[50]

Race, Class, Gender

Minority Youth Sentenced to Life without Parole

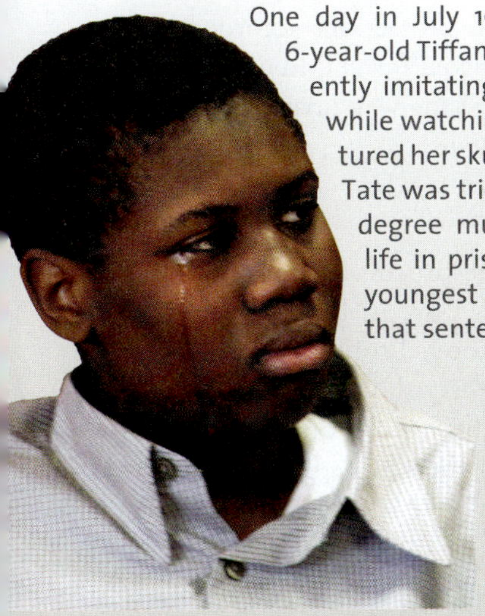

One day in July 1999, 12-year-old Lionel Tate killed 6-year-old Tiffany Eunick by stomping on her. Apparently imitating moves he had seen on television while watching professional wrestling, Tate fractured her skull and damaged her internal organs. Tate was tried as an adult and convicted of first-degree murder. When he was sentenced to life in prison without parole, he became the youngest person in the country to be serving that sentence.

Tate's case raised several important questions. Is it appropriate to try a 12-year-old as an adult and give him such a severe sentence? Tate had a history of aggression and other behavior problems. Why had the educational, social service, and juvenile justice systems not somehow prevented Tate's behavior? Many critics also claimed Tate's harsh treatment was just an extreme example of the justice system's pervasive mistreatment of Blacks. Even the prosecutor protested the severe sentence Tate received.

In January 2004, Tate's conviction was overturned because his competency had not been evaluated before he was tried. Instead of being retried, he accepted the plea deal he had initially been offered, but which his mother had rejected, of 1 year of house arrest plus 10 years of probation. Within a year, he had violated probation by leaving his house with a knife, and 5 years were added to his probation term. Only a few months later, Tate robbed a pizza deliveryman at gunpoint. He received a 30-year prison sentence for unlawful gun possession and 10 years for the robbery. Clearly his experience with incarceration had done little to rehabilitate him and may have taught him criminal behavior.

Observe Investigate Understand

- **If you were the prosecutor in the case of Lionel Tate, how would you have handled the case? Would you have referred it to juvenile court or to an adult court? State your reasons.**
- **What role do you think Tate's race played in the way he was processed in the criminal justice system?**
- **Do you think Tate's later criminal behavior would have been prevented by a juvenile court proceeding and disposition (sentencing)? Why or why not?**

SOURCES: "Lionel Tate gets 30 Years in Jail," KDKA.com, http://kdka.com/homepage/topstories_story_138103942.html (retrieved June 19, 2007); Abby Goodnough, "Youngster Given Life Term for Killing Gets New Trial," *The New York Times*, December 11, 2003.

A second objection to the use of waivers is that prosecutorial waiver results in uneven and unfair patterns of transfers. Because prosecutors are elected, they may choose to waive a case if they believe doing so is a politically popular decision. Thus the proportion and kind of cases waived under direct file may vary a great deal from one county to the next, depending on the philosophy of each county's prosecutors. In one study, fewer than 20 percent of the waived cases were crimes against persons.[51] On any given day in 2004, approximately 2,500 people under the age of 18 were confined in adult prisons. Forty percent of these youths had committed nonviolent crimes, and only 13 percent had committed homicide or sex offenses.[52]

A third major criticism is that waivers send children to adult jails and prisons.[53] Clearly children in prisons are vulnerable to sexual exploitation and physical injury. Furthermore, an increasing body of research demonstrates that children tried as adults are more likely to reoffend after release, as we saw in the case of Lionel Tate, described in the Race, Class, Gender box.[54]

Landmark U.S. Supreme Court Cases

For nearly seven decades after its inception, the juvenile court functioned more informally than adult courts. One result of this informality was that children were given virtually none of the due process protections adults receive. They were not permitted assistance of counsel, were not allowed to confront and cross-examine witnesses, and did not have the right to avoid self-incrimination. They did not have to be found guilty beyond a reasonable doubt, and judges rather than juries decided their fate. Due process rights were thought to be unnecessary because the court's goal was to treat, not to punish. The assumption was that due process requirements would actually impede juvenile courts' abilities to treat young offenders.

In theory, it made sense for wayward youths to trade due process rights for compassionate rehabilitation. But in reality, from the very beginning, most children received neither from courts too overwhelmed to provide careful consideration of individual cases. As the U.S. Supreme Court wrote in 1966, "[T]here may be grounds for concern that the child receives the worst of both worlds: that he gets neither the protections accorded to adults nor the solicitous care and regenerative treatment postulated for children."[55] As a result, in a series of cases the Supreme Court gradually changed the way juvenile courts operated by granting children certain rights.

In re Gault (1967)—Establishing Due Process for Juveniles

The Court decision that was key to the establishment of due process in the modern juvenile justice system was *In re Gault*, decided in 1967.[56] A Case in Point gives the details of this landmark case. Once *Gault* was decided, children brought before the juvenile court were entitled to several of the most basic rights adult defendants are guaranteed—the right to be notified of the charges against them, to confront and cross-examine witnesses, to remain silent, to obtain a transcript of the proceedings, and to appeal the court's decision. Perhaps most significant, juveniles were also entitled to the assistance of an attorney.

As a result of gaining these rights, what was once envisioned as an informal conversation between concerned parties now takes on many of the characteristics of an adult criminal trial. While in the past about a quarter of juvenile court judges did not have any formal training in law, a law degree is now essential.[57]

In re Winship (1970)—Proof Beyond a Reasonable Doubt for Juveniles

Three years after *Gault*, the Supreme Court considered another important issue: What should be the standard of proof in juvenile cases? While the long-standing common law rule had been that adults must be found guilty beyond a reasonable doubt, juvenile cases usually needed to be proven only by a preponderance of the evidence—the same standard used in civil cases. The case that brought this issue before the Court concerned 12-year-old Samuel Winship, who was sent to a training school for up to 6 years for stealing $112 from a locker.[58] In *In re Winship* the State of New York argued the lesser standard of proof was appropriate in juvenile cases because it was suited to the juvenile court's rehabilitative purposes. A majority of the Supreme Court disagreed, holding the due process clause in the Constitution requires proof beyond a reasonable doubt in juvenile as well as adult cases.

McKeiver v. Pennsylvania (1971)—No Jury Trials for Juveniles

After *Gault* and *Winship*, the juvenile system began to resemble the adult criminal system in many important respects. Advocates of the changes argued they were necessary to ensure young offenders were treated fairly. Critics feared they would interfere with the juvenile justice system's mission of rehabilitation and erase any meaningful distinction between the juvenile and adult systems. The Supreme Court discussed this controversy when it decided a third landmark case, *McKeiver v. Pennsylvania*, which centered on whether juveniles were entitled to jury trials.[59] *McKeiver* was actually several consolidated cases involving juveniles charged with a broad variety of offenses.

McKeiver was a contentious case—four Justices joined in one opinion, two Justices each wrote his own concurring opinion, and three Justices dissented. In the end, however, a majority agreed that children in juvenile proceedings are not entitled to juries. The Court admitted the juvenile justice system was a failure but was not ready to give up on it altogether. Justice Harry Blackmun wrote, "There is a possibility, at least, that the jury trial, if required as a matter of constitutional precept, will remake the juvenile proceeding into a fully adversary process and will put an effective end to what has been the idealistic prospect of an intimate, informal protective proceeding."[60]

Breed v. Jones (1975)—Double Jeopardy and Juvenile Cases

In 1975, the Supreme Court granted another important right to juvenile offenders. Gary Jones, 17, was accused of committing an armed robbery. The juvenile court judge ruled Jones had in fact committed robbery, but also that he was "unfit for treatment as a juvenile"—that is, he was not likely to be rehabilitated by the juvenile justice system. The judge ordered him tried in adult court, where Jones was found guilty of the robbery. When Jones appealed to the U.S. Supreme Court, the Court held the Fifth Amendment's double jeopardy clause applies to juvenile proceedings. A person cannot be tried in both juvenile and adult courts for the same offense.[61]

a Case in Point

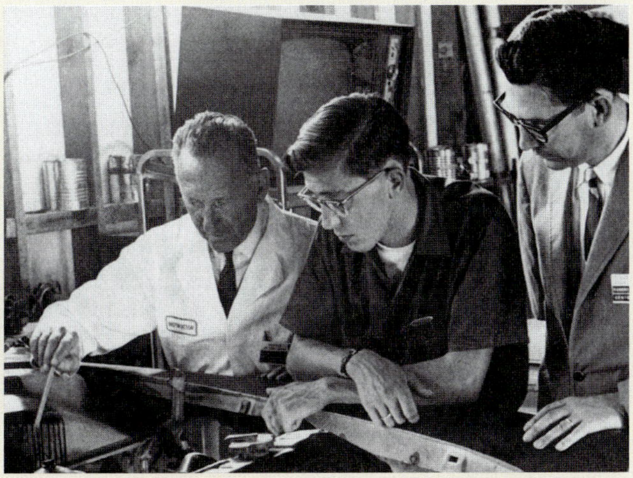

Gerald Francis Gault Has His Day in Supreme Court

On June 8, 1964, in Gila County, Arizona, a woman complained to police about sexually suggestive prank phone calls she had received. That afternoon, the local sheriff arrested her neighbor, 15-year-old Gerald Francis Gault, and took him to the juvenile detention facility. Gault's parents did not even know he had been arrested until they arrived home from work and could not find him.

The next day, a petition stating he had been delinquent was filed against Gault in juvenile court. He and his parents were not given a copy. Hearings were held that day and again 6 days later in front of a juvenile court judge. During the hearings, Gault was not read his rights before being questioned, no lawyers were present, and Gault was not given the chance to consult with one. The neighbor who issued the complaint was not there. Probation officers gave the judge a referral report, but Gault and his parents were not allowed to see it.

No record was made of the proceedings, at the end of which the judge found Gault delinquent. Although Gault's only previous run-in with the law was being present when a friend stole a wallet from a purse, the judge committed him to the state Industrial School until he was 21—a period of nearly 6 years. The maximum sentence an adult could have received for the offense was 2 months in jail or a $50 fine. Under Arizona law, Gault was not allowed to appeal to the state appeals court.

Gault filed a federal habeas corpus petition, which eventually reached the U.S. Supreme Court. Justice Abraham Fortas wrote an opinion for the Court that was highly critical of the state of juvenile justice in the United States. Justice Fortas wrote, "In view of this, it would be extraordinary if our Constitution did not require the procedural regularity and the exercise of care implied in the phrase 'due process.' Under our Constitution, the condition of being a boy does not justify a kangaroo court." The Court went on to grant juveniles several basic due process rights.

Gerry Gault was finally released after having been incarcerated for nearly 3 years. He had a long and successful military career, earned vocational degrees, and today is a heavy equipment operator who has been married for over 35 years.

Observe Investigate Understand

- **Why do you think young Gault was punished so much more severely for his offense than an adult would have been for the same offense?**
- **In your opinion, what is the most serious due process right that Gault was deprived of? State your reasons.**
- **If the juvenile justice system had been meeting its goals, do you think the Supreme Court would have been as likely to grant juveniles due process rights? Why or why not?**

SOURCES: *In re Gault*, 387 U.S. 1, 28-29 (1967); "Protecting America's Children—Assessing the Promise of *In Re Gault* 40 Years Later," Open Society Institute, OSI Forum, www.soros.org/initiatives/justice/events/gault_20070503/event_biography_folder_initiative_view (retrieved June 18, 2007).

Other Important Cases

MYTH/REALITY

MYTH: Minors cannot be interrogated without the presence of their parents or an attorney.

REALITY: Like adults, children may waive their *Miranda* rights and be questioned without lawyers present. In fact, unless a juvenile specifically asks for a parent, the parent need not even be notified that the child is being questioned.[62]

Several other cases are of particular importance to juvenile offenders. In *Fare v. Michael C.* (1979), the Supreme Court refused to extend extra protections to juveniles during police interrogations.[63] Under the Court's decision in this case, police may interrogate children without their parents' or an attorney's presence, and any statements the children make will be admissible in court (see the Disconnects box).

In 1984, in *Schall v. Martin*, the Court held that minors may be subjected to preventive detention.[64] That is, children accused of crimes may be held not only to ensure they appear in court, but also to protect them from adverse home conditions or prevent them from committing additional offenses while their case is pending.

DISConnects

Interrogating Children

There are several troubling cases of children confessing to murdering other children. In 1998, two boys ages 7 and 8 confessed to murdering an 11-year-old girl. In 1994, a 10-year-old boy was convicted of killing his elderly neighbor; almost the only evidence against him was his confession. In 1998, a 14-year-old boy and one of his friends confessed to murdering the boy's younger sister. In another case in 1998, a 12-year-old confessed to killing a 5-year-old girl. And in 1996, an 11-year-old admitted murdering a 2-year-old; she was convicted—twice, after the first conviction was overturned—and served 3 years of a 25-year sentence.

What these cases have in common is that each of these children uttered their confessions while being interrogated at length by police, sometimes for days. They all later recanted, and DNA evidence eventually exonerated most of them. These cases exemplify the risks of interrogating children.

For several decades, scholars and child advocates have argued that juvenile suspects should not be allowed to waive their *Miranda* rights to remain silent, and that police should not be permitted to question them unless their parents or attorneys are present. Two areas of research support these arguments. First, evidence indicates youths younger than 16 do not really understand *Miranda* warnings, even when they are of average intelligence or have prior experience with the justice system. Second, although people of all ages give false confessions, children are more likely than adults to admit to crimes they did not commit.

Despite the research, the Supreme Court has never ruled that special requirements are needed for interrogating children. Many critics point out that it is illogical that children who are too young to vote, drive, or enter into contracts are nonetheless permitted to be interrogated under the same conditions as adults. Some states do require that a parent or lawyer be present during interrogations of younger children, and the Wisconsin Supreme Court ruled in 2005 that all interrogations of juveniles in custody must be videotaped. In most states, however, the potential for young children to be persuaded to give confessions when a parent or lawyer is not present is still very real.

Observe Investigate Understand

- **What makes children more likely than adults to give false confessions to police?**
- **Do you think parents should always be present during interrogations of a juvenile? Why or why not? Are there any circumstances under which it might be permissible or understandable not to have a parent present? If so, describe the circumstances.**
- **Why do you think the Supreme Court has never ruled that there be special requirements for interrogating children?**

SOURCES: *Fare v. Michael C.*, 442 U.S. 707 (1979); Barry C. Feld, "Juveniles' Competence to Exercise *Miranda* Rights: An Empirical Study of Policy and Practice," *Minnesota Law Review* 91, no. 1 (2006): 26–100; Jeanne Galatzer-Levy, "Harris Case a 'Wake-up Call' on Kids' Confessions," *Chicago Tribune*, March 22, 2000, www.law.northwestern.edu/depts/clinic/Articles/newsarticleharriscase32200.htm (retrieved April 16, 2007); Lisa M. Krzewinski, "But I Didn't Do It!: Protecting the Rights of Juveniles during Interrogation," *Boston College Third World Law Journal* 22 (2002): 355–388; Allison D. Redlich and Gail S. Goodman, "Taking Responsibility for an Act Not Committed: The Influence of Age and Suggestibility," *Law and Human Behavior* 27 (2003): 141–156.

Until 2005, children could be sentenced to death. In 1944, 14-year-old George Stinney was put to death in the electric chair for killing two girls.[65] In cases decided in 1988 and 1989, the Supreme Court held that capital punishment was constitutional for offenders over 15.[66] Between 1976 and 2004, 22 people who were younger than 18 when they committed murder were executed in the United States, and 73 more were on death row.[67] Only a handful of other nations—Pakistan, Bangladesh, Rwanda, and Barbados—executed juveniles during this time.[68] However, in 2005 the Supreme Court held in *Roper v. Simmons* that the death penalty for people younger than 18 when they committed murder is cruel and unusual punishment.[69]

Finally, in a series of decisions the Supreme Court has ruled on children's Fourth Amendment search and seizure rights when they are in school. In general, these cases hold that school officials and school resource officers—police officers based inside public schools—must respect students' rights against unreasonable searches and seizures, but these rights are limited compared to those of adults. For example, reasonable suspicion, rather than probable cause and a search warrant, is sufficient to justify searches of students and their belongings.[70] Furthermore, schools may conduct random drug testing of all students engaged in extracurricular activities.[71] However, in 2009 the Supreme Court held that the strip search of a 13-year-old girl by school officials who believed she had prescription-strength ibuprofen and knives violated her Fourth Amendment rights.[72]

PROCESSING JUVENILE OFFENDERS

Describing how juvenile offenders are processed is difficult because there is considerable regional variation in the juvenile justice system. The process in one county or state may be quite different from the process elsewhere. Figure 15-5 shows the typical way in which cases flow through the juvenile justice system. We will discuss each of the major steps in detail. Although many juvenile court procedures closely resemble adult procedures, notice that they use different terminology to avoid the stigma associated with adult criminal convictions.

Arrest

A child may enter the justice system via a referral from parents, school officials, probation officers, or other adults. Most, however, enter the same way most adults do: they are arrested by police. In 2002, for example, 82 percent of all delinquency cases were referred by law enforcement.[73]

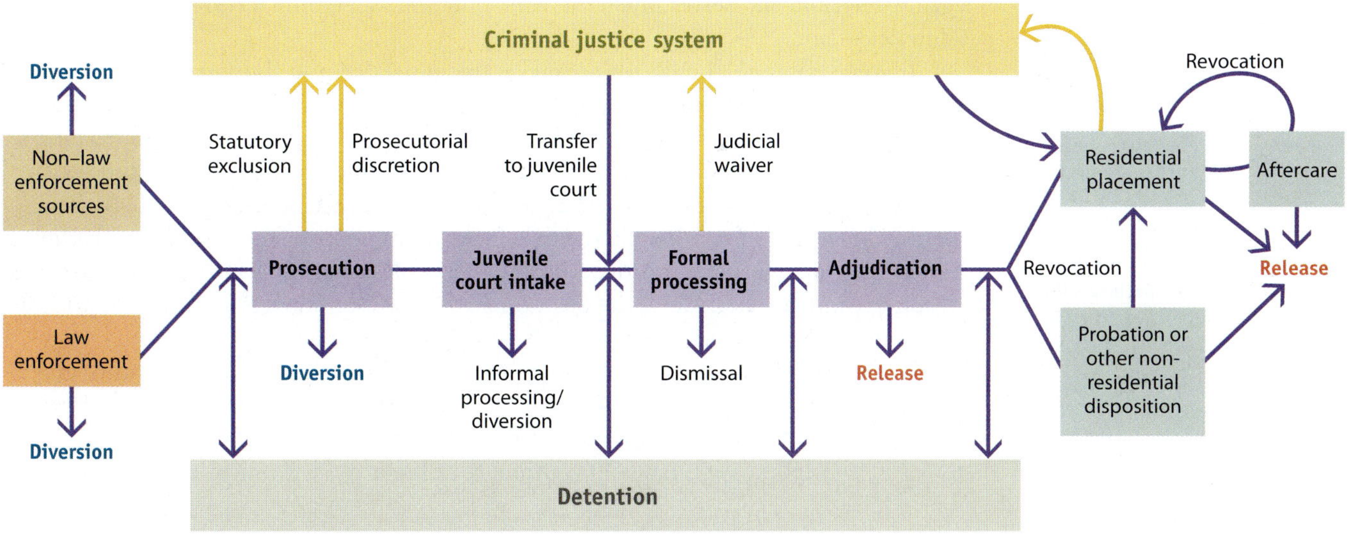

FIGURE 15-5 **Juvenile Case Flow**

▲ **Guards Restraining Feet of Juveniles**

On occasion, some juveniles in juvenile facilities must be restrained.

In 2003, one in five arrested juveniles was released by the police department. Ten percent were handled through other systems and agencies (including, in many cases, the adult criminal justice system). The remaining 70 percent had their cases recommended for prosecution within the juvenile court system.[74]

When police choose to pursue a case against a child, that child is usually taken to a juvenile detention center, known as a **juvenile hall**. However, children may sometimes be held in adult jails, particularly when no juvenile facility is available. An estimated 1 percent of the population in jails in 2004 was under age 18.[75] Children held in adult jails are more likely than children held in juvenile facilities to suffer violent or physical attacks, or to commit suicide.[76]

The 1974 Juvenile Justice and Delinquency Prevention Act prohibited holding juveniles in adult facilities, but with exceptions. Children may be housed with adults for up to 48 hours—or longer, if weekends or holidays intervene—while arrangements are made to transfer them to a juvenile facility. Children also may be housed in jails if they are separated from adult inmates or if they will be or have been tried as adults. The act, amended by Congress several times, currently seeks to address the disproportionate number of juveniles of color in the criminal justice system, encourage alternative sanctions for status offenders, and remove juveniles from adult jails and other adult facilities.[77]

juvenile hall
A juvenile detention center.

Unlike adult offenders, people held in juvenile detention facilities are not constitutionally entitled to a swift "probable cause" hearing (see Chapter 9). However, each state has a statute that mandates that a detention hearing occur within a certain amount of time—usually 24 hours.

Intake

intake
Process during which an official decides whether to release the juvenile or refer the case to court or put the juvenile under some other supervision.

delinquency petition
The formal document that initiates a juvenile case and lays out the specific allegations against the child; serves much the same function as a criminal complaint.

intake officer
The probation officer who makes the initial decision about whether to proceed with a case.

informal probation
A situation in which as long as the child obeys certain conditions and stays out of trouble, the case will not proceed any further, such as to court.

diversion programs
Programs that handle juvenile cases informally, rather than through the juvenile court.

Shortly after a juvenile is taken into custody, the **intake** process begins, during which an official decides whether to release the juvenile, refer the case to court, or put the juvenile under some other supervision. In most states, a prosecutor will consider the case. The prosecutor may choose not to proceed any further, in which case the child is released. Under some circumstances, the prosecutor may file charges against the child in adult court. The prosecutor may also refer the case to juvenile court. The formal document that initiates a juvenile case is called a **delinquency petition;** it lays out the specific allegations against the child and serves much the same function as a criminal complaint does for an adult defendant.

In some states, the **intake officer** makes the initial decision about whether to proceed with a case. Intake officers are usually probation officers. They may choose to handle the case informally by dropping it, placing the child on **informal probation** (as long as the child obeys certain conditions and stays out of trouble, the case will not proceed any further), or placing the child in a **diversion program**, such as substance abuse treatment. Or the intake officer can handle the case formally by recommending the case be heard in juvenile court. In some jurisdictions, the intake officer can also recommend a transfer to adult criminal court. However, the ultimate decision on waivers usually rests with the prosecutor.

The intake officer usually determines whether to release the child to parents or guardians or to detain the child in custody while waiting for the case to go to court. Bail is rarely used in juvenile cases, primarily because the juveniles' parents or guardians are expected to ensure the child's appearance in court, and children present much less of a flight risk than adults.

Nationwide, about half of all cases are settled informally at intake. The likelihood of a case being handled formally has increased since 1985, primarily due to policy changes demanding that the system get tough on crime and treat juvenile offenders more like adults.[78]

Diversion

When juvenile cases are handled informally, one option is to place the child in a diversion program. Diversion programs are meant to rehabilitate children, provide more effective early intervention for troubled youths, and reduce juvenile court caseloads, all without burdening offenders with the stigma associated with going to court. These programs are usually available for first-time, nonviolent offenders and may be aimed at specific groups, such as very young offenders or substance abusers.

One common program is the **teen court**, in which teenagers serve as jurors and often as judges, attorneys, and bailiffs as well. Although there are more than 600 teen courts in the United States, so far there has been little research on their effectiveness in reducing recidivism.[79] Another popular diversion option is a restorative justice program such as community service (see Chapter 13).

teen court
A court in which teenagers serve as jurors and often as judges, attorneys, and bailiffs as well.

Juvenile diversion programs produce mixed results. Some appear to reduce recidivism, whereas others appear to be no more effective than traditional juvenile court dispositions.[80] A diversion program that is no more effective than traditional methods may still be worth pursuing because it costs less, reduces court caseloads, and carries less of a stigma.

Preventive Detention

When the decision is made to take a juvenile to court, the question arises of what to do with the child until the court date. Should the child be released to parents or guardians or be kept in a detention center (serving the same purpose as the adult's jail)? About one in five arrested juveniles is held in **preventive detention** in a juvenile facility while awaiting a court appearance, either to ensure appearance at trial or to prevent the child from committing dangerous acts.[81]

preventive detention
Custodial holding of children accused of crimes to ensure they appear in court, but also to protect them from adverse home conditions or to prevent them from committing additional offenses while their case is pending.

Preventive detention of adults is permitted only when the adults are accused of violent felonies or have a previous record of dangerous behaviors.[82] Children can be detained under broader circumstances, such as when the intake staff determines they require diagnostic evaluation, pose a threat to the community, or will themselves be at risk if released.[83] Most juvenile detainees are not accused of violent crimes. In 2002, for example, 29 percent of detainees were accused of crimes against persons, 32 percent of property crimes, 27 percent of public order crimes, and 11 percent of drug offenses.[84]

A number of problems are associated with preventive detention of juveniles. One is that detention is used unequally. Boys are more likely than girls to be detained, even for the same offenses, and children who are not White are more likely to be detained than are White children. This is especially true for drug offenses: In 2002, only 16 percent of White juveniles charged with drug offenses were detained, but 33 percent of Black juveniles with drug charges were detained.[85]

A second problem with preventive detention is that it is difficult to determine accurately whether a youth will be dangerous if released. A large proportion of juveniles who are detained—perhaps 80 percent—would, in fact, have presented very little risk to the community, as evidenced by the fact that 62 percent of those found to be delinquent are given probation, and only 23 percent are placed in a facility of any kind.[86] The mistaken detention of low-risk youths creates problems for them because, among other effects, detained youths are more likely to be found delinquent and to receive a more severe sentence than those who are not detained.[87]

The third problem is that conditions within detention centers can be poor. Overcrowding is common. In 2002, 14 percent of juvenile detention centers were at capacity, and 18 percent were over capacity. In New Jersey, 31 percent of juveniles were in overcrowded facilities, and in Delaware 81 percent were overcrowded.[88] Youths in overcrowded conditions are more likely to be victimized by other youths, to suffer physical and mental health problems, to be maltreated by staff, and to lack adequate diagnosis and treatment.[89]

risk assessment instrument
A worksheet that measures the degree of risk present in a given case.

One promising solution to these problems is the standardized use of **risk assessment instruments.** These instruments (in the form of a worksheet) measure the degree of risk in a given case. The intake officer enters specific information about the case and the juvenile into the instrument, such as the number of prior arrests, previous violations, and absence of parental supervision. The resulting "score" predicts the likelihood that the juvenile will commit more crimes or fail to appear in court. The intake officer can then base a detention decision on this score. Risk assessment instruments may reduce the rate of detentions, as well as race and gender bias, without creating increased danger to the public.[90]

Adjudication

In 2005, more than 1.5 million juvenile cases were handled formally through filing a petition sending a juvenile to court. This was 46 percent more than in 1985.[91] The increase in formal petitions was likely a consequence of tough-on-crime policies.

adjudication hearing
A hearing to determine whether the juvenile committed the action as charged.

When the prosecutor files a petition in a juvenile case, the juvenile may plea bargain or not. If not, the court proceeding in which a judge determines whether a juvenile has committed an offense is an **adjudication hearing**, not a criminal trial.

In many respects, however, an adjudication hearing resembles a criminal trial. The case is brought by a prosecutor, who must prove the case beyond a reasonable doubt. The juvenile is entitled to be represented by an attorney, although in some jurisdictions, fewer than half of juveniles have a lawyer. (Some research suggests juveniles represented by counsel actually receive more severe treatment.[92]) Witnesses are sworn and evidence produced. A typical juvenile court judge may hear 30 to 50 cases each day, which means that each case will be given only a few minutes. Unlike criminal cases, juvenile cases in many states are closed to the public to avoid further stigmatization of the child. A recording or transcript of the proceedings is made, in case the juvenile later wishes to appeal.

adjudicated delinquent
The equivalent in the juvenile system of being found guilty in adult court.

The most striking difference from a criminal trial is the lack of a jury in an adjudication hearing. The judge determines whether the prosecution has met its burden of proof. If not, the petition will be dismissed, and, just as in criminal cases, the youth cannot be retried for the same offense. If the prosecution has met its burden, the youth is **adjudicated delinquent**, the juvenile equivalent of being found guilty. In 2004, about two-thirds of petitioned cases resulted in a delinquency adjudication.[93]

Disposition

dispositions
The results or outcome for those juveniles adjudicated delinquent.

Adults who are found guilty are given sentences and often a sentencing hearing. Once again, the terminology differs for juvenile court: those adjudicated delinquent are given **dispositions**, often at a disposition hearing. Before the hearing, a probation officer prepares a predisposition investigation report that outlines the juvenile's personal and family history. The probation officer may be present during the hearing along with a defense attorney (and perhaps a prosecutor), the child, the parents, social workers, and other interested parties.

Juvenile court judges have broad discretion over a wide variety of dispositions. The most common disposition, however, is probation. Other alternatives include private treatment centers, group homes, foster homes, shelters, boot camps, wilderness camps, and state-run training schools or secure facilities. Juveniles may be ordered to pay fines or restitution or to do community service.

Until the 1970s, instead of being given sentences of a fixed length as adults receive, juveniles were given indeterminate commitments. Their dispositions would continue as long it took to "cure" them of whatever problems led them to crime. Rather than being proportionate to the severity of the offense, the length of time juveniles spent as wards of the juvenile system was determined by the complexity of their problems and how well they responded to treatment. As a result, youths could be incarcerated significantly longer than adults who had committed the same offense. Gerry Gault, who would have spent nearly 6 years in a reform school for making lewd phone calls, is a good example. In recent years, however, many states have been making juvenile dispositions of fixed length and in proportion to the seriousness of the crime. Other states still use indeterminate commitments but limit them to the maximum time an adult could serve for the same crime.[94]

Sealing and Expunging Juvenile Records

Labeling theory states that if a person is stuck with a negative label, such as "criminal" or "delinquent," that label will negatively affect the person's future behavior.[95] For this reason, juvenile hearings are usually closed to the public. The media may be prohibited from publishing the names of juvenile offenders, and when court decisions about juveniles are published, the decisions often replace the juveniles' names with initials.

In addition, juvenile records may sometimes be sealed or expunged. When a juvenile record such as an arrest, court, or probation record is **sealed**, most people will be denied access to it, and the person who committed the offense can claim to have no criminal record. When a record is **expunged**, it may be destroyed entirely, or it may be accessible only by court order.

sealed
A juvenile record that is made inaccessible.

expunged
A process in which a court record is destroyed or made legally unavailable.

MYTH/REALITY

MYTH: All juvenile records are automatically erased when the person becomes an adult.

REALITY: Although some juvenile records may be sealed or expunged, the process is rarely automatic. Even sealed and expunged records may still remain available under some circumstances.

The laws concerning sealing and expunging juvenile records vary greatly by jurisdiction and may be available only for certain offenses, after a certain amount of time has passed, or if certain conditions are met (for instance, the offender has not been arrested since that offense). Some jurisdictions prohibit sealing or expunging offenses, sometimes for some crimes and sometimes for all offenses. In most jurisdictions, the sealing and expunging are not automatic; the offender must go through a particular process, and usually only after reaching adulthood.

Just because a record is sealed or expunged does not mean it disappears. For example, a state may seal its own records, but related records may remain in private or federal databases. Some law enforcement agencies may still have access to sealed or expunged records.

JUVENILE CORRECTIONS

Before the *Gault* decision, when establishing due process rights, juvenile courts took into account not only the offense but also such factors as school performance, family functioning, addiction problems, attitude, and prior history in order to serve the best interests of minors. Following *Gault*, juvenile courts became increasingly adversarial, legalistic, and less oriented toward social welfare.[96] Some states, such as Washington, took a step away from the original juvenile court philosophy and adopted sentencing guidelines that identified specific dispositions for specific offenses, regardless of the juvenile's social history.[97] Individualized rehabilitation programs and specified treatment plans lost importance. Although probation was still the most common sanction, incarceration became increasingly popular, especially with the media and the public.[98]

▲ **Juvenile Corrections Facility**

There are a variety of kinds of juvenile corrections facilities.

Incarceration

MYTH/REALITY

MYTH: Everyone locked up in juvenile institutions is, in fact, a juvenile.

REALITY: Juvenile correctional jurisdiction often extends into young adulthood; many people in juvenile institutions are actually in their early 20s.[99]

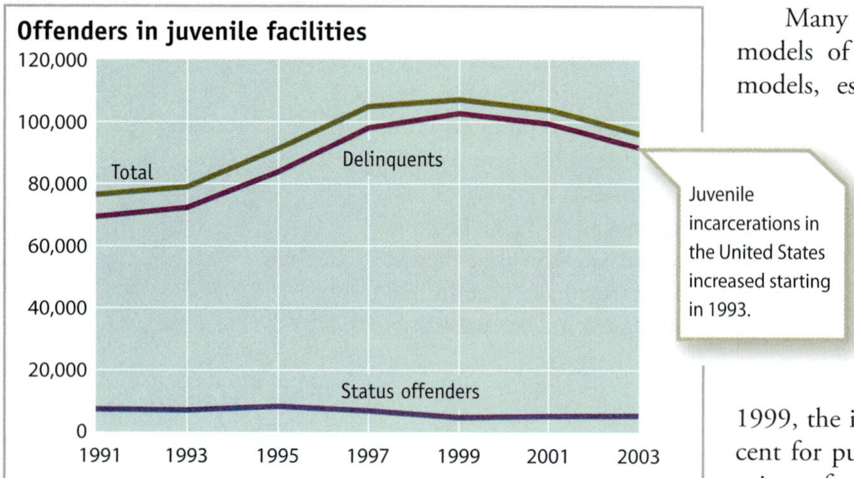

FIGURE 15-6 Juvenile Offenders in Residential Placement Facilities, 1991–2003

SOURCE: Howard N. Snyder and Melissa Sickmund, *Juvenile Offenders and Victims: 2006 National Report* (Washington, DC: U.S. Department of Justice, March 27, 2006), chap. 7, p. 199.

Many jurisdictions have moved from rehabilitation models of delinquency to more punishment-oriented models, especially for juveniles convicted of violent offenses. Juvenile court critics argue that punishment of juveniles must be longer and more severe.[100] In response, many states have implemented tough-on-crime policies including waivers that send juveniles to adult court and increased the use of incarceration. Figure 15-6 shows the increase in the numbers of juveniles in custody. Even with the decline after 1999, the increase between 1991 and 2003 was 36 percent for public facilities and 32 percent for public and private facilities combined.[101] Many people currently confined in juvenile correctional facilities are not children at all but young adults who are serving a term they began as a juvenile. In 2007, for example, the average age of wards within the California Department of Corrections and Rehabilitation's Juvenile Justice Division was 19.5 years.[102]

Blacks are disproportionately represented in juvenile correctional institutions. Figure 15-7 shows the rate of juveniles in custody by race for the year 2003.

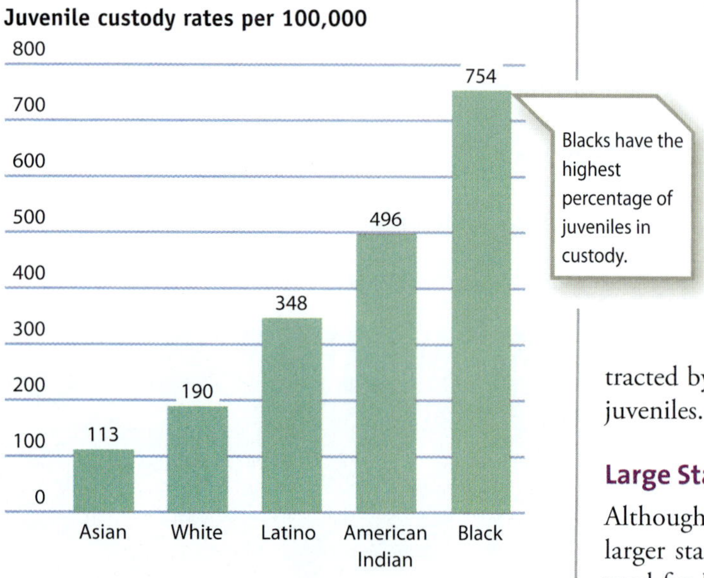

FIGURE 15-7 Juvenile Custody Rates (per 100,000), by Race, 2003

SOURCE: Howard N. Snyder and Melissa Sickmund, *Juvenile Offenders and Victims: 2006 National Report* (Washington, DC: U.S. Department of Justice, March 27, 2006), chap. 7, p. 213.

Types of Juvenile Correction Facilities

A juvenile court judge who believes a juvenile must be removed from home and placed in a correctional facility often has a choice between a community-based program or a larger custodial facility. Short-term detention facilities tend to be locally operated; long-term facilities are mostly run by the states. Group homes are mostly private but may be contracted by local, state, and federal agencies to provide services for juveniles.

Large State-Run Facilities

Although there are more local facilities in the United States, the larger state-run facilities house the majority of juveniles and are used for longer incarcerations.[103] They tend to be secure institutions, with locked gates and fences or razor-wire walls. Many state-operated facilities have treatment programs for drug abuse and education.

The larger juvenile facilities have been accused of gross mistreatment and abuse of youth, committed sometimes by inmates but mostly by staff.[104] Many social structures and interactions of male inmates are based on the power one inmate has over another and on physical attacks, coercion, and sexual exploitation.[105] Physical and sexual abuse of juveniles by staff in state custodial institutions has been well documented, largely because of the media attention that lawsuits and scandals generate. The sexual misconduct of staff against youth was reported at a rate of 11 percent for state institutions as opposed to a rate of 3 percent for local and private facilities.[106] Because people assume that state institutions might be safer than local ones, these statistics are troubling.

On April 10, 2007, the top two officials of the state juvenile facility in Texas were charged with having sexual contact with some of the juveniles under their care and control.[107] The investigation that followed uncovered a series of scandals and cover-ups at the institution and resulted in the firing of the entire Texas Youth Board.[108] Human Rights Watch and the American Civil Liberties Union issued a joint report in September 2006 indicating that young women were being neglected and abused in New York City's juvenile institutions. The report also charged that 56 percent of the reported incidence of sexual violence was staff-on-youth abuse.[109]

In adult correctional facilities, most of the abuse that occurs is inmate against inmate, whereas in juvenile facilities, the majority of abuse is perpetrated by staff members against the juveniles. The mistreatment of juveniles in custodial correctional facilities is not limited to the United States but rather seems rooted in the nature of total institutions themselves.

Real Careers

ERICA KNUTSEN

Work location: Austin, TX

College(s): University of Florida in Gainesville, 2006; University of Pennsylvania, 2007

Major(s): Criminology (B.A.); Criminal Justice (MS)

Job title: Policy Writer, Department of Policy and Accreditation, Texas Youth Commission

Salary range for job like this: $35,000–$42,000

Time in job: 2 years

Work Responsibilities

I am a Policy Writer for the Texas Youth Commission (TYC), which is the state's juvenile corrections agency. My primary function is to develop and maintain agency policies, procedures, and forms. I also post new policies online and transmit them agency-wide to staff and volunteers, maintain policy history, and serve as the agency's liaison with the *Texas Register*, the newspaper of record.

New leadership at TYC has made significant changes to improve the services provided to the youth in its care. As a result, during the past year I have been very busy writing case management standards and treatment policies.

Why Criminal Justice?

I originally decided to major in criminal justice because I wanted to be a special agent for the FBI. However, after taking several courses, I began considering a career in juvenile justice. I did not know much about possible careers in this field, so I sought relevant work experience. First, I interned at Project Payback, a restorative justice and restitution program housed within the Victim Services Division of the State Attorney's Office in Gainesville, Florida. My favorite aspect of this job was teaching juveniles the necessary skills for obtaining and maintaining a job.

In addition to the internship, I also worked part-time as a project assistant for the Florida Network of Victim Witness Services (FNVWS), which provides support and technical assistance for advocates in the emerging fields of victim assistance and witness management. My work in this job made me realize how recently the rights of crime victims have been established in the criminal justice system. With this experience, coupled with the experience that I've gained as a policy writer at the Texas Youth Commission, I hope to one day work in juvenile victim services.

Expectations and Realities of the Job

My understanding of the juvenile justice system has changed after working in both the Florida and Texas systems. I had expected the system to focus primarily on rehabilitation, but I have found a balance between services rendered and jail sentencing. But policies are always evolving, and in my current role as policy writer, I regularly work with local and state government officials. I have been glad to see that the treatment of youth in the criminal justice system is a concern for lawmakers.

My Advice to Students

First, be proactive in your job hunt. Contact employers, and if you do not hear from them, call them back and inquire about your application. Consider a broad range of opportunities. The glory of criminal justice is that it is such a broad field, and a connection with a government official, or even a psychologist, can sometimes yield a career possibility. Finally, consider graduate school. While many careers in criminal justice do not require a master's degree, having one can certainly strengthen any resume. If you decide to apply to graduate school, make sure to take a statistics course, a prerequisite for many programs.

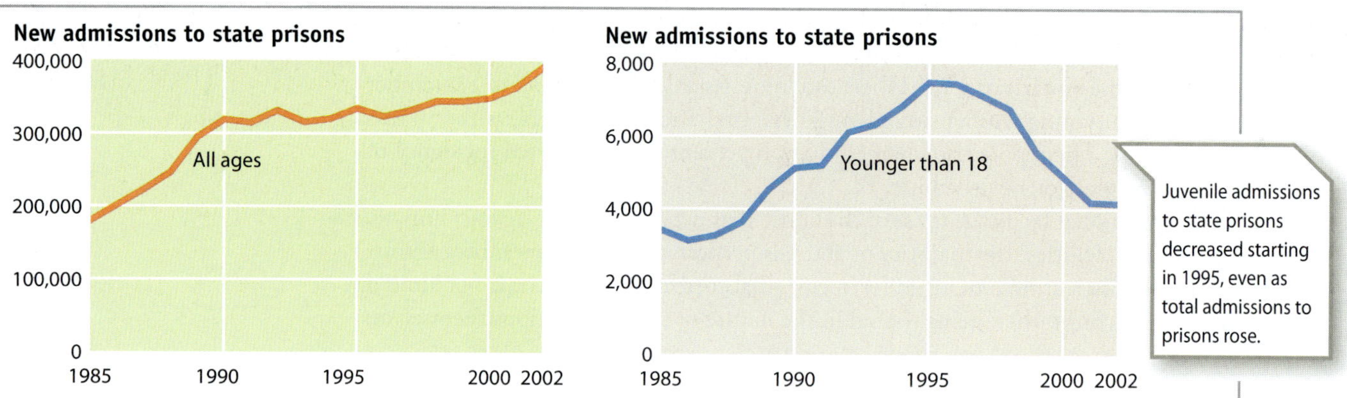

FIGURE 15-8 New Admissions to State Prisons, 1985–2002

SOURCE: Howard N. Snyder and Melissa Sickmund, *Juvenile Offenders and Victims: 2006 National Report* (Washington, DC: U.S. Department of Justice, March 27, 2006), chap. 7, p. 238.

As the Stanford Prison Experiment illustrates (see Chapter 12), institutions tend to bring out the worst in the keepers and the kept. A study in Israel found that victimization and violence by peers and by staff was commonplace in juvenile correctional facilities.[110]

Juveniles in Adult Prisons

Juveniles housed with adult prisoners can easily be victimized by adults. Victimization takes the form of stealing property and physical and sexual assaults.[111] These juveniles also are prone to recidivism. A study comparing 15- and 16-year-olds who were sentenced in adult court with those who were sentenced in juvenile court showed that the juveniles tried as adults reoffended and were reincarcerated at rates higher than those tried in juvenile court. Furthermore, there is reason to believe that juveniles who receive adult sentences experience greater stigma that can interfere with future work options.[112]

Between 1996 and 2002, the number of new admissions of persons under the age of 18 to state prisons decreased, while total admissions rose (see Figure 15-8).[113] This decrease in admissions mirrors the decrease in juvenile arrests discussed earlier (see Figure 15-1, page 432), underscoring the view that juvenile offenses have been declining since 1996.

There is a large racial disparity among the youths admitted to state prisons, as Figure 15-9 shows. Black youths admitted to prison outnumber all other racial groups. They are incarcerated in numbers out of proportion to their population in the general community.

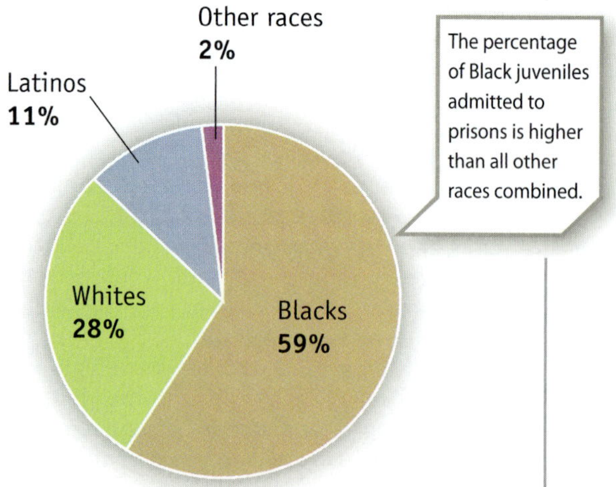

FIGURE 15-9 Race of Youth Admitted to Prison, 2002

SOURCE: Howard N. Snyder and Melissa Sickmund, *Juvenile Offenders and Victims: 2006 National Report* (Washington, DC: U.S. Department of Justice, March 27, 2006), chap. 7, p. 238.

Group Homes

A minor who does not need a secure custodial setting but cannot return home could be placed in a group home. Small community programs such as group homes have a significant advantage in that they allow the juvenile to live in the community, attend school, and take advantage of resources there. Research shows that combining services such as medical treatment and job training with good aftercare and reintegration services offers the juvenile offender the best chance of reducing postrelease arrests.[114]

▼ Juveniles in Group Counseling

Group counseling is common in juvenile corrections facilities.

Institutions for Female Juveniles

The first correctional facility for female juveniles was founded in Lancaster, Massachusetts, in 1856. Its emphasis on domestic work such as sewing and house-cleaning continues in many schools for females to the present day. Like adult female inmates, juvenile female inmates develop subcultures, called pseudo families, to cope with the stress and difficulties of confinement. The pseudo families provide incarcerated young women with a sense of affection and belonging and mimic the roles parents, spouses, siblings, and children play in the wider community.[115]

Although the number of juvenile female offenders is far below that of males, incarceration of female juveniles is increasing at a higher rate than for young males (see Figure 15-10).[116]

Alternatives to Incarceration

Probation

Most juvenile offenders are not incarcerated. The most common disposition is probation. Figure 15-11 shows the disposition of delinquency cases between 1985 and 2004, with probation clearly the most common sanction.

Juvenile courts order probation in almost 50 percent of the cases they hear.[117] A juvenile on probation is usually required to report to a probation officer at regular intervals and attend school and may be required to attend a specific program such as counseling or other treatment. The probation officer is responsible for supervising the juvenile and reporting any new violations to the court. Violations or new offenses can revoke probation and send the juvenile back to court on new charges. Probation officers also help the juvenile solve the problems that got her into trouble in the first place.

Probation officers act as both enforcer and social worker at the same time. But because probation caseloads in many jurisdictions are high, officers seldom are able to offer more than occasional guidance. Recidivism for juveniles on probation ranges from 40 percent to 70 percent.[118] Noninstitutional programs such as intensive supervision probation (ISP) use probation officers who closely monitor juveniles, especially those at high risk of recidivism. ISP might be coupled with regular or random drug testing. (See Chapter 13 for a discussion of ISP.)

Fines and restitution are usually conditions of probation, and the court orders the juvenile to make payments to the victim or the court, or requires the juvenile to work in some community project for a length of time.[119]

Female offenders in juvenile facilities

> The rate of female juveniles in custody is rising.

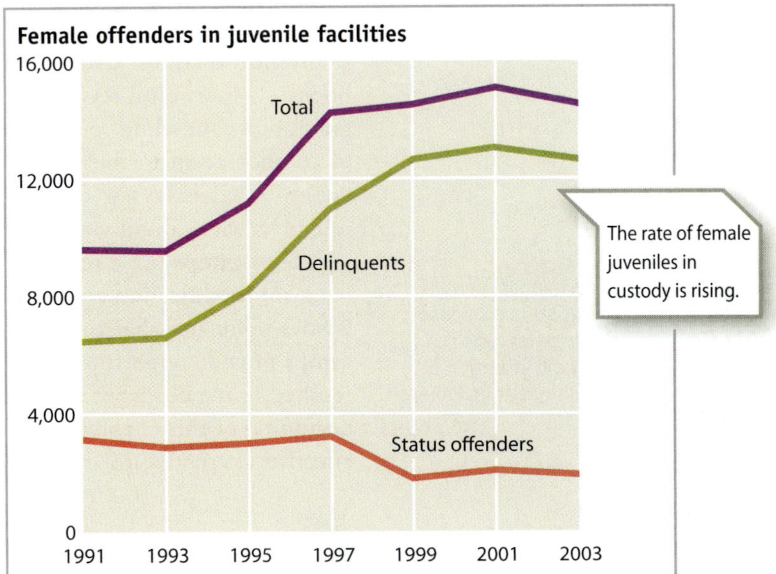

FIGURE 15-10 Female Juvenile Offenders in Custody, 1991–2003

SOURCE: Howard N. Snyder and Melissa Sickmund, *Juvenile Offenders and Victims: 2006 National Report* (Washington, DC: U.S. Department of Justice, March 27, 2006), chap. 7, p. 206.

Disposition of delinquency cases

> Juvenile probation is the most common sentence by the juvenile courts in the United States.

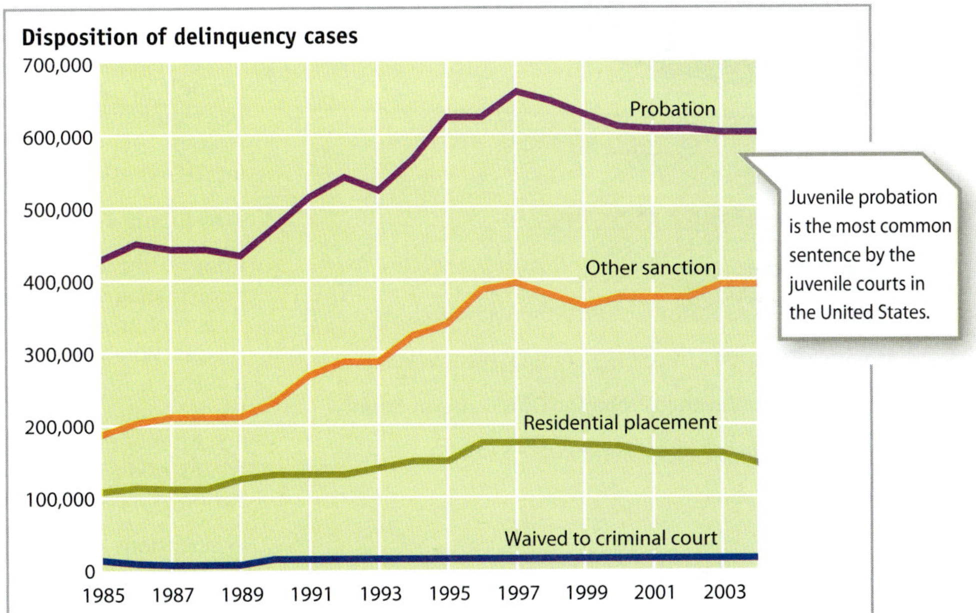

FIGURE 15-11 Disposition of Delinquency Cases, 1985–2003

SOURCE: Office of Juvenile Justice and Delinquency Prevention, *Statistical Briefing Book* (Washington, DC: Office of Juvenile Justice and Delinquency Prevention, 2007).

Other Programs

Many jurisdictions divert first-time offenders—especially those arrested for petty offenses—to a youth service bureau, a community-based agency, a school or church program, or a counseling center. Sometimes they just dismiss the case, often with some form of compensation to the victim or a mediation agreement between the juvenile and the victim. A Global View describes an alternative program in Denmark for juvenile male offenders who exhibit violent behavior, criminality, or drug abuse.

boot camps
Facilities that use a model of military basic training, strict discipline, rigid rules, and behavior modification to command the attention of out-of-control delinquent juveniles.

Boot camps use a model of military basic training, strict discipline, rigid rules, and behavior modification to command the attention of out-of-control delinquent juveniles. Critics point out that camps are only as good as the officers who operate them. These camps provide opportunities for physical abuse and injuries, and they have occasionally resulted in the deaths of juveniles, as in the case of Martin Lee Anderson discussed at the beginning of this chapter. Although boot camps are popular with the public and a cost-effective alternative to incarceration, studies have shown they are no more effective in

Real Careers

JULIA MARTINEZ MORRIS

Work location: San Antonio, TX

College(s): Texas State University–San Marcos (2005, 2007)

Major(s): Criminal Justice (BS); Criminal Justice (MS)

Job title: Senior Juvenile Probation Officer, Bexar County

Salary range for job like this: $30,000-$36,000

Time in job: 2 years

Work Responsibilities

I supervise 15 to 18 juveniles in the community on Intensive Supervision Probation and Intensive Community Based Probation. I maintain 5 to 7 face-to-face contacts with each juvenile per month through office, home, and school visits. I am responsible for making sure that juveniles adhere to the conditions of their probation. When juveniles violate a condition of probation, I refer them for additional services or submit a Motion to Modify Disposition to the Juvenile Court. After several violations, I can place the juvenile at the detention center.

During the court process I act as a representative for the Department of Juvenile Justice and make a recommendation to the court during the juvenile's disposition hearing. Recommendations include continued probation, probation with specialized programs, placement at a short or long term residential facility, or commitment to the Texas Youth Commission (for felony offenders only).

I typically work 40 to 50 hours a week, which includes detention visits, detention hearings, office visits, drug tests, home visits, curfew checks, and school visits. I can receive phone calls 24 hours a day regarding a juvenile. I often receive phone calls from parents reporting that their child missed curfew and sometimes from the Detention Center Intake reporting that a probationer was arrested.

Why Criminal Justice?

I started at a junior college and was interested in restaurant/hotel management. A peer who told me about a field trip his class took to a prison stirred my interest in Criminal Justice classes. When I transferred to Texas State University I took a Juvenile Justice class in which juveniles from the Texas Youth Commission in Giddings, Texas were guest speakers. After I heard these juveniles talk about their past, their crimes, and their rehabilitation I knew I wanted to be a probation officer.

Expectations and Realities of the Job

I have learned that you do not go into Criminal Justice for the money. There is job security, good benefits, and you can make a living but, you can sometimes feel overwhelmed, overworked, and underpaid. However, I get job satisfaction when one of my juveniles completes his or her probation. I had to wait a while for this to happen, but it makes it all worthwhile.

My Advice to Students

Be a team player. We have to assist when someone is away or needs to detain a juvenile or requires a partner for home visits. If you try and do a job in criminal justice alone you will burn out. You need the help and support of your coworkers. If you are a team player you will have people assisting you every step of your career.

A Global View

Ny Start: An Alternative to Incarceration in Denmark

The United States is not the only country that uses alternatives to incarceration for juvenile offenders. But what makes the Ny Start ("new start") program in Denmark different is that it targets persistent adolescent male offenders ages 12–18 who demonstrate aggressive and violent behavior, a pattern of criminality, or substance abuse. The 2-year treatment program has four phases:

Contact phase: The aim of the first week is to establish contact with the adolescents, to motivate them and their parents to become involved, and to obtain their agreement to participate.

Motivational phase: The aim of weeks 2 and 3 is to establish the group cohort. A 24-hour stay away from familiar surroundings enables the instructors and the young men to get to know each other. Each instructor has overall responsibility for three or four adolescents and will work with them for the full two years.

Social skills training phase: During weeks 4 through 20, for three days a week the participants learn to see themselves from past, present, and future perspectives and develop tools to enable them to function with their families, schools, and peers. Twenty-five scripted lessons cover management of problems and emotions as well as communication and assertiveness. Nineteen more lessons consist of "reality visits" to interesting occupation sites that enable the young men to talk to people who work in the real world. They are also exposed to other cultural and physical experiences to provide contact with other adolescents who have positive goals in their lives.

Reintegration phase: In the remaining 1½ years, each participant follows a personal target plan, developed at the end of the third phase, to use and develop his newfound skills in a realistic social world, with the support of parents and program instructors. Emphasis is on education, work, and constructive use of leisure time.

Ny Start was piloted for two years in four Danish municipalities with 21 offenders. Only one did not complete the program. Two-thirds of the participants showed diminished aggression, minimal substance abuse, cessation of criminality, appropriate social behavior, and markedly decreased problems with family, school, and peers. No positive changes occurred in a control group that was not treated. Parental involvement, other support, and the low ratio of instructors to offenders were key to the positive effects of this program.

Even though there are social and cultural differences between Denmark and the United States, Ny Start's promising results suggest we can learn much from other countries' practices when exploring ways to reduce delinquency.

Observe Investigate Understand

- **Which phase of the Ny Start program do you think is most crucial for its success? State your reasons.**
- **Describe some "reality visits" (other than vocational sites) that you think would be helpful for participants in this type of program.**
- **Would a program similar to Ny Start work with violent juvenile offenders in the United States? Why or why not?**

SOURCE: Gemma Buckland and Alex Stevens, *Review of Effective Practice with Young Offenders in Mainland Europe* (University of Kent at Canterbury: European Institute of Social Services, March 2001), 20–21.

reducing recidivism than traditional programs.[120] It seems better aftercare is needed if they are to be effective in reducing recidivism.[121]

Day treatment facilities (sometimes called day reporting centers) provide noninstitutional sanctions that are structured and community-based such as recreation, counseling, scholastic programs, and other activities, often after school. Structured activities with positive adult role models provide a stable environment that is lacking in the homes of many troubled juveniles. Some centers allow probation officers to monitor large numbers of juveniles efficiently.[122] Day treatment centers offer many of the same programs but are less expensive than residential facilities and have met with success in various jurisdictions.[123]

VICTIMIZATION AND VICTIM SUPPORT SERVICES

Juveniles are not just perpetrators of crime in the United States; they are often victims. A majority of crimes against juveniles ages 12–17 are not reported to the police or to other authorities. Even when the crimes are serious or involve weapons or injury, they are less

What about the Victim?

Consequences of Child Victimization

Teenagers are more than twice as likely as adults to be victims of violent crime. Homicide is the third leading cause of death among children under 12, and the fourth leading cause of death among teenagers. In general, younger children tend to be victimized by parents or other family members, whereas older teens tend to be victimized by other young people.

Violence against children is troubling, not only because of its immediate effects on the young victims but also because of the lingering effects of the trauma. One unsettling aftereffect is an increased suicide rate in juvenile victims. Rates of teen suicide are shockingly high: suicide is the third leading cause of death among teenagers. A recent study concluded that girls who were physically attacked by someone they dated are at increased risk of attempting suicide. Boys who were sexually assaulted were four times as likely as other boys to attempt suicide. Nearly 1 in 10 youths in this study had attempted suicide within the past year.

Children who are victims of crime are also at increased risk of committing offenses themselves. Ample research demonstrates that children abused or neglected by their parents are more likely than other children to become delinquent, and at earlier ages. Child victims of sexual abuse are more likely to later molest children, and most young people who kill have histories of serious abuse. Even witnessing violence can have an adverse effect on children. A recent study suggested children who see domestic abuse occur between their parents are more likely to bully other children.

All this research indicates how important it is to pay close attention to young victims of crime. Society seems increasingly eager to view children who engage in dangerous and illegal behavior as criminals instead of as victims of failures on the part of their families, the criminal justice system, and the child welfare system.

Observe Investigate Understand

- **Why do you think young victims of violent crime are so prone to attempt suicide?**
- **Would teenage crime victims in college be less vulnerable to suicidal tendencies than teenage victims in high school? Why or why not?**
- **Because the juvenile offender is often the product of childhood abuse, what steps should the criminal justice system take to deliver a fair and just verdict in such cases?**

SOURCES: Howard N. Snyder and Melissa Sickmund, *Juvenile Offenders and Victims: 2006 National Report, 7: Delinquency Prevention* (Washington, DC: Office of Juvenile Justice, 2006); Elyse Olshen, Katharine H. McVeigh, Robin A. Wunsch-Hitzig, and Vaughn I. Rickert, "Dating Violence, Sexual Assault, and Suicide Attempts among Urban Teenagers," *Archives of Pediatric and Adolescent Medicine* 161 (2007): 539–545; Joseph P. Ryan, "Dependent Youth in Juvenile Justice: Do Positive Peer Culture Programs Work for Victims of Child Maltreatment?" *Research on Social Work Practice* 16 (2006): 511–519; A. Scott Aylwin, Lea H. Studer, John R. Reddon, and Steven R. Clelland, "Abuse Prevalence and Victim Gender among Adult and Adolescent Child Molesters," *International Journal of Law & Psychiatry* 26 (2003): 179–190; Dorothy Van Soest, Hyun-Sun Park, and Toni K. Johnson, "Different Paths to Death Row: A Comparison of Men Who Committed Heinous and Less Heinous Crimes," *Violence & Victims* 18 (2003): 15–33; Carol Anne Davis, *Children Who Kill: Profiles of Pre-Teen and Teenage Killers* (London: Allison & Busby, 2003); Anna C. Baldry, "Bullying in Schools and Exposure to Domestic Violence," *Child Abuse & Neglect* 27 (2003): 713–732.

likely to be reported than if they had happened to an adult.[124] The different ways teens are affected by crime and violence are illustrated in What about the Victim?

The good news is that the victimization of juveniles declined between 1993 and 2003 for all types of crimes and among all racial groups.[125] Nonetheless, we can distinguish victimization patterns among juveniles. From 1993 to 2003, an African American juvenile was five times more likely to be the victim of a homicide than a White juvenile. Juvenile males were four and a half times more likely to be homicide victims than juvenile females.[126] Although males are more often victimized in violent crimes than females, females are six times more likely to be victims of rape or sexual assault. Younger juveniles have a greater chance of being victimized than older juveniles; African Americans are more likely to be victimized than Whites, but Latino and non-Latino juveniles have about the same likelihood of being victimized.[127]

◀ Adult Male Talking to Juvenile and His Mother

Probation officers and counselors often need to deal with both the juvenile and a parent.

Victim advocates within the juvenile justice system have established several types of laws to safeguard young people. Some services assist those already victimized; other services detect situations in which young people might find themselves vulnerable to victimization.

Child Protective Services

One way the justice system deals with young victims of crime is through **Child Protective Services (CPS)**, a county-level government organization in all 50 states whose trained staff investigates allegations of child abuse and neglect. It operates a 24-hour, 7-days-a-week hotline to receive anonymous calls. If CPS does not determine the child is at risk, the case will remain open, usually for 1 year. If there are no further calls of suspected abuse, the case will then be closed, but all cases can be reopened if necessary.

If CPS confirms abuse and neglect, the agency has several options. It can remove the child from the home and place him in foster care or with extended family members such as grandparents, older siblings, an aunt, or an uncle. CPS works to strengthen family bonds by mandating attendance at anger management, substance abuse, and parenting skill classes, as a preventive tool either before a child is removed or before family–child reunification can take place. After relocating a child, CPS continues its investigation, monitors the child's adjustment to the new home, and secures counseling, academic assistance, or other services. The agency determines when it is safe for the child to be reunited with the family, or whether a permanent placement outside of the home is needed instead. CPS staff members also prepare court reports and initiate criminal proceedings on behalf of the child. Finally, CPS trains foster parents and acts as an adoption agency to help them adopt foster children.

Mandatory Reporting Laws

Many professionals in the course of their work come in contact with young people who show signs of being victimized. A **mandatory reporting law** requires any professional who has regular contact with a child to report any reasonable suspicion of physical or sexual abuse or neglect to the proper law enforcement or protective services. The professionals required to report such suspicions include health care practitioners, law enforcement officers, school personnel, day care providers, spiritual leaders, social workers, mental health care practitioners, medical examiners and coroners, clergy, and lawyers. A mandated professional who fails to report an allegation of abuse or neglect is subject to sanctions outlined by state laws, such as civil penalties or loss of license. If no abuse or neglect is found, the person who reports it is immune from liability if he acted in good faith or had a reasonable suspicion of abuse.

The national mandatory reporting law was part of the Child Abuse Prevention and Treatment Act (CAPTA) of 1974 and has since been amended several times. In the late 1990s, all 50 states extended mandatory reporting requirements to include older and dependent adults because of their vulnerability to abuse and neglect.[128]

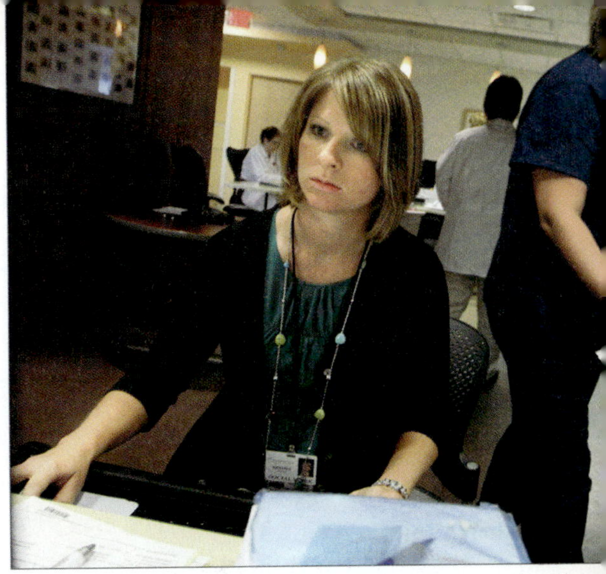

RealCrime Tech

COMPUTERS ARE DECIDING IF PARENTS WILL KEEP THEIR CHILDREN

Several counties in California are now using a computer program to help social workers make a decision about removing a neglected or abused child from a parent. The program, called structured decision making (SDM), helps child welfare workers assess the risks to children of remaining in the home or being returned to their home. The computer uses research-based information to determine the likelihood of future mistreatment. A Michigan study showed that using SDM allowed 40 percent fewer children to be removed from their homes, and 42 percent fewer children required medical assistance.

Since the removal and return of children is such an emotional issue, some workers seem to welcome the objective scoring of the computer to back up or help them with these difficult, sometimes traumatic, decisions. Intuition may indeed be helped by solidly based statistics showing the likelihood of a child being further abused.

SOURCES: Garrett Therolf, "How Computers Call the Shots for L.A. County Children in Peril," *Los Angeles Times*, March 9, 2009, www.latimes.com/news/local/la-me-childabuse8-2009mar08,0,753306,full.story (retrieved March 21, 2009); Department of Social Services, "Structured Decision Making," 2007, www.childsworld.ca.gov/PG1332.htm (retrieved March 21, 2009).

Court Appointed Special Advocates

A **Court Appointed Special Advocate (CASA)** is a volunteer selected by the courts to protect the rights and interests of child victims of abuse, neglect, or abandonment. Without CASAs, child victims might get lost in the large and often overburdened judicial and welfare systems. The appointment is normally for 2 years. During this time,

Child Protective Services
County-level government organizations in all 50 states whose trained staff investigates allegations of child abuse and neglect.

mandatory reporting law
Requires that professionals who have regular contact with a child report any reasonable suspicions of physical or sexual abuse or neglect to the proper law enforcement or protective services.

Court Appointed Special Advocate (CASA)
A volunteer selected by the courts to protect the rights and interests of child victims of abuse.

the volunteer visits the child at home, school, or other locations such as a day care facility, the public library, or a relative's home to talk with the child and determine what services the child needs to excel at home, in school, and in the community. The CASA volunteer contacts Child Protective Services (CPS) if there is a suspicion of abuse, if the child has to be removed from home, or if service referrals are needed. CASA volunteers are trained to speak on behalf of the child in all court proceedings.

SUMMARY

Juvenile justice was created as a way to deal informally with troubled and delinquent children. The original intent was rehabilitation rather than punishment, with the state or local authority acting as *parens patriae,* especially when the real parents were absent or abusive. But as the system grew and overwhelmed the judges, as due process rights granted to juveniles "legalized" the process of justice, and as public opinion backed "tough on crime" policies, the system became more formalized. It took on more and more aspects of the adult criminal justice process, with some juveniles even being tried in adult courts.

Most people agree that juvenile justice has yet to live up to its promise. There are, however, glimmers of hope. Many jurisdictions have implemented plans such as youth mentoring, teen courts, youth drug courts, and restorative justice programs, which may successfully prevent young people from offending or reoffending. What seems to work best are programs that best fit the original goals of the juvenile justice system: they are small; they are tailored to each youth's individual needs; they address the complexity of a youth's problems, rather than simplistically trying to fix one or two issues; they focus on offenders' successful reentry into the community; and they provide the opportunity for youthful offenders to achieve something meaningful.

OBSERVE Investigate Understand

Review

Describe the early treatment of youthful offenders.

- Until the nineteenth century, young offenders were usually treated the same as adults.
- The infancy defense prohibited prosecution of people under age 7.
- Delinquents in England could be bound out, placed in institutions, or sent to America.
- The first U.S. institution for juveniles opened in 1825.
- By the middle of the nineteenth century, many jurisdictions had created reform schools for wayward youths.

Analyze current juvenile crime rates and trends.

- Arrests are dropping, but the proportion of female arrests is rising.
- Arrest rates for Blacks are dropping faster than the average, but Blacks are still disproportionately represented.

Evaluate the philosophy behind the creation of juvenile courts.

- Special courts were created for youths because they were less culpable than adults and more likely to be rehabilitated.
- Juvenile courts were intended to treat delinquency rather than punish it.

- Juvenile courts were intended to be less formal than adult courts.
- The legal doctrine that supports juvenile courts is *parens patriae.*

Describe the breadth and limitations of juvenile court jurisdiction.

- Juvenile court jurisdiction is defined by age and behavior.
- Juvenile courts have the power to hear both delinquency and status offense cases as well as dependency cases.
- Certain actors in the juvenile justice system can choose to waive jurisdiction over juveniles and send them to adult courts.

Compare and contrast the constitutional rights of youthful offenders and adults.

- Juveniles' due process rights are more limited than adults' rights.
- Juveniles, like adults, have the right to an attorney, to be found guilty beyond a reasonable doubt, and to appeal.
- Juveniles do not have the right to a jury.
- Juveniles have no special rights regarding interrogation.
- Schoolchildren have limited Fourth Amendment rights (search and seizure).

Characterize the types of juvenile correctional facilities in the United States.

- Incarceration of juveniles is dropping.
- Community settings work better than large institutions in treating delinquents.
- Large juvenile institutions are prone to abuse of juveniles by both staff and inmates.
- Alternatives to incarceration include group homes, boot camps, and day treatment centers, all with varying degrees of success.

Analyze victimization of juveniles and the services to support them.

- Juveniles are often victims of crimes, many of which go unreported.
- Child Protective Services (CPS) investigates child abuse and neglect and decides whether to remove a child from a family setting.
- Mandatory reporting laws require professionals to report signs of child victimization.
- Court Appointed Special Advocates (CASAs) are volunteers who protect the rights and interests of child victims.

Key Terms

Study Questions

1. Approximately when were the first juvenile courts created?
   a. 1550
   b. 1800
   c. 1900
   d. 1950
2. In recent years, violent crime arrests of juveniles in the United States have
   a. increased.
   b. decreased.
   c. increased or decreased depending on the race of the juvenile.
   d. remained the same.
3. Over which of the following cases would a juvenile court typically have jurisdiction?
   a. A 15-year-old accused of stealing a car
   b. A 13-year-old who has not been attending school
   c. A 6-year-old who has been abandoned by her parents
   d. All of the above
4. The *Gault* decision
   a. was decided by the U.S. Supreme Court.
   b. granted juveniles the right to an attorney.
   c. allowed juveniles to confront and cross-examine witnesses.
   d. applies to all of the above.
5. Which of the following will *not* usually be allowed during a juvenile court case?
   a. Assistance from an attorney for the juvenile
   b. A jury
   c. Hearsay evidence
   d. Confrontation and cross-examination of witnesses
6. The juvenile equivalent of a criminal trial is called
   a. a delinquency petition.
   b. detention.
   c. an adjudication hearing.
   d. a disposition hearing.
7. The disposition most commonly used by the juvenile court is
   a. group homes.
   b. treatment facilities.
   c. probation.
   d. residential institutions.
8. An adjudication hearing
   a. is used for an informal decision by the juvenile court.
   b. is the juvenile court equivalent of sentencing in adult court.
   c. determines whether the juvenile has committed the offense.
   d. determines whether the juvenile is fit to be tried by the juvenile court.
9. A juvenile court waiver
   a. is used by the youth to waive the right to bail.
   b. permits a juvenile to be tried as an adult.
   c. permits a youth who is over the age of 18 but younger than 21 to be handled as a juvenile.
   d. is used by the juvenile court to waive extradition.
10. Which statement is correct?
    a. The number of female juveniles in custody is almost as great as the number of male juveniles in custody.
    b. The rate of female juvenile arrests is rising faster than the rate of male juvenile arrests.
    c. There is evidence that female juvenile delinquents are becoming increasingly more violent.
    d. All of the above

Critical Thinking Questions

1. How can we ensure a juvenile justice system that is fair, while still allowing it to achieve its original goals of treatment and rehabilitation?
2. Under what circumstances should a child be held criminally liable in adult court for his behavior?
3. What are likely to be the characteristics of successful juvenile correctional programs? How would these differ from adult programs?

Internet Sites

Office of Juvenile Justice and Delinquency Prevention
http://ojjdp.ncjrs.org/
The OJJDP has a comprehensive collection of reports on juvenile delinquency and juvenile justice, including the most recent statistics.

***Frontline:* "Juvenile Justice"; "When Kids Get Life"**
www.pbs.org/wgbh/pages/frontline/shows/juvenile/
www.pbs.org/wgbh/pages/frontline/whenkidsgetlife/
These two reports explore some recent dilemmas in juvenile justice, including when to try children as adults and whether child offenders should receive life sentences. Statistics and other information on these topics are provided, and you can watch the entire "When Kids Get Life" program online.

Human Rights Watch
www.hrw.org/children/justice.htm
Human Rights Watch provides extensive information on children's rights and juvenile justice around the world.

Suggested Readings

Edward Humes, *No Matter How Loud I Shout* (New York: Simon & Schuster, 1996).
A year's look at the Los Angeles Juvenile Court and the police, judges, attorneys, probation officers, prosecutors, juveniles, and parents connected to it.

Barry Krisberg, *Juvenile Justice: Redeeming Our Children* (Thousand Oaks, CA: Sage, 2005).
This book provides a historical context for and exposes truths about juvenile justice.

Mark Salzman, *True Notebooks: A Writer's Year at Juvenile Hall* (New York: Vintage Books, 2003).
This book describes the experiences of a creative writing teacher working with juveniles incarcerated at Central Juvenile Hall, a Los Angeles County detention facility for high-risk juveniles.

CHAPTER 16

Contemporary Challenges

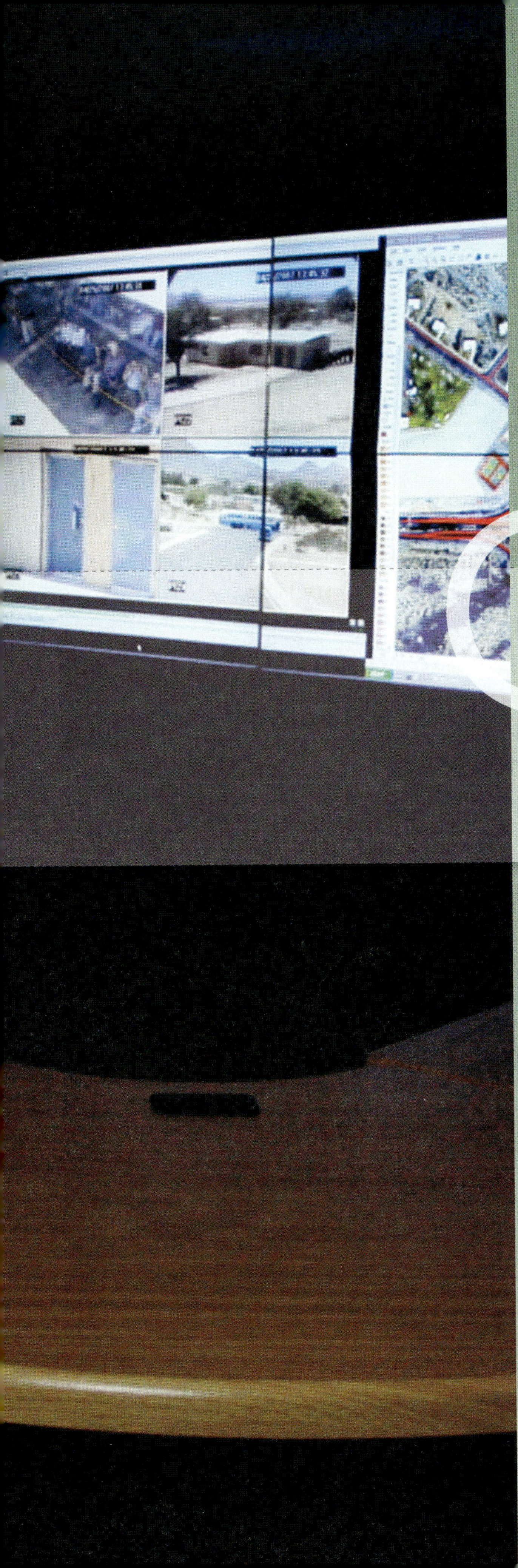

OBSERVE Investigate *Understand*

After reading this chapter, you should be able to:

- Describe the nature and extent of cybercrime, and identify some techniques used to investigate this type of crime.
- Discuss the nature and extent of identity theft, and describe some strategies used to contend with it.
- Explain the interaction between the law and intelligence gathering with regard to terrorism, and discuss some strategies employed to prevent terrorist activities.
- Define hate crime and explain its operation as a penalty enhancer.
- Identify the factors contributing to the emergence of civil disorder and strategies for prevention.
- Analyze the tension between safeguarding civil liberties and infringing on individual rights.
- Identify victimology challenges and treatment regimens for victims with a disability, immigrants, lesbian, gay, bisexual, transgendered, and questioning (LGBTQ) victims, and victims of hate crimes.

Realities and Challenges

The Great Power Blackout of 2003

August 14, 2003, was a typical late summer day in New York City—hot, hazy, and humid. Typical, that is, until shortly after 4:00 p.m. Then, all over the city, lights went out, computer screens blinked and went dark, subway and commuter trains stopped running, air conditioners fell silent, and elevators came to a standstill. Flights into and out of the city's airports were halted, stranding travelers. Passengers stuck in subway cars had to be evacuated through the tunnels, often in total darkness, to subway platforms or to escape hatches in the streets. Workers in high-rise office buildings—the fortunate ones who were not trapped in elevators—made their way down flights of stairs to the street. There they found the streets jammed with cars, buses, and trucks, most of them unable to move because no traffic lights were working. Hundreds of thousands of pedestrians spilled from the sidewalks onto the streets. Hotel lobbies filled with guests unable to use their keycards to enter their rooms.

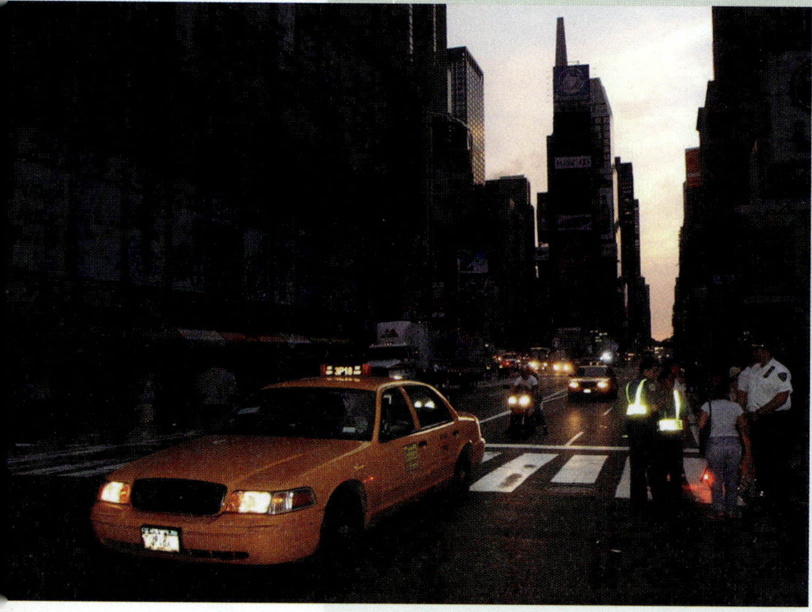

When the blackout enveloped the city, the New York Police Department initiated antiterrorism procedures that had been put in place following the terrorist attacks of September 11, 2001. A special command center was activated, helicopter and harbor fleet patrols were increased, and teams of heavily armed officers were deployed to potential targets, such as the New York Stock Exchange.

Apprehensive New Yorkers wondered—and feared—"was this blackout the result of another terrorist attack on the city?" After all, it had been less than 2 years since the 9/11 attacks. Soon it became apparent that if this blackout was the result of terrorism, New York City was not the only target. Parts of eight states in the Northeast and Midwest and parts of southern Canada, including the city of Toronto, were similarly affected. More than 50 million people felt the blackout's effects.

Fortunately, the blackout of August 2003 was not the result of terrorist activity, but rather the unintentional result of an electrical failure that triggered shutdowns in parts of the nation's power grid. Within 24 hours, power had been restored to most of the affected areas.

Imagine, however, what might have been the effects if terrorists had planned and controlled the blackout, allowing it to continue for days or even indefinitely. With backup generators able to supply only limited power to specific areas, food would spoil, court proceedings would be delayed, and medical treatment postponed. Outlying regions would not receive vital shipments, electronic messaging and document transfers would be halted, and media programming originating in New York would reach its worldwide audience only intermittently via auxiliary power.

If power interruptions were the intended actions of a terrorist or rogue nation-state, restoration likely would be far more difficult. The perpetrators would undoubtedly have calculated a strategy for maximizing the damage to computers and electronic networks that run our vital systems. A coordinated attack on critical infrastructures such as telecommunications, electrical power systems, transportation systems, and financial services could prove disastrous.

This chapter focuses on current and emerging issues in the criminal justice system. Cybercrime, terrorist activities, hate crimes, and certain types of civil disorder, for example, are paving new paths in the detection, investigation, prosecution, and prevention of crime and changing the way criminal justice professionals do their jobs. At the same time, the tension between ensuring public safety and safeguarding individuals' rights heightens, as new law enforcement technologies, methods, and procedures designed to protect the public may infringe on individuals' rights to privacy and other civil liberties. Another growing concern is recognizing the rights and needs of all victims of crime, including—perhaps especially—those whose victimization has been neglected, ignored, or minimized. In the sections that follow, we outline the issues surrounding crimes and victimization that represent new challenges for the criminal justice system.

Preview

FIGHTING CYBERCRIME

Information technology has produced unprecedented advances in productivity and the spread of information, but it has also triggered new forms of criminal behavior. Identity theft and electronic theft of proprietary information (economic espionage) were nonexistent only a few years ago but now account for extraordinary losses.[1]

Cybercrime is any crime that relies on a computer and an electronic network for its commission.[2] It exploits, for illicit purposes, the electronic highway upon which computer transmissions travel. The Internet has become the catalyst for many forms of criminal activity,[3] such as hacking, digital child pornography, identity theft, and online fraud. Even stalking and bullying are perpetrated online.

cybercrime
Any crime that relies on a computer and a network for its commission; crime that exploits the electronic highway over which computer transmissions travel.

Extent of Cybercrime

The extent of cybercrime is significantly underreported. Studies by the Computer Security Institute indicate only about one-third of illegal or unauthorized criminal activity in cyberspace is reported to law enforcement.[4] See What about the Victim? on the next page for a discussion of ways cybercriminals operate and who their victims are.

Detection and Investigation

Traditional investigative strategies do not readily apply to cybercrime, where the offender is often a faceless entity. Internet cafés, open wireless routers, libraries, and a host of other venues allow almost anyone access to the Internet with virtually complete anonymity. The place where the crime occurred is hard to identify: Did the crime occur where the perpetrator's computer is located? Or was the crime site that of the victim's computer, which may be in another state or even another country? Could the location of the Internet server be considered the place where the crime took place? Or was the crime location somewhere in between? Victims and offenders can be on different sides of the world. The new theory of

◀ Computer Forensics Analyst at Work

Computer forensic analysts recover data from electronic devices such as computers, e-mail, BlackBerries, and iPhones, and then give a thorough report on their findings relevant to a case.

What about the Victim?

Sexual Solicitation via the Internet

In June 2006, Katherine, a 16-year-old girl from Gilford, Michigan, met a man on the social network MySpace. The man described himself as a 25-year-old from the city of Jericho on the West Bank of the Palestinian territories. A short time later, Katherine asked her parents for a passport so she could accompany her friend on a family vacation to Canada. With her passport in hand and clothes for two weeks, she left home. She called her mother that day and the next, indicating she was okay and would be home the next day.

After two days, however, Katherine's parents called the police. The FBI tracked Katherine to the airport in Amman, Jordan, where authorities approached her and persuaded her to return home.

A Michigan news show broadcast a telephone interview with the man Katherine met on MySpace. He identified himself as Abdullah, a wealthy 20-year-old businessman who said he wanted to marry Katherine and had sent her money for a plane ticket to visit him.

Young people like Katherine are the victims of a variety of Internet crimes, including solicitations to engage in sexual acts for commercial gain through production and distribution of child pornography or for personal gratification. In 2001, the Crimes Against Children Research Center at the University of New Hampshire conducted a nationwide Youth Internet Safety Survey through telephone interviews with 1,501 youth 10 to 17 years old. Nearly 20 percent had received an unwanted sexual solicitation within the last year; two-thirds of the victims were female. Five percent received sexual solicitations that made them very upset or afraid; of these victims, 37 percent were between ages 10 and 13. Another 3 percent were asked to allow contact or a meeting offline. None of the solicitations resulted in a sexual contact or assault.

Given the anonymity afforded by the Internet, the true identity, age, and gender of the perpetrators may be different from what they told the victims. Victims believed nearly all the perpetrators were strangers and that almost half the solicitations, including the most aggressive, were from juveniles. Two-thirds of all solicitations came from self-described males.

Approximately two-thirds of solicitations occurred in chat rooms; 24 percent were Instant Messages. One-quarter of respondents had received unwanted sexual material, more boys (57 percent) than girls (42 percent). Nearly half of the victims did not tell anyone about the solicitation; of those who did, about a quarter informed a parent.

As access to Internet technologies expands via increased use of wireless and handheld technologies, monitoring Internet communications will become increasingly challenging. Prevention programs that acknowledge normal adolescent interest in romance and sex and provide adolescents with skills to recognize and avoid unwanted communications, rather than messages that emphasize parental control, are needed.

Observe Investigate Understand

- **Why do sexual predators solicit victims via the Internet?**
- **Why did only half the victims tell anyone about the unwanted messages they received?**
- **How can detection and prevention efforts be improved if reporting rates remain low?**

SOURCES: Janis Wolak, David Finkelhor, Kimberly J. Mitchell, and Michele L. Ybarra, "Online 'Predators' and Their Victims: Myths, Realities, and Implications for Prevention and Treatment," *American Psychologist*, 63, no. 2 (2008): 111–128; Associated Press, "Michigan Teen in Seclusion after Overseas MySpace Trip, Lawyer Says," June 13, 2006, www.foxnews.com; Helen Connelly, "Internet Crimes against Children," Office for Victims of Crime, 2001, www.ojp.usdoj.gov/ovc/; David Finkelhor, Kimberly Mitchell, and Janis Wolak, "Highlights of the Youth Internet Safety Survey," U.S. Department of Justice, 2000, www.ojp.usdoj.gov.

"faceless-oriented policing" explains how traditional policing and criminological theories do not apply to cybercrime.[5] To make investigation even more complicated, the laws in most countries, including those in the United States, have not kept up with technology.

computer forensics
Application of the knowledge and methods used in computer science to law enforcement purposes (such as recovery of deleted files or Web site activity).

The complexity of cybercrime demands technologically sophisticated investigative techniques that include computer forensics, collaboration, and training. **Computer forensics** is the application of the knowledge and methods used in computer science to law enforcement. Computer forensic experts are asked, for example, to recover deleted files, locate hidden files, trace Web site activity, and produce a variety of other forms of digital evidence for use in criminal and civil proceedings.[6] One expert estimates that 90 percent of legal evidence exists in computer systems rather than on paper.[7]

Multiple crime activities and locations are commonplace in cybercrime. Within networked environments, evidence may reside on any number of machines using a variety of operating systems, in many different physical or network locations, and in multiple jurisdictions. Yet search and seizure operations must adhere to legal requirements that minimize intrusions into network operations.[8]

Forensic analysis is also used to uncover evidence residing on hard drives and disks to investigate crimes not directly reliant on computers. The infamous "BTK" serial murderer, discussed in A Case in Point, was tripped up through evidence gathered from a church computer he used to compose a note mailed to a Wichita television station.

Prevention Strategies

Like investigation of cybercrime, prevention of cybercrime also requires collaboration among law enforcement, the private sector, and even international agencies. Much cybercrime is **transnational crime**, taking place across national boundaries. In 2008 the FBI detected a worldwide ATM scam that defrauded thousands of individuals via 130 ATMs in 49 cities inside and outside of the United States. The perpetrators used 100 fake ATM cards to access more than $9 million—within a span of 30 minutes.[9] Some cybercrime may be legal in one country, but illegal in another. For example, pornographic material depicting 16-year-olds is illegal in the United States but legal in Iceland and Germany.[10] In 2006, the United States ratified the Council of Europe Convention on Cybercrime, the

transnational crime
Crime orchestrated across a national boundary from where the crime actually occurs.

a Case in Point

Computer Forensics Uncovers a Serial Killer

The "BTK" serial killer terrorized the Wichita, Kansas, region for more than three decades, committing 10 homicides between 1974 and 1991. (BTK, standing for "Bind, Torture, Kill," was the killer's self-proclaimed nickname.) At first he communicated often with news outlets; then he stopped. Around the 30th anniversary of the first killings, however, BTK delivered a flurry of communiqués about his persona and exploits to the media and police. On February 16, 2005, he mailed a computer disk to Wichita's Fox News affiliate. Although the contents of the message disclosed little about the killer, examination by forensic analysts uncovered remnants of a newsletter and the words "Dennis" and "Christ Lutheran Church."

A search of the church's Web site revealed that an individual named Dennis Rader was the church president. Police went to the church to search its computers and found a disk Rader had given the pastor. The disk contained the agenda for an upcoming meeting—and the message BTK had mailed to the Wichita television station. Until this revelation, Dennis Rader had been considered another potential victim of BTK—certainly not a suspect.

The computer forensic evidence, including the use of DNA analysis and video surveillance, was instrumental in focusing the investigation on Rader, who had been married for 30 years and was a father, the president of his church, and a Boy Scout leader. Rader was convicted of the slayings and on August 17, 2005, was sentenced to 10 consecutive life sentences.

Computer forensics has become a crucial investigative tool with a reach as broad as cyberspace. In other cases, investigators using computer forensics have traced a spouse's mapping of the flow of currents before his pregnant wife's body drifted up on a remote shoreline and established that a murder suspect surfed the Web for information about poison formulations.

Observe Investigate Understand

- **Can computer forensic techniques become intrusive instead of investigative? When, or how?**
- **How do Fourth Amendment protections against unreasonable searches and seizures apply to computer forensic activity?**
- **Why is specific training in forensics important for law enforcement personnel engaged in computer forensic work?**

SOURCES: Kari and Associates, "BTK Killer Dennis Rader," http://karisable.com/skazbtk.htm (retrieved July 3, 2008); Gary C. Kessler, "The Role of Computer Forensics in Law Enforcement," (Burlington, VT: Champlain College Computer and Digital Forensic Program, 2006), www.officer.com (retrieved July 3, 2008); Robert Moore, "The Role of Computer Forensics in Criminal Investigation," in *Crime Online*, ed. Yvonne Jewkes (Portland, OR: Willan, 2007), 82.

first international treaty to address Internet crimes by coordinating national laws, improving investigative techniques, and increasing cooperation among nations.[11]

Within the United States, federal, state, and local law enforcement entities, as well as private sector professionals, often work together, exchanging information and hardening crime targets. To reduce the public's vulnerability to victimization, local law enforcement agencies' cybercrime units are increasingly using their Web presence to educate the public about and raise awareness of cybercrime.[12] The communications and information technology industries play a crucial cooperative role by designing products that are resistant to crime.[13] An initial federal statute to contend with fraud committed via computer was 18 U.S.C. 1030, the Computer Fraud and Abuse Act.[14] Other statutes have been enacted to combat child pornography and unauthorized access to computer-stored records.[15]

Some experts predict that by the year 2025 technology will have advanced by an equivalent of 5,000 years, paving the future path through cyberspace with possibilities—and threats—unimaginable today.[16] Unchecked growth in surveillance technology, for instance, could result in recording virtually all activity for retrieval and prosecution. However, just as today, the use of twenty-first-century technology for evidence gathering will come face-to-face with that eighteenth-century guarantor of protection against unreasonable government intrusion: the U.S. Constitution. The "duel" should be intriguing.

Identity Theft: A Particular Type of Cybercrime

identity theft
Unauthorized use of another person's identifying information to obtain credit, goods, services, money, or to commit a misdemeanor or felony.

Identity theft is "the unauthorized use of another person's identifying information to obtain credit, goods, services, money, or property, or to commit a felony or misdemeanor." Some criminologists consider identity theft to be "the" crime of the twenty-first century.[17] Typical offenses associated with identity theft include credit card fraud, fraudulently obtaining loans, and bank fraud. Fraudulently obtained funds may be used to finance larger criminal enterprises, including gang, drug, and terrorist activities.

MYTH/REALITY

MYTH: Those who refrain from purchasing goods or services online are protected from becoming victims of identity theft.

REALITY: Minimizing use of online purchases does not necessarily correlate with a decreased potential for victimization. Personal identifying information can be obtained offline (for example, via "dumpster diving" or eavesdropping) as well as online.[18]

We often underestimate how easy it is for one person to obtain another's personal data. In public places perpetrators can simply observe or overhear consumers providing personal identifying information. Some criminals engage in dumpster diving to obtain records or correspondence. The Internet has become an easily navigated avenue for obtaining

KEY CONCEPTS
Challenges to Fighting Cybercrime

Offenders are anonymous and can work from any private or public computer.

The location of the crime is difficult to identify and could range from being at the perpetrator's computer or the computer of the victim and a network server in between.

Cybercrime can be transnational and its prosecution complicated by conflicting laws and enforcement practices in different countries.

Detecting cybercrime is expensive and requires technologically sophisticated techniques and training.

Evidence for a crime may reside on many computers across many networks.

Search and seizure operations must meet legal requirements and minimally affect normal computer network operation.

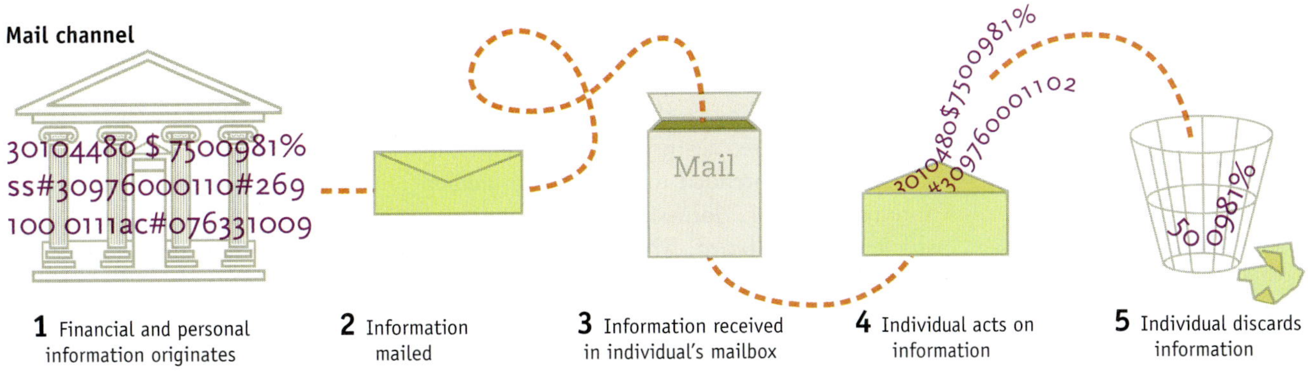

FIGURE 16-1 Channel-Interrupt Procedure

The channel-interrupt analytic procedure applied to the U.S. postal mail system to identify points of vulnerability. Within the channel are five points where identity theft could occur. Once the points have been identified, the individual or entity responsible for movement of information along the transmission channel must exercise diligence to prevent compromise of information flow.

SOURCE: Office of Community Oriented Policing Services, *A National Strategy to Combat Identity Theft* (Washington, DC: Office of Community Oriented Policing Services, 2006), 45.

passwords and banking information as unwary consumers unwittingly respond to spam and other fraudulent requests for information.[19]

It is difficult to total the specific losses incurred via identity theft because many occurrences are not reported and there is no single source of data on this type of criminal activity. Nonetheless, one survey put the losses associated with identity crime in 2007 at $45 billion.[20] The widespread occurrence of identity theft is due in large part to the technology revolution of the information age. The exponential rise in the use of computers to store personal data and of the Internet to communicate and transact business has provided new incentives and means to steal and misuse information.[21]

A significant difference between identity theft and other property crimes is that identity theft can continue for months, during which time the victim may feel helpless and experience a lack of control over her life. These stresses may result in psychological and physical illness.[22]

When identity theft was first recognized as a widespread problem, police agencies, victim assistance advocates, and private industry usually operated independently. In 2003, however, a joint effort of the U.S. Department of Justice's Office of Community Oriented Policing Services and the Major Cities Chiefs Association produced plans for state-level identity theft coordination centers. These centers facilitate the flow of information and promote collaboration among state, local, and federal law enforcement agencies, the Federal Trade Commission, and corporate entities.[23]

The U.S. Department of Justice has trained law enforcement officers to identify the points of vulnerability along an information flow and put safeguards in place at those points. This process is referred to as a "channel-interrupt analytic." Figure 16-1 illustrates the process via an item sent through the U.S. Postal Service mail "channel." In the mail channel, five points are identified as locations where identity theft could be perpetrated. For example, at Point 1, the place of origination for the dispatch of personal and financial information, a reasonable question to ask relative to safeguarding the mailed financial document is: "How can a financial institution prevent an employee from taking a statement from the mass mailing to use criminally?" Similarly, at Point 2, where the information enters the mail system, one might ask: "What safeguards does the U.S. Postal Service have in place to prevent unauthorized persons from taking information?" The same analysis would continue through the remaining three points of vulnerability within the mail system. The same method can be applied to cell phones and other transmission channels. Of course, all parties along the channel must collaborate for the channel-interrupt analytic to be successful.[24]

terrorism
Premeditated, politically motivated violence perpetrated against non-combatant targets by subnational groups or clandestine agents.

USA PATRIOT Act
"Uniting and Strengthening America by Providing Appropriate Tools Required to Intercept and Obstruct Terrorism Act" enacted by Congress following the 9/11 terrorist attacks, intended to deter and punish terrorist acts in the United States and around the world, to enhance law enforcement investigatory tools, and to strengthen measures to prevent and detect terrorism.

COMBATING TERRORISM

Terrorism, according to the United States Code, is "premeditated, politically motivated violence perpetrated against non-combatant targets by sub-national groups or clandestine agents, usually intended to influence an audience."[25] Terrorism has been categorized as "international" or "domestic." International terrorism against the United States is that which is foreign based, whereas domestic terrorism involves groups that are based and operate entirely within the United States.[26] There is, however, no universally agreed-upon definition of terrorism. Even within the United States, the FBI, Department of Homeland Security, and the Department of Defense definitions of terrorism differ, reflecting the priorities and particular interests of the specific agency. In the past, terrorism was easier to define because of some readily identifiable structure and chain of command. Today the "structural" aspect of many terrorist entities may consist only of a shared philosophy among close-knit autonomous cells, communicating as necessary via information age technologies. No matter which definition is used, the common thread is that all terrorist acts involve violence. "Through the publicity generated by their violence, terrorists seek to obtain leverage, influence, and power they otherwise lack to effect political change on either a local or an international scale."[27]

Although acts of terrorism against the United States had occurred prior to September 11, 2001, the attacks that took place on that date heightened the concern of the U.S. criminal justice system on terrorism as a serious criminal activity. Worldwide, attacks and deaths related to terrorism (exclusive of incidents occurring in Iraq) have increased annually. In 2005, attacks totaled 7,690 and deaths totaled 6,318; in 2008, attacks increased to 8,512 and the number of deaths climbed to 10,749. This increased lethality, with the number of deaths exceeding the number of attacks, is a most disturbing trend.[28] The U.S. State Department has also noted that terrorist groups and individuals are increasingly using the Internet for propaganda, recruiting, fundraising, and training.[29]

▼ World Trade Center Burning

Terrorist attacks can destroy property and life and alter our sense of safety. *What are some of the things we can do to prevent terrorist attacks?*

In its report released in 2008, the Commission on the Prevention of Weapons of Mass Destruction Proliferation and Terrorism, chartered by the U.S. Congress, warned that "America's margin of safety is shrinking, not growing."[30] Other observers note that Western nations are likely to be targets of further acts of terrorism because the terrorists perpetrating such acts regard the policies of those nations as being responsible for overcrowding, underemployment, resource scarcity, and other problems that plague developing nations.[31]

Terrorism and the Law

Acts of terrorism are prosecuted as offenses within existing laws. If a building is intentionally set on fire by terrorists, the charge against the perpetrators is arson, not terrorism. If someone dies in the blaze, the perpetrators will likely be charged with murder.

Following the 9/11 terrorist attacks, Congress enacted the **USA PATRIOT Act** (Uniting and Strengthening America by Providing Appropriate Tools Required to Intercept and Obstruct Terrorism). The act is intended to deter and punish terrorist acts in the United States and around the world, to enhance law enforcement investigatory tools, and to strengthen U.S. measures to prevent and detect terrorism. Congress reauthorized the act in March 2006,[32] and permanently extended 14 of its 16 expiring provisions. Critics of the act charge that the broad authority given to the government under the act's provisions amounts to an "overnight revision of the nation's surveillance laws that vastly expanded the government's authority to spy on its own citizens." They claim further that the act infringes on individuals' civil liberties by eliminating or reducing checks and balances on such powers as judicial oversight, public accountability, and the ability

Real Careers

AMY ZELSON MUNDORFF

Work location: New York, NY

College(s): Syracuse University, 1991; California State University, 1999; Simon Fraser University, 2009

Major(s): Archaeology (BA); Anthropology (MA); Archaeology (PhD)

Job title: Forensic Anthropologist, Office of Chief Medical Examiner, New York City

Salary range for job like this: $40,000–$120,000

Time in job: 5 years

Work Responsibilities:

From 1999 through September 2001, I was responsible for establishing protocol for all forensic anthropology-related matters for the City of New York. During this time, I analyzed more than 250 forensic anthropological cases, including standard medical examiner cases with bone trauma or pathology and unidentified, decomposed, burned, mummified, or skeletonized remains to help identify individuals. I participated in search and recovery of human remains, prepared case reports, and testified as an expert witness in court. I also provided training to medical examiners, medical students, fellows, and interns and lectured on forensic anthropology to law enforcement agencies and district attorneys.

Following the events of 9/11, I was primarily involved with the mortuary operations and identification efforts of the World Trade Center (WTC) victims. I was part of a team that established standards and procedures for the WTC Human Identification Project and developed protocols for handling and processing human remains, DNA sampling, and quality assurance procedures. I met with family members to review individual cases and attended "family group" meetings to update family members on the progress of the identification project. I was also part of the disaster identification team for the 2001 crash of American Airlines flight 587 and the Staten Island ferry crash in 2003.

Why Criminal Justice?

I fell into the field of forensic anthropology. As an undergrad, I was an archaeology major. During a summer archaeology field school in Jamaica in 1988, I helped excavate a skeleton and became fascinated with the stories human bones could tell. Following graduation, I worked as an archaeologist in Hawaii and California for about 5 years, where I participated in excavating skeletal remains. I returned to school for a master's, focusing in forensic anthropology. During my master's program, I volunteered one summer at the Office of Chief Medical Examiner, New York City; that was when I decided I wanted to do forensic anthropology full time.

Expectations and Realities of the Job:

It's both better and more frustrating than I expected. It's better in the sense that I work with every subfield of forensics, so I learn a tremendous amount. Unlike TV, forensic scientists don't work in a vacuum, solving every aspect of the crime themselves. I worked with brilliant forensic pathologists, odontologists, radiologists, fingerprint experts, toxicologists, histologists, biologists, detectives, and more. We pooled our expertise to help identify individuals or determine someone's cause and manner of death. On the other hand, it is more frustrating than I had anticipated because not every case is solved. Not being able to identify remains or help solve a homicide is one of the most difficult aspects of my work.

My Advice to Students:

Don't hesitate to ask for help or advice on the job. Actually being a practitioner, instead of a graduate student, was initially a big transition for me. When confronted with a particularly challenging case, I would often reach out to other colleagues with more experience and seek their opinion. Another piece of advice is to include something on your resume that separates you from your fellow graduates. This can be achieved in a number of ways, but for me, it was showing practical experience working at a medical examiner's office. During one of my summer breaks from graduate school, I called the medical examiner office where I wanted to work and offered my services for free. No one turns down free labor! I interned there for the summer, made fantastic contacts, and learned a tremendous amount. When I graduated, I wrote the Chief Medical Examiner a letter suggesting it was time to hire a forensic anthropologist full time, and that person should be me. And they did. I was the first full-time forensic anthropologist hired at New York City's Office of Chief Medical Examiner.

A Global View

France's Terrorism Strategy

France has had a history of terrorist attacks. In the 1980s terrorists set off bombs on trains and subways and in department stores. In 1995 Algerian radicals detonated a bomb in a Paris train station, killing 8 and injuring 150. In response to these attacks, the French enacted a series of harsh laws and an aggressive counterterrorism strategy. France's approach to countering terrorism involves a cooperative effort among prosecutors, investigative judges, intelligence personnel, and surveillance and communications intercepts. French law now makes even the intention to commit an act of terrorism a crime itself. Even mere association with someone suspected of terrorism is a crime.

The French have taken a preemptive approach, and judges have detained persons based on minimal information. Human Rights Watch, a worldwide independent organization dedicated to defending and protecting human rights, found that French authorities arrest persons with little, if any, evidence that they engaged in terrorist activities. When arrested, a suspect can see a lawyer only after 3 days of intense police questioning and then only for 30 minutes. Suspects' lawyers do not have access to files and can only provide minimal assistance, and the suspect can be held up to 6 days before being brought before a judge. When the suspect is before a judge, a decision is made about pretrial custody, which can result in long periods of incarceration before being tried.

Human Rights Watch also reports that the French use sleep deprivation, constant repetitive questioning, and physical abuse during investigations and interrogations. The organization charges that the long periods of custody, delayed access to legal counsel, and harsh interrogation without the presence of legal counsel hinder a defendant's right to a fair trial. Following release of the Human Rights Watch report, the UN enjoined the French government to revise its counterterrorism strategies so that they do not violate human rights.

The French claim that their system is the most efficient in Europe and that their approach has prevented many terrorist attacks. On the question of human rights, they maintain that the right not to die in a terrorist attack is a more primary human right than protection of the rights of a suspected terrorist.

Observe Investigate Understand

- **What are some arguments for and against a preemptive strategy?**
- **How does the U.S. counterterrorism strategy differ from France's? Should the United States follow the French model?**
- **Does the French approach trade civil rights for security? If so, is it a good trade-off?**

SOURCES: H.D.S. Greenway, "How France Confronts Terrorism," *The Boston Globe*, February 17, 2009; Human Rights Watch, "Preempting Justice: Counterterrorism Laws and Procedures in France", July 1, 2008, www.hrw.org/en/reports/2008/07/01/preempting-justice-0 (retrieved July 29, 2009); Elaine Sciolino, "France's Terrorism Strategy Faulted," *The New York Times*, July 3, 2008; Human Rights Watch, "France: UN Calls for Counterterrorism Reform: Government Should Ensure Laws Guarantee Rights for Security Suspects," September 22, 2008, www.hrw.org/en/news/2008/09/22/france-un-calls-counterterrorism-reform (retrieved July 29, 2009).

to challenge government searches in court.[33] Implementation of the PATRIOT Act has rekindled the long-standing debate between the crime control and due process models of justice (see Chapter 1). For a view of how another country combats terrorism, see A Global View.

Terrorism and Intelligence

intelligence
Product of the application of analytical reasoning to data in order to develop a reliable picture of the environment or a situation.

Law enforcement plays a threefold role against terrorism: protection of the community, emergency response, and intelligence gathering and sharing.[34] As depicted in Figure 16-2, **intelligence** is the product of the application of analytical reasoning to data or information to develop a reliable picture of the environment or situation. Often, the planning timelines of terrorist incidents and the proximity of terrorists to their targets are quite similar. Preparations usually begin less than 6 months before an attack and end with a flurry of actions a day or so before. Almost half of all terrorists reside within 30 miles of their targets.[35] These patterns are important for the intelligence-gathering activities of law enforcement entities. Early development of intelligence can give law enforcement personnel the opportunity to intervene before a terrorist incident occurs. For instance, information regarding one person's purchase of a large quantity of ammonium nitrate (fertilizer) in one part of a local region could be combined with information about another individual's purchase of fuel oil in another nearby locale to yield "intelligence" that the ingredients for a powerful explosive now reside in the local area. Combining this intelligence with other information such as a police agency's field interview report of an individual taking numerous photos

Data or Information + Analysis = Intelligence

FIGURE 16-2 Intelligence Recipe
"Intelligence" is refined information.

around the base of a bridge spanning a large river could result in markedly increased patrol of the bridge as well as surveillance of the individuals making the ammonium nitrate and fuel oil purchases.

Protection and emergency response have long been functions of the police, but the intelligence function of policing, which may be the most important law enforcement function of the twenty-first century, is still developing.[36] **Intelligence-led policing (ILP)** is the collaborative collection and analysis of data by intelligence analysts, field officers, and senior leaders to improve crime control strategies, allocation of police resources, and operations.[37] Intelligence analysts are individuals with expertise in discerning "intelligence" from "information." Analysts examine information brought to the attention of police agencies to look for patterns and associations. By linking otherwise unrelated pieces of data together, they can identify existing threats of terrorist activity and enforcement opportunities.[38] Field officers are law enforcement generalists who in the course of their duties come across information that should be forwarded to analysts for analysis. Senior leaders are law enforcement agency personnel who make operational decisions based on the intelligence provided to them by analysts. Occasionally, depending on organizational resources and the urgency of a situation, there are overlaps in the performance of these intelligence-related duties.

intelligence-led policing (ILP)
Collaborative collection and analysis of data by intelligence analysts, field officers, and senior leaders.

MYTH/REALITY

MYTH: "Intelligence" and "information" are the same thing.

REALITY: A crucial distinction is that collected information must be *analyzed* to produce intelligence.[39]

Intelligence is the lifeblood of antiterrorism operations, but only if it reaches the people who need to act on it. Local law enforcement agencies tend to be attuned to crime only within their own communities After the 9/11 terrorist attacks, nonfederal authorities began forming **fusion centers**, regional intelligence hubs that pool and analyze information from many jurisdictions and share it with those to whom it directly applies. National agencies, particularly the Department of Homeland Security (DHS) and the FBI, have become increasingly involved, with DHS providing personnel with intelligence and operational skills to the fusion centers.[40] Fusion centers now exist in nearly every state and in several large cities, including New York City, Los Angeles, and the Dallas-Fort Worth metro region.[41]

fusion center
Regional intelligence hub that pools and analyzes information from many jurisdictions and shares it with those to whom it directly applies.

Information from the community at large can be a vital ingredient in developing intelligence. Alert citizens help prevent conventional crime, and they can help prevent acts of terrorism as well. For example, a large number of individuals using a rented apartment on an irregular basis can trigger the landlord's suspicion. Purchases of large amounts of hydrogen peroxide or ammonium nitrate, both ingredients in improvised explosive devices, may cue a retailer or wholesaler to report such a transaction to the local authorities.

Prevention Strategies

The broken windows theory of crime (see Chapter 6), which suggests that targeting minor offenses and community disorder reduces crime by creating an unfriendly environment for criminals, may be effective in preventing acts of terrorism. In this context the theory has two components: hostile environment and precursor crimes.

Real Crime Tech

BORDER PATROL PREDATORS TAKE FLIGHT

Since 2007 U.S. Customs and Border Protection (CBP) has routinely deployed unmanned Predator aircraft over the U.S. southwestern border to help combat terrorism, help catch illegal immigrants, and stem the flow of illegal drugs. The electro-optical and forward-looking infrared camera systems aboard the Predators enable imaging with very high resolution, in any weather conditions. The moving target indicator system enables tracking of cars and vessels, and the aircraft can stay aloft for 34 hours without having to be refueled.[43] Deployment of the Predators enables extension of the CBP into remote areas where ground-based patrols cannot easily travel and detection systems cannot be installed.

Law enforcement can create a hostile environment that frustrates or thwarts terrorists by, for example, conducting drills and staging scenes that mimic terrorist attacks. For example, the NYPD, without announcement, randomly deploys massive numbers of officers in areas of New York City perceived to be targets of terrorist activity. This strategy prevented a plot to blow up the Brooklyn Bridge. An al-Qaeda operative sent to survey the bridge was recorded as saying "the weather was too hot" to complete the operation.[42] Surveillance cameras, random screenings, and sensors can create a hostile environment by conveying a sense that law enforcement is ever-present. The challenge, of course, is to ensure that these methods do not infringe on the privacy rights of law-abiding citizens.

Police need to be vigilant for **precursor crimes**, offenses committed for the purpose of enabling acts of terrorism. Forged documents, illegal border crossings, and other seemingly minor crimes may serve to support preparations for terrorism. Patrol officers should view vehicle stops and all preliminary investigations as opportunities to intervene in terrorism.

PROSECUTING HATE CRIMES

A **hate crime** is a criminal offense committed because of the victim's race, ethnicity, religion, sexual orientation, or other group affiliation. Despite the name, the offender need not actually hate the victim to be convicted. In some jurisdictions, hate crimes are known as bias crimes or ethnic intimidation crimes. Typical examples of hate crimes include burning a cross in the yard of a Black family, painting a swastika on a synagogue wall, or "gay-bashing" (beating a person assumed to be gay).

Crimes motivated by bias are ancient, but most laws against them are new, having been enacted in the 1980s and 1990s. Almost all states now have a hate crime law of some kind. In addition, federal law now requires the U.S. Department of Justice to collect specific data related to hate crimes from local law enforcement agencies. In 2004 police departments collected reports on 7,649 offenses that were classified as hate crimes; however, most hate crimes probably do not get reported to the police.[44]

KEY CONCEPTS

Policing Techniques Used to Prevent Terrorism

Intelligence-led policing (ILP) collects and analyzes data brought to the attention of police agencies.

Instructing the public and soliciting information about suspicious activity from the community at large helps to identify suspects.

Targeting minor offenses in the community (broken windows strategy) creates an unfriendly environment for criminals and potential terrorists.

Conducting drills (often unannounced) and staging scenes that mimic terrorist attacks can disrupt terrorist planning.

Detecting precursor crimes that might lead to terrorism, such as document forgery and illegal border crossings, can disrupt plots.

Using vehicle stops and other routine investigative work as opportunities to intervene provides information on terrorists.

precursor crime
Offense committed for the purpose of enabling acts of terrorism, such as illegal border crossings or forged documents.

hate crime
Criminal offense committed because of the victim's race, ethnicity, religion, sexual orientation, or other group affiliation.

penalty enhancer
Attribute that adds to the penalty for a crime.

civil disorder
Disturbance by a group of people that is symptomatic of a major sociopolitical problem.

MYTH/REALITY

MYTH: Most people who commit crimes based on hatred, bias, or discrimination face hate crime charges or longer sentencing.

REALITY: Prosecutors have extraordinary discretion regarding how to charge suspects and often do not seek hate crime penalties.[45]

Many hate crime laws operate as **penalty enhancers**, meaning they add to the penalty for the underlying criminal act. For example, vandalizing another person's property is ordinarily a Class B misdemeanor. If, however, the vandalism was determined to be motivated by the victim's race and prosecuted under hate crime laws, the charge can be raised to a Class A misdemeanor, thus increasing the potential punishment.

Hate crimes require evidence not only of *actus reus* and *mens rea* (see Chapter 4), but also of the offender's motive. To obtain a conviction for a hate crime, the prosecutor must prove the defendant's acts were motivated (at least in part) by the victim's race, ethnicity, religion, or sexual orientation. Because it is often difficult, if not impossible, to accurately assess another person's motives,[46] convictions for hate crimes are rare. Of the nearly 1,500 hate crimes reported to California police in 2004, only 139 resulted in convictions.[47]

Considerable controversy surrounds the topic of hate crimes, including debate about which groups need protection. Many states do not include victims' sexual orientation or gender identity as criteria for hate crimes, and only a few include disability or age.[48] The Race, Class, Gender box on the next page describes one case in which gender identity and sexual orientation contributed to the commission of a crime.

As shown in Figure 16-3, the majority of hate crimes are motivated by race; others are motivated by religion, sexual orientation, ethnicity, and victim disability.

The least violent hate crimes tend to be motivated by religious bias; these crimes are usually property-related crimes or vandalism. Jewish victims were targeted in 41 percent of the hate crimes based on religion.[49] Anti-Muslim hate crimes are also common, especially since 9/11. However, various jurisdictions may categorize these crimes differently, either as crimes based on religion (Islam), on ethnicity (Arab or Middle-Eastern) or even as "other." Thus the actual prevalence of these specific crimes is not always clear from the official data. Blacks are more likely than Whites to be victims of racially motivated hate crimes. Younger victims tend to be the target of violent hate crimes; more than half of all victims of violent hate crimes are under age 24. Approximately three-quarters of victims of property-related hate crimes are 25 or older, and 40 percent of victims of intimidation are 35 or older.[50]

▲ **Swastikas on Gravestones**

Hate crimes are widespread and send an intimidating message that targeted groups are unwelcome and unsafe in a community.

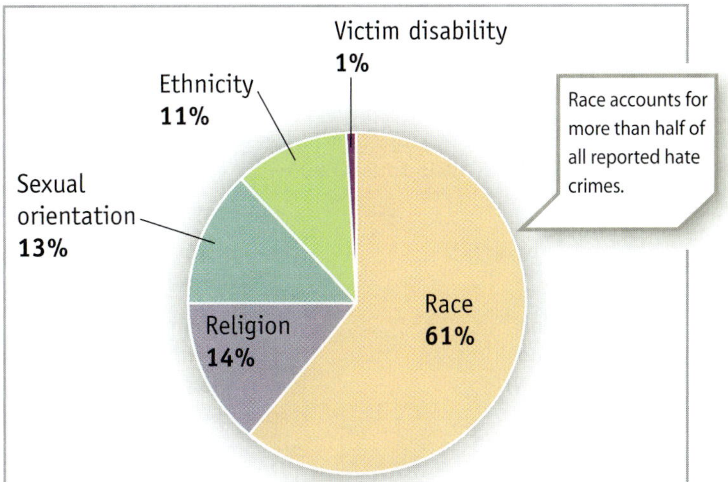

FIGURE 16-3 Types of Hate Crimes

SOURCE: U.S. Dept. of Justice, "Bureau of Justice Statistics: Advance Release of September 23, 2001," www.ojp.usdoj.gov/bjs/pub/press/hcrn99pr.htm.

CONTROLLING CIVIL DISORDER

Civil disorder is a disturbance by a group of people that is symptomatic of a major sociopolitical problem. Normally it arises from a spontaneous gathering in response to some perceived injustice. Any assembly of persons that poses a threat of collective violence or a breach of the peace is subject to laws against civil disorder.[51]

The severity of the disturbance usually corresponds to the degree of outrage among participants. Even

Race, Class, Gender

The Killing of Gwen Araujo

On October 3, 2002, a 17-year-old named Gwen Araujo attended a party near her home in Newark, California. During the party, some guests learned that, although she considered herself female and had been living as a female for some time, Gwen was biologically male. Reaction to this news was swift and violent: several young men attacked Gwen, beating her with their fists, a frying pan, and other objects. Then they strangled her with a rope. The men drove her body to the Sierra foothills, where they buried her in a shallow grave.

When brought to trial, the defendants in the case employed a "panic strategy," claiming that they "panicked," became enraged, and acted in a state of violent temporary insanity upon learning that Gwen, with whom they had engaged in sexual activity, was biologically male. The jury in a first trial was unable to reach a verdict, but eventually two men were convicted of second-degree murder, and two others pled guilty to voluntary manslaughter. The killers were not convicted of a hate crime because some members of the jury were not convinced the crime was committed because of Araujo's sexual identity. Most people, however, had little doubt that Araujo was killed because she was transgendered. Her death is an extreme example of what many researchers argue is an all-too-common event: hate crimes against lesbian, gay, bisexual, transgendered, and questioning, (LGBTQ) people.

According to the FBI, antigay bias is the third most common kind of hate crime. In 2004, more than 1,400 antigay hate crimes were reported, but this number probably underestimates the problem. Hate crimes against LGBTQ people often go unreported due to victims' fears of being "outed," as well as poor relationships between police departments and the LGTBQ community. In fact, one study found that one in four gay men and one in five lesbians had been the victim of a hate crime at some point. Despite the prevalence of antigay hate crimes and the well-publicized murders of LGTBQ people like Gwen Araujo, Matthew Shepard (a gay college student killed in Wyoming in 1998), Brandon Teena (a transgendered man killed in Nebraska in 1993), and Barry Winchell (killed by fellow soldiers in 1999 because he was gay), laws against antigay violence remain controversial. Only 30 states include crimes based on sexual orientation in their hate crimes laws, and only 7 states include crimes based on gender identity. In the wake of Araujo's murder, the California legislature passed a law addressing the use of panic strategies. According to this law, instructions to the jury in a criminal trial must state that use of a panic strategy to influence the proceedings of the trial is not permitted. This was the first such law in the United States.

OBSERVE Investigate Understand

- **Was the murder of Gwen Araujo a hate crime?**
- **If antigay hate crimes are so prevalent, why do laws against antigay violence remain controversial?**
- **Can hate crime laws help prevent crimes like the murder of Gwen Araujo? Why or why not?**

SOURCES: Greg Herek, Roy Gillis, and Jeanine Cogan, "Psychological Sequelae of Hate Crime Victimization among Lesbian, Gay, and Bisexual Adults," *Journal of Consulting and Clinical Psychology* 67, no. 6 (1999): 945–951; "Gwen Araujo Justice for Victims Act Becomes Law," www.transgenderlawcenter.org/gwen (retrieved March 22, 2009); Phyllis Gerstenfeld, *Hate Crimes: Causes, Controls, and Controversies* (Thousand Oaks, CA: Sage, 2004).

citizens not directly involved in a civil disorder may experience major disruptions in their daily lives. Chaos at the site may constrain travel and commerce; residents may fear for their safety. When public order is disrupted, the police act as a control force with a threefold mission: to preserve life, protect property, and restore order. They may suspend their response to routine criminal activities (such as taking a report of a burglary or theft) and encourage citizens to defer reporting less serious offenses until order has been restored.

Episodes of social unrest that have escalated to the level of civil disorder have occurred throughout U.S. history. From Shays's Rebellion in 1786–1787 (in which more than 2,000 western Massachusetts farmers participated in armed rebellion in protest over heavy taxation, high legal and court fees, and government waste)[52] through the civil rights disturbances during the 1960s, to demonstrations over wars, immigration, and the economic challenges of the modern era, people have used civil disorder to express the intolerability of perceived sociopolitical injustices.

Causes of Civil Disorder

Research on the riots of the 1960s examined the dynamics of crowds and mobs and identified some elements common to episodes of civil disorder. A **crowd** is defined as a group of individuals drawn together by common values and feelings about a current matter. A crowd, although unorganized and without leadership, is ruled by collective reason, is aware of the law, and generally respects its principles.

crowd
Leaderless group of individuals, generally respectful of the law, drawn together by common values about a current matter.

mob
Non–law-abiding group, with a leader, ruled by emotion.

Like a crowd, a **mob** is drawn together by common values, but otherwise it is quite different. First, a mob is not law-abiding. A mob usually is organized, has a leader, and is ruled by emotion. Its creation is usually sparked by a climactic event, such as an organized expression of sympathy or resentment. Zealots mill about from one small group to another, rousing emotions that build to a high state of collective tension and excitement. Mob members lose their personal identity and become anonymous in the large group, a psychological effect that absolves them of personal responsibility for any destructive acts that ensue.[53] Sports fans watching an athletic event, for instance, may become either angered at a loss or overjoyed by a win and then act collectively in ways that include breaking laws. At first, a few people begin to act and then others follow, spurred by their sudden anonymity in a large group of their peers.[54] Automobiles are overturned, bonfires set in streets, and businesses vandalized—usually with no premeditation.

Major riots often exhibit five phases: accumulated reservoir, precipitating incident, confrontation with authorities, "carnival," and "war."[55] Groups may congregate—and mob behavior result—because of the weight of accumulated grievances.[56] The Los Angeles riots that occurred following the 1992 acquittal of White police officers accused of beating Black motorist Rodney King took place in a climate of racial unrest. For months, television stations had played and replayed video footage of King's beating taken by a bystander, priming the public mood. Many people of color were experiencing what they believed to be social and economic inequities as well as discriminatory treatment by the justice system. All that was needed to ignite disorder was a precipitating incident; the acquittal of the White officers charged with beating King served that purpose.[57]

Soon after the precipitating incident, an angry confrontation between shouting crowds and the authorities may take place. Random acts of violence characterize the "carnival" phase of the situation. Then the situation quickly escalates to acts of serious violence, a phase referred to as "war."[58] These phases were prominent in the dynamics of the 1992 Los Angeles riot when angry protestors took to the streets, shooting, assaulting passersby, looting stores and other businesses, and setting fires. A strikingly similar situation had occurred in 1980 in Miami, Florida, when five White police officers were acquitted of charges related to their involvement in the beating death of Arthur McDuffie, a Black man. The acquittal touched off violent rioting, shootings, burglaries, looting, and numerous fires. In both the Los Angeles and Miami incidents, "the underlying reservoir of grievances and the precipitating incidents were virtually identical."[59]

▲ **Sports Fans Rioting**

Excitement, passion, adrenaline, and alcohol can turn a happy event like a sports team's title victory into a riot.

MYTH/REALITY

MYTH: Civil disorders are usually spontaneous and unpredictable occurrences.

REALITY: Civil disorders require some precipitating incident, which may be spontaneous. However, civil disorders are often predictable because the "tinder" upon which they are ignited has accumulated visibly over time.[60]

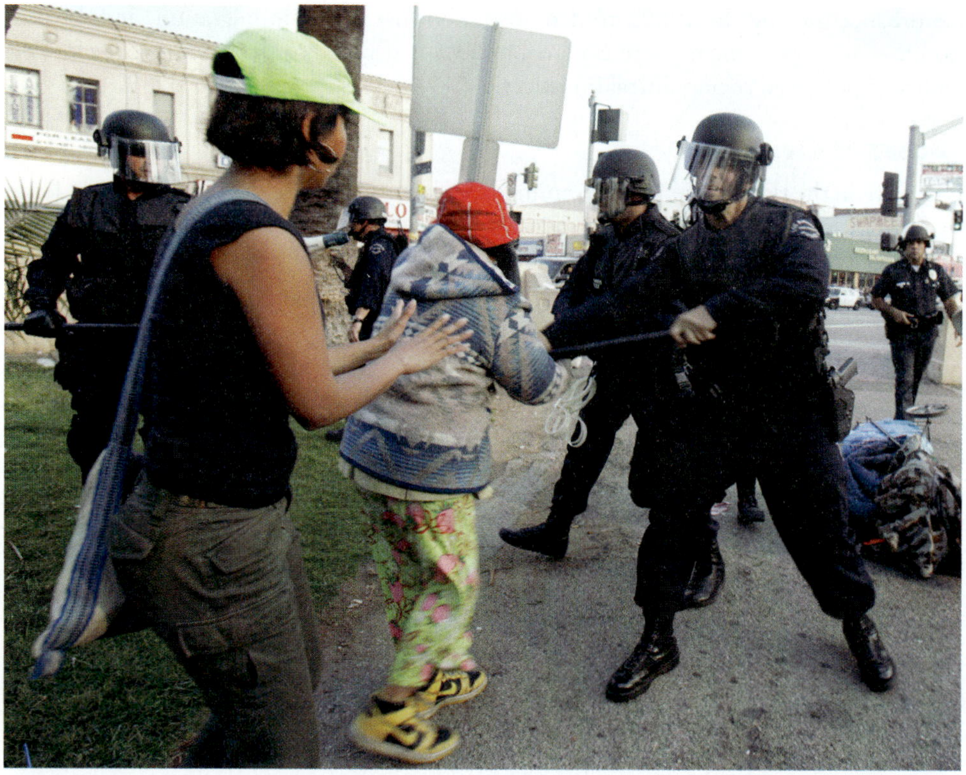

▶ LAPD at MacArthur Park Immigration Rally

After the immigration rally was declared an unlawful assembly, many thought the police used excessive force against protesters.

Social protests of today and the future will likely be carried out by groups better prepared and more organized than they have been in the past. Individuals sympathetic to every possible issue, some of whom may be located outside the community or even outside the country, can connect with one another online to participate in social protests.[61] Within the United States, the combination of soaring fuel prices and a tumultuous real estate market recently expanded the ranks of protesters. In Atlanta during the spring of 2008, a 30-vehicle trucker's convoy grew to three miles in length by the time it crossed through the city in a protest of high fuel prices.[62] The soaring cost of food staples "is the world's big story," reports the Columbia University Earth Institute. Riots over food shortages and rising costs have already occurred in developing nations, including Haiti and Bangladesh, but the United States and other Western nations are not immune to such problems. Even in those countries, "more and more poor families are feeling the pinch."[63]

KEY CONCEPTS

Five Phases of a Riot

Phase	Description
Accumulated reservoir	Grievances known by the public
Precipitating event	Government ruling, court decision, or street incident that ignites the buildup of "tinder" accumulated via the reservoir of grievances
Confrontation with authorities	Members of the public come face-to-face with law enforcement or other authorities trying to maintain control
Carnival	Random acts of violence, such as vandalism, break out
War	Situation escalates to include serious acts of violence, such as shootings, fighting, looting, and assault on innocent bystanders

Prevention Strategies

Commissions convened in the 1990s identified the quality of the relationship between the community and its police force as the most significant factor in preventing or resolving civil disorder.[64] Good relationships can enable quick and effective intervention when unrest develops. If unrest is allowed to progress to angry confrontation with authorities, the likelihood of violence is strong.[65] The character of the intervention is also vital. Contemporary strategies encourage "under-enforcement of the law (rather than rigid enforcement), complex procedures of negotiation, and large-scale gathering of information and intelligence."[66]

As part of its preparation for an unknown and perhaps dangerous future, the U.S. Department of Defense has committed to analyzing the most credible unconventional threats on the horizon. In its 2008 report, the Strategic Institute of the U.S. Army War College cautioned that the likeliest and most dangerous future shocks will be unconventional. The report warned that the United States may experience massive civil unrest in the wake of a series of crises (for example, unforeseen economic downturns or pervasive public health emergencies). The Department of Defense, in response to this report, has taken steps to ensure that it will act to preserve political authority in the event of a nationwide civil disturbance.[67]

SAFEGUARDING CIVIL LIBERTIES

A recurrent dilemma within the U.S. criminal justice system is protecting people and property without infringing on constitutionally guaranteed individual liberties. More and stricter laws, greater leeway for police officers and other criminal justice professionals, and harsher punishments might make us all safer, but perhaps at the cost of decreasing the freedoms we now enjoy. For example, police would likely catch more criminals if they were allowed to search houses whenever they wished without first getting search warrants, but then all people would be at perpetual risk of having their privacy invaded.

The U.S. Constitution prohibits the government from making laws that violate certain rights, among them the rights to freedom of expression, religion, and privacy. However, the Constitution does not specify the precise nature of those rights, nor the circumstances, if any, under which they may be overridden. Furthermore, individuals often disagree over whether freedom or safety is more valuable, so proposed laws and policies are frequently subject to vigorous debate.

Numerous times in the country's history a crisis has justified, at least for many people, fairly extensive infringements on individual liberties. The right to a writ of habeas corpus, which allows people to challenge their incarceration in court, was suspended or denied several times, including during and after the Civil War, during World War II, and following the 9/11 attacks. Rights of free assembly and free expression were frequently overlooked during the Red Scare of the 1950s, for fear of the spread of communism. During the war on drugs of the 1980s and 1990s, law enforcement was generally given more latitude to conduct warrantless searches. And during the war on terrorism after 9/11, Congress passed laws authorizing warrantless monitoring of telephone calls and Internet activity.

The extraordinary measures undertaken by law enforcement following 9/11 have, at times, called into question whether officials are adhering to the rule of law—the underpinning of the U.S. system of justice. The rule of law states that all people within the United States, regardless of their citizenship status, are covered by the provisions of the U.S. Constitution and all the statutory law (law enacted by authorized lawmaking bodies, such as Congress) that evolves from it. In essence, this means we must objectively consider the facts about any criminal act and disregard any bias toward or against an individual's race or status when making a decision to interfere with that person's freedom.

The war on terrorism has had considerable effects on immigrants and persons visiting the United States on a visa.[68] Law enforcement has detained many people fitting the

▲ **Acquitted Terror Suspect Shoue Hammod**

Shoue Hammod was charged with terrorist offenses and went to trial in Melbourne, Australia, because he made a comment to his wife over the telephone about terrorist training.

▼ **Victim with a Disability**

A victim in a wheelchair testifies in court.

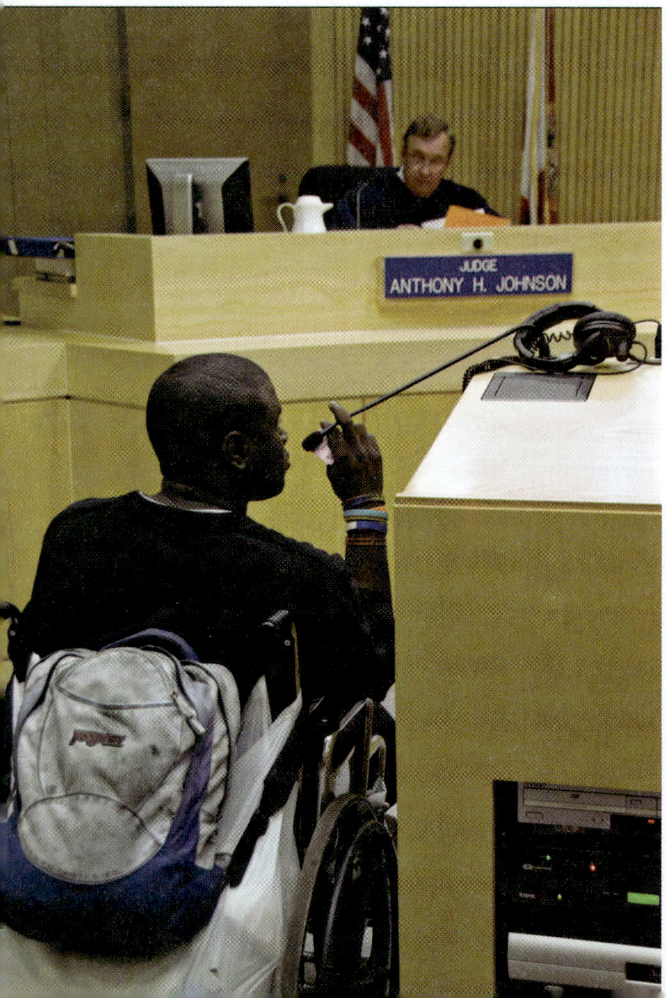

terrorist profile of Middle Eastern heritage, temporary visa status, Muslim faith, male gender, and young adult age. Critics vehemently condemn the practice of detaining suspects without formally charging them with a criminal offense.

In addition, the U.S. Department of Justice has expanded the FBI's authority to permit surveillance of religious institutions, Web sites, libraries, and organizations without any finding of criminal suspicion before the fact.[69] Critics of these surveillance guidelines contend they give the state too much power to infringe on individuals' privacy. They argue that the focus of these practices on individuals with a specific ethnic, national, or racial heritage constitutes racial profiling.[70]

MEETING EMERGING CHALLENGES IN VICTIMOLOGY

Victims of a specific crime may be easily recognized, but there are many others who have traditionally not been identified as victims, whose victimizations have gone unnoticed, or who have had limited access to programs that provide assistance. What does the future hold for addressing the needs of these people and the challenges they face?

Victims with Disabilities

As many as one of every five people in the United States may have a disability of some sort, such as mental illness, reduced mental functioning, limited mobility, or inability to communicate. Some people are born with a disability, and others' disabilities result from accident, disease, or a criminal victimization. People with a disability are more vulnerable to victimization, are typically less able to protect themselves, have more trouble contacting law enforcement, often find victim services inaccessible, and have more difficulty recovering. They also are more likely to experience repeat victimizations by the same offender than those who do not have disabilities.[71]

People with developmental disabilities are 4 to 10 times more likely to become crime victims than others. Women with a disability are twice as likely as other women to be victims of abuse. When the abuser is also a loved one or caretaker, victims suffer added stress due to their increased isolation, inability to seek outside services, and dependence on the abuser.[72]

In 2000, the Center for Research on Women with Disabilities conducted a study of victim service providers. The almost 600 respondents served victims with mental illnesses, physical disabilities, developmental disabilities, hearing impairments, and visual impairments. The services provided included access to shelter, individual counseling, group counseling, an interpreter, safety planning modified for persons with a disability, and staff disability awareness training. Nearly 20 percent of the responding agencies had one staff member assigned to provide services to victims with a disability, and 6 percent provided a specific care attendant to help the victim. When asked about outreach to victims with disabilities, most organizations said they conducted community presentations and training, distributed printed materials, formed collaborative partnerships with organizations serving persons with disabilities, and made referrals.[73]

Most crime victims, regardless of ability, experience some level of trauma and thus need services after the crime. Those with disabilities must be treated equitably and have the same access to services. Two federal laws prohibit discrimination on the basis of disability: the Americans with Disabilities Act (ADA), enacted in 1990, and Section 504 of the Rehabilitation Act of 1973. The former applies to state and local governments and the latter to entities receiving financial assistance from the federal government. Both laws require that law enforcement make reasonable modifications to enable crime victims with a disability to benefit equally from participating in all agency services, programs, and activities. When law enforcement responds to victims appropriately and compassionately, victims are more willing to cooperate by providing information vital to the investigation and prosecution of the offender.

In 2002, the U.S. Department of Justice created a handbook to assist law enforcement in responding to the specific needs of crime victims with disabilities. Some of the guidelines, which are helpful for law enforcement and anyone working with crime victims with a disability, follow:

- Rethink negative attitudes about people with a disability.
- Remember having a disability does not equate to being unhealthy or unintelligent.
- Use person-first language and do not label a person by disability. For example, it is more appropriate to say, "a person with a disability" rather than "a disabled person." In doing so, you are indicating the disability is secondary to the person.
- Speak directly to the victim even if a third party is present to assist, and ask victims how to most effectively communicate with them. Do not speak in a childlike or condescending manner.
- Ensure the victim is safe before leaving the scene. If not, provide an alternate caregiver or shelter. A victim advocate can provide vital information to assist in the situation.
- Do not assume family members, service providers, or caretakers are safe for the victim. Sometimes these individuals are the perpetrators, a situation that may inhibit a victim's ability to disclose the victimization and raise fears of retribution.
- Make sure to document the victims' disabilities, including specific communication, transportation, medication, or other accommodation needs.
- It is inappropriate to be curious about the disability outside the bounds of providing assistance, to express pity about the disability (such as "I'm sorry you are suffering from a mental illness"), to show admiration for the victim's ability to accomplish things despite having a disability, or to make insensitive comments (such as "She's disabled and he raped her anyway"). Such remarks can be very painful to a victim with a disability or members of the victim's family.[74]

Today more organizations are providing outreach and modified services for victims with disabilities, helping diminish the trauma and crisis associated with victimization. The future should bring greater collaboration between victim and disability service providers; more training for first responders, service providers, and caretakers; better screening for appropriate services; and greater accessibility to services. Each of these interventions will help victims with a disability move toward long-term healing and recovery. More remains to be done, however, as illustrated by the Disconnects box on the next page, which highlights some of the gaps in services for victims with disabilities.

Immigrant Victims

Most people think of trafficking in persons (TIP) when thinking about victimization against immigrants. In reality, immigrants are victims of many different crimes in the United States and in their home countries. No matter where the crime occurred, a number of programs and services exist to assist immigrant victims in the United States.

MYTH/REALITY

MYTH: Immigrant victims will be deported if they call the police or seek services after a crime.

REALITY: Federal and state laws protect immigrant victims from deportation if they contact the police. Some states provide benefits to those victimized by TIP, intimate partner violence, and other serious crimes.[75]

DISConnects

Helping or Hurting Victims with Disabilities?

Individuals with disabilities are victimized at higher rates than those without disabilities. Many of these crimes go unreported, and victims do not seek services. Those victims who do report their victimization may interact with law enforcement, service providers, prosecutors, and allied professionals who have limited training in working with this population. These victims must overcome not only the trauma of the crime but also the prevalent misperceptions, stereotypes, and myths about victims with disabilities.

Services for victims with disabilities may be limited, and victims may have difficulty accessing the services that are available. Organizations with ramps in the back or at the side of the building add an extra burden of access, are not welcoming, and raise concerns about safety in entering from an isolated access point. For safety reasons, victim services are often not located at a building's ground level. Thus the victim may have to move further through a building that may not have an elevator or large doors and hallways to accommodate wheelchairs and other assistive devices. Written materials may not be available in Braille or large print, causing additional disadvantages to victims who are visually impaired. Victims who have difficulties with speech may be asked to write about their victimization to help the officer or service provider understand the crime. This tactic, however, raises further difficulties for victims. The duty of a first responder or service provider is to help the victim, not cause greater trauma and anxiety. Having communication devices and access to sign language interpreters are necessary, but not always available.

Courthouses and other buildings victims may have to visit may be large, requiring victims to navigate long distances to reach their destination. Bathrooms may not be easily accessible and may be far from the safety afforded in the courtroom, contributing to the victim's vulnerability. Those with communicative disorders can benefit from assistive devices to ease giving testimony and victim impact statements. Victims who experience intimate partner violence may have difficulty leaving an abusive partner due to the lack of shelter services that provide assistive accommodations. Some shelters are older homes that have been converted and have limited services to assist those with physical disabilities. These shelters may only have availability on upper levels, the bathroom may be far from the bedroom, and the living space may not be accessible. Telecommunication devices (TTY/TTD, or Tele-typewriting Device for the Deaf/Tele-typewriter machines) may not be readily available to help victims keep in contact with loved ones. This isolation can contribute to further depression, fear, and anxiety.

To bridge these gaps, a three-pronged approach is needed. First, increasing the availability and accessibility of services assists with recovery and ensuring victims' rights. Next, multidisciplinary cross-training for service providers, criminal justice professionals, and those from the disability community contributes to efficient and effective provision of services. Finally, greater awareness of the needs of victims with disabilities will help promote the implementation of appropriate policies to help these victims.

OBSERVE Investigate Understand

- **What are some other identifiable gaps in services for victims with disabilities?**
- **What can be done to provide better outreach to crime victims with disabilities?**
- **If a victim with a disability requests prerecorded testimony or victim impact statements, should the request be granted? Why or why not?**

SOURCE: Cheryl Guidry Tyiska, "Working with Victims of Crime with Disabilities," U.S. Department of Justice, Office for Victims of Crime, October 1, 2008, www.ovc.gov/publications/factshts/disable.htm (retrieved July 24, 2009).

For an immigrant victim to be eligible for benefits, credible evidence indicating the person is a victim is required. Such evidence may be police reports, physical evidence, and documentation from social service or health care providers. If there is no evidence, the individual's sworn statements about the victimization may be sufficient. Victims who assist police in investigating TIP and work to prosecute traffickers may apply for a T visa or request continued presence in the United States through the U.S. Office of Refugee Resettlement (ORR). Individuals the office certifies as TIP victims are eligible for federal benefits.[76]

Immigrant victims of intimate partner violence are eligible for access to shelters, food banks, soup kitchens, Supplemental Nutrition Program for Women, Infants, & Children (WIC), emergency medical services including prenatal care and care during labor and delivery, community clinics, and services provided by nonprofit organizations. Children also are eligible for school breakfast and lunch programs and the Child Health and

Disability Prevention (CHDP) program. These benefits are available regardless of whether the victim contacts and cooperates with the police. Immigrants who have suffered substantial physical and mental abuse such as intimate partner violence, sexual assault, prostitution, female genital mutilation, kidnapping, servitude, false imprisonment, and other crimes can apply for U visas. This type of visa, which gives victims temporary legal status and eligibility for work in the United States, is granted only if victims cooperate in the investigation and prosecution of a crime.[77]

▲ **Immigrant Victims**

Family and relatives try to make sense of their loss after a shooting rampage at the American Civic Association, a nonprofit organization providing services to immigrants in Binghamton, New York, where a gunman killed 13 people, then took his own life.

Local, state, and federal programs for immigrant victims are intended to help the victims reestablish healthy and normal lives and support them if they wish to serve as witnesses in the prosecution of offenders. The labyrinth of immigrant services, government agencies, and applicable rules requires collaboration among agencies providing aid to immigrant victims. First responders, service providers, and government workers need training in the unique challenges of working with immigrant victims. Finally, outreach and educational programs are particularly important because immigrant victims are often unaware of services, do not believe they are eligible for them, and do not know how to access them. They often distrust law enforcement and government officials and fear reporting a crime will expose them to deportation.[78]

LGBTQ Victims

Members of the lesbian, gay, bisexual, transgender, and questioning (LGBTQ) community experience victimization, but there is little research on the prevalence of the problem and services for these victims are limited. One research effort is conducted each year by the National Coalition of Anti-Violence Programs (NCAVP), a national network of more than 35 community-based organizations that provide services to address violence against LGBTQ individuals, persons who are HIV-infected, and those affected by HIV/AIDS through family or friends. In 2007, the NCAVP released two reports on violence and another on intimate partner violence against people who identify as LGBTQ.

The first report focused on bias-motivated incidents in 2007. The data are based on reported incidents in 13 states: California, Colorado, Illinois, Massachusetts, Michigan, Minnesota, Missouri, New York, Ohio, Pennsylvania, Texas, Vermont, and Wisconsin. In 2007, the 2,430 victims who reported anti-LGBTQ violence represented a 24 percent increase from 2006. The number of reported murders doubled over the same 1-year period, from 10 in 2006 to 21 in 2007. Other increases occurred in reported sexual assaults (61 percent), noninjury incidents (28 percent), and the use of weapons (5 percent). Some decreases were noted as well: minor injuries fell by 6 percent, and serious injuries were down 11.7 percent.

Strangers were less likely than acquaintances to commit bias-motivated crimes against LGBTQ individuals. Strangers accounted for 809 incidents in comparison to 1,741 acquaintance incidents in 2007. Almost half the incidents implicated multiple offenders, and one-quarter were serial offenses; some offenders targeted the LGBTQ individual multiple times before the victim called for help. Nearly half the cases reported in the study did not result in a call to the police. When the victim did call law enforcement, just under a quarter of the cases resulted in an arrest.[79]

The NCAVP report on intimate partner violence, based on data received from 14 member organizations representing 11 states (Arizona, California, Colorado, Illinois, Massachusetts, Minnesota, Missouri, New York, Ohio, Pennsylvania, and Texas), revealed slightly more than 3,500 cases of intimate partner violence and four deaths in 2006, a

15 percent decrease over the previous year. It is unclear whether the decrease resulted from fewer cases of intimate partner violence, fewer people seeking services, or a combination of other unknown factors.[80]

Both reports called for changes at the local, state, and federal level to address victimization within the LGBTQ community. The recommendations include the following:

- Implement a comprehensive awareness campaign to create a societal climate that fosters respect and shuns violence against all people.
- Adopt LGBTQ-inclusive and nondiscriminatory policies and practices that are implemented and enforced.
- Establish and promote antibias units within law enforcement, including training and resources to investigate and sanction inappropriate police response.
- Increase funding for research, training, and provision of services to LGBTQ individuals.[81]

These recommendations as well as additional research can lead to a greater understanding of the prevalence and nature of violence within the LGBTQ community. The more we know, the more we can accomplish to raise awareness and offer a more effective response.

Hate Crime Victims

Increases in global migration have brought to many countries new groups of emigrants from different cultures, who speak different languages and practice different religions. Some native residents perceive the new immigrants and their differences as threats to the stability of the host countries, resulting in conflicts based on fear, frustration, and anger. Victims of hate crimes (discussed earlier in this chapter from a law enforcement perspective) often suffer as much, or more, pain and trauma as victims of street crimes. Official responses to hate crime victimizations include research;[82] passage of laws;[83] and training in cultural diversity and tolerance for law enforcement professionals,[84] communities, and students.[85]

Some observers predict a rise in the rate of hate crimes, an increase that will place greater demands on the limited resources available for assistance to hate crime victims. One of the major challenges of providing adequate services for hate crime victims is ensuring accurate reporting of these offenses. In compliance with the 1990 Hate Crime Statistics Act, the FBI added hate crimes to the National Incident-Based Reporting System (NIBRS).

Figure 16-4 shows the number of hate crimes reported from 1991 through 2006. This figure underestimates the actual number of hate crimes because only about half of the states participate in the NIBRS program. In 2006, however, in the 7,722 reported hate crime incidents, the Bureau of Crime Statistics listed 9,642 victims among those jurisdictions reporting nationwide.[86] All states must provide accurate reporting of hate crimes so that resources can be provided to meet the needs of all hate crime victims. This is one of the major challenges for the future of victim assistance.

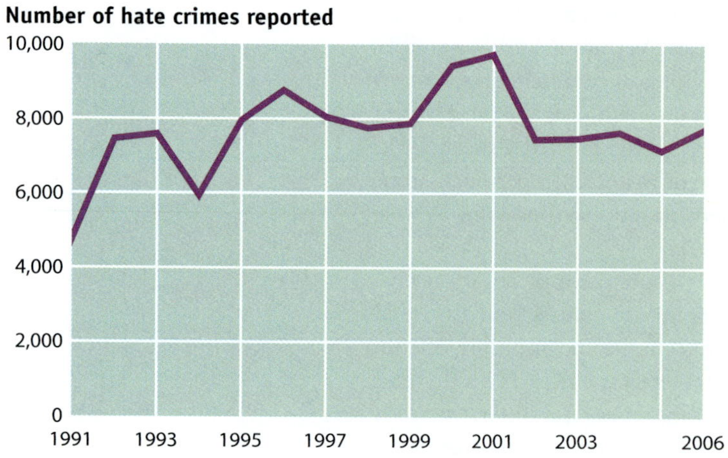

FIGURE 16-4 Hate Crime Statistics Collected by the FBI, 1991–2006

SOURCE: Federal Bureau of Investigation, Department of Justice, "Hate Crime Statistics," www.adl.org/issue_government/hate_crime_statistics_act.asp.

Treatment for Crime Victims with Post-traumatic Stress Disorder

Effective treatment methods for crime victims suffering from post-traumatic stress disorder (PTSD) include exposure therapy, cognitive therapy, anxiety management training, and psychoeducation. In exposure therapy the therapist directly introduces the trauma cues, like smells and sounds, while providing therapeutic support during the victim's fear responses. Cognitive therapy teaches victims

KEY CONCEPTS

Challenges to Victimology and Victim Services

Crime victims have been largely ignored in research, policy, and practice; access to services continues to be inadequate to their needs.

Some persons, especially those with disabilities, immigrants, LGBTQs, and the discriminated, have been recently identified as more vulnerable to being victimized. If they become victims, they have had more difficulty in accessing needed assistance.

New laws, policies, strategies, and practices have been developed to address needed services for crime victims.

New and innovative forms of treatment for crime victims with PTSD have emerged such as exposure therapy, cognitive therapy, anxiety management training, psychoeducation, and critical incident stress debriefing.

to identify and change the way they think about their traumatic event to strengthen their beliefs about safety, trust, power, competence, esteem, and intimacy. Anxiety management therapy, which relies on muscle relaxation and controlled breathing with a special emphasis on the physical symptoms of distress, helps victims cope with the anxieties related to their victimization. Psychoeducation emphasizes teaching victims adaptive coping techniques that can help them recover. This treatment method is often used with other interventions, as a starting point to help provide victims with accurate information about their victimization and typical responses to it.[87]

Research on the benefits of peer support groups has been sparse. Recent studies on the effectiveness of these groups have found that sharing or just having contact with other victims has not been very helpful and may actually be harmful.[88]

Another victim treatment that has gained some level of acceptance is psychological debriefing, especially the model referred to as "critical incident stress debriefing." This model was originally proposed as an early intervention method to help large numbers of persons who had been traumatized in emergency situations, for example, in disasters. The technique, used primarily to prevent or reduce posttraumatic stress, usually takes place in a group setting soon after the occurrence of the traumatic event. A facilitator encourages members of the group to describe what happened, their thoughts and emotions as the event was happening, and any physical or psychological responses to the event. The facilitator then provides tips on how to deal with these responses, summarizes the group meeting, and assesses the need for follow-up with any members of the group.[89] More rigorous and controlled studies are required before this treatment strategy can be supported as an effective method to prevent trauma from forming, especially among all disaster victims.[90]

One of the major challenges facing victim assistance practitioners today is professionalization of the craft. Professionalization essentially means the process of ensuring competence in one's field. Victims need competent treatment that enhances their chances for recovery. Care providers have the responsibility to use practices that are based on evidence and thus offer the best chance to reduce victims' suffering and facilitate their recovery.

SUMMARY

This chapter focused on just a few of the contemporary issues facing the criminal justice system and providers of victim services. Among these challenges are dealing with new types of crime, including cybercrime, terrorism, and hate crimes. The challenge of fighting these types of crime as well as controlling civil disorder often heightens the tension between providing safety and security for all people, prosecuting crimes, and safeguarding individuals' civil liberties. Crime victims whose victimizations have been ignored or gone unnoticed, or who have had limited access to programs that provide assistance, often require specialized services that recognize their particular needs and circumstances. New strategies are being developed to address crime and provide services for crime victims.

Observe Investigate Understand

Review

Describe the nature and extent of cybercrime, and identify some techniques used to investigate this type of crime.

- Cybercrime is any crime that relies on a computer and a network for its commission (for example, digital child pornography, identity theft, and online fraud schemes).
- The extent of cybercrime is significantly underreported (only about one-third is reported).
- The complexity of cybercrimes demands a technologically sophisticated investigative response that includes computer forensics, collaboration, and training.
- The communications and information technology industries play a crucial prevention role by designing products that are resistant to cybercrime and that help law enforcement detect and investigate it.

Discuss the nature and extent of identity theft, and describe some strategies used to contend with it.

- It is difficult to total the specific losses incurred via identity theft because many occurrences are not reported and there is no single source of data on this type of criminal activity.
- State-level identity theft coordination centers facilitate the flow of information and collaboration among state, local, and federal law enforcement agencies and the Federal Trade Commission and corporate entities in combating identity theft.

Explain the interaction between the law and intelligence gathering with regard to terrorism, and discuss some strategies employed to prevent terrorist activities.

- The terrorist attacks on the United States that occurred on September 11, 2001, heightened the concern of the U.S. criminal justice system on terrorism as a serious criminal activity.
- Acts of terrorism are prosecuted as offenses within existing laws.
- Implementation of the USA PATRIOT Act has rekindled the long-standing debate between the crime control and due process models of justice.
- Early development and communication of intelligence can give law enforcement personnel the opportunity to intervene before a terrorist incident occurs.
- Police need to be vigilant for precursor crimes, offenses committed for the purpose of enabling acts of terrorism.

Define hate crime and explain its operation as a penalty enhancer.

- A hate crime is a criminal offense committed because of the victim's race, ethnicity, religion, sexual orientation, or other group affiliation.
- Many hate crime laws operate as "penalty enhancers," meaning they add to the penalty for the underlying criminal act.

Identify the factors contributing to the emergence of civil disorder and strategies for prevention.

- Frequently, civil disorder arises from an accumulation of grievances and then progresses through a succession of stages: precipitating incident, angry confrontation with authorities, carnival phase, and, ultimately, war.
- The most significant factor in preventing or resolving civil disorder is the quality of the relationship between the community and its police force.

Analyze the tension between safeguarding civil liberties and infringing on individual rights.

- The rule of law states that all people within the United States, regardless of their citizenship status, are covered by the provisions of the U.S. Constitution and all the statutory law that evolves from it.
- Measures such as the USA PATRIOT Act have called into question whether officials are adhering to the rule of law.

Identify victimology challenges and treatment regimens for victims with a disability, immigrants, lesbian, gay, bisexual, and questioning (LGBTQ) victims, and victims of hate crimes.

- Individuals with developmental disabilities are 4 to 10 times more likely to become crime victims than others.
- In order for an immigrant victim to be eligible for benefits, there must be credible evidence such as police reports, physical evidence, and documentation from social service or health care providers to indicate the person is a victim.
- Members of the LGBTQ community experience victimization, but little is known about prevalence of the problem and services to LGBTQ victims are limited.
- Official responses to hate crime victimizations include research, passage of laws, and training in cultural diversity and tolerance for law enforcement professionals, communities, and students.
- Effective treatment methods for crime victims with post-traumatic stress include exposure therapy, cognitive therapy, anxiety management training, psychoeducation, and critical incident stress debriefing.

Key Terms

civil disorder 472
computer forensics 464
crowd 475
cybercrime 463
fusion center 471
hate crime 472
identity theft 466
intelligence 470
intelligence-led policing (ILP) 471
mob 475
penalty enhancer 472
precursor crime 472
terrorism 468
transnational crime 465
USA PATRIOT Act 468

Study Questions

1. Which of the following is a cybercrime?
   a. Online fraud
   b. Identity theft
   c. Digital child pornography
   d. All of the above
2. __________ is the collaborative collection and analysis of data to improve crime control strategies, allocation of resources, and operations.
   a. Channel-interrupt procedure
   b. Intelligence-led policing (ILP)
   c. A fusion center
   d. Critical incident stress debriefing
3. Intelligence is the product of the application of __________ to data or information.
   a. analytical reasoning
   b. computer forensics
   c. a moving target indicator system
   d. the rule of law
4. Which of the following is *not* a precursor crime?
   a. Forging documents
   b. Crossing a border illegally
   c. Drunken driving
   d. Money laundering
5. Which of the following is a hate crime?
   a. Beating a person because he is homosexual
   b. Painting a swastika on a synagogue wall
   c. Burning a cross on the property of a Black family
   d. All of the above
6. The majority of hate crimes are motivated by
   a. ethnicity.
   b. victim disability.
   c. race.
   d. religion.
7. The most significant factor in preventing civil disorders is
   a. a decisive chief law enforcement officer.
   b. a strong tie between the community and its law enforcement entity.
   c. a nation's laws.
   d. all of the above.
8. One law that prevents the discrimination of individuals based on disability is the
   a. American Discrimination Act.
   b. Americans with Disabilities Act.
   c. Disabilities and Rehabilitation Act.
   d. U.S. Disabilities Act.
9. Immigrant victims of intimate partner violence are *not* eligible to
   a. access shelters, food banks, soup kitchens.
   b. call the police because they will be deported.
   c. access emergency medical services including prenatal care and care during labor and delivery.
   d. automatically gain U.S. citizenship.
10. The treatment method used with crime victims suffering from posttraumatic stress that teaches victims to identify and change the way they think about their traumatic events is
    a. relational management therapy.
    b. cognitive therapy.
    c. psychoeducation.
    d. exposure therapy.

Critical Thinking Questions

1. How are cybercrime, terrorism, and certain types of civil disorder changing the way criminal justice professionals do their jobs?
2. What actions can law enforcement take to prevent terrorism? How should these actions be balanced against individuals' civil liberties and rights to privacy?
3. Which is more important, security or freedom? Why?

Internet Sites

Department of Homeland Security
www.dhs.gov/index.shtm
This Web site offers a variety of information about the department and issues related to terrorism.

Australian High Tech Crime Centre
www.ahtcc.gov.au/
This Web site provides information on Australian police efforts to combat cybercrime.

Computer Crime and Intellectual Property
www.cybercrime.gov/index.html
This Web site, maintained by the U.S. Department of Justice, provides a variety of useful information, including how to report cybercrime.

Suggested Readings

Daniel Beland, *States of Global Insecurity: Policy, Politics, and Society* (New York: Worth, 2008).
This book undertakes a comparative, historical, and political analysis of state protection and the politics of insecurity surrounding it.

Jamal Nassar, *Globalization and Terrorism: The Migration of Dreams and Nightmares* (Lanham, MD: Rowman & Littlefield, 2010).
This book illuminates the effects of globalization on the Middle East and other parts of the world, breaking down the causes and effects of terrorism in terms of the cycle of violence between those with power and their victims.

TF-CBT Web First Year Report, *Trauma-Focused Cognitive-Behavioral Therapy* (Charleston, SC: National Crime Victims Research and Treatment Center, February 2007).
This is a special report for teaching an innovative method of victim treatment, "trauma-focused cognitive-behavioral therapy," in a multimedia distance education format for mental health professionals.

Bill of Rights

Amendment I

Congress shall make no law respecting an establishment of religion, or prohibiting the free exercise thereof; or abridging the freedom of speech, or of the press; or the right of the people peaceably to assemble, and to petition the Government for a redress of grievances.

Amendment II

A well regulated Militia, being necessary to the security of a free State, the right of the people to keep and bear Arms shall not be infringed.

Amendment III

No Soldier shall, in time of peace, be quartered in any house, without the consent of the Owner, nor in time of war, but in a manner to be prescribed by law.

Amendment IV

The right of the people to be secure in their persons, houses, papers, and effects, against unreasonable searches and seizures, shall not be violated, and no Warrants shall issue, but upon probably cause, supported by the Oath or affirmation, and particularly describing the place to be searched, and the persons or things to be seized.

Amendment V

No person shall be held to answer for a capital or otherwise infamous crime, unless on a presentment or indictment of a Grand Jury, except in cases arising in the land or naval forces, or in the Militia, when in actual service in time of War or public danger; nor shall any person be subject for the same offence to be paid twice put in jeopardy of life or limb; nor shall be compelled in any criminal case to be a witness against himself, nor be deprived of life, liberty, or property, without due process of law; nor shall private property be taken for public use, without just compensation.

Amendment VI

In all criminal prosecutions, the accused shall enjoy the right to a speedy and public trial, by an impartial jury of the State and district wherein the crime shall have been committed, which district shall have been previously ascertained by law, and to be informed of the nature and cause of the accusation; to be confronted with the witnesses against him; to have compulsory process for obtaining witnesses in his favour, and to have the Assistance of Counsel for his defence.

Amendment VII

In suits at common law, where the value in controversy shall exceed twenty dollars, the right of trial by jury shall be preserved, and no fact tried by a jury, shall be otherwise reexamined in any Court of the United States, than according to the rules of the common law.

Amendment VIII

Excessive bail shall not be required, nor excessive fines imposed, nor cruel and unusual punishments inflicted.

Amendment IX

The enumerations of the Constitution, of certain rights, shall not be construed to deny or disparage others retained by the people.

Amendment X

The powers not delegated to the United States by the Constitution, nor prohibited by it to the States, are reserved to the States respectively, or to the people.

Glossary

A

actus reus The specific act required to convict a person for a specific crime.

adjudicated delinquent The equivalent in the juvenile system of being found guilty in adult court.

adjudication hearing A hearing to determine whether the juvenile committed the action as charged.

administrative segregation A special area in a prison in which inmates are deprived of the services available to the general population.

adolescence-limited offenders Young people who participate in antisocial behavior for a limited period of time during adolescence while maintaining school performance and respectful relationships with parents and teachers.

adult learning Method of learning that emphasizes engaging the learner by incorporating the learner's experiences in the curriculum.

Adult Protective Services Safeguards older people and dependent adults with disabilities who are in danger of being mistreated or neglected, are unable to protect themselves, or have no one to assist them.

aggressive order maintenance Policing activities that address noncriminal or minor offenses that affect residents' quality of life.

alternative sentence A sentence that is served in a treatment facility or in community service.

American Law Institute Rule A standard for insanity that asks whether the defendant lacked the substantial capacity to appreciate the criminality of the act or conform to the law.

anomie A feeling of alienation or a condition that leaves people feeling hopeless, rootless, cut off, alienated, isolated, disillusioned, and frustrated.

appellate brief Written document containing legal arguments in an appellate case, submitted to a court by attorneys for one party.

arraignment A hearing before a judge or magistrate during which the complaint is formally read.

arrest rates The number of arrests per 100,000 persons.

assault and battery A harmful or offensive physical attack by one person upon another.

atavism The belief that criminals are evolutionally primitive or subhuman people characterized by certain "inferior" identifiable physical and mental characteristics.

attenuation An exception to the exclusionary rule that applies when the link between the unconstitutional acts and the evidence becomes weak due to intervening time or events.

attorney general A state's head law enforcement officer; also the head of the U.S. Department of Justice.

attorney–client privilege The right of a person to prevent the government from asking his lawyer to provide evidence of the content of discussions between the person and his attorney.

Auburn system A system of prison administration in which prisoners were isolated in cells at night but allowed to congregate during the day for work duty and meals, but in total silence.

automobile exception An exception to the warrant requirement holding that police do not need warrants to search automobiles, just probable cause.

B

bail A sum of money deposited by a defendant with a court to ensure the defendant's appearance at trial.

bench trial A trial in which guilt is determined by a judge rather than by a jury.

beyond a reasonable doubt The standard of proof required to criminally convict a person.

bifurcated trial A two-part trial in which the first part decides guilt and the second decides the penalty or whether the defendant was insane.

binding out Sending children to live with relatively wealthy families who provided the child with the basic necessities of life in return for labor.

bipolar affective disorder A major mood disorder manifested by bouts of serious depression alternating with periods of extreme elation and exaggerated self-importance.

blue code of silence Adherence to a code of conduct that places loyalty to fellow officers above all other values.

booking The process of photographing and fingerprinting a suspect and creating the police record of personal information and the crime(s) with which the suspect is initially being charged when taken into custody.

boot camps Facilities that use a model of military basic training, strict discipline, rigid rules, and behavior modification to command the attention of out-of-control delinquent juveniles.

broken windows theory Theory proposing that disorder leads to crime because criminals assume a neighborhood that tolerates disorder will also ignore criminal acts.

burden of proof The burden falls on the party that must prove a particular thing in court.

burglary Entering another's property with the intent to commit a felony such as larceny.

C

capital crime An offense punishable by execution.

case law Decisions judges have made in previous court cases.

case-in-chief A stage in a criminal trial during which a party presents the main body of evidence.

chain of command The line of authority that extends throughout a police organization.

challenges for cause Excusing potential jurors from a jury because they might be biased in that case.

change of venue Relocation of a case to another court because the case has received too much publicity in the original jurisdiction for the defendant to receive a fair trial.

child abuse Neglect of and/or violence against children.

child neglect Chronic and repetitive failure to provide children with food, clothing, shelter, cleanliness, medical care, or protection from harm.

Child Protective Services County-level government organizations in all 50 states whose trained staff investigates allegations of child abuse and neglect.

child savers Women in the 1800s who lobbied for child labor regulations, laws against child abuse, and a specialized justice system that would focus on the needs of youths.

civil commitment A process in which a judge decides a person is mentally ill and is a danger to himself or others, and incarcerates that person indefinitely in a mental hospital rather than a prison.

civil disorder Disturbance by a group of people that is symptomatic of a major sociopolitical problem.

civil law (1) The system of laws, sometimes known as the Roman system, used in many countries that do not use the common law system; or (2) noncriminal law, or law that concerns disputes between individual parties.

civilianization A component of community policing that increases the number of community residents active in the profession of policing by assigning to civilians tasks previously performed by sworn officers.

classical school of criminology A system of thought that views the criminal as having free will to choose a criminal path.

classification Determination of which inmates go to which institutions and the specific conditions under which they will be confined.

clear and convincing evidence An intermediate standard of proof, sometimes required for certain defenses such as the insanity defense.

commissioners People who preside over the early stages of some criminal trials, or serve as judges in specialized courts.

common law The legal system created in England after the Norman Conquest and still used in the United States today.

communications interoperability The ability of police and other public safety agencies from different jurisdictions to talk and share data.

community corrections Court-imposed programs and sanctions that allow offenders to serve their sentences within the community instead of in jail or prison.

community policing Philosophy of policing that emphasizes crime prevention and focuses on developing positive relations between the police and the public.

community-oriented policing A policing strategy that depends on getting community members to address the problems that plague their neighborhoods.

compassion fatigue Occurs when a practitioner working with a victim experiences difficulty learning more about the crime and working with the victim.

complaint The document containing the initial crimes with which a defendant is charged.

CompStat A computerized statistical program that integrates information from crime maps across the city for department leaders' review.

computer forensics Application of the knowledge and methods used in computer science to law enforcement purposes (such as recovery of deleted files or Web site activity).

conflict perspective A view of crime as one outcome of a struggle among different groups competing for resources in their society.

conjugal visit program Allows an inmate a private extended visit with a partner or spouse.

consensus perspective A view of crime that sees laws as the product of social agreement or consensus about what criminal behavior is.

consent A defense against criminal liability because the victim actually gave the defendant permission to engage in the prohibited acts.

constitution A document that specifies the components of a government, the duties of each component, and the limits of their power.

containment theory Factors that keep behavior in check are personal, such as self-concept, self-control, goal-directedness, conscience, tolerance for frustration, sense of responsibility, realistic levels of aspiration, and identification with lawful norms.

contempt of court Violation of a court's order, punishable by fine, jail time, or both.

corpus delicti "The body of the crime"; the specific elements that must be proved to convict someone of a specific offense.

corrections The systematic, organized effort by society to punish offenders, protect the public, and change an offender's behavior.

corruption Misuse of authority for personal gain, such as skimming seized narcotics monies.

Court Appointed Special Advocate (CASA) A volunteer selected by the courts to protect the rights and interests of child victims of abuse.

court of general jurisdiction A court that can hear nearly any type of case.

court of last resort The highest court to which a case may be appealed.

courts of limited jurisdiction A specialty court that can hear only cases of a certain type.

crime analysis The application of processes designed to analyze information pertinent to crimes and develop correlations useful in crime prevention, resource deployment, investigations, and suspect apprehension.

crime control model A model of the criminal justice system that emphasizes the efficient arrest and processing of alleged criminal offenders.

Crime Index An officially compiled statistical measure of the incidence of crime in the United States.

crime mapping A technique used by police to pinpoint the locations and times of crimes.

crime victim compensation Programs administered at the state level to provide financial assistance to victims and their families.

crime victimization Injuring or killing a human being in the course of a crime; the term focuses on the victim rather than on the event.

crimes against morality Specific laws against public order crimes.

crimes against persons Attack or threats of an attack to a person's body, including murder and manslaughter (both mean taking a life), sexual assault, kidnapping, robbery (theft with force or the threat of force), and battery (the intentional unwanted touching of one person by another).

criminal intent The degree to which a defendant must have intended his or her actions or the consequences of those actions.

criminal justice system The interrelation of law enforcement agencies, the courts, the correctional system, and victim services.

criminal law A body of laws in which people are punished by the government for specific prohibited actions.

criminalistics The application of scientific techniques to recognizing, identifying, individualizing, and evaluating physical evidence in legal proceedings.

crisis intervention Immediate assistance after a traumatic event.

critical theory A branch of social conflict theory concerned with the way in which structural conditions and social inequalities influence crime.

cross-examination A stage in a trial when an attorney questions the opposing side's witness.

crowd Leaderless group of individuals, generally respectful of the law, drawn together by common values about a current matter.

cruel and unusual punishment A sentence or conditions of confinement that at that time period goes beyond what is acceptable to society.

cultural deviance theory Adoption of negative and antisocial values learned in neighborhoods and subcultures produces criminal behavior.

culture conflict When the norms of conduct for one group conflict with conduct norms of another group.

custody The incarceration of persons either accused or convicted of a crime.

custody level The degree of danger an inmate poses to other prisoners and to correctional staff.

cybercrime Any crime that relies on a computer and a network for its commission; crime that exploits the electronic highway over which computer transmissions travel.

D

damages Payments a defendant must make to a winning plaintiff in a civil lawsuit to compensate the plaintiff for the injuries or costs the defendant's actions have caused.

dark figure of crime The group of unreported and unrecorded crimes as revealed by crime victim surveys.

day fines Fines based on what is fair for a specific offender to pay, instead of the same penalty regardless of ability to pay. Also called structured fines.

decentralization of command The fanning out of substations in various areas so the police maintain a physical presence throughout the city.

defendant The person against whom criminal charges or a civil lawsuit are filed.

defense attorney The lawyer who represents the defendant in a criminal case.

delinquency petition The formal document that initiates a juvenile case and lays out the specific allegations against the child; serves much the same function as a criminal complaint.

deprivation model The perspective that the hardships prisoners endure lead to the development of a distinctive way of behaving in prison.

derivative evidence rule An extension to the exclusionary rule holding that evidence derived from something that is illegally searched or seized is itself inadmissible; also known as the "fruit of the poisonous tree" doctrine.

determinate sentence Specifies a precise period of time that the offender needs to serve.

deterrence A sentencing goal focused on convincing the offender or others not to commit crime.

deviance The violation of a norm.

***Diagnostic and Statistical Manual of Mental Disorders* (DSM)** The standard classification reference used by mental health professionals in the United States.

differential association theory Criminal behavior is learned during normal social interactions, and the same learning principles are involved in reinforcing criminal and law-abiding behavior.

direct examination A stage in a trial when an attorney questions his own witness.

direct file (prosecutorial waiver) A method that allows the prosecutor to choose whether to bring the juvenile's case to juvenile or adult court.

directed verdict A motion made by a defense attorney after the prosecution has rested its case; the motion asks for the judge to direct the jury to find the defendant not guilty due to the prosecution's failure to meet its burden of proof.

discovery The process in which an attorney requests that opposing counsel or other parties provide certain evidence or information.

discretion Authority to act in a manner that officers judge most appropriate for a given situation.

discretionary release A procedure by which a parole board decides whether the offender meets eligibility requirements and is ready to be released from prison.

dispositions The results or outcome for those juveniles adjudicated delinquent.

district attorney The lawyer who prosecutes criminal cases at the local level.

diversion An intermediate sanction that is used in place of incarceration.

diversion programs Programs that handle juvenile cases informally, rather than through the juvenile court.

double jeopardy The Fifth Amendment right that protects anyone from being tried twice for the same offense.

drug offenses Public order crimes that include the unlawful possession, use, manufacturing, selling, growing, making, or distributing of drugs classified as having potential for abuse.

dual arrest The arrest of *both* parties in a physical altercation instead of identifying and arresting only the primary aggressor.

due process The right, guaranteed by the Fifth and Fourteenth Amendments, that laws and processes be fair.

due process clause A clause of the U.S. Constitution that represents the proposition that government laws and proceedings must be fair.

due process model A model of the criminal justice system that emphasizes individual rights at all stages of the justice process.

duress A defense in which the defendant claims he or she was forced or coerced into committing a crime.

Durham Rule A standard for insanity that asks whether the defendant's conduct was the product of a mental disease or defect.

E

early warning systems Data-driven programs that identify police whose behavior suggests misconduct.

elder abuse Any knowing, intentional, or negligent act by a caregiver or another person that causes harm or serious risk of harm to a vulnerable adult 60 years of age or older.

electronic monitoring The use of technology to enforce house arrest or to monitor the whereabouts of an offender through electronic sensors, usually placed around the offender's ankle, that send a continuous signal.

Elmira Reformatory A New York reformatory that emphasized rehabilitation rather than punishment.

emotional abuse A form of victimization by means of power or control that harms the victim's sense of self and is sometimes referred to as psychological abuse, including verbal threats, social isolation, intimidation, exploitation, or routinely making unreasonable demands, terrorizing, shaming, and putting the victim down.

en banc An appeals case presided over by a larger than usual panel of judges (more than three judges).

entrapment Law enforcement officers or agents trap or trick a person into committing a crime that the person would not otherwise have committed.

exclusionary rule Illegally obtained evidence cannot be used against a criminal defendant at trial.

expert witnesses People who have specialized knowledge of some scientific or technical matter that may help in the decision of a case.

expunged A process in which a court record is destroyed or made legally unavailable.

F

faith-based prison programs Services provided when a private prison corporation builds or operates a prison under contract with a government agency and invites religious organizations to offer rehabilitation services to the inmates.

federal courts The system in which federal crimes are prosecuted consisting of district courts, appellate courts or circuit courts, and the Supreme Court.

felony A serious criminal offense that brings a potential punishment of a year or more in state or federal prison.

feminist criminology The application of feminist thought and analysis to the study of crime.

fines Payments, imposed by judges, that require offenders to pay or forfeit a specific sum of money as a penalty for committing an offense.

first-degree murder The most serious kind of murder. To be convicted of first-degree murder, an offender must have purposely killed the victim and must have planned the killing at least a short time in advance.

forensic science laboratories Facilities using scientific or technical methods to process and analyze evidence.

forensics The application of scientific knowledge and methods to criminal and civil investigations and legal procedures, including criminal trials.

forfeiture Confiscation by law enforcement of profits made by committing a crime and property used to commit a crime.

fragmentation The lack of coordination among law enforcement agencies in the same geographic region due to the existence of many small departments.

frankpledge Peacekeeping system in early England in which a group of 10 local families agreed to maintain the peace and make sure lawbreakers were taken into custody and brought to court.

fruit of the poisonous tree doctrine Another name for the derivative evidence rule, which excludes evidence derived from an illegal search or seizure.

fusion center Regional intelligence hub that pools and analyzes information from many jurisdictions and shares it with those to whom it directly applies.

G

geographic information systems (GIS) A technology that uses a computerized mapping system to produce descriptions of crime occurrence and analyzes the relationships between variables such as location and time.

global positioning system (GPS) A satellite-based system that can calculate users' exact locations, direction, and speed. Many states use GPS systems to monitor sex offenders while they are on parole.

going rate A generally agreed-upon sentence for a defendant based on the crime and prior record.

good faith exception Exception to the exclusionary rule allowing illegally obtained evidence to be used if officers relied in good faith on an invalid warrant.

good time Time taken off a prison sentence for satisfactory behavior or for participating in a prison program.

grand jury Panel of citizens who may investigate certain crimes and determine whether sufficient evidence exists to bring a defendant to trial.

guilty but mentally ill (GBMI) Verdict for a person recognized to be mentally ill but still considered criminally responsible for the crime.

H

habeas corpus A written judicial order requiring that a prisoner's case be reviewed in court to determine if he is being held unconstitutionally.

habitual offender statutes Laws that create enhanced penalties for repeat offenders.

halfway house A loosely structured pre-release, community-based residence that helps prisoners adjust to the community after total incarceration.

Hammurabi's Code The earliest known written laws, which were set down by Babylonian King Hammurabi (1792–1750 BCE). The core of the code was the principle that violators should suffer punishment equal to their offense.

hands-off doctrine An approach that made courts reluctant to interfere with prison management or prisoner rights.

hate crime Criminal offense committed because of the victim's race, ethnicity, religion, sexual orientation, or other group affiliation.

hearsay evidence Any statement made by a witness that is not based on that witness's personal knowledge.

hot spot Areas of concentrated crime or higher risk of victimization.

house arrest (home confinement) An intermediate sanction that restricts offenders to their homes during the time they are not working or attending treatment programs.

hulks Abandoned ships that functioned as enormous holding blocks within which offenders were chained.

hung jury A jury that is unable, after concerted effort, to reach a verdict.

I

identity theft Unauthorized use of another person's identifying information to obtain credit, goods, services, money, or to commit a misdemeanor or felony.

immigration offenses Violation of federal immigration law, which determines whether a person is an alien and stipulates all the legal rights, duties, and obligations aliens have in the United States.

importation model The perspective assuming that inmate subculture does not develop as a result of prison circumstances but rather is brought in, or imported, from the outside when offenders enter.

in chambers Meeting that occurs between attorneys and a judge in the judge's office rather than in the courtroom.

incapacitation A sentencing goal that aims to make it impossible for the offender to commit a future crime because he is imprisoned.

incarceration Imprisonment in the criminal justice system.

inchoate crimes Crimes that have been begun but not completed.

indentured servitude The practice of selling criminals as servants to private individuals instead of sentencing them to penal colonies.

independent source Exception to the exclusionary rule permitting the use of evidence discovered independent of any improper search or seizure.

indeterminate sentence The offender is given a range of time he can serve, such as 5 to 7 years, dependent on how he behaves while in prison.

indictment A document issued by a grand jury after if finds probable cause, formally listing the charges against the defendant.

industrial prisons Prison factories where the focus was on creating a productive work environment rather than the rehabilitation or reform of prisoners.

inevitable discovery Exception to the exclusionary rule allowing illegally obtained evidence to be admissible if it would inevitably have been discovered through legal means.

infancy A defense that sometimes protects very young offenders from criminal liability because they do not understand the consequences of their actions.

infancy defense A defense holding that children under age 7 could not be criminally prosecuted because they were too young to form *mens rea,* or criminal intent.

informal probation A situation in which as long as the child obeys certain conditions and stays out of trouble, the case will not proceed any further, such as to court.

information A document filed by a prosecutor after a preliminary hearing, formally listing the charges against the defendant.

infraction A minor violation of a local ordinance or state law that brings a potential punishment of fines.

inmate code Rules of behavior that inmates follow.

inmate subculture The norms, values, and beliefs that develop among prisoners.

insanity A defense in which the defendant admits committing the criminal act but claims not to be culpable due to mental illness.

institutional corrections Incarceration in jails and prisons.

institutionalization The state of being dependent on an institution to meet basic needs, such as for food, shelter, and friends, to the point of being unwilling—or unable—to function in the outside world.

intake Process during which an official decides whether to release the juvenile or refer the case to court or put the juvenile under some other supervision.

intake officer The probation officer who makes the initial decision about whether to proceed with a case.

integrity Adherence to moral principles and professional standards.

intelligence Product of the application of analytical reasoning to data in order to develop a reliable picture of the environment or a situation.

intelligence The capacity to learn or comprehend, manifested by the ability to solve problems and adapt to life's everyday experiences.

intelligence-led policing (ILP) Collaborative collection and analysis of data by intelligence analysts, field officers, and senior leaders.

intensive-supervision probation (ISP) A variety of probation programs characterized by smaller officer caseloads and closer surveillance.

intermediate sanctions Judicial punishments that do not require incarceration but stop short of allowing offenders to remain in the community on probation with minimal supervision.

intimate partner violence An assault on a person with whom the attacker is intimately involved.

involuntary manslaughter A killing that results from an offender's careless actions.

irresistible impulse test A standard for insanity that asks whether the defendant had a mental disease or defect, as a result of which the defendant was unable to control his or her behavior.

J

jail Municipal or regional facilities that house pretrial individuals believed to present a risk of danger or flight, those awaiting probation or parole revocation, and those sentenced to less than 1 year incarceration.

judicial waiver A means by which a juvenile is sent by a judge to be tried in adult court.

jurisdiction A court's legal power to hear a particular case.

jury nullification The power of juries to refuse to apply criminal laws when they feel applying them would be unjust.

justice of the peace A judge who handles matters such as warrants, infractions, and the early stages of a criminal case.

juvenile delinquency Criminal acts that are committed by juveniles.

juvenile hall A juvenile detention center.

juvenile justice system The justice system that attempts to address important distinctions between children and adults and differs from the adult system in many respects.

L

labeling theory The belief that the social process individuals experience has the potential to define them as "bad" or "good" and that some people become bad because others do not believe them to be good.

larceny A type of theft that includes both completed and attempted taking of cash or property from a location *without* attacking or threatening the victim and without obtaining permission.

law enforcement The police agency's application of the criminal code to specific situations.

laws Formal rules of conduct sanctioned by the state.

lay witness A person who has personally seen or heard information relevant to the case at hand; also called a fact witness or eyewitness.

life course persistent offenders Those who engage in delinquency at young ages and continue their criminal behavior throughout their lives.

line activities The principal activities performed by law enforcement officers, including patrol, follow-up investigation, and traffic operations.

local legal culture A shared understanding of how cases should be processed.

long-term therapy Focuses on the victim's responses to trauma, symptoms of PTSD, anxiety disorders, depression, terminal conditions, and dysfunctional behaviors that render victims vulnerable.

looking-glass self The idea that if we perceive that others see us in certain ways, we learn to see ourselves in those ways.

M

M'Naghten Rule A standard for insanity that asks whether the defendant was unable to understand the nature of his actions or to distinguish right from wrong.

magistrate A judge who handles matters such as warrants, infractions, and the early stages of a criminal case.

maintaining order Peace-keeping activities, including enforcement of quality of life laws such as no loitering.

mala in se A behavior categorized as morally wrong ("evil in itself").

mala prohibita A statutory crime that reflects public opinion at a moment in time.

mandatory arrest policy Requires officers to make an arrest when there is evidence of an assault.

mandatory release Early release mandated by law after an offender has served a specified time in prison.

mandatory reporting law Requires that professionals who have regular contact with a child report any reasonable suspicions of physical or sexual abuse or neglect to the proper law enforcement or protective services.

manslaughter A killing in which the offender is less blameworthy than for murder; it usually carries a less severe penalty than murder.

mass murder Multiple murders that occur at one place and at one time.

maximum-security prisons Institutions subject to high levels of control in which the mobility of prisoners is severely restricted by physical barriers.

medical model A viewpoint focusing on mental illness and behavioral problems, such as committing a crime, as diseases.

medium-security prisons Institutions in which inmates are under greater control than in minimum-security prisons, and their freedom of movement is restricted to areas that are under close surveillance.

mens rea The level of criminal intent, or the mental state, required to convict a person of a specific crime.

minimum-security prisons Institutions that hold offenders who have short sentences, are nonviolent, and are unlikely to attempt escape or pose risks to others in the institution.

***Miranda* warnings** Notifications that police must give suspects about their rights prior to beginning custodial interrogation.

misdemeanor A criminal offense that is punished by fines or a maximum of a year in a county or city jail.

missing children Children not accounted for by their next of kin because they were kidnapped, killed, wandered away due to a developmental disability, or are intentionally missing in order to escape violence at home.

mistrial A judge's ruling that declares a trial invalid, often because of a hung jury.

misuse of authority Police disregard for policies, rules, or laws in the performance of their duty.

mob Non–law-abiding group, with a leader, ruled by emotion.

Model Penal Code A suggested code of criminal law drafted by the American Law Institute and used to guide the states in modernizing their laws.

moral panic The reaction by a group of people based on exaggerated or false perceptions about crime and criminal behavior.

moral reasoning Application of a set of ethical principles based on what society views as good versus bad behavior.

motor vehicle theft A property crime that usually does not include contact with the offender and accompanying fear or trauma. It is less common than household burglary or larceny.

N

National Crime Victimization Survey (NCVS) A statistical sampling of households and individuals who have been personally victimized by specific crimes.

National Incident-Based Reporting System (NIBRS) A U.S. crime index (not yet fully national in scope) compiled by the FBI and the Department of Justice that tracks detailed information about 22 categories of crime incidents and arrests.

necessity A defense in which the defendant must demonstrate that he or she had to commit the crime to avoid more severe consequences.

neoclassical school of criminology Recognizes differences in criminal circumstances and assumes that some people, such as children, the insane, and the intellectually deficient, cannot reason. In such cases the criminal justice system must look at the needs of the offender in determining appropriate punishments.

neurotransmitter A chemical secreted by neurons that facilitates the transmission of information from one neuron to another.

neutralization theory If people break the law, they overcome their feelings of responsibility through rationalizations.

1974 Martinson report Indicated that rehabilitative efforts, for the most part, have had little to no effect on recidivism.

no contest (nolo contendere) A plea in which a defendant admits that sufficient evidence exists to convict him, but he does not actually admit his guilt.

noble cause Justification for wrongdoing committed by an officer based on the premise that the end justifies the means.

norm A rule that makes clear what behavior is appropriate and expected in a particular situation.

not guilty by reason of insanity (NGRI) A verdict in which the jury determines that the defendant is not criminally culpable due to mental illness.

O

opening statements Initial statements made by attorneys to a jury outlining the case they will present during the trial.

ordinances Laws enacted by local governments such as cities and counties.

organized crime An ongoing criminal conspiracy that exists to profit from providing illicit goods and services, using or threatening violence to facilitate its criminal enterprise and to maintain monopoly control of illicit markets.

P

pains of imprisonment The deprivations inmates experience such as liberty, autonomy, security, personal goods and services, and heterosexual relations.

parens patriae A legal doctrine that gives the government authority to step in and make decisions about children, even against the wishes of their parents, when doing so is in the children's best interests.

parole An early release from prison conditional on complying with certain standards while free.

parole boards Groups of persons authorized by law to grant permission for selected offenders—after serving a portion of time in prison—to serve their remaining sentence in the community.

peacemaking criminology A branch of criminology that views crime as a form of violence and urges criminology to advocate a nonviolent, peaceful society.

penalty enhancer Attribute that adds to the penalty for a crime.

penitentiary Term the Quakers coined from the word *penitent*—referring to a residence where offenders could be sorrowful for their wrongdoings.

Pennsylvania system A system of prison administration in which inmates lived in solitary confinement, total silence, and religious penitence as the way to prevent future criminal behavior.

peremptory challenges An attorney removes a prospective juror she feels will not be sympathetic to her side of the case.

petit jury Small groups of citizens who determine whether a criminal defendant is guilty of the crimes with which he is charged.

physical abuse The condition whereby an individual suffers serious physical injury, including intentionally assaulting, beating, biting, burning, strangulation, hitting, kicking, shaking, or pushing a victim.

plaintiff The party who initiates the lawsuit in a civil case.

plea A defendant's formal denial or admission of guilt.

plea bargains Agreements between defendants and prosecutors, in which defendants plead guilty to the original or reduced charges in exchange for reduced sentences.

police–community reciprocity A policing practice that relies on collaboration between police and community members to solve and prevent crime.

police occupational subculture Norms and beliefs embraced by most officers in a given country.

police organizational subculture Norms and beliefs particular to an individual department.

political crimes Violent or nonviolent acts that society perceives as threats to a government's survival.

positivist school of criminology Views criminal behavior as a product of biological, psychological, and social forces beyond a person's control.

postpartum psychosis A serious mental illness characterized by hallucinations, delusions, and obsessive thoughts about the baby.

precedent Previous court decisions that have binding authority on subsequent cases.

precursor crime Offense committed for the purpose of enabling acts of terrorism, such as illegal border crossings or forged documents.

preliminary hearing A proceeding in which a judge determines whether probable cause exists to bring the defendant to court to face trial for the crimes with which he has been charged.

preponderance of the evidence The standard of proof required to win a civil lawsuit.

Presentence Investigation Reports (PSI) Reports that provide the court with a basis for making a sentencing decision by including a personal history of the offender, often a victim impact statement, and a recommendation for sentencing.

presumptive sentencing models A sentencing model assuming that judges should sentence within sentencing guidelines, or within ranges specified for particular charges.

preventive detention The practice of holding a suspect without bail because he is believed to pose a potential danger to the community or at risk of fleeing the jurisdiction.

preventive detention (juvenile) Custodial holding of children accused of crimes to ensure they appear in court, but also to protect them from adverse home conditions or to prevent them from committing additional offenses while their case is pending.

preventive detention laws Legislation that allows the criminal justice system to prevent offenders from committing future crimes by lengthy incarceration or placement in mental health facilities.

preventive patrol Officers maintaining a visible presence in communities to serve as a deterrent to a variety of street-level crimes.

primary victim A person injured or killed as a direct result of a criminal act.

Prison Rape Elimination Act (PREA) Legislation that established the National Prison Rape Elimination Commission to develop national standards for detecting and preventing prison rape, as well as for punishing perpetrators.

prisonization A process of socialization whereby individuals adopt the norms, values, and beliefs of the inmate subculture as their own.

prisons State or federal facilities that hold offenders sentenced to 1 year or more incarceration.

private security Any individual, organization, or service—other than public law enforcement and regulatory agencies—engaged primarily in the prevention and investigation of crime, loss, or harm to specific individuals, organizations, or facilities.

privatization The transfer of government programs and functions to the private sector.

proactive foot patrol A component of community policing that leads to increased interactions between the police and community members to improve relationships.

probable cause The amount of evidence necessary to obtain a warrant or conduct most searches and seizures.

probation An alternative to jail or prison in which the offender remains in the community under court supervision, usually within the caseload of a probation officer who is an officer of the court.

probation kiosks Automated reporting machines, resembling an ATM, that monitor low-risk nonviolent offenders.

problem-oriented policing A policing strategy based on conducting specific and detailed research on a community's problems to discover the underlying dynamics of crime.

property crimes Taking money and/or material goods *without* the use of force.

prosecutorial discretion The prosecutor's power to determine when to bring criminal charges and which charges to bring.

psychic trauma Severe emotional stress that immobilizes the victim's mind and body and can result in long-lasting emotional injury.

psychopathy A personality disorder exhibited by a lifelong pattern of antisocial behavior about which the individual has no remorse.

psychoses Serious mental disorders that cause individuals to be out of touch with reality and unable to cope with the demands of everyday living.

public order crimes A wide variety of offenses considered immoral or public nuisances, including disorderly conduct, disturbing the peace, loitering, public intoxication, panhandling, bigamy, drunk driving, weapons violations, prostitution, obscenity, gambling, and possession of controlled substances.

public safety exception Exception to *Miranda* requiring police to interrogate suspects without first warning them of their rights if there is a significant threat to public safety.

punishment model A viewpoint that assumes the offender is inherently a bad person and deserves to be placed under correctional authority for punishment.

punitive segregation A special area in a prison that provides additional supervision and control of inmates for disciplinary reasons.

Q

qualified immunity The inability of officers to be sued for their actions under certain circumstances.

R

racial profiling Police contact with an individual initiated because of the person's skin color or ethnicity.

rape trauma syndrome The three phases (acute phase, outward adjustment phase, and resolution phase) of symptoms that many victims experience after a sexual assault.

rational choice theory Criminals choose to commit crime because they believe the benefits they will derive will overshadow the risks of getting caught.

reasonable suspicion Amount of evidence necessary for officers to conduct a stop-and-frisk, or *Terry* stop.

recidivism The habitual relapse into criminal behavior.

recidivist victims Persons who are victimized repeatedly.

recidivists Offenders who have been previously convicted of crimes.

recognizance Literally, "an obligation to the court" that usually requires the accused, if released on his own recognizance, to perform some act such as appearing at trial instead of being incarcerated.

recusal The act by which a judge removes herself from a case because she may be biased, or may have the appearance of being biased.

referees People who preside over the early stages of some criminal trials, or serve as judges in specialized courts.

reform schools Industrial schools that housed children who were delinquent, disobedient, or otherwise wayward.

rehabilitation A sentencing goal focused on aiding offenders in changing their lives.

rehabilitation model A viewpoint that assumes the offender is inherently a good person and focuses on changing an offender's behavior.

reintegration model A viewpoint that assumes that offenders must be helped to readjust and fit successfully back into the community.

remand The act by which an appellate court sends a case back to a lower court for further proceedings.

restitution In a criminal case, money a defendant must pay a victim to compensate the victim for damages.

restorative justice A perspective that focuses on the offender's responsibility to repair the hurt, damage, and injustice the crime victim experienced by making restitution and doing community service.

retribution A sentencing goal focused on punishing the convicted for the crime.

risk assessment instrument A worksheet that measures the degree of risk present in a given case.

risk classification An assessment of the level and kind of risk an individual presents to correctional staff and other inmates.

robbery A crime against persons in which the offender takes personal property from the victim by either using or threatening force.

routine activities theory Some individuals' daily activities make them more vulnerable to being crime victims.

rule of law The guiding principle of our legal system, which states that no single person is more powerful than the law.

S

sanctions Prescribed consequences intended to reinforce people's conformity to norms.

schizophrenia A mental illness characterized by an individual's split from reality.

sealed A juvenile record that is made inaccessible.

search incident to arrest A warrantless search of a person and the area around that person, conducted shortly after the person is arrested.

secondary victim Someone who experiences sympathetic pain as a result of a primary victim's suffering.

secondary victims Family and friends of an individual who has been victimized.

secondary victimization The suffering of a crime victim caused by his subsequent treatment by the police, the courts, or personal acquaintances.

security level The degree of danger associated with the inmates being housed in a prison.

security threat group (STG) Inmates who, when they collaborate, can jeopardize the institution's security.

self-report Surveys in which individuals (who are guaranteed confidentiality) reveal offenses that they have committed but may or may not have been arrested and held accountable for their crimes. These surveys uncover another part of the dark figure of crime.

sequestered A jury that is kept separate from outside contact during a trial.

serial murder Killing three or more people over an extended period of time.

service activities Non-law enforcement activities performed by officers on an as-needed basis.

sexual assault nurse examiner (SANE) Nurse who provides 24-hour first-response medical care and crisis intervention for rape victims in hospital and clinics.

sexual assault response team (SART) Made up of local police officers, victim advocates, SANE practitioners, and prosecutors, who in many states work together to determine the most effective way to work on sexual assault cases.

sexual victimization Forced or coerced sexual intimacy.

sexual violence A range of crimes including vaginal, anal, and oral penetration that can include the use of weapons and foreign objects to torture and terrorize the victim.

shock probation A combination of probation with short-term incarceration.

shock programs Short-term incarceration programs used to frighten the offender by instilling uncertainty about whether the offender will be released and, if so, when.

short-term therapy Usually administered by clinical psychologists, clinical social workers, and marriage and family counselors to address immediate mental health concerns.

siege mentality Police view of themselves as a "band of brothers"—or "sisters"—against everyone else in society.

simulation-based training Use of computers, media players, interactive screens, and authentic-looking replicas of police firearms and vehicles to simulate field conditions.

social bond theory The social bond people have with society consists of attachment, commitment, involvement, and belief.

social conflict theory Crime is the result of conflict between the wealthy and powerful and the poor and powerless in society.

social control theory An individual's belief system, the police, and parental supervision are important in preventing individuals from getting into trouble.

social disorganization theory Explains crime rates by examining city neighborhood characteristics.

social learning theory Behavior is learned and is maintained or extinguished based on the rewards or punishments associated with it.

social norm A rule that specifies how people are expected to behave.

social process theory Criminal behavior results from successive interactions with others and with society's institutions.

solitary confinement Isolation that denies the basic human need to interact with others.

solvability The likelihood that a crime will be solved.

span of control The extent of an individual's authority, or the number of individuals that one person is responsible for overseeing.

special prosecutor A prosecutor who is appointed specifically for one particular case, usually because of his specialized knowledge or experience.

spree murder Killing several people within a fairly narrow period, such as several hours or days.

stalking Willfully, maliciously, and repeatedly following or harassing another person and making a credible threat with the intent to place that person in reasonable fear for his or her safety, or for the safety of his or her family.

standing The legal ability to assert a particular constitutional claim.

state courts The system in which state crimes are prosecuted; it includes both trial and appellate courts.

status offense An offense that is illegal only because the defendant is a child, such as playing truant or running away.

statutes Laws enacted by state legislatures or by Congress.

statutory crime An act that is criminal because it is prohibited by law.

statutory exclusion A state law categorically excluding certain ages and offenses from juvenile court jurisdiction.

statutory minimum The minimum sentence set by a legislature that must be imposed for a particular crime.

stop-and-frisk Police action allowing the police, with reasonable suspicion, to briefly detain a person, question him about his activities, require him to show identification, and frisk him, or pat him down for weapons; also known as a *Terry* stop.

strain theory Extraordinary pressures make people more likely to commit crime.

strict liability offenses Crimes that have no mens rea requirement; a person who commits the requisite actus reus may be convicted of the offense regardless of intent.

student bullying A form of victimization in which a student is repeatedly exposed to harmful acts from other students over a period of time.

subculture A group that has some of the same norms, values, and beliefs as members of the dominant, mainstream culture but also other norms, values, and beliefs *not* held by society at large.

subpoena A legal document ordering a person to appear in court.

supermaximum-security (supermax) prisons Facilities that provide the highest level of security possible—solitary confinement—using the latest correctional technology.

support activities Additional policing activities that support line activities, such as communications, custody, and forensics.

survivor A relative or loved one of a person who has been killed; also, a crime victim who copes well and manages to resume a normal life.

sworn personnel Police department employees entrusted with arrest powers; usually referred to as "peace officers."

T

targeted integrity testing Strategy of using controlled opportunities to test for unlawful or unethical behavior.

teen court A court in which teenagers serve as jurors and often as judges, attorneys, and bailiffs as well.

terrorism Premeditated, politically motivated violence perpetrated against noncombatant targets by subnational groups or clandestine agents.

***Terry* stop** Another name for stop-and-frisk, in which the police, with reasonable suspicion, briefly detain a person, question him about his activities, require him to show identification, and frisk him, or pat him down for weapons.

testimonial evidence Words or statements made by a person.

torts Civil disputes in which one party sues another for the damages the defendant's actions have caused.

total institutions Facilities responsible for, and in control of, every aspect of life for those who live and work within them, including food, shelter, medical assistance, clothing, and safety.

transnational crime Crime orchestrated across a national boundary from where the crime actually occurs.

transportation The export of criminals to other lands to complete their sentences.

TRIAD A collaborative effort between police departments, sheriff's offices, and senior groups (like AARP) to reduce crime and the victimization of older adults.

U

unconditional release Releasing inmates from prison without parole.

Uniform Crime Reports (UCR) An annual series of U.S. statistical measures of the incidence of selected crimes reported by police departments and compiled by the FBI.

unity of command The requirement that each individual within an organization reports directly to a single individual higher in the chain of command.

USA PATRIOT Act "Uniting and Strengthening America by Providing Appropriate Tools Required to Intercept and Obstruct Terrorism Act" enacted by Congress following the 9/11 terrorist attacks, intended to deter and punish terrorist acts in the United States and around the world, to enhance law enforcement investigatory tools, and to strengthen measures to prevent and detect terrorism.

use of force continuum Guideline depicting the appropriate amount of force a law enforcement officer may use in particular kinds of situations.

V

vehicular manslaughter Death that results from careless driving.

venire A group of people called to be prospective jurors.

vicarious trauma Psychological distress experienced by persons who know about a traumatic event experienced by another person and who feel the victim's pain.

victim advocate A professional who assists the victim with every aspect of the postvictimization period.

victim impact statement A victim's statement about how his experiences with crime affected him.

victim recidivism Occurs when a person, household, or business is victimized more than once; also called repeat victimization.

victim services The promotion of victims' rights to participate in criminal proceedings and to enjoy personal safety; services include shelters and transitional housing programs, counseling services, and 24-hour hotlines.

victim surveys Interviews with individuals (including but not limited to actual victims) who have been personally affected by specific crimes.

victimless crimes Often called crimes against public order and considered victimless because they usually have no identifiable victim.

victim–offender mediation A process that brings victims and offenders face-to-face to work out a restitution and restorative strategy under the direction of a trained counselor or mediator.

victimology The scientific study of victims, which includes their behaviors, injuries, assistance, legal rights, and recovery.

vigilantism Use of volunteer, self-appointed committees organized to suppress crime and punish criminals.

voir dire The process of questioning prospective jurors about their background, opinions, and knowledge relevant to a particular case.

voluntariness test Rule that confessions are inadmissible unless made willingly.

voluntary manslaughter Killing in the heat of passion.

W

waiver A mechanism to permit the transfer of some juvenile offenders to adult court.

Walnut Street Jail The first public institution to specifically use imprisonment as the primary method of reforming offenders.

warrant A legal document, based on probable cause, permitting police to conduct a search or seizure, or to arrest someone.

watch system System in which particular men were assigned the job of watchman and became responsible for patrolling the streets, lighting lanterns, serving as a lookout for fires, and generally keeping order.

wedding cake model An explanation of the workings of the criminal justice system that shows how cases get filtered according to the seriousness of the offense.

white-collar crime Illegal or unethical acts that violate fiduciary responsibility or public trust, committed by an individual or organization, usually during the course of legitimate occupational activity, by persons of high or respectable social status for personal or organizational gain.

work release (furlough) Partial release of inmates to work for pay in the community and return to a correctional facility each night.

workhouse An institution that held jobless vagrants, debtors, and sometimes serious criminals.

writ of certiorari A request that a case be heard by an appellate court such as the U.S. Supreme Court.

Endnotes

CHAPTER 1

1. Jessica DiNapoli, "Two Men Charged in Fatal Stabbing of East Quogue Man," *The Southampton Press*, June 27, 2008; Vera Chinese, "Man Convicted of Second Degree Murder in Slaying of East Quogue Man," *The Southampton Press*, May 20, 2009.
2. Ibid.
3. Matthew Chayes, "Ronkonkoma Man Convicted of Murder in Stabbing Death" Newsday.com, May 19, 2009, www.newsday.com/news/local/crime/ny-listab-2012785388may19,0,7182553.story.
4. Hans Joachim Schneider, "The Media World of Crime: A Study of Learning Theory and Symbolic Interaction," in *Advances in Criminological Theory*, vol. 2, eds. William S. Laufer and Freda Adler (Piscataway, NJ: Transaction, 1990), 115–144.
5. William Chambliss, "A Sociological Analysis of the Law of Vagrancy," *Social Problems* (Summer 1964): 67–77.
6. Death Penalty Information Center, www.deathpenaltyinfo.org/ (retrieved July 3, 2009).
7. Andrew Karmen, *Crime Victims: An Introduction to Victimology*, 5th ed. (Belmont, CA: Wadsworth, Cengage Learning, 2004).
8. See Samuel Walker and Charles Katz, *The Police in America: An Introduction* (New York: McGraw Hill, 2008).
9. Ibid.
10. U.S. Department of Justice, Office of Justice Programs, Bureau of Justice Statistics, "Corrections Statistics," www.ojp.usdoj.gov/bjs/correct.htm#findings (retrieved July 3, 2009).
11. Harvey Wallace, *Family Violence: Legal, Medical, and Social Perspectives*, 4th ed. (Needham Heights, MA: Pearson, Allyn & Bacon, 2005).
12. Karmen, *Crime Victims.*
13. Denise Kindschi Gosselin, *Heavy Hands: An Introduction to the Crimes of Family Violence*, 3rd ed. (Upper Saddle River, NJ: Prentice Hall, 2005).
14. Thomas Underwood and Christine Edmunds, eds., *Victim Assistance: Exploring Individual Practice, Organizational Policy, and Societal Responses* (New York: Springer, 2003).
15. Thomas Cohen and Brian Reaves, "Felony Defendants in Large Urban Counties, 2002," *Bureau of Justice Statistics*, February 2006, NCJ 210818, www.ojp.usdoj.gov/bjs/pub/pdf/fdluc02.pdf (retrieved July 6, 2009).
16. Herbert Packer, *The Limits of the Criminal Sanction* (Stanford, CA: Stanford University Press, 1968).
17. Karmen, *Crime Victims.*
18. Bureau of Justice Statistics, "Number of Victimizations and Victimization Rates by Type of Crime and Victim-Offender Relationship," 2006, www.ojp.usdoj.gov/bjs/pub/pdf/cvus/current/cv0628.pdf (retrieved January 3, 2009).
19. See Jeffery Edleson and Claire Renzetti, *Violence against Women: Classic Papers* (Boston, MA: Allyn and Bacon, 2005); Esther Madriz, *Nothing Happens to Good Girls: Fear of Crime in Women's Lives* (Berkeley, CA: University of California Press, 1997).
20. Gallup. www.Gallup.com (retrieved February 4, 2008).
21. Dereck Chadee, Liz Austen, and Jason Ditton, "The Relationship between Likelihood and Fear of Victimization," *The British Journal of Criminology* 47 (2007): 133–153; Kenneth Ferraro, *Fear of Crime: Interpreting Victimization Risk* (Albany, NY: State University of New York Press, 1995).
22. Bureau of Justice Statistics, "Victmization Rates for Persons Age 12 and Over, by Gender and Age of Victims and Type of Crime, 2006," www.ojp.usdoj.gov/bjs/pub/pdf/cvus/current/cv0604.pdf (retrieved January 3, 2009).
23. Kenneth Ferraro, "Women's Fear of Victimization: Shadow of Sexual Assault?" *Social Forces* 75 (1996): 667.
24. Bureau of Justice Statistics, "Victmization Rates for Persons Age 12 and Over."
25. Wesley G. Skogan and William R. Klecka, "Fear of Crime," John Howard Society of Alberta 1999, www.johnhoward.ab.ca/PUB/C49.htm (retrieved May 15, 2006).
26. Ronald Weitzer and Charis Kubrin, "Breaking News: How Local TV News and Real-World Conditions Affect Fear of Crime," *Justice Quarterly* 21 (2004): 497.
27. R. Lance Holbert, Dhavan Shah, and Nojin Kwak, "Fear, Authority, and Justice: Crime Related TV Reviewing and Endorsements of Capital Punishment and Gun Ownership," *Journalism & Mass Communication Quarterly* 81 (2004): 343.
28. Lori Dorfman and Vincent Schiraldi, *Off Balance: Youth, Race, and Crime in the News* (Washington, DC: Building Blocks for Youth, 2001). Executive Summary, Berkeley Media Studies Group, www.buildingblocksforyouth.org/media.
29. There were an estimated 454.5 violent crimes per inhabitants in 2008. Federal Bureau of Investigation, *Crime in the United States*, 2008. Retrieved (Oct. 2, 2009), from http://www.fbi.gov/usr/cius2008/offenses/violent_crime/index.html.
30. Samuel Walker, Cassia Spohn, and Miriam Delone, *The Color of Justice: Race, Ethnicity and Crime in America* (California: Wadsworth, Cengage Learning, 2004).
31. Angela Davis, *Women, Race & Class* (New York: Vintage Books, 1983).
32. Bureau of Justice Statistics, "Percent Distribution of Single-Offender Victimizations, Based on Race of Victims, by Type of Crime and Perceived Race of Offender, 2006." www.ojp.usdoj.gov/bjs/abstract/cvus/race989.htm (retrieved August 17, 2009).
33. Jessie Klein, "Teaching Her a Lesson: Media Misses Boys' Rage Relating to Girls in School Shootings," *Crime Media Culture* 1 (2005): 90–97.
34. Heather West and William Sabol, "Prisoners in 2007." Bureau of Justice Statistics, U.S. Department of Justice Office of Justice Programs, December 2008, NCJ 224280.

35. Ibid.

36. Marc Mauer, *The Crisis of the Young African American Male and the Criminal Justice System* (Washington DC: U.S. Commission on Civil Rights, 1999).

37. Walker, Spohn, and Delone, *The Color of Justice.*

38. Diana Ahmad, *The Opium Debate and Chinese Exclusion Laws in the Nineteenth Century American West* (Nevada: University of Nevada Press, 2007).

39. National Center for Chronic Disease Prevention and Health Promotion, "National Youth Risk Behavior Survey, 2007," www.cdc.gov/HealthyYouth/yrbs/pdf/yrbs07_us_disparity_race.pdf (retrieved January 3, 2009); National Institutes of Health, "Drug Use among Racial/Ethnic Minorities," Report No. 95-3888 (Washington, DC: U.S. Government Printing Office, 1995); National Institute on Drug Abuse, "National Household Survey on Drug Abuse: Population Estimates 1990" (Washington, DC: U.S. Government Printing Office, 1991).

40. Sheryl Pimlott and Rosemary Sarri, "The Forgotten Group: Women in Prisons and Jails," in *Women at the Margins: Neglect, Punishment, and Resistance*, eds. Josefina Figueira-McDonough and Rosemary Sarri (New York: Haworth Press, 2002).

41. Joan E. Foltz, "Global Crime Case: Cybercrime and Counterfeiting," *The Futurist* 42, no. 6 (2008): 46.

42. National Institute of Justice, "Identity Theft—A Research Review," U.S. Department of Justice, July 2007.

43. Stephan Aguilar-Millan, Joan E. Foltz, John Jackson, and Amy Oberg, "Global Crime Case: The Modern Slave Trade," *The Futurist* 42, no. 6 (2008): 45.

44. Barry Kellman, "Bioviolence: A Growing Threat," *The Futurist* 42, no. 3 (2008): 26.

45. Heather C. West and William J. Sabol, "Prisoners in 2007," *Bureau of Justice Statistics Bulletin*, December 2008, NCJ 224280, 6–7.

46. Yan Zhang, Christopher D. Maxwell, and Michael S. Vaughn, "The Impact of State Sentencing Policies on the U.S. Prison Population," *Journal of Criminal Justice* 37, no. 2 (2009): 197.

47. Patrick A. Langan and David J. Levin, "Recidivism of Prisoners Released in 1994," *Bureau of Justice Statistics Special Report,* June 2002, NCJ 193427, 1.

48. William Kanapaux, "Guilty of Mental Illness," *Psychiatric Times* 21, no. 1 (2004): 1.

49. Michael Thompson, Fred Osher, and Denise Tomasini-Joshi, "Improving Responses to People with Mental Illness: The Essential Elements of a Mental Health Court," *Bureau of Justice Assistance* (2007): 10.

50. The Innocence Project, "News and Information: Fact Sheets," www.innocenceproject.org/Content/351.php (retrieved July 2, 2009).

51. http://dna.gov/backlog-reduction/ (retrieved July 3, 2009).

52. www.ojp.usdoj.gov/nij/topics/technology/less-lethal/welcome.htm (retrieved July 3, 2009).

CHAPTER 2

1. David Scott and Carl Hulse, "Idaho Senator Says He Did Nothing Wrong," *The New York Times*, August 28, 2007, ww.nytimes.com/2007/08/28/washington/28cnd-craig.html?_r=1&or ef=slogin&pagewanted=print (retrieved October 6, 2007); "Monday: Idaho Senator Fined for Lewd Behavior at Minneapolis Airport," *Star Tribune.com: Minneapolis–St. Paul, Minnesota,* August 29, 2007, www.startribune.com/587/v-print/story/1386023.html (retrieved October 6, 2007).

2. Federal Bureau of Investigation, *Crime in the United States*, 2008. Retrieved (Oct. 2, 2009), from http://www.fbi.gov/usr/cius2008/documents/aboutcius.pdf.

3. Keith Clement and John Barbrey, "Criminal Laws on the Fringe: An Analysis of Legislated Punishments for Morality Crimes in the Fifty States," *Critical Criminology* 16, no. 2 (2008).

4. Federal Bureau of Investigation, "Uniform Crime Reports," www.fbi.gov/ucr/ucrquest.htm (retrieved July 5, 2009).

5. Ibid.

6. Federal Bureau of Investigation, "Uniform Crime Report—Hate Crime Statistics, 2007," October 2008.

7. Federal Bureau of Investigation, "FBI Releases 2007 Hate Crime Statistics," 2007, www.fbi.gov/ucr/hc2007/summary.htm (retrieved July 5, 2009).

8. Bill Hanna, "James Byrd, Jr.: 10 Years Later, 'Horrific Death' in Jasper Won't Fade from Memory," *The Star Telegram (Texas),* June 8, 2008.

9. Federal Bureau of Investigation, "Uniform Crime Reports," www.fbi.gov/ucr/ucrquest.htm (retrieved July 5, 2009).

10. Federal Bureau of Investigation, "Variables Affecting Crime," www.fbi.gov/ucr/icus2007/about variables_affecting_crime.html (retrieved July 5, 2009).

11. Federal Bureau of Investigation, "NIBRS Frequently Asked Questions," www.fbi.gov/ucr/nibrs_general.html (retrieved July 5, 2009).

12. Federal Bureau of Investigation, "About CIUS 2007," www.fbi.gov/ucr/cius2007/about/index.html (retrieved July 5, 2009).

13. Federal Bureau of Investigation, "NIBRS Frequently Asked Questions."

14. Eugene H. Czajkoski and Laurin A. Wollan Jr., "Bureaucracy and Crime," *International Journal of Public Administration* 5, no. 2 (1983): 195–216.

15. Bureau of Justice Statistics, "Crime and Victim Statistics" (Washington, DC: Bureau of Justice Statistics, 2008), www.ojp.usdoj.gov/bjs/cvict.htm#Programs (retrieved July 6, 2009).

16. Bureau of Justice Statistics, "The Percentage of Crimes Reported to the Police Has Been Increasing" (Washington, DC: Bureau of Justice Statistics, 2006), www.ojp.usdoj.gov/bjs/glance/d_reporting type.htm (retrieved July 6, 2009).

17. Austin L. Porterfield, *Youth in Trouble: Studies in Delinquency and Despair, with Plans for Prevention* (Fort Worth, TX: Leo Potishman Foundation, 1946).

18. Federal Bureau of Investigation, *Crime in the United States, 2006* (Washington, DC: Department of Justice, 2006).

19. Federal Bureau of Investigation, *Crime in the United States, 2003* (Washington, DC: Department of Justice, 2004).

20. Ibid.

21. Federal Bureau of Investigation, *Crime in the United States, 2004* (Washington, DC: Department of Justice, 2005), www.fbi.gov/ucr/cius_04/offenses_reported/violent_crime/murder.html (retrieved June 26, 2006).

22. Diane Craven, *Sex Differences in Violent Victimization, 1994* (Washington, DC.: Bureau of Justice Statistics, 1997).

23. Ross Macmillan and Candice Kruttschnitt, "Patterns of Violence against Women: Risk Factors and Consequences," www.ncjrs.org/pdffiles1/nij/grants/208346.pdf (retrieved February 15, 2005).

24. Callie Rennison, *Intimate Partner Violence, 1993–2001* (Washington, DC: Bureau of Justice Statistics, 2003).

25. Denise Kindschi Gosselin, *Heavy Hands: An Introduction to the Crimes of Family Violence*, 3rd ed. (Upper Saddle River, NJ: Prentice Hall, 2005).

26. United States Department of Health and Human Services, *Child Maltreatment 2004* (Washington, DC: U.S. Department of Health and Human Services, 2005).

27. Bureau of Justice Statistics, "Crime Characteristics," www.ojp.usdoj.gov/bjs/cvict_c.htm retrieved February 23, 2005); "Criminal Victimization in the United States, 2005 Statistical Tables," *National Crime Victimization Survey*, www.ojp.usdoj.gov/bjs/pub/pdf/cvus0501.pdf (retrieved February 5, 2008).

28. National Center on Elder Abuse, "The National Elder Abuse Incidence Study: Final Report," www.aoa.gov/eldfam/Elder_Rights/Elder_Abuse/AbuseReport_Full.pdf (retrieved February 15, 2005).

29. Bureau of Justice Statistics, "Crime Characteristics."

30. John Curran, "Novice Hunter Gets 1–5 Years in Hunter's Death," *Boston Globe*, November 9, 2007, www.boston.com/news/local/vermont/articles/2007/11/09/novice_hunter_gets_1_5_years_in_hunters_death/ (retrieved March 10, 2008).

31. Federal Bureau of Investigation, *Crime in the United States, 2006*.

32. "Homicide Trends in the U.S.: Regional Trends," Bureau of Justice Statistics, July 11, 2007, www.ojp.usdoj.gov/bjs/homicide/region.htm (retrieved December 4, 2007).

33. "Murders (Most Recent) by Country," NationMaster.com, www.nationmaster.com/red/graph/cri_mur-crime-murders&b_printable=1 (retrieved December 4, 2007).

34. Harvey Wallace, *Victimology: Legal, Psychological, and Social Perspectives*, 2nd ed. (Boston: Pearson Education, 2007).

35. Candice Skrapec, "Defining Serial Murder: A Call for a Return to the Original Lustmörd," *Journal of Police and Criminal Psychology* 16 no. 2 (2002): 10–24.

36. Eric Hickey, *Serial Murderers and Their Victims* (Belmont, CA: Wadsworth, Cengage Learning, 2002), 3.

37. Ibid.

38. Ibid.

39. Ibid.

40. Federal Bureau of Investigation, *Crime in the United States*, 2008. Retrieved (Oct. 2, 2009), from http://www.fbi.gov/usr/cius2008/offenses/violent_crime/aggravated_assualt.html.

41. Joanne Belknap, *The Invisible Woman: Gender, Crime, and Justice*, 2nd ed. (Belmont, CA: Wadsworth, Cengage Learning, 2001).

42. Harvey Wallace, *Family Violence: Legal, Medical, and Social Perspectives*, 4th ed. (Massachusetts: Pearson Allyn and Bacon, 2005).

43. Callie Marie Rennison, "Rape and Sexual Assault: Reporting to Police and Medical Attention, 1992–2000," *U.S. Department of Justice*, 2002, www.ojp.usdoj.gov/bjs (retrieved June 15, 2006).

44. Ibid.

45. Ibid.

46. Bonnie S. Fisher, Leah E. Daigle, Francis T. Cullen, and Michael G. Turner, "Reporting Sexual Victimization to the Police and Others: Results from a National-Level Study of College Women," *Criminal Justice and Behavior* 30, no. 1, (2003): 6–38.

47. Rennison, "Rape and Sexual Assault."

48. Fisher, Daigle, Cullen, and Turner, "Reporting Sexual Victimization to the Police and Others."

49. Ibid.

50. Ibid.

51. Ann Burgess and Lynne Holmstrom, "Rape Trauma Syndrome," *American Journal of Nursing* 131 (1974): 981–986; *Rape Trauma Syndrome*, Rape, Abuse & Incest National Network, www.rainn.org (retrieved June 15, 2006).

52. Ibid.

53. Ibid.

54. Federal Bureau of Investigation, *Crime in the United States, 1999* (Washington, DC: Department of Justice, 2000).

55. Federal Bureau of Investigation, *Crime in the United States*, 2008. Retrieved (Oct. 2, 2009), from http://www.fbi.gov/usr/cius2008/offenses/violent_crime/robbery.html.

56. Andrew Karmen, *Crime Victims: An Introduction to Victimology*, 6th ed. (Belmont, CA: Wadsworth, Cengage Learning, 2007), 68.

57. Matthew R. Durone, Caoloine Wolf Harlow, Patrick A. Langan, Mark Motivans, Ramona R. Rantala, and Erica L. Smith, *Family Violence Statistics: Including Statistics on Strangers and Acquaintances* (Washington DC: U.S. Department of Justice, Bureau of Justice Statistics, 2005).

58. Henry Kempe, F. Silverman, B. Steele, W. Droegemueller, and H. Silver, "The Battered Child Syndrome," *Journal of the American Medical Association* 181 (1962): 107–112.

59. Murray Straus, *Beating the Devil Out of Them: Corporal Punishment in American Families* (New York: Lexington Books, 1994).

60. Matthew R. Durose, Caroline Wolf Harlow, Patrick A. Langan, Mark Motivans, Ramona R. Rantala, and Erica L. Smith, "Family Violence Statistics," www.ojp.usdoj.gov/bjs (retrieved June 30, 2007).

61. David Finkelhor, *Sexually Victimized Children* (New York: Free Press, 1979).

62. Jason L. Walker, Paul D. Carey, Norma Mohr, Dan J. Stein, and Soraya Seedat, "Gender Differences in the Prevalence of Childhood Sexual Abuse and in the Development of Pediatric PTSD," *Archives of Women's Mental Health* 7 (2004): 111–121.

63. Department of Justice, "Child Abuse," www.justice.gc.ca/en/ps/fm/childafs.html (retrieved May 31, 2007).

64. The National Clearinghouse on Family Violence, "Emotional Abuse," www.phac aspc.gc.ca/ncfv-cnivf/familyviolence/pdfs/emotion.pdf (retrieved May 31, 2007).

65. Nico Trocme et al., "Canadian Incidence Study of Reported Child Abuse and Neglect, 2003," *Child Abuse: A Fact Sheet from the Department of Justice Canada*, www.phac-aspc.gc.ca/cm-vee/csca-ecve/pdf/childabuse_final_e.pdf (retrieved January 1, 2009); Bruce D. Perry, Kevin Colwell, and Stephanie Schick, "Child Neglect," in *Encyclopedia of Crime and Punishment*, vol. 1, ed. David Levinson (Thousand Oaks, CA: Sage, 2002), 192–196, www.childtrauma.org/ctamaterials/neglect_in_childhood.asp (retrieved May 30, 2007).

66. Perry, Colwell, and Schick, "Child Neglect."

67. Sonia Sharp, David Thompson, and Tiny Arora, "How Long before It Hurts? An Investigation into Long-Term Bullying," *School Psychology International* 21 (2000): 37–46.

68. Dan Olweus, *Bullying at School: What We Know and What We Can Do* (Carlton, Australia: Blackwell, 1993).

69. John P. J. Dussich and Chie Maekoya, "Physical Child Harm and Bullying-Related Behaviors: A Comparative Study in Japan, South Africa and the United States," *International Journal of Offender Therapy and Comparative Criminology* 51, no. 5 (October 2007): 495–509.

70. Ronald Laney, "Parental Kidnapping," NLPOA Fact Sheet 34, 1995, www.nploa.org/Office_of_Juvenile_Justice_Parental_Kidnapping_1995_NLPOA.pdf.

71. National Crime Information Center Missing Person File. "NCIC Missing Person and Unidentified Person Statistics for 2006," www.fbi.gov/hq/cjisd/missing persons.htm (retrieved May 30, 2007).

72. The Carole Sund/Carrington Memorial Reward Foundation, www.carolesund foundation.com/sections/homicide (retrieved February 23, 2008).

73. Federal Bureau of Investigation, *Crime in the United States*, 2008. Retrieved (Oct. 2, 2009), from http://www.fbi.gov/usr/cius2008/offenses/property_crime/index.html.

74. Patsy Klaus, "National Crime Victimization Survey: Crime and the Nation's Households," (Washington, DC: U.S. Department of Justice, 2004), www.ojp.usdoj.gov/bjs (retrieved June 1, 2006).

75. U.S. Department of Justice, "Property Crime Victims (2004)," www.ojp.usdoj.gov/bjs (retrieved June 1, 2006).

76. Chester L. Britt, "Health Consequences of Criminal Victimizations," *International Review of Victimology* 8 (2001): 63–73.

77. Federal Bureau of Investigation, *Crime in the United States, 2007.*

78. Thomas A. Reppetto, *Residential Crime* (Cambridge, MA: Ballinger Press, 1974).

79. Irvin Waller and Norman Okihiro, *Burglary: The Victim and the Public* (Toronto: University of Toronto Press, 1978).

80. Federal Bureau of Investigation, *Crime in the United States, 2006.*

81. Ibid.

82. Federal Bureau of Investigation, *Crime in the United States*, 2008. Retrieved (Oct. 2, 2009), from http://www.fbi.gov/usr/cius2008/offenses/motor_vehicle_theft.html.

83. Richard A. Ball, "White-Collar Crime," in *Handbook of Criminal Justice Administration*, eds. M. A. DuPont-Morales, Michael K. Hooper, and Judy H. Schmidt (New York: Marcel Dekker, 2001).

84. Howard E. Williams, *Investigating White-Collar Crime* (Springfield, IL: Charles C Thomas, 2006).

85. National White-Collar Crime Center (NW3C), "2005 NW3C National Survey: Nearly One in Two Households Experienced at Least One Form of White-Collar Crime within the Past Year" (Glen Allen, VA: NW3C, 2006).

86. Williams, *Investigating White-Collar Crime*, 24, 52.

87. Federal Bureau of Investigation, www.fbi.gov/facts_and_figures/investigative_programs.htm (retrieved December 21, 2008).

88. Julie Appleby, "Many Who Lost Savings, Jobs Pleased," *USA Today*, May 26, 2006, www.usatoday.com/money/industries/energy/2006-05-25-enron-workers-usat_x.htm?loc+interstitialskip (retrieved July 5, 2006).

89. National White-Collar Crime Center (NW3C), "2005 NW3C National Survey."

90. Clifton Leaf, "Enough Is Enough," in *Annual Editions: Criminal Justice 2006/2007*, eds. Joseph L. Victor and Joanne Naughton (Dubuque, IA: McGraw-Hill, 2007), 46.

91. Ball, "White-Collar Crime."

92. *Loving v. Virginia*, 388 U.S. 1 (1967); *Lawrence v. Texas*, 539 U.S. 538 (2003).

93. Christine Alder, "'Passionate and Willful' Girls: Confronting Practices," *Women and Criminal Justice* 9, no. 4 (1998): 81.

94. Arlene McCormack, Mark-David Janus, and Ann W. Burgess, "Runaway Youths and Sexual Victimization: Gender Differences in an Adolescent Runaway Population," *Child Abuse and Neglect* 10 (1986): 387; Lisa Maher, *Sexed Work: Gender, Race, and Resistance in a Brooklyn Drug Market* (Oxford: Clarendon Press, 1997).

95. Randall G. Shelden, *Controlling the Dangerous Classes* (Boston: Allyn & Bacon, 2001).

96. Anti-Drug Abuse Act of 1988, Public Law 100-690, 21 U.S. Ct. 1501: Subtitle AA—Death Penalty, Sec. 001, Amending the Controlled Substances Abuse Act, 21 USC 848.

97. Craig Reinarman, Peter D. A. Cohen, and Hendrien L. Kaal, "The Limited Relevance of Drug Policy: Cannabis in Amsterdam and in San Francisco," American Journal of Public Health 94, no. 5 (2004): 836–842.

98. Peter Rydell and Susan Everingham, "Controlling Cocaine" (Santa Monica, CA: Rand Drug Policy Research Center, 1994); U.S. Department of State, "International Narcotics Control Strategy Report" (Washington, DC, February 1999); Juan Forero and Tm Weiner, "Latin American Poppy Fields Undermine U.S. Drug Battle," *The New York Times*, June 8, 2003, 1.

99. Peter Reuter, "The Limits of Drug Control," *Foreign Service Journal* 70 (2002): 1.

100. Ethan Nadelman, "Addicted to Failure," *Foreign Policy* (July/August 2003).

101. Juan Forero and Tim Weiner, "Latin American Poppy Fields Undermine U.S. Drug Battle," *The New York Times*, June 8, 2003, 1.

102. Lee Robins, *The Vietnam Drug User Returns*, Special Action Office for Drug Abuse Prevention Monograph, Series A, no. 2, May 1974, Contract No. HSM-42-72-75; Lee Robins and others, "Narcotic Use in Southeast Asia and Afterward: An Interview Study of 898 Vietnam Returnees," *Archives of General Psychiatry* 32, no. 8 (1975): 955–961.

103. Paige M. Harrison and Allen J. Beck, "Prison and Jail Inmates at Midyear 2004," *Bureau of Justice Statistics* (Washington, DC: U.S. Department of Justice, April 2005), 11.

104. Matthew Derose and Patrick Langan, "State Court Sentencing of Convicted Felons, 1998 Statistical Tables," *Bureau of Justice Statistics* (Washington, DC: Department of Justice, December 2001); David B. Mustard, "Racial, Ethnic, and Gender Disparities in Sentencing: Evidence from the U.S. Federal Courts," *The Journal of Law and Economics* 44 (2001).

105. See Joanne Belknap, *The Invisible Woman: Gender, Crime, and Justice* (Belmont, CA: Wadsworth, Cengage Learning, 2007); Paige Harrison and Allen Beck, *Prisoners in 2005* (Washington, DC: Bureau of Justice Statistics, 2007), 5; Allison T. Chappell and Scott R. Maggard, "Applying Black's Theory of Law to Crack and Cocaine Dispositions," *International Journal of Offender Therapy and Comparative Criminology* 51 no.3 (2007): 264–278.

106. John Irwin, Vincent Schiraldi, and Jason Ziedenberg, "America's One Million Nonviolent Prisoners" (Washington, DC: Justice Policy Institute, March 1999), 6–7; Harrison and Beck, *Prisoners in 2005*, 5; Natalie Sokoloff, "Women Prisoners at the Dawn of the 21st Century," *Women and Criminal Justice* 16 no. 1-2 (2005):127–137; Chappell and Maggard, "Applying Black's Theory of Law to Crack and Cocaine Dispositions."

107. "Women in Prison and Substance Abuse Fact Sheet," in *Women in Prison Project* (Correctional Association of New York, December 9, 2008), http://209.85.173.132/search?q=cache:djlxRRzQPisJ:www.correctionalassociation.org/publications/download/wipp/factsheets/Women_and_Substance_Abuse_Fact_Sheet_2008.pdf+Women+in+Prison+and+Substance+Abuse+Fact+Sheet+March+2008&hl=en&ct=clnk&cd=1&gl=us.

108. Amnesty International, *Not Part of My Sentence: Violations of the Human Rights of Women in Custody* (Washington, DC: Amnesty International, 1999), 26; Paige M. Harrison and Allen J. Beck, "Prisoners in 2004," Bureau of Justice Statistics (Washington, DC: US Department of Justice, October 2005), 11.
109. Lawrence A. Greenfield and Tracy L. Snell, "Women Offenders" (Washington, DC: Bureau of Justice Statistics, December 1999), 5.
110. Associated Press (US), "ACLU Report: U.S. Drug Laws Harm Women," March 17, 2005, www.novermber.org/stayinfo/breaking3/ACLU-Women.html (retrieved March 2, 2006).
111. Kelsey Kauffman, "Mothers in Prison," *Corrections Today* 63, no. 1 (2001): 62–65; Christopher Mumola, *Incarcerated Parents and Their Children* (Washington, DC: Bureau of Justice Statistics, 2000): 2, 4.
112. John M. Hagedorn, *The Business of Drug Dealing in Milwaukee* (Milwaukee, WI: Wisconsin Policy Research Institute, 1998), 3; Lorraine Maserolle, David Soole, and Sacha Rombouts, "Disrupting Street-Level Drug Markets," *Crime Prevention Research Reviews* (Washington, DC: U.S. Department of Justice, Office of Community Oriented Policing Services, 2007).
113. "Study Finds Rich Kids More Likely to Use Drugs Than Poor," Join Together: Advancing Effective Alcohol and Drug Policy, Prevention, and Treatment, www.jointogether.org/news/headlines/inthe-news/2007/study-finds-rich-kids-more.html. (retrieved December 10, 2008); Kauffman, "Mothers in Prison."
114. Leonard Saxe, Charles Kadushin, and Andrew A. Berveridge, et. al., "The Visibility of Illicit Drugs: Implications for Community-Based Drug Control Strategies," *American Journal of Public Health 1987–1994* 91 (December 2001): 12; Lisa Maher and Susan Hudson., "Women in the Drug Economy: A Metasynthesis of the Qualitative Literature," *Journal of Drug Issues* 37, no. 4.(2007): 805–826; S. Poret and C .Téjédo, "Law Enforcement and Concentration in Illicit Drug Markets," *European Journal of Political Economy* 22, no. 1 (2006): 99–114.
115. *Property Crime Victims (2004)*, U.S. Department of Justice, www.ojp.usdoj.gov/bjs (retrieved June 1, 2006).
116. Cornell School of Law, "Immigration Law: An Overview," 2006, www.law.cornell.edu/wex/index.php/Immigration (retrieved July 3, 2006).
117. Bureau of Justice Statistics, "Immigration Law Prosecutions Double During 1996–2000" (Washington, DC: Department of Justice, 2002).
118. Ibid.
119. 2007 State of the Union, *President Bush's Plan for Comprehensive Immigration Reform*, www.whitehouse.gov/stateofthe union/2007/initiatives/immigration.html (retrieved February 5, 2008).
120. Lawrence Downes, "Talking Points: The Terrible, Horrible, Urgent National Disaster That Immigration Isn't," *The New York Times*, June 20, 2006.
121. Jay S. Albanese, *Organized Crime in America* (Cincinnati, OH: Anderson, 1996), 3.
122. Ibid., 102–103.
123. Alan Wright, "Organised Crime," *Crime and Justice International* 23, no. 100 (2007): 23.
124. Michael D. Lyman and Gary W. Potter, *Organized Crime* (Upper Saddle River, NJ: Prentice Hall, 1997).
125. James A. Fagin, *Criminal Justice* (Massachusetts: Pearson Education, 2005).
126. Lyman and Potter, *Organized Crime*, 57.
127. James O. Finckenauer and Ko-lin Chin, *Asian Transnational Crime* (Washington, DC: National Institute of Justice, 2007), 1, 20.
128. Joan Belknap. *The Invisible Woman: Gender, Crime, and Justice* (Belmont, CA: Wadsworth, Cengage Learning, 2001).
129. National Center for Victims of Crime, "Stalking Technology Outpaces State Laws," www.ncvc.org/src/main.aspx?dbID=DB_Stalking_Technology_Outpaces_State_Laws 123 (retrieved May 30, 2007).
130. Penal Code § 646.9. "Stalking," 1990. Amended 2002. California Penal Code.
131. Patricia Tjaden and Nancy Thoennes, "Stalking in America: Findings From the National Violence Against Women Survey," *National Institute of Justice, Centers for Disease Control and Prevention—Research in Brief* (Washington, DC: U.S. Department of Justice, April 1998).
132. Ibid.

CHAPTER 3

1. www.trutv.com/library/crime/notorious_murders/women/andrea_yates/index.html
2. Deborah W. Denno, "Who Is Andrea Yates? A Short Story about Insanity," *Duke Journal of Gender Law and Policy* 10 (2003): 32–33.
3. Ibid., 38.
4. Ibid., 39.
5. Cesare Beccaria, *On Crimes and Punishments* (reprint for The Library of Liberal Arts Series), trans. Henry Paolucci (New York: Bobbs-Merrill, 1963).
6. Jeremy Bentham, *An Introduction to the Principles of Morals and Legislation* (corrected ed.) (Oxford: Clarendon Press, 1823).
7. Beccaria, *On Crimes and Punishments.*
8. Bentham, *An Introduction to the Principles of Morals and Legislation.*
9. James Q. Wilson and Richard J. Herrnstein, *Crime and Human Nature: The Definitive Study of the Causes of Crime* (New York: Simon & Schuster, 1985); James Q. Wilson, *Thinking about Crime*, rev. ed. (New York: Vintage Books, 1983); Dereck Cornish and Ronald Clarke, eds., *The Reasoning Criminal: Rational Choice Perspectives on Offending* (New York: Springer Verlag, 1986); Morgan Reynolds, *Crime by Choice: An Economic Analysis* (Dallas: Fisher Institute, 1985).
10. Marvin E. Wolfgang, "Cesare Lombroso," in *Pioneers in Criminology*, ed. Hermann Mannheim (Montclair, NJ: Patterson Smith, 1973), 232–291; Cesare Lombroso, *Crime: Its Causes and Remedies,* trans. H. P. Horton (Boston: Little Brown, 1911).
11. Mara Rose Williams, "Science Finds Neurological Clue to Teen Irresponsibility," *Philadelphia Inquirer*, November 24, 2000; Jay N. Giedd, "Structural Magnetic Resonance Imaging of the Adolescent Brain," *Annals of the New York Academy of Sciences* 1021 (2004): 77–85, http://intramural.nimh.nih.gov/research/pubs/giedd05.pdf (retrieved December 10, 2008).
12. Gail S. Anderson, *Biological Influences on Criminal Behavior* (New York: CRC Press, 2008).
13. Dorothy Otnow-Lewis, Shelly S. Shanok, Jonathan H. Pincus, and Gilbert H. Glaser, "Violent Juvenile Delinquents: Psychiatric, Neurological, Psychological, and Abuse Factors," *Journal of the American Academy of Child and Adolescent Psychiatry* 18 (1979): 307–319.
14. James M. Bjork, Donald M. Dougherty, Frederick Gerard Moeller, Donald R. Cherek, and Alan C. Swann, "The Effects of Tryptophan Depletion and Loading

on Laboratory Aggression in Men: Time Course and a Food-Restricted Control," *Pharmacology* 142, no. 1 (February 1999): 24–30.

15. Shitij Kapur, *Pathophysiology and Treatment of Schizophrenia: New Findings*, 2nd ed. (London: Taylor & Francis 2003).
16. Robert Sapolsky, *The Trouble with Testosterone and Other Essays on the Human Predicament* (New York: Simon & Schuster, 1998).
17. Keith McBurnett, Benjamin B. Lahey, Paul J. Rathouz, and Rolf Loeber, "Low Salivary Cortisol and Persistent Aggression in Boys Referred for Disruptive Behavior," *Archives of General Psychiatry* 57 (2000): 38–43.
18. Michael E. Roettger, Tianji Cai, and Guang Guo, "The Integration of Genetic Propensities into Social-Control Models of Delinquency and Violence among Male Youths," *American Sociological Review*, 73 (2008): 543–568.
19. David P. Farrington, Geoffrey C. Barnes, and Sandra Lambert, "The Concentration of Offending in Families," *Legal and Criminological Psychology* 1, no. 1 (1996): 47–63.
20. Han G. Brunner, M. Nelen, Xandra O. Breakefield, Hans-Hilger Ropers, and Bernard A. van Oost, "Abnormal Behavior Associated with a Point Mutation in the Structural Gene for Monoamine Oxidase A," *Science* 262, no. 5133 (1993): 578–580.
21. Adrian Raine, *The Psychopathology of Crime: Criminal Behavior as a Clinical Disorder* (San Diego: Academic Press, 1993).
22. For one of the most comprehensive adoption studies, see Raine, *The Psychopathology of Crime.* See also, S. A. Mednick, W. F. Gabrielli, and B. Hutchings, "Genetic Factors in the Etiology of Criminal Behavior," in *The Causes of Crime: New Biological Approaches*, eds. S. A. Mednick, T. E. Moffitt, and S. A. Stack (Cambridge, UK: Cambridge University Press, 1987).
23. A. Tengström, S. Hodgins, M. Grann, N. Långström, and G. Kullgren, "Schizophrenia and Criminal Offending: The Role of Psychopathy and Substance Use Disorders," *Criminal Justice and Behavior* 31 (2004): 367–391.
24. G. Gerbner, L. Gross, M. Morgan, and N. Signorielli, "Health and Medicine on Television," *The New England Journal of Medicine* 305 (1981): 901–904.
25. John Monahan, "Mental Disorder and Violent Behavior: Perceptions and Evidence," *American Psychologist* 47 (1992): 511–521.
26. J. Bonta, M. Law, and K. Hanson, "The Prediction of Criminal and Violent Recidivism among Mentally Disordered Offenders: A Meta-Analysis," *Psychological Bulletin* 123 (1998): 123–142.
27. Paula M. Ditton, *Mental Health Treatment of Inmates and Probationers* (Washington, DC: U.S. Department of Justice, Bureau of Justice Statistics, July 1999). For additional information about the many problems mentally ill offenders present to the prison system, see Jamie Fellner and Sasha Abramsky, *Ill-Equipped: U.S. Prisons and Offenders with Mental Illness* (New York: Human Rights Watch, October 2003).
28. American Psychiatric Association, *Diagnostic and Statistical Manual of Mental Disorders-IV-TR* (Washington, DC: American Psychiatric Association, 2000).
29. The DSM is currently in its fourth (IV), text-revised (TR) edition.
30. National Institute of Mental Health, 2006, www.nimh.nih.gov/publicat/numbers.cfm.
31. Adrian Raine, ed., *Crime and Schizophrenia: Causes and Cures* (New York: Nova Science, 2006).
32. National Institutes of Health, http://psychcentral.com/lib/2006/schizophrenia-and-violence/ (retrieved December 19, 2008).
33. Shitij Kapur, *Pathophysiology and Treatment of Schizophrenia: New Findings*, 2nd ed. (London: Taylor & Francis, 2003).
34. The National Alliance on Mental Illness reports information on mental disorders. Statistics pertaining to major depressive disorder in 2006 can be found at www.nami.org/Template.cfm?Section=By_Illness&Template=/TaggedPage/TaggedPageDisplay.cfm&TPLID=54&ContentID=23039.
35. Information on postpartum psychosis (and postpartum depression) can be found in Mark Levy, Deborah Sanders, and Stacy Sabraw, "Moms Who Kill: When Depression Turns Deadly," *Psychology Today*, November-December 2002.
36. Denno, "Who Is Andrea Yates? A Short Story about Insanity."
37. Jonathan H. Pincus, *Base Instincts: What Makes Killers Kill* (New York: Norton, 2001).
38. Robert D. Hare, *Manual for the Hare Psychopathy Checklist-Revised*, 2nd ed. (Toronto, ON: Multi-Health Systems, 2003).
39. Robert D. Hare, *Without Conscience: The Disturbing World of the Psychopaths among Us* (New York: Guilford Press, 1999), 83.
40. Ibid.
41. Ibid.
42. Laura A. King, *The Science of Psychology: An Appreciative View* (New York: McGraw-Hill, 2008), 338.
43. Timothy B. Jeffrey and Louise K. Jeffrey, "The Utility of the Modified WAIS in a Clinical Setting," *Journal of Clinical Psychology* 40, no. 4 (2006): 1067–1069; Charles L. Scott and Joan B. Gerbasi, *Handbook of Correctional Mental Health* (Arlington, VA: American Psychiatric Publishing, 2005).
44. Wilson and Herrnstein, *Crime and Human Nature.*
45. Peter Salovey and John Mayer, "Emotional Intelligence," *Imagination, Cognition, and Personality* 9 (1990): 185–211.
46. "50 Weeks of Planned Killing: A Profile in Mass *sic* Murder," directed by Bob Anderson (New York: American Broadcasting Companies, 1978).
47. Adrian Raine, J. Reid Meloy, Susan Bihrle, Lori LaCasse, and Monte S. Buchsbaum, "Reduced Prefrontal and Increased Subcortical Brain Functioning Assessed Using Positron Emission Tomography in Predatory and Affective Murderers," *Behavioral Sciences and the Law* 16 (1998): 319–332.
48. Jean Piaget, *The Moral Judgment of the Child* (New York: Free Press, 1965).
49. Daniel Tranel, "Long-Term Sequalae of Prefrontal Cortex Damage Acquired in Early Childhood," *Developmental Neuropsychology* 18, no. 3 (2000): 281–296.
50. Craig W. Haney, "The Good, the Bad, and the Lawful: An Essay on Psychological Injustice," in *Personality Theory, Moral Development, and Criminal Behavior*, eds. W. S. Laufer and J. M. Day (Lexington, MA: Lexington Books, 1983), 107–117.
51. Craig A. Anderson, "An Update on the Effects of Playing Violent Video Games," *Journal of Adolescence* 27 (2004): 113–122.
52. Sigmund Freud, *The Complete Works of Sigmund Freud*, Vol. 19 (London: Hogarth, 1961).
53. Robert Agnew, "Foundation for General Strain Theory of Crime and Delin-

quency," *Criminology* 30 (February 1992): 1, 47–87.

54. Émile Durkheim, *The Division of Labor in Society*, trans. George Simpson (Glencoe, IL: Free Press, 1933).

55. Johnathan Lawrence and Justin Vaisse, "Understanding Urban Riots in France," *New Europe Review* 1 (December 2005), www.brookings.edu/views/articles/fellows/Laurence_vaisse_20051201.htm (retrieved June 9, 2006).

56. Robert K. Merton," Social Structure and Anomie," *American Sociological Review* 3 (October 1938): 672–682; Robert K. Merton, *Social Theory and Social Structure*, rev. ed. (New York: Free Press, 1957); Albert Cohen, *Delinquent Boys: The Culture of the Gang* (New York: Free Press, 1955); Richard A. Cloward and Lloyd E. Ohlin, *Delinquency and Opportunity: A Theory of Delinquent Gangs* (Glencoe, IL: Free Press, 1960).

57. Cohen, *Delinquent Boys: The Culture of the Gang.*

58. Celeste Fremon, G-*Dog and the Homeboys* (Albuquerque: University of New Mexico Press, 2004); David De Cremer and Tom Tyler. "Am I Respected or Not? Inclusion and Reputation as Issues in Group Membership," *Social Justice Research* 18, no. 2 (2005): 121–153.

59. Robert Sampson and John Laub, *Crime in the Making: Pathways and Turning Points through the Life Course* (Cambridge, MA: Harvard University Press, 1993).

60. Terrie Moffit, "Adolescence-Limited and Life-Course-Persistent Antisocial Behavior: A Developmental Taxonomy," in *Life-Course Criminology: Contemporary and Classic Readings,* eds. Alex Piquero and Paul Maserolle (Belmont, CA: Wadsworth, Cengage Learning, 2001).

61. D. P. Farrington and D. J. West, "Criminal, Penal and Life Histories of Chronic Offenders: Risk and Protective Factors and Early Identification," *Criminal Behaviour and Mental Health* 3 (1993): 492–523; Zena Smith Blau, "The Life Cycle: Delinquency and Disrepute in the Life Course," in *Current Perspectives on Aging*, ed. J. Hagan (Greenwich, CT: JAI Press, 1995), 249–282.

62. Durkheim, *The Division of Labor in Society.*

63. Gresham Sykes and David Matza, "Techniques of Neutralization: A Theory of Delinquency," *American Sociological Review* 22 (December 1957): 664–670.

64. Ibid., 664–570.

65. Walter C. Reckless, *The Crime Problem*, 4th ed. (New York: Appleton-Century-Crofts, 1967).

66. Michael Gottfredson and Travis Hirschi, *A General Theory of Crime* (Stanford, CA: Stanford University Press, 1990); Robert J. Sampson and John H. Laub, *Crime in the Making: Pathways and Turning Points through the Life Course* (Cambridge, MA: Harvard University Press, 1993).

67. Sampson and Laub, *Crime in the Making.*

68. Gottfredson and Hirschi, *A General Theory of Crime.*

69. Ibid., 90.

70. Howard B. Kaplan, *Deviant Behavior in Defense of Self* (New York: Academic Press, 1980).

71. L. E. Wells, "Self-Enhancement through Delinquency: A Conditional Test of Self-Derogation Theory," *Journal of Research in Crime and Delinquency* 26 (1989): 3, 226–252.

72. M. Brent Donnellan, Kali H. Trzesniewski, Richard W. Robins, Terrie E. Moffitt, and Avshalom Caspi, "Low Self-Esteem Is Related to Aggression, Antisocial Behavior and Delinquency," *Psychological Sciences* 16, no. 4 (2005): 328–334; R. F. Baumeister, B. J. Bushman, and W. K. Campbell, "Self-Esteem, Narcissism, and Aggression: Does Violence Result from Low Self-Esteem or from Threatened Egotism?" *Current Directions in Psychological Science* 9 (2000): 26–29; R. F. Baumeister, J. D Campbell, J. I. Krueger, and K. E. Vohs, "Does High Self-Esteem Cause Better Performance, Interpersonal Success, Happiness, or Healthier Lifestyles?" *Psychological Science in the Public Interest* 4, no.1 (2003); R. F. Baumeister, L. Smart, and J. M. Boden, "Relation of Threatened Egotism to Violence and Aggression: The Dark Side of High Self-Esteem," *Psychological Review* 103 (1996): 5–33; B. J. Bushman and R. F. Baumeister, "Threatened Egotism, Narcissism, Self-Esteem, and Direct and Displaced Aggression: Does Self-Love or Self-Hate Lead to Violence?" *Journal of Personality and Social Psychology* 75 (1998): 219–229; J. M. Bynner, P. O'Malley, and J. G. Bachman, "Self-Esteem and Delinquency Revisited," *Journal of Youth and Adolescence* 10, (1981): 407–441; D. L. DuBois and H. D. Tevendale, "Self-Esteem in Childhood and Adolescence: Vaccine or Epiphenomenon?" *Applied and Preventive Psychology* 8 (1999): 103–117; Travis Hirschi, *Causes of Delinquency* (Berkeley: University of California Press, 1969); S. J. Jang and T. P. Thornberry, "Self-Esteem, Delinquent Peers, and Delinquency: A Test of the Self-Enhancement Thesis," *American Sociological Review* 63 (1998): 586–598; T. A. Judge, A. Erez, C. J. Thoresen, and J. E. Bono, "Are Measures of Self-Esteem, Neuroticism, Locus of Control, and Generalized Self-Efficacy Indicators of a Common Core Construct?" *Journal of Personality and Social Psychology* 83 (2002): 693–710; L. A. Kirkpatrick, C. E. Waugh, A. Valencia, and G. D. Webster, "The Functional Domain Specificity of Self-Esteem and the Differential Prediction of Aggression," *Journal of Personality and Social Psychology* 82 (2002): 756–767; J. D. McCarthy and D. R. Hoge, "The Dynamics of Self-Esteem and Delinquency," *American Journal of Sociology*, 90 (1984): 396–410; M. Rosenberg, C. Schooler, and C. Schoenbach, "Self-Esteem and Adolescent Problems: Modeling Reciprocal Effects," *American Sociological Review* 54 (1989): 1004–1018; J. B. Sprott and A. N. Doob, "Bad, Sad, and Rejected: The Lives of Aggressive Children," *Canadian Journal of Criminology* 42 (2000): 123–133.

73. Kaplan, *Deviant Behavior in Defense of Self.*

74. Susan Titus Reid, *Crime and Criminology,* 6th ed. (Austin, TX: Holt, Rinehart, & Winston, 1991); James A. Fagin, *Criminal Justice* (Boston: Pearson Education, 2005).

75. Judith R. Blau and Peter M. Blau, "The Cost of Inequality: Metropolitan Structure and Violent Crime," *American Sociological Review* 147 (1982): 114–129.

76. See, for example, Rosalyn Muraskin, *It's a Crime: Women and Justice*, 4th ed. (Upper Saddle River, NJ: Prentice Hall. 2006).

77. Sally S Simpson, "Feminist Theory, Crime and Justice," *Criminology* 27 (1989): 605–631.

78. Joanne Belknap, *Invisible Woman: Gender, Crime, and Justice*, 3rd ed. (Belmont, CA: Wadsworth, Cengage Learning, 2007).

79. See, for example, Freda Adler, *Sisters in Crime* (New York: McGraw-Hill, 1975).

80. See, for example, Meda Chesney-Lind, "Girls and Violence: Is the Gender Gap Closing," *Applied Research Forum* (National Electronic Network on Violence against Women, August 2004).

81. For an excellent example of recent such work, see Jody Miller, *Getting Played: African American Girls, Urban Inequality,*

and Gendered Violence (New York: New York University Press, 2008).

82. See Amanda Burgess-Proctor, "Intersections of Race, Class, Gender and Crime," *Feminist Criminology* 1, no. 1 (January 2006): 27–47.

83. J. Wozniak, "The Voices of Peacemaking Criminology: Insights into a Perspective with an Eye Toward Teaching," *Contemporary Justice Review* 3, no. 3 (2000): 267–289.

84. Richard Quinney, "Life of Crime: Criminology and Public Police as Peacemaking," *Journal of Crime and Justice* 16, no. 2 (1993): 3–9.

85. Richard Quinney, "The Way of Peace: On Crime, Suffering, and Service," in *Criminology as Peacemaking*, eds. Harold E. Pepinsky and Richard Quinney (Bloomington: Indiana University Press, 1991); Wozniak, "The Voices of Peacemaking Criminology."

86. M. Braswell, J. R. Fuller, and B. Lozoff, *Corrections, Peacemaking, and Restorative Justice: Transforming Individuals and Institutions* (Cincinnati, OH: Anderson, 2001).

87. Robert E. Park and Ernest W. Burgess, *The City* (Chicago: University of Chicago Press, 1925).

88. Clifford R. Shaw and Henry D. McKay, *Juvenile Delinquency in Urban Areas* (Chicago: University of Chicago Press, 1942); Clifford R. Shaw and Henry D. McKay, *Juvenile Delinquency and Urban Areas: A Study of Delinquents in Relation to Differential Characteristics of Local Communities in American Cities*, rev. ed. (Chicago: University of Chicago Press, 1969).

89. Marvin Wolfgang and Franco Ferracuti, *The Subculture of Violence* (London: Tavistock, 1967).

90. David Luckenbill and Daniel Doyle, "Structural Position and Violence: Developing a Cultural Explanation," *Criminology* 27 (1989): 419–436.

91. Thorsten Sellin, *Culture Conflict and Crime* (New York: Social Science Research Council, 1938).

92. Charles H. Cooley, *On Self and Social Organization*, ed. Hans-Joaquim Schubert (Chicago: University of Chicago Press, 1998).

93. Howard Becker, *Outsiders, Studies in the Sociology of Deviance* (New York: Macmillan, 1963).

94. Edwin M. Schur, *Labeling Deviant Behavior: Its Sociological Implications* (New York: Harper & Row, 1971).

95. Frank Tannenbaum, *Crime and the Community* (New York: Atheneum Press, 1938), 17–19.

96. Edwin Sutherland, *Principles of Criminology*, 3rd ed. (Philadelphia: J. B. Lippincott, 1939): 4–8.

97. Joanna Shapland, Johnathan Willmore, and Peter Duff, *Victims in the Criminal Justice System* (Brookfield, VT: Avebury, 1985).

98. William Tallack, *Reparations to the Injured and the Rights of Victims of Crime to Compensation* (London: Wertheimer, Lea, 1900).

99. Robert J. McCormack, "Compensating Victims of Violent Crime" *Justice Quarterly* 8, no. 3 (1991): 329–246, http://pdfserve.informaworld.com/330515_731200452_718864699.pdf (retrieved December 19, 2008).

100. Edwin H. Sutherland, *Criminology* (Philadelphia: J. B. Lippincott, 1924); Hans von Hentig, "The Criminal and His Victim," in *Studies in the Sociobiology of Crime* (New Haven: Yale University Press, 1948); Stephen Schafer, *The Victim and His Criminal: A Study in Functional Responsibility* (New York: Random House, 1968).

101. Chie Maekoya, "Victimization and Levels of Aggression in Intimate Partner Violence," *International Perspectives in Victimology* 3 no. 1 (March 2007): 42–49.

102. John P. J. Dussich, "The Victim Vulnerability Attributes Paradigm," unpublished class lectures, California State University, Fresno, 2005; John P. J. Dussich and Charles J. Eichman, "The Elderly Victim: Vulnerability to the Criminal Act," in *Crime and the Elderly*, eds. Jack Goldsmith and Sharon S. Goldsmith (Lexington, MA: Lexington Books, 1976), 93.

103. Graham Farrell and Ken Pease, "Once Bitten, Twice Bitten: Repeat Victimisation and Its Implications for Crime Prevention," Police Research Group, Crime Prevention Unit Series Paper No. 46 (London: Home Office Police Department, 1993); Gloria Laycock, "Hypothesis-based Research: The Repeat Victimization Story," *Criminology and Criminal Justice*, 1 (2001): 59–82; Terri L. Messman and Patricia J. Long, "Child Sexual Abuse and Its Relationship to Revictimization in Adult Women: A Review," *Clinical Psychology Review* 16, no. 5 (1996): 307–420.

104. Nina Schuller, "Disabled People, Crime and Social Inclusion," *Community Safety Journal* 4, no. 3 (2005): 4–15; Barbara Collier, Donna Ghie-Richmond, Fran Odette, and Jake Pyne, "Reducing the Risk of Sexual Abuse for People Who Use Augmentative and Alternative Communication," *Argumentative and Alternative Communication*, 22 (2006): 62–75; Virginia Aldigé Hiday, Marvin S. Swartz, Jeffrey W. Swanson, Randy Borum, and H. Ryan Wagner, "Criminal Victimization of Persons with Severe Mental Illness," *Psychiatric Services* 50 (1999): 62–68.

105. Reid Meloy, *The Psychology of Stalking: Clinical and Forensic Home Office Police Department Perspectives* (San Diego, CA: Academic Press, 1998).

106. Christopher A. Janicak, "Regional Variations in Workplace Homicide Rates," in *Compensation and Working Conditions* (Washington, DC: U.S. Department of Labor, 2003), 3.

107. Dee Wood Harper Jr., "Comparing Tourist's Crime Victimization," *Annals of Tourism Research* 28, no. 4 (2001): 1053–1056.

108. Yasmin Jiwani, "Vulnerabilities to Victimization at the Juncture of Intersecting Oppressions," in *Mapping Violence: A Work in Progress* (Vancouver, BC, Canada: FREDA Centre for Research on Violence against Women and Children, December 2000), www.harbour.sfu.ca/freda/articles/fvpi02.htm (retrieved December 17, 2008).

109. Martin E. P. Seligman, *Helplessness: On Depression, Development, and Death* (San Francisco: W. H. Freeman, 1975).

110. Andrew Karmen, *Crime Victims: An Introduction to Victimology*, 5th ed. (Belmont, CA: Wadsworth, Cengage Learning, 2004), 66.

111. Ibid.

112. George W. Holden and Kathy L. Richie, "Linking Extreme Marital Discord, Child Rearing, and Child Behavior Problems: Evidence from Battered Women," *Child Development* 62, no. 2 (1991): 311–327; Jacquelyn C. Campbell and Linda A. Lewandowski, "Mental and Physical Health Effects of Intimate Partner Violence on Women and Children," *The Psychiatric Clinics of North America*, 20, no. 2 (1997): 353–374; Kimberly J. Mitchell and David Finkelhor, "Risk of Crime Victimization among Youth Exposed to Domestic Violence," *Journal of Interpersonal Violence* 16, no. 9 (September 2001), 960.

113. National Center for Education Statistics, "Student Victimization at Schools" (Washington, DC: U.S. Department of

Education, October 1995), http://nces.ed.gov/pubs95/web/95204.asp (retrieved December 16, 2008).

114. Richard Sparks, *Research on Victims of Crime* (Washington, DC: U.S. Government Printing Office, 1982).

115. David F. Luckenbill, "Criminal Homicide as a Situated Transaction," *Social Problems* 25, no. 2 (1977): 176–186.

116. Carlene Wilson, Ted Nettlebeck, Robert Potter, and Caroline Perry, "Intellectual Disability and Criminal Victimisation," *Trends and Issues in Crime and Criminal Justice* 60 (Australian Institute of Criminology), www.aic.gov.au/publications/tandi/ti60.pdf (retrieved February 2, 2008).

CHAPTER 4

1. Jennifer Scholtes, "Former Chi Tau Men Become Roommates in Jail," *Orion*, December 9, 2005, www.orion online.net/media/storage/paper889/news/2005/12/09/APledgesDeath/Former.Chi.Tau.Men.Become.Roommates.In.Jail-1509019.shtml (retrieved July 3, 2006).

2. California Penal Code § 245.6.

3. L. W. King, "Hammurabi's Code of Laws," in *Ancient History Sourcebook*, www.fordham.edu/halsall/ancient/ham code.html#text (retrieved February 22, 2009.

4. Lawrence Friedman, *A History of American Law*, 3rd ed. (New York: Touchstone, 1993).

5. Bryan A. Garner, ed., *Black's Law Dictionary*, 8th ed. (St. Paul, MN: Thomson West 2004), 369.

6. Richard Bevin, "John Haigh (The Acid Bath Murderer)," www.thebiography channel.co.uk/biography_story/906:614/1/John_Haigh_The_Acid_Bath_Murderer_.htm (retrieved June 29, 2006).

7. Richard Bevin, The case of John George Haigh is documented on the Web site for The Biography Channel.

8. Florida Statutes § 837.02 (2008).

9. The case of Charles Manson and his followers is documented by the lead prosecutor in Vincent Bugliosi with Curt Gentry, *Helter Skelter: The True Story of the Manson Murders* (New York: W. W. Norton, 1994).

10. Included in the published writings of English jurist Edward Coke is a four-volume series on English law in the mid-seventeenth century. The third volume constitutes the first major study of English criminal law. E. Coke, *The Third Part of the Institutes of the Laws of England: Concerning High Treason, and Other Pleas of the Crown, and Criminal Causes*, 1644 (London: E. and R. Brooke, 1797), 107.

11. "Eric Smith: Inside the Mind of a Child Killer," produced by Claudia Pryor Malis (New York: ABC, 1998).

12. *Atkins v. Virginia* 536 U.S. 304 (2002).

13. Michael Keiter, "Just Say No Excuse: The Rise and Fall of the Intoxication Defense," *Journal of Criminal Law and Criminology* 87 (1997): 482–518.

14. *Regina v. Dudley and Stevens* (1881-85) All E.R. Rep. 61 (Queen's Bench, Dec. 9, 1884).

15. Andrew J. King, "Sunday Law in the Nineteenth Century," *Albany Law Review* 64 (2000): 675–772.

16. *United States v. Bailey*, 444 U.S. 394 (1980).

17. *Rex v. Arnold* (Court of Common Pleas 1724) in Thomas Bayly Howell, ed., *A Complete Collection of State Trials* (1812): 695, 765. This is the first known insanity trial for which the entire transcript exists. In this case, the defendant, Arnold, shot Lord Onslow who Arnold believed was inhabiting his body. Although Arnold was found guilty, his sentence was commuted to life by Onslow.

18. L. A. Callahan, H. J. Steadman, M. A. McGreevy, and P. C. Robbins, "The Volume and Characteristics of Insanity Defense Pleas: An Eight-State Study," *Bulletin of Psychiatry and the Law* 19 (1991): 331–338.

19. *Queen v. M'Naghten*, 8 Eng. Rep. 718 (1843).

20. Carl Elliott, *The Rules of Insanity: Moral Responsibility and the Mentally Ill Offender* (Albany, NY: State University of New York Press, 1996).

21. *Durham v. United States*, 214 F.2d 862 (1954).

22. Model Penal Code § 4.01, Proposed Official Draft (May 4, 1962).

23. Del Quentin Wilber, "Hinckley to Gain Driving Privileges, Longer Visits," *The Washington Post*, June 17, 2009, www.washingtonpost.com/wp-dyn/content/article/2009/06/16/AR2009061601761.html.

24. Gary B. Melton, John Petrila, Norman G. Poythress, and Christopher Slobogin, *Psychological Evaluations for the Courts: A Handbook for Mental Health Professionals and Lawyers*, 2nd ed. (New York: Guilford Press, 1997).

25. "Police Finish Bertuzzi Investigation," *CBC Sports*, April 16, 2004, www.cbc.ca/sports/story/2004/04/14/bertuzzi040413.html (retrieved October 5, 2007).

CHAPTER 5

1. Associated Press, "Kent State Riot," April 27, 2009.

2. Marilyn Miller, "Ohio Chief Defends Response to Kent State Riot," *The Akron Beacon Journal, Ohio*. April 28, 2009, www.officer.com/web/online/Top-News-Stories/Ohio-Chief-Defends-Response-to-Kent-State-Riot/1$46408 (retrieved May 8, 2009).

3. NBC News, "Kent State Riot Explained, April 27, 2009, www.nbcactionnews.com/content/aroundtheweb/story/Kent-State-Riot-Explained/hAdQiVmYykqIbdnz17kiOQ.cspx.

4. Associated Press, "Kent State Riot."

5. For more information, see www.may4.org/.

6. Egon Bittner, *Aspects of Police Work* (Boston: Northeastern University Press, 1990).

7. Eric Scott, *Calls for Service: Citizen Demand and Initial Police Response* (Washington, DC: Government Printing Office, 1981).

8. David Bayley, *Police for the Future* (New York: Oxford University Press, 1994); David Barlow and Melissa Hickman Barlow, *Police in a Multicultural Society: An American Story* (Prospect Heights, IL: Waveland Press, 2000).

9. Bittner, *Aspects of Police Work*.

10. See Rosemary Gido, Tammy Castle, Kimberly Dodson, Danielle McDonald, Christine Olsen, and Rebecca Boyd, "The Irish in Schuylkill County Prison: Ethnic Conflict in Pre- and Post-Civil War in Pennsylvania," *The Prison Journal* 86 (June 2006): 260–268.

11. Richard Maxwell Brown, "Vigilante Policing," in *Thinking about Police: Contemporary Readings*, ed. Carl B. Klockars and Stephen D. Mastrofski (New York: McGraw-Hill, 1991).

12. Ibid.

13. David Barlow and Melissa Hickman Barlow, *Police in a Multicultural Society: An American Story* (Prospect Heights, IL: Waveland Press, 2000); Samuel Walker, *A Critical History of Police Reform: The Emergence of Professionalism* (Lexington, MA: Lexington Books, 1977);
P. L. Reichel, "Southern Slave Patrols as a

Transitional Police Type," *American Journal of Policing* 7 (1988): 51–77.

14. Eugene Genovese, *Roll, Jordon, Roll: The World the Slaves Made* (New York: Vintage Books, 1976).

15. Julian Samora, Joe Bernal, and Albert Pena, *Gunpowder Justice: A Reassessment of the Texas Rangers* (Notre Dame, IN: University of Notre Dame Press, 1979).

16. Hubert Williams and Patrick Murphy, *The Evolving Strategy of Police: A Minority Perspective* (Washington, DC: National Institute of Justice, 1990).

17. Neil Websdale, *Policing the Poor: From Slave Plantation to Public Housing* (Boston: Northeastern University Press, 2001).

18. E. F. Foner, *Reconstruction: America's Unfinished Revolution, 1863–1877* (New York: Harper & Row, 1988), 4–5.

19. Barlow and Barlow, *Police in a Multicultural Society.*

20. Samuel Walker and Charles M. Katz, *Police in America: An Introduction* (New York: McGraw-Hill, 2005), 77.

21. Wilbur Miller, "Police Authority in London and New York City 1830–1870," *Journal of Social History* 9 (Winter 1975): 81–101.

22. Ibid.; George Kelling and Mark Moore, "The Evolving Strategy of Policing," *Perspectives on Policing* 4 (November 1988): 1–15.

23. Nathan Douthit, "August Vollmer, Berkeley's First Chief of Police, and the Emergence of Police Professionalism," *California Historical Quarterly* 54 (Spring 1975): 101–124.

24. Robert Lombardo and Todd Lough, "Community Policing: Broken Windows, Community Building, and Satisfaction with the Police," *The Police Journal* 80, no. 2 (2007): 119.

25. Robert Fogelson, *Big-City Police* (Cambridge, MA: Harvard University Press, 1977).

26. Jan Chaiken, Peter Greenwood, and Joan Petersilia, "The Criminal Investigation Process: A Summary Report," *Policy Analysis* 3, no. 2 (1977): 187–217.

27. Walker and Katz, *Police in America: An Introduction,* 77.

28. O. Elmer Polk and David W. MacKenna, "Dilemmas of the New Millennium: Policing in the 21st Century," *ACJS Today* 30, no. 3 (2005): 4.

29. Bureau of Justice Statistics, *Local Police Departments, 2003* (Washington, DC: Bureau of Justice Statistics, 2006), 1.

30. Dayton Kelley, "Ranger Hall of Fame," *FBI Law Enforcement Bulletin* 45, no. 5 (1976): 18.

31. Walker and Katz, *Police in America: An Introduction,* 72.

32. Bureau of Justice Statistics, *Local Police Departments, 2003,* 1.

33. Bureau of Justice Statistics, *Federal Law Enforcement Officers, 2004* (Washington, DC: Bureau of Justice Statistics, 2006), 11.

34. National Institute of Justice, *Policing on American Indian Reservations* (Washington, DC: National Institute of Justice, 2001), vi–x.

35. Walker and Katz, *Police in America: An Introduction,* 76–77.

36. Polk and MacKenna, "Dilemmas of the New Millennium: Policing in the 21st Century," 5.

37. Jacksonville Sheriff's Office, "History of the JSO Consolidated Law Enforcement." www.co.net/Departments/Sheriffs+Office/About+the+JSO/History+of+the+JSO.htm (retrieved March 30, 2007).

38. Walker and Katz, *Police in America: An Introduction,* 77–78.

39. Simon A. Andrew, "Interlocal Contractual Arrangements in the Provision of Public Safety" (presentation prepared for the Florida Department of Community Affairs under the auspices of Florida State University, 2004).

40. W. Dwayne Orrick, *Recruitment, Retention, and Turnover of Police Personnel: Reliable, Practical, and Effective Solutions* (Springfield, IL: Charles C. Thomas, 2008), 3.

41. Department of Justice, *Hiring and Keeping Police Officers* (Washington, DC: Department of Justice, 2004), 2.

42. Marvin J. Cetron and Owen Davies, "Trends Now Shaping the Future: Economic, Societal, and Environmental Trends," *The Futurist* 39, no. 2 (2005): 33–34.

43. Police Executive Research Forum, *The Cop Crunch: Identifying Strategies for Dealing with the Recruiting and Hiring Crisis in Law Enforcement* (Washington, DC: Police Executive Research Forum, 2005), 6.

44. Partnership for Public Service and National Academy of Public Administration, "Where the Jobs Are: The Continuing Growth of Federal Job Opportunities," *Partnership for Public Service—Research,* www.ourpublicservice.org/research/research_show.htm?doc_id=260717 (retrieved August 28, 2006).

45. California Employment Development Department, "Projections of Employment by Industry and Occupation," *California Labor Market Info,* www.calmis.ca.gov/FILE/OCCPROJ/cal$OccProj.xls (retrieved August 28, 2006).

46. Police Executive Research Forum, *The Cop Crunch,* 4.

47. Ibid., 8.

48. Ellen Scrivner, *Innovations in Police Recruitment and Hiring* (Washington, DC: Department of Justice, 2006), 15.

49. M. L. Dantzker and J. H. McCoy, "Psychological Screening of Police Recruits: A Texas Perspective," *Journal of Police and Criminal Psychology* 21, no. 1 (2006): 23.

50. National Advisory Commission on Criminal Justice Standards and Goals, *Police* (Washington, DC: Government Printing Office, 1973), 337.

51. U.S. Equal Employment Opportunity, *Recent Developments in Scored Test Case Law: By Lawrence Ashe,* Meeting of May 16, 2007.

52. Scrivner, *Innovations in Police Recruitment and Hiring,* 15.

53. Walker and Katz, *Police in America: An Introduction,* 128.

54. Sameshield.Com, "History of Policewomen," August 28, 2006, www.sameshield.com/history/sshistory16.html.

55. Ibid.

56. National Center for Women and Policing, *Hiring and Retaining More Women: The Advantages to Law Enforcement Agencies* (Arlington, VA: National Center for Women and Policing, 2003), 2.

57. Ibid., 1–16.

58. Ibid., 6.

59. Herbert Williams and Patrick Murphy, *The Evolving Strategy of Police: A Minority Perspective* (Washington, DC: National Institute of Justice, 1990).

60. Marvin Dulaney, *Black Police in America* (Bloomington, IN: Indiana University Press, 1996).

61. Bureau of Justice Statistics, *Local Police Departments, 2003,* iii.

62. Jihong Zhao, Ni He, and Nicholas Lovrich, "Predicting the Employment of Minority Officers in the U.S. Cities: OLS Fixed-Effect Panel Model Results for African American and Latino Officers for 1993, 1996, and 2000," *Journal of Criminal Justice* 33 (July-August 2005): 377–386.

63. Bureau of Justice Statistics, *Local Police Departments, 2003*, iii.

64. See David Fahrenthold, "The Blue and the Gay: DC Officer Links His 2 Communities," *The Washington Post*, October 22, 2001, B01.

65. www.gspoa.com/jobs.asp (retrieved January 17, 2009).

66. Allison T. Chappell, Lonn Lanza-Kaduce, and Daryl H. Johnston, "Law Enforcement Training Changes and Challenges," in *Critical Issues in Policing*, eds. Roger G. Dunham and Geoffrey P. Alpert (Long Grove, IL: Waveland Press, 2005), 72.

67. Polk and MacKenna, "Dilemmas of the New Millennium," 7.

68. David L. Carter, *The Police and the Community* (Upper Saddle River, NJ: Prentice Hall, 2002), 157.

69. Chappell, Lanza-Kaduce, and Johnston, "Law Enforcement Training Changes and Challenges," 72–73.

70. Mark R. McCoy, "Teaching Style and the Application of Adult Learning Principles by Police Instructors," *Policing: An International Journal of Police Strategies & Management* 29, no. 1 (2006): 78.

71. Commission on Peace Officer Standards and Training, *Integration of Leadership, Ethics, and Community Policing into the Regular Basic Course* (Sacramento, CA: Peace Officer Standards and Training, 2003), 120–121.

72. Sunny Simmonds, "Use of Computer Generated Imagery in Law Enforcement Weapons Training and Tactics" (paper presented at the National Institute of Justice Conference, July 19, 2006).

73. Chappell, Lanza-Kaduce, and Johnston, "Law Enforcement Training Changes and Challenges," 76–77.

74. Robert Worden, "The 'Causes' of Police Brutality: Theory and Evidence on Police Use of Force," in *The Police in America: Classic and Contemporary Readings*, eds. Steven G. Brandl and David S. Barlow (Belmont, CA: Wadsworth, Cengage Learning, 2004): 128–173; Geoff Coliandris and Colin Rogers, "Linking Police Culture, Leadership and Partnership-Working," *The Police Journal* 81, no. 2 (2008): 114.

75. Worden, "The 'Causes' of Police Brutality," 128–173.

76. Michael W. Quinn, *Walking with the Devil and the Police Code of Silence* (Minneapolis: Quinn and Associates, 2005) 118; Coliandris and Rogers, "Linking Police Culture, Leadership and Partnership-Working," 114.

77. William Westley, *Violence and the Police* (Cambridge, MA: MIT Press, 1970); David Weisburd, Rosann Greenspan, Edwin E. Hamilton, Hubert Williams, and Kellie Bryant, *Police Attitudes toward Abuse of Authority: Findings from a National Study* (Washington, DC: Government Printing Office, 2000).

78. Carl B. Klockars, "Police Code of Silence," in *Encyclopedia of Law Enforcement*, ed. Larry E. Sullivan (Thousand Oaks, CA: Sage, 2005), 334–335.

79. Bittner, *Aspects of Police Work.*

80. John Van Maanen, "The Asshole," in *Policing: A View from the Street*, eds. P. K. Manning and J. Van Maanen (Santa Monica, CA: Goodyear, 1978); Meghan Stroshine, Geoffrey Alpert, and Roger Dunham, "The Influence of 'Working Rules' on Police Suspicion and Discretionary Decision Making," *Police Quarterly* 11, no. 3 (September 2008): 315–337.

81. William V. Pelfrey, "The Inchoate Nature of Community Policing: Differences between Community Policing and Traditional Police Officers," *Justice Quarterly* 21, no. 3 (September 2004): 579–601.

82. William Terrill, Eugene Paoline, and Peter Manning, "Police Culture and Coercion," *Criminology* 41, no. 4 (2003): 1003–1034.

83. Robert Brown and James Frank, "Race and Officer Decision Making: Examining Differences in Arrest Outcomes between Black and White Officers," *Justice Quarterly* 23, no. 1 (March 2006).

84. Ibid.

85. Stroshine, Alpert, and Dunham, "The Influence of 'Working Rules' on Police Suspicion and Discretionary Decision Making," 315–337.

86. Brown and Frank, "Race and Officer Decision Making."

87. Robin Shepard Engel and Jennifer Calnon, "Examining the Influence of Drivers' Characteristics during Traffic Stops with Police: Results from a National Survey," *Justice Quarterly* 21, no. 1 (March 2004).

88. John Lamberth, "Traffic Stop Data Analysis Project of the Sacramento Police Department: Final Report for the Sacramento Police Department," August 2008.

89. Donald Black, "The Social Organization of Arrest," *Stanford Law Review* 23 (June 1971): 1087–1111.

90. Ibid.

91. International Association of Chiefs of Police, *Corruption Prevention* (Alexandria, VA: International Association of Chiefs of Police, 1996), 1.

92. Michael A. Caldero and John P. Crank, *Police Ethics: The Corruption of Noble Cause* (New York: Anderson, 2004), 2.

93. Sean W. Malinowski, "The Conceptualization of Police Corruption: An Historical Perspective," in *Police Corruption: Challenges for Developed Countries—Comparative Issues and Commissions of Inquiry*, ed. Menachem Amir (Huntsville, TX: Office of International Criminal Justice, Sam Houston State University, 2004), 37.

94. Caldero and Crank, *Police Ethics*, 30–31.

95. Darrell L. Ross, *Civil Liability in Criminal Justice* (Dayton, OH: LexisNexis, 2006), 5.

96. *Thurman v. City of Torrington* (595 F. Sup. 152, 1984).

97. Ibid.

98. Wendy L. Hicks, "Police Vehicular Pursuits: A Descriptive Analysis of State Agencies' Written Policy," *Policing: An International Journal of Police Strategies & Management* 29 (2006): 122.

99. Herman Goldstein, *Police Corruption: Perspective on Its Nature and Control* (Washington, DC: Police Foundation, 1975), 5.

100. International Association of Chiefs of Police, *Corruption Prevention*, 2.

101. Klockars, "Police Code of Silence," 334–335.

102. Jerome H. Skolnick, "Corruption and the Blue Code of Silence," *Police Practice and Research* 3 (2002): 8–12.

103. Laurence Miller, "'Good Cop—Bad Cop' Problem Officers, Law Enforcement Culture, and Strategies for Success," *Journal of Police and Criminal Psychology* 19, no. 2 (2004): 33.

104. Mark Chapin and others, "Training Police Leadership to Recognize and Address Operational Stress," *Police Quarterly* 11, no. 3 (2008): 338–341.

105. National Institute of Justice, *Enhancing Police Integrity* (Washington, DC: National Institute of Justice, 2005), 2.

106. Caldero and Crank, *Police Ethics*, 269.

107. Kim Michelle Lersch, Tom Bazley, and Tom Mieczkowski, "Early Intervention Programs: An Effective Police Accountability Tool, or Punishment of the Productive?" *An International Journal of Police Strategies & Management* 29 (2006): 59.

108. International Association of Chiefs of Police, *Internal Affairs Study* (Washington, DC: International Association of Chiefs of Police, 2009), 13.

109. Tim Prenzler, "Senior Police Managers' Views on Integrity Testing, and Drug and Alcohol Testing," *Policing: An International Journal of Police Strategies & Management* 29 (2006): 394.

110. Thomas D. Stucky, "Local Politics and Police Strength," *Justice Quarterly* 22 (2005): 164.

111. Darl Champion and Michael Hooper, *Introduction to American Policing* (New York: McGraw-Hill, 2003), 365.

112. David Shichor, *Punishment for Profit* (Thousand Oaks, CA: Sage,, 1995).

113. David Shichor and Michael J. Gilbert, *Privatization in Criminal Justice: Past, Present, and Future* (Cincinnati: Anderson, 2001), 1.

114. Joseph Straw, "Homeland Security," *Security Management* 52, no. 11 (2008): 24.

115. Polk and MacKenna, "Dilemmas of the New Millennium," 5.

116. Champion and Hooper, *Introduction to American Policing*, 192.

117. Polk and MacKenna, "Dilemmas of the New Millennium," 5.

118. Brian Forst, "Private Policing," in *Encyclopedia of Law Enforcement*, ed. Larry E. Sullivan (Thousand Oaks, CA: Sage, 2005), 364.

CHAPTER 6

1. Kareem Fahim and Christine Hauser, "Taser Use in Man's Death Broke Rules, Police Say," *New York Times*, September 26, 2008, http://www.nytimes.com/2008/09/26/nyregion/26taser.html?_r=1&sq=Iman%20Morales&st=cse&adxnnl=1&scp=1&adxnnlx=1240951932-eScYPZ9iPL3JoBdK+9EsKQ (retrieved April 28, 2009).

2. John Doyle, Jamie Schram, and Eric Lenkowitz, "Cops in Nude Taser Slay," *New York Post*, September 25, 2008, http://www.nypost.com/seven/09252008/news/regionalnews/cops_in_nude_taser_slay_130670.htm.

3. Statement from the New York City Police Department, September 25, 2008, http://www.nytimes.com/2008/09/25/nyregion/25taserletter.html?ref=nyregion (retrieved April 28, 2009).

4. Robert D. McFadden and Christine Hauser, "2nd Victim of Taser Fire: Officer Who Gave Order," *New York Times*, October 2, 2008, http://www.nytimes.com/2008/10/03/nyregion/03taser.html?scp=2&sq=Iman%20Morales&st=cse (retrieved April 28, 2009).

5. Thomas J. Sweeney, "Patrol," in *Local Government Police Management*, ed. William A. Geller and Darrel W. Stephens (Washington, DC: International City/County Management Association, 2003), 89.

6. National Research Council, *Fairness and Effectiveness in Policing* (Washington, DC: NRC, 2004), 58. Furthermore, when officers appear on the scene, they often find that no criminal activity has occurred. David A. Klinger and George S. Bridges, "Measurement Error in Calls-for-Service as an Indicator of Crime, *Criminology* 35 (1997): 707.

7. Eric Scott, *Calls for Service: Citizen Demand and Initial Police Response* (Washington, DC: Government Printing Office, 1981).

8. Bureau of Justice Statistics, *Reporting Crime to the Police, 1992-2000* (Washington, DC: Government Printing Office, 2003).

9. Ibid.

10. Michael Caldero and John P. Crank, *Police Ethics: The Corruption of Noble Cause* (New York: Anderson, 2004), 253.

11. James Q. Wilson, *Varieties of Police Behavior* (Cambridge, MA: Harvard University Press, 1968), 31.

12. George Kelling, Tony Pate, Duane Dieckman, and Charles Brown, *The Kansas City Preventive Patrol Experiment: A Summary Report* (Washington, DC: Police Foundation, 1974).

13. Ibid.

14. For more on this topic see John Eck and Edward Maguire, "Have Changes in Policing Reduced Violent Crime? An Assessment of the Evidence," in *The Crime Drop in America*, ed. Alfred Blumstein and Joel Wallman (Cambridge: Cambridge University Press, 2000).

15. Herman Goldstein, "Improving Policing: A Problem-Oriented Approach," *Crime & Delinquency* 25 (1979): 236–258.

16. Ibid.

17. Ibid.

18. Ibid.

19. Jerome Skolnick and David Bayley, *The New Blue Line* (New York: The Free Press, 1986).

20. Ibid.

21. Ibid.

22. Steven Mastrofski, "Community Policing: A Cautionary Tale," in *Community Policing: Rhetoric or Reality*, ed. Jack Greene and Stephen Mastrofski (New York: Praeger, 1988), 47–68.

23. Ibid.

24. Neil Websdale, *Policing the Poor: From Slave Plantation to Public Housing* (Boston: Northeastern University Press, 2001).

25. Department of Justice, Community Oriented Policing Services Office, http://cops.usdoj.gov/Default.asp?Item=34 (accessed January 31, 2009).

26. Department of Justice, Community Oriented Policing Services Office, "FY 2006 End of Year Report," http://www.cops.usdoj.gov/mime/open.pdf?Item=1952.

27. Matthew Hickman and Brian A. Reaves, "Community Policing in Local Police Departments, 1997 and 1999," *Bureau of Justice Statistics Special Report*, February 2001, NCJ 184794.

28. Edward Maguire, "Structural Change in Large Municipal Police Organizations during the Community Policing Era," *Justice Quarterly* 14 (1997): 547–576.

29. John Eck and Edward Maguire, "Have Changes in Policing Reduced Violent Crime? An Assessment of the Evidence," in *The Crime Drop in America*, ed. Alfred Blumstein and Joel Wallman (Cambridge: Cambridge University Press, 2000).

30. Marcia R. Chaiken, *COPS: Innovations in Policing in American Heartlands* (Alexandria, VA: LINC, 2001).

31. Kenneth Novak, Leanne Alarid, and Wayne Lucas, "Exploring Officers' Acceptance of Community Policing: Implications for Policy Implementation," *Journal of Criminal Justice* 31 (2003): 57–71.

32. John MacDonald, "The Effectiveness of Community Policing in Reducing Urban Violence," *Crime and Delinquency* 48, no. 4 (2002): 592–618.

33. Ling Ren, Liquen Cao, Nicholas Lovrich, and Michael Gaffney, "Linking Confidence in the Police with the Performance of the Police: Community Policing Can Make a Difference," *Journal of Criminal Justice* 33 (2005): 55–66.

34. James Q. Wilson and George Kelling, "Broken Windows: Police and Neighborhood Safety," *Atlantic Monthly* 249 (March 1982): 29–38.

35. Ibid.

36. Robert Sampson and Stephen Raudenbush, "Systematic Social Observation of Public Spaces: A New Look at Disorder in

Urban Neighborhoods," *American Journal of Sociology* 105, no. 3 (1999): 603–651.

37. Darrel W. Stephens, "Organization and Management," in *Local Government Police Management*, ed. William A. Geller and Darrel W. Stephens (Washington, DC: International City/County Management Association, 2003), 51.
38. Meghan Stroshine, Geoffrey Alpert, and Roger Dunham, "The Influence of 'Working Rules' on Police Suspicion and Discretionary Decision Making," *Police Quarterly* 11, no. 3 (2008): 334.
39. National Institute of Justice, *Crime Scene Investigation: A Reference for Law Enforcement Training* (Washington, DC: NIJ, 2004), 9–16.
40. Ibid.
41. Joan Petersilia, *The Influence of Criminal Justice Research* (Santa Monica, CA: Rand Corporation, 1987), 15.
42. Frank Horvath and Robert T. Meesig, *A National Survey of Police Policies and Practices Regarding the Criminal Investigation Process: Twenty-Five Years After Rand* (East Lansing, MI: Michigan State University, 2001), 2.
43. Albert Reiss, *The Police and the Public* (New Haven, CT: Yale University Press, 1974).
44. Federal Bureau of *Investigation,* Crime in the United States, 2007 (Washington, DC: Government Printing Office, 2008), http://www.fbi.gov/ucr/cius2007/offenses/clearances/index.html.
45. International Association of Chiefs of Police, *Training Key #58: Criminal Investigations* (Alexandria, VA: IACP, 2003), 2–4.
46. National Advisory Commission on Criminal Justice Standards and Goals, *Police* (Washington, DC: NACCJSG, 1973), 227.
47. Angelo Rao, "Transportation Services," in *Local Government Police Management,* ed. William Geller and Darrel W. Stephens (Washington, DC: International City/County Management Association, 2003), 207–238.
48. Ronnie L. Paynter, "Patrol Car Video," *Law Enforcement Technology* 26, no. 6 (1999): 34–35.
49. National Institute of Justice, *Communications Interoperability* (Washington, DC: NIJ, 2006), 1.
50. National Institute of Justice, *Education and Training in Forensic Science* (Washington, DC: NIJ, 2004), 31.
51. National Institute of Justice, *Crime Scene Investigation: A Reference for Law Enforcement Training,* (Washington, DC: NIJ, 2004), 9–16.
52. Kathleen M. Stephens, "The Changing Role of Forensic Science," *Police Futurist* 13, no. 2 (2005): 7–8.
53. http://www.nytimes.com/2008/11/10/opinion/10mon2.html (accessed January 25, 2009).
54. National Institute of Justice, *Solicitation: Forensic DNA Backlog Reduction Program* (Washington, DC: NIJ, 2008).
55. National Institute of Justice, *Education and Training in Forensic Science* (Washington, DC: NIJ, 2004), 2.
56. Darrel W. Stephens, "Organization and Management," in *Local Government Police Management*, ed. William Geller and Darrel Stephens (Washington, DC: International City/County Management Association, 2003), 52.
57. Daniel E. Marks and Ivan Y. Sun, "The Impact of 9/11 on Organizational Development among State and Local Law Enforcement Agencies," *Contemporary Criminal Justice* 23, no. 2 (2007): 162–163.
58. Thomas D. Stucky, "Local Politics and Police Strength," *Justice Quarterly* 22 (2005): 144.
59. Ibid., 144, 163–164.
60. Ibid.
61. National Institute of Justice, *Mapping Crime: Understanding Hot Spots* (Washington, DC: NIJ, 2005), 2.
62. National Institute of Justice, *Mapping the Path to Problem-Solving* (Washington, DC: NIJ, 1999), 3–4.
63. David Weisburd, Rosann Greenspan, Stephen Mastrofski, and James J. Willis, *CompStat and Organizational Change: A National Assessment*, DOJ-Funded Report, Document No. 222322 (April 2008): 6.
64. Christopher Bruce, "Redistricting and Resource Allocation: A Question of Balance," *Geography and Public Safety* 1, no. 4 (2009): 1.
65. Municipal Police Officers' Education and Training Commission, *Criminal Investigative Analysis: Implications for First Responders* (Hershey, PA: MPOETC, 2004), 1–2.
66. Jeffrey M. Jones, "Confidence in Police Drops to Ten Year Low," The Gallup Poll, November 10, 2005, http://www.galluppoll.com/content/Default.aspx?ci=19783&pg=1&VERSON=p (retrieved January 31, 2007).
67. The Gallup Poll, "Honesty/Ethics in Professions," December 8-10 2006, http://www.galluppoll.com/content/Default.aspx?ci=1654&pg=1&VERSON=p (retrieved January 31, 2007).
68. The Gallup Poll, "Confidence in Institutions," June 1-4, 2006, http://www.galluppoll.com/content/Default.aspx?ci=1597&pg=1&VERSON=p (retrieved January 31, 2007).
69. The Gallup Poll, "Crime," October 9–12, 2006, http://www.galluppoll.com/content/Default.aspx?ci=1603&pg=1&VERSON=p (accessed January 31, 2007).
70. Matthew Hickman, "Citizen Complaints about Police Use of Force," Bureau of Justice Statistics Special Report. U.S. Department of Justice, Office of Justice Programs, June 2006, NCJ 210296.
71. Steven Tuch and Ronald Weitzer, "Racial Differences in Attitudes toward the Police," *Public Opinion Quarterly* 61 (1997): 642–643.
72. Darren K. Carlson, "Racial Profiling Seen as Pervasive, Unjust," The Gallup Poll, July 20, 2004, http://www.galluppoll.com/content/Default.aspx?ci=12406&pg=1&VERSON=p (retrieved January 31, 2007).
73. See for example, *Bureau of Justice Statistics, Characteristics of Drivers Stopped by Police*, 1999.
74. Jeffrey M. Jones, "Confidence in Police Drops to Ten Year Low," The Gallup Poll, November 10, 2005, http://www.galluppoll.com/content/Default.aspx?ci=19783&pg=1&VERSON= (retrieved January 31, 2007).
75. Ronald Weitzer and Steven Tuch, "Perceptions of Racial Profiling: Race, Class, and Personal Experience," *Criminology* 40, no. 2 (2002): 435–456.
76. Ronald Weitzer, "Racialized Policing: Residents' Perceptions in Three Neighborhoods," *Law & Society Review* 34, no. 1 (2000): 129–156.
77. Joseph Carroll, "Majority of NOLA Residents Approve of Mayor's Response to Katrina: Blacks Much More Likely Than Whites to Approve of Job Done by Local Leaders," The Gallup Poll, March 1, 2006.
78. Ronald Weitzer, "Racialized Policing: Residents' Perceptions in Three Neighborhoods," *Law & Society Review* 34, no. 1 (2000): 129–156.

79. Ronald Weitzer and Steven Tuch, "Perceptions of Racial Profiling: Race, Class, and Personal Experience," *Criminology* 40, no. 2 (2002): 435–456.

80. John Reitzel, Stephen Rice, and Alex Piquero, "Lines and Shadows: Perceptions of Racial Profiling and the Hispanic Experience," *Journal of Criminal Justice* 32, no. 6 (2004): 607–616.

81. Ronald Weitzer and Steven Tuch, "Perceptions of Racial Profiling: Race, Class, and Personal Experience," *Criminology* 40, no. 2 (2002): 435–456; John Reitzel, Stephen Rice, and Alex Piquero, "Lines and Shadows: Perceptions of Racial Profiling and the Hispanic Experience," *Journal of Criminal Justice* 32, no. 6 (2004): 607–616.

82. Michael Mukasy, Jeffrey Sedgwick, and David Hagy, "Policing in Arab-American Communities After September 11," *National Institute of Justice: Research for Practice,* July 2008, NCJ 221706.

83. John Song, "Attitudes of Chinese Immigrants and Vietnamese Refugees toward Law Enforcement in the United States," *Justice Quarterly* 9 no. 4 (December 1992): 703–719.

84. http://www.ojp.usdoj.gov/nij/topics/crime/elder-abuse/welcome.htm (accessed January 25, 2009).

85. Etta Morgan, Ida Johnson, and Robert Sigler, "Public Definitions and Endorsement of the Criminalization of Elder Abuse," *Journal of Criminal Justice* 34 (2006): 275–276.

86. National Center on Elder Abuse, *The 2004 Survey of State Adult Protective Services: Abuse of Adults 60 Years and Older* (Washington, DC: NCEA, 2006), 9.

87. International Association of Chiefs of Police, *Training Key #518: Elder Victimization* (Alexandria, VA: IACP, 1999), 10–11.

88. Diana Koin, MD, "Issues to Be Addressed at the Scene of an Elder's Death," interview by Michael Hooper, PhD, April 15, 2004.

89. International Association of Chiefs of Police, *Training Key #518: Elder Victimization* (Alexandria, VA: IACP, 1999), 10.

90. American Bar Association Commission on Law and Aging, *The Availability and Utility of Interdisciplinary Data on Elder Abuse: A White Paper for the National Center on Elder Abuse* (Washington, DC: ABACLA, 2005), 44.

91. National Center on Elder Abuse, *The 2004 Survey of State Adult Protective Services: Abuse of Adults 60 Years and Older* (Washington, DC: NCEA, 2006), 15–23.

92. International Association of Chiefs of Police, *Training Key #518: Elder Victimization* (Alexandria, VA: IACP, 1999), 9.

93. Texas Attorney General, *Protecting Senior Texans* (Texas Office of the Attorney General, August 12, 2006), http://www.oag.state.tx.us/elder'elder.shtm.

94. Cheryl Guidry Tyiska, "Working with Victims with Disabilities," National Organization for Victim Assistance, http://www.trynova.org/victiminfo/ovc disabilities/ (retrieved February 16, 2007).

95. Linda Teplin, "Keeping the Peace: Police Discretion and Mentally Ill Persons," *National Institute of Justice Journal,* no. 244 (July 2000): 9–15.

96. Ibid.

97. Ibid.

98. Ibid.

99. Fred E. Markowitz, "Psychiatric Hospital Capacity, Homesslessness, and Crime and Arrest Rates," *Criminology* 44, no. 1 (2006): 45–72.

100. Mary Castle White, Linda Chafetz, and Gerri Collins-Bride, "History of Arrest, Incarceration and Victimization in Community-Based Severely Mentally Ill," *Journal of Community Health* 31, no. 2 (April 2006): 123–135.

101. Christopher Jencks, *The Homeless* (Cambridge, MA: Harvard University Press, 1994); National Alliance to End Homelessness, "Homelessness Counts," http://www.endhomelessness.org/content/article/detail/1440 (retrieved February 19, 2007).

102. Collen Cosgrove and Anne Grant, "National Survey of Municipal Police Departments on Urban Quality of Life Initiatives," in *Problem Oriented Policing,* ed. Tara O'Connor Shelley and Anne Grant (Washington, DC: PERF, 1998).

103. William King and Thomas Dunn, "Dumping: Police-Initiated Transjurisdictional Transport of Troublesome Persons," *Police Quarterly* 7, no. 3 (September 2004): 339–358.

104. Deborah Padgett, Elmer Struening, Howard Andrews, and John Pittman, "Predictors of Emergency Room Use by Homeless Adults in New York City: The Influence of Predisposing, Enabling and Need Factors," *Social Science Medicine* 41, no. 4 (1995): 547–556.

105. Kimberly Tyler and Katherine Johnson, "Trading Sex: Voluntary or Coerced? The Experiences of Homeless Youth," *The Journal of Sex Research* 43, no. 3 (August 2006): 208–216.

106. National Alliance to End Homelessness, "Homelessness Counts," http://www.endhomelessness.org/content/article/detail/1440 (retrieved February 19, 2007).

107. Phillip Taft, "Policing the New Immigrant Ghetto," *Police Magazine* (July 1982).

108. Refugees International, "Hmong Refugees Arrive in the U.S.: The Latest Chapter in a Long Odyssey," http://www.refintl.org/content/article/detail/3147/ (retrieved February 19, 2007).

109. Philip Taft, "Policing the New Immigrant Ghetto," *Police Magazine* (July 1982).

110. Ibid.

111. Matthew J. Hickman and Brian A. Reaves, "Local Police Departments, 2003," Bureau of Justice Statistics: Law Enforcement Management and Administrative Statistics, http://www.ojp.usdoj.gov/bjs/pub/pdf/lpd03.pdf (retrieved March 20, 2007).

112. Timothy O'Shea, "Community Policing in Small Town Rural America: A Comparison of Police Officer Attitudes in Chicago and Baldwin County, Alabama," *Police and Society* 9 (1999): 59–76.

113. Ralph Weishei, L. Edward Wells, and David N. Falcone, "Community Policing in Small Town and Rural America," *Crime & Delinquency* 40, no. 4 (October 1994): 549–567.

114. Bureau of Justice Statistics, "Victimization Rates for Persons Age 12 and Over, by Type of Crime, Region and Locality of Residence," 2005, http://www.ojp.usdoj.gov/bjs/pub/pdf/cvus/previous/cvus57.pdf (accessed January 31, 2009).

115. Federal Bureau of Investigation, Uniform Crime Reports 2008, http://www.fbi.gov/ucr/08aprelim/index.html (accessed June 4, 2009).

CHAPTER 7

1. Dan Klepal and Cindi Andrews, "Stories of 15 Black Men Killed by Police since 1995," *The Cincinnati Enquirer,* April 15, 2001.

2. "Timeline of Roach-Thomas Case," *The Cincinnati Enquirer,* March 20, 2002.

3. Karen Juanita Carrillo, "Cincinnati Cop Freed in Death of Young Teen; Groups Call for Boycott," *The New York Amsterdam News,* October 4, 2001.

4. Terry Kinney, "Officer Who Shot Unarmed Black Man Won't Face Federal

Charges," *Associated Press*, February 16, 2006.

5. Gregory Korte and Dan Horn, "City Settles 16 Police Suits for $4.5 Million," *The Cincinnati Enquirer*, May 22, 2003.
6. City of Cincinnati Police Department, "Collaborative Agreement," City of Cincinnati, www.cincinnati-oh.gov/police/pages/-5111-/.
7. See, for example, *United States v. Van Leeuwen*, 397 U.S. 249 (1970); *Katz v. United States*, 389 U.S. 347 (1967); *Stanley v. Georgia*, 394 U.S. 557 (1969); *Bond v. United States*, 529 U.S. 334 (2000).
8. *California v. Greenwood*, 486 U.S. 35 (1988); *Smith v. Maryland*, 442 U.S. 735 (1979); *Florida v. Riley*, 488 U.S. 445 (1989); *United States v. Place*, 462 U.S. 696 (1983).
9. In *Hiibel v. Sixth Judicial Dist.*, 542 U.S. 177 (2004), the Court held that a suspect who refuses to identify himself during a *Terry* stop may be arrested and taken to jail.
10. *Carroll v. United States*, 267 U.S. 132 (1925).
11. *California v. Carney*, 471 U.S. 386 (1985).
12. Barton Gellman, Dafna Linzer, and Carol D. Leonnig, "Surveillance Net Yields Few Suspects," *Washington Post*, February 5, 2006, A01.
13. In late 2005, a federal court permitted these searches in New York City. See *MacWade v. Kelly*, U.S. Dist. LEXIS 39695 (2005).
14. *Weeks v. United States*, 232 U.S. 383, 393 (1914).
15. *Mapp v. Ohio*, 367 U.S. 643 (1961); Crime Library, "Dolly Mapp." www.crimelibrary.com/gangsters_outlaws/cops_others/dolly_mapp/index.html (retrieved July 19, 2006).
16. *Mapp v. Ohio*. Eight years later, in *Stanley v. Georgia* 394 U.S. 597 (1969), the Supreme Court further held that private possession of obscene materials in the home, such as the materials for which Mapp was prosecuted, is protected by the First Amendment.
17. *Mapp v. Ohio*.
18. See, for example, Craig D. Uchida and Timothy S. Bynum, "Search Warrants, Motions to Suppress, and 'Lost Cases': The Effects of the Exclusionary Rule in Seven Jurisdictions," *Journal of Criminal Law and Criminology* 81 (1991): 1034–1036.
19. *United States v. Leon*, 468 U.S. 897 (1984).
20. *Arizona v. Evans*, 514 U.S. 1 (1995).
21. *Brown v. Illinois*, 422 U.S. 590 (1975).
22. *Wilson v. Arkansas*, 514 U.S. 927 (1995).
23. *Hudson v. Michigan*, 547 U.S. 1096 (2006).
24. See, for example, Graham Boyd, "Collateral Damage in the War on Drugs," *Villanova Law Review* 47 (2002): 839–850.
25. *Brown v. Mississippi*, 297 U.S. 278 (1936).
26. *Malloy v. Hogan*, 378 U.S. 1 (1964).
27. *Miranda v. Arizona*, 384 U.S. 486 (1966). Miranda was retried—this time without his confession being brought as evidence—and convicted again. After he was released from prison, he was stabbed to death in a bar fight at the age of 34.
28. Richard A. Leo, "Inside the Interrogation Room," *Journal of Criminal Law and Criminology* 86 (1996): 621–692.
29. *Dickerson v. United States*, 530 U.S. 428 (2000).
30. *Miranda v. Arizona*.
31. *Rhode Island v. Innis*, 446 U.S. 291 (1980).
32. *Fare v. Michael C.*, 422 U.S. 707 (1979); Solomon L. Fulero and Caroline Everington, "Assessing the Capacity of Persons with Mental Retardation to Waive Miranda Rights: A Jurisprudent Therapy Perspective," *Law & Psychology Review* 28 (2004): 53–69; Thomas Grisso, *Juveniles' Waiver of Rights: Legal and Psychological Competence* (New York: Plenum Press, 1981).
33. Saul M. Kassin and Rebecca J. Norwick. "Why People Waive Their Miranda Rights: The Power of Innocence," *Law and Human Behavior* 28 (2004): 211–221.
34. Innocence Project, "Causes and Remedies of Wrongful Convictions," www.innocenceproject.com/causes/index.php (retrieved August 3, 2006).
35. *Massiah v. United States*, 377 U.S. 201 (1964).
36. *Patterson v. Illinois*, 487 U.S. 285 (1988); *McNeil v. Wisconsin*, 501 U.S. 171 (1991).
37. *Nix v. Williams*, 467 U.S. 432 (1984). Williams was eventually convicted of first-degree murder and sentenced to life in prison.
38. See, for example, Michael R. Smith, "The Effectiveness of Force Used by Police in Making Arrests," *Police Practice and Research* 3 (2002): 201.
39. http://cityroom.blogs.nytimes.com/2008/07/28/police-investigate-officer-in-critical-mass-video/?scp=5&sq=police%20push%20bicyclist%20july%2028&st=cse (retrieved January 28, 2009).
40. *Tennessee v. Garner*, 471 U.S. 1 (1985).
41. *Graham v. Connor*, 490 U.S. 386 (1989).
42. *Saucier v. Katz*, 533 U.S. 194, 206 (2001).
43. *Brosseau v. Haugen*, 543 U.S. 194, 199 (2004).
44. William Terrill, "Police Use of Force: A Transactional Approach," *Justice Quarterly* 22 (2005): 108.
45. National Research Council, *Fairness and Effectiveness in Policing: The Evidence* (Washington, DC: The National Academies Press, 2004), 282.
46. Ibid., 282–283.
47. International Association of Chiefs of Police, *Use of Force* (Alexandria, VA: International Association of Chiefs of Police, 2001), 4.
48. "Los Angeles Mandates Officer to Act to Bar Another Officer's Use of Force," *Crime Control Digest*, October 8, 2004.
49. Bureau of Justice Statistics, *Contacts between Police and the Public: Findings from the 2002 National Survey* (Washington, DC: Bureau of Justice Statistics, 2005), v.
50. Liqun Cao, "Curbing Police Brutality: What Works? A Reanalysis of Citizen Complaints at the Organizational Level," NIJ Grant No. 98-IJ-CX-0064 (2001), 2–3.
51. National Institute of Justice, *Use of Force by Police: Overview of National and Local Data* (Washington, DC: National Institute of Justice, 1999), viii–ix.
52. Robert Worden, "The 'Causes' of Police Brutality: Theory and Evidence on Police Use of Force," in *And Justice for All: Understanding and Controlling Police Abuse of Force*, eds. W. Geller and H. Toch (Arlington, VA: Police Executive Research Forum, 1995), 31–60.
53. James McElvain and Augustine Kposowa, "Police Officer Characteristics and Internal Affairs Investigations for Use of Force Allegations," *Journal of Criminal Justice* 32, no. 3 (May–June 2004): 265–279.
54. Geoffrey Alpert and Roger Dunham, *Understanding Police Use of Force: Officers, Suspects, and Reciprocity* (New York: Cambridge University Press, 2004).
55. Katheryn Russell, "'Driving While Black': Corollary Phenomena and Collateral Consequences," in *Race, Class, Gender, and Justice in the United States*, eds. Charles Reasons, Darlene Conley, and

Julius Debro (Boston: Allyn & Bacon, 2002), 191–200.

56. National Research Council, *Fairness and Effectiveness in Policing,* 275–276.

57. Geoffrey P. Alpert, Dennis Jay Kenney, Roger G. Dunham, and William Smith, *Police Pursuits: What We Know* (Washington, DC: Police Executive Research Forum, 2000).

58. Chris Pipes and Dominick Pape, "Police Pursuits and Civil Liability," *FBI Law Enforcement Bulletin* 70, no. 7 (2001): 16–21.

59. *Scott v. Harris,* 550 U.S. *372* (2007).

60. Ryan Kim, "$3.15 Million in Settlement in High Speed Chase," *San Francisco Chronicle*, Saturday, March 26, 2005. www.sfgate.com/cgi-bin/article.cgi?f=/c/a/2005/03/26/BAGTBBV2751.DTL&feed=rss.bayarea.

61. Alpert, Kenney, Dunham, and Smith, *Police Pursuits: What We Know.*

62. See "Voices Insisting on Pursuit Safety," www.pursuitsafety.org/.

63. U.S. Department of Health, "2005 National Survey on Drug Use and Health" (Washington, DC: Government Printing Office, 2006), www.samhsa.gov.

64. Jerome Cartier, David Farabee, and Michael Prendergast, "Methamphetamine Use, Self Reported Crime, and Recidivism among Offenders in California Who Abuse Substances," *Journal of Interpersonal Violence* 21, no. 4 (2006): 435–445.

65. Governor's Office of Criminal Justice Planning, "Multi-Agency Partnerships: Linking Drugs with Child Endangerment" (Sacramento, CA: Governor's Office of Criminal Justice Planning, n.d.), 9.

66. Michael Scott and Kelly Dedel, "Clandestine Methamphetamine Labs, 2nd Edition," *Problem Oriented Guides for Police Series,* no. 16. Community Oriented Policing Services, U.S. Department of Justice, www.cops.usdog.gov (retrieved March 28, 2007).

67. Office of National Drug Control Strategy, "Table: Federal Drug Control Spending by Function,"www.whitehousedrugpolicy.gov/publications/policy/10budget/tbl_1.pdf (retrieved June 26, 2009).

68. Peter Reuter and Mark Kleiman, "Risks and Prices: An Economic Analysis of Drug Enforcement," in *Crime and Justice,* eds. Michael Tonry and Norval Morris (Chicago: University of Chicago Press, 1986), 289–340; Brian Lawton, Ralph Taylor, and Anthony Luongo, "Police Officers on Drug Corners in Philadelphia, Drug Crime, and Violent Crime: Intended, Diffusion, and Displacement Impacts," *JQ: Justice Quarterly* 22, no. 4 (December 2005): 427–451.

69. John Eck and Edward Maguire, "Have Changes in Policing Reduced Violent Crime?" in *The Crime Drop in America*, eds. Alfred Blumstein and Joel Wallman (Cambridge, UK: Cambridge Press, 2000); U.S. Department of Health, "2005 National Survey on Drug Use and Health" (Washington, DC: Government Printing Office, 2006), www.samhsa.gov.

70. U.S. Department of Health, "2005 National Survey on Drug Use and Health."

71. The Sentencing Project, "Drug Policy and the Criminal Justice System 2001" (Washington, DC: The Sentencing Project, 2001), www.sentencingproject.org/PublicationDetails.aspx?PublicationID=323 (retrieved March 30, 2007).

72. Donald Lynam and Richard Milich, "Project DARE: No Effects at 10-Year Follow-Up," *Journal of Consulting and Clinical Psychology* 67, no. 4 (1999): 590–593.

73. Robert J. Bursik Jr. and Harold G. Grasmick, "Defining and Researching Gangs," in *The Modern Gang Reader*, eds. Arlen Egley Jr. et al. (Los Angeles: Roxbury, 2006), 10.

74. Malcolm W. Klein, *Street Gangs and Street Workers* (Englewood Cliffs, NJ: Prentice Hall, 1971), 13.

75. National Institute of Justice, *Youth Gangs in Rural America* (Washington, DC: National Institute of Justice, 2004), 2.

76. Office of Juvenile Justice and Delinquency Prevention, *Gangs in Small Towns and Rural Counties* (Washington, DC: Office of Juvenile Justice and Delinquency Prevention, 2005), 1–2.

77. Institute for Intergovernmental Research, "National Youth Gang Survey Analysis," National Youth Gang Center, www.iir.com/nygc/nygsa/ (retrieved February 23, 2007).

78. Bureau of Justice Assistance, *2005 National Gang Threat Assessment* (Washington, DC: Bureau of Justice Assistance, 2006), 1.

79. Ibid., 2.

80. Ibid., 3.

81. Anthony Braga and David Kennedy, "Reducing Gang Violence in Boston," in *Responding to Gangs: Evaluation and Research*, eds. Winifred Reed and Scott Decker (Washington, DC: National Institute of Justice, July 2002), www.ojp.usdoj.gov/nij/pubs-sum/190351.htm.

82. "Juvenile Curfews and Gang Violence: Exiled on Main Street," *Harvard Law Review* 107, no. 7 (May 1994): 1693–1710.

83. Institute for Intergovernmental Research, "National Youth Gang Survey Analysis."

84. Noelle E. Fearn, Scott H. Decker, and G. David Curry, "Public Policy Responses to Gangs: Evaluating the Outcomes," in *The Modern Gang Reader,* 323.

85. Beth Bjerregaard, "Antigang Legislation and Its Potential Impact: The Promises and the Pitfalls," in *The Modern Gang Reader,* 385.

86. Callie Rennison and Susan Welschans, *Intimate Partner Violence* (Washington, DC: Bureau of Justice Statistics, 2003).

87. Eve S. Buzawa and Carol G. Buzawa, *Domestic Violence: The Criminal Justice Response* (Thousand Oaks, CA: Sage, 1996).

88. Ibid.

89. Lawrence Sherman and Richard Berk, "The Specific Deterrent Effect of Arrest for Domestic Assault," *American Sociological Review* 49, no. 2 (1984): 261–272.

90. Federal Bureau of Investigation, "Law Enforcement Officers Killed and Assaulted 2005," Uniform Crime Reports, www.fbi.gov/ucr/killed/2005/ (retrieved March 28, 2007).

91. Bureau of Justice Statistics Crime Data Brief, *Intimate Partner Violence, 1993–2001,* February 2003; Russell P. Dobash, R. Emerson Dobash, Margo Wilson, and Martin Daly, "The Myth of Sexual Symmetry in Marital Violence," *Social Problems* 39, no. 1 (1992): 71–91.

92. Violence Against Women and Department of Justice Reauthorization Act of 2005 (H.R. 3402), www.ncadv.org/publicpolicy/VAWA_2005_179.html (retrieved February 26, 2007).

93. www.ncadv.org/publicpolicy/VAWA_2005_179.html.

94. Violence Against Women and Department of Justice Reauthorization Act of 2005 (H.R. 3402).

95. Pamela Collins and A. C. Gibbs, "Stress in Police Officers: A Study of the Origins, Prevalence and Severity of Stress-Related Symptoms within a County Police Force," *Occupational Medicine* 53, no. 4 (2003): 256–264.

96. Jerome McElroy, Colleen Consgrove, and Susan Sadd, *Community Policing: The CPOP in New York* (Newbury Park, CA: Sage, 1993).

97. Jihong Zhao, Quint Thurman, and Ni He, "Sources of Job Satisfaction among Police Officers: A Test of Demographic and Work Environment Models," *Justice Quarterly* 16 (1999): 153–174; Mark Chapin, Stephen Brannen, Mark Singer, and Michael Walker, "Training and Police Leadership to Recognize and Address Operation Stress," *Police Quarterly* 11, no. 3 (September 2008): 338–352.

98. Collins and Gibbs, "Stress in Police Officers."

99. Merry Morash, Robin Haarr, and Dae-Hoon Kwak, "Multilevel Influences on Police Stress," *Journal of Contemporary Criminal Justice* 22, no. 1 (February 2006): 26–43.

100. Erik Meers, "Good Cop, Gay Cop," *The Advocate*, March 3, 1998, 26–34.

101. Stephen Leinen, *Gay Cops* (New Brunswick, NJ: Rutgers University Press, 1993); J. Violanti and F. Aron, "Ranking Police Stressors," *Psychological Reports* 75 (1994): 824–826.

102. Robin Shepard Engel, "Explaining Suspects' Resistance and Disrespect Toward Police," *Journal of Criminal Justice* 31, no. 5 (September–October 2003): 475–492.

103. Jeremy Davey, Patricia Obst, and Mary Sheehan, "It Goes with the Job: Officers' Insights into the Impact of Stress and Culture on Alcohol Consumption within the Policing Occupation," *Drugs: Education, Prevention & Policy* 8, no. 2 (May 2001): 141–149.

104. Judith A. Waters and William Ussery, "Police Stress: History, Contributing Factors, Symptoms, and Interventions," *Policing: An International Journal of Police Strategies & Management* 30 (2007): 176.

105. Ibid., 184.

106. Ibid., 180.

107. Mark Chapin, Stephen Brannen, Mark Singer, and Michael Walker, "Training and Police Leadership to Recognize and Address Operation Stress," *Police Quarterly* 11, no. 3 (September 2008): 338–352.

CHAPTER 8

1. "National Special Report: Oklahoma City Bombing Trial," *Washington Post.com*, www.washingtonpost.com/wp-srv/national/longterm/oklahoma/stories/chron.htm (retrieved February 20, 2009).

2. Bureau of Justice Statistics, *Compendium of Federal Justice Statistics, 2003* (Washington, DC: U.S. Department of Justice, 2003).

3. *Hamdan v. Rumsfeld,* 126 S. Ct. 2749 (2006).

4. Carson Fox and West Huddleston, "Drug Courts in the U.S.," http://usinfo.state.gov/journals/itdhr/0503/ijde/fox.htm (retrieved April 12, 2007); National Drug Court Institute, "Drug Courts: A National Phenomenon," www.ndci.org/courtfacts.htm (retrieved April 12, 2007).

5. Valerie Bryan, Matthew Hiller, and Carle Leukefeld, "A Qualitative Examination of the Juvenile Drug Court Treatment Process," *Journal of Social Work Practice in the Addictions* 6, no. 4 (2006): 91–114; J. Scott Sanford and Bruce Arrigo, "Lifting the Cover on Drug Courts: Evaluation Findings and Policy Concerns," *International Journal of Offender Therapy and Comparative Criminology*," 49, no. 3 (2005): 239–259; Nancy Rodriguez and Vincent Webb, "Multiple Measures of Juvenile Drug Court Effectiveness: Results of a Quasi-experimental Design," *Crime and Delinquency* 50, no. 3 (2004): 292–314.

6. Jeremy Travis, *But They All Come Back: Rethinking Prisoner Reentry, Research in Brief—Sentencing and Corrections: Issues for the 21st Century* (Washington, DC: National Institute of Justice, 2000); *Reentry Courts: Managing the Transition from Prison to Community, A Call for Concept Papers* (Washington, DC: U.S. Department of Justice, 1999).

7. Dale G. Parent, *Day Reporting Centers for Criminal Offenders: A Descriptive Analysis of Existing Programs* (Washington, DC: National Institute of Justice, 1990); *Reentry Courts: Managing the Transition from Prison to Community, A Call for Concept Papers;* (see also Shadd Maruna and Thomas P. LaBel, "Welcome Home? Examining the 'Reentry Court' Concept from a Strengths-based Perspective," *Western Criminology Review* 4, no. 2 (2003): 91–107.

8. Office of Juvenile Justice and Delinquency Prevention, *Teen Courts: A Focus on Research*, 2000, www.ncjrs.gov/pdffiles1/ojjdp/183472.pdf (retrieved November 25, 2007).

9. *Caperton v. A. T. Massey Coal Co.*, 129 S.Ct. 2252 (2009).

10. American[0] Bar Association, "National Database on Judicial Diversity in State Courts," www.abanet.org/judind/diversity/national.html (retrieved August 25, 2006); Pat K. Chew and Robert E. Kelley, "Myth of the Color-Blind Judge: An Empirical Analysis of Racial Harassment Cases," *Washington University Law Review*, 2009, http://ssrn.com/abstract=1273235 (retrieved February 15, 2009).

11. American Bar Association, "A Current Glance at Women in the Law," www.abanet.org/women/CurrentGlanceStatistics2006.pdf (retrieved August 25, 2006).

12. Benjamin Wittes, "Judges and Politics," *The Weekly Standard*, October 6, 2003, www.weeklystandard.com/Content/Public/Articles/000/000/003/173wfhlw.asp?pg=1 (retrieved February 26, 2007).

13. A. Goldstein and C. Babington, "Roberts Avoids Specifics on Abortion Issue," *Washington Post*, September 14, 2005, A01.

14. S. Goldman, "Judicial Confirmation Wars: Ideology and the Battle for the Federal Courts," *University of Richmond Law Review* 39, no. 3 (2005): 873; J. A. Segal and H. J. Spaeth, *The Supreme Court and the Attitudinal Model Revisited* (Cambridge: Cambridge University Press, 2002).

15. Mark Kozlowski, "What Judges Do: The Founders Saw that Laws Are Often Murky, So Judicial Beliefs Matter," *New Jersey Law Journal*, 167 (February 18, 2002): 20.

16. *Clark v. United States*, 289 U.S. 1 (1933).

17. Bureau of Justice Statistics, "State-Funded Indigent Defense Services, 1999" (Washington, DC: U.S. Department of Justice, 2001).

18. U.S. Department of Justice, *Defense Counsel in Criminal Cases* (Washington, DC: U.S. Department of Justice, 2000).

19. Ibid.

20. T. W. Church, "Examining Local Legal Culture," *American Bar Foundation Research Journal* (Summer 1985): 449.

21. Mary R. Rose, "The Peremptory Challenge Accused of Race or Gender Discrimination? Some Data from One County," *Law and Human Behavior* 23 (1999): 695–702; David Baldus, "Use of Peremptory Challenges in Capital Murder Trials: A Legal and Empirical Analysis," *University of Pennsylvania Journal of Constitutional Law* 3 (2001): 3.

22. Richard Seltzer, "Scientific Jury Selection: Does It Work?" *Journal of Applied Social Psychology* 36 (2006): 2417–2435.

23. Samuel Sommers, "Race and the Decision Making of Juries," *Legal & Criminological Psychology* 12 (2007): 171–187.

24. Gary Wells, Amina Memon, and Steven Penrod, "Eyewitness Evidence: Improving Its Probative Value," *Psychological Science in the Public Interest* 7 (2006): 45–75.

25. The Innocence Project, "Study of Year-Long Pilot Project Shows that Key Eyewitness Identification Reforms Are Effective," www.innocenceproject.org/press/index.php (retrieved August 29, 2006).

26. Wells, Memon, and Penrod, "Eyewitness Evidence: Improving Its Probative Value."

27. *In re Imbler*, 60 Cal.2d 554 (1963).

CHAPTER 9

1. Center on Wrongful Convictions, "Police Perjury and Jailhouse Snitch Testimony Put Rolando Cruz on Death Row," www.law.northwestern.edu/depts/clinic/wrongful/exonerations/cruz.htm(retrieved February 23, 2007); "Convicted Murderer Moved to DuPage Jail," *The Wheaton Sun.com*, www.suburbanchicagonews.com/wheatonsun/news/239282,6_1_NA02_WSRAIL_S1.article (retrieved February 23, 2007).

2. Court Statistics Project, *State Court Caseload Statistics, 2004* (Williamsburg, VA: National Center for State Courts, 2005).

3. Superior Court of California, County of Los Angeles, *2009 Felony Bail Schedule*, www.lasuperiorcourt.org/bail/pdf/felony.pdf (retrieved February 20, 2009).

4. *Powell v. Alabama*, 387 U.S. 45 (1932); Douglas O. Linder, "The Trials of the Scottsboro Boys," www.law.umkc.edu/faculty/projects/FTrials/scottsboro/SB_acct.html (retrieved July 8, 2006).

5. *Gideon v. Wainwright*, 372 U.S. 335 (1963).

6. Ibid., 344.

7. *Argersinger v. Hamlin*, 407 U.S. 25 (1972); *Ross v. Moffitt*, 417 U.S. 600 (1974); *McFarland v. Scott*, 512 U.S. 849 (1994).

8. Bureau of Justice Statistics, "Felony Defendants in Large Urban Counties, 2002," www.ojp.usdoj.gov/bjs/pub/pdf/fdluc02.pdf (retrieved February 23, 2007).

9. *Duncan v. Louisiana*, 391 U.S. 145 (1968).

10. Dennis J. Devine, Laura D. Clayton, Benjamin B. Dunford, Rasmy Seying, and Jennifer Pryce, "Jury Decision Making: 45 Years of Empirical Research on Deliberating Groups," *Psychology, Public Policy, and Law* 7 (2001): 622–727.

11. *Maryland v. Craig*, 497 U.S. 836 (1990).

12. *Benton v. Maryland*, 395 U.S. 784 (1969).

13. *Green v. United States*, 355 U.S. 184, 187-8 (1957).

14. *United States v. Felix*, 503 U.S. 378 (1992).

15. Malcolm Feeley, *The Process Is the Punishment: Handling Cases in a Lower Criminal Court* (New York: Russell Sage Foundation, 1979).

16. Niki Kuckes, "The Useful, Dangerous Fiction of Grand Jury Independence," *American Criminal Law Review* 41 (2004): 1–66. New York's Chief Judge once stated that a grand jury would indict a ham sandwich. *Grand Jury Subpoena of Stewart*, 545 N.Y.S.2d 974, 977 (N.Y. App. Div. 1989).

17. Bureau of Justice Statistics, *Felony Defendants in Large Urban Counties, 2004* (Washington, DC: Department of Justice, 2008).

18. Bureau of Justice Statistics, *Felony Defendants in Large Urban Counties, 2002* (Washington, DC: Department of Justice, 2006).

19. Bureau of Justice Statistics, *Violent Felons in Large Urban Counties* (Washington, DC: DOJ, 2006).

20. T. W. Church, "Examining Local Legal Culture," *American Bar Foundation Research Journal* (Summer 1985): 449.

21. Thomas Pyszczynski and Lawrence Wrightsman, "The Effects of Opening Statements on Mock Jurors' Verdicts in a Simulated Criminal Trial," *Journal of Applied Social Psychology* 11 (1981): 301–313.

22. *Gregg v. Georgia*, 428 U.S. 153 (1976).

CHAPTER 10

1. Adam Liptak, "Finding 11-Day Sentence Not Too Little but Too Late," *New York Times*, February 12, 2009, A12.

2. Ibid.

3. Ibid.

4. Brendan Kirby, "Federal Judge Sets Mississippi Man Free," *Alabama Press Register*, February 28, 2009.

5. *Trop v. Dulles*, 356 U.S. 86, 101 (1958).

6. Ibid.

7. *Penry v. Johnson*, 532 U.S. 782 (2001).

8. *Kennedy v. Louisiana*, 128 S. Ct. 2641 (2008).

9. *Robinson v. California*, 370 U.S. 660 (1962).

10. Lisa M. Seghetti and Nathan James, "Federal Habeas Corpus Relief: Background, Legislation, and Issues," *Congressional Research Service*, 2006, http://assets.opencrs.com/rpts/RL33259_20060201.pdf (retrieved February 15, 2009).

11. Paul F. Cromwell, Rolando V. Del Carmen, and Leanne F. Alarid, *Community Based Corrections*, 5th ed. (Belmont, CA: Wadsworth, 2002).

12. Timothy O'Shea, "Getting the Deterrence Message Out: The Project Safe Neighborhoods Public Private Partnership," *Police Quarterly* 10 (September 2007): 288–307.

13. Paul Brennan and Cassia Spohn, "Race/Ethnicity and Sentencing Outcomes among Drug Offenders in North Carolina," *Journal of Contemporary Criminal Justice* 24, no. 4 (November 2008): 371–393.

14. Brenda Sims Blackwell, David Holleran, and Mary A. Finn, "The Impact of the Pennsylvania Sentencing Guidelines on Sex Difference in Sentencing," *Journal of Contemporary Criminal Justice* 24, no. 4 (November 2008): 399–418.

15. John Scalia, "The Impact of Changes in Federal Law and Policy on the Sentencing of, and Time Served in Prison by, Drug Defendants Convicted in U.S. District Courts," *Federal Sentencing Reporter* 14, no. 3-4 (November/December 2001, January/February 2002): 52–158.

16. "An Overview of the United States Sentencing Commission," www.ussc.gov/general.htm (retrieved December 7, 2007).

17. *United States v. Booker*, 543 U.S. 220 (2005).

18. Margaret E. Leigey and Ronet Bachman, "The Influence of Crack Cocaine on the Likelihood of Incarceration for a Violent Offense: An Examination of a Prison Sample," *Criminal Justice Policy Review* 18 (December 2007): 335–352.

19. United States Sentencing Commission, *Amendments to the Sentencing Guidelines*, May 11, 2007, www.ussc.gov/ (retrieved December 12, 2007).

20. David Stout, "Retroactively, Panel Reduces Drug Sentence," *The New York Times*, December 12, 2007.

21. *United States v. Booker*, 543 U.S. 220 (2005); *Kimbrough v. United States*, 06-6330 (2007); *Gall v. United States*, 06-7949 (2007).

22. Paul H. Robinson, "Crime, Punishment, and Prevention," *Public Interest* (Winter 2001), http://newssearch.looksmart.com/p/articles/mi_m0377/is_2001_Wntr/

ai_69411630/pg_5 (retrieved June 29, 2006).

23. Elsa Chen, "Impacts of 'Three Strikes and You're Out' on Crime Trends in California and throughout the United States," *Journal of Contemporary Criminal Justice* 24 (November 2008): 345–372.

24. Matthew Crow and Katherine Johnson, "Race, Ethnicity, and Habitual-Offender Sentencing: A Multilevel Analysis of Individual and Contextual Threat," *Criminal Justice Policy Review* 19 (March 2008): 63–83.

25. Justine M. Nagurney, "Acts of Fear: An Analysis of the Constitutionality of the Civil Confinement of Sexually Violent Predators," *Dartmouth College Undergraduate Journal of Law* 3, no. 2 (Spring 2005): 29–34.

26. Nathan James, Kenneth R. Thomas, and Cassandra Foley, *Civil Commitment of Sexually Dangerous Persons* (New York: Novinka Books, 2008).

27. Washington State Psychiatric Association amicus curiae brief filed In the Matter of the Personal Restraint of *Andre Brigham Young v. David Weston, Superintendent of the Special Commitment Center* 122 Wn.2d 1, P.2d 989 at 10. The argument put forward by amicus asserted the common belief that, especially involuntarily, violent sex offenders cannot be successfully treated.

28. Peter W. Greenwood, C. Peter Rydell, Allan F. Abrahamse, Jonathan P. Caulkins, James R. Chiesa, Karyn E. Model, and Stephen P. Klein, "Estimated Benefits and Costs of California's New Mandatory-Sentencing Law," in *Three Strikes You're Out: Vengeance as Public Policy*, eds. David Shichor and Dale K. Sechrest (Thousand Oaks, CA: Sage, 1994), 53–90.

29. Peter W. Greenwood and Angela Hawken, "An Assessment of the Effects of California's Three Strikes Law," Working paper. (Greenwood & Associates, March 2002).

30. Special circumstances are, essentially, particular aggravating circumstances that, when present, limit the possible outcome of the penalty phase of a capital case to either life in prison without the possibility of parole or death. For an example of special circumstances in Texas, see http://tarlton.law.utexas.edu/vlibrary/outlines/deathpen.html.

31. James S. Liebman, Jeffrey Fagan, and Valerie West, "A Broken System: Error Rates in Capital Cases: 1973–1995," Columbia Law School, June 12, 2000.

32. Technically, capital punishment is also a possibility for a few crimes other than murder, including treason and some rapes. In practice, however, virtually everyone sentenced to death has been convicted of murder.

33. John Blume, Theodore Eisenberg, and Martin T. Wells, "Explaining Death Row's Population and Racial Composition," *Journal of Empirical Legal Studies* 1, no. 1 (March 2004): 165–207. These authors found a national death sentence rate of 2.2 percent of murders resulted in a death sentence. Viewed state by state, the national average death sentence rates from 1977 to 1999 was 2.5 percent, with a median of 2.0 percent. See also James R. Acker and David R. Karp, eds., "Introduction" in *Wounds That Do Not Bind: Victim-Based Perspectives on the Death Penalty* (Durham, NC: Carolina Academic Press, 2006), 4.

34. David McCord, "If Capital Punishment Were Subject to Consumer Protection Laws," *Judicature* 89, no. 5 (March–April 2006): 304–305.

35. "Death Penalty Information Center Fact Sheet," www.deathpenaltyinfo.org/FactSheet.pdf (retrieved March 1, 2009).

36. Craig Haney, *Death by Design: Capital Punishment as a Social Psychological System* (New York: Oxford University Press, 2005).

37. "Death Penalty Information Center Fact Sheet."

38. Tracy Snell, "Capital Punishment, 2007" (Washington, DC: U.S. Department of Justice, Bureau of Justice Statistics, 2008).

39. According to researchers at Columbia Law School, each year since 1984 (when executions resumed in earnest after the 1972 *Furman v. Georgia* decision) the number of inmates executed compared to the number of inmates on death row has averaged 1.3 percent; it has never exceeded 2.6 percent of inmates on death row. This and related information is detailed in Liebman, Fagan, and West, "A Broken System: Error Rates in Capital Cases: 1973–1995."

40. *Kennedy v. Louisiana*, 554 U.S. _____ (2008).

41. *Furman v. Georgia*, 408 U.S. (1972).

42. David Baldus, George Woodworth, and Charles Pulaski, *Equal Justice and the Death Penalty: A Legal and Empirical Analysis* (Boston: Northeastern University Press, 1990).

43. *Atkins v. Virginia*, 536 U.S. 304 (2002).

44. Jeffrey Kirchmeier, "Casting a Wider Net: Another Decade of Legislative Expansion of the Death Penalty in the United States," *Pepperdine Law Review* 34 (2006).

45. Snell, "Capital Punishment, 2007."

46. Jeffrey Jones, "Support for the Death Penalty 30 Years after the Supreme Court Ruling," Gallup News Service, June 30, 2006.

47. Samuel Walker, Cassia Spohn, and Miriam DeLone, *The Color of Justice*, 3rd ed. (Belmont, CA: Wadsworth, 2004).

48. Death Penalty Information Center, "Innocence and the Death Penalty," www.deathpenaltyinfo.org/innocence-and-death-penalty (retrieved March 1, 2009).

49. Richard Dieter, "A Death Penalty Information Report, September 2004," www.deathpenalty.org.

50. "Death Penalty Focus," www.deathpenalty.org (retrieved January 24, 2008).

51. "Illinois Suspends Death Penalty," CNN.com, January 31, 2000, http://archives.cnn.com/2000/US/01/31/illinois.executions.02/ (retrieved October 5, 2007).

CHAPTER 11

1. The Law Office of the Southern Center for Human Rights, "Violence and Abuse," www.schr.org/incarceration/abuse.

2. See www.prisoncommission.org.

3. Don Harris, *Good Morning America*, ABC News, June 7, 2006, http://abcnews.go.com/GMA/LegalCenter/Story?id=2048040&page=1.

4. John Gibbons and Nicholas de B. Katzenbach, *Confronting Confinement: A Report of the Commission on Safety and Abuse in America's Prisons* (New York: Vera Institute of Justice, 2006).

5. Doug Carlson, "Prisoners Reentering Society Given 'Second Chance,'" The Ethics & Religious Liberty Commission, April 8, 2008, http://erlc.com/article/prisoners-reentering-society-given-second-chance/ (retrieved February 28, 2009).

6. Marie Gottschalk, *The Prison and the Gallows: The Politics of Mass Incarceration in America* (New York: Cambridge University Press, 2006).

7. George Bernard Shaw, *The Crime of Imprisonment* (New York: Philosophical Library, 1946), 13; Lester Pincu and Ruth Masters, "Can Punishment and Rehabilitation Coexist? The Failure of U.S.

Correctional Philosophy," *Official Proceedings of the International Social Science Conference at KonKuk University, Seoul Korea* (May 2000).

8. Frank McLynn, *Crime and Punishment in Eighteenth-Century England* (New York: Routledge, 1989).
9. Bradley R. E. Wright, Avshalom Caspi, Terrie E. Moffitt, and Ray Patenoster, "Does the Perceived Risk of Punishment Deter Criminally Prone Individuals? Rational Choice, Self-Control, and Crime," *Journal of Research in Crime and Delinquency* 41, no. 2 (May 2004): 180–213.
10. David A. Anderson, "The Deterrence Hypothesis and Picking Pockets at the Pickpocket's Hanging," *American Law and Economics Review* 4, no. 2 (2002): 295–313.
11. Jeffery Fagan, Aaron Kupchick, and Akiva Liberman, *Be Careful What You Wish For: The Comparative Impacts of Juvenile versus Criminal Court Sanctions on Recidivism among Adolescent Felony Offenders* (New York: Columbia University, 2003); Jeffrey Fagan and Martin Guggenheim, "Preventive Detention and the Judicial Prediction of Dangerousness for Juveniles: A Natural Experiment," *Journal of Criminal Law and Criminology* 80 (1996): 415–448; Jeffrey Fagan, "The Comparative Advantage of Juvenile versus Criminal Court Sanctions on Recidivism among Adolescent Felony Offenders," *Law and Policy* 18 (1996): 77–115.
12. House of Commons Standing Committee on Justice, Human Rights, Public Safety and Emergency Preparedness, *Bill C-10* (Toronto, Canada: The John Howard Society of Canada, 2006), 4; Paula Smith, Clare Goggin, and Paul Gendreau, *The Effects of Prison Sentences and Intermediate Sanctions on Recidivism: General Effects and Individual Differences* (Saint John: Department of Psychology and Centre for Criminal Justice Studies, University of New Brunswick, Public Works and Government Services Canada, 2002).
13. House of Commons Standing Committee on Justice, Human Rights, Public Safety and Emergency Preparedness, *Bill C-10,* 5.
14. This followed a comparative study of 200 adolescents in New Jersey and New York.
15. Fagan, Kupchick, and Liberman, *Be Careful What You Wish For*; Fagan and Guggenheim, "Preventive Detention and the Judicial Prediction of Dangerousness for Juveniles: A Natural Experiment"; Fagan, "The Comparative Advantage of Juvenile versus Criminal Court Sanctions on Recidivism among Adolescent Felony Offenders."
16. K. M. Carismith, "The Roles of Retribution and Utility in Determining Punishment," *Journal of Experimental Social Psychology* 42, no. 4 (2006): 437–451.
17. Robert Johnson, *Hard Time: Understanding and Reforming the Prison*, 2nd ed. (Belmont, CA: Wadsworth, 1996).
18. Ibid.
19. George Ives, *A History of Penal Methods* (Montclair, NJ: Patterson Smith, 1970).
20. Thorsten Sellin, *Pioneers in Penology: The Amsterdam Houses of Correction in the 16th and 17th Centuries* (Philadelphia: University of Pennsylvania Press, 1944).
21. "Workhouse Life," www.institutions.org.uk/poor_law_unions/workhouse_life.htm#Workhouse%20Rules%20and%20Regulations (retrieved January 1, 2009).
22. James G. Houston, *Correctional Management*, 2nd ed. (Chicago, IL: Nelson-Hall, 1999).
23. William Parker, *Parole: Origins, Development, Current Practices and Statutes* (College Park, MD: American Correctional Association, 1975).
24. The Howard League for Penal Reform, "Short History of Prison," 2006, www.howardleague.org/index.php?id=historyofprison (retrieved August 15, 2006).
25. Thorsten Sellin, *Slavery and the Penal System* (New York: Elsevier, 1976).
26. Todd R. Clear and George F. Cole, *American Corrections*, 3rd ed. (Belmont, CA: Wadsworth, 1994).
27. Stephen A. Toth, *Beyond Papillon: The French Overseas Penal Colonies, 1854–1952* (Lincoln: University of Nebraska Press, 2006).
28. John Vincent Barry, "Alexander Maconochie," in *Pioneers in Criminology*, 2nd ed., ed. Hermann Mannheim (Montclair, NJ: Patterson Smith, 1973), 94.
29. Ibid., 101–102.
30. Charles F. Campbell, *The Intolerable Hulks: British Shipboard Confinement 1776–1857* (Tucson, AZ: Fenestra Books, 2001).
31. Ronald L. Goldfarb and Linda R. Singer, *After Conviction* (New York: Simon & Schuster, 1973).
32. Laura Magnani and Harmon L. Wray, *Beyond Prisons* (Minneapolis: Fortress Press, 2006).
33. Norman B. Johnston, "John Haviland," in *Pioneers in Criminology*, 2nd ed., ed. Hermann Mannheim (Montclair, NJ: Patterson Smith, 1973), 110.
34. Johnson: *Hard Time: Understanding and Reforming the Prison*.
35. H. Richard Phelps, *Newgate of Connecticut; Its Origin and Early History* (Hartford, CT: American, 1876).
36. Ronald L. Goldfarb and Linda R Singer, *After Conviction* (New York: Simon & Schuster, 1973).
37. Ibid.
38. Magnani and Wray, *Beyond Prisons*.
39. Goldfarb and Singer, *After Conviction*.
40. Howard Gill, "State Prisons in America: 1787–1937," in *Penology: the Evolution of Corrections in America,* 2nd ed., eds. George G. Killinger, Paul F. Cromwell Jr., and Jerry M. Wood (New York: West, 1979).
41. Charles Dickens, *Pictures from Italy, and American Notes for General Circulation* (London: Chapman and Hall, 1862).
42. Peter Scharff Smith, "The Effects of Solitary Confinement on Prison Inmates: A Brief History and Review of the Literature," *Crime and Justice* 34 (2006): 441–528.
43. Goldfarb and Singer, *After Conviction*.
44. David Fogel, *We Are the Living Proof: The Justice Model for Corrections*, 2nd ed. (Cincinnati, OH: Anderson, 1979).
45. Gill, *State Prisons in America: 1787–1937*.
46. Joycelyn M. Pollock, *Prisons and Prison Life* (Los Angeles, CA: Roxbury, 2004), 3.
47. Goldfarb and Singer, *After Conviction*.
48. Cayuga County Historian's Page, Early History of Cayuga County, Prison History, "Inside the Auburn Prison," http://co.cayuga.ny.us/history/cayugahistory/prison.htm (retrieved March 25, 2007).
49. Goldfarb and Singer, *After Conviction*.
50. Magnani and Wray, *Beyond Prisons*.
51. Gill, *State Prisons in America: 1787–1937*.
52. Fogel, *We Are the Living Proof*, 24.
53. Ibid.
54. Edgardo Rotman, "The Failure of Reform," in *The Oxford History of the Prison: The Practice of Punishment in Western Society*, eds. Norval Morris and David J. Rothman (New York: Oxford University Press, 1998), 155.
55. Ibid.
56. Johnson, *Hard Time: Understanding and Reforming the Prison*.

57. Goldfarb and Singer, *After Conviction.*
58. Johnson, *Hard Time: Understanding and Reforming the Prison,* 55.
59. Sue Titus Reid, *Crime and Criminology* (New York: Holt, Rinehart & Winston, 1976).
60. Rotman, "The Failure of Reform."
61. Peter Quinn, "The 'Penal Reformatory' That Never Was: Proposals to Establish Borstal Training in New South Wales, 1900–1948," *Journal of the Royal Australian Historical Society* (December 2002).
62. Goldfarb and Singer, *After Conviction.*
63. Rotman, "The Failure of Reform."
64. Reid, *Crime and Criminology.*
65. Johnson, *Hard Time: Understanding and Reforming the Prison*, 56.
66. Morgan O. Reynolds, *Factories Behind Bars* (Dallas, TX: National Center for Policy Analysis, 1996).
67. Rotman, "The Failure of Reform."
68. Gill, *State Prisons in America: 1787–1937.*
69. Reynolds, *Factories Behind Bars.*
70. Johnson, *Hard Time: Understanding and Reforming the Prison*, 254.
71. Robert Martinson, "What Works: Questions and Answers about Prison Reform," *Public Interest* 35 (1974): 25.
72. Pollock, *Prisons and Prison Life.*
73. Johnson: *Hard Time: Understanding and Reforming the Prison.*
74. Governor's Rehabilitation Strike Team, *Meeting the Challenges of Rehabilitation in California's Prison and Parole System* (Sacramento, CA: Office of the Governor, Rehabilitation Strike Team, December 2007), 10.
75. John W. Santrock, *Psychology*, 7th ed. (New York: McGraw-Hill, 2005).
76. Ruth E. Masters, *Counseling Criminal Justice Offenders,* 2nd ed. (Thousand Oaks, CA: Sage, 2004), 6.
77. Sheldon Zhang, Robert Roberts, and Valerie Callanan, "Preventing Parolees from Returning to Prison Through Community-based Reintegration," *Crime & Delinquency* 52, no. 4 (2006): 551–571.
78. Jeremy Travis, *But They All Come Back: Facing the Challenges of Prisoner Reentry* (Washington, DC: Urban Institute Press, 2005).
79. Todd R. Clear and George F. Cole, *American Corrections,* 3rd ed. (Belmont, CA: Wadsworth, 1994), 239–240.
80. Paul F. Cromwell, Rolando V. Del Carmen, and Leanne F. Alarid, *Community Based Corrections*, 5th ed. (Belmont, CA: Wadsworth, 2002); Restorative Justice Online, "Introduction," www.restorativejustice.org/intro (retrieved April 13, 2007).
81. Lauren Glaze and Thomas Bonczar, "Probation and Parole in the United States, 2006," December 2007, www.ojp.usdoj.gov/bjs/pub/ascii/ppus06txt (retrieved June 6, 2008); Bureau of Justice Statistics, "Corrections Statistics: Summary Findings," 2006, www.ojp.usdoj.gov/bjs/correct.htm (retrieved June 6, 2008).
82. Bureau of Justice Statistics, "One in Every 31 U.S. Adults Was in a Prison or Jail or on Probation or Parole at the End of Last Year," December 5, 2007, www.ojp.usdoj.gov/bjs/pub/press/p06ppus06pr.htm (retrieved June 6, 2008).
83. Roy Walmsley, *Findings: World Prison Population List*, 7th ed. (London: Research, Development and Statistics Directorate, 2006).
84. Paige M. Harrison and Allen J. Beck, *Prison and Jail Inmates at Midyear 2005* (Washington, DC: U.S. Department of Justice, Bureau of Justice Statistics, May 2006), 9.
85. Norval Morris, "The Contemporary Prison, 1965–Present," in *The Oxford History of the Prison: The Practice of Punishment in Western Society*, eds. Norval Morris and David J. Rothman (New York: Oxford University Press, 1998).
86. Ibid.
87. Ibid.
88. Ibid.
89. Paige M. Harrison and Allen J. Beck, *Prisoners in 2005* (Washington, DC: U.S. Department of Justice, Bureau of Justice Statistics, November, 2006).
90. Harrison and Beck, *Prison and Jail Inmates at Midyear 2005.*
91. Clear and Cole, *American Corrections,* 503–504.
92. Bureau of Justice Statistics, "Slower Growth in the Nation's Prison and Jail Populations," June 6, 2008, http://ojp.usdoj.gov/bjs/pub/press/prim07jim07pr.htm (retrieved June 6, 2008).
93. Harrison and Beck, *Prison and Jail Inmates at Midyear 2005.*
94. Harrison and Beck, *Prisoners in 2005.*
95. Ibid.
96. Legislative Analyst's Office, "A Primer: Three Strikes—The Impact after More Than a Decade," October 2005, http//www.lao.ca.gov/2005/3_Strikes/3_strikes_102005.htm (retrieved April 15, 2007).
97. Justice Policy Institute, "Still Striking Out: Ten Years of California's Three Strikes," www.justicepolicy.org/article.php?id=393 (retrieved April 23, 2007).
98. Ibid.
99. Harrison and Beck, *Prisoners in 2005.*
100. Federal Bureau of Prisons, "Quick Facts," March 24, 2007, www.bop.gov/news/quick.jsp#2 (retrieved April 26, 2008).
101. Harrison and Beck, *Prisoners in 2005.*
102. William J. Sabol and Heather Couture, "Inmates at Midyear 2007," *Bureau of Justice Statistics Bulletin* (Washington, DC: Department of Justice, June 2008), 3.
103. Ibid.
104. Ibid., 14.
105. Ibid., 15–16.
106. Ibid., 17.
107. Ibid., 18.
108. Bureau of Justice Statistics, July 30, 2006, www.ojp.usdoj.gov/bjs/pandp.htm (retrieved June 10, 2008).
109. Office of Victim Advocate, Pennsylvania Department of Corrections, www.cor.state.pa.us/victim/site/default.asp?portalNav=| (retrieved April 22, 2007).
110. Kyran P. Quinlan, Robert D. Brewer, Paul Siegel, David A. Sleet, Ali H. Mokdad, Ruth A. Shults, and Nicole Flowers, "Alcohol-Impaired Driving among U.S. Adults, 1993–2002," *American Journal of Preventive Medicine* 28, no. 4 (May 2005).
111. Michelle Polacsek, Everett M. Rogers, W. Gill Woodall, Harold Delaney, Denise Wheeler, and Nagesh Rao, "MADD Victim Impact Panels and Stages-of-Change in Drunk-Driving Prevention," *Journal of Studies on Alcohol* 62, no. 3 (2001): 344–350; Janet C'de Baca, Sandra C. Lapham, H. C. Liang, and Betty Skipper, "Victim Impact Panels: Do They Impact Drunk Drivers? A Follow-Up of Female and Male, First-Time and Repeat Offenders," *Journal of Studies on Alcohol* 62, no. 5 (2001): 615–620.
112. Karen L. Dunlap, Tracy G. Mullins, and Marilyn Stein, *Guidelines for Community Supervision of DWI Offenders* (Washington, DC: National Highway Traffic Safety Administration, March 2008).
113. National Center for Victims of Crime, "Rights of Survivors of Homicide," 1999, www.ncvc.org/ncvc/main.aspx?dbName=DocumentViewer&DocumentID=32470 (retrieved January 31, 2007).

114. Texas Department of Criminal Justice, "Victim Survivors Viewing Executions," www.tdcj.state.tx.us/faq/faq-victim.htm (retrieved January 31, 2007).

115. David Shichor, *Punishment for Profit* (Thousand Oaks, CA: Sage, 1995).

116. Phil Smith, "Private Prisons: Profits of Crime," *Covert Action Quarterly* (Fall 1993), http://mediafilter.org/caq/Prison.html.

117. Magnani and Wray, *Beyond Prisons*, 89.

118. Meredith Kolodner, "Immigration Enforcement to Benefit Detention Companies," *The New York Times*, July 26, 2006.

119. Douglas McDonald, Elizabeth Fournier, Malcolm Russell-Einhourn, and Stephen Crawford, "Private Prisons in the United States," Executive Summary (Cambridge, MA: ABT Associates, 1998), iv.

120. Travis C. Pratt and Jeff Maahs, "Are Private Prisons More Cost-Effective Than Public Prisons? A Meta-Analysis of Evaluation Research Studies," *Crime and Delinquency* 45, no. 3 (1999): 358–371.

121. Philip Mattera and Mafruza Khan, "Jailbreaks: Economic Development Subsidies Given to Private Prisons" (Washington, DC: Institute on Taxation and Economic Policy, October, 2001), www.goodjobsfirs.org/pdf/jailbreaks.pdf.

122. Magnani and Wray, *Beyond Prisons*, 89–93.

123. National Center for Policy Analysis, "Private Prisons Succeed" (Analysis based on testimony of Charles W. Thomas, Director of the Private Corrections Project at the University of Florida in Gainesville), 1995, www.ncpa.org/ba/ba191.html (retrieved June 28, 2008).

124. Scott D. Camp and Gerald Gaes, "Growth and Quality of U.S. Private Prisons: Evidence from a National Survey" (Washington, DC: Federal Bureau of Prisons, October 23, 2001).

125. Lonn Lanza-Kaduce, Karen F. Parker, and Charles W. Thomas, "A Comparative Recidivism Analysis of Releasees from Private and Public Prisons," *Crime & Delinquency* 45, no.1 (1999): 28–47.

126. McDonald, Fournier, Russell-Einhourn, and Crawford, *Private Prisons in the United States*, iv.

127. *Richardson v. McKnight*, 521 U.S. 410 (1997).

128. McDonald, Fournier, Russell-Einhourn, and Crawford, *Private Prisons in the United States*, vi.

129. George W. Bush, Executive Order, "Establishment of White House Office of Faith-Based and Community Initiatives," The White House, January 29, 2001, http://whitehouse.gov.news/reports/faith-based.html (retrieved August 24, 2006).

130. "Faith-Based Prison Programs Raise Eyebrows," FoxNews.com, December 9, 2004, www.foxnews.com/story/0,2933,14985,00.html.

131. Alan Cooperman, "An Infusion of Religious Funds in Fla. Prisons: Church Outreach Seeks to Rehabilitate Inmates," *Washington Post,* April 25, 2004, www.washingtonpost.com/ac2/wp-dyn?pagename=article&contentId=A39834-2004Apr24&notFound=true (retrieved August 22, 2006).

132. Joe Follick, "State Opens the Largest Faith-based U.S. Prison," Gainesville.com., November 23, 2005, www.gainesville.com/apps/pbcs.dll/article?AID=/20051124/ (retrieved August 11, 2006); Jacqui Goddard, "Florida's New Approach to Inmate Reform: A 'Faith-Based' Prison," CS Monitor.com, December 24, 2003, www.csmonitor.com/2003/1224/p01s04-usju.html (retrieved February 20, 2009).

133. Nancy La Vigne, Diana Brazzell, and Kevonne Small, *Evaluation of Florida's Faith- and Character-Based Institutions,* (Washington, DC: Urban Institute Justice Policy Center, 2007), 53.

134. Alan Cooperman, "Spiritual Prison Program Ruled Unconstitutional," *Washington Post*, June 3, 2006.

135. Amanda Paulson, "A Tighter Rein on Faith-based Initiatives," *The Christian Science Monitor,* June 12, 2006.

136. Cooperman, "Spiritual Prison Program Ruled Unconstitutional."

137. Neela Banerjee, "Court Rejects Evangelical Prison Plan over State Aid," *The New York Times*, June 3, 2006.

138. Neela Banerjee, "Court Bars State Effort Using Faith in Prisons," *The New York Times*, December 4, 2007.

139. David Crary, "Faith-based Prisons Multiply," Associated Press, October 13, 2007, www.usatoday.com/news/religion/2007-10-13-prisons_N.htm (retrieved June 24, 2009).

140. Vicki Mabrey and Sarah Rosenberg, "High Hopes for Faith-Based Prisons," ABC News.com, January 27, 2006, abcnews.go.com/Nightline/story?id=1550733.

141. Mark A. R. Kleiman, "Faith-Based Fudging," *Slate*, August 4, 2003, www.slate.com/id/2086617 (retrieved March 25, 2007); Lawrence T. Jablecki, "A Critique of Faith-Based Prison Programs," *The Humanist*, September 1, 2005, www.accessmylibrary.com/coms2/summary_0286-14864330_ITM.

142. "Private Prisons Expect a Boom," News21, A Journalism Initiative of the Carnegie and Knight Foundations, http://newsinitiative.org/story/2006/07/26private_prisons_expect_a_boom (retrieved June 28, 2008).

143. Associated Press, "Despite Lingering Questions, Faith-based Prison Programs Multiply across U.S.," *International Herald Tribune*, October 13, 2007.

144. Alexander Volokh, "Developments in the Law—The Law of Prisons: III. A Tale of Two Systems: Cost, Quality, and Accountability in Private Prisons," *Harvard University Law Review* (2002).

CHAPTER 12

1. An in-depth discussion, slide show, vignettes, Web links, and video clips of the Stanford Prison Experiment can be found at Zimbardo's Web site, www.prisonexp.org/slide-1.htm.

2. Bradley R. E. Wright, Avshalom Caspi, Terrie E. Moffitt, and Ray Patenoster, "Does the Perceived Risk of Punishment Deter Criminally Prone Individuals? Rational Choice, Self-Control, and Crime," *Journal of Research in Crime and Delinquency* 41, no. 2 (May 2004): 180–213.

3. Marc Mauer, "The Hidden Problem of Time Served in Prison," *Social Research* 74, no. 2 (2007): 701–706; Scott Decker, "The Relationship between the Street and Prison," *Criminology and Public Policy* 6, no. 2 (2007): 183–186; "Criminal Offender Statistics," Bureau of Justice Statistics, U.S. Department of Justice, 2007, www.ojp.usdoj.gov/bjs/crimoff.htm.

4. Mauer, "The Hidden Problem of Time Served in Prison"; Decker, "The Relationship between the Street and Prison"; David Weiman, "Barriers to Prisoners' Reentry into the Labor Market and the Social Costs of Recidivism," *Social Research* 74, no. 2 (2007): 575–611; Gail Hughes, "The Violation Population," *Corrections Today* 69, no. 6 (2007): 100–101.

5. Michael Welch, *Detained: Immigration Laws and the Expanding I.N.S. Jail Complex* (Philadelphia, PA: Temple University Press, 2003).

6. Douglas C. McDonald, "The Cost of Corrections: In Search of the Bottom Line," *Research in Corrections* 2, no. 1 (1989): 4.
7. Maris Eleno Domino, Edward C. Norton, Joseph P. Morrissey, and Neil Thakur, "Cost Shifting to Jails after a Change to Manage Mental Health Care," *Health Services Research* 39, no. 5 (October 2004): 1379–1402, www.pubmedcentral.nih.gov/articlerender.fcgi?artid=1361075 (retrieved August 13, 2009).
8. "Individuals with Mental Illnesses in Jail and Prison," The Bazelon Center for Mental Health Law, Fact Sheet #3, data from Bureau of Justice Statistics Special Report, *Mental Health Treatment of Inmates and Probationers,* August 2001, NCJ 174463, www.bazelon.org/issues/criminalization/factsheets/criminal3.html (retrieved March 28, 2007).
9. Dan Miller, "Counties Attack Problem of Jail Overcrowding," National Association of Counties, www.naco.org/Template.cfm?Section=justice_and_public_safety&template=/ContentManagement/ContentDisplay.cfm&ContentID=22354 (retrieved March 28, 2007).
10. *Schall v. Martin* (juveniles), 46f US 253 (1984); and *U.S. v. Salerno* (adults), 481 US 739 (1987).
11. Paige M. Harrison and Allen J. Beck, *Prison and Jail Inmates at Midyear 2005* (Washington, DC: Department of Justice, Bureau of Justice Statistics, 2006).
12. Ibid.
13. Ibid.
14. Human Rights Watch, *Ill-Equipped: U.S. Prisons and Offenders with Mental Illness* (New York: Human Rights Watch, 2003).
15. Harrison and Beck, *Prison and Jail Inmates at Midyear 2005.*
16. Andy Furillo, "Housing Prices Still Rising—at State Prisons," Sacbee.com, February 1, 2007, www.sacbee.com/111/story/116756.htm (retrieved February 10, 2007).
17. Ed Mendel, "More Beds, Transfers in $7.4 Billion Proposal," *Union-Tribune*, April 26, 2007, www.signonsandiego.com/uniontrib/20070426/news_1n26prisons.html (retrieved April 30, 2007).
18. "New Incarceration Figures: Thirty-Three Consecutive Years of Growth," The Sentencing Project, www.sentencingproject.org/Admin/Documents/publications/inc_newfigures.pdf (retrieved March 30, 2007).
19. "New Incarceration Figures: Thirty-Three Consecutive Years of Growth," The Sentencing Project.
20. "Facts about Prisons and Prisoners," The Sentencing Project, 2006, www.sentencingproject.org/Admin/Documents/publications/inc_factsaboutprison.pdf (retrieved March 17, 2007).
21. Jennifer Senior, "You've Got Jail, "*New York Magazine*, July 15, 2002, http://nymag.com/nymetro/news/crimelaw/features/6228/.
22. "Medium Security Prisons," *Encarta*, http://encarta.msn.com/encyclopedia_761573083_4/Prison.html (retrieved February 4, 2007).
23. Steven Stanko, Wayne Gillespie, and Gordon Crews, *Living in Prison: A History of the Correctional System with an Insiders' View* (Westport, CT: Greenwood Press, 2004): 151–152.
24. Ibid., 153.
25. "Third Quarter 2008 Facts and Figures," California Department of Corrections and Rehabilitation, www.cdcr.ca.gov/Divisions_Boards/Adult_Operations/Facts_and_Figures.html (retrieved February 9, 2008).
26. Jeffrey I. Ross, "Is the End in Sight for Supermax?" Forbes.com, April, 18, 2006, www.forbes.com/blankslate/2006/04/15/prison-supermax-ross_cx_jr_06slate_0418super.html (retrieved March 1, 2007).
27. Chase Riveland, *Supermax Prisons: Overview and General Considerations* (Washington, DC: National Institute of Corrections, 1999).
28. Laura Magnani and Harmon L. Wray, *Beyond Prisons* (Minneapolis: Fortress Press, 2006).
29. Rachael Kamel and Bonnie Kerness, *The Prison Inside the Prison: Control Units, Supermax Prisons, and Devices of Torture* (Philadelphia: American Friends Service Committee), 3.
30. Barbara Owen, "Prisons: Prison Women—The Contemporary Prison," Law Library-American Law and Legal Information, http://law.jrank.org/pages/1800/Prisons-Prisons-Women-contemporary-prison.html (retrieved February 14, 2009).
31. Ted Conover, *NEWJACK: Guarding Sing Sing* (New York: Vintage Books, 2001).
32. Mark Pogrebin, *Qualitative Approaches to Criminal Justice: Perspectives from the Field* (Thousand Oaks, CA: Sage, 2002), 274.
33. Lucien X. Lombardo, *Guards Imprisoned: Correction Officers at Work* (New York: Elsevier, 1981).
34. Ibid.
35. Conover, *NEWJACK: Guarding Sing Sing.*
36. Lombardo, *Guards Imprisoned: Correction Officers at Work.*
37. Robert Johnson: *Hard Time: Understanding and Reforming the Prison*, 2nd ed. (Belmont, CA.: Wadsworth, 1996).
38. Alexander B. Smith, Bernard Locke, and Abe Fenster, "Authoritarianism in Policemen Who Are College Graduates and Non-College Police," *The Journal of Criminal Law, Criminology and Police Science* 61, no. 2 (June 1970).
39. Don Josi and Dale Sechrest, *The Changing Career of the Correctional Officer: Policy Implications for the 21st Century* (Boston: Butterworth-Heineman, 1998).
40. Dana M. Britton, *At Work in the Iron Cage* (New York: New York University Press, 2003).
41. Evelyn Nieves, "California Examines Brutal, Deadly Prisons," *The New York Times,* November 7, 1998.
42. Craig Haney, W. Curtis Banks, and Philip G. Zimbardo, "Interpersonal Dynamics in a Simulated Prison," *International Journal of Criminology and Penology* 69 (1973).
43. Josi and Sechrest, *The Changing Career of the Correctional Officer: Policy Implications for the 21st Century.*
44. Ibid.
45. D. Carter, "The Status of Education and Training in Corrections," *Federal Probation* 55 (1991): 17–23.
46. Elena Saxonhouse, "Unequal Protection: Comparing Former Felons' Challenges to Disenfranchisement and Employment Discrimination," *Stanford Law Review* 56 (2004); "The Need for Reform of Ex-Felon Disenfranchisement Laws," *The Yale Law Journal* 83, no. 3 (January 1974).
47. *Cooper v. Pate*, 378 U.S. 546 (1964).
48. *Wolff v. McDonnell*, 418 U.S. 539 (1974).
49. *Estelle v. Gamble*, 429 U.S. 97 (1976).
50. *Daniels v. Williams*, 474 U.S. 327 (1986).
51. *Wilson v. Seiter*, 501 U.S. 294 (1991).
52. *Helling v. McKinney*, 509 U.S. 25 (1993).
53. *Procunier v. Martinez*, 416 U.S. 396, 412 (1974).
54. *Cruz v. Beto*, 405 U.S. 319 (1972).
55. *O'Lone v. Estate of Shabazz*, 482, U.S. 342 (1987).

56. Karen Abbott, "Muslim Inmate Wins Fight over Meals, Prayer Cap," *Rocky Mountain News, reprinted* in *The Muslim News,* www.muslimnews.co.uk/news/news.php?article=9605 (retrieved July 27, 2005).

57. "ACLU Secures Religious Freedom for Muslim Prisoners at Wyoming State Penitentiary," American Civil Liberties Union, November 20, 2008, www.aclu.org/racialjustice/gen/3783prs20081120.html.

58. *Cutter v. Wilkinson*, 544 U.S. 709 (2005); "The Supreme Court's Decision in *Cutter v. Wilkinson*," The Pew Forum on Religion & Public Life, June 2005, http://pewforum.org/publications/reports/RLUIPA-addendum.pdf (retrieved March 19, 2007).

59. Todd Clear and George Cole, *American Corrections*, 2nd ed. (Belmont, CA: Brooks/Cole, 1990).

60. Donald Clemmer, *The Prison Community* (New York: Holt, Rinehart & Winston, 1940).

61. Ibid.; Geoffrey Alpert, "A Comparative Study of the Effects of Ideology on Prisonization: A Research Note," *LAE Journal of the American Criminal Justice Association* 41, no. 1 (1978): 77–78.

62. Gresham M. Sykes, *The Society of Captives: A Study of a Maximum Security Prison* (Princeton, NJ: Princeton University Press, 1958).

63. John Irwin and Donald Cressey, "Thieves, Convicts, and the Social Inmate Culture," *Social Problems* 10 (Fall 1962): 142–155.

64. John Irwin, *The Felon* (Englewood Cliffs, NJ: Prentice Hall, 1979).

65. Joycelyn M. Pollock, *Prisons and Prison Life* (Los Angeles, CA: Roxbury, 2004).

66. *Reducing Racial Disparity in the Criminal Justice System: A Manual for Practitioners and Policymakers* (Washington, DC: The Sentencing Project, 2000).

67. Chad R. Trulson and James W. Marquart, "Inmate Racial Integration: Achieving Racial Integration in the Texas Prison System," *The Prison Journal* 82 (2002): 498–525.

68. Ronald J. Berger, Marvin D. Free Jr., and Patricia Searles, *Crime, Justice, and Society: Criminology and the Sociological Imagination* (New York: McGraw-Hill, 2001).

69. Cordon James Knowles, "Male Prison Rape: A Search for Causation and Prevention," *The Howard Journal* 38, no. 3 (August 1999).

70. Leanne Fiftal Alarid and Paul F. Cromwell, *Correctional Perspectives: Views from Academics, Practitioners, and Prisoners* (Los Angeles, CA: Roxbury, 2002).

71. Johnson, *Hard Time: Understanding and Reforming the Prison.*

72. Alarid and Cromwell, *Correctional Perspectives: Views from Academics, Practitioners, and Prisoners.*

73. Berger, Free, and Searles, *Crime, Justice, and Society: Criminology and the Sociological Imagination.*

74. Intelligence Report, "Behind the Walls," Southern Poverty Law Center, www.spleecenter.org/intel/intelreport/article.jsp?sid=55 (retrieved November 25, 2007).

75. Alarid and Cromwell, *Correctional Perspectives: Views from Academics, Practitioners, and Prisoners.*

76. Edwin L. Santana "Gang Culture from the Inside & Out, Part II," Corrections.Com, www.corrections.com/news/article/17132 (retrieved February 21, 2009); Louis Kontos and David Brotherton, *Encyclopedia of Gangs* (Westport, CT: Greenwood Press, 2008).

77. Alarid and Cromwell, *Correctional Perspectives: Views from Academics, Practitioners, and Prisoners.*

78. Geoffrey Hung, Sephanie Rigel, Tomas Morales, and Dan Waldorf, "Changes in Prison Culture: Prison Gangs and the Case of the Pepsi Generation," in *Correctional Perspectives: Views from Academics, Practitioners, and Prisoners*, eds. Alarid and Cromwell.

79. Magnani and Wray, *Beyond Prisons.*

80. Arjen Boin and Menno Van Duin, "Prison Riots as Organizational Failures: A Managerial Failure," *Prison Journal* 75, no. 3 (1995): 357; Reid Montgomery and Gordon Crews, *A History of Correctional Violence: An Examination of Reported Causes of Riots and Disturbances* (Lanham, MD: American Correctional Association, 1998).

81. Erich Fromm, *The Anatomy of Human Destructiveness,* rev. ed. (New York: Macmillan, 1992).

82. Robert A. Baron and Deborah R. Richardson, *Human Aggression* (New York: Springer, 2004).

83. Reid Montgomery Jr., "Bringing the Lessons of Prison Riots into Focus," *Corrections Today* 59, no. 1 (1997): 28–33.

84. Marvin Wolfgang and Franco Ferracuti, *The Subculture of Violence* (London: Tavistock, 1967); Susan Clayton and Gabriella Daley, "Mock Riot," *Corrections Today* (July 2000): 128–131.

85. Pollock, *Prisons and Prison Life.*

86. Steven Dillingham and Montgomery Reid, "Can Riots Be Prevented?" *Corrections Today* 44, no. 5 (1982); Reid and Crews, *A History of Correctional Violence: An Examination of Reported Causes of Riots and Disturbances.*

87. Bureau of Justice Statistics, "Prison Statistics: Summary Findings," http://www.pjp.usdoj.gov/bjs/prisons.htm (retrieved October 23, 2009); Human Rights Watch, "No Escape: Male Rape in U.S. Prisons," 2001, www.hrw.org/reports/2001/prison/report.html (retrieved March 18, 2007).

88. Allen J. Beck and Paige M. Harrison, *Special Report: Sexual Violence Reported by Correctional Authorities, 2005*, July 2006, www.ojp.usdoj.gov/bjs/pub/pdf/svrca05.pdf, (retrieved December 6, 2007).

89. Gerald G. Gaes and Andrew L. Goldberg, "Prison Rape: A Critical Review of the Literature," Working paper (Washington, DC: National Institute of Justice, 2004).

90. Associated Press, "Study: Sex Crimes in Prisons Underreported," *USA Today,* July 30, 2006, www.usatoday.com/news/washington/2006-07-30-prison-sex_x.htm (retrieved June 2, 2008).

91. Mary Bosworth, *The U.S. Federal Prison System* (Thousand Oaks, CA: Sage, 2002), 114.

92. Wayne S. Wooden and Jay Parker, *Men Behind Bars: Sexual Exploitation in Prison* (New York: Plenum, 1982).

93. Ibid.

94. Magnani and Wray, *Beyond Prisons.*

95. Pollock, *Prisons and Prison Life.*

96. Christian Parenti, "Rape as a Disciplinary Tactic," Salon.com, August 23, 1999, www.calon.com/news/feature/1999/08/23/prisons/ (retrieved May 24, 2008); Lewis Griswold, "Inmate Testifies about Corcoran Prison Rape," *The Fresno Bee*, October 19, 1999; Evelyn Nieves, "California Examines Brutal, Deadly Prisons," *The New York Times,* November 7, 1998, http://query.nytimes.com/gst/fullpage.html?res=9B03E6DE123EF934A35752C1A96E958260 (retrieved May 24, 2008).

97. Gary Marx, "When the Guards Guard Themselves: Undercover Tactics Turned Inward," *Policing and Society* 2, no. 3 (1992): 151–172; Stephen Sachs et al., *Report on Security Conditions at Maryland Penitentiary's South Wing Annapolis*

(Annapolis: Attorney General of Maryland, 1984).

98. U.S. Department of Justice, *Substance Abuse and Treatment, State and Federal Prisoners, 1997* (Washington, DC: Bureau of Justice Statistics, 1999), www.ojp.usdoj.gov/bjs/abstract/satsfp97.htm (retrieved April 30, 2007).

99. Jan Keene, "Drug Misuse in Prison: Views from Inside: A Qualitative Study of Prison Staff and Inmates," *The Howard Journal* 36, no. 1 (1997): 31.

100. Heinrich Andersen, D. Sestoff, and T. Lillegoek, "A Longitudinal Study of Prisoners on Remand: Repeated Measures of Psychopathology in the Initial Phase of Solitary versus Nonsolitary Confinement," *International Journal of Law and Psychiatry* 26, no. 2 (2003): 165–177; Tor Gamman, "The Detrimental Effects of Solitary Confinement in Norwegian Prisons," *Nordisk Tidsskrift for Kriminalvidenskab* 88, no. 1 (2001): 42–50.

101. Atul Gawande, "Hellhole," *The New Yorker*, March 30, 2009, p. 42.

102. Ibid., 36–45.

103. Ibid., 43–44.

104. William Sabol, Heather Couture, and Paige M. Harrison, *Prisoners in 2006* (Washington, DC: Bureau of Justice Statistics, 2007), 3.

105. Ibid.

106. Ibid., 4.

107. B. Keith Crew, "Sex Differences in Criminal Sentencing: Chivalry or Patriarchy?" *Justice Quarterly* 8, no. 1 (1991): 59–83.

108. Sabol, Couture, and Harrison, *Prisoners in 2006*, (6–8.

109. Ibid., 6.

110. Boalt Hall Prison Action Coalition, "Women in California Prisons," September 2000, www.boalt.org/PAC/stats/women-prison-fact-sheet.html (retrieved February 14, 2009).

111. Barbara Bloom, Barbara Owen, Stephanie Covington, and Myrna Raeder, *Gender-Responsive Strategies: Research, Practice, and Guiding Principles for Women Offenders* (Washington, DC: National Institute of Corrections, 2003).

112. K. van Wormer and L. Kaplan, "Results of a National Survey of Wardens in Women's Prisons: The Case for Gender-Specific Treatment," *Women and Therapy* 29, no. 1 (2006): 133–151.

113. S. Jiang and L. Winfree, "Social Support, Gender, and Inmate Adjustment to Prison Life: Insights from a National Sample," *The Prison Journal*, 86, no. 1 (2006): 32–55.

114. Bloom, Owen Covington, and Raeder, *Gender-Responsive Strategies: Research, Practice, and Guiding Principles for Women Offenders*; Karen Holt, "Nine Months to Life—the Law and the Pregnant Inmate," *Journal of Family Law* 20 (1982): 524–525.

115. Cheryl Hanna-Truscott and others, "A Photodocumentary Project at the WCCW," in *Her Hand Rocks the Cradle: A Photodocumentary Project at the Washington Corrections Center for Women*, www.residentialparenting.com/ (retrieved March 3, 2007).

116. Candace Kruttschnitt and Sharon Krmpotich, "Aggressive Behavior among Female Inmates: An Exploratory Study," *Justice Quarterly* 7 (1990): 371–389; Pollock, *Prisons and Prison Life*.

117. Kristin C. Carbone-Lopez and Candace Kruttschnitt, "Assessing the Racial Climate in Women's Institutions in the Context of Penal Reform," *Women and Criminal Justice* 15, no. 1 (2003): 55–79.

118. Lawrence Greenfeld and Tracy Snell, *Women Offenders* (Washington, DC: Bureau of Justice Statistics, 1999).

119. Marc Mauer, Cathy Potler, and Richard Wolf, *Gender and Justice: Women, Drugs, and Sentencing Policy* (Washington, DC: The Sentencing Project, 1999).

120. Shulamith Lala Ashenberg Straussner, "Gender and Substance Abuse," in *Gender and Addictions*, ed. Shulamith Lala Ashenberg Straussner and Elizabeth Zelvin (Norvale, NJ: Jason Aronson, 1997).

121. Bloom, Owen, Covington, and Raeder, *Gender-Responsive Strategies: Research Practice and Guiding Principles for Women Offenders*.

122. Ibid.

123. K. Kauffman, "Mothers in Prison," *Corrections Today* 63, no. 1 (2001): 62–65; Greenfeld and Snell, *Women Offenders*.

124. J. M. Pollock-Byrne, *Women, Prison, and Crime* (Pacific Grove, CA: Brooks/Cole, 1990).

125. C. E. Temin, "Let Us Consider the Children," *Corrections Today* 63, no.1 (2001): 66–68.

126. Caron Zlotnick, Lisa Nijavits, Damaris Rohsenow, and Dawn Johnson, "A Cognitive-Behavioral Treatment for Incarcerated Women with Substance Abuse Disorder and Posttraumatic Stress Disorder: Findings from a Pilot Study," *Journal of Substance Abuse Treatment* 25, no. 2 (2003): 99–105.

127. Cindi Banks, *Women in Prison* (Santa Barbara, CA: ABC-CLIO, 2003), 52–53; Abigail Groves, "Blood on the Walls: Self-Mutilation in Prisons," *Australian and New Zealand Journal of Criminology* (April 1, 2004).

128. Jo Borrill, Louisa Snow, Diana Medlicott, Rebecca Teers, and Jo Paton, "Learning from 'Near Misses': Interviews with Women Who Survived an Incident of Severe Self-Harm in Prison," *Howard Journal of Criminal Justice* 44, no. 1 (2005): 57–69; Jan Heney, *Dying on the Inside: Suicide and Suicidal Feelings among Federally Incarcerated Women* (Ann Arbor, MI: University Microfilms International, 1996).

129. U.S. Department of Justice, *Survey of Inmates in State and Federal Correctional Facilities, 1997.*

130. American Correctional Association Task Force on the Female Offender, *The Female Offender: What Does the Future Hold?* (Washington, DC: St. Mary's Press, 1990).

131. E. Lord, "The Challenge of Mentally Ill Female Offenders in Prison," *Criminal Justice and Behavior* 35, no. 8 (2008): 928–942.

132. Caroline Wolf Harlow, *Education and Correctional Populations* (Washington DC: Bureau of Justice Statistics, 2003).

133. Meda Chesney-Lind and Noelie Rodriguez, "Women under Lock and Key: A View from the Inside," in *Girls, Women, and Crime: Selected Readings*, 2nd ed., ed. Meda Chesney-Lind and Lisa Pasko (Newbury Park, CA: Sage, 2003), 200–201.

134. A. Blackburn, J. Mullings, and J. Marquart, "Sexual Assault in Prison and Beyond: Toward an Understanding of Lifetime Sexual Assault among Incarcerated Women," *The Prison Journal* 88, no. 3 (2008): 351–377.

135. Bloom, Owen, Covington, and Raeder, *Gender-Responsive Strategies: Research, Practice, and Guiding Principles for Women Offenders.*

136. Cindy Struckman-Johnson and David Struckman-Johnson, "Sexual Coercion Reported by Women in Three Midwestern Prisons," *The Journal of Sex Research* 39 (2002): 217–218.

137. Christopher Hensley, Richard Tewksbury, and Mary Koscheski, "The Characteristics and Motivations behind Female Prison

Sex," *Women and Criminal Justice* 13 (2002): 125–129.

138. Pollock, *Women, Prison, and Crime.*

139. "Prisons: Prisons for Women—Problems and Unmet Needs in Contemporary Women's Prisons," http://law.jrank.org/pages/1805/Prisons-Prisons-Women-Problems-unmet-needs-in-contemporary-women-s-prison.html (retrieved February 14, 2009).

140. Barbara V. Smith, "Sexual Abuse against Women in Prison," *American Bar Association Criminal Justice Magazine* 16, no. 1 (Spring 2001), www.wcl.american.edu/nic/Articles_Publications/Sexual_Abuse_Against_Women_in_Prison.pdf?rd=1 (retrieved March 18, 2007).

141. Allen J. Beck, and Page M. Harrison, "Sexual Violence Reported by Correctional Authorities," 2005, www.wcl.american.edu/nic/documents/Beckand-Harrison_BJSReport2005_000.pdf?rd=1 (retrieved April 2, 2007); Office of the Inspector General, *Deterring Staff Sexual Abuse of Federal Inmates* (Washington, DC: U.S. Department of Justice, April 2005), www.usdoj.gov/oig/special/0504/final.pdf.

142. See 18 U.S.C. § 2243 (c).

143. Office of the Inspector General, *Deterring Staff Sexual Abuse of Federal Inmates,* 21–22.

144. Prison Rape Elimination Act of 2003, 45 U.S.C. § 15601 (2003).

145. Brenda V. Smith, "Analyzing Prison Sex: Reconciling Self-Expression with Safety," *Human Rights Brief,* Westlaw (Spring 2006), www.spr.org/pdf/Analyzing%20Prison%20Sex.pdf (retrieved March 15, 2007).

146. Norval Morris, "The Contemporary Prison, 1965–Present," in *The Oxford History of the Prison: The Practice of Punishment in Western Society,* ed. Norval Morris and David J. Rothman (New York: Oxford University Press, 1998).

147. David Leonhardt, "As Prison Labor Grows, So Does the Debate," *The New York Times,* March 19, 2000, www.commondreams.org/headlines/031900-02.htm (retrieved March 19, 2007).

148. "Inmates Gladly Take on Jobs for Low or No Pay," in The Real Cost of Prisons Weblog (February 23, 2005), http://realcostsofprisons.org/blog/archives/2005/02/inmates_gladly.html (retrieved March 19, 2007).

149. "Academic, Vocational, and Substance Abuse Program Impacts," Florida Department of Corrections, www.dc.state.fl.us/pub/recidivismprog/execsum.html (retrieved March 28, 2007).

150. David B. Wilson, C. A. Galagher, and D. L. MacKenzie, "A Meta-Analysis of Corrections Based Education, Vocation, and Work Programs for Adult Offenders," *Journal of Research in Crime and Delinquency* 37 (2001): 347–368, cited by Shawn Bushway, "Employment Dimensions of Reentry: Understanding the Nexus between Prisoner Reentry and Work," *Urban Institute Reentry Roundtable* (New York University Law School, May 19–20), www.urban.org/UploadedPDF/410853_bushway.pdf (retrieved March 22, 2007).

151. Kathleen Scalise, "California Prison Factories Generate $150 Million in Sales Each Year, New U.C. Berkeley Report Finds," News Release, University of California Berkeley, June 25, 1998, www.berekeley.edu/news/media/releases/98legacy/06-25-1998.html (retrieved March 20, 2007).

152. Alarid and Cromwell, *Correctional Perspectives: Views from Academics, Practitioners, and Prisoners.*

153. D. A. Andrews, Ivan Zinger, Robert D. Hoge, James Bonta, Paul Gendreau, and Francis T. Cullen, "Does Correctional Treatment Work? A Clinically Relevant and Psychologically Informed Meta-Analysis," *Criminology* 28, no. 3 (1990): 369–404.

154. Johnson: *Hard Time: Understanding and Reforming the Prison.*

155. Maxwell Jones, *The Therapeutic Community: A New Treatment Method in Psychiatry* (New York: Basic Books, 1953).

156. Clayton Mosher and Dretha Phillips, "The Dynamics of a Prison-based Therapeutic Community for Women Offenders: Retention, Completion, and Outcomes," *The Prison Journal* 86, no. 1 (2006): 6–31.

157. James Inciardi, *A Corrections-based Continuum of Effective Drug Abuse Treatment* (Washington, DC: National Institute of Justice, 1996).

158. Madeline Ortiz, "Managing Special Populations," *Corrections Today* 62 (2000): 64–68.

159. Marc Mauer, Ryan S. King, and Malcolm C. Young, "The Meaning of 'Life': Long Prison Sentences in Context," The Sentencing Project, 2004, www.sentencingproject.org/Admin/Documents/publications/inc_meaningoflife.pdf (retrieved March 1, 2007).

160. National Correctional Industries Association, "Executive Summary: Major Findings," September 27, 1998, http://66.165.94.98/stories/eldst.pdf (retrieved March 1, 2007).

161. Linda Richardson, "Other Special Offender Populations," in *Correctional Mental Health Handbook,* eds. Thomas Fagan and Robert Ax (Thousand Oaks, CA: Sage, 2003).

162. Ibid.

163. Ibid.

164. National Correctional Industries Association, "Executive Summary: Major Findings."

165. Donald Pointer and Marjorie Kravitz, *The Handicapped Offender: A Selected Bibliography* (Washington, DC: Department of Justice, 1981).

166. Human Rights Watch, *Ill-Equipped: U.S. Prisons and Offenders with Mental Illness* (New York: Human Rights Watch, 2003).

167. Monica Davey and Abby Goodnough, "Doubts Rise as States Hold Sex Offenders after Prison Terms," *Herald Tribune,* March 4, 2007, www.heraldtribune.com/apps/pbcs.dll/article?AID=/20070304/ZNYT02/703041099 (retrieved March 1, 2007).

168. Shelia Holton, "Managing and Treating Mentally Disordered Offenders in Jails and Prisons," in *Correctional Mental Health Handbook,* eds. Thomas Fagan and Robert Ax (Thousand Oaks, CA: Sage, 2003).

169. Ibid.

170. Human Rights Watch, *Ill-Equipped: U.S. Prisons and Offenders with Mental Illness.*

171. Franca Cortoni and R. Carl Hanson, *Research Report: A Review of the Recidivism Rates of Adult Female Sexual Offenders* (Ottawa, Canada: Correctional Service of Canada, 2005).

172. Davey and Goodnough, "Doubts Rise as States Hold Sex Offenders after Prison Terms."

173. Ibid.

174. Lydia Long and Allen Sapp, "Programs and Facilities for Physically Disabled Inmates in State Prisons," *Journal of Offender Rehabilitation* 18 (1992): 191–204.

175. Ibid.

176. *Armstrong v. Wilson,* 124 F. 3d 1019 (9th Cir. 1997).

177. *Pennsylvania Dept. of Corrections v. Yeskey,* 524 U.S. 206, 209 (1998).

178. Josi and Sechrest, *The Changing Career of the Correctional Officer: Policy Implications for the 21st Century*, 103–105.

179. Ibid., 105–106.

180. Richardson, "Other Special Offender Populations," 199–216; Gene Draper and Michael Reed, *Criminal Alien Project for the State of Texas* (Austin: Texas Criminal Justice Council, 1995).

181. Richardson, "Other Special Offender Populations."

182. D. L. Saunders, D. M. Olive, S. B. Wallace, D. Lacy, R. Leyba, and N. E. Kendig, "Tuberculosis Screening in the Federal Prison System: An Opportunity to Treat and Prevent Tuberculosis in Foreign-Born Populations," *Public Health Reports* 116, no. 3 (2001): 210–218.

183. Laura Maruschak, *HIV in Prisons, 2006* (Washington, DC: Bureau of Justice Statistics, 2008), Tables 7 and 9.

184. T. Hammett, P. Harmon, and Laura Maruschak, *1996-1997 Update: HIV/AIDS, STDs, and TB in Correctional Facilities* (Washington, DC: National Institute of Justice, 1999).

185. Richardson, "Other Special Offender Populations."

186. A. A. Amankwaa, L. C. Amankwaa and C. O Ochie, "Revisiting the Debate of Voluntary versus Mandatory HIV/AIDS Testing in U.S. Prisons," *Journal of Health and Human Services Administration* 22, no. 2 (1999).

187. Jay Romano, "Plan for AIDS Testing in Prison Raises Questions," *The New York Times*, December 17, 1989.

188. Mary Sylla, "HIV Treatment in U.S. Jails and Prisons," San Francisco AIDS Foundation, www.sfaf.org/beta/2008_win/jails_prisons (retrieved February 27, 2009).

189. American Correctional Association, *Managing Special Needs Offenders* (Lanham, MD: American Correctional Association, 2004).

190. Kathleen Block and Margaret Potthast, "Girls Scouts Behind Bars: Facilitating Parent-Child Contact in Correctional Settings," in *Children with Parents in Prison: Child Welfare Policy, Program, and Practice Issues*, eds. Cynthia Seymour and Creasie Finney Hairston (New Brunswick, NJ: Transaction, 2001).

191. Kelsey Kauffman, "Mothers in Prison," *Corrections Today* 63, no. 1 (2001): 62–65; Greenfeld and Snell, *Women Offenders*; J. M. Pollack-Byrne, *Women, Prison, and Crime* (Pacific Grove, CA: Brooks/Cole, 1990); Bloom, Owen, Covington, and Raeder, *Gender-Responsive Strategies: Research, Practice, and Guiding Principles for Women Offenders*.

192. Christopher J. Mumola, *Incarcerated Parents and Their Children* (Washington, DC: Bureau of Justice Statistics, 2000).

193. Phyllis J. Baunnach, "Critical Problems of Women in Prison," in *The Changing Roles of Women in the Criminal Justice System*, ed. Imogene L. Moyer (Prospect Heights, IL: Waveland Press, 1985).

194. Temin, "Let Us Consider the Children."

195. G. Lane Wagaman, "Managing and Treating Female Offenders," in *Correctional Mental Health Handbook*, eds. Thomas Fagan and Robert Ax (Thousand Oaks, CA: Sage, 2003).

196. Patrick Rodgers, "Conjugal Visits: Preserving Family Bonds behind Bars," Legalzoom.com, www.legalzoom.com/articles/article_content/article12959.htm (retrieved March 2, 2007).

197. Federal Bureau of Prisons, "Conjugal Visits Information Page," www.bop.gov/inmate_locator/conjugal.jsp (retrieved April 17, 2007); Reginald A. Wilkinson and Tessa Unwin, "Visiting in Prison," *Prison and Jail Administration: Practice and Theory*, Peter M. Carlson and Judith Simon Garrett (Sudbury, MA: Jones & Bartlett, 2006), www.drc.state.oh.us/web/Articles/article46.htm (retrieved March 1, 2007).

198. Christopher B. Epps and Harley B. Barbour, "Conjugal Visits," Mississippi Department of Corrections, 2007, www.mdoc.state.ms.us/conjugal_visits.htm (retrieved March 2, 2007).

199. Adam Tanner, "California Allows Gay Conjugal Visits in Prisons," Reuters, June 1, 2007, www.reuters.com/article/lifestyleMolt/idUSN0134740420070601.

200. *Kentucky Dept. of Corrections v. Thompson*, 490 U.S. 454 (1989); Pollock, *Prisons and Prison Life*.

CHAPTER 13

1. William Booth, "Judgment Day in 'Malibu': Gibson's DUI Case is Closed," *Washington Post*, August 18, 2006.

2. Edward Latessa and Christopher Lowenkamp, "What Works in Reducing Recidivism," *St. Thomas Law Journal* 3 (2007): 521–535.

3. James Q. Wilson and Joan Petersilia, *Crime: Public Policies for Crime Control* (Oakland, CA: Institute for Contemporary Studies Press, 2002).

4. Lauren E. Glaze and Thomas P. Bonczar, "Probation and Parole in the United States, 2006," *Bureau of Justice Statistics Bulletin* (Washington, DC: U.S. Department of Justice, July 2, 2008) www.ojp.usdoj.gov/bjs/pub/pdf/ppus06.pdf (retrieved March 5, 2009).

5. *Burns v. U.S.*, 287 U.S. 216, 220 (1932).

6. Maurice Vanstone, *Supervising Offenders in the Community: A History of Probation Theory and Practice* (London: Ashgate, 2007).

7. Robert Panzarella, "Theory and Practice of Probation on Bail in the Report of John Augustus," *Federal Probation* 66, no. 3 (2002): 38–42.

8. Philip Whitehead and Roger Statham, *The History of Probation: Politics, Power and Cultural Change 1876–2005* (Crayford, Kent, UK: Shaw and Sons, 2006).

9. "Conditions of Probation," *U.S. Code Collection* (Ithaca, NY: Legal Information Institute, Cornell University Law School), www2.law.cornell.edu/uscode/uscode18/usc_sec_18_00003563——000-.html.

10. Norval Morris and Michael Tonry, *Between Prison and Probation: Intermediate Punishments in a Rational Sentencing System* (New York: Oxford University Press, 1990).

11. Billie S. Erwin and Lawrence A. Bennett, "New Dimensions in Probation: Georgia's Experience with Intensive Probation Supervision (IPS)," *Research in Brief* (Washington, DC: National Institute of Justice, January 1987).

12. Morris and Tonry, *Between Prison and Probation: Intermediate Punishments in a Rational Sentencing System.*

13. Joan Petersillia and Susan Turner, *Intensive-Supervision for High-Risk Probationers: Findings from Three California Studies* (Santa Monica, CA: RAND Corporation, November 1990).

14. Jodi Lane, Susan Turner, Terry Fain, and Amer Sehgal, "Evaluating an Experimental Intensive Juvenile Probation Program: Supervision and Official Outcomes," *Crime and Delinquency* 51, no. 1 (2005): 26–52.

15. Kelly L. Brown, "Effects of Supervision Philosophy on Intensive Probationers," *Justice Policy Journal* 4, no. 1 (Spring 2007).

16. New York State, Division of Probation and Correctional Alternatives, *Annual Report: Intensive-Supervision Program 2005 Operations*, December 2006,

dpca.state.ny.us/pdfs/isp2005report.pdf (retrieved October 20 2007).

17. Carnille Graham Camp and George W. Camp, *The Corrections Yearbook 2000* (Middletown, CT: Criminal Justice Institute, 2001).

18. Newsletter of the Federal Courts, Third Branch, FY 2004, *Costs of Incarceration and Supervision* 37, no. 7 (May 2005), www.uscourts.gov/ttb/may05ttb/incarceration-costs/index.html (retrieved April 26, 2007).

19. Glaze and Bonczar, "Probation and Parole in the United States, 2006."

20. Ibid.

21. M. Nieto, "Changing Role of Probation in California's Criminal Justice System," *National Criminal Justice Reference Service* (Washington, DC: U.S. Department of Justice, 1996).

22. John L. Wordall, Pamela Schram, Eric Hays, and Mathew Newmaan, "An Analysis of the Relationship between Probation Caseloads and Property Crime Rates in California Counties," *Journal of Criminal Justice* 32, no. 3 (May-June 2004): 231–241.

23. Lauren E. Glaze and Thomas P. Bonczar, "Probation and Parole in the United States, 2007, Statistical Tables," *Bureau of Justice Statistics* (Washington, DC: U.S. Department of Justice, December 2008). www.ojp.usdoj.gov/bjs/pub/pdf/ppus07st.pdf (retrieved March 2, 2009).

24. "Probation Officers," U.S. Courts, www.uscourts.gov/fedprob/officer/probation.html (retrieved March 3, 2009).

25. Bennet Mead, "Is There a Measure of Probation Success?" *Federal Probation* 69, no. 2 (December 2005). Originally published in *Federal Probation* (May-June 1937).

26. Glaze and Bonczar, "Probation and Parole in the United States, 2007, Statistical Tables."

27. Nancy Rodriguez and Vincent J. Webb, "Probation Violations, Revocations, and Imprisonment," *Criminal Justice Policy Review* 18, no. 1 (2007): 3–30.

28. E. F. Travis and A. Holsinger, *Evaluation of Ohio's Community Correctional Act Programs by County Size* (Cincinnati, OH: Division of Criminal Justice, University of Cincinnati, 1997).

29. *Gagnon v. Scarpelli,* 411 U.S. 778 (1973).

30. Heather C. West and William J. Sabol, "Prisoners in 2007," *Bureau of Justice Statistics* (Washington, DC: U.S. Department of Justice, December 2008; revised February 12, 2009), www.ojp.usdoj.gov/bjs/pub/pdf/p07.pdf (retrieved March 9, 2009).

31. Michael R. Geerken and Hennessey D. Hayes, "Probation and Parole: Public Risk and the Future of Incarceration Alternatives," *Criminology* 31, no. 4 (March 7, 2006).

32. "Annual Report, 2003—Probation: Its Past, Present and Future," Adult Probation Department, Arizona Superior Court, Pima County, 2004, www.sc/pima.gov/SC_Web/Portals/0/Library/Comm/AnnualReport2003.pdf (retrieved March 9, 2009).

33. Isiah Brown, "The Changing Role of Probation and Parole: A View to the Future," August 25, 2008, www.fdle.state.fl.us/Content/getdoc/dcc13209-622b49f4-8f68-7d5c7c4eec9/Brown-Isiah-paper.aspx (retrieved March 9, 2009).

34. Edward E. Rhine, Gary Hinzman, Ronald P. Corbett, Dan Richard Beto, and Mario Paparozzi, "The 'Broken Windows' Model of Probation: A Call for Transforming Community Supervision," 2001, garyhinzman.com/articles/Broken_Windows_Spring_2001.pdf (retrieved March 9, 2009).

35. Reid Montgomery Jr. and Steven Dillingham, *Probation and Parole in Practice* (Cincinnati, OH: Pilgrimage, 1983); Little Hoover Commission, *Back to the Community: Safe and Sound Parole Policies* (Sacramento, CA: Little Hoover Commission, 2003).

36. Todd Clear and George Cole, *American Corrections,* 2nd ed. (Pacific Grove, CA: Brooks/Cole, 1990); David Harding, "Jean Valjean's Dilemma: The Management of Ex-Convict Identity in the Search for Employment," *Deviant Behavior* 24, no. 6 (2003): 571–595.

37. Glaze and Bonczar, "Probation and Parole in the United States, 2007, Statistical Tables," 4.

38. Ibid.

39. Ibid., 6.

40. Ibid.

41. Little Hoover Commission, *Breaking the Barriers for Women on Parole* (Sacramento, CA: Little Hoover Commission, December 2004).

42. Barbara Bloom, Barbara Owen, Stephanie Covington, and Myrna Raeder, *Gender-Responsive Strategies: Research, Practice, and Guiding Principles for Women Offenders* (Washington, DC: National Institute of Corrections, 2003).

43. Glaze and Bonczar, "Probation and Parole in the United States, 2007, Statistical Tables," 6.

44. Joan Parkin, "Throwing Away the Key: The World's Leading Jailer," *International Socialist Review Online* 21 (2002), www.isreview.org/issues/21/prisons.shtml.

45. William Sabol and Heather Couture, *Prison Inmates at Midyear 2007* (Washington, DC: Bureau of Justice Statistics, 2008), 7.

46. "Reentry Trends in the U.S.: Characteristics of Releases," Department of Justice, Bureau of Justice Statistics, www.ojp.usdoj.gov/bjs/reentry/characteristics.htm (retrieved December 25, 2006).

47. RAND Research Brief, "Prisoner Reentry: What Are the Public Health Challenges?" 2003, www.rand.org/pubs/research_briefs/RB6013/index1.html (retrieved December 26, 2006).

48. Sabol and Couture, *Prison Inmates at Midyear 2007,* 7.

49. Peggy B. Burke, *Abolishing Parole: Why the Emperor Has No Clothes* (Lexington, KY: American Probation and Parole Association, 1995).

50. Office of Justice Programs Press Release, "One in Every 32 Adults Was in Prison, Jail, on Probation, or on Parole at the End of 2005," Bureau of Justices Statistics, 2005, www.ojp.usdoj.gov/bjs/pub/press/pripropr.htm (retrieved December 24, 2006).

51. Office of Justice Programs, "Summary Findings of Probation and Parole Statistics Office of Justice Programs," Bureau of Justice Statistics, 2005, www.ojp.usdoj.gov/bjs/pandp.htm (retrieved December 24, 2006).

52. Glaze and Bonczar, "Probation and Parole in the United States, 2007, Statistical Tables," 7–8.

53. Ibid., 6.

54. Jeremy Travis, "Back-end Sentences' Costs," *The National Law Journal Online*, April 11, 2005, www.law.com/jsp/wlj/PubArticleFriendlyNCJ.jsp?id=1112951108522 (retrieved April 12, 2007).

55. Jeremy Travis and Sarah Lawrence, *Beyond the Prison Gates: The State of Parole in America* (Washington, DC: Urban Institute Justice Policy Center, 2002).

56. Todd R. Clear and George F. Cole, *American Corrections*, 2nd ed. (Belmont, CA: Brooks/Cole, 1990), 442; Joan Petersillia, *When Prisoners Come Home: Parole*

and Prisoner Reentry (New York: Oxford University Press, 2003).

57. Amy Solomon, Vera Kachnowski, and Avinash Bhati, *Does Parole Work? Analyzing the Impact of Postprison Supervision on Rearrest Outcomes* (Washington, DC: The Urban Institute, 2005).

58. Douglas S. Lipton, Robert Martinson, and Judith Wilks, *The Effectiveness of Correctional Treatment: A Survey of Treatment Evaluation Studies* (New York: Praeger, 1975).

59. A Keith Bottomley, Michael Tonry, and Norval Morris, "Parole in Transition: A Comparative Study of Origins, Developments, and Prospects for the 1990s," in *Crime and Justice: A Review of Research*, eds. Michael Tonry and Norval Morris (Chicago: University of Chicago Press, 1990), 319–374.

60. *Morrisey v. Brewer,* 408 U.S. 471 (1972).

61. *Gagnon v. Scarpelli,* 411 U.S. 778 (1973).

62. *Greenholtz v. Inmates of the Nebraska Penal and Correctional Complex*, 442 U.S. 1 (1979).

63. Terryl Arola and Richard Lawrence, "Broken Windows Probation," *Perspectives* 24, no. 1 (2000): 27–33.

64. Jeff Jacoby, "The Real Meaning of Willie Horton," *Boston Globe*, January 20, 1999, http://graphics.boston.com/news/politics/campaign2000/news/The_real_meaning_of_Willie_Horton+.shtml (retrieved December 26, 2006).

65. Shela R. Van Ness, "Intensive Probation versus Prison Outcomes in Indiana: Who Could Benefit?" *Journal of Contemporary Criminal Justice* 8, no. 4 (1992): 351–364.

66. Morris and Tonry, *Between Prison and Probation: Intermediate Punishments in a Rational Sentencing System.*

67. James Turner Johnson and Daniel Van Ness, eds., *Handbook of Restorative Justice* (Cullompton, Devon: Willan, 2007).

68. Restorative Justice Online, "Introduction," www.restorativejustice.org/intro (retrieved April 13, 2007).

69. Laura Magnani and Harmon L. Wray, *Beyond Prisons* (Minneapolis: Fortress Press, 2006).

70. Bureau of Justice Statistics, "Criminal Victimization in the United States, 2004: Statistical Tables", Table 82, 2006, www.ojp. usdoj.gov/bjs/pub/pdf/cvus04.pdf (retrieved September 19, 2006); United States Delegation to the Intergovernmental Expert Group, "Response of the United States Delegation to the Intergovernmental Expert Group, Questionnaire on Fraud and the Criminal Misuse and Falsification of Identity (Identity Fraud)," 2006, 37, www.usdoj.gov/criminal/fraud/UNODCQuestionnaire USGResponse Final.pdf (retrieved September 15, 2006); Federal Bureau of Investigation, "Financial Crimes Report to the Public," 2005, www.fbi.gov/publications/financial/fcs_report052005/fcs_report052005.htm (retrieved September 26, 2006); Suzette Fromm, "Total Estimated Cost of Child Abuse and Neglect," (Washington, DC: Prevent Child Abuse America, 2001), 2, 3, www.preventchildabusenj.org/documents/index/cost_analysis.pdf (retrieved September 26, 2006).

71. U.S. Department of Justice, Office of Justice Programs, Office for Victims of Crime, "Promising Victim-Related Practices in Probation and Parole—A Compendium of Promising Practices," July 1999, www.ojp.usdoj.gov/ovc/publications/infores/probparole/ (retrieved January 31, 2007).

72. *Criminal Debt: Court-Ordered Restitution Amounts Far Exceed Likely Collections for the Crime Victims in Selected Financial Fraud Cases* (Washington, DC: U.S. Government Accountability Office, 2005).

73. "Legal Series #6 Bulletin. Ordering Restitution to the Crime Victim," U.S. Department of Justice, Office of Justice Programs. Office for Victims of Crime, November 2002, NCJ 189189.

74. Restorative Justice Online, "Restitution," Prison Fellowship International, www.restorativejustice.org/intro/tutorial/outcomes/restitution (retrieved October 20, 2007).

75. R. Barry Ruback, "The Imposition of Economic Sanctions in Philadelphia: Costs, Fines, and Restitution," *Federal Probation* 68, no. 1 (2004).

76. Patrick Mcgreevy, "State Closes Restitution Centers for White-Collar Prisoners," *Los Angeles Times*, January 13, 2009, http://articles.latimes.com/2009/jan/13/local/me-prison13 (retrieved March 6, 2009).

77. "How to Use Structured Fines (Day Fines) as an Intermediate Sanction," (Washington, DC: Department of Justice, November 1996).

78. Ronald J. Berger, Marvin D. Free Jr. and Patricia Searles, *Crime, Justice, and Society: Criminology and the Sociological Imagination* (New York: McGraw-Hill, 2001).

79. L. S. Abrams, M. Umbreit, and A. Gordon, "Young Offenders Speak about Meeting Their Victims; Implications for Future Programs," *Contemporary Justice Review; Issues in Criminal, Social and Restorative Justice* 9, no. 3 (2006): 243–256; J. Wemmers and K. Cyr, "Can Mediation Be Therapeutic for Crime Victims? An Evaluation of Victims Experiences in Mediation with Young Offenders," *Canadian Journal of Criminology and Criminal Justice* 47, no. 3 (2005): 529–544.

80. D. Springer and A. Roberts, eds., *Handbook of Forensic Mental Health with Victims and Offenders: Assessment, Treatment, and Research* (New York: Springer, 2007); S. Trankle, "In the Shadow of Penal Law: Victim-Offender Mediation in Germany and France," *Punishment and Society* 9, no. 4 (2007): 395–415.

81. Julian V. Roberts, *The Virtual Prison: Community Custody and the Evolution of Imprisonment* (Cambridge: Cambridge University Press, 2004); Josh Kuriantzic, "China, Burma and Sudan: Convincing Argument," *The New Republic Online,* May 11, 2006, www.carnegieendowment.org/publications/index.cfm?fa=pring&id=18329 (retrieved October 19, 2007).

82. Roberts, *The Virtual Prison: Community Custody and the Evolution of Imprisonment.*

83. Jeffrey Ulmer, "Intermediate Sanctions: A Comparative Analysis of the Probability and Severity of Recidivism," *Sociological Inquiry* 71 (2001).

84. Nancy Marion, "Effectiveness of Community-based Correctional Programs: A Case Study," *Prison Journal* 82 (2002).

85. Mary A. Finn and Suzanne Muirhead-Steves, "The Effectiveness of Electronic Monitoring with Violent Male Parolees," *Justice Quarterly* 19 (2002).

86. Ralph Kirkland Gable and Robert S. Gable, "Electronic Monitoring: Positive Intervention Strategies," *Federal Probation* 69, no. 1 (June 2005), www.uscourts.gov/fedprob/jun2005/intervention.html (retrieved March 9, 2009).

87. Tomer Einat, "Shock-Incarceration Programs in Israeli Sanctioning Policy: Toward a New Model of Punishment," *Israeli Law Review* 36, no. 1 (2002): 144–177.

88. "Youth Violence: A Report of the Surgeon General, Ineffective Tertiary Programs and Strategies," www.surgeongeneral.gov/library/youthviolence/chapter5/sec6.html (retrieved April 13, 2007).

89. National Institute of Justice, "Researchers Evaluate Eight Shock Incarceration Programs," Update October 1994, www.ncjrs.gov/pdffiles/shock.pdf (retrieved April 13, 2007).

90. Earnest Cowles and Laura Dorman, "Problems in Creating Boundaryless Treatment Regimens in Secure Correctional Environments: Private Sector-Public Agency Infrastructure Compatibility," *Prison Journal* 83, no. 3 (2003): 235–256.

91. Earnest Cowles, Thomas Castellano, and Laura Gransky, *'Boot Camp' Drug Treatment and Aftercare Intervention: An Evaluation Review* (Washington, DC: U.S. Government Printing Office, 1995).

92. New York State Division of Parole, *The Ninth Annual Shock Legislative Report: 1997* (Albany, NY: New York State Division of Parole, 1998).

93. Jane Ellen Steves, "Myths Cover Up Further Tragedies in Episodes of Child Molestation," *SFGate*, April 3, 2005, www.sfgate.com/cgi-bin/article.cgi?file=/chronicle/archive/2005/04/03/INGN4C224F1.DTL.

94. Sean Maddan and Paula Gray Stiz, *Sex Offender Registry Protocol Training Manual,* Arkansas Crime Information Center, www.acic.org/Registration/Sex%20Offender%20Manual%203rd%20edition.pdf (retrieved January 26, 2007).

95. "The Proper and Improper Use of Risk Assessment in Corrections," *Federal Sentencing Reporter* 16, no. 3 (February 2004), www.jfa-associates.com/publications/pcras/proper%20userand%20misuse%20of%20risk.pdf (retrieved March 9, 2009).

96. "Maine Killings Raise Questions about Sex Offender Registries," *Wheeling News Register*, April 4, 2007, www.oweb.com/news/story/044202007_newSexOffender-sSlain.asp (retrieved April 27, 2007).

97. Jamie Fellner, "The Wrong Sex Offender Laws," *Los Angeles Times*, September 18, 2007.

98. David Morgan, "N.J. Study Finds Registration Helps Locate Sex Offenders but Does Not Affect Recidivism," CBS News (CBS/AP), February 5, 2009, www.sdp123a.com/index.php?option=com_content&task=view&id=658&Itemid=58 (retrieved June 26, 2009).

99. Jeffery T. Walker, Sean Maddan, Bob E. Vasquez, Amy C. Van Houten, and Gwen Ervin-McLarty, "The Influence of Sex Offender Registration and Notification Laws in the United States," Arkansas Crime Information Center, www.acic.org/statistics/Research/SO_Report_Final.pdf (retrieved April 27, 2007); Bureau of Justice Assistance, Center for Program Evaluation and Performance Measurement, "What Have We Learned from Evaluations of Sex Offender Programs/Strategies?" October 25, 2006, www.ojp.usdoj.gov/BJA/evaluation/psi_sops/sops2.htm (retrieved January 20, 2007).

100. Fellner, "The Wrong Sex Offender Laws."

101. Center for Sex Offender Management, "Myths and Facts about Sex Offenders," August 2000, www.csom.org/pubs/mythsfacts.html (retrieved March 5, 2009).

102. Tracy M. L. Brown, Steven A. McCabe, and Charles Wellford, "Global Positioning System (GPS) Technology for Community Supervision: Lessons Learned," *Center for Criminal Justice Technology, Noblis Technical Report*, August 2007, www.ncjrs.gov/pdffiles1/nij/grants/219376.pdf (retrieved March 9, 2009).

103. National Institute of Justice, *Issues and Practices* (Washington, DC: Government Printing Office, 1990).

104. Voncile Gowdy, *Intermediate Sanctions* (Washington, DC: U.S. Department of Justice, 1993), 5.

105. Jeffrey A. Bouffard, Doris Layton MacKenzie, and Laura J. Hickman "Effectiveness of Vocational Education and Employment Programs for Adult Offenders: A Methodology-based Analysis of the Literature," *Journal of Offender Rehabilitation* 31 (2000).

106. Leonidas K. Cheliotis, "Reconsidering the Effectiveness of Temporary Release: A Systematic Review," *Aggression and Violent Behavior* 13, no. 3 (June 2008).

107. Karen Alexander, "Furlough Proposal Stirs Foes," *Los Angeles Times*, February 26, 2000, http://articles.latimes.com/2000/feb/26/local/me-2726 (retrieved March 7, 2009).

108. David Reyes, "Protest Derails Fountain Valley Halfway House," *Los Angeles Times*, May 3, 2000, http://articles.latimes.com/2000/may/03/local/me-26172 (retrieved March 7, 2009).

109. Tony Brecht, "Residents Fear Halfway House Plan," *Quad-City Times*, November 1, 2006, www.qctimes.com/articles/2006/11/01/news/local/doc454846b2a9189203300076.txt (retrieved March 8, 2009).

110. Nancy Marion, "Effectiveness of Community-based Correctional Programs: A Case Study," *Prison Journal* 82 (2002).

111. Susan Turner and Joan Petersilia, "Work Release: Recidivism and Corrections Costs in Washington State," *Research in Brief*, National Institute of Justice, 1996, www.ncjrs.gov/pdffiles/163706.pdf (retrieved March 27, 2007).

112. Monica G. Massarand, "Work Release Program Research Project," Final Report, Multnomah County, Oregon, June 30, 2004, www.lpscc.org/does/Work ReleaseProgram ResearchReportJune2004.pdf (retrieved March 7, 2009); Jillian Berk, "Does Work Release Work?" Brown University Micro Lunch Series, May 2, 2008, http://client.norc.org/jole/SOLEweb/8318.pdf (retrieved March 7, 2009).

113. Holly K. O. Sparrow, "Private Probation in Georgia: A New Direction, Service and Vigilance," Institute for Court Management, Administrative Office of the Courts, May 2001, www.ncsconline.org/D_ICM/Research_Papers_2001/Private_Probation_GA.pdf (retrieved January 27, 2007).

114. Clear and Cole, *American Corrections.*

CHAPTER 14

1. H. Gordon, *Hammurabi's Code: Quaint or Forward Looking* (New York: Rinehart Press, 1957).

2. Stephan Schafer, *The Victim and His Criminal* (New York: Random House, 1968).

3. Frederick Wertham, *The Show of Violence* (Garden City, NY: The Country Life Press, 1948).

4. Frederick Wertham, *A Sign for Cain: An Exploration of Human Violence* (New York: Hale Press, 1968).

5. Miroslav Volf, "Original Crime, Primal Care," in *God and the Victim: Theological Reflections on Evil, Victimization, Justice, and Forgiveness,* eds. Lisa Barnes Lampman and Michelle D. Shattuck (Grand Rapids, MI: William B. Eerdmans, 1999).

6. Frans W. Winkel, "Peer Support Groups: Evaluating the Mere Contact/Mere Sharing Model and Impairment Hypotheses," *International Perspectives in Victimology* 2, no. 1 (2006): 101–113.

7. Jeffrey T. Mitchell and George S. Everly, *Critical Incident Stress Debriefing: An Operations Manual* (Ellicott City: Chevron Press, 1995).

8. Ezzat A. Fattah, *Understanding Criminal Victimization: An Introduction to Theoretical Victimology* (Scarborough, Ontario: Prentice-Hall, 1991); William G. Doerner

and Steven P. Lab, *Victimology*, 4th ed. (New York: Anderson, 2005).

9. William V. Pelfrey Sr. and William V. Pelfrey Jr., "Fear of Crime, Age, and Victimization Relationships and Changes over Time," in *Current Issues in Victimological Research,* eds. Laura J. Moriarty and Robert A. Jerin (Durham, NC: Carolina Academic Press, 1998).
10. Susan Brownmiller, *Against Our Will: Men, Women and Rape* (New York: Simon & Schuster, 1975).
11. Frank Carrington, *The Victims* (New Rochelle, NY: Arlington House, 1975).
12. Judith Green, "Getting Tough on Crime: The History and Political Context of Sentencing Reform Developments Leading to the Passage of the 1994 Crime Act," in *Sentencing and Society: International Perspectives,* eds. Cyrus Tata and Neil Hutton (Farnham, Surrey, U.K.: Ashgate, 2002), 43–65.
13. Ibid.
14. Desmond S. Greer, "A Transatlantic Perspective on the Compensation of Crime Victims in the United States," *Journal of Criminal Law and Criminology* 85 (Fall 1994): 1–38.
15. Robert A. Jerin and Laura J. Moriarty, *The Victims of Crime* (Upper Saddle River, NJ: Pearson Education, 2010).
16. Graham Farrell, "Preventing Repeat Victimization," *Crime and Justice* 19 (1969): 469–534.
17. Graham Farrell and Ken Pease, "Once Bitten, Twice Bitten: Repeat Victimisation and Its Implications for Crime Prevention," *Crime Prevention Unit*, Paper 46 (1993).
18. Ken Pease, "Repeat Victimization: Taking Stock," *Crime Detection and Prevention Series,* Paper 90 (1998): 1–40.
19. John P. J. Dussich, "Concepts and Forms of Victim Services," in *Victim Services,* ed. John Dussich (Fresno, CA: Kennel Bookstore, California State University, Fresno, 2007).
20. Larry Bennett, Stephanie Riger, Paul Schewe, April Howard, and Sharon Wasco, "Effectiveness of Hotline, Advocacy, Counseling, and Shelter Services for Victims of Intimate Partner Violence: A Statewide Evaluation," *Journal of Interpersonal Violence* 19, no. 7 (July 2004): 815–829.
21. Ibid.
22. Federal Bureau of Investigation, "Victim Assistance: FBI Resources for Helping Victims," www.fbi.gov (retrieved April 23, 2007).
23. Bureau of Justice Statistics, "Victim Characteristics," www.ojp.usdoj.gov/bjs/cvict_v.htm (retrieved May 1, 2007).
24. Steven W. Perry, "American Indians and Crime: A BJS Statistical Profile, 1992–2002," U.S. Department of Justice, Bureau of Justice Statistics, December 2004, (NCJ 203097.
25. Ada Pecos-Melton, "Specific Justice Systems and Victims' Rights, Section 4, Tribal Justice," *National Victim Assistance Academy, Training Manual* (Washington, DC: Office for Victims of Crime, June 2002).
26. Bryan D. Byers, "Death Notification: The Theory and Practice of Delivering Bad News," in *Crisis Intervention in Criminal Justice and Social Service,* eds. James E. Hendricks and Bryan D. Byers (Springfield, IL: Charles C Thomas, 2002).
27. National Association of Crime Victimization Compensation Boards, "FAQ: Manager," www.nacvcb.org/ (retrieved April 24, 2007).
28. Ibid.
29. Ibid.
30. Ibid.
31. Ibid.
32. Office for Victims of Crime, *OVC Handbook for Coping after Terrorism: A Guide to Healing and Recovery* (Washington, DC: U.S. Department of Justice, Office of Justice Programs, September 2001).
33. David A. Alexander, "Early Mental Health Intervention after Disasters," *Advances in Psychiatric Treatment* 11 (2005): 12–18.
34. Ibid.
35. Ibid.
36. Kathleen M. Palm, Melissa A. Polusny, and Victoria M. Follette, "Vicarious Traumatization: Potential Hazards and Interventions for Disaster and Trauma Workers," *Prehospital and Disaster Medicine* 19, no. 1 (2004): 73–78.
37. Richard E. Adams, Joseph A. Boscarino, and Charles R. Figley, "Compassion Fatigue and Psychological Distress among Social Workers: A Validation Study," *American Journal of Orthopsychiatry* 76, no. 1 (2006): 103–108.
38. Anne Seymour and Christine Edmunds, "Mental Health Needs, Section 2, Stress Management," *National Victim Assistance Academy, Training Manual* (Washington, DC: Office for Victims of Crime, June 2002).
39. Alexander, "Early Mental Health Intervention after Disasters."
40. Rick A. Myer and Christian Conte, "Assessment for Crisis Intervention," *Journal of Clinical Psychology: In Sessio*n 62, no. 8 (2006): 73–79.
41. Larry Bennett, Stephanie Riger, Paul Schewe, April Howard, and Sharon Wasco, "Effectiveness of Hotline, Advocacy, Counseling, and Shelter Services for Victims of Domestic Violence: A Statewide Evaluation," *Journal of Interpersonal Violence* 19, no. 7 (July 2004): 815–829.
42. Albert L. Shostack, *Shelters for Battered Women and Their Children: A Comprehensive Guide to Planning and Operating Safe and Caring Residential Programs* (Springfield, IL: Charles C Thomas, 2001).
43. Janice Humphreys and Kathryn Lee, "Sleep Disturbance in Battered Women Living in Transitional Housing," *Journal of Mental Health Nursing* 26 (2005): 771–780.
44. Shostack, *Shelters for Battered Women and Their Children.*
45. Ibid.
46. Ibid.
47. John Devaney, "Chronic Child Abuse and Domestic Violence: Children and Families with Long-Term Complex Needs," *Child and Family Social Work* 13, no. 4 (November 2008): 443–453.
48. Betsy McAlister Groves, *Children Who See Too Much: Lessons from the Child Witness to Violence Project* (Boston, MA: Beacon Press, 2002).
49. Peter G. Jaffe, David A. Wolfe, and Susan Kaye Wilson, *Children of Battered Women* (Newbury Park, CA: Sage, 1990).
50. Devaney, "Chronic Child Abuse and Domestic Violence: Children and Families with Long-Term Complex Needs."
51. Rebecca M. Bolen, "Attachment and Family Violence: Complexities in Knowing," *Child Abuse and Neglect: The International Journal* 29 (August 2005): 845–852.
52. Jennifer E. Macomber, "An Overview of Selected Data on Children in Vulnerable Families," Urban Institute, August 10, 2006, www.urban.org/url.cfm?ID=311351 (retrieved February 12, 2009).
53. Bolen, "Attachment and Family Violence: Complexities in Knowing."
54. Bennett, Riger, Schewe, Howard, and Wasco, "Effectiveness of Hotline,

Advocacy, Counseling, and Shelter Services for Victims of Intimate Partner Violence: A Statewide Evaluation."

55. Ibid.
56. Ibid.
57. Elizabethann O'Sullivan and Abigail Carlton, "Victim Services, Community Outreach, and Contemporary Rape Crisis Centers: A Comparison of Independent and Multiservice Centers," *Journal of Interpersonal Violence* 16, no. 4 (2001): 343–360.
58. Ibid.
59. Rebecca Campbell, Debra Patterson, and Lauren F. Lichty, "The Effectiveness of Sexual Assault Nurse Examiner (SANE) Programs: A Review of Psychological, Medical, Legal, and Community Outcomes," *Trauma, Violence, and Abuse* 6, no. 4 (October 2005): 313–329.
60. Rupaleem Bhuyan and Kirsten Senturia, "Understanding Intimate Partner Violence Resource Utilization and Survivor Solutions among Immigrant and Refugee Women: Introduction to the Special Issue," *Journal of Interpersonal Violence* 20, no. 8 (August, 2005): 895–901.
61. National Center on Elder Abuse, *The 2004 Survey of State Adult Protective Services: Abuse of Adults 60 Years and Older* (Washington, DC: National Center on Elder Abuse, 2006).
62. Pamela B. Teaster, Tyler A. Dugar, Marta S. Mendiondo, Erin L. Abner, and Kara A. Cecil, *The 2004 Survey of State Adult Protective Services: Abuse of Vulnerable Adults 18 Years of Age and Older* (Washington, DC: National Center on Elder Abuse, March 2007).
63. *New Directions from the Field: Victims' Rights and Services for the 21st Century* (Washington, DC: U.S. Department of Justice, Office of Justice Programs, Office for Victims of Crime, May 1998).
64. Kris Henning and Lynette Feder, "Criminal Prosecution of Domestic Violence Offenses: An Investigation of Factors Predictive of Court Outcomes," *Criminal Justice Behavior* 32, no. 6 (December 2005): 612–642.
65. Nicole E. Allen, "An Examination of the Effectiveness of Intimate Partner Violence Coordinating Councils," *Violence against Women* 12, no. 1 (January 2006): 46–67; Melanie Shephard, "Twenty Years of Progress in Addressing Intimate Partner Violence: An Agenda for the Next 10," *Journal of Interpersonal Violence* 20, no. 4 (2005): 436–441.
66. O'Sullivan and Carlton, "Victim Services, Community Outreach, and Contemporary Rape Crisis Centers."
67. *New Directions from the Field: Victims' Rights and Services for the 21st Century.*
68. California Institute on Human Services, "Multi-Disciplinary Interview Centers & Team Directory 2005," July 2005, www.cihsinc.org/CATTA (retrieved February 12, 2009).
69. Mark S. Umbreit, *The Handbook of Victim Offender Mediation: An Essential Guide to Research and Practice* (San Francisco, CA: Jossey-Bass, 2001).
70. Ibid.
71. Kathleen Daly, "A Tale of Two Studies: Restorative Justice from the Victim's Perspective," in *Restorative Justice: Emerging Issues in Practice and Evaluation,* eds. E. Elliott and R. Gordon (Collompton, U.K.: Willan, 2004), 153–174; Kathleen Daly and Julie Stubbs, "Feminist Engagement with Restorative Justice," *Theoretical Criminology* 10, no. 1 (2006): 9–28.
72. Annalise Acorn, *Compulsory Compassion: A Critique of Restorative Justice,* (Vancouver, Canada: University of British Columbia Press, 2004); Daly and Stubbs, "Feminist Engagement with Restorative Justice."
73. John Braithwaite and Kathleen Daly, "Masculinities, Violence, and Communitarian Control," in *Men, Masculinity and Crime,* eds. Tim Newburn and Betsy Stanko (New York: Routledge, 1994); Daly and Stubbs, "Feminist Engagement with Restorative Justice."
74. Daly and Stubbs, "Feminist Engagement with Restorative Justice."

CHAPTER 15

1. "Marchers Protest Boot Camp Death: Jackson, Sharpton Decry Florida's Handling of 14-Year-Old's Death," CBS News, April 21, 2006, www.cbsnews.com/stories/2006/04/21/national/main1532198.shtml.
2. "Autopsy: Beating Killed Boot Camp Teen: Medical Examiner Says Boy, 14, Died from Suffocation by Guards," CBS News, May 5, 2006, www.cbsnews.com/stories/2006/02/16/national/main1325807.shtml.
3. Randall G. Shelden, *Controlling the Dangerous Classes* (Needham Heights, MA: Allyn & Bacon, 2001).
4. Matthew Lippman, *Contemporary Criminal Law: Concepts, Cases, and Controversies* (Thousand Oaks, CA: Sage, 2006).
5. Barry Krisberg, *Juvenile Justice: Redeeming Our Children* (Thousand Oaks, CA: Sage, 2005).
6. Shelden, *Controlling the Dangerous Classes.*
7. Lawrence M. Friedman, *Crime and Punishment in American History* (New York: Basic Books, 1993).
8. Ibid., 165.
9. Krisberg, *Juvenile Justice: Redeeming Our Children.*
10. Ibid.
11. Ibid.
12. Howard N. Snyder and Melissa Sickmund, *Juvenile Offenders and Victims: 2006 National Report* (Washington, DC: U.S. Department of Justice, March 27, 2006) chap. 3, p. 72, www.ojjdp.ncjrs.org/ojstatbb/nr2006/downloads/chapter3.pdf.
13. Rolf Loeber and Magda Stouthamer-Loeber, "Family Factors as Correlates and Predictors of Juvenile Conduct Problems and Delinquency," *Crime and Justice* 7 (1986): 29–149.
14. Denise C. Gottfredson, *Schools and Delinquency,* 2nd ed. (Cambridge: Cambridge University Press, 2001).
15. Joan McCord, Cathy Spatz Widom, Melissa I. Bamba, and Nancy A. Cromwell, eds., "Linking School Performance and Delinquency," in *Education and Delinquency: Summary of a Workshop,* Panel on Juvenile Crime: Prevention, Treatment and Control (Washington, DC: National Academy Press, 2000), www.nap.edu/openbook.php?record_id=9972&page=R1 (retrieved March 16, 2009), 13–15.
16. Richard A. Cloward and Lloyd E. Ohlin, *Delinquency and Opportunity* (New York: Free Press, 1960); Albert K. Cohen, *Delinquent Boys* (New York: Free Press, 1955); Walter B. Miller, "Lower Class Culture as a Generating Milieu of Gang Delinquency," *Journal of Social Issues* 14 (1958): 5–19.
17. James F. Short and F. Ivan Nye, "Extent of Unrecorded Juvenile Delinquency," *Journal of Criminal Law, Criminology and Police Science* 49 (1958): 296–302.
18. Margaret Farnworth, Terence P. Thornberry, Marvin D. Krohn, and Alan J. Lizotte, "Measurement in the Study of Class and Delinquency: Integrating Theory and Research," *Journal of Research in Crime and Delinquency* 31 (1994): 32–61.
19. Joanne M. Kaufman, "Explaining the Race/Ethnicity Violence Relationship: Neighborhood Context and Psychological

Processes," *Justice Quarterly* 22 (June 2005): 224–251.

20. Snyder and Sickmund, *Juvenile Offenders and Victims: 2006 National Report*, chap. 5, p. 132.
21. Robert Agnew, *Juvenile Delinquency: Causes and Control,* 2nd ed. (Los Angeles: Roxbury, 2005).
22. Charles Puzzanchera, "Juvenile Arrests 2007," *Juvenile Justice Bulletin* (Washington, DC: U.S. Department of Justice, April 2009), www.ncjrs.gov/pdffiles1/ojjdp/225344.pdf (retrieved July 12, 2009).
23. Statistical Briefing Book, "Juvenile Arrests 2007," *Juvenile Justice Bulletin* (Washington, DC: U.S. Department of Justice, October 2008), http://ojjdp.ncjrs.org/ojstatbb/crime/qa05101.asp?qaDate=2007 (retrieved July 12, 2009).
24. Joanne Belknap, *The Invisible Woman: Gender, Crime, and Justice*, 3rd ed. (Belmont, CA: Wadsworth, 2007).
25. Snyder and Sickmund, *Juvenile Offenders and Victims: 2006 National Report*, chap. 5, p. 129.
26. Ibid.
27. Puzzanchera, "Juvenile Arrests 2007," *Juvenile Justice Bulletin.*
28. Snyder and Sickmund, *Juvenile Offenders and Victims: 2006 National Report.*
29. Ibid.
30. Richard Lawrence, *School Crime and Juvenile Justice,* 2nd ed. (New York: Oxford University Press, 2007).
31. U.S. Department of Justice, Office of Justice Programs, Office of Juvenile Justice and Delinquency Prevention, "Juvenile Arrests 2007," *Juvenile Justice Bulletin,* April 2009, www.ncjrs.gov/pdffiles1/ojjdp/225344.pdf (retrieved August 31, 2009).
32. Meda Chesney-Lind and Randall G. Shelden, *Girls, Delinquency and Juvenile Justice* (Belmont, CA: Wadsworth, 2004).
33. Miriam Sealock and Sally S. Simpson, "Unraveling Bias in Arrest Decisions: The Role of Juvenile Offender Type-Scripts," *Justice Quarterly* 15 (1998): 427–457.
34. Samuel Walker, Cassia Spohn, and Miriam DeLone, *The Color of Justice*, 2nd ed. (Belmont, CA: Wadsworth, 2000).
35. S. A. Anderson, R. M. Sabatelli, and J. Trachtenberg, "Community Police and Youth Programs as a Context for Positive Youth Development," *Police Quarterly* 10, no. 1 (2007): 23–40.
36. G. T. Patterson, "The Role of Police Officers in Elementary and Secondary Schools: Implications for Police-School Social Work Collaboration," *School Social Work Journal* 31, no. 2 (Spring 2007): 82–99.
37. "About D.A.R.E.," D.A.R.E.: The Official D.A.R.E. Web Site, www.dare.com/home/abut_dare.asp (retrieved March 19, 2009).
38. D. M. Gorman, "The Irrelevance of Evidence in the Development of School-based Drug Prevention Policy, 1986–1996," *Evaluation Review* 22, no. 1 (1998): 118–146.
39. "Youth Illicit Drug Use Prevention: DARE Long-Term Evaluations and Federal Efforts to Identify Effective Programs," U.S. Government Accountability Office, GAO-03-172R, January 15, 2003, www.gao.gov/products/GAO-03-172R (retrieved March 19, 2009); full report available at http://archive.gao.gov/t2pbat6/149076.pdf.
40. Friedman, *Crime and Punishment in American History*; Krisberg, *Juvenile Justice: Redeeming Our Children*; Anthony Platt, "The Triumph of Benevolence: Origins of Juvenile Justice in the U.S.," in *Criminal Justice in America: A Critical Understanding,* ed. R. Quinney (Boston: Little, Brown, 1974).
41. Julian W. Mack, "The Juvenile Court," *Harvard Law Review* 23 (1909): 104–122.
42. *OJJDP Statistical Briefing Book*, http://ojjdp.ncjrs.gov/ojstatbb/structure_process/qa04101.asp?qaDate=2004 (retrieved April 9, 2007).
43. Ibid.
44. Office of Juvenile Justice and Delinquency Prevention, "Juvenile Offenders and Victims: 2006 National Report," http://ojjdp.ncjrs.gov/ojstatbb/nr2006/downloads/NR2006.pdf (retrieved April 9, 2007).
45. "7 Year Old Charged in Stabbing Death of Neighbor's Boyfriend Arraigned," www.wlextv.com/global/story.asp?s=3535254&ClientType=Printable (retrieved April 11, 2007); "Pint-Sized Threat Gets Adult Response," *Washington Post*, www.washingtonpost.com/ac2/wp-dyn?pagename=article&node=&contentId=A276882003Apr23&notFound=true (retrieved April 11, 2007); "Boys 7, 10, 11 Face Arson Charges," CNN.com, www.cnn.com/2007/US/03/13/boys.fire.ap/index.html (retrieved April 11, 2007).
46. "Little Criminals," *Frontline* (PBS), May 13, 1997, www.pbs.org/wgbh/pages/frontline/shows/little/etc/script.html (retrieved April 11, 2007).
47. Office of Juvenile Justice and Delinquency Prevention, *Juvenile Justice Reform Initiatives in the States, 1994–1996*, http://ojjdp.ncjrs.org/pubs/reform/contents.html (retrieved April 27, 2007).
48. *Kent v. United States*, 383 U.S. 541 (1966).
49. Jolanta Juszkiewicz, "Youth Crime/Adult Time: Is Justice Served?" (Washington, DC: Building Blocks for Youth, 2000); Office of Juvenile Justice and Delinquency Prevention, *Juvenile Court Statistics, 2000* (Washington, DC: Office of Juvenile Justice and Delinquency Prevention, 2000).
50. Benjamin Adams and Sean Addie, "Delinquency Cases Waived to Criminal Court, 2005," OJJPD Fact Sheet, June 2009, www.ncjrs.gov/pdffiles1/ojjdp/224539.pdf (retrieved August 29, 2009).
51. Donna M. Bishop, Charles E. Frazier, and John C. Henrietta, "Prosecutorial Waiver: Case Study of a Questionable Reform," *Crime & Delinquency* 35 (1989): 179–198.
52. Snyder and Sickmund, *Juvenile Offenders and Victims: 2006 National Report.*
53. Juszkiewicz, "Youth Crime/Adult Time: Is Justice Served?"; Office of Juvenile Justice and Delinquency Prevention, *Juvenile Court Statistics, 2000.*
54. Donna M. Bishop, Charles E. Frazier, and Lanza Kaduce Lonn, "The Transfer of Juveniles to Adult Court: Does It Make a Difference?" *Crime & Delinquency* 42 (1996): 171–191; Coalition for Juvenile Justice, *Childhood on Trial: The Failure of Trying and Sentencing Youth in Adult Criminal Court* (Washington, DC: Coalition for Juvenile Justice, 2005).
55. *Kent v. U.S.*, 383 U.S. 541, 556 (1966).
56. *In re Gault*, 387 U.S. 1 (1967).
57. Samuel M. Davis, Elizabeth S. Scott, Walter Wadlington, and Charles H. Whitebread, *Children in the Legal System: Cases and Materials*, 3rd ed. (New York: Foundation Press, 2004).
58. *In re Winship*, 397 U.S. 358 (1970).
59. *McKeiver v. Pennsylvania*, 403 U.S. 528 (1971).
60. *McKeiver v. Pennsylvania*, 403 U.S. 528, 545 (1971).
61. *Breed v. Jones*, 421 U.S. 519 (1975).
62. *Fare v. Michael C.*, 442 U.S. 707(1979).
63. Ibid.
64. *Schall v. Martin*, 467 U.S. 253 (1984).

65. Death Penalty Information Center, "Juveniles News and Developments, 2003," www.deathpenaltyinfo.org/article.php?did=2137 (retrieved April 27, 2007).

66. *Thompson v. Oklahoma*, 487 U.S. 815 (1988); *Stanford v. Kentucky*, 492 U.S. 361 (1989).

67. American Bar Association, "The Juvenile Death Penalty; Facts and Figures," March 16, 2004, www.abanet.org/crimjust/juvjus/dparticles/factsheetfactsfigures.pdf (retrieved April 27, 2007).

68. *Stanford v. Kentucky*, 492 U.S. 361 (1989).

69. *Roper v. Simmons*, 543 U.S. 551 (2005).

70. *New Jersey v. T.L.O.*, 469 U.S. 325 (1984).

71. *Pottawatomie v. Earls*, 536 U.S. 822 (2002).

72. *Safford United School District #1 v. Redding*, 2009 U.S. LEXIS 4735 (2009).

73. Office of Juvenile Justice and Delinquency Prevention, *Statistical Briefing Book* (Washington, DC: Office of Juvenile Justice and Delinquency Prevention, 2007), http://ojjdp.ncjrs.org/ojstatbb/structure_process/case.html (retrieved April 20, 2007).

74. Ibid.

75. Office of Juvenile Justice and Delinquency Prevention, *Juvenile Offenders and Victims: 2006 National Report.*

76. Krisberg, *Juvenile Justice: Redeeming Our Children.*

77. American Bar Association, Resolution, Adopted by the House of Delegates, August 11-12, 2003, www.abanet.org/leadership/2003/journal/101b.pdf (retrieved May 26, 2007).

78. Snyder and Sickmund, *Juvenile Offenders and Victims: 2006 National Report.*

79. Office of Juvenile Justice and Delinquency Prevention, "Teen Courts: A Focus on Research," 2000, www.ncjrs.gov/pdffiles1/ojjdp/183472.pdf (retrieved April 27, 2007).

80. Steven Patrick, Robert Marsh, and Susan Mimura, "Control Group Study of Juvenile Diversion Programs: An Experiment in Juvenile Diversion," *Social Science Journal* 41 (2004): 129–135; Steven Patrick and Robert Marsh, "Juvenile Diversion: Results of a 3-Year Experimental Study," *Criminal Justice Policy Review* 16 (2005): 59–73.

81. Snyder and Sickmund, *Juvenile Offenders and Victims: 2006 National Report.*

82. *United States v. Salerno*, 481 U.S. 739 (1987).

83. *Schall v. Martin*, 467 U.S. 253 (1984).

84. Snyder and Sickmund, *Juvenile Offenders and Victims: 2006 National Report* , chap. 6, p. 168.

85. Ibid, p. 169.

86. Jeffrey Fagan and Martin Guggenheim, "Preventive Detention and the Judicial Prediction of Dangerousness for Juveniles: A Natural Experiment," *Journal of Criminal Law and Criminology* 80 (1996): 415-448; Snyder and Sickmund, *Juvenile Offenders and Victims: 2006 National Report.*

87. Fagan and Guggenheim, "Preventive Detention and the Judicial Prediction of Dangerousness for Juveniles: A Natural Experiment."

88. Snyder and Sickmund, *Juvenile Offenders and Victims: 2006 National Report.*

89. American Medical Association Council on Scientific Affairs, "Health Status of Detained and Incarcerated Youths," *Journal of the American Medical Association* 263 (1990): 987–991.

90. Craig S. Schwalbe, Mark W. Fraser, Steven H. Day, and Valerie Cooley, "Classifying Juvenile Offenders according to Risk of Recidivism: Predictive Validity, Race/Ethnicity, and Gender," *Criminal Justice and Behavior* 33 (2006): 305–324.

91. Charles Puzzanchera and Melissa Sickmund, *Juvenile Court Statistics 2005: Report* (Washington, DC: National Center for Juvenile Justice, July 2008), www.ncjjservehttp.org/NCJJWebsite/pdf/jcsreports/jcs2005.pdf (retrieved July 12, 2009).

92. Barry C. Feld, "*In re Gault* Revisited: A Cross-State Comparison of the Right to Counsel in Juvenile Court," *Crime & Delinquency* 34 (1988): 393–424; Lori Guevara, Cassia Spohn, and Denise Herz, "Race, Legal Representation, and Juvenile Justice: Issues and Concerns," *Crime & Delinquency* 50 (2004): 344–371.

93. Office of Juvenile Justice and Delinquency Prevention, *OJJDP Statistical Briefing Book.*

94. Barry C. Feld, "The Juvenile Court Meets the Principle of Offense: Punishment, Treatment, and the Difference It Makes," *Boston University Law Review* 68 (1988): 821–896.

95. Joseph G. Weis, Robert D. Crutchfield, and George S. Bridges, *Juvenile Delinquency: Readings,* 2nd ed. (Boston: Pine Forge Press, 2001), 425; Edwin Schur, *Labeling Deviant Behavior: Its Sociological Implications* (New York: Harper & Row, 1971), 15–25.

96. Brandon Applegate, Michael Turner, Joseph Sanborn, Edward Latessa, and Melissa Moon, "Individualization, Criminalization, or Problem Resolution: A Factorial Survey of Juvenile Court Judges' Decisions to Incarcerate Youthful Felony Offenders," *Justice Quarterly* 17 (2000): 328, cited in Robert M. Regoli and John D. Hewitt, *Delinquency in Society,* 5th ed. (New York: McGraw-Hill, 2003).

97. Washington State Institute for Public Policy, "The Criminal Justice System in Washington State: Incarceration Rates, Taxpayer Costs, Crime Rates, and Prison Economics," January 2003, www.wsipp.wa.gov/rptfiles/SentReport2002.pdf (retrieved March 28, 2009).

98. Regoli and Hewitt, *Delinquency in Society.*

99. California Department of Corrections and Rehabilitation, "Youth Population Overview," Division of Juvenile Justice, 2009, www.cdcr.ca.gov/Juvenile_Justice/DJJ_Quick_Facts/Youth_Population_Overview.html (retrieved August 29, 2009).

100. Lloyd E. Ohlin, "The Future of Juvenile Justice Policy and Research," *Crime and Delinquency* 44 (1998): 143–153.

101. Snyder and Sickmund, *Juvenile Offenders and Victims: 2006 National Report.*

102. California Department of Corrections and Rehabilitation, "Summary Fact Sheet," www.cya.ca.gov/ReportsResearch/summarys.html (retrieved April 9, 2007).

103. Snyder and Sickmund, *Juvenile Offenders and Victims: 2006 National Report,* chap. 7, p. 218.

104. Peter W. Greenwood, "Responding to Juvenile Crime: Lessons Learned," in *Juvenile Delinquency: Readings,* 2nd ed., eds. Joseph G. Weis, Robert D. Crutchfield, and George S. Bridges (Boston: Pine Forge Press, 2001).

105. Eric Poole and Robert Regoli, "Violence in Juvenile Institutions," *Criminology* 21 (1983): 213–232.

106.Snyder and Sickmund, *Juvenile Offenders and Victims: 2006 National Report,* chap. 7, p. 230.

107. "Ex-Youth Prison Officials Charged with Inmate Abuse," CNN.com, April 10, 2007, http://nospank.net/n-q81r.htm (retrieved May 25, 2007).

108. Miguel Bustillo, "Texas Youth Prison Board Ousted amid Sex Abuse Scandal," *Los Angeles Times*, March 17, 2007, www.nospank.net/tyc-13.htm (retrieved May 25, 2007).

109. "Girls in the Juvenile Justice System," Facts Sheet: ACLU and Human Rights Watch, www.aclu.org/womensrights/crimjustice/26843 res20060925.html; "U.S.: Girls Abused in New York's Juvenile Prisons," Human Rights Watch, September 25, 2006, http://hrw.org/english/docs/2006/09/22/usdom14249_txt.htm (retrieved May 25, 2007).

110. Bilha Davidson-Arad and Miriam Golan, "Victimization of Juveniles in Out-of-Home Placement: Juvenile Correctional Facilities," *British Journal of Social Work* 1 (2006): 107–125.

111. Martin Frost, Jeffrey Fagan, and T. Scott Vivona, "Youth in Prisons and Training Schools," *Juvenile and Family Court Journal* 40 (1989): 1–14.

112. Jeffrey Fagan, "The Comparative Advantage of Juvenile versus Criminal Court Sanctions on Recidivism among Adolescent Felony Offenders," *Law and Policy* 18 (1996): 77–115.

113. Snyder and Sickmund, *Juvenile Offenders and Victims: 2006 National Report*, chap. 7, p. 238.

114. Peter W. Greenwood, "Responding to Juvenile Crime: Lessons Learned," in *Juvenile Delinquency: Readings.*

115. Agnew, *Juvenile Delinquency: Causes and Control.*

116. Snyder and Sickmund, *Juvenile Offenders and Victims: 2006 National Report,* chap. 7, p. 206; Office of Juvenile Justice and Delinquency Prevention, *Statistical Briefing Book*; Joanne Belknap, *The Invisible Woman: Gender, Crime, and Justice*, 3rd ed. (Belmont, CA: Wadsworth, 2007).

117. Office of Juvenile Justice and Delinquency Prevention, *Statistical Briefing Book.*

118. Agnew, *Juvenile Delinquency: Causes and Control*; Dean John Champion, *The Juvenile Justice System: Delinquency, Processing, and the Law* (Upper Saddle River, NJ: Pearson/Prentice Hall, 2004).

119. Andrew R. Klein, *Alternative Sentencing: A Practitioner's Guide* (Cincinnati: Anderson, 1988).

120. Doris MacKenzie, Angela Gover, Gaylene Armstrong, and Ojmarrh Mitchell, *A National Study Comparing the Environments of Boot Camps with Traditional Facilities for Juvenile Offenders* (Washington, DC: National Institute of Justice, 2001).

121. Jerry Tyler, Ray Darville, and Kathi Stalnaker, "Juvenile Boot Camps: A Descriptive Analysis of Program Diversity and Effectiveness," *The Social Science Journal* 38, no. 3 (Autumn 2001): 445–460.

122. Richard Lawrence, *School Crime and Juvenile Justice,* 2nd ed. (New York: Oxford University Press, 2007), 260.

123. Office of Juvenile Justice and Delinquency Prevention, *Day Treatment, Model Programs Guide, Version 2.5*, www.dsgonline.com/mpg2.5/intermediate_sanctions.htm (retrieved June 25, 2007).

124. David Finkelhor and Richard Ormrod, "Reporting Crimes against Juveniles," *Juvenile Justice Bulletin* (Washington, DC: Office of Juvenile Justice and Delinquency Prevention, November 1999), www.unh.edu/ccre/pdf/jvq/CV23.pdf (retrieved May 22, 2007).

125. Katrina Baum, "Juvenile Victimization and Offending, 1993–2003," *Bureau of Justice Statistics, Special Report* (Washington, DC: Office of Justice Programs, August 2005), www.ojp.usdoj.gov/bjs/pub/pdf/jvo03.pdf (retrieved May 22, 2007).

126. Ibid.

127. Agnew, *Juvenile Delinquency: Causes and Control.*

128. Child Welfare Information Gateway, www.childwelfare.gov (retrieved April 30, 2007).

CHAPTER 16

1. Sameer Hinduja, "Perceptions of Local and State Law Enforcement Concerning the Role of Computer Crime Investigative Teams," *Policing: An International Journal of Police Strategies & Management* 27 (2004): 341.

2. Robert Moore, *Cybercrime: Investigating High Technology Computer Crime* (Florence, KY: Anderson, 2005), 3.

3. Hinduja, "Perceptions of Local and State Law Enforcement Concerning the Role of Computer Crime Investigative Teams," 355.

4. Simpson Garfinkel, "The FBI's Cybercrime Crackdown," in *Annual Editions: Criminal Justice 04/05*, ed. Joseph L. Victor and Joanne Naughton (Dubuque, IA: McGraw-Hill/Dushkin, 2004).

5. Darin Walker, Deon Brock, and T. Ramon Stuart, "Faceless-Oriented Policing: Traditional Policing Theories Are Not Adequate in a Cyber World," *The Police Journal* 79 (2006): 169–175.

6. Robert Moore, "The Role of Computer Forensics in Criminal Investigation," in *Crime Online*, ed. Yvonne Jewkes (Portland, OR: Willan, 2007), 82.

7. Don Philpot, "Computer Forensics and Cyber Security," *Homeland Defense Journal* (2008), www.homelanddefensejournal.com (retrieved July 13, 2008), 2.

8. U.S. Department of Justice, Computer Crime and Intellectual Property Section, *Searching and Seizing Computers and Obtaining Electronic Evidence in Criminal Investigations* (Washington, DC: Department of Justice, 2002), 1–24.

9. http://securitydebrief.adfero.com/cyber-security-waiting-for-godot/?display=print (retrieved March 6, 2009).

10. Roderic Broadhurst, "Developments in the Global Law Enforcement of Cyber-crime," *Policing: An International Journal of Police Strategies & Management* 29 (2006): 408, 417.

11. Council of Europe, "Summary of the Convention on Cyber Crime," *European Treaty Series* no. 185 (2001), http://conventions.coe.int/Treaty/en/Summaries/Html/185.htm (retrieved July 3, 2008).

12. Sameer Hinduja and Joseph A. Schafer, "US Cybercrime Units on the World Wide Web," *Policing: An International Journal of Police Strategies & Management* 32 (2009): 288.

13. Broadhurst, "Developments in the Global Law Enforcement of Cybercrime," 412.

14. Moore, *Cybercrime: Investigating High Technology Computer Crime,* 3.

15. Ibid., 142.

16. Gene Stephens, "Cybercrime in the Year 2025," *The Futurist* 42, no. 4 (2008): 36.

17. Judith M. Collins, "Identity Theft and Identity Crimes, "in *Encyclopedia of Law Enforcement, Volume 1,* eds. Larry E. Sullivan and Marie Simonetti Rosen (Thousand Oaks, CA: Sage, 2005), 227.

18. "Identity Theft and Fraud." U.S. Department of Justice, www.usdo.gov/criminal/fraud/websites/idtheft.html (retrieved July 24, 2009).

19. "Ibid.

20. International Association of Chiefs of Police, *Identity Crime Update, Part I* (Alexandria, VA: International Association of Chiefs of Police, 2008).

21. Ibid.

22. Collins, "Identity Theft and Identity Crimes, 228.

23. Office of Community Oriented Policing Services, *A National Strategy to Combat Identity Theft* (Washington, DC: Office of Community Oriented Policing Services, 2006), 9.

24. Office of Community Oriented Policing Services, *A National Strategy to Combat Identity Theft,* 44–46.
25. Title 22 USC 2656f(d).
26. Title 18 USC 2331(1) & (5).
27. Bruce Hoffman, *Inside Terrorism: Revised and Expanded Edition* (New York: Columbia University Press, 2006), 40.
28. National Counterterrorism Center, "2008 Report on Terrorism," April 30, 2009, www.nctc.gov (retrieved July 24, 2009).
29. U.S. Department of State, "Country Reports on Terrorism 2008, Chapter 1 Strategic Assessment," April 30, 2009, www.state.gov/s/ct/rls/crt/2008/122411.htm (retrieved July 24, 2009).
30. Commission on the Prevention of Weapons of Mass Destruction Proliferation and Terrorism, *World at Risk* (New York: Vintage Books, 2008), xv.
31. Marvin J. Cetron and Owen Davies, "Trends Now Shaping the Future: Economic, Societal, and Environmental Trends," *The Futurist* 39, no. 2 (2005): 33.
32. U.S. Department of Justice, "Fact Sheet: USA Patriot Act Improvement and Reauthorization Act of 2005," 2006, 1.
33. American Civil Liberties Union, "Surveillance under the USA PATRIOT Act." April 3, 2003, www.aclu.org/printer/printer.php (retrieved April 27, 2006).
34. Gene Stephens, "Policing the Future: Law Enforcement's New Challenges," *The Futurist* 39, no. 2 (2005): 55.
35. Brent Smith, "A Look at Terrorist Behavior: How They Prepare, Where They Strike," *National Institute of Justice Journal* 260 (2008): 2–6.
36. George L. Kelling and William J. Bratton, "Policing Terrorism," *Civic Bulletin,* no. 43 (2006), www.manhattan-institute.org/cgi-bin/apMI/print.cgi.
37. Michael Barrett, "The Need for Intelligence-Led Policing," *DomPrep Journal* (June 21, 2006), www.manhattan-institute.org/cgi-bin/apMI/print.cgi.
38. Paul E. O'Connell, "The Chess Master's Game: A Model for Incorporating Local Police Agencies in the Fight against Global Terrorism," *Policing: An International Journal of Police Strategies & Management* 31, no. 3 (2008): 461.
39. Bureau of Justice Assistance, *Intelligence-Led Policing: The New Intelligence Architecture,* September 2005, NCJ 210681.
40. Paul Serluco, "Fusion Centers," *Homeland Defense Journal* 6, no. 3 (2008): 16.
41. Kelling and Bratton, "Policing Terrorism."
42. Ibid.
43. Paul Serluco, "Customs and Border Patrol Predators Take Flight," *Homeland Defense Journal* 6, no. 1 (2008): 18–21.
44. "Hate Crime Statistics, 2004," U.S. Department of Justice, www.fbi.gov/ucr/hc2004/openpage.htm (retrieved June 26, 2006).
45. Phyllis B. Gerstenfeld, *Hate Crimes: Causes, Controls, and Controversies* (Thousand Oaks, CA: Sage, 2004).
46. Ibid.
47. California Department of Justice, "Hate Crimes in California 2004," http://caag.state.ca.us/cjsc/publications/hatecrimes/hc04/preface.pdf (retrieved June 26, 2006).
48. Anti-Defamation League, "State Hate Crime Statutory Provisions," www.adl.org/learn/hate_crimes_laws/State_Hate_Crime_Statutory_Provisions_chart.pdf (retrieved February 10, 2005).
49. U.S. Department of Justice, "Bureau of Justice Statistics: Advance Release of September 23, 2001," www.ojp.usdoj.gov/bjs/pub/press/hcrn99pr.htm (retrieved July 6, 2006).
50. Ibid.
51. International Association of Chiefs of Police, "Training Key #588: Mass Demonstrations and Civil Disturbances" (Alexandria, VA: International Association of Chiefs of Police, 2005), 1.
52. James A. Conser, *Law Enforcement in the United States* (Sudbury, MA: Jones & Bartlett, 2005), 445.
53. Raymond M. Momboisse, *Riots, Revolts, and Insurrections* (Springfield, IL: Charles C Thomas, 1967), 5–21.
54. See Rick Ruddell, Matthew O. Thomas, and Lori Beth Way, "Breaking the Chain: Confronting Issueless College Town Disturbances and Riots," *Journal of Criminal Justice* 33 (2005): 549–560.
55. Michael K. Hooper, "Civil Disorder and Policing," in *Handbook of Criminal Justice Administration,* eds. M. A. DuPont-Morales, Michael K. Hooper, and Judy H. Schmidt (New York: Marcel Dekker, 2001), 159.
56. National Advisory Commission on Civil Disorders, *Report of the National Advisory Commission on Civil Disorders* (New York: Bantam Books, 1968[0]), 117.
57. Report by the Special Advisor, *The City in Crisis: A Report by the Special Advisor to the Board of Police Commissioners on the Civil Disorder in Los Angeles* (Washington, DC: Police Foundation, 1992), 42.
58. Bruce D. Porter and Marvin Dunn, *The Miami Riot of 1980: Crossing the Bounds* (Lexington, MA: D. C. Heath, 1984[0]), 173–174.
59. Hooper, "Civil Disorder and Policing," 163.
60. Porter and Dunn, *The Miami Riot of 1980: Crossing the Bounds*; (Hooper, "Civil Disorder and Policing," 163.
61. Ronald D. Hunter, Thomas Barker, and Pamela D. Mayhall, *Police-Community Relations and the Administration of Justice* (Upper Saddle River, NJ: Prentice-Hall, 2004), 405.
62. "Truckers Protest High Fuel Prices," MSNBC.MSN.Com, April 1, 2008, www.msnbc.msn.com/id/23903144/ (retrieved July 3, 2008).
63. "Riots, Instability Spread as Food Prices Skyrocket," CNN.Com, April 14, 2008, http://edition.cnn.com/2008/WORLD/americas/04/14/world.food.crisis/ (retrieved July 3, 2008).
64. Hooper, "Civil Disorder and Policing," 165.
65. Porter and Dunn, *The Miami Riot of 1980: Crossing the Bounds,* 174.
66. David Baker, "Policing, Politics, and Civil Rights: Analysis of the Policing of Protest against the 1999 Chinese President's Visit to New Zealand," *Police Practice and Research* 8 (2007): 221.
67. Nathan Freier, "Known Unknowns: Unconventional 'Strategic Shock,'" in *Defense Strategy Development,* Strategic Studies Institute (Carlisle, PA: U.S. Army War College, 2008), 32–36.
68. John P. Crank, *Counter-Terrorism After 9/11: Justice, Security, and Ethics Reconsidered* (Cincinnati, OH: Matthew Bender, 2005), 243–244.
69. Gus Martin, *Understanding Terrorism: Challenges, Perspectives, and Issues* (Thousand Oaks, CA: Sage, 2006), 511–512.
70. Ibid., 512.
71. "First Response to Victims of Crime Who Have a Disability: A Handbook for Law Enforcement Officers on How to Approach and Help Crime Victims Who Have Alzheimer's Disease, Mental Illness, Mental Retardation, or Who Are Blind or Visually Impaired, Deaf or Hard of Hearing," U.S. Department of Justice, Office of Justice Programs, October 2002, www.ojp.usdoj.gov/ovc/publications/infores/

firstrep/2002/welcome.html (retrieved July 17, 2008), NCJ 195500.

72. Sharon Milberger, Barbara LeRoy, Angela Martin, Nathaniel Israel, Linda Potter, and Pam Patchak-Schuster, "Michigan Study on Women with Physical Disabilities, Final Report," U.S. Department of Justice, National Institute of Justice, February 2002, NCJ 193769; "Facts about Programs Delivering Battered Women's Services to Women with Disabilities," Center for Research on Women with Disabilities www.bcm.edu/crowd/abuse_women/progfact1.htm (retrieved July 11, 2008).

73. "Facts about Programs Delivering Battered Women's Services to Women with Disabilities."

74. "First Response to Victims of Crime Who Have a Disability."

75. Tanya Broder and Sheila Neville, "Benefits for Immigrant Victims of Trafficking, Domestic Violence, and Other Serious Crimes in California," California Immigrant Policy Center, http://caimmigrant.org/source/TraffickingReportFinal%20(2).pdf (retrieved July 10, 2008).

76. Ibid.

77. Ibid.

78. "OVC Fact Sheet: International Activities," March 7, 2007, www.ojp.usdoj.gov/ovc/publications/factshts/interact.htm (retrieved July 12, 2008).

79. Avy A. Skolnik, Ivana Chapcakova, Kelly Costello, Chris Cozad, Tina D'Ellia, Kim Fountain, Rebecca Waggoner Kloek, Crystal Middlestadt, Lindsey Moore, Melissa L. Pope, Oscar Trujillo, Ardel Thomas, and Laura Velazquez, "Anti-Lesbian, Gay, Bisexual, and Transgender Violence in 2007," National Coalition of Anti-Violence Programs, 2008, www.avp.org/publications/reports/documents/2007HVReportFINAL_002.pdf (retrieved July 19, 2008).

80. Kim Fountain and Avy A. Skolnik, "Lesbian, Gay, Bisexual, and Transgender Domestic Violence in the United States in 2006: A Report of the National Coalition of Anti-Violence Programs," National Coalition of Anti-Violence Programs, 2007, www.avp.org/publications/reports/documents/2006NationalDVReport(Final).pdf (retrieved July 19, 2008).

81. Fountain and Skolnik, "Lesbian, Gay, Bisexual, and Transgender Domestic Violence in the United States in 2006"; Skolnik et al., "Anti-Lesbian, Gay, Bisexual, and Transgender Violence in 2007."

82. Brian Levin, Center for the Study of Hate and Extremism, www.civilrights.org/assets/pdfs/LLEHCPA-Levin-Ltr-4302007.pdf (retrieved July 24, 2008); Gregory M. Herek, "Preliminary Findings of the Psychological Impact of Hate Crimes Based on Sexual Orientation," Public Police Office, American Psychological Association, www.apa.org/ppo/issues/pherek.html (retrieved July 24, 2008).

83. ABC News, "FBI Reports Increases in Hate Crimes," http://abcnews.go.com/ (retrieved July 24, 2008).

84. *National Bias Crimes Training Manual for Law Enforcement and Victims Assistance Professionals* (Washington, DC: U.S. Department of Justice, 1995).

85. Michigan Department of Community Health, Crime Victim Services Commission and Michigan Department of Civil Rights, www.mi.gov/crimevictim/ (retrieved July 24, 2008).

86. U.S. Department of Justice, "2006 Hate Crime Statistics," www.fbi.gov/ucr/hc2006/methodology.html (retrieved July 24, 2008).

87. Ananda B. Amstadter, Michael R. McCart, and Kenneth J. Ruggiero, "Psychosocial Interventions for Adults with Crime-Related PTSD," *Professional Psychology: Research and Practice* 38, no. 6 (2007): 640-651.

88. Frans W. Winkel, "Peer Support Groups: Evaluating the Mere Contact/Mere Sharing Model and Impairment Hypotheses," *International Perspectives in Victimology* 2, no. 1 (2006): 101–113.

89. Jeffrey T. Mitchell and George S. Everly, *Critical Incident Stress Debriefing: An Operations Manual* (Ellicott City, MD: Chevron Press, 1995).

90. Jennifer Ormerod, "Current Research into the Effectiveness of Debriefing," in *Psychological Debriefing* (Leicester, UK: The British Psychological Society, May 2002), chap. 2; Zeev Kaplan, Iulian Iancu, and Ehud Bodner, "A Review of Psychological Debriefing after Extreme Stress," *Psychiatric Services* 52, no. 6 (2001).

Credits

PHOTO CREDITS

Chapter 1 p. 1, © Mario Tama/Getty Images; p. 2, © Michael Kelley/Stone/Getty Images; p. 3L, © AP/Wide World Photos; p. 3R, © Jordan Rooney/Alamy; p. 4, © AP/Wide World Photos; p. 6T, © Paula Bronstein/Getty Images; p. 6B, © Mario Tama/Getty Images; p. 7, © G&H Productions/The Kobal Collection; p. 9, © Michael Newman/PhotoEdit; p. 10, © AP/Wide World Photos; p. 11, © Marmaduke St. John/Alamy; p. 12, © The McGraw-Hill Companies Inc./Jaques Cornell; p. 13T, Columns: ©iStockphoto.com/John Woodcock; p. 13, © Elaine Thompson/Pool/epa/Corbis; p. 14, © Marco Baass/Fstop/PhotoLibrary; p. 15, © Joel Gordon; p. 17, D. Falconer/PhotoLink/Getty Images; p. 18, © David Hoffman/Alamy **Chapter 2** p. 24, © Arthur Turner/Alamy; p. 26, © AP/Wide World Photos; p. 30, © Fabienne Fossez/Alamy; p. 32, © Graham Morrison/Getty Images; p. 33, © Spemcer Grant/PhotoEdit; p. 35L, © Bettmann/Corbis; p. 35R, © Steve Eicher/WireImage/Getty Images; p. 37, © Nancy Scholz/Express-Times /Landov; p. 39, © Lucille Khornak/Taxi/Getty Images; pp. 43, 44, © AP/Wide World Photos; p. 46, © Justin Sullivan/Getty Images; p. 47, National Library of Medicine; p. 49, © Jared Moossy/Redux; pp. 50, 51, © Joel Gordon; p. 54, Courtesy David Steele Enterprises, Inc.; p. 55, © David R. Frazier Photolibrary, Inc./Alamy; p. 56, © Brand X Photography/Veer; p. 57, © AP/Wide World Photos **Chapter 3** pp. 64, 66, © AP/Wide World Photos; p. 67, © Dorling Kindersley/Getty Images; p. 69, James Woodson/Getty Images; p. 71, © Deco/Alamy; p. 72, PhotoDisc/age footstock; pp. 73, 74, © AP/Wide World Photos; p. 76, © PhotoDisc/Getty Images; p. 77T, © AP/Wide World Photos; p. 77B, © Bettmann/Corbis; pp. 80, 81, 84, © AP/Wide World Photos; p. 86T, © Bettmann/Corbis; p. 86B, Royalty-FreeCorbis; p. 88, © Ethan Miller/Getty Images; p. 90, © B. Tanaka/Photographer's Choice/Getty Images **Chapter 4** p. 96, © Tom Brakefield/Getty Images; p. 98, © Chuck Savage/Corbis; p. 99, © Time & Life Pictures/Getty Images; p. 100, Courtesy LexisNexis; p. 101TL, Private Collection/© The Stapleton Collection/The Bridgeman Art Library; p. 101ML, © Musee de la Tapisserie, Bayeux, France/Bridgeman Art Library/Getty Images; p. 101TR, © Time & Life Pictures/Getty Images; p. 101MR, © Sant'Apollinare Nuovo, Ravenna, Italy/The Bridgeman Art Library; p. 101BR, Private Collection/© The Bridgeman Art Library; p. 101B, Glasses: © Getty Images; p. 101B, Quill pen: © Ingram Publishing/Alamy; p. 102, VisionsofAmerica/Joe Sohm/Getty Images; p. 103, © Joel Gordon; p. 104, Castle Rock/Section Eight/The Kobal Collection; p. 106, © Marianne Barcellona/Time & Life Pictures/Getty Images; p. 107, © Daniel Allan/Taxi/Getty Images; p. 108T, © Popperfoto/Getty Images; p. 108B, © AP/Wide World Photos; p. 109, © AP/Wide World Photos; p. 111, StockByte/Fotosearch; p. 114, © AP/Wide World Photos; p. 117, © Bettmann/Corbis; p. 119, © Reuters/Corbis **Chapter 5** p. 124, © The Granger Collection, New York; p. 126, © Bettmann/Corbis; p. 128, © AP/Wide World Photos; p. 129, © The Granger Collection, New York; p. 131, Courtesy Berkeley Police Department Historical Unit; pp. 132, 133, © AP/Wide World Photos; p. 136, © Pat Canova/Alamy; p. 137, © John Moore/Getty Images; p. 141, © Ryan McGinnis/Alamy; p. 143T, © Spencer Platt/Getty Images; p. 143B, © AP/Wide World Photos; p. 147, © AP/Wide World Photos; p. 149, © Ralf-Finn Hestoft/Corbis; p. 151, © Getty Images; p. 153, Ryan McVay/Getty Images **Chapter 6** p. 158, © Joel Gordon; p. 160, © Robert Stolarik/The New York Times/Redux; p. 161, © AP/Wide World Photos; p. 163, © Hemis/Alamy; p. 165, age fotostock/Fotosearch; p. 167, PhotoDisc/Getty Images; p. 170, © Michael Matthews-Police Images/Alamy; p. 171, © AP/Wide World Photos; p. 172, © Darren Klimek/Digital Vision/Getty Images; p. 173, © AP/Wide World Photos; p. 174L, Digital Vision/Getty Images; p. 174R, © Alan Schein/Alamy; p. 175, © ThinkStock Images/Getty Images; p. 176, © Marco Di Lauro/Getty Images; p. 179, © Joel Gordon; p. 183, © Mitch Wojnarowicz/The Image Works; p. 184, Amos Morgan/Getty Images; p. 185, © Justin Sullivan/Getty Images; p. 186, ©iStockphoto.com/absolut_100 **Chapter 7** pp. 192, 194, 196, © AP/Wide World Photos; p. 198, Courtesy FEMA; p. 197, © Mikael Karlsson; p. 200, © AP/Wide World Photos; p. 203, © Darren Klimek/Digital Vision/Getty Images; pp. 204, 207, © AP/Wide World Photos; p. 210, © Jeff Greenberg/PhotoEdit; p. 212, © D. Hurst/Alamy; p. 213, © AP/Wide World Photos; p. 216, © Joel Rogers/Stone/Getty Images; p. 217, Fotosearch; p. 218, © AP/Wide World Photos; p. 219, Courtesy Case Western Reserve University **Chapter 8** p. 224, © Altrendo Images/Getty Images; p. 226, © J. Pat Carter/Getty Images; p. 227, © iStockphoto.com/Joel Carillet; pp. 230, 231, © AP/Wide World Photos; p. 232, © Royalty-Free/Corbis; p. 234, © Stock Montage/Hulton Archive/Getty Images; p. 235, © Alex Wong/Getty Images; p. 236, © Jim Arbogast/Digital Vision/Getty Images; p. 238, © Sam Diephuis/Corbis; p. 240, © Getty Images; p. 241, © Comstock/PunchStock; p. 242, Brand X Pictures; p. 243, © AP/Wide World Photos; p. 245, © Stockbyte/Getty Images **Chapter 9** p. 250, © Michael Newman/PhotoEdit; p. 252, © AP/Wide World Photos; p. 254, © Bettmann/Corbis; p. 255, © Zigy Kaluzny/Riser/Getty Images; p. 256, © Joel Gordon; p. 257, © AP/Wide World Photos; p. 260, © Gabriel Bouys/AFP/Getty Images; p. 262, © Justin Sullivan/Getty Images; pp. 266, 267, 268, © AP/Wide World Photos; p. 269, © Tim Pannell/Corbis; p. 264, © Mary Kate Denny/PhotoEdit; p. 265, StockByte/Fotosearch **Chapter 10** p. 276, © AP/Wide World Photos; p. 278, © Cheryl Gerber/The New York Times/Redux; p. 280, © Getty Images; p. 281, © Joe Raedle/Getty Images; p. 282, © Royalty-Free/Corbis; p. 283, © AP/Wide World Photos; p. 285, © Joel Gordon; p. 287, © iStockphoto.com/Stefan Klein; p. 288, © Shepard Sherbell/Corbis; p. 289, © Michael Newman/PhotoEdit; p. 291, © Getty Images; p. 293, © Jerry Cabluck/Sygma/Corbis; p. 294, © AFP/Getty Images; p. 296, © AP/Wide World Photos **Chapter**

11 p. 300, © Steve Starr/Corbis; p. 302, © AP/Wide World Photos; p. 303, © Hulton Archive/Getty Images; p. 304, © Mike Fiala/Getty Images; p. 305, © The Granger Collection, New York; p. 306, © AP/Wide World Photos; p. 307, © Corbis; p. 308, © AP/Wide World Photos; p. 309, © The Granger Collection, New York; p. 311, © AP/Wide World Photos; p. 312, © The Bridgeman Art Library/Getty Images; p. 313, © Bettmann/Corbis; p. 315, © AP/Wide World Photos; p. 317T, © Q. Sakamaki/Redux; p. 317B, © John Chiasson/Getty Images; p. 319, © Justin Sullivan/Getty Images; p. 323, © Tannen Maury/AFP/Getty Images; p. 324, © Mikael Karlsson/Alamy **Chapter 12** p. 334, © Stephen Ferry/Getty Images; p. 336, © Philip G. Zimbardo/Stanford University; p. 340, © iStockphoto.com/Alex Potemkin; pp. 341T, 341BL, © AP/Wide World Photos; p. 341BM, © Dirk Eisermann/laif/Redux; p. 341BR, © Peter Macdiarmid/Getty Images; p. 342, © AP/Wide World Photos; p. 345, © Joel Gordon; p. 346, © Royalty-Free/Corbis; pp. 347, 348, © AP/Wide World Photos; p. 351, © Joel Gordon; p. 353, © 2007 Keith Eng; p. 356, © Robin Nelson/PhotoEdit; p. 357, 360, © AP/Wide World Photos; p. 362, © Mark Peterson/Redux; pp. 365, 366, © Joel Gordon **Chapter 13** p. 370, © Joel Gordon; p. 372, © Getty Images; p. 374, © John Birdsall/The Image Works; p. 378, © Johnny Nunez/WireImage/Getty Images; p. 379, © Mikael Karlsson/Alamy; p. 381, © Joel Gordon; p. 385, © AP/Wide World Photos; p. 386, © Jeff Greenberg/The Image Works; p. 387, © Kathy McLaughlin/The Image Works ; p. 388T, © A. Ramey/PhotoEdit; pp. 388B, 389, © Joel Gordon; p. 391, © AP/Wide World Photos; p. 393, © Royalty-Free/Corbis **Chapter 14** p. 398, © Joel Gordon; p. 400, © AP/Wide World Photos; p. 403T, © Hamburger Kunsthalle, Hamburg, Germany/The Bridgeman Art Library; p. 403B, © Robert Altman/The Image Works; p. 405, © Robert Sciarrino/Star Ledger/Corbis; p. 406, © Paul Doyle/Alamy; p. 407, © AP/Wide World Photos; p. 408, © Joel Gordon; p. 409T, © Nicole Bengiveno/The New York Times/Redux; p. 409B, © Stockbyte/PunchStock; p. 412, © Scott Olson/Getty Images; p. 414, © Ilene MacDonald/Alamy; p. 415, © Mary Kate Denny/PhotoEdit; p. 417, © AP/Wide World Photos; p. 419, © Chip Somodevilla/Getty Images; p. 420, © Bob Daemmrich/The Image Works; p. 421, © Steve Healey/The Hamilton County Star **Chapter 15** p. 426, © Bonnie Kamin/PhotoEdit; p. 428, © AP/Wide World Photos; p. 430, © Bettmann/Corbis; p. 431T, © The Granger Collection, New York; p. 431B, © Denis Tangney Jr./Photodisc/Getty Images; p. 435, © Bob Daemmrich/PhotoEdit; p. 436, © Joel Gordon; pp. 438, 439, 440, © AP/Wide World Photos; p. 444, © Spencer Grant/PhotoEdit; p. 448, © Joel Gordon; p. 449, DigitalVision/Fotosearch; p. 450, © AP/Wide World Photos; p. 452, © Royalty-Free/Corbis; p. 454, © Joel Gordon; p. 455, © AP/Wide World Photos **Chapter 16** pp. 460, 462, 463, © AP/Wide World Photos; p. 464, IndexStock/Photolibrary; p. 465, © Getty Images; p. 467, © iStockphoto.com/John Woodcock; p. 468, © Gabe Palacio/Getty Images; p. 469, © Lisa Lanham/Getty Images; p. 472, © AP/Wide World Photos; p. 473, © Thomas Wirth/AFP/Getty Images; p. 474, © AP/Wide World Photos; p. 475, © Gerard Burkhart/Getty Images; p. 476, © AP/Wide World Photos; p. 478T, © AP/Wide World Photos; p. 478B, © Joel Gordon; p. 481, © AP/Wide World Photos **Repeating Design Elements** Police badge: © iStockphoto.com/Karen Mower; Passport: © iStockphoto.com/William Voon; Cut-out people: © iStockphoto.com/Timsa; Target: © iStockphoto.com/Andrew Johnson; Question mark: © iStockphoto.com/Deliormanli; File folder: © iStockphoto.com/Subjug; Polaroid: ©iStockphoto.com/Nic Taylor

TEXT/FIGURE CREDITS

Figure, box, and table credits appear on page in the text. Additional credit information is below:

Figure 3.1, p. 86: Robert E. Park, Ernest W. Burgess, and R. D. McKenzie, The City, p. 55. Copyright 1925 University of Chicago Press. Used with permission. **Figure 6.1, p. 164**: SARA figure found at http://www.popcenter.org/learning/60steps/index.cfm?stepNum=7 Copyright © Ronald Clarke and John E. Ecke. Used with permission. **Chapter 12, p. 351**: taken from http://prisonplace.com/forums/p/1252/6152.aspx#6152 **Table 15.4, p. 438**: taken from *Building Blocks for Youth* initiative_ Youth Law Center_1010 Vermont Avenue, N.W., Suite 310_Washington, DC 20005_Phone: 202 637-0377_ Fax: 202 379-1600_Email: info.bby@erols.com. http://www.buildingblocksforyouth.org/issues/transfer/transchart.html. Adapted from Griffin,P., Torbet, P., and Szymanski, L. 1998. *Trying Juveniles as Adults in Criminal Court: An Analysis of State Transfer Provisions*. Washington, DC: US. Department of Justice, Office of Justice Programs, Office of Juvenile Justice and Delinquency Prevention.

Case Index

Name and Subject Index

Note: Illustrations are indicated by page numbers in italic type. Figures and tables are indicated by "f" and "t," respectively, following page numbers.

T

U

Y

Z